THE WESTERN IDEA OF LAW

THE WESTERN IDEA OF LAW

By

J.C. SMITH
Professor of Law
University of British Columbia

and

DAVID N. WEISSTUB
Professor of Law
Osgoode Hall Law School
York University

BUTTERWORTHS

London; Toronto; Sydney; Singapore; and Durban.

The Western Idea of Law

Printed and bound in Canada by John Deyell Company

The Butterworth Group of Companies

Canada:
Butterworth & Co. (Canada) Ltd., Toronto and Vancouver

United Kingdom:
Butterworth & Co. (Publishers) Ltd., London

Australia:
Butterworths Pty Ltd., Sydney, Melbourne, Brisbane, Adelaide, and Perth.

New Zealand:
Butterworths of New Zealand Ltd., Wellington and Auckland

Singapore:
Butterworth & Co. (Asia) Pte. Ltd., Singapore

South Africa:
Butterworth Publishers (Pty) Ltd., Durban and Pretoria

United States:
Butterworth Legal Publishers, Boston, Seattle and Austin
Mason Publishing Company, St. Paul
D & S Publishers, Clearwater

Canadian Cataloguing in Publication Data

Main entry under title:
The Western idea of law

ISBN 0-409-86819-1

1. Law - Philosophy. 2. Law - History. I. Smith, J.C. (Joseph Carman), 1930- II. Weisstub, David N., 1944-

K215.E5W47 1983 340.1 C83-098905-6

To
Max, Melanie, Miriam
and
Jonathan and Jeremy

INTRODUCTION

The quest for a coherent philosophy of law has long haunted writers and jurists in the West. While Judeo-Christian influences have been felt, the heritage of Western law, in terms of language, logic and archetypes, may be traced primarily to Greco-Roman scientism and patriarchy. Law is a significant description of the way in which a society analyzes itself and projects its image to the world. It is a major articulation of a culture's self concept, representing the theory of society within that culture. It is the deepest and most generalized philosophical statement that a non-revolutionary or non-anarchistic culture can make about itself. The legal experience, in its most comprehensive form, is a multi-dimensional phenomenon, wherein mythic, dramatic, rhetorical, and philosophical elements play significant roles. In the West, the philosophic dimension of law has eclipsed the development of myth, drama, and rhetoric, to the detriment of cultural harmony.

In ancient Greek philosophy, and particularly the Platonic conception, law was the primary ordering principle. The philosophic ideas which governed public institutions were rationally and consciously stated. Socrates attacked the dramatic, the gods, and poetry; in short, he attacked everything which was uncertain. The poetic, for example, was thought unscientific and, therefore, ultimately unable to ascend the heights of the good, the just, and the beautiful. Under the Socratic influence philosophy aligned itself with absolutist scientific thought, change was viewed with suspicion, and the ideal of a predictable, certain, changeless world was embraced. Aristotle responded to this static concept merely by rearticulating it in terms of a theory of physical or natural science. He did not absent himself from the Platonic enterprise, as an examination of the tenth book of the *Nichomachean Ethics* or the *Metaphysics* will suggest. To posit a tension between Plato the idealist, and Aristotle the biologist, and to represent them as the principal exponents of opposing schools of thought is to engage in misleading oversimplification. They both adhered to a concept of scientific knowledge and philosophy; Greek philosophies of law were inseparable from general theories of society being developed at the time and, indeed, from general theories of society subsisting until the nineteenth century, when the technological era began.

Despite contemporary upheavals in theories of social ordering, the Greek philosophical legacy still persists in the West. Truth, like science, is seen as inherently provable; myth is seen as inferior to philosophy. Yet all cultures have their mythic structures, their non-rational or unconscious underpinnings which give rise to strongly held world views. It may be argued that law is, in fact, a major representation of the mythic dimension of civilization. If the constitutional life of nations defines the condition of nationhood, it would be impossible to think about legal cultures without considering the impact of myth.

Cultures have critical moments in history when their values are constitutionally structured according to a legal design. The Magna Carta and the

American Constitution are both examples of such an historical birth. These constitutional statements embody the most fundamental values that the society commits itself to at the time. When this is accomplished in law it means that the society undertakes to harness its energies to ensure that these values are protected and that the future of the society is shaped by them. The constitutional document then serves as a monitor of the society's conduct. The civic pedagogical function of the state and its legal apparatus is to educate all members of the society in these directives, thus allowing each citizen to share in a set of moral-legal assumptions. This lays such strong claims on man's developmental sense of morality and justice that the values become identified with social equilibrium. Law therefore is central to man's psyche and moral concerns. To admit this is to give law a critical place in the world view both of a culture and the individual life of its citizens. This is to say that law has the power of myth. Clearly, a mythic analysis involves more than an inquiry into a particular aspect of legal apparatus such as a constitution. Myth permeates law and mythic elements can be associated with various levels of legal phenomenology.

Myth operates at many levels within a society: the national, the familial, and the individual. Myth is the mediator between past and present and, once a culture loses sight of myth, it is disembodied from history. The classic ingredient of myth is ritual, yet increasingly contemporary Western cultures have purged ritual as they have demythologized their origins and systematized their beliefs. In current parlance "myth" has become the synonym for "the big lie," the story about the world which we know to be false. The realm of the mythic is the realm of the naive and myth is dismissed as having no real significance. Given the contemporary Western proclivity to demythologize, it may well be that ideology has become the modern replacement of myth. Legalism is the ordering principle and conservative force of Western culture. Being resistent to both change and disorder, "legalism" has corresponding mythic or ideological requirements of coherence and predictability, the two fundamental principles of "scientism."

The contesting mythic harmony in law and culture shows itself in the dramatization of conflicting or contradictory values. Drama, as a form of language and experience, is non-philosophical, operating through parable and paradox. It does not attempt to establish truth through proof and, therefore, does not behave scientifically. When the dramatic life of any society is so embedded in culture as to represent a state of normalcy, drama acquires the proportions of myth. Conversely, when mythic supremacy is undermined, it is challenged in the dramatic mode. If drama becomes too intense, complete revolution will result; one mythic structure will die and another will take its place.

Modern culture is out of touch with the dramatic modality of experiencing law. This is so because modern man finds himself depersonalized and abstracted from any relationship between himself and an extended community such as the family, or a religious congregation. His personal condition of character is so widespread that he is unable to express his defeat or accuse his tormentors. Anomie has flattered man's legal personality and political identity. In this sense, technological man is abstracted from law and its moral possibilities. For modern man law is indistinguishable from a maze of intricate bureaucratic regulations. It is rationality without life.

In his de-dramatized condition technological man invests, as a compensatory mechanism, in unaesthetic and unsatisfactory modes of communication. As his imagination is de-emphasized and his skills of efficiency are increased, he retreats further and further from dramatic expression and a personalized search for justice within a sustaining community. What he has gained in rational discourse he has lost in his sense of personhood.

The dramatic form is needed by law to create the conditions for change and to channel the resources and requirements of the imagination. When law loses its capacity to respond to these ingredients in the psychology of man and culture, it is caught in its tracks and atrophies. This can occur in mature civilizations as much as in primitive settings. When law becomes a closed system which feeds on itself and disengages from the demands of unique human experiences, it too loses its power of idealism. And, as a symbolic form of stating the higher values of civilization, loses its credibility and mass appeal.

When man finds himself dissociated from his legal-relatedness he will, before long, break out against the system and rack it asunder. When law becomes oppressive and unresponsive it, as an institution, is the target of revolutionary acts. Usually this happens when the stated values of the community, expressed mythically in its original constitutions or judicial institutions, are plainly contradicted by actual practice. Justice then requires either that the practitioners be accused or that the values or frameworks be destroyed in order that the society begin afresh.

Revolutions are the strongest examples of dramatic acts. Lesser examples are political trials and the testing in courts of changing social values such as privacy, the rights of children, the poor, and the sexually deviant.

The experience of the dramatic modality altogether is a response, on the rational plane, to man's search for personalized truth. Drama by its very definition is neither socially nor scientifically monolithic. Drama suggests a state of social disequilibrium devoid of a statement of uncontestable proof. In contrast, the mythic and scientific lives of nations carry with them equilibrium at the social level and rational propositions at the level of institutional discourse, as in law. In this sense the law is both mythic and philosophical. The rational life of law is mythic as demonstrated by its complete power as a socializing and harmonizing institution. It is the final adjudication of our shared values. In rational cultures, rational discourse is the conscious articulation of the shared values of the culture at large. The discourse is the message of the deep structure or mythic bendings of the culture.

In the ancient Near East and Asia Minor, law as an instrument of transaction, was described poetically. All types of agreements, rites, regulations, and other legal relationships worked through literary modalities. One of the most poignant illustrations in the Western tradition is the *Apology*. The dialogue is written in the classical sophistic literary form characteristic of ancient Greece. Socrates behaves like a lawyer, despite his recognition that the issues he confronts move far beyond the confines of law. Amidst his profound respect for law as a necessity of culture, we find Socrates struggling, through paradox, with the legal mythologies of his age.

The rhetorical dimension of law is the art of sophistry or persuasive reasoning. Perceived as the practical side of law, it has no general set of principles. Rhetoric lies somewhere between the rational-philosophical dimension and the ambiguity of drama. While necessary to allow a system of law to go forward in actual situations of conflict, rhetoric lacks the substance to explain the deeper implications of the pilosophical, mythic, or dramatic dimensions of law and culture.

Whether through fear of irrationality or the positive lure of the scientific paradigm, universal reason has evolved, in the West, as the antithesis to myth. The mythic, dramatic, and rhetorical dimensions of culture, and of law as a collective expression of culture, have paled into obscurity. If societal harmony is the product of the integration of world views, the unilateral evolution of scientism as a prevailing philosophy warns of serious social discord. Cohesion disappears. Law ceases to be part of an integrated theory of knowledge and experience; it becomes a splinter phenomenon which maintains the illusion that it exists in isolation from other institutions.

While universal rationality may be wrong-headed or incomplete, irrationality, though it exists in every so-called rational culture, is extremely threatening. It is clear that the equation of rationality with good and irrationality with evil in the Western theory and practice of law is uncontested. Unless there is a balance in a culture between these opposing archetypes, the culture will heat up and destroy itself. Any culture which becomes overly rationalist in concept or design is potentially dangerous. Whether the Inquisition, the Roman Empire or Nazi Germany are regarded as rational or irrational, the problem resided in the imbalance between rational and irrational forces in their cultures.

Suppose we acknowledge the fact that a rationalist philosophical representation of law is phenomonologically incorrect, that conflict can never be governed by a body of unchanging precepts. It becomes necessary to reject a theory which states that law does not change, that judges only discover the law and do not create it. Nazi and other totalitarian judges had no problem applying the law rationally and they applied it consistently. The problem with the German judicial system was that the relationship among those involved was objectified and the human content was removed. The person before the law was turned into an object of rationality.

One of the most interesting aspects of law during this century is the fact that most lawyers have no theory about what they do. Instead, they regard themselves as pragmatists. In a certain sense we have a theory without a profession and a profession without a purpose. Despite the fact that law may be viewed as a secularized theology with the lawyer as secularized high priest, many lawyers participate in legal institutions, without the remotest sense of their own or the institution's social purpose. If a church ceases to exhibit its function in society and becomes deritualized to the point where its congregation loses a sense of mystique and greater design, the institution is no longer viable. In many places throughout the world this is indeed what has happened and the same fate may well await the law. The classical image of the lawyer in Western literature is a central figure in society, a giver of order. We now have a fraternity of lawyers who do not know what the law is. They know how to lobby on behalf of a client but they lack a coherent theory about their work. Law, in this crippled state, is a pale imitation of an ordering principle of society.

In post-industrial states, legal systems are devoid of the contents of a mythic structure which is a working force within society. But we can safely distinguish the rational discourse of law from the mythologies of earlier or other cultures, making the argument that rationality is the opposing force to myth. Even if we are persuaded that law has been demythologized in the West, we must analyze the forces that have at once given law the aura of myth, and the forces that drive man back in the direction of his mythological, perhaps pre-conscious roots. Western law at its best, is a fragile artifact of history and, as a structure, is undoubtedly a high moment in man's historical creativity. Many centuries after the achievement of legal-rational discourse, man's needs on the level of the dramatic and mythic are sustained by the forces of a universal psychology. What demarcates humanness is man's profound desire for the personalizing of his self and his moral expression, through his private and public acts.

At this stage in history we should neither be impressed by man's total rationality nor by his total irrationality. Depending upon the culture his needs are variously expressed. And it is in the dialectical unfolding of the different aspects of human needs and consciousness of the mythic, dramatic, and philosophical, that the concept of law has evolved. To think of man as a unidimensional psychological figure, devoid of feelings, may in some way be the psychological error of the concept of the rational man produced by Western law. To be aware of man's multi-dimensional being may be the only avenue presently available to us in getting in touch with the historical cultural forces that reverberate through all our Western legal systems. Patriarchism, the church, familial ties, and group solidarity of many sorts continue to have their impact on the legal system, while utilizing the linguistic tools of persuasion, proof, and argument that are associated with rational law as we justify it. At this time we know of no alternative discourse to the one we have created. The important point is to acknowledge that rational law does not exist in pure form but is intertwined with culture, psychology, and history. To see this unravel may not produce answers. But it may describe a reality which we intuit in the life of the law but cannot comfortably lift to the level of consciousness. To experience dramatically the real limitations of law as a discourse is to expose the limitations of our cultural unity and ideals. We resist this at all costs for our fantasies carry us to places where the terrain is unfamiliar and foreboding. Our resistance represses our imagination but sustains a self-limiting artifact of our own doing, our rational law which makes all men equal and free before it. Is it the interpretation of this discourse with which we are dissatisfied or the vision itself? Do we wish to be born free before the law? Or at some deep level of culture and emotion are we in need of liberating ourselves from the law in order to be free? Unless world views, as reflected in cultural mythologies, are integrated, societal harmony is a dream. The task is one of restructuring history, of striking the delicate balance between rational law and psychology.

ACKNOWLEDGMENTS

The authors are grateful to The Law Foundation of British Columbia for their generous support of this project.

Acknowledgment is made for permission to reproduce extracts from the following works:

Ames, James Barr, "The Disseisin of Chattels." *Lectures on Legal History.* (Cambridge, Mass: Harvard University Press, 1913), pp. 172-191.

Aquinas, Thomas, *Summa Theologica* (Indiana: Regnery/Gateway, Inc., 1963), pp. 1-19.

Aristotle, *Ethics*, Book V, trans. J.A.K. Thompson (London: Penguin Books, 1955), pp. 157-159.

Aristotle, *Politics*, trans. Ernest Barker (Oxford: Clarendon Press, 1946), p. 146.

Attenborough, F.L., ed., "Laws of Alfred", in *The Laws of the Earliest English Kings* (Cambridge: Cambridge University Press, 1922), p. 507.

Bachofen, J.J., *Myth, Religion, and Mother Right* (New York and Princeton: Princeton University Press, 1967), pp. 75-161.

Bakan, David, *And They Took Themselves Wives* (New York: Harper & Row, 1980).

Barkun, Michael, *Law Without Sanctions* (New Haven: Yale University Press, 1968), pp. 127-132.

Bay, Christian, "From Contract to Community," in Fred R. Dallmayr, ed., *From Contract to Community* (New York: Marcel Dekker Inc., 1978), pp. 31-43.

Bay, Christian, "Hayek's Liberalism: The Constitution of Perpetual Privilege," *The Political Science Reviewer* 1 (Pennsylvania: Intercollegiate Studies Institute, 1971): 110-123.

Bell, Daniel, *The End of Ideology* (New York: The Free Press, 1962), pp. 37-42.

Bentham, Jeremy, "A Critical Examination of the Declaration of Rights," in John Bowring, ed., *The Works of Jeremy Bentham* (New York: Russell and Russell, 1962), pp. 497-503.

Bentham, Jeremy, *An Introduction to the Principles of Morals and Legislation* (New York: Hafner Publishing Co.), pp. 1-314.

Berle, A.A., "Economic Power and the Free Society," in Andrew Hacker, ed., *The Corporation Take-Over* (New York: Doubleday, 1965), pp. 86-102.

Berman, Harold J., *The Interaction of Law and Religion* (New York: Abingdon Press, 1974), pp. 52-65.

Berman, Harold J., "The Origins of Western Legal Science," *Harvard Law Review* 90 (1977): 900-931.

Black, Mr. Justice Hugo, "The Bill of Rights," in Irving Dilliard, ed., *One Man's Stand for Freedom* (New York: Alfred A. Knopf, 1963), pp. 31-48.

Blackstone, Sir William, *Blackstone's Commentaries*, vol. 1, ed. St. George Tucker (Philadelphia: Birch and Small, 1803), pp. 34-43.

Bohannan, P., *Justice and Judgment Among the Tiv* (Oxford University Press, 1957), pp. 111-112.

Bonnard, Andre, *Greek Civilization* (London: George Allen and Unwin Ltd., 1959), pp. 54-73.

Bonner, Robert, *Lawyers and Litigants in Ancient Athens* (Chicago: University of Chicago Press, 1927), pp. v-vi, 1-2.

Botsford, G.W., *The Develoment of the Athenian Constitution*, 1893 Reprint (New York: Cornell University Press, 1965), pp. 1-4.

Bracton, Henry de, *Bracton on the Laws and Customs of England*, Samuel E. Thorne, ed. (Cambridge, Mass.: Harvard University Press, 1968), pp. 305-306.

Campbell, Robert, ed., *Austin on Jurisprudence*, vol. 1 (London: John Murray, 1885), pp. 86-227.

Cassirer, Ernest, *The Myth of the State* (New Haven: Yale University Press, 1946), pp. 47-48, 53-77, 100-104, 282-295.

Ch'u, Tung-Tsu, *Law and Society in Traditional China* (The Hague, Netherlands: Mouton & Co. Publishers, 1961), pp. 20-287.

Cicero, *De Legibus*, translated by Clinton Walker Keyes (London: The Leob Classical Library (Harvard University Press: William Heinemann Ltd., 1928)), pp. 379-387.

Clarke, M.G. Lorenne, "Politics and Law: The Theory and Practice of the Ideology of Female Supremacy: Or, It Wasn't God Who Made Honky Tonk Angels," *Law and Policy*, ed. D.N. Weisstub (Toronto: Osgoode Hall Law School, 1976), pp. 37-49.

Cohen, Felix. "The Relativity of Philosophic Systems and the Method of Systematic Relativism," *The Legal Conscience: Selected Papers of Felix S. Cohen*, ed. Lucy Kramer Cohen (Hamden: Shoe String Press, 1970), pp. 95-110.

Cohen, Julius, "The Value of Value Symbols in Law," in *Essays on Jurisprudence from the Columbia Law Review* (New York: Columbia University Press, 1963), p. 332.

Coker, G.B.A., *Family Property Among the Yorubas* (London: Sweet and Maxwell Ltd., 1966), pp. 3-31, 29-34.

Denning, Alfred, Lord, *The Changing Law* (London: Stevens & Sons Ltd., 1953), pp. 99-122.

de Reincourt, Amaury, *Sex and Power in History* (New York: David McKay Company, 1974), pp. 17-87.

Derham, David P., "Theories of Legal Personality," in *Legal Personality and Political Pluralism*, ed. Leicester C. Webb (Victoria: Melbourne University Press), p. 5.

De Vaux, Roland, *Ancient Israel* (New York: McGraw-Hill Book Company, Inc., 1961), pp. 143-152.

Diamond, A.S., *Primitive Law, Past and Present* (London: Methuen & Co. Ltd., 1971), pp. 378-387.

Dicey, A.V., *Introduction to the Study of Law of the Constitution* (London: MacMillan & Co., 1959).

Djilas, M., *The New Class* (New York: Holt, Rinehart and Winston, Inc. 1957), pp. 1-170. Excerpted from *The New Class* by Milovan Djilas, © 1957 by Harcourt Brace Jovanovich, Inc. Slightly adapted and reprinted by the permission of the publisher.

Dodds, E.R., *The Greeks and the Irrational* (Berkeley: University of California Press, 1951), pp. 236-255.

Driver, G.R. and John C. Miles, eds., *The Babylonian Laws* (Oxford: Clarendon Press, 1952), p. 96.

Dworkin, Ronald, *Taking Rights Seriously* (Cambridge, Mass.: Harvard University Press, 1977), pp. 188-205.

Edwards, Chilperic, trans., *The Hammurabi Code and the Sinaitic Legislation* (Port Washington, N.Y.: Kennikat Press, 1971), pp. 29-30, 61-63, 73-76.

Elias, T. Olawale, *The Nature of African Customary Law* (Manchester: Manchester University Press, 1956), pp. 269-300.

Engels, Frederick, "Origin of the Family," in *The Woman Question* (U.S.A.: International Publishers Co., Inc., 1975), pp. 11-39.

Engnell, I., *Studies in Divine Kingship in the Ancient Near East* (Oxford: Basil Blackwell, 1967), pp. 4-16.

Eusden, J.D., *Lawyers and Politics in Early Seventeenth Century England* (New Haven: Yale University Press, 1958), pp. 1-125.

Figgis, J.V., *The Divine Right of Kings* (New York: Harper & Row, 1965), pp. 5-8.

Firth, Raymond, *Primitive Economics of the New Zealand Maori* (London: George Routledge & Sons Ltd., 1929), pp. 124-381.

Fisher, H.A.L., ed., *The Collected Papers of Frederic William Maitland*, vol. 1 (Cambridge: Cambridge University Press, 1911), p. 372.

Freeman, J.D., "On the Concept of Kindred," in *Kinship and Social Organization*, ed. Paul Bohannan and J. Middleton (Garden City, N.Y.: Natural History Press, 1968), pp. 263-266.

Freeman, Kathleen, "Legal Code and Procedure," in *The Murder of Heroes and Other Trials from the Athenian Law Courts* (New York: W.W. Norton & Company Inc., 1963), pp. 10-30.

Fromm, Erich, *Escape From Freedom* (New York: Holt, Rinehart & Winston, Inc., 1969), pp. 17-52.

Fuller, Lon. L. "Mediation — Its Forms and Functions," *Southern California Law Review* 44 (1971): 314-339.

Fuller, L.L., "Pashukanis and Vyshinsky: A Study in the Development of Marxian Legal Theory," *Michigan Law Review* 47 (1949): pp. 1159-1162.

Ganhi, M.K., *An Autobiography: The Story of My Experiments with*

Truth, trans. Mahadev Desai (Washington, D.C.: Public Affairs Press, 1948), pp. 165-168.

Golunskii, S.A. and M.S. Strogovich, "The Theory of the State and Law," trans. H.W. Babb, *Soviet Legal Philosophy* (Cambridge, Mass.: Harvard University Press, 1951), pp. 365-386.

Gouldner, Alvin W., *Enter Plato* (New York: Basic Books Inc., 1965), pp. 78-310.

Gough, J.W., *Fundamental Law in English Constitutional History* (Oxford: Clarendon Press, 1955), pp. 31-35.

Gulliver, Ashbel G., *Future Interests, American Casebook Series* (St. Paul, Minnesota: West Pub. Co., 1959), pp. 36-196.

Guth, De Lloyd J., "The Age of Debt, the Reformation and English Law," *Tudor Rule and Revolution: Essays for G.R. Elton From His American Friends,* ed. D.J. Guth and J.W. McKenna (N.Y.: Cambridge University Press, 1982), pp. 70-85.

Hansen, M.H., *The Sovereignty of the People's Court in Athens in the Fourth Century B.C. and the Public Action Against Unconstitutional Proposals* (Odense: Odense University Press, 1974), pp. 10-59.

Hart, H.L.A., "Law in the Perspective of Philosophy: 1776-1976," *New York University Law Review* 51 (1976): 538-551.

Havelock, Eric A., *The Liberal Temper in Greek Politics* (London: Jonathan Cape, 1957), pp. 379-403.

Hayek, Friedrich, *The Constitution of Liberty* (Chicago: The University of Chicago Press, 1960), pp. 54-175.

Hayek, Friedrich, *Law, Legislation and Liberty*, vol. 1 (Chicago: The University of Chicago Press, 1973), pp. 8-95.

Hertz, J.H., ed., *The Pentateuch and Haftorahs* (London: Oxford University Press, 1956).

Heschel, Abraham J., *The Prophets* (New York: Harper & Row, 1962), pp. 195-230.

Highwater, Jamake, *The Primal Mind* (New York: Harper & Row, 1981), pp. 18-19.

James, E.O., *The Cult of the Mother-Goddess* (London: Thames and Hudson, 1959), pp. 228-230.

Jolowicz, H.F., and B. Nicholas, *Historical Introduction to the Study of Roman Law*, 2nd ed. (Cambridge: Cambridge University Press, 1952), pp. 161-165.

Jones, J. Walter, *The Law and Legal Theory of the Greeks* (London: Oxford University Press, 1956), pp. 228, 293.

Kagan, Donald D., *The Great Dialogue: History of Greek Political Thought from Homer to Polybius* (New York: The Free Press, 1965), pp. 73-90.

Kasulis, Thomas T., "References and Symbol in Plato's *Cratylus* and Kukai's *Shojijissogi,*" *Philosophy East and West* 32 (1982): 404-405. Reprinted from *Philosophy East and West* by permission of the University of Hawaii Press.

Katz, Milton, *Government Under Law and the Individual* (American Council of Learned Societies, 1957), pp. 2-13.

Kaufmann, Y., *The Religion of Israel*, trans. Moshe Greenberg (Chicago: The University of Chicago Press, 1960), pp. 316-340.

Kenyon, J.P., ed., "James I on Monarchy: Speech to Parliament," in *The Stuart Constitution* (Cambridge: Cambridge University Press, 1966).

Kierkegaard, Soren, *Fear and Trembling and the Sickness unto Death*, trans. Walter Lowrie (Princeton: Princeton University Press, 1941), pp. 69-71.

Kline, Morris, *Mathematics in Western Culture* (New York: Oxford University Press, 1954), pp. 24-34.

Knox, T.M., trans., *Hegel's Philosophy of Right* (London: Oxford University Press, 1942), pp. 155-281.

Kocourek, Albert, and John H. Wigmore, *Evolution of Law Series: Sources of Ancient and Primitive Law*, vol. 1 (Boston: Little, Brown & Co., 1915), pp. 542-543.

Kocourek, Albert, and John H. Wigmore, eds., "The Lex Salica," in *Primitive and Ancient Legal Institutions*, vol. 1 (Boston: Little, Brown & Co., 1915), p. 507.

Kuhn, Thomas S., *The Structure of Scientific Revolutions*, 2nd ed. (Chicago: The University of Chicago Press, 1970), pp. 138-156.

Laslett, Peter, ed., *Patriarcha and Other Political Works of Sir Robert Filmer* (Oxford: Basil Blackwell, 1949), pp. 20-26, 57-229.

Lawson, F.H., *A Common Law Lawyer Looks at the Civil Law* (Ann Arbor: University of Michigan Law School, 1953), pp. 91-101.

Lawson, F.H., "The Creative Use of Legal Concepts," *New York University Law Review* 32 (1957): 913-916.

Lawson, F.H., *The Rational Strength of English Law* (London: Stevens & Sons Ltd., 1951), p. 79.

Lenin, V.I., *The State and Revolution* (Peking: Foreign Language Press, 1970), pp. 100-112.

Lenin, V.I., "Women and Society," in *The Woman Question* (U.S.A.: International Publishers Co. Inc., 1975), p. 52.

Marx, Karl, "The Materialist Conception of History," in T. Bottomore, trans., *Karl Marx* (New York: McGraw-Hill Book Co., 1956), pp. 51-227.

Marx, Karl, "On the Jewish Question," in David McLellan, ed. and trans., *Karl Marx Early Texts* (Oxford: Blackwell, 1971), pp. 104-108.

McIlwain, Charles H., *The High Court of Parliament* (New Haven: Yale University Press, 1910), pp. 109-166.

Miquel, Juan, "Stoic Logic and Roman Jurisprudence," trans. George H. Kendal, *Zeitschrift Der Savigny Stiftung für Rechtsgeschichte Romanistische Abteilung* 87 (1970): 85-122.

Morgan, Robin, ed., *Sisterhood is Powerful* (New York: Random House, 1970), pp. 31-36.

Muller, F. Max, ed., G. Buhler, trans., "The Laws of Manu," in *The Sacred Books of the East*, vol. 25 (Delhi: Motilal Banarsidass, 1967), pp. 1-217, 262-293, 301-304.

Nenner, Howard, *By Colour of Law* (Chicago: The University of Chicago Press, 1977), pp. ix-xi.

The New English Bible: The New Testament, 2nd ed. (Oxford and Cambridge: Oxford University Press, and Cambridge University Press, 1970).

Noda, Yosiyuki, "The Character of the Japanese People and their Conception of Law," in H. Tanaka, ed., *The Japanese Legal System* (University of Tokyo Press, 1976), pp. 301-310.

Northrop, F.S.C., "The Comparative Philosophy of Comparative Law," *Cornell Quarterly* 45 (1960): 617-658.

Northrop, F.S.C., *The Complexity of Legal and Ethical Experience* (Boston: Little, Brown and Company, 1959), pp. 177-221.

Nozick, Robert, *Anarchy, State, and Utopia*, (New York: Basic Books, Inc., 1974), pp. 4-5, 26-27, 51-53, 83, 113-115, and 119.

Oates, Whitney, "Discourses of Epictetus" and "Marcus Aurelius, Meditations," in *The Stoic and Epicurean Philosophers* (New York: Random House, 1940), pp. 243-294, 498-563.

Okin, S.M., *Women in Western Political Thought* (Princeton: Princeton University Press, 1979), pp. 5-9, 285-287, and 298-302.

Pashukanis, E.B., "The General Theory of Law and Marxism," *Soviet Legal Philosophy*, trans. H.W. Babb (Cambridge, Mass.: Harvard University Press, 1951), pp. 193-201.

Perry, J.W., *Lord of the Four Quarters: Myths of the Royal Father* (New York: George Braziller, Inc., 1966), pp. 3-18.

Plato, *The Apology*, trans. F.J. Church (New York: The Liberal Arts Press, 1948), pp. 34-37.

Plato, *Crito*, trans. F.J. Church (New York: The Liberal Arts Press, 1948), pp. 52-65.

Plato, *The Laws*, trans. A.E. Taylor (London: J.M. Dent & Sons, 1960), p. 1.

Pollock, Sir Frederick, and F.W. Maitland, *The History of the English Law* (Cambridge: Cambridge University Press, 1968), vol. 1, pp. 111-112, 232-233; vol. 2, pp. 29-38, 157-158, 184.

Pomeroy, Sarah B., *Goddesses, Whores, Wives and Slaves: Women in Classical Antiquity* (New York: Schocken Books, 1975), pp. 57-87. Copyright 1975. Sarah B. Pomeroy. Reprinted by permission of Schocken Books.

Post, E., trans., *The Institutes of Roman Law by Gaius*, 4th ed. (London: Oxford University Press, 1925), pp. 442-443.

Randall, J.H., *Hellenistic Ways of Deliverance and the Making of the Christian Synthesis* (New York: Columbia University Press, 1970), pp. 137-155.

Rawls, John, *A Theory of Justice* (Cambridge, Mass.: Harvard University Press, 1971), pp. 11-303.

Redfield, Robert, "Maine's Ancient Law in the Light of Primitive Societies," *The Western Political Quarterly* 3 (1950): 586-589.

Richardson, H.G., and G.O. Sayles, *Select Cases of Procedure Without Writ Under Henry III*, Vol. 40, Selden Society (London: Quaritch Pub., 1941), p. 25.

Sabine, George H., *A History of Political Theory* (New York: Holt, Rinehart & Winston, Inc., 1937), pp. 163-173.

Sambursky, S., *The Physical World of the Greeks* (London: Routledge & Kegan Paul Ltd., 1956, 1962), pp. 18-21.

Sambursky, S., "Structural and Dynamic Elements in the Greek Conception of Physical Reality," in Northrup and Livingston, eds., *Cross-Cultural Understanding* (New York: Wenner-Green Foundation, 1964), pp. 30-252.

Schulz, Fritz, *History of Roman Legal Science* (London: Oxford University Press, 1946), pp. 39-86.

Schulz, Fritz, *Principles of Roman Law* (London: Oxford University Press, 1936), pp. 6-161.

Scott, S.P., trans., "The Digests or Pandects," in *The Civil Law* (New York: AMS Press, 1973), pp. 279-283.

Scott, S.P., trans., "The Institutes of Gaius," in *The Civil Law* (New York: AMS Press, 1973), pp. 162-163.

Scott, S.P., trans., "The Laws of the Twelve Tables," in *The Civil Law* (New York: AMS Press, 1973), pp. 58-65.

Scott, S.P., trans., "The Opinions of Julius Paulus," in *The Civil Law* (New York: AMS Press, 1973), p. 259.

Scott, S.P., trans., "The Rules of Ulpian," in *The Civil Law* (New York: AMS Press, 1973), pp. 238-239.

Selden, John, *Table Talk*, ed. Pollock (London: Quaritch Press, 1927), pp. 157-158.

Shanks, E., ed., *Novae Narrationes*, Selden Society (London: Quaritch Pub. Co., 1963), p. 109.

Smith, J.C., "The Concept of Native Title," *University of Toronto Law Journal* 24 (1974): 1.

Smith, J.C., "The Theoretical Constructs of Western Contractual Law," in *Cross Cultural Understanding*, Northrop and Livingston (New York: Harper & Row, 1964), pp. 263-266.

Smith, J.C., "The Unique Nature of the Concept of Western Law," *Canadian Bar Review* 46 (May, 1968): 198-207.

Smith, Norman, *Maori Land Law* (Wellington: A.H. & A.W. Reed, 1960), pp. 94-96.

Lubman, Stanley, "Mao and Mediation: Politics and Dispute Resolution in Communist China," *California Law Review*, 55 (1967): 1289-1297.

Stein, Peter, *Roman Law and English Jurisprudence Yesterday and Today* (Cambridge: University Press, 1969).

Steiner, George, *In Bluebeard's Castle: Some Notes Towards the Redefinition of Culture* (New Haven: Yale University Press, 1971), pp. 42-56.

Stone, Julius, *Human Law and Human Justice* (Sidney: Maitland Publications Pty. Ltd., 1965), p. 18.

Stone, Merlin, *When God Was a Woman* (London: Sidgwick and Jackson, 1978), pp. xi-xiii, 196-197.

Sullerot, Evelyne, *Woman, Society, and Change* (New York: McGraw-Hill Book Co., World University Library, 1971), pp. 19-28.

Sumner Maine, Sir Henry, *Ancient Law* (London: Oxford University Press, reprinted 1959, copyright 1861), pp. 149-229.

Thomas, J.A.C., trans., *The Institutes of Justinian* (Cape Town: Juta and Company, 1975), pp. 2-5, pp. 65-66, pp. 84-85, pp. 87-90.

Tierney, Brian, "Bracton on Government" *Speculum* (1963): 295 in *Church Law and Constitutional Thought in the Middle Ages* (London: Variorum Reprints, 1979), iv.

Tierney, Brian, "The Prince Is Not Bound by the Laws: Accursius and Origins of the Modern State," Comparative Studies in Society and History 5 (1963): 378 in *Church Law and Constitutional Thought in the Middle Ages* (London: Variorum Reprints, 1979), III.

Tucker, Robert, *Philosophy and Myth in Karl Marx*, 2nd ed. (Cambridge: Cambridge University Press, 1972), pp. 218-232.

Ullmann, Walter, "Juristic Obstacles to the Emergence of the Concept of the State in the Middle Ages," *Annali di storia del diritto* (Studi in memoria Francesco Calasso) 13 (1969): 43, in *The Church and the Law in the Earlier Middle Ages* (London: Variorum Reprints, 1975), xii.

Unger, R.M., *Law in Modern Society* (New York: The Free Press, 1976), pp. 192-203.

Vinogradoff, Sir Paul, "Outlines of Historical Jurisprudence," vol. 2, *The Jurisprudence of the Greek City* (London: Oxford University Press, 1922), pp. 11-12.

Vyshinsky, Andrei, *The Law of the Soviet State* (New York: MacMillan and Co., 1954), pp. 5-8.

Westrup, C.W., *Introduction to Early Roman Law, Patria Potestas*, vol. 3, book 2 (London: Oxford University Press, 1939), pp. 143-186.

Whitehead, Alfred North, *Modes of Thought* (New York: The Free Press, 1969), pp. 41-63.

Wolff, Hans Julius, *Roman Law* (Norman: University of Oklahoma Press, 1951), pp. 3-166.

Wolff, Robert Paul, *In Defense of Anarchism* (New York: Harper & Row, 1970), pp. 3-72.

Wollstonecraft, Mary, *A Vindication of the Rights of Woman,* 1972, ed. Miriam Kramnick (London: Penguin Books Ltd., 1975), pp. 79-92.

Every effort has been made to contact authors and publishers to obtain permissions. If the publisher is made aware of any errors which may have been made in obtaining permissions, the publisher will take steps to ensure that proper credit be given at that time.

TABLE OF CONTENTS

CHAPTER I

LAW AND CULTURE

Legal systems emerge from cultural contexts and, depending on the period of history and the specific set of social relations, law codes and legal regulations assume distinctive forms. It is not surprising then that the laws of ancient India and classical Rome contributed to different social orders. In categorizing legal systems it is important to realize at the outset that law is a seminal institution in any given culture and that, therefore, in unpacking the cultural contours of a civilization we may hope to detect relations between the world view of that culture and its concepts of law. Neither anthropologists nor philosophers, in approaching this issue, have created entirely satisfactory tools for assessing the conflicting models that have occurred. The old debate whether tribal societies contain embryonic forms of more mature legal systems or whether they are inherently different continues to plague legal commentators. There is something disturbing about approaching legal systems with an analytical framework that is even covertly culturebound. And yet what appear to be neutral scientific measures of assessment may be added to the list of culturally determined models of analysis. Whatever the outcome of this problem, it is still possible to earmark a number of broad legal categories which distinguish "status" and "contract" systems of law. With this rough tool in hand, historical connections may be made among tribal, Eastern, and Western legal traditions.

There are, however, deeper questions to be raised. What is the relationship between the world view of a culture and its process of dispute resolution, apart from its emphasis on a particular sort of ordering ? Or, can the two ever be separated ? Even where certain societies share readily observable traits in common, such as kinship systems for the resolution of conflict, further differentiations may be made between matriarchal and patriarchal societies. Status systems become highly particularized. Tribal and Eastern societies may both share well-defined kinship structures, but, whereas tribal societies have functioned without codes, Eastern societies have produced them over time, albeit regarding them as inferior to mediation as a method of dispute resolution. The staunchly patriarchal systems of the ancient Mediterranean world also reveal social ordering based on status, but they developed systems of law which, apart from status aspects, produced unique criteria for adjudication.

The Western view, for the most part, has been to regard the Greco-Roman synthesis as a superior form of law. This is so because status systems predetermine the content of law according to such factors as lineage and sex, whereas the scientific legal systems of the West have, in theory, provided the tools for the Western concept of the individual man with his attendant legal rights and obligations.

Not all cultures have responded to disorder and chaos in the universe with the same predilection for rationality. In the East the non-rational world view was incorporated into a status system of law, a system which downplayed the role of fundamental rights and the need for a professional body of legal experts trained to apply general principles to concrete situations. In the West, by contrast, lawyering tools were manufactured whose purpose was to put into effect rational legal constructs only secondarily associated with genealogical status. There has been considerable reversion to status in determining the nature of rights in Western legal systems. Nonetheless, we must keep in mind that in the history of cultures fundamentally different world views have given rise to different principles of legal ordering.

Deficiencies in aspects of Western property and contract law are current objects of frustration. Legal procedures and concepts have become so rarified that commentators have condemned Western law, in retrospect, as amounting to nothing more than an elaborate defence of the status quo. Not only have the rights of orphan and widow paled beside those of corporation owners in Western legal economics, but massive webs of social and economic power have also been erected by complicated structures affecting business planning and property holding. These webs appear to surpass the social milieu of even tribal societies for rigidity. Technical law in the West, furthermore, has contributed to alienation within the context of large so-called rationalist bureaucracies. The individual may sense himself as having been cast into the role of passive observer of a pre-determined order of status relationships which are awesome and overpowering.

In this period of frustration Western societies have begun to experiment with techniques of conflict resolution such as mediation and conciliation which historically have been identified with tribal or Eastern societies. Similarly, kinship societies which have undergone sudden industrialization are turning to Western law to manage their wealth and changing social hierarchy. The implications of this legal transmigration are still unclear because we remain unaware of the causal relations between world views and legal forms. Costs, no doubt, will be incurred in the struggle. Kinship or patriarchal societies may want to adopt Western science and technology but may wish to reject some of the assumptions inherent in Western law, for example, notions of liberty and equality. If indeed these notions are fundamental, will the adoption of Western law in the area of commercial relations threaten the political fabric of these cultures and result in certain movements towards the Western models of government and legal ordering ? Similarly, when Western legal systems exhume mediation to remedy the deficiencies of precedent law in such areas as labour and matrimonial relations, will we begin to see an erosion not only of the tools but also of some long-standing assumptions about the nature of rational law and its capacity for organizing rights and obligations in complex industrial societies ? There are many who cling to the view that the problems with Western law lie in the distortions and misapplications of its ideals and principles. Other critics see law, whatever its structure, as the vehicle through which the most conservative set of status relations in a given culture is enforced.

What then is the world view which we share in industrial and post-industrial cultures ? The fact that certain scientific concepts or paradigms have come forward in history is, to some extent, reflected in the Western legal paradigm. But there is little evidence that man's rationality and his social institutions have been collectively integrated in even the most civilized of the Western societies. The dimensions of the interrelationship between legal theory and scientific knowledge have been of considerable concern to Western legal theorists. Scientific paradigms have altered dramatically as have our legal ways and concepts. Despite the fact that we may proceed with the overriding concept of rational law, it is hard to see that law, as a social institution, can direct itself according to scientific method. This is so because law is vulnerable to the psychological presuppositions of the decisionmaker who is called upon to react to conflict. Few would assert that the science of law is as exact and separable from psychology as the science of physics or mathematics.

The forms of Western law and other representative systems reflect aspects of the human condition which are connected to deeply rooted psychological needs and experiences. Whereas, arguably, scientific paradigms can be applied in pure form, legal paradigms often function alongside, or in relation to, conflicting views. That is, kinship and patriarchy are mixed with rationality in legal experiences at the levels of profession, institution, and theory. We are left with the realization that psychological explanations may best account for the historical differentiations which have occurred in law and which persist despite the availability of theories about the nature of law as a rational body of precepts. Perhaps we should not demand perfect rationality in phenomena which are fraught with non-rational or irrational content. Through its very embodiment of cultural world views, does law not thereby compromise its neutral or universal rationality ? From the standpoint of man's psychological condition and the history of world culture, the "rational world view" may be a misnomer.

Ultimately man's rationality is no more compelling than man's rational law or his rational culture. To see the matter otherwise is to avoid learning the lessons of comparative psychology and anthropology. There are serious differences among persons, societies, and cultures. But, more importantly, we must recognize the power of culture and psychology in dictating the direction of man's social and legal conduct. Why man fails in his rationality is the pressing issue of advanced civilizations. In exploring the non-rational or mythological we may come closer to understanding the depth of this question and possibly be better able to answer man's legal needs.

Western law will only survive if it can incorporate both the human desire for personalized justice and the view that the preservation of justice must be based on a definition of person as free and independent agent. Such a synthesis has never been properly attempted except in a manner which has denied "status" or distorted the principles of "rational justice."

In looking at the paradigms of Western law we must attempt to think of new models which respond to human and cultural needs. The balancing of these needs is psychologically turbulent and law, in its present form, may be unable to meet the challenge. If so the very notion of law, to which we are presently committed, may be radically transformed over the next millenium, just as the Greco-Roman and Judaic traditions of law represented quantum leaps over previous paradigms.

THE STRUCTURE OF SCIENTIFIC REVOLUTION[1]

Thomas S. Kuhn

Scientists are not, of course, the only group that tends to see its discipline's past developing linearly toward its present vantage. The temptation to write history backward is both omnipresent and perennial. But scientists are more affected by the temptation to rewrite history, partly because the results of scientific research show no obvious dependence upon the historical context of the inquiry, and partly because, except during crisis and revolution, the scientist's contemporary position seems so secure. More historical detail, whether of science's present or of its past, or more responsibility to the historical details that are presented, could only give artificial status to human idiosyncrasy, error, and confusion. Why dignify what science's best and most persistent efforts have made it possible to discard ? The depreciation of historical fact is deeply, and probably functionally, ingrained in the ideology of the scientific profession, the same profession that places the highest of all values upon factual details of other sorts. Whitehead caught the unhistorical spirit of the scientific community when he wrote, "A science that hesitates to forget its founders is lost." Yet he was not quite right, for the sciences, like other professional enterprises, do need their heroes and do preserve their names. Fortunately, instead of forgetting these heroes, scientists have been able to forget or revise their works.

The result is a persistent tendency to make the history of science look linear or cumulative, a tendency that even affects scientists looking back at their own research....

But that is not the way a science develops. Many of the puzzles of contemporary normal science did not exist until after the most recent scientific revolution. Very few of them can be traced back to the historic beginning of the science within which they now occur. Earlier generations pursued their own problems with their own instruments and their own canons of solution. Nor is it just the problems that have changed. Rather the whole network of fact and theory that the textbook paradigm fits to nature has shifted....

Those theories, of course, do "fit the facts," but only by transforming previously accessible information into facts that, for the preceding paradigm, had not existed at all. And that means that theories too do not evolve piecemeal to fit facts that were there all the time. Rather, they emerge together with the facts they fit from a revolutionary reformulation of the preceding scientific tradition, a tradition within which the knowledge-mediated relationship between the scientist and nature was not quite the same.... [pp. 138-141]

. . . Since new paradigms are born from old ones, they ordinarily incorporate much of the vocabulary and apparatus, both conceptual and manipulative, that the traditional paradigm had previously employed. But they seldom employ these borrowed elements in quite the traditional way. Within the new paradigm, old terms, concepts and experiments fall into new relationships one with the other. The inevitable result is what we must call, though the term is not quite right, a misunderstanding between the two competing schools. [p. 149]

. . . Practicing in different worlds, the two groups of scientists see different things when they look from the same point in the same direction. Again, that is not to say that they can see anything they please. Both are looking at the world, and what they look at has not changed. But in some areas they see different things, and they see them in different relations one to the other. That is why a law that cannot even be demonstrated to one group of scientists may occasionally seem intuitively obvious to another. Equally, it is why, before they can hope to communicate fully, one group or the other must experience the conversion that we have been calling a paradigm shift. Just because it is a transition between incommensurables, the transition between competing paradigms cannot be made a step at a time, forced by logic and neutral experience. Like the gestalt switch, it must occur all at once (though not necessarily in an instant) or not at all.

How, then, are scientists brought to make this transposition ? Part of the answer is that they are very often not. Copernicanism made few converts for almost a century after Copernicus' death. Newton's work was not generally accepted, particularly on the Continent, for more than half a century after the *Principia* appeared. Priestley never accepted the oxygen theory, nor Lord Kelvin the electromagnetic theory, and so on. The difficulties of conversion have often been noted by scientists themselves. Darwin, in a particularly perceptive passage at the end of his *Origin of Species*, wrote : "Although I am fully convinced of the truth of the views given in this volume, ... I by no means expect to convince experienced naturalists whose minds are stocked with a multitude of facts all viewed, during a long course of years, from a point of view directly opposite to mine... [B]ut I look with confidence to the future, — to young and rising naturalists, who will be able to view both sides of the question with impartiality."[2] And Max Planck, surveying his own career in his *Scientific Autobiography*, sadly remarked that "a new scientific truth does not triumph by convincing its opponents and making them see the light, but rather because its opponents eventually die, and a new generation grows up that is familiar with it."[3]

These facts and others like them are too commonly known to need further emphasis. But they do need re-evaluation. In the past they have most often been taken to indicate that scientists, being only human, cannot always admit their errors, even when confronted with strict proof. I would argue, rather, that in these matters neither proof nor error is at issue. The transfer of allegiance from paradigm to paradigm is a conversion experience that cannot be forced. Lifelong resistance, particularly from those whose productive careers have committed them to an older tradition of normal science, is not a violation of scientific standards but an index to the nature of scientific research itself. The source of resistance is the assurance that the older paradigm will ultimately solve all its problems, that nature can be shoved into the box the paradigm provides. Inevitably, at times of revolution, that assurance seems stubborn and pigheaded as indeed it sometimes becomes. But it is also something more. That same assurance is what makes normal or puzzle-solving science possible. And it is only through normal science that the professional community of scientists succeeds, first, in exploiting the potential scope and precision of the older paradigm and, then, in isolating the difficulty through the study of which a new paradigm may emerge.... [pp. 150-152]

Probably the single most prevalent claim advanced by the proponents of a new paradigm is that they can solve the problems that have led the old one to a crisis. When it can legitimately be made, this claim is often the most effective one possible. In the area for which it is advanced the paradigm is known to be in trouble. That trouble has repeatedly been explored, and attempts to remove it have again and again proved vain. "Crucial experiments" — those able to discriminate particularly sharply between the two paradigms — have been recognized and attested before the new paradigm was even invented. Copernicus thus claimed that he had solved the long-vexing problem of the length of the calendar year, Newton that he had reconciled terrestrial and celestial mechanics, Lavoisier that he had solved the problems of gas-identity and of weight relations, and Einstein that he had made electrodynamics compatible with a revised science of motion.... [p. 153]

All the arguments for a new paradigm discussed so far have been based upon the competitors' comparative ability to solve problems. To scientists those arguments are ordinarily the most significant and persuasive. The preceding examples should leave no doubt about the source of their immense appeal. But, for reasons to which we shall shortly revert, they are neither individually nor collectively compelling. Fortunately, there is also another sort of consideration that can lead scientists to reject an old paradigm in favour of a new. These are the arguments, rarely made entirely explicit, that appeal to the individual's sense of the appropriate or the aesthetic — the new theory is said to be "neater," "more suitable," or "simpler" than the old. Probably such arguments are less effective in the sciences than in mathematics. The early versions of most new paradigms are crude. By the time their full aesthetic appeal can be developed, most of the community has been persuaded by other means. Nevertheless, the importance of aesthetic considerations can sometimes be decisive. Though they often attract only a few scientists to a new theory, it is upon those few that its ultimate triumph may depend. If they had not quickly taken it up for highly individual reasons, the new candidate for paradigm might never have been sufficiently developed to attract the allegiance of the scientific community as a whole. [pp. 155-156]

NOTES

1. Thomas S. Kuhn, *The Structure of Scientific Revolutions*, 2nd ed. (Chicago : University of Chicago Press, 1970), pp. 138-156.

2. Charles Darwin, *Origin of Species*, 6th ed., vol. 2 (New York : 1889), pp. 295-296.

3. Max Planck, *Scientific Autobiography and Other Papers*, trans. F. Gaynor (New York : 1949), pp. 33-34.

MODES OF THOUGHT[1]

Alfred North Whitehead

The specialization which is necessary for the development of civilized thought had in the last century a most unfortunate effect on the philosophic outlook of learned people, and thence on the development of institutions for the promotion of learning. The various departments of universities emphasized their independence of each other. Also a university gained reputation in proportion to its expansion in terms of such subdivision.

As science grew, minds shrank in width of comprehension. The nineteenth century was a period of great achievement, suggestive of an anthill. It failed to produce men of learning with a sensitive appreciation of varieties of interest, of varieties of potentiality. It criticized and exploded, where it should have striven to understand. The detailed setting of its interest is, in every age, a crude mixture of depth of understanding and of triviality of setting, when looked at from beyond that age. And yet to understand the nature of existence, we must grasp the essential character of that depth which, beyond all mistaken details, is the mainspring of the ascent of life discernible in its own age. And here another qualification must be added, namely — If ascent there be.

The very Renaissance itself, of which the last century was the final phase in the agonies of begetting its successor, carried in itself limitations which obstructed the proper expansion of intellectual interest. It was rooted in Greek learning, conceived as the only begetter of civilization. Undoubtedly, the debt of Europe to Greece is beyond words to express. But, after all, Grecian thought, even when expanded into Greek-Hebrew-Egyptian thought, only presents one finite aspect of the many-sided modes of importance which are pressing upon the outskirts of human consciousness.

We must enlarge our effort at understanding. In the nineteenth century, the Greek scholars were somewhat narrower than the best of the Greeks, the Christian scholars were somewhat narrower than the best of the early Popes, and the men of science were somewhat narrower than the founders of the study of mathematics and of physical science. The nineteenth century in the aggregate knew immeasurably more than the Greeks, and the Popes, and the founders of science, all put together. But the moderns had lost the sense of vast alternatives, magnificent or hateful, lurking in the background, and awaiting to overwhelm our safe little traditions. If civilization is to survive, the expansion of understanding is a prime necessity.... [pp. 44-45]

There is one moral to be drawn. Apart from detail, and apart from systems, a philosophic outlook is the very foundation of thought and of life. The sort of ideas we attend to, and the sort of ideas which we push into the negligible background, govern our hopes, our fears, our control of behaviour. As we think, we live. This is why the assemblage of philosophic ideas is more than a specialist study. It moulds our type of civilization. [p. 63]

NOTE

1. Alfred North Whitehead, *Modes of Thought* (New York : The Macmillan Company, The Free Press, 1969), pp. 44-63.

THE VALUE OF VALUE SYMBOLS IN LAW[1]

Julius Cohen

The utilization of symbolic constructs is common to the disciplines of both scientist and lawyer. To be sure, there is a vast difference, on the one hand, between such constructs as energy, mass, motion, space and acceleration, and, say, negligence, proximate cause, property and due process, on the other. But the difference is not in the fact of their use but in the nature of the use to which they are put. The scientist builds his structures on hypothetical, symbolic elements, hoping ultimately to translate them into propositions that correspond to events observable by direct sense experience. The end he seeks is the establishment of reliable *is* or *fact* judgments. The lawyer starts with facts, especially as they have a bearing on human relationships in society, but the end he seeks is the imposition of *ought* or *normative* judgments concerning them. The symbols that he utilizes, though they relate to facts, are value-charged. Their purpose is evaluative and incitive ; they are the means of deciding between competing claims of individuals or groups in society. Unlike the symbols of science, they are not instruments for discovering ; rather they are, in the main, instruments for ordering, for creating. Their primary use is not as a means of seeking answers to the mysteries of nature, but rather as one of maintaining or changing human relationships in society. They are in brief, value symbols.... [p. 332]

NOTE

1. Julius Cohen, "The Value of Value Symbols in Law," in *Essays on Jurisprudence from the Columbia Law Review* (New York : Columbia University Press, 1963), p. 332.

THE PRIMAL MIND[1]

Jamake Highwater

An examination of Western anthropology and archaeology reveals the numerous ways in which Western people have conceived of themselves in relation to other peoples and how they have devised an image of progress placing themselves at the pinnacle of creation. This viewpoint has had a very important impact upon the dominant culture's evaluation of the various "pagans" and "barbarians" encountered during wide-flung explorations beyond the very narrow boundaries of its European homelands.

This consensus established a highly ethnocentric anthropological error : the farther back in the "ancestral cave" you live the more "primitive" you are and, therefore, the more lowly by comparison to the white male who places himself at the crown of creation. It is immediately clear how readily this error has served the political and economic aggressiveness of the West.

Though this theory of evolution has been abandoned in most professional circles, it persists as a prevalent conviction of lay people and is so subtly and deeply rooted in an unconscious racism that it ideally condones the tendency in the West to measure all things by the very high regard the dominant world has of itself.....[pp. 18-19]

NOTE

1. Jamake Highwater, *The Primal Mind* (New York : Harper & Row, 1981), pp. 18-19.

REFERENCE AND SYMBOL IN PLATO AND KUKAI[1]

Thomas P. Kasulis

The assumption that people in different cultures actually think differently in some inherent way is untenable.....[T]he difference among traditions derives not from variance in inherent thinking patterns, but from differences in what is thought *about*...

In summation, there is no *prima facie* reason to abandon the hypothesis that the logical form of rationality is the same around the world. Rather, the divergence between cultures lies in the traditional concerns of rationality, and therefore, the experiences to which logic is applied. Human experience is too complex to be analyzed all at once. A tradition must be selective, choosing certain points to be examined first and others deferred until some later time. But once the initial topics are chosen, their complexity leads to ever further analysis and enrichment. New terms are developed and the answer to one question carries in its wake the beginnings of the next question. A tradition seldom has the leisure to return to those experiences initially bracketed from consideration. At the same time, in each culture certain forms of human experience come to be understood as being particularly profound or revealing. The experiences even become intensified as they are self-consciously named and analyzed. In short, each culture specializes, as it were, in the cultivation and analysis of particular human possibilities. This is why intellectual traditions diverge as much as they do.

NOTE

1. Thomas P. Kasulis, "Reference and symbol in Plato's *Cratylus* and Kukai's, *Shojijissogi*", *Philosophy East and West* 32, (1982) : 404-405.

THE RELATIVITY OF PHILOSOPHICAL SYSTEMS AND THE METHOD OF SYSTEMATIC RELATIVISM[1]

Felix Cohen

The thesis which I wish to defend is that....statements which, if made within the same system, would be incompatible propositions, may be both true in two different but compatible systems, and may even be identical within two such systems. [p.96]

The Relativity of Philosophic Systems

We may perhaps find some light on the interrelations of philosophic systems if we consider the field in which rational system-making has had its longest career, that is, the field of geometry. Euclid himself used a great many terms for which no rigorous definitions were offered. The euclidean geometry has been restated in more adequate form by Hilbert, who uses only five undefined terms, *point, straight line, plane, between, congruent.*[2] The mathematician Veblen has succeeded in reducing the number of undefined terms in euclidean geometry to two, namely, *point* and *order.*[3] In Veblen's system of euclidean geometry, lines, angles, circles, and all the other elements of euclidean geometry are logical constructs of *point* and *order.* The mathematician Huntington has formulated a system of euclidean geometry in which the only geometric elements which are undefined are *sphere* and *inclusion.*[4]

Suppose now that certain bad manners that obtain among philosophers were taken over by geometricians. Each of these system-makers would feel constrained to assert that the geometrical world in reality consists of the basic concepts which are the starting points of his system. Each system-maker would show that the terms used as starting points by other system-makers are not in reality basic, and can be analyzed and explained in terms of his own basic concepts. Our bad-mannered geometrician might go on to argue that each rival system puts the cart before the horse, or stands the world on its head, or runs into a vicious circle, because it assumes as postulates propositions which presuppose the very theorems they are designed to prove, and which, in his own system, are derived and deduced from those theorems. From all of which our bad-mannered geometrician would conclude that the crisis in contemporary geometry is the result of not looking at first principles first and thus failing to see that in reality the world of space consists of points and order or of spheres and inclusion or some other sufficient set of geometric elements.

In fact, however, we find that geometricians who have elaborated different systems of euclidean geometry are perfectly willing to recognize the logical equivalence of these systems. Formulae of translation have been worked out which permit any proposition in one of these systems to be equated with some proposition in any of the other equivalent systems.

Can the same principle of logical tolerance be applied to the diversity of philosophic systems?

I believe that this question is to be answered in the affirmative. Let me say at the outset, however, that I cannot offer a rigorous proof of this thesis....

From the standpoint of the natural history of philosophies we may trace the growth of philosophic systems along the line of development that recurs again and again. In the beginnings is the idea that gives a system its distinctive character and importance. Applied to some current problem or to some field of experience the idea enlightens us. A broader formulation or application of the idea is attempted. Facts appear that do not conform to the scheme. For a time these facts may be ignored or bent to fit the idea. But at some point this becomes impossible. The idea is revised to take account of the new facts. As systems grow more inclusive they tend to incorporate more and more qualifications. In this manner divergent systems tend to approximate each other as they grow more inclusive. A philosophy of aesthetics, if it treats of the narrow realm of life in studios, museums, and concert halls, may have no relevance to other branches of philosophy, but if the field of aesthetics is viewed in broader proportions, as Kant viewed it, covering the entire field of perceptual experience, then a doctrine that covers that field must be vitally relevant to the problems of epistemology, ethics, and cosmology. In the field of physics the classical conflict between the Ptolemaic and the Copernican systems vanishes into a non-existent ether if enough qualifications are laid upon the earlier system. Political systems that appear to be diametrically opposed may approximate identity as each qualifies its distinctive idea to take account of a common world of fact.

One may suggest a geometric analogy. Take any two distinct points in a given plane. It is possible to draw about these points as centres two mutually exclusive circles, enclosing no space in common. But increase the diameter of the two circles, and no matter how far apart, they will eventually overlap. Increase the diameter further, and the common space grows proportionately while the relative fraction of space governed by one and not the other approaches zero. If finally we speak of the system of all points which are included in circles having point A as a centre, and the system of all points included in circles having point B as a centre, we find that the two systems are no longer mutually exclusive, or even overlapping, but are in fact identical, both including all the points of the given plane. So, I suggest, two philosphic systems may be so restricted in scope and so far apart in origin as to have no content in common. But increase the diameter or scope of the two systems and you have an increasing common content. And what is perhaps more important, you have no content in either system which cannot be reached and included by an extension of the other system.... [pp. 97-99]

Materialist and Idealist Interpretations of History

Consider . . . the supposed opposition between materialism and idealism as philosophies of history. The historical materialist, in defending his position, will show how each significant event in history has been a product of economic developments, technology, material resources, the natural history of earth, air, fire, and water. The idealist counters by demonstrating that the role of material things in history can always be explained in terms of human will, knowledge, belief. Things are not resources in themselves : they become resources as men grow more resourceful. The economic order is itself an order of human wants and sacrifices, satisfactions and acts of will. Technology is a form of knowledge.

It seems to me that in this argument both parties are right in what they affirm and both parties are wrong in believing that they have "cornered" reality.

If both parties agree that there is a determinate relationship between human ideas and environmental realities, it is immaterial that one says, "The idea creates the environment," and the other says, "The environment creates the idea." Whatever can be said in one language can be said in the other.

I do not mean to suggest that materialists and idealists necessarily agree with each other on all historical questions. After all, materialists do not always agree among themselves, nor any more do idealists. What I do suggest is that disagreements in appraising certain historical events are not a necessary consequence of the fact that one formulates explanations in terms of ideas and the other in terms of material things. Every historical statement that is put forward by a materialist may be accepted by an idealist, and vice versa. The formula of translation would run roughly as follows : "Wherever the idealist ascribes importance, imminence, or causal efficacy to an idea, the materialist is to ascribe importance, imminence, or causal efficacy to the material things that accompany the idea, and vice versa.... [pp. 102-103]

The Relativity of System

The method of analysis which we have called systematic relativism is applicable, I believe, not only to systems of philosophy but to all rational systems. It offers, I think, an organon for eliminating unreal questions and false alternatives in the jungles of politics as well as in the Elysian fields of philosophy. Broadly stated, the viewpoint of systematic relativism may be summed up in the thesis that every assertion and every concept depends for its significance upon a systematic context which is not uniquely determined by the assertion or concept itself.

Except within a given context an assertion is neither true nor false, neither probable nor improbable, neither *a priori* nor derivative. Except within a given context a concept is neither simple nor complex, neither one nor many. Except within a single context one assertion cannot be said either to support or to contradict another assertion. Order, causality, proof, analysis, all have significance only within a system. And many systems are possible.

This viewpoint compels a reformulation of significant categories. With some trepidation I offer a few suggestions for this task of reformulation.

The Relativity of Simplicity

Any ordered system begins with undefined terms which are used to define other terms. For purposes of the system, the undefined terms are ultimate simples, and all other concepts in the system can be explained, analyzed, or defined in terms of these simples. Different systems, however, may locate simplicity in different parts of the universe. Within the system of chemistry the physical elements are the base points of analysis, but within the system of physics each of the elements is a composite structure of forces. For economics a human want is an ultimate datum. For psychology the want is something to be analyzed and explained. No significant term is in itself simple or complex. Simplicity and complexity are relative to context.

If this view is sound, the search for First Elements or Atomic Facts, whether carried on by metaphysicians or by antimetaphysicians, is, ... doomed to failure, unless the seeker recognizes that things are "first" or "atomic" only within the framework of a given system and that no given system monopolizes reality.

Explanation or analysis involves direction. In any concrete situation analysis can proceed along alternative lines. You can divide a piece of pie into six equal portions, or into five equal portions, or into fat, protein, and carbohydrates, or into carbon, hydrogen, and various other physical elements. Does the pie now, in reality, consist of sixths, fifths, chemical compounds, or physical elements ? I think this question is parallel to the question whether law is the creature of the state or the state the creature of law, or the question whether the world in reality consists of material things, ideas, substance and attributes, things in relations, events, or atomic facts. The viewpoint of systematic relativism suggests that the process of analysis, whether applied to the cosmos, the nature of the state, or apple pie, can begin at different points, proceed in different directions, use different instruments, and still produce equally exhaustive results, with no crumbs left over.

The Relativity of Proof

The same viewpoint that suggests that the direction of analysis and the location of simplicity and complexity are functions of a contextual system, also suggests that the direction of proof, generalization and particularization and the location of probability and the *a priori* are functions of such a system.

In the field of deductive proof, systematic relativism asserts only what I think we should all maintain, namely, that propositions or theorems are proved with reference to assumptions or postulates, and that no proof is conclusive if you reject the assumptions, which you can always do, logically, though as a moral human being you may find certain assumptions indispensable.

The viewpoint of relativism is equally applicable, I believe, to so-called inductive proof.

To the absolute pluralist induction is a mystery. If the falling of apple A is intrinsically and ineluctably a particular, distinct from the falling of apple B, then no sum of these particulars can establish a general proposition about the falling of apples, or about gravity in general.

But induction is not a mystery if one accepts the relativistic view that what is particular is also general — in another context. From this standpoint, the physicist does not have to traverse the infinite distance from the particular to the universal, because he does not start with the particular in the first place. He views only those aspects of the universe which are common to apples and other material things, namely, such universals as mass, velocity, acceleration, weight, shape, colour. The process of induction is not an addition of particulars but a subtraction of universals. It is a process of eliminating irrelevant elements. The hypothesis that colour or shape or weight influences velocity may be experimentally disproved, thus permitting a progressive abstraction in what the physicist observes. From the standpoint of systematic relativism, then, induction is the process of abstracting from experience the elements relevant to a given system and of eliminating elements which are not relevant. The so-called assumption of the uniformity of nature is nothing more than a recognition of the fact that particularizations which may be very important to us as human beings may be quite irrelevant to the cosmic process. The assumption that the future will be like the past is only a recognition of the fact that the systemic distinction that each of us makes at each instant between two segments of time, however important it may be to us at the moment, is irrelevant to certain cosmic processes which govern us and which, if we are scientifically inclined, we can observe. Systematic relativism is, in this sense, a safeguard against the naive assumption that I am the centre of the world and that Now is the critical moment of history.

This viewpoint with respect to the relativity of proof throws light, I think, on the problem of probability. No fact has, in itself, an assignable probability. It either exists or does not exist. And what is true of one fact is true, a thousand times, of a thousand facts. The empirical frequency of a certain occurrence is a fact and not a probability. To be specific, there is no probability that I *as an individual* will live another ten years. Different insurance companies may assign different degrees of probability to this possible event, depending upon whether they classify me with respect to age, health, weight, occupation, and heredity, or disregard one or more of these factors, or weigh the factors differently. A degree of probability can be assigned only within a system that selects certain elements as relevant, disregards others, and deals with the characteristics of classes defined by these relevant elements. There is no absolute system with which these selective systems can be compared, and if there were an absolute system there would be no probability. The system which any insurance company adopts may fail. The probability that any insurance company will fail is itself a risk that a reinsurer may take, and this risk will be variously calculated by different reinsurers. The human acceptance of a system of selective elements cannot be uniquely determined by any criterion of truth, but must inevitably involve an element of convention or purpose.

The problem of the *a priori* is subject, I think, to the same type of analysis... Since the notion of the relative *a priori* has been developed with some care in Professor Cohen's *Reason and Nature* and in Professor Lewis's *Mind and the World Order*, I shall not offer more than a summary note of explanation. That is *a priori* to a system which cannot be proved or disproved within the limits of the system but is assumed in the development of the system. This assumption may be embodied in a postulate or in a definition. I know, *a priori*, that colour involves space if I have defined colour in such a way that a phenomenon not involving space would not be called a colour. If I define colour in some other way, the proposition that colour does involve space may be provable, capable of disproof, or indeterminate in truth value. I know of no material proposition which is *a priori* for all rational systems, and I am inclined to believe that such a proposition does not exist. Of the purely logical or analytic *a priori* I do not speak.

The Relativity of Classification

Applied to the notion of class, the viewpoint of systematic relativism suggests that classification is relative to context, that no entity contains within itself a unique principle of classification. Any entities may be grouped together in a class. If certain classes seem more "natural" than others this is largely the result of language and habits of thought that change with changing cultures and vary in various contexts. Failure to recognize the relativity of classification to purpose or system is a fruitful source of empty argument. Thus people argue for or against the proposition that international law is a kind of law, or that the social sciences are sciences, or that man is an animal, as if these were propositions with a fixed meaning, true or false, and are continually surprised because such arguments never convince their adversaries. Recognition that such assertions are merely ordering principles for systematic thinking, in the nature of definitions, shifts argument to the level of testing the comparative usefulness for agreed ends of alternative methods of systematizing experience.

The Relativity of Causation

Applied to the notion of *cause*, the method of systematic relativism points to the plurality of systems in which lines of causation can be traced. If the question is asked, in the system of physics, "What causes the periodic rearrangement of these pages ?" an answer in terms of my desire to get to the next page is quite irrelevant.

The notion of the relativity of causation throws light, I think, upon a central problem of jurisprudence. When we seek to impose a liability upon the person who has caused an injury, a science that utterly ignores ethics can never fasten responsibility upon any one individual. An event in society typically involves antecedent events by many persons, including persons no longer alive at the time of the event. If, as a matter of fact, we fasten the thread of causation to one person it is because here is a point in the myriad strings of historical connectedness where social pressure accomplishes some approved social purpose.

The relativity of causation implies the relativity of the accidental. The pure accident does not exist. A hurricane may be an accident in a social system but not in a system of meteorology.

If causation is relative to system, the whole problem of chance and determinism must be reformulated. Any event is determinate within a system that postulates the sufficient conditions of the event, and indeterminate in any other system. The fact that an act of a human being is determined in the system of physical motion does not mean that the act is determined in another kind of system. No event is in itself determinate or indeterminate.

The Relativity of Individuality

I think that a good deal of confusion in political life as well as in philosophy has been caused by an absolutistic view of individuality. In the system of psychology, or at least in some systems of psychology, I am an individual. From the viewpoint of the biology of unicellular organisms, I suppose I am a cooperative society of several million members, the membership of which is constantly changing. From the sociologist's viewpoint, I suppose I am only a part of a community or society, perhaps a part of many concentric or overlapping societies.

Is it significant to ask whether I am *really* an individual or a great many individuals or only a part of some bigger individual ? The thesis here advanced would require us to maintain that this question is invalid, that individuality is relative to system, that any group may be an individual from some viewpoint, that any individual may be a group from some viewpoint.

This, of course, is merely an example of what might be called the relativity of number to the unit of operation. In its everyday form this relativity is accepted by common sense. A quart is two pints and is at the same time a fourth of a gallon. The same liquid thus partakes of plurality, unity, and partiality, with reference to different standards. So, when the monistic lamb in Professor Strong's philosophic fable, refusing to recognize a real distinction between the nutritious and the poisonous, told its mother that, after all, the universe is one, the lamb's mother, being a thorough-going systematic relativist, replied "One what ?"[5]

What we call a principle of individuation is, in effect, a formula for designating units of operation within a rational system. If alternative systems are valid, alternative principles of individuation are likewise valid.

This viewpoint dissolves a good many philosophic problems that seem otherwise insoluble. The metaphysical problem of the personality of groups which runs through political philosophy and jurisprudence vanishes once we recognize that the term "person" may be defined to cover various units in the segmentation of human activity. There remains the question of what definitions are useful for certain purposes, but this is no longer a problem of metaphysics.

This notion of the relativity of the individual person or thing suggests the thought that what is substance in one context may be quality or relation in another context. The distinction between essence and attribute, between substance and quality, between entity and relation, is, like the distinction between the individual and the society that includes the individual or the environment that surrounds the individual, relative to the contextual system in which the distinction is drawn.

Conclusion

The method of systematic relativism, applied in the jungles of politics, frequently demonstrates that what appear to be bitter differences of opinion on practical matters are actually differences of terminology or perspective. Rational argument in this situation becomes possible only when, through some emotional shift, one party comes to accept the postulates and definitions of his adversary and to talk in the same system, or when a third party (i.e., a "politician" or "statesman") is found who can talk to each of the disputants in his own system and thus offer each a practical solution which is what he wanted all along and was convinced his adversary did not want, but which, as a matter of fact, his adversary does not object to if only it is phrased in the proper way.

It is the chief purpose of this paper to suggest that a similar process of resolution may be applied to philosophical controversies. The pragmatic or operational meaning of systematic relativism may be summed up in these proposals for dealing with philosophical controversy :

1. Never assume that a philosophical doctrine is a true-or-false proposition. Its significance may lie in its function in organizing inquiry.
2. Be aware of assuming that any particular perspective is pre-eminent or that any philosophy is unavoidable or that any truth can be expressed in only one language.
3. Never assume that two philosophers who use the same symbol mean the same thing, or that those who make apparently contradictory assertions really disagree. They may be talking different languages.
4. In order to determine whether two philosophical doctrines are compatible, incompatible, or indentical, look for a formula of translation by which propositions within one philosophical system may be correlated with equivalent propositions in the other. [pp. 103-110].

NOTES

1. Felix Cohen, "The Relativity of Philosophic Systems and the Method of Systematic Relativism," in *The Legal Conscience : Selected Papers of Felix S. Cohen*, ed. Lucy Kramer Cohen (Shoe String Press : 1970), pp. 96-110.

2. D. Hilbert, *Foundations of Geometry*, trans. Townsend (1902), p.3.

3. O. Veblen, "A System of Axioms for Geometry," *Transactions of the American Mathematical Society* 5 (1904) : 343-384.

4. Huntington, "A Set of Postulates for Abstract Geometry," *Mathematischeische Annalen* 73 (1912-1913) : 522-559.

5. C.A. Strong, *The Wisdom of the Beasts* (1921), p. 60. The answer of the lamb was : "I am not quite sure ; but if I have correctly understood my illustrious teachers, it is one Lamb."

1. Law of Agreements

THE UNIQUE NATURE OF THE CONCEPTS OF WESTERN LAW[1]

J.C. Smith

Like ownership, the concept of contract was unknown in primitive and ancient cultures untouched by the classical Roman law. The term contract is commonly used in three different ways by both laymen and lawyers. It is used to refer to the factual operative acts of agreement, to a piece of paper on which the agreement is recorded, and to the imageless theoretical relations to which the act of agreement gives rise. It is the latter which is not to be found in primitive and archaic law. According to Seagle, "But no one has been able to find even in any archaic legal system, whether Ashanti, Babylonian, Hebrew, early Roman, or Germanic, an example of the enforcement of transactions which were purely executory on both sides — that is, when parties had merely exchanged promises with each other and no transfer of possession or partial performance had yet taken place...."[2] Even in early Roman law, "not only the word-'contractus' but also the idea or concept of contract was unknown,"[3] writes Professor Collinet. He further states that, "In the beginning of every civilization there was no contract," and that "the agreement of two or more persons never gave rise to an obligation....[4]

This does not mean that primitive and archaic societies were without commercial transactions. These consisted, however, principally of exchanges of land, commodities, or money. Barter and sale, it must be noted, did not give rise to contractual relations but to new relationships of physical possession. Immediately the transaction was completed, the parties had no further relationship to each other.

Stability of expectation in regard to patterns of trade were maintained by personal relationships, custom or by a ritualization of trading patterns such as the economic institution of the Kula described by Malinowski in *Argonauts of the Western Pacific.*

The closest these systems approached the concept of contract was an incomplete conveyance where one party gave goods but did not immediately receive value in return. Such a transaction, however, did not set up a legal relation between the creditor and debtor, but a common practice was for the debtor to give a hostage or his own body to insure that he completed the transaction. There was no concept of a legal obligation but a failure to pay was considered a wrongful detention of the creditor's property, and a failure to repay a loan, a wrongful detention of the creditor's money.... In the early common law, for instance, the action brought for a wrongful refusal to surrender a chattel to which the plaintiff was entitled was detinue, while the action for money owed was the closely related action of debt wherein the plaintiff would plead that the defendant "has detained his money until the present time, wrongfully and to his damages etc."[5]

In a number of societies legal remedies were available when someone broke his oath or pledge. The reason was not, however, because giving one's oath gave rise to a legal duty to perform one's agreement. Such a concept is to be found only in classical Roman and related legal systems. A remedy was available because to break one's pledge to another was to commit a wrong to him. There is no distinction made in primitive and archaic law between the wrongs of injuring another or his property, or failing to keep one's pledge or oath. The division between property, contract, and tort did not exist in such legal systems. Instead, their law was a law of wrongs rather than rights.

Rather than attempting to fit primitive law "into European categories like tort, contract, property rights, etc., thus hiding the most important thing about them ... "[6] a number of authorities on archaic and primitive law find the concept of "debt" useful to describe the legal situation arising when a wrong has been committed. The advantage of this concept over the categories of Western law is that it preserves the unified approach to wrongs, whatever their source, which was taken in archaic and primitive law. Seagle writes in regard to archaic law :

> . . .archaic law knows not so much a law of contracts as a law of debt. Indeed, its creative power seems to be exhausted in devising machinery for recording or enforcing a debt irrespective of its cause of origin. The Babylonian law recognized the *i'iltum* or obligation note which could be employed to incorporate any cause of debt. Medieval English law developed a general action of debt.[7]

Thus we see that the concepts of primitive and archaic law, in marked contrast to classical Roman and modern law, get their meaning directly in terms of sensed experience. The conceptions applied to the property and commercial relationship of these societies are factual rather than abstract. Their legal codes all follow a basic pattern of specifying patterns of behaviour to be or not to be performed, and a penalty for failure to comply.

The lack of theoretical concepts in, or what some writers have termed the "materialism," of archaic and primitive law is merely a reflection of the naive realism of primitive and archaic peoples as reflected in their languages. Although the conceptual structures of such societies differ greatly from one to another, they appear to have at least one factor in common, and that is the inability to organize experience in terms of highly abstract concepts and categories having logically rather than empirically known properties. This is not because of any inherent deficiency in the mind of primitive man but because he interprets new experience in terms of his own inherited conceptual structure which provides a different kind of logic and set of principles for organizing experience than the theoretical constructs of Western mathematics and science.

Primitive and archaic law is a law of empirically known, psychologically sensed wrongs rather than theoretically conceived rights and duties having no existence in the material world of the senses. These legal systems were therefore static and past oriented, since they dealt basically with wrongs and compensation, that is, the restitution as far as possible of a previously existing situation which had been wrongfully disturbed. Classical Roman and modern law, on the other hand, is future oriented and a law of movement concerned with the creation, transfer, and extinction of legal relations and prediction of this future movement. Through the use of these constructs it is possible to control future human behaviour in regard to physical resources to a degree not possible by using only concepts having a referent in sensed experience.

The most basic construct, the right, for instance, is not a thing nor can it be empirically known in the same way as an object such as a tree. Most constructs of modern law such as estates, trusts, or contracts, and so on are collections or bundles of rights or jural relations. These concepts are empty forms, the parts of which are variables into which people and patterns of behaviour are put in order to accomplish certain purposes. Take, for instance, the situation where John wishes to have his fence painted by Richard but does not wish to pay until the job is completed, and Richard is willing to paint the fence but wishes to be certain of being able to collect. By use of the concept of the contract, filling in the variables with themselves and the patterns of behaviour of painting a fence and paying money, they are able to gain some control of each other's actions. [pp. 202-207]

NOTES

1. J.C. Smith, "The Unique Nature of the Concepts of Western Law," *Canadian Bar Review* 46, No. 2 (May, 1968) : 202-207.
2. Seagle, *The History of Law* (1946), p. 256.
3. Collinet, "The Evolution of Contract as Illustrating The General Evolution of Roman Law", *Law Quarterly Review*, 48 (1932) : 488.
4. *Ibid.*
5. Selden Society, vol. 80 (1963), Novae Narratinnes B 209.
6. Bohannan, *Justice and Judgment Among the Tiv* (1957), p. 102.
7. Seagle, *op. cit.*, p. 260.

JUSTICE AND JUDGMENT AMONG THE TIV[1]

Paul Bohannan

... We have discovered that Tiv use a single concept 'debt' (*injo*) to cover instances and cases which we, in our folk system, classify into several different categories. Tiv take those *jir* which, in our classification, might be called contract and they see the debt aspect rather than the contract aspect as the most important point. From the viewpoint of the comparative jurist, there is a contract between a man who owns a goat and the man who keeps it. One could also speak of a contract between a pledgor and a pledgee. Tiv agree with such statements if made and explained to them. But they do not use this aspect of the relationship for purposes of classification. In their own folk system, the idea of contract takes, for purposes of classification, a subordinate position to the idea of the debt involved.

Tiv can be said to have a right against the world for their crops to be protected from molestation by other people's livestock, and it can be said — accurately in one sense — that it is a tort for a man to allow his livestock to harm another's crops. But Tiv classify this idea also under debt : if a man's livestock injures a farm, he falls into debt to the farmer. Debt is an aspect of both this sort of contract and this sort of tort : it is the aspect on which Tiv classify. Needless to say, our categories of contract and of tort are not coterminous with the Tiv category of debt. [pp. 111-112]

NOTE

1. P. Bohannan, *Justice and Judgment Among the Tiv* (Oxford University Press, 1957), pp. 111-112.

PRIMITIVE LAW PAST AND PRESENT[1]

A.S. Diamond

. . .In many ages, but chiefly in the most developed of these economies, men have taken or exacted oaths to do or refrain from acts, especially such acts as are outside the sphere of law, and have uttered curses upon those who should pass a threshold, deface a boundary stone or sepulchral monument, or seek to upset a transaction, and kings have enacted imprecations upon any successor who should annul or alter a code, but these phenomena are irrelevant to the history of contract.

. . . The law of contract starts with simple and practical beginnings. Law does not develop by giving unwanted remedies. In the law of the Late Codes, in England, Rome, Babylonia, and Assyria, in India and China, in Hebrew and Islamic law, we must still talk not of contract but of transactions, that is to say, transfers. The history of primitive contract is the history of primitive commerce, and the progress is small till the close of the primitive era.

In the Food Gatherers we found no evidence of trade because there were no goods surplus to requirements.

Among the Hunters and Early Agriculturists we found some animals and goods (mainly natural produce) surplus to the immediate needs of subsistence, and some trade in this almost everywhere. It takes place by barter, that is to say contemporaneous exchange of one thing for another — though in a few places there are imperishable articles in use as a medium of exchange. Trade takes many forms, sometimes it is between individuals, sometimes between permanent "partners" belonging to different tribes or other social groups. In some areas types of goods and return goods go from hand to hand over thousands of miles on permanent routes. Some of this is enveloped in ritual and much exemplifies gift-exchange, that is to say, gifts for which a return of similar value is expected. This we can hardly call trade.

In the peoples of our Second Agricultural Grade trade has largely increased both in barter and sale, and now includes a quantity of partly manufactured goods. Again there are individual transactions between a man and his trade friend, and also exchange between neighbouring communities, for example, of the vegetable product of horticulturalists in return for the fish of a neighbouring coastal village. Apart from this there is the exchange of standard trade goods travelling over vast distances on regular routes. There is also in some areas (especially the Kula Ring in Melanesia) the ritual exchange of two highly prized, imperishable commodities, travelling in opposite directions, that seems to serve no commercial but only social purposes, and is not called "trade" but by another name. Rarely do we find, as among the Kapauku, a developed system of credit, savings, loans at interest, hire, and leases of land.

In the first stage of the Third Agricultural Grade there is trade by contemporaneous barter, and cattle, goats, and often grain play a prominent part in the estimation of values and as medium of exchange. There are also smiths engaged to make an article, often on terms of being supplied with the metal and charcoal needed and grain for subsistence during the work and a lump-sum payment at the close in the form of a cow or goat. There are rarely any markets, for these people live mainly in isolated homesteads.

In the peoples of the Early Codes there is still hardly a market till the close of this period. There is some trade in produce and manufactured articles and there are traditional value-relations for the purposes of exchange, expecially between cattle, sheep and goats. When a metal currency is adopted it bears a fixed relation to them, so that a shilling in England is at first the price of a cow and a sceata or penny the price of a sheep. There are some foreign merchants, but the chief transactions remain contemporaneous barter, cash sale, loans between friends and arrangements between friends for agistment of cattle. There is still little or no hiring or commercial deposit and little engagement of specialists.

At the close of the Early Codes and among the peoples of the Central Codes there is substantial economic development. There is a great increase in trade, especially in manufactured goods. There are in most peoples, markets, market towns, tolls and dues on goods for sale, and a port reeve, or market chief, in control. There are currencies of some kind (mainly metal) everywhere, but money is in little use in the countryside. For large transactions cattle are usually the means of payment, except in barter. There is hire of goods, especially farm animals and carts in the ancient world. Artisans number some 3 per cent of the working population and there is some hire of agricultural workers (paid in kind) and artisans in the towns (paid in money) and at the close of the age some fixing of prices of goods and hire charges, for the value of money is beginning to fall. Loan of money for a lump-sum payment begins. There is suretyship and pledging by debtors of their dependents. There is a familiar situation where A sees an animal or article in B's possession and claims that it is his and has been stolen from him, and B denies this and alleges he bought it from a third party. He is required to produce his vendor. Sales of goods of any value take place in a market town before a group of witnesses, and the law endeavours to insist on this practice but it is nowhere essential to validity.

The great and quickening development in the Late Codes has been outlined, and there is no space for details. The number of craftsmen and artisans is some 5 per cent of the working population and the traders some 6 per cent. The variety of skilled occupations is large. Agricultural workers are paid in kind, artisans in the towns often in money. Guilds of artisans and traders and markets and market courts show great development and foreign trade is considerable and kings engage in it. There is commercial hire and deposit (including banking), investment in commercial expeditions and enterprises, partnership, agency, suretyship and leases of land. There is pledging of dependants, and mortgages of land and crops,at first by pledge (where the occupier parts with possession on loan) and later by hypothec (where he loses possession only on failure to repay). There is some registration of title to land. And there is, of course, the law of marriage.

Yet in spite of this development, sale is still by far the most common transaction, and all that has happened to contemporaneous barter (which survives) is the substitution of money for the commodity on one side and the conversion of the transaction to cash sale. Nothing remains to be done or claimed (except that the law may give the buyer a claim to recover the price if a certain disease or defect in the thing sold appears within a certain period or, of course, it if turns out not to have been the vendor's to sell). This is considered a distinct type of transaction. Even at the end of this age in the Old Babylonian period, no transaction was considered a sale unless it was for cash, otherwise it was not recorded in a sale tablet alone. So, the Roman *vendere* originally signified a cash sale, and *emere* ("to take") a cash purchase. Even modern English records the same situation, for "sell" originally meant "deliver," and "sale" still primarily denotes an instantaneous and completed transaction. Indeed, in even a modern market, a retail sale which is not for cash must be an unusual event.

All important transactions are conducted before a substantial number of witnesses. We have seen this in the Central Codes, and throughout our period it is universal in England, Africa, Rome, Jerusalem, India and everywhere else. We have seen the reason for this — to meet a possible claim by a third person (or the seller) that the propery is his and has been stolen from him. If we had any doubts that this was still the reason, the Codes of Eshnunna and Hammurabi, the Assyrian Laws and the tablets tell us so in the plainest terms. As in modern times, even writing (where writing is in use) is not thought to obviate the necessity for witnesses (especially as neither party can usually write or read) but the number of witnesses is larger than with us because fraud is perhaps more rife and life more uncertain and the courts demand that evidence. In Babylonia there may be anything between one witness and twenty or more, and five or six is an average number, but neither tablet nor form nor witnesses are essential to validity. In West Africa today we have the further advantage of being able to observe that the witnesses in some places at least, receive a customary gift-payment for their pains, which may be a fixed proportion of the price.

This, then, is the universal type of the most familiar and important commercial transaction — a ready-money sale (in the more advanced economies, the metal currency weighed out at the time) before some five or six witnesses. The witnesses (and the writing, if any) are for the benefit of the buyer, not the seller (as indeed they must be on a cash sale). So, in the Mesopotamian tablet in this Old Babylonian period, the transaction is always expressed from the buyer's point of view : "So-and-so has taken for so much silver such-and-such a thing," not "So-and-so has given," and the seal is always the seal which will be of use to the buyer, namely the seller's seal. The early Romans called the transaction *mancipium,* a "taking," not a "giving."

Everywhere, too, among the most developed economies, the important sales tend to be of the same subject-matter — in Rome, Mesopotamia, Egypt, and elsewhere, land, cattle, and slaves or serfs, and among a people who engage largely in a water-borne trade, like the Babylonians and Egyptians, ships also ; and in Babylonia and Egypt, where the temples retain their records for centuries, sacred offices and the income from them. We have already sought to set out steps by which land had become saleable in the middle of the Late Codes and a ready market in land appeared at the close. We are not told much in the Codes or deeds of the consents required from near kin or their rights or pre-emption and redemption.

These sales are all sales of specific items of property — in such-and-such a field (naming it) a particular slave, bull, or cow, and so on. Thus it is that in Rome by the year 270 B.C. a rule is evolved by the conservative Roman mind that land in Italy, cattle and slaves are only properly transferred in the presence of five Roman citizens and a man holding a copper balance, and the buyer ("taker") declares : "I say this (slave etc.) is mine by Roman law, and he be taken by me with this copper and copper balance" — and he strikes the balance with the copper and gives it to the transferor. The Romans were then still generally illiterate, but this transaction in later days remained an oral transaction long after writing was in general use. The Sumerians, Babylonians, and Assyrians, and to a lesser extent the Hebrews and Egyptians, used writing to evidence their important transactions, the Egyptians and Hebrews mainly papyrus, and the Mesopotamians clay tablets. In twelfth and thirteenth-century England, and among all these peoples who used writing, the general form of the document was the same. The parties were illiterate and the document was written by a scribe, witnessed, and sealed by a party....

There is little barter of specific valuables, either in Rome or Babylon or elsewhere : these are normally disposed of in the towns and by way of sale, in the way we have seen. There is no sale of a large quantity of non-specific-goods — that is to say, of produce; such transactions usually take place in the country and by barter. When a large estate disposed of its produce, say, its present produce of oil, to another estate which would deliver a quantity of its produce of corn after next harvest, this credit-barter was recorded in a loan-tablet. It was not a sale. In Rome, indeed, the transaction retained the name of *muutum* ("exchange," "barter") in classical times.

So much for the cash sale, but less commonly there are also sales (of specific goods) on credit, where the purchaser is to pay in the future. These were so much less common that the Babylonians did not regard them as mere sales: they drew up two tablets, one a sale-tablet recording a cash sale, and the second a tablet recording that the seller has lent the buyer such-and-such a sum (the amount of the price), which the buyer will repay on such-and-such a date; or recording a deposit by the seller with the buyer of the amount of the price, or an account declaring the buyer to be in debit to the seller in that amount, and recording that he will repay on a certain date. Similarly, if the transaction were one under which the buyer paid in advance and the seller agreed to deliver in the future, a sale-tablet was drawn up recording a cash sale, and a second tablet recorded the seller's debt in respect of the goods. In Rome by 200 B.C. they had arrived at the practice-book rule (which survives in the fragments of the Twelve Tables) that any of these extra terms, if orally stated at the time of the *mancipium*, would be binding.

There were no mere agreements to sell, in which payment and delivery were both to take place in the future — what the English law calls an executory agreement of sale — the people of this stage do not do business that way. But there is quite a little here and there of the giving of "earnest." X may want to consider whether he will buy a certain article from Y. Y lets him consider the matter till, say, the following day, on condition that he pays him a small sum which he will forfeit if he decides not to buy. We see this practice in West Africa and England, but it is not sufficiently important to find its way into the Old Babylonian tablets or the Roman forms of transactions of our period.

In Bechuanaland and West Africa loan of money at interest was not known. Among the Hebrews it was just creeping in — a loan of money remunerated by money — that is to say, by interest. Hence, in the Old Testament, religion exercising its normal function of resisting innovation (in this case, salutary if impracticable) prohibited usury, and the rule survived in England with wide exceptions till 1865. Muhammadan law struggles to maintain a consistent and practical attitude. But in all the more developed economies of the Late Codes, thirteenth-century England, Rome, Babylon, Assyria, Ethiopia, China and India, the loan of money at interest is common. In England, kings, monasteries and landowners are widely borrowing at interest, and loans upon a rent-charge of 10 per cent per annum are normal. In Babylon the rate was as high or higher — 20 per cent and more could be got. Loans by a moneylender or landlord on the security of a crop or a field (a form of security corresponding to the letting of land on the *metayage* system) were very common, and Hammurabi was concerned to check its abuses. In Rome (as elsewhere) the money lent was weighed out as in the *mancipium*, at the time of the transaction.

Then there are the bailments of goods which will be returned in the future, free loans of goods to friends for use, deposit (in the East especially of silver) and hire of ploughs, wagons and oxen, with or without drivers. The process seen in the Central Codes continues : the ordeal by oath is brought into use to meet the case where the borrower or hirer says the ox has died or was eaten or the property destroyed without his privity. These clauses are more numerous and more detailed in the Codes, the more advanced is the economy.

We have seen enough to realize that there has been a large-scale development in this branch of law, and there are now a good many types of transactions, but there is not yet nearly enough of this in Babylon, Rome, England or elsewhere, to call for a general theory of contract : that, for example, a contract is made by an offer and an acceptance in the same terms, or that it must be carried out, or a breach compensated by the amount of the loss incurred. It is not that these peoples do not think that a promise should be performed, but that at this stage commerce does not proceed on that basis : no one relies on a mere agreement on both sides to do something in the future, and consequently no one can be damaged by a failure to carry it out. Law does not pretend to compensate where there is no loss, and there are few, if any, cases where the loss to the plaintiff is tried and estimated. In a modern court the usual remedy for breach of a contract to buy or sell goods is the difference between the contract price and the market price and if there is no difference there is no loss and no remedy. In the times of which we speak market prices do not fluctuate to the extent so that even if parties relied on a mere executory agreement it would usually be difficult to say what loss has been incurred by a breach. In England and elsewhere, there are claims in debt to recover money owing to the plaintiff (for work done, or the return of the price paid for goods or of bridewealth) and claims in detinue to recover his goods (hired and not returned, for example) but in England it is probably the sharp drop in the value of the coinage and the sharp fluctuations in market prices in the sixteenth century that create the necessity to rely on executory contracts and develop the action of assumpsit. [pp. 378-387]

NOTE

1. A.S. Diamond, *Primitive Law, Past and Present* (London : Methuen & Co. Ltd., 1971), pp. 378-387.

HISTORICAL INTRODUCTION TO THE STUDY OF ROMAN LAW[1]

H.F. Jolowicz & B. Nicholas

Justinian defines an obligation as "a legal bond by which we are placed under the necessity of performing some duty in accordance with the laws of our state," and this definition describes with considerable accuracy the developed Roman and the modern conception of an obligation. But it must be realized that this apparently simple conception is by no means primitive, and that its elaboration by the Roman jurists was an achievement not less difficult and not less important than the development of the absolute conception of ownership. When we say today that A is under an obligation to B, we imply that, if A does not voluntarily perform his duty in accordance with that obligation, B can bring an action in the courts against him and, after getting judgment, have A forced by state authorities either to do what he should have done originally or, if that is impossible or undesirable, to do something else instead, generally to pay him money....

In the early stages of law, on the other hand, these two things,duty and liability, are by no means necessarily combined. At a time when the state has not yet undertaken generally the enforcement of duties between private persons, it by no means follows that because a duty is recognized, therefore it will be enforced, and the primitive creditor consequently asks for something tangible which will serve as security for the performance of the duty by the debtor; he wants to have in his power some person or some thing which will be liable; in other words, he wants a hostage or a pledge with whom or with which he can do what he likes if he does not get his rights. It must be noted especially that it is not a question (originally) of getting the hostage to do what the debtor ought to do, or of selling the pledge and paying oneself out of the proceeds; it is a question of having the hostage or pledge in one's power and, in the case of the hostage, of being able to wreak vengeance on him.

A further difference between developed and primitive law is that primitive systems have not yet made the distinction, common to advanced systems, between delict and contract as sources of obligation. In the developed Roman and in modern law we can say that if A is under an obligation to B it is usually (by no means always) either because A has agreed to perform the act which forms the content of the obligation (contract), or because he has committed some wrong (delict) against B for which he must pay B damages. In early law, on the other hand, the idea of wrong is still undifferentiated, and it is only very gradually that the particular sort of wrong which consists in not doing what one has agreed to do is separated from other wrongs. Further, the natural reaction against wrong is a desire to take vengeance on the wrongdoer, and the recognition that such vengeance is permissible and not itself a wrong is the beginning of the law of obligations. The next step is that the person wronged may agree to forgo his vengeance if the wrongdoer will pay him composition, and it is precisely in these agreements for composition that we find the clearest example of the distinction between duty and liability, as well as, obviously, the germ of contract. Suppose that A has committed a delict against B — has stolen his property — B is justified in avenging himself on A, and if he is strong enough, will capture A for the purpose. A may then promise to pay composition and B may agree to accept it, but it may easily happen that A will be unable to collect the money so long as he remains in custody, whereas B, having once got hold of him, does not want to let him go. A therefore gets a child or kinsman to be hostage for him in the meanwhile. The result of this is that although A owes the money, he is no longer liable, whereas the hostage, who does not owe the money, is liable, because liability is something quite physical; it means being in the power of the creditor. Then, in some systems, at any rate, comes a stage when A can become hostage for himself or, rather, as one can now say, surety. That is to say B lets him go on his undertaking to be liable, which means that B shall be allowed to take him again if he does not pay. The physical binding is replaced, for the time being, by a metamorphical bond, which may in certain circumstances be converted into a real one again....

Now, at the time of the Twelve Tables the law was no longer in its most primitive condition. The state had already restricted self-help very considerably, but the time when it would take upon itself the task of seeing that people carried out their duties to each other was still in the far distant future ; the most it could do was to say when one man was liable to another, to decide in some, indeed in most, cases how that liability could be redeemed, and to provide methods for preventing unauthorized enforcement of liability. Thus, so far as what is later called delict is concerned, it already provides generally that a certain penalty is to be paid by the wrongdoer to the person wronged, in other words, that the person wronged must forgo his right to vengeance if he receives a certain sum by way of composition, but in other cases the right to take vengeance (though in a restricted form) is expressly preserved, and it is for the person wronged to consider whether he will accept composition instead and, if so, at what rate. Contract is still in its infancy. The agreement to pay and accept composition for delict is recognized, and so are forms of suretyship. Of two old types of surety, *vas* and *praes*, the former was certainly mentioned in the Twelve Tables. Since the discovery of the new fragments of Gaius we know that stipulation also goes back to this period, i.e., that an oral promise preceded by a question could create an actionable obligation. But it is not certain that stipulations could yet be made for anything except a definite sum of money (as in the example Gaius gives), and the survival of *nexum*, a form of loan which "bound" the debtor to the creditor, seems to show that the mere "obligation" (in the later sense) produced by a stipulation was by no means always considered sufficient.

It seems at first sight inconceivable that a society could exist at all in which the idea of contract was as little developed as this. How, it may be asked, could men do without at least sale and hire, loan of chattels, and deposit ? The answer is twofold. First one must distinguish the question of the existence of the economic relationship covered by each of these contracts of the later law from the question whether there arose as yet any liability from promises made or implied in such relationships, and secondly one must realize that many of the results achieved later by the idea of contract can be, and were, achieved by that of delict. Thus it is quite clear that the economic relationship of sale or barter existed, that people in fact exchanged goods for the primitive equivalent of money (especially uncoined metal), or for other goods, but this proceeding did not result in any obligations and was not a contract because the two parties almost always carried out their respective parts of the bargain simultaneously. Thus mancipation, before the weighing out of the copper became purely symbolical, was clearly, from the economic point of view, a sale — the exchange of a thing for money of a sort — but it was no sale in the sense of the later contract, for in that sense a sale means an agreement to transfer a thing in return for a money payment,and when the agreement is once reached the seller is under an obligation to do what he has promised to do, as the buyer on the other hand is under an obligation to pay the price that he has promised. In the mancipation there was no scope for these obligations because the transfer of the thing and the weighing out of the copper were both parts of the same transaction ; the property in the thing passed only when the copper was given, and the copper was only given when the property in the thing passed. Once the mancipation is complete there is nothing left for either party to do, and before it is complete no legal effect is produced. When the weighing out became symbolical it did become possible to mancipate property without receiving an equivalent at once ; in other words it became possible to give credit, but there is no reason to think that, at the time of the Twelve Tables, a seller who had thus given credit had an action for the price. It may well be that he could secure himself by making a nexum whereby the price was treated as a loan from him to the buyer, though there is no direct evidence of this practice. Further, if there was a rule that property did not pass until the price was paid, the seller was protected by his ability to vindicate the property. The converse case — that the buyer should pay the price before the transfer of the thing — would presumably be very rare indeed. If a mancipation had taken place, but the thing had remained in the possession of the seller, it would none the less belong to the buyer, who would thus be protected by his power to vindicate.... [pp. 161-165]

NOTE

1. H.F. Jolowicz and B. Nicholas, *Historical Introduction to the Study of Roman Law*, 2nd ed. (Cambridge : Cambridge University Press, 1952), pp. 161-165.

THE LAW AND LEGAL THEORY OF THE GREEKS[1]

J.W. Jones

Despite the obscurity of the not very abundant material which has come down to us, there is good ground for supposing that Greek law, like early Roman and English law, considered sale as essentially an exchange of land or goods for money, a cash transaction giving no right to enforce payment on the one side or delivery on the other. It was a two-sided affair ; but there could be no question of any outstanding obligations arising from the simple fact of agreement. In law the sale was complete or it was nothing, and it was not complete until the price had been paid : "Paying down the forty minae, I made the purchase," says a buyer. While Roman and English law eventually came to recognize the binding force of mutual promises, Greek law clung throughout its history to the conception of sale as a purely ready-money business. Further, the passing of the seller's rights to the buyer was brought about by payment of the price. In English law ownership of the goods depends upon agreement ; in classical Roman law agreement followed by delivery was probably enough ; in Greek law delivery was irrelevant, in the matter of passing the title, and payment decisive, provided that any regulations as to publicity were satisfied. And payment, though it divested the seller of his ownership, did not necessarily vest it in the buyer ; the loan of the money to the buyer seems to have given a lender some sort of proprietary right over the thing bought with or out of the money lent. On the other hand, the giving of a surety or a pledge, even in the earlier period when it replaced rather than reinforced the earlier claim of the seller by giving him a power of enforcement hitherto lacking, was inoperative to deprive him of his title to the goods since, for this, payment of the price was both indispensable and sufficient. [p. 228]

NOTE

1. J.W. Jones, *The Law and Legal Theory of the Greeks* (Oxford : Clarendon Press, 1956), p. 228.

THE HISTORY OF ENGLISH LAW[1]

Sir Frederick Pollock and Frederic W. Maitland

The law of contract holds anything but a conspicuous place among the institutions of English law before the Norman Conquest. In fact it is rudimentary. Many centuries must pass away before it wins that dominance which we at the present day concede to it. Even in the schemes of Hale and Blackstone it appears as a mere supplement to the law of property. The Anglo-Saxon dooms tell us but little about it ; they tell us less the more carefully we examine them. For example, certain provisions which may seem at first sight to show a considerable development in this department turn out, on closer scrutiny, to have a wholly different bearing. There are many ordinances requiring men who traffic in cattle to make their purchases openly and before good witnesses. But they really have nothing to do with enforcing a contract of sale between the parties. Their purpose is to protect an honest buyer against possible claims by some third person alleging that the beasts were stolen from him. If the Anglo-Saxon team was an ancestor of the later law of warranty in one line, and of rules of proof, ultimately to be hardened into rules of the law of contract, in another, the results were undesigned and indirect. Anglo-Saxon society barely knew what credit was, and had no occasion for much regulation of contracts. We find the same state of things throughout northern and western Europe. Ideas assumed as fundamental by this branch of law in modern times and so familiar to modern lawyers as apparently to need no explanation had perished in the general breaking up of the Roman system, and had to be painfully reconstructed in the Middle Ages. Further, it is not free from doubt (though we have no need to dwell upon it here) how far the Romans themselves had attained to truly general conceptions. In any case the Germanic races, not only of the Karolingian period, but down to a much later time, had no general notion whatever of promise or agreement as a source of civil obligation. Early Germanic law recognized, if we speak in Roman terms, only *formal* and *real* contracts. It had not gone so far as to admit a *consensual* contract in any case. Sale, for example, was a real, not a consensual transaction. All recent inquirers seem to concur in accepting this much as having been conclusively established. [p. 184]

NOTE

1. Sir Frederick Pollock and Frederic W. Maitland, *The History of English Law*, 2nd ed., vol. 2 (Cambridge : Cambridge University Press, 1968), p. 184.

THE AGE OF DEBT The Reformation and English Law[1]

De Lloyd J. Guth

[T]he Tudor era can be viewed as a pivotal point for the centrality of debt in English legal development. If the two centuries following the Civil War brought the 'Age of Contract', then one might label the preceding three centuries the 'Age of Debt'. By Henry VIII's reign, the judicial system available to Englishmen interwove the king's common law across the crazyquilt of local customary and ecclesiastical jurisdictions. Debt, with its correlative action of trespass, had come to dominate late-medieval litigation. This courtroom reality, in fact, only mirrored a broader social truth : late-medieval language and its metaphors were supersaturated with the imagery of debt.

'Give us this day our daily bread. And forgive us our debts even as we forgive our debtors.' So read the English version of the Lord's Prayer in use from the fourteenth through the sixteenth centuries, from Wycliffe in 1390 through Bishop Pecock's biblical paraphrases in the 1450s to the Geneva Bible of 1557. The Scottish version in Matthew's Gospel was 'And forgif to us our dettis, as we forgef to our dettouris', while Luke's more succinct text became 'And forgeve to us our synnis : as we forgeve to ilk man that aw to us.' Bishop John Fisher of Rochester, shortly before joining Sir Thomas More at the Tower block in 1535, preached on Christ's Passion and reinforced this meaning : 'But the dampned sinner that must paye his own debtes in hell, shal suffer everlasting death... [and] shalt come to that place to pay thy debtes of thine own sinnes... [so] that the debtes of thy sinnes shall be throughly payde.'[2] A common theological manual added that the Seventh Commandment against stealing applied to those 'that nell not pay hare dette that thei oweth....'[3] [pp. 70-73]

With typical Middle English variety, debt also had a sensual meaning, sanctioning sexual pleasures. Geoffrey Chaucer's Wife of Bath asserted 'that a man shall yelde to his wyf hire dette,'[4] referring to his obligation to have sexual intercourse with his wife whenever she so desired. This derived from St. Paul's First Letter to Corinthians, VII, as found in all English and Scottish translations before and after the Reformation : 'ye woman paie her fleischli dette to her husbond asking it, and biddeth ye husbond paie his fleischli dette to his wiyf asking it'....

Common law, meaning royal law common to the entire realm, divided itself from the thirteenth century into courts of Common Pleas, King's Bench, and Exchequer. Their plea rolls have survived from the 1190s. By the pre-Reformation era three hundred years later, the Court of Common Pleas produced parchment plea rolls one foot thick for each of any year's four law terms (Michaelmas, Hilary, Easter, Trinity). In Easter term, 12 Edward IV (1473), two-thirds of the 4970 case entries were actions mainly of debt or scatterings of detinue, another twenty percent alleged trespass, and less than one lawsuit in ten qualified directly as a real action. Ten years later in the same Common Pleas, Michaelmas term 1482 generated 6204 case entries on its roll, seventy-one percent being actions of debt, twenty percent were for trespass and only five percent were real actions.

If we look to the other two common law courts of King's Bench and Exchequer, real actions were all the more absent. In King's Bench, litigants battled mainly over allegations of trespass, with actions of debt noteworthy but a distant second in quantity. On the plea side of the King's Bench roll for Michaelmas 1507, there were a total of 782 case entries : 509, or two-thirds, were actions of trespass, to which one can add 121 so-called *quare* actions, better known to lawyers as trespass on the case. This left only 44 actions of debt, six percent of the total, but even fewer real actions were on the record. In Henry VII's Exchequer, the action of debt accounted for virtually all litigation, not a surprising figure since it was the royal revenue chasing court. There the King's Remembrancer annually enrolled less than two hundred prosecutions, usually against smugglers evading customs duties. Common law courtrooms at Westminster Hall, then, mirrored accurately the England that contemporary writers so inexorably immersed in metaphors of debt....

Debt is central to the Anglo-Saxon dooms which from the seventh century record schedules of elaborate fines (wer-geld) for homicide and theft weighted entirely to the victim's status. Every Anglo-Saxon had his price, as did every part of him. These violent acts thus created clear indebtedness, with the wer-geld being a money substitute for vengeance, *lex talionis,* as well as for any stolen goods. Debt had been made an instrument for the control of violence, with all values translated to a money standard. These early medieval dooms spoke with one voice from the perspective of debt and duty. With the arrival of eleventh-century feudalism, and its mainly unwritten military, personal, and mutual sets of obligations, the concept of debt-duty must have penetrated even deeper into ordinary human consciousnes.... [pp. 77-78]

What happened to dethrone debt (duty), as well as trespass (wrong), and ultimately lead to an age of contract three centuries later can only be outlined here. Central to this legal development was the English Reformation, specifically the attendant impulses it unleashed in royal administration and parliaments to organize, re-define, and especially further to formalize and to secularize polity and law. The fact that debt and trespass had multiplied into common denominators for litigation left both actions vulnerable to demands for more precise and specific legal protections. The resort to equity, with its early Tudor judicialization and its expanded Elizabethan respectability, was only symptomatic of the common law's problem with such a simple system of remedies....

What the sixteenth century witnessed was the steady unravelling of the debt-duty basis for moral obligation which had overtly buttressed the English legal system. Obligation remained in law, to be sure, but it gradually came to be defined, in a sense secularized, as contractual and consensual agreements enforceable *per se* by the common law and customary courts. Simple obligations made in debt, whether oral or written, had previously been made for accomplished exchanges of benefits, usually money for goods ; such obligations had to be translated, in the eyes of later law, into formalized contracts based on future performance. By the seventeenth century and the later age of contract, obligation was strictly limited to this world, where benefit and promise could be measured in terms of enforceability and where the obligation remained personally externalized, no longer one reserved to moral duty and conscience....

Again, the history of ideas provided suggestive correlations with legal realities, for the Reformation century and its aftermath. Martin Luther's pessimism about man's irrevocable unworthiness before God had made it impossible for man to connect his salvation with repayment of debts, whether before or after death. It was also Luther who led rejection of the more crass application of debtor metaphors, peddled in the theology of Tetzel and the pre-Reformation papacy. No doubt Luther and later English reformers, particularly so-called "covenant" theologians like Bullinger and the early seventeenth-century Puritans, were appalled by purgatorial, debt-ridden beliefs that made God the final accountant. By the Elizabethan era, Calvin's doctrine of double predestination made purgatory an unnecessary abomination because debts could neither damn the debtor to hell nor could repayment ever provide the cachet into heaven, whose inhabitants God must know (even will ?) to be there.

The metaphors of debt, along with the dominance of the action of debt, gave way to newer metaphors associated with the emerging law of contract. If one may speculate further, these new legal realities accompanied, and perhaps made necessary, the seventeenth century's creation of 'society' in earth-bound minds, as the reason and root for enforcing obligations. The transcendancy of moral duty in the nature of pre-Reformation debt gave way to the grounding, after the sixteenth century, of post-Reformation contractual obligation within society. It was no accident, then, that Thomas Hobbes, John Locke, Adam Smith, and others articulated social contract theories, in much the same metaphorical way as William Langland, Robert Fabyan, Bishop John Fisher and others had written about debt. The age of contract would be a world of formalized obligation, of temporal and specific mutuality, of concrete and tangible terms based on future promise that would allow such contractual debts to be discounted and negotiable. [pp. 83-85]

NOTES

1. De Lloyd J. Guth, "The Age of Debt, The Reformation and English Law," D.J. . Guth and J.W. McKenna, eds., *Tudor Rule and Revolution : Essays for G.R. Elton From His American Friends.* (Cambridge : Cambridge University Press, 1982), pp. 70-85.

2. J.E.B. Mayor (ed.), *The English Works of John Fisher,* Early English Text Society, extra series, XXVII (London : 1876), 426 (11. 10-12) and 427 (11. 14-16, 33-34).

3. J.H.L. Kengen (ed.), *Memoriale Credencium : A Late Middle English Manual of Theology for Lay People edited from Bodley McTanner 201* (Nijmegen, The Netherlands, Dept. of Middle English, [1980]), 45 (11. 18-19).

4. Walter W. Skeat (ed.), *The Complete Works of Geoffrey Chaucer* (Oxford, 1894), IV, 324 (1.130).

NOVAE NARRATIONES[1]

E. Shanks (Editor)

Debt on a Loan

B 209. A etc. lays before you this : that B etc. wrongfully detains from him and does not render to him ten shillings in silver which he owes him. And wrongfully because, whereas he lent him these ten shillings on Easter day, the year etc. in his own house in N, to [repay] the aforesaid ten shillings the day of Pentecost in the same year at the same place : at which (224r) day A came and awaited his payment at the same place from morning until evening, B did not pay him anything nor did any man in his name ; but he has detained his money until the present time, wrongfully and to his damages etc.

Another Form

B 210. Or as follows : and wrongfully because the aforesaid John bound himself to this same W, for grain which he bought from him, namely wheat etc., at such a day, such a year, such a place, in twenty marks to be paid on such a day in such a place ; at which day W came to the place agreed upon and asked for his money, [but] he could not have it ; but he detained it and still does, wrongfully etc.

Debt

B 210A. J de C, who is here, lays before you this : that Roger de W, who is there, wrongfully detains from him and does not render to him forty shillings in silver. And wrongfully because this same Roger bought from him ten ells of blue [cloth] the Monday after etc. in the vill etc. in the house etc. for forty shillings in silver to be paid at such a day [following] in the same place, on which day this J awaited his payment etc ; but this Roger paid him nothing,but ever since has detained this money from him and still detains it, wrongfully etc.

Another Form

B 210B. [B] etc. this etc. : that J, the bishop of N by his attorney etc. to [whose hands] the goods and chattels of H de C came as to the ordinary of the place because the aforesaid [H] died intestate, wrongfully detains from him and does not render to him ten pounds in silver, which the aforesaid [H] owed him. And wrongfully because on the Monday next etc. in the vill of N in a street called etc. in the house of this same B where he is resident, this same B sold to the aforesaid H, a horse for ten pounds in silver, the money to be paid at the feast etc. in the same year and in the same place ; on which day this same B awaited his payment in the place assigned [but] could not have it ; wherefore he approached this same H and often during his lifetime asked him to pay his money, [but] he would not pay it ; wherefore often since his death [B] has come to this same bishop, as to the ordinary of the place, into whose hands the goods and chattels of the aforesaid H came because he died intestate, and asked him etc. he etc. and to [his] etc. [p. 109]

NOTE

1. E. Shanks, ed., *Novae Narrationes*, Selden Society (London : Quaritch Pub. Co., 1963), p. 109.

THE LAWS OF MANU[1]

47. When a creditor sues (before the king) for the recovery of money from a debtor, let him make the debtor pay the sum which the creditor proves (to be due).

48. By whatever means a creditor may be able to obtain possession of his property, even by those means may he force the debtor and make him pay.

49. By moral suasion, by suit of law, by artful management, or by the customary proceeding, a creditor may recover property lent ; and fifthly, by force.

50. A creditor who himself recovers his property from his debtor, must not be blamed by the king for retaking what is his own. [p. 262]

215. A hired (servant or workman) who, without being ill, out of pride fails to perform his work according to the agreement, shall be fined eight *krishnalas* and no wages shall be paid to him.

216. But (if he is really) ill, (and) after recovery performs (his work) according to the original agreement, he shall receive his wages even after (the lapse of) a very long time.

217. But if he, whether sick or well, does not (perform or) cause to be performed (by others) his work according to his agreement, the wages for that work shall not be given to him, even (if it be only) slightly incomplete.

218. Thus the law for the non-payment of wages has been completely stated ; I will next explain the law concerning men who break an agreement.

219. If a man belonging to a corporation inhabiting a village or a district, after swearing to an agreement, breaks it through avarice (the king) shall banish him from his realm.

220. And having imprisoned such a breaker of an agreement, he shall compel him to pay six *nishkas*, (each of) four *suvarnas*, and one *satamana* of silver. [p. 293]

NOTE

1. F. Max Muller, ed., G. Buhler, trans., "The Laws of Manu," in *The Sacred Books of the East*, vol. 25 (Delhi : Motilal Banarsidass, 1967), pp. 262-293.

THE LEX SALICA[1]

1. If any freeman or leet have made to another a promise to pay, then he to whom the promise was made shall, within 40 days or within such term as was agreed when he made the promise, go to the house of that man with witnesses, or with appraisers. And if he (the debtor) be unwilling to make the promised payment, he shall be sentenced to 15 shillings above the debt which he had promised. [p. 507]

NOTE

1. Albert Kocourek and John H. Wigmore, eds., "The Lex Salica," in *Primitive and Ancient Legal Institutions*, vol. 1, (Boston : Little, Brown & Co., 1915), p. 507.

LAWS OF ALFRED[1]

Section 1, Subsection 2

I, then, Alfred, King of the West Saxons, have shewn these to all my councillors, and they have declared that it met with the approval of all, that they should be observed.

1. In the first place we enjoin you, as a matter of supreme importance, that every man shall abide carefully by his oath and his pledge.

s. 1. If anyone is wrongfully constrained to promise either of these : to betray his lord or to render aid in an unlawful undertaking, then it is better to be false [to the promise] than to perform it.

s. 2. If, however, he pledges himself to something which it is lawful to carry out and proves false to his pledge, he shall humbly give his weapons and possessions to his friends to keep, and remain 40 days in prison at a royal mannor, and undergo there whatever [sentence] the bishop prescribes for him ; and his relatives shall feed him if he himself has no food. [p. 63]

NOTE

1. F.L. Attenborough, ed., "Laws of Alfred," in *The Laws of the Earliest English Kings* (Cambridge : Cambridge University Press, 1922), p. 507.

2. Law of Property

THE RATIONAL STRENGTH OF ENGLISH LAW[1]

F.H. Lawson

Now the law of property, and more especially the law of real property, presents in almost every respect a marked contrast to the rest of the law as so defined. It is logical and orderly, its concepts are perfectly defined, and they stand in well recognized relations to one another. It is no longer easy to make any remarkable inventions, though new combinations of concepts are constantly being worked out. Above all, this part of the law is intensely abstract and has become a calculus remarkably similar to mathematics. The various concepts had, and still have, when properly understood, a very necessary relation to the economic facts of life, but once created and defined they seem to move among themselves according to the rules of a game which exists for its own purposes. So extreme are these various characteristics that they make of this part of the law something more logical and more abstract than anything that to my knowledge can be found in any other law in the world. More than anything else we seem to be moving in a world of pure ideas from which everything physical or material is entirely excluded.... [p. 79]

NOTE

1. F.H. Lawson, *The Rational Strength of English Law* (London : Stevens, 1951), p. 79.

THE UNIQUE NATURE OF THE CONCEPTS OF WESTERN LAW[1]

J.C. Smith

. . .[U]nlike modern law, primitive and archaic law contain few abstract or theoretical concepts. Most concepts in such legal systems derive their meaning directly from, or in terms of sensed experience. This difference can be illustrated by comparing the modern law concepts of contract and property with their closest counterparts in archaic law. While every society has a concept or concepts relating to property and commercial transactions carried out upon the basis of mutual consensus, the concepts of "ownership" and "contract" in the sense of abstract bundles of jural relations exist only in classical Roman and modern law.

In modern law the term "property" has two meanings, the land or chattels, and the imageless, theoretical legal relations through which human behaviour is controlled in regard to them. The concept of "ownership" as a bundle of legal relations *in rem* by which people's conduct is regulated in regard to resources is unknown in both archaic and primitive law. In primitive legal systems an individual's personal property such as wearing apparel, ornaments, tools, weapons, and horses were his not because of any legal conception of ownership, but because of the directly sensed physical connexion between the individual and his personal goods. A number of writers have suggested that this type of property was conceived as being a part of the individual, or a manifestation or extension of his personality.

Equally the concept of property in archaic law was that of physical possession. The early Roman or Greek family was inseparably connected to their land through their religion. The family occupied it, and it was the location of the family hearth and sacred fire which was not to be moved. The souls of their dead who were buried there possessed the fields. Thus the soil and the home belonged to the family in the sense of those dead, the living, and those yet to be born. The slaves, flocks, and herds were not owned by the family but were part of the family in a similar way as were the children. The element which held the various parts together and welded them into a single unit was the relationship of the patriarchal family head to the members. His power was practically without limit and was exercised over persons, slaves, flocks, and herds alike.

The primitive and archaic concepts of property are generally found to have two constituents, the empirically known physical relationship of possession, and an introspected feeling that something belongs to oneself, which springs from such factors as actual possession, the religion, and the family. This relationship and feeling would be often expressed by the equivalent of the English phrase "this is mine." The languages of such societies do not contain a word which corresponds to "ownership" : or the "dominium" of classical Roman law. The words which connote property usually mean the equivalent of physical possession or the taking of possession.

When property was wrongfully taken from the possession of a person or family who considered it their own, the physical relationship of possession would be broken and that relationship would then exist towards the wrongful taker. Before the development of classical Roman law, no question of ownership could arise for a tribunal to decide as the corresponding concept to ownership was possession. The removal of possession from the prior possessor destroyed his relationship. When each of two people claimed that a certain object belonged to them, the question for the tribunal to decide was not who had the proprietary rights, but instead who had the older or the prior possession. Although the fact of the previous possession and the wrongful removal gave the original possessor an action in law, this action did not connote ownership.

The concept of property of the early common law was similar to that of archaic law. In disputes regarding property, the issue was never "who owned the property ?" — theoretical constructs being foreign to the people's conceptual structure — but rather "has a wrong been committed to possession ?" For instance, if a dispute arose in regard to a cow, the claimant would grasp the animal in dispute by the ear and swear that the animal had been stolen from him. The possessor then had to show that either he had possessed the animal since birth or had purchased it from a third party. If the latter was true the third party would be accused of theft and would then become the defendant. A nearly identical procedure existed in such diverse cultures as the Babylonian, Greek, Continental Saxon, and Welsh.

The first recorded appearance of the word "owner" in our language is 1340, and the first instance of the appearance of ownership is 1583. Neither owner nor ownership became common legal terminology until the seventeenth century. The word "possession" was not introduced into legal terminology until Littleton borrowed it from Roman law in order to distinguish possession of chattels from possession of land. There was only one word used to describe an individual's relationship to his property and that was the word "seisin" which meant simply physical possession and was used equally of chattels as of land. The person of this period who was seised of land had the land itself and did not conceive of himself as holding abstract legal rights as against other people, which allowed him to enjoy his land. When he was disseised he had nothing but his legal remedies. Thus, if John came upon Blackacre and disseised Richard, John, since he was the person seised, could :

1. convey the estate to anyone else ;
2. his heir would succeed to the property ;
3. his widow was entitled to dower ;
4. if Richard died without heirs, the land would not escheat to the lord ;
5. John and not Richard owed the feudal dues to the lord.

Richard on the other hand :

1. had nothing to alienate ; he could not convey the land ;
2. his wife was not entitled to dower ;
3. he could not after five days from his disseisin retake possession of the land by force.

Although Richard could bring an action to recover the land, he could not convey or assign this remedy, as it was based on the directly sensed relationship of possession which only Richard had had with the land.

The empirical concept of property of the early English common law can be illustrated by the methods of conveying land. Since the relationship between people and their property was the physical relationship of possession rather than the legal rights between individuals, the only way an object could be conveyed was to transfer possession. This process was termed livery of seisin ; that is, delivery of possession. The two parties would come upon the land, each with his witnesses, and the one would hand the other a twig or piece of turf which would symbolize the land passing from the possession of the one person to the other. Then the *feoffor,* as the grantor was called, would vacate the land, taking his goods with him, and the *feoffee* would take possession. Other methods of conveying land such as the use of the fine, common recovery, or lease and release, equally revolved around a delivery of possession, without which there could be no conveyance. [pp. 198-202]

NOTE

1. J.C. Smith, "The Unique Nature of the Concept of Western Law," *Canadian Bar Review* 46 (1968) : 198-202.

THE HISTORY OF ENGLISH LAW[1]

Sir Frederick Pollock and Frederic Maitland

Leaving out of sight for a while the cases in which there has been a bailment, we may consider the position of the owner whose goods have been taken from him, in order that we may if possible come to some understanding of that puzzling phenomenon, the ascription of property to the trespasser and even to the thief, which we find in the later Year Books.

Cattle lifting is our starting point. It is a theme to which the Anglo-Saxon dooms and the parallel "folk laws" of the continental nations are ever recurring. If only cattle lifting could be suppressed, the legislators will have done all or almost all that they can hope to do for the protection of the owner of movables. The typical action for the recovery of a movable is highly penal. It is an action against a thief, or at any rate it is an action which aims at the discovery and punishment of a thief as well as at the restitution of stolen goods. An action we call it, but it is a prosecution, a prosecution in the primary sense of that word, a pursuit, a chase ; a great part of the legal procedure takes place before any one has made his way to a court of law. My cattle have been driven off ; I must follow the trail ; it is the duty of my neighbours to assist me, to ride with me. If we catch the marauder still driving the beasts before him, we take him as a "hand-having" thief and he is dealt with in a summary fashion ; "he can not deny" the theft. The practice of ear-marking or branding cattle, and the legal duty that I am under of publicly exposing to the view of my neighbours whatever cattle I have, make it a matter of notoriety that these beasts, which this man is driving before him, have been taken from me. Even if we cannot catch a thief in the act, the trail is treated as of great importance. If it leads into a man's land, he must show that it leads out again ; otherwise it will "stand instead of a foreoath" ; it is an accusing fact. If the possessor has no unbroken trail in his favour, then, when he discovers the thing, he lays his hand upon it and claims it. He declares the ox to be his and it falls upon the possessor to say how he came by it. The possessor has to give up the thing or to answer this question. He may perhaps assert that the beast is his by birth and rearing ; a commoner answer will be that he acquired it from a third person whom he names. Then the pursuer with his left hand grasping one of the beast's ears, and his right upon a relic or a sword, swears that the beast is his and has been stolen from him, and the possessor with his left hand grasping the other ear swears that he is naming the person from whom he purchased.

Now at length there may be proceedings before a court of law. The possessor must produce this third person in court ; he has vouched a warrantor and must find him. If this vouchee appears and confesses the warranty, then the beast is delivered over to him, and the accusation is made against him. He can vouch another warrantor, and so, by following backwards the course along which the beast has passed, we may come at length to the thief. The rules about proof we need not here consider, only we must notice that the possessor, though he is not convicted of theft, may often have to give up the thing to the pursuer. The elaborate law of warranty, the attempts made in England and other countries to prevent undue delay by a restriction of the process to some three or four vouchers, these show plainly enough that the man whose beasts have been stolen can claim them from any one in whose possession they are. If the possessor can name no warrantor, it is still possible that he should protect himself against the charge of theft by showing that he purchased the thing in open market before the proper witnesses ; but he will have to surrender that thing ; it is not his though he bought it honestly. Sales and purchases ought to take place before official witnesses, and the possessor who has neither warrantor nor witness has himself to blame if he is treated as a thief. [pp. 157-158]

NOTE

1. Sir Frederick Pollock and Frederic Maitland, *The History of English Law*, 2nd ed., vol. 2 (Cambridge : Cambridge University Press, 1968), pp. 157-158.

SELECT CASES OF PROCEDURE WITHOUT WRIT UNDER HENRY III[1]

H.G. Richardson and G.O. Sayles

Curia Regis Roll, No. 131

And Geoffrey comes and says that Richard sold a horse to Hugh of Ossulstone and Hugh sold it to William son of Reiner and William sold it to Henry of Hambleton. And then Ralph Day came and said that the horse was his. And so each of them vouched the other to warranty until it came to Richard. And Richard came into open county court and said that he had a good warrantor. And, because he did not have him present in court, the sheriff arrested Richard. And the sheriff agrees that Ralph Day said only that the horse was his and was removed from his possession.

Afterwards Ralph came. And he is told to find pledges if he wishes to sue. And let the sheriff take pledges from Richard and, if he can try that plea in his own court, let him do so, but otherwise let him take good pledges from Richard until the arrival of the justices. [p. 25]

NOTE

1. H.G. Richardson and G.O. Sayles, *Select Cases of Procedure Without Writ Under Henry III*, vol. 40, Selden Society (London : Quaritch Pub., 1941), p. 25.

THE CODE OF HAMMURABI[1]

9. If a man has lost anything, and finds it in the hands of another ; if the holder says, "A seller sold it me ; before the elders I bought it." And if the claimant says, "I can produce witnesses who will recognize my property." Then the purchaser shall bring the vendor who gave it him, and the elders before whom he bought it ; and the claimant the witnesses recognizing his lost property. The judge shall weigh their evidence. The elders before whom the purchase was made, and the witnesses recognizing the property, shall affirm before God what they know. The seller shall be held for a thief, and slain : the claimant shall receive back his lost property ; and the purchaser shall receive back the money he paid from the house of the seller.

10. If the purchaser has not produced the seller from whom he received it, and the elders before whom he bought it ; but the claimant has brought witnesses recognizing the property ; then the purchaser shall be held for a thief, and slain ; and the owner shall take his lost property.

11. If the claimant has not brought his witnesses recognizing the property, he has acted in bad faith, he has calumniated ; he shall be slain.

12. If the seller has gone to his fate, then from his house the purchaser shall claim five-fold as the penalty in the case.

13. If that man has not the elders at hand, the judge shall give him a time, up to six months. If in six months his witnesses do not appear, he has acted in bad faith ; the penalty of that case he shall bear. [pp.29-30]

NOTE

1. Chilperic Edwards, trans., *The Hammurabi Code and the Sinaitic Legislation* (Port Washington, N.Y. : Kennikat Press, 1971), pp. 29-30.

THE BABYLONIAN LAWS[1]

G.R. Driver and John C. Miles (Editors)

The typical movable of those days was cattle. If a man's beast has been carried off, he must follow the trail with the assistance which was due from his neighbours and, when he finds it, he lays his hand upon it and claims it. The possessor must either give up the beast or assert that it is his own, when the usual answer is that he has bought it of someone, whom he names. Then the owner grasps an ear of the beast and swears on a relic that it is his, and the person grasping the other ear swears that he has acquired it from the person named. The parties then go before a court and the possessor must produce the seller whom he has "vouched to warranty," if the seller or vouchee confesses the warranty, the beast is handed to him and the accusation is brought against him. He, too, can vouch to warranty the person from whom he has acquired the beast. Hence "sales and purchases ought to take place before official witnesses and the possessor who has neither warrantor nor witness has himself to blame if he is treated as a thief." [p. 96]

NOTE

1. G.R. Driver and John C. Miles, eds., *The Babylonian Laws* (Oxford : Clarendon Press, 1952), p. 96.

LAWS OF HOWEL DDA[1] [Ancient Laws of Wales]

33. Whosoever may will to swear to the property, is to do it in this manner. If he swear to what is inanimate let him swear to it, with his left hand upon any part thereof. If it be a living animal, let him swear to it, with his left hand upon the right ear of the animal, and his right hand upon the relics : and let the defendant place his right hand upon the left ear of the animal ; and so let him swear to the plaintiff, that there was no owner to it, who ought either to purchase or to sell it, excepting himself, by right ; and, moreover, that he did not part with it, either by gift, or loan, or deposit, or sell it ; but that, either by theft, or surreption, or straying he lost it ; naming the day or night in the week, and naming the week in the month, and naming the month in the season, and naming the season in the year, when it was missing.

34. There are three *arddelws* (vouchees of defences) to an animal : birth and rearing ; possession before loss ; and *arwaesav* (person, or authority, a defendant avouches to be the guarantor of the right to property with which he is charged to be unlawfully possessed). To inanimate things there are only two : possession before loss ; and *arwaesav.*

35. If a person seek his *arddelw* on birth and rearing, let him proceed thus : let him have guardians to speak to the mother's being his property, and that the animal was born and bred in his possession, and was not out of his possession since its birth until that day. The guardians to be produced by him are, a neighbour above his hand, and another below his hand ; that is, a man above his rank and another below his rank ; and, if he can obtain these, it will be sufficient for him.

36. If he choose his *arddelw* on possession before loss, let him swear to it, according to the form we have previously mentioned. After he has sworn to it, let him say that the animal was in his possession, either a week, or a month, or two, or a season, before the other had it ; and that he has guardians lawfully to prove its being in his possession, whether a week, or a fortnight, or a month, or a season, before he lost it : if he can do this, it is sufficient for him.

37. If his *arddelw* is by *arwaesav*, let him say : "Who will *arddelw* or *arwaesav* this ?" And if one be in the field, let his *arwaesav* take it, let the claimant swear to it in his hand ; and he is, if so minded, to seek another *arwaesav*, or another lawful *arddelw;* or let him fail in the cause.

38. It is not right that there should be a raith, after detention and swearing, only *arwaesav*, or custody before loss, or birth and rearing. [pp. 542-543]

NOTE

1. Albert Kocourek and John H. Wigmore, eds., *Evolution of Law Series : Sources of Ancient and Primitive Law*, vol. 1 (Boston : Little, Brown & Co., 1915), pp. 542-543.

FAMILY PROPERTY AMONG THE YORUBAS[1]

G.B.A. Coker

Basic Principles of Land Tenure in Nigeria

It is necessary to understand that the basis or unit of landholding in Nigeria is the family. Some writers have described the unit of holding as tribal or communal apart from being family. It is easy to demonstrate the error of their observations. Apart from the sources which are more or less strictly legal, there is abundant testimony from other writers of repute to the contrary. Lord Lugard, who carried out extensive fieldwork in the study of the people of Northern Nigeria, in describing the native land tenure has stated as follows :

> Title to land accrued to the latest conquerors and where land has become derelict as a result of extermination, slave raids, migration or pestilence, the individual who first reclaimed it claimed ownership of it for himself and his descendants. The title to such land was vested in the head of the family and further areas reclaimed by its members were added to the family lands. [2]

And, despite his own conclusions about the relationship of the chief to the land, from which he conjectures that land may also have been held in common by the tribe, Lord Lugard agrees that :

> It is clear from this description that African land tenure is not communal in the sense of tenure in common. Its fundamental characteristic seems rather to be an individual tenure of land derived from the common stock at the disposal of the tribe or family.[3]

It is not difficult to appreciate the difficulties which beset a foreigner trying to comprehend a complicated scheme of native life against an English background. In early communities it was extremely unlikely that the distinction between the family and the tribe should be sufficiently clear, for the members of such communities considered themselves to be of the same stock or lineage. The interrelation between the organization of the family and that of the tribe made, and indeed in some areas still makes, it possible to assume that the juristic powers possessed by one are coterminous with those of the other. Dr. Meek has described the same subject among the Jukum tribes in Northern Nigeria. He has pointed out that among these tribes all unoccupied land is free to any person to farm without any reference to anyone, not even the king or chief, and there is no "communism" as regards ownership of land in the modern sense of that word. But then he was faced with the fact, all too obvious to be ignored, that isolated parcels of land were held by persons who almost invariably claimed to have descended from a common ancestor. He explained this by pointing out that members of the same household generally endeavour to farm in one locality and also that a farmer was obliged to obtain permission from the members of the family of a deceased farmer if he intended to farm within the site of the other farmer's house. Dr. Meek's explanation, however, reveals that, whilst it may be correct that unoccupied land was free to the members of the tribe, there was still a unit of control, that being the family. In any case, no other form of control or administrative unit was suggested and it was positively stated that there was no "communal" or tribal holding in the modern sense.

Land, probably the most important source of wealth in a developing country, can always be the subject of a great many interests and derivative rights. These are often difficult to elucidate and, where land is subject to native customary tenure, it is always the subject of rights and interests vested in both the individual and the group, and such rights and interests are frequently co-existent with each other. This, to a very large extent, must be responsible for the erroneous conception, peculiar to some writers and fieldworkers in anthropology, that the ownership of land under native law and custom is vested in the community as such. Ancestral worship on common grounds and many forms of social and religious ceremonies held on land commonly held have also helped to make more obscure an already entangled subject. It is, of course, clear, on closer analysis, that the control exercised by the community as a group on lands is mostly social or political and does not extend beyond the limits necessary to maintain the group solidarity of the community. Actual physical control of native lands is vested in the families and, speaking generally, only in the sense that it is an aggregate of the constituent family groups could the community or tribe be said to own the land.

That this is so is further proved by the fact that, although the king or the chief is held among the Nigerians to be the head of the tribe or community, yet he has no powers by himself to sell or alienate the lands at his disposal. He is bound by native law and custom to allocate to the several families for their own use portions of such lands ; in many cases he can also allocate to strangers portions of the lands at his disposal, against the payment of tribute. At no period of history was this the function of the entire community or tribe and no evidence is recorded by which any such system of allocation could be described as a general sharing between the members of the community or tribe concerned. . . .

> The chief is everywhere regarded as the symbol of the residuary reversionary and ultimate ownership of all land held by a territorial community. He holds on behalf of the whole community in the capacity of a caretaker or trustee only but he allocates portions of land to family heads according to need and these in turn reallocate among their members.[4]

Such a system of land-holding, almost always confused with land ownership, is bound to create, and has indeed created, a very complex situation within the compartment of property law in Nigeria. The rights possessed by the members of the family over its land are more often confused with the rights of the family as a corporate entity and, worse still, with those of the chief or the head of the family as a caretaker in the comprehensive structure. It is, of course, inevitable that this should be so, for the compartment of the law of succession frequently intrudes into that of strict property law.

It is perhaps apposite to discuss, at this juncture, the customary ideas of the legal conceptions of ownership and possession. In an ordinary fee simple estate, according to English law, the radical or absolute ownership of the land, the subject of the estate, is vested in the Crown. This is in theory an ascription of the absolute ownership of all lands to the Crown or sovereign and the estates and interests possessed by the subjects are merely derivative. In practice the effect of this is hardly realized, for the average owner of a fee simple estate considers himself the absolute owner for all purposes. This consideration, rightly or wrongly, supports the manner in which the multitude of rights comprising a freehold estate is exercised, one such instance being the well-known right that such an owner is not obliged, except in certain defined cases, to obtain any permission from the Crown before exercising any of the rights vested in him. That is why he is, in popular language, referred to as the owner of the land. Under native law and custom, however, the connotation of the word "owner," as far as land is concerned, is entirely different. Far more different from its counterpart in the English legal system is that fluid and erratic legal concept which lawyers call "possession." It is not intended here to discuss the abstract division of possession into mediate or immediate, or indeed the more abstruse analysis of that concept familiar to students of the Austinian theory of law, but only the common everyday usage and acceptance of that word. In the English legal system possession is a relationship between the owner and the subject which is recognized and protected by law. Within this wide ambit of definition it is possible to employ the term to suit all the different purposes to which it has been applied by generations of lawyers. Under native law and custom, however, possession is the only relationship into which all forms of holding could be tidily reduced.

To begin with, it is futile to try to apply the common law conception of ownership of land to a holding under native law and custom. This is perhaps a reasonable way of putting the subject, for it is not possible to group together all the rights akin to ownership within any well-known legal terminology. The aggregate of rights vested in a land-owning family over the family land is probably no less than the aggregate of rights vested in an owner *in stricto sensu* but those several rights are not identical. It is appropriate to point out that it is more correct to state that a family or a person possess rights over land than to say that he owns the land. That this is so is proved by the fact that, although in loose language the family is always referred to as the "owner" of the land, yet it is not possible, except under certain conditions, to deprive any of the members of his customary rights. This is also demonstrated by the fact that the individual members of the family cannot by themselves divest themselves of their own customary rights. It is impossible to resist the fact that these several rights may differ among different tribes and, as pointed out before, the divergencies affect substantially the law of succession. It is sufficient to observe here that the rights of the members of the family do not derive from the corporate rights of the family as such, but exist by operation of law. Hence it is that the several rights of the members could be inferior to, coterminous with, or indeed superior to the sum total of the rights of the family. Dr. Elias has described the position in this way :

> What we have said so far, as well as what we shall say later, will show that the land-holding recognized by African customary law is neither "communal" holding nor "ownership" (in the strict English sense of the term). The term "corporate" would be an apter description of the system of land-holding, since the relation between the group and the land is invariably complex in that the rights of the individual members often co-exist with those of the group in the same parcel of land. But the individual members hold definitely ascertained and well recognized rights within the comprehensive holding of the group. [5]

Native law and custom does not, therefore, vest ownership in the strict sense in the family but ascribes to the family the aggregate of the rights which could be described (for want of a better terminology) as "ownership." To all intents and purposes the family is the owner and in modern conveyancing the family is usually recited as possessing "an estate of inheritance." In practice no harm is contemplated or even done by employing these terms, but the precautionary need to guard against an underestimation of the competing rights of the members, equally recognized by law and not merely derivative, cannot be overstressed.

It only remains to emphasize that possession is a much more important conception in native law and custom with regard to property holding. It embraces all forms of legal relationships existing between the family and/or its members and the property belonging to the family. We shall see later that possession, more than anything else, is a characteristic phenomenon of native jurisprudence, and the employment of the concept in native law and custom completely obviates the difficulty, otherwise insurmountable, of relating the various legal rights of members as well as of the family to existing forms of action for the purposes of litigation. An example of this will be found in the settled practice that an action for trespass is almost always preferred in the case of an infraction of family rights over lands. Actual physical occupation by the family is probably a legal impossibility and, in any case, such possession as is necessary to ground an action for trespass in the strict legal acceptation could hardly ever exist in the family as such. However, no anachronism exists when it is realized that the rights of the family are always vested in possession ; it would equally be understandable that an invasion of any or all of those rights must be a trespass thereon. [pp. 29-34]

NOTES

1. G.B.A. Coker, *Family Property Among the Yorubas* (London : Sweet and Maxwell Ltd., 1966), pp. 29-34.

2. Sir F.J.D. Lugard, *The Dual Mandate in British Tropical Africa* (London : William Blackwood & Sons, Ltd., 1926), p. 283.

3. *Ibid.*, p. 285.

4. T.O. Elias, *The Nature of African Customary Law*, (Manchester : Manchester University Press, 1956), p. 164.

5. *Ibid.*

PRIMITIVE ECONOMICS OF THE NEW ZEALAND MAORI[1]

Raymond Firth

Social Structure and Economic Organization

To begin with local grouping — the Maori dwelt in villages, each of which was the centre of the economic life of the people of the surrounding district. Among the most important *foci*, or rallying points, for the activities of the community were the *marae*, or public square, and the *whare whakairo*, the carved meeting-house, each a centre of "intensive sociality." The former was the stage for important socio-economic events, the latter an object of tribal sentiment and a valued possession, embodying the finest results of artistic taste and technical skill. It was produced, too, by a complex form of organization of labour, involving preliminary accumulation of wealth, careful integration of work, and a lavish system of apportionment of goods. Each village was composed of households, which functioned as economic units.

In respect of kinship grouping, in general, the persons in a household comprised the members of the *whanau,* a group of people closely related by descent from some person three or four generations distant from the youngest member. Such a family group was the basic unit of the Maori economy. The individual family certainly existed, and appears to have constituted at times a separate economic group. Its importance has been somewhat underestimated by writers on Maori sociology, owing to the prominence of the *whanau* ; the latter certainly assumed wider social functions. In the economic sphere the special importance of the individual family law in the reciprocal obligations of husband and wife in respect of food, clothing, domestic duties, and care of the children ; the new set of ties created between two kinship groups now allied by marriage ; and the rules of succession and inheritance, the one concerned with rank and its accompanying privileges of wealth, the other with the distribution of property. The *whanau* held group-ownership of certain types of property, and also as a body exercised rights to land and its products. Tasks requiring a small body of workers and co-operation of a not very complex order were performed by the *whanau,* and the apportionment of food was largely managed on this basis. Each family group was a cohesive, self-contained unit, managing its own affairs, both social and economic, except as these affected village or tribal policy. Members of a *whanau,* on the whole, worked, ate, and dwelt together in a distict group.

The more inclusive kinship group, the *hapu,* was correlated with the major village activities. More important species of property, such as a war-canoe, a meeting-house, a large eel weir, were regarded as the property of the whole *hapu* and were used by the members as a body. All the land surrounding the village, incorporating, of course, the rights of individuals and of *whanau,* was under the ownership of this group, while important tasks involving considerable labour power saw a muster of all its members. At large tribal feasts, too, and on similar occasions of ceremony the *hapu* functioned as a united body.

The economic functions of the tribe (*iwi*) were confined almost solely to participation in huge feasts and to an all-embracing over-right to the land within its borders ; the latter was made manifest in the rallying of *hapu* to defend the tribal land at any point invaded. The *waka* was a loose political aggregation of tribes, and had no economic function.

It is plain that in Maori society the economic structure is to a large extent coincident with the kinship grouping ; there are, for instance, no economic associations of any importance which are not based upon it. This is to be expected, once the fundamental value attached by natives to the kinship tie is realized.

The interrelation between the economic and other aspects of social life has been shown in the examination of various institutions. The rank and position of the chief, determined primarily by his eminence of birth, was buttressed by his accumulation and distribution of wealth. This in turn depended to quite a large extent upon his plurality of wives. There is then a definite correlation between rank, wealth, and polygyny, each of which reacts upon and supports the others. Marriage, also, had its definite economic aspect, both in regard to the relations of husband and wife, and the wider circle of their kin. The inquiry might have been extended to some of the more spectacular institutions, such as the *hakari* (feast), the custom of *muru* (compensation by plunder), and the gift-exchange ;it could be shown how each is connected with social structure, with kinship ties, and ideas of communal solidarity, besides displaying an economic side as well....

... [T]he economic organization of any community is very closely bound up with the social structure in such manner that each serves to reinforce the other. It is a very sober principle, but one which has not yet wholly found its way into the economic organon, and which it is essential to realize both for theoretical analysis and descriptive method.

. . .Kinship organization appears to be rather a determinant than an outcome of economic structure. The family, the primary group, has its roots in the biological and social, rather than in the purely economic sphere.... The central theme which it is so essential both for economist and anthropologist to grasp is that of the deep interaction between these two fundamental aspects of culture.... [pp. 124-127]

Seen in true perspective the system of ownership in a community is essentially the mechanism which standardizes and gives stability to the relation between members of the society and the body of material culture and natural resources which they have at command. It stands therefore at the base of economic welfare, and reacts strongly upon the efficiency of production. This has already been demonstrated in considering the effects of the concentration of certain types of wealth in the hands of the chief men of the Maori community.

A problem which for some decades has occupied the attention of anthropologists and other workers in the field of social science is the mode of holding property which characterized man in the primeval economic state. It is a question which has aroused considerable controversy, and as yet none of the proffered solutions has met with any general acceptance. Neither in the guise of a hard-headed individualist nor as the disciple of a pure and untrammelled communism — the two most popular roles for which he has been cast — does original man appear to be wholly pleasing to the more critically minded of his descendants. . . . All that is attempted here is to examine the Maori system of ownership as it worked in relation to the other elements of the economic structure.

It must be realized in considering the problem of the control of man over material goods that such terms as "property" and "ownership," which are employed to indicate a certain set of relationships in our own society, do not necessarily preserve the same connotation when applied in a native community. The essential factors in the situation — the individual, the goods, and the other members of his community — remain unchanged, but the set of concepts by which these are related has been formed against a different cultural background. Hence the impression that is conveyed to a European by the simple and satisfying statement that an object is "owned" by a certain person may be entirely divorced from reality through his ignorance of all those rights and qualifications which to the native form an integral part of the situation. The practical truth of this has been demonstrated many times by the misunderstandings which have thus arisen in regard to the alienation of native land.

In consequence of this difference in the native viewpoint and terminology from our own the effort is made here to describe the Maori system of the holding of property at first in terms of use and control of goods, until the underlying principles have been sufficiently well elaborated to allow of a more explicit formulation of the native theory. The most satisfactory method would undoubtedly be to give an inventory of the main specific types of goods in a community, studying in each case the people who had rights over each item, the reason, nature, and extent of their control, and whether they exercised it as individuals or in virtue of being members of some definite group. From such an ideal field worker's description the basic principles of the institution of property could be deduced.... [pp. 330-331]

The modes by which rights to land were acquired and retained may now be considered. These were of three main types — conquest, occupation, and ancestral right.

Conquest and Discovery

In days of old wars were frequent, and large areas of land changed hands as the result of conquest of the original owners, accompanied in many cases by a literal absorption of them by the victorious tribe. Such land was termed *whenua raupatu,* and the nature of the original title would not be forgotten. When the territory was left entirely open for occupation the method of *taunaha whenua,* bespeaking of land, was sometimes followed as a means of acquiring title among the conquerors . . . . This practice also obtained, according to tradition, on the first discovery of certain districts of New Zealand by the fourteenth century immigrants. It is recorded in the story of the coming of the Arawa canoe that the shore was distinctly seen one morning at daylight. Tama-te Kapua, the leader, at once sprang up and called out, "That point there (Maketu point) is the bridge of my nose." Tai, another chief, eagerly arose and said, "that hillock to the south there, and hitherward to the mountain is the belly of Tapuika" (his son), while Hei interrupted by saying, "From behind the mountain there extending to that range of mountains indistinctly seen in the north is the belly of my son Waitaha." It was for this reason that the other chiefs on landing proceeded to the south ; the district had all been annexed by those three men. Rights to land seem also to have been established by those early discoverers on the basis of a kind of prospecting trip during which they travelled over and named the land. To traverse a district in this manner for the purpose of establishing possession was termed *takahi,* meaning literally to "tread" the land.

Occupation

For a title to land obtained by conquest or discovery to be valid, occupation had to be effective. If one tribe were defeated by another and their lands occupied, the original owners, if thoroughly dispossessed or enslaved, had no further claim to the land, unless in future years they could win back their territory again by intermarriage or force of arms. But invasion and driving out of the inhabitants was not sufficient to establish a title if the land were not permanently occupied. Again, even if the land were settled for a time by invaders but the dispossessed tribe still managed to maintain itself in freedom within its own borders, scattered in the forest or in hiding in the mountains, their title to the whole of the land still held good. "*I ka tonu taku ahi i runga i toku whenua*" (my fire has ever been kept alight upon my land) was the saying, indicating that their rights had not been extinguished. The proof of this continuity was sufficient to establish ownership in later years.

In ordinary times periodical visits were made to the borders of tribal territory, where small pieces of ground were cultivated, birds snared, or rats trapped in order by such acts to keep up the rights of possession in these lands. This also served as a challenge to neighbouring tribes to contest the claim. Thus at the time of Cook's arrival, Ngati Whanaunga, according to Horeta te Taniwha, were living at Whitianga. "Our tribe was living there at that time. We did not live there as our permanent home, but were there according to our custom of living for some time on each of our blocks of land to keep our claim to each, and that our fire might be kept alight on each block so that it might not be taken from us by some other tribe."[2] Certain areas lying on the borders between two tribes were *whenua tautohe,* debatable lands, claimed by both sides, and were often hotly contested, each party endeavouring to establish ownership, though not actually occupying the land.

Ancestral Right

One most important basis of ownership to land was ancestral right (*take tipuna).* This leads to the consideration of the rules of inheritance in land. As this subject has already been dealt with fairly fully by a number of writers, all that need be given here is a summary of the main principles involved. A Maori could inherit land through either parent, so that if his father and mother happened to belong to different hapu or different tribes, he would become possessed of land rights in both. In regard to the actual apportionment of landed property a diversity of custom seems to have obtained, varying, perhaps, according to district. Thus it has been stated that land descended from a father to each of his sons in turn, and that it was only on the death of the last surviving son that the children of the eldest could inherit. At the same time, the land was always tended to revert to the eldest branch. It is in this light that one can understand the statement made by early writers that a Maori always preferred to trace his claim to land through his grandfather rather than through his father. In regard to the inheritance of land by girls, a diversity of opinion is found. Sometimes it is said that they inherited equally with their brothers, at others that they received no land at all, but shared only in the movable property of the deceased, it being added as a corollary that they were given a piece of land by their brothers on marriage. It seems probable that either might occur according to circumstances. The crux of the problem in regard to the inheritance of land by women lay in the fact of marriage. For if a girl married a man from a stranger tribe and went to live with his relatives, as was usual, those people, through her children, would gain a footing in any lands she possessed. This was contrary to the best interests of her own kinsfolk, hence we find that the opinion of the brothers of a girl had great weight in affecting the decision as to her marriage. If she were insistent, then she might be sent off landless to wed. "The woman goes, and goes without her girdle" is the proverb. If the dowry of land was given, and there was no issue of the marriage, the land reverted on the woman's death to her brothers. In any case the husband could acquire no interest in it beyond cultivation during his wife's lifetime.

Disputes sometimes occurred between members of the same tribe over the ownership of a piece of land, or the right to exercise certain privileges on it. The question was generally thrashed out in open assembly of the people, each party endeavouring to prove his claim by the recitation of his *whakapapa* or genealogy, substantiating it by citing acts of ownership or occupation performed without opposition by his ancestors, such as cultivation, taking of game, putting a mark upon a tree or rock, or some similar deed by which priority was established. A mark or sign of this kind was termed *tohu whenua* (land token). To provide evidence of ownership sometimes the *iho* or umbilical cord of a newly born child of rank was hidden together with a small stone on the land or the boundary thereof, so that in future years it could be referred to in case of dispute. Spots where these were concealed were *whare pito tamariki* (shelters for the umbilical cords of children) or *takotoranga iho tamariki* (receptacles of the umbilical cords of children).

It will have been noted that conquest, occupation, and ancestral right are not mutually exclusive grounds of ownership, but may be concurrent or supplementary. In addition to these main bases of claims to land, there are a number of others, depending upon special circumstances, and very often simply of individual concern. A few of these may be enumerated. Thus a person might have a certain right in the lands of another tribe or *hapu* if he happened to have been born thereon, if his blood had been shed there, if an ancestor of his were buried there, or if his umbilical cord had been severed there. Once the chief from whose head-dress a feather had been brushed while travelling stopped and built a little fence around it with twigs, thereby establishing a claim to the land. Another who was pleased with the catch of eels in the river of a stranger tribe took the albatross-down tuft from his ear and threw it into the water, by this act securing an interest in the land and in the periodical eel fishing. On the Tamaki River near Auckland is a place called Te Pupu-a-Kawau. Here a chief of Ngati-Paoa, Te Kawau (the shag) by name, combed his hair and left the combings in a small bundle on a pole. He thereby made the locality *tapu* to himself and occupied it. Hence some of the *Ngati-Paoa* were dwelling in that place when Europeans first arrived. Many similar performances have been recorded. When the owners made no objection on the spot, these acts have been used later to found claims to the land which have been admitted by the proprietors. Both here and in the former instances the essential underlying idea seems to have been that by this occurrence the personality of the man became connected with the land, and he was therefore entitled to a share in it. No explicit native theory, however, seems to have been formulated on this point. There is no doubt that in post-European times this principle has often been unduly extended by claimants in the Native Land Court. In the ordinary way, when a man established a right of this specific type, he exercised it by periodically visiting the land to work it, by receiving a portion of the produce from the actual occupiers, or by obtaining compensation if the land were alienated. [pp. 377-381]

NOTES

1. Raymond Firth, *Primitive Economics of the New Zealand Maori* (London : George Routledge & Sons Ltd., 1929), pp. 124-381.

2. John White, *Ancient History of the Maori*, 6 vols. (Wellington : 1887-1890), vol. 5, p. 121.

MAORI LAND LAW[1]

Norman Smith

. . .If a Maori left his tribe and went to live in another district either through marriage or otherwise, and he and his descendants remained away for three generations, they would forfeit all rights to the land so abandoned ; their claims would become *ahi-mataotao.* The meaning of this term is cold or extinguished fire and as applied to the instance just given would signify that the rights of the claimants had become cold and their claims extinguished. The same rule applied to voluntary migrations of a whole family group or *hapu.* They may have allied themselves with some enemy and been forced to leave. If, however, the claimants who had voluntarily abandoned the land sent some of their children back at intervals to occupy the lands, or to exercise some right of ownership, and there was no objection from the tribe, that would be sufficient to relight the flame and so keep their fires burning, and their rights alive. In the example just given, if the Maoris remained away without exercising their rights continuously for one generation, their claims would not be materially affected, but absence for two generations would seriously weaken the claims and render them subject to some recognition by the tribe ; they would not entirely cease until after an absence for three generations.

Where a group of Maoris had abandoned or lost their interest in the manner just referred to, it would be possible for those rights to be restored again upon their acceptance of an invitation from the tribe to which they belonged, to return and reoccupy the land. Such an invitation, however, must emanate from the tribe as a whole, and an overture from an individual member alone would, in most cases, hardly be sufficient to effectively bring about restoration of the lapsed rights unless it could be shown he acted with the concurrence of his tribe.

The incidence of occupation being abandoned and restored is illustrated in the following statements from judgments of the Court : "It was also admitted that Turaki's descendants from whom Karaitiana sprang, lived in the district of Te Piripiri and other places until the days of Rangikamahuru, who married a man belonging to Heretaunga, where she settled and her descendants after her. Her children, grandchildren, and great grandchildren were all born and married at Heretaunga, and no satisfactory evidence was adduced to show that any of them returned to the district until Karaitiana Akamoana was invited to return by Te Hirawanu about 1850. With regard to the Native custom affecting cases of this kind, there is possibly no definite rule that can be made applicable to all cases and to all districts, but this rule appears to be applicable everywhere, that when a woman of one tribe or *hapu* marries into another tribe or *hapu* and leaves the land of her own tribe or *hapu,* her rights become extinguished, unless some act of ownership is exercised either by herself or her immediate descendants. It is said that she leaves her *ahi-ka* (burning fire) and becomes an *ahi-tere* (unstable fire). The fire she has left remains smouldering but unless fresh fire is supplied to it, it ultimately dies out and the ashes become cold. If she or her children return before the ashes become cold, it becomes again an *ahi-ka,* but there is a difference of opinion whether the grandchildren can recover their rights in that way, but there is no doubt that the great grandchildren cannot do so unless they are expressly invited and welcomed by the tribe."

Ahi-mataotao applies to cases where the descendants of the territorial ancestor voluntarily abandon the land and none of the progeny return to keep their rights alive for a period of three generations. Absence for one generation would not materially affect the rights of the absent parties. Absence for two generations would diminish their claim, and absence for three generations would entirely obliterate it. As regards *ahi-tere* it is a recognized principle of Maori custom that if a woman marries out of the tribe she forfeits all rights to land in her parents' tribe, and her children have no right of succession without other members of the family bring the children back and adopt them, in that case they would be reinstated in the tribal rights which their mother had forfeited....[2] [pp. 94-95]

NOTES

1. Norman Smith, *Maori Land Law* (Wellington : A.H. & A.W. Reed, 1960), pp. 94-95.
2. Nap. Appellate Court Minute Book, 48/78.

THE HISTORY OF ENGLISH LAW[1]

Sir Frederick Pollock, and F.W. Maitland

Every acre of English soil and every proprietary right therein have been brought within the compass of a single formula, which may be expressed thus : *Z tenet terram illam de ... domino Rege.* The king himself holds land which is in every sense his own ; no one else has any proprietary right in it ; but if we leave out of account this royal demesne, then every acre of land is "held of" the king. The person whom we may call its owner, the person who has the right to use and abuse the land, to cultivate it or leave it uncultivated, to keep all others off it, holds the land of the king either immediately or mediately. In the simplest case he holds it immediately of the king ; only the king and he have rights in it. But it well may happen that between him and the king there stand other persons ; Z holds immediately of Y, who holds of X, who holds of V, who holds ... of A, who holds of the king. Let us take one real instance : in Edward I's day Roger of St. German holds land at Paxton in Huntingdonshire of Robert of Bedford, who holds of Richard of Ilchester, who holds of Alan of Chartres, who holds of William le Boteler, who holds of Gilbert Neville, who holds of Devorguil Balliol, who holds of the king of Scotland, who holds of the king of England. A feudal ladder with so many rungs as this has, is uncommon ; but theoretically there is no limit to the possible number of rungs, and practically, as will be seen hereafter, men have enjoyed a large power, not merely of adding new rungs to the bottom of the ladder, but inserting new rungs in the middle of it. The person who stands at the lower end of the scale, the person who seems most like an owner of the land, and who has a general right of doing what he pleases with it, is said to hold the land in demesne. . . . We suppose that he holds it of Y ; in that case Y is the lord of Z, and Z is the tenant of Y. But Y again is said to hold the land ; he holds it however not in demesne but in service . . . and Y again must hold it of someone — let us say of X — whose tenant he will be, who will be his lord, and who also will be said to hold the land in service. Ultimately we shall reach the king : A, or some other person, will hold the land immediately of the king and be his tenant in chief. Every person who stands between the king and him who holds in demesne, every mesne lord or mesne, is both lord and tenant lord as regards those who stand below him, tenant as regards those who stand above.... [vol. 1, pp. 232-233]

In the history of our law there is no idea more cardinal than that of seisin. Even in the law of the present day it plays a part which must be studied by every lawyer ; but in the past it was so important that we may almost say that the whole system of our land law was law about seisin and its consequences.

Seisin is possession. A few, but only a few words about etymology may be ventured. The inference has been too hastily drawn that this word speaks to us of a time of violence, when he who seized land was seised of it, when seizing land was the normal mode of acquiring possession. Now doubtless there is an etymological connexion between "seizing" and being "seised," but the nature of that connexion is not very certain. If on the one hand "seisin" is connected with "to seize," on the other hand it is connected with "to sit" and "to set" : the man who is seised is the man who is sitting on the land ; when he was put in seisin he was set there and made to sit there. Thus seisin seems to have the same root as the German *Besitz* and the Latin *possessio.* To our medieval lawyers the word *seisina* suggested the very opposite of violence ; it suggested peace and quiet.

. . . To this day we call the person who takes possession of land without having title to it a "mere squatter" ; we speak of "the sitting tenant," and such a phrase as a "country seat" puts us at the right point of view. The seated man is in quiet enjoyment. We reverence the throne, the bishop's see, "the Right Reverend Bench," the bench of judges, we obey the orders of the chair ; the powers that be are seated.

Now in the course of time seisin becomes a highly technical word ; but we must not think of it having been so always. Few, if any, of the terms in our legal vocabulary have always been technical terms. The licence that the man of science can allow himself of coining new words is one which by the nature of the case is denied to lawyers. They have to take their terms out of the popular speech ; gradually the words so taken are defined ; sometimes a word continues to have both a technical meaning for lawyers and a different and vaguer meaning for laymen ; sometimes the word that lawyers have adopted is abandoned by the laity. Such for a long time past has been the fate of seisin.

The process by which words are specified, by which their technical meaning is determined is to a first glance a curious, illogical process. Legal reasoning seems circular : for example, it is argued in one case that a man has an action of trespass because he has possession, in the next case that he has possession because he has an action of trespass ; and so we seem to be running round from right to remedy and then from remedy to right. All the while, however, our law of possession and trespass is being more perfectly defined. Its course is not circular but spiral ; it never comes back to quite the same point as that from which it started. This play of reasoning between right and remedy fixes the use of words. A remedy, called an assize, is given to any one who is disseised of his free tenement : in a few years lawyers will be arguing that X has been disseised of his free tenement because it is an established point that a person in his position can bring an assize. The word seisin becomes specified by its relation to certain particular remedies.

What those remedies were it will be our duty to consider. But first we may satisfy ourselves that, to begin with, seisin simply meant possession. Of this we may be convinced by two observations. In the first place, it would seem that for at least three centuries after the Norman Conquest our lawyers had no other word whereby to describe possession. In their theoretical discussions, they, or such of them as looked to the Roman books as models of jurisprudence, could use the words *possessio and possidere* ; but these words are rarely employed in the formal records of litigation, save in one particular context. The parson of a church is "in possession" of the church : but then this is no matter for our English law or our temporal courts ; it is a matter for the canon law and the courts Christian ; and it is all the more expedient to find some other term than "seised" for the parson, since it may be necessary to contrast the rights of the parson who is possessed of the church with those of the patron who is seised of the advowson. In the second place, this word "seisin" was used of all manner of things and all manner of permanent rights that could be regarded as things. At a later date to speak of a person as being seised, or in seisin, of a chattel would have been a gross solecism. But throughout the thirteenth century and in the most technical documents men are seised of chattels, and in seisin of them, of a fleece of wool, of a gammon of bacon, of a penny. People were possessed of these things ; law had to recognize and protect their possession ; it had no other word than "seisin" and therefore used it freely. It may well be, as some think, that the ideas of seisin and possession are first developed in relation to land ; one sits, settles, squats on land and in early ages, preeminently during the feudal time, the seisin of chattels was commonly interwoven with the seisin of land. Flocks and herds were the valuable chattels : "chattel" and "cattle" are the same word ; and normally cattle are possessed by him who possesses the land on which they are levent and couchant. Still when the possession of chattels was severed from the possession of land, when the oxen were stolen or were sold to a chapman, there was no word to describe the possession of this new possessor, this thief or purchaser, save seisin. Sometimes we meet with the phrase "vested and seised," which was common in France ; this however seems to mean no more than "seised," and though we may now and then read of "investiture," chiefly in relation to ecclesiastical offices, this does not become one of the technical terms of the common law.... [vol. 2, pp. 29-33]

Then we must consider the ascending series of lords and tenants. Let us suppose that Ralph holds in fee and in free socage of the earl, who holds in fee by knight's service of the king. If all is as it should be, then both Ralph and the earl may be said to be seised of the land. Ralph, who is occupying the land by himself, his servants, his villein tenants or his termors, is seised in demesne. The earl, to whom Ralph is paying rent, also is seised ; he is seised of the land, not in demesne but in service. We have here to remember that if the feudal idea of seignorial justice had been permitted to develop itself freely, this ascending series of seisins would have had as its counterpart an ascending series of courts. The king's court would have known of no seisin save that of the earl, the tenant in chief. The seisin of Ralph, the earl's immediate tenant, would have found protection — at least in the first instance — only in the earl's court ; and so downwards, each seisin being protected by a different court. The seisin of the tenant in villeinage protected only in the manorial court is an illustration of this principle. [vol. 2, p. 38)

NOTE

1. Sir Frederick Pollock and F.W. Maitland, *The History of the English Law* (Cambridge : Cambridge University Press, 1968), vol. 1, pp. 232-233 ; vol. 2, pp. 29-38.

THE DISSEISIN OF CHATTELS[1]

James Barr Ames

. . .In substance, however, the law of disseisin was common to both realty and personalty.

A disseisor of land, it is well known, gains by his tort an estate in fee simple. "If a squatter wrongfully incloses a bit of waste land and builds a hut on it, and lives there, he acquires an estate in fee simple in the land which he has inclosed. He is seised, and the owner of the waste is disseised.... He is not a mere tenant at will, nor for years, nor for life, nor in tail ; but he has an estate in fee simple. He has seisen of the freehold to him and his heirs."[2] Compare with this the following, "Note if one takes my goods, he is seised now of them as of his own goods, adjudged by the whole court,"[3] or Finch's definition : "Trespass in goods is the wrongful taking of them with pretence of title, and therefore altereth the propertie of those goods."[4] This altering of the property by a trespass is pointedly illustrated by a case from the *Book of Assizes.* The plaintiff brought a bill of trespass for carrying off his horse and killing it. "The defendant prayed judgment of the bill, since you have confessed the property to be in us at the time of the killing, and so your bill is repugnant ; for by the tortious taking, the property was devested out of you and vested in us, and therefore we could not kill our own horse *contra pacem.*"[5] The bill was adjudged bad. Furthermore, incredible as it may appear, a disseisin by theft vested the property in the stolen chattel in the thief. *John v. Adam* was a case of replevin in the *detinet* for sheep. Avowry that the sheep were stolen from the plaintiff by M, who was driving them through the defendant's hundred ; that M, to avoid arrest, fled to the church and abjured the realm, and so the defendant was seised by virtue of his franchise to have the goods of felons. Certain formal objections were taken to the avowry, to which Herle, C.J. answered : "Whatever his avowry be, you shall take nothing ; for he has acknowledged that the property was once in you, and afterward in him who stole them ; and now he affirms the property in himself, and therefore, although he cannot maintain the property in himself for the reason alleged, still you shall not have the sheep again, for he gives a mesne ; namely, the felon in whom the property was."[6] The opinion of this distinguished judge is confirmed by numerous cases in which stolen goods were forfeited by the thief, under the rule of law that gave to the Crown the chattels of felons. The goods, having become by the theft the property of the felon, were forfeited as a matter of course with the rest of his chattels.

These examples are sufficient to bring out the analogy between the tortious taking of chattels and the wrongful ouster from land. But in order to appreciate fully the parallel between disseisin of chattels and disseisin of land, we must consider in some detail the position of the deisseisor and disseisee in each case.

The disseised owner of land loses, of course, with the *res* the power of present enjoyment. But this is not all. He retains, it is true, the right *in rem* ; or, to use the common phrase, he has still a right of entry and a right of action. But by an inveterate rule of our law, a right of entry and a chose in action were strictly personal rights. Neither was assignable. It follows, then, that the disseisee cannot transfer the land. In other words, as long as the disseisin continues, the disseised owner is deprived of the two characteristic features of property : he has neither the present enjoyment nor the power of alienation.

These conclusions are fully borne out by the authorities. The common law was, as we read in Plowden, "that he who was out of possession might not bargain, grant, or let his right or title ; and if he had done it, it should have been void."[7] It was not until 1845 that by statute the interest of the disseisee of land became transferable....

A right of entry and action is now everywhere devisable. But until 1838 in England and 1836 in Massachusetts, a disseise had nothing that he could dispose of by will.... [pp. 172-175]

One more phase of the non-assignability of the disseisee's right of action is shown by another recent case. It was decided in Rhode Island, in 1879, in accordance with a decision by the King's Bench, in the time of James I, that a disseised owner of land had nothing that could be taken on execution.

The position of the disseisor of land is, in most respects, the direct opposite of that of the disseisee. The strength of each is the weakness of the other. The right of the disseisee to recover implies the liability of the disseisor, or his transferee, to lose the land. But so long as the disseisin continues, the disseisor, or his transferee, possesses all the rights incident to the ownership of an estate in fee simple. If he is dispossessed by a stranger, he can recover possession by entry or action. . . . If he wishes to transfer his estate in whole or in part, he may freely do so. He may sell the land, or devise it, or lease it. He may convey it with the usual limitations, i.e., for life, in tail, etc., or subject to trusts. His interest is subject also to the rules of involuntary transfer. Accordingly, it may descend to his heir, escheat to his lord, or be taken on execution, and would doubtless pass to his assignee in bankruptcy. The husband of the disseisor has curtesy, and the wife dower, and a disseisin by a villein must have enured the benefit of his lord at the latter's election. The disseisor is entitled to common (but not advowson ?), he has presentment, may insure realty, may grant a rent charge, and may distrain for damage feasant.

The legal effects of the disseisin of chattels are most vividly seen by looking at the remedies for a wrongful taking. The right of recaption was allowed only *flagrante delicto.* This meant in Britton's time the day of the taking. If the owner retook his goods afterwards, he forfeited them for his "usurpation." If the taking was felonious, the despoiled owner might bring an appeal of larceny, and by complying with certain conditions, obtain restitution of the stolen chattel. . . .

But such was the rigour and hazard of these conditions, that from the middle of the thirteenth century the appeal was largely superseded by the new action of trespass. If the taking was not criminal, trespass was for generations the only remedy.

Trespass, however, was a purely personal action ; it sounded only in damages. The wrongful taking of chattels was, therefore, a more effectual disseisin than the ouster from land. The dispossessed owner of land, as we have seen, could always recover possession by an action. Though deprived of the *res,* he still had a right *in rem.* The disseisor acquired only a defeasible estate. One whose chattel had been taken from him, on the other hand, having no means of recovering it by action, not only lost the *res*, but had no right *in rem*. The disseisor gained by his tort both the possession and the right of possession ; in a word, the absolute property in the chattel taken.

What became of the chattel afterwards, therefore, was no concern of the victim of the tort. Accordingly, one need not be surprised at the following charge given by Brian, C.J. and his companions to a jury in 1486 : "If one takes my horse *vi et armis* and gives it to S, or S takes it with force and arms from him who took it from me, in this case S is not a trespasser to me, nor shall I trespass against him for the horse, because the possession was out of me by the first taking ; then he was not a trespasser to me, and if the truth be so, find the defendant not guilty." Brooke adds this gloss, "for the first offender has gained the property by the tort...."[8] [pp. 177-180]

So long as the adverse possession continues, the dispossessed owner of the chattel has, manifestly, no power of present enjoyment. Has he lost also the power of alienation ? His right *in rem*, if analyzed, means a right to recover possession by recaption or action. But these rights are as personal in their nature as the corresponding rights of entry or action in the case of land. It follows, then, that they were not transferable. And such was the law.... [p. 185]

Not much is to be found in the books as to one's power to dispose, by will, of chattels adversely held. It is plain, however, that before 1330 the disseisee had nothing that he could bequeath. At that time the only remedies for a wrongful taking were trespass and the appeal of felony, both of which actions died with the person wronged.... [p. 187]

Finally, the disseisee of a chattel, like the disseisee of land, has at common law nothing that can be taken on execution. In a valuable book published in 1888 we read : "When personal property is held adversely to its owner, his interest therein is a mere chose in action and cannot be reached by execution, unless by the provisions of some statute...."[9]

The position of the disseisor of a chattel was the converse of that of the disseisee. The converter, like the disseisor of land, had the power of present enjoyment and the power of alienation. If dispossessed by a stranger he might proceed against him by trespass, replevin, detinue or trover. He could sell the chattel or bail it. It would go by will to the executor or be cast by descent upon the administrator, was forfeited to the Crown for felony, and was subject to execution. A conversion by the wife,unless the property was destroyed, was necessarily to the use of the husband, as a disseisin by a villein must have profited his lord if the latter claimed it.

We have thus far considered only the resemblances between land and chattels in the manner of seisin and disseisin. But our comparison would be incomplete if attention were not called to one point of difference. One in possession of a horse or cow was seised of the chattel itself, without more. There could, therefore, be but a single seisin of it at any given moment. If, for instance, a chattel was loaned for a term, the bailee alone was seised of it. He and he only could be disseised of it. To this day the bailor for a term cannot maintain trespass or trover against a stranger for a disseisin of the bailee. But, on the other hand, there was no such thing as seisin of land simpliciter. The seisin was always qualified by the mode of possession.... Accordingly, wherever there was a term there were necessarily two distinct seisins in one and the same land, at one and the same time. Both of these seisins were lost by the tortious entry of a stranger upon the land under a claim of right, and the disseisor was exposed to two actions — the assize of novel disseisin by the freeholder, and the *ejectio firmae* by the termor. This difference between land and chattels is obviously artificial and of feudal origin.

But if this historial sketch has been accurately drawn, the disseisin of land finds its almost perfect counterpart in the conversion of chattels, notwithstanding the difference here indicated. It is still true that the doctrine of disseisin belongs not to feudalism alone, but to the general law of property. . . . [T]his doctrine is not a mere episode in English legal history . . .it is a living principle, founded in the nature of things, and of great practical value in the solution of many important questions. [pp. 189-191]

NOTES

1. James Barr Ames, "The Disseisin of Chattels," in *Lectures on Legal History*, (Cambridge, Mass. : Harvard University Press, 1913), pp. 172-191.
2. Williams, Seisin, 7.
3. Fitzherbert. Abridgement — Trespass 153.
4. Finch, Law, Book III, c. 6.
5. 27 Ass. pl. 64.
6. Year Book 8 Ed. III, 10,30.
7. *Partridge v. Strange*, Plow. 88 per Montegue, C.J.
8. Brookes, Abridgement-Trespass 358.
9. Freeman, *Executions*, 2nd ed., s. 112.

FUTURE INTERESTS[1]

Ashbel G. Gulliver

. . . Chronologically, conveyances of land fall into three classes : "common law" conveyances, conveyances under the Statute of Uses, and conveyances by the modern statutory deed.

Common Law Conveyances

The ubiquitous and ambiguous term "common law" means in this context the conveyances that were possible during the period after the Norman Conquest up to the Statute of Uses of 1536. The use of these conveyances did not end when the Statute of Uses was enacted, but they were continued after that statute as alternative methods of transfer, and were employed in addition to the new types of transfer made possible by the statute.

Two basic ideas underlie the common law conveyances : First, and of vital importance, in understanding future interests doctrine, was a thoroughly materialistic attitude, which Maitland attributed to "a mental incapacity, an inability to conceive that mere rights can be transferred."[2] Because of this attitude, the essential dispositive act in these conveyances was a transfer of physical possession of the land ; the way to transfer a physical thing was to transfer "it." This may be explained in modern terms by saying that it was impossible for "title" to pass without a simultaneous transfer of "possession" ; but this would not accurately represent the early thinking, since the failure to think in terms of such two separate concepts was probably the chief reason for the requirement of a physical transfer of the subject matter.

The second idea was the desirability of publicity. This was an age which not only had no recording system, but did not even require a writing for transfers of land. It was therefore obviously very important for future proof of ownership to have the facts of the transfer either made known to a group of people at the time or officially preserved in some way.

The *feoffment* (creation or a feud or fief, i.e., a feudal state) with livery of *seisin* (delivery of possession) was the standard way of creating a freehold estate (fee simple, fee tail, life estate). "Fee," in fee simple and fee tail, is etymologically synonymous with feud and fief, but has always been confined in the law to an inheritable estate, and was thus more limited in coverage than "feoffment," which included the creation of life estates. The procedure of the feoffment is no doubt familiar. The feoffor and feoffee, or agents empowered to act as attorneys for either or both of them, would come to the land and declare the terms of the transfer to assembled witnesses, who could later provide proof, perhaps as jurors under the early system of the jury furnishing evidence. The feoffor would customarily make some symbolic delivery, such as handing the feoffee a twig or piece of turf — "they are the land in miniature and thus the land passes from hand to hand." (2 P. & M. 85) The parties might perambulate the boundaries, and there might be other ceremonies to dramatize the occasion in the minds of the witnesses. But the vital requirement was that the feoffor vacate the land, taking his people and goods with him, and the feoffee occupy it. "There must be in very truth a change of possession, and rash is the feoffee who allows his feoffor's chattels to remain upon the land or who allows the feoffor to come back into the house, even as a guest, while the feoffment is yet new" (2 P. & M. 84).... [pp. 36-37]

For about a century and a half before the enactment of the Statute of Uses in 1536, agreements to hold land for the use of another were not recognized by the law courts but were enforced by the Chancellor on ethical principles similar to the theories of consideration that were later developed for contracts. The outstanding characteristic of the Chancellor's enforcement was a simple liberality that was entirely free of the technicalities of the common law. When the Statute of Uses converted the former equitable passive uses of real estate into legal interests, thus transferring jurisdiction over that type of use to the law courts, the latter carried on the tradition of the Chancellor in dealing with these interests. The law courts also adopted the same attitude toward devises of land after they were authorized by the Statute of Wills of 1540. . . .

The original method of creating a use interest was to employ a common law conveyance. If A wished to create such an interest in C, A would transfer the land to B by feoffment, fine, or common recovery, B agreeing to hold the land to the use of C. This same method still prevailed after the Statute of Uses, the transfer from A to B being controlled by the principles of the common law conveyances, but the interest of C being controlled by the liberal principles initiated by the Chancellor and followed after the statute by the law courts.

The system of uses, however, also inaugurated new methods of transfer which were responsible for the shift from conveying by transfer of physical possession to conveying by deed.... [pp. 39-40]

. . . Vested and contingent remainders were the two types of future interests in transferees that the law courts allowed to be created by the common law conveyances. . . before the Statute of Uses. This statement refers only to the results in the law courts ; if the common law conveyance was accompanied by an agreement by the transferee to hold the use of others, the Chancellor would enforce such an agreement without regard to the technical rules of the law courts and would simply carry out the stated intent. After the Statute of Uses of 1536 and the Statute of Wills of 1540, the law courts followed this liberal tradition of the Chancellor for executory interests created either by an *inter vivos* transfer in the form of a passive use of real estate (executed into a legal interest by the Statute of Uses and thus transferred into jurisdiction from the Chancellor to the law courts), or by a will, the law courts having jurisdiction over wills of real property. Such *inter vivos* transfer might be either a common law conveyance to the use of others, or a conveyance operating entirely under the Statute of Uses (bargain and sale, covenant to stand seised, lease, and release), the latter being the original form of a deed of land. But the category of executory interests and the liberality of construction characteristic thereof were confined by the law courts to dispositions that they would have held void before the Statute of Uses ; they continued to construe vested and contingent remainders in the same way as they had done before that statute.

The two types of future interests in transferees that were held void by the law courts before the Statute of Uses and thus became executory interests thereafter were those that were certain to follow a gap (which became springing executory interests) and those that would divest the interest of another transferee (which became shifting executory interests). Vested remainders were interests that would not be preceded by any gap and that would not divest the interest of another transferee. Contingent remainders were interests that might or might not be preceded by a gap (the gap being possible but not certain), and that would not divest the interest of another transferee. These bases for classification still hold.

There is no question whatever about these results, but the problem is to explain how they came to pass, and this is largely guesswork, in view of the paucity of material available for precise documentation. Even the date of origin of the concept of a contingent remainder is uncertain. But some attempt at explanation, even if not wholly reliable, seems desirable in order to put some rational content into what would otherwise be empty verbalisms.

Interests certain to be preceded by a gap : void in the law courts before the Statute of Uses ; valid thereafter as springing executory interests if created by a transfer operating under the Statute of Uses or by deed or by will. One example would be an *inter vivos* transfer from *A to C and his heirs after A's death.* Why would this be held nugatory by the law courts before the statute, a result often expressed by the statement that it was then impossible to create a freehold to commence in the future ?

It has been suggested that this result was due to the general principle then prevailing that there should never be a gap in the seisin, and that a disposition purporting to create such a gap was therefore void as violating that principle. This explanation, however, is not convincing. There seems no doubt about the proposition that there should at all times be someone seised of the land. This was a period during which seisin represented the real ownership of land, and it was necessary that such ownership be continuous for various purposes. There had to be somebody seised to respond to lawsuits about the land. Responsibility for feudal services and incidents was in the person who had seisin ; the feudal manor could only operate efficiently if the services due from the land were regularly performed (it could not be defended against attack if the tenants owing military services could not be found, the crops and cows and chickens needed continuous attention, etc.), and the lord's revenues would be substantially impaired if those owing feudal incidents could not be identified. But, granting the legal, economic and political necessity of continuity of seisin, it does not as such explain the invalidity of the above transfer because, if there were no other objection to it, it could easily have been held that the grantor, A, remained seised up to the time that the gift to C took effect in possession. In other words, the courts could have held then, for the purpose of meeting this objection alone, as they do today for this type of disposition that A retained a fee simple subject to be divested by C's interest.

A much more convincing explanation is that the materialistic philosophy and requirements of the common law conveyances made such a transfer impossible. "Title" was not separated from "possession" ; if you wanted to transfer land, you had to transfer "it" physically, which meant that you had to get off the land entirely and your grantee had to occupy it ; anachronistically, the law of that time may be expressed by saying that it was impossible to create an interest in land without simultaneously transferring possession.... The example of a feoffment will illustrate the impossibility of creating a freehold in the future like that of C in the above example. The procedure of the feoffment would require that A and C meet on the land for livery of seisin, but how could this be carried out in such a way as to accomplish the intent that C should not have possession until A's death ? To do this, A would have to remain in possession after the feoffment ; but, if this should happen, the feoffment would be nullified. To make the feoffment effective, it would be necessary for C to stay on the land, but this would nullify the intent. It is impossible to reconcile the idea of creating a freehold to commence in possession in the future with the concept that title cannot be divorced from possession and therefore must pass simultaneously with it. Reverting to the analogy of juvenile mental processes this would be the equivalent of a father telling his son Johnny to give his ball to Freddy now, but not to give it to him until next week, a remark not calculated to reduce Johnny's skepticism concerning the rationality of his progenitor's mental processes. So, in the old days, if A and C should meet on the land, and A should hand over a twig telling C that he should have the land when A died and C should then leave, the legal thinking of the time would say, "A has given C nothing, but because A still has the land."

Another example of the same type of interest would be a grant from *A to B for life, and one year after B's death to C and his heirs.* Before the Statute of Uses, the law courts would hold that this effectively created a life estate in B, but that the gift to C was void ; today C would have a springing executory interest, A having a reversion subject to be divested by C's interest. Here again, the necessity of always having some person seised of the land for legal and feudal purposes has been offered as an explanation of the invalidity of C's interest before the Statute of Uses ; but again the explanation is not convincing, since it would have been possible to hold that A had the seisin during the interval between the end of the life estate and the beginning of C's possession, just as it was held after the recognition of executory interests that A had a reversion entitling him to possession during that interval. There was never any problem about a grant from A to B for life, leaving a reversion in A ; the fact that the above disposition would limit A's seisin after the life estate to a shorter period would not seem to make it any more difficult to hold that A would have the seisin during that shorter period.

Materialism again furnishes the most probable explanation. At the end of B's life estate, the land would go back to A (or his successors in interest). Once the land returned to the transferor, a new transfer of possession was necessary to get it away from him again. The original statement of intent that C should have the land after the one-year period was ineffective to transfer the seisin from A to C, because the seisin could only be transferred by an actual physical change in occupancy. Johnny gives his ball to Freddy ; Freddy gives it back to Johnny ; if Johnny now wants Dick to have the ball, he has to hand it over to him ; whatever he might have said when he gave it to Freddy about Dick having it after he got it back makes no difference because Dick doesn't get the ball until he gets it. [pp. 193-196]

NOTES

1. Ashbel G. Gulliver, *Future Interests*, American Casebook Series (St. Paul, Minnesota : West Pub. Co., 1959), pp. 36-196.

2. Maitland, "The Mystery of Seisin," *Law Quarterly Review* (1886) : 489.

THE COLLECTED PAPERS OF FREDERIC WILLIAM MAITLAND[1]

H.A.L. Fisher (Editor)

The Mystery of Seisin

The true explanation of the foregoing rules will I believe be found in no considerations of public policy, no wide views of social needs, but in what I shall venture to describe as a mental incapacity, an inability to conceive that mere rights can be transferred or can pass from person to person. Things can be transferred ; that is obvious ; the transfer is visible to the eye ; but how rights ? You have not your rights in your hand or your pocket, nor can you put them into the hand of another nor lead him into them and bid him walk about within their metes and bounds. "But," says the accomplished jurist, "this is plain nonsense ; when a gift is made of a corporeal thing, of a sword or a hide of land, rights are transferred ; if at the same time there is a change of possession, that is another matter ; whether a gift can be made without such a change of possession, the law of the land will decide ; but every gift is a transfer of ownership, and ownership is a right or bundle of rights ; if gift be possible, transfer of rights is possible." That, I should reply, doubtless is so in these analytic times ; but I may have here and there a reader who can remember to have experienced in his own person what I take to be the history of the race, who can remember how it flashed across him as a truth, new though obvious, that the essence of a gift is a transfer of rights. You cannot give what you have not got : this seems clear ; but put just the right accent on the words give and got, and we have reverted to an old way of thinking.

You can't give a thing if you haven't got that thing, and you haven't got that thing if some one else has got it. A very large part of the history of Real Property Law seems to me the history of the process whereby Englishmen have thought themselves free of that materialism which is natural to us all. [p. 372]

NOTE

1. H.A.L. Fisher, ed., *The Collected Papers of Frederic William Maitland*, vol. 1 (Cambridge : Cambridge University Press, 1911), p. 372.

SELECTIONS FROM : THE CONCEPT OF NATIVE TITLE[1] AND LEGAL OBLIGATION[2]

J.C. Smith

Property is a social institution whereby people regulate the acquisition and use of the resources of our environment according to a system of rules.If we lived in an environment where there was an inexhaustible supply of resources which could be appropriated and used without labour, there would be absolutely no need for any society to have an institution of property. If everyone could have all the food, clothing, shelter, etc. that he wished without in any way affecting the supply available to others, and without effort on anyone's part, there would be no need for regulating the acquisition of resources, nor any need even to have a concept such as "theft." Where, for instance, land has been in abundance, and the use of the land has not required the expending of labour, land will generally be considered to be open to inclusive enjoyment. Thus, nomadic tribes in an area of abundant land used only for grazing purposes generally don't recognize property in land, nor have such a concept as "trespass." Scarcity of labour can thus be said to be the foundation of the institution of property.

Every society, without exception, has institutions of property because no society exists in an environment where there are not at least some resources which are scarce, and some which require labour to appropriate or be useable. Man is, by the structure of his brain, a rule-making animal, and it is in the best long-term interests of all to regulate the acquisition of resources by rules, and to give community protection to the fruits of one's labour, rather than to let a man's relation to the resources of his environment be determined solely in terms of naked power.

In order to have an institution of property, there must be, at least, the following :

(1) a community,
(2) a quantity of limited or scarce resources,
(3) a set of rules regulating the acquisition, access to, and use of those resources. This set of rules will be made up of at least the following sub-sets,
 (A) a set of rules which provides the manner in which the property relation is created,
 (B) a set of rules which provides for the transfer of this relation from one member of the community to another,
 (C) a set of rules which determines how and when the property relation is terminated so that the resources are open to acquisition by others,

(4) a set of possessive pronouns such as "mine," "yours," "his," "hers," and "theirs," etc. whereby this relation can be expressed,
(5) a set of rules protecting the property relation by, for instance, providing sanctions when it is wrongfully interfered with.

Resources, by their nature, may be shareable or non-shareable. Where the use and enjoyment of a resource may best be maximized by sharing, the rules of property may prohibit exclusive appropriation and provide for mutual access for members of the community.

The rules of any particular institution of property will reflect the basic goals of the related social system in regard to the relation between people and resources. To the degree that different property institutions reflect similar goals, a similarity will generally be found between the rules of those systems. Certain minimal rules can be said to be almost universal in that they can be found in any system of property whatsoever. This would indicate that there are certain basic ends common to nearly every institution of property. The minimal rules relating to resources subject to exclusive appropriation are :

(1) *Resources which are unused and unclaimed may be acquired.* This rule reflects the overriding goal of an institution of property to enable persons to use the resources of their environment.
(2) *Resources which are used and claimed may not be acquired.* This rule reflects the goal of the institution of property that a person's enjoyment of resources is to be protected from the interference of others.
(3) *Unused and unclaimed resources may be acquired by use and the expending of labour upon them.* This rule reflects the goal of an institution of property to allow people to enjoy the fruits of their own labour.
(4) *Resources which once were acquired by one person may be acquired by someone else if they have been permanently abandoned.* This rule reflects the ends of the institution of property to maximize the use of scarce resources.
(5) *Resources once acquired by one peson may be voluntarily transferred to another.* This rule reflects the goal of the institution of property to maximize the access to resources for all persons by enabling them to share and exchange.

Although every collection of people which can be called a society will have an institution of property, not every society may have a legal system. Where a legal system and a system of property co-exist in the same society, the system of property will generally be incorporated into the legal system in that most of the property rules will be rules of law. When an institution of property is incorporated into a legal system the methods of acquiring property and transferring it from one person to another tend to become formalized. In more modern times, with the population growth within societies, and the development of the nation state, land has become such a scarce resource that it has either all been acquired or its allocation is supervised by the state itself.

Transfer by gift, purchase, or inheritance, therefore, are generally the only methods by which land can be acquired. Where land is to be transferred by any of these methods the law provides strict procedures. When these have been complied with a person is said to have title to the land. Title, therefore, is the recognition afforded by an institution of property to the property relation. This recognition is based on the existence of that state of affairs specified by the rules of the system as a necessary condition for the property relation to exist between a particular person and a particular resource or "thing."

It is the set of rules providing for the creation of the property relation which provides the basis for title. Every property institution will have rules which provide that a particular state of affairs is a necessary condition for the property relation to exist. A statement that a person P has title to an object X,

(1) presupposes that P is a member of a community, the members of which share a common set of rules constituting the institution of property,
(2) assumes that those rules contain a rule providing that if condition R exists, X will belong to P,
(3) asserts that condition R does in fact exist.

Whether in North America, Africa, New Zealand, or the Pacific Islands, the property institution of tribal societies generally have the following properties or features :

(1) The property relation is that of physical possession and is expressed in terms of possessive pronouns such as "ours" or "yours."
(2) Title is based on long uninterrupted possession and use.
(3) The property relations in regard to land are viewed in terms of groups rather than of individuals.
(4) These groups are conceived of as including the dead, and the yet to be born, as well as the living.
(5) The property relation reflects and parallels the patriarchal or matriarchal social ordering of the society.

The group which is inclusive of the social system is generally the tribe. Each tribe is normally divided into major lineages, and each of these into minor lineages. The minor lineages are made up of the extended families, and the extended families, of the nuclear families consisting of parents and children. Each of the above groups is conceived of as possessing an area of land and the land of each group in the social ordering will include the land of the groups which are included within itself. There is thus a hierarchy of layers of possession to correspond with the hierarchical social order. The tribe will possess its lands, which will include the lands possessed by the major lineages, each of which will include the lands of its minor lineages, which in turn will be made up of the lands of its extended families, and so on.

There are, of course, many differences between the various tribal societies, and consequently many differences in their legal systems. There are also, however, many similarities. What is most striking is the unity of each individual within a larger group. A person is first a member of a race, tribe, lineage group, or family. His identity and meaning is to be found in these large groups. His own individuality is nacent and secondary. Secondly, these groups feel a unity with the earth, their land, their cattle, and possessions.

This perspective can be illustrated by two incidents told to one of the authors by the judge of the land court in the Cook Islands. In one dispute between two families over land, the one litigant said to the other, "the bones of your father still stick in my teeth." The title claimed by the litigant was based on an early conquest by his forefathers of the ancestors of the other litigant. But notice the identity of the man with his blood line, and the timelessness of his view of his relationship to his family. He is and was the family and the family lives on in him. A similar perspective is reflected in the statement of another litigant when he said to his protaganist, "Were you in the canoe?" Here title was being claimed on the basis of early occupation by his ancestors.

An interesting parallel may be drawn between the levels of possession in a tribal society and that in the early English feudal system after the Norman Conquest. The king was seized of all of England. He then parcelled out large areas to the various lords who in turn were seized of their portion. They then let out the land to vassals, and so forth down to the individual farmer. There was thus a hierarchy of seisin reflecting or paralleling the feudal structure just as in tribal societies there is a hierarchy of possession reflecting the kinship structure.

The history of the English law of real property reflects the conceptual shift from commonsense empiricism to the use of abstract theoretical constructs for regulating the use of land. The original grants of land under the feudal system were for life. While the feudal tenant's heir was always put into possession, it was done by an actual conveyance or feoffment in which physical possession was passed from the lord to the tenant. The reason why there was no direct transfer of possession from the feudal tenant to his heir on his death was probably in order to require the new tenant personally to swear the oaths of service and fealty to his lord.

Just as in a tribal society if a family died out their land would revert to the extended family, on the basis that their occupation as the larger kinship group included the occupation of the particular nuclear families, so the occupation of the land included all the areas occupied by his tenants, so that if a tenant died without heirs his land would revert to his lord, the person having the next higher layer of seisin.

It later became possible to create a fee simple or fee tail, rather than a life estate by granting to the tenant and his heirs or the heirs of his body. It, as well, later became possible to grant to a tenant for life, without it having to go to the tenants, heirs on his death. This marks the beginning of the English doctrine of estates. When the lord had granted a life estate to someone such that the land would revert back to him on the tenant's death, the lord's interest was known as a reversion in that the land would revert back to him in possession. It was the lord's higher level of seisin which supported his reversion. It could be said to be seised of the reversion because it formed a part of the overall lands of which he was seised as a tenant of his lord in the feudal hierarchy.

When the transfer of estates became possible a lord could grant various estates in possession to tenants and later convey to another his interest in the land, represented by his higher level of seisin. Later still he could grant an estate to a tenant for life and then, rather than transfer all his lands, convey to another merely his reversion in the land granted in possession to A. Thus a grant to A for life, then to B became possible. B's interest became known as a vested remainder.

A vested remainder is defined as an interest which is not preceded by a gap in the seisin and does not divest the interest of another transferee. A grant from A to B for life and then to C and his heirs gives B a life estate and C a vested remainder because when B dies C will go into possession and thus does not divest B's interest nor is there a gap in the seisin.

If the grant is, however, by A to B for life and then *to the heirs of C*, rather than to C, C being alive at the time of transfer, a gap in the seisin might develop. If C is still alive on B's death his heirs will not yet be ascertained and consequently there will be a gap in the seisin until C dies and his heirs are then known and they can then go into possession. If C dies before B, however, his heirs will be known, and they can go directly into possession on B's death, thus no gap in the seisin.

An interest which may or may not be preceded by a gap in the seisin is known as a contingent remainder. If the gap does occur the interest is destroyed. A contingent remainder is therefore destroyed if it does not become vested by the time of the termination of the preceding estate.

An interest which will be proceeded by a gap in the seisin, such as a gift from A to B for life and one year after B's death to C, would be void in common law as equally would be a gift which divested the interest of another, such as a transfer from A to B and his heirs but, if C reaches 21, then to C. Such gifts were valid, however, in equity if made by a conveyance operating under the Statute of Uses. Why would a gap in the seisin be fatal at common law but not in equity? The answer likely is that the Chancellors of Equity, who were generally trained in Roman law, were operating on the basis of the concept of ownership rather than seisin and were thus viewing the property relationship as a bundle of legal rights rather than as physical possession. The understanding of the shift from the empirically known relationship of physical possession to the theoretical construct of property as a bundle of rights makes much sense of the history of the law of English real property, which otherwise appears as irrational and incomprehensible.

Once we conceive of property as a bundle of rights to enjoy our property and duties on others to refrain from interfering with our enjoyment, we might next reason that the value of our property lies as much in what we can do with 'things' and prevent others from doing with them as in the actual objects themselves. An object which a person can be prevented from using or which a person cannot prevent others from using would be of little value to him. Any object beyond a person's control is valueless to him so long as it remains so and he has no expectation of gaining any control. It is our actual or potential use and enjoyment of objects and resources which measures their value. If, for instance, a state announced that the law would no longer enforce the legal relation of ownership which a particular citizen had to a large diamond which belonged to him, the diamond would greatly decrease in value to that person, especially if he was unable to protect his physical possession. One could no longer say he "owned" the diamond, at least not in a strictly legal sense. We therefore can have a dual concept of value not just in terms of the thing itself but also of the control over the behaviour of others which we can exercise through the machinery of the legal system, in respect of the thing. We thus create a conceptual structure of legal relations in regard to land and chattels which is related to the physical world by the rules of the system. "Property" would now have two meanings, the commonsense land and objects and a technical sense of the conceptual legal structure of rights, duties, powers, and privileges, which allow the owner to enjoy the land or physical objects.

As well as a series of such relations which place duties on other persons in regard to one's property, the absence of duties on the part of the owner can be viewed as negative relations which are termed in law liberties or privileges. The owner of a thing can do anything in regard to it that he has no obligation not to do. Anything which he has no obligation not to do, or an obligation to do, he is at liberty to do. All the obligation relations which impose duties on others, and all the privilege relations in regard to which others have no rights as to what the owner does with his property, can be conceived as a set in a way similar to that in which a group of relations created by agreement are treated as a set which is termed a contract. The set of relations can now be conceived as "property." A set of rules prohibits people from interfering with the owner's property. Other rules specify the limitations on the owner's use and enjoyment of his land so as not to cause harm or interference with others. From these rules we infer a set of rights and duties. A further set of rules provide how property (viewed as bundles of legal relations) can be acquired, transferred, or destroyed. One such rule might be :

Taking possession of an object	constitutes acquiring ownership	under conditions (a) the object is not owned by anyone else, (b) is not taken out of any other person's possession
	or	
The signing of a deed	constitutes a conveyance of property	under conditions that (a) the person conveying is the owner (b) the deed is witnessed (c) is under seal, etc.

The existence of such rules as the latter create in the owner a power to transfer his property to others. This power can be conceived of as a legal relation whereby the owner has a privilege to transfer his 'bundle' of relations to others. Such powers form a part of the set of relations in regard to the object. Ownership can now be defined in terms of such sets. To say that a person owns a particular object X means that the person has, in regard to the object, the bundle of rights, privileges and powers as described above. To say that John Doe owns Blackacre would mean that Doe can observe a wide variety of patterns of behaviour in regard to Blackacre and prevent others, through the law, from acting likewise. When John Doe sells Blackacre to Richard Roe he is selling his expectations as to the beneficial options of behaviour he has in regard to Blackacre, and the control he can exercise over the behaviour of others in regard to the land. What he sells therefore is his bundle of legal relations.

In order that sets of legal relations can be transferred from one person to another we must be able to conceive of those sets in the abstract. We might say that the sets must be seen as groups of relations between variables which take a material constant when held by a particular person or persons. Legal relations generally are either *in personam* or *in rem*. A legal relation *in personam* is one which holds between particular persons, and a legal relation *in rem* is one which generally holds between a particular person and anyone else in the legal system. There is no theoretical reason why both kinds of sets cannot be made transferrable. The right to collect a debt as well as certain other contractual rights are examples of assignable sets of relations *in personam* to be found in the common law.

The conception of property in terms of abstract sets of relations opens up possibilities of relations between persons and the physical resources of our environment which would be totally inconceivable within a social system where property was conceived of only in terms of physical things. Sets of relations can now be created and tailored to fit any particular social need and these sets can be created in several ways. For example, we can create a variety of sets of relations by splitting the set of ownership up into sub-sets as follows.

A. Firstly, we can conceive of the legal relations of the ownership set on a time plane. The rights can then be fragmented in terms of periods of time. Rather than having to lay out the capital required for full ownership, a person can acquire the bundle of rights constituting ownership for a limited period of time for a smaller capital outlay. Ownership sets conceived in terms of a period of time are termed estates in the common law and may be had in regard to land or funds. There is, however, no theoretical reason why a legal system should not have estates in regard to anything which can be the subject of property rights.

An estate may be infinite or limited to a finite period of time. A set having an infinite duration would be the basic set out of which sets of a lesser time period can be carved. In the common law this estate is called a fee simple. All other estates are created by a fragmentation of the fee simple and eventually, with the disappearing of estates of a finite period by the passage of time, a fee simple will be left. The time limitation may be definite or indefinite. An estate of a definite duration will be limited in terms of exact periods of time, usually months or years. An estate of an indefinite time period will be either of infinite duration or limited by an event which will occur at an unascertainable time such as the death of a particular person. The legal term for an estate of a definite period is a leasehold estate and estates limited for an indefinite period are called freehold estates and are either fee simples or life estates. An estate may be absolute or defeasible. If an estate is absolute the time limitation must always run its full course. If the estate is defeasible, the time limitation may not always run its full course but may be subject to termination by the happening of a particular stated event which may or may not take place. An estate may be in possession in the sense that the holder of the estate may immediately possess, use and enjoy the subject of the relations, or the estate may be in expectancy in the sense that the estate which a person has will not give him rights of enjoyment until a future date. A hypothetical example will illustrate. A man may by his will leave a fund of five million dollars to his wife. He dies at the age of eighty. Two million dollars go in estate tax, leaving his seventy-eight year old wife a fund now worth three million dollars. The wife dies one year later and by her will leaves the three million dollars to an only child. Estate tax now takes a further million and the child receives two million dollars. Let us say, however, that in the original will the husband gives his wife a life estate in the five million dollar fund and an estate in expectancy to the child. The wife will get the income from the fund for her life and the capital will be paid to the child on her death. The government will, on the husband's death, still take two million in estate taxes. On the death of the wife, however, no further estate taxes would be payable as the child takes nothing under her will but took an estate in expectancy under the father's will. While his mother was alive he had property in the sense of a bundle of rights which could be dealt with like any other property. One million dollars in estate tax would thus be saved by splitting the rights of ownership into an estate in possession and an estate in expectancy.

All estates have one of each of these four pairs of properties. An estate in fee simple will be (a) infinite, (b) indefinite, (c) present, (d) absolute. A fee simple defeasible will have properties (a) to (c) but will be defeasible. An estate in expectancy may be finite or infinite, definite or indefinite, absolute or defeasible. When a fee simple is divided up into smaller estates, the last estate on the plane of time will always be infinite in length.

B. Another way in which the ownership set of legal relations might be split is to separate all the rights, privileges or powers relating to control from those relating to beneficial enjoyment. These two sets could then be held in different people. This, in effect, is what happens when a trust is created. Those legal relations which allow control are held by the trustee and those which relate to beneficial enjoyment are held by the beneficiary of the trust.

C. The rights of ownership could also be fragmented by allowing the withdrawal of specific legal relations from the ownership set and permitting them to be held by persons other than the owner of the object. A person, for instance, who wished to subdivide a piece of land and retain a piece to which access could be gained only through the piece he wished to sell could do so by selling the complete bundle of rights, except for a privilege to cross the land, which he would retain. Such rights are known in the common law as easements. A holder of the rights of ownership could sell out of his set of relations the right to come on the land and take out minerals or crops, cut and remove trees, or take any other product of the land. Such rights are known as *profits a prendre.* The power to transfer the bundle of rights could also be separated by virtue of a person giving to another the power to appoint to whom his own property should go on his death or at the termination of a particular estate.

All the sets of property relations described above are *in rem.* One can also have interests *in personam* or contractual rights in regard to an object. Agreements to sell and options to purchase are examples. Rights *in personam* can also be united with sets of rights *in rem.* Thus while a landlord and tenant both have estates in regard to the same piece of land, certain rights *in personam* will also hold between them.

D. A further level of complexity is possible in that sets of legal relations themselves can be considered as things or the subject of ownership rights. For example, just as the object of an estate set of relations is generally a piece of land or a fund, the estate itself can be the object of a further set of relations of ownership not conceived in relation to time. The rights, duties, and privileges will relate to the estate and only indirectly to the subject of the estate. Thus, the owner of an estate in expectancy may not have the privilege of possession and enjoyment until the termination of the estate in possession. His ownership of the estate, however, is not future but present and he may sell his estate or grant it as a gift even though his enjoyment of the subject of his estate is postponed. Shares, bonds, copyrights, patents, bills of exchange, promissory notes are but a few of the various sets of legal relations which can be treated, like things, as the subject of rights of ownership.

The subject of rights of ownership need be neither a particular thing or set of relations but could be a set of things and relations, the content of which could vary from time to time, such as a fund invested at a particular time in land, equipment, shares, debentures, etc., which things could be sold at any time and other things bought, the fund still keeping its identity. The subject matter of most trusts is generally an income-producing fund, the particular units of which it is composed varying from time to time.

There can be numerous different forms of ownership or different kinds of sets of relations by which other sets of relations or things are held. Many of these, such as mortgages, function to furnish security for a debt. When an estate in land is mortgaged, for instance, the mortgagee who has the mortgage has a set of relations which give him certain rights against the land which, at common law, include title, while the mortgagor has a set of relations known as the right of redemption. Both these sets are property and can be assigned or sold. The mortgage set of relations, like the lease, enable a person to have most of the advantages of full ownership without the capital outlay.

E. Another set of relations allows people to own property jointly. They thus can be said to have concurrent rights. All property held in partnership is of this type. The common law has two kinds of sets available, joint tenancy and tenancy in common. In the former a co-owner's interest will go, on death, to the survivors in the joint tenancy while in the latter a co-owner's share can be passed on to a successor by will or on an intestacy.

F. The most complex form of ownership is that which is made possible by the complex set of relations known as a corporation. Such sets of relations enable the accumulation of large amounts of capital, physical resources and skills and, consequently, production on a scale seldom possible by other means of carrying on business enterprises. Through the use of shares (a sub-set of relations) ownership of such accumulations of wealth can be spread a large number of people. It further enables the development of a skilled managerial class, separate from those enjoying the profits of their ownership. We may tabulate some of these possibilities as follows :

(A) We can start with the primary object of ownership such as a piece of land.

(B) We postulate a primary set of ownership relations which will include all the rights, privileges, and powers relating to the control or use of the land.

(C) We then create sub-sets by fragmenting the primary set in the following ways :

- (1) on the plane of time (estates),
- (2) in terms of dividing beneficial enjoyment from control (trusts),
- (3) by isolating specific relations of sub-sets (easements, profits, powers of appointment).

(D) The above interests may be the subject of various forms of ownership such as :

(1) a secondary set of ownership relations,
(2) various security interests such as mortgages, agreements of sale,
(3) forms of co-ownership.

(E) These again may be owned by a company.

(F) The company itself may be owned by another company or by people in the form of shares.

A person, John Doe, may own (D1) shares (F) in a company (E) which owns (D1) an equity of redemption (D2) in a fee simple (C1) in Blackacre (A). Thus there may be as many as six (or even more) sets of legal relations between John Doe and Blackacre. This analysis looks only at the way the common law handles legal relations. Many different techniques and kinds of sets of relations are to be found in the civil law systems.

Let us take the situation where a client comes to his lawyer and asks him to draft his will. There are a number of legal constructs which the lawyer may use in passing the property from a testator to the beneficiaries. The ones selected will depend upon what the testator wishes to accomplish. The client tells the lawyer that he wishes to leave his property to his wife, but he is concerned that she will not be able to manage it properly. Further he wants to ensure that some property will be left for his adult children after his wife's death, but he does not want his infant son John to have anything unless and until he reaches the age of twenty-one. The draftsman then uses the construct of the trust which enables the giving of the legal relations relating to control of the property to a trust company and the relations relating to beneficial enjoyment to his wife. To ensure that there will be some property left for the children upon the death of the wife, he uses the construct of the estate by which the legal relations of ownership can be divided on the plane of time to give the wife a life estate with power to encroach on the capital. The adult children will then be given a vested remainder except for son John who will be given a contingent remainder upon the condition that he reaches twenty-one. What the legal draftsman has done is to have made a selection of certain empty legal forms developed by the law of property, in order to accomplish certain ends, and then to have filled in the variables on these forms with the appropriate persons and patterns of conduct. Such constructs of the English common law of real property are a part of almost a calculus where the lawyer is "moving in a world of pure ideas from which everything physical or material is entirely excluded."[3]

The advantages of dealing indirectly with people and resources through the use of such concepts are many. By their use a wider sharing and distribution of a particular resource is possible. In relation to a piece of land, Blackacre for instance, the legal system creates a bundle of jural relations which altogether are termed "ownership." Thus if A owns Blackacre, that is, he is the holder of the rights and powers of the jural relations, he can divide these various relations into their separate parts. He can give the right to possession by lease to B, the right to remove minerals to C, an easement to D, and so forth. He can also divide these jural relations along the plane of time into estates. He can give a life estate to B, and on his death a life estate to C, and on C's death a vested remainder to D, subject to be divested by a shifting executory interest given to E. He can also further divide his jural relations into legal relations and equitable relations, thus creating a trust. He can as well use two or all three of these methods of divisions at the same time. Thus he may give to B the right to remove minerals from the land, in trust for C for life, and on his death to D.

The use of such concepts allows a much greater flexibility. Ease of transfer of property is facilitated. Whereas now property can be transferred by mere agreement or deed, in legal systems where the property concept was that of physical possession property could be conveyed only by the actual transfer of that possession. A vast number of factual situations can be dealt with by the use of a minimum number of concepts. Such constructs, being theoretical, can be formulated to fit practically any human need. Their properties can be defined with much more precision than can the concepts of the world of fact. The increasing complexity of modern society, requiring a high degree of stability of expectations in regard to individual behaviour, could be possible only through such highly technical jural constructs.

NOTES

1. J.C. Smith, "The Concept of Native Title," *University of Toronto Law Journal* 24 (1974) : 1.

2. J.C. Smith, *Legal Obligation* (London : University of London, Athlone Press, 1976).

3. F.S. Lawson, *The Rational Strength of English Law* (London : 1951), p. 79.

3. Law of Persons

THE LAWS OF MANU[1]

147. By a girl, by a young woman, or even by an aged one, nothing must be done independently, even in her own house.

148. In childhood a female must be subject to her father, in youth to her husband, when her lord is dead to her sons ; a woman must never be independent.

149. She must not seek to separate herself from her father, husband, or sons ; by leaving them she would make both (her own and her husband's) families contemptible.

150. She must always be cheerful, clever in (the management of her) household affairs, careful in cleaning her utensils, and economical in her expenditures.

151. Him to whom her father may give her, or her brother with the father's permission, she shall obey as long as he lives, and when he is dead, she must not insult (his memory).

152. For the sake of procuring good fortune to (brides), the recitation of the benedictory texts and the sacrifice to the Lord of creatures are used at weddings ; (but) the betrothal (by the father or guardian) is the cause of (the husband's) dominion (over his wife).

153. The husband who wedded her with sacred texts, always gives happiness to his wife, both in season and out of season, in this world and in the next.

154. Though destitute of virtue, or seeking pleasure (elsewhere), or devoid of good qualities, (yet) a husband must be constantly worshipped as a god by a faithful wife.

155. No sacrifice, no vow, no fast must be performed by women apart (from their husbands) ; if a wife obeys her husband, she will for that (reason alone) be exalted in heaven.

156. A faithful wife, who desires to dwell (after death) with her husband, must never do anything that might displease him who took her hand, whether he be alive or dead.

157. At her pleasure, let her emaciate her body by (living on) pure flowers, roots and fruit ; but she must never even mention the name of another man after her husband has died.

158. Until death let her be patient (of hardships), self-controlled, and chaste, and strive (to fulfil) that most excellent duty which (is prescribed) for wives who have one husband only.

159. Many thousands of Brahmanas who were chaste from their youth, have gone to heaven without continuing their race.

160. A virtuous wife who after the death of her husband constantly remains chaste, reaches heaven, though she have no son, just like those chaste men.

161. But a woman who from a desire to have offspring violates her duty towards her (deceased) husband, brings on herself disgrace in this world, and loses her place with her husband (in heaven).

162. Offspring begotten by another man is here not (considered lawful), nor (does offspring begotten) on another man's wife (belong to the begetter), nor is a second husband anywhere prescribed for virtuous women.

163. She who cohabits with a man of higher caste, forsaking her own husband who belongs to a lower one, will become contemptible in this world, and is called a remarried woman *(parapurva).*

164. By violating her duty towards her husband, a wife is disgraced in this world (after death) she enters the womb of a jackal, and is tormented by diseases (the punishment of) her sin.

165. She who, controlling her thoughts, words, and deeds, never slights her lord, resides (after death) with her husband (in heaven), and is called a virtuous (wife).

166. In reward of such conduct, a female who controls her thoughts, speech, and actions, gains in this (life) highest renown, and in the next (world) a place near her husband.

167. A twice-born man, versed in the sacred law, shall burn a wife of equal caste who conducts herelf thus and dies before him, with (the sacred fires used for) the Agnihotra, and with the sacrificial implements.

168. Having thus, at the funeral, given the sacred fires to his wife who dies before him, he may marry again, and again kindle (the fires).

169. (Living) according to the (preceding) rules, he must never neglect the five (great) sacrifices, and, having taken a wife, he must dwell in (his own) house during the second period of his life. [pp. 195-198]

267. A Kshatriya, having defamed a Brahmana, shall be fined one hundred *(panas)* ; a Vaisya one hundred and fifty or two hundred, a Sudra shall suffer corporal punishment.

268. A Brahmana shall be fined fifty *(panas)* for defaming a Kshatriya ; in (the case of) a Vaisya the fine shall be twenty-five *(panas)* ; in (the case of) a Sudra twelve.

269. For offences of twice-born men against those of equal caste (*varna,* the fine shall be)also twelve (*panas*) ; for speeches which ought not to be uttered, that (and every fine shall be) double.

270. A once-born man (a Sudra), who insults a twice-born man with gross invective, shall have his tongue cut out, for he is of low origin.

271. If he mentions the names and castes (*gati*) of the (twice-born) with contumely, an iron nail, ten fingers long, shall be thrust red-hot into his mouth.

272. If he arrogantly teaches Brahamanas their duty, the king shall cause hot oil to be poured into his mouth and into his ears.

273. He who through arrogance makes false statements regarding the learning (of a caste-fellow), his country, his caste (*gati*), or the rites by which his body was sanctified, shall be compelled to pay a fine of two hundred (*panas*).

274. He who even in accordance with the true facts (contemptuously) calls another man one-eyed, lame, or the like (names) shall be fined at least one *karshapana.*

275. He who defames his mother, his father, his wife, his brother, his son, or his teacher, and he who gives not the way to his preceptor, shall be compelled to pay one hundred (*panas*).

276. (For mutual abuse) by a Brahmana and a Kshatriya a fine must be imposed by a discerning (king), on the Brahmana the lowest amercement, but on the Kshatriya the middlemost.

277. A Vaisya and a Sudra must be punished exactly in the same manner according to their respective castes, but the tongue (of the Sudra) shall not be cut out ; that is the decision.

278. Thus the rules for punishment (applicable to cases) of defamation have been truly declared; I will next expound the decision (of cases) of assault.

279. With whatever limb a man of a low caste does hurt to (a man of the three highest castes), even that limb shall be cut off; that is the teaching of Manu.

280. He who raises his hand or a stick, shall have his hand cut off; he who in anger kicks with his foot; shall have his foot cut off.

281. A low-caste man who tries to place himself on the same seat with a man of a high caste, shall be branded on his hip and be banished, or (the king) shall cause his buttock to be gashed.

282. If out of arrogance he spits (on a superior), the king shall cause both his lips to be cut off; . . .

283. If he lays hold of the hair (of a superior), let the (king) unhesitatingly cut off his hands, likewise (if he takes him) by the feet, the beard, the neck, or the scrotum.

284. He who breaks the skin (of an equal) or fetches blood (from him) shall be fined one hundred (*panas*), he who cuts a muscle six nishkas, he who breaks a bone shall be banished. [pp. 301-304]

NOTE

1. F. Max Muller, ed., G. Buhler, trans., "The Laws of Manu," in *The Sacred Books of the East*, vol. 25 (Delhi : Motilal Banarsidass, 1967), pp. 301-304.

THE CODE OF HAMMURABI[1]

195. If a son has struck his father, his hands shall be cut off.

196. If a man has destroyed the eye of a free man, his own eye shall be destroyed.

197. If he has broken the bone of a free man, his bone shall be broken.

198. If he has destroyed the eye of a plebeian, or broken a bone of a plebeian, he shall pay one mina of silver.

199. If he has destroyed the eye of a man's slave, or broken a bone of a man's slave, he shall pay half his value.

200. If a man has knocked out the teeth of a man of the same rank, his own teeth shall be knocked out.

201. If he has knocked out the teeth of a plebeian, he shall pay one-third of a mina of silver.

202. If a man strike the body of a man who is great above him, he shall publicly receive sixty lashes with a cowhide whip.

203. If a man strike the body of the son of a free man of like condition, he shall pay one mina of silver.

204. If a plebeian strike the body of a plebeian, he shall pay ten shekels of silver.

205. If a man's slave strike the body of the son of a free man, his ear shall be cut off.

206. If a man has struck another man in a dispute and wounded him, that man shall swear, "I did not strike him knowingly" ; and he shall pay for the doctor.

207. If he die of his blows, he shall swear likewise ; and if it be the son of a free man, he shall pay half a mina of silver.

208. If he be the son of a plebeian, he shall pay a third of a mina of silver.

209. If a man strike the daughter of a free man, and causes her foetus to fall ; he shall pay ten shekels of silver for her foetus.

210. If that woman die, his daughter shall be slain.

211. If he has caused the daughter of a plebeian to let her foetus fall through blows, he shall pay five shekels of silver.

212. If that woman die, he shall pay half a mina of silver.

213. If he has struck the slave of a man, and made her foetus fall ; he shall pay two shekels of silver.

214. If that slave die, he shall pay a third of a mina of silver. [pp. 61-63]

NOTE

1. Chilperic Edwards, trans., *The Hammurabi Code and the Sinaitic Legislation* (Port Washington, N.Y. : Kennikat Press, 1971), pp. 61-63.

ON THE CONCEPT OF THE KINDRED[1]

J.D. Freeman

. . .[B]efore discussing the ways in which kindred relations become important I would like to refer briefly to what I shall call the moral basis of the kindred. Kindred relations cannot, I believe, be accounted for as simple extension of the sentiments which develop in the nuclear family. This is not to deny the importance of consanguinity ; evidence from a number of bilateral societies suggests that what is basic is the fact that relations between kindred are governed by a special morality arising from the recognition of common descent.... Thus it is usual for kindred to admit a special obligation toward one another : an obligation to give help and support in culturally determined ways....

. . ."Kindred and kindness go together — two words whose common derivation expresses in the happiest way one of the main principles of social life."[2] It is a principle seen in the Iban utterance : "Though angered at us he took no action out of kindness on seeing kindred...." ; or in the old Germanic maxim, "The blood of friends boils even though it be but a drop" — friends here, as among other ancient Teutonic peoples, meaning kindred.

The existence of a special morality is demonstrated among the Iban in the not uncommon occurrence of two individuals hitherto unknown to one another meeting for the first time and establishing to their mutual satisfaction that they are members of the same stock, or turun. At once their relationship is changed for, on the moment, they recognize obligations to one another as kindred. Thus, an Iban traveller in some remote quarter of his tribal territory will always endeavour to trace consanguineal ties, for once these be established he is no longer a stranger and enters the ambit of what Morgan called "the natural faith of kindred." This is not to claim, let me make it plain, that those who are kindred dwell in a state of mystical concord ; on the contrary, as among the Iban, quarrelling and litigation may be frequent happenings, but these cases (which I cannot here discuss) are all shaped by the fact that it is kindred who are in conflict and not strangers. It is also important to note that the morality of the kindred is commonly of a restricted kind and quite distinct from the morality of the wider society, a point well illustrated by Maude in his discussion of the *utu*, or kindred of the Gilbertese. "On one occasion", writes Maude, "a man mentioned in my presence that on crossing the lagoon an hour before he had passed a woman endeavouring to swim for the shore with a baby (evidently her canoe had sunk) and he expressed the opinion that she would never make it. When asked why he had not stopped to pick her up his reply was, to all except me, perfectly reasonable : *tikai kain au utu* (she was not a member of my *utu*)."[3]

In any examination of the moral basis of the kindred one is soon confronted by the problem of whether the rights and obligations of kindred exhibit any kind of gradation and whether they can be said to terminate at any precise point. The ethnographic evidence suggests that a sharp line of demarcation is never drawn, but rather (in Seebohm's words) there is a "shading off as degrees of relationship become more distant"[4] the outer limits of recognition varying, as we have seen, from one society to another, and within a society, even from individual to individual. Thus, in the absence of arbitrary demarcation it is merely the cessation of inter-communication, for whatever reasons, that tends to terminate kindred relations and the moral obligations associated with them. It is, in other words, a *de facto* and not a *de jure* termination. Indeed, it is always possible, where circumstances make it advantageous, for a dormant relationship to be revived if those concerned are ready to recognize it.

As many writers have noted, some degree of gradation in obligation, within the kindred, is usual. Among the Melanau, for example, obligations "vary with the closeness of relationship and the generation of the people concerned." So writes Morris, "If an 'invitation' comes from a parent's sibling to accompany a work party to the sago gardens, an individual would need a better excuse for refusing, if he wished to avoid a disobliging reputation, than he would if the 'invitation' came from a parent's cousin who is rated as a 'side uncle.'[5]

It must not be supposed, however, that kindred relations are dominated by this notion of gradation. An even more important feature of the kindred in bilateral societies is that it presents an individual with a wide range of optative relationships — relationships, which, in the absence of any binding descent principle, it is possible for him to accentuate as he pleases or as suits his special interests. Thus, among the Iban, a man's kindred represents a field in which he is able to move largely at will, and it frequently happens that in economic, ritual, and other spheres a man's closest ties are by choice with "distant" rather than "near" members of his kindred. Similarly, as Pehrson demonstrates, "the Lapp's membership in the flexible kindred provides him with a wide range of alternative courses of action."[6] Kindred relationships then, are, to a marked extent, optative, a fact of fundamental importance in the functioning of bilateral societies like those of the Lapps and the Iban. [pp. 263-266)]

NOTES

1. J.D. Freeman, "On the Concept of Kindred," in *Kinship and Social Organization*, ed. Paul Bohannan & J. Middleton, (Garden City, N.Y. : Natural History Press, 1968), pp. 263-266.

2. E.B. Taylor, *Anthropology : An Introduction to the Study of Man and Civilization*, 2nd ed. (London : John Murray and Co., 1881), p. 405.

3. H.E. Maude, "The Evolution of the Gilbertese 'Boti,'" paper presented at the 10th Pacific Scientific Congress (Honolulu : 1961).

4. F. Seebohm, *The Tribal System in Wales* (London : Longmans, Green and Co., 1904), p. 101.

5. C.W. Morris, *Report on a Melanau Sago Producing Community in Sarawak* (London : H.M. Stationary Office, 1953), p. 105.

6. Robert N. Pehrson, *The Bilateral Network of Sacral Relations in Konkama Lapp District* (Bloomington : Indiana University Publications, Slavic and East European Series), p. 96.

FAMILY PROPERTY AMONG THE YORUBAS[1]

G.B.A. Coker

Among the Yorubas the conception of the family is perhaps the most dearly cherished and certainly the oldest. The origin of the principles which govern dealings in, by and with the family is lost in history. There are but few recorded accounts of these principles and even those available records are deeply embellished with legend and mythology. The whole life of the Yorubas is dominated by religion and the conception of man by the Yorubas is essentially religious. This conception involves an acceptance common to the Yorubas of the possession by man of both a material and an ethereal body, the latter capable after his death of continuing existence. Unless it is understood that this belief is fundamental among the Yorubas, it may be difficult to appreciate many of the rules which apply not only to the preservation of family properties but also to the distribution of the properties generally in Yorubaland. Once it is realized that the deceased ancestor continues to exist in another form and that from such state of existence he is still capable of watching the affairs of those still alive in the flesh, it is natural to maintain only a course of conduct which would not only benefit the offsprings but also to a greater extent placate the living spirit of the deceased. The law governing the establishment and the maintenance of family properties has today assumed a magnitude which the progenitors of the Yorubas could not possibly have anticipated or envisaged, but it should be understood that most of the rules of that system of jurisprudence have come to us in our own days more or less completely unscathed by the vicissitudes,legal and otherwise, through which they had passed. The modern lawyer may justly claim to have found these rules of law relating to the family, but he certainly has not made them. There has certainly been a growth of law by an unconscious and organic process from the easily grasped legal relations characterizing the families in remote communities to the greater complexity which those rules manifest today.

It is however not open to doubt that at some time in history some kind of family law was administered among the Yorubas, because in remote days (and even in recent times among primitive communities) almost every known legal concept began and ended with the family. The individual is only thought of in so far as he belongs to a family.

In the language of the learned writer :

> There is no such thing as succession in the proper English manner, in a family owning ancestral property. The whole family, consisting of males and females constitutes a sort of corporation ; some of the members being co-partners . . .and others who are dependents, and are entitled to reside in the dwelling house for life, such as sons and daughters, subject to good conduct and not disputing right of the family. Partition being extremely rare the idea of heirship scarcely presents itself to the mind of any member of the family. The members are entitled to reside in the ancestral house and to enjoy that amount of affluence and consideration which springs from their belonging to a family possessed of greater or lesser wealth.[2]

. . .[A]ll along the West Coast of Africa, there is a universally accepted conception of the family set up, involving identical or at least similar characteristics and, in any case, exhibiting a marked reflection of family dependence. Among these communities a broader view is taken of the composition of the family than the average Westerner would, and instances are not unknown where even the slaves or domestics of a man have become regarded as members of his family. Such an elastic composition is capable of expansion to intolerable dimensions, at any rate in the comprehension of someone unacquainted with the actual facts or the way of life of the members of such communities. It is however the position that established and recognized methods of identification have always been applied to determine the extent of the family and limit it to within traditionally accepted bounds. The family unit is after all maintained together by a common adoption and a kindred consciousness of an inward oneness. This state of existence is not unknown in other communities and students of historical jurisprudence have explained the position as resting on the assumption characteristic of early communities that their members were banded together by common lineage. In ancient patriarchal times, people hardly appreciated that any difference existed between the king and the father, for they regarded the king of a country as the father and/or progenitor of his people. Sir Henry Maine has summarized the position :

> The history of political ideas begins in fact with the assumption that kinship in blood is the sole possible ground of community in political functions : nor is there any of those subversions of feeling, which are termed empathetically revolutions so startling and so complete as the change which is accomplished when some other principle — such as that, for instance, of local contiguity — establishes itself for the first time as the basis of common political action. It may be affirmed then of

early commonwealths that their citizens considered all the groups to which they claimed membership to be founded on common lineage.[3]

A clear example of Sir Henry Maine's proposition could be found among the Yorubas and this would account for what would otherwise appear to be a marvellous (if not impossible) instance of fecundity in any king, like, for instance, Oranyan, traditionally believed to be the father of all Yorubas.... [pp. 3-6]

Land, probably the most important source of wealth in a developing country, can always be the subject of a great many interests and derivative rights. These are often difficult to elucidate and, where land is subject to native customary tenure, it is always the subject of rights and interests vested in both the individual and the group, and such rights and interests are frequently co-existent with each other. This, to a very large extent, must be responsible for the erroneous conception, peculiar to some writers and fieldworkers in anthropology, that the ownership of land under native law and custom is vested in the community as such. Ancestral worship on common grounds and many forms of social and religious ceremonies held on land commonly held have also helped to make more obscure an already entangled subject. It is, of course, clear, on closer analysis, that the control exercised by the community as a group on lands is mostly social or political and does not extend beyond the limits necessary to maintain the group solidarity of the community. Actual physical control of native lands is vested in the families and, speaking generally, only in the sense that it is an aggregate of the constituent family groups could the community or tribe be said to own the land.

That this is so is further proved by the fact that, although the king or the chief is held among the Nigerians to be the head of the tribe or community, yet he has no powers by himself to sell or alienate the lands at his disposal. He is bound by native law and custom to allocate to the several families for their own use portions of such lands ; in many cases he can also allocate to strangers portions of the lands at his disposal, against the payment of tribute.At no period of history was this the function of the entire community or tribe and no evidence is recorded by which any such system of allocation could be described as a general sharing between the members of the community or tribe concerned. The position has been described by a learned writer :

> The chief is everywhere regarded as the symbol of the residuary reversionary and ultimate ownership of all land held by a territorial community. He holds on behalf of the whole community in the capacity of a caretaker or trustee only but he allocates portions of land to family heads according to need and these in turn reallocate among their members.[4] [pp. 30-31]

NOTES

1. G.B.A. Coker, *Family Property Among the Yorubas* (London : Sweet & Maxwell Ltd., 1966), pp. 3-31.
2. J.M. Sarbah, *Fanti Customary Laws*, 2nd ed., (London : Wm. Clowes & Sons, 1904), p. 100-101.
3. Sir Henry Maine, *Ancient Law*, (London : John Murray, 1930), p. 145.
4. T.O. Elias, *The Nature of African Customary Law*, (Manchester : "Manchester University Press", 1956), p. 164.

MAINE'S ANCIENT LAW IN THE LIGHT OF PRIMITIVE SOCIETIES[1]

Robert Redfield

The acknowledgement of greatest worth should be made with regard to Maine's most comprehensive and summary statement : that the general trend of history has been from status to contract, that, on the whole, society began as a collection of families and has become an aggregation of individuals, that a man's rights and obligations were once fixed by the familial relationships in which he found himself, and that they have come to depend upon his own free and contractual undertakings. Maine develops this generalization, which is true whether the comparison be between modern society and ancient Greco-Roman society, as Maine made it, or between modern society and the hundreds of tribal and peasant societies as made by the writer of this paper. Maine made the generalization stick by a historical study of Western juridical institutions. The same generalization illuminates and brings into orderly comprehension otherwise heterogeneous facts from the primitive societies. If Maine was wrong in thinking of patriarchal society as something historically primary and more or less universal, he was right in thinking of familial institutions as universal and, in a sense, primary. For the relations of kinship do provide a sort of basic pattern of human association. Later students than Maine have shown that a territorial bond as well as a kinship bond holds together the men and women of simple societies. This qualification, however, is minor : the simplest societies are, in quality of social relationships, essentially families or family-like groups. Maine expressed this general truth alternatively in his conclusion that originally status, and only later contract, fixed a man's obligations. The anthropologist again recognizes the intellectual value of the insight offered. For primitive societies exist as networks of right and obligation and attitude between child, shaman and layman, elder man and younger. A man's conduct follows from his place in this constellation of relationships. This is as true for the patriarch-less Andamanese as it is for the patriarchal early Romans.

We think of contract especially in connection with material goods, with matters of purchase and sale. In our modern societies most goods are made to be put into a market in which their value is fixed by a pricing mechanism, and most goods are distributed by contracts entered into by sellers and buyers who, as a rule, make their agreements to buy and sell as the profit motive suggests. The market system of modern times is largely independent of the status system of the society.But in primitive societies the opposite is true. There economic systems are imbedded in social relations. Men work and manufacture not for motives of gain. They tend to work because working is part of the good life and often of a man's religious obligations. Goods are distributed not by means of the market, but as an aspect of relations between men that are personal, conventional and moral. Thus, for example, the Australian hunter who kills a wild animal is expected to give one certain part of it to his elder brother, other parts to his younger brother and still other parts of the animal to defined relatives. He does this, knowing that he is a younger brother to his elder brother who, when the latter is successful in hunting, will make a corresponding distribution of meat to him. In many societies in which descent in the maternal line is stressed, a man gives the food he collects or grows to his sister's children who are not members of his own household. His own children are fed by his wife's brother. Moreover, a great deal of the distribution that takes place in primitive society is incidental to the tribal organization. It is customary in many Melanesian tribes for every worker to put some of the yams he grows into the yam-storehouse of the chief. The more yams in the storehouse, the greater the pride of the community. The yams are known as the chief's yams, but he is not free to eat them all himself, still less to sell them. He is expected to give them away, on certain festal occasions, to people of his own community, and to their guests from other communities.

In such a system of living, where is contract and freedom of contract? Maine was right in seeing that contract, as we know it, is not an original important feature of society. It is true that there are instances, in primitive societies, of trading between two tribes without established personal relations between the two groups. The Congo Pygmies bring game they have killed to certain clearings, knowing that Bantu tribesmen, with whom they are not so friendly, will come and put down bananas beside the meat and so, in effect, make an offer to exchange the bananas for the meat. After the Bantu have withdrawn, the Pygmies return. If satisfied with the number and quality of the bananas, they take them away; then the Bantu once more come to the clearing and take the meat. This is a kind of contract, without status relations, in primitive society. This — the silent trade — does occur. But it is not typical.

Much more usual in primitive societies is exchange of goods upon what has been called a principle of equivalent goodwill. The Andamanese — to mention a primitive group that has been cited before as an illustration — from time to time go visiting, a group from one band calling upon a neighbouring and friendly band. The visitors take with them pots, bows, and woven ornaments. Arrived in the other camp, each visitor presents articles he has brought with him to one or another of the host encampments. The recipient then knows he is expected to reciprocate with a gift made to the giver and visitor. Emphasis is upon the equivalence of the generous gesture, not upon equivalent value of the object given. This is not a market. It is a party of visitors making friends. It is the personal relationship of friendliness that is important — it is status that matters, not contract. Yet the affair has something in it that has to do with our idea of contract, for the man who accepts a gift is under an obligation to make a gift in return. It is contract-like only in that an obligation arises to return something for what has been received. It is different from contract in that the one party has no real choice — he cannot decently refuse the gift. And it is different from contract in that there is no law, no formal sanction, to enforce the obligation to make a counter-gift. Only the informal social controls have influence: public opinion, personal conscience, and the pleasure derived from participating in the friendly giving.

Primitive societies are characteristically like families rather than like markets. From early documents and from the history of western law Maine saw that this must be so, and although he knew little about primitive societies, in this respect he was right about them too. The primitive society is a family in that rights and obligations are largely fixed by the position of the individual — a position determined at birth. Economic institutions follow from social institutions and are subordinate to them. Men rarely contract, independent of these traditional and personal obligations. Barter is far from being a primary form of exchange of goods — it is secondary. On the whole, the broad history of humanity, the narrower history of Europe, and the transformation of tribal society under the influences of contact with other societies, fulfill the generalization. The society becomes less dependent on inherited personal status as an aspect of family and family-like relationships, and more dependent on the deliberate choices and undertakings of separate individuals. It is particularly in this respect that Maine's book justifies Hoebel's statement, with which this paper began, that "Maine's Ancient Law still remains . . . the pre-eminent work on the origin and nature of primitive legal institutions." [pp. 586-589]

NOTE

1. Robert Redfield "Maine's Ancient Law in the Light of Primitive Societies," *The Western Political Quarterly* 3 (1950) : 586-589.

THE CREATIVE USE OF LEGAL CONCEPTS[1]

F.H. Lawson

Legal personality is not the same as human personality, an estate in fee simple does not exist physically in the same way as the land over which it exists, nor is a contract the same as the agreement of which it is the legal manifestation. Legal personality, estates, and contracts are part of a world of their own, which is in some way related to the world of fact but is separate from it.

It is an artificial world, whose members are to some extent arbitrarily, though not irrationally, created to serve certain purposes. Thus they can be defined with fair exactness, much more satisfactorily than the facts of everyday life. In a sense they are created to conform to predetermined definitions. Again, their relations to each other are much more clearly fixed than relations in the world of fact. This is not invariably true, but it is usually true of that part of the world of law which is the main concern of the business lawyer.

It would be very odd if it were not so. For the business lawyer could hardly use instruments with the individuality and uncertain definition of natural objects. He could not predict the effects to be obtained from using them. He would be working with the hopeful (or hopeless) uncertainty of a man who guides his future conduct merely by predicting the probable conduct of his fellow men in accordance with his view of their temperament and character. The whole object of the business lawyer's activities is to exclude that uncertainty as far as he can.

Thus he must work with artificial concepts. Sooner or later the results he gets must be translated from the world of law into that of fact, for "business law" exists only to achieve practical results. It is perhaps for that reason that legal concepts start by looking as much as possible like their counterparts in the world of fact. This is apt to lead to some confusion in the mind of the analyst, though it must be admitted that neither the practical business lawyer nor the business man is troubled by it.

It is indeed easy to see that all legal relations are abstract and exist not in fact but only in contemplation of law. Rights and duties do not belong to the physical world, though the infringement of a right may involve the wrongdoer in a loss of physical goods or in a physical interference with his body. It is a little harder to see that the persons between whom relations exist do not themselves live in the physical world but play parts in the drama of the law. But that is certainly so. If relations are abstract, the persons who are the ends of them are abstract also. If the law can choose which rights or other relations to create or at least recognize, it can also choose which persons to create or recognize. This truth is obscured by the fact that in the modern world few distinctions are made between human beings as possible subjects of rights, and by the possibility of expressing variations as variations in the relations of one person to another rather than as variations in the nature of either person. Thus, if it is convenient to do so, an infant can be considered not to differ as a person from an adult, and the whole weight of the difference in his legal position can be thrown on the varying relations that arise from his infancy. But it is probably better for the law to admit variations in legal personality instead of working legal relations to death. The law is not bound to resemble a game of draughts or *halma*, where position is everything. It can enjoy the greater complexity of chess, where the pieces are of different kinds.

It has long been recognized that such a conception of legal personality greatly facilitates the analysis of corporate personality. As long as the legal personality of a human being is regarded as existing in the world of fact it is hard to avoid being anthropomorphic in all one's dealings with legal personality. Any characteristic attributed to a corporation which could not be attributed to a human being is apt to shock. Conversely, any characteristic which is too human to be attributed to a nonhuman person also shocks, for obviously a corporation is not actually flesh and blood. Indeed the legal person was an abstraction that was not easily come by, for the Romans themselves, who seem to have been the first to use it, often confused the nonhuman corporation with its human members, and the same confusion, happily one of words only, is evident in the official title of a municipal corporation like the City of Oxford as the Mayor, Aldermen and Citizens of the City of Oxford, or of Brasenose College as the Principal and Scholars of the King's Hall and College of Brasenose in Oxford.

All that is necessary for the existence of a person is that the lawmaker be he legislator, judge, or jurist, or even the public at large, should decide to treat it as a subject of rights or other legal relations. It is sufficient for it to be recognized as a possible person of inherence or of incidence, according to the language of the English analytical jurists. Once this point has been reached, a vista of unrestricted liberty opens up before the jurist, unrestricted, that is, by any need to make a person resemble a man or collection of men. If in any scheme of legal relations it suits him to interpolate a person at any point, he can do so and he can give it the characteristics he wants. No doubt entities are not to be invented beyond necessity, but necessities grow out of each other. Doubtless also the business lawyer will find it convenient to make his artificial persons imitate the characteristics of human beings, for those characteristics are familiar to us and we can move from the known to the unknown more easily if such imitation is allowed ; but this only means that the farther the legal person diverges from the natural human being the more particularized its description must be. The internal and external constitution of an American state or an English limited company is in fact defined in such detail that the analogy to a human being is hardly noticed.

Legal personality and legal persons are, as it were, mathematical creations devised for the purpose of simplifying legal calculations. Just as unknown quantities denoted by algebraical symbols such as X are used to simplify problems which could, with a great expenditure of time and labour, be solved by purely arithmetical methods, so legal problems which ultimately concern human beings and physical objects are often more easily solved by interpolating an artificial legal person between the human being or beings and their relation to another person or thing.

The kinds of legal persons are many. They include not only collections of human beings associated for various purposes — from such all-purpose organizations as the state, through churches, local authorities, colleges and universities, clubs and trade unions, to trading corporations such as the English limited company — but also successions of persons known as corporations sole, idols, funds devoted to charitable or other purposes.... There is a steady drop in resemblance to human persons, until in the end personality is attributed to various kinds of things, whether individual or collective, and even to disembodied purposes. There is no reason to suppose that other kinds of legal persons may not be created at will, though the intervention of a legislature may be needed.

Nor is there any limit in logic, though there may be in policy, to the number of legal persons that may be interpolated at any point in human relations. Thus in America before the New Deal "pyramiding," a process by which one company in effect controlled subsidiary companies which in their turn controlled other subsidiaries and so on, had become extraordinarily complicated. It was a new form of feudalism with legal persons taking the place of human beings. What is more, suggesions such as those pilloried by the late Dr. Martin Wolff, that such pyramiding was inadmissible on the ground that it involved the enslavement of one person by another, strike all but the most pedantic of jurists as ludicrous.

This is not the place to examine the ways in which legal personification facilitates the calculations of both law and business, or the extent to which it may be chosen in preference to some other device. It is enough for the present to emphasize the extraordinary freedom that it has given to the business lawyer, most of all to the corporation lawyer or company draftsman. It seems as indispensable as money or the infinitesimal calculus, though it has not become so elaborate as either.

There is an enormous juristic literature about legal personality, but it is mainly concerned with its relation to the world of fact and the extent to which it should be governed by human personality. There is no doubt about its position in the legal world and it no longer causes real difficulty to the pure analyst. [pp. 913-916]

NOTE

1. F.H. Lawson, "The Creative Use of Legal Concepts," *New York University Law Review* 32 (1957) : 913-916.

THEORIES OF LEGAL PERSONALITY[1]

David P. Derham

All legal systems (at least so far as I am aware) are concerned with the control and organization of relations between human beings by means of general rules.

So soon as there is any system, any organization, with a logic of its own, just so soon must there be some constants, some reference points given, on which to base the logic of the system. Just as the concept "one" in arithmetic is essential to the logical system developed and yet is not one something (e.g., apple or orange, etc.), so a legal system (or any system perhaps) must be provided with a basic unit before legal relationships can be devised which will serve the primary purpose of organizing the social facts. The legal person is the unit or entity adopted. For the logic of the system it is just as much a pure "concept" as "one" in arithmetic. It is just as independent from a human being as one is from an "apple." [p.5]

NOTE

1. David P. Derham, "Theories of Legal Personality," in *Legal Personality and Political Pluralism*, ed. Leicester C. Webb (Victoria : Melbourne University Press), p. 5.

4. Law Without Rules

AN AUTOBIOGRAPHY : THE STORY OF MY EXPERIMENTS WITH TRUTH[1]

M.K. Gandhi

The year's stay in Pretoria was a most valuable experience in my life. Here it was that I had opportunities of learning public work and acquired some measure of my capacity for it. Here it was that the religious spirit within me became a living force, and here too I acquired a true knowledge of legal practice. Here I learnt the things that a junior barrister learns in a senior barrister's chamber, and here I also gained confidence that I should not after all fail as a lawyer. It was likewise here that I learnt the secret of success as a lawyer.

Dada Abdulla's was no small case. The suit was for £40,000. Arising out of business transactions, it was full of intricacies of accounts. Part of the claim was based on promissory notes, and part on the specific performance of promise to deliver promissory notes. The defence was that the promissory notes were fraudulently taken and lacked sufficient consideration. There were numerous points of fact and law in this intricate case.

Both parties had engaged the best attorneys and counsel. I thus had a fine opportunity of studying their work. The preparation of the plaintiff's case for the attorney and the sorting of facts in support of his case had been entrusted to me. It was an education to see how much the attorney accepted, and how much he rejected from my preparation, as also to see how much use the counsel made of the brief prepared by the attorney. I saw that this preparation for the case would give me a fair measure of my powers of comprehension and my capacity for marshalling evidence.

I took the keenest interest in the case. Indeed I threw myself into it. I read all the papers pertaining to the transactions. My client was a man of great ability and reposed absolute confidence in me, and this rendered my work easy. I made a fair study of book-keeping. My capacity for translation was improved by having to translate the correspondence, which was for the most part in Gujarati.

Although, as I have said before, I took a keen interest in religious communion and in public work and always gave some of my time to them, they were not then my primary interest. The preparation of the case was my primary interest. Reading of law and looking up law cases, when necessary, had always a prior claim on my time. As a result, I acquired such a grasp of the facts of the case as perhaps was not possessed even by the parties themselves, inasmuch as I had with me the papers of both the parties.

I recalled the late Mr. Pincutt's advise — facts are three-fourths of the law. At a later date it was amply borne out by that famous barrister of South Africa, the late Mr. Leonard. In a certain case in my charge I saw that, though justice was on the side of my client, the law seemed to be against him. In despair I approached Mr. Leonard for help. He also felt that the facts of the case were very strong. He exclaimed, "Gandhi, I have learnt one thing, and it is this, that if we take care of the facts of a case, the law will care of itself. Let us dive deeper into the facts of this case." With these words he asked me to study the case further and then see him again. On a re-examination of the facts I saw them in an entirely new light, and I also hit upon an old South African case bearing on the point. I was delighted and went to Mr. Leonard and told him everything. "Right," he said, "we shall win the case. Only we must bear in mind which of the judges takes it."

When I was making preparation for Dada Abdulla's case, I had not fully realized this paramount importance of facts. Facts mean truth, and once we adhere to truth, the law comes to our aid naturally. I saw that the facts of Dada Abdulla's case made it very strong indeed, and that the law was bound to be on his side. But I also saw that the litigation, if it were persisted in, would ruin the plaintiff and the defendant, who were relatives and both belonged to the same city. No one knew how long the case might go on. Should it be allowed to continue to be fought out in court, it might go on indefinitely and to no advantage of either party. Both, therefore, desired an immediate termination of the case, if possible.

I approached Tyeb Sheth and requested and advised him to go to arbitration. I recommended him to see his counsel. I suggested to him that, if an arbitrator commanding the confidence of both parties could be appointed, the case would be quickly finished. The lawyers' fees were so rapidly mounting up that they were enough to devour all the resources of the clients, big merchants as they were. The case occupied so much of their attention that they had no time left for any other work. In the meantime mutual ill will was steadily increasing. I became disgusted with the profession. As lawyers the counsel on both sides were bound to rake up points of law in support of their own clients. I also saw for the first time that the winning party never recovers all the costs incurred. Under the Court Fees Regulation there was a fixed scale of costs to be allowed as between party and party, the actual costs as between attorney and client being very much higher. This was more than I could bear. I felt that my duty was to befriend both parties and bring them together. I strained every nerve to bring about a compromise. At last Tyeb Sheth agreed. An abitrator was appointed, the case was argued before him, and Dada Abdulla won.

But that did not satisfy me. If my client were to seek immediate execution of the award, it would be impossible for Tyeb Sheth to meet the whole of the awarded amount, and there was an unwritten law among the Porbandar Memans living in South Africa that death should be preferred to bankruptcy. It was impossible for Tyeb Sheth to pay down the whole sum of about £37,000 and costs. He meant to pay not a pie less than the amount, and he did not want to be declared bankrupt. There was only one way. Dada Abdulla should allow him to pay in moderate instalments. He was equal to the occasion, and granted Tyeb Sheth instalments spread over a long period. It was more difficult for me to secure this concession of payment by instalments than to get the parties to agree to arbitration. But both were happy over the result, and both rose in the public estimation. My joy was boundless. I had learnt the true practice of law. I had learnt to find out the better side of human nature and to enter men's hearts. I realized that the true function of a lawyer was to unite parties riven asunder. The lesson was so indelibly burnt into me that a large part of my time during the twenty years of my practice as a lawyer was occupied in bringing about private compromises of hundreds of cases. I lost nothing thereby — not even money, certainly not my soul. [pp. 165-168]

NOTE

1. M.K. Gandhi, *An Autobiography : The Story of My Experiments with Truth*, trans. Mahadev Desai (Washington, D.C. : Public Affairs Press, 1948), pp. 165-168.

THE NATURE OF AFRICAN CUSTOMARY LAW[1]

T. Olawale Elias

In the conditions obtaining in many African societies, the margin of social security is often too narrow for peremptory, unilateral penalties to be fashionable. That is why the judges often follow up the payment of fines or compensation with a ceremonial reconciliation of the parties so that personal rancour and clan feud might not have free rein to the detriment of the social order.... "The object of the elders was not punishment, but settlement of the dispute ; not a declaration of strict legal rights, but reconciliation. The tender of amends (*mpatse*) by the wrongdoer implied an apology for the wrong done ; its acceptance meant forgiveness and forgetting. . . ."[2]

If we may quote Lambert's *Kiambu Guide* once more, "The native method would tend to adjust disturbances of the social equilibrium, to restore peace and goodwill, and to bind or rebind the two disputing groups together in a give-and-take reciprocity. The European method would tend to widen the gulf between the two groups by granting all the rights to one of them to the exclusion of the other, because it would in general concern itself with facts and legal principles and take no cognizance of social implications. . . ."[3]

. . .When one comes to think seriously about the matter, one soon realizes how utterly unsatisfying it must be that in a case where neither all the rights nor all the wrongs of the case are on one side or the other, one of the parties should be made to carry away "the whole loaf" while the other retires embittered and disgruntled, but is powerless to show his exasperation only because of the state force behind the judges. Confidence in the judicial process cannot but be slightly undermined by such happenings and the general impression of the layman is that the state's "law is an ass." Society becomes increasingly estranged from this type of "lawyer's law" as argued and interpreted by professional bench and bar between them. The litigant is often a mere bewildered onlooker in court.

But how different is a system in which the twin elements of cognoscibility and publicity are present, in that everyone or nearly everyone knows the main rules of customary law, and the arguments as well as counter-arguments are publicly marshalled and weighed one against the other, sometimes with the aid of symbols such as sticks or stones or handclaps, and sometimes by the preponderance of evidence. The judgments take the form of apportioning blame and praise for particular acts or omissions of the litigants as they unfold their stories and buttress them by witnesses or other evidence. It is the one who, on balance, has more points against him that finally gets mulcted in fine or compensation for the benefit of the other. Restoration of the parties to the *status quo ante* is the keynote of the judicial process, and nothing must be left in the possession of the one which legitimately belongs to the other. Even where the final point is scored by only one party so that fine or compensation is imposed on the other, the latter goes away at least satisfied by the open handed way in which the various aspects of the respective rights and wrongs have been acknowledged and appraised in the course of the judgment(s). The verdict, where it goes against him, does not strike him as the command of an all-powerful judge laying down an inexorable law which he hardly understands, or which can hardly be regarded as the expression of the common consciousness of the community.

In the vast majority of cases the general atmosphere of the African judicial process is not one of enforced awe or sullen resentment but is, as Krige has said of the Lovhedu system, one of peaceful debate of the issues dividing the litigants in the sure belief that some kind of acceptable solution will be found out of the elder's fund of wisdom and sense of justice. The criminal is similarly made to pay compensation for his misdeeds if such a composition will be adequate to the damage done to his victim. Banishment, hanging, drowning, and the other indigenous modes of getting rid of the outlaw and the recidivist are resorted to only when all other means have been exhausted of re-incorporating such in society as useful members thereof. Only in these few cases is the judicial process prompt, definite, and inexorable.

Generally, African judges are wont to indulge in end-of-trial judicial homilies to the parties. In these they attempt to state and enunciate the norms of social behaviour expected of right-minded members of the community, to condemn departures from these objective standards, and to praise such acts as tend to maintain and enhance the general well-being of the community. The delivery of these sermons in the course of judgment often affords the listeners a measure of vicarious pleasure. It would be superfluous to add that they are invariably as instructive as they are edifying.

All this very well accords with the character of the African judge as a peace-maker anxious to effect a reconciliation, if necessary by making one to pay fine or compensation to the other or to restore such other's property being illegally withheld, but always by the gentle process of arguments and persuasion leading gradually and inevitably to a verdict that is at once clear and fair. The judge's reasoning and statements are punctuated at appropriate stages with allusions to the legal principles involved and to wise laws and apt aphorisms intended to elucidate his meaning.

But running through it all is his transparent duty to reconcile the disputants with each other, to re-incorporate the minor criminal in society at large, and to show the necessity for elimination of the malefactor and the antisocial. In this often difficult task the judge or judges must apply the law to the facts as found and do so in such a way as to command the respect and approval of the overwhelming majority of the people. All technicality is eschewed in his earnest endeavour to do justice, fair play, and equity. It is this motive of the judge to do equity that is the most persistent characteristic of the African judicial process. Did not Aristotle in his *Rhetoric* write :

> It is equity to pardon human failings, to look to the lawgiver and not to the law . . . to wish to settle a matter by words rather than by deeds ; lastly, to prefer arbitration to judgment, for the arbitrator sees what is equitable, but the judge only the law, and for this an arbitrator was first appointed, in order that equity might flourish.[4]

It remains to conclude that only in this sense is the African judge an arbitrator.... [pp. 269-279]

The African litigant is naturally bewildered by many aspects of the British judicial innovations. For example, an illiterate African offender was once brought before a Nigerian magistrate and asked to plead "Guilty or Not Guilty" to the charge of riding his bicycle, after sunset, without a lighted lamp. He grinned at the magistrate, shook his head, and retorted somewhat acidly, "What a question ! Is that not what I have been dragged before you to find out ?" We may laugh at him for his ignorance of English criminal procedure but, on second thought, logic will not be found to be entirely on our side. Again, a man negligently killed another by running him down with his limousine car, and a Tanganyika judge sentenced him to six months' imprisonment for manslaughter. The deceased man's relatives went away more disconsolate and embittered than before, as they were told that that was all English law could do for them. One of them was heard to shout as he walked out of the courtroom, "He may work for the government, but he has yet to pay us the usual compensation as blood-money. Until that is done we are unrequited." How much more satisfying to these persons the customary judicial method would have been ! Compensation to the bereaved, not imprisonment by the authorities, would have been ordered by the elders. Of course, as we have seen, the modern statutory native courts everywhere have their own way of avoiding this piece of English legal humbug by first sentencing the offender in such a case to prison and then, on his coming out, making him pay a reduced rate of compensation according to the tribal tariff schedule of penalty.

To quote a third instance, it often happens in the case of technical offences under some ordinance, that a sophisticated offender employs a lawyer to defend him, in a frame of mind which seems to imply that the white man's law ought to be confronted with the white-man-trained lawyer (they should understand each other better). Then, after long and often protracted arguments back and forth, the African offender is let off on a technicality, substantive or procedural. He breaks out irrepressibly into protestations of his guilt ! And he is hustled away —

an innocent man — even though he admits his guilt and is ready and willing to pay for it. [pp. 299-300]

NOTES

1. T. Olawale Elias, *The Nature of African Customary Law* (Manchester : Manchester University Press, 1956), pp. 269-300.

2. J.N. Matson, "The Supreme Court and the Customary Judicial Process in The Gold Coast," *International and Comparative Law Quarterly*, 2, Pt. 1 : 48.

3. A. Phillips, ed., *Survey of African Marriage and Family Life.* (London : Oxford University Press, 1953), p. 39.

4. Apud. Ethi. Nic. 1.13.1374b Grant's Translation (London : Dent, 1953).

THE CHARACTER OF THE JAPANESE PEOPLE AND THEIR CONCEPTION OF LAW[1]

Yosiyuki Noda

The Conception of Law Among The Japanese

The meaning represented by the Japanese word *ho* as we use it today is a translation of such words as "law," "Recht," or "droit." The Japanese did have the word *ho* for many centuries but it was of Chinese origin. Today the Japanese word "*ho*" is supposed to correspond to the Western concept of law. Such a conception of law is not something that arose naturally out of the traditional character of the ordinary Japanese. Therefore , when a Japanese views the law from his tradition-tinted perspective, he tends to see it in a different light. In fact, there is a significant difference between the jurist's concept of law and that of the layman. It therefore follows that when a set of modern laws of the Western style is applied to the day-to-day activities of the people, distortions and variations are bound to develop. . . .

The concept underlying Western law has been profoundly influenced by the Roman concept of law. I therefore believe that a comparison with the Roman concept of law will bring into relief the characteristics of the Japanese concept of law. . . .

(1) Japanese Attitude toward Law

When I lectured at the University of Paris some years ago, I began the fourth part of my lecture with a sentence, *"On n'aime pas le droit au Japon."* We find an unequivocal pronouncement of this feeling in a comment by Shusui Kotoku who was subsequently executed on charges of treason. In an article carried in the *Heimin Shimbun* (The Plebian Chronicle), he stated that "We detest the law and look forward to the day when the law is rendered useless."

I would call such an attitude an emotional anarchism. Proponents of this kind of anarchism give little thought to how the social order can be maintained without law. In their view, all society's troubles are of the law's own making ; the less we are bothered by the law, the better off we are ; they therefore crane their necks to see the day when they will be freed from the encumbrance of the law and believe that if they persist in their wish, a law-free society will arrive some day. Implicit in this kind of emotional attitude is not just a reasoned denial of the significance of law but also an instinctive abhorrence of the very idea of law. Ordinary Japanese therefore feel ashamed of being subpoenaed by, or of taking somebody to, a court. To them, the ideal life is one in which they have no truck whatsoever with either the court or the law. This attitude is also another sign revealing the lack of norm consciousness.

By contrast, the Romans took a great pride in the fact that their daily life was governed by law. Marcus Tullius Cicero (106-43 B.C.), the great Roman orator, author and statesman, boasted that Rome had the world's finest system of law, while the neighboring people had only very primitive law. The Romans were very sensitive to law and keen on acquiring a knowledge of law. They considered learnedness in law as an indispensable part of cultural refinement. Cicero proudly relates how persistently he, while still a child, was exhorted to learn the Twelve Tables by rote. The Law of the Twelve Tables was a sort of code adopted around 450 B.C., called as such because its provisions were engraved on twelve wooden tablets. Its first provision states : "When you are subpoenaed by the court, answer the subpoena." The fact that average Roman families introduced their children early in their lives to a fairly large number of articles of laws like this testifies to the importance they attached to the law.

Their interest in law was not confined to a mere knowledge about it ; they strongly believed in abiding by the law. The reverse is true with the Japanese. The Japanese feel they are better off when not bothered by law. If they can do without law, so much the better. Law is something to be shunned and it is regarded as quite natural for a man to try to violate the laws when he believes that his violation will not be noticed. When a stringent punishment is meted out in relation to a violation of law in a case where the violation is noticed, the Japanese people often label the punishment an inhuman act, or an act contrary to *ninjo* (human feeling). In Japan, one who tries to enforce the law leniently is considered a man with an understanding heart. Stretching the law in favor of violators is considered a virtue. This attitude is in sharp contrast with the uncompromising way in which Romans applied the law....

(2) Japanese Conception of Rights

The term "right" is generally defined as a legally protected interest. The Romans insisted on their rights as an interest protected by the law. But that something is protected by the law implies that it is protected by an objective standard. It therefore follows that the rights of all people are to be protected equally by an objective standard called law. So, when one asserts his right he impliedly assumes the existence of law and therefore he must be prepared to accept the assumption that other persons can also assert their rights on the basis of the same law. In other words, in order for a given concept of right to be valid, it must be applicable to others just as it is applicable to him....

In Japan, the concept of right did not exist until the end of the Tokugawa period (1603-1867). Early in the Meiji period (1867-1912) a man named Rinsho Mitsukuri, who was commissioned to translate the French Civil Code, racked his brain to find a Japanese equivalent of "*droit*" and finally came up with a Japanese coinage "*kenri.*" This episode serves to show that the concept of right was first introduced only in the early years of the the Meiji period. It may be said that the concept of right is still too new to have struck a deep root in our conceptions. To borrow the words of Jhering, we have just started our toddling steps toward the recognition of others' rights. I venture to say that the concept of right still has a long and tortuous way to go before taking firm root in this country. To casual observers it may seem that members of the younger Japanese generation have become aggressively assertive of their rights, but a closer examination would soon make it plain that what the younger generation is doing is often nothing but a naked assertion of their own interests, falling far short of the assertion of rights in the proper sense of this term as their assertions do not premise any recognition of the rights of others.

(3) The Conception of Adjudication

Next, I would like to examine the Japanese concept of adjudication. In the context of Roman law, adjudication in a civil lawsuit is to be defined as the determination of who has the right between the parties in dispute, the plaintiff or the defendant. The right, to be sure, is a concept which is accompanied by quantitative delimitation. One cannot make an assertion without such a clear-cut delimitation, so that one cannot say simply that "he is a villain because he impaired my interest." Let us suppose that A lent a sum of one million yen to B. When A demands the repayment of the one million yen from B, A is actually making a definitive claim and the hearing must determine whether or not A has a contractual right. This is what we call adjudication. If A's claim is established, A wins the case and B loses. If A wins the case, B inevitably loses. This is a situation of *Entweder-oder* (a choice between the two), and there is no other way of settling disputes if we use adjudication. It is inconceivable that both win or both lose.

This kind of resolution, however, goes against the grain with most Japanese. We seek to establish a harmonious situation with which both parties are neither satisfied nor dissatisfied, where there is no loser or winner. This is the ideal we expect of adjudication. In Japan, we have a story called *Sambo Ichiryo Zon* (all three lost one pound each). This is a story about a trial during the Tokugawa period which is suggestive of the Japanese concept of adjudication. One day, so the story goes, a plasterer picked up on the road a purse containing three *ryo*. [A *ryo* is an old Japanese gold coin.] The purse also contained a piece of paper identifying a certain carpenter as its owner. The plasterer took the trouble of locating the carpenter to return the purse. For all his pains the plasterer was told by the carpenter : "Since the purse elected to slip out of my pocket, I don't want such ungrateful money. Go away with the money." The plasterer insisted that the money belonged to the carpenter. Thereupon a brawl started and finally they agreed to take the case to arbitration by the Lord Ooka of Echizen. Having heard the story from both sides, the Lord added one *ryo* to the three *ryo*, split the sum into two, handed two *ryo* to each party, and announced : "My good men, this is my decision. The plasterer could have gained three *ryo* if he had walked away as the carpenter told him to do. By this decision, he will end up with two *ryo*, so he is to lose one *ryo*. The carpenter could have recovered all three *ryo* if he had accepted the plasterer's kindness with a good grace. Instead he refused to accept the purse. By this decision, he is to lose one *ryo*. I also have to contribute one *ryo*. So, each of the three is to end up with one *ryo* less." Of course, this is just a fiction but still it is suggestive of a notion of the function of a lawsuit which is peculiar to the Japanese.

This is in a sense really an ingenious settlement of the dispute. Everybody came out as neither a winner nor a loser. Even the judge went out of his way to contribute one *ryo* in the interest of all round amicability. The standards of law had no role to play here. Incoherent though it may seem to us students of law, such a decision appeals to the Japanese as demonstrating the most humane considerateness. We Japanese tend to feel uncomfortable with a black-or-white type of adjudication. If a Japanese loses in a lawsuit, being of emotional inclination, he is bound to be embittered against the winner, and even against the judge. We do not want to leave the embers of a grudge smouldering. We would rather pay a small price, if such a price rounds off the edges, and let bygones be bygones. This explains why a large majority of cases that are brought to the court are settled through compromise. This is very indicative of the peculiar character of the Japanese.

(4) The Conception of Contract

We Japanese were agrarian people and settled ourselves in large numbers in a given locality as tillers of land from the early days of our history. We therefore felt no particular need for a contract. In order to cooperate among ourselves, we did not need a contract whose violation invoked sanctions. People got together and talked things over to enlist the cooperation of their neighbors. This tradition has bred in the minds of the Japanese a very easy-going attitude toward contracts. We Japanese do not go so far as to consider a breach of a contract to be a virtue but we are certainly not very serious about honoring contracts. One might say that a breach of contract is not often accompanied by a sense of guilt. In fact we view contracts in such a light-hearted manner that a contract is often regarded as a sort of tentative agreement [which may be reformed as the circumstances change]. If a party to a contract is subsequently urged by the other party to perform his contractual obligations to the letter, he considers such a demand to be an inhumane act. We used to hear people say : "The *samurai* (the warrior) never goes back on his word." The *samurai* is supposed to have abided by contracts. Could it be that the samurai class was an exception ? I should think not, for they abided by contracts for reasons other than a belief that contracts as such must be observed.

In this connection, I might tell you an anecdote of Yukichi Fukuzawa which he himself related in his autobiography, *Fuku-o Jiden.* Shortly before Edo (Tokyo) was thrown into confusion he had bought a piece of real estate and promised that he would pay the price on such and such a date. On the appointed day, he called on the vendor to make the payment. As it happened, Edo was then on the verge of great confusion and land prices threatened to go down drastically. Accordingly, the vendor suggested to Fukuzawa that he might be better to defer the payment until the land price went down still further, and then ask to pay a smaller amount. But Fukuzawa insisted that "as a member of the *samurai* class, I cannot allow myself to do such a demeaning thing. Since I have made a promise to you, I must pay you the money here and now." In such a manner, he forced the money on the vendor. Later he explained in his autobiography that his pride as a *samurai* compelled him to insist on making the payment. "It was beneath me, as a *samurai,*" he said, "to allow myself to be swayed by a pecuniary gain. The very idea was detestable." This remark typifies the *samurai's* concept of contract. He made the payment as promised not because he believed that the contract was a thing he had to abide by but because he did not want there to be any suspicion that he had been blinded by a small monetary gain, an act he would have been very much ashamed of.

To Western thinking, however, the concept that the contract must be adhered to is a matter of principle basic to natural law. To Westerners, observance of a contract is based upon the concept of duties which every human being has as a matter of reason. They observe the contract simply because it is a contract and they need no other reason for observing it. The Japanese view the institution of the contract differently. True, the *samurai* did abide by contracts, not because they were contracts but rather because they did not want to compromise their honor or their face as a *samurai.* In other words, they were motivated not by the sense of obligation but by the need to satisfy their sense of self-respect. In this sense, Ruth Benedict, author of the widely read book, *The Chrysanthemum and the Sword,* was correct in characterizing the Japanese culture as a "shame culture" as opposed to a "guilt culture"

Given the difference in the cultural backgrounds, it is not surprising that Europeans find it difficult to understand the Japanese concept of contract. For instance, contracts drawn up by large Japanese trading companies invariably contain a "good-faith clause" or an "amicability clause." Typical of these clauses is a clause which states that "in case a dispute arises between the parties hereto with respect to their rights and obligations under this contract ..., the parties hereto shall discuss the matter among themselves with good faith," or "it shall be resolved amicably." This seems to indicate that the contract sets forth only a tentative agreement, and if something goes wrong the parties should renegotiate the terms and conditions of the contract. By contrast, once the parties have agreed to the specific terms and conditions of the contract, Europeans think that they are entitled to take the other party to court if he fails to perform his contractual obligations. This is often a source of misunderstanding between Japanese and Westerners in relation to contracts they sign. The Japanese assumes that even if he did not perform his part of the contract it just would not happen that the other party would immediately take an action for the enforcement of the contract. The Westerner on the other hand thinks it is simply a matter of course that he can proceed in such a manner to enforce the contract as it is written. The difference between Japanese and Westerners in their concepts of contract has caused a number of sad misunderstandings. [pp. 301-310]

NOTE

1. Yosiyuki Noda, "The Character of the Japanese People and their Conception of Law," in H. Tanaka, ed., *The Japanese Legal System,* (University of Tokyo Press, 1976) pp. 301-310.

MAO AND MEDIATION : POLITICS AND DISPUTE RESOLUTION IN COMMUNIST CHINA[1]

Stanley Lubman

Dispute Resolution in Traditional China : A Summary

In traditional China, ideology interacted with institutions to produce a characteristic mediational style of dispute resolution which is best described by focusing on two aspects : philosophical conceptions of disputes and their settlement and the institutions utilized for dispute resolution.

Confucian Views of Social Conflict and Dispute Resolution

Confucianism, which dominated traditional Chinese political thought, postulated the existence of a harmony extending throughout heaven and earth. On earth harmony was manifested in a hierarchical order that began with the emperor and extended downward to the lowest level of society. The aim of government, and indeed of all human relations, was to preserve natural harmony, which was the source of, and was expressed in, ethical behaviour. Primary ethical rules lay in the *li*, a variety of moral and customary principles for ceremonial or polite behaviour. More concretely, *li* was a collection of "rules of behaviour varying in accordance with one's status" which differentiated behaviour according to age and rank in family and society. The function of *li* was "preserving status differences in a hierarchically organized society."[2] The Confucians viewed law, *fa*, as a clumsy system of punishments directed only at strengthening the state and lacking proper regard for "an ordered world of peace, harmony, and simple contentment," and the cultivation of the individual. *Fa* was associated with the radically different philosophical school of Legalism. This school regarded *li* and all ethical principles as irrelevant to government, whose essence was seen to lie in uniform and harsh regulation. *Fa* was further discredited when Legalist ideas were implemented by the harsh Ch'in dynasty. After Ch'in rule was dissolved in 210 B.C., Confucianism became the orthodox philosophy of the state.

In Chinese legal history from the Ch'in to the Ch'ing dynasty, overthrown in 1911, Confucian and Legalist strands of thought were interwoven : *li* was insufficient to govern the empire, and regulation was used to reinforce it. Much of the *li* was infused into substantive rules of law, thereby "Confucianizing" it so that, for instance, criminal penalties were differentiated according to status, membership in privileged groups like the *literati*, and position within the family. Further, Confucianism clearly influenced the interpretation of laws by officials charged with applying them. As Max Weber wrote, the Chinese magistrate "judged persons according to their concrete qualities and in terms of the concrete situation, or according to equity and the appropriateness of the concrete results."[3]

The dominant Confucian view of morality and law produced a haracteristic view of disputes and their resolution. Disputes were viewed as disruptions of the natural harmony which linked individual, group, society, and the entire universe. As one scholar put it, "the spheres of man and nature were inextricably interwoven to form an unbroken continuum."[4] Yielding (*jang*) was virtuous because it prevented friction and disharmony. Moreover, customary ethical rules of behaviour which emphasized status and the necessity of preserving group harmony greatly inhibited the assertion of rights and caused such claims to be regarded as disruptive violations of fundamental ethical rules. These philosophical tenets, the structure of Chinese society, and the operation of imperial governmental institutions combined to produce a striking preference for mediated settlement of disputes.... [pp. 1289-1291]

Families, Clans, Guilds, and Other Social Units

The basic unit of traditional Chinese society was not the individual but the groups to which he belonged. Most basic of all was the family, in which rules of customary behaviour emphasized the precedence and authority of older over younger generations. The families themselves were organized into kinship groups or clans, a "transitional grouping between the family and village,"[5] which instructed members on Confucian morality, assisted poor and aged members, maintained schools and ancestral halls, and settled disputes among members.

Yet another collective grouping was the guild, an organization of merchants or artisans in the same trade or craft. The guilds controlled prices, competition, training and admission to callings. They also engaged in some charitable ventures and represented common commercial interests in dealing with government officials.

Ordinary social and commercial relationships between persons unrelated to each other by family or common membership in a group also had a distinctive quality — different from friendship — known as *kan-ch'ing*. The existence of *kan-ch'ing* between two persons meant that they had regard for each other and could ask favours from each other. In these relationships, persons did not want to lose "face" — their reputation for integrity and dignity. Personal relationships formed a tightly woven web.

Family, clan, village, gentry and officials dominated the individual. The pressure to maintain proper *kan-ch'ing* and "face" further conditioned his behaviour. Moreover, institutions and ideology reinforced each other. For instance, a system was devised to indoctrinate the illiterate masses in the Confucian virtues. Lectures stressing piety, respect for elders and superiors, maintenance of harmony among neighbours, diligence, the necessity to instruct youth, and obedience to the law were given by officials, gentry and local headmen at frequent compulsory meetings called "village pacts" or *hsiang-yueh*, attended by the common people. Although the efficacy of these "sonorous platitudes" in guiding the populace along virtuous paths may be doubted, and although the entire "village pact" system disintegrated well before the end of the Ch'ing dynasty, the use of these lectures illustrates the extent to which Confucian ideology permeated governmental techniques. Ideology combined with the institutional structure to create strong pressures for mediation of disputes.

The Preference for Mediation

1. The Perils of Litigation

Most civil disputes were settled extrajudicially rather than through litigation in traditional China. Not only did the official philosophy stress the virtue of yielding and the superiority of noncontentiousness, but the administration of justice discouraged and sometimes ruined litigants. The magistrate's *yamen*, or office, was usually far from the disputants' residence. Magistrates were not law-trained experts but generalists often ignorant of the law and "corrupt, cruel, and lazy."[6] Because the magistrates were inexpert and occupied with other functions of government, they relied heavily on their clerks and other underlings for assistance. The corruption and greed of these "tigers or wolves" was "legendary and frequently well-deserved." The "customary fees" which had to be paid to the *yamen* employees imposed extraordinarily heavy burdens on litigants. Extraordinary, too, were the delays and "errors" which could beset a litigant hapless enough to fall afoul of a *yamen* employee. Furthermore, trials were humilitating for litigants and witnesses and occasionally involved the use of torture to obtain evidence. Litigation was, in short, time-consuming, degrading and costly. It was no wonder that "[t]o involve someone in a lawsuit was a way of ruining him,"[7] and that, according to a Chinese saying, "[t]o enter a court of justice is to enter a tiger's mouth."[8] The perils of litigation, widely publicized in popular lore, undoubtedly restrained many persons from bringing suit at the magistrate's *yamen* and impelled them to settle disputes through extrajudicial mediation closer to home.

2. Availability of Social Units as Dispute-Settling Forums

A number of factors combined to cause disputes to be settled, as much as possible, within the basic nuclei of traditional Chinese society : the hazards of litigation ; widespread fear of involvement with government officials ; the dominant ethic ; and the primacy of the nuclei themselves — family, clan, village and guild. Particularly in the settlement of disputes these social units exercised considerable independence from the *yamen*. If disputes could not be settled within the unit, relatives, friends and local leaders outside the group, but still closer to the disputants than the magistrate, would often resolve them by mediation. These groups generally strove to avoid involving government officials in quarrels between their members. Recourse to the magistrate without prior attempts to settle disputes within groups was actively discouraged and sometimes, as in the case of clans and guilds, prohibited by the group's internal regulations. In sum, "the local group generally required the parties to exhaust their remedies within the group before looking to the magistrate for relief."[9]

Generally speaking, disputes within families were settled by elders. While the authority of the *paterfamilias* was theoretically absolute, there was undoubtedly much mediation by older relatives, friends, and clan leaders — especially when the family was small. Disputes between members of a clan were settled by clan leaders and sometimes by other respected local leaders. Disputes within a village not coterminous with one clan were mediated not only by relatives, friends and neighbours, but by official village headmen and unofficial leaders, whether gentry or other respected figures. Within the guilds, disputes between members were settled if not by friends, witnesses of a transaction, or middlemen, then by guild officers.... [pp. 1294-1297]

NOTES

1. Stanley Lubman, "Mao and Mediation : Politics and Dispute Resolution in Communist China," *California Law Review*, 55 (1967) : 1289-1297.

2. Cohen, "Chinese Mediation on the Eve of Modernization," *California Law Review*, 54, Pt. 2 (1966) : 1208.

3. M. Weber, *The Religion of China*, (1951).

4. Bodde, "Basic Concepts of Chinese Law : The Genesis and Evolution of Legal Thought in Traditional China," *Proceedings of the American Philosphical Society*, 107 (1963) : 375.

5. M. Yang, *A Chinese Village : Taitou, Shantung Province* (1945), p. 134.

6. Cohen, *op. cit.*, p. 1212.

7. S. Van Der Sprenkel, *Legal Institutions in Manchu China* (1962).

8. R. Douglas, *Chinese Society* (1901), p. 104.

9. Cohen, *op. cit.*, p. 1223.

LAW WITHOUT SANCTIONS[1]

Michael Barkun

The lineage system does not in and of itself prescribe conduct ; conduct is the business of rules of behaviour. On the other hand, conduct sets down various social relationships, and norms cannot be meaningfully applied without taking these relationships into account. Putative genealogical distance determines the meaning and consequences of action.

Whatever the oughts are, they exist only in reference to specific lineage relationships. The norms are meaningless if they are divorced from the applicable fact-situations. The legal process has long been recognized as a matching of norms and facts, and lineage provides the latter half of this relationship. A jural community, as we have said, is the area within which an all-inclusive organizing idiom is used, be it lineage, sovereignty, or something else. Thus the largest area that comprehends an overall, common lineage framework constitutes a jural community because everyone within this area shares approximately the same map of the society.

That this map is only approximately the same for everyone is the crucial point. It should be clear by now that the conventional separation between a lineage system and a legal system is purely analytic and in no way specific and mutable. Neither could exist in reality independently of the other. From an anthropological perspective it may be useful to regard them as separate (because analytic categories, in their own way, are a species of fiction) ; from a legal standpoint, however, such separation deprives a legal system of an essential component. Without the lineage framework, legal decision-making at any level of complexity is impossible. Therefore we must regard the lineage framework as an integral part of the legal system of segmentary societies ; to fail to do so would be equivalent to studying our own legal system without reference to "person" or "state."

Segmentary societies, in the schematic view we have presented, seem to be extremely rigid, but the rigidity tends to disappear under closer scrutiny. Part of this impression results from the learning process itself : although anthropologists learn genealogy systematically and as an interrelated whole, a Tiv, for example, learns his genealogy piecemeal and never learns all there is to know. Indeed, the overriding structuralism of, say, British social anthropology has concentrated on symmetry and homogeneity at the expense of flux and variation, but the true picture lies somewhere in between. Discretionary acts also are important, for the conflict-management process often goes beyond the mechanical and ritualistic. Our Supreme Court, after all, combines the flexibilities of discretion and the constraints of precedent. In fact, there are hints of subsurface complexities even within the classical ethnographic literature. Between closely related Nuer, disputes rarely are simple transgressions of general rules ; they also involve qualifying considerations of kinship, affinity, and age. In light of this we may proceed on the assumption that inasmuch as disputes differ in complexity their handling also will vary.

Ethnographers frequently refer to mediators as possessing some kind of expertise but there are two reasons why a mediator is used. Utilization manifests the respect the parties have for community ties while testifying to the fact that such a figure as the Nuer leopard-skin chief is a "ritual expert." Clearly, through his utilization of ritual, the leopard-skin chief performs mediative functions. Evans-Pritchard's tendency to emphasize ritual at the expense of mediative expertise doubtless is based partly on the fact that his evidence for actual conflict-management situations was largely hearsay. A British colonial administrator who worked among the Nuer and was a close student of Nuer law suggests that Evans-Pritchard undervalued the leopard-skin chief's influence and persuasive powers. Among the Chiga, another segmentary people, the "judge" (whose decision is not binding) hears the accounts of both parties ; then he listens to the deliberations of an *ad hoc* "jury." When he is satisfied that he has heard everything of importance, he gives his decision, which will be followed if the parties agree to it.

Frequently the third party is a tribal elder, as is the case with the Chiga, the Tiv, the Konkomba, and the Lugbara. Tiv elders are those who are learned in genealogical lore, and the younger men come to them for advice. The availability of such experts seems sufficient inasmuch as the elders feel no necessity for systematically imparting their expertise to others. Younger and less expert or less knowledgeable Tiv seem not to object to this ; it is enough for them to know that, should need arise, there will be an elder who can answer the pertinent questions. There is no more reason for a Tiv to learn the complete tribal genealogy than there is for a resident of Illinois to commit the state statutes to memory. This, incidentally, is not a matter of nonliteracy being a bar to systematic learning and teaching ; the vast amounts of knowledge that nonliterate people communicate orally and relatively intact over many generations demonstrate that such means exist even if the motivation to use them does not.

Although segmentary societies manifest little role differentiation, the need for genealogical expertise parallels the need for what in Western societies we would call traditional legal expertise. Weber contended that the growth of the legal profession was stimulated by a demand for special skills, above all for "the capacity to state clearly and unambiguously the legal issues involved in a complicated situation." The fusion of genealogical expertise and law is even more interesting when we recall that law is the symbolic representation of a social structure. A third party in a segmentary society could no more resolve a dispute without genealogical expertise than a U.S. federal judge could hand down a ruling without a good working knowledge of earlier decisions and the statutes. Both sets of symbols provide the respective societies with manageable, manipulable terms.

Many Tiv law cases hinge on genealogy ; therefore the availability of expertise is essential, and, in the belief that the problems being dealt with have determinate solutions, it is permissible to question an individual's genealogical knowledge. For the Tiv, the assumptions that above conflicting views of the moment there is a true and knowable genealogy, and that someone somewhere knows it, are beyond argument. Again, we come up against the fiction of completeness — the belief, translated into genealogical terms, that beyond the uncertainties of the moment there is perfect and complete knowledge. That the fiction is one of genealogy does not make it any less a legal fiction inasmuch as the foundations for behavioural rules would crumble if the genealogical fiction were acknowledged. As we have seen, however, completeness is unattainable ; no symbol system that purports to represent a portion of the observable world can achieve perfect success. (The only enduring symbol systems are mathematical systems, which are far removed from the forces of change.) Thus genealogical-legal systems are at the mercy of changing patterns of interaction that may render portions of them empirically irrelevant. Tiv genealogy is reciprocally related to the real world in which the Tiv live. In principle, present relationships receive their validity from a genealogy, which in turn is proved correct by the existence of these relationships.

This one-to-one matching, however, is an ideal that is only partially adhered to. In every case the search is for the applicable genealogy. If the genealogy does not fit the case a search for an alternative ancestry begins. How, logically, can alternative genealogies exist ? They can exist because no one is sufficiently certain of the "true" genealogy that alternatives can be ruled out. Alternative lineage patterns in fact exist, and this fact bestows discretionary power on mediators, just as alternative lines of precedent expand the discretion of a court judge. The inconsistent versions of a genealogy that are in general circulation — with the inconsistencies masked by piecemeal learning — permit ample latitude. It is, moreover, an observable fact that genealogies — rather, perceptions of them — do change. They must change because Tiv society, despite its generally static quality, alters the levels of specificity with which genealogy deals.

Significantly, the rate of change seems to vary inversely with the size of the units involved. Genealogies that validate the existence of large groups change slowly, for two reasons. First, genealogy changes with alterations in relative size, territorial distribution, and power positions, whose nature it is to change slowly ; in addition, the perception of change is presumed to lag behind the event. Second, the number of persons involved, given the consensual basis of a system, prevents rapid change as if by fiat. The converse also is true : the smaller the size of the groups the more rapidly genealogy changes, both because it must and because it can. There is a crucial congruence between this relationshp and our earlier concentration upon the differences between smaller-unit complex core areas and large-unit simple peripheral areas.

The effect of this is twofold. First, the third party receives a measure of discretion because he must manipulate ambiguous symbols and there is apt to be disagreement about the precise meanings of the genealogical-legal symbols he will deal with. Second, expertise endows the third party with control over society's legitimation processes. Because the choice of the third-party is made according to qualities of persuasiveness and mediative skill and ritual-symbolic status, the status criterion means, in effect, that the leopard-skin chief (or a comparable figure) possesses knowledge of societal symbols and has the skills to manipulate them to bestow legitimacy on present relationships. Even Evans-Pritchard acknowledged the mutability of Nuer lineage.

The time-depth recorded in the lineage is limited and is fixed at a few generations, which hardly is adequate for historical record. The lineage distance between groups seems to be strikingly similar to the political distance between them, implying that lineage is adjusted to hew closely to day-to-day power relationships. It also is likely that a lineage would cease to be part of a society's oral record if it ceased to have political significance. These considerations suggest that actual-descent records are a medium on which political relationships can work their will.

These observations raise the problem of efficacy : the mediator changes a society's socio-political map, but are these not simply changes after the fact, belated bestowal of blessings on the status quo ? The relationship, in reality, is reciprocal ; the decisions in the legal process are both effects and causes. As the former, they legitimate present relationships ; as the latter they exert influence on future relationships. Lineage is the idiom that expresses and directs social relations. . . . [T]o the extent members of a society adopt the same symbols that are used by the mediator in conflict management, to this extent are apparently *post facto* symbolic changes projected into the world of future action.

Who really makes decisions ? It seems not to be the mediator, for he can only cajole and suggest, but experts have an authority that far surpasses their tangible resources. Technically, decisions are made by the disputants themselves, but there is a critical nexus between disputants and the mediator. Although the mediator gives no orders, as a repository of vital knowledge he in fact directs those who come before him. The legal process is not, of course, the only nor even necessarily the primary agent of change ; many different forces work to change present relationships, and these changes must be assimilated if societal integrity is to be preserved. The alternatives perceived in future decision making will be structured in terms of the categories that have been inherited. Thus every decision, joining mediator and disputants, becomes a precedent for the future — just as every decision also is shaped by the alternatives that have been passed down through innumerable series of prior conflict-management situations. [pp. 127-132]

NOTE

1. Michael Barkun, *Law Without Sanctions* (New Haven: Yale University Press, 1968), pp. 127-132.

MEDIATION — ITS FORMS AND FUNCTIONS[1]

Lon L. Fuller

It is fairly obvious that mediation has scarcely any role to play in human relationships fluidly organized on what may be broadly described as the market principle. If X finds A, B, and C all competing to supply his needs through rival contractual arrangements, he may need the services of an expert adviser, but he will scarcely have occasion to call on those of a mediator. Likewise, in a society where transient and freely terminable sexual alliances took the place of marriage it is hardly likely that there would develop any institutional practice comparable to "marriage therapy." Mediation by its very nature presupposes relationships normally affected by some strong internal pull toward cohesion; this is true whether the mediative efforts in question be directed toward the formation, modification or dissolution of such relationships. . . .

A serious study of mediation can serve, I suggest, to offset the tendency of modern thought to assume that all social order must be imposed by some kind of "authority." When we perceive how a mediator, claiming no "authority," can help the parties give order and coherence to their relationship, we may in the process come to realize that there are circumstances in which the parties can dispense with this aid, and that social order can often rise directly out of the interactions it seems to govern and direct. [pp. 314-315]

It is time now to bring mediation into some closer relation with the order-producing and order-restoring processes of society as a whole and in particular with those of state-made law. . . . I spoke of the "central quality of mediation, namely, its capacity to reorient the parties toward each other, not by imposing rules on them, but by helping them to achieve a new and shared perception of their relationship, a perception that will redirect their attitudes and dispositions toward one another." This suggests a certain antithesis between mediational processes, on the one hand, and the standard procedures of law, on the other, for surely central to the very notion of law is the concept of *rules.*

Insofar as our concern is with the problem of bringing laws into existence, this "antithesis" presents no difficulty at all. It is a commonplace of democratic government that statutes quite generally express some measure of compromise between opposing points of view. Individual legislators often find themselves, at times with some reluctance, cast in the essential mediative role that will effect this compromise. The crucial problem arises when we ask, not what role mediation should play in creating law, but how far and in what respects should it enter into the administration of laws. A general answer to this question is easy: once a law has been duly enacted its interpretation and enforcement is for the courts; courts have been instituted, not to mediate disputes, but to decide them.

It is not difficult to see why, under a system of state-made law, the standard instrument of dispute settlement should be adjudication and not mediation. If the question is whether A drove through a red light, or has paid his grocery bill, or has properly reported his earnings to Internal Revenue, even the most ardent advocate of conciliative procedures would hardly recommend mediation as the standard way of dealing with such problems. A pervasive use of mediation could here obliterate the essential guideposts and boundary markers men need in orienting their actions toward one another and could end by producing a situation in which no one could know precisely where he stood or how he might get where he wanted to be. As between black and white, gray may sometimes seem an acceptable compromise, but there are circumstances in which it is essential to work hard toward keeping things black and white. Maintaining a legal system in functioning order is one of those occasions.

It is, then, not in the making of legal rules, but in their enforcement and administration that a certain incompatibility may be perceived between mediative procedures and "the rule of law." We may express something of the nature of this incompatibility by saying that, whereas mediation is directed toward *persons,* judgments of law are directed toward *acts*; it is acts, not people, that are declared proper or improper under the relevant provisions of law. This distinction is not quite so simple as it seems on the surface, for there are routine occasions within the operations of a legal system when judgment must be passed on persons. This necessity arises, for example, when a court must decide whether a convicted criminal should be admitted to probation or when a judge must determine which of two contesting parents should be given custody of a child. But in its core operations, in deciding, for example, whether a man has committed a crime or broken a contract, the standards of legal judgment are derived from rules defining the consequences of specific acts or failures to act ; these rules do not attempt to invite any general appraisal of the qualities or dispositions of the person, exception being made, of course, for cases where the problem of legal accountability is raised, as when the defence of insanity is pleaded. . . .

In seeking now to delineate, within the processes of society as a whole, the proper domain of mediation, I suggest that we may usefully apply two tests ; the first of these tells us when mediation *should not* be used, the second tells us when it *cannot* be used. The two tests are as follows : *First,* is the underlying relationship such that it is best organized by impersonal act-oriented rules ? If so, then mediation will generally be out of place except as it is employed to create or modify rules. *Second,* is the problem presented amenable to solution through mediation processes ? Mediation is itself subject to intrinsic limitations ; I have discerned two of these : (1) it cannot generally be employed when more than two parties are involved ; (2) it presupposes an intermeshing of interests of an intensity sufficient to make the parties willing to collaborate in the mediational effort. . . . [pp. 327-330]

Perhaps the aspect of mediation discussed here which seems most remote from early forms of social ordering is that I have described as an adjustment of interests designed to obtain optimum "pay-offs" for the participants. Yet Malinowski discerned in the principle of reciprocity a fundamental aspect of the ordering systems of "savage societies."[2] If he had in mind an explicit trade in which one party withholds his contribution until an opposite number has promised some reciprocal benefit, he would seem to be contradicted by his own report of relationships among the Trobriand Islanders. But we must remember that the silent slowdown is a more ancient phenomenon than the openly declared strike and that tacit contracting and trading were known and practiced centuries before the explicit verbal contract was perceived as an available expedient for arranging human affairs.

If we were to distinguish broadly among the various processes that contribute to social ordering we might discern six : legislation, adjudication, administrative direction, mediation, contractual agreement, and customary "law" — it being recalled of the last of these that it is often the intended product of a relegation of emergent issues to the tacit accommodations foreseen as developing out of future interactions. Even in modern societies these forms are interrelated in various complex ways and at times tend to shade into one another. In primitive society, I would suggest, they appear in still more mixed and muted forms ; generally any scruple about blending or mixing them seems to be absent, perhaps because they are simply not perceived as separate processes.

Something of the ambiguity of the social processes by which primitive societies are ordered is suggested in Barton's famous study of the Ifugao *monkalun* or "go-between." Barton refers to the parties who invoke the *monkalun's* office as "litigants"; the services rendered by the *monkalun* himself are described as follows :

> The office of the *monkalun* is the most important one to be found in Ifugao society. The *Monkalun* is a whole court, completely equipped, in embryo. He is judge, prosecuting and defending counsel, and the court record. His duty and his interest are for a peaceful settlement . . . . To the end of peaceful settlement he exhausts every art of Ifugao diplomacy. He wheedles, coaxes, flatters, threatens, drives, scolds, insinuates . . . . The *monkalun* has no authority. All he can do is to act as a peace making go-between. His only power is in his art of persuasion, his tact and his skillful playing on human emotions and motives.[3]

What appears to us as hopelessly confusing ambiguities of role were probably not perceived as such either by the occupant of the role or by those subject to his ministrations. In analysing the social processes of primitive societies this often makes it an exercise in futility, as Gluckman has cogently observed, to try to sort out those processes that deserve to be called "law."[4]

One might have been inclined to assume that as, in the course of history, the various forms of social ordering and dispute-settlement became separated in practice, they would become the subject of an earnest discussion among scholars as to their distinctive functions and their most appropriate applications. Instead of this, however, we find the substitution of one simplifying obfuscation for another. Now the tendency is to convert every form of social ordering into an exercise of the authority of the state, or, among sociologists, into a projection of "norms" by an abstract entity called "society." Legislation, adjudication, and administrative direction, instead of being perceived as distinctive interactional processes, are all seen as unidirectional exercises of state power. Contract is perceived, not as a source of "law" or social ordering in itself, but as something that derives its whole significance from the fact that the courts of the state stand ready to enforce it. Custom is passed over in virtually complete silence by sociologists and is viewed by legal scholars as becoming worthy of attention only when it has been recognized by the courts and thus been converted into "law." Only mediation seems to resist this tendency to subsume every kind of ordering under the rubric of "power" or "authority." Perhaps the attempt made in this essay — tentative and imperfect as it is — to analyze the forms and functions of mediation may help in some small measure to stimulate a more general interest in the analysis and comparison of the competing forms of social ordering. [pp. 337-339]

NOTES

1. Lon L. Fuller, "Mediation — Its Forms and Functions," *Southern California Law Review* 44 (1971), 314-339.
2. B. Malinowski, *Crime and Custom in Savage Society* (1926).
3. R. Barton, *Ifugao Law* (1969) p. 87.
4. M. Gluckman, *Politics, Law, and Ritual in Tribal Society* (1965), pp. 211-216.

5. Cultural Values and Legal Structure

THE COMPARATIVE PHILOSOPHY OF COMPARATIVE LAW[1]

F.S.C. Northrop

. . . Notwithstanding the different meanings which the words "good" and "just" have in different cultures and even for different people in any one nation or culture, comparative law and comparative cultural philosophy have shown that the different legal procedures and normative legal postulate sets, used to settle disputes the world over and throughout human history, fall into three major types. Sir Henry S. Maine in his classic work, *Ancient Law*, described two of these three types. The third is equally well known and of very ancient origin. These three major species of law are : (1) law of status, (2) law of contract and (3) mediational law. Types (1) and (2) have one characteristic in common. Both rest on the ethical assumption that the moral goodness or the legal justice of any particular act is to be determined by measuring the *de facto* character of the act against a determinate codified or codifiable rule which applies qualitatively in principle, although only statistically in fact, to all people in the culture in question. The method of carrying through this measuring process is called "litigation." Consequently in any law of status or law of contract society, the settling of disputes by litigation is regarded as good conduct. It was because Sir Henry Maine was concerned in his classic study only with codified or codifiable law that this study specified but two of the three major species of law.

Mediational Law

That there is a third type of ethical and legal conduct is shown by the following considerations : (a) Confucius taught that the superior or moral man does not indulge in litigation. Put concretely, this means that, according to the highest ethical and legal ideal and practice of classical Confucian Chinese society it was regarded as immoral to settle a dispute over some act by measuring the facts of the act against a determinate normative rule or principle. To be sure, Confucian society had codified law. Examination of it shows, however, that it was of the law-of-status type. Nevertheless, subject to certain restrictions to be noted shortly, the guidance of one's personal conduct or the settling of any dispute with one's adversary by recourse to determinate normative commandments or rules was regarded as a moral "second-best." The "first-best" moral and legal way was that of mediation in which the final settlement of the normative dispute is fitted uniquely in each particular case to the existential feelings and assents of both parties to the dispute ; also the final settlement is proposed and agreed upon by the parties themselves. (b) The Buddhist peacemaking of the "middle path" expresses the same ethic and type of law. (c) Another example is the lawyer Gandhi's rejection, during his South African period, of a favourable litigational victory for his client, which would have financially ruined the other party to the dispute, in favour of a mediated solution less remunerative to his client which enabled the other party to survive financially, and Gandhi's subsequent moral rebellion against litigation under the codified law of either the status or the contractual type.

More and more parties to legal disputes in the United States have found that the litigational method of settling disputes by recourse to legislative statutes and to judicial decisions which appeal to precedents may be relevant to the present dispute only in a verbal and artificial way and have concluded that the litigational method of codified law is not merely unnecessarily expensive and time-consuming, dragging on often, due to successive appeals, over years, but also frequently unsatisfactory in the final verdict to all the parties concerned. Hence many American business and labour leaders have set up mutual procedural agreements in which a mediationally agreed upon middle man is appointed to serve two functions : (i) to listen passively to the claims of both parties in the hope that the mere presentation of the rival claims to one another before a neutral observer will enable the disputants to reach a settlement themselves, and (ii) in case the latter event does not occur, to give a verdict which the parties agree ahead of time to accept.

This American example is not a pure instance of the mediational type of ethics and law, since it combines mediation with arbitration. The sign of arbitration is the decision by the middle man. In the mediational theory of ethics and law in its pure form, the mediator never gives a decision ; he merely serves as a go-between for the different parties and the dispute is not settled until both parties become so psychologically and intuitively sensitive to the other party's feelings, circumstances and standpoint in the matter that they agree upon the mutual adjustment and settlement, i.e., the middle path, which meets the *esse est percipi* relativities and the existential particularity of the situation. Because a dispute is not regarded as settled until the disputants themselves agree, the mediational type of law does not require physical sanctions.

Point (i) above shows that even in the present American procedure, which combines arbitration with mediation, the pure mediational normative ideal is there as the first-best. It is hoped that the parties themselves will come to a mutually satisfactory solution of their dispute, which they themselves propose. Arbitration enters only if this fails. Item (ii) shows that in this American method, even when arbitration is required, the ethic of the middle path, i.e., of mediation, must be used by the middleman. Actual practice in concrete cases shows also that the middleman is not bound by, nor do the parties want him to be bound by, past solutions of "similar" disputes. This means that the criterion of the good and the just is broken loose entirely from the concept of a dispute as a member of a common class and from the concept of the ethically good and the legally just as identifiable with being an instance of a universal determinate code or law which is applied consistently and syllogistically to all "similar" cases. The ideal, instead, is to get the present dispute settled as quickly as possible in the light of its unique characteristics.

Philosophically this means that the ethical ideal of the mediational type of law assumes a nominalistic, radically empirical, and existential philosophy. Each legal judgment, each moral choice, each dispute and each individual is regarded in its essential normative nature to be unique rather than an instance of a universal scientific law or a determinate normative ethical and legal commandment or rule. Expressed in terms of the pragmatic and problematic American philosophy of Dewey, this existentialism of the mediational type of law is the affirmation that the key to morality and law is to be found, not in the constancy and absoluteness of universal codes, commandments and principles which resolve the problematic situations, but in denotatively immediate, here-and-now, intuitive sensitivity to the the unique particularity of the present particular problematic situation in every dimension of its human and social characteristics....

That each fact in experience and any case in law is in part unique, no one can deny. That it is wholly so, however, may be open to question. The prevalence throughout the world and its history of codified law and its litigational method forces us to take the latter possibility seriously. That this possibility is an actuality becomes evident when one notes that every culture which has embraced the mediational type of ethics and law also has codified law and a personal and social ethics of principles which cannot be compromised if one is to be a moral or a just person.

Law of Status

Even with the first-best ethic of Confucian societies there were certain things taken for granted and expressed in determinate rules which applied to everyone and which were not regarded as subject to mediation in either theory or practice. These universal, wholly non-nominalistic and nonchanging ethical and legal principles appear in the five "proper" social relations laid down by Confucius as the requirements for a good and just society or government.

These five determinate principles are a *"proper" relation* between :

(1) Father and son,
(2) Husband and wife,
(3) Elder brother and younger brother,
(4) Sovereign and subject, and
(5) Friend and friend.

Unfortunately, most scholars who translate these principles into English and comment upon them tell a non-classically Chinese person very little about what they mean, since the word "proper" is never defined.

To any anthropologist or student of comparative law who looks at a society with respect to the three types of law which it may exemplify, the meaning of the word "proper" is evident in the words chosen to state the five relations. A "proper" relation between the persons referred to is one that characterizes the joint families of a law-of-status society which is predominantly patriarchal in character. The patriarchal character of the status type of ethic and law which Confucian ethics and culture exemplifies appears most blatantly in relation (3). Why should the question as to whether one is an elder or a younger brother have anything whatever to do with one's moral, legal or political duties ? The answer is that it has no relevance unless the society is that of a law-of-status type in which the family structure is predominantly patriarchal. One legal requirement in most patriarchal societies is that in the inheritance sons are favoured ; whereas daughters are favoured if the family is matriarchal. Also if patriarchal, the eldest brother inherits more than the younger brothers ; moreover upon the death or retirement of the father, it is the eldest son's duty to take over the headship of the family. Clearly in such a society, if there is not a "proper" relation between the eldest brother and the younger brother that is grounded in this status ethic of patriarchal primogeniture, such an ethical and legal theory will not work.

Moreover, in a patriarchal law-of-status society, the head of the family legally and morally is the male and usually is the male who is the eldest son of the family head of the previous generation. A "proper" relation between elder brother and younger brother means, therefore, a willingness upon the part of the younger brothers and their families and all the sisters to accept the biological priority of birth of the eldest brother as the criterion of their legal and moral rights and duties. It means, conversely, a willingness upon the part of the eldest son, when he succeeds his father in the headship of the joint family, to accept the responsibility for properly marrying his sisters and for caring for the families of all his younger brothers. Socially and practically it entails what is a commonplace throughout traditional Asian cultures and what was a commonplace in ancient Greek and Roman society before the creation of Western legal science and its ethic of the law of contract — namely a society of joint families.

The characteristic of a joint family is that it is a family of families in which, if the society is patriarchal, to be the eldest son means to be the head not merely of the family of one's own wife and children, but of all the families of one's younger brothers and their children's families. It means also the moral and legal duty to care for one's father's family upon his retirement and also the families of all his younger brothers.

The import of the word "proper" as it applies to the five relations specified by Confucius is that one's moral, familial, legal and social responsibilities and duties are defined by one's biologically bred status in the patriarchal joint family.

The meaning of the Confucian relation (1) now becomes evident. A "proper" relation between father and son is one in which all the sons and especially the eldest accepts the responsibilities and filial piety loyalties of a predominantly patriarchal joint family. Similarly a "proper" relation between husband and wife is one in which the primary obligation of the wife is to produce a son to head the husband's family and the joint family in the next generation. So great is this obligation in a "proper" relation between husband and wife that it often becomes the moral duty in case no son is born of the first wife for the husband to take a second wife.

The Confucian relation (4) defines the moral and political criterion of political leadership. It, too, is a function of objective biological facts having nothing to do with personal choices or with popular elections. If the society is patriarchal, the political leader is normally a king; if matriarchal, normally a queen. Furthermore, if it is not to become ambiguous about which joint family is to be the royal family, the relation of the joint families in the society as a whole must be hierarchical with a privileged first family at the top of the hierarchy.

The foregoing considerations suffice to make clear what the word "status" means in any law-of-status society. The meaning is that all normative words such as "personally good", "legally just" or "politically good" are defined in terms of natural history, biological facts having little if anything to do with the personal preferences or with the consent of the individual. "Status" means biologically bred, temporal order-of-birth status in an objectively determinable, genealogical table. It has nothing to do with the status that occurs in a law-of-contract society when certain people become more successful than others and separate into social groups. Just as the hedonistic theory of ethics and law defines the meaning of the words "good" and "just" in terms of the immediately inspected concept of pleasure of introspective psychology, so the ethics of a law-of-status society defines these words in terms of the concepts of natural history and biology. Consequently, to ask in any law-of-status society whether a given person is a "good" person is equivalent to asking for that person's pedigree....

The prevalent practice of political usurpers in law-of-status societies, of investing one's own family with a purity of biological descent from the first founder of the nation and the culture, which in fact it does not possess, is of considerable anthropological and philosophical importance. It shows that what matters is not *the fact* of one's purity of line of breeding, but *the belief* in this theory of personal, familial and political authority. This suggests that even in law-of-status societies, where kinship relations are of the essence in understanding ethics and law, the philosophical belief is the key to the *de facto* kinship and political relations ; the kinship relation is not the key to the philosophical belief. This conclusion is confirmed by the additional fact that otherwise neither Western civilization with its novel ethic of the law of contract, nor the Asian mediational ethic and law conceived as a first-best, would be possible. For if the *de facto* biological kinship relation determines every belief in philosophy, ethics and law, then, since one's genetic ancestry is fixed, it would have been impossible to make the shift as did ancient Asia in part at least from status to mediation and as did the West, also only in part as yet, from status to contract. Similarly it would be impossible for the people of Asia and Africa today to replace their old joint-familial and tribally focused ways with those prescribed by the quite different ethic of their new law-of-contract political constitutions which they have imported recently from the West.

The crucial question, therefore, arises : What is the belief system, i.e., the philosophy, which initially led practically every people on the earth's surface to find the meaning of the words "good" and "just" in the concepts of genealogical and racial biology ?

The Philosophy of the Law of Status

The answer to the foregoing question begins to appear if we ask what the ethics of the law of status assumes a moral, legal or political act to be. Clearly, the assumption is that every normative event or judgment is the act of a person whose scientific and philosophical defining properties are completely known when his biological sex, primogeniture of birth and tribal ancestry are specified. In other words, the ethic of the law of status rests upon the empirically scientific and philosophical belief that fully known man or woman is commonsense-object, biologically bred man or woman.

The word "object" in the last sentence is important for several reasons : (1) It explains why a law-of-status ethic is an absolute ethic for those who hold it. One's sex is not a matter of one's choice ; nor is one's temporal order of birth. Nor is the tribe of one's ancestors. (2) The word "object" also expresses the fact that the ethic of the law of status assumes a realistic epistemology rather than a nominalistic, radically empirical epistemology....

[T]he essential connection between colour of skin and morality in a law-of-status community is . . . an epistemological rather than an anthropological point. This epistemological point is that the objective realism of the philosophy of the law of status is *naive* realism, where "realism" means that one knows objects which exist independently of their relation to the observer and "naive" means that both the objects and their defining properties are directly sensed. To use the conceptual language of the writer's *The Logic of the Sciences and the Humanities,* naive realism affirms that external objects and public substantial selves, purporting to be directly observable and to exist and persist independently of their relation to the percipient, are completely denotable or definable in terms of "concepts by intuition," where by "a concept by intuition" one means any idea the complete meaning of which refers to something naively, i.e., directly or radically empirically sensed, introspected or immediately experienced.

Experience in societies unaffected by Western legal science indicates that without law of contract it is impossible to obtain political unity and authority over wide geographical areas at the national level without a racially privileged first family whose claim to political authority depends on racial purity and primogeniture of breeding and birth. This calls for a law-of-status ethic and for the definition of the political and legal duties of provincial and federal public officials in terms of the naively realistic philosophy of such a theory of law and politics.

The reason for this conclusion will become more evident if we compare the Laws of Manu of Aryan Hindu India with the codified law of Western legal science after its creation by the Stoic Roman lawyers. Certain contrasts are obvious. (1) The words of the former have commonsense meanings that are concrete ; those of the latter have formal, technical meanings which only a lawyer trained in Western legal science can fully understand and which are for the most part emotively dull and abstract. (2) The focus of the criterion of justice in codified law of the status type is more in the concrete material substance of what the code says ; in codes of the law-of-contract type, the formal and procedural properties of the codes rather than their concrete substance tends to become more and more the decisive criterion of what is just. To use the language of pure mathematics and contemporary symbolic logic, in the codes of any law-of-status society the criterion of what is just turns for the most part around the material constants in the legal sentences, whereas in those of the law-of-contract, the particular concrete person and the concrete content of the dispute tend to function merely as an instance of a variable. The law of contract expresses this conceptually different mentality by its dictum that the law is no respecter of persons.

In the Laws of Manu what is just for a given person cannot be separated from his or her sex or promogeniture of birth in the joint family or from the tribal origins and hierarchical status, i.e., caste, of his or her joint family in the society as a whole. What is just in a case which the law-of-contract would call a "trespass" is a function of the caste of the person's family or the species of animal which commits the trespass. The penalty is one thing in the case of a third-caste Sudra and another in the case of a second-caste Kshatriya ; one thing in the case of a horse and, because of its sacredness for Hindus, a different thing in the case of a cow. In the law-of-contract, on the other hand, the normative ideal, still imperfectly realized, is to substitute technical, abstract words like "delict" and "trespass" for concrete specific classes of persons or animals who commit the delict or the trespass, making the concrete object which instances what is unjust irrelevant to the criterion of goodness or justice.

Another contrast is that the law-of-status codes of different tribes and societies are exceedingly pluralistic and incompatible, varying in normative content from tribe to tribe, whereas in Western contractual legal science the legal words and more and more the substantive content of the contractual codes of the law tend to be characterized first by formal and later by substantive universalism.

As suggested above, however, the most notable contrast between status and contract appears in the political sphere at the federal level. The law of contract achieves provincial and federal legal and political unity by substituting (1) contractually introduced written or unwritten constitutions in which consent is of the essence of political authority and legal obligation for (2) the determination of political leadership by biology of breeding from a first family of the tribe or of the caste system of tribes. The practical significance of this contrast will become evident if we return to the difficulty in any law-of-status society of obtaining national unity over a wide geographical area when the people in the area are of different racial stocks or the cultural tradition is such that there is no religiously designated, privileged first family.

The achievement of national unity on a law-of-status basis was relatively easy in Japan since, for the most part, the people are of but one racial stock and the Shinto religion not merely specified the unique first family within this common stock from whom the political leader is selected by patrilineal primogeniture, but also prescribed absolute obedience of every one to the eldest son of the royal joint family in each generation. This gave each citizen a greater loyalty to the nation than to his own joint family.

In India, however, the many races made such an easy solution impossible. If national unity within the ethic of a patriarchal law-of-status procedure for determining political leadership was to be achieved, one of the tribes had to be given a higher status in the community than any other tribe. The Aryan Hindu conquerors of India acquired this social, political and religious priority for themselves first by force of conquest and later by being captured in significant part by the philosophical system of the pre-Aryan Indians' living law. Consequently the *de facto* national legal and political institutions of classical and medieval Hindu India are the synthesis of (1) the pre-Aryan Indian living law and (2) the new positive and living legal customs of the Aryan conquerors.

These ways in which the problem of federal political and legal unity have been solved in societies which possess only the mediational or the status types of law point up the unique contribution of the law of contract. It provides a method of achieving political unity at the federal level without recourse to a privileged race and a privileged first family. In short, it provides constitutional law in which the source of political authority is not in the biology of one's breeding or the sex and temporal priority of one's birth, and thereby makes a democratic political government possible.

Another contrast between status and contract appears if we note what happened when the Western legal science of the Stoic Roman Scaevolas and their successors made its impact upon the exceedingly patriarchal law-of-status societies of the ancient Western world :

(1) The law-of-status codes of the non-Roman tribes and ancestral joint families were given the same status under the national law as the law-of-status codes of the conquering Roman tribes. In short, the attempt to achieve national unity under codified law by setting up a privileged political and legal tribe or first joint family was rejected.

(2) Lawyers and statesmen began immediately to look for what is common to the law-of-status codes of the different tribes and different varieties of joint

families as well as to the differences. Those law-of-status codes of the different tribes or joint families which were peculiar to one particular tribe they called the *jus civile*. Those law-of-status rules which were common to the different tribes they called the *jus gentium*. The history of Western law from the Scaevolas to Justinian is the story of the increasing triumph of the universalism of the *jus gentium* over the pluralism and the normative incompatibilities of the diverse examples of the *jus civile*.

(3) The process was begun of breaking the status of the individual person, before the codified law, away from the primogeniture, elder brother-younger brother relation, the male-female and brother-sister sexual criterion, and the father-son patriarchal headship status of the individual in the joint family. This had the effect of making the moral and legal person the individual person *qua* person. In other words, to use the language of the Stoic Roman philosophers and lawyers, moral and just man is transformed from joint-family and tribal man into universal or cosmopolitan man.

Point (2) concerning the *jus civile* expresses the previously noted fact that the codes of law-of-status nations and cultures are pluralistic and frequently incompatible, generating either the caste system or many nations, when the people are of different racial stocks. The *jus gentium* of Roman law points up, by way of contrast, the *universalism* that characterizes the law of contract when it achieves its ideal.

Point (3) shows that this universalism involves much more than merely finding what is common to every instance of the *jus civile*. Such a cultural common denominator of the codes of the many law-of-status tribal nations would have left one with codes which were too weak to define any Western legal and political system. Moreover, this common denominator would have made slavery just, since every law-of-status society in the ancient West took for granted the moral and political justice of slavery. Clearly, therefore, a new philosophical conception of what the words "good" and "just" mean was also involved. What is this philosophy ?

The Philosophy of Law of Contract

The fact that codified law is retained gives part of the answer. Codified law means that the moral and legal person is conceived as an instance of a universal law. Thus existentialism and nominalism are rejected. Concepts of the person or of anything else are real rather than nominalistic universals. But the real universal which is the moral and legal person is broken free from any sensible biological or tribal criteria. This is the meaning of the Stoic Roman philosophers' thesis that moral and just man is a universal or cosmopolitan human being. When this is the belief of one's ethics and law, the individual stands before the law *qua* person, not *qua* this sensible tribal or sexual kind of person, nor *qua* the head of his joint family. In short, codified law is made, not found. And being made by men, all men are born free and equal so far as the law is concerned. It is to be noted, therefore, that the first sentence of the Declaration of Independence in the contractual constitutional law of the United States is not, as so many suppose, a proposition in biology or the comparative psychology of newly born babies ; it is, instead, an axiom of contractual legal science.

The moment, however, that the person is not born to his moral, legal and political duties, rights and responsibilities, but makes them, a new procedure for specifying the laws and selecting those who administer them is necessary. This procedure is freely-assented-to contract. Hence, Sir Henry Maine's name for our third type of law. Its content, moreover, is for the parties concerned to determine. Thus substance tends to become secondary in defining the morally good and the legally just. Procedural rules instead which specify when the contracting parties have consented and who is to administer or adjudicate, in case of a dispute, what they have consented to, become of the essence. Hence the aforementioned abstract character of the terminology of the law of contract. Hence, also, the importance of the variable rather than the material constant ; also the postulational (in the sense of the formally hypothetical) character of the law of contract. And being thus procedurally hypothetical rather than categorically descriptive, there is no obligation without consent.

This emphasis upon hypothetically introduced, formal procedural rules means not merely that a formal, technical language in terms of abstract Latin nouns replaces the more commonsense concrete language of law-of-status codes, but also that sensible properties tend to be rejected in the definition of normative words. Philosophically this means that not only a nominalistic radical empirical, but also a naively realistic philosophy is being replaced in the law of contract by an epistemological philosophy of a different kind.

Two characteristics of this philosophy are evident. (1) *The concept of the moral and just individual is that of an entity which instances a universal law and is, therefore, the concept of a real* (rather than a nominalistic) *universal,* but (2) *this real universal is not defined,* as in naive realism, *in terms of directly sensed properties.*

Two questions remain : (a) Why would anyone choose to define a universal in this way ? (b) How is it possible to do it, i.e., how is it possible to define an object of knowledge without recourse to any empirically given properties ?

We shall get an answer to the first of these two questions if we note the conclusion which mediational law and the law of contract hold in common, and inquire concerning the reason. This conclusion is that the ethic of the law of status is a false ethic and law. The reason is that it assumes and requires a naively realistic epistemology for its validity and this epistemological theory of conceptual meaning is false. The following three facts make these statements evident : (1) Every people in the world at one time in their history believed in and practiced the ethic of the law of status, and most people still do in considerable part. (2) The philosophy of the law of status is naive realism. (3) Sooner or later in every culture, scientists, philosophers and sages arise who (a) demonstrate that naive realism is a false philosophy and (b) convince a statistically high percentage of their people that this is the case.

There must be a good reason why philosophical movements, originating as distant from one another in space and time, should agree that the naively realistic epistemology is a false philosophy. This reason is not hard to find and, Aristotelian Thomists and Feuerbachian Marxists to the contrary notwithstanding, is unanswerable. Empirical and logical considerations show that naive realism is a self-contradictory theory....

The empirical and logical reason why the three major philosophies of classical Asia, three of the four major philosophies of ancient Greece and classical Rome, and every modern and contemporary Western theory of natural science, philosophy, ethics, law and politics, except that of the Feuerbachian Marxists, regard naive realism as a false philosophy should now be both clear and irrefutable. The believer in this epistemology purports to know objects and events with scientifically defined properties that exist independently of their relation to the perceiver and the particular moment of perception, yet he defines these supposedly public spatio-temporal events and objects in terms of sensed events, qualities, objects and relations of simultaneity, all of which are relative to the percipient. Since it is self-contradictory to define objects of knowledge, that purport to be independent of their relation to the percipient, in terms of items of knowledge all of which are relative to the percipient, the naive realistic concept of anything, whether it be a person or a chemical atom, is a self-contradictory and hence a false theory.

Also the ethic of the law of status which assumes and requires a naively realistic epistemology for its meaningfulness is a false theory. It is false because it confuses the accidental *esse est percipi* effects of another person upon the percipient with the essential and objective human being him- or herself.

When this self-contradictory character of the naively realistic epistemology in philosophy, natural science and law becomes evident, two alternatives are possible : (a) One can retain the naivete, i.e., the radical empiricism, and reject the realism, or (b) one can retain the realism by finding a new way to define the realistic epistemological object of knowledge, which has no recourse to sensed or introspective qualities or events, except in the operational testing of the theory.

Applied to the normative sciences, alternative (a) generates the shift from status to mediation, whereas alternative (b) creates Western legal science and initiates its "shift from status to contract." Applied to psychology, ontology and religion, alternative (a) leads to the Nirvana non-dualistic Vedantic field or *chit* consciousness theory of the self and the Divine. Applied to the natural sciences, alternative (a), by removing the belief in a realistic epistemological world, substitutes impressionistic and relativistic aesthetic and introspective psychology for physics, thereby taking the mathematical physical sciences into decline as occurred in Asia, the Middle East and medieval Europe, whereas alternative (b) caused the Western type of mathematical physics and its technology to flourish and generated, as the sequel will show, the creation of Western legal science by the Stoic Roman lawyers and philosophers.

. . . The Romans created no physics ; their physics was that of the Greeks whom they conquered. There must be something novel, therefore, in Greek physics which, when discovered and applied to the normative sciences, leads to the creation of Western legal science and the ethic of its unique law of contract.

It will help us to become clear as quickly as possible concerning what this new epistemology of Greek science is by reference to a statement which Whitehead made to the writer in the early 1920s. His statement was to the following effect : The two greatest achievements of the Western human mind were (1) the discovery of the concept of the variable by the Greek mathematical physicists and (2) Eudoxus' use of the universally quantified variable to define equality of ratios for any relata whatever in Definition 5 of the Book V of Euclid.

Let us begin with the meaning of the former discovery first. Briefly its significance is that it gives an entirely new logical, scientific and philosophical concept of the individual, whatever the individual may be. Previous scientific and philosophical thought had but two concepts of the individual. One was that designated by the proper name. This is the concept of the individual of a strictly nominalistic radically empirical, existential philosophy. Since the radically empirical individual is unique, only the proper name designates it in a non-misleading way. The other previous concept of the individual is that of the member of a class, the defining properties of which are given through the senses. This is the concept of the individual of a naively realistic epistemology. It is this concept of the individual which leads, for people in a society uninfluenced by the law of contract, to the ethics of the law of status.

The concept of the individual in the idea of the variable combines elements of both of the former concepts. It is like that of the nominalists' proper name in that one individual and one only is referred to. But it is like that of the naively realistic class name in that any one contained in what is called the range of the variable will do. Thus, the heart of the nature of an individual when conceived with the idea of the variable is *any-one-ness*. This is the individual in the law of contract. The law is not just, unless *any one* individual has the privileges, the rights and the duties prescribed by the content of the law.

But more also is involved. There is also the novel way in which *the range* of the *any-one-ness* is made determinate. Determinate concepts by intuition referring to sensed or introspected factors of any kind are not used ; otherwise one would be back in the old naively realistic epistemology which is self-contradictory. Also the objects, the events and the laws of natural science would have lost all objectivity, and in the normative sciences one would have obtained the *for-any-one-ness* which is the heart of the ethic of the law of contract only at the cost of identifying the range of the *any-one-ness* with the naive realistically sensed colour-of-skin type of definition of the ethic of the law of status. As just noted, this is precisely what occurred with Aristotle and his Middle Eastern and Western Jewish, Christian and Islamic successors with their racially privileged Patriarchs, Kings and Sultans.

Hence, if the self-contradictory, naively realistic epistemological theory of the *range* of the *any-one-ness* is to be avoided, all introspected or sensed qualities must be rejected in the specification of its determinateness. To use the language of Socrates, one must "drop all images." How is this to be done ?

Those who have analyzed Western mathematical physics or who understand Russell and Frege's interpretation of Peano's Fifth postulate know the answer. The variable *qua* variable is conceived as nothing but a relatum in an imageless, logical, or purely mathematical, formally constructed relation. Apart from this relation there is nothing to distinguish one entity-variable from another. Furthermore, if we are not to fall back in the definition of our relations or laws on sensed or introspected events, properties or objects which are relative to the percipient, the relations must not be imageful. In short, they must be defined in terms of imageless, formal, logical properties or procedural rules rather than in terms of sensed qualities, sensed relations or sensed events. This means that the concept of an individual which the discovery of the variable gives is that of an entity which has no scientific properties except as it is conceived as a relatum of a formally constructed relation with specific imageless formal properties. By laying more and more complex formal properties on these imageless relations, one can define individuals which, or who, instance imageless formal laws with any degree of specificity.

Because such an individual has no determinate meaning apart from the non-empirical, i.e., imageless, formal properties of the relations or laws in which he is a relatum, it follows that such laws are universally quantifiable by definition, i.e., applicable to all by virtue of the axiomatically constructed formal properties of the relations which specify their properties. One does not have to take the individuals one by one, as is the case in a radically empirical or a naively realistic epistemology, to see whether all of them have the properties which the universal law affirms....

Without this concept of an individual, the problem in recent Western law of clarifying what is meant by a "corporate personality," such as the General Motors Corporation, which has baffled American legal realists with their radically empirical theory of the meaning of all legal concepts, is insoluble. Clearly the legal meaning of the General Motors Corporation is not the radically empirical images of its factories ; nor is it the naively realistic personality of its former top official, the former United States Secretary of Defence, Mr. Charles E. Wilson. But if not this, what scientific meaning does this legal entity have ? The answer is that it is a personality of the concept by postulation type. In other words, like one of Frege's natural numbers, the General Motors Corporation is an instance of an entity-variable in the state legislative statutes which created this legal construct and specified its legal properties. The legal philosophy of the present Regius Professor of Jurisprudence at Oxford expresses this same theory of the meaning of legal language.

The same is true of the original theory of the moral and the just human person according to the law of contract. He or she is *qua* person a merely meaningless entity-variable, p, apart from the contractually constructed rules preceded by the universal quantifier, (p), to which implicitly or explicitly he or she gives consent. Negatively this novel epistemological concept of an individual eliminates sensed or introspected qualities from the definition of what is politically good or legally just. Positively, it gives one half but not the whole of the Roman Stoics' thesis that moral man and just man is universal or cosmopolitan man, i.e., *any one* human being whatever, standing equally with any other under a common, determinate law whose authority rests in principle on consent to what is contained in the contract. Also it probably gives part at least of Kant's categorical imperative which is : Act so that the substance of one's act may be generalized for *any one.*

Buddhist and Hindu philosophy obtain something similar to the universalism of the law of contract in their concept of the true self which Confucius called "*jen,*" the Buddhists call "Nirvana" and which the non-dualistic Vedantists call the "*chit* consciousness." As previously noted, according to this theory all human beings are not merely equal morally, but they are, strictly speaking, either identical in their true nature, as in Buddhism or non-dualistic Hinduism, or they possess a common human-heartedness as in the *jen* of Confucianism. But, being radically empirical and immediate and also indeterminate or formless, this Confucian, Buddhist and Hindu type of moral and religious universalism cannot be expressed in determinate propositions or codes and hence has to be brought forth merely existentially by yogic or other psychological exercises or by the fostering of mutual warm-heartedness in the mediational process. This is why the Confucian, Buddhist or non-dualistic Vedanta Hindu universalism takes one legally from status to mediation.

Consequently, the uncodifiable universalism of the classical Asian philosophy and the codifiable universalism of the law of contract are both empirically valid and though different, they supplement one another. Furthermore, both components of what is universal to all human beings, when carried out and applied consistently, are incompatible with the family and tribally centred ethic of biologically bred status and provide positive and living law support for democratic legal and political nations....

Some Practical Implications

The foregoing comparative study is of considerable contemporary practical significance. First, it shows that in introducing foreign legal and political norms into any society, those norms will become effective and take root only if they incorporate also a part at least of the norms and philosophy of the native society. Second, this means that the present practice of imposing purely Western secular legal and political systems on African, Middle Eastern and Asian societies, without incorporating into those systems at least some basic factors in the traditional philosophy of the living law of the native people, is likely to end in failure. Recent events in Turkey and South Korea illustrate such failures. Third, the practical problem, therefore, if success is to occur, consists in finding a criterion for determining those factors in the traditional living law which are to be incorporated and synthesized with the new positive codified law of contract from the modern West, and those factors of the old living law which must go because they are incompatible with modern contractual legal and political institutions and social ways. In the case of free democratic modern contractual law and politics, the foregoing study specifies the portion of the traditional philosophy of the living law of Confucian, Buddhist and Hindu Asian societies which, though different from, is, nevertheless, compatible with the philosophical concept of the person in any free democratic contractual legal and political system. Any contemporary Asian leader whose aim is the free democratic modernization of his nation will be wise to make this portion of the living law of his people as essential and explicit a part of his legal and political system as is the new free democratic positive law and politics which he is importing from the modern West. Otherwise, the maximum support from the living law that is necessary to make his new positive legal and political reforms effective is not likely to be forthcoming.

NOTE

1. F.S.C. Northrop, "The Comparative Philosophy of Comparative Law," *Cornell Law Quarterly* 45 (1960) : 617-658.

CHAPTER II

THE MYTHOLOGICAL ORIGINS OF LAW

Myth is an uncommon word in modern legal systems. Indeed, lawyers, perhaps more than other social scientists, are likely to embrace the perjorative use of myth, as falsification or story telling which has little or no relevance to the tasks of lawyering or judging. Yet it is a fact of history that law emerged from mythology and was at one time doubtlessly intertwined with mythopeic conceptions of the universe. Myth simply understood has to do with the human attempt to fashion order out of chaos, to describe the world in such a manner that the parts are interrelated and result in subduing the threatening aspects of human existence. In early history nature was an imposing and awesome force in which man's place was precarious and unexplainable. The rational dimension of thought lay as a potent force in the human psyche but scientific logical categorizing of nature was preceded by historical periods which can be best described as mythic. Some commentators have associated myth with religion while others have preferred psychological explanations. These descriptions have suggested at times a universalism about myth while empirically oriented scientists have resisted structural analysis to concentrate more on the internal culture-specific mythologizing of particular groups. In all cultures the resolution of conflict, and the law as the embodiment and systematization of basic principles around which to organize authority, may be seen as the rationalizing processes according to which obedience and respect for hierarchy are developed.

In the Platonic period the relationship between *mythos* and *logos* was clarified. Myth at that point in history became identified with the Western use of myth as stories the truth of which could not be assured. In the *Republic*, Plato understood *muthoi* as forms of untruth, even though there could be elements of truth associated with them (2.377a). Plato, as the father of modern philosophical thinking evolved his theory of scientific justice against a long background of non-scientific, mythological, conceptualization of law in the context of nature. In so doing his theories contained a high degree of ambivalence towards the tradition of myth and law. Since Plato the Western legal imagination has been preoccupied with purifying the logic of law, improving on the lucidity of legal argumentation, and documenting the predictable quality of legal craftmanship and the rationality of its institutions.

Plato was displeased with the allegorical mode of explanation and despite his fascination with dialectical method sought to dissociate law from its non-rational, mythological roots. Shall we thus regard post-platonic legal theory as part of an evolutionary growth of legal concepts away from the irrational? Whether we move to adopt such a perspective or not, it is instructive to study the foundation of law in prerational history in order to delineate the extent to which law's involvement with rationality has been successful; it is further instructive to examine the extent to which the recurrence of mythic expression is natural and psychologically necessary to the human condition.

All cultures have a mythic dimension and it is through myth that man organizes and experiences history. Myth, as expressed through law, thus mediates between the past and the present. As a culture reconstructs its mythology, history evolves but, so too, as a culture loses touch with its mythology that culture becomes disembodied from history. We, in the twentieth century West, lacking mythological perception, have turned to ideology as a myth replacement.

Myth, through its offspring, law, is the most powerful statement of values to which any society commits itself. Law, furthermore, is the most conservative statement of these values, bearing an intimate relationship to the existing power structure. In all cultures the resolution of conflict and law, as the embodiment of systematic principles around which authority is organized, may be seen as the rationalizing process according to which obedience and respect for hierarchy are developed. Myth, in functional terms, is a pragmatic reaction to the resolution of problems which affect the individual in the social environment ; it legitimates institutions and their rituals. An unsympathetic analysis of this process interprets myth as a device of propaganda and social control.

Views of myth, however, differ widely. Empirically oriented scientists have resisted structural analysis in favour of examining the specific mythological patterns of particular cultural groups. Others have taken a more universalist approach. Writers, such as Bergson, view myth as an expression counteracting the imbalance of intelligence that alienates man from society and nature. Both Bergson and Cassirer agree that myth is the common source of morality and religion. Law, broadly conceived, should be added to this list.

Jung approached myth as an exemplary experience of the human psyche. He contended that there are predictable biological and historical factors which have consistently demonstrated the efficacy and universalism of myth. For Jung, myth could not be superseded by science. He, therefore, came to the conclusion that many of our basic social motives and beliefs are inseparably bound to recurring mythic patterns of human experience. Myth is beyond being proven or disproven ; it simply exists as part of our theories and ideals. Because it is unconscious, it has a profound effect upon our institutions and conduct.

Recently, in the face of heightened consciousness about male-female relations, historians and psychologists have turned their attention to the earliest periods of history in order to clarify the division of labour between matriarchal and patriarchal systems of control. Matriarchy appears to have been the first and most prolonged stage of human consciousness. Although matriarchy, which persisted until the end of the Bronze Age, was not equipped with a legal system, as such, woman nonetheless predominated, her power emanating from her role as giver of life. As Earth Mother, woman controlled the reproductive cycles ; man, whose biological function in reproduction was unknown, was given a subsidiary status. Once man perceived his essential role, a historical threshold was crossed and the symbolic ordering of the universe was replaced with man's struggle for dominion, a struggle which in history was also linked to rationality. Man's task became one of remaking history, of redefining the male as the embodiment of order and will. Male gods appeared, followed by royal kings and the *paterfamilias.* To the female were attributed the weak and passive virtues. Law and will were earmarked as qualities of the male ; justice and mercy were attached to the female.

1. The Rise of Patriarchy

It is impossible, at this stage in history, to prove with any degree of scientific accuracy the universal existence of matriarchal civilizations. Compelling observations, however, have been made about ancient mythologies as they pertain to a dominant female figure. The earliest portion of the Bible is the Song of Deborah which describes a military victory under the leadership of a woman. It has been suggested that the disorder in the text of the Noah story indicates that someone tampered with it, substituting a male for a female Noah.[1] There are scholars who go so far as to suggest that the Bible is an elaborate response to the scientific discovery of the male's role in conception. The great mother is central in the historical traditions, for example, of Babylonia, Phoenecia, the Celts, and the Egyptians. In addition, figurines have been discovered in many parts of the world which express the female form as dominant. These precede their male counterparts both in mythologies and art.

Whether of universal proportion or not, it is significant that matriarchal history was unconnected to organized systems of law. There is, however, no indication that matriarchal communities lacked rules, customary practices, and various forms of effective social control. There is no reason to dispute the existence of social institutions designed to cope with the exigencies of property holding, trade relations, or even marital bonds. We cannot, however, locate in our historical records a body of knowledge and social practices which can be identified as law. We have no evidence that the matriarchal cultures were conscious of an overriding set of rules which regulated transactions among individuals and maintained a hierarchy of social relations.

With the advent of patriarchy (either rational or non-rational), we see the first large-scale emergence of legal institutions which protected patriarchal domination and, as a consequence, justified ownership and property rights of the male. This critical development has been viewed as the manifestation of a dimension of consciousness. Femaleness is thus identified with the cyclical flow of nature, that is, fertility and natural growth, and maleness with the structuring and ordering of relations. Whether this historic condition of maleness is connected to man's disassociation from the natural act of carrying and giving birth is a matter of conjecture. What we can conclude, however, is that the ancient legal systems were part of a male psychology which gave rise to our histories of law.

An examination of legal imagery reinforces this suggestion. Law is spoken of as having been handed down or laid down. There is a certain fascination with phallic or vertical symbolism in the concept of the sceptre or the divine right of kings. The psyche of justice, as opposed to law, on the other hand, is represented in the image of the scales or, to continue the sexual metaphor, breasts. The imagery reveals a more horizontal dynamic, involving balance and moderation.

In the contemporary West we are witnessing a breakdown in our authority structure coupled with the demythologizing of the male figure and a delegitimizing of law. There are too many laws, too many regulations, and too many complications in their application for the traditional model to retain any meaning.

Not surprisingly, there has been an escalation in the field of administrative law, legal reform, and informal methods of dispute resolution such as arbitration, mediation, and conciliation. This too has been an imperfect revolution as there is a dialectical process at work. Currently there are tensions and uncertainties in world society between the patriarchal and matriarchal archetypes and, as yet, equilibrium is elusive. While we cannot return to the patriarchal structure of sovereignty and the divine right of kings, the rationality of Kant, or the concept of legal principles and axioms of Rome, we are incapable of experiencing the non-scientific or non-patriarchal instrument.

One of the problems is language itself. Forms of language, found in the tradition of literacy and rationality, have definite patriarchal associations. Nonverbal communication, the sensitive, the poetic, the dramatic, the non-rational side of consciousness, have all been developed and identified with the feminine. How can we experience an ideological expression of a dimension of history which has been repressed and distorted to the point where we no longer know what its representative forms are ? Also, there is fear of expansion of the intuitive. Those who propound intuition as a theoretical basis may well be attacked as being unjust, uncertain, and illegal. The profession protects itself by moving back in the direction of structure and rigidity in times of uncertainty. Given these historical conditions and patterns, the question presently to be addressed is whether law's association with maleness and the protection of patriarchal privilege is inherently part of the structure of law or, rather, a matter of vestigial content, which can be corrected according to what might be termed "androgynous universalist law."

NOTE

1. This has been recently documented in David Bakan, *And They Took Themselves Wives* (New York : Harper & Row, 1980).

THE MYTH OF THE STATE[1]

E. Cassirer

In mythical thought and imagination we do not meet with *individual* confessions. Myth is an objectification of man's social experience, not of his individual experience. It is true that in later times we find myths made by individuals, as for instance, the famous Platonic myths. But here one of the most essential features of the genuine myths is missing. Plato created them in an entirely free spirit ; he was not under their power, he directed them according to his own purposes : the purposes of dialectical and ethical thought. Genuine myth does not possess this philosophical freedom ; for the images in which it lives are not known as images. They are not regarded as symbols but as realities. This reality cannot be rejected or criticized ; it has to be accepted in a passive way. But the first preliminary step on the new road that finally will lead to a new goal has been made. For even here emotions are not simply felt. They are "intuited" ; they are "turned into images." These images are crude, grotesque, fantastic. But it is just for this reason that they are understood to uncivilized man because they can give him an interpretation of the life of nature and of his own inner life.

Myth and religion in general, have often been declared to be a mere product of fear. But what is most essential in man's religious life is not the *fact* of fear, but the *metamorphosis* of fear. Fear is a universal biological instinct. It can never be completely overcome or suppressed, but it can change its form. Myth is filled with the most violent emotions and the most frightful visions. But in myth man begins to learn a new and strange art : the art of expressing and that means of organizing, his most deeply rooted instincts, his hopes and fears. [pp. 47-48]

NOTE

1. E. Cassirer, *The Myth of the State* (New Haven : Yale University Press, 1946), pp. 47-48.

MYTH, RELIGION AND MOTHER RIGHT[1]

J.J. Bachofen

Since the beginning of all developments lies in myth, myth must form the starting point for any serious investigation of ancient history. Myth contains the origins, and myth alone can reveal them. It is the origins which determine the subsequent development, which define its character and direction. Without knowledge of the origins, the science of history can come to no conclusion. A distinction between myth and history may be justified where it refers merely to a difference in mode of expression, but it has neither meaning nor justification when it creates a hiatus in the continuity of human development. The success of our undertaking depends essentially on the abandonment of any such distinction. The forms of family organization prevailing in the times known to us are not original forms, but the consequences of earlier stages. Considered alone, they disclose only themselves, not their causality ; they are isolated data, elements of knowledge at most, but not of understanding. The strictness of the Roman patriarchal system points to an earlier system that had to be combatted and suppressed. And the same applies to the paternal system of Athens, the city of Athene, motherless daughter of Zeus. With all its Apollonian purity, it too represents the peak of a development, the first stages of which must have belonged to a world characterized by entirely different ideas and institutions. How then shall we understand the end if the beginnings remain a riddle to us ? But where are these beginnings to be found ? The answer is not in doubt. In myth, the faithful picture of the oldest era, and nowhere else.

The thirst for systematic knowledge has inspired many attempts to arrive at a picture of the origins by philosophical speculation, to fill in the great gaps in our historical records with the shadowy figures of abstract reasoning. A strange inconsistency : to reject myth as invention and to accept one's own utopias so confidently. . . .

It has been said that myth, like quicksand, can never provide a firm foothold. This reproach applies, not to myth itself, but only to the way it has been handled. Multiform and shifting in its outward manifestation, myth nevertheless follows fixed laws, and can provide as definite and secure results as any other source of historical knowledge. Product of a cultural period in which life had not yet broken away from the harmony of nature, it shares with nature that unconscious lawfulness which is always lacking in the works of free reflection. Everywhere there is system, everywhere cohesion ; in every detail the expression of a great fundamental law whose abundant manifestations demonstrate its inner truth and natural necessity. [pp. 75-76]

. . . And we have still another highly remarkable allusion to the existence of mother right in archaic Attica. I am referring to the *Eumenides* of Aeschylus. The two principles, mother right and father right, are here championed by the Erinyes on the one hand, by Apollo and Athene on the other. Orestes kills his mother in order to avenge his father. Which of the two stands closer to the child ? Athene ordains a court of justice. The most respected of her citizens shall decide. The Erinyes testify against the matricide ; Apollo, who commanded Orestes to act and purged him of blood guilt, is his defender. The Erinyes argue the cause of Clytaemnestra while Apollo takes the part of Agamemnon. The Erinyes are the champions of mother right, Apollo the advocate of father right. The position of the Erinyes is made clear in their dialogue with Orestes :

CHORUS : The Prophet guided you into this matricide ?
ORESTES : Yes. I have never complained of this. I do not now.
CHORUS : When sentence seizes you, you will talk a different way.
ORESTES : I have no fear. My father will aid me from the grave.
CHORUS : Kill your mother, then put trust in a corpse ! Trust on.
ORESTES : Yes. She was dirtied twice over with disgrace.
CHORUS : Tell me how, and explain it to the judges here.
ORESTES : She murdered her husband, and thereby my father too.
CHORUS : Of this stain, death has set her free. But you still live.
ORESTES : When she lived, why did you not descend and drive her out ?
CHORUS : The man she killed was not of blood congenital.
ORESTES : But am I then involved with my mother by blood-bond ?
CHORUS : Murderer, yes. How else could she have nursed you beneath Her heart ? Do you forswear your mother's intimate blood ?

It is plain that the Erinyes do not recognize the law of the father and husband, for they leave Clytaemnestra's deed unpunished. They know only the law of the mother, the rights of the mother's blood ; they demand the punishment of the matricide in accordance with old law and custom. Not so Apollo. He ordered the deed to avenge the father, having received his own orders from Zeus, the god of heaven. And now he defends Orestes against the Erinyes, championing father right against mother right. He reveals himself as Patroos (paternal god), and indeed this was his epithet as tutelary god of Athens. He speaks to the judges as follows :

> I will tell you, and I will answer correctly. Watch. The mother is no parent of that which is called her child, but only nurse of the new-planted seed that grows. The parent is he who mounts. A stranger she preserves a stranger's seed, if no god interfere. I will show you proof of what I have explained. There can be a father without any mother. There she stands, the living witness, daughter of Olympian Zeus, she who was never fostered in the dark of the womb, yet such a child as no goddess could bring to birth.

Thus Apollo champions the right of the begetter, while the Erinyes defend the rights of the blood, of the maternal matter. Apollo's is the new law, theirs is the old. To Apollo's arguments the Erinyes reply :

> You won the ancient goddesses over with wine and so destroyed the orders of an elder time.

and further on :

> Since you, a young god, would ride down my elder age . . . .

Now the judges, enlightened by the arguments on both sides, step up to the voting urn. Athene also takes up a stone from the altar, holds it in her hand, and speaks :

> It is my task to render final judgment here. This is a ballot for Orestes I shall cast. There is no mother anywhere who gave me birth, and but for marriage, I am always for the male with all my heart, and strongly on my father's side. So, in a case where the wife has killed her husband, lord of the house, her death shall not mean most to me. And if the other votes are even, then Orestes wins.

Thus it is the father, protector of the house, and not the mother, who has the superior right. According to this right, which comes from Zeus, father of both Apollo and Athene, Orestes is acquitted. In this first trial for murder ever to have been held among mortals, an equal number of votes is cast on each side and the decision is carried by the *calculus Minervae* [Minerva's stone]. But this is the new law of the new gods. Of Apollo it is said that he "blighted age-old distributions of power," and "destroyed the orders of an elder time." The semichorus of the Erinyes sings :

> Gods of the younger generation, you have ridden down the laws of the elder time, torn them out of my hands.

The old juridical state of mankind is now deprived of every support, the foundation of all well-being is shattered. No longer shall anyone cry out : "O Justice! Throned powers of the Erinyes." Fuming with rage, the goddesses, childless daughters of the night, resolve to hide in the subterranean depths to destroy the fertility of the earth and the growth of the infant in the womb. But Athene wins them over and reconciles them with the new law. Henceforth they shall serve piously by her side. They are not banished, they are not fallen. No :

> And you, in your place of eminence beside Erechtheus in his house shall win from female and from male processionals more than all lands of men beside could ever give.

And gladly they agree to dwell and serve beside Pallas ; henceforth, beloved of maidens, they will prepare nuptial joys — they, the primordial goddesses, now spirits of peace and concord. The throng of pious maidens and aged mothers then conducts the reconciled corulers of the land back to their realm, down to Hades, the dark abode of the dead. For the people of Athens, Moira and Zeus the all-seeing are joyfully united.

The child's predominant connection with its mother is relinquished. Man is raised above woman. The material principle is subordinated to the spiritual principle. Thus marriage for the first time attains its true height. For the Erinyes, as Apollo held up to them, failed to honour Hera's decree, the sacred marriage bond. Clytaemnestra's infringement of it was nothing to them : in their eyes it could not excuse Orestes' just, though bloody, deed. In this sense father right is tantamount to marriage right, hence the starting point of a new era, an era of fixed order in family and state, which bore within it the germs of a great unfolding and flowering. [pp. 158-161]

NOTE

1. J.J. Bachofen, *Myth, Religion, and Mother Right* (New York and Princeton : Princeton University Press, 1967), pp. 75-161.

THE CULT OF THE MOTHER-GODDESS[1]

E.O. James

Whether or not this reflects a primeval system of matriarchal social organization, as is by no means improbable, the fact remains that the Goddess at first had precedence over the Young God with whom she was associated as her son or husband or lover. A number of causes may have contributed to her enhanced status in society and in the pantheon, but the starting-point in the institution of the family and its wider ramifications in kinship can hardly have been other than the relationship of mother and child in the first instance. That an infant is the offspring of its mother never could be in doubt, however its origin and generation may have been explained, if, indeed, there was any speculation on the subject in its physical aspects. The role of the father might be very obscure and even nonexistent, but that of the mother was not open to question, being merely a matter of observation. Therefore, around the maternal centre a network of emotions and sentiments arose — the care and protection of the offspring and their sense of dependence upon their parents giving rise to respect for parental authority and guidance — all of which were essential for the survival and well-being of the human race and the right ordering of family life. And, as Marett says, "fear tempered with wonder and submissiveness and thus transmuted into reverence is the forerunner of love."

Woman with her inexplicable nature and unaccountable attributes and functions, such as menstruation, pregnancy, childbirth, and lactation, has been a mysterious person, calling forth a numinous reaction and evaluation, permeated with religious sentiments, rendering her at once sacred and tabu. Regarded as the sole source of the family, the parental instinct doubtless from the first was primarily female, descent invariably following the distaff. This probably explains to a considerable extent the priority of mother-right in primitive society, sometimes as a unilateral organization in which the woman may have remained among her own people and the husband was little more than a visitor and stranger in her kin. The mother alone then became the fountain-head and the self-sufficing source of the family and, by implication, the personification of the principle of life.

When these more extreme forms of matrilocal marriage did not obtain, the husband and the sons would be occupied chiefly within the chase, the pursuit of game, warfare, or tending the flocks and herds, while the mother and her daughters attended to the domestic chores, and after the discovery and practice of agriculture (for which in all probability women were mainly responsible), hoeing and the cultivation of the crops on a small scale around the homestead. The fertility of the soil and that of women has been one of the salient features in agricultural society at all times, and it was not until sowing and reaping expanded, involving heavy manual labour, that it was transferred to the male section of the community. It was then that the plough acquired a phallic significance, being the instrument employed to break up the earth and make it fertile. But originally the soil was exclusively the domain of Mother Earth, and to disturb it was a perilous undertaking, usually demanding appeasement by a sacrificial oblation of some kind. Even when the ground was cleared and farmed by men the breaking of the soil and the planting was done by women, who as the child-bearers alone could enable the earth to bring forth abundantly. [pp. 228-230]

NOTE

1. E.O. James, *The Cult of the Mother-Goddess* (London : Thames and Hudson, 1959), pp. 228-230.

WHEN GOD WAS A WOMAN[1]

Merlin Stone

Few people who live in societies where Christianity, Judaism, or Islam are followed remain unaware of the tale of Eve heeding the word of the serpent in the Garden of Eden, eating the forbidden fruit and then tempting Adam to do the same. Generally, during the most impressionable years of childhood, we are taught that it was this act of eating the tasty fruit of the tree of knowledge of good and evil that caused the loss of Paradise, the expulsion of Adam and Eve, thus all humankind, from this first home of bliss and contentment. We are also made to understand that, as a result of this act, it was decreed by God that woman must submit to the dominance of man — who was at that time divinely presented with the right to rule over her — from that moment until now.

The expulsion of Adam and Eve from the Garden of Eden is not exactly the latest news, but few contemporary happenings have affected women of today any more directly. In the struggle to achieve equal status for women, in a society still permeated by the values and moralities of Judeo-Christian beliefs (which have penetrated deeply into even the most secular aspects of our contemporary civilization) we soon realize that a thorough examination of this creation legend, alongside its historical origins, provides us with vital information. It allows us to comprehend the role that contemporary religions have played in the initial and continual oppression and subjugation of women — and the reasons for this.

In prehistoric and early historic periods of human development, religions existed in which people revered their supreme creator as female. The Great Goddess — the Divine Ancestress — had been worshipped from the beginnings of the Neolithic periods of 7000 B.C. until the closing of the last Goddess temples, about A.D. 500. Some authorities would extend Goddess worship as far into the past as the Upper Paleolithic Age of about 25,000 B.C. Yet events of the Bible, which we are generally taught to think of as taking place "in the beginning of time," actually occurred in historic periods. Abraham, first prophet of the Hebrew Christian god Yahweh, more familiarly known as Jehovah, is believed by most Bible scholars to have lived no earlier than 1800 B.C. and possibly as late as 1550 B.C.

Most significant is the realization that for thousands of years both religions existed simultaneously — among closely neighbouring peoples. Archaeological, mythological, and historical evidence all reveal that the female religion, far from naturally fading away, was the victim of centuries of continual persecution and supression by the advocates of the newer religions which held male deities as supreme. And from these new religions came the creation myth of Adam and Eve and the tale of the loss of Paradise....[pp. xi-xiii]

We have seen that the orders for the destruction of the religion of the Goddess were built into the very canons and laws of the male religions that replaced it. It is clear that the ancient reverence for the female deity did not simply cease to be but that its disappearance was gradually brought about, initially by the Indo-European invaders, later by the Hebrews, eventually by the Christians, and even further by the Mohammedans. Along with the ultimate acceptance of the male religions throughout a large part of the world, the precepts of sexual "morality," that is, premarital virginity and marital fidelity for women, were incorporated into the attitudes and laws of the societies which embraced them.

There is no question about the antagonism expressed by the Levite patriarchs toward the religion of the female deity. Accounts, perhaps originally remembered in oral form, taken from other Hebrew scripts or even some other language, became part of the biblical texts which are assumed to have first been written as we know them in about 1000 B.C. From the time of Moses onward, the Levites appear to have made the decision to destroy the shrines and sanctuaries of the earlier worship. From that time on until the fall of the two Hebrew nations in 722 and 586 B.C., we read in the Bible of the actual massacres and desecrations, claimed to be executed at the command of the male deity. We cannot avoid observing the continual emphasis upon the female sexuality as acceptable only when women were safely designated as the property of one specific male and that any deviation from that rule was denounced as harlotry or adultery and subject to punishment by death, making the sexual customs of the older religion rather difficult to follow. . . .

Within the legend of the creation of all existence and life by Yahweh, the story which supposedly explained what happened at the very beginning of time, the image of woman as the dangerously seductive temptress, who brought about the fall of all humanity, may have been inserted. Knowing all that we do about the sacred sexual customs in the religion of the Goddess, the continual presence of these customs among the Hebrews even in Jerusalem, the use of dragon or serpent myths, often in conjunction with creation stories, by the Indo-Europeans and the vestiges of the Leviathan myth in the Old Testament, we may gain a most clarifying and enlightening insight into the symbolism and message contained in the biblical myth of Adam and Eve. [pp. 196-197]

NOTE

1. Merlin Stone, *When God Was a Woman* (New York : Harcourt Brace Jovanovich, 1978), pp. xi-xiii, 196-197.

SEX AND POWER IN HISTORY[1]

Amaury de Reincourt

> In the beginning the Great Mother created the heaven and the earth ... And the Great Mother said, let there be light : and there was light ... and the Great Mother divided the light from the darkness.

Had the biblical Genesis been written some tens of thousands of years ago, this would probably have been its rendering, since every evidence points to the fact that the male stood in awe of the female, as he did of all natural phenomena — storms, lightning, earthquakes, volcanic eruptions. Weak, relatively defenceless, and more or less isolated in small, scattered groups, yet increasingly capable of abstract thought, primitive man was afraid of nature's mysterious displays of grandiose power. In exactly the same way, he stood in awe of the mysteries of gestation and childbirth because they were natural manifestations of creative power. Social forces he understood, since he, as a hunting male, was the originator of social organizations and customs, but all natural phenomena were invested by him with magic significance — they were mysteries. Men's rites were social customs, but all rights of protective isolation, applicable to women were men's social attempts to cope with, and control, natural mysteries. The weird menstrual cycle, the flow of blood, the magical birth of new life made woman part of those forces of nature that he did not understand and feared, and the necessary intermediary, not only between man and man (via the incest taboo) but also between man and nature.... [p. 17]

In Bronze Age matriarchal symbolism, placid and optimistic, the motherly stress was on unification and conservation ; in the subsequent patriarchal era, the stern, fatherly stress would be on dissociation and change. The fundamental psychological reason is obvious : a girl gradually approaches her ultimate role of motherhood with rising sureness, thanks to identification with her mother. A "girl finds that the reinterpretation of impregnation and conception and birth fits easily into her early experience with the intake of food, while the boy with the same initial experience can at most use it to interpret the female role, but will find himself heavily confused if he attempts to use it to interpret his own."[2] For the boy, the process is reversed ; he must realize himself as different from his mother, must "turn out of himself" and find expression through the bodies of others. As Margaret Mead states it, a girl's femininity is "concealed deep within her, nothing that she can touch and see, depend upon, or flaunt .... The small boy struts, sometimes with emphasis on his penis, more often carrying hatchet, knife, stick, pole, in upward position as he marches, parries, performs. His behaviour, however symbolic, is to the extent that he is male a concentrated phallic exaggeration, while his sister's is more diffuse and involves the whole body. The little boy is sure about his specific maleness, but seems not to be so sure of his adequacy to operate it. He supplements with various symbolic objects."[3]

A further difference lies in the fact that a woman experiences sharp and dramatic cleavages in her life course, sharp transitions between defloration, pregnancy, childbirth, and menopause ; man's life course knows no such abrupt thresholds, its various stages shading imperceptibly into one another from childhood to old age. As a result, woman places greater emphasis on being, and man on doing, on proving that he is a man, that he is different. The female-motherly outlook, cyclical and rhythmic, dissolves all duality, including life and death, in a warm, consoling embrace ; nature and spirit are not divorced, immanence and mystical feeling prevail. Life and death are only two episodes in the essential being of Mother Earth — life merely implying a temporary detachment from the planet's womb, death a return home.

Keeping this view in mind makes it easier to understand what happened when, at the end of the Bronze Age, a monumental psychological shift took place and the prevailing female-oriented outlook disintegrated. In remote times, the mysterious menstrual cycle, pregnancy, and the birth of new life out of woman's body made a profound impression on the masculine mind, greatly enhanced by the fact that pregnancy and the sexual act were not understood to be connected. Apparently, man had no part in the creation of new life. It was female magic and the reincarnation of ancestral spirit that thrust new life into the woman's womb, not man's semen. Even in the advanced civilization of early Minoan Crete, where divinity was worshipped in the shape of sacred motherhood — the heavy-buttocked clay figures prefiguring the forthcoming Great Goddess were usually in a state of advanced pregnancy — the biological role of the father does not seem to have been fully understood.

Man was therefore father only in a legal and social sense. Men were related through mothers, not fathers : until very recently, for instance, among matrilineal Bantu tribes, kinship ties were based on the fact of being "born from the same womb" or "suckled at the same breast." All the father did was to legitimize, as it were, almost adopt his own children. And the fact that they thought that the fetus was merely a seed placed in woman's womb through contact between her and some animal or sacred object stripped man of all participation in the life-creating process. Since they believed that before birth their soul or spirit dwelt in caves, trees, wells, or rock crevices, before being ushered into woman's womb by some magic or other, they were far more closely related to, and yet fearful of nature than they have been ever since : "We might say in a sense that man was not yet born, that he did not yet realize that he belonged wholly to the biological species he represented. It might be better to consider that at this stage his life was in a pre-natal phase : a man still continued to share, directly, in a life that was not his own, in a 'cosmico-maternal' life."

This seems to have been a worldwide fact. In Athens, traditional lore had it that, before Cecrops (the mythical founder of the city), children were ignorant of their fathers. In early China, it was commonly believed that a woman could become pregnant from a dragon's saliva. Even in contemporary times, the Trobriand islanders' language had no word for "father" because the very concept did not exist. It was the missionaries who taught the incredulous islanders the facts of procreation, which they had believed, until then, to be attributable to the entrance of a ghost, *baloma,* into the womb, usually when the woman was bathing. New Zealand's Maoris claimed that "the moon is the real husband of all women." Some Australian tribes restrict the role of the husband to merely "opening the woman," while Hudson Bay's Eskimos believe that, although the child actually crawls into the womb, man's semen is required to "feed the child." Other Central Australian aborigines, the Arunta, Luritcha, and Ilpirra, understand the connection but claim that the child is not the direct result of coitus ; as far as they are concerned, sexual congress does not cause pregnancy but is merely a required preparation for the introduction of the child's spirit in the womb.

It seems quite probable that, under those circumstances, the woman did not suffer from any Freudian penis envy but that the men suffered from "uterus envy," a female-protest within men who were awed by the apparently exclusively female power of creation of new life. This is perhaps the origin of the widespread ritual known as *couvade*, which was highly popular in many parts of the world, from France to China, and was mentioned in Roman times by Diodorus and Strabo. The ritual still survives among some South American Indian tribes : either before or at the birth of a child, the father takes to his bed or hammock for days or weeks and receives the kind of care usually reserved for women in an advanced stage of pregnancy. This ancient tradition was probably inspired by such uterus envy, as well as by a desire to affirm, however artificially, the existence of a bond between father and child which nature alone did not seem to establish. Those were times when woman's main desire was not marital bliss but fertility and procreation.

One modern psychologist, Karen Horney, even asserts that this male envy of female procreativity has served, and still serves, "as one, if not as the essential, driving force in the setting up of cultural values." And she adds :

> Is not the tremendous strength in men of the impulse to creative work in every field precisely due to the feeling of playing a relatively small part in the creation of new living beings, which constantly impels them to an over-compensation in achievement ?[4]

Undoubtedly. And even more so when, in ancient times, they believed that they played no part at all. And this in turn explains why cultural production and symbol making became an almost exclusively male function. In the remote days when the Great Mother ruled supreme, there was little cultural outlet for the humbled male. It is only when phallic symbolism appeared that it became evident that a profound psychological shift was taking place and that a culturally induced "penis envy" began to haunt female psychology.

In the early stages of Minoan art, divinity was thought of so exclusively in terms of motherhood that the typically divine couple was mother and son — Mother Earth giving birth without need of a male assistant. The slender, youthful boy-god depicted so often in earlier Minoan art represents the annual birth, growth, and decay of vegetation, the typically cyclical conception of a gardening culture. In the early stages, Cretan art portrays the boy-god seated on his mother's lap, then growing up toward puberty. And then, in the Late Minoan Age, the boy-god "seems to have lost prominence before the slow advance of procreative ideas"[5] — probably the very beginning of an understanding of the crucial role played by the sexual act in the procreating process. The boy-god is replaced by a full-fledged consort ; the Great Mother acquires a spouse — first step on her way to ultimate dethronement. Some similar shift took place in Sumer ; from being the supreme deity, ranking before Enki in the god-lists, the goddess Minhursag slowly declined in prestige and influence before the air god, Enlil — originally her son.

There appears, therefore, to be a close connection between the disintegration of the female-oriented outlook and increasing knowledge of man's biological role in the procreating process. In order to understand the psychological nature of this dawning awareness, it is essential to remember that early man did not think in logical terms as we do ; causality was unknown to him. Even when some connection between sex and procreation was finally established, this connection was not, at first, a causal one. Prelogical thinking is not exclusively focused on practical aims ; its main goal is to satisfy intellectual requirements. Primitive man, then and now can no more live in mental chaos than we can ; an intellectual frame of reference is required at all times. The greatest curse, that which induces insanity and has destroyed many primitive cultures under the impact of an alien civilization, is mental disorder, the inability to classify things and ideas, and connect them, and thus introduce some order in man's mental picture of the universe. Any form of classification is preferable to chaos, even classifying at the level of mere appearances is a step in the direction of rational order.... [pp. 28-32]

It seems clear, therefore, that the gradual awareness of man's biological role in determining pregnancy, understood in terms of rough causality, implies that sometime between the fifth and third or second millenia B.C. (depending on the culture and the geographic location), man crossed a mental threshold from magico-symbolic thought processes to rational thinking : the same fact (connection between coitus and pregnancy) that had been observed for some time was now understood quite differently in causal, and no longer magical, terms. It gradually dawned on Late Bronze Age man that this connection was not only essential but was also the only one that created new life. To give an instance of the conclusions reached by relatively primitive cultures when that mental threshold was reached, we have the widely prevalent view among the Lepchas of Sikkim (but also known to the Turks, Mongols, ancient Chinese, and Indians since the distant days of the Mahabharata) that the bones and brain come from the father's semen and the flesh and blood from the mother's vaginal secretions — hence the necessity of the prohibition of incest, in the light of this new knowledge, failing which it is presumed that bones become brittle and the offspring sickly.

Crossing this threshold must have also implied that man began to realize that he belonged to his own specific biological species. His relationship with the whole of nature was changing under the spur of the Neolithic revolution and its technical discoveries. Man left the "cosmico-maternal" life that had been his for hundreds of thousands of years. One of the most significant symbols of this metamorphosis in mental outlook was a complete change in burial customs, the beginning of cremation, of the swift and utter destruction of the physical body which appeared in Neolithic times among the Aryan tribes. This signified a typically male urge to escape from the timeless bondage to the earth, an attempt to get away from Mother Earth's eternal clutches so that the soul could soar toward the wide-open spaces of the firmament rather than descend into her bowels. Instant destruction of the body freed the imprisoned soul whereas customary burial left it attached to a slowly rotting body of flesh and bones, haunting the earth as an unhappy ghost, chained to a decomposing corpse being slowly reabsorbed into the muddy bosom of Mother Earth. Cremation was a male revolt, a decisive symbol of masculine emancipation from thraldom to the Great Mother — the opposite of the earthbound outlook of female-oriented cultures in which the corpses were carefully buried in fetal position as if returning to the womb.

When man became fully aware, in a rational sense, of his biological role in the process of creating new life, he must have completely reevaluated the importance of his part in conjugal life and come to the conclusion that, through this knowledge, he was, in fact, in full control of the fate of woman. By now, male agriculture had replaced female horticulture, enhancing the male's economic importance. Just as the farmer plowing the Earth Mother's soil sows his seed purposefully, knowing that a plant will grow out of it, so does the male penetrate the female and discharge his semen (from the Latin "to sow") in the full knowledge that an offspring will grow out of it. The identification of the plow with the phallus and of semen with seed became widespread in all agricultural communities, that is, quasi-universal. While the Indian *Videvadat* compares fallow land to a barren woman, in many Eastern and Western tales the woman who cannot beget children cries that she is like a field on which nothing grows. The great Syrian god Ba'al was termed "the spouse of the fields" and the Qur'an of Muhammad states that "your women are unto you as fields." The Indians Laws of Manu bluntly declared that "the woman is the field and the male is the bestower of the seed." By and large, woman was identified with a furrow and the phallus with spade and plow — which came into being as "anthropo-telluric" concepts only when the true nature of conception was understood. The Hindus compared the vulva *(yoni)* with the furrow, the spade or plow and the male organ *(lingam),* with the semen virile. When the Hindu god Indra marries Urvara, her meaning is "fertile land" — symbol standing for the invasion and undertaking over a foreign country, implying the marriage between the invading kind and the plowed land.

It is in the amazing metamorphosis of the old matriarchal mythologies that the depth and importance of this profound psychological revolution can be best understood. All the mythologies were taken over and stood on their head ; all the female-oriented myths were reinterpreted patriarchally. What had been good became bad, former heroes became demons, and the remarkable coincidence was that this metamorphosis happened more or less simultaneously, over a period of time, in the Indo-European and Semitic worlds, in Greece as in India, and in China as well as in Palestine and Mesopotamia. It is to this exceptional conjunction of a changing male outlook in the ancient agricultural societies and an irresistible tidal wave of nomadic patriarchal invaders that history owes this global revolution.... [pp. 33-35]

It is easy to recapitulate the metamorphosis of the concepts of cosmic creation — from the universe born of a goddess without a spouse, to that born of a Great Goddess in need of a male consort, and through the concept of the universe formed out of the earth body of the slain goddess by a male deity (the Babylonian concept), to the ultimate downfall of the goddess in the biblical account. In conjunction with the gradual fade-out of the female principle and the rise of the male principle to mythological supremacy, another striking development takes place : the increasing strength of the male *per se,* in that the son becomes invariably more powerful than the father. The begotten one overcomes the begetter, implying the birth of the masculine notion of progress : Enlil, the air god, become stronger than his father, An, god of heaven ; later, Marduk, the great god of the Semitic Babylonians, becomes mightier than his father, Enki.

Finally, in the biblical account, the universe is created by the male godhead alone, unassisted by a female deity ; even matter, the earth, was created by God since, as John tells us in his Gospel, "In the beginning was the Word." It is, perhaps, by studying the remote origins of the "Word" as creative power that one can see the gradual emergence of the supremacy of man's autonomous mental power over that of the female's physiological, material creativity. As far back as one can see, it appears to have started with the Sumerian expression for "word," *enem,* the voice of Enlil, "Lord of the Storm," among other things. However, the same pictogram is also used for *gu,* "voice" or "thunder." In later Canaanite mythology, this assimiliation is amplified : the storm god, Ba'al or *Haddu (Hadad),* creates the thunderbolt, *baraqu,* so that his subjects may hear his commands. The Semites translated the Sumerian *enem* by *awatu,* and it is at this juncture, it seems, that a decisive shift of concept took place. The vague notion of "Creative Word" acquired added precision when associated with thunder. The "Sumerian" *enem* is therefore the most likely root of the Greek *logos,* although the same concept began to appear more or less simultaneously in Egypt, as stated in the Memphite text : "Ptah the Great is the heart and tongue of the gods" — heart meaning "mind" and tongue the "spoken word." The creator god Ptah "pronounced the names of all things" and thus created them *ex nihilo :* from now on, cosmic creativity belongs to the mind rather than the womb. Eventually, the Stoic philosophers of the Hellenistic Age went one step further and conceived "creative reason," *logos spermatikos,* as the origin of the supreme divine element. From now on, the power of original creation was assigned to man's natural ability for *seminal thought.*

In Freudian terms, this revolutionary "transference upward," this sublimation, was to be symbolically represented in Greek mythology by the birth of Athene from the forehead of Zeus ; and, henceforth, sexuality and spirituality were to be sharply opposed as irreconcilable enemies.

What happened in the Semitic Middle East found its echo in Greece during the transition from Minoan-Mycenaean culture to post-Homeric times. In Minoan Crete, as in the entire Aegean world, the pre-Homeric outlook on life was essentially female-oriented, a peaceful acceptance of the entire cosmic process, an organic, unheroic view of human destiny that was in stark contrast with the dramatic Homeric vision to come. The iron-bearing Dorian invaders, patriarchal to the core, despised this world outlook and consigned it to the netherworld. In classical Greece, as in Hebrew Palestine, the reversal was total ; in Greece, as in Palestine, all the old elements were taken over and turned upside down. In the new patriarchal myths, all that was good belonged to the new heroic male gods, shifting the Great Mother Goddess's natural powers to the murky underworld of Tartarus — Mother Earth's now-despised bowels. Needless to add, even the social position of women began to suffer in this new mythological environment.

It is easy to follow, in the dreamlike sequence of the Homeric myths, the overthrow of the old order by the shining knights of the new patriarchal one : the victory of Zeus over Typhon, youngest son of Gaea (Mother Earth), and the crushing defeat of the Titans, her sons, defeat which secured sovereign rule for the new gods on Olympus while the defeated Typhon was hurled into Tartarus — from where he revenged himself and his mother by stirring up dreadful storms, volcanic eruptions, and earthquakes. And so it was, too, in Vedic India after the Aryan invasions when Indra, the Indian counterpart of Zeus, triumphed over the cosmic serpent, Vritra.

From then on, in Greece, as in Palestine, as in India, in the throes of barbaric invaders who patriarchally upheld the warlike value of the male individual and the unique worth of the autonomous personality, the old female-oriented order disappeared or went underground ; in the dark mystery cults of classical Greece, we can find all the distorted remains of the old outlook. But from now on, the prevailing outlook focused on the principles of free will and moral responsibility of the individual : the revolution was directed against the worship of the Earth and its natural fertility. Man's attention in Greece focused on himself (leaving woman to her closer affinity with nature), or on his relationship with the godhead in Palestine. But there was a difference : while the biblical outlook expelled all traces of feminine influence, and through its onesided, uncompromising monotheism, all references to earlier worships, classical Greece proved more tolerant. In the mysteries of Demeter and the Orphics, the earlier, pre-Homeric deities survived and retained part of their former influence. Greek religion became a blend of the emotional, mystical temper of the pre-Hellenic population and the more sober, intellectual faiths of the Indo-European patriarchs who had invaded the land. Indeed, the Olympic gods married the female deities of the land, rather than annihilating them in biblical fashion — although even in Palestine,the Great Mother retained some of her hidden power for a long time, to the great displeasure of the prophets. And in the rest of the Middle East she survived quite successfully into the Christian era as Isis, Ishtar, Cybele, Diana, Venus-Aphrodite, and many other incarnations. But henceforth it is the patriarchal, transcendental God that rules supreme and makes history, relegating the immanent goddesses and female immanentism to the dark underground of the unconscious and subterranean caves of the earth.

In the new patriarchal *Weltanschauung*, the female principle has been systematically degraded, as if in revenge for its former redominance. Nothing illustrates this better than the mythology surrounding the epic Trojan War ; in the Judgment of Paris, the feminine is debased in an atmosphere of beauty contest, cheating, and bribery, which has left its stamp on the Western conception of true femininity — a concept to which Western women ever since have tried to live up, in spite of temporary revolts.

The downfall of the Great Mother some three to four thousand years ago was a psychological event of the first magnitude. It took place in the collective unconscious of these early cultures and shaped the relationship of the sexes of the species in such a way as to assure the complete predominance, not always or necessarily of men, but of the masculine principle — in the West far more than in the East. Even more than the great invasions of the iron-wielding warrior tribes, it was the crossing of this mental threshold that set the stage for the beginning of history proper — some four thousand years of turbulent rise and fall of civilizations, of wars and revolutions, of strife and anguish and catocylsmic progress.... [pp. 38-41]

The emancipation of human thought from the "feminine" mode of understanding was an exceedingly slow process. It required, at the outset, a true mental revolution within the context of the mythologies in which the traditional wisdom of the various cultures was expressed. In this mythopoeic view of the world, a gradual shift had to occur — and it did take place — which dethroned the female principle in favour of the male. After this, and then only, did it become possible for the masculine mode to come to the fore and begin the steady progression that was to lead to an entirely different *Weltanschauung.* The first step was the emergence of reflective thought, *reflection,* the ability of an individual consciousness to turn around and look upon itself as an *object,* no longer simply to know but to become conscious of the fact of knowing, to think that one is thinking ; this involves detachment from external circumstances and emotional participation. This triumph of Greek speculative philosophy consisted of focusing on the *ob- jectum* as something alien projected against the thoughtful subject, that is, its opposite. What surrounds the subject becomes an objective environment, independent from it.

From an I-thou relationship based on the fact that "thou" is always unique, unclassifiable, and unpredictable, and has to be experienced intuitively in a reciprocal relationship, the human mind progressed slowly to a "subject-object" form of understanding based on the fact that, stripped of the "thou" personalism, the objectified "it" can be scientifically related to other objects, become part of a series, and be amenable to universal, impersonal laws — again, an essentially masculine approach. Man questions the external world, no longer in terms of "who" but of "what."

True myth, the expression of the collective dream world of a given culture, is not mere childish fantasy but is endowed with the compelling authority that always springs from the unconscious. In this outlook, or psychological disposition, the contrast between reality and appearance becomes meaningless ; whatever moves feelings, will, mind is automatically considered real and has to be dealt with as such — in which case, dreams are at least as real as impressions received in the waking state. From the spontaneous symbolism of the dream world springs the religious and artistic symbolism expressed in mythological thought. It is in mythology, first of all, that the momentous patriarchal revolution took place, long before it began to become visible in historical events — in the deep, dark unconscious of Bronze Age men : "Myth is a form of poetry which transcends poetry in that it proclaims a truth ; a form of reasoning which transcends reasoning in that it wants to bring about the truth it proclaims ; a form of action, of ritual behaviour, which does not find its fulfilment in the act but must proclaim and elaborate a poetic form of truth...."[6] [pp.70-71]

The great patriarchal revolution at the dawn of the Iron Age set the stage for the rise of the higher cultures, and for what Karl Jaspers calls the "Axial Period." This was the era that started with Zoroaster and the Magians of Persia, a relatively short era during which the most momentous events that started history proper on its course were concentrated — the age of Confucius, Lao-tzu, and the great Chinese schools of philosophy ; the age of *Upanisads* and the Buddha in India ; of Socrates, Plato, and Periclean Athens ; of the great Hebrew prophets in Palestine, Elijah, Isaiah, and Jeremiah — all between 800 and 200 B.C., "the most deepcut dividing line in history."

In this new patriarchal age, mythology, the mythology that had prevailed in the old days of the Great Mother's pre-eminence, was put to flight by a new, masculine, unmythical thought process, relying increasingly on rationalism and logic : it was *logos* against *mythos,* male abstract thought against female concrete feeling, conscious thinking instead of unconscious myth making. Religion became ethical ; myths were reshaped into parables ; and uncertainty, spiritual questing took the place of the quiet, passive acceptance of nature and destiny. In Jasper's words, "the calm of polarities becomes the disquiet of opposites and antinomies."[7] It was the first stage of *philosophy*, of speculative thought. The overthrow of the female-centred outlook allowed mankind as a whole to take a giant step forward : tension replaced repetitive rhythm. Everything was now in flux : the first "universal empires" and male-oriented cultures appeared, along with the new historical consciousness, and catastrophic and eschatological views of life and death, original sin, heaven and hell, final judgment. From now on, all was guilt, effort, struggle, danger, violence — but also thirst for individual freedom, quest for personal development, enlightenment, and spiritual salvation. Power of creation was mythically transferred from the womb (the lotus goddess, Padma, in India) to the navel (Vishnu's) or to the brain (Athene springing from Zeus's head). Hence the creative power of the "word," *logos* or its Indian equivalent, *manasa putra* ("mind-born child" according to the Puranas) ; the transfer was quite a natural one, the mouth being assimilated to the vagina and the "word" to the newborn child. In all patriarchal myths, whenever they survived the onslaught of the discursive thought, the significance and function of the female were systematically downgraded in a cosmological and symbolic sense. But this revolution was also a major breakthrough, the birth of a new man endowed with Promethean drive to master the forces of nature and dominate the earth.

Detached and psychologically free of the powers of nature in whose psychological clutches he left woman, man at last became conscious of consciousness, able to reflect on himself and, simultaneously, to ask radical questions concerning his destiny. Set loose from the mythical age with its calm and gentle stagnation, he set out on an anxiety-filled journey of exploration and armed with the essential tools of masculinity : philosophic thought in Greece, cosmological thought in Iran, driving willpower among the Hebrews. Even in India and China, philosophers were basically unmythical in their creative intellectual power although tolerant of surviving mythologies. Men began to rely on themselves in an individual sense as free, autonomous personalities : "Man proved himself capable of contrasting himself inwardly with the entire universe."[8] The sharp opposition between *subject* and *object* finally dawned on him, along with a newborn mystical urge to overcome this sharp opposition which his increasingly acute mind has been able to perceive for the first time since mankind came into existence. In fact, as Jaspers points out, "this overall modification of humanity may be termed spiritualization."[9]

Inasmuch as Persian culture had a profound impact on Judaism after Cyrus freed the Jews from their captivity in Babylon, the Zoroastrian creed must be viewed as probably the first one to have achieved the decisive spiritual breakthrough — the overthrow of the cyclical fertility cults tied to the rhythm of seasonal change and female physiological laws. For the first time, a purely "masculine" concept of the unidirectional flow of time achieved a breakthrough by dramatically emancipating itself from the tight grip of the lunar-vegetal cycle and setting up the flow of time, history as the great battlefield between good and evil. In Greece and China, historical happenings were still viewed as cyclical and without metaphysical meaning ; in India, historical insight was altogether smothered in much vaster cosmological schemes, equally based on endless cyclical repetition of *yugas* and astronomical *mahayugas* — all of them unconscious metaphysical extensions of fertility concepts based on the rhythmic alternation of seasons and crops.

Now, for the first time, history is viewed as a linear progression with a beginning, a middle — the present — and an end, and therefore with profound, metaphysical significance. The distinction between past, present, and future, hitherto blurred by endless cyclical repetitions, is now sharply perceived. Emancipated from nature's grip, from the primeval "once upon a time," man begins to see history as a linear development of unique and unrepeatable events, all endowed with moral significance. . . . [pp. 79-81]

Originally, all Semites were organized in matrilinear clans ; the mother's, and not the father's, bloodline determined kinship. Goddesses rather than gods were worshipped as prime deities. But at some point in history a massive transfer altered the sex of most deities from female to male ; the rule of kinship also changed from matrilinear to patrilinear.

In the earlier days of female kinship and widespread polyandry, the Great Mother was supreme ; under one guise or another, she survived for a long time in the patriarchal era. The Carthaginians worshipped a Great Mother identified with Tanith-Artemis — the "heavenly Virgin" which Augustine, much later, reidentified with the unmarried mother of the gods in *De Civitate Dei.* The Arabian goddess al-Lat was worshipped by the Nabateans at Petra, as described by Epiphanius :

> Divine motherhood, like the kinship of men and gods in general, was to the heathen Semites a physical fact, and the development of the corresponding cults and myths laid more stress on the physical than the ethical side of maternity, and gave a prominence to sexual ideas which was never edifying, and often repulsive.[10]

The change in kinship laws transferred authority from uncle to father, from brother to husband. Women fell under the authority of their new lord and master from another family ; their children became members of his kinship group not of theirs. And along with this social metamorphosis in sexual relations went the theological metamorphosis already alluded to in Canaan and elsewhere, Ishtar reappeared as Astarte (Ashtoreth to the Hebrews), but now only as a subservient consort to the supreme, all powerful, masculine Ba'al. Whenever the identity of the goddess was too well established to be altogether discarded or associated with a new male deity, she changed her sex, as in southern Arabia where Ishtar was transmuted into the masculine 'Athtar. Whatever emotionalism there was in Semitic paganism always focused on the worship of goddesses, both in the sexual and the motherhood aspects. The male deity appealed rather to more austere and rigidly ethical feelings — and it was among the Hebrews, latter-day beneficiaries of this vast upheaval in the Semitic world, that this ethical aspect of religion received its most uncompromising formulation.

The struggle toward monotheism among the Hebrews implied far more than the mere elimination of polytheism ; it suggested intense concentration on morality and, as a consequence, on a degradation of the feminine element that found its natural counterpart in woman's low status in ancient Israel. A wife called her husband *ba'al* (master) or *'adon* (lord), addressing him as a slave addresses his master ; the Decalogue ranks a wife among her husband's possession. While he could repudiate her, she could not ask for divorce and remained legally a minor through life. Wives and daughters did not inherit, except in the absence of male heirs.

From all this, it should not be gathered that women were without protection or influence ; again, as in Persia, they were well protected by law and tradition in their capacity as generators of new life. As is still the case under rabbinic law, children's Jewishness was determined by the mother's bloodline, not the father's. Women performed most of the hard work at home, but in times of national stress they often took part in public life — heroines such as Deborah and Jael, rulers like Athaliah in Judah, prophetesses after the pattern of Huldah who was consulted by the king's ministers, national saviours in the mould of Judith and Esther. The wife won increasing respect when she became a mother, especially of male children :

> The social and legal position of an Israelite wife was, however, inferior to the position a wife occupied in the great countries round about. In Egypt the wife was often the head of the family, with all the rights such a position entailed. In Babylon she could acquire property, take legal action, be a party to contracts, and she even had a certain share of her husband's estate.[11]

In fact, only among Jewish colonies in foreign lands, such as Elephantine in Egypt, was the social position of women improved. [pp. 86-87]

NOTES

1. Amaury de Reincourt, *Sex and Power in History* (New York : David McKay Company, 1974), pp. 17-87.
2. Margaret Mead, *Male and Female* (London : 1950), pp. 143-144.
3. *Ibid*, p. 86.
4. C.C. Zimmerman and and S.J. Cervantes, *Marriage and the Family* (Chicago : 1956), p. 400.
5. A.C. Vaughan, *The House of the Double Axe* (New York : 1959), p. 198.
6. H. Frankfort, *Before Philosophy* (Baltimore : Penguin Edition, 1954), p. 16.
7. K. Jaspers, *The Origin and Goal of History* (London : 1958), p. 3.
8. *Ibid.*
9. *Ibid.*
10. W.R. Smith, *The Religion of the Semites* (New York : 1959), pp. 156-158.
11. R. de Vaux, *Ancient Israel* (New York : 1961), p. 40.

WOMAN, SOCIETY, AND CHANGE [1]

Evelyne Sullerot

Three main traditions have held sway in Europe and have eventually merged : the Greco-Latin system, the Judaic, and the Scandinavian-German patterns. The latter prevailed in the north and the west of Europe before and during the Roman conquest, and spread during Rome's decline. It was Christianity which modified and unified these three social systems. On the other hand, the Confucian, Hindu and later the Islamic traditions held sway over the East with hardly any contact with the West until the nineteenth century. This extremely simplified picture should not lead us to forget that none of these patterns remained stable over time. For example, considerable change in family life occurred between Peloponnesian Greece and pre-Christian Rome. It would be too much of a generalization to state that the position of women improves with the development of civilizations ; sometimes the opposite appears to be the case. As a rule it is in the early periods of each civilization that the least difference exists between the position of men and that of women. As a civilization asserts and refines itself, the gap between the relative status of men and women widens ....

While Prometheus had to steal fire from the gods to make himself their equal, woman — who alone can give life — had no need of the Promethean fire. But did her fecundity give her power, did it confer on her a supremacy in ancient societies ? Did a true matriarchy really precede patriarchy as a system of family organization ? Many have been the theories about the primitive matriarchy, many are the traces left behind by matrilineal societies in Africa, Melanesia, and South America, and many also have been the myths and legends, at times corroborated by archaeological discoveries, of the rule of women in ancient civilizations. It is uncertain whether these legends describe reality or whether they have merely become exaggerated and distorted in the process of telling. It is difficult to interpret the legend of the Amazons, or that of the Chinese Kingdom known as "the Country of Women" (where a queen and a minor queen ruled) or finally the Czech legend of the Kingdom of Vlasta, the woman who repelled Charles Martel, founded Drewin, the City of Women, and governed Bohemia until it was forcibly recaptured by men. Such stories of female rule are always relegated to the distant past and one may wonder whether they are not used to counterbalance the pattern of patriarchy. However, it is unclear if these legends have been invented after the event to provide a parallel to what exists now and thus to satisfy the tendency of the human mind to think in binary terms, by imagining an opposing reign succeeding another. In any case the link which would explain how the rule of men succeeded that of women has always been missing.

Historically the strictest partriarchal pattern has dominated the Greco-Roman, Semitic, Indian, Chinese, and Japenese civilizations. In this system, the reproductive function of women has appeared at he same time both as their justification in the world and the reason for their subordination. From this follow all the other features of woman's position and it is interesting to see which elements of this chain, when modified, bring about a change in the whole structure. But while answering this question, an assesment should be made of what remains of this legacy of the past.

Fertility and Adultery

Before all else, the wife was considered as a breeding machine to perpetuate the male line of the husband, the tribe, and the race. Therefore the punishments for female adultery were extremely severe, as by this act the wife asserted her individuality, her free will, her right to choose. Such an assertion was seen as a threat to the whole male-centred structure. In Judaic society the adulterous wife was stoned ; in Greek society, if she was not put to death she became infamous and was forced to dress in a way which would enable others to recognize her transgression ; in China and Vietnam she passed through the Seven Hells. Despite these variations, the husband everywhere had the power of life or death over his adulterous wife. The severity of this condemnation did not arise so much from emotional jealousy as from the fact that the preservation of the system required the wife to fulfil her reproductive role in accordance with strict rules. If she were to assert her individuality by committing adultery, she would destroy the fabric of the system, and the family name, property, titles, power, nationality and other prerogatives would no longer be transmitted by the male line.

Love as a sentiment is so lacking in this system that the wife was bequeathed or lent in order to perpetuate the race. Thus in Greece, Israel, and India, the widow was part of the husband's estate and was left to his eldest male relative like a chattel. The barren wife was sometimes approached by the brother of her husband, with his consent, so that the future of the line could be guaranteed. The rules of repudiation were related to this overriding goal. Thus, according to the Manu Code of India, if a wife had no children, she could be banished after eight years ; if all her children were dead, she could be dismissed after ten years ; if she had nothing but girls, she could be repudiated after the eleventh year. Modern science in fact shows that it is the odd chromosome in the male semen which determines the sex of the child, so that the mother does not influence it. Yet thousands of women have been repudiated for this reason, at the time when the patriarchal system was alleged to embody the natural order.

According to Mosaic law, the Israelite had the right to repudiate his infertile wife and to father children with his servant. The legitimate wife, if kept in the conjugal home, would help and aid the servant in her delivery. The story of Abraham and Sarah illustrates this practice. In Greece, the man — even though he had only one legitimate wife — could nevertheless surround himself by a swarm of slave mistresses and have children by them. In the East, the present practice of polygamy witnesses the same idea of the wife as a breeding machine placed at the service of the male, his group, family, tribe, and people. In the old Germanic tribes, the adulterous wife was also put to death or mutilated, and a widow, when she did not commit suicide on the death of her husband — a practice which also occurred in India — was given to her brother-in-law. This kind of ritual suicide did not reflect private grief or desperation, but expressed obedience to social constraints.

Thus the system might be monogamous or polygamous, but this made little difference to the overall patriarchal society.

Domestic Confinement

A direct consequence of the system described above was the desire to confine women in the home, to restrict their movements and to prevent them showing themselves outside. These customs have determined women's activities for centuries and may account for the presence of many acquired characteristics, now considered as innate. The wives were strictly confined to their quarters in Greece, whereas the courtesans, whose job was to give pleasure to man and not to produce his children, were free. Woman was confined indoors, turned into a recluse and often hidden, like the Chinese behind screens and the Moslem behind veils, while man alone had the freedom of the outside world. Socrates claimed that it was thus that the gods had decreed. But this territorial division quickly became a moral one — "the house is for the good woman, the street is for the wicked one," said Menander, repeating a popular cliche. Consequently activities within the house are feminine, those which take place outside — business, politics, war — are masculine. This polarity of inside-outside, interior-exterior, imperceptibly became a distinction between inferiority-superiority. Gradually activities conducted inside were considered inferior to those performed outside. Female tasks, just as necessary in life as those accomplished outside, soon became despised. The spatial division between the man and the woman is not an unavoidable consequence of their physiological differences, but only an important element of the patriarchal system whose legacy endures in our own civilization.

Property

A third and related characteristic of the system is that women were excluded from owning and disposing of property. The Manu Code of India specified that everything acquired either by the wife or the slave belonged to the husband or the master. In Greece the wife could never dispose of her property. She passed from the tutelage of her father to that of her husband, or of his male relative on widowhood, or finally of her own son if he was the only man left in the family. She could be given a dowry, but this would not become her property. Such was not the case in Sparta or in early Rome, where barbarian family customs still prevailed. But when Rome became prosperous a patriarchal system was enforced, and attempts were made to limit women's right of possession. The Oppian law, which sought to restrict women's ownership of clothing and jewellery, caused a female rebellion and had to be abrogated. Shortly afterwards Cato supported the adoption of a law forbidding women to inherit more than 100,000 sesterces. Again, the Jewish tradition excluded the daughter from her father's estate, unless he had no sons. In that case she had to marry a member of her own tribe and credit him with the money, land, or property that she had inherited. Moreover, the Jewess was not considered a legitimate wife but a concubine unless she brought property to the marriage, nor did she have any control over her portion.

Civic Rights

The fourth link in this chain was that women had no civic role. In Greece they had no more public rights than slaves, minors, or foreigners. Solon regulated even their right to travel. Within the city they could not even cross the streets unless they were in a carriage preceded by a torch-bearer. The only right they were granted was that of defending themselves in court or being witnesses in trials. Even this prerogative became more and more restricted and was finally withdrawn in Rome by Justinian. In the predominantly religious Jewish community, this deprivation of civic rights extended to the majority of religious observances, from which women were excluded. However, Greek and Roman women joined in many religious celebrations and had specific roles to play in the religious life of their community. Their creeds and mythologies were not uniformly hostile to women nor derogatory about the female character. On the other hand, Judaism, accusing woman of the original sin, reduced her to something impure and untrustworthy, responsible for the fall of man. Hence she is forbidden to touch the Book of Laws, excluded from religious learning in the temple and, in this respect, treated like a male slave. The temple ceremonies can only be celebrated by men and for men, since ten male witnesses must be present, regardless of the number of women. Giving birth to a son leaves the the wife impure for a week, giving birth to a daughter leaves her impure for two. The woman is sullied and she contaminates. "Blessed be Thou, O God, who did not make me a woman !" exclaims man.

Islam too makes use of this notion of impurity and uncleanliness to exclude women from the city and from religion, where they are nothing more than subdued onlookers. Oriental religions are even more emphatic in their denunciation of female uncleanliness. In China during the early historial period it was the custom for the family to take on mourning when a daughter was born. The girl was placed on the ground next to bricks and tiles, which represented "symbols of the abjection and the evils which were to accompany her throughout her life!" Pan Hoei Pan explains tiles were used because they were exposed to damage from above and bricks because they were meant to be crushed under foot. To kill a daughter was not classed as a crime and girl children were often left to die from exposure or were simply sold. Pan Hoei Pan wrote in *Seven Articles Intended for Women*, a book which appeared in the first century A.D. : "Never let us forget that we belong to the lowest form of human life. We must expect only contempt. There will never be disillusionment for a woman so long as she remembers that she will always be made to suffer by those with whom she lives." [pp. 19-28]

NOTE

1. Evelyne Sullerot, *Woman, Society, and Change* (New York : McGraw-Hill Book Co., World University Library, 1971), pp. 19-28.

SISTERHOOD IS POWERFUL[1]

Robin Morgan (Editor)

Know Your Enemy : A Sampling of Sexist Quotes

The glory of a man is knowledge, but the glory of a woman is to renounce knowledge.
— Chinese proverb

Do not trust a good woman, and keep away from a bad one.
— Portuguese proverb

Women are sisters nowhere.
— West African proverb

Whenever a woman dies there is one quarrel less on earth.
— German proverb

Never trust a woman, even though she has given you ten sons.
— Chinese proverb

In childhood a woman must be subject to her father ; in youth, to her husband ; when her husband is dead, to her sons. A woman must never be free of subjugation.
— The Hindu Code of Manu, V

I thank thee, O Lord, that thou hast not created me a woman.
— Daily Orthodox Jewish Prayer (for a male)

There is a good principle which created order, light, and man, and an evil principle which created chaos, darkness, and woman.
— Pythagoras

We may thus conclude that it is a general law that there should be naturally ruling elements and elements naturally ruled . . . the rule of the freeman over the slave is one kind of rule ; that of the male over the female another . . . the slave is entirely without the faculty of deliberation ; the female indeed possesses it, but in a form which remains inconclusive . . . .
— Aristotle (*Politics*)

If thy wife does not obey thee at a signal and a glance, separate from her.
— Sirach, 25:26

When a woman thinks . . . she thinks evil.
— Seneca

Creator of the heavens and the earth. He has given you wives from among yourselves to multiply you, and cattle male and female. Nothing can be compared with Him.
— *Holy Koran of Islam*

And the rib, which the Lord God had taken from man, made he a woman and brought her unto the man. And Adam said, "This is now bone of my bone, and flesh of my flesh, she shall be called Woman, because she was taken out of man."
— *Genesis*, 2:22-23

How can he be clean that is born of a woman ?
— *Job*, 4:4

Suffer women once to arrive at an equality with you, and they will from that moment become your superiors.
— Cato the Elder, 195 B.C.

Let the women learn in silence with all subjection . . . I suffer not a woman to usurp authority over men, but to be in silence.
— St. Paul

Wives, submit yourselves unto your husbands . . . for the husband is the head of the wife, even as Christ is the head of the church.
— *Ephesians*, 5:23-24

The first worst infirmities that afflict the female are indocility, slander, jealousy, and silliness . . . . Such is the stupidity of woman's character, that it is incumbent upon her, in every particular, to distrust herself and to obey her husband.
— *Confucian Marriage Manual*

God created Adam lord of all living creatures, but Eve spoiled it all.
— Martin Luther

All witchcraft comes from carnal lust, which is in women insatiable.
— Kramer and Sprenger, Inquisitors (*Malleus Maleficarum*, c. 1486)

A man in general is better pleased when he has a good dinner than when his wife talks Greek.
— Samuel Johnson

The whole education of women ought to be relative to men. To please them, to be useful to them, to make themselves loved and honoured by them, to educate them when young, to care for them when grown, to counsel them, to console them, and to make life sweet and agreeable to them — these are the duties of women at all times and what should be taught them from their infancy.
— Jean Jacques Rousseau

Women have no moral sense ; they rely for their behaviour upon the men they love.
— La Bruyere

Most women have no characters at all.
— Alexander Pope

I never knew a tolerable woman to be fond of her own sex.
— Jonathan Swift

Man for the field and woman for the hearth : Man for the sword and for the needle she : Man with the head and woman with the heart : Man to command and woman to obey ; All else confusion.
— Alfred Lord Tennyson

Men are men, but Man is a woman.
— G.K. Chesterton

Nature intended women to be our slaves . . . they are our property ; we are not theirs. They belong to us, just as a tree that bears fruit belongs to a gardener. What a mad idea to demand equality for women ! . . . Women are nothing but machines for producing children.
— Napoleon Bonaparte

To men a man is but a mind. Who cares what face he carries or what he wears ? But woman's body *is* the woman.
— Ambrose Bierce

Regard the society of women as a necessary unpleasantness of social life, and avoid it as much as possible.
— Count Leo Tolstoy

A woman who is guided by the head and not the heart is a social pestilence : she has all the defects of the passionate and affectionate woman, with none of her compensations ; she is without pity, without love, without virtue, without sex.
— Honore de Balzac

And a woman is only a woman, but a good cigar is a smoke.
— Rudyard Kipling

Women have great talent, but no genius, for they always remain subjective.
— Arthur Schopenhauer

One must have loved a woman of genius to comprehend the happiness of loving a fool.
— Talleyrand

If the feminine abilities were developed to the same degree as those of the male, her (woman's) maternal organs would suffer and we should have a repulsive and useless hybrid.
— P.J. Moebius (German scientist, 1907)

The greatest question that has never been answered, and which I have not yet been able to answer despite my thirty years of research into the feminine soul, is : What does the woman want ?
— Sigmund Freud

The woman's fundamental status is that of her husband's wife, the mother of his children.
— Talcott Parsons

Man's superiority will be shown, not in the fact that he has enslaved his wife, but that he has made her free.
— Eugene V. Debs

Women should receive a higher education, not in order to become doctors, lawyers, or professors, but to rear their offspring to be valuable human beings.
— Alexis Carrel, *Man, the Unknown*

Woman as a person enjoys a dignity equal with men, but she was given different tasks by God and by Nature which perfect and complete the work entrusted to men.
— Pope John XXIII

The only position for women in SNCC is prone.
— Stokeley Carmichael, 1966

It would be preposterously naive to suggest that a B.A. can be made as attractive to girls as a marriage license.
— Dr. Grayson Kirk (former President, Columbia University)

Women, in general, want to be loved for what they are and men for what they accomplish. The first for their looks and charm, the latter for their actions.
— Theodor Reik

My secretary is a lovable slave.
— Morris Ernst, attorney, on the fiftieth anniversary of his having hired Paula Gross, secretary

The only alliance I would make with the Women's Liberation Movement is in bed.
— Abbie Hoffman

Women are usually more patient in working at unexciting, repetitive tasks .... Women on the average have more passivity in the inborn core of their personality .... I believe women are designed in their deeper instincts to get more pleasure out of life — not only sexually but socially, occupationally, maternally — when they are not aggressive. To put it another way I think that when women are encouraged to be competitive too many of them become disagreeable.
— Dr. Benjamin M. Spock, *Decent and Indecent*

Women? I guess they ought to exercise Pussy Power.
— Eldridge Cleaver, 1968

AND

A woman's place is in the home/Housewives are such dull people/ Women's talk is all chatter/Intelligent women are emasculating/ If you're so smart why aren't you married/Can you type ?/If you want to make decisions in this family, go out and earn a paycheque yourself/Working women are unfeminine/A smart women never shows her brains/It is a woman's duty to make herself attractive/ All women think about are clothes/Women are always playing hard to get/No man likes an easy women/Women should be struck regularly like gongs/ Women like to be raped/Women are always crying about something/Women don't understand the value of a dollar/Women executives are castrating bitches/Don't worry your pretty little head about it/Dumb broad/It is glorious to be the mother of all mankind/A woman's work is never done/All you do is cook and clean and sit around all day/Women are only interested in trapping a man/ A woman who can't hold a man isn't much of a woman/Women hate to be with other women/Women are always chattering with each other/Some of my best friends are women. . . . [pp. 31-36]

NOTE

1. Robin Morgan, ed., *Sisterhood is Powerful* (New York : Random House, 1970), pp. 31-36.

2. Divine Law and Kingship

Voluntary compliance is a necessary condition for an effective and efficient social order. Compliance will be voluntary where people believe the social order to be good, right, or justified. The difference between the exercise of lawful authority and the wielding of naked power is legitimacy ; a social hierarchy of domination and obedience will be legitimate if those who obey consider obedience to be justified. The most common form of justification of the social order is that it reflects the natural order, which is assumed to be right or proper, nature being one of the oldest and most universal ethical norms.

The earliest world view was mythological in that creation and natural phenomena were generally explained in terms of the activities of the gods. Domination over the female in ancient cultures generally coincided with a shift in mythology which reflected a shift from a matriarchal to a patriarchal consciousness. The sky god or heavenly father replaced the great or earth mother as the dominant mythological persona. The authority of kings was rooted in the mythology of the gods. The king's right to rule was derived from his relationship to the sky god or ruling male in the hierarchy of the gods, either in terms of his genealogical descent from the god, or a belief that the king himself was a god incarnate. The legitimacy of monarchy is rooted in the mythological foundation of divine right.

Law usually received its legitimacy in terms of a mythological derivation from God or the gods, or a king of divine origin. Thus law was often justified on the grounds that it directly or indirectly reflected the will of God or the gods.

LORD OF THE FOUR QUARTERS : MYTHS OF THE ROYAL FATHER[1]

J. W. Perry

. . .In archaic times it was typical for a society to establish a powerful focal point where the world of myth met and entered the world of human community. This point served as a cosmological system's centre in which man reached divinity and divinity entered man. This central channel of interpenetration of worlds was personified in the figure of the sacral king. At first he was usually the sole intermediary between men and the gods, however much of this function might be delegated to his priestly representatives.

The king as the Royal Father was the acme of all father figures. In these days of prevalence of psychoanalytic thinking, we might be inclined to think of him as a surrogate father, created out of the reminiscences of the parents of individuals' childhood, and engendering the same emotions as those of early life. However, there is a larger sense of the term "father figure" than that which implies a re-creation of the father of one's youngest years. This Royal Father in history was not only shepherd of the people, but also centre of the realm, a functionary endowed with a magical or numinous potency concentrating in his person the properties of the masculine principle. This constellation of attributes involved emotions that reached far beyond the limits of childhood and family into the more awesome plane of spiritual and cosmic and timeless issues. The king was mediator of the life force itself, giving fertility and virility ; carrier of the power of authority, giving order and integrity ; and bearer of the aggressive might of the executive function, giving chastisement to disorder and encouragement to obedience. He thus embodied male qualities so intensely valued that they were experienced by the people as divine. [pp. 3-4]

Since the divine kingship was first pointed out by Sir J.G. Frazer,[2] many illuminating investigations of the theme of kingship have been carried forward by the proponents of the "myth and ritual" schools of England and of the Scandinavian countries. The opinion was first put forward by Robertson Smith at the end of the last century[3] that myth was the secondary, spoken part of ritual, and that the community rather than the individual was the essential unit in ceremonial life. Gronbech, with an admirable capacity for poetic insight, described at the start of this century[4] the Teutonic creation rite in such a way as to bring to life the myth in its relation to the ceremonial action, while Gunkel[5] placed the Royal Psalms in their organic setting in the royal cultus of Jerusalem. Following the impetus of these pioneers, the Scandinavian school has carried out explorations in many directions, with Mowinkel's[6] further analysis of the Royal Psalms, and with Engnell[7] and Widengren[8] probing the sacral kingships of other Near Eastern cultures, particularly to throw light on the meaning of the Israelite kingship and the Messianic ideology that derived out of it.

Some twenty years after the magnificent elucidation of Greek myth and ritual at the hands of Jane Harrison,[9] Gilbert Murray,[10] and Francis Cornford,[11] the English "myth and ritual" school got its start in the lectures which made a stir in the field in 1933, published under the title *Myth and Ritual in the Ancient Near East*,[12] and its sequel *The Labyrinth*.[13] These lectures had their inspiration from the vision of S.H. Hooke, who perceived a ritual pattern in the various cultures of that part of the world centering upon the kingship and its seasonal festivals. The further work of this movement has been reviewed more recently in a symposium entitled, *Myth, Ritual, and Kingship,*[14] and E.O. James has in the last few years brought out several volumes[15] integrating with succinct clarity the studies of these practices throughout the orbit of the Near East and the Mediterranean.

Against this view of a ritual pattern and its diffusion, the Chicago school has emphasized the distinctness and difference of the forms of kingship in the various cultures of the Near East ; from here came Thorkild Jacobsen's influential work[16] on early Mesopotamian concepts and Henri Frankfort's brilliant work, *Kingship and the Gods.*[17]

Two distinguished masters of the exposition of the myth and ritual of kingship remain to be mentioned. Theodor Gaster, whose Thespis[18] is a veritable mine of rich comparative material covering the texts of the Near East, and Marcel Granet, whose *Chinese Civilization*[19] is a work of intuitive artistry in illuminating the wealth of legends concerning the early origins of Chinese kingship.

I would say in comment upon the myth and ritual viewpoint only that it becomes somewhat superfluous to claim priority for either ritual or myth once it becomes apparent whence these phenomena arise. It had seemed in the last century that, as in the view of Tylor,[20] myth was the outcome of primitive man's attempt, with his untutored mind, to account for his universe, and that ritual was then the expression of this ; after Robertson Smith's[21] reversal of this order, it seemed that emotional ritual action, with the intent of preserving the integrity of the social group, was the basic source of communal action. Now that we are discovering that the psyche is the *fons et origo* of all such imagery and action, we may regard myth and ritual as coequal, simultaneous, and mutually interdependent expressions of the psychic propensities in spoken and in acted form. Only we must qualify such a summary statement with the recognition that times plays a part in the fate of this interrelation, for as the psyche develops and differentiates, the myth becomes increasingly a matter of acknowledged fantasy or at best beliefs that need not be attached to any ritual or social practice. . . . [pp. 5-7]

The age of genuineness and fullness of the archaic kingship was ... the "archaic era of incarnated myth." Its main characteristic was that the king embodied in himself the life-principle and the principle of order. Both principles belonged essentially to the cosmic dimension with which he was in a state of magical participation and oneness, notably a state of identity or of kinship with the gods of order and of life.

Usually this phase of the kingship lasted only a few centuries, by the end of which time there might be one of several outcomes. In many civilizations around the Mediterranean it led into a democratization of its functions, which amounted to a reassertion of the "primitive democracy" out of which the kingship had arisen in the first place (in which the head of the assembly had been voted into office) while only the priestly function of the former kingship survived with the attributes of royalty.

A different kind of eventuality was the distortion of the divinity of the kingship forcing it to serve other ends. When the naturalness of the presupposition that order and life depended upon the person of the king began to fall away, the divinity concept was turned to strategic advantage to bolster the prestige of ambitious monarchs. This late and decadent deification bore the marks of political opportunism and contrivance, even of frank megalomania at times, and certainly of artificiality in the claims to suprahuman powers. By this time it became a conceit in both senses of the word, both a notion snatched from tradition and a puffing up of the person of the ruler to yield him an aggrandizement intended to impress the world.

A third fate of the sacral kingship was perhaps the most common, that of being overrun and dominated by an alien people, which would sometimes be the occasion for a shift from a genuine and indigenous sacral kingship to the decadence of its borrowed form in the hands of the conquerors who applied it.

The era of genuineness of the sacral kingship is sometimes difficult to identify and to delimit, as I noted ; therefore I have gone entirely by an intuitive sense of the real and the archaic in it. This is particularly hazardous in the case of Iran, which established its renowned sacral kingship both late and in the form of customs borrowed from the Assyrian Empire which it subdued and emulated ; yet from Iran this practice of divine kingship was taken over by the Greek Alexander,and by Rome to the west and India to the east.

By the same token, the mythology of kingship as the counterpart of its ceremonial can be said to pass through the same stages. There was an early form at the time of the supremacy of the clan chiefs when the deity was the representation in myth of the ritual function of the priest-father. When, however, a culture reached its fullness and the sacral kingship its zenith of numinosity, then the myth also was possessed of an aesthetic unity and fullness of cosmic imagery. In the myth there was too the feeling of real events being related — real because they were still being enacted in the ritual and still giving rise to real eventualities in the world of society and of nature, renewals that were vital and indispensable to the welfare of the people and of all growing things. It was not long, however, before myths, like other aspects of the ceremonial of royalty, became secularized and were told as tales that might have value both for their literary form and for their entertaining function.

In either the ceremonial or the mythology of kingship, the most genuine and fruitful evolution was in the direction of its elevation to a spiritual and internal plane. The role of the spiritual kingship became in some cases a matter for the individual to achieve within himself, while that of its mythology was to expand and differentiate the imagery of the psychic world and to give expression to the values and meanings of its culture. . . .

To obtain a grasp of the function of the sacral kingship in its typical threefold form, with the king as head of the priesthood, the judiciary, and the military, we must take into account the broad philosophy of order and the life principle as part of its context. In the archaic era with which we are dealing, order was primarily a cosmological matter, a principle intrinsic to the heavens and to terrestrial nature and personified in the king in common with the king god. Since the life principle was something that had a source and the connection to it was in need of constant refreshment, the whole set of beliefs about the nature of life and death must be comprehended as part of the ideology of the kingship.

Where we can, we will take special note of a culture's formulation of the principle of order, such as the Egyptian Maat, or Rita or Dharma in India, or the Chinese Tao, for characteristically it connotes the regularity of the relationships of time and space and movement which holds the universe in its ordered ways and at the same time motivates man to be guided in his ethical life by right ways, that is, the ways of nature. The god of the sky was the very embodiment of right order and authority, and this frequently took the form of a Sun God whose regularity or rhythmic progress in running his daily and seasonal course was the epitome of right order. The codification of law belonged to the gradual process of differentiation of the functions of the kingship and their consequent secularization. Until then the king was the embodiment of right order itself; his very essence was at one with the cosmic source. His obligation as the earthly representative of such a divine power was to maintain a stringent regularity of life in his personal actions throughout the hours of the day and the months of the year — for what he did was identical with what happened in the world of nature, inasmuch as both were in a state of mutual *participation mystique* (Levy-Bruhl's term).[22] In the period of archaic genuineness of incarnated myth, then, the king upheld justice by living it, and only secondarily did he enforce it.

The other kind of rulership proper, the enforcement of justice by armed might, found its representation in the heavens in a mythological personage other than the Sky God, or at least in a different aspect of him. This was typically the Storm God, who wielded the thunderbolt with might, whose anger made his opponents quake with fear, but who in his more beneficent mien was the sender of rain and fertility. He was by the same token the War God, in the sense that he was the mythological model of the kingly function of wielding executive power, defending the right and chastising the wrong, and enforcing the law inherent in the god of the high heaven. Policing and military expeditions had the same basic significance in this archaic mentality, that of acting on behalf of the deity to promote order and to oppose disorder and chaos or disruption.

For in the typical archaic mode of conceiving the organization of things, the kingdom was so identified with the world that one was coequal and coextensive with the other, the outer margin of one containing also the other, and both schematically symmetrical in their symbolic arrangement, as I will point out shortly. What lay outside these confines belonged to chaos and darkness, and thus to the demon, associated with desiccation and death; those outer lands were then the representation of the "King's Enemies," which played a role in the ritual combat or cosmic conflict. Therefore the cosmological meaning of chastisement within and without the realm were the same, in both cases designed to promote order and life on behalf of the god of the kingship.

Life and order went hand in hand in the make-up of the social organism and of the king who personified it. On this account the broad philosophy of life and death, the meaning of the cessation of life and of its passage over into the Beyond, and of its rejuvenation or of its elevation into the status of deification, were all elements in the ideology of the sacral kingship which cannot be bypassed if one is to grasp the wholeness of its meaning. To be an effective giver of livingness was the king's prime concern, and hence the mythology of fertility played a large part in this nurturant function of the kingship. Nurturance required nutrition : sustaining life involved providing food. Now only through the beneficent influences of the dead dwelling within the earth could this living matter grow from it, and only through death and the dead could renewal of life be given to the realm of the living. Thus we find the king's nature to be in part of the incarnation of an ancestral divine king, and his duties to involve a faithful ritual attentiveness to the Chthonic Father. I will be referring to this figure as the First Ancestor-Founding King, or Ancestral Founding King, an image of which the Primordial Man and the Culture Hero were variants. This Ancestral King coincided in greater or lesser degree from culture to culture with the dying god who, as the embodiment of the life potency, fostered fertility.

This aspect of the kingship reaches back into the most hoary antiquity, when presumably the king was the very embodiment of the potency of earth as its fertility *daemon.* The indications are that, in most parts of the world, these earth cults had preceded the sky powers, and had belonged to the matriarchal era when the god was merely instrumental in serving the Great Mother as her lover and fructifier. The attributes frequently associated with the kingship in this life-engendering aspect were the Tree of Life and the Water of Life (perhaps set in the Garden of God or Paradise or Sacred Grove), and the Divine Bull who had more specifically phallic implications in the generation of life and of revivification and yet who primarily served the goddess. The latter may be said also of the serpent imagery abounding among all these.

We are in a position now to risk a generalization in regard to functions of the kingship, one which, while it has the vice of imprecision as do all such abstractions, nonetheless has the virtue of bringing to light some of the meanings inherent in the profusion of forms. We have already noted that in the main, the agricultural community came first, with all its emotional investment in the fructification of the earth and the promotion of life, whether plant or beast; Mother Earth and the Ancestors within her bosom were then the principal objects of worship and supplication, because they were the source of greatest potency. We noted that the industrial community that later evolved was a different matter, with its new capacity to accumulate wealth and provisions and to give time to metallurgic crafts, for with it the urban society and the city kingdom came into being. The point of interest is that the emotional investment was now shifted from the survival of the physical man to that of the social organism, thus maintaining the cohesion of a more subtly structured body politic than that which had prevailed before in the form of tribal groupings with their clans and moieties and exogamous systems and totems. With this step in cultural evolution came the supremacy of the god over the goddess, of the sky powers over the earth, and of patriarchal and patrilineal practices superseding the matriarchal and matrilineal; above all, the principal objective of kingship and its mythological representation of the masculine principle was to promote order and organization. For as the nutritional virtue of the earth gave life to the physical body, so the ethical virtue of the sky safeguarded the life of the social body. The upward trend of culture was from the survival of the biological man to the expansion of the powers of man's spirit, expressed symbolically as the trend from earth to sky.

This era of genuineness of the archaic sacral kingship, of incarnated myth, was one in which the two kinds of potency were embodied with equal measure in the Royal Father; the fostering of life and the promotion of order. The king was the embodiment of or the son of the First Ancestor-Founding King, living in the world of the dead, the earth, or the underworld. This ancestral forebear was divine in a chthonic idiom, and was the mediator of the vital principle, in keeping with the archaic view that life emerges out of death, its pushing up out of the soil being fostered by the dead ancestors within the earth. At the same time the sacral king held a special relation to the Sky God, whether of identity or of sonship by adoption, and was this god's special representative on earth. He then held the same relation to the society of men that this deity did to the company of the gods — the one was the reflected image of the other. We may thus think of a typical dual potency of the sacral kingship, with a dual sonship, the one dark, mysterious, and earthy, the other light, bright, and celestial — the chthonic derived from below, the spiritual from above. [pp.12-18]

NOTES

1. J.W. Perry, *Lord of the Four Quarters : Myths of the Royal Father* (New York : George Braziller, Inc., 1966), pp.3-18.
2. J.G. Frazer, *The Golden Bough* (London : Macmillan, 1890), Part I ; *Idem, The Magic Art and the Evolution of Kings*, Chapters 2, 6, 7.
3. W. Robertson Smith, *The Religion of the Semites* (London : Black, 1901 ; Republished New York : Meridian, 1956), p. 18 ff.
4. Vilhelm Gronbech, "Essay on Ritual Drama," in *The Culture of the Teutons*, trans. W. Worster (London : Oxford University Press, 1931).
5. H. Gunkel, *Schopfung und Chaos, Willzeit und Endzeit* (Gottingen : Vandenboeck und Ruprecht, 1895).
6. S. Mowinkel, *Psalmenstudien, Videnskapsselskapetz Skrifter II*, His. Filos. Klasse (Kristiania, Oslo : 1921-24).
7. Ivan Engnell, *Studies in Sacral Kingship* (Uppsala : Almquist & Wiksells, 1943).
8. George Widengren. See the various titles in his series *King and Saviour* in the *Uppsala Universitets Arsskrift.*
9. Jane Harrison, *Themis* (Cambridge : Cambridge University Press, 1927).
10. Gilbert Murray, *Five Stages of Greek Religion* (New York : Columbia University Press, 1925).
11. F.M. Cornford, *From Religion to Philosophy* (New York : Harper, 1957).
12. S.H. Hooke, *Myth and Ritual* (London : Oxford University Press, 1933).
13. S.H. Hooke, *The Labyrinth* (New York : Macmillan, 1935).
14. S.H. Hooke, *Myth, Ritual, and Kingship* (Oxford : Clarendon, 1958).
15. E.O. James, *The Ancient Gods : The History and Diffusion of Religion in the Ancient Near East and the Eastern Mediterranean* (New York : "The Putnam History of Religion," Putnam, 1960).
16. Thorkild Jacobsen, "Mesopotamia," in *Before Philosophy : The Intellectual Adventure of Ancient Man*, Henri Frankfort, ed. (London : Penguin Books, 1949. First published Chicago : University of Chicago Press, 1946).
17. Henri Frankfort, *Kingship and the Gods : A Study of Ancient Near East Religion as the Integration of Society, and Nature* (Chicago : University of Chicago Press, 1948).
18. Theodor H. Gaster, *Thespis : Ritual, Myth and Drama in the Ancient Near East* (Garden City : Anchor Books, Doubleday, 1961).
19. M. Granet, *Chinese Civilization* (New York : Meridian Books, 1958).
20. E.B. Tylor, *Researches into the Early History of Mankind* (London : Macmillan, 1881).
21. Smith, *op. cit.*
22. Levy-Bruhl, *Primitive Mentality*, trans. L.A. Clair (London : Allen and Unwin, 1923).

STUDIES IN DIVINE KINGSHIP IN THE ANCIENT NEAR EAST[1]

I. Engnell

The central position occupied by the king in the religion of Ancient Egypt, thanks to the modern researches, stands out more and more clearly. . . .

We may state at once with Wainwright : "Nothing is more certain than that the Pharaoh was divine."[2] The king is thus of divine origin. This fundamental fact is expressed in two ways, which in reality imply the same thing, though in the former case the personal or dynastic point of view may be said to dominate, and in the second a more institutional, hierarchic one.

The king is divine from birth or even in a pre-natal existence. The crown prince is begotten by the god — corporealized in the king — and the queen. The child is formed by the gods in the womb of the mother, and at its birth the life-fluid throws itself from the god to the royal child.... On account of this divine, non-human origin the king is therefore described as the one who has neither father nor mother.

According to the other train of thought the future king is raised to the divine sphere through the crown-prince enthronization. At this solemn act of state the royal "friends," the nobles, the dignitaries, the court slaves, etc., are "transferred" to the crown prince. Then these, the heir apparent having received his crown-prince name, recognize him as such and swear their allegiance to him. He has now been changed into a new numinous man.

The enthronization of the crown prince, which is actually only a renewed confirmation of the rank already held — according to the former train of thought — in virtue of the divine birth, is confirmed under still more solemn forms by the enthronement of the king, into the ritual details of which we shall not enter here, as well as by the state-jubilee festival, and by the daily cult, which may be characterized as a shortened and simplified enthronement ritual.

In the cult, the king functions as high priest *par excellence.* Pictures and texts describe him again and again as performing the ritual tasks in the daily cult as well as at the great festivals. As a rule, he must of course be replaced by a priest, but the latter is then the principal identical with the king, and the ideology connected with the king is, therefore, transferred to him.

The character of this cult is only to be understood in the light of the king's identity with the god ; and here, at least formally, two different lines may be distinguished.

The king is identical with Re, the sun-god. This identity, going back, no doubt, to the earliest times, is expressed in the king's so-called Horus name, and through it the king is characterized in his "regulative function."

Thus, what is characteristic of the high god is also said of him. He is a creator through the words of his mouth, the upholder of the right order of nature, of jurisdiction and justice, he is all-seeing and all-hearing.... [pp. 4-6]

Also according to the Sumero-Acadian king ideology the monarch is of divine origin. The kingship is from eternity, is pre-existent. It belongs from the beginning to the highest god — Anu or Enlil — it descends to the earth as *anutu* or *enlilutu* and is maintained there by the king who is from the womb of his mother chosen and nominated to uphold it. This "pre-earthly" investiture from the mother's womb takes place from the earliest Sumerian times by means of a threefold confirmation : the divine regard, the utterance of the name, and the fixing of the good destiny. The latter is performed by the congregation of the gods, the *puhar ilani*, and is often celebrated in the hymns.

So the king is born of the goddess, and has for his father Anu, Enlil or some other god, who is called *abu banu*, "the father — begetter." This is why the king has no father and no mother, but often calls himself "the creation of the fingers of the god." In his mother's womb the king's body as well as his soul is endowed with divine qualities, first of all strength and wisdom.... [p. 16]

NOTES

1. I. Engnell, *Studies in Divine Kingship in the Ancient Near East* (Oxford : Basil Blackwell, 1967), pp. 4-16.
2. G.A. Wainwright, *The Sky Religion in Egypt* (Cambridge : 1938), p. 14.

THE ANCIENT CITY[1]

Fustel de Coulanges

The origin of ancient laws appears clearly. No man invented them. Solon, Lycurgus, Minor, Numa might have reduced the laws of their cities to writing, but they could not have made them. If we understand by legislator a man who creates a code by the power of his genius, and who imposed it upon other men, this legislator never existed among the ancients. Nor did ancient law originate with the votes of the people. The idea that a certain number of votes might make a law did not appear in the cities till very late, and only after two revolutions had transformed them. Up to that time laws had appeared to men as something ancient, immutable, and venerable. As old as the city itself, the founder had established them at the same time that he established the hearth. He instituted them at the same time that he instituted the religion. Still it could not be said that he had prepared them himself. Who, then, was the true author of them ? When we spoke above of the organization of the family, and of the Greek and Roman laws which regulated property, succession, wills, and adoption, we observed how exactly these laws corresponded to the beliefs of ancient generations. If we compare these laws with natural equity, we often find them opposed to it, and we can easily see that it was not in the notion of absolute right and in the sentiment of justice, that they were sought for. But place these laws by the side of the worship of the dead and of the sacred fire, compare them with the rules of this primitive religion, and they appear in perfect accord with all this.

Man did not need to study his conscience and say, "This is just ; this is unjust." Ancient law was not produced in this way. But man believed that the sacred hearth, in virtue of the religious law, passed from father to son ; from this it followed that the house was hereditary property. The man who had buried his father in his field believed that the spirit of the dead one took possession of this field forever, and required a perpetual worship of his posterity. As a result of this, the field, the domain of the dead, and place of sacrifice, became the inalienable property of a family. Religion said, "The son continues the worship — not the daughter" ; and the law said, with the religion, "The son inherits — the daughter does not inherit ; the nephew by the males inherits, but not the nephew on the female side." This was the manner in which the laws were made; they presented themselves without being sought. They were the direct and necessary consequence of the belief; they were religion itself applied to the relations of men among themselves.

The ancients said their laws came from the gods. The Cretans attributed their laws, not to Minos, but to Jupiter. The Lacedaemonians believed that their legislator was not Lycurgus, but Apollo. The Romans believed that Numa wrote under the dictation of one of the most powerful divinities of ancient Italy — the goddess Egeria. The Etruscans had received their laws from the god Tages. There is truth in all these traditions. The veritable legislator among the ancients was not a man, but the religious belief which men entertained....

From this we can understand the respect and attachment which the ancients long had for their laws. In them they saw no human work, but one whose origin was holy. It was no vain word when Plato said, "To obey the laws is to obey the gods...." [pp. 188-189]

NOTE

1. Fustel de Coulanges, *The Ancient City*, trans. by Willard Small (New York : Doubleday & Co. Inc., Copyright 1873), pp. 188-189.

THE LAWS OF MANU[1]

1. The great sages approached Manu, who was seated with a collected mind and, having duly worshipped him, spoke as follows :

2. "Deign, divine one, to declare to us precisely and in due order the sacred laws of each of the (four chief) castes *(varna)* and of the intermediate ones."

3. "For thou, O Lord, alone knowest the purport, (i.e.,) the rites, and the knowledge of the soul, (taught)in this whole ordinance of the Self-existent (Svayambhu), which is unknowable and unfathomable."

4. He, whose power is measureless, being thus asked by the high-minded great sages, duly honoured them, and answered, "Listen !"

5. This (universe) existed in the shape of Darkness, unperceived, destitute of distinctive marks, unattainable by reasoning, unknowable, wholly immersed, as it were, in deep sleep.

6. Then the divine Self-existent (Svayambhu, himself) indiscernible (but) making (all) this, the great elements and the rest, discernible, appeared with irresistible (creative) power, dispelling the darkness.

7. He who can be perceived by the internal organ (alone), who is subtile, indiscernible, and eternal, who contains all created beings and is inconceivable, shone forth of his own (will).

8. He, desiring to produce beings of many kinds from his own body, first with a thought created the waters, and placed his seed in them.

9. That (seed) became a golden egg, in brilliancy equal to the sun; in that (egg) he himself was born as Brahman, the progenitor of the whole world.

11. From that (first) cause, which is indiscernible, eternal, and both real and unreal, was produced that male (Purusha), who is famed in this world (under the appellation of) Brahman.

12. The divine one resided in that egg during a whole year, then he himself by his thought (alone) divided it into two halves ;

13. And out of those two halves he formed heaven and earth, between them the middle sphere, the eight points of the horizon, and the eternal abode of the waters.

14. From himself *(atmanah)* he also drew forth the mind, which is both real and unreal, likewise from the mind egoism, which possesses the function of self-consciousness (and is) lordly ;

15. Moreover, the great one, the soul, and all (products) affected by the three qualities, and in their order, the five organs which perceive the objects of sensation.

22. He, the Lord, also created the class of the gods, who are endowed with life, and whose nature is action ; and the subtile class of the Sadhyas, and the eternal sacrifice.

31. But for the sake of the prosperity of the worlds, he caused the Brahmana, the Kshatriya, the Vaisya, and the Sudra to proceed from his mouth, his arms, his thighs, and his feet.

32. Dividing his own body, the Lord became half male and half female ; with that (female) he produced Virag.

87. But in order to protect this universe He, the most resplendent one, assigned separate (duties and) occupations to those who sprang from his mouth, arms, thighs, and feet.

88. To Brahmanas he assigned teaching and studying (the Veda), sacrificing for their own benefit and for others, giving and accepting (of alms).

89. The Kshatriya he commanded to protect the people, to bestow gifts, to offer sacrifices, to study (the Veda), and to abstain from attaching himself to sensual pleasures ;

90. The Vaisya to tend cattle, to bestow gifts, to offer sacrifices, to study (the Veda), to trade, to lend money, and to cultivate land.

91. One occupation only the lord prescribed to the Sudra, to serve meekly even these (other) three castes.

92. Man is stated to be purer above the navel (than below) ; hence the Self-existent (Svayambhu) has declared the purest (part) of him (to be) his mouth.

93. As the Brahmana sprang from (Brahman's) mouth, as he was the first-born, and as he possesses the Veda, he is by right the Lord of this whole creation.

94. For the Self-existent *(svayambhu)*, having performed austerities, produced him first from his own mouth, in order that the offerings might be conveyed to the gods and manes and that this universe might be preserved.

95. What created being can surpass him, through whose mouth the gods continually consume the sacrificial *viands* and the manes the offerings to the dead ?

96. Of created beings the most excellent are said to be those which are animated ; of the animated, those which subsist by intelligence ; of the intelligent, mankind ; and of men, the Brahmanas ;

97. Of Brahmanas, those learned (in the Veda) ; of the learned, those who recognize (the necessity and the manner of performing the prescribed duties) ; of those who possess this knowledge, those who perform them ; of the performers, those who know the Brahman.

98. The very birth of a Brahmana is an eternal incarnation of the sacred law ; for he is born to (fulfil) the sacred law, and becomes one with Brahman.

99. A Brahmana, coming into existence, is born as the highest on earth, the lord of all created beings, for the protection of the treasury of the law.

100. Whatever exists in the world is the property of the Brahmana ; on account of the excellence of his origin the Brahmana is, indeed, entitled to it all.

101. The Brahmana eats his own food, wears but his own apparel, bestows but his own in alms ; other mortals subsist through the benevolence of the Brahmana.

102. In order to clearly settle his duties and those of the other (castes) according to their order, wise Manu sprung from the Self-existent, composed these Institutes (of the sacred law). [pp. 1-26]

Chapter VII

1. I will declare the duties of kings (and) show how a king should conduct himself, how he was created, and how (he can obtain) highest success.

2. A Kshatriya, who has received according to the rule the sacrament prescribed by the Veda, must duly protect this whole (world).

3. For, when these creatures, being without a king, through fear dispersed in all directions, the Lord created a king for the protection of this whole (creation),

4. Taking (for that purpose) eternal particles of Indra, of the Wind, of Yama, of the Sun, of Fire, of Varuna, of the Moon, and of the Lord of Wealth (Kubera).

5. Because a king has been formed of particles of those lords of the gods, he therefore surpasses all created beings in lustre ;

6. And, like the sun, he burns eyes and hearts ; nor can anybody on earth even gaze on him.

7. Through his (supernatural) power he is Fire and Wind, he Sun and Moon, he the Lord of Justice (Yama), he Kubera, he Varuna, he great Indra.

8. Even an infant king must not be despised, (from an idea) that he is a (mere) mortal ; for he is a great deity in human form.

9. Fire burns one man only, if he carelessly approaches it, the fire of a king's (anger) consumes the (whole) family, together with its cattle and its hoard of property.

10. Having fully considered the purpose, (his) power, and the place and the time, he assumes by turns, many (different) shapes for the complete attainment of justice. [pp. 216-217]

NOTE

1. F. Max Muller, ed., G. Buhler, trans., "The Laws of Manu," in *The Sacred Books of the East*, vol. 25 (Delhi : Motilal Banarsidass, 1967), pp. 1-217.

THE CODE OF HAMMURABI[1]

Hammurabi, the protecting king, am I. I have not withdrawn myself from the blackheaded race that Bel has entrusted to me, and over whom Merodach has made me shepherd. I have not reposed myself upon my side ; but I have given them places of peace. Difficult points have I made smooth, and radiance have I shed abroad. With the mighty weapon that Zamama and Ishtar have lent me ; with the penetration with which Ea has endowed me ; with the valour that Merodach has given me, I have rooted out all enemies above and below ; and the depths have I subjugated. The flesh of the land I have made rejoice : the resident people I have made secure ; I have not suffered them to be afraid. It is I that the great gods have elected to be the Shepherd of Salvation, whose sceptre is just. I throw my good shadow over my city. Upon my bosom I cherish the men of the lands of Sumir and Akkad. By my protecting genius, their brethern in peace are guided : by my wisdom are they sheltered. That the strong may not oppress the weak ; that the orphan and the widow may be counselled ; in Babylon, the city whose head has been lifted up by Anu and Bel ; in E Saggil, the temple whose foundations are as solid as heaven and earth : to proclaim the law of the land : to guide the procedure of the land ; and to sustain the feeble ; I have written my precious words upon my pillar, and before my image as king of justice I have placed it.

I am the monarch who towers above the kings of the cities. My words are well weighed ; my valour has no equal. By command of Shamash, the great judge of heaven and earth, justice shall glisten in the land. By direction of Merodach, my lord, my monument shall never see destruction. In E Saggil that I love, my name shall ever be spoken. The oppressed, who has a lawsuit, shall come before my image as king of justice. He shall read the writing on my pillar, he shall perceive my precious words. The word of my pillar shall explain to him his cause, and he shall find his right. His heart shall be glad [and he shall say], "The Lord Hammurabi has risen up as a true father to his people. . . ." [pp. 73-74]

In after days and for all time, the king who is in the land shall observe the words of justice which are written upon my pillar. He shall not alter the law of the land which I have formulated, or the statutes of the country that I have enacted ; nor shall he damage my sculptures. If that man has wisdom, and desires to keep his land in order, he will heed the words which are written upon my pillar. The canon, the rule, the law of the country which I have formulated, the statutes of the country that I have enacted, this pillar shall show to him. The blackheaded people he shall govern ; their laws he shall pronounce, their statutes he shall decide. He shall root out of the land the perverse and the wicked ; and the flesh of the people he shall delight.

Hammurabi, the king of justice, am I, to whom Shamash has granted rectitude. My words are well weighed : my deeds have no equal, levelling the exalted, humbling the proud, expelling the haughty. If that man heeds my words that I have engraved upon my pillar, departs not from the laws, alters not my words, changes not my sculptures, then may Shamash make the sceptre of that man to endure as long as I, the king of justice, and to lead his people with justice.

But if that man heeds not my words that I have written upon my pillar ; if he has scorned my malediction, nor feared the curse of God ; if he has annulled the law that I have given, or altered my words, or changed my sculptures, or erased my name in order to write his own. Or if, from fear of these curses, he has commissioned another ; then that man, whether he be king, or prince, or feudatory, or citizen, whatever his title, may the great Anu, the father of the gods, who has decreed my reign, may he extinguish the splendor of his royalty, may he shatter his sceptre, may he curse his end. [pp. 75-76]

NOTE

1. Chilperic Edwards, trans., *The Hammurabi Code and the Sinaitic Legislation* (Port Washington, N.Y. : Kennikat Press, 1971), pp. 73-76.

THE PENTATEUCH AND HAFTORAHS[1]

Genesis I, 1

Chapter I

1 In the beginning God created the heaven and the earth.

2 Now the earth was unformed and void, and darkness was upon the face of the deep ; and the spirit of God hovered over the face of the waters.

3 And God said : "Let there be light." And there was light.

4 And God saw the light, that it was good ; and God divided the light from the darkness.

5 And God called the light Day, and the darkness He called Night. And there was evening and there was morning, one day.

6 And God said : "Let there be a firmament in the midst of the waters, and let it divide the waters from the waters."

7 And God made the firmament, and divided the waters which were under the firmament from the waters which were above the firmament ; and it was so.

8 And God called the firmament Heaven. And there was evening and there was morning, a second day.

9 And God said : "Let the waters under the heaven be gathered together unto one place, and let the dry land appear." And it was so.

10 And God called the dry land Earth, and the gathering together of the waters He called Seas ; and God saw that it was good.

11 And God said : "Let the earth put forth grass, herb-yielding seed, and tree-bearing fruit after its kind, wherein is the seed thereof, upon the earth." And it was so.

12 And the earth brought forth grass, herb-yielding seed after its kind, and tree-bearing fruit, wherein is the seed thereof, after its kind ; and God saw that it was good.

13 And there was evening and there was morning, a third day.

14 And God said : "Let there be lights in the firmament of the heaven to divide the day from the night ; and let them be for signs, and for seasons, and for days and years ;

15 and let them be for lights in the firmament of the heaven to give light upon the earth." And it was so.

16 And God made the two great lights : the greater light to rule the day, and the lesser light to rule the night ; and the stars.

17 And God set them in the firmament of the heaven to give light upon the earth,

18 and to rule over the day and over the night, and to divide the light from the darkness ; and God saw that it was good.

19 And there was evening and there was morning, a fourth day.

20 And God said : "Let the waters swarm with swarms of living creatures, and let fowl fly above the earth in the open firmament of heaven."

21 And God created the great sea-monsters, and every living creature that creepeth, wherewith the waters swarmed, after its kind, and every winged fowl after its kind ; and God saw that it was good.

22 And God blessed them, saying : "Be fruitful, and multiply, and fill the waters in the seas, and let fowl multiply in the earth."

23 And there was evening and there was morning, a fifth day.

24 And God said : "Let the earth bring forth the living creature after its kind, cattle, and creeping thing, and beast of the earth after its kind." And it was so.

25 And God made the beast of the earth after its kind, and the cattle after their kind, and every thing that creepeth upon the ground after its kind ; and God saw that it was good.

26 And God said : "Let us make man in our image, after our likeness ; and let them have dominion over the fish of the sea, and over the fowl of the air, and over the cattle, and over all the earth, and over every creeping thing that creepeth upon the earth."

27 And God created man in His own image, in the image of God created He him ; male and female created He them.

28 And God blessed them ; and God said unto them : "Be fruitful, and multiply, and replenish the earth, and subdue it ; and have dominion over the fish of the sea, and over the fowl of the air, and over every living thing that creepeth upon the earth."

29 And God said : "Behold, I have given you every herb-yielding seed, which is upon the face of all the earth, and every tree, in which is the fruit of a tree-yielding seed — to you it shall be for food ;

30 and to every beast of the earth, and to every fowl of the air, and to every thing that creepeth upon the earth, wherein there is a living soul, [I have given] every green herb for food." And it was so.

31 And God saw every thing that He had made, and, behold, it was very good. And there was evening and there was morning, the sixth day.

Chapter II

1 And the heaven and the earth were finished, and all the host of them.

2 And on the seventh day God finished His work which He had made ; and He rested on the seventh day from all His work which He had made.

3 And God blessed the seventh day, and hallowed it ; because that in it He rested from all His work which God in creating had made.

4 These are the generations of the heaven and of the earth when they were created, in the day that the Lord God made earth and heaven.

5 No shrub of the field was yet in the earth, and no herb of the field had yet sprung up ; for the Lord God had not caused it to rain upon the earth, and there was not a man to till the ground ;

6 but there went up a mist from the earth, and watered the whole face of the ground.

7 Then the Lord God formed man of the dust of the ground, and breathed into his nostrils the breath of life; and man became a living soul.

8 And the Lord God planted a garden eastward, in Eden; and there He put the man whom He had formed.

9 And out of the ground made the Lord God to grow every tree that is pleasant to the sight, and good for food; the tree of life also in the midst of the garden, and the tree of the knowledge of good and evil.

10 And a river went out of Eden to water the garden; and from thence it was parted, and became four heads.

11 The name of the first is Pishon; that is it which compasseth the whole land of Havilah, where there is gold;

12 and the gold of that land is good; there is bdellium and the onyx stone.

13 And the name of the second river is Ginon; the same is it that compasseth the whole land of Cush.

14 And the name of the third river is Tigris; that is it which goeth toward the east of Asshur. And the fourth river is the Euphrates.

15 And the Lord God took the man, and put him into the garden of Eden to dress it and to keep it.

16 And the Lord God commanded the man, saying: "Of every tree of the garden thou mayest freely eat;

17 but of the tree of knowledge of good and evil, thou shalt not eat of it; for in the day that thou eatest thereof thou shalt surely die."

18 And the Lord God said: "It is not good that the man should be alone; I will make him a help meet for him."

19 And out of the ground the Lord God formed every beast of the field, and every fowl of the air; and brought them unto the man to see what he would call them; and whatsoever the man would call every living creature, that was to be the name thereof.

20 And the man gave names to all cattle, and to the fowl of the air, and to every beast of the field; but for Adam there was not found a help meet for him.

21 And the Lord God caused a deep sleep to fall upon the man, and he slept; and He took one of his ribs, and closed up the place with flesh instead thereof.

22 And the rib, which the Lord God had taken from the man, made He a woman, and brought her unto the man.

23 And the man said : "This is now bone of my bones, and flesh of my flesh ; she shall be called Woman, because she was taken out of Man."

24 Therefore shall a man leave his father and his mother, and shall cleave unto his wife, and they shall be one flesh.

25 And they were both naked, the man and his wife, and were not ashamed.

Chapter III

1 Now the serpent was more subtle than any beast of the field which the Lord God had made. And he said unto the woman : "Yea, hath God said : Ye shall not eat of any tree of the garden ?"

2 And the woman said unto the serpent : "Of the fruit of the trees of the garden we may eat ;

3 but of the fruit of the tree which is in the midst of the garden, God hath said : 'Ye shall not eat of it, neither shall ye touch it, lest ye die."

4 And the serpent said unto the woman : "Ye shall not surely die ;

5 for God doth know that in the day ye eat thereof, then your eyes shall be opened, and ye shall be as God, knowing good and evil."

6 And when the woman saw that the tree was good for food, and that it was a delight to the eyes, and that the tree was to be desired to make one wise, she took of the fruit thereof, and did eat ; and she gave also unto her husband with her, and he did eat.

7 And the eyes of them both were opened, and they knew that they were naked ; and they sewed fig-leaves together, and made themselves girdles.

8 And they heard the voice of the Lord God walking in the garden toward the cool of the day ; and the man and his wife hid themselves from the presence of the Lord God amongst the trees of the garden.

9 And the Lord God called unto the man, and said unto him : "Where art thou ?"

10 And he said : "I heard Thy voice in the garden, and I was afraid, because I was naked ; and I hid myself."

11 And He said : "Who told thee that thou was naked ? Hast thou eaten of the tree, whereof I commanded thee that thou shouldest not eat ?"

12 And the man said : "The woman whom Thou gavest to be with me, she gave me of the tree, and I did eat."

13 And the Lord God said unto the woman : "What is this thou hast done ?" And the woman said : "The serpent beguiled me, and I did eat."

14 And the Lord God said unto the serpent : "Because thou hast done this, cursed art thou from among all cattle, and from among all beasts of the field ; upon thy belly shalt thou go, and dust shalt thou eat all the days of thy life.

15 And I will put enmity between thee and the woman, and between thy seed and her seed ; they shall bruise thy head, and thou shalt bruise their heel."

16 Unto the woman He said : "I will greatly multiply thy pain and thy travail ; in pain thou shalt bring forth children ; and thy desire shall be to thy husband, and he shall rule over thee."

17 And unto Adam He said : "Because thou hast hearkened unto the voice of thy wife, and hast eaten of the tree, of which I commanded thee, saying : Thou shalt not eat of it ; cursed is the ground for thy sake ; in toil shalt thou eat of it all the days of thy life.

18 Thorns also and thistles shall it bring forth to thee ; and thou shalt eat the herb of the field.

19 In the sweat of thy face shalt thou eat bread, till thou return unto the ground ; for out of it wast thou taken ; for dust thou art, and unto dust shalt thou return."

20 And the man called his wife's name Eve ; because she was the mother of all living.

21 And the Lord God made for Adam and for his wife garments of skins, and clothed them.

22 And the Lord God said : "Behold, the man is become as one of us, to know good and evil ; and now, lest he put forth his hand, and take also of the tree of life, and eat, and live for ever."

23 Therefore the Lord God sent him forth from the garden of Eden, to till the ground from whence he was taken.

24 So He drove out the man ; and He placed at the east of the garden of Eden the cherubim, and the flaming sword which turned every way, to keep the way to the tree of life.

Exodus

Chapter XX

1 And God spake all these words, saying :

2 I am the Lord thy God, who brought thee out of the land of Egypt, out of the house of bondage.

3 Thou shalt have no other gods before Me.

4 Thou shalt not make unto thee a graven image, nor any manner of likeness, of any thing that is in heaven above, or that is in the earth beneath, or that is in the water under the earth;

5 thou shalt not bow down unto them, nor serve them; for I the Lord thy God am a jealous God, visiting the iniquity of the fathers upon the children unto the third and fourth generation of them that hate Me;

6 and showing mercy unto the thousandth generation of them that love Me and keep My commandments.

7 Thou shalt not take the name of the Lord thy God in vain; for the Lord will not hold him guiltless that taketh His name in vain.

8 Remember the sabbath day, to keep it holy.

9 Six days shalt thou labour, and do all thy work;

10 but the seventh day is a sabbath unto the Lord thy God, in it thou shalt not do any manner of work, thou, nor thy son, nor thy daughter, nor thy man-servant, nor thy maid-servant, nor thy cattle, nor thy stranger that is within thy gates;

11 for in six days the Lord made heaven and earth, the sea, and all that in them is, and rested on the seventh day; wherefore the Lord blessed the sabbath day, and hallowed it.

12 Honour thy father and thy mother, that thy days may be long upon the land which the Lord thy God giveth thee.

13 Thou shalt not murder. Thou shalt not commit adultery. Thou shalt not steal. Thou shalt not bear false witness against thy neighbour.

14 Thou shalt not covet thy neighbour's house; thou shalt not covet thy neighbour's wife, nor his man-servant, nor his maid-servant, nor his ox, nor his ass, nor any thing that is thy neighbour's.

15 And all the people perceived the thunderings, and the lightnings and the voice of the horn, and the mountain smoking; and when the people saw it, they trembled, and stood afar off.

16 And they said unto Moses: "Speak thou with us, and we will hear; but let not God speak with us, lest we die."

17 And Moses said unto the people: "Fear not; for God is come to prove you, and that His fear may be before you, that ye sin not."

18 And the people stood afar off; but Moses drew near unto the thick darkness where God was.

19 And the Lord said unto Moses: "Thus thou shalt say unto the children of Israel: Ye yourselves have seen that I have talked with you from heaven.

20 Ye shall not make with Me — gods of silver, or gods of gold, ye shall not make unto you.

21 An altar of earth thou shalt make unto Me, and shalt sacrifice thereon thy burnt-offerings, and thy peace-offerings, thy sheep, and thine oxen ; in every place where I cause My name to be mentioned I will come unto thee and bless thee.

22 And if thou make Me an altar of stone, thou shalt not build it of hewn stones ; for if thou lift up thy tool upon it, thou hast profaned it.

23 Neither shalt thou go up by steps unto Mine alter, that thy nakedness be not uncovered thereon."

NOTE

1. *The Pentateuch and Haftorahs*, ed. J.H. Hertz, (London : Oxford University Press, 1956).

THE LAWS, BOOK[1]

Plato

A Visitor from Athens : To whom is the merit of instituting our laws ascribed, gentlemen ? To a god, or to some man ?

Clinias : Why, to a god, sir, indubitably to a god ; in our case to Zeus, in the case of Lacedaemon, to which our friend here belongs, I believe, according to their own story, to Apollo. That is so, is it not ?

Megillus : Certainly. [p. 1]

NOTE

1. Plato, *The Laws*, trans. A.E. Taylor (London : J.M. Dent & Sons, 1960), p.1

THE RECONSTRUCTION OF LEGAL THOUGHT IN ISLAM[1]

Syed Riazul Hassan

The basic source of Islamic Law is Divine Revelation. This has been given to us by the Prophet (Peace be upon him) in two forms. One is the direct speech of God — the Quar-an, the other is the indirect speech of God — the Sunnah. These two forms of Revelation are called the roots of Islamic Law.... [p. 7]

NOTE

1. Syed Riazul Hassan, *The Reconstruction of Legal Thought in Islam* (Lahore, Pakistan : Law Publishing Co., 1974), p. 7.

THE DIVINE RIGHT OF KINGS[1]

J.N. Figgis

The theory of the divine right of kings in its completest form involves the following propositions :

(1) *Monarchy is a divinely ordained institution.*

(2) *Hereditary right is indefeasible.* The succession to monarchy is regulated by the law of primogeniture. The right acquired by birth cannot be forfeited through any acts of usurption, of however long continuance, by any incapacity in the heir, or by any act of deposition. So long as the heir lives, he is king by hereditary right, even though the usurping dynasty has reigned for a thousand years.

(3) *Kings are accountable to God alone.* Monarchy is pure, the sovereignty being entirely vested in the king, whose power is incapable of legal limitation. All law is a mere concession of his will, and all constitutional forms and assemblies exist entirely at his pleasure. He cannot limit or divide or alienate the sovereignty, so as in any way to prejudice the right of his successor to its complete exercise. A mixed or limited monarchy is a contradiction in terms.

(4) *Non-resistance and passive obedience are enjoined by God.* Under any circumstances resistance to a king is a sin and ensures damnation. Whenever the king issues a command directly contrary to God's law, God is to be obeyed rather than man, but the example of the primitive Christians is to be followed and all penalties attached to the breach of the law are to be patiently endured.

The following passages set the doctrine forth in the language of the time :

> We will still believe and maintain that our Kings derive not their title from the people, but from God ; that to Him only they are accountable ; that it belongs not to subjects, either to create or censure, but to honour and obey their sovereign, who comes to be so by a fundamental hereditary right of succession, which no religion, no law, no fault or forfeiture can alter or diminish.[2]
>
> Obedience we must pay, either Active or Passive ; the Active in the case of all lawful commands ; that is whenever the Magistrate commands something which is not contrary to some command of God, we are then bound to act according to that command of the Magistrate, to do the thing he requires. But when he enjoins anything contrary to what God hath commanded, we are not then to pay him this Active Obedience ; we may, nay we must refuse thus to act (yet here we must be very well assured that the thing is so contrary, and not pretend conscience for a cloak of stubbornness), we are in that case to obey God rather than man. But even this is a season for the passive obedience ; we must patiently suffer what he inflicts on us for such refusal, and not, to secure ourselves, rise up against him.[3]
>
> If Adam himself were still living and now ready to die it is certain there is one man, and but one in the world who is next heir, although the knowledge who should be that one man be quite lost.[4]

The theory is commonly supported by a number of biblical illustrations and texts, of which some of the most important may be mentioned : Samuel's description of a king, on the Jewish nation demanding one ;[5] David's refusal to touch "the Lord's annointed" ; the text "by me kings reign and princes decree justice" ;[6] the passage describing the vision of Nebuchadnezzar, asserting that, "the Most High ruleth in the kingdom of men, and giveth it to whomsoever he will, and setteth up over it the basest of men" ;[7] the command to "render unto

Caesar the things that are Caesar's" ;[8] Christ's words to Pilate, "thou couldest have no power at all against me except it were given thee from above" ;[9] the behaviour of the primitive Christians ; and above all the direct enjoining by both St. Peter and St. Paul of obedience to constituted authority. "The powers that be are ordained by God. Whosoever therefore resisteth the power, resisteth the ordinance of God. And they that resist shall receive to themselves damnation." "Ye must needs be subject, not only for wrath, but for conscience' sake."[10] "Submit yourselves to every ordinance of man for the Lord's sake — whether it be to the king as supreme...."[11] [pp. 5-8]

NOTES

1. J.N. Figgis, *The Divine Right of Kings* (New York : Harper & Row, 1965), pp. 5-8.
2. From an address of the University of Cambridge to King Charles II in 1681, printed in *The History of Passive Obedience,* p. 108.
3. *Whole Duty of Man,* Sunday xiv. s.5. The passage is quoted by Hobbes as giving the best expression of "the doctrine of the King's party." (Behemoth, Part I, p. 80.)
4. Filmer's *Patriarcha.* Chap. 1, s. 9.
5. 1 Sam. 7 : 10-18.
6. Prov. 8 : 15.
7. Dan. 4 : 17.
8. Luke 20 : 25.
9. John 19 : 11.
10. Rom. 13 : 1-7.
11. 1 Pet. 2 : 13-17.

PATRIARCHA AND OTHER POLITICAL WORKS OF SIR ROBERT FIMLER[1]

Peter Laslett (Editor)

Introduction

. . . Why, it might be asked, were the works of Sir Robert Filmer of any importance at all ? Why, above all, should a thinker of the stature of John Locke have found it necessary to analyze Filmer almost word for word before he could present his own argument ? *Patriarcha* cannot bear comparison as philosophy or as history with the *Leviathan,* with Harington's *Oceana,* or even with many of the ephemeral tracts of the times. What, then, is it doing alongside all these illustrious names in English thinking and English politics ?

It must be pointed out at once that such a reflection does far less than justice to the thesis, or rather the implied thesis, of Filmer's thinking. No less an authority than J.W. Allen has stated that "as a political thinker he was far more profound and far more original than was Locke."[2] His critique of the assumptions his contemporaries were making about political obligation went to the bottom of the most difficult problem in the whole field of inquiry. It will be seen that neither Locke nor Sidney nor any of a host of others who attacked *Patriarcha* ever attempted to meet the force of these criticisms and that none of them even realized what he meant by his naturalism....

. . .[The] writings of Filmer have a significance in the history of European social thinking which is quite independent of the relation they bear to Locke's theory of obligation and of the position of the English Tories in later Stuart times. The value of *Patriarcha* as a historical document consists primarily in its revelation of the strength and persistence in European culture of the patriarchal family form and the patriarchal attitude to political problems. It was because of patriarchalism that Sir Robert Filmer was read, not because of his literary or philosophical ability. It was because of patriarchalism that Locke and Sidney had to answer him, for in appealing to the power of the father and the relevance of the family to the state he touched the assumptions of all his own readers and of most of Locke's. Some attention must be given to patriarchalism as a feature of European culture in general, and of Sir Robert's generation and class in particular, if his importance and effectiveness are to be properly understood....

The seventeenth-century patriarchal family, moreover, had many of the features of the patriarchal household. It included not only wife and children, but often younger brothers, sisters, nephews, and nieces : male superiority and primogeniture were unquestioned. More striking was the presence of a very large number of servants, whose subjection to the head of the household was as absolute and unquestioned as that of the infant heir. The size of the household varied with the wealth and importance and profession of its master. A gentleman like Sir Robert would have in his domestic society not only manservants and maidservants for the house, but also many of the workers on the home farm, the carters, the huntsman, the coachmen, perhaps a brewer, a carpenter, or even a blacksmith. If the head of the family were a nobleman, the number of such dependents would be proportionately larger, but the landed gentry were not the only heads of patriarchal households. The merchant in the city had a similar entourage of apprentices and journeymen : even a professional man like Pepys refers to his "family," which on New Year's Day 1661 was "myself, my wife, Jane, Will, Hewer, and Wayneman, my girl's brother." The tenant farmer had an establishment smaller in size but similar in arrangement. In fact there can have been few individuals in seventeenth-century England who did not belong to one or other of these patriarchal households. All but a very small number were in "natural subjection" to men to whom they were not necessarily connected by blood. The smaller tradesfolk cannot be reckoned as members : otherwise the only exceptions were the patriarchs themselves, who were, of course, the directive minority. Nevertheless, in most of the places where the word "people" is mentioned in the political writings of the time, even in such authors as Milton himself, it is possible to substitute the word "patriarchs" or "heads of households."

It has been seen how important a part such a patriarchal household played in Sir Robert's own experience. It is obvious from the contents of *Patriarcha* that he assumed in his readers the presuppositions of the head of East Sutton Park. It must also be remembered that in the traditions and even in some of the practice of the royal household, where his brother and son held posts of ceremonial importance, he and his readers had before them an example which certainly lent itself to the view that political society at large was nothing more than an extension of the patriarchal household. The officers of the king's household had become the heads of the national civil service, and the subjection of the whole of the nobility with their own households derived in part from the personal service which they did in the household of the king. The medieval, even the primitive and barbaric, origins of these customs were important illustrations of the European tradition which placed the patriarchal household at the very centre of society. To this day the royal household is a survival of the greatest significance in the history of social institutions : it is preserved not only in the constitutions of Great Britain and other European monarchies, but also over the whole range of European dramatic literature. The modern reader is only familiar with the patriarchal household in such contexts as the court of Hamlet, king of Denmark, and it is this archaism which makes Filmer's work so anachronistic. It is worth pointing out, however, that the descendants of the Virginian planters, who became the slaveowners of the southern states, were the heads of a classic type of patriarchal household, so that it survived until the middle of the nineteenth century even in such a rationalistic and egalitarian society as the U.S.A. [pp. 20-26]

NOTES

1. Peter Laslett, ed., *Patriarcha and Other Political Works of Sir Robert Filmer* (Oxford : Basil Blackwell, 1949), pp. 20-26.

2. Hearnshaw, ed., *The Social and Political Ideas of Some English Thinkers of the Augustan Age* (London : 1928).

PATRIARCHA[1]

Sir Robert Filmer

...[C]reation made man Prince of his posterity. And indeed not only Adam, but the succeeding Patriarchs had, by right of fatherhood, royal authority over their children. . . . For as Adam was lord of his children, so his children under him had a command over their own children, but still with subordination to the first parent, who is lord paramount over his children's children to all generations, as being the grandfather of his people.

I see not then how the children of Adam, or of any man else, can be free from subjugation to their parents. And this subordination of children is the fountain of all regal authority, by the ordination of God himself. From whence it follows, that civil power, not only in general is by Divine institution, but even the assigning of it specifically to the eldest parent. Which quite takes away that new and common distinction which refers only power universal or absolute to God, but power respective in regard of the special form of government to the choice of the people. Nor leaves it any place for such imaginary pactions between Kings and their people as many dream of.

This lordship which Adam by creation had over the whole world, and by right descending from him the Patriarchs did enjoy, was as large and ample as the absolutest dominion of any monarch which hath been since the creation. For power of life and death we find that Judah, the Father, pronounced sentence of death against Thamar, his daughter-in-law, for playing the harlot, "Bring her forth" (saith he) "that she may be burnt."[2] Touching war, we see that Abraham commanded an army of 318 soldiers of his own family. And Esau met his brother Jacob with 400 men at arms. For matter of peace, Abraham made a league with Abimelech, and ratified the articles with an oath. These acts of judging in capital crimes, of making war, and concluding peace, are the chiefest works of sovereignty that are found in any monarch. Not only until the Flood, but after it, this patriarchal power did continue, as the very name of Patriarch doth in part prove.

The three sons of Noah had the whole world divided amongst them by their Father ; for of them was the whole world overspread, according to the benediction given to him and his sons : "Be fruitful and multiply and replenish the earth." Most of the civilest nations of the world labour to fetch their origin from some one of the sons or nephews of Noah, which were scattered abroad after the confusion of Babel. In this dispersion we must certainly find the establishment of regal power throughout the kingdoms of the world.

It is a common opinion that at the confusion of tongues there were seventy-two distinct nations erected. All which were not confused multitudes, without heads or governors, and at liberty to choose what governors or governments they pleased, but they were distinct families, which had Fathers for rulers over them, whereby it appears that even in the confusion God was careful to preserve the fatherly authority by distributing the diversity of languages according to the diversity of families. For so it plainly appears by the text. First, after the enumeration of the sons of Japhet, the conclusion is : "By these were the isles of the Gentiles divided in their hands ; every one after his tongue, after their families, in their nations."[3] So it is said : "These are the sons of Ham after their families, after their tongues, in their countries, and in their nations." The like we read : "These are the sons of Shem after their families, after their tongues, in their lands, after their nations. These are the families of the sons of Noah after their generations in their nations, and by these were the nations divided in the earth after the Flood." [pp. 57-59]

It may seem absurd to maintain that Kings now are the fathers of their people, since experience shows the contrary. It is true, all Kings be not the natural parents of their subjects, yet they all either are, or are to be reputed, as the next heirs of those progenitors who were at first the natural parents of the whole people, and in their right succeed to the exercise of supreme jurisdiction. And such heirs are not only lords of their own children, but also of their brethren, and all others that were subject to their Fathers....

As long as the first Fathers of families lived, the name of Patriarchs did aptly belong unto them. But after a few descents, when the true fatherhood itself was extinct, and only the right of the Father descended to the true heir, then the title of Prince or King was more significant to express the power of him who succeeds only to the right of that fatherhood which his ancestors did naturally enjoy. By this means it comes to pass, that many a child, by succeeding a King, hath the right of a Father over many a grey-headed multitude, [and hath the title of *Pater Patriae*].... [pp. 60-61]

If we compare the natural duties of a Father with those of a King, we find them to be all one, without any difference at all but only in the latitude or extent of them. As the Father over one family, so the King, as Father over many families, extends his care to preserve, feed, clothe, instruct, and defend the whole commonwealth. His wars, his peace, his courts of justice, and all his acts of sovereignty tend only to preserve and distribute to every subordinate and inferior Father, and to their children, their rights and privileges, so that all the duties of a King are summed up in an universal fatherly care of his people.... [p. 63]

If the nature of laws be advisedly weighed, the necessity of the Prince's being above them may the more manifest itself. We all know that a law in general is the command of a superior power. Laws are divided . . . into written and unwritten. The Common Law unwritten, the statute law written. The Common Law is called unwritten,not for that it is not written at all, but because it was not written by the first devisers or makers of it. The Common Law (as the Lord Chancellor Egerton teacheth us) is the *common custom of the realm.* Now concerning customs, this must be considered, that for every custom there was a time when it was no custom, and the first precedent we now have had no precedent when it began. When ever custom began, there was something else than custom that made it lawful, or else the beginning of all customs were unlawful. Customs at first became lawful only by some superior power which did either command or consent unto their beginning. And the first power which we find (as is confessed by all men) is Kingly power, which was both in this and in all other nations of the world long before any laws or any other kind of government was thought of. From whence we must necessarily infer that the Common Law itself, or common customs of this land, were originally the laws and commands of Kings at first unwritten.... [pp. 106-107]

Since this is the common condition of Laws, it is most reasonable that the lawmaker should be trusted with the application or interpretation of the laws. For this cause anciently the Kings of this land have sitten personally in courts of judicature and are still representatively present in all courts. The judges are but substituted and called the King's justices, and their power ceaseth when the King is in place.... [p. 109] ...[T]here is no form of government, but monarchy only....[T]here is no monarchy, but paternal. [T]here is no paternal monarchy, but absolute, or arbitrary. [T]here is no such thing as an aristocracy or democracy. [T]here is no such form of government as a tyranny. [T]he people are not born free by nature. [p. 229]

NOTES

1. Peter Laslett, ed., *Patriarcha and Other Political Works of Sir Robert Filmer* (Oxford : Basil Blackwell, 1949), pp. 57-229.
2. Gen. 38 : 24.
3. Gen. 10 : 5.

3. Patriarchal Law

An effective social order requires certainty as well as legitimacy. The law must be known and easily recognizable by clear and public tests. One of the oldest and most widespread methods of maintaining certainty in social control is to vest the right to legislate in the hands of particular persons who become the designated law makers or rulers. Certainty requires public consensus as to whom these people are to be, or how they are to be chosen. Legitimacy demands justifiction of their selection in terms of their suitability to make the law or to dominate.

Authority, therefore, furnishes two necessary conditions for voluntary conduct : legitimacy and certainty, which, in turn, produce efficient and economic social control. The criteria of authority will not only identify the hierarchy of domination and obedience but will also reflect the ideology which justifies the hierarchy.

The biological criteria of race, colour of skin, tribe, family, order of birth, and sex are natural indications for social differentiation and hierarchical ordering. The dominant race or colour will justify its suppression of different peoples in terms of a natural superiority and inferiority. Tribes will be ordered along kinship lines. Common ancestry will knit groups together to the exclusion of others. Chosen or royal families will dominate and justify their rule in terms of their genealogical origins. Thus, the law of status reflects the criteria of authority. The natural biological properties which define status furnish the criteria of certainty, and an ideology of domination will legitimatize the law in terms of its reflection of the natural order.

There are two biological criteria, however, which are truly universal : the bi-polarity of sex and the relationship of parent to child. The sexual difference has been used for many centuries to justify male domination. The ideology of male superiority and female inferiority, coupled with the advantage of strength often enjoyed by the male and the natural dependence of a child on its parents, has served to place authority in the father. The wisdom born of age and experience furnishes the justification for patriarchal rule.

The patriarchal family has been the archetype of social hierarchy from one end of the world to the other. Gods and kings are seen as the fathers of people who, as children, are their subjects. Law has been the arm or tool of patriarchy and its authority has rested on a patriarchal ideology. The evolution of ideologically based patriarchal law as a means to suppress the female would indicate that male domination was, in fact, not a part of the natural order from the beginning but a form of control to facilitate social organization. It was effective because it furnished the two requirements for authority : clearly identifiable criteria for social hierarchy, and a justification in terms of the natural order. Because it was effective it became universal. With the shift from myth to science, the ideology of patriarchy is no longer persuasive. Yet its implications are so embedded in our institutions, religions, and language that male domination and patriarchal values have yet to be relegated to historical obscurity.

THE DEVELOPMENT OF THE ATHENIAN CONSTITUTION[1]

G.W. Botsford

It was the belief of the ancients that the family was the primitive society out of which the state developed. They were led to this view partly by observing that the institutions of their state and family were throughout of a similar character — as were also the relations sustained by the individual to family and state — but more directly by the fact that each ascending group in the gentile organization of the ancient city had, as its protecting deity and centre of its common religious life, an eponymous (name-giving) hero, from whom the members of the respective groups were supposed to have derived their lineage. Thus Aristotle says, "That society which nature has established for daily support is a household.... But the society of many households for lasting and mutual advantage is called a village naturally composed of members of one family. When many villages join themselves perfectly together into one society, that society is a state. . . .[2]

The Aryan (Indo-European) household (or family), as it appears at the dawn of history, possessed a political, social, and religious organization which rendered it capable of an isolated, independent existence, and was held in partial subjection only by the superior power of the city. The tendencies were centrifugal, the family possessed large individuality and freedom of action, and the ties of kindred and home were stronger than love of country (city) or loyalty to the king. Thus the Greek house was monarchical in government — its *pater* was priest and king — while a considerable judicial authority, afterwards exercised by the central government, was, in the Homeric age, vested in the near kin. Thus the kinsmen of a murdered man wreaked vengeance in person, accepted a compensation in money, or voluntarily offered their case to the arbitration of the state. The initiative was taken by the *anchisteis*; the clansman, *phrateres*, and kings were helpers. The Roman household is a more striking example of a society organized on the monarchical principle and tending to isolation and independence. The Roman *pater* was, in a stricter sense, priest, judge, and king. He had power of life, death, and sale over his children, lasting while he lived. His authority was antagonistic to that of the state. The latter could not, therefore, have created the *patria potestas* but, finding it already existing, a sovereignty within its borders, tolerated this institution because unable to suppress it and succeeded in modifying it only in the course of centuries. The *patria potestas*, then, seems to point to a time when the family was an independent community under the absolute rule of its *pater*, while agnation, cutting off the wife from her kin, gave to woman an inferior place and promoted isolation. The patriarchal theory, resting on this strong basis, would be further strengthened, if an example could be found of a family actually existing in remote antiquity as a separate and autonomous community and if the genesis of higher units could be traced from it as a beginning. The advocates of this view have thought that this first point of growth existed in the patriarchal family as we see it, e.g., among the Hebrews. From the family of Abraham developed the tribes and finally the city and kingdom. Another example of the isolated family is found in the Homeric picture of life among the Cyclopes. These are a pastoral people with "neither gatherings for council nor oracles of law, but they dwell in hollow caves on the crests of high hills, and each one utters the law to his children and his wives, and they reck not one of another."[3] While these examples of the patriarchal family are, indeed, non-Aryan, there are reasons for believing that it existed also among the Aryans in a period preceding that of the clan. [pp. 1-4]

NOTES

1. G.W. Botsford, *The Development of the Athenian Constitution* (New York : Cornell University Press, reprinted 1965, copyright 1893), pp. 1-4.
2. Aristotle, *Politics* 1.2.1252b12.
3. Homer, *Odyssey* 9.112-115.

INTRODUCTION TO EARLY ROMAN LAW
Patria Potestas[1]

C.W. Westrup

The Patriarchal Joint Family

Among the Aryan-speaking peoples the family was in early times everywhere autonomous : law is virtually formed through customs created within the family by concrete judicial interpretation of justice. The Roman *patria potestas* itself, according to the classical juris-consults, had its origin in custom. And the instrument of this autonomy is the head of the house. The house-father is the interpreter of the legal traditions (*mores* of the Romans) handed down from father to son. What the father had learnt as the custom of his forefathers he again taught his son. The *paterfamilias* does not create law. But as the person who, by virtue of the higher insight accorded him by the gods, had uncontested and incontestable knowledge of ancestral customs, of the legal usages, he had to interpret, to "show," to say, to dictate what was Law *(jus dicere).* It is this fundamental feature, common to the primitive family everywhere, this hereditary personal authority of the *paterfamilias* which, despite all differences in the cultural stage, is described in the Homeric tale about "the primitive habits of the *Kyklopes,*" to use Plato's expression. They have neither common political assemblies nor universal laws common to all. "Each (father of a family) gives his own law to sons and wives without recking of others."[2] In the third book of the *Laws* Plato, like Aristotle in his *Politics,* with true intuition gives an account — no doubt in accordance with historical reality — of the primitive community and its first political development, and quotes just this Homeric passage in order to characterize the form of government in the early Greek family : "Those born in that age lived by following custom and what is called patriarchal law."[3] They lived in scattered families says Aristotle, "and that is the way, in which people used to live in early times."[4] [When the individual families and settlements later by a union formed cities, each of them brought with them their peculiar customs and usages which then constituted the common law, in so far as they were consistent with the new larger community.]. . . The head is the eldest of the household. Aristotle says in his *Ethica Nicomachea* that, while in Lakedaimon the state by its laws has taken charge of the education and mode of life of the citizens, such matters were entirely neglected in most other cities. Each (house-father) lives his life according to his own will and like the *Kyklopes* gives laws to sons and wives.[5] According to the Greek tradition each peasant family, even after Theseus had founded the Athenian state, lives scattered in separate households, isolated from others and autonomous.

Through the natural autonomy of the house, with the head of the house as the hereditary personal interpreter and upholder of the traditions, the family took shape as a legal institution....

[Within the family it was right down into historical times the *paterfamilias* who, as the intermediary of the legal traditions, decided what was law. Even long after the family chief had been deprived of his autonomous power — in Greece as far back as the earliest historical times — it was in general not by means of statutorily formulated laws but, as hitherto, through "self-grown" customary laws arising within the family, through unwritten customs only later enacted in writing, that the law arose.]

The maxim still having formal constitutional validity among the Romans as late as the time of the classical juris-consults, that the internal controversies of the family should be settled *intra domum* or, in judicial terms, that the state should not in principle interfere by statutory measures for control or direct restriction in the family's private concerns, is not, in its primitive form, a particular national Roman, legal axiom. According to Dionysios this principle was also known in historical Sparta : the State neither cared nor concerned itself with what happened within the family. The door of the house was to everyone a boundary where a life in liberty began. The same principle of family autonomy is supposed to have dominated the old Teutonic cultivating community : "Each family in the township was governed by its own free head of the family or *paterfamilias.* The precinct of the family dwelling-house could be entered by nobody but himself, not even by the officers of the law, for he himself made law within, and enforced the law made without.'"[6] It was merely that, among the Romans, this principle, legally and juridicially developed, acquired a greater fundamental importance. In all law it marks the point of departure. But in early Rome the customs *(mores)* arising and handed down within the family, with the *paterfamilias* as the upholder of the traditions in connection with sacral law *(fas)*, entirely dominated the historical development of the law.

The earliest traditions of the various Aryan-speaking peoples would seem to suggest that a house community comprising several generations, the joint undivided family, was the primitive common Aryan form of family. And what comparative law would seem to show is strengthened by linguistic evidence....

The economic and social conditions which, in connection with the religious ideas, created the house-community of the joint undivided family, were bound to give its individual fundamental institutions their essential stamp and, in particular, must necessarily determine the form of government. Where the family consisted not only of parents and children, but of several generations living in the same house and joined together through common worship, common work, and common property into a social-political unit, a single person must be invested with authority and power to gather into his hand *(manus)* the government of the family *(domus).* A single person (normally, we may assume, the eldest male of the eldest line) must by virtue of a natural monocratic principle be the manager of the house, the head of the "joint family", must — in Roman legal terms — *in domo dominium habere.* And this headship belonged to him, we may suppose, in the first place as the religious head of the family.

As the priest of the family it was a sacred duty for the head of the house to take charge of the ancestral cult. At the paternal hearth, *focus patrius,* whose ever-burning flame was a symbol of the perpetuation of the race, he had to perform the death sacrifices and offer up the prayers enjoined by the rites handed down from generation to generation. And as the person who was thus the intermediary between the departed "fathers" *(divi parentes)* and the coming generations (and hence responsible for the continued existence of the family), he must have power to decide and dispose in all religious matters. Just as it certainly was not the common cult which alone founded the family, the house, thus it was not either, we may suppose, the religious authority alone which made the house-father the primitively peculiar *paterfamilias.* But, in everything that concerned the *sacra* of the family, the decision must be with the family chief. He must decide who was to be admitted to the family and who excluded from it. It was only by his solemn strongly religiously stressed recognition *(liberum tollere)* that the new-born child was adopted as a child of the house, and so admitted into the family and its cult. Only by virtue of the house-father's decision could the sons, and the grandsons, bring their wives into the paternal family and let them share in its *sacra.* His decision was required for the marriage of the daughters (sons' daughters) which, because of the agnatic character of the cult community, implied an emancipation *(detestatio)* from the paternal *sacra.* As the person liable for the perpetuation of the ancestral cult, and hence of the race, it was his duty to see that the sons (and grandsons) were married in due course.

As the person entrusted with the charge of upholding the ancestral customs, as *judex domesticus* he must, however, also have authority *(imperium)* to maintain order and discipline within the family among the freemen and slaves of the house community. And as the economic head of the house, whose duty it was to keep together the family property, so that it might constantly serve as a basis for the spiritual and material subsistence of the family, the house-father must be invested with the authority to decide — on behalf of the house and in the interest of the family — how the work should be divided and the proceeds be applied *(administratio bonorum),* and must have that power to act which was required by the concrete economic system, created by the material development. What the sons — and grandsons — acquired through their work for the needs of the house must also be subject to the disposal of the head of the house for the common benefit of the family.

In relations with the outside world he alone could act for the family, contract valid obligations and appear in lawsuits. Only the *paterfamilias* was — in Roman legal terms — *sui juris.* For the obligations of a delictual nature, too, incurred by the individual members of the family, he must consequently, in principle, be liable on behalf of the house. For the unjust acts (delicts) of the family he was responsible as for his own guilt. In terms of Roman law : *noxa caput sequitur....* [pp. 143-152]

That the house-father should, as generally assumed, have possessed the same power in the house in his capacity of religious authority, of magistrate and judge, and of manager of the family estate is a *petitio principii* which has had a fatal influence on the historical investigation of the whole "legal" structure of the early Aryan and especially the Roman family. The material legal and juridical contents of the house-father's *potestas* in its various relations cannot be deduced by general logical inferences, but must, as far as possible, be determined, in certain fundamental features, by concrete sociological investigations into the material character of the individual functions assigned to the *paterfamilias* in his capacity of priest, judge, and economic manager of the family.

As the religious head of the family he was indeed bound by the precepts of the sacral Law, but as the person who was alone responsible to the gods for the due performance of the ancestral cult and hence for the perpetuation of the race he must in carrying out the concrete sacral act — in his interpretation of the sacred law — as a matter of course be justified in performing it as his own conscientious judgment dictated. As the manager of the family estate, on the other hand, he alone had certainly the ability and power to act *(potestas),* but in all important dispositions he was, as long as the ancient community of property persisted, of necessity positively limited by the customary rules, created by the joint rights of the descendants — in different ways in the various stages of the economic development (community of use, community of property, co-existent or successive).... [pp. 158-159]

If we would seek to form a historical conception of the actual binding norms of the primitive *patria potestas,* we must first try to gain an idea of the general social character of the system of precepts that — securing law and order — dominated the early Roman commonwealth.

In the primitive community there is no differentiation between those manifestations which are, by the discrimination of later times, termed respectively religious commandment, moral precepts, and legal rules (*jus*). In the regulating and binding rules of conduct that dominated the legal fellowship which, by virtue of a law of necessity, made up the primitive community too, religion, morals, and law, in consequence of their common divine origin, are not yet or are but very little separated. Only by degrees, and very slowly, a differentiation begins to be made. A legal order which had developed into an independent system of precepts belongs to a relatively late age.... [pp. 177-178]

If we would try to form an idea of the primitive *patria potestas,* we must refrain from all abstract constructions on the basis of the dogmatically evolved definitions of a later jurisprudence. It is in other ways that we must seek to form a historical, a sociologically founded historical conception. One-sided juridical reconstructions, which entirely leave out of consideration the very real forces, the peculiar and powerful factors, that once dominated social life and especially the family, and secured obedience to the law by other means than external direct compulsion, must be replaced by an — unprejudiced — historical understanding, built up by and founded on juridical sociology, supported by logical and psychological arguments.

On the basis of the conception that a house community comprising several generations, the joint undivided family, was the primitive common Aryan form of family, we have by logical conclusions combined with linguistic evidence thought it possible to determine the primitive Aryan *patria potestas* in general as a simple logical consequence of the ancient patriarchal house community joined together into a social unit through a common cult, common work, and common property. Just as the point of crystallization of the family was the house, so the existence of the household and its power of action were embodied in the person of the master of the house. The house-father was in a representative form "the man in the house" — "himself." The house-father was the family : in the small political-social organism made up by the family the actual exercise of the power in the house *(dominium in domo)* belonged to the head of the family, *princeps familiae.* All the authority and the power to act which was given by the law was concentrated in the hand *(manus)* of the master of the house. Just as he was the religious head of the family and its *judex domesticus,* so also he had, as the manager of the house property, that economic *potestas* which was required by the concrete economic system of law created by the material evolution. But this, in reality merely formal, definition of the general legal character of early *patria potestas* has as yet settled nothing about the material — juridical content of this power.

These investigations supported by the evidence of comparative law and the history of languages seem, however, to let us faintly descry certain primary legal notions and legal institutions, which are hardly reconcilable with the current definition of the *patria potestas* in early style as being in its essence simply arbitrariness. Just as the family organization itself, the house community, united through a common cult and common property, was not merely, in primitive law, an actual form of common life, but a community of law under a patriarchal government organized through ancient customs, so also the *potestas* of the *paterfamilias* was, we may assume, not in its nature an arbitrary display of power, but a distribution of justice founded and bound by ancestral legal traditions handed down from generation to generation by the head of the house. And this surely applies to primitive Roman law more than to any other early law. [pp. 185-186]

NOTES

1. C.W. Westrup, *Introduction to Early Roman Law, Patria Potestas*, vol. 3, book 2 (London : Oxford University Press, 1939), pp. 143-186.
2. Homer *Odyssey* 9.112 ff.
3. Plato *Nomoi* 3.680a (Bury).
4. Aristotle l.c.
5. Aristotle *Nichomachean Ethics* 10.9, 13.
6. Maurer in Maine, *Village Communities in the East and West* (1871), p. 78.

LAW AND SOCIETY IN TRADITIONAL CHINA[1]

T'Ung-Tsu Ch'u

The Chinese family was patriarchal. The grandfather or father was the ruling head and had authority over all the members of the family, including his wife and concubines, his sons and grandsons, their wives and children, his unmarried daughters, his collateral relatives who were junior to him and who shared his domicile, his slaves and servants. His control of the family economy and his power to make financial decisions strengthened his authority. In addition, since the concept of ancestor worship was central to the perpetuation and solidarity of the family, the authority of the family head, who was also the family priest, was further enhanced. Finally, his authority was recognized and supported by the law.

In a family of two generations, which includes only parents and children, the father is the absolute head. In a family of three generations, the grandfather is the supreme authority. Every family, large or small, has a recognized head who exercises absolute and permanent authority over his male descendants. Even when sons and grandsons are of age they have no right to independence.... [p. 20]

The above facts indicate the almost absolute power of the parent over his child. The government merely acted as agent, framed the regulations and saw to it that they were carried out. But the will of the parents was decisive and, generally speaking, a child's freedom or lack of it depended on that will. The law was the chief instrument through which the parental will was recognized and implemented.... [p. 27]

Obviously, whether he was to be beaten or banished depended entirely on the will of his parents. The authorities merely acted as punishing agents.

As noted above, when parents asked to have an unfilial son prosecuted, the authorities demanded no evidence, nor did they raise any objections to the punishment asked. The law states clearly : "When a father or mother prosecutes a son, the authorities will acquiesce without question or trial." "No parents in the world are wrong" is a very popular adage in China.

Thus, parents in China had absolute power to control and punish their children. According to Confucian ethics a son should "obey and never show resentment." It was all a question of filial piety. Right and wrong were a matter of position : I am wrong because I am my father's son ; what he says or does is right because he is my father. A son should not argue with his parents. Nor should the authorities question the reason given by the parents and investigate whether the accused child was actually unfilial. If they did, it would have meant that the parents might be wrong. It would also have meant that the father's absolute authority was not recognized.... [pp. 28-29]

In conclusion, the father, or whoever was the family head, was then the supreme authority within the family. His will was a command, and every member of the family was expected to obey it. Ssu-ma Kuang (1019-1086) said, "All the inferiors and the younger ones must consult the head of the family about every event, large or small. How dare an inferior do anything without asking permission from his parents ? You must ask permission from the head of the family, even though he is not your parent, before you do anything ; then the orders will come from one person only, and the family will be in order."

Generally speaking, a mother had the same authority over her children as had the father. Society and the law also demanded that a son respect and be filial to his mother. Disobedience to either parent was punishable and in the same degree. Nevertheless, speaking strictly, the father's authority was supreme. The mother's derived from her position as his wife : "When she is not the wife of Chi, she is not the mother of Pai." The mother's authority was therefore neither permanent nor absolute. She was expected to follow her husband's will in every respect. Theoretically speaking this should assure continual agreement. Actually this was not always the case and, when conflict arose, the husband's authority took precedence. The mother was expected to assist her husband in ruling over their immediate family and over those other family members who were his inferiors. A father could beat or punish his offspring whenever he believed he was justified in so doing, and this despite his wife's feelings to the contrary. A son would not oppose his mother's choice of his mate, but it was his father who made the final decision. Thus the ancients said, "There are no two supremes in a family." It was usually expressed thus, "Mother is dear but not superior...."

Only a male could hold the position of family head. Usually it was a grandfather or a father, but at times it might be a grandfather's brother, father's brother, an elder brother, or cousin. Whoever was the recognized head exercised the "father's"authority. When a family head died his son would take over, never his wife, whether she were grandmother or mother. She was expected to "follow" her son, unless he was too young to function adequately, in which case some male of a senior generation in a collateral line would exercise a father's authority.... [pp. 30-31]

According to Ming and Ch'ing law, one who scolded his elder paternal cousins in the fourth degree (great-grandfather's brother's great grandson or granddaughter) was punished by fifty strokes ; for elder cousins in the third degree (grandfather's brother's grandson or granddaughter) by sixty strokes ; for elder cousins in the second degree (father's brother's son and daughter) by seventy strokes ; and to scold one's own elder brother and sister by one hundred strokes. When the person was an elder in a higher generation the punishment was increased one degree according to the scale just noted. Thus to scold a fourth-degree great-granduncle, granduncle, uncle (great-grandfather's brother, their sons, and their grandsons), and their wives, a third-degree granduncle, uncle (grandfather's brothers and their sons), and their wives, or first-degree uncle (father's brothers), and their wives was punished by sixty, seventy, and one hundred strokes respectively, together with one year's imprisonment in each case.

Punishment for striking one's elder relative was granted on the same basis. For striking one's own elder brother or sister the punishment was increased to a five-year punishment during the time of Wei (220-265). A more elaborate system was worked out in later times. The T'ang, Sung, Ming, and Ch'ing law stated that to strike a fourth-degree cousin, regardless of whether or not he was harmed, would be punished by one hundred strokes ; for a third-degree cousin one year's imprisonment ; for one in the second degree one and a half year's imprisonment. If severe injury resulted in any of the above cases the punishment was generally one degree more severe than in ordinary cases (one degree more severe for fourth-degree cousins, two degrees more severe for third-degree cousins, and three degrees more severe for second-degree cousins). When the wound occasioned disability the offender was strangled. If death resulted the offender was beheaded.

The punishment for striking an elder brother or sister was imprisonment for two and a half years when no injury resulted, or three years' imprisonment if the victim was wounded. If a tooth, finger, toe, or rib was broken by the blow, the punishment was banishment to a distance of three thousand *li* ; if a wound was caused by a sharp-bladed instrument or if a limb was broken or an eye blinded, the offender was strangled ; if death resulted, the punishment was beheading.

If the victim was of a higher generation, the punishment in each case was more severe by one degree than that for the same generation. Thus anyone who struck his fourth-degree granduncle or uncle was punished by one year in prison, by one and a half year's confinement if the individual was in the third degree ; by two years if he was in the second degree. If the elder was wounded, the punishment was two degrees, three degrees and four degrees more severe than in ordinary cases, depending upon the degree of relationship. In case of disability or death, the punishment was the same as that for striking an elder cousin.

For striking one's father's brothers and their wives or a father's sister, the punishment was one degree more severe in each one of the cases than in the case of striking an elder brother or sister.

The punishment for killing one's father's brother or his wife, father's sister, one's own elder brother or sister with intent to kill was, according to the law of Ming and Ch'ing, dismemberment.... [pp. 54-55]

But man's superiority over woman was well established in the basic Chinese philosophy of ancient times and it was this philosophy that underlay the relations between men and women in traditional Chinese society. Under the principle of the "three dependencies" a woman could never act autonomously. On her wedding day her parents gave her the final instructions, saying, "Be respectful and cautious, do not disobey your husband." The husband's authority replaced the father's, and "the husband was a leader to his wife" in much the same way as the ruler was a leader to his minister, the father to his son.

In the family the division of labour between the sexes also rested on man's recognized superiority to woman. It had long been orthodox for man to rule outside the household, woman within it. Care of the children, cooking, washing, sewing, cleaning, and directing the maid servants were all inside tasks — in their final analysis services for the husband. Such expressions, "to stand by with towels and combs" and "to hold a broom" were commonly used by the wife to underline her humble position vis-a-vis her husband. The story of Huai-ying who held a basin for prince Ch'ung-erh reveals that even in a princely family, humble labours of this kind were performed by the wife and not by domestics.

The character of "woman" is a combination of *nu* "female" and *chou* "broom." It has the meaning "to serve" and "to submit."

Within the household, all the women and children who lived in the inner quarters were under the control of the mistress. Included were the younger sisters-in-law, concubines, unmarried sisters of the husband, daughters, daughters-in-law, nieces, servants, and little boys. Nevertheless, the position of the mistress was also a submissive one. Whenever her ideas or wishes conflicted with her husband's, she had to bow to his authority.

Under the principle of no two authorities in one family, woman was eliminated from being the head of a family. The wife was to submit to the husband. Even after his death, her son, or some other male member of her husband's family, succeeded to his position ; and although a mother or grandmother was senior to her son or grandson, she could never become the family head. An ancient proverb says, "If a hen rules at morning, the family comes to an end."

A wife's authority was controlled and limited by her husband. To be sure, she had the right to discipline her children and arrange for their marriages, but she could not go counter to her husband's will. And while she had authority to control the household and the household property, this authority also derived from her husband. Any activity over and above routine matters had to be approved by him. This was clearly stated by the Supreme Court as late as 1916. Undoubtedly, it reflected a traditional viewpoint.

A wife owned no property. Usually, she received a limited sum of money for household expenses and this she spent as she saw fit but she had no power to dispose over the family property. Most important, this family property descended directly to her son or adopted heir after her husband's death. If her son was not yet grown, she could manage the property in his behalf until he reached maturity. In Ch'ing times a widow who remarried was prohibited from taking either her former husband's property or even her dowry with her. Both remained with the latter's family. As late as 1918 the Supreme Court maintained that the wife's own property was subject to the husband's authority....

It has been shown that within a family, seniors and juniors are not treated as equals under the law. As far as husband and wife are concerned, the former is regarded as the senior, the latter as the junior....

A wife who accused her husband was "offending against status and right principles" *kan-ming fan-i* and was accorded the same punishment as a junior who accused a senior.... [pp. 102-105]

Men of different social status in a capitalist society may buy the same things and live the same way ; or a man of superior status, who is not wealthy or who prefers to live simply, may have a lower standard of living than one who is his social inferior. Such behaviour is not thought to disturb the social order and nothing is done about it. In such a society there is no legal restriction on consumption.

The situation in Chinese society prior to 1912 was the exact opposite. Consumption was positively correlated with status, and a man's status determined his standard of living. It was recommended in the *Kauntzu* that restrictions be placed, in accordance with status, on food, clothing, housing, domestic animals, attendants, boats, carriages. and utensils ; that during life there should be differences in hats, clothing, salaries, land, and houses and after death in coffins, funeral clothes, and graves.

The *Hsin-shu* also remarked that since the statuses differed there should be differences in titles, power, salaries, flags, hats, shoes, clothing, belts, ornaments, carriages, horses, wives, houses, beds, mats, utensils, food drinks, sacrifices, and funerals. Thus, "by looking at a man's dress it can be seen whether he is noble or humble and, by looking at a man's flag, his power can be ascertained." In such a society property alone did not give prestige nor did it guarantee the right to consume. A man of superior status might be unable to possess something to which he was entitled because he lacked the wherewithal to buy it, but a wealthy man was not permitted to possess goods to which his status did not entitle him.

Different styles of life, corresponding to different statuses, were regarded as prerequisites for maintaining the social and political order, and an administration was judged good or bad according to its success in maintaining these differences. From time to time imperial edicts warned those who had violated the regulations concerning dress and ornament. Many officials also memorialized, asking for investigation of such violations, since they were considered dangerous to the social order. For this reason, these regulations were not only set down in the patterns of behaviour which distinguished the noble from the humble and which were enforced by education, ethics, custom, and social sanction,but they were also incorporated in the law. Obviously these sumptuary laws and the penalties meted out in case of violation served to guarantee that the privileged status group could enjoy exclusively a particular style of life and that it would not be threatened by a propertied class.... [pp. 135-136]

In the typical Chinese society, as shown above, class distinctions were based on social and political factors. However, in conquest dynasties a line was drawn between different ethnic groups. The conquerors always regarded themselves as superior to the conquered, and the latter were discriminated against. The inequalities were expressed socially, politically, and legally.

When the Ch'i-tan, Jurchen, Mongols, and Manchus conquered and ruled over China, the inequalities were extremely significant. The conquering group considered itself the superior one. Differences were also recognized among the conquered groups : those who submitted first were usually considered superior to those who submitted later. Under Liao, the status of the Ch'i-tan was superior to that of the Chinese and the Po-hai. Under Chin, the Jurchen ranked highest among the various peoples of the empire ; next came those who had been taken over from Liao, the "Han people." The lowest rung was occupied by the southern people, the Chinese in what is now Shantung and Honan, who were the last to submit. Under Yuan, four strata were clearly defined : the Mongols at the top, then the Se-mu, the people of the western regions who had submitted in Chingis Khan's time, the Han, who had been taken over from Chin, and the Southerners, who had submitted after the Southern Sung dynasty was overthrown. In Ch'ing times, the Manchus were always superior to the Chinese (Han people).... [p. 201]

To the Confucianist the differences in nearness and remoteness, in superiority and inferiority, and in seniority and juniority which operated within a kin group, and the differences in superiority and inferiority which operated in the society at large were of equal importance. Both classes of differences were indispensable to the maintenance of the social order. To them the social order was but the sum total of these two kinds of social differences. Confucius said, "Benevolence is (the chief element in) humanity, and the greatest exercise of it is in the honour paid to the worthy."[2] A society in which honourableness and humbleness, superiority and inferiority, seniority and juniority, nearness and remoteness were clearly defined constituted the ideal society ; and conversely, a lack of distinction between these various features was extremely repugnant to the Confucianists. It was said that the main reason for Confucius' writing the *Ch'un-chi'iu* was to censure those rebellious officials and sons who disregarded the prescribed distinctions. Hsun-tzu says, "Not to differentiate causes the greatest injury to human beings. To differentiate forms the basic advantage of the world." He lists three kinds of misfortune : the young who are not willing to serve their elders ; the humble who are not willing to serve the noble ; and the unworthy who are not willing to serve the virtuous.

Therefore the most essential thing is that men's statuses shall be clearly defined, and that their expected roles shall be properly carried out. This depends upon the presence of a body of approved behaviour patterns. The *li*, which may be defined as the rules of behaviour varying in accordance with one's status defined in the various forms of social relationships, were formulated by the Confucianists for this purpose. They are the means by which differences in status and role are maintained. "When a person's title and position are different, the *li* used are also different."[3]

Unlike music, whose function is to achieve homogeneity, the function of *li* is to achieve differentiation. We find the following in the Classics :

> Music aims at homogeneity ; *li* aim at differentiation.[4]
> Music embraces what is equal ; *li* distinguish between what is different.[5]
> Music unites the homogenous ; *li* distinguish between differences.[6]
> *Li* are not the same.[7]

This function of the *li* to discriminate between persons according to their different statuses has been formulated by Hsun-tzu. "Wherein is it that man is truly man ? Because he makes distinctions . . . . Hence the path *(tao)* of human life cannot be without its distinctions ; no distinction is greater than social divisions ; no social division is greater than the rule for proper conduct *[li]*."[8] Similar emphasis on this point is also found in many other sources :

[Li] are the rules of propriety that furnish the means of determining the (observances towards) relatives as near and remote ; of settling the points which may cause suspicion or doubt of distinguishing where there should be agreement, and where difference, and of making clear what is right and what is wrong.[9]

The decreasing measures in the love of relatives, and the steps in the honour paid to the worthy, are produced by (the principle of) propriety *[li]*.[10]

Hence the rules of proper conduct *(li)* are to educate and nourish. When the superior man has gotten its education and nourishment, he also esteems its distinctions. What are meant by its distinctions ? There are classes of the noble and the base ; there are the inequalities of the senior and the younger ; there is what is appropriate to those who are poor and those who are rich, to those who are unimportant and those who are important.[11]

Hence the ancient kings invented the rules of proper conduct *(li)* and justice *(yi)* for men in order to divide them, causing them to have the classes of noble and base, the disparity between the aged and the young, and the distinction between the wise and the stupid, the able and the powerless ; all to cause men to assume their duties and each one to get his proper position.[12]

The ancient kings hated any disorder, and hence established the rules of proper conduct *(li)* and justice *(yi)* to divide the people, to cause them to have the classes of poor and rich, of noble and inferior, so that everyone would be under someone's control.[13]

The *li* are for the purpose of distinguishing the superior from the inferior, and of discriminating between the noble and the humble.

[Li] are the interactions between the ruler and his ministers, between the father and his sons, through which the noble and the humble, the virtuous and the unworthy are distinguished from each other.

[Li] arrange the rank of the superior and the inferior, of the noble and the humble, and the great and the small in order to distinguish the grades of the external and internal, the remote and the near, and the new and the old.[14]

There is justice between the upper and the lower ; there is distinction between the noble and the humble, there are grades between the elders and the young. There is a [difference in] standing between the rich and the poor. The above eight are the essentials of *li*.

Li arrange people in their ranks.[15]

[*Li* are used] to order the upper and the lower, to regulate the ways of human life.[16]

To advance and to retire within boundaries, to have distinction between the superior and the inferior, this is called *li*.... [pp. 229-233]

How were the *li* implemented ? How were the violations handled ? The Confucianist believed that no matter whether human nature was good or bad, it was possible to bring about improvement by moral and educational influences. To improve the heart through education enabled a man to become good and to become conscious of shame without, however, suffering from evil intentions. To the Confucianist this was the most thorough, the most fundamental, and the most successful way to attain their social aims....

Since moral influence could function so broadly and so permanently, the Confucian School strongly advocated ruling by virtue. Confucius drew an analogy between governing by virtue and the character of the north polar star which remains fixed in its place while all others turn toward it. "If the people be led by laws, and uniformity sought to be given them by punishments, they will try to avoid punishment, but have no sense of shame," said the master. "If they be led by virtue, and uniformity sought to be given them by the rules of propriety [*li*], they will have the sense of shame and moreover will become good."[17]

Even if the people violate the rules, the Confucianists do not feel that these erring ones should be punished by law, for law can never be effective in keeping a society from deteriorating. It can neither prevent evils from occurring nor remedy them after they have occurred. It would be as little effective as an effort to stop water from boiling by adding hot water or an attempt to extinguish a fire by adding a bundle of wood. Moreover, when people are guilty the fault is not theirs, but the ruler's, for their guilt is due to an inoperative or only partially operative system of education. "To put the people to death without having instructed them — this is called cruelty. To require from them, suddenly, the full task of work, without having given them warning — this is called oppression."[18] Therefore Confucius maintained that to govern properly, a country must rid itself of punishment and killing, and the ruler must exercise greater moral influence to attain the ideal political order....

The relation of the ruler to his subjects was also compared to the relation of the sun dial and the shadow to the source and the stream and to the mould and the molten metal. If the sun dial was correct, the shadow would be correct. If the source was clear, the stream would be clear. And it was the mould which determined the shape of the metal in the pot. In short, the behaviour of the inferior was merely a response to the behaviour of the superior....

The Legalists' position, as noted before, was diametrically opposed to that of the Confucianists. The former denied that moral influence alone could determine the social order and that some one or two persons could wield enough power to transform the customs of the land and create either order or disorder within the state.... [pp. 247-257]

The distinction between the superior and the inferior was strongly emphasized by the Confucianists. It was basic in the development of the *li.* Therefore the regulations governing special considerations as regards punishments as well as requests for the emperor's approval were incorporated into the law. The noble and the mean were subject to different punishments, and the officials were permitted to use their rank to cancel their punishments. Also, according to *li,* clothing, ornaments, houses, horses and carriages, marriage rites, funeral rites, and sacrifices varied with political and social status. Thus all manner of sumptuary laws found their way into the codes.

The Confucianists also emphasized familism and gave importance to distinctions between seniority and juniority among family members, and between nearness and remoteness. All these features were, therefore, given consideration in law, and the degree of punishment adjusted to them. The mourning system, which made explicit these varying degrees of relationship, became an important factor in litigation.

Filial piety implicit in the familistic ideal was also strongly stressed by the Confucianists. The *Hsiao ching* reads, "There are three thousand offences against which the five punishments are directed, and there is not one of them greater than being unfilial." Therefore the punishment for being unfilial was necessarily severe. Not only were special articles on this point formulated in the codes, but the crime of "not being filial" was even included in the Ten Offences listed in the introductory chapter of the codes from the time of Northern Ch'i to that of Ch'ing. According to *li,* children should serve their parents dutifully. Therefore "not supporting the parents" was defined in the law. According to *li,* children should not have private property. Therefore "having private property" was punishable. According to *li*, three years' mourning was required of a son on the death of his parents. Therefore, to marry, to be an official, or to be entertained with music during the period of mourning was punishable. Confucius said that the father should conceal the crimes of his sons, and the sons, the crimes of their father. Therefore, such concealment was permissible, and the law did not ask that a man's children bear witness against him. Nor were children permitted to bring accusations against their parents. According to *li*, a man could not live under the same sky as his father's enemy. Therefore, although the law failed to mention the subject, cases of blood revenge were often pardoned. And also according to *li*, there were seven conditions for divorcing a wife and three conditions under which a wife could not be divorced, and these conditions became the legal basis of divorce. The *li*, then, formed the basis for all laws dealing with the family, marriage, and inheritance. The *ssu-kk'u ch'uan-shu tsung-mu t'i-yao* notes that the T'ang code was based entirely on the *li*. This is obviously correct, but we must remember that this observation is equally applicable to many other ancient Chinese codes. Originally, these rules of behaviour were regulated in detail in the books of *li*. Later, when the law was formulated, the behaviour prescribed by *li* was incorporated into the codes. What was approved by *li* was thus also approved by law and considered as legal; and what was not tolerated and was tabooed by *li* was also prohibited and punished by law. Thus Ch'en Ch'ung, the Minister of Justice in the first century, said, "What is left by *li* is covered by punishment. To go beyond *li* means to enter punishment. The two are but the outside and the inside of the same thing."

The ancient people frequently mentioned *li* and law together, and such terms as *li fa* or *li lu (li* and law) were common in their writings. The relation between *li* and law was obviously close.

We may say that originally *li* were enforced by social sanction, and later by legal sanction. A rule of behaviour enforced by social sanction is *li*; the same rule of behaviour is law when legal sanction is introduced. It is obvious that the same behaviour pattern may be subsumed under *li* and law at the same time. Thus the later Confucianists used political and legal power to enforce their rules of behaviour, but these norms were still included in their books of *li*, and they still sought to enforce them by morality and education. *Li* and law, while separate entities, were supplementary to each other. As the norms were simultaneously sustained by both social and legal sanctions, they imposed a strong compulsion on the members of the society.... [pp. 278-279]

The most significant development in the legal system of China, prior to the twentieth-century modernization of Chinese law, was the Confucianization of law. The law codes of the state of Wei, and of Ch'in and Han were compiled by the Legalists who won dominance over Confucianists and controlled the government. But with the triumph of the Confucianists in the second century B.C., when Confucianism became the state philosophy, they began to use their influence to interpret and apply the law in accordance with Confucianist doctrines and, most important of all, to revise the law by incorporating *li* into it. As shown in this study, Confucianization was a gradual process, one which began in the Han dynasty and continued through the Southern and the Northern Dynasties. Such important laws as not permitting sons to live separately from their parents, *pa-i* (eight conditions for consideration), Ten Offences, punishment based upon the five degrees of mourning, criminals reprieved from execution in order to serve their aged parents, concealment, and *kuan-t'ang* (cancellation of punishment by surrendering one's official post) — all were introduced in this period, between the third and sixth centuries. By the time of the Sui and the T'ang, the process of Confucianization was more or less completed. The T'ang law represented the fullest development of Confucianization. Confucian doctrines, especially the essential themes of *li*, then came to dominate the law.

The main characteristic of Chinese law, after it had become Confucianized, was its emphasis on the status factor which found expression both in the kinship system and the system of stratification. This study shows clearly that the family and the stratification order were fundamental features in traditional Chinese law. This law fully recognized the parents' authority in controlling and chastising their children. The latter had no independent right to own private property, to live separately from their parents, or to choose their own spouses. The law also recognized the supremacy of seniors and husbands over junior relatives and wives. Disputes between and persecution of family members were always judged according to an individual's status in the kinship group. The law of concealment and other laws . . . similarly indicate the dominance of family ethics in Chinese law.

The law also recognized the differing status of nobles, officials, commoners, and the "mean" people. There existed sumptuary laws, which regulated a person's mode of life in accordance with his social and legal status. Above all, people of different status were not treated alike before the law. Nobles and officials enjoyed certain legal privileges, whereas the "mean" people were legally unprivileged.

. . .No substantial change occurred in the kinship system. Not only did the father remain the supreme authority within the family, but his authority was even increased. Similarly, the increase in the husband's authority strengthened the status relationship between the husband and wife.

There was also no significant change in the stratification system. Officials, commoners, and the "mean" people remained the three major social classes throughout the history of China. Their statuses were clearly defined. The laws governing their rights of consumption, marriage, legal privileges (or disabilities) were maintained. The removal of certain regionally defined groups from the "mean" category should not be seen as the emancipation of the "mean" people as a class. Not only did the slaves remain "mean" people, but prostitutes, entertainers, and government runners were also included. The fact that special laws dealing with the hired servants, whose status was somewhat between the slaves and the free men, were formulated in the Ming and the Ch'ing was an indication that the lawmakers were very much concerned with the delicate differences in social status. All these laws consolidated rather than weakened the stratification order.

In conclusion, after the law had been crystallized by the Confucianists, there were no fundamental changes in it up to the nineteenth century, as far as family and social classes are concerned. In spite of various changes in law, the fundamental characteristics of Chinese law remained the same. This law was dominated by the *li*, with great emphasis on status in the kinship system and in the stratification system, both of which were considered by the Confucianists as the essential themes of the *li* and the backbone of the social and political order. Within this frame of reference, we may speak of a law as being relatively stable.

It is not difficult to understand why there were no fundamental changes in the law, a fact which seems rather surprising at first glance. An explanation is to be found in the value system, for there is a close relation between norms and values. The essential doctrines of *li*, namely royalty, filial piety, three bonds (*san-kang*), five cardinal human relationships, generally labelled as *li-chiao* (doctrines of *li*), *ling-chiao* (doctrines of status), *lun-ch'ang* (the constant principles of five relationships) or *kang-ch'ang* (the constant principles of the three kang) were basic values long dominant in society, centuries before the law was Confucianized. The specific rules of behaviour, *li* and law, were norms designed to maintain and enforce these values. Since the Confucian values, accepted by society as ultimate, remained unchanged, the norms were also basically unchanged. Moreover, a social change always involves a change in the value system, an essential component of social structure; such a change is likely to have far-reaching consequences for the social system. On the other hand, no significant social change can take place without a change in social values. This explains why there was a remarkable continuity in the history of China. As the Confucian values dominated both law and society, we find stability in law and society.

This body of law, being consistent with the basic values, functioned more or less effectively in society. Since the *li* and the law were closely integrated and were enforced by social and legal sanctions simultaneously, an extremely strong compulsion was imposed on the members of society.

Now we should ask : what did this kind of law mean in society ? What was the role of law in society ?

First, in accordance with the Confucian concept of law, the latter, as an instrument for implementing *li*, was subordinated to *li* and ethics. It was mainly regulative and punitive. Law was seen as more or less identical to punishment, which was invoked whenever *li* or moral principles were violated. Consequently law played only a secondary role in society. It failed to develop a body of rules independent of *li* and ethics.

Secondly, the emphasis on status led to the development of a part of the law which was specific as to familial or social status (and thus was burdened with detailed provisions). It was this part of the law that was given first consideration. The general law (law not particularized as to status) was invoked only when a specific law could not be applied. Primary importance was given to particularism. The status of the parties involved became the main consideration in the administration of justice. Right or wrong was not an absolute standard, but relative to one's status ; this notion corresponded to the Confucian principle of "rectification of names," which emphasized that a person must act in accordance with his status as defined in the social relationships.

As a result, the law was primarily concerned with status relationship and the corresponding obligations, paying little attention to such matters as individual rights, which were incompatible with particularism. Specifically, it was particularism which prevented the development of a universal law and abstract legal principles. The emphasis on particularism shaped the characteristics of Chinese law ; it also set a limit on the development in Chinese law.

Thirdly, the law played a limited role in society, mainly because the law, essentially a penal code, included only a few provisions on family, marriage, adoption, inheritance, property, and debts. In fact, the law mainly dealt with violations and penalties for such violations. Many of these matters, which would be considered civil laws in modern concepts, were very much neglected and largely left to custom or *li* (the part which was not incorporated into the legal code). These two played a more important role than the law code in regulating social activities of the people. While *li* were usually in written form, customs which varied from area to area, were unwritten. In addition, there were rules of behaviour, often in written form, which were applicable to members of a particular group, for instance, family or *tsu* rules, guild rules, and the like.

Moreover, litigation was discouraged. Since the law was punitive, and since the people were treated in a humiliating manner before the court, it was disgrace to be involved in a legal case. Litigation was also costly, for parties involved were usually subject to extortion by clerks and runners. Consequently, there was a tendency among the people to avoid litigation. They preferred to settle disputes outside of the court. Many cases were settled within the family or *tsu*, the village, or the guild. Elders and gentry members often acted as arbitrators. Only cases which failed to be settled by these means went to court. As litigation was generally disapproved, reputable persons were not willing to get involved in another's litigation. The only group handling law suits for others were the notorious pettifoggers (*sung-shih* or *sung-kun)* who usually fomented litigation for their own profit, and for this reason they were looked down upon by society and dealt with harshly by the officials.

No significant change occured until the early twentieth century when the Chinese government began to revise and modernize its law. The modernization of Chinese law is beyond the scope of this study. However, several relevant points may be made in this conclusion to indicate how strong the traditional force was and to what degree it affected the modernization of Chinese law.

The revision of law was the result of the presence of new influence from outside, that is, the impact of modern Western law. However, it was not because the government and its people felt that the traditional law was inferior to Western law, and hence that the latter should be accepted as a model. Instead, the purpose of formulating a code basically similar to Western law was to urge the Western powers and Japan to surrender their rights to extraterritoriality.

The drafts of criminal and civil law, compiled by Japanese legal advisors and copied in the main from European and Japanese law, brought about radical changes. The Draft Criminal Code of 1907, except for a few articles dealing with the injury or murder of parents and grandparents, contained no clause dealing specifically with family status, social status, and the corresponding privileges. This Draft certainly introduced a basic change in the social structure : in terms of the family, it meant the weakening of patriarchy and the reduction of a husband's authority over his wife. The father's authority was weakened by the omission of any provision for punishing a child who had been disobedient or had scolded or accused his seniors. A parent who killed his child, on the other hand, was held guilty. Moreover, a junior was given the right of self-defence, nor was he punished more severely when he injured or killed an uncle, elder brothers, or other senior relatives than if his crime had been against a non-relative. Neither could such senior relatives have their punishments reduced for injuring or killing a junior relative. A husband's superiority was no longer recognized. To beat or kill a wife did not allow a reduced punishment. On the other hand, a wife was no longer punished for scolding or accusing her husband, nor was she subject to heavier punishment for injuring or killing her husband. In short, under the Draft, husbands and wives were given equal treatment.

The Draft also put an end to the legal recognition of class differences. No sumptuary laws were included in it ; no legal privilege was granted to nobles and officials in actions involving commoners ; and there was no law dealing with slaves and other "mean" people.

A comparison of the traditional law and the Draft shows clearly that "particularism" gave way to "universalism." In other words, the Draft was a body of law applicable to all regardless of familial or social status.

As the revised law was not consistent with the existing values and the social order a basic conflict model emerged between the modern school of thought as embodied in the modern law, and the prevailing values found in the traditional ethics. The conflict of values was clearly indicated in the arguments advanced by such scholar-officials as Chang Chi-Tung (1837-1909), Lao Nai-hsuan (1843-1921), and others who protested vehemently against the Draft. They severely attacked it on the ground that it was contrary to the Chinese doctrines of *li (li-chiao),* for it contained no special regulations on such matters as the scolding and accusing of seniors and husbands, the disobeying of parents' orders, the killing of one's children and junior relatives, the fighting or killing of a spouse, the fighting, theft, or illicit intercourse between relatives, an exemption of punishment because of aged parents, illicit intercourse between a man and an unmarried woman, etc.

They all held that the Chinese law, based on the principles of *li,* was superior to Western law, in which the five cardinal human relationships and the concept of the three bonds *(san-kang)* are neglected. Therefore, they saw no reason for abandoning the good teachings and copying an inferior law. The conflict was for them beyond compromise.

However, it may be noted that, while the conservatives found that revision in connection with the family was unacceptable, they did not formally oppose (though of course they did not approve) the abolition of sumptuary laws and those dealing with the "mean" people. As a matter of fact, the buying of slaves had been made unlawful in 1909, and these special laws applying to slaves had been eliminated from the revised Criminal Code of 1910 (the *Ta-ch'ing hsien-hsing hsing-lu).* The contrasting reaction toward these two areas of the law (the family and social classes) implies that, although both components were essential in the traditional social order, the kinship system, which had deeper roots in the society, was the most conservative element and the one most resistent to change.

The scholar officials were emotionally committed to the Confucian values which had long been accepted as ultimate truth. They considered these basic principles of the *li* the universal, unalterable principles. Once these were abandoned, the existing socio-political order would collapse, and the Chinese culture would come to an end. They took it upon themselves to defend these values passionately. [pp. 280-287]

NOTES

1. T'ung-Tsu Ch'u, *Law and Society in Traditional China* (The Hague, Netherlands : Mouton & Co. Publishers, 1961), pp. 20-287.

2. *Li Chi Chu-Su,* 52, 10b, Legge, *Texts of Confucianism,* IV, 312 ; Couvreur, *Li ki,* II, 449-450.

3. *Tso Chuan Chu-Su*, 9, 8b. *Cf.* Legge, *Chinese Classics*, V, Pt. 1, Couvreur, *Tso Tchouan*, 1, 168.

4. *Li Chi Chu-Su*, 47, 6b-7a. *Cf.* Legge, *Texts of Confucianism*, IV, 98 ; Couvreur, *Li Ki*, II, 55.

5. *Lio Chi Chu-Su*, 38, 9a. *Cf.* Legge, *Texts of Confucianism,*, IV, 114 ; Couvreur, *Li Ki*, II, 83.

6. *Hsun-Tzu*, 14, 5a. *Cf.* Dubs, *Works of Hsuntze*, 254.

7. *Li Chi Chu-Su*, 23, 8b. Cf. Legge, *Texts of Confucianism*, IV, 401 ; Couvreur, *Li Ki* I, 550.

8. *Hsun-Tzu*, 3, 5b-6a ; Dubs, *Works of Hsuntze*, 71-72.

9. *Li Chi Chu-Su*, 1, 6a ; Legge, *Texts of Confucianism*, III, 63 ; Couvreur, *Li Ki*, I, 3.

10. *Li Chi Chu-Su*, 52, 10b ; Legge, *Texts of Confucianism*, IV, 312-313 ; Couvreur, *Li Ki*, II, 450.

11. *Hsun-Tzu*, 13, 1b-2a ; Dubs, *Works of Hsuntze*, 214.

12. *Hsun-Tzu*, 2, 22a ; Dubs, *Works of Hsuntze*, 65.

13. *Hsun-Tzu*, 5, 4a ; Dubs, *Works of Hsuntze*, 124.

14. *Chu'Un-Ch'Iu Fan Lu*, 9, 6b.

15. *Tso Chuan Chu-Su*, 4, 13b. *Cf.* Legge, *Chinese Classics*, V, Pt. I, 33 ; Couvreur, *Tso Tchouan*, I, 60.

16. *Pai-Hu T-Ung*, 2, 6b-7a.

17. *Lun Yu Chu-Su*, 2, 1a-b ; Legge, *Chinese Classics*, I, 9.

18. *Lun Yu Chu-Su*, 20, 2b ; Legge, *Chinese Classics*, I, 217.

ANCIENT LAW[1]

Sir Henry Sumner Maine

The movement of progressive societies has been uniform in one respect. Through all its course it has been distinguished by the gradual dissolution of family dependency, and the growth of individual obligation in its place. The Individual is steadily substituted for the Family, as the unit of which civil laws take account. The advance has been accomplished at varying rates of celerity, and there are societies not absolutely stationary in which the collapse of the ancient organization can only be perceived by careful study of the phenomena they present. But, whatever its pace, the change has not been subject to reaction or recoil, and apparent retardations will be found to have been occasioned through the absorption of archaic ideas and customs from some entirely foreign source. Nor is it difficult to see what is the tie between man and man which replaces by degrees those forms of reciprocity in rights and duties which have their origin in the Family. It is Contract. Starting, as from one terminus of history, from a condition of society in which all the relations of Persons are summed up in the relations of Family, we seem to have steadily moved towards a phase of social order in which all these relations arise from the free agreement of Individuals. In Western Europe the progress achieved in this direction has been considerable. Thus the status of the Slave has disappeared — it has been superseded by the contractual relation of the servant to his master. The status of the Female under Tutelage, if the tutelage be understood of persons other than her husband, has also ceased to exist ; from her coming of age to her marriage all the relations she may form are relations of Contract. So too the status of the Son under Power has no true place in the law of modern European societies. If any civil obligation binds together the Parent and the child of full age, it is one to which only Contract gives its legal validity. The apparent exceptions are exceptions of that stamp which illustrate the rule. The child before years of discretion, the orphan under guardianship, the adjudged lunatic have all their capacities and incapacities regulated by the Law of Persons. But why? The reason is differently expressed in the conventional language of different systems, but in substance it is stated to the same effect by all. The great majority of Jurists are constant to the principle that the class of persons just mentioned are subject to extrinsic control on the single ground that they do not possess the faculty of forming a judgment on their own interests ; in other words, that they are wanting in the first essential of an engagement by Contract.

The word Status may be usefully employed to construct a formula expressing the law of progress thus indicated, which, whatever be its value, seems to me to be sufficiently ascertained. All the forms were derived from, and to some extent are still coloured by, the powers and privileges anciently residing in the Family. If then we employ Status, agreeably with the usage of the best writers, to signify these personal conditions only, and avoid applying the term to such conditions as are the immediate or remote result of agreement, we may say that the movement of the progressive societies has hitherto been a movement *from Status to Contract....* [p. 149]

But Ancient Law, it must again be repeated, knows next to nothing of Individuals. It is concerned not with Individuals, but with Families, not with single human beings but groups. Even when the law of the State has succeeded in penetrating the small circles of kindred into which it had originally no means of penetrating, the view it takes of Individuals is curiously different from that taken by jurisprudence in its maturest stage. The life of each citizen is not regarded as limited by birth and death ; it is but a continuation of the existence of his forefathers, and it will be prolonged in the existence of his descendents. [p. 229]

NOTE

1. Sir Henry Sumner Maine, *Ancient Law* (London : Oxford University Press, reprinted 1959, copyright 1861), pp. 149-229.

CHAPTER III

THE FOUNDATIONS OF WESTERN LAW

Western legal cultures are broadly grounded in two highly distinctive traditions : the Judeo-Christian and the Greco-Roman. The biblical understanding of justice and law is derived from revealed sources of knowledge which contain the moral basis for law and posit a direct relationship between man and God. The Greco-Roman scientific cultures, on the other hand, emphasize the necessary connection between reason and law. The many attempts of philosophers and jurists to unite moral content with scientific syllogism reveal both the strength and weakness of Western jurisprudence. Notwithstanding the medieval Christian theologians who saw no inherent difficulty in accommodating these two strands, the dilemma of unification persists to this day. Is it possible in the West to retain the constitutive elements of an existential law which incorporates the drama of particular life situations and the sense of higher purpose while, at the same time, preserving the structures necessary for the coherent management of large industrial states ?

In one sense the traditions are conflicting. In another sense, however, the dialectics of Western law, that is, the movements between reason and emotion, continue to suggest that the human experience of dispensing justice requires both traditions to flourish, one often at the expense of the other. It is possible that attempts at unifications have been resisted by the phenomenology of law itself and that it is the destiny of law to exist in a twilight zone between the two historical frameworks.

The accommodation that Western law has achieved may be most sympathetically expressed through suggesting that its sense of justice is derived from its religious roots, while its form and structure is defined in terms of Greco-Roman science and philosophy. Through the doctrine of precedent the common law has fashioned justice for the individual case on the basis of the consistent application of rules. Nevertheless, it is readily observed by commentators on our contemporary legal system that "hard cases make bad law". Such statements again reflect the recurring tension between particular justice and abstract consistency, a tension apparent throughout the history of legal theory and expressed in such phrases as posivitism and natural law, the spirit and letter of the law, and forgiveness and retribution.

1. Jerusalem

The Judaic tradition encompasses a complex dialectic between a powerful legalism and an equally powerful prophetic tradition. The priest represented a ritualistic approach to law, whereas the prophets accentuated justice and mercy. The synthesis of the priest-prophet dialectic furnished Hebrew law with values unique in the context of the ancient Near East, stressing charity, humanism, and the relief of suffering. Christianity perpetuated these values, emphasizing the spirit or purpose of the law as contrasted with literal ritualistic obedience.

Law performs a repressive civilizing function : man, outside the gates of Paradise, is thrust into conflict and needs guidelines for resolution. Psychologically, therefore, man both resists law as a necessary evil and depends on law as a necessary good. The Old Testament world was profoundly legalistic, but no more surely than subsequent Christian communities or our own modern nation-state. Law in the Old Testament, in view of prophecy and the ambiguous status of monarchy, lays out the psychological range of conflicts that are part and parcel of any community living with law.

The story of Abraham and Isaac is one of the most poignant and dramatic expositions of this conflict. Just as law is both good and evil, in a psychological sense, so too is there a bright and dark side to even the most intimate of human relationships. Without exploration of the dark side, life in the light is, at best, an illusion. The story of Abraham and Isaac juxtaposes justice in a deep psychological and existential sense with justice adorned in its universal trappings — the greater good and the grand design. As the story evolves, it becomes apparent that by choosing to order a universe according to a higher purpose, man may sacrifice the emotions nearest to him ; thus his self is denied and his very existence is threatened. On the order of God, and in God's name, Abraham was capable of the murder of his son on both the social and emotional level. In short, he was willing to embrace the universal while abandoning all existential particularity : himself, his tribal and familial identification.

Despite conflicts and divergent strands, the ancient Hebraic civilization was bound together by the concept of covenant. In the legal tradition covenant meant obedience ; in the prophetic tradition it meant commitment of the heart and soul. The Hebrews began with the simple structure of God and man. This then advanced to encompass a covenantal undertaking between God and the patriarchal fathers and, later, between God and the people of Israel. The concept of covenant is reflective of man's need to align himself with a moral personality who has a relationship with each individual and with the community at large.

The covenant obligated the people of Israel to a specific role in history. Even if the people strayed from the law they remained bound, as God was bound to them. Their practical laws affecting every aspect of their daily lives, from family law to commercial transactions, were enlightened by this covenant. The covenant, though, was not static in its design, for God's demands upon the people of Israel could be altered in the light of their conduct. This meant that in significant respects both moral and legal relationships could be altered, even redefined, in the light of changing social circumstances. As an "existential" law the Hebraic covenant was distinguishable from the law of contract, which, in contrast, defined legal relationships in a depersonalized and abstract form.

Jewish law and the prophetic and Christian traditions have provided a rich source for many of the higher values of Western law. Through the Christianization of natural law, the influence of canon law and the interaction between law and religion, the conflict within Judaism between legalism and existential justice was introduced into Western law. Law in the twentieth-century Western tradition lacks an anthropomorphic moral personality. If it can be said that the ancient Hebrews harmonized the legal and the prophetic, can it not also be said that in the modern industrial West, law is levitical and its priests are without the power of prophecy ?

ANCIENT ISRAEL[1]

Roland de Vaux

The Law, *Torah*, means in the first place a teaching, a doctrine, a decision given for a particular case. Collectively, the word means the whole body of rules governing men's relations with God and with each other. Finally the word comes to mean the first five books of the Bible, the Pentateuch, containing God's instructions to his people, the prescriptions which his people had to observe in their moral, social and religious life. All the legislative codes of the Old Testament are found in the Pentateuch.

(a) The *Decalogue* contains the "Ten Words" of Yahweh, the essential precepts of morality and religion. It is set out twice (Exod. 20 : 2-17 and Deut. 5 : 6-21) with some significant variants, but the two texts stem from a shorter primitive form which may justifiably be assigned to the Mosaic Age.

(b) The *Code of the Covenant* (Exod. 20 : 22-23 : 33) is a composite collection, in which one can easily distinguish a central portion (Exod. 21 : 1-22 : 16), where "sentences" or "judgments," *mishpatim* of civil and criminal law are grouped together : it is a law for a community of shepherds and peasants. The present context (cf. Exod. 24 : 3-8) connects it, like the Decalogue which precedes it, with the Sinaitic Covenant, but the directions about slaves, cattle, fields, vineyards, and houses can only apply to an already settled population. This code has obvious connections with the curses of Deut. 27 : 15-26, the "law" (Deut. 27 : 26) which was to be proclaimed on Mount Ebal (or Garizim ?) after the entry into Canaan (Deut. 27 : 11-14). This command of Moses was carried out by Josue, according to Josh. 8 : 30-35, the opening words of which recall in turn the law of the altar with which the *Code of the Covenant* begins (Exod. 20 : 24-25). But this passage in Josh. 8 does not fit in with its present context nearly so well as with the assembly at Shechem, where Joshua gave the people a law (*mishpat*) written in a "book of the law" (Josh. 24 : 25-26). We cannot be certain that the Code of the Covenant, in the form in which it has come down to us, is the actual law promulgated by Josue at Shechem, but we can say that internal evidence and the witness of tradition agree in dating this Code from the early days of the settlement in Canaan, before the organization of the state. It is the law of the tribal federation.

(c) *Deuteronomy*, in its legislative part (Deut. 12-26), forms another code which brings together, in ill-defined order, some short collections of laws which may have originated in different ways. Some of them repeat the directions of the Code of the Covenant, others, e.g., the laws on the one sanctuary and on the slaves, modify them, and many others are added. This code seems designed to replace the old code by taking account of a whole social and religious evolution ; it also reveals a change of spirit by its appeals to the heart and by the tone of exhortation in which its prescriptions are often couched. Fundamentally, it is certainly the "law" discovered in the Temple in the time of Josias (2 Kings 22:8f). It contains ancient elements which seem to stem, at least in part, from the Northern Kingdom, but it is difficult to say how long before the reign of Josias they were collected and completed. One plausible hypothesis is that they were brought to Judah after the fall of Samaria and put together under Ezechias.

(d) *The Law of Holiness* (Lev. 17-26) is also a compilation, containing a number of doublets. But it constitutes a unity which, like Deuteronomy, begins with rules about sacrifices and ends with blessings and curses. It differs from it by its strong preoccupation with rites and priesthood, and its constant reminders of the holiness of Yahweh and his people. It may represent the customs in vogue at the end of the monarchy, originating in a different milieu from that of Deuteronomy, and codified during the Exile. It may well have received some additions before or after its inclusion in the Pentateuch.

(e) *The Priestly Code.* The rest of Leviticus is composed of other collections : laws about sacrifices (Lev. 1-7) ; the ritual for the installation of priests (Lev. 8-10) ; the law of purity (Lev. 11-16), to which must be added the legislative texts scattered throughout Exod. and Num. and associated with events of the desert period. The sum total of these enactments and the narratives in which they are set, together with the Law of Holiness, form what critics call the Priestly Code. It contains some rules which are very ancient and others which are much more recent, and it received its final form only in the Jewish community after its return from Exile.

This brief survey is enough to make clear how inorganic was the legislation of Israel, how it varied with the background and time, and how much more closely connected it was with religious than with civil life. These are points to which we shall have to return, but before embarking on them we must compare this body of law with those of the other peoples in the ancient East.

It is a remarkable fact that Egypt, where there was so much writing and so much litigation, has left us no body of laws (the Edict of Horemheb is only an administrative document) ; nor is there any record of any Egyptian king's having been a law-giver, apart from some traditions collected at a very late date by Diodorus of Sicily, which we cannot check. It was a foreign conqueror, Darius, who issued the only codification recorded by an Egyptian text. Egypt seems to have felt no need for a written law because it had a living law, the Pharaoh, son of Ra, a god upon earth, whose word laid down the law. The language has no word to denote law as such. The nearest term is *ma'at,* which covers the concepts of truth and justice and is an attribute, itself divine, of the Pharaoh. The judges gave their decisions according to the principles of this "truth which is justice" and by applying the unwritten customs or the directive of the sovereign.

Babylonia, on the other hand, has bequeathed several collections of laws ascribed to the initiative of a king or placed under his name, and they are very ancient. The Code of Ur-Namu or Ur is to be dated about 2050 B.C., that of Lipit-Ishtar of Isin, about 1850 ; the law of the city of Eshnunna was promulgated by an unknown king long before Hammurabi and perhaps before Lipit-Ishtar ; lastly, the Code of Hammurabi of Babylon, issued about 1700, was the first to be discovered and is the most complete. These are not, strictly speaking, "codes" in our modern sense, i.e., bodies of law to which the judge is obliged to refer in giving judgment. It is noteworthy that in Mesopotamian texts we never come across expressions like "by application of the law" or "in virtue of such and such a law." There is not even any word meaning "law" in general. The king governs and the judges decide according to "justice" *(mesharu)* or "the truth" (*kittu*), following the accepted custom in similar cases. The practice was therefore not very different from that in Egypt, but in Mesopotamia this legal tradition or jurisprudence was, in certain circumstances, collected and put into writing, rather for the benefit of the people, it seems, than for that of the judges. These "codes," however, were not binding texts, as is evident from the number of divergent solutions given to the same cases by contemporary juridical acts.

The Collection of Assyrian Laws, compiled about 1100 but making use of older material, has long been recognized as a book of law, a manual of jurisprudence, but it covers only certain fields, and does not attempt to set forth the general law of the state. It is perhaps the work of a private jurist ; but even if it was compiled for the use of the judges by an official authority, it would still be a reference book rather than an authoritative code.

The Hittite laws are preserved in copies probably dating from the thirteenth century B.C., but they were compiled, apparently, about 1500. They frequently contrast "what must be done" now with "what was done formerly," the change being usually a reduction of the penalty. They are based, then, on an older customary law. They do not constitute a code ; they form an even looser collection than that of the Assyrian laws. They refer mostly to very particular cases, the presumption being that ordinary cases will be settled by simple and generally accepted rules.

No similar collection is forthcoming from Syria or Palestine, where juridical texts are extremely rare, apart from the two lots recently discovered in northern Syria, at Ras Shamra and Alakakh. Their principal characteristic is the special place assigned to the king, acting as representative of public authority : judgment is represented as his personal act, without reference to a law of the state. Their usages and formularies have certain peculiar features, but on the whole they have little which is not found in some other province of the ancient East, whether in Asia Minor, Babylonia, or more distant Elam.

This fundamental unity of Eastern law is of greater importance than the variations to be found between regions and epochs. It is the expression of a common civilization, in which the application of the same juridical principles has produced a similar customary law.

The civil legislation of the Old Testament belongs to the same ancient world, though it certainly has an originality which will be emphasized later. The very close connections and even the occasional identity of expression which we find between Israelite law and the Code of Hammurabi, the Assyrian Collection of the Hittite laws, is not to be explained by direct borrowing but by the influence of a single widespread customary law.

The legislative codes of the Old Testament are collections of particular rules, like the Eastern "codes," and they are even less unified than the latter. They are also more heterogeneous ; ethical, religious, or ritual prescriptions are found side by side with articles of civil or criminal law. The laws fall into two groups according to their style. There are laws in casuistical form, in which the conjunction "if" or "supposing that" introduces a typical case, followed by the solution. "If you take a man's cloak as security, you must return it to him at nightfall" (Exod. 22 : 25). "Supposing that a bull gores a man . . . that bull shall be stoned" (Exod. 21 : 28, etc.) Other laws are in an apodictic form and lay down commands or prohibitions in the second person future. "You shall not allow a witch to live" (Exod. 22 : 17). "You shall not boil a kid in its mother's milk" (Exod. 23 : 19 ; Deut. 14:21, etc.) The casuistic form is used chiefly for secular law, the apodictic form chiefly for laws covering worship. But we must observe that the distinction of styles and their use is less rigid than is usually thought.

What was the origin of these forms ? A theory at present in favour holds that "casuistic law" is a wholesale borrowing from the Canaanite legislation which the Israelites encountered when they settled in the land, and that the "apodictic" law represents the strictly Israelite tradition. It is mere guesswork to speculate about the formulation of Canaanite law so long as we possess none of the legislative texts which embodied it, and the juridical texts of Alakakh and Ras Shamra suggest that it hardly differed at all from other oriental laws. The fact remains that the Mesopotamian codes are compiled in casuistic form, and part of the Israelite law closely resembles them in style. Like these codes, the legislative collections of Israel bring together customary decisions.

The apodictic form is not found in these codes. But the originality of Israel in this respect is less striking if we compare it with the treaties imposed by the Hittite kings on their vassals. The treaties very frequently contain clauses introduced by "if", and also imperative clauses, as for example : "You shall keep the land which I have given you and shall not covet any territory of the land of Hatti." The form is like that of the Decalogue : "You shall not covet your neighbour's house, etc." (Exod. 20:17). We also have the remains, though badly damaged, of three Assyrian treaties of vassalage, and an important part of a treaty in Aramaic, found at Sfire near Aleppo ; and a treaty of vassalage imposed by Asarhaddon on certain princes of Media has recently been discovered. The essential points of the Hittite treaties are also found in these Assyrian ones ; the texts date from the first millenium and may be compared with the legislation of the Old Testament. The structure of Old Testament legislation, however, is much closer to that of the Hittite documents, which date from the second half of the second millenium. In addition, Ras Shamra has yielded fragments of treaties which were imposed on the king of Ugarit by a Hittite sovereign.

These resemblances are not accidental. The Covenant between Yahweh and his people had to be sealed by a treaty, and between God and men this could only be a treaty of vassalage. The ancient legal codes of Israel do in fact read like the clauses of such a treaty. The Decalogue is the deed of the Sinaitic covenant, inscribed on large stones entrusted by God to Moses (Exod. 24:12), which are the tables of the law (eduth : Exod. 31 : 18), or the tables of the covenant (b'rith : Deut. 9 : 9). The Code of the Covenant, as we have seen, may be connected with the pact at Shechem, where Josue concluded a covenant between Yahweh and the people, and gave the people a statute and a law (Josh. 24 : 25-26). The Code of Deuteronomy is also the expression of a pact : it is set forth as the sum total of the conditions accompanying the gift of the Holy Land (Deut. 12 : 1 ; cf. 11 : 31-32), and after the curses and blessings it culminates in these words : "These are the words of the covenant which Yahweh commanded to Moses to make with the children of Israel, in the land of Moab, in addition to the covenant he had made with them at Horeb" (Deut. 28:69) ; the Deuteronomic law is thus connected with the Decalogue, by-passing the Code of the Covenant, which it professes to replace. Under Josias, this Deuteronomic law was accepted by the king and the people as a covenant with Yahweh (2 Kings 23 : 2-3). The fiction of a treaty is still maintained in the Law of Holiness, which ends by recalling the covenant (Lev. 26 : 42-45), and concludes : "These are the customs, rules and laws which Yahweh established between himself and the Israelites" (Lev. 26:46).

If this is granted, other points of resemblance appear between the legal codes of the Old Testament and Oriental treaties. The latter begin with a historical introduction, sometimes fairly long, recalling the events leading up to the treaty. Similarly, the two promulgations of the Decalogue are introduced by a very short summary of previous facts (Exod. 20 : 1 ; Deut. 5 : 4-5). This is more developed in the narrative of the pact at Shechem (Josh. 24 : 2-13), to which we assigned the Code of the Covenant ; in the first chapters of Deuteronomy it becomes a record of the entire history of the people. Oriental treaties end with formulas of cursing and blessing, as sanctions for the keeping or breaking of the engagements undertaken. So too the Law of Holiness and the Code of Deuteronomy conclude with blessings and curses (Lev. 26 : 3-41 ; Deut. 28). The Code of the Covenant has no similar conclusion in its present context, but this context is not the original one, and if we were right in associating this Code with the pact at Shechem, it too involved curses and blessings (cf. Josh. 8 : 34 ; Deut. 11 : 26-29 ; 27 : 12-13) : the curses would then be those recorded in Deut. 27 : 15-26, which, as we have already noted, were closely connected with the Code of the Covenant.

Oriental treaties were inscribed on tablets, or engraved on a stele, and placed in a sanctuary in the presence of the gods. The Decalogue was engraved on two tablets and deposited in the sacred tent, in the Ark "of the Covenant" or "of the Law." The pact at Shechem was written in a book, according to Josh. 24:26, on stones according to Josh. 8:35, Deut. 27 : 2-4, and the record of this pact was preserved in the sanctuary of Yahweh (Josh. 24 : 26-27). Again, the "book of the law," Deuteronomy, was discovered in the Temple at Jerusalem (2 Kings 22 : 8).

Finally, several Hittite treaties order the text to be read periodically before the vassal king and his people. So too Deut. 31 : 10-13 prescribes a public reading of the law every seven years. It is very likely that such readings actually took place, perhaps even more often, e.g., in connection with an annual ceremony for renewing the Covenant, similar to that recorded by the Dead Sea scrolls among the Qumran sect. The historical books have recorded only readings which took place in certain exceptional circumstances, at the reform of Josaphat (2 Chron. 17:9), after the discovery of the Deuteronomy (2 Kings 23:2), and after the promulgation of the law by Esdras (Neh. 8 : 4-18).

But since these pacts governed the relations of Israel's dependence on Yahweh, not on a human suzerain, the Israelite law, for all its resemblances in form and content, differs radically from the clauses of Oriental "treaties" and the articles of their "codes." It is a religious law. It established the principles of the Covenant with Yahweh : its aim was to ensure that this Covenant remained in force. It is perfectly true that the Hittite and Assyrian treaties invoke their gods as guarantors, and that in the prologue and epilogue of their codes Lipit-Ishtar purports to be the interpreter of Enlil, and Hammurabi to be "the king of justice to whom Shamash has entrusted the law" ; but God was not merely a guarantor of the Covenant, he was a party to it, and no Oriental code can be compared with the Israelite law, which is ascribed in its entirety to God as its author. If it contains, and often mingles, ethical and ritual prescriptions, this is because it covers the whole field of the divine Covenant, and because this Covenant governed the relations of men with one another as well as their relations with God.

The law was the charter of the covenant with God ; hence it contained the obligations undertaken by the people, but it was also a body of teaching directed to them. From this notion another characteristic of Israelite legislation proceeds. Unlike all other Eastern laws, its prescriptions are often supported by a justifying motive. This may be a simple explanation based on common sense : if a man has violated an already betrothed girl in the town, both are put to death, "the girl because she did not call for help, the man because he has abused his neighbour's wife" (Deut. 22:24). Alternatively, the motive may be moral : in judicial actions, gifts must not be accepted "because gifts blind the eyes of the clear-sighted" (Exod. 23 : 8). Often it is a religious motive, as in the Decalogue itself : idolatry is forbidden, "for I, Yahweh your God, am a jealous God" (Exod. 20:5) : this is often found in the Law of Holiness, where the prescriptions are punctuated with the refrain, "I am Yahweh, your God." Finally, it may be an appeal to history, especially the remembrance of the deliverance from Egypt (Exod. 23:9 ; Lev. 19 : 36 ; Deut. 5:15 ; 24:18, etc.).The examples quoted show that these motives are attached to apodictical and casuistical laws alike and are found in different collections. They are proportionately more numerous in Deuteronomy and the Law of Holiness, but they are found as early as the Decalogue and the Code of the Covenant, and they are certainly a primitive feature of the law of Israel.

This connection between the law and religion explains one last characteristic of Israelite legislation. Because it is designed to safeguard the Covenant, it enjoins severe penalties for all crimes against God, idolatry and blasphemy, and for crimes which tarnish the holiness of the chosen people, e.g., bestiality, sodomy, and incest. But it is further distinguished from other Eastern codes (even the Hittite, which is the most lenient) by the humaneness of its sentences. Bodily mutilation is exacted only in one very special case (Deut. 25 : 11-12) which the Assyrian law punishes in the same way. Flogging is limited to forty strokes, "lest the bruises be dangerous and your brother be degraded" (Deut. 25:3). Certain dispositions in the Code of the Covenant, more developed in Deuteronomy, protect the stranger, the poor, the oppressed, the widow and the orphan, even the personal enemy (Exod. 22 : 20-26 ; 23 : 4-9 ; Deut. 23 : 16, 20 ; 24 *passim*). Exemptions from military service are very generous (Deut. 20 : 5-9). The law of retaliation, however, the *lex talionis,* is expressed in all its crudeness : "life for life, eye for eye, tooth for tooth, hand for hand, foot for foot, burning for burning, bruise for bruise, wound for wound" (Exod. 21 : 23-25 ; *cf.* Lev. 24 : 19-20 ; Deut. 19 : 21). But this formula seems to have lost its force, merely asserting the principle of proportionate compensation. In the oldest text, that of Exodus, it is in fact followed immediately by a law which orders the liberation of a slave in compensation for the loss of an eye or a tooth (Exod. 21 : 26-27), and it is preceded by a law which, for a wound inflicted in a fight, orders only the payment of compensation and medical expenses (Exod. 21 : 18-19). Only in one case is strict retaliation exacted : the guilty murderer must die and cannot buy his freedom. This rigour is justified by religious reason : the blood which has been shed has profaned the land in which Yahweh dwells (Num. 35 : 31-34). Thus again we meet the religious sanctions mentioned in the beginning of this paragraph. The Israelites could repeat with pride these words of Deuteronomy : "What great nation is there whose laws and customs are so just as all this Law ?" (Deut. 4:8).

The "codes" which have come down to us from Mesopotamia are all attributed to a king. As we have seen, they were rather collections of customary law than laws of the state, decreed by the sovereign, but they were at least promulgated by royal authority. In Israel, granted the religious nature of the law and its connection with the Covenant, nothing of the sort was possible, and in fact the historical books never allude to any legislative power of the king. The nearest example is the order said to have been given by David, to share the booty between the combatants and those who had been left to guard the baggage, which became "a rule and a custom" for Israel (1 Sam. 30 : 24-25). But David was not then king : as commander, he decided a particular case, and his decision became a custom. During the seige of Jerusalem, Sedecias ordered that all slaves should be freed ; but this was after he had consulted the people — he did not act on his own authority (Jer. 34 : 8). The king had of course an extensive administrative authority ; he organized his kingdom, appointed his officials, and made decrees, but he did not enact law. It is remarkable that the two "laws of the king" (1 Sam. 8 : 11-18 ; Deut. 17 : 14-20) make no allusion to any power of the king to lay down laws. On the contrary, the first warns the people against his arbitrary acts, and the second orders him to have a copy of the divine law and obey it to the last detail. It is also noteworthy that apart from this passage the king is nowhere mentioned in the Deuteronomic Code. When Josaphat reformed the administration of justice, he told his judges to apply the law of Yahweh (2 Chron. 19 : 5-7), and his envoys were to take with them, and to explain everywhere, not a law of the king, but "the law of Yahweh" (2 Chron. 17:9). The king was not even in the full sense the promulgator of this law, as if it became the law of the state by his authority. That is not the meaning to be ascribed to the reading of Deuteronomy by Josias in the Temple (2 Kings 23 : 1-2). Josias was the human intermediary in the covenant between God and his people ; he published its clauses and watched over its observance. He performed the same function as Moses on Sinai (Exod. 24 : 7-8), as Josue at Shechem (Josh. 24 : 25-26), and Esdras in days still to come at Jerusalem (Neh. 8). But the king could add nothing to the authority of a law to which he himself was subject (Deut. 17:19 ; 1 Kings 8 : 58 ; 2 Kings 23 : 3). There was no such thing as state law in Israel, and it was only under the foreign rule of Artaxerxes that "the law of God brought by Esdras" was imposed as "the law of the king" (Esd. 7 : 26).

On the other hand, the king was a judge, and held judicial power. This is an essential function of the chief : every sheikh wields it in his tribe and Moses exercised it in the desert (Exod. 18 : 16). Josue, Moses' successor at the head of the people "was filled with the spirit of wisdom" and everyone obeyed him (Deut. 34 : 9 ; *cf.* Num. 27 : 18-23). He acted as a judge in condemning Akan (Josh. 7 : 19-25). This was, of course, an exceptional case, but it was natural that the man who determined the law of the people (Josh. 24 : 25) should also see to the enforcement. Between the death of Josue and the institution of the monarchy came the period of the "judges." This title has been wrongly extended to the heroes who saved some part of the people from oppression, but it seems to belong properly to the "lesser" judges, whose names are given in Judg. 10 : 1-5 ; 12 : 8-15, along with whom we should count at least Jephthah (*cf.* Judg. 12 : 7), who combined this role with that of a great "saviour" judge. It seems that these judges were a permanent institution of the tribal federation : instead of a political head, it had a judge to whom all could appeal. Samuel performed the same function when he judged Israel at his home-town, Ramah, and also at Bethel, Gilgal, and Mispah (1 Sam. 7 : 16-17) ; he claimed that no one could accuse him of denying any man justice or taking bribes (1 Sam. 12 : 3-5). In his old age he appointed his two sons as judges at Beersheba, but they accepted his gifts and bent justice to their own ends (1 Sam. 8 : 1-3).

It was then that the Israelites begged Samuel to give them a king, "that he may be our judge" (1 Sam. 8:5). There is no reason to suspect this passage, which represents the king as heir to an office which already had a long history in Israel. The same passage says that the people asked for a judge-king "to be like other nations." Among the texts lately discovered at Ras Shamra and Alalakh there are, in fact, judgments given by the king and contracts guaranteed by his seal. On a wider scale, the preambles of Mesopotamian codes, the poems of Ras Shamra and Aramaean and Phoenician inscriptions all demand as the first quality of a king the virtue of justice. In Israel, too, men prayed that the king might be given justice (Ps. 72 : 1-2), the foundation of his throne (Prov. 16 : 12 ; 25 : 5 ; 29 : 14 ; cf. Isa. 9 : 6). The list of David's senior officials (2 Sam. 8:15) is introduced with these words : "David reigned over all Israel, doing right and justice to all his people," which seems to reserve the administration of justice to the sovereign. In the same way, the list of Solomon's senior officials (1 Kings 4 : 1-6) is immediately preceded by the story of the famous judgment which proved to all that there was in the king "a divine wisdom for doing justice" (1 Kings 3 : 28), i.e., both to settle quarrels and to assist every man to obtain his rights. This was the wisdom for which Solomon had prayed, to "judge the people" (1 Kings 3 : 9). Thus "to judge" was almost a synonym for "to govern" (cf. again 2 Kings 15 : 5), and "governors" could be called "judges" (Ps. 2 : 10 ; 148 : 11). It is the king who is called the "judge of Israel" in Mic. 4 : 114, following what is still the likeliest interpretation.

When Absalom exclaimed : "Ah ! who will make me judge in this land ? If everyone who had a lawsuit and a judgment were to come to me, I would do them justice" (2 Sam. 15 : 4), he was coveting the crown itself. The whole story shows that there was at Jerusalem a king's court, to which every man in Israel could appeal. So too, Solomon's palace contained a "porch of judgment" where the king administered justice (1 Kings 7 : 7). The real or fictitious cases recorded in the historical books show that appeal was made to the king even in cases which we should leave to lower courts : the theft of a sheep (2 Sam. 12 : 6), a family blood feud (2 Sam. 14 : 4-11), the substitution of a child (1 Kings 3 : 16-28), the recovery of a house and land (2 Kings 8:3). The woman of Teqoa is supposed to be appealing from a judgment given by her clan (2 Sam. 14 : 4-11), and the king here appears as the judge in the final court of appeal, which he certainly was, but the other examples presume that recourse could also be made to him in the first instance. [pp. 143-152]

NOTE

1. Roland de Vaux, *Ancient Israel* (New York : McGraw-Hill Book Company, Inc., 1961), pp. 143-152.

THE RELIGION OF ISRAEL[1]

Y. Kaufmann

The moral conceptions of the Bible have been crystallized in two parallel but distinct traditions : Torah and prophecy on the one hand, and the wisdom literature on the other. Prophetic morality is rooted in that of the Torah and is its culmination. Biblical wisdom literature exhibits hardly a trace of the influence of either ; it runs as a parallel and independent stream of thought. These traditions differ fundamentally with regard to the source, the ground, and the bearers of moral responsibility.

For Torah and prophecy, the source of morality is the will of God, and the basis of moral obligation is the command of God communicated to man through prophecy. God gave man a just and moral law and made a historical covenant with him, binding him to observe it. With Israel, God made a national covenant involving a special moral-religious law which is the basis of Israel's special obligations. The prophetic denunciations of Israel take their departure from this notion.

Biblical wisdom literature is pervaded with the idea that morality stems from wisdom. Its source is not prophetic revelation, but understanding and discernment. To be sure, morality is rooted also in the fear of God, who requites men according to their deserts. Yet, for all that, it is primarily conceived of as the child of wisdom, human and divine. This viewpoint dominates Proverbs, which, as the book of wisdom's instructions, may be regarded as a counterpart to the Torah, the book of divine laws. In Job, God's providence is a speculative problem which it is the task of wisdom to solve. In prophecy, it is a matter of faith and trust (Jer. 12 : 1 ff. ; Hab. 1:2 — 2 : 4 ; cf. Ps. 73 ; Lam. 3). Wisdom literature makes no allusion to covenants having moral content between man and God. It conceives of morality rather as a kind of natural law that God implanted in the hearts of men.

Conceptions of morality thus crystallized in two distinct literary corpora : a prophetic — humanistic and national, and a sapiential — humanistic alone. The one speaks in categorical imperatives ; the other appeals to prudence and utilitarian considerations. The Torah legislates and commands ; the prophets exhort and censure ; both call for faith and trust in God. Proverbs counsels and warns on the basis of observation and experience ; it does not know of any disturbing problems. Job (like the later Ecclesiastes) speculates upon the moral order. Psalms contains something of the sapiential outlook, but by and large it is a book of faith and trust.

The Decalogue (Exod. 20 : 1 ff.; Deut. 5 : 6 ff.), doubtless part of the earliest Israelite traditions, lays down broad principles of justice and morality that are detailed and elaborated upon in the other law corpora : the inviolability of life and person, the sanctity of marriage, of one's utterance, and of property rights. Exodus 21 : 12 ff. distinguishes the murderer from the accidental homicide, condemning the first to death and providing the second with asylum. Numbers 35 : 9 ff. and Deuteronomy 4 : 41 ff ; 19 : 1-13 institute cities of refuse for the accidental slayer, though outside the laws only the alter-asylum is referred to (1 Kings 1:50 ff. ; 2:28 f.). The murder of a slave, even by his owner, was to be avenged (Exod. 21 : 20f.). For goring a slave to death, a bull known to be a gorer was stoned, and its owner compelled to pay a fine. If the slain was a freeman, the owner was put to death (Exod. 21 : 28-32). Even indirectly causing death imposes guilt on a person (Deut. 22:8). Maiming is punished by the *lex talionis* : "an eye for an eye, etc." (Exod. 21 : 24 f. ; Lev. 24:19 f.). According to Deuteronomy 19:21, this law was applied to the false witness as well. A man who maims his slave must set him free (Exod. 21 : 26 f.).

A man's freedom is his supreme right. Kidnapping for sale into slavery is punishable with death (Exod. 21 : 16 ; Deut. 24 : 7). In the conception of Adam — the progenitor of all men — as created in God's image, the idea of the equality of all men is implicit. This idea, however, never attains full expression ; women are subservient to men, and — what is worse — slaves to their masters. Slavery is regarded as a curse laid especially on the offspring of Canaan (Gen. 9 : 25 ff.), though by no means limited to them. A Hebrew who sells himself into slavery must be released after six years. If he refuses to be freed, he is formally branded as a perpetual slave (Exod. 21 : 2 ff.). Leviticus 25 : 39-43, on the other hand, does away with Israelite bondage entirely, for Israelites are "slaves of YHWH," whose lordship excludes subservience to human masters. This lofty conception, unparalleled elsewhere in antiquity, is, however, limited in its application to Israelites and does not embrace foreigners (vss. 44 ff.). Moreover, it seems that in pre-exilic times it was a utopian ideal without practical effect. From the equality of all men before God, Job 31 : 13-15 infers only that justice and compassion must be shown to slaves ; it does not repudiate slavery in principle. A foreign slave who fled to the land of Israel must not be surrendered to his owner (Deut. 23 : 16 f.), although it appears that there was in fact an international convention to surrender fugitive slaves (1 Kings 2 : 39 f.). Israelite slaves could acquire property and might even have slaves of their own (2 Sam. 9 : 2, 9 f.). Bondwomen usually became concubines of their master or his sons (Exod. 21:7 ff.)....

To do what is right and just is the way of YHWH (Gen. 18:19). In Israel, as elsewhere, justice was the special virtue of the king, the quality in which he gloried (2 Sam. 8 : 15 ; 1 Kings 3 : 6 ff. ; Pss. 45 : 5, 8 ; 72 : 1 ff.). But every Israelite is enjoined from showing partiality, taking bribes, and perverting justice (Exod. 23 : 3, 7 ff. ; Lev. 19 : 15, 35 ; etc.). The duty of dealing rightly with the poor and helpless is emphasized (Exod. 23 : 6 ; Deut. 24 : 17 ; 27 : 19) ; God himself is the model of this virtue (Deut. 10 : 18 ; Ps. 10 : 18). Equality before the law is implicit in biblical justice. It was long ago observed that the Covenant Code does not discriminate between men and women and recognizes that even slaves have certain basic rights. The Pentateuch enjoins equal treatment of alien and native-born in religious, as in non-religious, matters (Lev. 24 : 16 and elsewhere ; Num. 35:15). Despite the existence of class divisions among the people, particularly in late monarchic times, Israelite law — as distinct from other ancient Near Eastern law — recognizes no class privileges. Slaves apart, the law makes no distinction between patrician and plebeian, rich and poor, propertied and proletariat. There are no restrictions on intermarriage between classes. The king is ideally chosen "from among his brothers" (Deut. 17 : 15) and is charged not to let his "heart be exalted over his brothers" (vss. 19 ff.). His rule is based on a covenant with the people (2 Sam. 5 : 3 ; 2 Kings 11 : 17).

Going beyond the demands of strict justice is a class of laws aimed at placing the relations between men on a footing of propriety and mutual respect. Patriarchal society was founded on the respect shown to parents and other persons of experience, wisdom, or age. Honour and reverence of both father and mother is one of the basic commands. (Exod. 20 ; 12 ; Lev. 19 : 3 ; cf. Exod. 21 : 15, 17). An insubordinate, dissolute son is punished with death (Deut. 21 : 18 ff.). Chief and king must not be cursed (Exod. 22 : 27 ; 2 Sam. 16 : 5-13 ; 19 : 22 ; 1 Kings 2:8 f.). Respect is due to gray hairs (Lev. 19 : 32). Concern for the dignity of persons in general is expressed in the proscription of dealing out excessive stripes, lest "your brother become despised in your eyes" (Deut. 25:3). A captive woman taken to wife may never afterward be sold, "inasmuch as you have humiliated her" (Deut. 21 : 14).

Compassion is a quality of YHWH who is "a merciful and gracious God" (Exod. 34 : 6 ; Ps. 86 : 15 ; etc.). A creditor must not keep the pledged garment of a poor man overnight, for "if he cries out to me I will hear him, for I am gracious" (Exod. 22 : 26). Both compassion and love are embodied in the social legislation. "You shall love your neighbour as yourself" — a positive extension of "You shall not hate your brother in your heart" — is the climax of biblical morality (Lev. 19 : 17, 18). What is meant by this is not a mere state of mind, but its actualization in deeds of generosity and kindness. This becomes clear from verses 33 f., "You must not wrong the alien . . .but love him as yourself." Repeated in Deuteronomy 10 : 19, its meaning is elucidated in verse 18 where God, who "loves the alien," is said "to give him bread and clothes." All the laws that obligate men to stand by each other in the time of need, or which forbid exploiting poverty and distress, are based on this law of love. The Israelite is required to go out of his way, if necessary, to restore lost property or help unload an overburdened ass, even one belonging to his enemy (Exod. 24 : 4 f.). He is repeatedly bidden to aid the poor, the alien, the orphan, and the widow, as, e.g., in the obligation to be openhanded toward the needy ; the ban upon taking interest on loans (Exod. 22 : 24 ; Lev. 25 : 35 ff. ; Deut. 23 : 20 f.) ; the (surely utopian) sabbatical cancellations of debts (Deut. 15 : 1ff.) ; the right of redemption of real property and the jubilee law (Lev. 25 : 8 ff.) ; the poor dues — the spontaneous growth of the fallow year (Exod. 23 : 10 f.), the corners of the field, and gleanings of vineyard and field (Lev. 19 : 9 f. ; cf. Deut. 24 : 19 ff.).

Related to the law of love is the proscription of revenge, grudgebearing, and talebearing. (Lev. 19 : 16, 18). Compassion forbids cursing the deaf and placing a stumbling block before the blind (*ibid.* vs. 14). Beasts, too, are embraced by biblical compassion. They must be given rest on the Sabbath (Exod. 20 : 10 ; 23 : 12) ; the ox may not be muzzled while threshing (Deut. 25 : 4). Hospitality is not expressly enjoined, but it is considered an ancient and universal obligation. Abraham and Lot are depicted, in contrast to the Sodomites, as exemplary hosts (Gen. 18-19). Ammon and Moab are excluded from the Israelite community, because they refused to show elementary decency to the wandering tribes on their journey through the wilderness (Deut. 23 : 4 f.). The Israelite took care to be hospitable (2 Sam. 12 : 1 *ff.* ; *cf.* Job 31 : 32 : "No stranger had to lodge outside, I opened my door to the wayfarer").

Meekness is one of the virtues of Moses (Num. 12 : 3) ; in prophetic and wisdom literature, the meek are the mass of simple folk, over against the wealthy and luxurious classes....

While Torah and prophecy know of a universal moral law, the basis of Israel's moral obligation is the covenant, with its special moral-legal code. Several prescriptions of the universal moral law were given anew to Israel as national-religious obligations. Biblical morality is societal and national. Nation and society are responsible for its maintenance; their welfare is conditioned upon its observance.

Even the fundamental moral injunction, "You shall not murder," which in Genesis 9 : 5 f. has a general sanction ("for man was made in the image of God"), was given anew to the people of Israel at Sinai and supplied with a national motive : bloodshed defiles the land of Israel in which God dwells (Num. 35 : 31 ff.). A hanged man must not be exposed overnight lest the land be polluted (Deut. 21 : 22 f.). Several social laws are grounded in the fact that Israel was "a stranger in the land of Egypt" and knows what it means to be helpless : the injunction against wronging an alien (Exod. 22 : 20 ; 23:9) ; the duty to love him (Lev. 19 : 34 ; Deut. 10 : 19) ; bestowal of gifts on the emancipated slave (Deut. 15 : 13 ff.) ; the sharing of the festal banquet with the poor (16 : 11 f.) ; the injunction against perverting the cause of alien and orphan and taking a widow's pledge (24 : 17 f.) ; the poor dues (vss. 19-22). Even the Sabbath rest is supplied with this national motive (5:12 ff.). Violations of the sexual prohibitions of Leviticus 18 and 20 defile the land so that it will spew Israel forth. To take back a divorced wife after she has remarried also brings guilt upon the land (Deut. 24 : 4).

Various moral laws are grounded on Israel's religious distinction, Israelites may not be enslaved, because they are the slaves of God (Lev. 25 : 42, 55). The law of land redemption is linked with the sanctity of the jubilee year and with the fact that the land belongs to God (vss. 10 ff.). Some laws are framed in language applicable to Israel or Israelite only : the Sabbath law, the poor dues, the ban on cultic prostitution, those which speak of "your neighbour," "your brother" or which explicitly exclude the non-Israelite. The produce of the seventh year is set aside for "the poor of your people" (Exod. 23 : 10 f.) ; "you shall not go about as a talebearer among your people . . . you shall not hate your brother in your heart. . . you shall not take vengeance or bear a grudge against the members of your people" (Lev. 19 : 16 ff.). Boundary stones "in the inheritance which you hold in the land" (Deut. 19 : 14) must not be removed. The slanderer is guilty for having defamed "a virgin of Israel" (22:19). It is a duty to lend aid to "your needy brother" (15 : 7 ff). Usury may be exacted from the foreigner (23 : 20 f.). Only the Hebrew bondman is freed after six years (Exod. 21:2 ; Deut. 15 : 12 *ff.*), while the slavery of the foreigner is perpetual (Lev. 25 : 44 *ff.*).

In sum, then, the morality of the Torah is prophetic, given by God in a revelation. Though basically universal, it is fixed in a national framework.

The morality of biblical wisdom is catholic and humanistic, without any national or distinctly Israelite colouring. Its monotheism is the legendary monotheism of primeval times. Job is a patriarchal monotheist (Ezek. 14 : 14, 20). Proverbs speaks of the non-Israelite Agur and Lemuel (30 : 1 ; 31 : 1), both apparently conceived of as early monotheists (cf. Agur's lofty credo 30 : 5 ff.). The cult reflected in this literature consists of sacrifice, vow, and prayer. Like the cult of patriarchal times, it lacks priests, temples, and national festivals. Biblical wisdom retains the style and mood of ancient Near Eastern wisdom out of which it sprang. Like its antecedents, it grounds morality on prudence and "god-fearing," rather than on a historical covenant. Its doctrine of individual retribution resembles that of general Eastern wisdom ; like the latter, it too has little to say about cultic matters.

The nature of biblical wisdom stands out clearest in the book of Proverbs, the book of wisdom's teaching — a counterpart to the Torah, the book of divine commands.

Proverbs is suffused with optimism and complacency ; it knows no real problems. God's just providence and a moral world order are presuppositions it does not question. Do not envy the prosperous wicked man, it exhorts, for "the lamp of the wicked will be extinguished" (24 : 19 f.). If the righteous suffers, he is being chastened by God as a son by his father ; let him not reject God's reproof or hold himself wise or be lax in devoutness (3 : 5-12). An unmistakable utilitarianism pervades Proverbs, as in the wisdom literature of the ancient East in general. Morality is the way to success. Thus adultery is, of course, a sin (2:17) ; but is also ruinous to one's substance (29:3). Drunkenness involves one in blows and wounds (23 : 29-35). Even the religious basis of Proverbs' exhortations — the fear of God who requites men according to their deserts — is tinged with a certain utilitarianism. Since God oversees all the acts of men and knows their innermost thought, doing good will benefit man,while doing bad will harm him. How can man know what is good and bad ? Wisdom teaches him. Not personal wisdom — "Rely not on your understanding" (3:5 ; etc.) — but traditional wisdom tried and tested through the ages. It is a spark of the same divine wisdom through which God created the world (3 : 19 f.), which indeed preceded creation (8:22 ff.). And its first teaching is "fear of YHWH."

Sapiential morality coincides in many ways with that of the Torah. All of the rules of the Decalogue, excepting the ban on idolatry and the law of the Sabbath, are to be found here. Murder is an abomination to God (6 : 17, etc.) ; adultery is evil and disgraceful, a disregard of the divine convenant between husband and wife (2 : 16 ff. ; 5 : 1 ff. ; 6:20 ff. ; 7 : 1 ff. ; etc.). Theft is despicable (6 : 30 f.) and a profanation of God's name (30 : 9). False testimony is frequently condemned (6 : 19 ; 12 : 17 ; etc.). Following Egyptian models, the obligation of obedience to parents is dealt with even more fully than in the Torah.

There are points of contact with the other law corpora as well. False weights are an abomination to YHWH (11 : 1 ; 20 : 10, 23), for fixing weights is the work of his hands (16:11). Perversion of justice, biased judgment, taking bribes are also loathsome to YHWH (15 : 27 ; 17 : 15, 23, etc.). To do what is right and just is preferred by YHWH to sacrifice (21:3). The perversion of the poor man's cause is severely censured (22 : 22 f. ; 31 : 5, 9). The king above all is bound to be righteous in judgment (8:15 ; 16 : 10, 12 f.).

Among the virtues of the righteous sage are compassion and kindness (11 : 17 ; 14 : 22 ; 16 : 6 ; etc.). The righteous man withholds no good from his fellow (3 : 27 f.), gives unstintingly (21 : 26), has compassion even on beasts (12:10). He does not oppress the poor, for God is their avenger (14 : 31 ; 21 : 13 ; 22 : 16 ; etc.). He does not return evil for evil (20:22 ; 24 : 29). He regards it as a sin to deride the poor and rejoice in another's misfortune (17:5), to go about as a talebearer and betray confidences (11 : 13 ; 20 : 19). If he can, the God-fearing man saves his fellow from death and does not turn a blind eye to those in distress (24 : 10 f.). Humility characterizes the righteous man, as pride does the wicked (6 : 17 ; 8 : 13 ; 14 : 3 ; etc.).

The slave is mentioned in Proverbs alongside of the poor, the orphan, and widow. One must not inform on a servant to his master (30 : 10) ; at the same time, servants must not be overindulged (29:21) ; an occasional beating is in order (vs. 19). Only "patriarchal" slavery is mentioned, in which the slave is a permanent part of the household, at times shares a patrimony with brothers (17:2), may even rise to rule over nobles (19:10) and become king (30:22). The "Hebrew bondman" in the sense of the laws of Exodus is unknown.

Many maxims are intended to educate sons (daughters are unmentioned). The entire first collection (chaps. 1-9) and fragments of other collections are formally pedagogical. The son is warned away from women and wine; he is exhorted not to be greedy and gluttonous. An application of the rod is frequently recommended to lead youth into good ways.

In later wisdom literature (from Ben-Sira onward), Torah and wisdom were identified. This has not yet occurred in biblical times. Proverbs speaks of Torah and commandment, but they are (as always in Oriental wisdom) the instruction and commands of father, mother, sage, or of wisdom personified. There is nothing about a revealed Torah, concerning which a covenant has been made. The first chapters of Proverbs are full of the image of a father instructing his son, exhorting him to obey wisdom and get understanding. But according to Exodus 13:3 ff., Deuteronomy 4:9, etc., what the Israelite must teach his children is the story of the Exodus and the laws given Israel at that time. Proverbs 1 : 9 ; 3 : 3, 22 : 7 : 3 urge the wearing of wisdom as a graceful chaplet on one's head, as a necklace, writing them on the tablets of one's heart, binding them to one's fingers. Nothing is said of binding the words of God on the hands or placing them as "frontlets" between the eyes and on doorposts (Deut. 6 : 8 f. ; 11 : 18 ff.). In striking contrast with the Torah, the moral rules of Proverbs are never provided with a historical or national motive. Not only is the cultic aspect of the Sabbath never referred to, its social-moral aspect of giving rest to slave and animal is equally ignored. The poor dues, the sabbatical cancellation of debts, the jubilee, the gift to the emancipated slave, all go unmentioned. Proverbs frequently warns against the "strange woman" and her wiles, but it has not a word for the duty of the Israelite to guard the chastity of his daughter (Lev. 19:29 ; Deut. 23 : 18). Despite its solicitude for depressed classes, Proverbs lacks the great command of loving the stranger — in fact, there is no word at all about *gerim*, that class which the Torah takes pains to protect. Biblical wisdom altogether lacks the national-religious basis which is the distinctive feature of Israelite morality.

The abundant material of cognate cultures at our disposal today shows beyond question that Israelite wisdom belongs to the common sapiential legacy of the ancient Near East. Hardly anything in biblical wisdom (apart from its monotheistic viewpoint) cannot be paralleled in the literatures of Egypt and Mesopotamia. Inasmuch as Oriental wisdom was individual, universal, and humanistic, the presence of these features in Israelite wisdom must not be taken for signs of lateness, as if they are the end product of a long, internal development, showing the influence of classical prophecy, the national calamity, the Exile, and so forth. The very contrary is to be inferred : individual and universal morality was the earlier, and the societal-national morality the offspring of a later, inner Israelite development.

Indeed, biblical wisdom has preserved its ancient character intact far more successfully than have the materials of the Torah. Like its non-Israelite counterparts, biblical wisdom is not a prophetic revelation, but the teaching of reason. Nor is it addressed to the people as a whole or linked with the national destiny.

Biblical, like Egyptian, wisdom displays slight interest in cultic matters — an indifference which has nothing to do with prophetic influence. The materials that have entered the Torah, on the other hand, have been fundamentally recast. Just as state law was transformed in the Torah into a national-religious law, so the ancient individual and universal morality was given a national framework. The people became collectively accountable for its observance, and national destiny is made to depend upon the fulfilment of this moral-legal Torah. Special prescriptions affecting Israel and related to its land develop. The whole is given a religious cast, the old framework of rulings by a king or sage being replaced by prophecy. The laws of the Torah are the word of God through his prophet. Legal-moral prescriptions are frequently interspersed with a cultic element.

Such a profound transformation did not take place in the wisdom literature. Hence, the absence of a distinctively Israelite element in wisdom morality. That the moral covenant of God with Israel has no echo in biblical wisdom indicates the antiquity of the style of that literature. To be sure it was so far inspirited with Israelite conceptions as to bear the imprint of the monotheistic idea. But throughout the biblical period, wisdom remained a self-contained realm, and until the time of Ben-Sira scarcely a single national, or cultic, recognizably Israelite element penetrated it. True to its ancient forms, it maintained its similarity to the wisdom of Egypt, Mesopotamia, and the "Easterners." It was in the Torah and prophets that the creative force of the Israelite idea found fullest expression. The individual, universal wisdom of the sapiential literature is thus the crystallization of an earlier style, whatever be the date of its final compilation.

Torah and prophecy, then, distinguish two moral realms : Israelite and universal ; wisdom knows only the latter. Beside the special obligations laid on Israel by the covenant, Torah and prophecy recognize a primeval moral law obligatory upon all nations. This peculiar duality of moral realms, which is ignored by Israelite (as by Oriental) wisdom, is further evidence that the conceptions of Torah and prophets are the later. Far from being primitive, it is a new, national version of the ancient, individual-universal morality. What new idea is embodied in this national version ?

The conception of morality and justice as a branch of wisdom is part of the mythological world view of paganism.... While paganism roots moral and natural law alike in the primordial realm and understands it as the task of human and divine wisdom to discover and teach it, Israelite religion conceives of all law as an expression of the will of God, his absolute command. Israel's God created not only the realm of the is, but the realm of the ought as well. Whether goodness is intrinsic and therefore willed by God, or whether it is so only because God willed it, is not discussed in the Bible. Goodness is simply a quality of God ("YHWH, a God merciful and gracious. . .and abounding in love and fidelity" [Exod. 34:6]). While the Bible does not recognize the subjection of God to any compulsion, it does depict him as observing the moral law. But this is not conceived of as an autonomous law, to which God is subject, but rather as itself a manifestation of God's will. What is has been created by the goodness of God. This goodness has been revealed to man, and man has been commanded to realize it in his own life. Man must "create" here on earth the world of moral goodness that ought to be. But he has the freedom to defy God's will, and this freedom is the root of sin and evil. The moral demand thus reaches its highest intensity as an expression of the will of God ; at the same time, the moral responsibility of man reaches its full justification in the idea of human freedom.

The new idea is embodied in the concept found in the Torah and prophetic literatures that morality is a covenant between God and man. Since morality is now a statement of the divine will, all men ought to be obliged to observe it. Hence the biblical notion, expressed most clearly in the Pentateuch that primeval man (Noah and his sons [Gen. 9 : 1-7]) had already received a moral law. But this was, after all, only a legend. A historical covenant with a real people was made with Israel alone ; of Israel alone, then, could the new covenant morality be required.

Because of this historical reality, the new morality was incorporated in a national-moral law, given together with a new religious-cultic law. Because Israel alone knows YHWH, it especially is obliged to recognize and obey his will. The divine dictate is to be a kingdom of priests and a holy nation (Exod. 19:6); the reward is national well-being. In the account of the Sinaitic covenant, the moral-legal element is the very core. Exodus 18 relates the establishment of a judicial procedure for the people. In the Decalogue, the moral imperatives are the end and purposes of the initial declaration of God's sovereignty and the demand to be loyal to him. In the larger book of the covenant, too, the moral-legal element predominates. There is no need to look for later prophetic influence to account for this. The prophets' insistence that God's covenant had a moral-legal, rather than a cultic purpose (Amos 5 : 25; Isa. 5:7; Jer. 7 : 22 ; 34 : 13 f.), was not their own invention ; it is implied as well in this early literature.

The covenant calls into being a new moral entity : the people Israel. The laws of the Torah are given to the whole nation at once ; all as one are obliged to carry them out. The community to which God manifested himself becomes corporately responsible, becomes, as it were, a new moral person. The individual's responsibility derives from his membership in the Israelite community ; as such, the covenant binds him personally. On the other hand, the community as a whole is accountable for each of its members. The Torah addresses not the family, the tribe, the state, but the people of the covenant. The people are commanded to be just and righteous, must appoint judges, and extirpate evil out of their midst ; must keep sanctity of the land from being profaned by bloodshed, sexual immorality, and violence. The "you" of the laws shifts imperceptibly from the individual to the people ; at times, both are meant.

In the conception of the entire people receiving as a man the moral-legal covenant at the mouth of God, the unique essence of the Israelite idea of morality found its ultimate expression ; it is the absolute command of God, revealed and imposed on mankind by him. Its presupposition is the freedom of the human will. Sin is not a tragic necessity ; it is always the fruit of will, and its guilt is always deserved. True, there is suffering for the sin of another, but such suffering — let it be noted — is always attendant upon some deserved punishment ; it has, moreover, a counterpart in God's dispensation of grace, with which it is combined (Exod. 20 : 6 ; 34:7). The important point is that the ultimate causes of sin and punishment lie always in the will and act of man. Because man can choose to do good, he is answerable for his evil-doing. Hence the unparalleled moral passion of the Bible. Pagan morality and biblical wisdom utter their sage and prudent counsels in deliberate, reasonable accents. The Torah and prophets, however, speak impassionedly of guilt and the consequences of wrongdoing and demand that Israel choose life. Punishment is not merely a danger or threat, but a necessary part of the moral order. This moral passion is evident in the admonitions of the Torah, in the stories concerning Nathan (2 Sam. 12 : 1-12), Elijah (1 Kings 21 : 17-24), and especially in the writings of the literary prophets. Not the individualistic morality of wisdom literature, but the national morality of Torah and prophets is the sphere of the sublime prophetic passion.

The intense passion of the national morality is the final demonstration that is not primitive, but rather the highest stage of a morality transcending the individual. It is no longer satisfied with individual responsibility ; morality is not "a private matter." Society has a duty to educate each member and look after his deeds, not because there are crimes that produce a miasma and rouse the fury of the Erinyes against men, but because society as a whole is under a covenant obligation to eradicate evil from its midst and cause justice to prevail. Communal responsibility springs from the ardent desire to realize the demands of morality — a societal task which lies beyond the power of any individual to accomplish. This new moral conception, especially as it was expressed by the prophets, was beyond the scope of the ancient, sapiential morality that had never heard of a claim upon society as a whole.

It is a widespread opinion that the doctrine of individual retribution is a late development of Israelite religion. Ezekiel is thought to have been the first to transcend the "primitive, collective morality" of the old religion and discover the significance of the individual. Since Proverbs and Job deal with the individual and his fate, these works must necessarily come later than Ezekiel and be based on his revolutionary idea. This opinion is a compound of errors. The notion of individual retribution is to be reckoned among the ideas that Israel inherited from the ancient cultures. It is found, alongside the idea of collective punishment, in Egypt and Mesopotamia as well. That a man is requited for his own deeds is a theme of the earliest sources. He is not, however, conceived of as an isolated entity, but as inextricably bound up with his family, tribe, people, city, and land. And since his life extends in effect beyond his own person, the scope of his reward and punishment may also.

The first mention of retribution in the Bible is individual. Adam and Eve, who were, as we have seen, created not as ancestors of the race, but as individuals, are warned they will die if they sin. (Indeed Adam is warned of death even before Eve is created). Strictly individual requital is meted out to Noah and his generation. The individual members of Lot's family are requited variously in accord with their deserts ; some are saved ; Lot's wife is turned to salt for violating the angel's command ; Lot's scoffing sons-in-law are destroyed with Sodom and Gomorrah. The Egyptian midwives who saved the Hebrew children (Exod. 1:20 f.), the generation of the wilderness, Caleb and Joshua (Num. 14 : 20-34), Zelophehad (see Num. 27 : 3), and David (in the opinion of Shimei, 2 Sam. 16 : 8) are all rewarded or punished individually — to mention but a few instances. When all of a group are involved in sin all are punished, as, e.g., the generation of the Flood and the Sodomites. Various laws of the Torah, though set in a national framework, reflect the concept of individual requital (e.g., the individual sin and guilt offerings, laws of vows and dedications, nearly all of the moral injunctions).

However, there is also a belief in collective retribution and in collective responsibility. The stories about the ancestors of the race and of Israel assume collective retribution. The punishments of Adam, Eve, and the serpent were individual, as were the rewards of the tribe of Levi and of Phinehas, yet their effects endured throughout the generations. Especially close are the bonds of collective responsibility between members of the family. Children and wives are embraced by the retribution meted out to fathers and husbands. Although the custom of punishing children for fathers was eventually abolished (Deut. 24 : 16 ; 2 Kings 14:6), in Israel as elsewhere in antiquity, this custom seems to have been practised (Josh. 7 : 24 ff. ; Judg. 21:10 ; I Sam. 21 : 6 ff. ; cf. Code of Hammurabi, par. 210). The collective responsibility of the family before God remained fundamental. God visits the iniquity of parents on children and keeps mercy to the thousandth generation (Exod. 20 : 5f. ; 34 : 7 ; Deut. 5 : 9 f. ; 7:9). Amos prophesies to Amaziah not only that his children would die, but that even his wife would play the harlot in the city (7:17).

The scope of collective responsibility before God might extend even to a large group, a city or kingdom. A king's sin is particularly apt to bring calamity on his entire realm (Gen. 20 : 9 ; 26:10 ; etc.). Many of the calamities that befell Israel are explained as caused by royal sin. Saul's sin occasioned the subjection of Israel to the Philistines (1 Sam. 28 : 19) ; David's sin with Bathsheba brought on the rebellion of Absalom ; Solomon's sins were the cause of the division of the kingdom.

The people of Israel constitute a special sphere of collective responsibility. The basis of this responsibility is not natural, like that of the family or tribe, but artificial ; it is the covenant that God made with the people and which was made in terms of eternal obligations (Deut. 29:13 f.). There is, therefore, a common responsibility not only among all members of a given generation, but among all generations as well. This idea underlies the whole historial outlook of the Bible. Every sin committed by part of the people is counted against Israel and serves to explain the fate of the entire people.

Yet there is the feeling that the most fitting and just retribution is that which befalls the sinner himself; the more restricted the scope of collective responsibility, the more just the deserts meted out. Complaints are lodged against collective responsibility : "Will one man sin, and you be angry with the whole congregation ?" (Num. 16:22) ; "Lo, I have sinned and I have acted wickedly, but these sheep, what have they done ?" (2 Sam. 24:17). In the stories about Jonathan (1 Sam. 14 : 24 ff.) and Jonah, only the strictest individual retribution is regarded as just ; yet even in Jonah, one finds the notion that the doom of one man is liable to envelop so random an assemblage as the travellers on a ship.

Biblical thought attempted to account for the workings of divine justice by setting up various circles of retribution. Each man's destiny is bound up with that of his fellow ; the course of his life may be influenced by distant events. The deeds of his father, his relatives, his countrymen, and his king can all affect him. Other auxiliary assumptions were also at hand to explain God's ways. God afflicts men in order to test their loyalty to him ; this was the case of Abraham, of Job, of the people of Israel in the wilderness and in the land. Evil may go unpunished because God is patient with the wicked, or because he changed his mind about destroying them (Exod. 34:6 ; Jon. 4 : 2). At times, he waits until the measure of sin has been filled before inflicting punishment (Gen. 15:16). One way or another, biblical man justified his belief in a morally ordered world. Because he knew of no judgment after death, only this world could serve as the scene of divine justice. If the righteous suffer and the wicked prosper, he prays to God and entreats him to manifest his judgment.

Yet the contrast between reality and the religious-moral ideal could not be disregarded, and ever disturbs biblical thought. The Bible as a whole may well be called the book of the justification of God. To biblical writers, the fate of the righteous and the wicked is a distressing and perplexing problem. They question the disaccord between what befalls men and the religious-moral demand. But more often than ask they answer. They always justify God ; they always feel the need to justify him.

Theodicy is confronted with three basic issues. The first, the origin of primary, natural evils — death, sickness, pain, and toil — is dealt with in the legends of Genesis. Second is the issue of religious evil — idolatry and, its corollary, the weakness of Israel among heathen empires. Third is the issue of moral evil. This last has two aspects : social evil — the prevalence of violence and wickedness among men, the crushing of the righteous by the wicked ; and second, divine evil — the sufferings of the righteous at the hand of God. How can faith in a beneficient, just providence be maintained in the teeth of these phenomena ?

Complaints about the evil in the world, especially about moral evil, are voiced by pagan thinkers as well. Job and Ecclesiastes have their counterparts in the literatures of Egypt and Babylonia. Here, too, men vacillate between faith in a just providence and doubt and despair, to the point even of denying a moral order. Only in Israel, however, does the question touch the very essence of God. The existence of evil is not in itself a problem to paganism, which posits primordial evil principles. The presence of evil does not, therefore, condemn the good gods. Indeed, evil may also overwhelm the good gods themselves. They too are subject to its onslaught, and combat it like men ; they fall into sin and are punished. The pagan, faced by undeserved suffering, can suppose that the gods envy man and, therefore, injure him ; or out of caprice, they destroy him, or stand aside, indifferent to his fate. Pagan man complains, becomes embittered, and reviles the gods, or resigns himself in despair to their decrees. It was otherwise in Israel. On the one hand, there was no evil principle ; good and evil came from YHWH. On the other hand, Israelite religion tolerated no fault or blame in God. He was altogether good and just. When harsh reality challenged the conventional view of divine justice, concern for the honour of God violently disturbed the devout. They could not break out in insults or surrender to despair ; they could only complain and question and go on seeking an answer. At bottom, it is not so much the human side of undeserved suffering that agitates the Bible as the threat it poses to faith in God's justice. Hence the tremendous pathos of Israelite theodicy that has no pagan parallel.

The foundation of Israelite theodicy is the idea of human sin and rebellion. In the absence of divine sin, it is necessarily human sin which is forever at the root of all evil. In the stories of Genesis the sins of primeval man accounted once and for all for the existence of natural and religious evil. But the problem of the continual national-religious distress and the problem of ever present moral evil had constantly to be wrestled with anew at every fresh encounter.

The destiny of Israel among the nations was a perplexing enigma. Did not Israel's material failure before the eyes of the pagans discredit its religion as well ? The problem is ancient. It is given naive, direct expression in the prayers of Moses in Exodus 32:11 ff., Numbers 14 : 13 f., and Deuteronomy 9:28 f. : Israel's fate and the fate of YHWH's name in the world are inseparable. Several psalms, stemming no doubt from some period of war and suffering in pre-exilic times, give voice to the same concern. The enemy has humiliated Israel; YHWH's name has been desecrated. The psalmist fears for the honour of God; for the sake of his name, he begs for deliverance (Pss. 44 : 16 f. ; 74:10, 18, 22 f. ; 79:10 ff. ; 115:1 ff). This enigma gave birth to the legend of the national sin of Israel, whereby God was invariably justified. This sin is more a requirement of biblical theodicy than a historical reality....

In the individual moral sphere, it was equally impossible to escape the gap between what was and what should have been. The prosperity and success of the wicked flew in the face of belief in divine justice. Like their counterparts in Egypt and Babylonia, the poets and sages of Israel decry this wrong, but their plaint has a peculiar religious motive — concern for the good name of God. The prospering villain boasts, "There is no God," and denies divine providence and justice (Pss. 10:3 ff. ; 12:5 ; 14:1 ff. ; 36:2 ; 73:4 ff.). At times, even the faithful man falters ; envy of the wicked overcomes him ; what sense is there in his righteousness and integrity (Ps. 73:2 ff.) ? Yet, in the end, nothing can shake the faith in divine justice. Even the prophet who complains of the tranquillity of the wicked knows that God is "right" (Jer. 12 : 1f.). Biblical man has no refuge other than faith (Pss. 37:1 ff. : 73 : 17 ff. ; cf. Hab. 1:2-2:4).... [pp. 316-333]

The moral ideal of early Israel makes piety and God-fearing the basis of a life of righteousness, truth, love and compassion, humility and toil. Happiness and the pleasures of life are valued ; fertility — human, animal, and agricultural — is the supreme blessing of God ; to rejoice is a divine command. The flesh becomes evil only when it leads man astray and makes him forget God.

The honest man toils ; he is a herdsman or a farmer. The morality of the Bible is that of a folk living off its soil. Charity takes the form of produce of farm and orchard ; money is never mentioned. "The woman of valour" (Prov. 31) raises her own crops, buys a field, and plants a vineyard. Poverty, mendicancy, and suffering are not considered moral or religious virtues. The sage prays : "Give me neither poverty nor riches...lest I be full and deny, and say, 'Who is the Lord ?' Or lest I be poor, and steal, and profane the name of my God" (Prov. 30 : 8 f.). Integrity and closeness to God are absolute values to be desired even more than prosperity (Pss. 37 : 16 ; 73 : 25 ff. ; etc.). To judge from the Bible, commerce played a negligible role in the life of the people. It is a foreign characteristic (Canaanite = merchant), though it is not considered sinful.

The ancient narrative sources (the Torah and histories) count one religious-cultic sin against the people : straying after foreign gods. Violations of other religious laws are not mentioned there, nor in the psalms, and only incidentally in the latter prophets. Sabbath and festival, sacrifice and sacred dues, matters of purity and impurity were all part of popular life and popular piety. Sins were committed, of course, intentionally and unintentionally, but their remedy was also at hand in rites of propitiation and atonement. For this, one turned to the priest and his Torah. Certain of the moral prescriptions were supported by antique taboos. The early narratives illustrate how great was the fear of violating oaths (e.g., the story of Jephthah). Sexual taboos also doubtless inhibited grosser crimes under this head. The violation and murder of a concubine touched off a bloody intertribal battle (Judg. 19-20). David's adultery with Bathsheba stirred up a storm. Later, the morals of the aristocracy degenerated, but the common folk seem to have preserved their old ways.

In the relationships between man and man, however, the rift between ideal and reality was very great. One need only read what is narrated of Abimelech, Saul, David, Absalom, Joab, or Solomon to see how far the admonition "You shall not bear a grudge nor take vengeance" was from being a reality. Before the reign of Amaziah, the law "Fathers shall not be put to death for sons, nor sons for fathers" appears to have had no legal force (2 Kings 14:5 f.). The literature of the Torah takes its departure from the life of the people, but it contains a large idealistic and utopian element. Though it championed the weak and poor, it was not the law of the land ; it was merely an edifying literature to which were joined some legal elements. The basic social laws of the Torah were essentially no more than moral sanctions and exhortations, as is clear from the fact that no penalties are prescribed for their violation. The Torah provided no real legal recourse for the oppressed.

Moreover, the fact that the social background of the Torah was the early tribal and patriarchal polity tended to render it obsolete as the centuries passed. It says next to nothing of the monarchy ; it wholly ignores the royal officialdom ; its concept of land ownership is based exclusively on tribes and clans. No wonder, then, that actual practice was quite at variance with its idea. The Torah forbids taking usury or the clothes of a poor man in pledge. Yet, in the time of the monarchy, a creditor could take the children of his debtor as slaves (2 Kings 4 : 1). The Torah provides for a sabbatical emancipation of Hebrew slaves ; but when, in the time of Zedekiah, this law was (obviously as a novelty), put into effect by a special covenant, the slaves were soon re-enslaved by their owners (Jer. 34:8 ff.). Even the community of the Restoration took debtors' children into slavery (Neh. 5:1 ff.). There were many varieties of exploitation and expropriation, persecution and oppression. This provided the basis of the division between "righteous" and "wicked" in ancient Israel ; in the Torah, prophets, wisdom and psalm literature the distinction is a socio-moral, not a religious one.

In the twilight of the northern kingdom, the social cleavage and the evils that it entailed grew more acute. Masses of people became impoverished, and the rift between ideal and reality became critical. Out of this rift, classical prophecy was born. [pp. 338-340]

NOTE

1. Y. Kaufmann, *The Religion of Israel*, trans. Moshe Greenberg (Chicago : University of Chicago Press, 1960), pp. 316-340.

THE PENTATEUCH AND HAFTORAHS[1]
Genesis

Chapter XV

1 After these things the word of the Lord came unto Abram in a vision, saying : "Fear not, Abram, I am thy shield, thy reward shall be exceeding great."

2 And Abram said : "Oh Lord God, what wilt Thou give me, seeing I go hence childless, and he that shall be possessor of my house is Eliezer of Damascus ?"

3 And Abram said : "Behold, to me Thou hast given no seed, and, lo, one born in my house is to be mine heir."

4 And, behold, the word of the Lord came unto him, saying : "This man shall not be thine heir ; but he that shall come forth out of thine own bowels shall be thine heir."

5 And He brought him forth abroad, and said : "Look now toward heaven, and count the stars, if thou be able to count them" ; and He said unto him : "So shall thy seed be."

6 And he believed in the Lord ; and He counted it to him for righteousness.

7 And He said unto him : "I am the Lord that brought thee out of Ur of the Chaldees, to give thee this land to inherit it."

Chapter XXII

1 And it came to pass after these things, that God did prove Abraham, and said unto him : "Abraham" ; and he said : "Here am I."

2 And He said : "Take now thy son, thine only son, whom thou lovest, even Isaac, and get thee into the land of Moriah ; and offer him there for a burnt-offering upon one of the mountains which I will tell thee of."

3 And Abraham rose early in the morning, and saddled his ass, and took two of his young men with him, and Isaac his son ; and he cleaved the wood for the burnt-offering, and rose up, and went unto the place of which God had told him.

4 On the third day Abraham lifted up his eyes, and saw the place afar off.

5 And Abraham said unto his young men : "Abide ye here with the ass, and I and the lad will go yonder ; and we will worship, and come back to you."

6 And Abraham took the wood of the burnt-offering, and laid it upon Isaac his son ; and he took in his hand the fire and the knife ; and they went both of them together.

7 And Isaac spoke unto Abraham his father, and said : "My father." And he said : "Here am I, my son." And he said : "Behold the fire and the wood ; but where is the lamb for a burnt-offering ?"

8 And Abraham said : "God will provide Himself the lamb for burnt-offering, my son." So they went both of them together.

9 And they came to the place which God had told him of; and Abraham built the altar there, and laid the wood in order, and bound Isaac his son, and laid him on the altar, upon the wood.

10 And Abraham stretched forth his hand, and took the knife to slay his son.

11 And the angel of the Lord called unto him out of heaven, and said : "Abraham, Abraham." And he said : "Here am I."

12 And he said : "Lay not thy hand upon the lad, neither do thou any thing unto him ; for now I know that thou art a God-fearing man, seeing thou hast not withheld thy son, thine only son, from Me."

13 And Abraham lifted up his eyes, and looked, and behold behind him a ram caught in the thicket by his horns. And Abraham went and took the ram, and offered him up for a burnt-offering in the stead of his son.

14 And Abraham called the name of that place Adonaijireh ; as it is said to this day : "In the mount where the Lord is seen."

15 And the angel of the Lord called unto Abraham a second time out of heaven,

16 and said : "By Myself have I sworn, saith the Lord, because thou has done this thing, and hast not withheld thy son, thine only son,

17 that in blessing I will bless thee, and in multiplying I will multiply thy seed as the stars of the heaven, and as the sand which is upon the sea-shore ; and thy seed shall possess the gate of his enemies ;

18 and in thy seed shall all the nations of the earth be blessed ; because thou hast hearkened to My voice."

19 So Abraham returned unto his young men, and they rose up and went together to Beer-sheba ; and Abraham dwelt at Beer-sheba.

NOTE

1. *The Pentateuch and Haftorahs*, ed. J.H. Hertz, (London : Oxford University Press, 1956).

FEAR AND TREMBLING[1]

S. Kierkegaard

The difference between the tragic hero and Abraham is clearly evident. The tragic hero still remains within the ethical. He lets one expression of the ethical find its *telos* in a higher expression of the ethical ; the ethical relation between father and son, or daughter and father, he reduced to a sentiment which has its dialectic in its relation to the idea of morality. Here there can be no question of a teleological suspension of the ethical itself.

With Abraham the situation was different. By his act he overstepped the ethical entirely and possessed a higher *telos* outside of it, in relation to which he suspended the former. For I should very much like to know how one would bring Abraham's act into relation with the universal, and whether it is possible to discover any connection whatever between what Abraham did and the universal . . . except the fact that he transgressed it. It was not for the sake of saving a people, not to maintain the idea of the state, that Abraham did this, and not in order to reconcile angry deities. If there could be a question of the deity being angry, he was angry only with Abraham, and Abraham's whole action stands in no relation to the universal, is a purely private undertaking. Therefore, whereas the tragic hero is great by reason of his moral virtue, Abraham is great by reason of a purely personal virtue. In Abraham's life there is no higher expression for the ethical than this, that the father shall love his son. Of the ethical in the sense of morality there can be no question in this instance. In so far as the universal was present, it was indeed cryptically present in Isaac, hidden as it were in Isaac's loins, and must therefore cry out with Isaac's mouth, "Do it not! Thou art bringing everything to naught."

Why then did Abraham do it? For God's sake, and (in complete identity with this) for his own sake. He did it for God's sake because God required this proof of his faith; for his own sake he did it in order that he might furnish the proof. The unity of these two points of view is perfectly expressed by the word which has always been used to characterize this situation: it is a trial, a temptation (*Fristelse*). A temptation — but what does that mean? What ordinarily tempts a man is that which would keep him from doing his duty, but in this case the temptation is itself the ethical . . . which would keep him from doing God's will. But what then is duty? Duty is precisely the expression for God's will.

Here is evident the necessity of a new category if one would understand Abraham. Such a relationship to the deity paganism did not know. The tragic hero does not enter into any private relationship with the deity, but for him the ethical is the divine, hence the paradox implied in his situation can be mediated in the universal.

Abraham cannot be mediated, and the same thing can be expressed also by saying that he cannot talk. So soon as I talk I express the universal, and if I do not do so, no one can understand me. Therefore if Abraham would express himself in terms of the universal, he must say that his situation is a temptation (*Anfechtung*), for he has no higher expression for that universal which stands above the universal which he transgresses. [pp. 69-71]

NOTE

1. S. Kierkegaard, *Fear and Trembling and the Sickness unto Death*, trans. Walter Lowrie, (Princeton : Princeton University Press, 1941), pp. 69-71.

FEAR AND TREMBLING[1]

D.N. Weisstub

Isaac,
look up
it is early morn

God's task requires
a journey while the
dew yet kisses babes,
and eucalyptic trees
scratch branches
in waking yawns.

Go
before the desert light,
(go before the sun shows the deed).

Abraham,
clasp the knife that
circumcized this holy firstborn,
hide it well
before the sun and trees.

Mount yourselves, all
for the mountain ram
waits anxiously, and the sun
waits behind the ridges.
Angels, bring the host
and guested company
to the judgment hill,
where Isaac will free his father
from God's will.

Record the document that
God's eyes feared and trembled
in Isaac's quivering lip.
No man could take
his son again
to slide the knife at judgment hill.

NOTE

1. D.N. Weisstub, "Fear and Trembling," in *Heaven Take My Hand* (Toronto : McClelland and Stewart, 1968), p. 16.

THE PROPHETS[1]

Abraham J. Heschel

Sacred fire is burning on the altars in many lands. Animals are being offered to the glory of the gods. Priests burn incense, songs of solemn assemblies fill the air. Pilgrims are on the roads, pageantries in the sacred places. The atmosphere is thick with sanctity. In Israel, too, sacrifice is an essential act of worship. It is the experience of giving oneself vicariously to God and of being received by Him. And yet, the pre-exile prophets uttered violent attacks on sacrifices (Amos 5:21 -27 ; Hos. 6:6 ; Isa. 1 : 11-17 ; Mic. 6 : 6-8 ; Jer. 6:20 ; 7 : 21-23 ; Isa. 61 : 1-2 ; Pss. 40:7 ; 50 : 12-13). Samuel insisted : "Has the Lord as great delight in burnt offerings and sacrifices, as in obeying the voice of the Lord ? Behold, to obey is better than sacrifice, and to hearken than the fat of rams" (1 Sam. 15:22). However, while Samuel stressed the primacy of obedience over sacrifice, Amos and the prophets who followed him not only stressed the primacy of morality over sacrifice, but even proclaimed that the worth of worship, far from being absolute, is contingent upon moral living, and that when immorality prevails, worship is detestable. Questioning man's right to worship through offerings and songs, they maintained that the primary way of serving God is through love, justice, and righteousness.

This is a paradox to be sure and, like every paradox, its opposite is a view that is orthodox. It contains both a negation and an affirmation, the negation being more intelligible than the affirmation. It is difficult for us today to appreciate the boldness and defiance contained in these pronouncements. The distinction between the holy and the profane, between the divine and the mundane, is the basis of religious thinking. A line is drawn between the interests of man and the demands of God. What is it that all gods demand ? Sacrifice, incense, reverence for their power. Sacrifice, the strength and the measure of piety, acts wherein God and man meet — all this should be called obnoxious ?

Of course, the prophets did not condemn the practice of sacrifice in itself; otherwise, we should have to conclude that Isaiah intended to discourage the practice of prayer (Isa. 1 : 14-15). They did, however, claim that deeds of injustice vitiate both sacrifice and prayer. Men may not drown the cries of the oppressed with the noise of hymns, nor buy off the Lord with increased offerings. The prophets disparaged the cult when it became a substitute for righteousness. It is precisely the implied recognition of the value cult that lends force to their insistence that there is something far more precious than sacrifice.

These feasts and assemblies, offerings and rites, hallowed by the loyalty of many generations, had become the essence of piety. One cannot doubt the sacred authenticity of the cult. It had a place and a procedure of its own, a sacred nimbus, a mysterious glory. It differed from all other pursuits ; exceptional, striking, set apart, it conferred unique blessings. In the sacrificial acts something happened, something sacred was evoked, conjured up, initiated ; something was released or cast away. The person was transformed, a communion vital to man and precious to God established.

In the sacrifice of homage, God was a participant ; in the sacrifice of expiation, God was a recipient. The sacrificial act was a form of personal association with God, a way of entering into communion with Him. In offering an animal, a person was offering himself vicariously. It had the power of atonement.

How supremely certain ancient man was that sacrifice was what the gods most desired may be deduced from the fact that fathers did not hesitate to slaughter their own children on the altar. When Mesha, the king of the Moabites, was hard-pressed in war, he sacrificed his own son, who would have reigned as his successor, for a burnt offering upon the wall (2 Kings 3:27).

To add paradox to sacrilege : all this grandeur and solemnity are declared to be second rate, of minor importance, if not hateful to God, while deeds of kindness worrying about the material needs of widows and orphans, commonplace things, platitudinous affairs are exactly what the Lord of heaven and earth demands ! To give up a thousand fertile vineyards for an acre of barren ground ? To find the presence of God in the shape of righteousness ?

What they attacked was, I repeat, supremely venerable : a sphere unmistakably holy ; a spirituality that had both form and substance, that was concrete and inspiring, an atmosphere overwhelming the believer — pageantry, scenery, mystery, spectacle, fragrance, song, and exaltation. In the experience of such captivating sanctity, who could question the presence of God in the shape of a temple ?

Let us go to His dwelling place ;
Let us worship at His footstool !
Arise, O Lord, and go to Thy resting place,
Thou and the ark of Thy might.
Let Thy priests be clothed with righteousness,
And let Thy saints shout for joy. . .
For the Lord has chosen Zion ;
He has desired it for His habitation :
This is My resting place forever ;
Here I will dwell, for I have desired it.
Ps. 132:7-9, 13-14

It is hard for us to imagine what entering a sanctuary or offering a sacrifice meant to ancient man. The sanctuary was holiness in perpetuity, a miracle in continuity ; the divine was mirrored in the air, sowing blessing, closing gaps between the here and the beyond. In offering a sacrifice, man mingled with mystery, reached the summit of significance : sin was consumed, self abandoned, satisfaction was bestowed upon divinity. Is it possible for us today to conceive of the solemn joy of those whose offering was placed on the altar ?

Then I will go to the altar of God,
To God my exceeding joy ;
I will praise Thee with the lyre,
O God, my God.
Ps. 43:4 ; cf. Deut. 12:18-19 ;
31:11 ; Exod. 34:23 f. ; Isa. 1:12

Why should religion, the essence of which is worship of God, put such stress on justice for man ? Does not the preoccupation with morality tend to divest religion of immediate devotion to God ? Why should a worldly virtue like justice be so important to the Holy One of Israel ? Did not the prophets overrate the worth of justice ?

Perhaps the answer lies here : righteousness is not just a value ; it is God's part of human life, God's stake in human history. Perhaps it is because the suffering of man is a blot upon God's conscience ; because it is in relations between man and man that God is at stake. Or is it simply because the infamy of a wicked act is infinitely greater than we are able to imagine ? People act as they please, doing what is vile, abusing the weak, not realizing that they are fighting God, affronting the divine, or that the oppression of man is a humiliation of God.

He who oppresses a poor man insults his Maker,
He who is kind to the needy honours Him.
Prov. 14:31 ; cf. 17:5

The universe is done. The greater masterpiece still undone, still in the process of being created, is history. For accomplishing His grand design, God needs the help of man. Man is and has the instrument of God, which he may or may not use in consonance with the grand design. Life is clay, and righteousness the mould in which God wants history to be shaped. But human beings, instead of fashioning the clay, deform the shape.

The world is full of iniquity, of injustice and idolatry. The people offer animals ; the priests offer incense. But God needs mercy, righteousness ; His needs cannot be satisfied in the temples, in space, but only in history, in time. It is within the realm of history that man is charged with God's mission.

Justice is not an ancient custom, a human convention, a value, but a transcendent demand, freighted with divine concern. It is not only a relationship between man and man, it is an act involving God, a divine need. Justice is His line, righteousness His plummet (Isa. 28:17). It is not one of His ways, but in all His ways. Its validity is not only universal, but also eternal, independent of will and experience.

People think that to be just is a virtue, deserving honour and rewards ; that in doing righteousness one confers a favour on society. No one expects to receive a reward for the habit of breathing. Justice is as much a necessity as breathing is, and a constant occupation.

Power, omniscience, wisdom, infinitude are the attributes that man associates with the Supreme Being. Justice is not necessarily regarded as an essential attribute of God, nor is charity considered in all religions an essential part of piety. The holy men of India, for example, stand aloof from moral issues, and the highest goal of Indian philosophy and piety is to shed the fetters of action by overcoming the inclination to be active. Indeed, books on religion in which no reference is made to morality are as common as books on morality in which no reference is made to religion.

Greek religion did not stress the connection between religion and morality. It offered no precepts for the regulation of human conduct. Each god had his appointed sphere within which he exercised control. The gods were jealous to avenge any infringement of their privileges. But the sinner was punished, not as a moral offender, but as a trespasser against a divine power. In the tragedies the gods were considered guarantors of human injustice, which consisted primarily of submission to destiny ; but the gods in turn were not required to observe justice in their conduct toward mortals.

Occasionally we find the belief that certain gods who were the sources of the skills and wisdom of man had also given laws to him. In popular Greek religion there was a belief that specific laws were revealed by a god ; among Cretans it was said to have been Zeus, and in Lacedaemon, Apollo. According to Homer, Minos, the Cretan lawgiver, "went every ninth year to converse with his Olympian sire" ; his laws were derived from Zeus. The difference, however, is that the laws, like the skills, are not regarded as being an expression of the personal will of the god ; they are something that the gods have dealt out rather than something to which they remain personally committed.

There are few thoughts as deeply ingrained in the mind of biblical man as the thought of God's justice and righteousness. It is not an inference, but an *a priori* of biblical faith, self-evident ; not an added attribute to His essence, but given with the very thought of God. It is inherent in His essence and identified with His ways.

> The rock, His work is perfect ;
> For all His ways are justice.
> O God of faithfulness and without iniquity,
> Just and right is He.
>
> Deut. 32:4

> Righteous art Thou, O Lord,
> And right are Thy judgments.
>
> Ps. 119:137

God is the source of right (Deut. 1:17) ; judge of all the earth. It is inconceivable that He shall not do the right (Gen. 18:25), that He shall pervert justice (Job 8:3), or do wickedly (Job 34:12). "For the Lord is a God of justice" (Isa. 30:18). "The Lord is righteous, He loves righteousness" (Ps. 11:7). That "God is a righteous judge" is the incontestable premise of Jeremiah's question, "Why does the way of the wicked prosper ?" (Jer. 12:1).

The two key elements are *tsedakah (tsedek)* and *mishpat.* The word *mishpat* means the judgment given by the *shofet* (judge) ; hence the word can mean justice, norm, ordinance, legal right, law. The word *tsedakah* may be rendered by "righteousness." While legality and righteousness are not identical, they must always coincide, the second being reflected in the first.

It is exceedingly difficult to establish the exact difference in meaning of the biblical terms *mishpat,* justice, and *tsedakah,* righteousness (which in parallelism are often used as variants). However, it seems that justice is a mode of action, righteousness is a quality of the person. Significantly, the noun derived from *shafat* (to judge) is *shofet,* which came to mean a judge or arbitrator ; while the noun from *tsadak* (to be just) is *tsaddik,* a righteous man.

Righteousness goes beyond justice. Justice is strict and exact, giving each person his due. Righteousness implies benevolence, kindness, generosity. Justice is form, a state of equilibrium ; righteousness has a substantive associated meaning. Justice may be legal ; righteousness is associated with a burning compassion for the oppressed. When you extend a loan to a poor man, "you shall not sleep in his pledge ; when the sun goes down, you shall restore to him the pledge, that he may sleep in his cloak and bless you ; and it shall be righteousness to you before the Lord your God" (Deut. 24 : 10-13).

It would be wrong to assume that there was a dichotomy of *mishpat* and kindness ; "Justice was not equal justice but a bias in favour of the poor. Justice always leaned toward mercy for the widows and the orphans." Divine justice involves His being merciful, compassionate.

> Therefore the Lord is waiting to be gracious to you ;
> Therefore He exalts Himself to show mercy to you.
> For the Lord is a God of justice ;
> Blessed are all those who wait for Him.
>
> Isa. 30:18

Justice dies when dehumanized, no matter how exactly it may be exercised. Justice dies when deified, for beyond all justice is God's compassion. The logic of justice may seem impersonal, yet the concern for justice is an act of love.

If intense regard and concern for man is the mark of a moral act, then inspiration of the prophets in which God's regard and concern for man are disclosed and in which the prophet is entrusted with a mission to help the people, must be viewed as an eminently moral act. The moral aspect sets the prophetic act apart from intellectual, artistic, and mystical experiences.

In archaic religions the relationship between man and his gods and the relationship between man and his fellow men represented two areas unrelated to each other. Man owed certain duties toward the gods — he must offer prayer and sacrifice, the neglect of which is sin — but these duties did not concern his relations to his fellow men. In performing the rites, in his search to share sanctity or to attain salvation, the religious man might experience the power and grandeur of the divine, the bestowal of grace, or the assumption of insight, but not the concern of the god for someone else.

Religious experience, in most cases, is a private affair in which a person becomes alive to what transpires between God and himself, not to what transpires between God and someone else ; contact between God and man comes about, it is believed, for the benefit of the particular man. In contrast, prophetic inspiration is for the sake, for the benefit, of a third party. It is not a private affair between prophet and God ; its purpose is the illumination of the people rather than the illumination of the prophet....

The phenomenon of prophecy is predicated upon the assumption that man is both in need of, and entitled to, divine guidance. For God to reveal His word through the prophet to His people is an act of justice or an act of seeking to do justice. The purpose of prophecy is to maintain the covenant, to establish the right relationship between God and man.

The fact that filled the prophets with dismay was not the absence of adequate laws, but the absence of righteousness. Judges were active in the land, but their judgments were devoid of righteousness. The prophets were shocked not only by acts of injustice on the part of scoundrels but also by the perversion of justice on the part of the notables. When warped and garbled, justice yields strife and distrust.

> Do horses run upon rock ?
> Does one plow the sea with oxen ?
> But you have turned justice into poison,
> The fruit of righteousness into wormwood. . .
> O you who turn justice to wormwood,
> And cast down righteousness to the earth !
>
> Amos 6:12 ; 5:7 ;
> cf. Deut. 29:17 ;
> Jer. 8:14 ; 9:14 ; 23:15 ;
> Lam. 3:15 ; 19 ;
> Prov. 5:4

> They utter mere words ;
> With empty oaths they make covenants ;

So judgment springs up like poisonous weeds
In the furrows of the field.
Hos. 10:4

Israel was the vineyard that the Lord had planted. He looked for it to yield grapes, but it yielded wild grapes. He looked for it to yield justice, but it yielded perversion of justice; for righteousness, but it yielded outrage (Isa. 5:2).

The prophets consistently singled out the leaders, the kings, the princes, the false prophets, and the priests as the ones responsible for the sins of the community. (See Hos. 4:6, 8 f.; 7:3, 16; 9:15; Jer. 2:26.)

Hear this, O priest!
Give heed, O house of Israel!
Hearken, O house of the kings!
For the judgment pertains to you.
Hos. 5:1

The Lord enters into judgment
With the elders and princes of his people:
It is you who have devoured the vineyard,
The spoil of the poor is in your houses.
What do you mean by crushing the people,
By grinding the face of the poor?
Says the Lord of hosts.
Isa. 3:14-15

After declaring that no one in the streets of Jerusalem did justice or sought truth, Jeremiah added:

Then I said, These are only the poor,
They have no sense;
For they do not know the way of the Lord,
The Torah of their God.
I will go to the great,
And will speak to them;
For they know the way of the Lord,
The Torah of their God.
But they all alike had broken the yoke,
They had burst the bonds.
Jer. 5 : 4-5

"The shepherds are stupid" (Jer. 10:21). "Thus says the Lord God: Behold, I am against the shepherds; I will require My sheep at their hand" (Ezek. 34:10).

The prophet's preoccupation with justice and righteousness has its roots in a powerful awareness of injustice. That justice is a good thing, a fine goal, even a supreme ideal, is commonly accepted. What is lacking is a sense of the monstrosity of injustice. Moralists of all ages have been eloquent in singing the praises of virtue. The distinction of the prophets was in their remorseless unveiling of injustice and oppression, in their comprehension of social, political, and religious evils. They were not concerned with the definition, but with the predicament, of justice, with the fact that those called upon to apply it defied it.

Justice may be properly described as "the active process of remedying or preventing what should arouse the sense of injustice." What is uppermost in the prophets' mind is not justice, "an ideal relation or static condition or set of perceptual standards," but the presence of oppression and corruption. The urgency of justice was an urgency of aiding and saving the victims of oppression. In the words of the psalmist :

From the heavens Thou didst utter judgment
The earth feared and was still,
When God arose to establish judgment
To save all the oppressed of the earth.
Ps. 76:9-10

Justice is scarce, injustice exceedingly common. The concern for justice is delegated to the judges, as if it were a matter for professionals or specialists. But to do justice is what God demands of every man : it is the supreme commandment, and one that cannot be fulfilled vicariously.

Righteousness must dwell not only in the places where justice is judicially administered. There are many ways of evading the law and escaping the arm of justice. Only a few acts of violence are brought to the attention of the courts. As a rule, those who know how to exploit are endowed with the skill to justify their acts, while those who are easily exploited possess no skill in pleading their own cause. Those who neither exploit nor are exploited are ready to fight when their own interests are harmed ; they will not be involved when not personally affected. Who shall plead for the helpless ? Who shall prevent the epidemic of injustice that no court of justice is capable of stopping ?

In a sense, the calling of the prophet may be described as that of an advocate or champion, speaking for those who are too weak to plead their own cause. Indeed, the major activity of the prophets was interference, remonstrating about wrongs inflicted on other people, meddling in affairs which were seemingly neither their concern nor their responsibility. A prudent man is he who minds his own business, staying away from questions which do not involve his own interests, particularly when not authorized to step in — and prophets were given no mandate by the widows and orphans to plead their cause. The prophet is a person who is not tolerant of wrongs done to others, who resents other people's injuries. He even calls upon others to be the champions of the poor. It is to every member of Israel, not alone to the judges, that Isaiah directs his plea :

Seek justice,
Undo oppression ;
Defend the fatherless,
Plead for the widow.
Isa. 1:17

To the king as well as to the people, the prophet proclaims : "Thus says the Lord : Do justice and righteousness, and deliver from the hand of the oppressor him who has been robbed. Do no wrong or violence to the alien, the fatherless, and the widow, nor shed innocent blood in this place" (Jer. 22:3). "Amend your ways and your doings ; . . .execute justice one with another ;. . .do not oppress the alien, the fatherless, or the widow" (Jer. 7:5 f.).

In the *Iliad* gods as well as men are indifferent to wrongs inflicted, not upon themselves, but on others. Quite a number of homicides are mentioned. However, "outside the circle of the dead man's kinsmen and friends, there is no indication of any popular sentiment against ordinary homicide. Odysseus, in his character of Cretan refugee, had told a tale to Eumaeus in which he represented himself as the slayer of the son of Idomeneus. It would be hard to imagine a more cowardly murder than this. And yet Eumaeus receives the supposed murderer with all the respect due to a stranger in accordance with the prevailing customs. Several murderers are mentioned as living as honoured members of communities to which they had come as exiles.

It was long after the time of the early prophets of Israel that a law of Solon's (d. 559 B.C.E.) was promulgated in Athens which presupposed the readiness of the citizens to interfere when wrongs were inflicted on others. Solon "believed that the best-governing state was that in which those who had suffered no wrong were as diligent in prosecuting and punishing the wrongdoers as those who had suffered wrongs." The first appearance of "advocates" was at a trial in 489 B.C.E. It was in Rome that the advocate, more through his oratorical art than through his knowledge of law, achieved outstanding eminence.

An act of interfering in a case in which a wrong was inflicted upon someone else is reported from the time of David. After King David's sin with Bathsheba, the wife of Uriah, the prophet Nathan went to David and told him a parable.

There were two men in a certain city, the one rich and the other poor. The rich man had very many flocks and herds ; but the poor man had nothing but one little ewe lamb, which he had bought. And he brought it up, and it grew up with him and with his children ; it used to eat of his morsel, and drink from his cup, and lie in his bosom, and it was like a daughter to him. Now there came a traveller to the rich man,and he was unwilling to take one of his own flock or herd to prepare for the wayfarer who had come to him, but he took the poor man's lamb, and prepared it for the man who had come to him. Then David's anger was greatly kindled against the man ; and he said to Nathan, "As the Lord lives, the man who has done this deserves to die ; and he shall restore the lamb fourfold, because he did this thing, and because he had no pity." Thereupon Nathan said to David : "You are the man." (2 Sam. 12 : 1-6)

Ahab, the king of Israel (875-853 B.C.E.), insisted upon securing the property of Naboth of Jezreel. When the latter refused to sell it, he was put to death on false accusation. For this outrage, Elijah the prophet said to Ahab : "Have you killed, and also taken possession ?. . . Thus says the Lord : In the place where the dogs licked up the blood of Naboth shall dogs lick your own blood" (1 Kings 21 : 1-19).

The demand is not only to respect justice in the sense of abstaining from doing injustice, but also to strive for it, to pursue it.

> Seek the Lord, all you humble of the land,
> Who do His commands ;
> Seek righteousness, seek humility ;
> Perhaps you may be hidden

On the day of the anger of the Lord.
Zeph. 2:3

"Righteousness, and only righteousness you shall pursue" (Deut. 16:20). The term "pursue" carried strong connotations of effort, eagerness, persistence, inflexibility of purpose. This implies more than merely respecting or following justice, walking in the way of righteousness ; righteousness may be hard to attain ; it may escape us if we do not pursue it. (See Isa. 16:5).

Hearken to me, you who pursue righteousness,
You who seek the Lord.
Isa. 51:1

"You who pursue righteousness, you who seek the Lord" — what greater praise is possible than is given by the juxtaposition of these phrases ?

The imperative includes more than doing ; it asks for love ; beyond justice, it refers to good and evil. "Seek good and not evil. . . . Hate evil and love good and establish justice in the gate" (Amos 5:14,15).

"It has been told you, O man, what is good, and what does the Lord require of you but *to do justice* and *to love kindness* (*hesed*), and *to walk humbly with your God*" (Mic. 6:8) — *doing* justice as well as *loving* kindness. The prophets tried to excite fervour, to make *hesed* an object of love.

What the Lord requires of man is more than fulfilling one's duty. To love implies an insatiable thirst, a passionate craving. To love means to transfer the centre of one's inner life from the ego to the object of one's love.

Is this all the prophet came to teach us — social justice ? Are there no other demands to be satisfied, no other goals to be attained ?

God not only asks for justice : He demands of man "to regard the deeds of the Lord, to see the work of His hands" (Isa. 5 : 12 ; cf. 22:11), "to walk in His paths" (Isa. 2:3). "If you will not believe, you will not abide" (Isa. 7:11). Give thanks to the Lord,

Call upon His name,
Make known His deeds among the nations,
Proclaim that His name is exalted.
Sing praises to the Lord,. . .
Shout, sing for joy,. . .
For great in your midst is the Holy One of Israel.
Isa. 12:3-6

It is not only action that God demands, it is not only disobedience to the law that the prophet decries.

They do not cry to Me from the heart.
Hos. 7:14
This people draw near with their mouths
And honour Me with their lips,
While their hearts are far from Me ;
Their fear of Me is a commandment of men learned by rote.
Isa. 29:13

The fault is in the hearts, not alone in the deeds.

Their heart is false;
Now they must bear their guilt.
Hos. 10:2

Thou art near in their mouth,
And far from their heart. . .
Break up your fallow ground,
Sow not among thorns.
Circumcize yourselves to the Lord,
Remove the foreskin of your hearts,
O men of Judah and inhabitants of Jerusalem.
Jer. 4:3-4

Amos condemns the rich who revel in luxuries for not being pained or grieved over the afflictions of the people (6:6).

For the fool speaks folly,
And his mind plots iniquity;
To practice ungodliness,
To utter error concerning the Lord,
To leave the craving of the hungry unsatisfied,
And to deprive the thirsty of drink.
Isa. 32:6

The Lord alone is holy; "let Him be your fear, let Him be your dread" (Isa. 8:13). To fear God is to be unafraid of man. For God alone is king, power, and promise. "Yet even now, says the Lord, return to Me with all your heart, with fasting, with weeping, and with mourning, and rend your hearts and not your garments" (Joel 2:13).

Thus says the Lord:
Cursed is the man who trusts in man and makes flesh his arm,
Whose heart turns away from the Lord.
He is like a shrub in the desert,
And shall not see any good come.
He shall dwell in the parched places of the wilderness,
In an uninhabited salt land.
Blessed is the man who trusts in the Lord,
Whose trust is the Lord.
He is like a tree planted by water,
That sends out its roots by the stream,
And does not fear when heat comes,
For its leaves remain green,
And is not anxious in the year of drought,
For it does not cease to bear fruit.
Jer. 17:5-8

If justice be the mere relationship of a person to what he deserves, then why should it take precedence over the relationship of a person to what he desires? Obviously the situation of one who deserves contains an element not present in the situation of one who desires, namely, having a claim, being entitled to something. An individual's desire is his private affair, an individual's claim involves other selves. The claim of one person to attain justice is contingent upon the assumption that there is another person who has the responsibility to answer it. Justice, then is an interpersonal relationship, implying both a claim and a responsibility.

Justice bespeaks a situation that transcends the individual, demanding from everyone a certain abnegation of self, defiance of self-interest, disregard of self-respect. The necessity of submitting to a law is derived from the necessity of identifying oneself with what concerns other individuals or the whole community of men. Justice is valid because of the community that unites all individuals. The sense of justice is outgoing, transitive, inclusive.

There is an interpersonal correlation of claim and responsibility, but there is also an inner personal correlation of right and duty. Ancient Israel "does not distinguish between right and duty," and *mishpat,* the word for justice, denotes what a person may claim as well as what he is bound to do to others. In other words, it signifies both *right and duty.*

Justice is an interpersonal relationship, involving a claim and a responsibility, a right and a duty, applied, according to the Bible, to both God and man. In its fundamental meaning, *mishpat* refers to all actions which contribute to maintaining the covenant, namely, the true relationship between man and man, and between God and man.

Thus, justice in the Bible must not be taken in a legal sense as the administration of law according to the rules of law by a judge. One constantly "judges" in the daily life because one must constantly act so as to uphold the covenant, i.e., the whole of the common life of the community. Everything in which this kind of judging manifests itself is called *mishpat.*

Why and for what purpose was Abraham chosen to become a great and mighty nation, and to be a blessing to all the nations of the earth ? Not because he knew how to build pyramids, altars, and temples, but "in order that he may charge his children and his household after him to keep the way of the Lord by doing righteousness and justice" (Gen. 18 : 18-19). Righteousness is foremost among the things God asks of man. "Thus says the Lord : Let not the wise man glory in his wisdom, let not the mighty man glory in his might, let not the rich man glory in his riches ; but let him who glories, glory in this : that *he understands and knows Me, that I am the Lord Who does kindness, justice, and righteousness in the earth* ; for in these things I delight says the Lord" (Jer. 9:23-24).

This is sublime knowledge, sublime understanding, a new grammar of experience. What we encounter in the world is not neutral, impersonal being, things, forces, forms, colours. What we encounter is full of God's kindness, justice, and righteousness. "The earth is full of the kindness (*hesed*) of the Lord" (Ps. 33:5). "He is the Lord our God ; His judgments are in all the earth" (Ps. 105:7). "The heavens declare His righteousness. . . .and all the people behold His Glory" (Pss. 50:6 ; 97:6). "Thy love, O Lord, extends to the heavens, Thy faithfulness to the clouds" (Ps. 36:6).

God's love and kindness indicate a road. It is a road not limited to a particular area in space nor to exceptional miraculous happenings. It is everywhere, at all times.

Kindness, justice, and righteousness are heaven's part in life. Its perception is the prophet's daily experience and the spring of joy. And this is why celebration is man's first response to life and being. Beauty and grandeur are not anonymous ; they are outbursts of God's kindness.

In the passage quoted above (Jer. 9:23-24), knowledge of God is knowledge of what He does : kindness, justice, righteousness. In another passage, knowledge of God is equated with what man does : justice, righteousness. In exhorting King Jehoiakim, Jeremiah contrasts him with his father :

> Did not your father eat and drink
> And do justice and righteousness ?
> Then it was well with him.
> He judged the cause of the poor and needy ;
> Then it was well.
> Is not this to know Me ?
> Says the Lord.
>
> Jer. 22:15-16

Here knowledge is not the same as thought, comprehension, gnosis or mystical participation in the ultimate essence. Knowledge of God is action toward man, sharing His concern for justice ; sympathy in action.

Inner identification with God's will and concern is the goal of the new covenant :

> I will put My Torah within them,
> And write it on their hearts ;
> And I will be a God to them,
> And they to Me a people.
>
> Jer. 31:32

The world is overwhelmingly rich ; the human mind is incapable of paying attention to all its aspects. The painter sees the world in colour, the sculptor in form ; the musician perceives the world in sounds, and the economist in commodities. The prophet is a man who sees the world with the eyes of God, and in the sight of God even things of beauty or acts of ritual are an abomination when associated with injustice.

The world is overwhelmingly rich, but the prophet perceives the whole world in terms of justice or injustice ....

Justice is usually defined as giving every person his due. It connotes a conformity, a congruence, a proportion of some kind. This is reflected in the numerical symbols employed by the Greeks to express as the essence of justice the relation of parity between two contraposited terms : the dyad, also the number 8, which has 2 for its root, because of its peculiar divisibility. The idea of balancing two sides against one another is expressed in the most common symbol of justice, namely, the scales. When the sword is added to the scales, it is a symbol not only of power, but also of precision ; it seeks not so much to strike as to cut clearly the matter of controversy into two equal parts.

In sharp contrast to these symbols, expressing calmness, congruence and precision, stands the prophetic image :

> Let justice roll down like waters,

And righteousness like a mighty stream.
Amos 5:24

One is uncertain of the exact meaning of this bold image. It seems to combine several ideas : a surging movement, a life-bringing substance, a dominant power.

A mighty stream, expressive of the vehemence of a never-ending, surging, fighting movement — as if obstacles had to be washed away for justice to be done. No rock is so hard that water cannot pierce it. "The mountain falls and crumbles away, the rock is removed from its place — the waters wear away the stones" (Jon. 14:18 f.). Justice is not a mere norm, but a fighting challenge, a restless drive.

Balancing is possible when the scales are unimpaired, and the judge's eyes sound. When the eyes are dim and the scales unsure, what is required is a power that will strike and change, heal and restore, like a mighty stream bringing life to the parched land. There is a thirst for righteousness that only a mighty stream can quench.

Righteousness as a mere tributary, feeding the immense stream of human interests, is easily exhausted and more easily abused. But righteousness is not a trickle ; it is God's power in the world, a torrent, an impetuous drive, full of grandeur and majesty. The surge is choked, the sweep is blocked. Yet the mighty stream will break all dikes.

Justice, people seem to agree, is a principle, a norm, an ideal of the highest importance. We all insist that it ought to be — but it may not be. In the eyes of the prophets, justice is more than an idea or a norm : justice is charged with the omnipotence of God. What ought to be, shall be !

Righteousness is a vast and mighty stream because God is its unfailing source.

But the Lord of hosts shall be exalted in justice,
The Holy One of Israel sanctified in righteousness.
Isa. 5:16

This is a staggering assertion. Why should His justice be the supreme manifestation of God ? Is not wisdom or omnipotence a mode of manifestation more magnificent and more indicative of what we associate with the divine ? It would have been more plausible to declare : The Lord of hosts is exalted in majesty, the Holy One of Israel is sanctified in omnipotence. Omnipotence is an attribute which no mortal shares with God, while justice is a quality to which human beings, too, lay claim ; It is a quality devoid of sublimity and mystery, elementary and undistinguished.

Isaiah's declaration is humble compared with the words the Lord spake to Job out of the whirlwind. How trite and prosaic are justice and righteousness when matched against the transcendent majesty and the crushing mystery of the Creator of the universe ; a still, small voice compared with a thunderbolt. Job's answer to the words spoken out of the whirlwind was :

I had heard of Thee by the hearing of the ear,
But now my eye sees Thee ;
Therefore I despise myself

And repent in dust and ashes.
Job 42:6

In contrast, Isaiah was able to exclaim :

O house of Jacob,
Come, let us walk
In the light of the Lord.
Isa. 2:5

Perhaps this is the deeper meaning of the words, "The Holy One of Israel is sanctified in righteousness." The holy is all mystery, inscrutable, dwelling in "thick darkness." Yet beyond the darkness is righteousness. Mystery is not the ultimate. Mystery is surpassed by meaning.

Cloud and deep darkness are round about Him ;
Righteousness and justice are the foundations of His throne.
Ps. 97:2

History, what happens here and now, is the decisive stage for God's manifestation. His glorious disclosure is not in a display of miracles, evoking fascination, but in establishing righteousness, evoking appreciation.

Exalted is the Lord,
He who dwells on high,
He has filled Zion with justice and righteousness.
He will be the permanence of your times,
Abundance of salvation, wisdom, and knowledge.
The fear of the Lord is His treasure.
Isa. 33 : 5-6

The grandeur and majesty of God do not come to expression in the display of ultimate sovereignty and power, but rather in rendering righteousness and mercy. "He exalts Himself to show mercy to you" (Isa. 30:18).

For Thou has been a stronghold to the poor,
A stronghold to the needy in his distress.
Isa. 25:4

Isaiah's declaration does not speak about values, and its intention is not to assert that holiness and justice are very much alike, or that justice is holy, or that holiness is just. Isaiah speaks about God, and his intention is to say that the Lord of heaven and earth, of nature and history, finds His true exaltation in justice. Isaiah does not pronounce a theory, he proclaims what is to come. He does not teach what ought to be, he predicts what shall be.

The importance of moral ideas was known to people everywhere. Yet linked with the awareness of their importance was an awareness of their impotence. The prophets proclaimed that justice is omnipotent, that right and wrong are dimensions of world history, not merely modes of conduct. The existence of the world is contingent upon right and wrong, and its secret is God's involvement in history.

History is a turmoil. Survival and perdition are equally possible. But justice will decide ; righteousness will redeem.

> Zion shall be redeemed by justice,
> And those in her who repent, by righteousness.
> Isa. 1:27

Justice will not fail. Addressing himself to Assyria while she is at the height of her power, the prophet exclaims :

> Woe to you, destroyer,
> Who yourself have not been destroyed ;
> You treacherous one,
> With whom none has dealt treacherously !
> You will be destroyed.
> When you have made an end of dealing treacherously,
> You will be dealt with treacherously.
> Isa. 33:1

If justice is but a category, a conformity, then injustice must be regarded as an irregularity, a deviation from a norm. But justice is like a mighty stream, and to defy it is to block God's almighty surge. The moralists discuss, suggest, counsel ; the prophets proclaim, demand, insist.

To sum up, the image of scales conveys the idea of form, standard, balance, measure, stillness. The image of a mighty stream expresses content, substance, power, movement, vitality.

Justice represented as a blindfolded virgin, while conveying the essential thought of the rightful caution of the mind against illusions and partiality of the heart, conceives of the process of justice as a mechanical process, as if the life of man were devoid of individuality and uniqueness and could be adequately understood in terms of inexorable generalizations. There is a point at which strict justice is unjust.

Immutable justice — the principle *fiat justitia, pereat mundus* — raises justice to a position of supremacy, denying to any other principle the power to temper it, regarding it as an absolute ; the world exits for the sake of maintaining justice rather than justice for the sake of maintaining the world. Carried to the extreme, the principle sets up a false dichotomy of world and justice, betraying the truth that the survival of the world is itself a requirement of justice.

God's concern for justice grows out of His compassion for man. The prophets do not speak of a divine relationship to an absolute principle or idea, called justice. They are intoxicated with the awareness of God's relationship to His people and to all men.

Justice is not important for its own sake ; the validity of justice and the motivation for its exercise lie in the blessings it brings to man. For justice, as stated above, is not an abstraction, a value. Justice exists in relation to a person, and is something done by a person. An act of injustice is condemned, not because the law is broken, but because a person has been hurt. What is the image of a person ? A person is a being whose anguish may reach the heart of God, "You shall not afflict any widow or orphan. If you do afflict them, and they cry out to

Me, I will surely hear their cry . . . if he cries to Me, I will hear, for I am compassionate" (Exod. 22:22-23, 27).

When Cain murdered his brother Abel, the words denouncing his crime did not proclaim : "You have broken the law." Instead we read : "And. . . the Lord said : What have you done ? The voice of your brother's blood is crying to Me from the ground" (Gen. 4:10).

For all the centrality of ethos in the prophetic understanding of God, it is incorrect to say, as is often done, that "justice to the Israelitish mind was such an indispensable thing in the universe that it sometimes seems to stand out as some irresistible power independent even of God, as something which God Himself needs obey."[2]

In an effort to prove the similarity of Judaism and Kantian ethics, it was often maintained that, according to Judaism, "the moral law is autonomous because it originates in the nature of the human mind alone.... That autonomy implies the absence of every extraneous will in the creation of morality, every external power.... This exalted purity and this dignity of the moral are independent of every sort of theistic notion, because they spring from the very nature of the human mind." "Ethical holiness may be thought of detached from religious holiness. It has value and dignity of its own, without reference to God, the ordainer of morality ; that is, the moral idea has an existence independent of the recognition that it is actualized in God."[3]

The prophets did not conceive of the ethos as an autonomous idea, as a sovereign essence, higher in the scale of reality than God Himself, standing above Him like a supreme force. God to them was more than a moral principle or a moral exemplar.

The central achievement of biblical religion was to remove the veil of anonymity from the workings of history. There are no ultimate laws, no eternal ideas. The Lord alone is ultimate and eternal. The laws are His creation, and the moral ideas are not entities apart from Him ; they are His concern. Indeed, the personalization of the moral idea is the indispensable assumption of prophetic theology. Mercy, grace, repentance, forgiveness, all would be impossible if the moral principle were held to be superior to God. God's call to man, which resounds so frequently in the utterances of the prophets, presupposes an ethos based, not upon immutable principles, but rather upon His eternal concern. God's repenting a decision which was based on moral grounds clearly shows the supremacy of pathos.

Crime is not a violation of a law, but a sin against the living God. "Against Thee, Thee only have I sinned, and done that which is evil in Thy sight," confesses the psalmist (51:6). "If Thou, O Lord, shouldst mark iniquities, who could stand ?" (Ps. 132:3.)

To identify God with the moral idea would be contrary to the very meaning of prophetic theology. God is not a mere guardian of the moral order. He is not an intermediary between a transcendental idea of the good and man. The prophet does not think of Him as a being whose function it is to supervise the moral order and to bring about the realization of an autonomous morality. As love cannot be identified with the values found in it, so the relation between God and man cannot be simply equated with the value of the moral idea. The *pathos* structure of divine *ethos* follows from the unlimited sovereignty of God. If the moral law were something absolute and final, it would represent a destiny to which God Himself would be subject. Far from being sovereign, God would then fall into dependence on rigid, objective norms.

For a long time the importance of the prophets was seen to lie in the fact that they raised the religion of cult to a religion of morality. Ethical monotheism was "their contribution to the spiritual growth of their race."[4] The religion introduced by the prophets was a sort of protestantism, directed against all sorts of "paganism" and ritualism, with the main emphasis placed upon faith. The image of the prophets was that of preachers of morals and spiritual religion as opposed to ceremonialism and ritual. This view has not been questioned. "The prophets have been isolated in too high a degree, and made makers of ideas which in reality were common Israelite stock, and modern scholars have in a one-sided way stressed certain ideas of the prophets which acquired importance for posterity, and to which there might be found a special connection in the nineteenth century."[5]

Ethical monotheism must not be regarded as the contribution of the classical prophets, since it was known in Israel long before the time of Amos. Nor is "the primacy of morality" to be regarded as the chief characteristic of prophetic thought.

Divine ethos does not operate without pathos. Any thought of an objectivity, or a Platonic self-subsistence of ideas, be it the idea of beauty or of justice is alien to the prophets. God is all-personal, all-subject. His *ethos* and *pathos* are one.

The preoccupation with justice, the passion with which the prophets condemn injustice, is rooted in their sympathy with divine *pathos.* The chief characteristic of prophetic thought is the primacy of God's involvement in history. History is the domain with which the prophets' minds are occupied. They are moved by a responsibility for society, by a sensitivity to what the moment demands.

Since the prophets do not speak in the name of the moral law, it is inaccurate to characterize them as proclaimers of justice, or *mishpat.* It is more accurate to see them as proclaimers of God's *pathos,* speaking not for the idea of justice, but for the God of justice, for God's concern for justice. Divine concern remembered in sympathy is the stuff of which prophecy is made.

To the biblical mind the implication of goodness is mercy. *Pathos,* concern for the world, is the very *ethos* of God. This ethical sensitivity of God — not the ethical in and for itself — is reflected in the prophets' declarations. Prophetic morality rests upon both a divine command and a divine concern. Its ultimate appeal is not to the reasonableness of the moral law, but to the fact that God has demanded it and that its fulfilment is a realization of His concern.

Is the prophetic message to be reduced to a simple, plausible prescription : *Do ut des,* "I give so that thou mayest give" ? "Be moral, and I shall make you happy," says the Lord.

What the prophets proclaim is God's intimate relatedness to man. It is this fact that puts all of life in a divine perspective, in which the rights of man become, as it were, divine prerogatives. Man stands under God's concern.

It is a thought staggering, and hardly compatible with any rational approach to the understanding of God, that the Creator of heaven and earth should care about how an obscure individual man behaves toward poor widows and orphans. And if God is so powerful, and this concern so profound, why do the wicked prosper ? (Cf. Jer. 12:1).

Pathos is, indeed, righteousness wrapped in mystery, togetherness in holy otherness. Is the word of God irrational ? But by what reason do we measure the word of God ? By the reason expressed in our thoughts. But do we always understand our own thoughts ? Can we always express what we mean ? This, then, is our plight : What is most rational to the prophets seems irrational to us.

That incompatibility, however, is not ultimate. The goal is to establish compatibility, to refute idolatry and presumption that separate and antagonize man from what is supremely meaningful ; to destroy illusions and to inspire realism.

God rules the world by justice and compassion, or love. These two ways are not divergent, but rather complementary, for it is out of compassion that justice is administered. But again and again His compassion, or love, is manifested in the world. Cain, slaying his brother, does not receive the punishment he deserves. Though justice would require that Abel's blood be avenged, Cain is granted divine pardon and protection.

A father is disqualified to serve as a judge. Yet the judge of all men is also their Father. He would be unjust to His own nature were He to act in justice without being compassionate.... [pp. 195-220]

The decisive importance of the idea of divine pathos emerges clearly when we consider the possible forms in which God's relation to the world may present itself. A purely ethical monotheism in which God, the guardian of the moral order, keeps the world subject to the law, would restrict the scope of God's knowledge and concern to what is of ethical significance. God's relation to man would, in general, run along the lines of a universal principle. The divine *pathos* alone is able to break through this rigidity and create new dimensions for the unique, the specific, and the particular.

It is not law and order itself, but the living God who created the universe and established its law and order, that stands supreme in biblical thought. This differs radically from the concept of law as supreme, a concept found, for example, in the *Dharma* of Mahayana Buddhism. Before the Torah, the covenant was.

In contrast to our civilization, the Hebrews lived in a world of the covenant rather than in a world of contracts. The idea of contract was unknown to them. The God of Israel "cares as little for contract and the *cash nexus* as He cares for mere slavish obedience and obsequiousness. His chosen sphere is that of covenant."[6] His relationship to His partner is one of benevolence and affection. The indispensable and living instrument holding the community of God and Israel together is the law.

Prophecy is a reminder that what obtains between God and man is not a contract but a covenant. Anterior to the covenant is love, the love of the fathers (Deut. 4:37 ; 10:15), and what obtains between God and Israel must be understood, not as a legal, but as a personal relationship, as participation, involvement, tension. God's life interacts with the life of the people. To live in the covenant is to partake of the fellowship of God and His people. Biblical religion is not what man does with his solitariness, but rather what man does with God's concern for all men.

The idea of divine *pathos* throws light on many types of relations between God and man unknown in apathetic religion. The covenant between God and Israel is an example. The category of divine *pathos* adds a new dimension to it. The covenant is an extraordinary act, establishing a reciprocal relation between God and man ; it is conceived as a juridical commitment. *Pathos*, on the other hand, implies a constant concern and involvement ; it is conceived as an emotional engagement. From the point of view of the unequivocal covenant-idea, only two forms of relationship between God and people are possible : the maintenance or the dissolution of the covenant. This rigid either-or is replaced by a dynamic multiplicity of forms of relationship implied in *pathos*.[7] [pp. 229-230]

NOTES

1. Abraham J. Heschel, *The Prophets* (New York : Harper & Row, 1962), pp. 195-230.
2. M. Lazarus, *The Ethics of Judaism*, vol. 1 (Philadelphia : 1900-1901), pp. 135-136.
3. *Ibid.*, vol. 22, p. 13.
4. A. Kuenen, *The Prophets and Prophecy in Israel* (London : 1877), p. 589.
5. See J. Pedersen, "The Role Played by Inspired Persons Among the Israelites and the Arabs," in H.H. Rawley, ed., *Studies in Old Testament Prophecy* (Edinburgh : 1950), pp. 127 ff.
6. *Ibid.*, vol. 2, pp. 9-10.
7. W.F. Lofthouse, "Hen and Hessed in the Old Testament," *Zaw* (1933), pp. 29 ff.

HUMAN LAW AND HUMAN JUSTICE[1]

Julius Stone

Matthew Arnold was right to detect a sharp difference in interest and in emphasis between Greek and Hebrew traditions of thought about law and justice. Whether we think of the Torah as transmitted through Moses, or of the prophetic writings, the classical Hebrew teachings were rather precepts for man's daily social conduct, than ideas to prod or satisfy their intellectual questings. Justice and righteousness were to emerge not so much from arguments in the academies, as from living, whether in the home, or at the royal court, on the field of grain, or in the market place, at the gates of the city, or in the wilderness, week in week out, divided only by the sabbatical and jubilee years.

Comparisons of the Mosaic Code with that of Hammurabi show that the latter was more elaborated in its commercial aspects, and obviously designed for a society of more commercial maturity. It is no less clear that the Mosaic code addresses itself with a firm and practical didactic purpose, to correcting the individual and social moralities and customs of its age. This practical drive appears in ordinances of animal sacrifice which seek to adapt existing customs, while abolishing human sacrifice and worship of idols. It appears no less in its precepts concerning those who lived to a greater or lesser degree at the whim of others. The domestic animal, the slave, the servant, the wife, the child, the orphan, the widow, the people themselves are the subject no doubt of broad and noble protective proclamations based on the "blessed" nature of all creation. Yet these are but generalizations upon practical minutiae about not seething the kid in its mother's milk, about the sabbath rest and eventual emancipation of the slave, about connubial rights and duties, about leaving for the poor the unreaped corners of the field (and grain dropped in gathering the corn into sheaves, and sheaves forgotten in gathering in the sheaves, and the three-yearly tithe), and about the duties of kingship. The prophetic teachings were addressed centuries later to a people already weaned from the crudest and cruellest customs of the region ; for that reason they appear more orientated to principle than to precept. Yet even there the principles will most often be found to be principles of action in human relations rather than cosmological principles, and the precepts, for instance concerning the orphan and the widow, will be found embedded in the poetry and the allegory. And, of course, above all, the Hebrew tradition unlike the Greek appears to have been presented by its authors and redactors as well as by its rabbinic interpreters as a revealed and rather concrete system of regulation.

These and other features can be correctly urged to support the differentiation of the Hebrew from the Greek tradition. But it is all the more necessary not to accept uncritically the characterization of the distinction usually given. The Hebrew concept, it is sometimes said, is of a retaliatory justice, a justice of vengeance ; indeed, the maxim "an eye for an eye and a tooth for a tooth" the *lex talionis*, is often spoken of as if it comprised the essence of "the Mosaic law." Even if this were taken as correct, this differentiation from Greek law would not be very clear ; for in Greek thought, too, the retaliatory aspect of justice has been seen to be important.

The truth is that the element of vengeance is a convenient *starting-point* for a study of the Jewish concept of justice, but neither a fruitful nor correct *conclusion*. Undoubtedly Jehovah is seen by the prophets of the Old Testament as a God of vengeance. *Sometimes* this implied that His people, too, should seek vengeance, not of course for their own wrongs, but for wrongs against the divine law ; yet at other times the implication is precisely the contrary, that since vengeance belongs to the Lord it should be *left* to the Lord. In the 19th Chapter of *Leviticus* Moses is told : "Thou shalt not hate thy brother in thine heart. . . . Thou shalt not avenge, nor bear any grudge against the children of thy people, but thou shalt love thy neighbour as thyself." According to the rabbinical interpretation of this commandment, even a criminal remains our neighbour. The precept enjoining men to love each other is independent of any physical, intellectual, or moral attributes of the particular person ; it is based on the fact that all men are God's children, made in his image. This concept, if any single one is to be chosen, is the distinctive Jewish contribution to thought about justice. "Love thy neighbour as thyself," said Rabbi Akiba, "is the supreme principle of the Torah. You must not say, since I have been put to shame (by a fellow man), let him be put to shame ; since I have been slighted, let him be slighted. . . . If you do so, know whom ye put to shame, for in the likeness of God made He him."

The *lex talionis* itself, be it added, appears not to have been, in any case, the bloodthirsty principle that vulgar usage has conjured up. With gently ironic reflection on the *lex talionis* as somehow setting apart the Mosaic law, the historical meaning of this law best emerges when it is interpreted in the light of Aristotle's mean. What is prescribed is that an injury is to be requited by a reciprocal injury, perhaps no less *and certainly no more*. . . .

At any rate it is clear that by an astonishing variety of arguments, some as subtle as others were direct and even disingenuous, the talmudic interpreters effectually abolished and prohibited the *talio*, despite the biblical text prescribing it no less than three times. The oral law substituted money damages on a basis not very different from that of the modern common law. And it was to be a fifth-century Greek, and not a fifth-century Jew, who said that "it is the business of intelligence to guard against a threatened injustice, but it is the mark of insensibility not to avenge it when it has happened." [pp. 18-22]

NOTE

1. Julias Stone, *Human Law and Human Justice* (Stanford : Stanford University Press, 1965), p. 18.

2. Athens

Where the social order is legitimated in terms of its conformity to, or reflection of, the natural order, a radical change in a society's view of the natural order will give rise to new interpretations of the social order. When, in ancient Greece, there was a shift in world perception from a mythological to a scientific rationalist understanding of nature, a fundamental revolution in the social order followed. That revolution was described by Sir Henry Maine as a shift from status to contract.

With the birth of Western science in Greece came a new way of conceiving of the world ; nature was viewed in terms of universal laws, some of which could even be stated mathematically. Their success in discovering mathematical laws of harmony and astronomy led the Greeks to an optimistic search for universals in every field of knowledge. They concluded that the laws of human conduct were as universal as the laws of the natural sciences. This view of morality and law is the foundation of Greek natural law, moral, legal, and political theory.

One of the primary characteristics of a universal law is that it encompasses the widest possible spectrum of discourse. A universal law of human conduct was, for the Greeks, one which applied to every rational person whatsoever. This differs absolutely from a law of status — moral, legal, or political rules which apply to only a limited range of human beings. Universal laws of human conduct evolve into a notion of equality before the law and a radically new view of justice as equal treatment. A denial of moral and legal obligation based on the incidents of birth leads to a perception that man is free. Thus, the basic assumptions of democracy are derived from a new theory of authority based on the new world view of rationalistic science. It was no mere accident of history that Western science and democracy were born together in the age of Athen's greatness.

Grecian mathematical science represents as unique a contribution to abstract thinking as the Judeo-Christian approach to morality. The Greeks departed from other ancient Near Eastern societies, both in science and morality, by applying universal laws to man's moral nature and thus establishing, for the first time in history, the link between the natural and normative sciences. This postulation proceeded from the assumption that in moral and legal conduct there is a uniformity of causation ; laws exist to facilitate our ordered understanding of behaviour and are directed to bring about desirable results. Using the model of science, the Greeks founded the terms of reference for good legal and moral reasons for action in the principle of universalizability. Uniformity of cause led them to formal justice, which differentiates the Greco-Roman concept of law from all others. Formal justice simply stated demands that all persons found in relevantly similar situations are entitled to the same legal protection, or are obliged to do the same acts.

The development of Greek law was tempered by a liberal polis, which allowed for the widest participation of its citizenry. This meant that there was little pressure to produce a special class of legal technicians and that emphasis was placed on techniques of persuasion. Rhetoricians flourished in the domocratic polis. It was left to the Roman civilization to take the philosophical framework for rational systematization and apply it in accordance with the requirements of practical lawyering and thc demands for theoretical justifiction in the building of an empire which had universal designs.

Although the philosophical apparatus of ancient Greece was extremely rarified, the link between Greek science and everyday law was in fact neither attempted nor accomplished. Although rhetoric was a high art form and may be looked upon as the continuation of the dramatic and epic dimensions of the Greek imagination, its place in ancient Greek legal culture remains puzzling. For at times sophistry appeared to be both the undoing of art and philosophy in the sense that at its best it was merely a high form of craftsmanship and at its worst the debasement of real philosophy. This is born out in the trial of Socrates. What is exposed in the *Apology* is that the public forum was disinterested in procedural fairness and the legal requirement of clearly stated allegations. True, there was an appearance of fairness but, in the final analysis, the Athenian legal system was bound by persuasion rather than by precedent and the trial itself was a testimonial to the invasion of law by political rhetoric. Socrates was thrust into the midst of this confusion and emerged as a tragic hero who, despite the fact that he would have been the first to acknowledge the shortcomings of rhetorical justice at the expense of philosophical wisdom, sacrificed his own life in the name of presuming a philosophical and systematic basis for legal justice.

A persistent difficulty in Western civilization, which most surely was not resolved in Greek culture, is whether justice can be achieved through the vehicle of populism. Is technical training in the law, if not a guarantee, at least a necessary condition for realizing justice in highly evolved societies ? Socrates remained committed to higher truths as the bases for legal ordering. Ironically in his own trial he did not inform his judges of the principles upon which such a system would be based.

Our confusion deepens when we realize that his manipulation of language was so subtle that he managed to provoke his jurors by placing before them a parody of sophistry, which illustrated the limitations of rhetoric as the foundation of law. Socrates knew that no unassailable abstract system of justice could be simply produced, but his conscious choice of death informs us of the extent of his commitment to go beyond the non-rational elements of his day in the direction of a rational law. His genius lay in his capacity to demonstrate through his own life situation the spectrum of legal phenomenology, ranging from the dramatic to the philosophic.

Plato and Aristotle persevered in this quest for a rational legal discourse and, in so doing, have come under attack for having sacrificed liberalism to the attainment of the good and the just. On reflection, however, we should admit that their philosophical categorizations became the mainstay of a new intellectual movement in the West which wedded ethical principles to legal procedures and made the whole of the legal system the subject of teleological understanding.

There was undoubtedly an undemocratic flavour to their projects. This was so because Greek liberal society appeared unjust at the level of a philosophical understanding of law, given its populist orientation. The tension that was experienced in the Greek culture between legal justice and the liberal society continues until this day.

Law for Plato and Aristotle, as much as for the Greek culture at large, was integrated into a general world view which related nature, politics, and law. The disentanglement of law from all-encompassing theories of nature was left to subsequent civilizations.

For the Greek philosophers, the perfect law was a mirror of the perfect state. It is of interest that centuries later philosophers and pragmatists alike perceived that such fundamental principles as liberty and equality could only be realized by separating law from dominant state institutions.

The interpenetration of law and state brings with it the direct association between law and state power. The inherent difficulty with this is that personal autonomy and the legal personality are cast under the shadow of state authority. The interests of the collectivity and the ends of the state thus become the premise around which to organize legal entitlements and obligations. Whether or not law can evolve as an independent structure of principles and rules is the most critical subject of modern jurisprudence.

GREEK CIVILIZATION[1]

Andre Bonnard

There are moments in the history of mankind when new forms of thought or action appear so abruptly that they seem like explosions. Such was the appearance of science, that is of rational, scientific knowledge in Ionia at the end of the seventh century B.C. with Thales of Miletus and his school. This birth of science, with the appearance of the first scientists or "philosophers" as our books call them, was, if you like, spectacular but in no way astonishing or miraculous. It seems, by the way, that the word "philosopher" only appeared in the age of the sophists and was not in widespread use before the fourth century, when it was popularized by Plato. Of course the scientific attitude to nature was familiar to the most primitive of the Greeks, even to the men most naked and unequipped. Odysseus was typical of this questioning attitude, an attitude which in his case is combined with the most authentic and also the most practical of religious feelings. The poet calls him the man "of many devices."

It would in fact be a mistake to treat rational science and myth as if they were contraries that exclude each other; as if both were not for a long time closely intermingled, as if both were not seeking by different paths to surmount the obstacles and difficulties which the cosmos and its unknown laws present to man. All thought, at the outset, took the form of image or story, and we know that towards the end of the classical age Plato frequently uses myth to express his thoughts. He interprets ancient myths in his own way, and he invents myths of his own.

Greek science at its birth was much more like our science than appears at first sight. Naive as it may be, it knows that man is the product of natural evolution, it holds speech and thought to be the fruit of life in the social state, it regards itself as part of the technique : it is science itself that permits man to master his natural environment. Such a conception of science — an extremely bold one — definitely arose towards the year 600, in the time of Thales ; and in the course of two centuries it was to develop with a breadth of outlook and a quest for cohesion which astonish even today.... [pp. 54-55]

Many currents of thought, many interests and enquiries encountered each other in Ionia, which might be called the Babel of the Greek world. Thales lived at the centre where these multiple currents converged. For him and his fellow citizens the problem of living resided in an unknown domain, which they had to know if they were to live in it. So they formulated new questions. Thales put these questions in accordance with a method which is his own and in a language still unusual in such matters — in fact, in the language in which merchants transacted their business. He was a merchant and an engineer, and if he dealt with "meteors," it was in any event not in order to tell himself "stories," but to assign "reasons" to phenomena, to know how things happen as they do with the elements with which he was acquainted, namely, air, earth, water, and fire.

The rational science which was appearing and the character of demonstration which the whole of Greek science was to assume, seem to have been the result of a multitude of actions and gestures made by these observant sailors in steering their ships, when they observed, at every movement of their arms, that this movement was followed by a certain effect, and when they sought to establish a rigorous connexion between cause and effect, without leaving to chance the part that belongs to it.

The results obtained by Thales in his research were no doubt slight, problematical and often erroneous ; but his way of observing the world and his way of thinking were those of a true scientist. Not perhaps in the modern sense of the word, according to which the scientist practises a science closely bound up with experiment or experience, but in the simple sense of practising a science that is wholly one of observation, the sense in which he takes account of what he observes without using myths and with the greatest possible amount of exactness. On the basis of his observations he constructs hypotheses that seem to him plausible ; he builds up a theory which, in the course of time, will be subjected to experience.

So, instead of regarding the stars as gods — which they were before him and were to remain long after his time, for Plato and others — Thales was the first to treat them as natural objects. In his view, their nature was earthy or fiery. He was the first to say that when the moon, which is of earthy nature, was placed in a straight line between the sun and the earth, the sun was eclipsed. Did he really predict an eclipse of the sun, the eclipse of 610, or 585, or some other, as Greek tradition asserts ? Perhaps, by relying on the calculations of Babylonians, he indicated the year of a probable eclipse ; his knowledge of astronomy would scarcely permit of greater precision. Much more important than the results was the method of his research. Neither when treating of the stars, nor when treating of water, did Thales invoke gods or myths. He spoke of those phenomena as of purely physical and material things. When the modern chemist puts the question : "Whence comes water ?" he replies : "from a combination of hydrogen and oxygen." Thales' reply could not be identical ; ignorance weighed on him as too "heavy a burden" ; he was conscious of this and said so. But when he puts the question of the origin of water, he does not answer with a myth, but in an objective way, that is, by seeking to formulate a law of nature that will correspond to the reality of nature and may one day be verified by experience.

This form of thought, which is so novel, is sometimes extremely audacious in its enterprises, so audacious as to appear naive. Thales and the first Ionian scientists were trying to discover what matter the world is made of. It seemed to them that there must be a material element from which the other elements are engendered by a process not mythical, as in the old cosmogonies, but physical. For Thales, water was primitive, and from this primordial water was born earth which is, so to speak, its residue, and also air and fire which are vapours of exhalations from water. Everything is born of water and returns to water.

It was probably the techniques of fire that suggested to these scientists the notion of a transformation of one element into another, which other takes on another appearance while remaining identical. They had observed the various effects produced by the action of fire. Fire changes water into steam ; it changes other matter into ash ; in the foundry, it liquefies metal ; in the processes of metallurgy it separates and purifies it. Conversely, it unites in the processes of alloying and soldering. Thus, by observing his own techniques, man arrives at the notion of a transformation of elements or of the appearance of these elements. But these observations entail a share of suffering. Fire is not only a great educator, but also a pitiless despot who demands blood, sweat, and tears. "I have seen the blacksmith working at his furnacemouth," wrote a satirical poet of Egypt. "His fingers are like crocodile skin ; he stinks like fish roe." An observation of this kind, while implying a share of pain, also implies, in the formation of the theory, a share of error.

His conception of water as the origin of the other elements may have been suggested to Thales by simple facts of nature. The fact that water deposits mud or alluvium, for example in the flooding of the Nile and the formation of the Delta, or again the formation of sea-fogs, or perhaps the appearance of will-o'-wisps floating over ponds — all these things roused the scientist's attention. The important point is that the scientist began to observe nature or human techniques, while freeing himself from any supernatural explanations. In this process of observing and of verifying his observations, for example, in the very important technique of casting statues in bronze, the scientist was taking the first steps in what was to deserve, much later, the name of the experimental method. It was as yet only the stammering of a beginner, but of one who is inventing a new language.

About the same time the same scientists and, notably, Thales himself, discovered another scientific method, which men mastered from the outset better than any other. This was the mathematical method, in the form of geometry. In the eighth century the vases of Dipylon had already displayed the passion which the Greeks felt for the plain, bare style of geometry. The men and horses who move round the linear decoration of the vases are themselves geometry : they are like angles and segments of circles that have been assembled.

But, as always, the Greeks, whose imaginations had been filled with geometrical figures, invented this science by starting from precise techniques. The Egyptians and Assyrians, it is true, had already established the foundations of what was to become mathematical science. For example, when they wanted to re-establish the boundaries of their fields after they had been flooded by the Nile which buried them under a layer of mud, the Egyptians knew certain methods of land surveying which might initiate the discovery of certain theorems. Thus they knew that, for a right-angled triangle of which the shorter sides measure 3 and 4, while the hypotenuse measures 5, the squares of 3 and 4 together have the same area as the square of the hypotenuse. They knew this and measured it out on the ground, because they knew that 3 x 3 = 9, plus 4 x 4 = 16, is the same thing as 5 x 5 = 25. But they did not know that this proposition is true of any right-angled triangle and they were incapable of demonstrating it. Their geometry was not yet strictly a science.

For centuries what was to become the mathematical method was only a collection of rules. These were already sometimes very complicated and in certain cases, for example, allowed one to predict the position of the stars. But this collection of rules did not constitute a science. They were not all related to each other, they were valid only for particular cases and no one thought of demonstrating that they derived from certain simple principles which are imposed on the mind by experience ; as, for example : "A straight line is the shortest distance between two points." No one demonstrated that these rules are laws of nature and are necessarily what they are. Now the Greeks needed to develop their geometry for two main purposes : navigation — and no doubt shipbuilding, because in this period their ships had ceased to be mere canoes or primitive barges — and temple-building.

One day, we are told, Thales made a geometrical discovery which seems to relate exactly to the construction of the drums on temple columns. He showed not only that the angle inscribed in a semicircle is a right angle, but that it must necessarily be so, that is to say, that if you join the extremities of a half-circumference to any other point on the circumference, the two lines must always contain a right angle. In the same way Pythagoras, or some member of his school, but at an early date, showed that the square on the hypotenuse of a right-angled triangle is necessarily equal to the sum of the squares on the other sides, whatever the dimensions of the triangle. Thus the particular cases known to the Orientals became the universal properties of geometrical figures. The Greeks therefore invented a science of geometry, which is ours, a science in which the properties of straight lines, circles, and a few other curves could be demonstrated by reasoning and verified by the application of technique. And I am thinking especially of architecture which, by this means, they raised to a high degree of solidity and beauty.

In this way the Greeks built up a science of geometry closely connected with navigation and the art of building. The whole tradition relating to Thales ascribed to him a quite concrete knowledge of the distance of a ship in the open sea from a raised point on the shore ; the same tradition ascribes to him the geometrical knowledge, abstract and rational, of the properties of figure whose construction alone allows one to measure this distance.... [pp. 60-64]

Xenophanes, who was exiled from Ionia when the Persians conquered that country, went to Italy. He wandered from town to town, declaiming in the market-places his poem *Of Nature* ; in this he criticized the traditional mythology and mocked at the anthropomorphic conception of the divine. He wrote these astonishing lines : "If oxen, horses, and lions had hands and could paint pictures and carve statues, they would represent the gods under the guise of oxen, horses, and lions, in the manner of men who represent them in their own image." This Xenophanes was a scientist whose curiosity looked to the most diverse horizons.

It led him to make discoveries of great significance, as for example, in recognizing the presence of sea shells on mountains and the imprint left by fishes on stones on Malta, on Paros, and in the quarries at Syracuse.

In the fifth century scientists like Anaxagoras and Empedocles seem to have gone still further in this direction. The former was interested in all kinds of astronomical and biological phenomena. He observed the existence of parhelia, those strange luminous phenomena over the Black Sea, and tried to explain them. He also considered the cause for the flooding of the Nile. Empedocles has recently been described as a "real forerunner of Bacon." He devised original experiments in order to account, by analogy, for several phenomena that are natural, or that he believed to be. These attempts of his, revealing as they do a great deal of ingenuity, mark the birth of scientific experimentation.

All these efforts on the part of Thales' successors, efforts which, in the absence of adequate documents, are insufficiently known to us, led up to the two great discoveries in physics which were made in the fifth century. One was the exact knowledge of the annual movement of the sun in the heavens, on a plane which is oblique in relation to the plane in which the sun accomplishes, or appears to accomplish, its movement in a day. The other was the determining of the mathematical value of musical intervals, a value already familiar to one or two scientists at the end of the fifth century.

Such then is a rough summary of the scientific achievements of the successors of Thales.... [p. 66]

Democritus, as the ancients say, had "written about everything." If we do not possess his works, we at any rate have a list of their titles, and they confirm the assertion. He had written remarkable treatises on mathematics, according to Archimedes who gives examples of Democritus' discoveries in that art. He had written on biology, on which he spoke as a scientist who had practised dissection, a fact almost unique at that time. He had written on physics, ethics, philology, literary history and music. Above all, he had formulated his own system of nature. . . .

Democritus launched the great word "atom" — as a hypothesis. But because this hypothesis answered the problems raised by his predecessors and by his age better than any other, the word he launched was destined to traverse the centuries. Modern science has taken it up ; and if modern science uses it in a less narrow sense, if it is in a position to reveal the internal structure of the atom, it none the less derives from that spontaneous intuition of Democritus : the existence of atoms. J.C. Feinberg, a modern physicist, shows the striking parallelism between Democritus' atomic forecasts, if we may so call them, and Einstein's. He writes :

> In 1905, merely with paper, a pencil, and his brain, and many years before anyone succeeded in disintegrating an atom and destroying matter, Einstein predicted that matter could be destroyed and that, when it was, it would liberate terrifying quantities of energy.
>
> In the fifth century before our era, merely with a wax tablet, a stylet, and his brain, many centuries before science learned how to explore the interior of a substance, Democritus predicted that all substance was made of atoms.

Democritus therefore admits only two primordial realities in his system : atoms and vacuum. With regard to the vacuum we may note that the hypothesis of its existence in nature has today been entirely demonstrated. For a long time both philosophers and scientists declared in a peremptory manner that "Nature abhors the vacuum." But they were really attributing to nature a horror they felt themselves. Today it is admitted and has been demonstrated that there is a vacuum inside the atom as there is also between atoms. Professor Joliot-Curie writes : "There are great empty spaces in matter. When account is taken of the dimensions of the particles that constitute matter, these empty spaces are comparable to interplanetary spaces."

Democritus defines atoms as solid corpuscles, indivisible and indissoluble (their name means "insecable" : Democritus contested the possibility of splitting the atom). They are infinite in number, and eternal. They move in the void. This movement is not external to them, but coexists with matter and, like matter, is primordial. Atoms have no qualities other than a certain form, differing from one to another, and a weight connected with their dimensions.

The qualities we perceive in things by means of our senses are for Democritus purely subjective and do not exist in atoms. He had the merit of trying to found a science of nature, starting from the notion of quantity and then deducing from it sensible (or perceptible) qualities. The atoms are then like points, not mathematical but material, extremely small and which completely escape our sensory perception. They still escape it, today, in their structure, although they are decomposed and utilized by scientists. These atoms move about, "they jostle each other in every direction," without there being in the universe either top or bottom or middle or end. This affirmation of Democritus contains one of the clearest signs of the soundness of his spontaneous intuition. Nature for him is a "splashing of atoms in all directions." Their trajectories cannot fail to "cross each other," so that there are produced "grazings, shocks, reboundings, blows and collisions, and also interlacings" ; lastly, "formations of masses".... [pp. 68-70]

Democritus' position in the theory of knowledge is a form of sensationalism. But, in his explanations, he ran against difficulties and even contradictions. His consciousness of the difficulties in the way of knowledge does not mean that we should class him among the sceptics : he was not a sceptic but a mind conscious of the immensity of the task lying before the scientific enquirer. He therefore at times expresses feelings of doubt and reservation, feelings which, in any age, every honest seeker inevitably experiences when he compares the results obtained with what remains to be attained. In one of such moments he declares that the vocation of a seeker is the finest of vocations and that to devote oneself to giving a causal explanation of natural phenomena is better suited to make a man happy than the possession of a king's throne.

Here, as an example, is a passage in which we see Democritus involved in one of the contradictions which his system, as he invented it, led up to. The great physician, Galen, wrote :

> After discrediting the appearance of things by saying : "Colour is a convention, the sweet is a convention, the bitter is a convention, there are in reality only atoms and vacuum," Democritus makes the senses speak as follows to reason : "Poor reason, after depriving us of the means of proof, you want to beat us down. Your victory is also your defeat."

The mere fact that the admitted contradiction leads to a dialogue is a sign of the robust vitality of the thinker who seeks only one solution, the truth.

Democritus' system, as one sees, is remarkable for the variety of problems it strives to solve and for the solidity of the principles on which it rests. As M. Robin in his conclusion on Democritus, observes : "This original and coherent solution . . . might, had the philosophy of ideas not prevailed, have furnished the science of nature . . . with a methodological hypothesis suited for the organization of its researches."

Certainly, we must not deceive ourselves as to the resemblances between ancient atomic theory and that of modern science. In consequence of the immense progress that has been realized in experimental techniques and in mathematics, the atom is today no longer the indivisible unit which Democritus envisaged. It is a system formed of a certain number of corpuscles of negative electricity — the electrons — gravitating round a nucleus with a positive charge, exactly as planets gravitate round the sun. To quote the conclusion of M. Solovine's work on Democritus :

> And yet, in the last analysis, the picture of the universe is the same for us as it was for Democritus : an inconceivable number of corpuscles disseminated in limitless space and moving eternally. [pp. 72-73]

NOTE

1. Andre Bonnard, *Greek Civilization*, vol. 2, (London : George Allen and Unwin Ltd., 1959), pp. 54-73.

MATHEMATICS IN WESTERN CULTURE[1]

Morris Kline

Thales, along with most of the early Greek mathematicians, learned the elements of algebra and geometry from the Egyptians and the Babylonians. In fact, many of these scholars came from Asia Minor, which inherited the Babylonian culture. Others, born on the Greek mainland, went to Egypt and studied there. Despite the unquestioned influence of Egypt and Babylonia on Greek minds, the mathematics produced by the Greeks differed radically from that which preceded it. Indeed, from the point of view of the twentieth century, mathematics and, it may well be added, modern civilization began with the Greeks of the classical period, which lasted from about 600 to 300 B.C.

The mathematics that existed before Greek times has already been characterized as a collection of empirical conclusions. Its formulas were the accretion of ages of experience, much as many medical practices and remedies are today. Though experience is no doubt a good teacher, in many situations it would be a most inefficient way of obtaining knowledge.

Is experience the only way of obtaining knowledge ? Not for beings endowed with a reasoning faculty. Reasoning can follow many routes, among which is the commonly travelled one of analogy. The Egyptians, for example, believed in immortality and so they buried their dead with clothes, utensils, jewellery, and other things that might be of use in the next world. Their reasoning was that since life on Earth required these articles, the after-life would also.

Reasoning by analogy is useful, but it also has its limitations. There may not be an analogous situation at all ; airplanes, radios, and submarines could hardly have been invented by reasoning by analogy. Or, there may be an analogous situation that differs slightly but enough to matter a great deal. Though human beings resemble apes, some conclusions about humans cannot be drawn from a study of the apes.

A more commonly used method of reasoning is known as induction. A farmer may observe that heavy rains during several successive springs were followed by excellent crops. Hc concludes that heavy rains are beneficial to crops. Again, because a person may have had unfortunate experiences in dealing with lawyers, he concludes that all lawyers are undesirable people. Essentially, the inductive process consists in concluding that something is always true on the basis of a limited number of instances....

Though the conclusions obtained by inductive reasoning seem warranted by the facts, they are not established beyond all doubt. Logically, these conclusions are not any better established than the generalization drawn from the observation of four hundred million Chinese that all human beings are yellow-skinned. In other words, we cannot be certain of any conclusion obtained by inductive reasoning. There are other limitations to this type of reasoning. We cannot conclude inductively what the effect on society of an untried law may be. Nor can we conclude inductively, as one uncritical observer did, that all Indians walk single file by seeing one do so !

The several methods of obtaining conclusions, each undoubtedly useful in a variety of situations, possess a common limitation : even if the facts of experience, or the facts on which reasoning by analogy or induction are based, are entirely correct, the conclusion obtained is not certain, and where certainty is vital these methods are practically useless.

Fortunately, there is a method of reasoning that does guarantee the certainty of the conclusions it produces. The method is known as deduction. Let us consider some examples. If we accept the facts that all apples are perishable and that the object before us is an apple, we must conclude that this object is perishable. As another example, if all good people are charitable and if I am good, then I must be charitable. And if I am not charitable then I am not good. Again, we may argue deductively from the premises that all poets are intelligent and that no intelligent people deride mathematics, to the inevitable conclusion that no poet derides mathematics.

It does not matter, in so far as the reasoning is concerned, whether we agree with the premises. What is pertinent is that if we accept the premises we must accept the conclusion. Unfortunately, many people confuse the acceptability or truth of a conclusion with the validity of the reasoning that leads to this conclusion. From the premises that all intelligent beings are humans and that readers of this book are human beings, we might conclude that all readers of this book are intelligent. The conclusion is undoubtedly true but the purported deductive reasoning is invalid because the conclusion does not necessarily follow from the premises. A moment's reflection shows that even though all intelligent beings are humans there may be human beings who are not intelligent, and nothing in the premises tells us to which group of human beings the readers of this book belong.

Deductive reasoning, then, consists of those ways of deriving new statements from accepted facts that compel the acceptance of the derived statements. We shall not pursue at this point the question of why it is that we experience this mental conviction. What is important now is that man has this method of arriving at new conclusions and that these conclusions are unquestionable if the facts we start with are also unquestionable.

Deduction, as a method of obtaining conclusions, has many advantages over trial and error or reasoning by induction and analogy. The outstanding advantage is the one we have already mentioned, namely, that the conclusions are unquestionable if the premises are. Truth, if it can be obtained at all, must come from certainties and not from doubtful or approximate inferences. Second, in contrast to experimentation, deduction can be carried on without the use or loss of expensive equipment. Before the bridge is built and before the long-range gun is fired, deductive reasoning can be applied to decide the outcome. Sometimes deduction has the advantage of being the only available method. The calculation of astronomical distances cannot be carried out by applying a yardstick. Moreover, whereas experience confines us to tiny portions of time and space, deductive reasoning may range over countless universes and aeons.

With all of its advantages, deductive reasoning does not supersede experience, induction, or reasoning by analogy. It is true that 100 per cent certainty can be attached to the conclusions of deduction when the premises can be vouched for 100 per cent. But such unquestionable premises are not necessarily available. No one, unfortunately, has been able to vouchsafe the premises from which a cure for cancer could be deduced. For practical purposes, moreover, the certainty deduction grants is sometimes superfluous. A high degree of probability may suffice. For centuries the Egyptians used mathematical formulas drawn from experience. Had they waited for deductive proof the pyramids at Giza would not be squatting in the desert today.

Each of these various ways of obtaining knowledge, then, has its advantages and disadvantages. Despite this fact, the Greeks insisted that *all mathematical conclusions be established only by deductive reasoning.* By their insistence on this method, the Greeks were discarding all rules, formulas, and procedures that had been obtained by experience, induction, or any other non-deductive method and that had been accepted in the body of mathematics for thousands of years preceding their civilization. It would seem, then, that the Greeks were destroying rather than building; but let us withhold judgment for the present.

Why did the Greeks insist on the exclusive use of deductive proof in mathematics? Why abandon such expedient and fruitful ways of obtaining knowledge as induction, experience, and analogy? The answer can be found in the nature of their mentality and society.

The Greeks were gifted philosophers. Their love of reason and their delight in mental activity distinguished them from other peoples. The educated Athenians were as much devoted to philosophy as our smart-set is to night-clubbing; and pre-Christian fifth-century Athens was as deeply concerned with the problems of life and death, immortality, the nature of the soul, and the distinction between good and evil as twentieth-century America is with material progress. Philosophers do not reason, as do scientists, on the basis of personally conducted experimentation or observation. Rather their reasoning centres about abstract concepts and broad generalizations. It is difficult, after all, to experiment with souls in order to arrive at truths about them. The natural tool of philosophers is deductive reasoning, and hence the Greeks gave preference to this method when they turned to mathematics.

Philosophers are, moreover, concerned with truths, the few, immaterial wisps of eternity that can be sifted from the bewildering maze of experiences, observations, and sensations. Certainty is the indispensable element of truth. To the Greeks, therefore, the mathematical knowledge accumulated by the Egyptians and Babylonians was a house of sand. It crumbled to the touch. The Greeks sought a palacc built of ageless, indestructible marble.

The Greeks preference for deduction was, surprisingly, a facet of the Hellenic love for beauty. Just as the music lover hears music as structure, interval, and counterpoint, so the Greek saw beauty as order, consistency, completeness, and definiteness. Beauty was an intellectual as well as an emotional experience. Indeed, the Greek sought the rational element in every emotional experience. In a famous eulogy Pericles praises the Athenians who died in battle at Samos not merely because they were courageous and patriotic, but because reason sanctioned their deeds. To people who identified beauty and reason, deductive arguments naturally appealed because they are planned, consistent, and complete, while conviction in the conclusions offer the beauty of truth. It is no wonder, then, that the Greeks regard mathematics as an art, as architecture is an art though its principles may be used to build warehouses.

Another explanation of the Greek preference for deduction is found in the organization of their society. The philosophers, mathematicians, and artists were members of the highest social class. This upper stratum either completely disdained commercial pursuits and manual work or regarded them as unfortunate necessities. Work injured the body and took time from intellectual and social activities and the duties of citizenship.... [pp. 24-29]

Had the Greeks done no more to the character of mathematics than to convert it from an empirical science into a deductive system of thought their influence on history would still have been enormous. But their contributions only began there.

A second vital contribution of the Greeks consisted in their having made mathematics abstract. Earlier civilizations learned to think about numbers and operations with numbers somewhat abstractly, but only in the unconscious manner in which we as children learned to think about and manipulate them. Geometrical thinking, before Greek times, was less advanced. To the Egyptians, for example, a straight line was quite literally no more than either a stretched rope or a line traced in the sand. A rectangle was a fence bounding a field.

With the Greeks not only was the concept of number consciously recognized but also they developed *arithmetica*, the higher arithmetic or theory of numbers ; at the same time mere computation, which they called *logistica* and which involved hardly any appreciation or abstractions, was deprecated as a skill in much the same way as we look down upon typing today. Similarly in geometry, the words *point, line, triangle,* and the like became mental concepts merely suggested by physical objects but differing from them as the concept of wealth differs from land, buildings, and jewelry and as the concept of time differs from a measure of the passage of the sun across the sky.

The Greeks eliminated the physical substance from mathematical concepts and left mere husks. They removed the Cheshire cat and left the grin. Why did they do it ? Surely it is far more difficult to think about abstraction than about concrete things. One advantage is immediately apparent — the gain in generality. A theorem proved about the abstract triangle applies to the figure formed by three match sticks, the triangular boundary of a piece of land, and the triangle formed by the earth, sun, and moon at any instant.

The Greeks preferred the abstract concept because it was, to them, permanent, ideal, and perfect whereas physical objects are shortlived, imperfect, and corruptible. The physical world was unimportant except in so far as it suggested an ideal one ; man was more important than men.... [pp. 30-31]

The Greek preference for idealizations and abstractions expressed itself in philosophy and mathematics. It showed itself just as clearly in art. Greek sculpture of the classical period dwelt not on particular men and women but on ideal types. . . . This idealization extended to standardization of the ratios of the parts of the body to each other. No finger or toenail was overlooked in Polyclitus' prescriptions of these ratios. . . .

The Greeks standardized their architecture as they did their sculpture. Their simple and austere buildings were always rectangular in shape ; even the ratios of the dimensions were fixed. The Parthenon at Athens. . . is an example of the style and proportions found in almost all Greek temples. The insistence on ideal dimensions is, incidentally, closely related to the Greek insistence on form, form in the abstract, a concept not alien to our day, in which art and abstraction are practically synonymous. [pp. 33-34]

NOTE

1. Morris Kline, *Mathematics in Western Culture* (London : George Allen and Unwin Ltd., 1954), pp. 24-34.

STRUCTURAL AND DYNAMIC ELEMENTS IN THE GREEK CONCEPTION OF PHYSICAL REALITY[1]

S. Sambursky

The fundamental significance of Greek science for the understanding of our contemporary civilization, based on science and technology, stems from two facts. One is that the Greeks were the first to discover the scientific method and to inaugurate the rational approach to reality. Many of the great achievements of their classical period, such as epic literature and art, have counterparts in several ancient cultures all over the world, but the emergence of a logical mode of thought out of mythology in the comparatively short stretch of two hundred years is a unique phenomenon of fateful significance for all subsequent developments. There can be no doubt as to the Greek parentage of modern civilization in all that concerns its mode of scientific cognition and its striving toward an objectivization of reality.

The second fact of significance for our problem is that the Greeks, in the four hundred years from the Milesian philosophers of nature until the Alexandrian period, have to their credit hardly any technical achievements comparable to the enormous strides they made in science. European civilization, on the other hand, has in a shorter span of time seen the rise of a technology not less imposing and formidable than the parallel advances in the field of the sciences. Our civilization is characterized by an intertwining and integration of science and technology, a factor decisive for the rapid development of both components, whereas the Greeks were fundamentally interested only in understanding the physical world and felt no need to conquer it or to change it. The basic difference in attitude toward nature, the contemplative and the aggressive, which is also expressed in the fact that the ancient Greeks, with few exceptions, did not practice any systematic experimentation, has an important bearing on the problem of the specific character of their mode of cognition. While being logically realistic, like ours, it was essentially governed by a structural conception, by an approach largely defined in terms of harmony, proportion, and symmetry. As we shall see there were some notable exceptions to this, showing the beginnings of a dynamic conception of reality, but they remained rudimentary as compared with the structural one. It was only from the times of Galileo and Newton that the logic of scientific thought and discovery was determined by the dynamic conception and that man began to think in terms of change and forces instead of harmony and structures....

It is well known that it was Plato who assigned to geometry an exalted place among the sciences. In the *Gorgias* (508a), for instance, Socrates reproaches Callicles and says that he seems never to have observed that geometrical equality is mighty among both gods and men. Plato alludes here to equality expressed in geometrical proportions which for the Greek mind symbolized harmony and order by which heaven and earth are bound together forming an ordered whole, the cosmos. From the context it is clear, moreover, that Plato saw in geometrical proportions also a symbol of justice, in a more general way even than this is expressed and illustrated in our days by the scales of justice. It was a conception which lasted throughout antiquity and lived on in the tradition of the celebrated lines believed to have been written above the entrance of Plato's academy :

> Nobody ignorant of geometry should enter my roof.
> That is, no unjust person should pass these portals
> Because geometry is equality and justice.

If one finally remembers the great importance of the theory of proportions and of the concept of symmetry for Greek art, one will realize the singular significance held by geometry as a link between art, science, and ethics. There is another aspect to this problem, most revealing of the Greek attitude to geometry, and to mathematics in general. All fundamental mathematical constructs, like numbers, lines, and shapes, had their origin in empirical beings and were part of material entities. Arithmetic developed from the Pythagorean practice of representing numbers by a row of pebbles, and the beginnings of geometry went back to geodesy applied by the Egyptians to practical ends, whereby points were represented by stones or holes and lines by furrows or other material patterns. It thus seemed quite natural to regard mathematics, and geometry in particular, as perceptible things seen in abstraction from their material qualities. This was indeed the gist of Aristotle's philosophy of mathematics, whose view was that the objects of mathematics are abstractions of material entities. According to him the difference between a snub nose and a concave line is "that snub is a combination of matter and form whereas concavity is independent of perceptible matter."[2]

The Aristotelian conception, however, was rejected by the long Platonic tradition which prevailed for about 900 years, from Plato until the last Neoplatonists, and which was the essential moving spirit behind the spectacular development of geometry. Plato assigned to mathematics an autonomous position as a separate entity in the intermediate region between the intelligible world of pure forms and the material world of perceptible things. Mathematics is thus both eternal and permanent in essence and accessible to the human mind. Proclus in the introduction to his commentary on Euclid's *Elements* (fifth century) again and again emphasizes that to assume the subsistence of mathematical forms by material abstraction would mean in fact a dependence of the soul on material shapes, debasing her below the level of matter. On the contrary, the cogency of mathematical reasoning and the beauty and exactitude of mathematical forms are clear evidence of the fact that mathematics has its primary subsistence in the soul, which is the creator of all mathematical species.

The Platonic conception of the intermediate place held by mathematics between the permanent realm of the intelligible world and the changing world of physical phenomena formed the basis for the firm belief of its adherers in mathematics as a language suitable for the description and explanation of physical reality. Its roots go back to the first great success of applied mathematics — the Pythagorean theory of musical harmony. In the century preceding Plato it was discovered that simple musical consonances, like the octave, the fifth, or the fourth, are related to simple numerical proportions exhibited by the relative length of the sounding strings, or generally, the relative dimensions of sounding bodies. The respective proportions 1:2, 2:3, 3:4 became the starting point for a rich and ramified theory of harmony as well as for further developments in arithmetic which led to the definition of the three means, the arithmetic, geometric, and harmonic, and the three corresponding proportions.

But still more important from the viewpoint of the history of ideas was the Pythagorean attempt — so typical of a scientific train of thought — to extend the successful application of mathematics to other realms of the physical world. By a bold association of ideas, acoustics and music, based on the periodic phenomena of vibration, were connected with the revolutions of the planets and their periods, and thus gave rise to the idea of the harmony of the spheres and led to a systematic search after regularities in celestial motions, expressible in terms of mathematics. Mathematical astronomy, which evolved from this, was the second great creation of Greek science. It was strictly geometrical discipline, beginning under Plato's influence in the middle of the fourth century B.C. and rising to the heights of the Ptolemaic system five hundred years later. Greek astronomy is the most striking example for the structural approach of the Greeks to reality. . . . However, it is worthwhile quoting here a later source, the Neoplatonic philosopher Iamblichus (A.D. 300) in order to show how these developments were connected in retrospect with the Pythagoreans, who had been the first to apply mathematics to physics : "The Pythagoreans found out what is possible and impossible in the structure of the universe from what is possible and impossible in mathematics, and they derived the celestial revolutions from causal rules according to commensurable numbers, by defining the measures of heaven by certain mathematical laws and, generally, by establishing the prognostic science of nature through mathematics and by making mathematics a principle for all that can be observed in the cosmos...."[3] [pp. 237-240]

The theoretical constructs of Greek science, and of mathematical physics in particular, are distinct characteristics of a logically realistic culture. In this respect the Greeks are undoubtedly the ancestors of the present Western civilization. There are, however, some significant differences within the limits of this definition. The Greek attitude toward reality was a predominantly cognitive one lacking all the signs of aggressiveness toward nature which in modern times has brought about systematic experimentation and a rapid development of technology. One of the reasons for the fact that Greek civilization was scientific and nontechnical was indicated in this paper : The Greek mode of logical thought was essentially structural and showed only rudimentary beginnings of a dynamic approach. This restriction seems to have grown from deep psychological roots. The Greeks, always careful not to transgress the boundaries of moderation and to avoid hubris, were reluctant to interfere with nature and to provoke its revenge. It was further unthinkable that a living organism like the cosmos should be dissected and analyzed by the unnatural methods of experimentation, which consist in the artificial isolation of a narrow section of reality from the integral body of physical events. This tendency was enhanced by the Greek mentality with its definite bias for deductive reasoning, a neglect of induction combined with a lack of interest in applications. The consequences of these limitations were a gradual decline of science in later antiquity when the scientific spirit succumbed to the hostile attitude of the early church to Greek science as part of pagan civilization as well as to Neoplatonism and the influx of Oriental mysticism. [p. 252]

NOTES

1. S. Sambursky's "Structural and Dynamic Elements in the Greek Conception of Physical Reality," in Northrop and Livingston, eds., *Cross-Cultural Understanding* (New York : Harper & Row, 1964), pp. 30-252.
2. Aristotle, *Metaphysica*, 1025b 32.
3. Iamblichus, *De Communi Mathematica Scientia*, ed. N. Festa, p. 73 1, 22f.

THE PHYSICAL WORLD OF THE GREEKS[1]

S. Sambursky

One of the principal undertakings of early Greek philosophy was to give a rational interpretation to natural occurrences which had previously been explained by ancient mythologies. Greek science's achievement of independence through the struggle of *logos* against *mythos* is in many respects similar to the birth of modern science from the assault on petrified medieval scholasticism. With the study of nature set free from the control of mythological fancy, the way was opened for the development of science as an intellectual system. Similarly, the release of science from the domination of the philosophical dogmatism of the Middle Ages paved the way for the rise of modern science as an autonomous province of human culture.... [pp. 18-19]

But about one fundamental fact there can be no doubt : we have here before us an application of the scientific principle that a maximum of phenomena should be explained by a minimum of hypotheses. It may be regarded as a criterion of the simplicity of a theory if its succeeds in asserting the largest possible number of facts from the smallest possible number of assumptions. Every step in that direction can be taken as a scientific progress, and the ultimate objective, the Platonic ideal of every science, would be to derive from a single root the sum total of its data. Although modern science obviously makes far more exacting demands as regards the synthesis of induction and mathematical deduction than its ancient forerunner, the two are the same in principle. [p. 21]

NOTE

1. S. Sambursky, *The Physical World of the Greeks* (London : Routledge & Kegan Paul Ltd., 1956, 1962), pp. 18-21.

"LOGOS" AND "MYTHOS" IN EARLY GREEK PHILOSOPHY[1]

Ernest Cassirer

A rational theory of the state came to light in Greek philosophy. Here, as in other fields, the Greeks were the pioneers of rational thought. Thucydides was the first to attack the mythical conception of history....

> The absence of romance in my history will, I fear, detract somewhat from its interest ; but if it be judged useful by those inquirers who desire an exact knowledge of the past as an aid to the interpretation of the future, which in the course of human things must resemble if it does not reflect it, I shall be content. My history has been composed to be a possession for all time, not the show-piece of an ephemeral hour.[2]

But the Greek conception of history was not only based on new facts and on a much deeper and more comprehensive psychological insight than had preceded it. The Greeks had also found a new method that enabled them to see the problem in an entirely new light. Before studying politics they had studied nature. In this domain they had made their first great discoveries. Without this preliminary step it would not have been possible for them to challenge the power of mythical thought. The new conception of nature became the common ground for a new conception of man's individual and social life.

The victory could not be won at one blow. Here too we find the same slow and methodical procedure that was one of the most characteristic features of the Greek mind. It is as if the individual thinkers were following a preconceived strategic plan. One position after another is conquered ; the firmest fortifications are laid low, till, at last, the stronghold of mythical thought is shaken to its foundations. All the great thinkers and different philosophical schools have their share in this common work. The first Greek thinkers, the thinkers of the Milesian school, are described by Aristotle as the "ancient physiologists." Nature (*physis*) is the only object that attracts their attention. Their approach to nature is the very opposite of the mythical interpretation of natural phenomena. It is true that, in early Greek thought, the boundaries between the two types of thought were not yet clearly determined but were vague and vacillating. Thales said that "all things are full of gods," and that the magnet is alive, because it has the power of moving iron. Empedocles describes nature as a great struggle between two opposite forces — the forces of love and strife. At one time all things unite in one through love, at another each is borne in different directions by the repulsion of strife. Undoubtedly these are mythical conceptions. As a matter of fact a distinguished historian of Greek philosophy has written a book in which he tries to show that Greek natural philosophy was first conceived in a mystical rather than in a scientific spirit. But this view of the problem is misleading. It is true that the mythical elements could not be overthrown at once; but they were offset and counterbalanced by a new tendency of thought that steadily developed and won an ever-increasing weight. The thinkers of the Milesian school — Thales, Anaximander, Anaximenes — inquired into the beginning or "origin" of things. That is not a new trend of thought; what was really new was their definition of the very term "beginning" (*arche*). In all mythical cosmogonies the origin means a primeval state that belongs to the remote immemorial mythical past. It has faded away and vanished; it has been replaced and superseded by other things. The first Greek natural philosophers understand and define the beginning in quite a different sense. What they are asking for is not an accidental fact but a substantial cause. The beginning is not simply a commencement in time but a "first principle"; it is logical rather than chronological. According to Thales the world not only was water, it is water: water is the abiding and permanent element of all things. From the element of water or air, from the "Apeiron" of Anaximander, things have developed not in a haphazard way, according to the whims and caprices of supernatural agents, but in a regular order and according to general rules. The concept of such inalterable and inviolable rules is perfectly strange to mythical thought.

But nature is, after all, only the periphery of the mythical world; it is not its centre. It was a much bolder enterprise and required a much greater intellectual courage to direct the attack against this centre — against the mythical conceptions of the gods. The two opposite forces that built up Greek philosophy — the philosophy of "Being" and the philosophy of "Becoming" — were united in this attack. The same arguments were used by the Eleatic thinkers and by Heraclitus against the Homeric gods. Heraclitus did not shrink from saying that Homer should be turned out of the lists and whipped because of his misconstruction of the divine. Behind the veils that the imagination of the poets and the myth makers had spun around the nature of divinity, the philosophers attempted to discover its true face. The poets and the myth makers yielded to the common temptation of men; they made their gods in their own image. The Ethiopians, says Xenophanes, make their gods black and snub-nosed, the Thracians give them blue eyes and red hair. And if oxen and horses or lions had hands and could paint with their hands, horses would paint the forms of gods like horses, and oxen like oxen. Xenophanes rejected this mythical imagery for a double reason, speculative and religious. As a speculative thinker he insists that a plurality of gods is inconceivable and contradictory. In a passage of Aristotle's *Metaphysics* Xenophanes is styled "the first partisan of the One." According to the fundamental dogma of the Eleatic school "Being" and "Unity" are convertible terms: *ens et unum convertuntur.* If God has true being, he must have a perfect unity. To speak of many gods who are struggling one against the other, who have their combats and feuds, is absurd from a speculative point of view and blasphemous from a religious and ethical point of view. Homer and Hesiod have ascribed to their gods all things that are a shame and disgrace among mortals: stealing and adultery and deception of one another. To these pseudo-gods Xenophanes opposes his own new and sublime religious ideal: the conception of a deity that is free from all the limitations of mythical and anthropomorphic thought. There is

One god, the greatest among gods and men, who is neither in form nor in thought like unto mortals. He sees all things, thinks of everything, and hears all things whatsoever ; and without toil he swayeth all things by the thought of his mind.

But the new conceptions of physical nature introduced by the Milesian school and of divine nature by Heraclitus and the Eleatic thinkers, were only the first and preliminary steps. The greatest and most difficult task still remained to be done. Greek thought had created a new "physiology" and a new "theology" ; it had fundamentally changed the interpretation of nature and the conceptions of the deity. But all these victories of rational thought remained precarious and uncertain so long as myth was still in undisputed possession of its firmest stronghold. Myth was not really defeated so long as it had full sway over the human world and dominated man's thoughts and feelings about his own nature and destiny.

We meet with the same historical paradox here as in the criticism of the Homeric gods. The problem could only be solved by a combined and concentrated effort of thought that united two entirely different and diametrically opposed intellectual forces. Here, as in other fields, the unity of Greek thought proved to be a dialectic unity. To put it in the words of Heraclitus, it was an attunement of opposite tensions, like that of the bow and the lyre. In the development of Greek intellectual culture there is perhaps no stronger tension, no deeper conflict than that between sophistic and Socratic thought. Yet in spite of this conflict the sophists and Socrates were in agreement upon one fundamental postulate. They were convinced that a rational theory of human nature was the first desideratum of any philosophic theory. All the other questions that had been treated in pre-Socratic thought were declared to be secondary and subordinate. From then on man was no longer regarded as a mere part of the universe ; he became its centre. Man, said Protagoras, is the measure of all things. This tenet holds, in a sense, both for the sophists and for Socrates. To "humanize" philosophy, to turn cosmogony and ontology into anthropology, was their common goal. Yet however agreeing in the end itself, they entirely disagreed in their means and methods. [pp. 53-57]

The fundamental difference between Socrates and the sophists appears also in their attitude toward mythical thought. If we take things at their face value it seems that here, at last, we have found a bond linking Socratic to sophistic thought. However opposed the one to the other they were both fighting for a common cause ; they had to criticize and purify the traditional conceptions of Greek popular religion. But in this combat, too, their strategy was widely different. The sophists invented a new method that promised a "rational" explanation of the mythical tales. In this field they proved once more the versatility and adaptability of their minds. They became the virtuosi of a new art of allegorical interpretation. By this art every myth, however strange and grotesque, could suddenly be turned into a "truth" — a physical or a moral truth. But Socrates rejected and derided this subterfuge.... [p. 59]

We cannot hope to "rationalize" myth by an arbitrary transformation and re-interpretation of the old legends of the deeds of gods or heroes. All this remains vain and futile. In order to overcome the power of myth we must find and develop the new positive power of "self-knowledge." We must learn to see the whole of human nature in an ethical rather than a mythical light. Myth may teach man many things; but it has no answer to the only question which, according to Socrates, is really relevant: to the question of good and evil. Only the Socratic "logos," only the method of self-examination introduced by Socrates, can lead to a solution of this fundamental and essential problem.

All the great intellectual tendencies that formed Greek culture were preserved in the doctrine of Plato — none of them in its original shape, however. They were molded into a new form by Plato's genius.... The same independence of mind appears also in Plato's attitude toward Socrates. He was the most faithful and devoted pupil of Socrates and accepted both his method and his fundamental ethical ideas. Yet even in his first period, in the so-called "Socratic Dialogues," there is one element alien to the thought of Socrates. He had convinced Plato that philosophy had to begin with the problem of man. But according to Plato we cannot answer this Socratic question without enlarging the field of philosophical investigation. We cannot find an adequate definition of man so long as we confine ourselves within the limits of man's individual life. Human nature does not reveal itself in this narrow compass. What is written in "small characters" in the individual soul, and is therefore almost illegible, becomes clear and understandable only if we read it in the larger letters of man's political and social life. This principle is the starting point of Plato's *Republic.* From now on the whole problem of man was changed: politics was declared to be the clue to psychology. This was the last and decisive step necessary to the development of Greek thought which had begun with an attempt to conquer nature and continued by asking for rational norms and standards of ethical life. It culminated in a new postulate of a rational theory of the state.... [pp. 60-62]

It is this "categorical imperative," this demand for order and measure, that determines Plato's attitude toward mythical thought. The clearest expression of this fundamental tendency is to be found in his dialogue *Gorgias.* As Plato points out, the triad of *logos, nomos, taxis* — reason, lawfulness, order — is the first principle both of the physical and the ethical world. It is this triad that constitutes beauty, truth, morality. It appears in art, in politics, in science, and in philosophy. If regularity and order are found in a house it will be a good and beautiful one; if it appears in a human body we call it health or strength; if it appears in the soul we call it temperance *(sophrosyne)* or justice. The virtue of each thing, whether of an implement or of a body, or again of a soul or any live creature, does not arrive by accident but by an order of rightness or art that is apportioned to each. "And wise men tell us that heaven and earth and gods and men are held together by communion and friendship, by orderliness, temperance, and justice; and that is the reason why they call the whole of this world by the name of order (*kosmos*), not of disorder or dissoluteness. The principle of this universal order appears, in a clear and striking way, in geometry. Here it is expressed by the concept of "geometrical equality," of the right proportion between the elements that constitute a geometrical body. We need only transfer this principle from geometry to politics to discover the true constitution of the state. Plato never thought of political life as a detached province, as an isolated part of Being; he finds in it the same fundamental principle that governs the Whole. The political cosmos is only a symbol, and the most characteristic one, of the universal cosmos.

That leads us immediately to the very centre of Plato's criticism of mythical thought. It may appear, at first sight, that Plato in his views on popular Greek religion is not very original. All he says had been repeated over and over again since the first beginning of Greek philosophy. He simply resumes the arguments of Xenophanes by saying that the fundamental character of divine nature is its goodness and unity. But he adds a new and very specific feature. He insists that without having found a true and more adequate conception of his gods man cannot hope to order and rule his own human world. As long as we think of the gods, in the traditional way, as fighting or deceiving each other, cities will never cease from ill. For what man sees in the gods is only a projection of his own life — and vice versa. We read the nature of the human soul in the nature of the state — we form our political ideals according to our conceptions of the gods. One thing implies and conditions the other. To the philosopher, to the ruler of the state, it is therefore of vital importance to begin his work at this point. The first step to be taken is to replace the mythical gods by what is described by Plato as the highest knowledge : the "Idea of the Good."

That accounts for one of the most paradoxical features of Plato's *Republic.* Plato's attack on poetry always proves a stumbling block to his critics and commentators. Not only the fact and the manner but also the place of this attack is strange and unusual. No modern writer would ever think of inserting his objections to poetry and art into a work dealing with politics. We see no connection between the two problems. This connection becomes evident, however, if we bear in mind the connecting link : the problem of myth.Obviously we cannot think of Plato as an enemy of poetry. He is the greatest poet in the history of philosophy. In their artistic value many of his dialogues — *Phaedo, Symposium, Gorgias, Phaedrus* — are not inferior to the great Greek works of art. Even in the *Republic* itself Plato could not forbear professing his love and deep admiration for the Homeric poems. But here he was no longer speaking as an individual, and he does not allow himself to be influenced by personal inclinations. He speaks and thinks as a lawgiver who estimates and judges the social and the educational values of art. "You and I," says Socrates addressing Adeimantus, "are not, for the moment, poets, but founders of a commonwealth. As such, it is not our business to invent stories ourselves, but only to be clear as to the main outlines to be followed by the poets in making their stories, and the limits beyond which they must not be allowed to go." What are these limits that no poet, neither the epic nor the lyric and tragic poet, is allowed to transgress ? What is combated and rejected by Plato is not poetry in itself, but the myth-making function. To him and to every other Greek both things were inseparable. From time immemorial the poets had been the real myth makers. As Herodotus said, Homer and Hesiod had made the generations of the gods ; they had portrayed their shapes and distinguished their offices and powers. Here was the real danger for the Platonic *Republic.* To admit poetry meant to admit myth, but myth could not be admitted without frustrating all philosophic efforts and undermining the very foundations of Plato's state. Only by expellng the poets from the ideal state could the philosopher's state be protected against the intrusion of subversive hostile forces. Plato did not entirely forbid mythical tales ; he even admitted that, in the education of a young child, they are indispensable. But they must be brought under a strict discipline. From now on they are to be measured by a higher standard, by that of the "Idea of the Good." If this idea is the essence and the very core of divine nature the conception that God is the author of evil becomes absurd. Such a conception is no longer to be said or sung or heard, neither in verse nor in prose. It is declared to be impious, self-contradictory, and disastrous to the commonwealth.

But all this gives only the negative aspect of Plato's thesis. What compensation was possible for the highest and noblest force that hitherto had determined the form of Greek life and Greek culture ? What could be substituted for the work of Homer, Hesiod, Pindar, and Aeschylus ? The loss seemed, indeed, to be irreparable. To compete with the *Iliad* and the *Odyssey* and with the great Greek tragedies seemed to be an attempt that was doomed to failure. Yet Plato did not recoil from this attempt. For he was in possession of a new conception that he thought to be far superior to all the previous Greek ideals.

Long before Plato there had appeared Greek thinkers and statesmen who were inspired by the will to reform the state and who were endowed with deep political wisdom. In this sense Solon may be styled the "creator of Athenian political culture." What distinguished Plato from these first pioneers of political thought was not so much the answer given by him as the question itself. As to the answer we may criticize it very severely. Many features of the Platonic doctrine that he himself thought to be eternal and universal may now easily be recognized as accidental. They depend upon special conditions of Greek social life. Plato's tripartite division of the human soul, and the corresponding division of the social classes, his views about the community of property or the community of wives and children — all this is open to grave objection. But all these objections cannot detract from the fundamental value and merit of his political work. Its greatness depends on the new postulate introduced by Plato. This postulate was unforgettable. It stamped the whole future development of political thought.

Plato began his study of the social order with a definition and an analysis of the concept of justice. The state has no other and no higher aim than to be the administrator of justice. But in Plato's language the term justice does not mean the same as in common speech. It has a much deeper and more comprehensive meaning. Justice is not on the same level with other virtues of man. It is not, like courage or temperance, a special quality or property. It is a general principle of order, regularity, unity, and lawfulness. Within the individual life this lawfulness appears in the harmony of all the different powers of the human soul; within the state it appears in the "geometrical proportion" between the different classes, according to which each part of the social body receives its due and cooperates in maintaining the general order. With this conception Plato became the founder and the first defender of the idea of the legal state.

Plato was the first to introduce a "theory" of the state, not as a knowledge of many and multifarious facts, but as a coherent system of thought.... [pp. 65-69]

. . . Plato had to solve a problem very different from that of any other political reformer. He could not simply replace one political system or form of government by another and better one. He had to introduce a new method and a new postulate into political thought. In order to create the rational theory of the state, he had to lay the axe to the tree : he had to break the power of myth. But here Plato encountered the greatest difficulties. He could not solve the problem without, in a certain sense, surpassing himself and going beyond his own limits. Plato felt the whole charm of myth. He was endowed with a most powerful imagination that enabled him to become one of the greatest myth makers in human history. For we cannot think of Platonic philosophy without thinking of the Platonic myths. In these myths — in the myths of the "supercelestial place" of the prisoners in the cave, of the soul's choice of its future destiny, of the judgment after death, Plato expressed his most profound metaphysical thoughts and intuitions. And at the end he gave his natural philosophy in an entirely mythical form : he introduced, in *Timaeus*, the conceptions of the demiurge, of the good and the evil world soul, of the twofold creation of the world.

How is it to be accounted for that the same thinker who admitted mythical concepts and mythical language so readily into his metaphysics and his natural philosophy spoke in an entirely different vein when developing his political theories ? For in this field Plato became the professed enemy of myth. If we tolerate myth in our political systems, he declared, all our hopes for a reconstruction and reformation of our political and social life are lost. There is only one alternative : we have to make our choice between an ethical and a mythical conception of the state. In the legal state, the state of justice, there is no room left for the conceptions of mythology, for the gods of Homer and Hesiod. "Shall we simply allow our children to listen to any stories that anyone happens to make up, and so to receive into their minds ideas often the very opposite of those we shall think they ought to have when they are grown up ? No, certainly not. It seems, then, our first business will be to supervise the making of fables and legends, rejecting all which are unsatisfactory ; and we shall induce nurses and mothers to tell their children only those which we have approved, and to think more of moulding their souls with these stories than they now do of rubbing their limbs to make them strong and shapely." If we continue to speak of the wars in heaven, of the plots and fighting of the gods against one another, of the battles of the giants and all the innumerable other quarrels of gods and heroes with their friends and relatives, we shall never find order, harmony, unity in our own human world.... [pp. 71-72]

All this shows us once more the unbroken unity of Plato's thought. In his philosophical doctrine we do not find that specialization which was introduced by later thinkers. His whole work was from the same mould. Dialectic, theory of knowledge, psychology, ethics, politics, all this was fused together in one coherent and inseparable whole. It bears the stamp of Plato's philosophical genius and of his personality. This holds also for Plato's attitude toward mythical thought. His struggle against myth followed from his conception and his very definition of dialectic. In the dialogue *Philebus* Plato points out that all things whatever are composed of two different and opposed elements : of "limit" (*peras*) and the "unlimited" or "undeterminate" (*apeiria*). It is for dialectic to bridge the gulf between these two opposite poles : to determine the undeterminate, to reduce the infinite to fixed measures, to set bounds to the boundless. If we accept this definition of philosophy and dialectic it becomes clear why Plato had to exclude myth from his *Republic*, that is to say, from his system of education. Of all things in the world myth is the most unbridled and immoderate. It exceeds and defies all limits ; it is extravagant and exorbitant in its very nature and essence. To banish this dissolute power from the human and political world was one of the principal aims of the *Republic*. Plato's logic and dialectic teach us how to classify and systematize our concepts and thought ; how to make the right divisions and subdivisions. Dialectic, says Plato, is the art of dividing things by classes, according to their natural joints, and not trying to break any part after the manner of a bad carver. Ethics shows us how to rule over emotions ; how to moderate them by virtue of reason and temperance. Politics is the art of unifying and organizing human actions and directing them to a common end. Thus the Platonic parallel between the individual soul and the soul of the state is by no means a mere figure of speech or a simple analogy. It is the expression of Plato's fundamental tendency : the tendency to unify the manifold, to bring the chaos of our minds, of our desires and passions, of our political and social life into a cosmos, into order and harmony. [p. 77]

NOTES

1. Ernest Cassirer, *The Myth of the State* (New Haven : Yale University Press, 1946), pp. 53-77.

2. Thucydides, *The Peloponnesian War*, Bk. I, Chap. XXII, trans. Richard Crawley (New York : E.P. Dutton & Co., Everyman's Library, 1910), p. 15.

THE GREAT DIALOGUE : HISTORY OF GREEK POLITICAL THOUGHT FROM HOMER TO POLYBIUS[1]

Donald D. Kagan

The emergence of a democratic constitution in Athens in the fifth century was a development of the greatest importance in the history of political thought. It is not absolutely certain that the Athenians invented democracy, and Athens, of course, was not the only democracy in classical Greece. Nevertheless it was the Athenian democracy which made the greatest impact on the contemporary scene, and it is the Athenian constitution which remains the paradigm of ancient Greek democracy. It is to Athens, therefore, that we must look for an account of the democratic political ideas of the Greeks.

It is no easy task to present a coherent picture of Greek democratic theory. Indeed, there are those who deny its very existence. They point to the fact that we possess no systematic treatment of democratic theory from the ancient world an suggest that ancient democracy developed naturally, without self-consciousness, making no theoretical analysis of its principles and implications. To be sure, "Democratic political theory can only be tentatively reconstructed from scattered illusions." Yet for two reasons the task seems possible, even if difficult and uncertain. First it is *a priori* unlikely that the Athenian democracy in the period from Cleisthenes to Demosthenes — almost two centuries — should not have had occasion to contemplate and discuss its basic principles. Each year during that period elections were held, political campaigns were waged, and speeches made. Political clubs of both the oligarchic and democratic persuasion discussed the questions of the day. During that period democracy in general and the Athenian brand in particular were attacked from every conceivable angle. Surely it is highly unlikely that the leading democratic statesmen would have no occasion, not to say obligation, to defend the system they represented.

The second reason is more persuasive. We do have, albeit in "scattered allusions," examples of such a defence from which it is possible to obtain a reasonably broad and certain picture of the theory of Athenian democracy. We have seen that the plays of Aeschylus teem with references to the virtues of popular rule. We have seen that Herodotus, in particular in the speech of Otanes, yields more evidence. The rest of the fifth and fourth centuries provides many more documents with which to recreate the democratic theory. One excellent source is the praise of democracy offered in the speeches of Athenian statesmen and orators. Pericles' funeral oration in Thucydides, the funeral speech attributed to the orator Lysias, some references in Isocrates, Demosthenes, Aeschines, and lastly that "curious document of this class . . . the skit on a funeral speech contained in Plato's *Menexenus,* which seems close enough to type to be used — with reservations — as a statement of general principles."[2] A second source is the criticism of democracy by its enemies. Often such attacks state principles which would be accepted and defended by a democrat. Sometimes they contain summaries of democratic doctrines which we may accept as accurate. A third source is the Athenian constitution itself, from which general principles can sometimes be deduced.

We must begin with a working definition of democracy before we can consider its principles and characteristics. Such a definition should be as simple and basic as possible, for the forms and variations of any constitution may be innumerable, and democracy more than any other system is open to various interpretations. In our age, which has seen the name applied to such different governments as that of the United States and the Soviet Union, Great Britain and China, the confusion is especially apparent. To begin with, democracy, as opposed to oligarchy or monarchy, is a system of government in which the majority is legally and constitutionally sovereign. Its citizens "enjoy the right of sharing in deliberative or judicial office" (Aristotle, *Politics,* 1275b). Its legislators and magistrates are chosen for a relatively short term of office and depend on the continuing consent of the people at large. Ultimate authority rests with the citizens and it is exercised freely. It goes without saying that coercion might produce the appearance of such a system but would negate its reality. These seem to be the minimal requirements for a democratic state, and it is clear that they were fully met in Athens from the time of Cleisthenes to that of Demosthenes, with only few and brief interruptions.

What were the characteristics which its proponents claimed as virtues of democracy ? First and foremost was liberty in its various aspects : freedom to take part in public life, freedom to live one's private life according to one's own wishes, freedom from arbitrary action by private citizens or public officials, and, perhaps most important, freedom of speech. Even in Cleisthenes' time all male citizens could vote in the assembly and serve on the juries, but after the reform of Pericles jurors were paid, as were magistrates and members of the Council ; in the fourth century even attendance at the meetings of the assembly was compensated. This particular feature of Athenian democracy came under heavy attack from its critics as a corrupting element, for they claimed it made the Athenians "idle, cowardly, talkative and avaricious" (Plato, *Gorgias,* 515E) ; but we need only to turn to the greatest statement of democratic theory in our possession — the funeral oration of Pericles — to explain its purpose. It is to fulfil the democratic ideal which guarantees freedom to take part in public affairs to all its citizens, "nor again does poverty bar the way, if a man is able to serve the state, he is not hindered by the obscurity of his condition" (Thucydides ii, 371). Pericles goes on to proclaim yet another sphere of liberty basic to the democratic way of life, the realm of private life. Sparta might regulate every detail of the daily routine of its citizens to produce a uniform product, but a democracy must tolerate and even welcome variety. The critics of democracy found this freedom appalling. In extreme democracies, says Aristotle, "each man lives as he likes — or as Euripides says, "For any end he chances to desire." This is a mean conception of liberty" (*Politics*, 1310a). The consequence of this deplorably "excessive" freedom is that the citizens, instead of being all of one type, are various, and it becomes impossible to distinguish citizens from resident aliens or slaves; even women have freedom and approach equality (Plato, *Republic* 557b, 563b; Pseudo-Xenophon, *Athenian Constitution*, i, 10-12). A democrat would find his concept of personal freedom well worth the price of these inconveniences and might proudly support the claim of Pericles that "the freedom which we enjoy in our government extends also to our ordinary life. There, far from exercising a jealous surveillance over each other, we do not feel called upon to be angry with our neighbour for doing what he likes, or even to indulge in those injurious looks which cannot fail to be offensive, although they inflict no positive penalty" (Thucydides ii, 37.2).

Freedom of speech is in one sense of the private liberties, but its greater significance is in the public realm. We have seen that so far back as the time of Solon it had been realized that the well-being of the *polis* depended on a sensible, well-informed citizenry. The freedom to speak out on public matters was, therefore, no mere private convenience but a public necessity if the *demos* was to benefit from the best counsel. The praise of free speech by Aeschylus and Herodotus has already been noted, and free speech was to be the subject of pride for democrats throughout Athenian history. Demosthenes points out that in Sparta it is impossible to praise the laws of Athens or of any other state, whereas in Athens a man may say what he will (*Against Leptines*, 106). But once again it is Pericles who makes clear precisely the role played by free speech in a democratic state:

> We Athenians are able to judge at all events if we cannot originate, and instead of looking on discussion as a stumbling block in the way of action, we think it an indispensable preliminary to any wise action at all. (Thucydides ii, 40.2.)

A second characteristic feature of democracy is the principle of equality. More than any other, this was basic to the democratic idea, and Athenian literature is filled with references to its virtues. Theseus, the legendary founder of Athenian democracy, is made to speak in its defence; the principle of equality stands out as of major importance:

> This city is free, and ruled by no one man.
> The people reign in annual succession.
> They do not yield the power to the rich;
> The poor man has an equal share in it.
> (Euripides, *The Suppliant Women*, 405-408)

One of the greatest faults of tyranny is that where it exists "equality is no more."

> With written laws,
> People of few resources and the rich
> Both have the same recourse to justice. Now
> A man of means, if badly spoken of,
> Will have no better standing than the weak.
> And if the baser if in the right he wins

Against the great.

(*The Suppliant Women*, 432-437)

The close connection between democracy and equality is clearly shown by the frequent substitution for the word *democratia* of the word *isonomia* or *isegoria.* It is the latter term which is used by Herodotus to describe the Athenian constitution established by Cleisthenes, whose miraculous powers made Athens suddenly great (*History*, ii, 78), and the former, "the fairest name of all", by which Otanes designated popular government (iii, 80). *Isegoria* emphasizes the idea of free speech, that is the equal opportunity to speak, but generally means equality before the law. About *isonomia* there has been some disagreement. One view derives it from *isos* and *nemein*, and takes it to mean "equal distribution." If the things to be shared are understood to be rights and privileges rather than property this interpretation would accord well with the ideas of both opponents and proponents of Greek democracy, yet it is better, I think, to take it to mean, "*not* equality of distribution but equality of law." It will be seen that *isonomia* had several shades of meaning in Greek democracy, but at the very least it meant equality before the law. This point is stressed by the democratic orators. Demosthenes conjectures that Athenian public-spiritedness and liberality results from "the reflection that under a democracy each man has his share of just and equal rights" (*Against Medias*, 67). Elsewhere he praises an Athenian law which forbids the bill of attainder because "It forbids the introduction of any law that does not affect all citizens alike — an injunction conceived in the true spirit of democracy. As every man has an equal share in the constitution generally, so this statute asserts his equal share in the laws" (*Against Timocrates*, 59). Again, Pericles does not fail to mention this aspect of the Athenian democracy in his encomium of its institutions : "If we look to the laws, they afford equal justice to all in their private differences" (Thucydides, ii, 37.1).

This penchant for equality was no mere subject for political orations but was embedded in the very fabric of the Athenian constitution. We have seen that even in the time of Cleisthenes all citizens could vote for all state offices and all were eligible for jury duty. By the time of Pericles, election to the magistracies was possible for the top three classes in society in theory, and in practice probably to all. Payment for these services made such benefits actual rather than theoretical. The greatest tribute of all to the theory of equality was the widespread use of the lot for choosing public officials. Jurymen, minor officials, members of the council, even archons were chosen in this way.

This equality in all aspects of life, but particularly in political matters, was the target of the severest attacks by critics of democracy. Plato pointed out that democracy "distributes a sort of equality to equal and unequal alike" (*Republic*, 558C). Aristotle said that to the democrat justice is "the enjoyment of arithmetical equality, and not the enjoyment of proportionate equality on the basis of merit" (*Politics*, 1317b). This is a basic complaint of the critics of democracy and, of course, rests on the old conviction that somehow there are native distinctions among men which make them differ in *kind.* It is the view of Theognis which lingers on ; it is a view rejected by democrats. The critics, however, levelled more pointed and practical attacks on political equality. Socrates, for instance, pointed out the absurdity of the system of appointing public officals by lot, "when none would choose a pilot builder or flautist by lot" (Xenophon,

Memorabilia, i, 2.9). In more general terms he is made to criticize the free exercise of political action by any and all citizens. Like the other Greeks he concedes the wisdom of the Athenians. When they meet in the assembly to discuss technical questions such as construction, shipbuilding, etc., they are not content with any but expert advice and call in builders, shipwrights, and other craftsmen. To no one else will they listen regardless of his personal attractions. Such is their method of treating professional questions.

> But when the question is an affair of state, then everybody is free to have a say — carpenter, tinker, cobbler, sailor, passenger ; rich and poor, high and lower — anyone who likes gets up, and no one reproaches him, as in the former case, with not having learned, and having no teacher, and yet giving advice. (Plato, *Protagoras*, 319C-D)

The defender of democracy is here faced with a more serious challenge. Is it not absurd to argue that all men are equally competent to govern ? Is it not equally foolish to assert that all are able to consider policies and to give sound advice ? Democratic theory would respond to each attack differently : it would deny that it upheld the first claim and admit and defend the second. The Athenian democrats never asserted that all men were equally qualified to govern, and the history of their constitution makes this plain. So long as the archons were the chief officials of the state they were elected, not allotted. When they were chosen by lot they had lost their significance and the really important governors were the generals. These were always elected, chosen, presumably for their skill and talent. When we recall the men who held this position in the fifth century — Themistocles, Aristides, Xanthippus, Pericles, Phormio, Demosthenes, Nicias — we can hardly doubt that the Athenian democracy appreciated and utilized men of unusual merit. The officals chosen by lot did not exercise any functions requiring special talent or training ; their duties were routine and a mistake was not vital. Even then there were checks against the worst incompetence. The candidate for a magistracy had to undergo a preliminary examination ; he was liable to deposition by the assembly ten times each year and subject to prosecution for any malfeasance at the end of his year in office. As Jones has put it, "It is unlikely that many rogues or nincompoops would expose themselves to these risks."[3]

The spokesman for the Athenian democracy, moreover, emphasized its recognition of the difference in the abilities of men and boasted of its rewards to those who excel. Its slogan was not "a political career for any and all," but rather it offered and boasted of "the career open to talents." Pericles emphasized that although the Athenians were equal in the eyes of the law, "Advancement in public life falls to reputation for capacity, class considerations not being allowed to interfere with merit" (Thucydides ii, 37.1). The same sentiment is echoed in the funeral speech humorously attributed by Plato to Aspasia in the *Menexenus*. Whether this puzzling performance was intended as a satire, an epideictic display, or a serious attempt to address the Athenians is beside the point. In any case its ideas are those of the defender of democracy and may be taken as typical of democratic theory. In it the speaker attempts to describe the Athenian constitution which produced the heroes who died so nobly.

> Then as now, and indeed always, from that time to this, speaking generally, our government was an aristocracy — a form of government which receives various names, according to the fancies of men, and is sometimes called democracy, but is really an aristocracy or government of the best, which has the approval of the many. For kings we have always had, first hereditary and then elected, and authority is mostly in the hands of the people, who dispense offices and power to those who appear to be the most deserving of them. Neither is a man rejected from weakness or poverty or obscurity of origin, nor honoured by reason of the opposite, as in other states, but there is one principle — he who appears to be wise and good is a governor and ruler. (Plato, *Menexenus*, 238C-D)

We have here what must surely have been one of the most potent replies to the criticism by oligarchs. Far from being absurd, the democratic system which opens all offices to all citizens, with talent alone as the criterion, is the only sensible way to achieve good government. In oligarchies, birth, wealth, influence, all accidental circumstances, may stand in the way of excellence. Only under democracy is true *arete* given free play. Democracy not only permitted each man to participate in political life, it expected him to. As Pericles put it, "Unlike any other nation . . . [we regard] him who takes no part in the duties not as unambitious but as useless . . ." (Thucydides ii, 40.2). It is characteristic of Greek democracy, unlike the modern variety, that it insists on the positive participation of its citizens in its administration. Proponents of democracy seem to have feared no excess of popular participation. Such was their confidence in the resources of the people that this policy was viewed not as one which would be a levelling agent, but as one which would permit the cream to rise to the top. . . . [pp. 73-80]

In order to understand fully what the democratic idea of equality was, it is important to make clear what it was not. We have seen that the democratic constitution recognized that all men were not equal in ability and therefore not equally able to govern. So, too, does the subtlest expounder of democratic thought realize the natural inequality of men's talents. In spite of frequent assertions that Protagoras believed that all men share *equally* in the political art, there is no evidence whatever for such a view. Protagoras regularly and uniformly assumes and states the opposite : aptitude and talent for political virtue vary among men, though no man is wholly without them. Democracy, then, did not mean the senseless, absolute equality attributed to it by its critics. It also emphatically did not mean economic equality. In the troubled period of Solon in the sixth century the Athenian peasantry, to be sure, had demanded the redistribution of the land and *isomoiria,* "equal portions" of the land of Attica (Solon Fr. 23). That demand was not met, and never was it part of the program of the Athenian democrats. On the contrary, the Athenian democracy, even in its most radical phase, asserted and defended the right of private property and made no effort to change its unequal distribution. Demosthenes reads into the record an official version of the judicial oath taken by all jurors which contains the following statement : "I will not allow private debts to be cancelled, nor lands nor houses belonging to Athenian citizens to be redistributed" (*Against Timocrates,* 149). The Eponymous Archon, moreover, swore on his induction "that everyone will have and hold to the end of his term of office whatever he possessed at the beginning of his office" (Aristotle, *Constitution of Athens*, 56.2). From all this it is clear that the equality of Athenian democratic theory was purely political and not economic. It was no part of that theory to destroy the distinction between rich and poor, but rather to guarantee to both equal power to guide and advise the state.

A third basic tenet of Greek democratic thought was that democracy, more than any other constitution, represented and ensured the rule of law. This may seem paradoxical in the light of the critics' attacks on the lawless, undisciplined nature of the democratic state, yet one of the proudest claims of Greek democracy was its adherence and subjection to the law. It was a commonplace among the orators to point to the rule of law as the basis of all good in Athenian life. Demosthenes asserted that "no man living will attribute the prosperity of Athens, her liberty, her popular government to anything rather than to the laws" (*Against Timocrates,* 5). But it was no less common to see the rule of law as an exclusive attribute of democracy. To the orator Lycurgus it was the first of the three chief things which uphold democracy (*Against Leocrates,* 4). Demosthenes sharply contrasted the democratic respect for law with the lawlessness of other constitutional forms. Tyranny or monarchy, for instance, are incompatible with legal procedures, "For every king and every tyrant is the bitter enemy of freedom and law" (*Second Philippic,* 25). Oligarchy he likewise contrasts with "government by law," meaning democracy (*Ibid.,* 75-76). The fullest and strongest statement of this idea is made by Aeschines, who, incidentally, shows that it was common coin among Athenian speakers by apologizing in advance for repeating a commonplace :

> It is acknowledged . . . that there are in the world three forms of government, autocracy, oligarchy, and democracy : autocracies and oligarchies are administered according to the tempers of their lords, but democracies according to established laws. And be assured, fellow citizens, that in a democracy it is the laws that guard the person of the citizen and the constitution of the state whereas the tyrant and the oligarch find their protection in suspicion and in armed guards.
>
> (*Against Timarchus,* 4-5)

Again Pericles does not fail to mention this cardinal aspect of democratic theory. "But all this ease in our private relations does not make us lawless as citizens. Against this fear is our chief safeguard, teaching us to obey the magistrate, and the laws. . ." (Thucydides ii, 37.3).

This emphasis on the rule of law in democracy raises the question as to what the Greeks meant by the term "law," which in the fifth century and thereafter is usually rendered by the word *nomos.* That they could mean something different from the modern conception is clear from the statement of Aristotle. In describing the characteristics of radical democracy he says that "here, the people, and not the law, is the final sovereign. This is what happens when popular decrees (*psephismata*) are sovereign instead of the laws (*nomoi*)" (*Politics,* 1922a). He equates democracy of this sort with despotism ; neither is ruled by law, both attack the upper classes, and the decrees of democracy are analogous to the edicts of the tyrant. Aristotle seems to understand the law as an immutable code established in the past by some impartial legislator and not subject to change. Subsequent legislation must accord with this code, and where there is conflict legislation must yield to "law." Now although such a doctrine of the immutability of the law would seem to favour the oligarchic point of view and serve as a bulwark against change, it was widely held among Athenian democrats.

After the restoration of the democracy on the departure of the Thirty Tyrants, a commission was appointed to draw up a law code based on the ancient legislation of Solon and Draco. Careful provision was made for the proposal and approval of new laws and it was then ruled that "No decree, whether of the Council or Assembly, shall override a law" (Andocides, *On the Mysteries* 81-87). Furthermore, the constitution provided that anyone proposing a decree to alter the laws was liable to the *graphe paranomon,* the "indictment for illegal proceedings." If such an indictment was supported by the courts it abrogated the decree and exposed the mover to heavy punishment. This apparent paradox can be resolved by looking at the peculiar history of Athens. There democracy was a system of long standing, hallowed by time, seeking its founding father in Solon. The laws of Solon and Cleisthenes were the established laws of Athens and sanctioned democracy. It was for the enemies of democracy to deny the validity of these *nomoi,* a task, as we shall see, which some of them were glad to undertake.

Not all democrats, however, were content with this traditionalist interpretation of law. In the fifth and fourth centuries some of them — pressed, no doubt by their critics — sought a more satisfactory definition which could support democratic practice with something other than tradition and antiquity. Xenophon puts a conversation in the mouths of Pericles and Alcibiades which, even if it is imaginary, indicates the direction in which democratic thought on the nature of law was moving. The young Alcibiades asks Pericles to tell him what a law is and receives the following definition : "Laws are the rules approved and enacted by the majority in assembly, whereby they declare what ought and what ought not to be done." Alcibiades finds this definition less than satisfactory and presses for clarification. What, he asks, if, as under an oligarchy, such rules are enacted by a minority, not a majority ? Pericles answers that whatever is enacted by the sovereign (*to kratoun*) in the state is known as law. What if a tyrant is in control ? What, then, is violence and lawlessless ? Pericles must admit that it is when the stronger "constrains the weaker to do whatever he chooses, not by persuasion but by force." He is compelled to amend his definition to insist that the sovereign must impose its wishes by persuasion, not force, and is trapped by the logic of Alcibiades into facing the conclusion that the rule of the majority over an unpersuaded minority is the rule, not of law, but of force. The anecdote is ended on a humorous note when Pericles tells Alcibiades that, "at your age. . .we too, were clever at this sort of thing." To which Alcibiades replies, "Ah, Pericles, if only I had known you intimately when you were at your best" (*Memorabilia,* 1.2, 40-46).

Xenophon, of course, was an enemy of democracy, and the story scores at the expense of Pericles and points up a weakness in democratic theory. Yet it probably reflects the changing ideas of the democrats. For one thing the distinction between the laws and decrees has disappeared. Pericles is made to define the *nomoi* as simply the action of the assembly — that is, they are identified with *psephismata.* In the second place, there is increased emphasis on persuasion, as a necessary part of the rule of law, and this element at least was central in democratic thought. We have already seen how prominent a place the idea of persuasion held in the thinking of Aeschylus ; the democratic orators of the fourth century stressed it, too. Demosthenes, arguing against retroactive legislation, defines the laws of a free state as prescribing "what shall be done in the future, such laws having been enacted by *persuading* people that they will be beneficial to those who live under them" (*Against Timocrates,* 76). And this aspect of the democratic process is given an honourable place in the high praise of Athenian democracy contained in the funeral oration of Lysias :

> They were the first and the only people in that time to drive out the ruling classes of their state and to establish a democracy, believing the liberty of all to be the strongest bond of agreement ; by sharing with each other the hopes born of their perils they had freedom of soul in their civic life, and used law for honouring the good and punishing the evil. For they deemed that it was the way of wild beasts to be held subject to one another by force, but the duty of men to delimit justice by law, to convince by reason, and to serve these two in act by submitting to the sovereignty of law and the instruction of reason.
> (*Funeral Oration,* 18-19)

Thus persuasion and reason were seen to be vital components of the rule of law. The problem presented by Alcibiades — majority rule versus minority rights — was not solved by the democratic theorists, nor, it might be pointed out, has anyone solved it yet.

Another aspect of the rule of law emphasized in the political thought of the Greek democrats was the doctrine of political responsibility. It was widely recognized that the greatest threat to freedom lay in the usurpation, abuse, or arbitrary exercise of political power. For this reason the democracies employed the law on ostracism to head off any citizen whose power seemed to threaten the freedom of the state. In almost every case the victim was the leader of a political faction. For the same reason the Athenian constitution placed the tightest reins on its elected or allotted magistrates, who were chosen for short terms of office, subjected to regular examination during their tenure, and put through the most rigorous and searching scrutiny when they rendered their accounts at the end of their term. Even Pericles, who was elected general in Athens every year for three decades, the most powerful and secure politician in the history of democratic Athens, took the greatest care to meet these responsibilities. Plutarch tells us that one day Alcibiades was turned away when he tried to visit Pericles. He was told that the master could not be disturbed, for "he was studying how to render his accounts to the Athenians." To which Alcibiades answered with a characteristic quip that shows why he richly merited the distrust felt toward him by the Athenians. "Would it not be better for him," he said, "to study how not to render his accounts to the Athenians ?" (*Alcibiades,* 7.2). We have seen that this doctrine of responsibility was a hallmark of popular government and perhaps its finest aspect for Aeschylus and Herodotus, and the juror's oath cited by Demosthenes proves that it continued to be central to democratic theory and practice in the fourth century. Among other things each juror swore "I will not confirm the appointment to any office, of any person still subject to audit [*hypeuthynon*] in respect to any other office . . . I will not suffer the same men to hold the same office twice, or two offices in the same year" (*Against Timocrates,* 149-150).

The two great democratic principles, equality and the rule of law, were not unrelated in democratic theory. We are indebted to Gregory Vlastos for an insight into the relationship between them in the minds of Greek democrats. In his subtle and original analysis of the meaning of *isonomia* he points out :

> The junction of equality and law may be read not only in the sense of law as the guarantee of equality, but also in the converse sense of equality as the guarantee of

> law. In the former sense . . . law appears as the means to the end of political equality ; in the latter, law, or the rule of law, is the end, political equality is the means to this end. To take the word in this latter sense is to assert that its conformity to law will be ensured by its egalitarian distribution of political power.
>
> (*Isonomia*, 356-257)

The orator Aeschines simply assumes the connection in his contrast between "the oligarchs and those governed by an unequal constitution" and the Athenians, "who have the equal and law-abiding constitution" (*Against Timarchus*, 4-5), but the best reasoned statement of it is to be found in Otanes' speech in the constitutional debate reported by Herodotus. The greatest virtue of popular rule, apart from its beautiful name, is that it provides the rule of law free from lawless tyranny. He goes on to explain the cause for the lawlessness : it is the nature of monarchical power itself. "Give this power to the best man on earth, and his wonted mind must leave him. The advantage which he holds breed insolence. . ." (iii. 80). In this way he departs from all traditional explanations of the perversion of justice which have, up to this time, been based on personal morality. Hesiod explains the injustice of his *basileis* by their folly or naturally evil dispositions. Solon blames the *hybris* of the demagogue-tyrant and the ignorance and gullibility of the *demos*. Otanes, however, realizes that all men are liable to such weaknesses and that not envy but unchecked power creates *hybris*. Vlastos does not exaggerate when he sees in this analysis "a revolutionary advance in man's understanding of the problem of government" (*Isonomia*, 358). When he defends popular rule, Otanes does not argue for the special virtue or wisdom of the masses. He asserts only that such rule will be based on equality and responsibility. "He believes that the power of any man in office, when counterpoised against the equal power of his fellows to bring him to judgment under the law, will be held under constraint of equality within the just limits of lawful rule" (*Isonomia*, 359). [pp. 84-90]

NOTES

1. Donald D. Kagan, *The Great Dialogue : History of Greek Political Thought from Homer to Polybius* (New York : The Free Press, 1965), pp. 73-90.
2. A.H.M. Jones, *Athenian Democracy* (Oxford : 1960), p. 42.
3. *Ibid.*, p. 48.

ENTER PLATO[1]

Alvin W. Gouldner

It is widely agreed that Western individualism has one of its great burgeonings with the development of Greek culture. Although one might wish that there was as much clarity about the nature of this individualism as there is agreement about its occurrence, only pedantry would insist that we be clear about the details before acknowledging the broad pattern. The fact is that individualism, in a sense grossly familiar to Westerners, is one of the basic features of Greek culture ; in the context of the contest system, it commonly expresses itself as an ambition for personal fame, and in its heroic form it is a quest for a fame undying.

While Greek individualism is clearly evident at the beginning of the classical period, there are tentative indications of its emergence at least as early as Hesiod, who begins his narrative by giving his name and then continues in the first person. Sappho's lyric poetry around the end of the seventh century B.C. also centres attention on the individual, on his situation, emotions, and states of mind. Indeed it may be that the Delphic injunction "Know thyself," echoed in Heraclitus' proud claim, "I have searched myself," serves to legitimate the increasing interest in the individual self. The culmination of this trend occurs in the fifth century when Protagoras avers that "Man is the measure of all things," and when Socrates directs men not only to know their own selves but to take responsibility for reconstructing it.

Bruno Snell's linguistic analysis of Homeric literature suggests that men of that early period still had little knowledge of the self in the modern sense. That is, they did not yet regard it as the source of the emotions (or of the accomplishments of the person), especially those that were strong or abnormal in some manner. Agamemnon, for example, explains his behaviour toward Achilles in this way : "Not I was the cause of this act, but Zeus and my portion of the Erinyes who walk in darkness ; they it was who in the assembly put wide *ate* [divine temptation] in my understanding on that day when I appropriated Achilles' prize from him." The Homeric Greeks, says Snell, did not yet possess a term for the whole of man's mental equipment or for the mind or soul as an entity in our sense. The soul was not yet regarded as distinct from and, in particular, opposed to the body.

In early Greek art the physical body itself was not, according to Snell, comprehended as an organ unity but as an aggregate of parts. It is not until the classical art of the fifth century B.C. that efforts to depict the body as an integrated organism are found. Homer speaks of fleet legs and sinewy arms, but he has no one word for characterizing the mind or the self. Only gradually do men come to view themselves as the source and author of their feelings and actions, becoming increasingly aware of their powers and conscious of self ; only gradually is what we might call the "authority" of the self recognized.

It is well known that Greek sculpture presents an ideal, conventionalized portrait of individuals, as anyone can see who visits a museum in which there is a sampling of Greek sculpture that can be compared with the much more individuated features on the busts of Roman notables. It is not until the second half of the fifth century B.C. that serious literary efforts at individualized characterization are attempted and that Athenians develop a lively interest in personal character.

To understand this emergence of individualism, it must be remembered that from about the ninth to the sixth century B.C., there occurred the greatest social revolution that Europe has yet experienced : the breakdown of tribalism and the emergence of the urban community organized on the basis of territorial propinquity — in short, the state. Men came increasingly to depend upon the state's legal and administrative machinery to protect contracts and right wrongs, and began operating independently of their tribes and families. Important as kinship undoubtedly remains in subsequent Western societies, it will never again be the all-embracing matrix that it was in tribal societies.

In tribal societies kinship arrangements permeate the most diverse and basic involvements : they define a man's fundamental loyalties, determine when and against whom he is to wage war, establish the locales within which he will pursue his subsistence-getting activities, rigorously regulate whom he must or must not marry, from whom he gets justice, and from whom he learns ritual requirements and work skills.

With the decline of tribalism men leave a society in which their diverse activities are integrated within a single institutional framework, in which the bonds between men are multiple rather than segmentalized, and in which the basic paradigm of human relations is that of the family or of kinship ties. Leaving tribalism they come to live among those with whom they are, for the most part, unrelated by real or fictive kinship ties, and thus in effect relinquish the support and protection of a group that is viewed much as if it were a large family.

To leave the tribalism is to leave a world in which most decisions are closely regulated by a network of unexaminable rules. To leave tribalism is to enter a world of greater choices — concerning marriage, trade, and personal and political alliances. It is to enter a world in which the very rules governing decisions are themselves regarded as things concerning which decisions may be made. Men increasingly view themselves as rule-makers, as "the measure of all things," rather than simply as rule-followers or rule-breakers. It is a move, therefore, toward an open and unstructured social situation which can be more exciting but, at the same time, more uncertain and anxiety inducing.

In this new world, one way that men for whom established tradition and its interpreters have lost authority may know the right and the real is by referring to the opinion of those around them. It becomes increasingly important for men to secure consensual validation of their impulses, beliefs, and, indeed, of their very worth, when the traditional verities wane and the ways of the world no longer seem ordained.

Under tribalism men might chafe and rebel against the traditional rules but these rules constitute, nevertheless, the visible pivot of their choices. With the breakdown of tribalism the choice is no longer the relatively simple one of conformity with or deviance from received rules, of rules that are taken as given ; there is now a question of choices, concerning the rules themselves. The rules become problematic. The *dike,* or "the way," of the group becomes unclear to the detribalized Greeks ; they begin to ask themselves : what is *dike* ? What is the right way ? What is justice ? What rules should we follow ? What is the good ? Are there any limits to the rules we can make ? Is there a latent (or "natural") order underlying and limiting the diversity of the alternative rules by which one might be guided ?

The growing concern with problems of ethics and morality — already evident in Hesiod and culminating in Socrates — marks the emergence of men who have to improvise new rules of the game even as they are playing it. With the breakdown of the familiar and complex system of tribal tradition the Greeks face the problem of making decisions in new ways, of reconstructing the very groundwork of decision-making. In particular, they come to assign special importance to the response, the judgment, and the opinion of others as a guideline for decision-making. [pp. 78-81]

The development of law in ancient Greece moves along two parallel lines : first, toward universalism, that is, equal treatment for persons identified as belonging to the same category or class, and, second, toward individual as against family responsibility for crimes. Individual responsibility means that punishments can be inflicted only on the person doing them and that there is no imputation of the collective responsibility of the *genos.* The individual alone becomes the legal agent who, by himself, can make claims and who, by himself, is to be punished for his wrongs. There is, for example, an increasing tendency not to exile entire families (or to confiscate their property) but only the offending individuals. Justice becomes something that only the individual can seek and that only the individual can earn.

The former trend, toward universalistic law, entails the constitution of a public authority. It implies that all those belonging to the same legal category shall in principle have the same obligations toward, and the same privileges to influence, the public authority. Thus, following Cleisthenes, all males in the legal category of citizen were in principle entitled to an equal opportunity to vote and to hold office, and all were obligated to do military training and service at age eighteen.

Legal categories, as well as legal obligations and rights, are those explicitly stipulated by a public authority, and in the Greek case they are commonly regarded as those that are written down. The action of public authorities, such as the magistrates and *heliastai* (jurors), is to be based on an imputation of the individual's legal identity and the rights and obligations which are expressly stipulated for this category. All other aspects of the individual's social status — his kinship or friendship ties, his position in the system of social stratification, his relation to the judging authority — are defined as irrelevant to the legal decisions of the public authority. In its mature development, this implies that a firm distinction has been drawn between the public authority and the family system and in which public authority is not the special privilege of a leading family or families.

All persons publicly defined as belonging to the same legal category are to be treated in the same manner by the public authority and are defined as having the same relationship to it, and it is in this sense that Greek legal arrangements are increasingly universalistic. At any rate, this is the direction in which Greek legal institutions were drifting, though, in practice, the defendant in a trial often believes it legitimate to win the jury's sympathy by indicating his many services to the state or by pleading that a verdict against him would impose severe hardship on his family.

A universalistic conception of law is common to both the oligarchical and the democratic viewpoints in Greece. It is common to the Spartan no less than the Athenian, and even the Spartan conceives himself a "free man" because he lives under this system of laws. Such a view of the law is one of the shared premises pervading Hellenic culture and contributes importantly to the maintenance of social order within the *polis.*

Although both democrats and oligarchs concur on the importance of a rule of law universalistically conceived, they nonetheless differ on how they conceive universalism. In general, democrats stress an egalitarian conception of law ; they more typically want all citizens to have equal rights, and to this extent theirs is a larger and more open conception of the community. Oligarchs, in contrast, commonly seek to establish a more stratified and differentiated set of legal identities in relation to the public authority, and tend to establish property qualifications as a basis for defining different legal statuses among the citizenry. To this extent, theirs is a narrower and more closed conception of the community. Basically, oligarchs are concerned to limit the public influence of those with less property

— of the many — so that they cannot use their franchise to tax the property or impair the privileges of the upper classes.

The democratic view of legal universalism stresses the equality of all citizens and minimizes the number of legal identities that will be established. It insulates the public domain from influence by the upper classes and utilizes the legal system as a way of redressing existent social disadvantages. In the oligarchical view of legal universalism, emphasis is on maintaining the existent socio-economic differences among citizens and on developing diverse and unequal legal categories. In general the oligarch seeks to establish legal rights and categories isomorphic with established social differences. He uses the legal system to protect the established system of stratification.

To democrats, all reasonable men of mature years are seen as belonging to the same legal category and are viewed as entitled to the same relation to the public authority. Here, in the democratic interpretation of universalism, emphasis is on the similarities among men in one category. If the democrat leans toward a Dionysian oneness, the oligarch has an Apollonian impulse to separate men and to establish boundaries that kept them apart. To oligarchs, the spirit of legalism is in the making of distinctions among classes of men ; at its political root, these distinctions are aimed at separating those who vote or rule from those who do not. The oligarch's interpretation of universalism has an exclusive disposition ; governed by an elite impulse, it continually restricts the group to whom political power is available. The oligarch presses toward distinctions between those classes of men who have full political powers and those who have second-class membership in the polity.

If the democratic interpretation of universalism focuses on the similarities among all those in one category, the oligarchical interpretation focuses on the multiplicity of categories and on the differences between men who belong to different categories. In the oligarchical view, any category of public identity is legitimate, even though its members have more or less political power than those in others, so long as all those in one category are treated alike. From an oligarchical standpoint, then, a property qualification or an ethnic category is not felt to be intrinsically dissonant with legal universalism.

The oligarchical interpretation of universalism in Greece permits a compromise to be effected. Under the slogan of "equality of laws," *isonomia,* it provides a kind of partial compliance with the demands of the *demos* for distributive equality, i.e., *isomoiria ;* for now all those within one legal category are indeed to be aided equally by the public authority. At the same time, however, it formulates a system of unequal categories which reflects and safeguards the established system of social stratification.

In one sense, *isonomia* seems to mean equality before the law, which implies that whatever laws exist are to be upheld equally and impartially. In another sense, *isonomia* may also be taken to mean equality upheld through the law ; here the laws do not sanction unequal political powers but insist on and protect the equality of all within the public domain. In the oligarchic sense of *isonomia,* there is an implication that whatever social and economic differences exist should be upheld and protected equally by the laws. In the democratic sense of *isonomia,* the implication seems to be that all citizens should share equally in governing the state. If, on the one hand, the oligarch's view of *isonomia* conceals his intent to maintain social and economic inequality under the guise of allowing legal and political equality, *isonomia* is probably useful also to "liberal" democrats by allowing their demands to be distinguished from those of the "radical" democrats who seek *isomoiria.* "If this interpretation is correct," says Gregory Vlastos, "*isonomia* is the record of a defeat for the poorest section of the *demos.* It signalizes the paradox of Greek democratic society : the astonishing fact that the man who, as citizen, shares the kingly dignity, the sovereign power of the *demos,* may yet as a private individual labour under the indignity of utter destitution."[2] [pp. 308-310]

NOTES

1. Alvin W. Gouldner, *Enter Plato* (New York : Basic Books Inc., 1965), pp. 78-310.
2. Gregory Vlastos, *American Journal of Philology,* 74 (1953) : 355.

THE ETHICS OF ARISTOTLE, BOOK V[1]

Now of political justice. There are two forms of it, the natural and the conventional. It is natural when it has the same validity everywhere and is unaffected by any view we may take about the justice of it. It is conventional when there is no original reason why it should take one form rather than another and the rule it imposes is reached by an agreement, after which it holds good. It might, for instance, be agreed that the ransom of a prisoner of war shall be fixed at one pound, that the sacrifice in a certain ritual be one goat and not two sheep. Such are the rules prescribed by law in particular cases — I might instance the ritual observed in the worship of Brasidas — and details calling for special legislation. Some philosophers are of opinion that justice is conventional in all its branches, arguing that law of nature admits no variation and operates in exactly the same way everywhere — thus fire burns here and in Persia — while rules of justice keep changing before our eyes. This last statement, however, needs qualification. (It can hardly be true of justice among the gods.) But in this world of ours, while natural justice undoubtedly exists, the rules under which justice is administered are everywhere being modified. Thus a man's right hand is naturally defter than his left, yet he can always make himself as clever with the one as with the other. And it will be found that a distinction of this kind can always be made. It is not obvious what rules of justice are natural, and what are legal and conventional, in cases where variation is possible and equally possible. Yet it remains true that there is such a thing as natural, as well as conventional, justice.

Rules of justice established by convention and on grounds of convenience may be compared to standard measures. Thus the measures in general use in the wine and corn trade are not invariably the same, being larger in the wholesale and smaller in the retail business. The same is true of purely man-made laws. They are not the same everywhere, because forms of government are not the same. This does not alter the fact that there is only one natural form of government, namely, that which is best.

The rules of law and justice are in each case related to the actions performed in conformity with them as is universal to particular, for the actions are many, the law governing them only one, being universal.

We have now discussed just and unjust actions. It remains to observe that it is only when they are voluntary that they have the character of just or unjust.

When a man acts involuntarily his action cannot be called just or unjust in itself, though it may come about that circumstances make it have the effect of a just or unjust action. Therefore the injustice of an unjust, and the justice of a just, act are determined by its voluntariness. It is when the act is voluntary that the moral issue presents itself. We blame the doer and, with that, his deed becomes an unjust act. [pp. 157-159]

NOTE

1. Aristotle, *Ethics*, Book V, trans. J.A.K. Thompson (London : Penguin Books, 1955), pp. 157-159.

THE POLITICS OF ARISTOTLE, BOOK III[1]
Chapter XVI

. . .The rule of law is therefore preferable, according to the view we are stating, to that of a single citizen. In pursuance of the same view it is argued that, even if it be the better course to have individuals ruling, they should be made "law-guardians" or ministers of the law. There must, it is admitted, be offices of state ; but these it is urged, cannot be vested in one man, consistently with justice, when all are equals and peers.

Further consideration may be added in favour of the rule of law. If there are a number of cases which law seems unable to determine, it is also true that a person would be equally unable to find an answer to these cases. Law does the best it can : it trains the holders of office expressly in its own spirit, and then sets them to decide and settle those residuary issues which it cannot regulate, "as justly as in them lies." It also allows them to introduce any improvements which may seem to them, as the result of experience, to be better than the existing laws. He who commands that law should rule may thus be regarded as commanding that God and reason alone should rule ; he who commands that a man should rule adds the character of the beast. Appetite has that character ; and high spirit too, perverts the holders of office, even when they are the best of men. Law may thus be defined as "Reason free from all passion. . . ." [p. 146]

NOTE

1. Aristotle, *Politics*, Book III, trans. Ernest Barker (Oxford : Clarendon Press, 1946), p. 146.

THE LIBERAL TEMPER IN GREEK POLITICS[1]

Eric A. Havelock

In the liberal vision, all human beings, whatever their varieties of endowment or temper, were equal partners in the societies they formed. This egalitarianism did not mean that "one man was as good as another." The identity between human beings lay not in technical capacity or in moral character but in the common drive for safety, for sociality, and for pleasure. Men were in fact all "equal in the law" rather than "before the law," because law merely represented the usage of that form of society which happened to be the one that all members had collectively formed to satisfy their needs. Aristotle's text, even if unwillingly, preserves a stirring assertion of this principle :

> It is held that there inheres a principle of right between any one human being and any other who is capable of communal participation in custom-law and contract. Amity and moral right are found at a minimum in despotic relationships. They are maximized in democracies. For between beings treated as equals communal interests are also maximized. [EN. 8.11.7].

The conception of equality was not invented in the fourth century. We know from other sources (Herodotus and Thucydides) what a grip it had obtained over the Greek mind in the fifth. It responded to the Greek capacity to view reality — in this case the human reality — in mathematical terms. It had also controlled the thinking of the Elder Sophists, who rationalized the democratic process of government. Perhaps they did not even choose to argue it, simply because in their day it was accepted as self-evident. Aristotle's semantic contortions undertaken, in his *Ethics,* to construct a system of "proportional equality" show how even he never dared to dismiss the notion — which he logically should have done — but was compelled instead to keep it and render it as innocuous as possible.

Though the principle of equality was identified with that of moral right (*dikaion*) it was never linked with any inalienable rights theoretically possessed by any and every human being. Indeed, the whole doctrine of natural rights (in the plural) is modern ; and while in spirit and temper it recalled Greek liberalism, the form in which it was cast reflected the long influence of the doctrine of the independent existence of the soul of man, a doctrine which grew up outside the circle of liberalism, but was afterwards mated to liberal theory, as for example in Locke. Greek naturalism relied, instead, on a more generalized and scientific perception of the human being. He is a member of a species and between him and his fellow members the natural similitudes are therefore basic while the personal differences are incidental. The similitudes take effect in the common drive to survive, to enjoy oneself, and to express amiability. The instruments, social and technical, which make survival, enjoyment, and amiability possible are all genetically identical and procurable only by co-operation. Therefore, society exists only as the framework of supply, each and every man having an equal vested interest and at bottom a biological interest in the maintenance of its mechanism. His biological demand upon it for services is identical with that of any other man. It follows, said the liberals, that while his personal function in operating the machinery, his kind of work, may have special characteristics, there would always be others resembling him — he is never alone — and the inherent value of his contribution is identical with that of any other man's. It must be, because all contributions are evoked only by response to basic needs and these are all identical. No room here for moral hierarchies within the community membership.

The accents of Antiphon are discernible : "We all breathe the same air. . . ." His fierce naturalist rejection of classes and orders in society must have sharpened the focus of egalitarian theory in the fourth century. At the level of daily politics, it found increasing practical application. With the passage of the Athenian empire, the legal relationships of all free Greeks with each other tended to become formally identical. In municipal government, a democracy of equals was the norm. Tyrants might seize power, but classes, principalities, and powers validated by the state apparatus tended to disappear. The Athenian decree of *circa* 330 B.C. forbidding purchase of free Greeks captured in war is significant of the growing temper. Hence it is that, when Aristotle includes a working account of the legal system as it actually operated, he is forced to drop his "proportional justice" and describe a situation in which "the laws deal with men as equals" and in which law operates to "restore equality" between persons. His own report, that is to say, testifies to the growing influence of liberal temper upon administration and to his own personal distance from what was actually going on in the cities of his epoch. He, like Plato, lived mentally in a political vacuum which for him was partial and for Plato total. The vigour of their preoccupations with problems of education and of intellectual authority robbed them of any interest in or feeling for the actual democratization of the Hellenic society of their day. . . . [pp. 379-381]

Many as were the areas of conflict between Greek political liberalism and the classicism of Plato and Aristotle, no debate divided them so keenly as that which was held over the origin and character of law and justice. Even to name these names is to accord the honours to classicism. For law and justice inevitably evoke in the modern mind concepts of a majesty and authority which is imposed on common men for their good, even in their own despite, rather than of a kindly convenience invented by men to serve their own deepest impulses. In the liberal language, custom-and-law (*nomos*) remained hyphenated and tied to social usage and convention. "Law," as a set of principles independent of time and place, was a concept forbidden by the very structure of liberal thinking. Nor could "that which was right and proper" for men to claim from each other in given situations ever be moulded into the shape of an abstract and unchanging "justice." Yet so profound has been the influence of Platonism, so successfully has it seized on notions of usage and right dealing, and converted them into the shape of eternal verities above and beyond history and not to be elicited from the historical process, that it becomes almost impossible to describe the liberal doctrine of *nomos* and *dikaion* except as a reflex of its metaphysical rival.

Yet liberalism was in the field first. The beginnings of a historical critique which traced the roots of law in social usage are already perceptible in Democritus. For him, lawful action is primarily a device — perhaps a main one — invented by human beings to serve their need of security. He sees it in its grim primitive beginnings — the agreement to kill "the enemy." He is aware of its historical varieties, its growing complication, as the exceptions to killing multiply. He recognizes that it can have a positive quality in releasing human energies and benefiting the historical process — if men consent to be benefited. But this insight is not pursued far. At least, the growth of complex political partnerships involving compassion and consensus is not linked with "law."

Antiphon's impassioned attack upon "lawful usage" produced a turning point in the development of liberal theory. In effect he fastened precisely upon that one of its functions which Democritus had viewed as historically effective — its power to bring social pressure upon the members of the group. While in the thinking of Democritus this pressure was directed to prevent aggression, in Antiphon's it becomes a compulsion to commit aggression. Law for him is the legal system of a civilized state, with its apparatus of litigation and judicial process and its perils of imprisonment and fine, exile and execution, its opportunities for manoeuvring for position, its encouragement of enmity, its fundamental principle of fending off aggression by aggression. And Antiphon detests it. The court of true justice to which he appeals against it is "nature," meaning the biological hedonism and the fundamentally amiable instincts of individual men. Law, he cried, is only a compact (*syntheke*) and a convention (*homologia*) man-made, artificial, temporary, a violation of nature to whose spontaneous impulses it applies cruel and forceful pressure (*bia*).

Liberalism after him, as is clear from Aristotle's testimonies, so far from being content with this negativism, set about reconstructing a theory of custom-law which would stand up to this attack. First the historical analysis of Democritus is reaffirmed and amplified. An operative society is recognizable by the fact that it has a system of law and legal rights in which all its members "partake." This indeed, for practical purposes, is what their citizenship in the community amounts to. Any two human beings can enter into a relationship which becomes a "law, a system of rights." They create it by their association, and their essential humanity is guaranteed by their partnership in it. Law is an arrangement entered into with the initial purpose of furnishing them with "freedom from fear." It also identifies that machinery which allows mutual wrongs to be righted.

This keeps the character of law at a purely descriptive level. Its modes of regulative operation were then clarified further, in the light of those egalitarian convictions which had been exploited by the Elder Sophists. Law, negatively speaking, as a protective device is an "equalizer." For various reasons (what they are is not explained) the mutual equality of men is distributed by unequal distribution of advantage ; meaning the subtraction of a natural benefit from A and its addition to B. Law through equalization restores the original relation. Thus it is not properly designed to punish for the sake of punishment, but only to correct and to restore the previous equilibrium of nature.

But then, turning to Antiphon's assertion that law is only a non-natural compact or convention, the liberals accept this, but deleted the qualification "non-natural." For, with a more thorough historical method, they were prepared to see the growth of compact and convention as itself inherent in the historical process. Democritus had said : "Men form social shapes." And perhaps the notion of shape gave him a special interest in the city-state. Liberalism of the fourth century said : "Men form covenanted agreements," and these become society.

How firmly they applied this insight can be seen from the treatment of the example of weights and measures and of money. These illustrate social instruments, invented it is true, but dependent for their existence and substantiality on human compact and convention. If you change the agreement, the instrument dissolves back into its primal formlessness. Even so is law itself an invented instrument, wholly substantiated by human agreement and negotiation. The analogy is not accidental. Just as currency, rightly named as "current convention" (*nomisma*), maximizes association through the acceleration of exchange, so does all lawful convention (*nomos*). The degrees and intensities of "law" are like those of amity. Both increase with the increasing socialization of relationships. Again, a currency when stored becomes a "guarantor" of future purchase that future need will be met. Even so, law is our general "guarantor" that our rights will be always met. Its validity, therefore, for us lies in its capacity of temporal extension into the future. Society rests not merely on topographical contiguity but on expectation of future stability.

Yet this stability must never be over-played, till it becomes a monolithic and unchanging set of principles. Since law is human convention historically applied, there is no one unique law or set of laws, but only an unending series of arrangements and integrations. These must retain flexibility, for they have work to do as yet unforeseen, and their shapes may change as the needs of men require. Positive written law, therefore, as increasingly made by vote and decree in the fourth century, takes on a new historical importance, as against the unwritten law of conservative custom and past tradition. Plato and Aristotle, with the unerring instinct of metaphysical conservatives, gave their preferred allegiance to unwritten law.

Lastly, when law is named a "compact" (*syntheke*) and a common agreement (*homologia*) this naming is true to its nature, for law is really valid only as it is an emanation from the common communication held between equal and similar human beings. There can, strictly speaking, be no law that is not democratic law. For it represents that coincidence of real interest and that joining of natural amity which emerge in joint thinking, joint opinion, and political consensus, the last stage of which is that decision which implements, and so adds to, the legal pattern.

Yet are all human conventions and all civic law formed in accordance with this process ? The liberals must have had an answer to this — some critical weapon by which to disentangle apparent law from true. What they had to say here is largely hidden from us. Yet there is a hint. A crucial passage of the *Politics* calls attention to that custom-law which allowed the victors in war to enslave free men. If Aristotle's own mind had not been so ambiguous on this point, the report of how the liberals met the problem might have come through more clearly. But it can be inferred how they would have met it. Behind all laws of men stands the rule of "natural right" (*dikaion*) or natural justice. This it is which supplies the criterion of their validity. How then, if they should violate this *dikaion*, can they be true "conventions" of human beings, true "agreements" ? We suspect the liberals said that they were not, and that they failed of being true compacts because they were maintained only by superior pressure applied by one party to another. Such would be the kind of spurious usage which recognizes slavery itself, as well as hierarchies of privilege, wealth, and power.

This would mean that the positive and historical methodology of the liberals led them into a stringent social criticism of some aspects of contemporary society. They could never reject society as Antiphon did. The great meaning of their reassertion of the historical logic of law is that they did not turn away into a theoretic Utopia of saints. But they could not have escaped some necessity of passing moral judgment upon slavery and war. And it is to be expected that precisely for this reason did the classic thinkers find liberalism so disagreeable that it had to be ignored.

We say "moral judgment," even though their method was so descriptive, because they too, like Plato and Aristotle, had their standards of natural and true justice. But while classic philosophy identified these standards with the disciplined social guidance exercised by the superior over the inferior, liberalism named them simply the rule of "amity." Now, this is not just an inspirational statement. The emotion of amity and the behaviour pattern we call justice are both processes, not fixed quantities : they have evolved in parallel, as historical mechanisms, psychological and social which mark the growth of the "civility" of our race. The most part of justice is held to be amity : "indeed amity is enough without justice, but what use justice without amity ?" And again : "As the integration of society increases, so do justice and amity." And again : "When one is maximized, so is the other."

This kind of formula is not aspirational in the sense that it seeks to find the laws of human decency written in the geometry of the heavens. But is it any the less grandiose for being woven out of those uncounted years of human invention which came slowly to terms with elemental swamp and primeval forest in order to prepare a place of habitation, and a society of men, which would be gracious and kindly and good ? [pp. 399-403]

NOTE

1. Eric A. Havelock, *The Liberal Temper in Greek Politics* (London : Jonathan Cape, 1957), pp. 379-403.

WOMEN IN CLASSICAL ANTIQUITY[1]

Sarah B. Pomeroy

In the sixth century B.C. the Athenian lawgiver Solon institutionalized the distinction between good women and whores. He abolished all forms of self-sale and sale of children into slavery except one : the right of the male guardian to sell an unmarried woman who had lost her virginity. As part of his extensive legislation covering many aspects of Athenian life, Solon regulated the walks, the feasts, the mourning, the trousseaux, and the food and drink of citizen women. He also established state-owned brothels staffed by slaves, and made Athens attractive to foreigners who wanted to make money, including craftsmen, merchants, and prostitutes. In the Classical period, Solon's laws continued to exert tremendous influence over the lives of Athenian women. [p. 57]

As a logical consequence of the woman's duty to Athens, marriage and motherhood were considered the primary goals of every female citizen. The death of a young girl often elicited lamentations specifically over her failure to fulfill her intended role as a wife. Epitaphs express this feeling, and some vases of the shape used to transport water for a prenuptial bath mark the graves of girls who died unwed. The dead maiden is portrayed dressed as a bride on these memorial *loutrophoroi* vases.

Citizen women were perpetually under the guardianship of a man, usually the father or, if he were dead, the male next-of-kin. Upon marriage a woman passed into the guardianship of her husband in most matters, with the important limitation that her father, or whoever else had given her in marriage, retained the right to dissolve the marriage. If the husband predeceased the wife, the guardianship of her dowry and perhaps of her person passed to her sons if they were of age, or to their guardians. If a widow had no children, she would return to the power of her original guardian or his heirs. A widow was protected by the archon, who could prosecute offenders in her behalf.

Responsible fathers in Classical Athens did not raise female babies unless they foresaw a proper marriage for them at maturity. The initial consideration of the father was financial. Custom dictated that a dowry commensurate with the father's economic status be provided for a woman's maintenance. Vase paintings representing women seated on clothing chests allude to the dowries possessed by brides. A father would not raise more girls than he could provide with dowries, and larger dowries tended to attract wealthier and more desirable suitors. In cases where the father had not shown proper foresight or had suffered reverses, dowries were contributed from other sources. The wealthy frequently dowered their poorer relatives. We are told without further explanation that the law required that dowries be provided for poor girls of even passably attractive appearance, and a few times Athens provided dowries for daughters of men who had served the state. Lack of a dowry gave a hostile orator a chance to assert that no legal marriage had taken place, or gave self-righteous husbands an opportunity to boast that they had been compassionate enough to marry without the promise of a dowry....

A betrothal was contracted between the guardian of the bride and the groom or, if the latter was still young, the guardian of the groom. Marriage arrangements were made by men on the basis of economic and political considerations, and girls were always obliged to marry the men their male relatives selected for them. The bride and groom may have never set eyes upon one another, but there were many marriages between first cousins or other relatives, who presumably would have seen each other at such family ceremonies as funerals. Marriage to relatives was attractive especially among the wealthier families in democratic Athens, when inroads were constantly made against the fortunes of the wealthy : such marriages provided a way of consolidating the resources of the family, facilitated agreement between parties who knew and trusted each other, gave relatives preferential access to brides, and forestalled enforcement of the law of the epiklerate.

The purpose of marriage was procreation, within the limits of the economic resources of the family. Before the groom joined her on their wedding day, the bride ate a fruit with many seeds, symbolizing fertility. The birth of a child, especially a son, was considered a fulfillment of the goal of the marriage.

A girl was ideally first married at fourteen to a man of about thirty. The necessity that the bride be a virgin, coupled with the ancient belief that young girls were lustful, made an early marriage desirable. The husband who married at thirty could well be dead at forty-five, having begotten two or three children within the marriage and leaving his wife a candidate for remarriage. Late marriage of men in Athens can be attributed to their duty to serve as soldiers for ten years, but it appears also to have been an adaptation to the low proportion of females in the population. A young widow could serve as wife in a number of serial marriages. Since marriage was the preferable condition for women, and men were protective of their women, a dying husband, like a divorcing husband, might arrange a future marriage for his wife.

Divorce was easily attainable, either by mutual consent or through action on behalf of either one of the spouses, and there was no stigma attached. When the divorce was initiated by the husband, he was required merely to send the wife from his house. When the wife wished a divorce, she needed the intercession of her father or some other male citizen to bring the case before the archon. There are only three cases known from the Classical period where an Athenian divorce proceeded from the wife's side. Two are from the fourth century, and were negotiated exclusively among men. The third case was remarkable in that a woman attempted to obtain a divorce on her own initiative. During the stress of the Peloponnesian War, Hipparete attempted to divorce Alcibiades. She left her husband's house and moved in with her brother Callias. She then set off to register her divorce with the archon, evidently unaccompanied by her brother, for at the tribunal she was seized by Alcibiades and forcibly carried back to his house.

Since children were produced to perpetuate the father's house, they were the property of their father, and remained in his house when marriages were dissolved through death and probably also in cases of divorce. The divorcée or widow was thus entirely free to remarry and to bear children to a new husband. [pp. 62-65]

Socrates' blunt dismissal of his wife Xanthippe from his deathbed and his desire to die among his male companions is a dramatic, if exaggerated, indication of the emotional gulf between husband and wife. The distance between husbands and wives extended to other spheres. Athenian men and women lived separate lives, and most of our information is about men's lives. It is almost easier to describe the activities of men and then simply say women did not do most of these things.

The separation of the sexes was spatially emphasized. While men spent most of their day in public areas such as the marketplace and the gymnasium, respectable women remained at home. In contrast to the admired public buildings, mostly frequented by men, the residential quarters of Classical Athens were dark, squalid, and unsanitary.

Women stayed home not only because their work did not allow them much chance to get out but because of the influence of public opinion. Many families were likely to own at least one female slave, but even a woman with slaves was tied down by the demands of her household, husband, and infants.... Wealthier women were most likely to stay home and send their slaves on errands. But poor women, lacking slaves, could not be kept in seclusion, and in fact women found pleasure in the company of other women, for they gossiped while fetching water, washing clothes, and borrowing utensils....

The separation of the sexes was expressed in private architecture by the provision of separate quarters for men and women. Women usually inhabited the more remote rooms, away from the street and from the public areas of the house. If the house had two stories, the wife along with female slaves lived upstairs. The sexes were separated to restrain the household slaves from breeding without the master's permission. [pp. 79-80]

The sexual behaviour of citizen women was regulated by laws — mostly those attributed to Solon, who was himself a homosexual. The guardian of an unmarried woman caught *in flagrante delicto* had the right to sell her into slavery. I do not know of any case where this sale actually occurred, whether because the severity of the penalty was a deterrent, or because the father was reluctant to make the scandal in his family public. Since the aim of marriage between citizens was the production of legitimate children, adultery was a public offense because it could result in the introduction of a child unrelated to the husband — and possibly the offspring of a non-Athenian — into the husband's house and kinship-group cults and onto the rolls of Athenian citizens. Both parties were severely punished, but, despite the penalties, cases of adultery are recorded....

Interestingly, Athenian law governing sexual behavior was not limited to what one must not do, but also concerned itself with what one should do. Thus the husband of an heiress was to consort with her three times a month. While this suggests that the main purpose of their union was to produce an heir, Plutarch adds another dimension to the relationship when he says that any husband ought to show affection to a good wife three times a month because the result will be a reduction in marital tensions. [pp. 86-87]

NOTE

1. Sarah B. Pomeroy, *Goddesses, Whores, Wives and Slaves : Women in Classical Antiquity* (New York : Schocken Books, 1975), pp. 57-87.

THE MYTH OF THE STATE[1]

Ernst Cassirer

Yet all these discriminations between free men and slaves, between Greeks and barbarians, were called into question and finally swept away by the development of Greek ethical thought. In the system of Stoicism there arose a new intellectual and moral force. From a merely theoretical point of view Stoicism has little claim to originality. In their physics, logic, and dialectic the Stoics borrowed much of their theories from other sources. Their philosophy seems to be a mere eclecticism. They select doctrines from Heraclitus, Plato, and Aristotle. But in their general conception of man and his place in the universe the Stoic philosophers did open a new way. They introduced a principle that proved to be the turning point in the history of ethical, political, and religious thought. To the Platonic and Aristotelian ideal of justice there was added an entirely new conception : the conception of the *fundamental equality of man.*

The principal ethical demand of the Stoics was "to live in accordance with nature." But the "law of nature" to which they appeal is a moral not a physical law. Of course the Stoics never denied that, in a physical sense, there are innumerable differences between men ; differences of birth, rank, temperament, intellectual talents. But from an ethical point of view all these differences are declared to be of no account. They are a matter of indifference because they do not affect the form of human life. What matters alone, what determines a man's personality, are not the things themselves but his judgment about things. These judgments are not bound to any conventional standards. They depend upon a free act which creates a world of its own. The Stoics draw a sharp line between what is necessary and what is accidental in human nature. Only those things are necessary that regard the "essence," that is to say, the moral value of man. Whatever depends on external circumstances, on conditions that are not in our own power, is to be left out ; it does not count.

To obliterate or minimize the most important differences between men seems, at first sight, to be only a utopian thought, a philosopher's dream. But we must not forget that such thoughts were expressed by Marcus Aurelius, who was not only a philosophical thinker but also one of the great statesmen of antiquity and ruler of the Roman Empire. That there ever was a time in which such a connection was possible is one of the most remarkable facts in the history of human civilization.

Stoicism could not have fulfilled its historical mission without that clear alliance between philosophic and political thought. The conquest of Roman public life by the Stoic doctrines began very early. We can trace it back to the flowering season of the Roman republic. Many of the great political leaders were then imbued with Stoic thoughts.... If we study the classical works of Greek ethics, for instance Aristotle's *Nicomachean Ethics,* we find there a clear and systematic analysis of the different virtues, of magnanimity, temperance, justice, courage, and liberality (*humanitas*). Even the term seems to be missing from the Greek language and literature. The ideal of *humanitas* was first formed in Rome ; and it was especially the aristocratic circle of the younger Scipio that gave its firm place in Roman culture. *Humanitas* was no vague concept. It had a definite meaning, and it became a formative power in private and public life in Rome. It meant not only a moral but also an aesthetic ideal ; it was the demand for a certain type of life that had to prove its influence in the whole of man's life, in his moral conduct as well as in his language, his literary style, and his taste. Through later writers such as Cicero and Seneca this ideal of *humanitas* became firmly established in Roman philosophy and Latin literature.

This coalescence of political and philosophic thought was a fact of paramount importance. It was calculated to change the whole conception of social life. In its beginning, Stoicism was not especially concerned with social problems. Most of the Stoic thinkers were determined individualists. If the wise man has to free himself from all outward bonds, he must begin with emancipating himself from all social conventions and obligations. How could the Stoic philosopher maintain his independence of mind, his self-reliance, his firm and imperturbable judgment in the turmoil of political passions and in the arena of political struggles ? But that was not the manner in which the Roman writers, men like Cicero, Seneca, or Marcus Aurelius, understood and interpreted the Stoic ideal. They admitted no cleft between the individual and the political sphere. For they were convinced that reality taken as a whole, physical reality as well as moral life, was one great "republic." This republic is the same for all nations, the same for gods and men. All rational beings are members of the same commonwealth. "*Universus hic mundus,*" said Cicero, "*una civitas communis deorum atque hominum existimanda est.*" He who lives in harmony with himself, with his "demon," says Marcus Aurelius, lives in harmony with the universe. The personal and the universal order are but different manifestations of a common underlying principle.

That this view was pregnant with the most important practical consequences becomes evident in the treatment of the problem of slavery. No Stoic writer could accept the saying of Aristotle that there are slaves "by nature." "Nature" means ethical freedom, not social bondage. It is not nature but fortune that makes a man a slave. "It is a mistake," says Seneca, "to imagine that slavery pervades a man's whole being ; the better part of him is exempt from it : the body indeed is subjected and in the power of a master, but the mind is independent and indeed is so free and wild that it cannot be restrained even by this prison of the body, wherein it is confined." The mind remains free, independent, *sui juris.* The history of Stoic thought confirms and elucidates this maxim. Of the great Stoic thinkers one, Marcus Aurelius, was the Emperor of Rome, whereas another, Epictetus, was a slave....

The Stoic maxim of the fundamental equality of men was generally and easily accepted and it became one of the cardinal points of the medieval theory. It was not only taught by the Christian Fathers ; it was also established and confirmed by the Roman Jurists of the *Digests* and *Institutes.* On this point there was scarcely any disagreement between the various trends of thought and the philosophic schools of the Middle Ages. All of them could cooperate with each other in a common task. It was a general maxim of medieval theology and jurisprudence that according to "nature" and in the original order of things all men are free and equal.... The Stoic conception that all men are free because they are all endowed with the same reason found its theological interpretation and justification in the added dictum that this very reason is the image of God. Augustine declared in the *City of God* that God had made man the master of the animals but had given him no power over other human souls. Every attempt to usurp such a power would be an intolerable arrogance. Here as well as in Stoic thought every soul is declared to be *sui juris*; it cannot lose or renounce its original freedom.

It follows that the authority of no political power can ever be absolute. It is always bound to the laws of justice. These laws are irrevocable and inviolable because they express the divine order itself, the will of the supreme lawgiver. [pp. 100-104]

NOTE

1. Ernst Cassirer, *The Myth of the State* (New Haven : Yale University Press, 1946), pp. 100-104.

ROMAN STOICISM[1]

E. Vernon Arnold

Stoic ethics are not based on the needs of the individual, but on the demands of the supreme law. "If there is a universe, then there is a universal law, bidding us to do this and refrain from that." "If there are gods, there is virtue." . . . Zeno's earliest work was "On the State," and it is an attempt to show how a state can be ordered by wise laws. The whole theory of the *logos* leads up to the same point. The same eternal wisdom through which the primal stuff took shape is, in another function, the right rule which commands and forbids. Right rule and common law are terms of identical meaning, by which a standard of supreme authority is set up; state law and conventional morality, though always of narrower range, and often of inferior purity, are yet a reflection of universal law. The moral law must therefore first be studied in its bearings on man as a political and social animal.

The root-principle of the Stoic state is that it is worldwide, a cosmopolis. This title arose from the practice, attributed to Socrates and Diogenes (as well as others), of replying to the current question, "Of what city are you ?" by the answer, "Of the universe." We must therefore regard ourselves as members not of a clan or city, but of a worldwide society. In this society all distinctions of race, caste, and class are to be subordinated to the sense of kinship and brotherhood. This principle is equally opposed to the nationalist prejudices which rank Hellene above barbarian, to philosophical theories (such as that of Aristotle) which distinguish intelligent peoples fitted by nature to rule and others only fitted to obey and to ideal states (such as that of Plato) in which a ruling class is to be developed by artifice and schooling. Only the brute animals are excluded from this community, for they are not possessed of reason; they have therefore no rights, but exist for the service of men. All human beings are capable of attaining to virtue, and as such are natural-born citizens of the cosmopolis. Loyalty to this state, however, in no wise hinders a due loyalty to existing states which may be regarded as partial realizations of it. Socrates submitted to the laws of Athens even when they bade him die; Zeno and Cleanthes declined the citizenship of that famous city, lest they should be thought to hold cheap the places of their birth; and amongst the Romans Seneca frequently insists that every man is born into two communities, the cosmopolis and his native city.

The world-state is not held together either by force or by state-craft, but by goodwill. We must be able to say, "Love is god there, and is a helpmate to make the city secure." This feeling of love and friendship grows up naturally between wise men, because they partake in the reason of the universe; so that we may equally well say that the bond of the state is the *logos* (*ratio atque oratio*). Since reason and the universal law exist in the community from the beginning, law does not need to be created; it exists of itself, and by natural growth. The writing down of laws is only a stage in their development.

We must therefore maintain that the true Stoic state, whether it be called monarchy or democracy, calls for a revolt against nationalism, antiquity, custom, pride, and prejudice; and a new construction based upon universal reason and individual liberty. For the realization of this state it is first necessary to build up the individual, to fill his mind with the conception of reason and love, to strengthen his will to a true independence: for it is not buying or selling that makes the slave, but the will within. All are in truth slaves except the wise man; for freedom is the power of directing one's own actions. Here then we pass from the community to the individual, from politics to ethics in the narrower sense.... [pp. 273-281]

Although up to this point it has been our main purpose to set forth the doctrines of Stoicism, we have seen incidentally that these came to exercise a wide influence in Roman society, and that the later teachers are far less occupied in the attainment of truth than in the right guidance of disciples who lean upon them. In the present chapter we propose to describe more particularly the practical influence of Stoicism. Our information, whether drawn from history or from poetry, refers generally to the upper classes of Roman society; as to the influence of the sect amongst the poor we have no sufficient record. But although it is very generally held that the Stoics made no effort to reach the working classes of Rome, or met with no success in that direction, the evidence points rather to an opposite conclusion, at any rate as regards all that development of the system which was coloured by Cynicism, the philosophy of the poor. Our actual records are therefore rather of the nature of side-lights upon the system; the main stream of Stoic influence may well have flowed in courses with which we are imperfectly acquainted, and its workings may perhaps come to light first in a period of history which lies beyond our immediate scope.... [p. 380]

From the "humane" movement sprang the Gracchan reforms, which all alike aimed at deposing from power the class to which the reformers by birth belonged. To the temper of mind which made such a desire possible Stoic doctrine had largely contributed. The Greeks had taught their Roman pupils to see in the nascent Roman empire, bearing the watchword of the "majesty of the Roman name" (*maiestas nominis Romani*), at least an approximation to the ideal cosmopolis: and many Romans so far responded to this suggestion as to be not unfriendly towards plans for extending their citizenship and equalizing the privileges of those who enjoyed it.

Scaevola . . . a Stoic. . . is regarded as the father of Roman law, for he was the first to codify it, which he did in eighteen volumes. He also wrote a special work on definitions, which no doubt reflected the interest which the Stoics took in this part of logic.

It seems beyond dispute that the systematic study of law, which developed in later centuries into the science of Roman jurisprudence, and as such has exercised a weighty influence on the development of Western civilization, had its beginnings amongst a group of men profoundly influenced by Stoic teaching. It does not therefore follow that the fundamental ideas expressed by such terms as *ius gentium, lex naturae* are exclusively Stoic in origin. The former phrase appears to have been in common use at this time to indicate the laws generally in force amongst the peoples that surrounded Rome ; the latter is a philosophical term derived from the Greek, denoting an ideal law which ought to exist amongst men everywhere. The principle of obedience to nature is not peculiar to the Stoic philosophy, but belongs to the common substratum of all philosophical thought. It does however seem to be the case that the Stoic theory of the "common law" was in fact the stimulus which enabled the Romans to transform their system of "rights," gradually throwing over all that was of the nature of mechanical routine or caste privilege, and harmonizing contradictions by the principle of fairness. The successor of Scaevola was C. Aquilius Gallus, praetor in 66 B.C. with Cicero, of whom it is specially noted that he guided his exposition of law by the principle of equity ; and after him S. Sulpicius Rufus, the contemporary and intimate friend of Cicero. We do not know that he was a Stoic, but he was a student of dialectic under L. Lucilius Balbus, who as well as his brother belonged to this school ; and he followed Stoic principles in studying oratory just enough to make his exposition clear. He was the acknowledged head of his profession, and compiled 180 books on law. [pp. 382-385]

NOTE

1. E. Vernon Arnold, *Roman Stoicism* (Oxford : Clarendon Press, 1936), pp. 273-385.

DISCOURSES OF EPICTETUS[1]

Book 1, Chapter XI

"Well, do you think you were right to do it ?"

"It was natural," he said.

"Nay," said the master, "only convince me that it was natural, and I will convince you that everything that is natural is right." [p. 243]

Book II, Chapter VIII

God is beneficent, but the good also is beneficent. It is natural therefore that the true nature of the good should be in the same region as the true nature of God. What then is the nature of God ? Is it flesh ? God forbid. Land ? God forbid. Fame ? God forbid. It is intelligence, knowledge, right reason. In these then and nowhere else seek the true nature of the good. Do you look for it in a plant ? No. Or in an irrational creature ? No. If then you seek it in what is rational why do you seek it elsewhere than in what distinguishes it from irrational things ? Plants have not the faculty of dealing with impressions ; therefore you do not predicate "good" of them.

The good then demands power to deal with impressions. Is that all it demands ? If that be all, you must say that other animals also are capable of good and of happiness and unhappiness. But you do not say so and you are right, for whatever power they may have to deal with impressions, they have not the power to understand how they do so, and with good reason, for they are subservient to others, and are not of primary importance. [p. 294]

MARCUS AURELIUS, MEDITATIONS[1]

Book II : 9

This thou must always bear in mind, what is the nature of the whole, and what is my nature, and how this is related to that, and what kind of a part it is of what kind of a whole ; and that there is no one who hinders thou from always doing and saying the things which are according to the nature of which you are a part. [p. 498]

Book V:3

Judge every word and deed which are according to nature to be fit for thee ; and do not be diverted by the blame which follows from any people nor by their words but, if a thing is good to be done or said, do not consider it unworthy of thee. For those persons have their peculiar leading principle and follow their peculiar movement ; do not regard these things, but go straight on, following thy own nature and the common nature ; and the way of both is one. [p. 517]

Book V:14

Reason and the reasoning art are powers which are sufficient for themselves and for their own works. They move then from a first principle which is their own, and they make their way to the end which is proposed to them ; and this is the reason why such acts are named *catorthoseis* or "right acts," which signifies that they proceed by the right road. [p. 521]

Book VII : 55, 56

Do not look around thee to discover other men's ruling principles, but look straight to this, to what nature leads thee, both the universal nature through the things which happen to thee, and thy own nature through the acts which must be done by thee. But every being ought to do that which is according to its constitution ; and all other things have been constituted for the sake of rational beings, just as among irrational things the inferior for the sake of the superior, but the rational for the sake of one another.

The prime principle then in man's constitution is the social. And the second is not to yield to the persuasions of the body, for it is the peculiar office of the rational and intelligent motion to circumscribe itself, and never to be overpowered either by the motion of the senses or of the appetites, for both are animal ; but the intelligent motion claims superiority and does not permit itself to be overpowered by the others. And with good reason, for it is formed by nature to use all of them. The third thing in the rational constitution is freedom from error and from deception. Let then the ruling principle holding fast to these things go straight on, and it has what is its own.

Consider thyself to be dead, and to have completed thy life up to the present time; and live according to nature the remainder which is allowed thee. [pp. 540-541]

Book VIII:7

Every nature is contented with itself when it goes on its way well; and a rational nature goes on its way well when in its thoughts it assents to nothing false or uncertain, and when it directs its movements to social acts only, and when it confines its desires and aversions to the things which are in its power, and when it is satisfied with everything that is assigned to it by the common nature. For of this common nature every particular nature is a part, as the nature of a leaf is a part of the nature of a plant; except that in the plant the nature of the leaf is part of a nature which has not perception or reason, and is subject to be impeded; but the nature of man is part of a nature which is not subject to impediments, and is intelligent and just, since it gives to everything in equal portions and according to its worth, times, substance, cause, activity, and incident. But examine, not to discover that any one thing compared with any other single thing is equal in all respects, but by taking all the parts together of one thing and comparing them with all the parts together of another. [p. 545]

Book VIII:13

Constantly and, if it be possible, on the occasion of every impression on the soul, apply to it the principles of physic, of ethic and of dialectic. [p. 546]

Book IX:1

He who acts unjustly acts impiously. For since the universal nature has made rational animals for the sake of one another to help one another according to their desserts, but in no way to injure one another, he who transgresses her will is clearly guilty of impiety toward the highest divinity. And he too who lies is guilty of impiety to the same divinity: for the universal nature is the nature of things that are; and things that are have a relation to all things that come into existence. And further, this universal nature is named truth, and is the prime cause of all things that are true. He then who lies intentionally is guilty of impiety inasmuch as he acts unjustly by deceiving; and he also who lies unintentionally, inasmuch as he is at variance with the universal nature, and inasmuch as he disturbs the order by fighting against the nature of the world; for he fights against it who is moved of himself to that which is contrary to truth, for he had received powers from nature through the neglect of which he is not able now to distinguish falsehood from truth. And indeed he who pursues pleasure as good, and avoids pain as evil, is guilty of impiety. For of necessity such a man must often find fault with the universal nature, alleging that it assigns things to the bad and the good contrary to their desserts, because frequently the bad are in the enjoyment of pleasure and possess the things which procure pleasure, but the good have pain for their share and the things which cause pain. And further, he who is afraid of pain will sometimes also be afraid of some of the things which will happen in the world, and even this is impiety. And he who pursues pleasure will not abstain from injustice, and this is plainly impiety. Now with respect to the things toward which the universal nature is equally affected — for it would not have made both, unless it was equally affected toward both — toward these they who wish to follow nature should be of the same mind with it, and equally affected. With respect to pain, then, and pleasure, or death and life, or honour and dishonour, which the universal nature employs equally, whoever is not equally affected is manifestly acting impiously. And I say that the universal nature employs them equally, instead of saying that they happen alike to those who are produced in continuous series and to those who come after them by virtue of a certain original movement of Providence, according to which it moved from a certain beginning to this ordering of things, having conceived certain principles of the things which were to be, and having determined powers productive of beings and of changes and of such like successions. [p. 553]

Book X:2

Observe what your nature requires, so far as you are governed by nature only : then do it and accept it, if your nature, so far as you are a living being, shall not be made worse by it. And next you must observe what your nature requires so far as you are a living being. And all this you may allow yourself, if your nature, so far as you are a rational animal, shall not be made worse by it. But the rational animal is consequently also a social animal. Use these rules, then, and trouble yourself about nothing else. [p. 562]

Book X:6

Whether the universe is atoms or a system, let this first be established : I am part of the whole which is governed by nature ; next, I am in a manner intimately related to the parts which are of the same kind with myself. For remembering this, inasmuch as I am a part, I shall be discontented with none of the things which are assigned to me out of the whole ; for nothing is injurious to the part, if it is for the advantage of the whole. For the whole contains nothing which is not for its advantage ; and all natures indeed have this common principle, but the nature of the universe has this principle besides, that it cannot be compelled even by any external cause to generate anything harmful to itself. By remembering, then, that I am a part of such a whole, I shall be content with everything that happens. And inasmuch as I am in a manner intimately related to the parts which are of the same kind with myself, I shall do nothing unsocial, but I shall rather direct myself to the things which are of the same kind with myself, and I shall turn all my efforts to the common interest, and divert them from the contrary. Now, if these things are done so, life must flow on happily, just as you may observe that the life of a citizen is happy, who continues a course of action which is advantageous to his fellow citizens, and is content with whatever the state may assign to him. [p. 563]

NOTE

1. Whitney Oates, ed., "Discourses of Epictetus" and "Marcus Aurelius, Meditations," in *The Stoic and Epicurean Philosophers* (New York : Random House, 1940), pp. 243-294 ; 498-563.

LEGAL CODE AND PROCEDURE[1]

Kathleen Freeman

The legal code of Athens, very complicated and exact in historical times, had its origin in a remote past of custom and tradition. In the days of monarchy, the king was supreme judge in peace and war ; but when the government passed from the hands of a hereditary monarchy into those of the nobles, the king's power of jurisdiction passed with all his other powers to the supreme council of state, which met on the low rocky hill called the Areopagus. Some of the powers of jurisdiction were vested in magistrates, who all had to be of the noble class ; and the law they administered was the old law of custom (the Greek word for "law," *nomos,* means "custom") which had grown up with the community and had been altered and added to as circumstances required, but which had never been fixed or codified or written down or even published. Knowledge of it was believed to belong by divine dispensation first to the king, and then to the aristocracy of birth, the heads of the chief families. Such a law, devised and administered by the ruling class, was bound to be one-sided ; and when in addition the common people did not know exactly what the laws were except by tradition and observation, there was bound to be great hardship and injustice.

In the seventh century B.C., economic distress in Athens and the neighbourhood brought popular discontent to a climax. A great increase in commerce brought great prosperity to the already wealthy and powerful, and greater poverty to the poor. The inequality between the classes became glaring ; and in particular it was seen how severely the administration of the law bore upon the common people. Their discontent gave an ambitious adventurer his chance. In 630 B.C. a nobleman named Cylon, who had married the daughter of a neighbouring ruler, endeavoured to establish himself as dictator in Athens. He actually seized the Acropolis with the help of foreign troops sent by his father-in-law ; but the time was not ripe. The people, especially the farmers, would not rise against the governing class, and the attempt was a failure. Cylon himself escaped ; but his supporters were starved out and eventually slaughtered in cold blood by the authorities. However, the nobles were alarmed ; and in 621 B.C. they made a great concession : they appointed one of their own class to draw up for the first time a written code of the existing law.

This was the famous code of Dracon. The Athenians had a saying that the laws of Dracon were written not in ink but in blood. It was found that the penalty for almost all offences was death, no distinction being made between those who stole fruit or vegetables, and those who robbed a temple or murdered a man. The adjective "Draconian" is still used of harsh and cruel laws ; but this is unfair to Dracon. He did not invent these laws ; he merely collected and recorded the current practice. However, once the laws were written down, it could no longer be denied how harsh they were, and reform could not long be delayed.

The man chosen for the work of revision was Solon, one of the greatest law-givers of all times. He was appointed in 594 B.C., as chief magistrate with extraordinary powers, for one year only, and was asked to reform the whole constitution of Athens, including the administration of justice and the legal code. He was a man of aristocratic family, who had travelled and had also engaged in commerce ; by great good fortune he was the very man they needed, for he was born with the principle of justice in his soul. He carried out his work with commendable fairness and thoroughness, and fully earned the title of mediator which was bestowed upon him. His new constitution, intended to give a fair share of power to all classes, did not survive and did not end class warfare ; but he cured the worst of the people's troubles by abolishing all debts contracted on the security of personal freedom and so saving many from enslavement and exile ; he also restored all mortgaged land. His greatest and most enduring gift to the Athenian people was his new legal code and new law courts. This was the system, with certain necessary changes, which was used throughout the whole of the three succeeding centuries ; under it Athens grew to be an imperial power, and the Romans themselves, when compiling their own legal code, the Twelve Tables, sent a commission to Athens in 454 B.C. to examine the laws of Solon.... [pp. 14-15]

Apart from homicide and allied causes, the bulk of the work of jurisdiction came before the popular jury-courts. Solon was the first to institute a jury-court, called the Heliaea ; this was open to all citizens, and was chosen by lot from the citizen body. He intended it to hear appeals against the sentences pronounced by magistrates ; but it very rapidly developed into the supreme judicial power in the state ; and all cases except those of bloodshed and arson came before it. By the time that our speeches were delivered — two centuries later, more or less — the immense panel of jurymen (six thousand) was divided into bodies of different sizes according to the particular cases with which they had to deal. Their size is one of the most remarkable features about them : an Athenian jury for an important case would number five hundred and one members, and could be as many as two thousand. In the fifth and fourth centuries before Christ, they were not only chosen by lot from the whole body of adult male citizens : they were paid. Their verdict was given by a majority vote. It was usual to arrange that an odd number should be present ; but if by chance the voting was equal, the defendant was acquitted. The verdict of the jury's vote was final : there was no appeal from it to a higher court. A magistrate or some official presided ; but he had no power to direct the jury or to pronounce judgment. In most cases the penalty was prescribed by law ; but if there was any choice of alternatives, the prosecution could propose one penalty, and the defendant another ; the result was again decided by taking vote of the jury. This happened in the trial of Socrates. After he had been voted guilty, the question of the penalty arose. The prosecution proposed death. Socrates, when asked for his suggestion, amazed the jury, who were used to appeals for mercy, by saying that his true reward would be maintenance in the city hall, because he was a benefactor and a poor man who needed leisure to carry on his work ; but if they did not see eye to eye with him, he did not mind paying a small sum of money, which, as he could not afford it himself, would be contributed by his friends. The jury voted for the death penalty ; and so with a few final words to them on the nature of death and the reasons why men should not fear it, Socrates went his way, remarking : "Which of us, you or I, is going to the better fate, is unknown to all except God."

The Athenian jury-court, therefore, owing to its composition, its size, and its manner of functioning, was not, like our own jury, a handful of men ignorant of the law presided over by an expert, addressed by experts, and with its powers strictly circumscribed. To come before it was like addressing a public meeting ; and feeling very often ran high. In the speeches that have come down to us it is common to find the litigant appealing to the jury "not to raise a din," or "not to shout me down." The art of playing on the jury's feelings of pity and vanity by every possible means was taught in the schools of rhetoric. It was customary for defendants to bring their small children into court and to shed tears ; the best people considered this to be shameful and undignified, but it was often done, so that it must have been effective. The jurymen took a solemn oath, said to have been instituted by Solon, that they would hear both sides impartially ; but the atmosphere did not conduce to judicial calm ; and it was also possible to use bribery. This abuse reached such proportions that at the end of the fifth century B.C. elaborate arrangements were made to prevent jurors from knowing to which court they would be allotted on any given day until just before the trial opened. Intimidation was also practised ; and the new arrangements included a complicated scheme for ensuring the secrecy of the ballot, which was done by placing pebbles or other tokens into urns. The ordinary courts met in buildings which were mostly in or near the Agora or market place. The buildings have perished without leaving a trace, but some of the names of the courts have come down to us : the middle court, the greater court, the red court, the green court, and others. The atmosphere of the Areopagus Court was calmer and more dignified than that of the ordinary courts, and the oath its members swore was more solemn, invoking destruction on them and theirs if they did not judge fairly.

The legal code administered in all courts was the code of Solon, together with such alterations and additions as time had made necessary and the supreme Assembly of the People decreed. The Athenians were chary of altering their laws ; it had been one of Solon's principles that the law should remain unaltered, so that the whole structure should not be weakened or brought into contempt. When new legislation was proposed, a state official was appointed to defend the existing law ; and there were severe penalties for proposing laws which were contrary to the existing code. Alterations did of course occur ; ambiguities arose with the passage of time, for instance in Solon's testamentary law, which was giving much work to the jury-courts two and a half centuries later, in Aristotle's day ; and several times a complete revision was made. But on the whole the great code stood firm ; its archaic wording was appealed to and quoted and argued upon in the courts ; and its provisions always remained the basis of all legal administration in the Athenian state....

This brings us to the actual laws. One or two general principles must first be stated.

To begin with, there was no public prosecutor. The state took no cognizance of any crimes, not even murder, unless committed against itself : that is to say, the state did not prosecute for offences now commonly regarded as committed against the community, but only for offences against the actual administration, such as treason or cheating the public treasury. Until Solon's day, prosecution was allowed only to the person injured or his next-of-kin ; under Solon's reforms, any citizen who wished could bring an indictment against another, except in cases of homicide, where the right of prosecution was left as before in the hands of the relatives of the deceased. The penalty imposed was, however, executed by the state, which had its prison under the administration of annually chosen officers called "the eleven" ; these officials also supervised the infliction of the death penalty, usually the merciful method of giving the condemned man a fatal dose of hemlock. The state also watched over the rights of certain unprotected persons, the care of whom was allotted to certain magistrates, as for instance, wards unjustly treated by their guardians ; and the Court of the Areopagus was supposed to exercise a general supervision over public morals.

Another point to remember is that only free male citizens of full Athenian parentage of both sides could address the courts ; women could not plead, and had to be represented by their guardian — husband, father, eldest son, or other male relative. A slave, though he could not plead, could not be put to death by his master without a decree of a jury-court. There were special courts for foreigners.

Thirdly, one must always bear in mind that the litigants had each to conduct his own case : no hired lawyer was allowed in court or at the preliminary inquiries. Since, however, cross-examination of witnesses was not allowed in court, this stipulation was not such a hardship as at first appears. Each side had merely to make a speech, and bring forward his own witnesses to support him at the relevant points.... [pp. 17-20]

The magistrates of Athens, who presided over the courts, were elected annually by lot from the body of free Athenian citizens. Fifty names were put forward from each of the ten administrative divisions of Attica, which were called tribes. From these five hundred men, nine were chosen as chief magistrates : they were called the nine archons. Of these, the head was called the eponymous archon, because his name was given to his year of office ; events were said to have taken place "in the archonship of so-and-so" at Athens. Judicially, he had special charge of cases concerning married women, wards and "heiresses," that is, the family. Next in importance was the archon polemarchus, that is, field marshal archon, who had once been supreme commander in war, but who now was a magistrate whose special charge was cases concerning aliens. Next came the archon basileus or king archon, a relic of monarchy, who under the democracy had charge of state sacrifices, and who dealt with cases in which religion was concerned : this included homicide, because of the religious importance of blood-pollution. The six other members of the board of magistrates were called thesmothetae, "legislators" ; they shared out the less important work between them. In some cases the magistrates had summary jurisdiction ; but their chief function was to preside, first over the preliminary investigation, and then over the trial before the jury-court. Each was allowed two assessors to help him. The democratic state, while making use of the lot as a means of choice, protected itself from the holding of office by unworthy persons : any man so selected had to pass an examination of his character, or scrutiny, before entering upon office ; and also to submit to a review of his conduct during office at the end of the year when he retired. There were special rules for the king archon, whose duties concerned religion : his wife, to whom certain functions of this office were assigned, had to have been a virgin before marriage. The magistrates had no powers of jurisdiction when sitting with a jury-court ; the verdict of the jury was supreme.

In legislation, the assembly of the people (*ecclesia*), consisting of all male citizens over thirty years of age, was supreme. Business was prepared for the assembly, and resolutions framed, by the council of five hundred, consisting of five hundred citizens chosen by lot, fifty from each of the ten administrative divisions or tribes. The councillors sat in committees of fifty members, each comittee in turn for one-tenth of the year ; a different member, chosen by lot, presided each day. The periods of session of these committees were called "the first presidency," "the second presidency", and so on, dividing the official year into ten : the order of session was also decided by lot. They had no power to legislate, but they had charge of the state finances, and could even sit as a court of justice in certain cases, such as those which concerned the treasury.

Throughout the period covered by the following trials, jurymen were paid a sum of three *obols* (about two shillings) a day, so that even the poorest could afford to sit when chosen. The use of the lot as the method of choice for jurymen, councillors, and all officials except the ten chief generals, arose out of a primitive belief that though such means look like chance, the divine will is given an opportunity of expressing itself through them ; nevertheless, common sense demanded that a close watch should be kept on those thus chosen, by means of the scrutiny of incoming councillors and magistrates. The fact that offices were open to all citizens might seem to open the door to a flood of incompetents ; but actually the average free Athenian managed such official duties quite easily, as he was used from boyhood to taking an interest in public life, and expected to have his share of public activities. Also, in such a small community it was easy for every man to be well informed, when he could meet his friends every morning in the market place and discuss the latest news. Thus the system, though it had obvious faults and made glaring mistakes, was nevertheless a remarkably intricate and effective piece of machinery, the like of which the world had never seen, for the dispensation of justice equally to all.

It was typical of all Hellenic thought, as opposed to Oriental ideas of absolute obedience to a personal ruler, that in every rightly constituted state the law must stand above human caprice and ambition. "The people must fight to defend their laws as they would their fortifications," says Heraclitus. In the Athenian democracy, the constitution was designed to ensure that supreme power remained in the hands of the people, whose duty it was to defend the law : no single person or group of persons must ever rise so far above his fellows as to be out of control by the people, and above the law.... [pp. 28-30]

[T]he forensic speeches which have come down to us not only embody true stories and actual characters ; they happen to be works of art. This has come about owing to that provision in the Athenian legal code by which in any law suit the principals were obliged to deliver their speeches to the jury in person ; no hiring of an advocate to speak for one was permitted. The result of this stipulation was that men who lacked self-confidence or experience or the ability to compose a speech were driven to getting an expert to do this for them ; and so the profession of *logographos*, speechwriter, grew up in Athens in the fifth century B.C. Men who seldom or never appeared on a public platform made fortunes by writing speeches for clients, and running schools where the arts of composition and delivery were taught ; and so it came about that elegant phrases and subtle arguments dropped from the lips of farmers and business men who were rich enough to buy these goods from men cleverer than themselves. The best speech-writers considered the character of the client when composing the speech for him to deliver ; and the result is a dramatic monologue in the first person. In particular, there is a section of every speech called the narrative, in which the speaker puts the facts of the case before the jury. Some of these are models in the art of story-telling : the tale of the seduction of Euphiletus's wife, for instance, and the tale of Lysia's escape from his captors, are among the world's best short stories ; but because they occur as part of a forensic speech, they have not been recognized as early examples of this art — an art of which the Greeks were as much masters as they were of the lyric, the epic, and the drama. [p. 10-11]

NOTE

1. Kathleen Freeman, "Legal Code and Procedure," in *The Murder of Heroes and Other Trials from the Athenian Law Courts* (New York : W.W. Norton & Company Inc., 1963), pp. 10-30.

THE JURISPRUDENCE OF THE GREEK CITY[1]

Sir Paul Vinogradoff

The Greeks did not allow their law to lapse into obtruse technicality and to become a tool of professional jurists. Greek law in its application was meant to be a frame for public opinion. In Athens, at any rate, the remarkable experiment was made of handing over the administration of justice and the application of legal rules to batches of 201, 401, 1,001 jurors. The principle of which heliasts were called to decide cases was the same as that which has made the institution of the jury the usual device for deciding questions of fact in modern criminal procedure. It is the view that justice should be administered to the members of a community in accordance with the standards of morality and common sense prevailing in this community. But the Greeks went much further than we do, and entrusted to their many-headed juries not only questions of fact and responsibility, but questions of law which affected the distribution and enforcement of rights. It is most instructive to watch the results of this experiment on a large scale. Opinions differed among the experimenters themselves. We need not lay much stress on the contemptuous estimate of Plato, for he condemns all the democratic institutions of Athens, and yet Athenian democracy had formed the background for the greatest achievements of Greek genius. The extant speeches of pleaders indeed show that the experiment led to a somewhat capricious application of the law, opened the door for sentimentalism, prejudice, and sophistry. The heliasts were often circumvented, "bamboozled" by crafty pleaders, as Wyse, one of our authorities on the subject, has irreverently expressed it. But, on the whole, I confess that the wonder seems to be not that the heliasts should have been sometimes led astray or that they proved unable to analyze doctrine in the same way as this was done by Roman jurists, but rather that they should have grappled with their tasks as well as they did. These large tribunals were admittedly free from corruption, and, what is more, they were well able to appreciate the acute dialectics of Isaios or the refined literary skill of Hypereides. Apart from that, although learned jurisprudence in the sense of the Romans could not arise on such soil, the courts succeeded in treating problems of property, possession, obligation, association, etc. in the light of advanced notions of justice, fairness, and social expediency. This explains why Greek legal rules, instead of disappearing before the more strict and technical doctrines of Roman jurists, came to modify the latter in many ways : the more we study Roman law, the larger is the share we have to assign to the influence of Greek custom and Greek legislation. [p. 11-12]

NOTE

1. Sir Paul Vinogradoff, "Outlines of Historical Jurisprudence," vol. 2 *The Jurisprudence of the Greek City* (London : Oxford University Press, 1922), pp. 11-12.

THE LAW AND LEGAL THEORY OF THE GREEKS[1]

J. Walter Jones

No one who reads the extant legal orations of the Greek pleaders will feel that they were unduly hampered by respect for relevance, but there can be little doubt that when legal development is left, as it was at Athens, for the most part to the accidents of litigation before courts, there is likely to be an emphasis on casuistic at the expense of systematic treatment of legal questions. And this probability will be strengthened where there is a belief that democracy requires the members of the courts to be chosen by lot from the citizens at large, who would inevitably be without legal training ; and especially in Athens where there was little written enacted law, and despite a number of books few if any legal textbooks treating the law professionally and systematically ; and where such lawyers, in our own sense, as did exist, for the most part confined their activities to the notarial work of preparing legal documents for commercial purposes. The practice which eventually prevailed of putting almost all legal transactions into writing provided them with sufficient scope for their specialized knowledge, and the recurrence of the same clauses in contracts and loans which have come down to us shows that something resembling a notarial style had been evolved. The pleaders were chosen for their oratorical reputation rather than for legal learning though occasionally orators of the rank of Isaeus and Antiphon would devote themselves mainly to some particular branch of law, such as inheritance or homicide. It was only with the Roman conquest that the law became the subject of professional instruction and training for those who aimed at making a career as lawyers, for the most part in the service of Roman officials ; so that after the middle of the first century A.D. when the Romans ceased to send their sons to Athens to study philosophy, the Greeks began to send their sons to Rome to study law. [p. 293]

NOTE

1. J. Walter Jones, *The Law and Legal Theory of the Greeks* (London : Oxford University Press, 1956), p. 293.

LAWYERS AND LITIGANTS IN ANCIENT ATHENS[1]

Robert Bonner

Nowhere has popular sovereignty been so completely realized in practice as in ancient Athens. The sovereign people exercised their power not merely at intervals ; they actually wielded it at all times. The national assembly, composed of all citizens, debated and decided all questions of public policy. The legislative, executive, and judicial functions of government were exercised by commissions drawn from the citizen body by lot. Thus the people actually administered justice, interpreting and applying the law in each case as they saw fit. No trained jurist on the bench balked the popular will be citing inconvenient precedents. In theory, a judicial decision rendered today could be reversed in a similar case tomorrow.

Ever jealous of the expert, as democracy always is, the Athenians even tried to prevent the rise and development of a legal profession. The law required every man to plead his own case in court and permitted any man to prosecute a public offender. There were no official public prosecutors. The law did not forbid one citizen to aid another by making a plea in his behalf in court, but it did forbid the acceptance of fees for such service. No attempt, however, was made to prevent a litigant from reciting as his own a speech composed for him by an expert. Such a prohibition would have been quite futile. The attempt to prevent professionalism in the administration of justice was not altogether successful. At any rate, the considerable number of citizens — professional prosecutors (sycophants), speech-writers, and advocates — who devoted themselves almost exclusively to prosecuting wrongdoers and aiding those who were involved in litigation rendered services to the community similar to those performed by members of the modern bar, and are entitled to be regarded as professional lawyers.... [pp. v-vi]

The Athenians claimed the credit of being the first to establish regular processes of law, a claim which Cicero seems inclined to admit. The administration of justice in Athens was mainly conducted by amateurs. In the fifth and fourth centuries magistrates selected by lot held preliminary hearings and presided over the trials before popular courts. The requirement that each litigant should conduct his own case with such assistance as relatives and friends could render was not so unreasonable in a community where all citizens participated in the deliberations of the sovereign assembly and were free to address their fellow citizens on all public questions. In such conditions the proportion of citizens who could speak in public was much larger than in a modern community. But when about the middle of the fifth century the theory of rhetoric was developed and systematically taught, those who had the inclination and the means to acquire the "art of persuasion," as the Greeks called oratory, had an immense advantage over their untrained opponents in the law courts. As a consequence, expert rhetoricians began to compose speeches for clients to be recited in court as their own. Many orations of these speech-writers were published. An effective speech was a good professional advertisement for an ambitious speech-writer. About sixty orators are known to us by name, but practically all the extant orations have been transmitted as the work of ten men, the so-called "Canon of the Ten Orators," or the "Decade of the Orators." Contemporary interest in these speeches was due to their practical value as models for litigants, lawyers, and students of rhetoric. But later scholars and critics became interested in them because of the material they furnished for the study of the development of Attic prose style. And so they selected ten typical orators for study. The earliest record of the list is the *Lives of the Ten Orators,* wrongly attributed to Plutarch, the great biographer of antiquity, and included in his miscellaneous works. The *Lives of the Ten Orators* are now cited as the work of Pseudo-Plutarch. They were composed in the first century A.D., but it seems probable that the list was drawn up in the second century B.C. by a scholar at Pergamum, a centre of learning that rivaled the famous Museum of Alexandria. [pp. 1-2]

NOTE

1. Robert Bonner, *Lawyers and Litigants in Ancient Athens* (Chicago : University of Chicago Press, 1927), pp. v-vi ; 1-2.

THE SOVEREIGNTY OF THE PEOPLE'S COURT IN ATHENS IN THE FOURTH CENTURY B.C. AND THE PUBLIC ACTION AGAINST UNCONSTITUTIONAL PROPOSALS[1]

Mogens H. Hansen

In the second half of the *Constitution of Athens,* Aristotle makes a detailed analysis of the bodies of government existing in Athens at the end of the fourth century. He takes as his starting point a tripartition of the bodies, and accordingly his account is divided into the following three parts :

sections 43-49 : The Council of the Five Hundred and the Assembly
sections 50-62 : The magistrates
sections 63-69 : The Popular Courts....

Many works connect explicitly or implicitly Aristotle's tripartition of the bodies of Athens with modern theories of sovereignty and separation of powers such as are worked out especially by Bodin and Montesquieu. It is true that all authors make reservations, expressly warning against applying modern political concepts when analysing ancient Greek institutions ; still, in spite of all reservations, the result usually is that, consciously or unconsciously, the tripartition of the bodies in the *Constitution of Athens* is associated with the tripartition of the functions of government in recent times : the Assembly has the legislative, the magistrates the executive, and the courts the judicial power. Furthermore, usually with reference to Aristotle's description of radical democracy in his *Politics,* books iv-vi, it is maintained that it was the Assembly which was the sovereign democratic body in Athens....

The theory of the sovereignty of the Assembly might be justified as far as the fifth century is concerned, but the sources which mainly date from the fourth century and refer to conditions in the fourth century show that it cannot be upheld any longer after the restoration of the democracy in 403/2. [pp. 10-12]

On the face of it, the power of the state is equally divided between the Assembly and the courts, the Assembly having only a very limited prerogative in that it is sometimes able to decide when the court is to be convened. However, things look quite different when it comes to the mutual control of the two bodies and to the power of one body to reverse the decisions of the other....

1. Any decree may be overruled by the court by an indictment for unconstitutional proposal.
2. Any law may be reversed by the court by an indictment for proposing a law contrary to the interests of the state.
3. Certain sentences (for criminal offences) may be reversed by the Assembly through reprieve or amnesty. However, both reprieve and amnesty are granted in the form of a decree and may therefore, in turn, be appealed against to the court and overruled by a *graphe paranomon.*

The only decision made by the Assembly which has not the character of a decree and which cannot, therefore, be the object of a *graphe paranomon* is appointment of magistrates, but even here the court may exert its control through the obligatory examination of incoming magistrates and reverse the appointment made by the Assembly. We must conclude that any decision made by the Assembly may ultimately be reversed by the courts, whereas no decision made by the courts can ultimately be reversed by the Assembly. This state of affairs is best described by means of a terminology which is sometimes used in modern political science in connection with the concept of sovereignty, but which might with more reason be applied to Athenian conditions in the fourth century : while both the Assembly and the courts are immediate sovereigns, the courts alone have the ultimate sovereignty. [pp. 16-17]

In a study of the respective powers of the Assembly and of the courts it is important to emphasize the fact that there is no separation in the contemporary sense. In Greek political theory and practice we find no traces of any such concepts as separation of functions or separation of persons. No claim was ever made that each agency of government must perform only one function of government, nor was it ever forbidden any citizen to attend the Assembly while being at the same time a juror of the court and a magistrate. In the fifth century the judicial power in Athens was divided between the Assembly and the court, just as in the fourth century the legislative power was divided between the courts (passing laws as *nomothetai*) and the Assembly (passing decrees). Also, it was largely the same persons who voted by show of hands in the Assembly and by pebbles in the court. In forensic speeches we find numerous examples of the personal pronoun in the second person, and the verb in the second person plural applied in addresses to the jurors even when the speaker is referring to a decision actually made by the Assembly. Correspondingly, in the third book of the *Politics,* Aristotle defines a citizen, especially in a democracy, as a person who has the right to vote both in the Assembly and in the court. [p. 19]

A *graphe paranomon* might be brought by any citizen against any decision passed by the Assembly, with the exception of appointment of magistrates, and thus entailed a twofold treatment of the proposal. The indictment might be brought either prior to or after the passing of the decree by the Assembly, and the trial would either cause the proposal attacked to be upheld or overruled definitively. Thus, we have four variants of the process :

1. A decree is appealed against prior to being passed by the Assembly and is overruled.

2. A decree is appealed against after being passed by the Assembly and is overruled.
3. A decree is appealed against prior to being passed by the Assembly and is upheld.
4. A decree is appealed against after being passed by the Assembly and is upheld.

When we consider the relation between the Assembly and the courts, 1. and 4. are without special interest, whereas 2. and 3. clearly show the definite sovereignty of the courts over the Assembly

Re 2 : We know of five examples where a decree which has been passed by the Assembly is attacked for being unconstitutional and is subsequently overruled by the court. This and similar instances most clearly demonstrate the sovereignty of the laws and of the court over the Assembly . . . . Laws supersede decrees, since decrees must accord with laws, and no decree must override any law. The sovereignty of the law takes precedence over the sovereignty of the people, and the court must defend the law. What induced the Athenians to deprive the people of their sovereignty and to confer the ultimate decision on a body consisting of, for instance, 500, 1,000, or 1,500 citizens appointed by lot ? It is not possible to give a definite answer. The sources frequently refer to the law or to the court as the sovereign proper, but they do not state any reason for doing so. The answers I am going to suggest here, therefore, must be taken with the reservation that they are based on considerations which are supported only indirectly by the sources :

a. The jurors were sworn, whereas no oath should be taken prior to attendance in the Assembly. Furthermore, a citizen was allowed to attend the Assembly from the age of eighteen, but he could be appointed a juror by lot from the age of thirty only. If taking for our basis the number of citizens in the population census made by Demetrios of Phaleron and the normally accepted population distribution according to age groups, we find that at the end of the fourth century, 21,000 Athenians were able to attend the Assembly, whereas only 14,000 were eligible as jurors in court. The Greeks' respect for oaths and for the greater maturity and experience of old age is, in my opinion, a factor which should not be underrated. It has the effect that the Assembly and the court are comparable to some extent with a bicameral system in which the court is the controlling chamber.

b. The very fact that proposals were occasionally treated twice made a more well-founded decision possible. Probably the majority of the jurors in a *graphe paranomon* had already attended the session of the Assembly during which the proposal was discussed, and no doubt the decree was the subject of public debate in the interval between the hearings of the case by the Assembly and by the court. Two hearings meant time gained and constituted a safeguard against the effect of mass psychosis which a clever *rhetor* was able to whip up in a critical situation.

c. In the Assembly, the proposal treated has been one item on the agenda only, and the fact that everybody was allowed to speak might no doubt give rise to chaotic debates. In court, an entire day was set aside for the treatment of the proposal ; the debate took place between parties who had both prepared their speeches. In some respects the Assembly is comparable to a representative chamber in a multiparty system, the court to a chamber in a two-party system.

d. The frequent application of the process is no doubt due to the rather bitter conflict which was often seen in Athens between different groups of politicians. The party which was defeated in a vote in the Assembly would often refuse to admit defeat and therefore resort to an appeal to the court. Thus, the court obtained much greater influence through *graphe paranomon* than would have been the case if political conditions in Athens had been more settled....

The conclusion is that in a *graphe paranomon* the court not only had to decide if the decree attacked was unconstitutional, the jurors also had to decide whether the decree should be passed or not. This is most conclusively established in the instances where a decree in the form of a *probouleuma* has been appealed against to the court. An approval of the decree meant not only that it was in accordance with law, but also that it had been passed. In these instances the court seems to have assumed the right of the Assembly to carry decrees. Therefore, when the court tries a *graphe paranomon* it acts not only as a judicial body, but also as a political body : all sections of the preserved speeches that are concerned with the beneficial or harmful aspects of a proposal are, therefore, extremely relevant to the decision of the jurors and are not mere rhetorical devices meant to influence the jurors. [pp. 49-52]

A decree which is at variance with certain laws is also at variance with the principle underlying these laws. This principle will be specifically democratic since, according to Greek notion, legislation always reflects and conforms with the constitution. Accordingly, an unconstitutional decree is an attempt to overthrow the democratic constitution. For instance, a proposal to execute without trial is not only contrary to the law, but also contrary to the principles underlying the law : mildness and humanity. These principles are specifically democratic.

A decree which is contrary to certain laws constitutes a breach of the law as such, and the sovereignty of the laws is a distinctive feature of democracy as opposed to oligarchy and tyranny. Consequently, an unconstitutional proposal is an attempt to overthrow the democratic constitution, and a *graphe paranomon* constitutes a defence of democracy....

An examination of the preserved speeches and fragments of speeches delivered in connection with *graphe paranomon* shows that the plaintiff acts not only as a defender of the laws, but also as a defender of democracy, willingly denouncing the indicted proposer and his fellow fellow-partisans as public enemies and oligarchs.... [pp. 55-56]

Graphe paranomon was undoubtedly a safeguard of moderate, not radical, democracy. The most characteristic feature of a radical democracy was a sovereign Assembly which, led by demagogues, carried decrees that superseded laws. In contrast, *graphe paranomon* was the type of process which protected the law by granting the court power to overrule the unconstitutional decrees the demagogues had persuaded the Assembly to pass. Consequently, *graphe paranomon* was a moderate democratic institution aimed at oligarchs as well as radical democrats. [p. 59]

NOTE

1. M.H. Hansen, *The Sovereignty of the People's Court in Athens in the Fourth Century B.C. and the Public Action Against Unconstitutional Proposals* (Odense : Odense University Press, 1974), pp. 10-59.

THE APOLOGY[1]

Plato

Socrates : But in truth, Athenians, I do not think that I need say very much to prove that I have not committed the act of injustice for which Meletus is prosecuting me. What I have said is enough to prove that. But be assured it is certainly true, as I have already told you, that I have aroused much indignation. That is what will cause my condemnation if I am condemned ; not Meletus nor Anytus either, but that prejudice and resentment of the multitude which have been the destruction of many good men before me, and I think will be so again. There is no prospect that I shall be the last victim.... [p. 34]

Do not interrupt me, Athenians, with your shouts. Remember the request which I made to you, and do not interrupt my words. I think that it will profit you to hear them. I am going to say something more to you, at which you may be inclined to protest, but do not do that. Be sure that if you put me to death, I who am what I have told you that I am, you will do yourselves more harm than me. Meletus and Anytus can do me no harm : that is impossible, for I am sure it is not allowed that a good man be injured by a worse. He may indeed kill me, or drive me into exile, or deprive me of my civil rights. Perhaps Meletus and others think those things great evils. But I do not think so. I think it is a much greater evil to do what he is doing now, and to try to put a man to death unjustly. And now, Athenians, I am not arguing in my own defence at all, as you might expect me to do, but rather in yours in order you may not make a mistake about the gift of the god to you by condemming me. For if you put me to death, you will not easily find another who, if I may use a ludicrous comparison, clings to the state as a sort of gadfly to a horse that is large and well-bred but rather sluggish because of its size, so that it needs to be aroused....

Perhaps it may seem strange to you that, though I go about giving this advice privately and meddling in others' affairs, yet I do not venture to come forward in the assembly and advise the state. You have often heard me speak of my reason for this, and in many places : it is that I have a certain divine guide, which is what Meletus has caricatured in his indictment. I have had it from childhood. It is a kind of voice which, whenever I hear it, always turns me back from something which I was going to do, but never urges me to act. It is this which forbids me to take part in politics. And I think it does well to forbid me. For, Athenians, it is quite certain that, if I had attempted to take part in politics, I should have perished at once and long ago without doing any good either to you or to myself. And do not be indignant with me for telling the truth. There is no man who will preserve his life for long, either in Athens or elsewhere, if he firmly opposes the multitude, and tries to prevent the commission of much injustice and illegality in the state. He who would really fight for justice must do so as a private citizen, not as a political figure, if he is to preserve his life, even for a short time.... [pp. 36-38]

And now I wish to prophesy to you, Athenians, who have condemmed me. For I am going to die, and that is the time when men have most prophetic power. And I prophesy to you who have sentenced me to death that a far more severe punishment than you have inflicted on me will surely overtake you as soon as I am dead. You have done this thing, thinking that you will be relieved from having to give an account of your lives. But I say that the result will be very different. There will be more men who will call you to account, whom I have held back, though you did not recognize it. And they will be harsher toward you than I have been, for they will be younger, and you will be more indignant with them. For if you think that you will restrain men from reproaching you for not living as you should, by putting them to death, you are very much mistaken. That way of escape is neither possible nor honourable. It is much more honourable and much easier not to suppress others, but to make yourselves as good as you can. This is my parting prophecy to you who have condemned me.

With you who have acquitted me I should like to discuss this thing that has happened, while the authorities are busy, and before I go to the place where I have to die. So, remain with me until I go : there is no reason why we should not talk with each other while it is possible. I wish to explain to you, as my friends, the meaning of what has happened to me. An amazing thing has happened to me, judges — for I am right in calling you judges. The prophetic guide has been constantly with me all through my life till now, opposing me even in trivial matters if I were not going to act rightly. And now you yourselves see what has happened to me — a thing which might be thought, and which is sometimes actually reckoned, the supreme evil. But the divine guide did not oppose me when I was leaving my house in the morning, nor when I was coming up here to the court, nor at any point in my speech when I was going to say anything ; though at other times it has often stopped me in the very act of speaking. But now, in this matter, it has never once opposed me, either in my words or my actions. I will tell you what I believe to be the reason. This thing that has come upon me must be a good ; and those of us who think that death is an evil must needs be mistaken. I have a clear proof that that is so ; for my accustomed guide would certainly have opposed me if I had not been going to meet with something good. [pp. 46-47]

NOTE

1. Plato, *The Apology*, trans. F J. Church (New York : The Liberal Arts Press, 1948.), pp. 34-37.

CRITO[1]

Plato

Crito : O my good Socrates, I beg you for the last time to listen to me and save yourself. For to me your death will be more than a single disaster ; not only shall I lose a friend the like of whom I shall never find again, but many persons who do not know you and me well will think that I might have saved you if I had been willing to spend money, but that I neglected to do so. And what reputation could be more disgraceful than the reputation of caring more for money than for one's friends ? The public will never believe that we were anxious to save you, but that you yourself refused to escape.

Socrates : But my dear Crito, why should we care so much about public opinion ? Reasonable men, of whose opinion it is worth our while to think, will believe that we acted as we really did.

Crito : But you see, Socrates, that it is necessary to care about public opinion, too. This very thing that has happened to you proves that the multitude can do a man not the least, but almost the greatest harm, if he is falsely accused to them.

Socrates : I wish that the multitude were able to do a man the greatest harm, Crito, for then they would be able to do him the greatest good, too. That would have been fine. But, as it is, they can do neither. They cannot make a man either wise or foolish : they act wholly at random.

Crito : Well, as you wish. But tell me this, Socrates. You surely are not anxious about me and your other friends, and afraid lest, if you escape, the informers would say that we stole you away, and get us into trouble, and involve us in a great deal of expense, or perhaps in the loss of all our property, and, it may be, bring some other punishment upon us besides ? If you have any fear of that kind, dismiss it. For of course we are bound to run these risks, and still greater risks than these, if necessary, in saving you. So do not, I beg you, refuse to listen to me.

Socrates : I am anxious about that, Crito, and about much besides.

Crito : Then have no fear on that score. There are men who, for no very large sum, are ready to bring you out of prison into safety. And then, you know, these informers are cheaply bought, and there would be no need to spend much upon them. My fortune is at your service, and I think that it is adequate ; and if you have any feeling about making use of my money, there are strangers in Athens whom you know, ready to use theirs ; and one of them, Simmias of Thebes, has actually brought enough for this very purpose. And Cebes and many others are ready, too. And therefore, I repeat, do not shrink from saving yourself on that ground. And do not let what you said in the court — that if you went into exile you would not know what to do with yourself — stand in your way ; for there are many places for you to go to, where you will be welcomed. If you choose to go to Thessaly, I have friends there who will make much of you and protect you from any annoyance from the people of Thessaly.

And besides, Socrates, I think that you will be doing what is unjust if you abandon your life when you might preserve it. You are simply playing into your enemies' hands ; it is exactly what they wanted — to destroy you .... [pp. 52-54]

Socrates : Let us examine this question together, my friend, and if you can contradict anything that I say, do so, and I shall be persuaded. But if you cannot, do not go on repeating to me any longer, my dear friend, that I should escape without the consent of the Athenians. I am very anxious to act with your approval and consent. I do not want you to think me mistaken. But now tell me if you agree with the premise from which I start, and try to answer my questions as you think best.

Crito : I will try.

Socrates : Ought we never to act unjustly voluntarily ? Or may we act unjustly in some ways, and not in others ? Is it the case, as we have often agreed in former times, that it is never either good or honourable to act unjustly ? Or have all our former conclusions been overturned in these few days ; and did we at our age fail to recognize all along, when we were seriously conversing with each other, that we were no better than children ? Is not what we used to say most certainly the truth, whether the multitude agrees with us or not ? Is not acting unjustly evil and shameful in every case, whether we incur a heavier or a lighter punishment as the consequence ? Do we believe that ?

Crito : We do.

Socrates : Then we ought never to act unjustly ?

Crito : Certainly not.

Socrates : If we ought never to act unjustly at all, ought we to repay injustice with injustice, as the multitude thinks we may ?

Crito : Clearly not.

Socrates : Well, then, Crito, ought we to do evil to anyone ?

Crito : Certainly I think not, Socrates.

Socrates : And is it just to repay evil with evil, as the multitude thinks, or unjust.

Crito : Certainly it is unjust.

Socrates : For there is no difference, is there between doing evil to a man and acting unjustly ?

Crito : True.

Socrates : Then we ought not to repay injustice with injustice or to do harm to any man, no matter what we may have suffered from him. And in conceding this, Crito, be careful that you do not concede more than you mean. For I know that only a few men hold, or ever will hold, this opinion. And so those who hold it and those who do not have no common ground of argument ; they can of necessity only look with contempt on each other's belief. Do you therefore consider very carefully whether or not you agree with me and share my opinion. Are we to start in our inquiry from the premise that it is never right either to act unjustly, or to repay injustice with injustice, or to avenge ourselves on any man who harms us, by harming him in return ? Or do you disagree with me and dissent from my premise ? I myself have believed in it for a long time, and I believe in it still. But if you differ in any way, explain to me how. If you still hold to our former opinion, listen to my next point.

Crito : Yes, I hold to it, and I agree with you. Go on.

Socrates : Then, my next point, or rather my next question, is this : Ought a man to carry out his just agreements, or may he shuffle out of them ?

Crito : He ought to carry them out.

Socrates : Then consider. If I escape without the state's consent, shall I be injuring those whom I ought least to injure, or not ? Shall I be abiding by my just agreements or not ?

Crito : I cannot answer your question, Socrates. I do not understand it.

Socrates : Consider it in this way. Suppose the laws and the commonwealth were to come and appear to me as I was preparing to run away (if that is the right phrase to describe my escape) and were to ask, "Tell us, Socrates, what have you in your mind to do ? What do you mean by trying to escape but to destroy us, the laws and the whole state, so far as you are able ? Do you think that a state can exist and not be overthrown, in which the decisions of law are of no force, and are disregarded and undermined by private individuals ?" How shall we answer questions like that, Crito ? Much might be said, especially by an orator, in defence of the law which makes judicial decisions supreme. Shall I reply, "But the state has injured me by judging my case unjustly ?" Shall we say that ?

Crito : Certainly we will, Socrates.

Socrates : And suppose the laws were to reply, "Was that our agreement ? Or was it that you would abide by whatever judgments the state should pronounce ?" And if we were suprised by their words, perhaps they would say, "Socrates, don't be surprised by our words, but answer us ; you yourself are accustomed to ask questions and to answer them. What complaint have you against us and the state, that you are trying to destroy us ? Are we not, first of all, your parents ? Through us your father took your mother and brought you into the world. Tell us, have you any fault to find with those of us that are the laws of marriage ?" "I have none," I should reply. "Or have you any fault to find with those of us that regulate the raising of the child and the education which you, like others, received ? Did we not do well in telling your father to educate you in music and athletics ?" "You did," I should say. "Well, then, since you were brought into the world and raised and educated by us, how, in the first place, can you deny that you are our child and our slave, as your fathers were before you ? And if this be so, do you think that your rights are on a level with ours ? Do you think that you have a right to retaliate if we should try to do anything to you ? You had not the same rights that your father had, or that your master would have had if you had been a slave. You had no right to retaliate if they ill-treated you, or to answer them if they scolded you, or to strike them back if they struck you, or to repay them evil with evil in any way. And do you think that you may retaliate in the case of your country and its laws ? If we try to destroy you, because we think it just, will you in return do all that you can to destroy us, the laws, and your country, and say that in so doing you are acting justly — you, the man who really thinks so much of excellence ? Or are you too wise to see that your country is worthier, more to be revered, more sacred, and held in higher honour both by the gods and by all men of understanding, than your father and your mother and all your other ancestors ; and that you ought to reverence it, and to submit to it, and to approach it more humbly when it is angry with you than you would approach your father ; and either to do whatever it tells you to do or to persuade it to excuse you ; and to obey in silence if it orders you to endure flogging or imprisonment, or if it sends you to battle to be wounded or to die ? That is just. You must not give way, nor retreat, nor desert your station. In war, and in the court of justice, and everywhere, you must do whatever your state and your country tell you to do, or you must persuade them that their commands are unjust. But it is impious to use violence against your father or your mother ; and much more impious to use violence against your country." What answer shall we make, Crito ? Shall we say that the laws speak the truth, or not ?

Crito : I think that they do.

Socrates : "Then consider, Socrates," perhaps they would say, "if we are right in saying that by attempting to escape you are attempting an injustice. We brought you into the world, we raised you, we educated you, we gave you and every other citizen a share of all the good things we could. Yet we proclaim that if any man of the Athenians is dissatisfied with us, he may take his goods and go away wherever he pleases ; we give that privilege to every man who chooses to avail himself of it, so soon as he has reached manhood, and sees us, the laws, and the administration of our state. No one of us stands in his way or forbids him to take his goods and go wherever he likes, whether it be to an Athenian colony or to any foreign country, if he is dissatisfied with us and with the state. But we say that every man of you who remains here, seeing how we administer justice, and how we govern the state in other matters, has agreed, by the very fact of remaining here, to do whatsoever we tell him. And, we say, he who disobeys us acts unjustly on three counts : he disobeys us who are his parents, and he disobeys us who reared him, and he disobeys us after he has agreed to obey us, without persuading us that we are wrong. Yet we did not tell him sternly to do whatever we told him. We offered him an alternative ; we gave him his choice either to obey us or to convince us that we were wrong ; but he does neither.

"These are the charges, Socrates, to which we say that you will expose yourself if you do what you intend ; and you are more exposed to these charges than other Athenians." And if I were to ask, "Why ?" they might retort with justice that I have bound myself by the agreement with them more than other Athenians. They would say, "Socrates, we have very strong evidence that you were satisfied with us and with the state. You would not have been content to stay at home in it more than other Athenians unless you had been satisfied with it more than they. You never went away from Athens to the festivals, nor elsewhere except on military service ; you never made other journeys like other men ; you had no desire to see other states or other laws ; you were contented with us and our state ; so strongly did you prefer us, and agree to be governed by us. And what is more, you had children in this city, you found it so satisfactory. Besides, if you had wished, you might at your trial have offered to go into exile. At that time you could have done with the state's consent what you are trying now to do without it. But then you gloried in being willing to die. You said that you preferred death to exile. And now you do not honour those words : you do not respect us, the laws, for you are trying to destroy us ; and you are acting just as a miserable slave would act, trying to run away, and breaking the contracts and agreement which you made to live as our citizen. First, therefore, answer this question. Are we right, or are we wrong, in saying that you have agreed not in mere words, but in your actions, to live under our government ?" What are we to say, Crito ? Must we not admit that it is true ?

Crito : We must, Socrates.

Socrates : Then they would say, "Are you not breaking your contracts and agreements with us ? And you were not led to make them by force or by fraud. You did not have to make up your mind in a hurry. You had seventy years in which you might have gone away if you had been dissatisfied with us, or if the agreement had seemed to you unjust. But you preferred neither Sparta or Crete, though you are fond of saying that they are well governed, nor any other state, either of the Greeks or the Barbarians.

You went away from Athens less than the lame and the blind and the crippled. Clearly you, far more than other Athenians, were satisfied with the state, and also with us who are its laws ; for who would be satisfied with a state which had no laws ? And now will you not abide by your agreement ? If you take our advice, you will, Socrates ; then you will not make yourself ridiculous by going away from Athens.

Reflect now. What good will you do yourself or your friends by thus transgressing and breaking your agreement ? It is tolerably certain that they, on their part, will at least run the risk of exile, and of losing their civil rights, or of forfeiting their property. You yourself might go to one of the neighboring states, to Thebes or to Megara, for instance — for both of them are well governed — but, Socrates, you will come as an enemy to these governments, and all who care for their city will look askance at you, and think that you are a subverter of law. You will confirm the judges in their opinion, and make it seem that their verdict was a just one. For a man who is a subverter of law may well be supposed to be a corrupter of the young and thoughtless. Then will you avoid well-governed states and civilized men ? Will life be worth having, if you do ? Will you associate with such men, and converse without shame — about what, Socrates ? About the things which you talk of here ? Will you tell them that excellence and justice and institutions and law are the most valuable things that men can have ? And do you not think that that will be a disgraceful thing for Socrates ? You ought to think so. But you will leave these places ; you will go to the friends of Crito in Thessaly. For there is found the greatest disorder and license, and very likely they will be delighted to hear of the ludicrous way in which you escaped from prison, dressed up in peasant's clothes, or in some other disguise which people put on when they are running away, and with your appearance altered. But will no one say how you, an old man, with probably only a few more years to live, clung so greedily to life that you dared to break the highest laws ? Perhaps not, if you do not annoy them. But if you do, Socrates, you will hear much that will make you blush. You will pass your life as the flatterer and the slave of all men ; and what will you be doing but feasting in Thessaly ? It will be as if you had made a journey to Thessaly for a banquet. And where will be all our old arguments about justice and excellence then ? But you wish to live for the sake of your children ? You want to bring them up and educate them ? What ? Will you take them with you to Thessaly, and bring them up and educate them there ? Will you make them strangers to their own country, that you may bestow this benefit of exile on them too ? Or supposing that you leave them in Athens, will they be brought up and educated better if you are alive, though you are not with them ? Yes, your friends will take care of them. Will your friends take care of them if you make a journey to Thessaly, and not if you make a journey to

Hades ? You ought not to think that, at least if those who call themselves your friends are worth anything at all.

"No, Socrates, be persuaded by us who have reared you. Think neither of children nor of life, nor of any other thing before justice, so that when you come to the other world you may be able to make your defence before the rulers who sit in judgment there. It is clear that neither you nor any of your friends will be happier, or juster, or more pious in this life, if you do this thing, nor will you be happier after you are dead. Now you will go away a victim of the injustice, not of the laws, but of men. But if you repay evil with evil, and injustice with injustice in this shameful way, and break your agreements and covenants with us, and injure those whom you should least injure, yourself and your friends and your country and us, and so escape, then we shall be angry with you while you live, and when you die our brothers, the laws in Hades, will not receive you kindly ; for they will know that on earth you did all that you could to destroy us. Listen then to us, and let not Crito persuade you to do as he says."

Be sure, my dear friend Crito, that this is what I seem to hear, as the worshippers of Cybele seem, in their passion, to hear the music of flutes ; and the sound of these arguments rings so loudly in my ears, that I cannot hear any other arguments. And I feel sure that if you try to change my mind you will speak in vain. Nevertheless, if you think that you will succeed, speak.

Crito : I have nothing more to say, Socrates. [pp. 58-65]

NOTE

1. Plato, *Crito*, trans. F.J. Church (New York : The Liberal Arts Press, 1948), pp. 52-65.

3. Rome

Classical Roman law was radically different from the laws of any other people at that time, including even the laws of ancient Rome, of the Twelve Tables. Roman law was a system and a science. Explanations of its sudden evolution responding to needs of an expanding empire, while relevant, cannot possibly explain its sudden appearance and universal nature. It was the product of a group of technical legal craftsmen who were steeped in Stoic physics, ethics, and logic. While scholars may argue about the degree to which Hellenic culture influenced the creation of classical Roman law, there is little question of the existence of many parallels in terms of commitment to universality, logical structure and formal properties, and the use of the scientific method.

Unlike the Greeks, the classical Roman lawyers distrusted codification. The great codification of Roman law under Justinian took place after the zenith of classical Roman law and in the Hellenic Eastern Empire.

If, as many believe, the catalyst for the creation of classical Roman law was certain elements of Hellenic culture, one might well ask why Greek law was not systematic and scientific. One might explain the difference in terms of the complexity of law needed to govern a city-state as compared to an empire, and again this may be relevant. A critical aspect, however, is the fact that Greece had no lawyers or legal technicians. The Greek view of the role of the citizen in the governance of the state required that each citizen be cognizant of the law and argue his own case before a jury of citizens. A class of highly trained legal technicians, so characteristic of Rome and so necessary for a highly technical legal system, thus had no chance to flower in Greece.

One of the aspects of the scientific method is to account for the widest range of phenomena with as few laws as possible. Therefore, the Stoics, who defined law as rational and universal, saw an affinity between mathematics and legal science. Stoicism provides the link between Greek science and Roman law. The creation of classical Roman law was a result of a scientific method of organizing knowledge, through dialectical analysis, to explain individual cases through organizing principles. In Roman law, the legal personality surfaces as a tool of science. Legal constructs exist for the first time and simplicity is achieved through abstraction. The Romans informed the world that a legal system could be profitably composed out of the smallest possible number of variables ; this allowed for the combination of consistency, refinement, and a flexible pragmatism. Without the preceding efforts of Stoical science, Roman law would not have emerged in the same form. The concept of the variable implicit in Stoic logic allowed the Romans to conceive of law as abstract relations which could be made concrete in terms of any citizen or pattern of behaviour.

Abstract universalism stands in direct conflict with legal systems which are attached to kinship or patriarchal bonds. It is irrelevant in classical Roman law, for ownership, whether the parties shared a specific covenant or belief with respect to a deity. Roman law defined ownership as a bundle of rights and duties which could be applied to any person in regard to the objects in question. In the biblical society, by contrast, one is born with moral and legal duties which are determined by biological factors and birth. Suddenly, with the Stoics, man is born free, subject to no inherent moral or legal duties. Some commentators have proposed that the dividing line between ancient and modern legal and political theory should be sought in the period between Aristotle and Cicero. In this spirit, it was Lord Acton who remarked that it was the Stoics who emancipated mankind from despotic rule and enlightened the path of Western law to freedom. In the balance of history it is the Greco-Roman conception of law that has dominated both civil and common law systems in the West, relinquishing the moral content to important incursions from the commandments of the religious Testaments.

Although the Romans could not isolate their law from economic, religious, and political influences, they undertook to purify law as a theoretical structure independent of extra-legal considerations. The Romans proceeded from the assumption that a rational law could be made consistent with the reason and order of nature. In so doing they participated in the Grecian philosophical perspective on nature and law. Of course, with the benefit of hindsight, we can see that both the *ius gentium* and the *lex naturalae* were convenient tools to consolidate the economic and political presence of the Roman Empire. But this does not detract from the momentus impact that the concept of a legal science has had on Western jurisprudence. For it was the Romans who conceived of law as an autonomous structure upon which the concept of an autonomous legal person could be based. The natural sequence in this progression was to present the notion of the rule of law predicated on the existence of an independent and autonomous citizenry.

Stoic universality was the most comprehensive and encompassing statement of a world order yet received in the West. The Stoics presented a model of rational man of such force that it allowed the conquering Romans to rationalize their political authority with an aura of mythic proportion. But what must be recognized, in the final analysis, is that the Romans derived their authority from postulating a world order according to a universal rule of law.

THE LAWS OF THE TWELVE TABLES[1]

Table II

Concerning Judgments and Thefts

LAW I

When issue has been joined in the presence of the judge, sureties and their substitutes for appearance at the trial must be furnished on both sides. The parties shall appear in person, unless prevented by disease of a serious character ; or where vows which they have taken must be discharged to the gods ; or where the proceedings are interrupted through their absence on business for the state ; or where a day has been appointed by them to meet an alien.

LAW II

If any of the above mentioned occurrences takes place, that is, if one of the parties is seriously ill, or a vow has to be performed, or one of them is absent on business for the state, or a day has been appointed for an interview with an alien, so that the judge, the arbiter, or the defendant is prevented from being present, and the furnishing of security is postponed on this account, the hearing of the case shall be deferred.

LAW III

Where anyone is deprived of the evidence of a witness let him call him with a loud voice in front of his house, on three market days.

LAW IV

Where anyone commits a theft by night, and having been caught in the act is killed, he is legally killed.

LAW V

If anyone commits a theft during the day, and is caught in the act, he shall be scourged, and given up as a slave to the person against whom the theft was committed. If he who perpetrated the theft is a slave, he shall be beaten with rods and hurled from the Tarpeian Rock. If he is under the age of puberty, the praetor shall decide whether he shall be scourged, and surrendered by way of reparation for the injury.

LAW VI

When any persons commit a theft during the day and in the light, whether they be freemen or slaves, of full age or minors, and attempt to defend themselves with weapons, or with any kind of implements ; and the party against whom the violence is committed raises the cry of thief, and calls upon other persons, if any are present, to come to his assistance ; and this is done, and the thieves are killed by him in the defence of his person and property, it is legal, and no liability attaches to the homicide.

LAW VII

If a theft be detected by means of a dish and a girdle, it is the same as manifest theft, and shall be punished as such.

LAW VIII

When anyone accuses and convicts another of theft which is not manifest, and no stolen property is found, judgment shall be rendered to compel the thief to pay double the value of what was stolen.

LAW IX

Where anyone secretly cuts down trees belonging to another, he shall pay twenty-five *asses* for each tree cut down.

LAW X

Where anyone, in order to favour a thief, makes a compromise for the loss sustained, he cannot afterwards prosecute him for theft.

LAW XI

Stolen property shall always be his to whom it formerly belonged ; nor can the lawful owner ever be deprived of it by long possession, without regard to its duration ; nor can it ever be acquired by another, no matter in what way this may take place.

Table IV

Concerning the Rights of a Father and of Marriage

LAW I

A father shall have the right of life and death over his son born in lawful marriage, and shall also have the power to render him independent, after he has been sold three times.

LAW II

If a father sells his son three times, the latter shall be free from paternal authority.

LAW III

A father shall immediately put to death a son recently born, who is a monster, or has a form different from that of members of the human race.

LAW IV

When a woman brings forth a son within the next ten months after the death of her husband, he shall be born in lawful marriage, and shall be the legal heir of his estate. [pp. 58-65]

NOTE

1. S.P. Scott, trans., "The Laws of the Twelve Tables," in *The Civil Law* (New York : AMS Press, 1973), pp. 58-65.

ROMAN LAW[1]

Hans Julius Wolff

Roman law occupies a unique place in the history of our civilization. Originally the law of a small and insignificant rural community, then that of a powerful city-state, it became in due course the law of an empire which embraced almost the whole of the known civilized world of its time. When political, economic, and military exhaustion and the invasions of Huns and Germanic tribes put an end to this greatest political organization the world has ever seen, its law remained in force both in its eastern half, where the Byzantine Empire as the direct continuation of the old Roman Empire survived till 1453, and in its western regions, where new kingdoms under Germanic rule came into existence. In fact, it was only then — in Constantinople, the new, eastern Rome — that Roman law was for the first time laid down in a final and comprehensive statement.

Later many of its conceptions and institutions lived on in the legal systems which evolved in the Orthodox church in the East and in the Catholic church in the West. In the late Middle Ages it was considered as the supreme law of the new empire in the West, which claimed to be the successor of the Roman Empire of old. It was studied in the universities of Europe ; and through the medium of university-trained jurists in chancelleries and courts, it exerted a deep influence on the development of legal institutions and doctrine in all continental European countries inside and outside the Empire, from Spain to Poland. Only in England was this influence kept within narrow limits because of the early rise of a national legal profession and the early organization of a national common law.

The influence of Roman law, moreover, in original or adapted form, extended into modern times. The *Corpus Iuris Civilis,* as the codification made in Constantinople under the auspices of Emperor Justinian in the sixth century was called in more recent times, remained an immediate source of law in wide areas of Germany until 1900. Modified forms of Roman law are even now the law of the land in Scotland, in Ceylon, and in the Union of South Africa (where it is called the Roman Dutch law). Less direct but no less important was the impact of Roman doctrines on the great codifications of private law which have come into existence in Europe, America, and Asia since the eighteenth century.

The achievement of the Romans in the field of law has thus become one of the foundations of civil law, i.e., of one of the two main groups of legal systems governing the nations of Western civilization (the other being Anglo-American common law). We are therefore entitled to call Roman law one of the strongest formative forces in the development of Western civilization. [pp. 3-5]

In their early days the Romans, like every primitive people, lived by unwritten, customary laws. It is not known when legal rules were first laid down in written form. We hear of *leges regiae*, i.e., regal laws, which are supposed to have emanated from some of the early kings....

The first true Roman legislation of which we know — and very likely really the first ever undertaken by the Romans — occurred about the middle of the fifth century B.C. It grew out of the struggle between patricians and plebeians. Roman historians give us the following account of this legislation : In 451 B.C. ten patricians, the so-called *decemviri* (ten men), were charged with writing down the laws of the Roman people. They were granted extraordinary powers ; the whole machinery of government, including even the right of the tribunes to intercede against their decisions, was suspended while they were in office. Their appointment was the result of years of agitation by the plebeians who felt oppressed by biased patrician magistrates, and it was made only after long delays due to the dilatory tactics of the patricians.

The *decemvirs* issued a code of laws written on ten (probably wooden) tablets. As these laws were considered incomplete, a second group of *decemvirs* — this time including some plebeians — was elected, who wrote two more tablets of laws....

As a matter of fact, no other period of Roman history offered conditions more propitious for such a codification than the time in which later Roman tradition placed it. The cleavage between patricians and plebeians, then at its peak, was not only political but also social and economic, at least as regards the majority of the plebeians. Many plebeians were small and poor people, often heavily indebted to the patricians. The procedure for enforcement of obligations, as in all primitive law, was harsh. It might lead to slavery and death for the debtor and his family. The magistrates who supervised the enforcement were members of the same class as the creditors. It was therefore only natural that the plebeians were interested in a clear statement of the limits to which creditors might go, and to which magistrates might allow them to go, in enforcing their claims. This is exactly what was done by the Twelve Tables. Their law of enforcement was still pitiless. But they also contained, right in the first sentences, elaborate provisions concerning the methods to be used in bringing a defendant to court, the periods of grace to be granted a debtor, and so on. These provisions were obviously devised to protect debtors against unfair treatment and excessive cruelty.

The Twelve Tables, it is true, also contained much which had nothing to do with the question of how to protect the poor and the weak. But this affords no argument against our statement. The Twelve Tables represent an effort to codify the total of the rights and duties of the Roman citizen. The need of such a codification arose from the tension between the classes ; but once the task was undertaken, the provisions necessary to alleviate this tension were perhaps the first and most important, but not the only, concern of those who wrote these laws. Solon's codification of the laws of Athens offers a close parallel regarding both its occasion and its execution.

The original text of the Twelve Tables is lost. In fact, it is said that the original tablets perished in the great fire of Rome which was caused by the Gallic invasion of 390-389 B.C. Roman literature, however, gives us a good deal of information about their contents, including a number of direct quotations....

The provisions of the Twelve Tables have the form of terse commands and prohibitions, sometimes brief to the point of obscurity. They concern procedure in court actions and enforcement, the law of family, of wills, succession, property, contracts, and torts, as modern lawyers would classify them. Others deal with questions of sacral law, public law, and criminal law, to adopt again a modern mode of classification. Some regulate the behaviour of citizens, such as several provisions prohibiting, in the typical manner of ancient city-states, the display of excessive luxury in funerals. The Twelve Tables reflect the life of a primitive agricultural society which believed in witchcraft and had rigid and often harsh concepts of liability. Yet, while archaic in form and thought, the law of the Twelve Tables had advanced considerably beyond the most primitive stage. It shows some development in legal technique ; uncontrolled self-help was repressed and replaced by orderly forms of procedure ; private vengeance was in some cases limited by the principle of retaliation, and in other cases public punishment or private composition had taken its place. Some ability to make more subtle distinctions appears in the different treatment provided for wilful and accidental homicide.... [pp. 54-59]

The magnificent structure of the mature Roman law could never have come into existence nor could Roman law have achieved its worldwide influence had it not been for a class of legal experts who, in counseling parties and advising magistrates and judges, developed from early times a special skill in appraising new situations produced by the increasing complexity of Roman life and in suggesting solutions consistent with the order of the legal system as a whole.

It was these men who actually stood behind the progress of both the *ius civile* and the *ius honorarium*, by finding new doctrines and by showing new ways of utilizing doctrines already recognized. From the time of the middle Republic, some of them prepared in literary form restatements of, and commentaries on, the legal system. Under the Principate, their activities culminated in that great, scientific treatment of the law which enabled Roman law, in a manner unique in ancient times, to combine consistency, theoretical refinement, and a high degree of practical elasticity, thus causing historians to call this period of Roman legal history the "classical period."

Historically, this classical science of law was the outstanding particular contribution of Rome to the cultural evolution of mankind. For the first time in the history of human thought, legal phenomena were approached in the spirit of true legal scholarship, which combines systematic analysis with constant attention to practical results. It was this attitude which not only attained for Roman law its place as the first of the leading legal systems of the world, but made the great Roman jurists of the Principate the inspiration to legal scholarship in succeeding centuries.

It is true that Greek philosophers and rhetoricians also had included questions of law in the range of their investigations. But their interest had been concerned with such problems as the nature of justice, the purpose and place of law in state and society, ethics and psychology, and the art of presenting a convincing forensic argument. Accordingly, discussion of legal matters had been only incidental with them. They had little interest in satisfactory and practical decisions of disputes within the order defined by a specific legal system. Thus their writings had little, if any, influence on the daily practice of the courts in the Greek cities and monarchies.

Roman jurists, on the contrary, for all their philosophical and rhetorical education, never showed more than a superficial interest in purely philosophical problems. The originality of their approach lay in their interest in, and intimate connection with, the practical application of Roman law as it was. Their efforts were directed not at building a purely theoretical jurisprudence, but at demonstrating from every possible angle the practical use to which the institutions of their law could be put....

The need of legal experts was felt early in Rome because the insistence of the primitive law on the strict observance of prescribed forms compelled the average Roman to seek the assistance of men familiar with those forms. This assistance came from the "college" of the *pontifices* (pontiffs), a board of priestly officials who maintained an archive in which descriptions of the various rites and phrases were kept on file. Since none but the *pontifices* themselves had access to this archive, they were able to preserve a monopoly of legal advice....

The *pontifices* laid the ground for the later development of a legal science. For they were more than mere keepers of half-secret formulas. When they supplied inquirers with the proper phrases to be recited in transactions and court actions, they not only taught them the words but also indicated that these would have the desired effect. They were thus in a position to enable magistrates and parties to cope with new situations by showing them that traditional formal acts and phrases could be made applicable to them, and sometimes perhaps by altering or supplementing the traditional words in order to make them suit the circumstances of the case....

... Theirs was not a mechanical activity but required knowledge and skill. When in the third century B.C. the function of advising people about the law slipped out of their hands, the law had already reached such a high degree of intellectual and technical elaboration that only experts were then able to carry on their work....

The strict formalism and ever growing intricacy of the law made ready aid by the *iuris consultus* (he whose advice is sought on questions of law) indispensable, even after the forms themselves had become public knowledge. By the same token, they resulted in the formation of a distinct class of professional experts. To be sure, there was nothing formal or fixed about this. Anybody might engage in the giving of legal advice, no special training or examinations were required, and the success of the jurisconsult depended entirely on the quality of his work. But it is clear that only specialists who through experience had gained knowledge and skill could succeed.

Thus a kind of informal legal instruction came into being. Young men would, in the manner of apprentices, attend the consultations of an outstanding jurisconsult and afterward discuss the cases with him for further information. It was probably not long after the disclosure of the pontifical records that this type of instruction began....

It is not easy for us to realize fully the importance of these legal specialists in republican Rome. Though practicing as private citizens with no official position, they enjoyed a prestige far greater than that of even the most respected lawyer in modern society. This fact was due to the social function performed by them. The Roman jurisconsult did not practice law in the manner we understand by this expression. He would not ordinarily try cases in court or aid parties in their pleading before magistrates and judges. He confined himself to giving advice on questions of law. Moreover, his advice was free. He did his work, not as a way of earning a living, but rather as a gentleman's hobby. It was this very circumstance which gave the legal profession its unusual standing.

The consultative activities of the lawyers were part of the leadership supplied to the people by the aristocracy and were of equal prestige with the holding of high political office. As a matter of fact, most of the men engaged in this work came from the senatorial class and followed the usual political career of this class....

The importance of this role can hardly be overstated. It was during their time that Rome rose to political and economic leadership in the world. The adaptation of Roman law to new conditions — in particular the building up of the *ius honorarium* — was chiefly their work. As has already been said, their activities consisted primarily in giving individuals the technical means to realize their economic aims and in informing them about the legal implications of given situations (*respondere*) in order that they might pursue their rights in court.

As most of the praetors and aediles were not trained jurists but mere politicians, they leaned heavily on the suggestions and opinions of the jurisconsults. The *responsa* (opinions) of the most outstanding jurisconsults enjoyed an authority which for all practical purposes was equal to that of the law itself. In addition to the more indirect influence exerted through their *responsa,* many lawyers also had a direct hand in shaping the principles enforced by the magistrates by sitting on the *consilium,* the advisory council with which, according to immemorial custom, each magistrate surrounded himself; and some of the leading jurists occupied the office of praetor themselves, thus finding a direct opportunity for putting their own new ideas into effect.... [pp. 91-97]

This new approach owed much to the influence of Greek literature, which, from the closing years of the third century B.C., was becoming known in Rome. From Greek philosophical and rhetorical writers, Roman legal experts learned the "dialectical" method and brought it to bear on their specific subject. This method was a mode of logical analysis that both distinguished the various concepts and united under common heads those sharing the same essential traits. No longer content with simply applying existing rules and forms to given situations or with inventing new forms that responded to new needs, the jurists began to seek the logical connections between their institutions by creating a set of theoretical concepts for purposes of definition and classification.

The Roman jurisconsults naturally needed time for the assimilation and full use of the new method. Unfortunately, the details of this intellectual process are unknown to us, since we possess very little information about the actual achievements of the jurists of the second century B.C., although many of them are known to us by name. For some time philosophical interests and traditional methods of dealing with legal problems seem to have been followed by the same men, but with little connection between them. The first who really succeeded in combining the two may have been the younger Quintus Mucius Scaevola (the *pontifex*) who, about 100 B.C., wrote a comprehensive treatise on the *ius civile,* in eighteen books, in which he assembled related legal phenomena and principles under common headings, while at the same time distinguishing the various forms of appearance of these broader categories. For instance, he first defined the general characteristics of what was called possession and then described the various individual forms (*genera*) of possession found in the legal system. The method may have been further perfected in the next generation by Servius Sulpicius Rufus, who is credited by his close friend Cicero with having been the first to introduce the dialectical method into the law.

In determining the significance of this intellectual movement for the history of Roman law, the fact should be borne in mind that the adoption of Greek methods of scientific analysis did not lure the Roman jurists away from their traditional activities or from the case-by-case approach connected with them. Their interest and work remained practical. They did not use the dialectical method for its own sake, for the mere joy of indulging in theoretical analysis, but for the purpose of gaining a deeper understanding of the practical aspects of the law. It was precisely their combination of practical aims with their interest in systematic analysis which enabled the jurists of the last century of the Roman Republic to keep abreast of the problem posed by the rapidly growing Empire.

For the first time, Roman lawyers were really able to see their system as a whole. Familiarity with Greek logic and ethics made them more fully aware of the sociological function of legal institutions and, consequently, enabled them to look behind, and overcome, the rigid formalism of the old *ius civile.* This was the most progressive period in the whole history of Roman law, the time when most of the principles of the praetorian law were conceived and put into force. The realization of all the implications of both *ius civile* and *ius honorarium* — in other words, the erection of the great and intricate structure which *we* know as Roman law — was the work of the "classical" jurists of the imperial period. But the foundations of that structure were laid by the *veteres* (the ancient jurists), as they were called by their classical successors — that is to say, the jurisconsults of the second and first centuries B.C.

Unfortunately, only insignificant remnants of the writings of these legal scholars have been preserved, so that it is impossible to follow in detail the developments just described. But in other respects their period is one of the best-known from contemporary sources, among which the writings and letters of Cicero take a high place. It was also a period when Roman culture in general reached its peak, and a period of growing individualism....

The classical period lasted over two hundred years. Its inception coincided with the coming of the Principate, its end with the beginning of the collapse of the Principate around the middle of the third century A.D. It is the best-known period of Rome's legal history because a considerable part of its immense literary production, in contrast with that of the preceding epoch, has been preserved.... [pp. 100-103]

The degree to which the ideal of a full education in classical law was realized varied, of course, from time to time and from place to place. In early post-classical times — i.e., in the late third and early fourth centuries — a considerable amount of scholarly interest in the law seems to have existed in the West, in all probability centring chiefly in the law school of Rome. The assumption that most, if not all, of the literary activities described took place in the West may very well be correct. This aftermath of classical jurisprudence apparently reached its end under Constantine, when Constantinople became the seat of the government — and thereby the meeting place of the best legal minds — and when the East began generally to overshadow the West. Legal culture in the West took a sharp downward trend, which was aggravated by the confusion and decline of general culture caused by the barbaric invasions.... [p. 144]

At the two outstanding places of legal learning, Berytus and Constantinople, the study of the old authors gave rise in the fifth century to a new type of truly scientific jurisprudence. The revival of legal learning apparently was in the main confined to the two places named. This at least seems to be the conclusion called for by the following circumstances : that the names of several scholars of these two schools are still known, while no name of any professor of any other law school has survived ; and that Justinian allowed only these two schools to carry on under the new plan of instruction introduced by him in connection with the enactment of the Digest.

In their time the professors of the two great Byzantine schools — the "teachers of the universe," as they were admiringly called — enjoyed a tremendous prestige. There is no better proof for this than the fact that Justinian entrusted them with carrying out his plans for the final codification of the whole law. The first in the line of distinguished scholars at Berytus was perhaps Cyrillus, in the early years of the fifth century. A younger contemporary of Cyrillus may have been Patricius, now recognized as the most outstanding among the men of Berytus. Other noted jurists of the fifth century were Demosthenes, Eudoxius, Amblichus, and Leontius. It is known that these men wrote commentaries on imperial rescripts and statutes, as well as on a few works of classical scholars. Nothing of their work has been preserved, but some of it is known from quotations by Justinian's contemporaries, whose works were in part transmitted along with the *Basilica.*

The Byzantine legal science, as we call it, was not, to be sure, the creative and practical kind of jurisprudence the classical period had known. The representatives of this new legal science were teachers, not practitioners. Their ambition was not to produce new legal ideas but to obtain a real knowledge of what the classical jurists had left to posterity and to explain the doctrinal contents of classical decisions. There is, moreover, no doubt that Byzantine legal science was characterized by an utter lack of originality and productivity. In the discovery of doctrinal concepts underlying the practical work of the classical jurists, it can at best be credited with a very modest beginning.

However, this did make it a forerunner of the medieval and modern science of Roman law. Furthermore, whatever its flaws, Byzantine science did succeed in getting back genuine familiarity with the whole of the classical achievement. Its efforts bore rich fruit. Their new insight into the workings of the old law enabled men coming from these schools to improve on the technique of imperial legislation, so that the statutes of Justinian and his immediate predecessors differ favourably, in clarity of both thought and style, from those of the fourth and early fifth centuries. Last but not least, Byzantine legal science was capable of crowning its work by producing that comprehensive compilation and condensation of the law which is known as Justinian's *Corpus Iuris....* [pp. 146-147]

The purpose of the codification was twofold : to serve as an authoritative statement, with legally binding force, of the whole of Roman law ; and as the one and only text to be studied in the schools. It was to replace and did replace all former statements of law, both in literature and in legislation. It was to be the only source of law in the whole Empire. In this way Justinian hoped to make the law uniform throughout the Empire and to displace the diffuse mass of legal materials that had caused so much confusion.

The *Corpus Iuris* consists of three parts : (1) a brief introductory survey of the whole system in four books, called the Institutes ; (2) a collection in fifty books of excerpts from classical literature, called the Digest (*Digesta* ; Latin for "systematic arrangement") or Pandects (*Pandectae* ; Greek for "books containing everything") ; and (3) a collection in twelve books of imperial constitutions, called the Code (*Codex Iustinianus*). In the following discussion the three parts will be described in accordance with the actual course of the codification ; that is to say, in an order opposite to that in which they are listed above.... [p.164]

The Digest or Pandects ... is the most important part of the *Corpus Iuris.* The commission for its compilation was appointed on December 15, 530, and completed its work within three years, so that the Digest could be made public on December 16, 533, with legal force as of December 30 of the same year. It consists of thousands of excerpts from works by (or attributed to) legal writers of the first century B.C. to the fourth century A.D. — in other words, mainly of the classical period. The earliest author used is Quintus Mucius Scaevola, the *pontifex* ; and the latest writers are Arcadius Charisius and Hermogenianus. The majority of the books drawn upon came from the later classical period ; Ulpianus alone furnished about one-third of the whole, Paulus one-sixth. Altogether, the compilers claimed to have examined more than two thousand books with more than three million lines and to have condensed these to about 150,000 lines. [p.166]

NOTE

1. Hans Julius Wolff, *Roman Law* (Norman : University of Oklahoma Press, 1951), pp. 3-166.

HISTORY OF ROMAN LEGAL SCIENCE[1]

Fritz Schulz

From the close of the Second Punic War Roman legal science entered on a new phase which should be called "the Hellenistic period of Roman jurisprudence." In no period known to us was Roman legal science exempt from Greek influence, but it was only in the last two centuries of the Republic that it came to terms with the specific intellectual movement which we call "Hellenism." There was no sudden revolution ; the change took place with true Roman caution and deliberation. But gone were the days when honest Sextus Aelius could shrug his shoulders in humorous contempt of the new learning. The last two centuries of the Republic are the period in which Roman legal science, and indeed Roman civilization as a whole, was faced with the necessity of determining its relations with Hellenism. We shall obtain no comprehensive view of this process if, like the so-called "school of elegant jurisprudence," we are content to inquire in what particulars this or that juristic doctrine was derived from Greek philosophy and rhetoric. What we have to establish, in its totality and complexity, is the attitude of Roman jurisprudence towards Hellenism. In this matter what Roman jurisprudence took over from Hellenism was quite as important as what it rejected or modified. The Hellenistic wave arrived in Rome at a happy moment. On the other hand, Roman legal science was sufficiently developed not to be overwhelmed by Greek influences ; on the other hand, it was still young and far from being petrified, capable of being and prepared to be stimulated and moulded by Greek thought. Roman legal science contained in itself great potentialities but to release them and bring them into activity there was needed the solvent energy of Greek forms. The immensely important result was nothing less than that of Roman legal science developed into a professional science of the Hellenistic type, within the framework of Hellenstic science. This new science was not a *commixtio* of Greek and Roman elements but an organic unity. The formative discipline of Greece enabled the natural and national energy of the Roman science to reveal itself.... [p. 38-39]

The most considerable effect of Greek philosophy on Roman jurisprudence was the adoption by jurisprudence of the dialectical method, an event which has proved of decisive and lasting importance particularly in the science of private law. Here we are concerned with forms and methods, not with contents and results. The characteristic feature of the Hellenistic period is precisely that Hellenism provided the mould of theory into which the Romans poured their national life.

The influence of other non-Roman factors was small. The intensity of Roman nationalism was greater in jurisprudence than in the other professional sciences. [pp. 85-86]

NOTE

1. Fritz Schulz, *History of Roman Legal Science* (London : Oxford University Press, 1946), pp. 39-86.

A COMMON LAW LAWYER LOOKS AT THE CIVIL LAW[1]

F.H. Lawson

Roman law has long been recognized as something of an oddity. It is not very like any other ancient system and, surprisingly enough, its general character is often more like that of English law than of any modern civil law system....

A well-marked and well-known characteristic of Roman law is its tendency to become steadily more universal. Even the most archaic parts of Roman law are peculiarly practical and almost rational. In the beginning Roman law was as formal as any other law, more formal than many. Certain forms were prescribed in accordance with which acts were to be done. Thus certain kinds of things could be conveyed only by a piece of play-acting with copper and scales, known as mancipation. Most promises could be made only by a combination of question and answer called stipulation. There were only certain ways of bringing an action, all highly formal. In all these and other cases, failure to observe the prescribed form made the act invalid, whatever its substantial merits and whatever the intention of the parties.

This sort of formalism is very common in early law. In most countries, the forms have tended to be complicated and elaborate and, whatever they may have been to start with, have rapidly come to look irrational. It is easy to make mistakes ; indeed, sometimes the forms almost seem to have been devised in order to make it hard to avoid slips. There is nothing of this at any time in Roman law. The acts were almost always simple, and their rational character, if not perfectly obvious upon their face, can always be seen as it were just around the corner.

The words were always simple, so simple that it would argue extreme incompetence not to be able to use them without mistake.

Most of the formal acts could only be done by Roman citizens. Indeed, there seems no doubt that in the beginning Roman law was purely a law for Roman citizens. It did not govern the relations of foreigners among themselves or even with Roman citizens. As, however, Rome became a centre of world trade, some way had to be found of deciding disputes in which visiting merchants were concerned. There are many ways of dealing with such problems. The way we have become familiar with is the subject of an important and difficult branch of law, private international law or the conflict of laws. In every modern country this body of law makes two assumptions : first, that any given issue must be tried according to a single system of law and not by a mixture of systems ; and secondly, that this system is not necessarily that of the country where the issue is tried. Another way of dealing with the question would be simply to try all issues in accordance with the law of the court itself, the *lex fori,* but to apply the whole of that law, or, to speak more exactly, any appropriate rule of that law, whatever its origin.

Now the Romans did neither of these things. They did not adopt the former solution because they applied Roman law to all disputes. On the other hand, they did not adopt the latter because from a very early date, perhaps from the very beginning, Roman law provided an apparatus containing not only the formal acts of which examples have been given, but also informal acts, such as the transfer of property by a mere physical delivery based upon some appropriate understanding arrived at between transferor and transferee, or the simple loan of money or of other goods intended to be consumed. This apparatus of informal acts was made available to non-Romans as well as to Romans, and they were allowed to use all varieties of the stipulations except a single one which was reserved for the use of Roman citizens.... [pp. 91-94]

However, this is not the end of the story for Roman law, for from the third century A.D. onwards almost all the free inhabitants of the Empire were Roman citizens, and by a parallel process the more formal and less rational elements of Roman law disappeared, leaving the universal elements, which were also the more rational, to stand alone. There is little or nothing that is purely national in the Roman Law contained in Justinian's *Corpus Juris.* It was ready for reception by any people that had reached a state of civilization which demanded it and was capable of using it....

Another remarkable characteristic of Roman law is that it was a law of movement. By this I mean that little of the law in the books is concerned to describe what is. Everywhere the question is how does a particular legal situation come into existence and how will it disappear ? This is most obvious, as has often been remarked, in the Institutes of Gaius.... [p. 96]

. . . Roman law is really very remarkable. Most early laws devote most of their attention to the static elements, especially problems of kinship and marriage and of crime ; and they are composed mainly of prohibitions. But the element of taboo, which is so strong in them, is hardly visible in Roman law. Changes are regarded as normal, to be provided for by the appropriate legal instruments. Even in family law this is the point that is emphasized. Even the arrangements inside the family, where stability might be expected to reign, where subjected in theory to the absolute control of an enlightened despot, the *pater-*

familias, and anything that might have operated as a legal check, such as the continuance of a joint family under the headship of brothers whose consent might be needed for any act, was frowned upon, and indeed excluded. Even persons were made to approximate in many ways to things, as particles capable of moving and being moved with great freedom according to a very simple set of rules and principles.... [p. 101]

NOTE

1. F.H. Lawson, *A Common Law Lawyer Looks at the Civil Law* (Ann Arbor : University of Michigan Law School, 1953), pp. 91-101.

THE COMPLEXITY OF LEGAL AND ETHICAL EXPERIENCE[1]

F.S.C. Northrop

The essential connection between language and ethical and legal norms becomes evident in a concrete way when one compares the symbolism of mathematical physics with that of ordinary language with respect to the ethical implications of each. In mathematical physics individual entities are not regarded as truly known unless the universal laws — that is, the complex relations — which define their properties and which they satisfy are specified. This means that a truly known individual, even a truly known man, is always an entity which in its essential nature is an instance of a universal law. Directly experienced man is of a quite different character, as the ethics and the legal procedures of cultures which have never discovered the mathematical physicist's way of knowing clearly demonstrate. In all such cultures, where only the ordinary languages are used, moral man is always inductively observed, family and tribal man. Never, in the social norms for ordering human relations, is he conceived as universal man. Thus, the notion that colour of skin or family connection or tribe has nothing to do with the norms of a moral society is in fact foreign to peoples and cultures which have not discovered the way of knowing individuals by means of the linguistic universalism of deductively formulated mathematical physics, a mode of knowing which occurred first with ancient Greeks.

It was this way of knowing, passing over through Greek philosophy into Roman law, which gave rise to the Western law of contract and to the novel moral idea that no rule for ordering personal or social conduct is truly moral unless any human being whatever can be substituted for an instance of the rule. Then, for the first time, moral and political man was broken loose from Roman, Greek, Hebrew, Arab, Hindu, or Chinese family and tribal man. And even with the Romans, the break was made largely as an ideal and only in part in fact. The point to be noted, however, is that prior to the philosophers of ancient Greek mathematical physics and the Stoic Romans the idea of moral man being universal man had not been conceived even as an ideal. In the case of Hinduism and its Laws of Manu, this is unequivocally clear. Different legal penalties are applied for identical offences according to the caste to which one belongs, and a higher moral quality is assigned to the patriarchal families descended from Manu than any other patriarchal families in the Hindu-Aryan community.... [pp. 177-178]

The distinction between the different conceptions of scientific method in the common law and the civil and Roman law traditions has considerable historical and philosophical importance. It means that the conceptual generalization in the *jus gentium* of Roman law and the eventual triumph of the concepts of the *jus gentium* over those of the *jus civile* in the Digest of Justinian did not have its origin solely in the practical needs of the Romans to carry on trade with non-Romans, as some legally positivistically minded students of Roman law would like to suggest. It finds its basis instead in a novel scientific way of thinking about these and all other practical transactions and disputes....

A "verbal contract" was called by the Romans a "stipulation" and took a question-and-answer form. It contained two elements : form and agreement. The form required that the same principle verb be used in the question put by the questioner and in the answer given that sealed the commitments of the agreement as expressed in the question. The stipulation or verbal contract had two important implications quite apart from the verbal constancy of its form. First, it placed the burden of specifying the contact upon the questioner. Second, it required the agreement of the person who answered.... The key, however, to the mentality of Roman law and civil law shows in another characteristic of the stipulation, which Professor Lawson describes as follows :

> If we consider the content of the stipulation, we shall see at once that it must have been infinitely variable. The stipulation was not a contract but a contractual form, a mould for contracts.

Expressed in terms of mathematical logic, this means that the stipulation in Roman law entailed two technical concepts : (1) the concept of the variable, designated in modern mathematical and logical notation by the symbol x and meaning "any one" as opposed to the proper name of a specific one, on the one hand, and to the class concept of all the sensuously similar ones on the other hand ; (2) the concept of the matrix, or propositional form, in which the material commonsense concepts, called by modern logicians "material constants," are replaced with variables. The scientific importance of these two logical concepts is that they break scientific statements loose from specific material examples of the formal properties of the statements. This is precisely what the stipulation did with respect to the rigid codes with their specific law of status content of the pre-Stoic Roman Twelve Tables. Anything whatever could be contracted regardless of its common sense material content provided that the form by which the content was specified possessed certain formal properties. The second scientific importance of the notion of the variable is that it enables one to achieve generality for more than one individual or instance while at the same time preserving the fact that one is dealing with one particular individual and one particular instance. Thereby justice is done to the individuality of the case as well as to its generality. In short, the concept of the variable brings both the concept of univeral formal lawfulness and the notion of equity into Roman legal science.... [pp. 219-221]

NOTE

1. F.S.C. Northrop, *The Complexity of Legal and Ethical Experience* (Boston : Little, Brown and Company, 1959), pp. 177-221.

THE THEORETICAL CONSTRUCTS OF WESTERN CONTRACTUAL LAW[1]

J.C. Smith

The fundamental division of all actions in classical Roman law into *actiones in rem* and *actiones in personam* ... reflects a fundamental division in kinds of rights. Rights *in rem* are usually referred to as rights against all the world and rights *in personam* as rights against specific persons. Thus a person who has a proprietary right in relation to a specific object has a right against everyone in the legal system, all of whom are under a correlative duty to refrain from interfering with the object and the owner's enjoyment of it, while a person who has a contractual right has it only against the other party to the contract. This description is not completely accurate, however, since one can only have rights against individuals jointly, but not against everyone in the legal system in mass. This fact was recognized by Professor Hohfeld, who defined a right *in rem* as "one of a large class of fundamentally similar yet separate rights . . . residing in a single person (or a group of persons) but availing respectively against persons constituting a very large and indefinite class of people."[2] This definition also, however, does not accurately describe the right *in rem*, as the most fundamental characteristic of these relations is that the holder of the duty need not be named, but this definition forces one to name every single person in the legal system as holders of similar duties in order to indicate fully the range of the relation....

To say that a specific person A owns object X is to say that A has a right against "universal" man, or man conceived as a universally quantified variable for whom anyone in the legal system may be substituted, and thus, if A has a right *in rem* against any one person in the legal system, he has the same right against anyone else.... [T]he division of legal relations into those *in rem* and those *in personam* is fundamental to Western ... legal science.... The ancient form of Roman procedure ... was the *legis actiones*, the earliest and most important of which was the *actio sacramenti*, wherein the parties would challenge each other to stake a wager as to the correctness of their claim, and the question tried was which of the two parties had been correct in their wager. This same procedure could be and was used whether the action was to recover property, a debt, or for compensation.

Under the formulary procedure of classical law, however, all actions were either *in rem* or *in personam*. The crux of this procedure was the formula drawn up by the *praetor*, in which were stated the issues the *judex* was to decide. The two basic parts of the formula were the *intentio*, which set out the claim of the plaintiff, and the *condemnatio*, delegating to the *judex* power to condemn or acquit the defendant. The basic procedural difference between an action *in rem* and an action *in personam* is that in the former the defendant was not mentioned in the *intentio*, while in the latter he was. An example of an *intentio* is as follows :

> Titius be judge. Should it appear that the slave Stichus, about whom this action has been raised, belongs to A.A. in quiritary right,

The *condemnatio* would then follow :

> then, unless the slave be restored, whatever be his value, in that, Judge, you will condemn N.N. to A.A. should it not so appear, you will acquit him.[3]

Whereas the *intentio* of a formula *in personam* would read :

> Titius be judge. Should it appear that N.N. ought to pay 50,000 sesterces to A.A., in that sum,

The *condemnatio* would then follow :

> Judge, condemn N.N. to A.A. ; should it not so appear, acquit him.[4]

In any action there are usually two questions to be answered : First, whether the plaintiff has the right claimed, and second, whether there has been a breach of that right. Usually the answer to one of these questions is self-evident, and the other forms the main basis of the dispute. If the dispute concerned the existence of a right *in rem*, then the action would be an action *in rem*, since the identity of the defendant was irrelevant to the answer to this question. In a property dispute, for instance, the basic issue was not whether the plaintiff had a better claim to the object than the defendant, but whether the plaintiff owned the object, that is had rights *in rem* concerning it ; and the identity of the defendant was irrelevant to the answer to this question, since the duty rested upon anyone in the legal system. If the plaintiff did have such a right, the breach of it was self-evident, because the property was usually in the possession of the defendant, who needed only to be mentioned in the *condemnatio.* If, however, the existence of the right *in rem* was self-evident such as in delictual actions, where if the right exists in the legal system anyone will have it, the basic issue set out in the *intentio* was whether there had been a breach of that right by the specific defendant, who therefore had to be named.

The formulary procedure was introduced into the *jus civile* by the *lex Aebutia,* which, according to Professor Girard, could not have been passed before 149 B.C., and evidences of which begin to appear abundantly during the time of Q.Mucius Scaevola. Since the distinction between *actiones in rem* and *actiones in personam* was made by the time of Cicero, it can be said with a fair degree of certainty that contractual legal science was created in the period of the Scaevolas, which is the same period that, according to Professor Westrup, the concept of ownership first appears.

A most significant reference is made by Aulus Gellius in regard to the *lex Aebutia,* where he records the statement of a lawyer that, "all the ancient lore of the Twelve Tables . . . was put to sleep by the Aebutian law."[5] The only explanation which gives meaning to this statement is that the *lex Aebutia,* by introducing a new flexible procedural system, made it possible for a new type of susbtantive law to replace the old law of the Twelve Tables. [pp. 263-266]

NOTES

1. J.C. Smith, "The Theoretical Constructs of Western Contractual Law," in Northrop and Livingston, eds., *Cross Cultural Understanding* (New York : Harper & Row, 1964), pp. 263-266.
2. W.N. Hohfeld, *Fundamental Legal Conceptions* (New Haven : Yale University Press), p. 72.
3. James Muirhead, *Historical Introduction to the Private Law of Rome,* 3rd ed., (London : A & C Black, 1916), p. 327.
4. *Ibid.,* p. 325.
5. Aulus Gellius, *The Attic Nights of Aulus Gellius,* III, 16.X.1-6.

STOIC LOGIC AND ROMAN JURISPRUDENCE[1]

Juan Miquel

The inquiry into the logical skills of Roman jurists is linked to the following two tasks : to determine the effect of Hellenistic learning on Roman law, and the method of reasoning of Roman jurists....

Schulz described the fruitful encounter of Roman scientific thought with Greek dialectics in compelling words. He characterizes it as an event of the utmost importance in the history of the humanities, for, as he says, "if Plato's enthusiastic account of dialectics applies anywhere at all, it is here : For Roman jurisprudence dialectics was indeed the fire of Prometheus."[2] This last phrase is significant, as Schulz almost exclusively speaks of the influence of Platonic dialectics.

All these views use the word "dialectics" as if it referred to a given, definite entity. As opposed to this, the question surely should be : What was "dialektikē" for the Greeks ? Has the meaning of this term remained unchanged throughout the course of time ? What distinguishes Platonic dialectics on the one side and the Aristotelian on the other from Stoic dialectics ? What meaning had the word "dialectica" when used by the Romans of the late Republic (especially Cicero) ? I shall limit myself to the last question. I believe one should begin by assuming that the term "dialectica" denoted Stoic logic, and I shall, therefore, in the course of these inquiries use the latter expression to avoid misunderstandings which could easily arise.

The problem of finding criteria for the difference between Aristotelian and Stoic logic received a fundamental clarification by Lukasiewicz. It was the merit of this great Polish logician to have been the first to demonstrate that the Aristotelian syllogism is a system of true principles, while Stoic logic is the ancient form of propositional logic. Stoic logic is propositional logic, Aristotelian logic is a logic of names (predicates). The basic difference is that in the former only propositional variables occur, while in the latter there are variables which stand for names. By way of an example, Lukasiewicz makes use of the inference formula which the Stoics placed at the head of their dialectics as the first "indemonstrable" inference syllogism :

If the first, then the second, but now the first, hence the second.

"In this formula," Lukasiewicz notes, "the words 'the first' and 'the second' are variables, for the Stoics used ordinal numbers to mark variables. It is clear that here the variables can only be meaningfully replaced by propositions, f.i., 'it is day' and 'it is light'. Having replaced the variables by these propositions, the result is a sentence that recurs again and again as a textbook example in Stoic writings : "If it is day, then it is light."[3]

Lukasiewicz stressed a further important difference which distinguishes the Aristotelian from the Stoic syllogisms : "Aristotelian syllogisms are logical principles, and a logical principle is a statement in which, beside logical constants, only propositional variables or named variables appear and which is true for all values of the variables occurring in it. Stoic syllogisms are inference schemata which have the import of inference rules, and an inference rule is a prescription which enables the person drawing the inference to derive new propositions from accepted propositions."[4]

These two conceptions of Lukasiewicz form the foundation stones for my investigation. Accordingly, I shall apply modern logic to the Roman sources, as this will give us an insight into the logical structures which provide the basis for some of the decisions made by Roman jurists. I believe that, with the help of modern logic, certain passages in the original texts can be explained whose authenticity has been impugned by modern scholarship in Roman law, although these passages bear eloquent witness to logical acuity and scientific exactitude. The aim of this study is to answer the question of the form of the logic which Roman jurists used, and to solve the problem whether they were able to think "axiomatically"....

As facile generalizations are the basic fault of the ongoing discussion of the influence of Hellenistic science on Roman jurisprudence, it will be useful to abstain, for the time being, from making generalizations when we apply modern logic to Roman sources, and to begin instead with concrete determinations. In order not to contravene this methodological rule right at the outset, the following three exegeses should be considered only as samples :

A. Proculus on the Disjunction

D. 50, 16, 124, Proculus, Epistles, Book II[5]

> The following words, "So-and-So or So-and-So," are not only disjunctive, but subdisjunctive in their signification. They are disjunctive ; for example, when we say, "It is either day or night," for having suggested one of two things, it is necessary to cancel the other, since to suppose one disposes of the other. Therefore, by a similar form of words, an expression can be subdisjunctive. There are, however, two kinds of subdisjunctives ; one where in a molecular proposition both atomic propositions cannot be true, and neither of them may be ; as, for instance, when we say, "He is either sitting or walking," for as no one can do both these things at the same time, neither of them may be true, for example, if the person should be lying down.
>
> The other kind of disjunctive occurs in a statement where of two things neither may be true, but both of them can happen to be ; for instance, when we say "Every animal either acts or suffers," for there is no animal which neither acts nor suffers, but an animal may act and suffer at the same time.

This passage, which has been somewhat neglected in modern research, is of fundamental significance for the question of the logical skills of Roman jurists. At the same time it is also an important item of evidence for an historical account of Stoic logic as such : In the area of the (incomplete) disjunction we have at our disposal only fragmentary source materials.

It is almost certain that the quoted passage contains an item of Stoic dialectics. First of all, it contains propositional logic, for the two blank spaces "this one, that one" are being filled by propositions. Furthermore, it can easily be documented that the propositions "it is either day or night" and "he either sits or walks" are typical examples of Stoic logic....

Proculus discusses the phrase *this one or that one* which can have three different meanings in ordinary language. These are clearly distinguishable from each other with the help of Stoic logic. If one considers the facts which Proculus has in mind, namely *let this one or that one be my heir, to this one or that one give*

I the bequest etc., it seems at first glance surprising that not names (perhaps Titius, Maevius) are inserted for the variables *this one — that one*, but propositions, like *it is day — it is night.* Upon further consideration this is, however, explainable. Because, to quote Wittgenstein, "Names are like points, sentences are like arrows, they make sense."

Stoic logic is propositional logic. Hence it shows how composite propositions can be formed out of simple propositions with the help of logical constants like "not, and, or, if . . . so." Consequently, *this one or that one* is a molecular expression. It consists of two atomic expressions which are linked by the constant *or. This one, that one* are propositional variables, because they can only be replaced meaningfully by propositions. These variables have a dual purpose : First they indicate the blank space, secondly they express generality. As they are isomorph, this second purpose is only incompletely achieved. A fundamental contrast exists between the variables *this one — that one* and the constant *or* : while *this one — that one* are complete expressions *per se*, the expression *or* is obviously incomplete and requires an addition, indeed it is so incomplete and in need of supplementation that it carries two blank spaces.

At the very beginning, Proculus distinguishes the disjunctive (complete exclusionary disjunction) from the subdisjunctive clause ; the latter, in turn, is subdivided into two categories : a first category (the incomplete exclusionary disjunction) and a second (the incomplete inclusionary disjunction)....

Yet another question arises : Which facts had Proculus in mind in considering matters of logic ? A fragment from the Codex informs us about that :

4. C.6, 38, 4 : The Same to John, Praetorian Prefect[6]

When anyone appoints an heir, leaves a bequest, creates a trust, makes a grant of freedom, or establishes a guardianship, in the following words : "Let either So-and-So, or So-and-So be my heir," or "I give and bequeath to So-and-So or So-and-So," or "I wish property to be given to So-and-So," or "I desire that So-and-So, or So-and-So, shall become free, or act as guardian," or "I order this to be done," a doubt arose whether the appointment, the bequest, the trust, the grant of freedom, or the appointment of a guardian made in this way was not void ; and whether the position of the party in possession was the better ; or whether both parties were called to enjoy or assume benefits or burdens of this kind, and whether they should be admitted to any order, or whether both should be admitted without distinction.

In the case of the appointment of heirs, some authorities thought that the first one named should be considered as the designated heir, and the second as the substitute ; and others held that in the case of trusts, only the last one mentioned would have the right to accept it, as availing himself of the final intention of the testator.

Anyone who desires to succinctly dispose of the disputes of these jurisconsults will have no insignificant number of volumes to examine, as there is a great variety of opinions to be reconciled, for not only the legal authorities, but also the Imperial Constitutions which the said authorities have cited, are known to differ.

Therefore having rejected all this verbosity, it has seemed to us preferable that the conjunction "or" should be taken to mean "and," so that it may be understood in a certain sense to be copulative, and hence admit the first person mentioned without excluding the second ; just as, for the sake of example, in the interdict *Quod vi aut clam*, the conjunction *aut* is clearly used in the sense of *et* ; and, in all cases of this kind having reference to either the appointment of heirs or of the beneficiaries of a trust, or to grants of freedom, or to guardianships, it may be understood that both parties are entitled to equal shares of the estate, and can, in like manner, receive legacies, and that both will be entitled to their freedom, and that both can discharge the duties of guardianship, so that no one will be prevented from enjoying the liberality of the testator, and greater protection will be afforded to wards, and when a doubt exists as to who are entitled to the guardianship, the property of the wards may not, in the meantime, be lost.

We order that these rules shall be observed when the instrument in question has reference to persons. Where, however, only one person is mentioned, but property is left as follows, "I do give and bequeath such-or-such property to So-and-So," or "I leave it to So-and-So in trust," then, in accordance with the ancient regulations, and the provisions of antiquity, the laws remain unimpaired, no change having been introduced in them by this Constitution.

We order that this rule shall also apply to contracts.

Given at Constantinople, on the day before the *Kalends* of May, after the fifth Consulate of Lampadius and Orestes. 531.

Justinian informs us on a controversy among classical jurists. If somebody had given instructions for the appointment of an heir, a legacy, a trust, a manumission or a guardianship using the words :

"Let either So-and-So or So-and-So by my heir" or "I bequeath to So-and-So or So-and-So" or "I wish property to be given" or "I desire So-and-So or So-and-So to be free" or "to act as guardian', or 'I desire this to be done"

it was contested whether :

a) the appointment of an heir, the bequest, the trust, the grant of freedom and the appointment of a guardian be void
b) the position of the party in possession be better
c) both parties were to enjoy the benefits or to assume the burdens

and

a') they should be admitted in any order
b') both parties without distinction
because

1. In the case of the appointment of heirs some authorities thought that the first one named should be considered as the designated heir, and the second as substitute
2. and others held that in the case of trusts only the last one mentioned would have the right to accept it, as availing himself of the final intention of the testator ;

The last-mentioned two opinions do not seem to exclude but rather to complement each other.

Basically Justinian reaches the same result as Proculus : *Therefore it seemed to us .... that the connective "or" should be taken to mean "and" ....*

However, this legislative intervention is no more than a dictate, because Justinian confuses the purely possible (*or*) with the necessary (*and*), in contrast to Proculus who skilfully uses logic as an instrument of thought to achieve a more just decision in the case : *both parties without distinction.*

Thus, the entire decision rests on two pillars :

1. Taking the disjunction to be inclusionary (p or q);
2. Symmetry of the disjunction (p or q is equivalent to q or p).

B. Scaevola and the Logical Square
D. 14, 1, 129, Scaevola, Questions, Book XII[7]

Where anyone stipulates as follows, "Will you pay ten aurei if a ship arrives and Titius becomes Consul?" The money will not be due unless both of these events take place. The same rule applies to the opposite case, "Do you promise if a ship does not arrive, and Titius does not become Consul," for it is essential that neither of these things should occur. The following written agreement resembles this, namely, "If a vessel does not arrive, and Titius is not made Consul." When, however, the stipulation is in the following terms, "Will you pay if a ship arrives, or Titius becomes Consul?" it is sufficient for one of these events to take place. On the other hand, if it is expressed as follows, "Will you pay if a ship does not arrive, or Titius does not become Consul?" it will be sufficient if only one of these things does not occur....

The result of our exegeses of the texts is that Proculus, Julianus and Scaevola had a thorough education in logic. The following question, regarding which I can do no more than to provide some hints, then is: Were these jurists capable of thinking axiomatically?

. . . I shall ... start out by contrasting topics and axiomatics. Let us take as example: *he either sits or walks.*

a) When we apply the rule *having suggested one of two things the other is necessarily cancelled* to this rule, the result is the implication *if he is sitting, he does not walk.*

We now examine this implication according to the rule quoted by Sextus Empiricus:

b) We form the contradictory antithesis of the consequent: *he walks.*
c) It must be incompatible with the antecedent: *he is sitting*; this irreconcilability (*conflict*) is to be understood as impossibility: *he cannot.* Since *he is sitting, he walks = both,* the result is *both cannot be the case.* Since this incompatibility is only a partial one (*incomplete conflict*), we can proceed in the following way:
b1) We form the contradictory antithesis of the antecedent: *he is not sitting.*
c1) We compare it with the consequent *he is not sitting, not walking = neither.* Both can exist together: *neither could be the case.*

Now we apply the *since to suppose one disposes of the other* to *(every animal) either may act or suffer.*

a) *if it does not act, it suffers;*
b) *it does not suffer;*
c) *it does not act, it does not suffer = neither : neither cannot be the case;*
b1) *it acts;*
c1) *it acts, it suffers = both : it could be so that both is the case.*

We have now to add to these formulae of modal logic the truth-functional connectives of the predicate calculus:

1. *he cannot = no one can (respectively nothing);*
2. *he could = someone can.*

If we apply 1. to *both cannot be the case* and to *it cannot be so that neither can be the case* and 2. to *neither could be the case* and to *it could be so that both could be the case* the result is : *no one can both (i.e. occurring at the same time) ; someone can neither ; no (animal) can neither (i.e. there is none that neither acts nor suffers*).

There is no need to repeat that the formulae obtained in this way can be applied to the text by Scaevola and that further rules can be derived from them ; neither is it necessary to repeat that the passage by Julianus presents a correct, consequential evolution of the logical square. This is axiomatics in the sense of this term in which Viehweg uses it, for we started out with a basic truth (*having suggested one thing, the other is necessarily cancelled* respectively : *and besides having denied one it is necessary to affirm the other*) and then proceeded in a purely deductive way in the footsteps of Proculus. [pp. 85-122]

NOTES

1. Juan Miquel, "Stoic Logic and Roman Jurisprudence," trans. George H. Kendal, *Zeitschrift Der Savigny Stiftung fur Rechtsgeschichte Romanistische Abteilung* 87 (1970) : 85-122.

2. F. Schulz, *History of Roman Legal Science* (Oxford : Clarendon Press, 1946), p. 68.

3. Lukasiewicz, "To the History of Propositional Logic," 5 *Erkenntnus* (1935) : 111.

4. *Ibid.*, p. 114.

5. S.P. Scott, trans., The Digests or Pandects, Book L, Title XVI, 124, vol. 2, *The Civil Law* (New York : AMS Press, 1973), p. 276.

6. S.P. Scott, trans., The Code of Justinian, Book VI, Title XXXVII,4, vol. 14, *The Civil Law, op. cit.* p. 39.

7. S.P. Scott, trans., The Digests or Pandects, Book XLV, Title I, 129, vol. 10, *The Civil Law, op. cit.* p. 133.

PRINCIPLES OF ROMAN LAW[1]

Fritz Schulz

The volume of Roman legal material based on such state legislation is revealed on examination as surprisingly small. It is true that, when in a nation's youth or in a community living in a primitive state of law, the state-enacted law is found to play a minor part, it must not be concluded that such peoples are averse to this form of law. When, however, in the course of the 500 years or so of the highly developed culture (particularly in the sphere of law) in the epoch from the end of the Second Punic War to Diocletian, state legislation is found very much in the background and is confined to certain functions, then we may assume that a Roman principle existed which read : Romans are basically opposed to codification and maintain a strict reserve in regard to statutes. The "law-inspired nation" is not statute-inspired.

We must not allow ourselves to be confused by the fact that the codification of the Twelve Tables marks the beginning of Roman legal history. Apart from the consideration that the work in question does not belong to our period, it stands entirely alone in Roman legal history and arose — as is obvious both from its general conception and its form — under the influence of Greek codifications. Moreover, not only did Roman legislation never again revert to the laconic style used for the Twelve Tables, which by its very nature laid no claim to absolute accuracy, but the idea of a code embodying the entire law was never even seriously considered up to the end of the classical period. When, towards the end of his life, Julius Caesar entertained the idea of codification this, like others of his later measures, only shows how strongly he had become influenced by the spirit of Hellenism. In any case it cannot have been more than a fleeting notion, for no attempt to put into execution was ever made. Not till about 450 years later — at the time of the East Roman Empire under Theodosius II (429) — did the codification plan appear again, a fact which is as significant as that the plan failed. What was accomplished in 438 was merely an official collection of imperial legislation intended only to supplement existing private collections and to contain the constitutions since Constantine. The first complete codification after the Twelve Tables is to be found at the end of Roman legal history proper : plainly though Justinian's codification (529-34) bears a Roman stamp, it is, nevertheless, as a whole a Greek-inspired piece of work. Codifications of special legal departments such as constitutional law, civil law, or criminal law were never even attempted. It is only the municipal laws of the Roman and Latin townships that might be classed as codifications of local administrative law.

Side by side with this fundamental rejection of codification we find a general basic disinclination to accept any kind of legal enactment by the state.... [pp. 6-8]

In his famous work... *On the Mission of our Time in Regard to Legislation and Legal Science* Savigny in 1814 formulated the task of the legislator as follows : Codes are bad and should be avoided. It is impossible to avoid enacting some statutes, but these should be confined within narrow limits ; they should be employed when "higher political purposes demand the modification of the existing law" or the law gives rise to doubts or when a decision has to be given of so positive a nature that state legislation is essential (e.g., the determination of the period of prescription). Savigny's contentions have often been attacked, but they certainly are the exact counterpart of Roman principles, the views held for hundreds of years by the men in whose hands lay the development of Roman law and in which Savigny had steeped himself so thoroughly. The reasons which determined the attitude of the Romans must have been similar to those influencing Savigny, their line of thought being as follows. Codification is apt to lead to literal interpretation and to deflect attention from the nature of the matter itself ; a code purports to be a complete and finished whole, which it is not ; it demands abstract formulation of legal rules, a process which seems full of danger to the Roman mind and is too rigid as a system to be capable of adaptation. Similar, though weaker, objections are entertained against single statutes ; these may be indispensable on occasion, but should only be enacted in case of necessity.

In the republican and classical periods practice guided by jurisprudence was considered the best method of producing legal rules ; this applies to civil law, law of civil procedure, but also to criminal and constitutional law. The traditional rules emerging from this combination of legal decisions and practice may be called customary law, but it must not be forgotten that this "customary law" of the era up to the end of the classical period is not identical with the customary law of Justinian or modern continental theory.... [pp. 12-14]

Whatever one may think of the legal nature of Roman "customary law," though it may be admitted that it contains legal rules, it is, as already mentioned, something basically different from state-enacted laws in that it need not, like the latter, be scrupulously observed even by such as disapprove of their content. A long-established rule may therefore be attacked in juristic discussions on account of its inadequacy and an attempt made to replace it by another, a proceeding which is out of the question in the case of a statutory rule on which the magistrates have taken the oath. Everything, then, was in a state of flux and it is possible to apply to the customary law of republican and classical times the words in which Munroe Smith describes American case law, excepting only that in the case of America the guidance of legal science — so important in Rome — is lacking :

> In their effort to give to the social sense of justice articulate expression in rules and in principles, the method of the law finding experts has always been experimental. The rules and principles of case law have never been treated as final truths, but as working hypotheses, continually rested in those great laboratories of the law, the courts of justice. Every new case is an experiment ; and if the accepted rule which seems applicable yields a result which is felt to be unjust, the rule is reconsidered. It may not be modified at once . . . but if a rule continues to work injustice, it will eventually be reformulated. The principles themselves are continually retested ; for if the rules derived from a principle do not work well, the principle itself must ultimately be re-examined.

In principle this was the kind of legal development preferred in republican and classical times, i.e., a gradual progressive formation by means of cases and juristic discussion — not fixed by the rigid rules of statutes or binding customary law — and in co-operation with the magistrate entrusted with jurisdiction who can in individual cases either apply or refuse the legal remedy.... [pp. 16-17]

Private Roman law as portrayed by classical writers attains an extraordinary, almost logical, definiteness. The number of juristic conceptions which play a part in it is comparatively small, as all which pertain to special or non-Roman variations are set aside. The legal rules take on the character of apodictic truths, as any limitations imposed by public law or extra-legal duties are ignored. Often the jurists' statements almost give the impression of a mathematical treatise or rather of a treatise on a law of nature, a law, however, not so generally applicable as was claimed for the Stoical law of nature, but one within the framework of Roman legislation and retaining certain traditional principles and axioms — in short, a Roman law of nature lacking the speculative airiness of the Greek conception. The Roman jurists' aim is to find — within the specified framework — the rule arising out of the nature of the thing itself, out of conditions as they are. Take, for example, the legal matters not — or scarcely — regulated by statute : acquisition of possession and ownership and also the law relating to sale and hire, capacity to contract, doctrine of degree of liability, and so forth. In all these matters it may be observed that legal writers are not satisfied with describing the positive Roman law in force at the time, but that they are at pains to evolve a law of nature. This is the determining cause for the peculiar manner in which legal science is presented ; it does not actually prove the rules stated, but derives them direct from the contemplation of life, from the *ratio iuris.* This accounts for its dogmatic assurance, but also for its occasional shortsighted orthodoxy....

In the doctrine of private law, particularly Roman private law, the leaning shown by Roman jurists towards a law of nature appeared once more ; this in despite of the historical school, nay, particularly in the case of its leaders. In Jherings' inimitable phrasing the trend of legal science was towards "a dialectical jurisprudence seeking to clothe the positive in the shining garments of logic, to strengthen as far as possible the autonomy of juristic thought and to raise the positive till it reached the ideal heights of logical juristic truth." Jhering, however, rightly recognized that German legal science was in this "dazzled by the scintillating logic with which Roman law is imbued." The manner in which Roman law scholars, such as Puchta and his successors, described certain Roman conceptions as the only possible ones, rejecting others (such as direct agency, assignment of claims, acquisition of ownership from a non owner, positive duties running with the land, such as rent charges, etc.) as unreasonable, as incompatible with the *ratio iuris,* as impossible of contruction, is in truth reminiscent of the orthodoxy of Roman jurisprudence.... [pp. 34-38]

Inherent in the Roman conception of liberty are certain limitations ; in Rome, therefore, it is possible for liberty to be one of the principles on which the law is based. "Freedom," to the Romans, never meant the capacity to do or leave undone what one pleased, to live at one's own sweet will ; only such were not free as were subject to a *dominus,* a master who reigned over them and in relation to whom they were deprived of all rights of self-determination. Thus the individual was not free when he was a slave, a whole nation was not free when at its head was an absolute monarch or when it was subject to a foreign yoke. Where there was no "master" in this sense the Romans as individuals or as a people were free, however the degree of *libertas* might vary....

Therefore the Romans designated as free even a community which, by joining the Roman alliance, was deprived of internationally recognized sovereignty ; in such a case Roman paramountcy was not in the form of a Dominate. *Libertas* is a truly Roman conception : clear, limited, practical, somewhat matter-of-fact.

This freedom the Romans accounted their greatest privilege, and to this they clung tenaciously for a long period. They considered their strivings after liberty to be a national peculiarity ; all other nations could in their opinon endure a state of servitude, but not the Roman nation ; their state appeared to them as a "paradise of freedom," and in their struggles against the monarchs of the East they considered themselves to be the champions of liberty.

The Roman principle of liberty is first apparent in the history of Roman constitutional law. It is unnecessary to describe the vehemence with which in republican and classical times the absolute monarchy (*regnum*) was rejected. Nor was the Principate a *regnum.* The founder of the Principate was honoured with the name of "Augustus," and not, as had been suggested, with that of the first Roman king ; the decision with which both Augustus and Tiberius rejected the title *dominus,* even as a form of address, is most significant.... [pp. 140-143]

The Roman principle of liberty led to extreme individualism in the domain of private law. It is true that the Romans probably passed through a medieval period of fettered rights, but in the era which we have selected for our investigations, beginning with the second century B.C., the individualistic nature of Roman private law is undeniable and has never been denied....

The relation of husband and wife, for example, was extremely individualistic (except in the case of the *manus* marriage). Marriage and divorce were accomplished without the intervention of the state. No restrictions were placed on divorce — it was not even necessary for the parties to agree on divorce, a unilateral declaration sufficed.... [pp. 146-147]

. . .[B]oth under private and under public law, the bounds of ownership were very wide, much wider than in German law. A Roman principle must have existed to the effect that the right of ownership was to be as unrestricted as possible and the greatest possible latitude given to individual action and initiative. Both real and personal property could be freely alienated and divided ; under republican law statutory provisions prohibiting alienation and limiting the right of disposal were entirely unknown ; in the classical imperial era they existed only in a very few cases ; post classical law increased their number and finally recognized even the restrictive effect of acts-in-the-law prohibiting disposal.... [p. 153]

The law of succession, finally, was also individualistic in character. Statutory rules of succession were of minor importance in Roman eyes ; they were significantly described as the law of intestate succession, i.e., they were only applied in cases when there was no testamentary succession, the latter being considered the normal case.... [p. 156]

Thus Roman private law is in very truth a *monumentum aere perennius* of the Roman principle of liberty.

In the year 1848, when Theodor Mommsen was 31, he made a speech containing the following passage : "The liberty of the citizen as reflected in Roman civil law is so great that no extension, but on the contrary some limitation, is needed.... If, therefore, we are endeavouring to develop a law suitable for free citizens, we may rely absolutely as regards civil law in this respect on the Roman law of the classical era and be certain of discovering therein a spirit which may often conflict with the principle of solidarity as between the citizens, but never with that of the liberty of the individual." The young speaker even said : "The revival of classical civil law in Germany is equivalent to the beginning of the revolution which has started the work of leading European peoples to freedom."

In the face of the liberal nature of Roman private law it is not superfluous to stress the fact that none of the characteristic legal institutions of modern capitalism are derived from Roman law, such institutions being annuity bonds, bearer securities, shares, bills of exchange, trading companies (in their modern capitalistic form), mortgages (as capital investment, direct agency).[2]

The liberty thus accorded in private law does not, however, mean that within the limits of private law everybody could do as he pleased. Quite apart from the restrictions of public law, those imposed by *pietas, fides, humanitas* (in short, by the *officium*) were exceedingly real and powerful. Even though the general rule *male nostro iure uti non debemus* may not have been formulated till post classical times, it was already recognized in the republican and the classical era that abuse of the law could not be permitted : this is shown by the *exceptio doli generalis* and many another legal rule, but was also a living principle in such cases where abuse of the law was not expressly forbidden in legal form. Public opinion operated, for example, to restrict the freedom accorded to a testator to the limits imposed in good sense. The contents of private wills were of general interest ; they were looked upon as mirroring contemporary customs. A will which surprisingly showed the testator to have been better in death than in life, *quod pietas fides pudor scripsit,* was discussed in Rome for many days ; if these powers had been flouted, the discussion would have been still more animated. The character of the Romans made this a very effective check. A coheir could, as we said above, dispose of his quota of the estate, but the *officium* demanded that he should not do so without the consent of his coheirs, unless a higher duty absolved him from such obligation.

The principle of liberty was observed also in the relationship of the individual to the state. Great as were the demands made by the Roman state on its citizens in military matters and (in the early years of the Republic) by taxation, the liberty accorded to them in relation to the community was also very considerable. Roman history can show no period of totalitarian Polis, because Greek democracy was as unknown to Rome as Spartan camp life. Thus the "individual existence" of the Roman citizen, "an existence apart from the state and from public life," of which Jacob Burckhardt said that, "the men of our race demand it, as soon as they emerge from barbarism — an undisturbed home and an independent domain of thoughts and feelings," was respected in principle in the republican and classical eras. Liberty of opinion, of creed and worship were accorded, not entirely without restriction, but within very wide limits. The rights of the home were respected. The right to *provocatio* and the statutory limits set to corporal pubishment were also looked upon in Rome as measures for the protection of liberty. There was considerable freedom of movement, both in a physical and an economic sense. When, as happened occasionally (increasingly in post classical times), we come upon a shackled economy in the provinces with monopolies and compulsory guilds, these are "legal institutions which are basically opposed to the conception of Roman law" and derived from Greco-Hellenistic law. Above all, the Roman state refrained on principle from interference with existing private rights of individuals. It is significant that the legal institution of expropriation, in the sense of a compulsory alienation of private rights by the state in the public interest, is almost unknown to Roman law.... [pp. 157-161]

NOTES

1. Fritz Schulz, *Principles of Roman Law* (London : Oxford University Press, 1936), pp. 6-161.
2. Max Weber, *Wortschaftsgeschichte,* 2nd ed. (1924), p. 292.

DE LEGIBUS[1]

Cicero

Marcus : I find that it has been the opinion of the wisest men that Law is not a product of human thought, nor is it any enactment of peoples, but something eternal which rules the whole universe by its wisdom in command and prohibition. Thus they have been accustomed to say that Law is the primal and ultimate mind of God, whose reason directs all things either by compulsion or restraint. Wherefore that Law which the gods have given to the human race has been justly praised ; for it is the reason and mind of a wise lawgiver applied to command and prohibition.

Quintus : You have touched upon this subject several times before. But please make the character of this heavenly Law clear to us, so that the waves of habit may not carry us away and sweep us into the common mode of speech on such subjects.

Marcus : Ever since we were children, Quintus, we have learned to call, "If one summon another to court," and other rules of the same kind, laws. But we must come to the true understanding of the matter, which is as follows : this and other commands and prohibitions of nations have the power to summon to righteousness and away from wrong-doing ; but this power is not merely older than the existence of nations and States, it is coeval with that God who guards and rules heaven and earth. For the divine mind cannot exist without reason, and divine reason cannot but have this power to establish right and wrong.... For reason did exist, derived from the Nature of the universe, urging men to right conduct and diverting them from wrong-doing, and this reason did not first become Law when it was written down, but when it first came into existence ; and it came into existence simultaneously with the divine mind. Wherefore the true and primal Law, applied to command and prohibition, is the right reason of supreme Jupiter.

Quintus : I agree with you, brother, that what is right and true is also eternal, and does not begin or end with written statutes.

Marcus : Therefore, just as that divine mind is the supreme Law, so, when [reason] is perfected in man [that also is Law ; and this perfected reason exists] in the mind of the wise man ; but those rules which, in varying forms and for the need of the moment, have been formulated for the guidance of nations, bear the title of laws rather by favour than because they are really such. For every law which really deserves that name is truly praiseworthy, as they prove by approximately the following arguments. It is agreed, of course, that laws were invented for the safety of citizens, the preservation of States, and the tranquillity and happiness of human life, and that those who first put statutes of this kind in force convinced their people that it was their intention to write down and put into effect such rules as, once accepted and adopted, would make possible for them an honourable and happy life ; and when such rules were drawn up and put in force, it is clear that men called them "laws." From this point of view it can be readily understood that those who formulated wicked and unjust statutes for nations, thereby breaking their promises and agreements, put into effect anything but "laws." It may thus be clear that in the very definition of the term "law" there inheres the idea and principle of choosing what is just and true. I ask you then, Quintus, according to the custom of the philosophers : if there is a certain thing, the lack of which in a State compels us to consider it no State at all, must we consider this thing a good ?

Quintus : One of the greatest goods, certainly.

Marcus : And if a State lacks Law, must it for that reason be considered no State at all ?

Quintus : It cannot be denied.

Marcus : What of the many deadly, the many pestilential statutes which nations put in force ? These no more deserve to be called laws than the rules a band of robbers might pass in their assembly. For if ignorant and unskilful men have prescribed deadly poisons instead of healing drugs, these cannot possibly be called physicians' prescriptions ; neither in a nation can a statute of any sort be called a law, even though the nation, in spite of its being a ruinous regulation, has accepted it. Therefore Law is the distinction between things just and unjust, made in agreement with that primal and most ancient of all things, Nature ; and in conformity to Nature's standard are framed those human laws which inflict punishment upon the wicked but defend and protect the good. [pp. 379-387]

NOTE

1. Cicero, *De Re Publica, De Legibus*, trans., Clinton Walker Keyes (London : William Heinemann, 1928), pp. 379-387.

A HISTORY OF POLITICAL THEORY[1]

George H. Sabine

Cicero and the Roman Lawyers

Cicero's true importance in the history of political thought lies in the fact that he gave to the Stoic doctrine of natural law a statement in which it was universally known throughout western Europe from his own day down to the nineteenth century. From him it passed to the Roman lawyers and not less to the fathers of the church. The most important passages were quoted times without number throughout the Middle Ages. It is a significant fact that, though the text of *The Republic* was lost after the twelfth century and not recovered until the nineteenth, its most striking passages had already been excerpted into the books of Augustine and Lactantius, and so had become matters of common knowledge. The ideas were, of course, in no sense original with Cicero but his statement of them, largely in Latin expressions of his own devising to render the Stoic Greek, became incomparably the most important single literary means for spreading them through western Europe. A few of Cicero's great passages must be kept in mind by anyone who wishes to read political philosophy in the centuries that followed.

First of all, there is a universal law of nature arising equally from the fact of God's providential government of the world and from the rational and social nature of human beings which makes them akin to God. This is, as it were, the constitution of the world-state ; it is the same everywhere and is unchangeably binding upon all men and all nations. No legislation that contravenes it is entitled to the name of law, for no ruler and no people can make right wrong :

> There is in fact a true law — namely, right reason — which is in accordance with nature, applies to all men, and is unchangeable and eternal. By its commands this law summons men to the performance of their duties ; by its prohibitions it restrains them from doing wrong. Its commands and prohibitions always influence good men, but are without effect upon the bad. To invalidate this law by human legislation is never morally right, nor is it permissible ever to restrict its operation, and to annul it wholly is impossible. Neither the senate nor the people can absolve

> us from our obligation to obey this law, and it requires no Sextus Aelius to expound and interpret it. It will not lay down one rule at Rome and another at Athens, nor will it be one rule today and another tomorrow. But there will be one law, eternal and unchangeable, binding at all times upon all peoples; and there will be, as it were, one common master and ruler of men, namely God, who is the author of this law, its interpreter, and its sponsor. The man who will not obey it will abandon his better self, and in denying the true nature of a man, will thereby suffer the severest of penalties, though he has escaped all the other consequences which men call punishments.[2]

In the light of this eternal law all men, as Cicero insists in the most unequivocal terms, are equal. They are not equal in learning, and it is not expedient for the state to try to equalize their property, but in the possession of reason, in their underlying psychological make-up, and in their general attitude toward what they believe to be honourable or base all men are alike. Indeed Cicero goes so far as to suggest that it is nothing but error, bad habits, and false opinions that prevents men from being in fact equal. All men and all races of men possess the same capacity for experience and for the same kinds of experience, and all are equally capable of discriminating between right and wrong.

> Out of all the material of the philosophers' discussions, surely there comes nothing more valuable than the full realization that we are born for justice, and that right is based, not upon man's opinions, but upon nature. This fact will immediately be plain if you once get a clear conception of man's fellowship and union with his fellow men. For no single thing is so like another, so exactly its counterpart, as all of us are to one another, Nay, if bad habits and false beliefs did not twist the weaker minds and turn them in whatever direction they are inclined, no one would be so like his own self as all men would be like all others.[3]

Professor A.J. Carlyle has said that "no change in political theory is so startling in its completeness"[4] as the change from Aristotle to a passage such as this. The process of reasoning is, in truth, the exact opposite of that which Aristotle had used. The relation of free citizenship for Aristotle can hold only between equals, but because men are not equal, he had inferred that citizenship must be restricted to a small and carefully selected group. Cicero on the contrary infers that, because all men are subject to one law and so are fellow citizens, they must be in some sense equal. For Cicero equality is a moral requirement rather than a fact; in ethical terms it expresses much the same conviction that a Christian might express by saying that God is no respecter of persons. There is no implication of political democracy, though without some such moral conviction democracy would be hard to defend. What is asserted is that some measure of human dignity and respect is due to every man; he is inside and not outside the great human brotherhood. Even if he were a slave he would not be, as Aristotle had said, a living tool, but more nearly as Chrysippus had said, a wage-earner hired for life. Or, as Kant rephrased the old ideal eighteen centuries later, a man must be treated as an end and not as a means. The astonishing fact is that Chrysippus and Cicero are closer to Kant than they are to Aristotle.

The political deduction which Cicero draws from this ethical axiom is that a state cannot exist permanently, or at least cannot exist in any but a crippled condition, unless it depends upon, and acknowledges, and gives effect to the consciousness of mutual obligations and the mutual recognition of rights that bind its citizens together. The state is a moral community, a group of persons who in common possess the state and its law. For this reason he calls the state, in a fine phrase, the *res populi* or the *res publica*, "the affair of the people," which is practically equivalent in meaning to the older English use of the word "commonwealth." This is the ground for Cicero's argument, against the Epicureans and Skeptics, that justice is an intrinsic good. Unless the state is a community for ethical purposes and unless it is held together by moral ties, it is nothing, as Augustine said later, except "highway robbery on a large scale." A state may of course be tyrannous and rule its subjects by brute force — the moral law does not make immorality impossible — but in the measure that it does so, it loses the true character of a state.

> The commonwealth, then, is the people's affair ; and the people is not every group of men, associated in any manner, but is the coming together of a considerable number of men who are united by a common agreement about law and rights and by the desire to participate in mutual advantages.[5]

The state, then, is a corporate body, membership in which is the common possession of all its citizens ; it exists to supply its members with the advantages of mutual aid and just government. Three consequences follow. First, since the state and its law is the common property of the people, its authority arises from the collective power of the people. A people is a self-governing organization which has necessarily the powers required to preserve itself and continue its existence : *Salus populi suprema lex esto.* Second, political power when rightfully and lawfully exercised really is the corporate power of the people. The magistrate who exercises it does so by virtue of his office ; his warrant is the law and he is the creature of the law.

> For as the laws govern the magistrate, so the magistrate governs the people, and it can truly be said that the magistrate is a speaking law, and the law a silent magistrate.[6]

Third, the state itself and its law is always subject to the law of God, or the moral or natural law — that higher rule of right which transcends human choice and human institution. Force is an incident in the nature of the state and is justified only because it is required to give effect to the principles of justice and right.

These general principles of government — that authority proceeds from the people, should be exercised only by warrant of law, and is justified only on moral grounds — achieved practically universal acceptance within comparatively a short time after Cicero wrote and remained commonplaces of political philosophy for many centuries. There was substantially no difference of opinion about them on the part of anyone in the whole course of the Middle Ages ; they became a part of the common heritage of political ideas. There might, however, be considerable differences of opinion about the application of them, even among men who had not the remotest doubt about the principles themselves. Thus everyone agrees that a tyrant is despicable and his tyranny a bitter wrong against his people, but it is not obvious just what the people are entitled to do about it, or who is to act in their behalf in doing it, or how bad the abuse must be before measures are justified. In particular, the derivation of political authority from the people does not of itself imply any of the democratic consequences which in modern times have been deduced from the consent of the governed. It does not say who speaks for the people, how he becomes entitled to speak, or exactly who "the people" are for whom he speaks — all questions of the utmost practical importance. The use of the ancient principle that political authority comes from the people to defend the modern forms of representative government was merely the adaptation of an old idea to a new situation.

The classical period in the development of Roman jurisprudence fell in the second and third centuries after Christ, and the writings of the great jurists of that age were excerpted and compiled into the Digest (or Pandects), which the Emperor Justinian caused to be published in 533. The political philosophy which is embedded in this body of legal writing is a repetition and elaboration of the theories found in Cicero.

Political theory forms an insignificant proportion of the whole work, the relevant passages being neither very numerous nor very extensive. The lawyers were jurists, not philosophers. For this reason it is often hard to tell just how seriously a philosophical idea is to be taken when it occurs ; one does not know whether the writer himself regarded it as a polite embellishment or whether it really influenced his legal judgment. Obviously it was never part of the lawyers' purpose to formulate a political philosophy or to inject a philosophy into the law. The philosophy of the Roman lawyers was not philosophy in a technical sense but certain general social and ethical conceptions, known to all intelligent men, which were in some way considered to be useful for their own juristic purposes. This makes it the more striking that they uniformly selected philosophical ideas belonging in the Stoic and Ciceronian tradition. The ideas of egoistic individualism, contained in the writings of the Epicureans and the Skeptics, must have been equally at their disposal, but the lawyers found no use for them. The fact that their interest in political theory was desultory and unsystematic does not mean that what they had to say was unimportant. The enormous authority attached to the Roman law throughout western Europe gave weight to any proposition which was a recognized part of it. Moreover, any general conception embedded in the law was certain to be known to all educated men as well as to lawyers, and ultimately by common report to many who were not scholars at all. In the end the Roman law became one of the greatest intellectual forces in the history of European civilization, because it provided principles and categories in terms of which men thought about all sorts of subjects and not least about politics. Legalist argumentation — reasoning in terms of men's rights and of the justifiable powers of rulers — became and remained a generally accepted method of political theorizing.

The lawyers excerpted in the Digest, as well as those who formulated Justinian's Institutes in the sixth century, recognized three main types of law, the *ius civile*, the *ius gentium* and the *ius naturale.* The *ius civile* is, of course, the enactments or the customary law of a particular state, what would now be called positive municipal law. The other two classes are not quite so clear, either in respect to the distinction between *ius gentium* and *ius naturale* or in respect to the relation of both to the *ius civile.* Cicero had used both these terms but had apparently made no distinction of meaning between them. In origin, as was said in the preceding chapter, the term *ius gentium* belonged to the lawyers, while *ius naturale* was a rendering of Greek philosophical terminology. In meaning the two apparently coalesced, both for the earlier lawyers and for Cicero. They signified indifferently principles that were generally recognized and therefore common to the law of different peoples and also principles that were inherently reasonable and right without reference to their occurrence in any system of law. The distinction was easy to overlook because common consent was taken as a test of validity. It seemed a fair presumption that what many peoples have arrived at independently is more likely to be right than what is peculiar to any single people.

As time went on the lawyers apparently saw a reason for distinguishing *ius gentium* from *ius naturale.* Gaius, writing in the second century, continued to use the terms synonymously, but Ulpian and later writers in the third century made a distinction, as did also the lawyers who prepared the Institutes in the sixth. The distinction added precision to legal definition, but it perhaps signified also a more penetrating ethical criticism of the law ; even what is generally practiced may still be unjust and unreasonable. The main point upon which *ius gentium* and *ius naturale* are distinguished is slavery. By nature all men are born free and equal, but slavery is permitted according to the *ius gentium.* It is hard to tell just what this natural liberty meant to the lawyers who asserted its reality so flatly, but in view of the efforts made, not without success, to throw legal safeguards about slaves and other oppressed classes, it seems reasonably to construe it as representing some moral reservation about practices whose legality was unquestionable according to all known codes. Perhaps the idea was, as Professor Carlyle suggests, that in some purer or better form of society slavery had not existed, or would not exist. At all events, such passages would be so understood after Christianity had made the story of the fall of man a common belief.

Whether or not they distinguished between *ius gentium* and *ius naturale,* none of the lawyers doubted that there is a higher law than the enactments of any particular state. Like Cicero they conceived of the law as ultimately rational, universal, unchangeable, and divine, at least in respect to the main principles of right and justice. The Roman law, like the English common law, was only in small part a product of legislation. Hence the presumption was never made that law expresses nothing but the will of a competent legislative body, which is an idea of quite recent origin. It was assumed that "nature" sets certain norms which the positive law must live up to as best it can and that, as Cicero had believed, an "unlawful" statute simply is not law. Throughout the whole of the Middle Ages and well down into modern times the existence and the validity of such a higher law were taken for granted. As Sir Frederick Pollock says, the central idea of natural law, from the Roman Repubic to modern times, was "an ultimate principle of fitness with regard to the nature of man as a rational and social being, which is, or ought to be, the justification of every form of positive law."[7]

In theory, therefore, the positive law is an approximation to perfect justice and right ; these represent its objects and form its standards. It is, as Ulpian says, quoting Celsus, *ars boni et aequi.*

> Justice is a fixed and abiding disposition to give to every man his right. The percepts of the law are as follows : to live honorably, to injure no one, to give to every man his own. Jurisprudence is a knowledge of things human and divine, the science of the just and the unjust.[8]

Hence the lawyer is a "priest of justice," "the practitioner of a true philosophy, not a pretender to an imitation." It is not necessary to take Ulpian's rhetoric as a literal statement of fact. But it remains true that the Roman jurists did build up a more enlightened body of law than had ever existed, and though the changes they wrought had their economic and political causes, it is not to be imagined that they came about without reference to the ideals of the profession.

Natural law meant interpretation in the light of such conceptions as equality before the law, faithfulness to engagements, fair dealing or equity, the superior importance of intent to mere words and formularies, the protection of dependents, and the recognition of claims based on blood relationship. Procedure was more and more freed from mere formality ; contracts were made to rest on agreement rather than on words of stipulation ; the father's absolute control over the property and persons of his children was broken ; married women became the full legal equals of their husbands in the control of their property and children ; and finally great progress was made in throwing legal safeguards about slaves, partly by way of protecting them against cruelty, partly by making their manumission as easy as possible. A modern exponent of "just law," Rudolf Stammler, has regarded this belief in justice as the crowning glory of Roman jurisprudence.

> This, in my opinion, is the universal significance of the classical Roman jurists ; this, their permanent worth. They had the courage to raise their glance from the ordinary questions of the day to the whole. And in reflecting on the narrow status of the particular case, they directed their thoughts to the guiding star of all law, namely the realization of justice in life.[9]

It should be noted that these reforms in the Roman law, though they were completed after the beginning of the Christian era, were not due to Christianity. The effective humanizing influence was Stoicism and there seems to be no evidence whatever of any effect of the Christian communities upon the great jurists of the second and third centuries. At a later date, in the time of Constantine and after, Christian influence can be seen, but it was not exerted in the directions mentioned above. Its purpose was to secure in one way or another the legal position of the church or of its officials, or to aid in carrying out policies of the church. Typical legal changes which the church secured for the protection of its interests were the right to receive property by will, the establishment of the jurisdiction of bishops' courts, the power to supervise charities, the repeal of the laws against celibacy, and the enactment of laws against heresy and apostasy.

Finally, the Roman law crystallized the theory, already contained in Cicero, that the authority of the ruler is derived from "the people." The theory was summed up in a sentence by Ulpian, repeatedly quoted, and there is no dissent by any of the lawyers either of the Digest or the Institutes :

> The will of the Emperor has the force of law, because by the passage of the *lex regia* the people transfers to him and vests in him all its own power and authority.[10]

The theory is to be understood, of course, in a strictly legal sense and it is couched in terms that had a definitely technical significance. In itself it justifies neither the implication of royal absolutism, which was sometimes derived from the first clause, nor of representative government, which the sovereignty of the people came to signify later. The latter meaning would have been especially absurd in the Roman Empire when Ulpian wrote. The idea behind Ulpian's statement is that expressed by Cicero, that law is the common possession of a people in its corporate capacity. This idea appears in the theory that customary law has the consent of the people, since custom exists only in the common practice. It appears also in the classification of the sources from which law is derived. Thus law might arise by the enactment of a popular assembly (*leges*), or by the vote of some authorized part of the people such as the plebeian assembly (*plebescita*), or by a decree of the Senate (*senatus consulta*), or by a decree of the emperor (*constitutiones*), or by the edict of an ordinance-issuing official. In all cases, however, the source must be authorized and in the last resort all forms of law go back to the legal activity inherent in a politically organized people. In a sense every established organ of government does "represent" the people in some degree and some capacity, but there is obviously no implication that representation has anything to do with voting and still less that voting is a right inherent in every person. The "people" is an entity quite different from the persons who happen at any given time to be included in it.

At the same time some essence has been preserved from the ancient doctrine that law is an "impersonal reason" and that in consequence there is a broad moral distincion between lawful government and successful tyranny. Even though the former be often bad and the latter sometimes efficient, subjection to law is not imcompatible with moral freedom and dignity, while subjection to even the kindliest master is morally degrading. The Roman law preserved the spirit of Cicero's striking phrase : "We are servants of the law in order that we may be free."[11] And indeed, there is no more astonishing evidence of the strength that this conviction had come to have in European morals than the fact of its preservation in a system of law which reached its maturity at a time when the personal power of the emperors was often unlimited and when their authority rested frequently on nothing better than force. Yet the fact remains that in the long run the ideal embedded in the law was a permanent factor in European political civilization — a distillation from the old free life of the city-state — which was able to endure through and beyond an age in which all the servility of oriental despotism had apparently been transplanted to Rome. [pp. 163-173]

NOTES

1. George H. Sabine, *A History of Political Theory* (New York : Holt, Rinehart and Winston, 1937), pp. 163-173.
2. Cicero, *Republic*, 3, 22, trans., Sabine and Smith.
3. Cicero, *Laws*, trans., C.W. Keyes, 1, 10, 28-29.
4. A.J. Carlyle, *A History of Mediaeval Political Theory in the West*, vol. 1 (1903), p. 8.
5. Cicero, *Republic*, 1, 25.
6. Cicero, *Laws*, 3, 1, 2.
7. Sir Frederick Pollock, "The History of the Law of Nature," in *Essays in the Law* (1922), p. 31.
8. *Digest*, 1,1, 10.
9. Rudolf Stammler, *The Theory of Justice*, Eng. trans. (1925), p. 127.
10. *Digest* 1,4, 1.
11. *Pro Cluentio*, 53, 146.

THE INSTITUTES OF JUSTINIAN[1]

Book 1

Title I
Concerning Justice and Law

Justice is the constant and perpetual desire to give to each man his due right.

1. Jurisprudence is acquaintance with things human and divine, the knowledge of what is just and what unjust.

2. This posited, it is very much our view, as we begin our exposition, that the law and rights of the Roman people can most conveniently be set forth, if the individual elements be stated first in a light and elementary manner, the more careful and precise exposition following thereafter. If, following a different course, we were, from the outset, at once to burden the, as yet, immature and unready mind of the student with a multitude and variety of matters, one of two things would happen : either we would cause him to abandon his studies or we would lead him — with great toil on his part and often with lack of confidence (which frequently affects students) — with greater delay to the standard which he could have attained earlier, if led there by a gentler path without great labour and diffidence.

3. These are the precepts of law : to live justly, not to injure another and to render to each his own.

4. There are two aspects of this study, public and private. Public law is that which pertains to the Roman state, private that which concerns the well-being of the individual. One then has to observe of private law that it is threefold ; for it consists of natural precepts, those observed generally by nations and those of a given state.

Title II
Concerning Natural Law, the Law of Nations, and the Civil Law

Natural law is that which nature instils in all animals. For this law is not peculiar to humankind but is shared by all animals which are born on land or in the air or sea. From it derives that association of man and woman that we call marriage ; so also the procreation and rearing of issue : for we see that animals also are imbued with experience of this law.

1. Civil law and the law of nations, however, are distinguished in this way. All peoples who are governed by law and customs use law which is in part particular to themselves, in part common to all men : the law which each people has established for itself is particular to that state and is styled civil law as being peculiarly of that state : by what natural reason has esbablished among all men is observed equally by all nations and is designated *ius gentium* or the law of nations, being that which all nations obey. Hence the Roman people observe partly their own particular law, partly that which is common to all peoples. Which is which, we shall explain whenever it is desirable to do so.

2. However, civil law derives its name from each individual state, for example, Athens : for one would commit no error in calling the laws of Solon and Draco the civil law of Athens. In like manner, the law observed by the Roman people is termed Roman civil law or the law of Quirites, being applicable to Quirites — the Romans being called Quirites after Quirinus. However, whenever we do not add the name of a state, we are talking of our own (i.e., Roman) law ; in the same way that, when we speak of "the poet" without adding his name, the Greek will understand that it is the great Homer, while we know that it is Virgil. The law of nations, on the other hand, is common to all humankind. For through force of circumstances and human needs, people have developed certain measures for themselves : wars have arisen with subsequent captivity and slavery — which is contrary to natural law (for, by natural law, originally, all men were born free). From the law of nations also come virtually all the contracts, such as sale, hire, partnership, deposit, loan, and countless others.

3. Our law comes either from written or from unwritten sources, just as among the Greeks : some laws are written, others unwritten. Written law comprises legislation, *leges* (enactments of the *comitia*), plebiscites, resolutions of the Senate, the will of the Emperor (in its various manifestations), the edicts of magistrates, and the answers of the learned.

NOTE

1. J.A.C. Thomas, trans., *The Institutes of Justinian* (Cape Town : Juta and Company, 1975), pp. 2-5.

THE INSTITUTES OF ROMAN LAW

by Gaius[1]

Fourth Commentary

1. We have now to treat of actions, which, according to the better view, fall into two classes, being either real or personal : for those who count four classes, including the forms of *sponsio*, commit the error of co-ordinating sub classes with classes.

2. A personal action is an action which seeks to enforce an obligation imposed on the defendant by his contract or delict, that is to say, is an action by which one claims in the *intentio* of the formula that he is bound to convey some property to one, or to perform for one some service, or to make some other kind of performance.

3. A real action is an action by which one claims as one's own in the *intentio* some corporeal thing or some particular right in the thing, as a right of use or usufruct of a thing belonging to a neighbour, or a right of horseway, or carriageway through his land, or of fetching water from a source in his land, or of raising one's house above a certain height, or of having the prospect from one's windows unobstructed ; or, when the opposite party (that is the owner) brings the negative action, asserting that there is no such right in the thing.

4. Real and personal actions being thus distinguished, it is clear that I cannot demand my own property from another in the following form : "If it be proved that the defendant is bound to convey such property to me." For what is already my own cannot be conveyed to me, since conveyance to me makes a thing mine, and what is already mine cannot be made more mine than it is. Yet, to show the law's detestation of thieves, in order to make them liable to a greater number of actions, it is received doctrine that besides the penalty of twice the value of the thing stolen awarded against the thief not caught in the act, and the penalty of four times the value against the thief caught in the act, damages for the thing itself may be recovered by a personal action in which the contention is thus worded : "If it be proved that the defendant ought to convey the thing in question," although they are also liable to be sued by an action with the *intentio* thus formulated : "If it be proved that the plaintiff is owner of the thing in question."

5. A real action is called *vindicatio*; a personal action, whereby we contend that some property should be conveyed to us or some service performed for us, is called *condictio.*

NOTE

1. E. Post, trans., *The Institutes of Roman Law by Gaius*, 4th ed. (London : Oxford University Press, 1925), pp. 442-443.

THE INSTITUTES OF JUSTINIAN[1]

Book II

Title I

. . . Now let us consider things. These are either capable of being owned (*in nostro patrimonio*) or not capable of being owned (*extra nostrum patrimonium).* Some, again, are common to all by natural law, others are public, yet others the property of a community, and some belong to no one : then there are many things which belong to individuals, which they acquire on a variety of grounds, as will appear from what follows.

1. Now the things which are, by natural law, common to all are these : the air, running water, the sea, and therefore the seashores. Thus, no one is barred access to the seashore, provided he refrain from entry into houses, monuments, and buildings ; for they are not subject to the law of nations as also the sea.

2. Rivers, on the other hand, and ports are public ; hence the right to fish is open to all in ports and rivers.

3. Now, the seashore is as far as the winter tide reaches its furthest extent.

4. Again, public access to river banks is a matter of the law of nations as also is the use of the actual river : accordingly, it is open to anyone to steer a ship toward them, to moor ships by ropes to trees growing on the banks or to lay some cargo upon the banks as also to sail on the river itself. Ownership of the banks, however, vests in the riparian owners : hence trees growing on the banks belong to them.

5. Similarly, the use of seashores is also public by the law of nations, as also of the sea itself : and there it is open to anyone to put a house there to which to repair for the drying of nets or to draw up from the sea. But seashores are regarded as the property of no one but as being of the same legal status as the sea itself and as things lying under the sea, earth, or sand.

6. Things belonging to a community, not to individuals, are, for instance, those in cities — theatres, stadia, and the like, and anything else which is the common property of the community....

11. Now things become the property of individuals in many ways : for of some things ownership arises by natural law which, as we have said, is called the law of nations, and of others at civil law. It is more convenient to start with the older law and, obviously, the older law is natural law which the nature of things introduced with humankind itself : civil laws began to exist when cities began to be founded, magistrates to be created and statutes to be enrolled.

12. Hence, wild animals, birds and fish, i.e., all animals born on land or in the sea or air, as soon as they are caught by anyone, forthwith fall into his ownership by the law of nations : for what previously belonged to no one is, by natural reason, accorded to its captor. Nor does it matter whether the animals and birds be taken on one's own land or on someone else's. Of course, anyone entering another's land to hunt or for fowling can be stopped by the owner, if he be aware of it. But any of these things that you take is considered to be yours so long as it is regulated by your control : but, once it escapes from your custody and resumes its natural state, it ceases to be yours and again becomes open to the next taker. It is regarded as resuming its natural state when either it disappears from your sight or, though you can still see it, pursuit of it is difficult.

NOTE

1. J.A.C. Thomas, trans., *The Institutes of Justinian* (Cape Town : Juta and Company, 1975), pp. 65-66.

THE RULES OF ULPIAN[1]

Title XIX

Concerning Owners and Their Acquisition of Property

1. All property is either mancipable, or not mancipable. Mancipable property is land situated in Italy, both rustic, such as a field, and urban, such as a house ; likewise all rights attaching to rustic estates, as the right of way, to pass, or drive ; the right to conduct water, and also slaves, and quadrupeds broken to yoke or saddle, as for instance, oxen, mules, horses, and asses. All other property is not mancipable, for elephants and camels, although they are trained to haul loads and carry burdens, do not come under this category, as they are classed among wild beasts.

2. The ownership of individual articles of property is acquired by us by mancipation, by delivery, by surrender in court, by usucaption, by adjudication, and by law.

3. Mancipation is a kind of alienation peculiar to property of this kind, which is made by the use of certain words in the presence of a balance-holder and five witnesses.

4. Mancipation takes place between Roman citizens, Latin colonists, Junian Latins, and those aliens to whom commercial privileges have been granted.

5. Commerce is the right of reciprocal purchase and sale.

6. Movable property cannot be mancipated, unless the parties are present, and not more than can be taken in the hand should be disposed of; several tracts of immovable property can, however, be mancipated at one time, even though they be situated in different places.

7. Delivery is a species of alienation peculiar to property which cannot be mancipated. We acquire the ownership of property of this kind by mere delivery, provided it is transferred to us by a legal title.

8. By usucaption we obtain the ownership of property which is either susceptible, or not susceptible of mancipation. Moreover, usucaption is the acquisition of ownership by uninterrupted possession for one or two years; for one year in the case of movable property, for two in the case of property which is immovable.

9. Surrender in court is a kind of alienation common to property which can be mancipated as well as to that which cannot. It is effected by the agency of three persons, the one who surrenders, the one who claims, and the one who awards it.

10. The owner surrenders the property in court, the party to whom it is surrendered claims it, the praetor awards it.

11. Incorporeal property, as, for instance, a usufruct, an inheritance, and the legal guardianship of a freedwoman, can also be surrendered in court.

12. An estate is surrendered in court either before or after it has been entered on.

13. Before it is entered on, it can be surrendered in court by the heir-at-law; after it has been entered on, it can be surrendered either by the heir-at-law or by the testamentary heir.

14. If an estate is surrendered in court before it is entered on, the party to whom it is surrendered becomes the heir, just as if he himself was the heir-at-law.

15. If it is surrendered in court after it has been entered on, he who surrendered it remains the heir, and for this reason continues to be liable to the creditors of the deceased ; but the debts are extinguished, that is, the debtors of the deceased are discharged from liability ; the corporeal property, however, passes to the party to whom the estate was surrendered, just as if the articles had been transferred to him, one at a time.

16. We obtain ownership through adjudication, by means of the proceeding in partition which is instituted among co-heirs ; by that for the division of common property which applies to partners ; and by that for the establishment of boundaries, which is employed by neighbours. For if a judge should adjudicate any property to one of several heirs, partners, or neighbours, it will immediately be acquired by the latter, whether it is susceptible of mancipation or not.

17. Property is acquired by us by law, for example, where it has lapsed or been forfeited under the *Lex Papia Poppeae*, and also where it has been bequeathed under the law of the Twelve Tables ; whether it is susceptible of mancipation or not.

NOTE

1. S.P. Scott, trans., "The Rules of Ulpian," in *The Civil Law* (New York : AMS Press, 1973), pp. 238-239.

THE INSTITUTES OF JUSTINIAN[1]

Book II

Title II
On Incorporeal Things

Now, some things are corporeal, others incorporeal. 1. Corporeal things are those which, by their nature, can be touched, e.g., land, a slave, a garment, gold, silver, and, indeed, countless other things. 2. Incorporeal things, on the other hand, are such as cannot be touched but exist in law : for instance, an inheritance, usufruct, and obligations, however contracted. It matters not that an inheritance comprises corporeal things : for, again, the fruits reaped from land are corporeal as also, usually, is that which is due to us under some obligation, e.g., land, a slave, or money. But the actual right of inheritance, the right to use and enjoy and the obligation as such are incorporeal. 3. Such things include the rustic and urban praedial rights which are known as servitudes.

Title III
On Servitudes

The rights of rustic land are these : the rights of way, *iter, actus* and *via*, and the right to bring water through (*aquae ductus*). *Iter* entitles a man to walk and go on foot but not to drive animals or to go in a vehicle. *Actus* is the right to drive animals or take a vehicle. Hence, a person who has *iter* does not have *actus* but one who has *actus* also has *iter* for he can exercise his right even without animals. *Via* is a general right of passage, including in itself both *iter* and *actus. Aquae ductus* is the right of bringing water through another's land.

1. The servitudes of urban lands are those which pertain to buildings and so they get their name ; for all buildings are called urban estates, even though they be built in the country. And the servitudes of urban land are these : that one neighbour shall have the right of support as against the other ; that he shall allow his neighbour to insert a beam or rafter into his wall ; that a person may, or may not, allow rainwater to drip from another's eaves on to his own house or land ; and that he shall not build his premises above a certain height nor obscure the light for his neighbour.

2. Some properly include among the servitudes of rustic land the right to draw water, the right of pasturing cattle, lime-burning and the digging of gravel or sand.

3. Now these rights are called praedial servitudes because they cannot exist without land. For no one can have a rustic or urban praedial servitude unless he has land nor can anyone be subject to one if he does not have land.

4. Anyone wishing to create some right for his neighbour should do so by pacts and stipulations. He can also, by will, charge his heir not to build beyond a given height or not to obstruct the light of a neighbour's premises or to allow the latter to insert a beam into the wall or to accept raindroppings ; as also to allow the neighbour a right of passage over his land or to draw water there.

NOTE

1. J.A.C.Thomas, trans., *The Institutes of Justinian* (Cape Town : Juta & Co., 1975), pp. 84-85.

THE DIGEST OR PANDECTS[1]

Book VIII

Title I
Concerning Servitudes

1. Marcianus, Rules, Book III

Servitudes are either personal, as use and usufruct ; or real, as the servitudes of rustic and urban estates.

2. Ulpianus, On the Edict, Book XVII

One of the owners of a house held in common cannot impose a servitude upon it.

3. Paulus, On the Edict, Book XXI

Some servitudes are attached to the soil, others to the surface.

4. Papinianus, Questions, Book VII

Servitudes cannot be created by direct law from a certain time, or until a certain time, or under a condition, or on a certain contingency ; (for example, "as long as I wish,") nevertheless, if such provisions as these are added, and a party brings suit for the recovery of the servitude, in violation of the terms of the contract, an exception may be interposed on the ground that the claim is contrary to what had been agreed upon, or for fraud, and this Cassius states was the opinion of Sabinus in which he himself concurred.

(1) It is established that limitations can be added to servitudes ; as, for instance, with reference to what kind of transactions shall be permitted, or shall not be permitted upon a roadway, as, for instance, that it must only be traversed by a horse, or that only a certain weight shall be transported, or such-and-such a flock shall be driven over it, or that charcoal shall be carried.

(2) Where intervals of a certain number of days and hours are mentioned, this does not relate to the question of time, but only to the manner in which a servitude created in accordance with law shall be enjoyed.

5. Gaius, On the Provincial Edict, Book VII

Servitudes granted for a driveway, a pathway, the passage of cattle, and the conduct of water, are created in almost the same manner as those in which we have stated that usufruct is created.

(1) The enjoyment of servitudes may be limited with reference to time ; for example, where a party may make use of the servitude from the third until the tenth hour, or on alternate days.

6. Paulus, On the Edict, Book XXI

A servitude can be either released or created with reference to a certain part of the land.

Title II
Concerning Servitudes of Urban Estates

2. Gaius, On the Provincial Edict, Book VII

The following are the rights to which urban estates are subject, namely : that of raising a house and obscuring the lights of a neighbour, or of preventing a raising of this kind ; that of allowing the dripping of rainwater on the roof or the ground of a neighbour ; and also that of not allowing the right of inserting beams into the wall of a neighbour, and that of the projection of a building ; and others similar to these.

3. Ulpianus, On Sabinus, Book XXIX

A servitude providing against obstructing a view also exists.

4. Paulus, Institutes, Book II

Where a servitude of lights is created, it is held that what is acquired is that a neighbour must not interfere with our lights, but if the servitude imposed is to prevent the obscuring of lights, we seem to have especially acquired the right that a neighbour shall not raise his building any higher against our will, so as to lessen the amount of light in our house.

NOTE

1. S.P. Scott, trans., "The Digests or Pandects," in *The Civil Law* (New York : AMS Press, 1973), pp. 279-283.

The Institutes of Justinian[1]

Book II

Title IV
On Usufruct

Usufruct is the right to use and enjoy the things of another, their substance remaining unimpaired. It is a right in a corporeal thing and so, if the thing be removed, of necessity the usufruct is ended.

1. Usufruct is separated from ownership and arises in a variety of ways. Suppose that someone bequeath a usufruct to another, his heir will have bare title to the thing and the legatee will have the usufruct : conversely, if he devise land with the reservation of a usufruct, the legatee will have bare title and the heir will have the usufruct : similarly, it is possible to bequeath the usufruct to one person and the land, with the reservation of the usufruct, to another. If someone wishes to create a usufruct for another other than by will, he should do it by pacts and stipulations. But, so that ownership might not be wholly meaningless by reason of a permanently detached usufruct, it became settled that usufruct may be extinguished in certain ways and be reincorporated with title.

Title V
On Use and Habitation

Bare use (*usus*) can be created and extinguished in the same ways as is usufruct.

1. Naturally, the right conferred is less in use than is usufruct. For a person who has mere use of land is understood to have no more than the right to use vegetables, fruit, flowers, grass, straw and wood for his daily needs : and he may stay on the land only in so far as he is not troublesome to the owner thereof nor a hindrance to those engaged on agricultural work ; nor can he make available to anyone else the right he has by sale or hire thereof or, indeed, for nothing. A person with a usufruct can do all these things.

2. Again, a person who has the use of a house, is seen to have only the right to live in it himself and he cannot transfer that right to another : it was, indeed, only with difficulty accepted that he might receive guests there and have the right of living there with his wife and children, his freedmen and other free persons whom he employs no less than his slaves ; and, conversely, whether a woman who has the use of a house may live there with her husband.

NOTE

1. J.A.C.Thomas, trans., *The Institutes of Justinian* (Cape Town : Jutax Co., 1975), pp. 87-90.

THE INSTITUTES OF GAIUS[1]

Third Commentary

88. Let us now pass to other obligations, the principal divison of which is into two classes, for every obligation either arises from a contract, or from an offence.

89. And first, let us examine those which arise from contracts, of which there are four different kinds ; for an obligation is contracted either by delivery of property, verbally, by writing, or by consent.

90. An obligation by the delivery of property is contracted, for example, in the case of a loan for consumption. This generally takes place with reference to articles which are susceptible of being weighed, counted, or measured ; such as money, wine, oil, grain, bronze, silver, and gold. This kind of property we transfer either by counting, measuring or weighing it with the understanding that it shall belong to him who receives it, and that, at some time or other, not the same article, but another of the same nature, shall be returned to us, and therefore an obligation of this kind is called *mutuum*, because what was given to you by me, from being mine becomes yours.

91. He also who received something that was not due from a person who paid him through mistake, is liable under a contract of this description, for a personal action can be brought against him under the formula, "If it appears that he was required to give" ; just as if he had received the property as a loan for consumption. Hence certain authorities hold that a ward or a woman to whom payment was made of something which was not due, through mistake, and without the authority of his or her guardian, is not liable to a personal action ; any more than they are for a loan for consumption. This species of obligation does not, however, appear to arise from a contract, for a party who gives with the intention of paying a debt, rather desires to discharge an obligation than to incur one.

92. An obligation is verbally contracted by question and answer, as for instance : "Do you solemnly agree to give it to me ?" "I do solemnly agree." "Will you give it ?" "I will give it." "Do you promise ?" "I do promise." "Do you pledge your faith ?" "I do pledge my faith." "Do you guarantee ?" "I do guarantee." "Will you do this ?" "I will do it."

NOTE

1. S. P. Scott, trans., "The Institutes of Gaius," in *The Civil Law* (New York : AMS Press, 1973), pp. 162-163.

THE OPINIONS OF JULIUS PAULUS[1]

Book I

Title I
Concerning Agreements and Contracts

1. We can enter into agreements with reference to matters which are lawful, and from them alone the obligation of a contract arises.

2. In *bona fide* contracts one agreement is dissolved by another and, although it may give ground for an exception, it is, nevertheless, barred by a replication.

3. The Aquilian stipulation is usually added to an informal agreement, but it is preferable to also add a penalty to it, for the reason that, if the agreement should be rescinded in any way, the penalty can be recovered under the stipulation.

4. We cannot make a contract which is contrary to the laws or to good morals.

5. We can make agreement and settlement with reference to matters in litigation.

5a. An agreement entered into after a case has been decided should not be observed, unless it is introduced for the purpose of making a donation.

NOTE

1. S.P. Scott, trans., "The Opinions of Julius Paulus," in *The Civil Law* (New York : AMS Press, 1973), p. 259.

4. The Hellenic and Judeo-Christian Synthesis

There is a long-standing belief in Western Christian theology that a formidable integration of science and faith was brought about by Hellenized Christianity. The natural law theoretical corpus reached its pinnacle in the writings of St. Thomas Aquinas. In his philosophy of Being, the hierarchy of order in the universe culminated in the motionless and unchanging source of all authority, the Deity. Aquinas' notion of law may be regarded as a revealing medieval paridigm, perfectly consistent with medieval physics, where all natural motions are aspirations to reach the changeless. Untimately it is only God who is motionless ; it is thus the inherent tendency of all motion and things to try to attain God, and everything is seen as instrumental to that highest good.

Aquinas' theory of law is the offspring of Hellenized Christianity. All laws are derived from the eternal law ; man is subject to the eternal law in the mode appropriate to him through knowledge. Man participates in the eternal law through his participation in the natural law, in which the eternal law resides. The obligatory character of human law is found in the natural law, and any human law which is not in accord with the law of nature is seen as a corruption of legal justice. Aquinas' theory of law is completely dependent on the commandments of God, correlated through man's reason. His theory of psychology, which states that man's basic inclination is towards the good, and therefore God, is uniform and simplistic. For Aquinas, the man most suited to rule is the most virtuous. It is a curious irony of history that Christianity provided the justification for the punishment of heresy, the divine right of kings, and the complete interpenetration of law and state.

Medieval theologians and philosophers came to believe that reason was simply a complementary discourse to that of revealed truth. The medieval world, through the doctrine of divine revelation, reinstated the mythical patriarchy of earlier times. Jesus the prophet was transformed into Jesus the redeemer and, finally, Jesus the king in his identification with the Heavenly Father in the mystery of the Holy Trinity. In linking the natural law to the will of deity, the medieval Christian world returned law to its anthropomorphic and patriarchal roots. This then furnished an ideological rationale for territorial conquest and the enforced conversion of heathen and heretic.

Are we justified in concluding that Hellenized Christianity, in the name of natural law theory, distorted both the Hebraic law and abstract science and forestalled a meaningful historical equilibrium between the two ? Christian philosophers and theologians held to the belief in the reconcilability of science, true philosophy, and religion. In fact the Hellenization of Christianity strengthened and brought to fruition the already existing universalist values in Judaism. The identification of the natural law with the will of God furnished the passageway through which the historic human values of prophetic Judaism enriched Western law.

THE NEW ENGLISH BIBLE[1]
The Sermon on the Mount

Matthew

5 When he saw the crowds he went up the hill. There he took his seat, and
when his disciples had gathered round him he began to address them. And this is
the teaching he gave :

How blest are these who know their need of God ;
the kingdom of Heaven is theirs.
How blest are the sorrowful ;
they shall find consolation.
How blest are those of a gentle spirit ;
they shall have the earth for their possession.
How blest are those who hunger and thirst to see right prevail ;
they shall be satisfied.
How blest are those who show mercy ;
mercy shall be shown to them.
How blest are those whose hearts are pure ;
they shall see God.
How blest are the peacemakers ;
God shall call them his sons.

How blest are those who have suffered
persecution for the cause of right;
the kingdom of Heaven is theirs.

"How blest you are, when you suffer insults and persecution and every kind of calumny for my sake. Accept it with gladness and exultation, for you have a rich reward in heaven; in the same way they persecuted the prophets before you.

"You are the salt to the world. And if salt becomes tasteless, how is its saltness to be restored? It is now good for nothing but to be thrown away and trodden underfoot.

"You are light for all the world. A town that stands on a hill cannot be hidden. When a lamp is lit, it is not put under the meal-tub, but on the lamp-stand, where it gives light to everyone in the house. And you, like the lamp, must shed light among your fellows, so that, when they see the good you do, they may give praise to your Father in heaven.

"Do not suppose that I have come to abolish the Law and the prophets; I did not come to abolish, but to complete. I tell you this: so long as heaven and earth endure, not a letter, not a stroke, will disappear from the Law until all that must happen has happened. If any man therefore sets aside even the least of the Law's demands, and teaches others to do the same, he will have the lowest place in the kingdom of Heaven, whereas anyone who keeps the Law, and teaches others so, will stand high in the kingdom of Heaven. I tell you, unless you show yourselves far better men than the Pharisees and the doctors of the law, you can never enter the kingdom of Heaven.

"You have learned that our forefathers were told, 'Do not commit murder; anyone who commits murder must be brought to judgment.' But what I tell you is this: Anyone who nurses anger against his brother must be brought to judgment. If he abuses his brother he must answer for it to the court; if he sneers at him he will have to answer for it in the fires of hell.

"If, when you are bringing your gift to the altar, you suddenly remember that your brother has a grievance against you, leave your gift where it is before the altar. First go and make your peace with your brother, and only then come back and offer your gift.

"If someone sues you, you come to terms with him promptly while you are both on your way to court: otherwise he may hand you over to the judge, and the judge to the constable, and you will be put in jail. I tell you, once you are there you will not be let out till you have paid the last farthing.

"You have learned that they were told 'Do not commit adultery.' But what I tell you is this: If a man looks on a woman with a lustful eye, he has already committed adultery with her in his heart.

"If your right eye is your undoing, tear it out and fling it away; it is better for you to lose one part of your body than the whole of it to be thrown into hell. And if your right hand is your undoing, cut it off and fling it away; it is better for you to lose one part of your body than for the whole of it to go to hell.

"They were told, 'A man who divorces his wife must give her a note of dismissal.' But what I tell you is this: If a man divorces his wife for any cause other than unchastity he involves her in adultery; and anyone who marries a divorced woman commits adultery.

"Again, you have learned that our forefathers were told, 'Do not break your oath,' and 'Oaths sworn to the Lord must be kept.' But what I tell you is this : You are not to swear at all — not by heaven, for it is God's throne, nor by earth, for it is his footstool, nor by Jerusalem, for it is the city of the great King, nor by your own head, because you cannot turn one hair of it white or black. Plain 'Yes' or 'No' is all you need to say : anything beyond that comes from the devil.

"You have learned that they were told, 'eye for eye, tooth for tooth.' But what I tell you is this : Do not set yourself against the man who wrongs you. If someone slaps you on the right cheek, turn and offer him your left. If a man wants to sue you for your shirt, let him have your coat as well. If a man in authority makes you go one mile, go with him two. Give when you are asked to give : and do not turn your back on a man who wants to borrow.

"You have learned that they were told, 'Love your neighbour, hate your enemy.' But what I tell you is this : Love your enemies and pray for your persecutors ; only so can you be children of your heavenly Father, who makes his sun rise on good and bad alike, and sends the rain on the honest and the dishonest. If you love only those who love you, what reward can you expect ? Surely the tax-gatherers do as much as that. And if you greet only your brothers, what is there extraordinary about that ? Even the heathen do as much. There must be no limit to your goodness, as your heavenly Father's goodness knows no bounds.

6 "Be careful not to make a show of your religion before men ; if you do, no reward awaits you in your Father's house in heaven.

"Thus, when you do some act of charity, do not announce it with a flourish of trumpets, as the hypocrites do in synagogue and in the streets to win admiration from men. I tell you this : they have their reward already. No : when you do some act of charity, do not let your left hand know what your right hand is doing ; your good deed must be secret, and your Father who sees what is done in secret will reward you.

"Again, when you pray, do not be like the hypocrites ; they love to say their prayers standing up in the synagogue and at the street-corners for everyone to see them. I tell you this : they have their reward already. But when you pray, go into a room by yourself, shut the door, and pray to your Father who is there in the secret place ; and your Father who sees what is secret will reward you.

"In your prayers, do not go babbling on like the heathen, who imagine that the more they say the more likely they are to be heard. Do not imitate them. Your Father knows what your needs are before you ask him. This is how you should pray :

'Our Father in heaven,
thy name be hallowed ;
thy kingdom come,
thy will be done,
on earth as in heaven.
Give us today our daily bread.
Forgive us the wrong we have done,
as we have forgiven those who have
wronged us.

And do not bring us to the test,
but save us from the evil one.'

For if you forgive others the wrongs they have done, your heavenly Father will also forgive you ; but if you do not forgive others, then the wrongs you have done will not be forgiven by your Father.

"So too, when you fast, do not look gloomy like the hypocrites : they make their faces unsightly so that other people may see that they are fasting. I tell you this : they have their reward already. But when you fast, anoint your head and wash your face, so that men may not see that you are fasting, but only your Father who is in the secret place ; and your Father who sees what is secret will give you your reward.

"Do not store up for yourselves treasures on earth, where it grows rusty and moth-eaten, and thieves break in to steal it. Store up treasure in heaven, where there is no moth and no rust to spoil it, no thieves to break in and steal. For where your treasure is, there will your heart be also.

"The lamp of the body is the eye. If your eyes are sound, you will have the light for your whole body ; if the eyes are bad, your whole body will be in darkness. If then the only light you have is darkness, the darkness is doubly dark.

"No servant can be the slave of two masters ; for either he will hate the first and love the second, or he will be devoted to the first and think nothing of the second. You cannot serve God and Money.

"Therefore I bid you put away anxious thoughts about food and drink to keep you alive, and clothes to cover your body. Surely life is more than food, the body more than clothes. Look at the birds of the air ; they do not sow and reap and store in barns, yet your heavenly Father feeds them. You are worth more than birds ! Is there a man of you who by anxious thought can add a foot to his height ? And why be anxious about clothes ? Consider how the lilies grow in the fields ; they do not work, they do not spin, and yet, I tell you, even Solomon in all his splendour was not attired like one of these. But if that is how God clothes the grass in the fields, which is there today, and tomorrow is thrown on the stove, will he not all the more clothe you ? How little faith you have ! What shall we wear ? All these things for the heathen to run after, not for you, because your heavenly Father knows that you need them all. Set your mind on God's kingdom and his justice before everything else, and all the rest will come to you as well. So do not be anxious about tomorrow ; tomorrow will look after itself. Each day has troubles enough of its own.

"Pass no judgment, and you will not be judged. For as you judge others, so you will yourselves be judged, and whatever measure you deal out to others will be dealt back to you. Why do you look at the speck of sawdust in your brother's eye, with never a thought for the great plank in your own ? Or how can you say to your brother, 'Let me take the speck out of your eye,' when all the time there is that plank in your own ? You hypocrite ! First take the plank out of your own eye, and then you will see clearly to take the speck out of your brother's....

23 Jesus then addressed the people and his disciples in these words :

"The doctors of the law and the Pharisees sit in the chair of Moses : therefore do what they tell you ; pay attention to their words. But do not follow their practice ; for they say one thing and do another. They make up heavy packs and pile them on men's shoulders, but will not raise a finger to lift the load themselves.

Whatever they do is done for show. They go about with broad phylacteries and with large tassels on their robes; they like to have places of honour at feasts and the chief seats in synagogues, to be greeted respectfully in the streets, and to be addressed as 'rabbi.'

"But you must not be called 'rabbi'; for you have one Rabbi, and you are all brothers. Do not call any man on earth 'father'; for you have one Father, and he is in heaven. Nor must you be called 'teacher'; you have one Teacher, the Messiah. The greatest among you must be your servant. For whoever exalts himself will be humbled; and whoever humbles himself will be exalted.

"Alas, alas for you, lawyers and Pharisees, hypocrites that you are! You shut the door of the kingdom of Heaven in men's faces; you do not enter yourselves, and when others are entering, you stop them.

"Alas for you, lawyers and Pharisees, hypocrites! You travel over sea and land to win one convert: and when you have won him you make him twice as fit for hell as you are yourselves.

"Alas for you, blind guides! You say, 'if a man swears by the sanctuary, that is nothing; but if he swears by the gold in the sanctuary, he is bound by his oath.' Blind fools! Which is the more important, the gold, or the sanctuary which sanctifies the gold? Or you say, 'If a man swears by the altar, that is nothing; but if he swears by the offering that lies on the altar, he is bound by his oath.' What blindness! Which is the more important, the offering, or the altar which sanctifies it? To swear by the altar, then, is to swear both by the altar and by whatever lies on it; to swear by the sanctuary is to swear both by the sanctuary and by him who dwells there; and to swear by heaven is to swear both by the throne of God and by him who sits upon it.

"Alas for you, lawyers and Pharisees, hypocrites! You pay tithes of mint and dill and cumin; but you have overlooked the weightier demands of the Law, justice, mercy, and good faith. It is these you should have practised, without neglecting the others. Blind guides! You strain off a midge, yet gulp down a camel!

"Alas for you, lawyers and Pharisees, hypocrites! You clean the outside of cup and dish, which you have filled inside by robbery and self-indulgence! Blind Pharisee! Clean the inside of the cup first; then the outside will be clean also.

"Alas for you, lawyers and Pharisees, hypocrites! You are like tombs covered with whitewash; they look well from outside, but inside they are full of dead men's bones and all kinds of filth. So it is with you: outside you look like honest men, but inside you are brimful of hypocrisy and crime.

"Alas for you, lawyers and Pharisees, hypocrites! You build up the tombs of the prophets and embellish the monuments of the saints, and you say, 'If we had been alive in our father's time, we should never have taken part with them in the murder of the prophets.' So you acknowledge that you are the sons of the men who killed the prophets. Go on then, finish off what your fathers began!

"You snakes, you vipers' brood, how can you escape being condemned to hell? I send you therefor prophets, sages, and teachers; some of them you will kill and crucify, others you will flog in your synagogues and hound from city to city. And so, on you will fall the guilt of all the innocent blood spilt on the ground, from innocent Abel to Zechariah, son of Berachiah, whom you murdered between the sanctuary and the altar. Believe me, this generation will bear the guilt of it all."

MARK

7 A group of Pharisees, with some doctors of the law who had come from Jerusalem, met him and noticed that some of his disciples were eating their food with "defiled" hands — in other words, without washing them. (For the Pharisees and the Jews in general never eat without washing the hands, in obedience to an old established tradition ; and on coming from the marketplace they never eat without first washing. And there are many other points on which they have a traditional rule to maintain, for example, washing of cups and jugs and copper bowls). Accordingly, these Pharisees and the lawyers asked him, "Why do your disciples not conform to the ancient tradition, but eat their food with defiled hands ?" He answered, "Isaiah was right when he prophesied about you hypocrites in these words : 'This people pays me lip-service, but their heart is far from me : their worship of me is in vain, for they teach as doctrines the commandments of men.' You neglect the commandment of God, in order to maintain the tradition of men."

He also said to them, "How well you set aside the commandment of God in order to maintain your tradition ! Moses said, 'Honour your father and your mother,' and, 'The man who curses his father or mother must suffer death.' But you hold that if a man says to his father or mother, 'Anything of mine which might have been used for your benefit is Corban' (meaning, set apart for God), he is no longer permitted to do anything for his father or mother. Thus by your own tradition, handed down among you, you make God's word null and void. And many other things that you do are just like that."

On another occasion he called the people and said to them, "Listen to me all of you, and understand this : nothing that goes into a man from outside can defile him ; no, it is the things that come out of him that defile a man."

When he had left the people and gone indoors, his disciples questioned him about the parable. He said to them, "Are you as dull as the rest ? Do you not see that nothing that goes from outside into a man can defile him, because it does not enter into his heart but into his stomach, and so passes out into the drain ?" Thus he declared all foods clean. He went on, "It is what comes out of a man that defiles him. For from inside, out of a man's heart, come evil thought, acts of fornication, of theft, murder, adultery, ruthless greed, and malice ; fraud, indecency, envy, slander, arrogance, and folly ; these evil things all come from inside, and they defile the man."

NOTE

1. *The New English Bible : The New Testament*, 2nd ed. (Oxford and Cambridge : Oxford University Press, and Cambridge University Press, 1970).

HELLENISTIC WAYS OF DELIVERANCE AND THE MAKING OF THE CHRISTIAN SYNTHESIS[1]

J.H. Randall

The building of the Christian synthesis was one assimilation after another of all the strands of Hellenistic experience by what started as a rather minor sect. Ever since disintegration of this system set in at the Reformation, and even before, among the pre-reformers, this process has often been viewed as a kind of corruption of an original purity, which men have felt ought somehow to be regained. But to the historian, there is little doubt, if the teachings of Jesus, or if the simple religious life of the primitive church, had remained pure, they would never have been heard of by later generations. They certainly would never have been taken over by our western European ancestors. They were rather accidentally incorporated in the final synthesis of Hellenistic experience. From time to time, they have been rediscovered by individuals, or by small groups, whose insistence on them has always produced a great shock to Christians. But they have never been taken very seriously by the church — or by Christianity — at least, not by any church that has ever been taken very seriously. Only minor sects, like the Friends or Quakers, have ever made them very central. The other churches have been, not followers of Jesus, but "Christian" — which has historically always been quite another thing. And again and again it has been authoritatively proclaimed by Christian thinkers — by many Christian realists in our century — that to attempt to follow the teachings of Jesus literally is heresy — the heresy of perfectionism.

No, the making of the Christian synthesis was hardly a corruption, a dilution, but rather an enriching. It meant the building of an entire culture, of a whole round of activities, feelings, and beliefs. Naturally, the greater the success of this synthesis in incorporating and expressing the needs of one type of social experience, the more there was present that had to be reconstructed when Christianity was used to organize and express another and alien social experience : when it was employed for that purpose, for instance, by the barbarian peoples of western Europe. And again and again, since that culture gave way to its many successors, it has happened once more. Each elaborate adaptation has in turn demanded further extensive revision.

This Christian synthesis was the work of generation after generation of modernists, who succeeded in bringing in new values and new ideals in the face of the traditionalists. All the great theologians, prophets and statesmen of the church have been essentially assimilators of novelty into the Christian tradition. In Hellenistic times they succeeded in building up a tremendous system, the final synthesis of ancient culture, drawing on Egypt, Syria, Persia, as well as on Palestine, Greece, and Rome.

How did this synthesis of Christian thought take form ? Let us try to enumerate the major stages in its making. It is well to remember that there is no single line of development, especially at the outset : the lines are many that happened to come together and fuse. The synthesis really began centuries before the life of Jesus. And the roots of the Christian system are to be found, not only in Judaism : they are located equally in Persian dualism, in Syrian mystery cults, in Stoic ethics, in Platonistic thought. It was mainly the accident of the inclusion of the Hebrew scriptures in the Christian canon, and hence in the synthesis, that has led to an undue emphasis on the Jewish background of Christianity, though Jesus himself was of course a Jew. After these earlier roots have been explored, there are :

1. The Jewish religion of righteousness, transformed in Jesus and the Gospels into purity of heart ; that is, into what moderns have often called prophetic monotheism.

2. There ensues a double line of growth. On the one hand, Christianity first appears as a kind of universalized Judaism, as a moral law and a promise of immortality. At the same time, Paul started conceiving of Christianity, and furnished its first theological formulation, as a mystery religion, an interpretation pushed in the second century by the Gnostics. This conception, minor at first, made Christianity the Jewish way of personal deliverance and salvation.

3. There follows the rationalization of Christianity in terms of the common Hellenistic Platonic religious philosophies. There was, first, the necessity of providing an intellectual justification in the Hellenistic world : this was undertaken by those thinkers we know as the Apologists. There then developed, secondly, genuinely philosophical interests in the great Neo-Platonic Alexandrian theologians and doctors, the first systematizers of a Christian rational theology, who were defending and extending Greek conceptions and values against the Syrian ascetics and dualists of the School of Antioch. Thirdly, there followed the determination of what was to remain Christian orthodoxy in the great councils, especially those of Nicaea and of Chalcedon. In themselves these involved many political compromises, much like those familiar in recent experience among the determinations of "correct" doctrine among the Russian Marxian-Leninists.

4. Next came the incorporation of much of the Stoic ethics, so popular in the West, at the hands of the Latin Fathers, especially Ambrose, who wrote the classic document of Christian Stoicism, *De Officiis Ministrorum.*

5. The chief achievement of the Latin Fathers was to work out the intellectual formulation of the cardinal Roman experiences of sin and salvation and deliverance ; here Ambrose and Augustine are the chief thinkers.

6. The doctrine of the church as an administrative system was elaborated especially by Cyprian and Augustine and consummated by Vincent of Lerins.

7. Almost a millennium later, in the Middle Ages, Christianity absorbed Aristotelian science, at the hands of the Schoolmen, following its earlier appropriation by the Moslems Avicenna and Averroes, and the Jewish Maimonides.

8. The church managed to organize medieval society, with the aid of Roman law and Greek political philosophy.

9. The disintegration, and concentration on certain selected strands of the Christian synthesis began with the pre-reformers and the mystics, long before the rush came with the Protestant Reformation or Revolt.

10. In modern times there have followed a series of radical reinterpretations, adding quite contradictory elements. This process includes the Humanists of the Renaissance as well as the Reformers, and the long line of Humanists down to the present day ; the Humanitarians, who came to the fore in the eighteenth century ; and the liberals and modernists from the nineteenth century on, including the three great Romantic reinterpretations of Hegel, of Kant, Fichte and Ritschl, and of Schleiermacher.

The Gospel of Jesus and the Mystery Cult of Paul

Jesus of Nazareth appears in the three synoptic Gospels as a fairly typical Hebrew prophet. But there has never yet been agreement on just what he taught. The tradition has remained split, and since the birth of critical scholarship in the eighteenth century (going back, indeed,to Spinoza), there has been unending discussion and argument on this issue. The precise definition of the message of Jesus remains still a task for interpretation in the light of one's own ideals and religious commitments, even more than for historical scholarship. If we ask, however, not what Jesus intended, but what the Christian tradition has found there, the answer is clear : it has found many and diverse lights. For all these conflicting views, the Gospels seem to furnish some authority.

The early Jewish Christians remained Jews, with no thought of embracing a new religion ; they were merely convinced that Jesus was the "Messiah" or the "Christ," and they regarded his Messiahship as much more important than any new moral message he might be bringing. That is, they believed in Jesus, rather than that what Jesus taught was true — an attitude that remained characteristic of most Christian thought until the nineteenth century. This conviction involved certain intellectual beliefs or expectations : notably that only righteous, law-observing Jews who accepted Jesus as the Messiah would share in the kingdom he would set up on his second coming. But their faith in Jesus was primarily a commitment to Jesus : it was practical rather than intellectual.

The second stage of the making of the Christian synthesis occurred when Christianity became a Greco-Oriental religious cult, offering individual salvation, with a Lord, a Kyrios, who had died and then risen again. By magic union with him, the initiates or baptized might also rise with him. "Lord" meant a divine saviour : the "Kingdom of God" was identified with the sacramental cult or "church" ; the Hebrew scriptures were turned into a Christian allegory. Jesus of Nazareth as a personal moral prophet and teacher was largely forgotten, and Christianity was spread by men who had never seen him, and cared little about his personality. They preached "Christ crucified" not the Sermon on the Mount.

It was Saul of Tarsus — known to posterity as Paul — who was the formulator of the whole Christian system of salvation from sin. His conception of the nature of Christianity, however, had very little influence among Christians for at least a hundred years. Paul suffered an intense personal experience of moral struggle and sin : the seventh chapter of Romans is probably autobiographical. Paul was unable to keep the Jewish law : his besetting sin, it seems, was that he could not help getting angry. Generalizing from his own personal experience, he felt that man is by nature evil and wicked, because of the desires of the flesh, which persist despite all man's efforts to struggle against them. Hence derives man's bitter need of release from the flesh, that is, from his natural desires, his need for a transformation of his very nature that can only be supernatural and magical.

Such a form of experience was common in that Hellenistic world, and was stamped on Christianity by Paul. For Paul himself, it was an intensely personal and practical moral experience. Paul doubtless exaggerated it and made it central in the moral life. The exaggeration is clearly an aberration, and, according to our modern lights, perhaps even pathological. But it was probably inevitable in any Hellenistic religion that could hope to become widespread and popular. Then, the vision of the Risen Christ or the Living Christ on the road to Damascus did transform the nature of Paul himself. This was a fact of his experience, however we may try to explain it, psychologically or otherwise.

Now, Paul was a Hellenized Jew who had to understand what he believed. And he understood his experience and its fruits in terms familiar to one with a Hellenistic upbringing. The whole framework of the redemptive system, in terms of which he proceeded to interpret the salvation he had won on the road to Damascus, is paralleled in, if not actually borrowed from, the many mystery cults of the time, with their widespread myth of a dying and rising Saviour or Lord. But above all Paul had to construe his own experience in terms that would seem intelligible to him. Why ? How ? Why could he not keep the Hebrew law ? Who and what was the "Living and Divine Christ" who had saved him ? What was the character of his supernatural "life in Christ" and "in the Spirit" after he had "risen with Christ" ? To answer these questions he had to work out a whole theology....

The vision of the Living Christ on the road to Damascus meant to Paul : Christ is the Messiah, a Divine Spirit, who put on the flesh, then died, and was released from the flesh. That is, Christ was a Mystery Lord, a *Kyrios.* By accepting and believing in the Christ, man can be identified with him in a mystic union, man can die to the flesh with him, and rise with him, completely transformed in his own nature. He can rise to a new and divine life "in the Spirit" or "in Christ." The work of Christ is hence not to found the kingdom, but to save individual souls.

Christianity, at the hands of Paul, became a mystical system of redemption, much like the cult of Isis, and the other sacramental or mystery religions of the day. Salvation is not forgiveness of sin, as it is for Jesus himself, but a transformation of human nature from the flesh to the spirit, from human to divine : it is literally a process of deification. The life of the Christian is literally supernatural, a life "in Christ." And it is a present reality, freeing the saved from sin. It carries with it a future life for the saved ; but for Paul resurrection is essentially a spiritual thing. Men "rise with Christ" in this human life, they rise when they accept Christ. When he is so saved in Christ, the Christian leads a divine life. He is freed literally from the need to obey any law, freed from the moral or Mosaic law as well as from the ceremonial law of the Jews. The law, both ceremonial and moral, Paul held, was given to the Jews only to convince men that they are quite unable to keep it by their own efforts alone : they need a transformation of their human nature in order not to sin. The law is hence "a school master" teaching men that they need Christ. The Christian is literally a supernatural being, who needs no law to tell him what is right, or to compel him to do it, for he can do no wrong. Paul is thus a complete antinomian, freed from any legalistic conception of the moral life. Naturally he was sadly puzzled by the goings-on of the not completely sinless Christians in the churches he had organized.

Paul's scheme differed from those of the other mystery cults, save that of Mithras, in his moral emphasis, which derives from his Jewish background : the salvation gained through accepting and rising with Christ is a moral freedom to love and serve one's fellows. Hence Paul adopted much of the ethical teaching of the Gospels. Ever since the eighteenth century Paul has been much disliked by liberal Christians, who differ with him on their estimate of the powers of human nature, and the need for a supernatural transformation of it. But such liberals have at the same time welcomed Paul's strong social emphasis : like the body and its members, Christians are all one in Christ, and should therefore serve each other. This is of course Stoic teaching, absorbed from the Hellenistic culture of the day, even to the figure Paul employs, a familiar Stoic image. [pp. 137-155]

NOTE

1. J.H. Randall, *Hellenistic Ways of Deliverance and the Making of the Christian Synthesis* (New York : Columbia University Press, 1970), pp. 137-155.

CHRISTIANITY AS A JEWISH SECT[1]

Jean Danielou

Primitive Christianity, like the early history of Israel and Judah, has a form and structure very different from our conventional picture of it. In both cases the reason is the same : retrospective editing of historical texts by the victorious party. The conceptual framework of the New Testament writers led them to present history as a successful launching of Christianity upon the Greco-Roman world after a little local difficulty, stemming from a handful of conservative "Judaizers," and easily settled. In fact the documents contained in the New Testament relate mainly to the "Hellenist" party. Until A.D. 70, when its centre at Jerusalem was destroyed, a Jewish form of Christianity was dominant, and the Hellenizing tendencies represented by Paul were followed only by a minority.

The Judaeo-Christian and "pagano-Christian" churches differed sharply from each other. In the former, Jewish religious regulations, such as circumcision, were still held to be obligatory, and the faith was expressed less in theological and metaphysical formulae than by a symbolic system of mystic letters and numbers, secret rites and signs, and the esoteric names and doctrines. In recent years a number of relics of the Judaeo-Christians have been recovered in Palestine.... They reveal that many early Christian images, which are usually thought to be the legacy of Hellenistic Christianity, in fact derive from Judaeo-Christian milieux. Two examples are the martyr's crown of palm, which derives from those offered at the Feast of Tabernacles ; while the cross was linked in Judaeo-Christian minds with the ancient Jewish symbols of the plough and the axe, as several discoveries have recently confirmed.

Judaeo-Christianity had no future and has died out completely, so much so that its history and the relevant mentality are only now being painfully pieced together. The "Church of the Circumcision," originally an equal partner, has vanished, leaving the field to the "Church of the Gentiles." Personifications of the two churches are seen. . . in the mosaics from the Church of Santa Sabina in Rome.... [p. 262]

The official documents which tell us about the origins of Christianity — the writings of the New Testament — were written in Greek and are connected with Hellenistic Christianity. This has been a long-persisting obstacle to the recognition that Christianity, which arose in a Semitic milieu, was, to start with, deeply involved both sociologically and culturally in the Jewish world. The rediscovery of this Jewish Christianity is one of the achievements of recent scholarship; it was made possible by the combined effect of a number of discoveries concerning both the Jewish culture of that age — illustrated by the Qumran manuscripts — and the Judaeo-Christian culture — illustrated by the manuscripts found at Nag Hammadi and by the Judaeo-Christian inscriptions at Palestine.

The pioneer scholars were each concerned with a particular aspect of the problem. S.G.F. Brandon and Bo Reicke placed early Christianity in the context of the anti-Roman agitation of the Zealots. Herbert Braun studied its links with the Essene movement. H.J. Schoeps identified it with Ebionism. Marcel Simon defined Judaeo-Christianity by its adherence to ritual observances. I characterized it as a particular kind of culture, the apocalyptic kind. These approaches are all valid, and help to arrive at a description of the full complexity of Judaeo-Christianity, a complexity which reflects that of contemporary Judaism.

Christianity belonged to the Jewish world because its founder did: born of a Jewish mother, Jesus spoke Hebrew and Aramaic like all Jews at the time. He was circumcized on the eighth day after his birth, observed the Sabbath, and went to worship in the Temple; he was well versed in the Jewish scriptures and he used the rabbinical method of teaching, as Gerhardsson has shown. The difficulty lies in locating him in the complex currents of the Judaism of his time. The Gospels make it clear that he ran into a collision with the Sadducaean aristocrats, who stood for a compromise with the Romans who were in occupation; but he also opposed the Pharisees; he reproved them for their casuistry and their compromises. The movement which he created round himself had affinities with the radical reformist movements of the Zealots and the Zadokites, yet was independent of them.

The essential characteristic of the Zealots, whose ideals were both religious and military, was their implacable determination to liberate the Holy Land from the yoke of a pagan occupation. Josephus' picture of them does them less than justice. There are some indications that Jesus shared this ambition; there were Zealots among his disciples, and some dramatic acts of his that are reported in the Gospels, such as the cleansing of the temple and the triumphal entry into Jerusalem, are counterparts of Zealot demonstrations. Brandon is no doubt right in saying that Mark, and the other evangelists after him, writing, as they were, for a Roman audience, had every reason to play down Jesus' sympathy for the revolt against Rome, rather than to underline it. All the same, Jesus' possible sympathy for the Zealots stopped short of action. In his activities there was none of the violence that was characteristic of theirs.

Points in common with the Zadokite movement are more striking. Jesus shared with them the fundamental idea that the end of the world was at hand, and like them he interpreted Old Testament prophecies in that sense. However, granting that the context is in truth the same, Braun has convincingly shown that the attitudes were different. For the Zadokites, reform meant a stricter observance of the law; for Jesus it meant going beyond the law. The Zadokites' movement was separatist. They held that the temple had been profaned. Jesus addressed his message to all, and went to worship in the Temple like the majority of the Jews. The Zadokites saw "the Last Things" through the eyes of Ezekiel: the people of of Israel were to achieve a state of ritual sanctity and were to be installed in a purified terrestrial Jerusalem, world without end. The goal of

Jesus' vision was the everlasting Kingdom of God, preceded by the resurrection — a kingdom to which all are called.

What is certain is that the context of Jesus' preaching is to be found in these reformist movements. He never attacked them, as he did attack the Sadducees and the Pharisees, and this is why the Zadokites are never mentioned. We have to start from these movements if we are to understand his activity by locating it in its place in history. It went far beyond these movements in its universalism and in its radicalism, but it presupposes their existence. This explains the difficulty that early Christianity found in extricating itself from this political and religious context and in bringing out, to the full, the implacations of Jesus' teaching.

The conflict between official Judaism and the reformist Jewish movements is the framework within which the trial and death of Jesus must be envisaged. They end the first phase of the history of Judaeo-Christianity, which is the ministry of Jesus himself. The next phase opens after his resurrection, the little group of apostles which he had gathered round himself begins to organize itself. They saw in the resurrection of Jesus "the Last Things" proclaimed by the prophets of Israel, and therefore they called upon all Jews to recognize this epoch-making event. They regarded themselves as being the true Israel, the community of the New Testament. Actually, they ran into a collision with a persistent hostility on the part of official Judaism, as represented by both the Sadducees and the Pharisees. In consequence they were no more than a minority group, on a par with the other Jewish dissenting sects, but they continued to be a Jewish sect all the same. They continued to be faithful observers of the law and of the worship in the temple.

This situation did not create any problems as long as the Christian community consisted solely of Jews ; but very soon the question arose of the attitude to be adopted towards converts from the pagan world. A very early practice, which was sanctioned in the year 49 by the Council of Jerusalem, was to exempt pagan converts from circumcision and from all Jewish observances except the so-called "precepts given to Noah," but many Judaeo-Christians refused to countenance this concession. Moreover, a more radical current of opinion, represented by Paul, held that even the Judaeo-Christians themselves were not bound by the rules of ritual purity and that, in particular, they could sit at the table with uncircumcized Christians. This is the significance of the incident at Antioch in the same year 49. Paul regarded circumcision, the Sabbath, and the worship in the temple as being obsolete from now on, even for Jews. Christianity had to liberate itself from its religious and political ties with Judaism if it was to open its doors to the gentiles.

In the political and religious climate of the rising tide of Jewish revolt against Rome, Paul's attitude was bound to seem treasonable to the Judaeo-Christians, since these remained loyal Israelites. We find this in later Judaeo-Christian literature : in the writings of Pseudo-Clement, Paul is "the enemy," and the Judaeo-Christian document used by the Tabhbit Dala accused Paul of tactical duplicity. From this date onward a rift began to open between Judaeo-Christians and pagano-Christians, and this rift was never re-closed. But the essential fact for us, a fact which Brandon has emphasized, is that until the year 70 the Judaeo-Christian wing of the church was the majority and Paul remained isolated....[pp. 275-276]

Though originally Judaeo-Christianity had been coextensive with the whole church, and though it continued to be a power till about the year 140, in the West it rapidly forfeited its supremacy to Pauline Christianity, which succeeded in severing its ties with Judaism. From the end of the second century onwards, Judaeo-Christians were regarded as being heretics. It is they who are censured under the names Ebionites, Quartodecimans, Encratites, Millenarianists, or, more commonly, Judaizers. Cut off, as they were from the Great Church, they very soon died out in the West. But their survival in the East can be traced from the third to the fourth century, particularly in Palestine, Arabia, Transjordan, Syria, and Mesopotamia. Some were absorbed by Islam, which is itself in some ways an heir of Judaeo-Christianity ; others adopted the orthodoxy of the Great Church, while retaining their Semitic culture, and something of their influence survives in the churches of Ethiopia, Syria, and Chaldaea.

There remains one final question : does Judaeo-Christianity have any future ? St. Paul saw, with profound insight, that Christianity had to extricate itself from its Jewish matrix if it was to achieve universality and not remain a Jewish sect. But, now that Christianity has achieved that universality, the terms of the question have been changed and indeed reversed. Christianity's current problem is actually the deficiency of its Judaic expression, which is one of the necessary aspects of its universality. [pp. 281-282]

NOTE

1. Jean Danielou, "Christianity as a Jewish Sect," in Arnold Toynbee, ed., *The Crucible of Christianity* (New York : World Publishing Company, 1969), pp. 262-282.

THE NEW ENGLISH BIBLE[1]

Matthew

8 When he had entered Capernaum a centurion came up to ask his help. "Sir," he said, "a boy of mine lies at home paralyzed and racked with pain." Jesus said, "I will come and cure him." But the centurion replied, "Sir, who am I to have you under my roof ? You need only to say the word and the boy will be cured. I know, for I am myself under orders, with soldiers under me. I say to one, 'Go,' and he goes ; to another, 'Come here,' and he comes ; and to my servant, 'Do this,' and he does it." Jesus heard him with astonishment and said to the people who were following him, "I tell you this : nowhere, even in Israel, have I found such faith."

"Many, I tell you, will come from east and west to feast with Abraham, Isaac, and Jacob in the Kingdom of Heaven. But those who were born to the kingdom will be driven out into the dark, the place of wailing and grinding of teeth.

10 "You must not think that I have come to bring peace to the earth ; I have not come to bring peace, but a sword. I have come to set a man against his father, a daughter against her mother, a son's wife against her mother-in-law ; and a man will find his enemies under his own roof.

"No man is worthy of me who cares more for father or mother than for me ; no man is worthy of me who cares for son or daughter ; no man is worthy of me who does not take up his cross and walk in my footsteps. By gaining his life a man will lose it; by losing his life for my sake, he will gain it...."

12 He was still speaking to the crowd when his mother and brothers appeared; they stood outside, wanting to speak to him. Someone said, "Your mother and your brothers are here outside; they want to speak to you." Jesus turned to the man who brought the message, and said, "Who is my mother? Who are my brothers?"; and pointing to the disciples, he said, "Here are my mother and my brothers. Whoever does the will of my heavenly Father is my brother, my sister, my mother...."

28 The eleven disciples made their way to Galilee, to the mountain where Jesus had told them to meet him. When they saw him, they fell prostrate before him, though some were doubtful. Jesus then came up and spoke to them. He said: "Full authority in heaven and on earth has been committed to me. Go forth therefore and make all nations my disciples; baptize men everywhere in the name of the Father and the Son and the Holy Spirit, and teach them to observe all that I have commanded you. And be assured, I am with you always, to the end of time."

Acts

10 At Caesarea there was a man named Cornelius, a centurion in the Italian Cohort, as it was called. He was a religious man, and he and his whole family joined in the worship of God. He gave generously to help the Jewish people, and was regular in his prayers to God. One day about three in the afternoon he had a vision in which he clearly saw an angel of God, who came into his room and said, "Cornelius!" He stared at him in terror. "What is it, my lord?" he asked. The angel said, "Your prayers and acts of charity have gone up to heaven to speak for you before God. And now send to Joppa for a man named Simon, also called Peter: he is lodging with another Simon, a tanner, whose house is by the sea." So when the angel who was speaking to him had gone, he summoned two of his servants and a military orderly who was a religious man, told them the whole story, and sent them to Joppa.

Next day, while they were still on their way and approaching the city, about noon Peter went up on the roof to pray. He grew hungry and wanted something to eat. While they were getting it ready, he fell into a trance. He saw a rift in the sky, and a thing coming down that looked like a great sheet of sail-cloth. It was slung by the four corners, and was being lowered to the ground. In it he saw creatures of every kind, whatever walks or crawls or flies. Then there was a voice which said to him, "Up Peter, kill and eat." But Peter said, "No Lord, no: I have never eaten anything profane or unclean." The voice came again a second time: "It is not for you to call profane what God counts clean." This happened three times; and then the thing was taken up again into the sky.

While Peter was still puzzling over the meaning of the vision he had seen, the messengers of Cornelius had been asking the way to Simon's house, and now arrived at the entrance. They called out and asked if Simon Peter was lodging there. But Peter was thinking over the vision, when the Spirit said to him, "Some men are here looking for you; make haste and go downstairs. You may go with them without any misgiving, for it was I who sent them." Peter came down to the men and said, "You are looking for me ? Here I am. What brings you here ?" "We are from the centurion Cornelius," they replied, "a good and religious man, acknowledged as such by the whole Jewish nation. He was directed by a holy angel to send for you to his house, and to listen to what you have to say." So Peter asked them in and gave them a night's lodging. Next day he set out with them, accompanied by some members of the congregation at Joppa.

The day after that, he arrived at Caesarea. Cornelius was expecting them and had called together his relatives and close friends. When Peter arrived, Cornelius came to meet him, and bowed to the ground in deep reverence. But Peter raised him to his feet and said, "Stand up ; I am a man like anyone else." Still talking with him he went in and found a large gathering. He said to them, "I need not tell you that a Jew is forbidden by his religion to visit or associate with a man of another race ; yet God has shown me clearly that I must not call any man profane or unclean. That is why I came here without demur when you sent for me. May I ask what was your reason for sending ?"

Cornelius said, "Four days ago, just about this time, I was in the house here saying the afternoon prayers, when suddenly a man in shining robes stood before me. He said : 'Cornelius, your prayer has been heard and your acts of charity remembered before God. Send to Joppa, then, to Simon Peter, and ask him to come. He is lodging in the house of Simon the tanner, by the sea.' So I sent to you there and then ; it was kind of you to come. And now we are all met here before God, to hear all that the Lord has ordered you to say."

Peter began : "I now see how true it is that God has no favourites, but that in every nation the man who is godfearing and does what is right is acceptable to him. He sent his word to the Israelites and gave the good news of peace through Jesus Christ, who is Lord of all, I need not tell you what happened lately all over the land of the Jews, starting from Galilee after the baptism proclaimed by John. You know about Jesus of Nazareth, how God anointed him with the Holy Spirit and with power. He went about doing good and healing all who were oppressed by the devil, for God was with him. And we can bear witness to all that he did in the Jewish countryside and in Jerusalem. He was put to death by hanging on a gibbet ; but God raised him to life on the third day, and allowed him to appear, not to the whole people, but to witnesses whom God had chosen in advance — to us, who ate and drank with him after he rose from the dead. He commanded us to proclaim to the people, and affirm that he is the one who has been designated by God as judge of the living and the dead. It is to him that all the prophets testify, declaring that everyone who trusts in him receives forgiveness of sins through his name."

Peter was still speaking when the Holy Spirit came upon all who were listening to the message. The believers who had come with Peter, men of Jewish birth, were astonished that the gift of the Holy Spirit should have been poured out even on Gentiles. For they could hear them speaking in tongues of ecstasy and acclaiming the greatness of God. Then Peter spoke : "Is anyone prepared to withhold the water for baptism from these persons, who have received the Holy Spirit just as we did ourselves ?" Then he ordered them to be baptized in the name of Jesus Christ. After that they asked him to stay on with them for a time.

11 News came to the Apostles and the members of the church in Judaea that Gentiles too had accepted the word of God ; and when Peter came up to Jerusalem those who were of Jewish birth raised the question with him. "You have been visiting men who are uncircumcized," they said, "and sitting at table with them!" Peter began by laying before them the facts as they had happened.

"I was in the city of Joppa," he said, "at prayer; and while in a trance I had a vision: a thing was coming down that looked like a great sheet of sail-cloth, slung by the four corners and lowered from the sky till it reached me. I looked intently to make out what was in it and I saw four-footed creatures of the earth, wild beasts, and things that crawl or fly. Then I heard a voice saying to me 'Up, Peter, kill and eat.' But I said, 'No, Lord, no: nothing profane or unclean has ever entered my mouth.' A voice from heaven answered a second time, 'It is not for you to call profane what God counts clean.' This happened three times, and then they were all drawn up into the sky. At that moment three men, who had been sent to me from Caesarea, arrived at the house where I was staying; and the Spirit told me to go with them. My six companions here came with me and we went into the man's house. He told us how he had seen an angel standing in his house who said, 'Send to Joppa for Simon also called Peter. He will speak words that will bring salvation to you and all your household.' Hardly had I begun speaking, when the Holy Spirit came upon them, just as upon us at the beginning. Then I recalled what the Lord had said: 'John baptized with water, but you will be baptized with the Holy Spirit.' God gave them no less a gift than he gave us when we put our trust in the Lord Jesus Christ; then how could I possibly stand in God's way?"

When they heard this their doubts were silenced. They gave praise to God and said, "This means that God has granted life-giving repentance to the Gentiles also."

15 Now certain persons who had come down from Judaea began to teach the brotherhood that those who were not circumcized in accordance with Mosaic practice could not be saved. That brought them into fierce dissension and controversy with Paul and Barnabas. And so it was arranged that these two and some others from Antioch should go up to Jerusalem to see the apostles and elders about this question.

They went on their way by the congregation, and travelled through Phoenicia and Samaria, telling the full story of the conversion of the Gentiles. The news caused great rejoicing among all the Christians there.

When they reached Jerusalem they were welcomed by the church and the apostles and elders, and reported all that God had done through them. Then some of the Pharisaic party who had become believers came forward and said, "They must be circumcized and told to keep the Law of Moses."

The apostles and elders held a meeting to look into this matter; and, after a long debate, Peter rose and addressed them. "My friends," he said, "in the early days, as you yourselves know, God made his choice among you and ordained that from my lips the Gentiles should hear and believe the message of the Gospel. And God, who can read men's minds, showed his approval of them by giving the Holy Spirit to them, as he did to us. He made no difference between them and us; for he purified their hearts by faith. Then why do you now provoke God by laying on the shoulders of these converts a yoke which neither we nor our fathers were able to bear? No, we believe that it is by the grace of the Lord Jesus that we are saved, and so are they."

At that the whole company fell silent and listened to Barnabas and Paul as they told of all the signs and miracles that God had worked among the Gentiles through them.

When they had finished speaking, James summed up : "My friends," he said, "listen to me. Simeon has told how it first happened that God took notice of the Gentiles, to choose from among them a people to bear his name ; and this agrees with the words of the prophets, as Scripture has it :

> "Thereafter I will return and rebuild
> the fallen house of David ;
> even from its ruins I will rebuild it,
> and set it up again,
> that they may seek the Lord — all the
> rest of mankind,
> and the Gentiles, whom I have
> claimed for my own.
> Thus says the Lord, whose work it is,
> made known long ago."

"My judgment, therefore, is that we should impose no irksome restrictions on those of the Gentiles who are turning to God, but instruct them by letter to abstain from things polluted by contact with idols, from fornication, from anything that has been strangled, and from blood. Moses, after all, has never lacked spokesmen in every town for generations past ; he is read in the synagogues Sabbath by Sabbath."

Then the apostles and elders, with the agreement of the whole church, resolved to choose representatives and send them to Antioch with Paul and Barnabas. They chose two leading men in the community, Judas Barsabbas and Silas, and gave them this letter to deliver :

"We, the apostles and elders, send greetings as brothers to our brothers of gentile origin in Antioch, Syria, and Cilicia. Forasmuch as we have heard that some of our number, without any instructions from us, have disturbed you with their talk and unsettled your minds, we have resolved unanimously to send to you our chosen representatives with our well-beloved Barnabas and Paul, who have devoted themselves to the cause of our Lord Jesus Christ. We are therefore sending Judas and Silas, who will themselves confirm this by word of mouth. It is the decision of the Holy Spirit, and our decision to lay no further burden upon you beyond these essentials : you are to abstain from meat that has been offered to idols, from blood, from anything that has been strangled, and from fornication. If you keep yourselves free from these things you will be doing right. Farewell."

GALATIANS

3 For through faith you are all sons of God in union with Christ Jesus. Baptized into union with him, you have all put on Christ as a garment. There is no such thing as Jew and Greek, slave and freeman, male and female ; for you are all one person in Christ Jesus. But if you thus belong to Christ you are the "issue" of Abraham, and so heirs by promise.

NOTE

1. *The New English Bible : The New Testament*, 2nd ed. (London : Oxford University Press, 1970).

SUMMA THEOLOGICA[1]

Thomas Aquinas

Treatise on Law

Question 90 : Of The Essence of Law

1. Law is a rule and measure of acts, whereby man is induced to act or is restrained from acting : for *lex* (law) is derived from *ligare* (to bind) because it binds one to act. Now the rule and measure of human acts is the reason, which is the first principle of human acts . . . since it belongs to the reason to direct to the end, which is the first principle in all matters of action, according to the philosopher....

Reason has its power of moving from the will ... for it is due to the fact that one wills the end, that the reason issues its commands as regards things ordained to the end. But in order that the volition of what is commanded may have the nature of law, it needs to be in accord with some rules of reason. And in this sense is to be understood the saying that the will of the sovereign has the force of law ; otherwise sovereign's will would savour of lawlessness rather than of law.

2. The law belongs to that which is a principle of human acts, because it is their rule and measure. Now as reason is a principle of human acts, so in reason itself there is something which is the principle chiefly and mainly law must needs be referred — Now the first principle in practical matters, which are the object of the practical reason, is the last end : and the last end of human life is bliss or happiness.... Consequently the law must needs regard principally the relationship to happiness. Moreover, since every part is ordained to the whole, as imperfect to perfect ; and since one man is a part of the perfect community, the law must needs regard properly the relationship to universal happiness. Wherefore the philosopher, in the above definition of legal matters, mentions both happiness and the body politic : for he says (Ethic v. 1) that we call those legal matters just, which are adapted to produce and preserve happiness and its parts for the body politic : since the state is a perfect community, as he says in Polit. i. I....

3. A law, properly speaking, regards first and foremost the order to the common good. Now to order anything to the common good, belongs either to the whole people, or to someone who is the viceregent of the whole people, and therefore the making of a law belongs either to the whole people or to a public personage who has care of the whole people : since in all other matters the directing of anything to the end concerns him to whom the end belongs....

A private person cannot lead another to virtue efficaciously : for he can only advise, and if his advice be not taken, it has no coercive power, such as the law should have, in order to prove an efficacious inducement to virtue, as the philosopher says (Ethic x.9). But this coercive power is vested in the whole people or in some public personage, to whom it belongs to inflict penalties.... Wherefore the framing of laws belongs to him alone.

As one man is a part of the household, so a household is a part of the state : and the state is a perfect community, according to Polit. i.

And therefore, as the good of one man is not the last end, but is ordained to the common good ; so too the good of one household is ordained to the good of a single state, which is a perfect community. Consequently he that governs a family, can indeed make certain commands or ordinances, but not such as to have properly the force of law....

4. A law is imposed on others by way of a rule and measure. Now a rule or measure is imposed by being applied to those who are to be ruled and measured by it. Wherefore, in order that a law obtain the binding force which is proper to a law, it must needs be applied to the men who have to be ruled by it. Such application is made by its being notified to them by promulgation. Wherefore promulgation is necessary for the law to obtain its force.

Thus from the preceding, the definition of law may be gathered ; and it is nothing else than an ordinance of reason for the common good, made by him who has care of the community, and promulgated.

The natural law is promulgated by the very fact that God instilled it into man's mind so as to be known by him naturally.

Question 91 : Of the Various Kinds of Law

1. As stated above, a law is nothing else but a dictate of practical reason emanating from the ruler who governs a perfect community. Now it is evident, granted that the world is ruled by Divine Providence, ... that the whole community of the universe is governed by Divine Reason. Wherefore the very idea of the government of things in God the Ruler of the Universe has the nature of a law. And since the Divine Reason's conception of things is not subject to time but is eternal, according to Prov. viii, 23, therefore it is that this kind of law must be called eternal....

Promulgation is made by word of mouth or in writing, and in both ways the eternal law is promulgated : because both the Divine Word and the writing of the Book of Life are eternal. But the promulgation cannot be from eternity on the part of the creature that hears or reads....

2. Since all things subject to Divine Providence are ruled and measured by the eternal law, as it was stated above ; it is evident that all things partake somewhat of the eternal law, in so far as, namely, from its being imprinted on them, they derive their respective inclinations to their proper acts and ends. Now among all others, the rational creature is subject to Divine Providence in the most excellent way, in so far as it partakes of a share of providence, by being provident both for itself and for others. Wherefore it has a share of the Eternal Reason, whereby it has a natural inclination to its proper act and end : and this participation of the eternal law in the rational creature is called the natural law. Hence the psalmist after saying (Ps. iv.6) : Offer up the sacrifice of justice, as though some asked what the works of justice are, adds : Many say, who showeth us good things ? In answer to which question he says : the light of Thy countenance, O Lord, is signed upon us : thus implying that the light of natural reason, whereby we discern what is good and what is evil, which is the function of the natural law, is nothing else than an imprint on us of the Divine light. It is therefore evident that the natural law is nothing else than the rational creature's participation of the eternal law....

3. As stated above, a law is a dictate of the practical reason. Now it is to be observed that the same procedure takes place in the practical and in the speculative reason : for each proceeds from principles to conclusions.... Accordingly we conclude that just as, in the speculative reason, from naturally known indemonstrable principles, we draw the conclusions of the various sciences, the knowledge of which is not imparted to us by nature, but acquired by the efforts of reason, so too it is from the precepts of the natural law, as from general and indemonstrable principles, that the human reason needs to proceed to the more particular determination of certain matters. These particular determinations, devised by human reason, are called human laws, provided the other essential conditions of law be observed, as stated above. Wherefore Tully says in his Rhetoric (De Invent. Rhet. ii) that justice has its source in nature ; thence certain things came into custom by reason of their utility ; afterwards these things which emanated from nature and were approved by custom, were sanctioned by fear and reverence for the law.

The human reason cannot have a full participation of the dictate of the Divine Reason, but according to its own mode, and imperfectly. Consequently, as on the part of the speculative reason, by a natural participation of Divine Wisdom, there is in us the knowledge of certain general principles, but not proper knowledge of each single truth, such as that contained in the Divine Wisdom ; so too, on the part of the practical reason, man has a natural participation of the eternal law, according to certain general principles, but not as regards the particular determinations of individual cases, which are, however, contained in the eternal law. Hence the need for human reason to proceed further to sanction them by law.

Human reason is not, of itself, the rule of things : but the principles impressed on it by nature, are general rules and measures of all things relating to human conduct, whereof the natural reason is the rule and measure, although it is not the measure of things that are from nature.

The practical reason is concerned with practical matters, which are singular and contingent : but not with necessary things, with which the speculative reason is concerned. Wherefore human laws cannot have that inherency that belongs to the demonstrated conclusions of sciences. Nor is it necessary for every measure to be altogether unerring and certain, but according as it is possible in its own particular genus.

NOTE

1. Thomas Aquinas, *Summa Theologica* (Indiana : Regnery/Gateway, Inc., 1963), pp. 1-19.

TABLE TALK[1]

John Selden

Law of Nature

I cannot fancy to myself what the law of nature means but the Law of God. How should I know I ought not to steal, I ought not to commit adultery, unless somebody had told me so ? Surely 'tis because I have been told so ? 'Tis not because I think I ought not to do them, nor because you think I ought not : if so, our minds might change, whence then comes the restraint ? From a higher power nothing else can bind. I cannot bind myself, for I may untie myself again ; nor an equal cannot bind me, for we may untie one another : it must be a superior power, even God Almighty. If two of us make a bargain, why should either of us stand to it ? What need you care what you say, or what need I care what I say ? Certainly because there is something about me that tells me *fides est servanda* ; and if we after alter our minds and make a new bargain there's *fide servanda* there too. [pp. 157-158]

NOTE

1. John Selden, *Table Talk*, ed. Pollock (London : Quaritch Press, 1927), pp. 157-158.

BLACKSTONE'S COMMENTARIES[1]

This then is the general signification of law, a rule of action dictated by some superior being ; and, in those creatures that have neither the power to think, nor to will, such laws must be invariably obeyed, so long as the creature itself subsists, for its existence depends on that obedience. But laws, in their more confined sense, and in which it is our present business to consider them, denote the rules, not of action in general, but of human action or conduct : that is, the precepts by which man, the noblest of all sublunary beings, a creature endowed with both reason and freewill, is commanded to make use of those faculties in the general regulation of his behaviour.

Man, considered as a creature, must necessarily be subject to the laws of his creator, for he is entirely a dependent being. A being, independent of any other, has no rule to pursue, but such as he prescribes to himself ; but a state of dependence will inevitably oblige the inferior to take the will of him, on whom he depends, as the rule of his conduct : not indeed in every particular, but in all those points wherein his dependence consists. This principle therefore has more or less extent and effect in proportion as the superiority of the one and the dependence of the other is greater or less, absolute or limited. And consequently, as man depends absolutely upon his maker for everything, it is necessary that he should in all points conform to his maker's will.

This will of his maker is called the law of nature. For as God, when he created matter, and endued it with a principle of mobility, established certain rules for the perpetual direction of that motion ; so, when he created man, and endued him with freewill to conduct himself in all parts of life, he laid down certain immutable laws of human nature, whereby that freewill is in some degree regulated and restrained, and gave him also the faculty of reason to discover the purport of those laws.

Considering the creator only as a being of infinite power, he was able unquestionably to have prescribed whatever laws he pleased to his creature, man, however unjust or severe. But as he is also a being of infinite wisdom, he has laid down only such laws as were founded in those relations of justice that existed in the nature of things antecedent to any positive precept. These are the eternal, immutable laws of good and evil, to which the creator himself in all his dispensations conforms ; and which he has enabled human reason to discover, so far as they are necessary for the conduct of human actions. Such among others are these principles : that we should live honestly, should hurt nobody, and should render to every one his due ; to which three general precepts Justinian has reduced the whole doctrine of law.

But if the discovery of these first principles of the law of nature depended only upon the due exertion of right reason, and could not otherwise be obtained than by a chain of metaphysical disquisitions, mankind would have wanted some inducement to have quickened their inquiries, and the greater part of the world would have rested content in mental indolence and ignorance, its inseparable companion. As therefore the creator is a being, not only of infinite power, and wisdom, but also of infinite goodness, he has been pleased so to contrive the constitution and frame of humanity, that we should want no other prompter to inquire after and pursue the rule of right, but only our own self-love, that universal principle of action. For he has so intimately connected, so inseparably interwoven the laws of eternal justice with the happiness of each individual, that the latter cannot be attained but by observing the former ; and, if the former be punctually obeyed, it cannot but induce the latter. In consequence of which mutual connection with justice and human felicity, he has not perplexed the law of nature with a multitude of abstracted rules and precepts, referring merely to the fitness or unfitness of things, as some have vainly surmised ; but has graciously reduced the rule of obedience to this one paternal precept, "that man should pursue his own true and substantial happiness." This is the foundation of what we call ethics or natural law. For the several articles into which it is branched in our systems amount to no more than demonstrating that this or that action tends to man's real happiness, and therefore very justly concluding that the performance of it is a part of the law of nature ; or, on the other hand, that this or that action is destructive of man's real happiness, and therefore that the law of nature forbids it.

This law of nature, being coeval with mankind and dictated by God himself, is of course superior in obligation to any other. It is binding over all the globe in all countries, and at all times ; no human laws are of any validity, if contrary to this : and such of them as are valid derive all their force, and all their authority, mediately or immediately, from this original.

But in order to apply this to the particular exigencies of each individual, it is still necessary to have recourse to reason ; whose office it is to discover, as was before observed, what the law of nature directs in every circumstance of life ; by considering, what method will tend the most effectually to our own substantial happiness. And if our reason were always, as in our first ancestor before his transgression, clear and perfect, unruffled by passions, unclouded by prejudice, unimpaired by disease or intemperance, the task would be pleasant and easy ; we should need no other guide but this. But every man now finds the contrary in his own experience; that his reason is corrupt, and his understanding full of ignorance and error.

This has given manifold occasion for the benign interposition of divine providence; which, in compassion to the frailty, the imperfection and the blindness of human reason, hath been pleased, at sundry times and in diverse manners, to discover and enforce its laws by an immediate and direct revelation. The doctrines thus delivered we call the revealed or divine law, and they are to be found only in the Holy Scriptures. These precepts, when revealed, are found upon comparison to be really a part of the original law of nature, as they tend in all their consequences to man's felicity. But we are not from thence to conclude that the knowledge of these truths was attainable by reason, in its present corrupted state; since we find that, until they were revealed, they hid from the wisdom of ages. As then the moral precepts of this law are indeed of the same origin with those of the law of nature, so their intrinsic obligation is of equal strength and perpetuity. Yet undoubtedly the revealed law is of infinitely more authenticity than that moral system, which is framed by ethical writers, and denominated the natural law. Because one is the law of nature, expressly declared so to be by God himself: the other is only what, by the assistance of human reason, we imagine to be that law. If we could be as certain of the latter as we are of the former, both would have an equal authority; but, till then, they can never be put in any competition together.

Upon these two foundations, the law of nature and the law of revelation, depend all human laws; that is to say, no human laws should be suffered to contradict these. There are, it is true a great number of indifferent points, in which both the divine law and the natural leave a man at his own liberty; but which are found necessary for the benefit of society to be restrained within certain limits. And herein it is that human laws have their greatest force and efficacy; for, with regard to such points as are not indifferent, human laws are only declaratory of, and act in subordination to, the former. To instance in the case of murder; this is expressly forbidden by the divine, and demonstrably by the natural law; and from these prohibitions arises the true unlawfulness of this crime. Those human laws that annex a punishment to it do not at all increase its moral guilt, or superadd any fresh obligation *in foro conscientiae* to abstain from it's perpetration. Nay, if any human law should allow or enjoin us to commit it, we are bound to transgress that human law, or else we must offend both the natural and the divine. But with regard to matters that are in themselves indifferent, and are not commanded or forbidden by those superior laws; such, for instance, as exporting of wool into foreign countries; here the inferior legislature has scope and opportunity to interpose, and to make that action unlawful which before was not so.

If man were to live in a state of nature, unconnected with other individuals, there would be no occasion for any other laws than the law of nature and the law of God. Neither could any other law possibly exist; for a law always supposes some superior who is to make it; and in a state of nature we are all equal, without any other superior but him who is the author of our being. But man was formed for society; and, as is demonstrated by the writers on this subject, is neither capable of living alone, nor indeed has the courage to do it. However, as it is impossible for the whole race of mankind to be united in one great society, they must necessarily divide into many ; and form separate states, commonwealth and nations entirely independent of each other, and yet liable to a mutual intercourse. Hence arises a third kind of law, to regulate this mutual intercourse, called "the law of nations" which, as none of these states will acknowledge a superiority in the other, cannot be dictated by any but depends entirely upon the rules of natural law, or upon mutual compacts, treaties, leagues, and agreements between these several communities : in the construction also of which compacts we have no other rule to resort to but the law of nature ; being the only one to which all the communities are equally subject : and therefore the civil law very justly observes, that *quod naturalis ratio inter omnes homines constituit, vocatur jus gentium.* [pp. 39-43]

NOTE

1. Sir William Blackstone,*Blackstone's Commentaries,* vol. 1, ed. St. George Tucker (Philadelphia : Birch and Small, 1803), pp. 34-43.

THE INTERACTION OF LAW AND RELIGION[1]

Harold J. Berman

For Judaism, the centre of gravity of human history is the history of the Jewish people and of the Judaic law that binds it to God and its members to each other ; whereas for Christianity, the church from the time of St. Paul, though conceived to be a historical continuation of the Jewish people, was intended to embrace all other peoples as well, each with its own law. Therefore a new law was required within the church itself, as a religious community, to govern its relationships with God as well as the relationships of its members with each other ; also new attitudes and policies were required with respect to the secular law by which individual Christians were governed in their nonreligious activities and by which the church as a whole was governed in its relationships with "the world"....

With the conversion of the Roman emperors to Christianity in the fourth century, the church came to operate within the power structure. Now it faced a quite different aspect of the question of the relationship between law and religion — namely, whether the emperor's acceptance of the Christian faith had anything positive to contribute to his role as a legislator. The answer given by history was that the Christian emperors of Byzantium considered it their Christian responsibility to revise the laws, as they put it, "in the direction of greater humanity." Under the influence of Christianity, the Roman law of the postclassical period reformed family law, giving the wife a position of greater equality before the law, requiring mutual consent of both spouses for the validity of a marriage, making divorce more difficult (which at that time was a step toward women's liberation !) and abolishing the father's power of life or death over his children ; reformed the law of slavery, giving a slave the right to appeal to a magistra`e if his master abused his powers and even, in some cases, the right to freedom `the master exercised cruelty, mutiplying modes of manumission of slaves, and permitting slaves to acquire rights by kinship with freemen ; and introduced a concept of equity into legal rights and duties generally, thereby tempering the strictness of general prescriptions. Also the great collections of laws compiled by Justinian and his successors in the sixth, seventh, and eighth centuries were inspired in part by the belief that Christianity required that the law be systematized as a necessary step in its humanization. These various reforms were, of course, attributable not only to Christianity, but Christianity gave an important impetus to them as well as providing the main ideological justification. Like civil disobedience, law reform "in the direction of greater humanity" remains a basic principle of Christian jurisprudence derived from the early experience of the church.

In contrast to the Byzantine emperors, who inherited the great legal tradition of pagan Rome, the rulers of the Germanic, Slavic, and other peoples of Europe during roughly the same era (from the fifth to the tenth centuries) presided over a legal regime consisting chiefly of primitive tribal customs and rules of the blood feud. It is more than coincidence that the rulers of many of the major tribal peoples, from Anglo-Saxon England to Kievan Russia, after their conversion to Christianity promulgated written collections of tribal laws and introduced various reforms, particularly in connection with family law, slavery and protection of the poor and oppressed, as well as in connection with church property and the rights of clergy. The Laws of Alfred (about A.D. 890) start with a recitation of the Ten Commandments and excerpts from the Mosaic law ; and in restating and revising the native Anglo-Saxon laws Alfred includes such great principles as : "Doom [i.e., judge]very evenly ; doom not one doom to the rich, another to the poor ; nor doom one to your friend, another to your foe."

The church in those centuries, subordinate as it was to emperors, kings, and barons, sought to limit violence by establishing rules to control blood feuds ; and in the tenth and eleventh centuries the great Abbey of Cluny, with its branches all over Europe, even had some success in establishing the so-called Peace of God, which exempted from warfare not only the clergy but also the peasantry, and the so-called Truce of God, which prohibited warfare on the weekends. Here, too, are influences of religion on law that have bearing for our time.

Nevertheless, despite the reforms and innovations of Christian kings and emperors, the prevailing law of the West remained — prior to the twelfth century — the law of the blood feud, and of trial by battle, and by ordeals of fire and water, and by ritual oaths. There were no professional judges, no professional lawyers, no law books, either royal or ecclesiastical. Custom reigned — tribal custom, local custom, feudal custom. In the households of kings and in the monasteries there was civilization to a degree ; but without a system of law it was extremely difficult to transmit civilization from the centres to the localities. To take one example : the church preached that marriage is a sacrament which cannot be performed without the consent of the spouses, but there was no effective system of law by which the church could overcome the widespread practice of arranging marriages between infants. And not only were civilized values crushed by a hostile environment, but the church itself was under the domination of the same environment : lucrative and influential clerical offices were bought and sold by feudal lords who appointed brothers and cousins to be bishops and priests.

In the latter part of the eleventh and first part of the twelfth century, there took place in the West a great revolution which resulted in the formation of a visible, corporate, hierarchical church, a legal entity independent of emperors, kings, and feudal lords, and subordinate to the absolute monarchical authority of the bishop of Rome. This was the Papal Revolution, of whose enormous significance medieval historians both inside and outside the Catholic church are becoming increasingly aware. It led to the creation of a new kind of law for the church as well as new kinds of law for the various secular kingdoms.

Previously the relationship between the spiritual and secular realms had been one of overlapping authorities, with emperors and kings (Charlemagne and William the Conqueror, for example) calling church councils and promulgating new theological doctrine and ecclesiastical law, and with popes, archbishops, bishops, and priests being invested in their offices by emperors, kings, and lords. In 1075, however, Pope Gregory VII proclaimed the complete political and legal independence of the church and at the same time proclaimed his own supreme political and legal authority over the entire clergy of Western Christendom. It took forty-five years of warfare between the papal and the imperial parties — the Wars of Investiture — and in England it took the martyrdom of Thomas Becket before the papal claims were established (albeit with some substantial compromises).

The new visible, hierarchical, corporate Roman Catholic church needed a systematic body of law, and in the twelfth and thirteenth centuries this was produced — first in a great treatise written about 1140 by the Italian monk Gratian and, eighty years later, after a succession of jurist-popes had promulgated hundreds of new laws, by Pope Gregory IX in his Decretals of 1234. The Decretals remained the basic law of the Roman church until 1917.

Of course there had been ecclesiastical canons long before Gratian, but they consisted of miscellaneous scattered decisions, decrees, teachings, etc., mostly of a theological nature, pronounced by various church councils and individual bishops, and occasionally gathered in chronologically arranged collections. There were also traditional procedures in ecclesiastical tribunals. However, there was no systematized body of ecclesiastical law, criminal law, family law, inheritance law, property law, or contract law, such as was created by the canonists of the twelfth and thirteenth centuries. The canon law of the later Middle Ages, which only today, eight centuries later, is being called into question by some leading Roman Catholics themselves, was the first modern legal system of the West, and it prevailed in every country of Europe. The canon law governed virtually all aspects of the lives of the church's own army of priests and monks and also a great many aspects of the lives of the laity. The new hierarchy of church courts had exclusive jurisdiction over laymen in matters of family law, inheritance, and various types of spiritual crimes, and in addition it had concurrent jurisdiction with secular courts over contracts (whenever the parties made a "pledge of faith"), property (whenever ecclesiastical property was involved — and the church owned one-fourth to one-third of the land of Europe), and many other matters.

The canon law did not prevail alone, however. Alongside it there emerged various types of secular law, which just at this very time, in the twelfth and thirteenth centuries, began to be rationalized and systematized. In about 1100, the Roman law of Justinian, which had been virtually forgotten in the West for five centuries, was rediscovered. This rediscovery played an important part in the development of the canon law, but it also was seized upon by secular rulers who resisted the new claims of the papacy. And so in emulation of the canon law, diverse bodies of secular law came to be created by emperors, kings, great feudal lords, and also eventually in the cities and boroughs that emerged in Europe in the twelfth and thirteenth centuries, as well as among merchants trading in the great international fairs. The success of the canon law stimulated secular authorities to create their own professional courts and a professional legal literature, to transform tribal, local, and feudal custom, and to create their own rival legal systems to govern feudal property relations, crimes of violence, mercantile transactions, and many other matters.

Thus it was the church that first taught Western man what a modern legal system is like. The church first taught that conflicting customs, statutes, cases, and doctrines may be reconciled by analysis and synthesis. This was the method of Abelard's famous *Sicet Non* (Yes and No), which lined up contradictory texts of Holy Scriptures — the method reflected in the title of Gratian's *Concordance of Discordant Canons.* By this method the church, in reviving the study of the obsolete Roman law, transformed it by transmuting its complex categories and classifications into abstract legal concepts. These techniques were derived from the principle of reason as understood by the theologians and philosophers of the twelfth century as well as by the lawyers.

The church also taught the principle of conscience — in the corporate sense of that term, not the modern individualist sense : that the law is to be found not only in scholastic reason but also in the heart of the lawgiver or judge. The principle of conscience in adjudication was first stated in an eleventh century tract which declared that the judge must judge himself before he may judge the accused, that he must, in other words, identify himself with the accused, since thereby (it was said) he will know more about the crime than the criminal himself knows. A new science of pleading and procedure was created in the church courts, and later in secular courts as well (for example, the English Chancery), "for informing the conscience of the judge." Procedural formalism was attacked. (In 1215 the Fourth Lateran Council effectively abolished trials by ordeal throughout Europe forbidding clergy to participate in them.) The right to direct legal representation by professional lawyers and the procedure for interrogation by the judge according to carefully worked out rules were among the new institutions created to implement the principle of conscience. Conscience was associated with the idea of the equality of the law, since in conscience all litigants are equal ; and from this came equity — the protection of the poor and helpless against the rich and powerful, the enforcement of relations of trust and confidence, and the granting of so-called personal remedies such as injunctions. Equity, as we noted earlier, had been part of the postclassical Roman law as well, but it was now for the first time made systematic, and special procedures were devised for invoking and applying it.

And so the church sought both to legalize morality and to moralize legality ; it took legal jurisdiction over sins, and it influenced the secular law to conform to moral principles. As in ancient Israel the distinction between law and morality was minimized. On the other hand, standards of right and wrong were reinforced by legal procedures and legal sanctions ; on the other hand, a divine righteousness was attributed to legal standards which they by no means always had. Universal celibacy of the priesthood, for example, was made a legal requirement in the eleventh century in order to insulate the clergy from clan and feudal politics, but it acquired an aura of sanctity that made it survive long after it had ceased to be necessary. The law of heresy is another example of the evil of confusing immorality with illegality. Excommunication for disobedience to ecclesiastical authority was a legal remedy which could deprive a person of his entire moral security.... [pp. 52-61]

The key to the renewal of law in the West from the sixteenth century on was the Protestant concept of power of the individual, by God's grace, to change nature and to create new social relations through the exercise of his will. The Protestant concept of the individual will became central to the development of the modern law of property and contract. Nature became property. Economic relations became contract. Conscience became will and intent. The last testament, which in the earlier Catholic tradition had been a means of saving souls by charitable gifts, became a means of controlling social and economic relations. By the naked expression of their will, their intent, testators could dispose of their property after death and entrepreneurs could arrange their business relations by contract. The property and contract rights so created were held to be sacred and inviolable, so long as they did not contravene conscience. Conscience gave them their sanctity. And so the secularization of the state, in the restricted sense of the removal of ecclesiastical controls from it, was accompanied by a spiritualization, and even a sanctification, of property and contract. [pp. 64-65]

NOTE

1. Harold J. Berman, *The Interaction of Law and Religion* (New York : Abingdon Press, 1974), pp. 52-65.

THE CHANGING LAW[1]

Alfred Lord Denning

The Influence of Religion

In primitive societies, the influence of religion on law was obvious, but it is not so obvious in modern societies. In primitive communities religion, morals, and law were indistinguishably mixed together. In the Ten Commandments, for instance, you find the first Commandment which is *religious* : "God spake these words and said, 'I am the Lord thy God : Thou shalt have none other Gods but me.'" You find the fifth Commandment which is a *moral* precept : "Honour thy father and thy mother : that thy days may be long in the land which the Lord thy God giveth thee." You find the eighth Commandment which is a *legal* duty : "Thou shalt not steal." This intermingling is typical of all early communities. The severance of the three ideas — of law from morality, and of religion from law — belongs very distinctly to the later stages of mental progress.

This severance has gone a great way. Many people now think that religion and law have nothing in common. The law, they say, governs our dealings with our fellows : whereas religion concerns our dealings with God. Likewise they hold that law has nothing to do with morality. It lays down rigid rules which must be obeyed without questioning whether they are right or wrong. Its function is to keep order, not to do justice.

The severance has, I think, gone much too far. Although religion, law and morals can be separated, they are nevertheless still very much dependent on each other. Without religion there can be no morality : and without morality there can be no law. I will try to show you how many of the fundamental principles of our law have been derived from the Christian religion : and in so doing I will try to indicate how they are challenged by a changing world which knows no religion, or at any rate treats religion as something which is of no moment in practical affairs.... [pp. 99-100]

Let us now turn from truth to justice. No one here doubts, I hope, that it is his duty to be just and fair in all his dealings. But our conception of justice is only the Christian teaching of love. Such at least was the view of William Temple, Archbishop of Canterbury, one of the greatest thinkers of the present century. "It is axiomatic," he said, "that love should be the predominant Christian impulse and that the primary form of love in social organization is justice." The Christian standpoint is summed up in the Gospel when a certain lawyer asked our Lord, "Master, what shall I do to inherit eternal life ?" He said unto him, "What is written in the law ? How readest thou ?" And he answering said, "Thou shalt love the Lord thy God with all thy heart, and with all thy mind, and thy neighbour as thyself." And he said unto him "Thou hast answered right : this do and thou shalt live." This precept — love towards God and love towards your neighbour — is a precept of religion, but nevertheless in many affairs of life, love can only find expression through justice. William Temple gave this illustration : "Imagine a Trade Union Committee negotiating with an Employers' Federation in an industrial crisis on the verge of a strike. This committee is to be actuated by love. Oh, yes, by all means, but towards whom ? Are they to love the workers or the employers ? Of course — both. But then that will not help them much to determine what terms ought to be either proposed or accepted .... Love, in fact, finds its primary expression through justice which, in the field of industrial disputes, means in practice that each side should state its case as strongly as it can before the most impartial tribunal available, with determination to accept the award of that tribunal. At least that puts the two parties on a level, and is to that extent in accordance with the command "Thou shalt love thy neighbour as thyself."

Such being the view of the theologian, let me now turn to the judge, whose task it is to be the tribunal. He must do justice between the parties. But how is he to know what is justice ? Let me tell you how one great judge answered it. It arose in a case where a manufacturer of ginger beer had made it so carelessly that he left a snail in one of the bottles. He sold it as part of a consignment to a shopkeeper, who in turn sold a bottle to a man whose wife drank it and was injured. At one time the law held that the manufacturer was not liable to pay compensation because he had made no contract with the ultimate purchaser or his wife. But in 1932 the House of Lords held that the manufacturer was liable. In a judgment of great importance in the law, Lord Atkin took the Christian precept as the underlying basis of the decision in these words : "The rule that you are to love your neighbour becomes in law you must not injure your neighbour : and the lawyer's question 'Who is my neighbour ?' receives a restricted reply. You must take reasonable care to avoid acts or omissions which you can reasonably foresee would be likely to injure your neighbour. Who then in law is my neighbour ? The answer seems to be — persons who are so closely and directly affected by my act that I ought reasonably to have them in contemplation as being so affected when I am directing my mind to the acts or omissions which are called in question."

It is, I suggest to you, a most significant thing that a great judge should draw his principles of law, or rather his principles of justice, from the Christian commandment of love. I do not know where else he is to find them. Some people speak of natural justice as though it was a thing well recognizable by anyone, whatever his training and upbringing. But I am quite sure that our conception of it is due entirely to our habits of thought through many generations. The common law of England has been moulded for centuries by judges who have been brought up in the Christian faith. The precepts of religion, consciously or unconsciously, have been their guide in the administration of justice.... [pp. 106-109]

Conclusion

This brings me to the end. And what does it all come to ? Surely this, that if we seek truth and justice, we cannot find it by argument and debate, nor by reading and thinking, but only by the maintenance of true religion and virtue. Religion concerns the spirit in man whereby he is able to recognize what is truth and what is justice ; whereas law is only the application, however imperfectly, of truth and justice in our everyday affairs. If religion perishes in the land, truth and justice will also. We have already strayed too far from the faith of our fathers. Let us return to it, for it is the only thing that can save us. [p. 122]

NOTE

1. Alfred Lord Denning, *The Changing Law* (London : Stevens & Sons Ltd., 1953), pp. 99-122.

CHAPTER IV

LAW AND STATE

For the Greeks the natural order of things was a moral order which set the bounds of justice according to ordained destiny. In Homer and Hesiod, Moira or Destiny was the key to their legal cosmology. The pre-Socratic philosophers elaborated this view through a philosophy of nature based on dynamic principles of predetermined structures of natural order. Against this background, Plato, in the history of Western jurisprudence, represented a further turning away from the unconscious, the mythical, and the irrational. In his theory of justice in the *Republic* and the modification of that doctrine found in the *Laws,* Plato discerned an ideal realm, *sub species aeternitatis,* a theory of geometric certainty neither dependent upon man for its statement of truth nor upon a personal divinity for its salvation. Western legal theory was thereby grounded in rationality, based on a rigid and abstract definition of human nature. Justice was defined as a receptacle of pure reason, without passion or error. The emphasis of Platonic justice was on perfection, absolutism, and static science. This Greek contribution, a metaphysical explanation of the impersonal "fates" of the universe developed into a "unitary" theory of justice, remains the point of departure for Western legal theory's involvement with rationality as the basis for a theory of law.

In juxtaposition is the inheritance of the biblical imagination which stressed the existentialist or personal dimension of justice. The biblical lore is filled with the evocation of law through the dream, the parable, and the prophecy. The interpretation of law, however much related to the mundane responsibilities of priestly functions and ordinary transactions among men, is correlated and understood from the standpoint of the relationship that was struck between the children of Israel and a personal deity. The Hebrews were far removed from the Grecian orientation in legal theory ; for, although the transcendentalism of the divine was expressed, they assumed his transitive purpose and interaction with all the members of the community to whom he revealed his doctrine of law.

The commitment of these two ancient cultures, Greek and Hebrew, to dialectically opposed theories of law contains the seed of a historic antagonism in legal theory which remains until this day. The history of Western jurisprudence may be seen as the movement between universalizability and reason on the one hand, and individuation and personality on the other. The commitment to law as the manifestation of pure reason represents a rebuff to the psychodynamic dimension of law, fraught with uncertainty and discretion. It became the burden of Western metaphysics to create a framework where rationality, psychology, and law could be fixed as consistent parts of a symmetrical universe, in short, to accommodate Jerusalem to Athens.

Over the centuries jurisprudence appears to have developed a self-correcting mechanism which allows it, as a posited science, to acknowledge its debt to various revolutions of thought while preserving to remain a closed system. In this respect the ordinary language analysis of analytical jurisprudence may be seen as part of a long-standing historical pattern. Somehow, legal systems manage, with the help of philosophical modelling, to at once legitimatize and control the perimeters of judicial creativity. Our Anglo-American legal systems have preserved their historic stability through a model in which the legal system is dominated by legal values and structures which have survived over an extended period of application. They have avoided emphasizing the particular personality of the judge, his unique prejudices and the complex psychodynamics that occur among the various participants in the legal process.

The separation of powers that marks the achievement of social democratic justice establishes the ground rules for applying basic legal values to the elected members who constitute the group designated as official sovereign. Community expectations in a stable legal society are interpreted in the light of the balance between established rules and principles and the focus of changing social conditions. The common law reflects widely shared community norms fashioned according to received bodies of legal maxims and precedents. Thus, analytical jurisprudence has focused on the paradigm of the game as a departure point for describing the rule of law. In such a model, the judge functions as an umpire and the sense of justice is kept tidy because all the participants are accountable to the rules, including the judges. The discretion of the umpires is limited by the rules and, although there are moments when they might respond to emotion or probing self-conscious analysis, such occasions, according to official legalism, are regarded as rare and are permitted only because there are broad general principles which are believed to serve as signposts for the evolution of justice. Such model building, fulfilling the criteria of scientific systematization, turns jurisprudence into a legal science. In liberal democracies a commitment to the structured rule of law is deeply held.

The law cannot rest easily with its criteria of rationality, for, it is expected to respond to the Judeo-Christian principle of "individuation" as well. For centuries Western legal theorists have encountered the tension that comes between prophetic justice and universalizability. If a man and his needs are individual, is it possible for a legal system to apply its rules mechanically with the force of scientific coherence ? The historic debates of legal theory have centred around this very controversy. The conflict between abstraction and uniqueness has never been resolved because prima facie the heightening of one occurs at the expense of the other. No legal system can be perfectly rational nor can it achieve perfection by treating cases according to their existential particularity. These first principles, which have been inherited from the Judeo-Christian and Greek cultures, must attempt to mirror social realities while aspiring to the realm of science.

A radical paradigmatic shift took place in ancient Greece with the evolution of philosophy and science. The development of deductive and abstract mathematics, and the discovery of the scientific method led to the replacement of a mythological world view with a rational approach to reality. The universe was no longer conceived as a product of the will of the gods, or of magical and mystical forces, but was perceived as a rational natural order. Given that man legitimizes his social order in terms of the natural order, the shift from mythos to logos in ancient Greece has profound and far-reaching repercussions for morality and law. The mythic world view associated with status, and particularly patriarchy, came into conflict with an opposing archetypal life force, associated with rationality and the individual citizen. Centuries later, the majority of nation states may still be archetypally characterized as patriarchal; this is most pronounced in reversions to "monarchic dictatorships" and dependencies on charismatic leadership.

In theory, the rational paradigm brought with it the implied invalidity of the positivistic will-oriented patriarchal legal systems. The change in man's view of nature required a change in legal archetype, since the nature to which man was now to appeal was a universe of natural laws. The laws of nature became the paradigm for the laws of social order. The Greeks were conscious that they were appealing to nature as a source of legitimacy of their laws. This process in itself became the subject of analysis and thought, and hence the birth of the first legal philosophy, natural law.

The most fundamental assumptions of natural law are first that man is born free, and secondly that he is born equal. As empirical assertions, both are false; but most natural law theorists are quick to argue that these have never been meant to be factual propositions. They are simply a denial of the patriarchal-will theory of legal, political and social order. They follow implicitly from the shift from a mythological to a rational-scientific view of nature. The first is the biological order of birth, genealogy, and common descent. When man moved toward the order of the scientific laws of nature, he had, at least in theory, to oppose the validity of the biological order as the source of legitimacy for his social order, since each of the paradigms entailed attributes inconsistent with the other.

The postulate that man is born free means only that he comes into the world without rights and duties attached to him on the basis of his sex, family, colour, race or order of birth. Legal and moral obligations are in other words human artifacts, creations of social practices. They are not a part of the order of nature. Man is born equal in that no one has priority or ascendancy on the basis of birth. The state of nature suggested by natural law theory is not a mythical ancient Golden Age, but a state of human relations where we conceptually remove the structures of human social order, such as the state, the legal system, and the family. In such a conceptually possible world there are no rights or duties because they are not an intrinsic part of human beings. Everyone is free insofar as no one may be subjected to obligations or domination, and everyone is equal in precisely this way.

The two premises of nearly all Western political and legal theory that all men are born free and all men are born equal lead inevitably to the fundamental paradox of how to reconcile liberty or autonomy with community. While one may perceive law as a necessary condition for liberty within a community, law in order to be effective also entails coercion and power. Some commentators, in order to reconcile this seeming conundrum have fastened upon the notion of legitimacy, thus drawing the distinction between pure force and rightful authority. Fundamental to legitimacy are the dual concepts of consensus, as sought through the political process, and rationality, as embodied in the science of legal precept. Law, politics, and state are inextricably intertwined in a series of dialectical tensions. The reconciliation of liberty with community is seen in the tensions between libertarianism and egalitarianism as reflected in the spectrum between the minimum and maximum state. The dialectical tensions between consensus and power or coercion are seen in political processes ranging from the democratic to the totalitarian. The stress between rationality and consensus is reflected in the range between autonomous law such as judge-made law and externally determined law such as legislation and executive decree.

Legal and political theory from the time of the Greeks to the twentieth century reveal Western man's attempts to resolve the paradoxes which arise with the decline of patriarchy, a regime in which these tensions were minimal or absent altogether. When the tensions become extreme or aggravated, release is often sought in reversion to patriarchal forms. Western law, in and of itself, reflects the various dialectical dimensions of the tensions between prophetic and formal justice, liberty and community, liberty and power, liberty and equality, rationality and consensus, and liberty and equality versus patriarchy.

1. Constitutional Authority and the Rule of Law

If Athens may be viewed as the birthplace of modern science, Rome, in the same vein, may be viewed as the birthplace of Western law. While significant change in intellectual and cultural norms have affected both the scientific and legal traditions, an important continuity nonetheless exists. The relative influence of Roman law on the two principal legal systems in the West — the continental civil law and the English common law — has been the subject of controversy ; it is evident, however, that neither system has escaped the Roman experience.

Both systems engage in a dialectical method of interpretation, are committed to developing an autonomous legal set of values and principles, and move in as exacting a fashion as possible from the particular to the universal. Many of the basic ingredients of Western legal systems, stretching from ownership to contract and delict, find their origins in Roman sources. Legal conceptualization flourished in Roman law and, with the emergence of complex social and economic relations in the Middle Ages, national customary laws were placed under the scrutiny of Roman legalism.

There is little doubt that modern political theory has, too, been influenced by the Roman legal tradition — particularly through its medieval exegesis. Scholars, however, are in disagreement as to precisely what that influence has been. There are some who suggest that Roman law — and, consequently, Roman medieval jurisprudence — was the single most important element in retarding the recognition and emergence of the modern notion of statehood.

On the other hand, both positivists and constitutionalists have looked to Rome for their ideological roots. Positivists, rejecting the notion that a sovereign government may be subjected to any kind of legal limitations have pointed to Roman law texts as precursors to Austinian theory. Such celebrated Roman phrases as "the Prince is not bound by the laws" and "what has pleased the Prince has the force of law" have attracted commentary in this regard.

Constitutionalists, by contrast, have sought to establish a lengthy genealogy beginning with Roman republicanism as derived from Greek stoicism, evolving in the English common law tradition through Bracton and Coke, and culminating in the American Constitution with its Bill of Rights and powers of judicial review. Roman jurisprudence is thus viewed as a source for a theory of law as a separate and discrete entity over and against state control. There is no doubt that

Bracton, in writing the first scientific exposition of the English common law in the thirteenth century, implanted the seeds of Romanism in the common law heritage ; whether or not a theory of a constitutional state can be extracted from his work is questionable. Arguably, however, the theoretical foundations for Western constitutionalism were at hand. By the seventeenth century constitutional ideas were seized upon by Sir Edward Coke in the struggle with the Stuarts and the doctrine of Whiggism was born. The power of the king was thus perceived as subservient to the power of the law. Later, Thomas Jefferson was to claim, in referring to Coke, "a sounder Whig never wrote."

The debate will, no doubt, continue as to whether Roman legal theory provided the justification for political authority and power as opposed to the rule of law, the sanctity of the individual, and the rights of man. Genealogies, too, will differ as theorists of the various schools attempt to establish their historical origins. What remains to be examined are the implications for the individual in living in contemporary circumstances, under the rule of law or the rule of the state.

THE ORIGINS OF WESTERN LEGAL SCIENCE[1]

Harold J. Berman

The term *legal system* is used here to mean something more narrow and more specific than a *legal order.* There was, of course, a legal order in England and elsewhere in the West prior to the eleventh and twelfth centuries, in the sense that there were legally constituted authorities which applied law. Indeed, we know of no time in the history of the peoples of Western Europe when there was not a legal order in that sense : the earliest written records of their history are collections of laws, and Tacitus, writing in the first and second centuries A.D., describes Germanic assemblies acting as courts. Also, ecclesiastical authorities from early times declared laws ("canons") and established procedures for deciding cases. Lacking, however, in the secular sphere was a clear differentiation of law from social custom and from political and religious institutions generally. Similarly, the law of the church was largely diffused in the whole life of the church — in its theology, its moral precepts, its liturgy — and it, too, was primarily local and regional rather than centralized or enacted. In addition, secular and ecclesiastical law were intermingled with each other. No one had attempted to organize the prevailing laws and legal institutions into distinct structures. Very little of the law was in writing. There was no independent, integrated, developing body of legal principles and procedures, clearly differentiated from other processes of social organization, and consciously cultivated by a corps of persons specially trained for that task.

The relatively unsystematized character of legal regulation and the relatively underdeveloped state of legal science in the West prior to the twelfth century were closely connected to the prevailing political, economic, and social conditions. These included the predominantly local character of tribal, village, and feudal communities ; their relatively high degree of economic self-sufficiency ; the fusion of authorities within each ; the relative weakness of the political and economic control exercised by the central imperial and royal authorities ; the essentially military and religious character of that control ; and the relative strength of informal community bonds of kinship and soil and of military comradeship.

In the late eleventh and twelfth and early thirteenth centuries, however, a fundamental change took place in Western Europe in the very nature of law both as a political institution and as an intellectual concept. Politically, there emerged, for the first time, strong central authorities whose control reached down, through delegated officials, from the centre to the localities; partly in connection with that there also emerged a class of professional jurists, including professional judges and practicing lawyers. Intellectually, Western Europe experienced at the same time, the creation of its first law schools, the writing of its first legal treatises, the conscious ordering of the huge mass of inherited legal materials, and the development of a concept of law as an autonomous, integrated, developing body of legal principles and procedures.

A combination of these two factors, the political and the intellectual, helped to produce modern Western legal systems, of which the first was the new canon law of the Roman Catholic church. On the background of the new canon law, and often in rivalry with it, the European kingdoms began to create their own new secular legal systems. At the same time, there emerged in many parts of Europe free cities, each with its own governmental and legal institutions, forming a new type of urban law. Also in these centuries feudal and manorial legal institutions underwent systematization, and a new system of mercantile law was developed to meet the needs of merchants engaged in intercity, interregional, and international trade. The emergence of systems of feudal law, manorial law, mercantile law, and urban law strongly indicates that not only political and intellectual but also social and economic factors were at work in producing what can only be called a revolutionary development of legal institutions. In other words, the creation of modern legal systems in the late eleventh, twelfth, and early thirteenth centuries was not only an implementation of policies and theories of central elites, but also a response to social and economic changes " on the ground."

Religious factors were also at work. The creation of modern legal systems was, in the first instance, a response to a revolutionary change within the church and in the relation of the church to the secular authorities. And here the word "revolutionary" has all the modern connotations of class struggle and violence. In 1075, after some twenty-five years of agitation and propaganda by the papal party, Pope Gregory VII declared the political and legal supremacy of the papacy over the entire Western church and the complete independence of the clergy from secular control. Gregory also asserted the ultimate supremacy of the pope in secular matters, including the authority to depose emperors and kings. Increasingly these events have been recognized as constituting the Papal Revolution. The emperor — Henry IV of Saxony — responded by military action. Civil war between the papal and imperial parties raged sporadically throughout Europe until 1122, when a final compromise was reached by a concordat signed in the German city of Worms. In England and Normandy, the Concordat of Bec in 1107 had provided a temporary respite, but the matter was not finally resolved there until the martyrdom of Archbishop Thomas Becket in 1170.

It was out of the explosive separation of the ecclesiastical and the secular politics that there emerged the modern Western legal tradition. I propose in this essay to tell one part of the story, namely the origins of Western legal science.

To say that law was taught and studied in the West as a distinct science, at a time when the prevailing legal orders were only beginning to be clearly differentiated from politics and religion, raises a number of questions. What did the first law teachers teach ? How was it possible to teach law when the prevailing laws and legal institutions, both ecclesiastical and secular, were largely local and customary and largely merged in religious beliefs and practices and in political, economic, and social life generally ?

The answer surely sounds curious to modern ears. The law that was first taught and studied systematically in the West was not the prevailing law ; it was the law contained in an ancient manuscript which had come to light in an Italian library toward the end of the eleventh century. The manuscript reproduced the enormous collection of legal materials which had been compiled under the Roman Emperor Justinian in about 534 A.D. — over five centuries earlier.

The Roman law compiled under Justinian in Constantinople had at one time prevailed in the Western Roman Empire as well as the Eastern. In 476, however, the last of the Western Emperors was deposed, and even before then Roman civilization had been superseded in the West by the primitive, tribal civilization of the Goths, the Vandals, the Franks, the Saxons, and other Germanic peoples. After the sixth century Roman law survived in the West only in fragments, although it continued to flourish as a system in the Eastern Empire, called Byzantium (including southern Italy). Some of its individual rules and concepts appear in the occasional enactments of Western ecclesiastical and secular authorities as well as in the customary law of the peoples inhabiting what we call today France and (northern) Italy. The Carolingian and post-Carolingian idea of the succession of the Frankish king to the authority of the Roman emperors also fostered the survival of individual maxims and rules of Roman law, especially some concerning imperial authority. But Roman law as such, that is, as a system, had no validity in Western Europe when Justinian's work was rediscovered in Italy. The texts had disappeared. There were no Western counterparts to the Roman magistrates (praetors), legal advisers (jurists), or advocates (orators). The prevailing legal institutions were largely Germanic and Frankish. Thus it was the legal system of an earlier civilization as recorded in a huge book or set of books that formed the object of Europe's first systematic legal studies.

Two other ingredients were also necessary to the creation of the Western legal tradition. One was the method of analysis and synthesis which was applied to the ancient legal texts — a method which in modern times has been called, somewhat disparagingly, "scholasticism." The second was the context in which the scholastic method was applied to the books of Roman law — namely, the context of the university.

These three elements — the rediscovery of the legal writings compiled under the Roman Emperor Justinian, the scholastic method of analyzing and synthesizing them, and the teaching of law in the universities of Europe — are at the root of the Western legal tradition. The Roman law gave all Europe (including England) its basic legal vocabulary. The scholastic method has remained the predominant mode of legal thought throughout the West to this day. The universities brought together legal scholars — teachers and students — from all over Europe ; brought them in contact not only with each other but also with teachers and students of theology, medicine, and the liberal arts ; and made of them a calling or, as we would say today, a profession.

The newly discovered texts of Roman law were copied and began to be studied in various cities of Italy and elsewhere at the end of the eleventh century. Students would come together and hire a teacher for a year to expound them; the legal form adopted was that of a partnership (in Roman law, *societas*) of professor and students. One teacher in particular, named Guarnerius but historically known as Irnerius (about 1055-1130), who taught at Bologna in northern Italy, gained preeminence, and students began flocking to him from all over Europe. Eventually, thousands came each year to him and to the other teachers who joined him. By about 1150 there were some ten to thirteen thousand law students in Bologna.... [pp. 894-900]

What was taught from the beginning at Bologna was the manuscript of the Roman law compiled by Justinian's jurists in the sixth century. Indeed, it is likely that the law school was founded primarily for the purpose of studying that manuscript.

The manuscript consisted of four parts : (1) the Code *(Codex)*, comprising twelve books of ordinances and decisions of the Roman emperors before Justinian, (2) the Novels *(Novellae)*, containing the laws promulgated by Emperor Justinian himself, (3) the Institutes *(Institutiones)*, a short textbook designed as an introduction for beginning law students, and (4) the Digest *(Digestum)*, whose fifty books contained a multitude of extracts from the opinions of Roman jurists on a very wide variety of legal questions. In a modern English translation, the Code takes up 1,034 pages, the Novels 562 pages, the Institutes 173 pages, and the Digest 2734 pages.

While the outlook of the medieval European jurists . . . dictated that they treat all these writings as a single body, the *Corpus Iuris Civilis* ("Body of Civil Law"), primary focus was placed on the Digest (also called the Pandects *[Pandectae]*). The Digest was a vast conglomeration of the opinions of Roman jurists concerning thousands of legal propositions relating not only to property, wills, contracts, torts, and other branches of what we today call civil law, but also to criminal law, constitutional law, and other branches of law governing the Roman citizen. It was "municipal" law (*ius civilis*, "the law of the city"), covering everything except "the law of nations" (*ius gentium)*, which applied to non-Romans. The Digest was not a code in the modern sense; it did not attempt to provide a complete, self-contained, internally consistent, systematically arranged set of legal concepts, principles, and rules. It was only in the West, after the founding of the universities, that together with the Code, Novels, and Institutes it came to be called *Corpus Iuris Civilis* — "the body" of civil law.

The legal propositions which the Digest set forth were very often "holdings," as we would say today, in actual cases. Others were statements ("edicts") of magistrates, called praetors, of how they would rule in prospective cases. For example :

> The Praetor says, "If you or your slaves have forcibly deprived anyone of property which he had at that time, I will grant an action only for a year, but after the year has elapsed I will grant one with reference to what has [subsequently]come into the hands of him who dispossessed the complainant by force."[2]

Such propositions are then followed by quotations from opinions of various jurists. For example, concerning the statement of the praetor presented above, the jurist Ulpian is quoted as saying :

> This interdict was established for the benefit of a person who has been ejected by force, as it is perfectly just to come to his relief under such circumstances. This interdict was devised to enable him to recover possession . . . This interdict does not have reference to all kinds of violence but only to such as issued against persons who are deprived of possession. It only relates to atrocious violence, and where the parties are deprived of the possession of soil, as, for instance, to a tract of land, or a building, but to nothing else....[3]

Other jurists also comment on the same interdict — for example, Pomponius is quoted as saying : "If, however, you are ejected by armed force, you will be entitled to recover the land, even if you originally obtained possession of it either by force (*vi*), or clandestinely (*clam*), or under a precarious title (*precario*).[4]

The Roman jurists, as John P. Dawson has written, directed most of their attention,

> not to theoretical synthesis, but to the consistent and orderly treatment of individual cases . . . Their whole impulse was toward economy, not only of language, but in ideas. Their assumptions were fixed, the main purposes of the social and political order were not to be called in question, the system of legal ideas was too well known to require much discussion. They were problem-solvers, working within the system and not called upon to solve the ultimate problems of mankind's needs and destiny. They worked case by case, with patience and acumen and profound respect for inherited tradition.[5]

Professor Dawson notes the Roman jurists' "intense concentration on specific cases," sometimes hypothetical but often drawn from actual litigation :

> The cases are briefly stated, likewise the jurists' own conclusions. No elaborately reasoned justification was needed, for to persons outside the elite group the jurists' own authority was enough and those inside would understand the reasons well enough. There were many assumptions that were unspoken or merely hinted at and that have only been disclosed through centuries of later patient study. The primary task of the jurists as they conceived it was to provide solutions for cases that had arisen or might arise, testing and revising their central ideas by observing their effects on particular cases.[6]

Modern European law students, who study Roman law as it has been systematized by Western university professors since the twelfth century, sometimes find it hard to believe that the original texts were so intensely casuistic and untheoretical. They are able to show that *implicit* in the myriad of narrow rules and undefined general terms was a complex system of abstract concepts. It is this very conceptualism of Roman law that is held up by way of contrast to the alleged particularism and pragmatism of English and American law. But that is to view the Roman law of Justinian through the eyes of later European jurists ; it is they who first drew the conceptual implications, who made a theory of contract law out of the particular types of Roman contracts, who defined the right of possession, who elaborated doctrines of justification for the use of force, and who, in general, systematized the older texts on the basis of broad principles and concepts.

The curriculum of the twelfth-century law school consisted in the first instance of the reading of the texts of the Digest. Since the text was very difficult, it would have to be explained. Therefore, after reading the text the teacher would "gloss" it, that is, interpret it, word by word, line by line. (*Glossa,* in Greek means both "tongue," or "language," and "unusual word.") The glosses were copied by the student between the lines of the text ; as they became longer they spilled over into the margins. Soon written glosses had authority almost equal to that of the glossed text itself.

The glosses were of several kinds. Some (called *notabilia)* gave short summaries of the contents of the passage glossed. Others (nicknamed *brocardica)* were statements of broad legal rules (maxims) based on the part of the text that was being glossed. In addition, the teachers would annotate the text by classifications called *distinctiones* : they would start with a general term or broad concept and then divide it into various subordinate species, which in turn would be subdivided and further subdivided, the writer "following these ramifications of sense and terminology into the most minute details." Finally, in addition to making "distinctions," the teacher would pose *quaestiones,* testing a broad doctrine by its application to particular problems or "questions."

In addition to the readings of the texts and the glosses and the analysis of them through distinctions and questions, the curriculum at Bologna and other medieval law schools included the *disputatio,* which was a discussion of a question of law in the form of a dispute between two students under the guidance of a professor or else a dispute between professors and students. It has been compared to a modern moot court, but the questions were always questions of law, but actual or hypothetical fact situations.

As time went on, the law curriculum at Bologna, Paris, Oxford, and other universities of Europe expanded to include more than the Roman law contained in the *Corpus Iuris Civilis.* The principal new subject added in the latter half of the twelfth century was the newly developed canon law of the church ; in contrast to Roman law, canon law was current, prevailing law, replenished by decrees of church councils and applied by ecclesiastical courts. Also as the secular legal systems of the cities, principalities, and kingdoms of Europe developed — usually under the guidance of jurists trained at Bologna or elsewhere — the curriculum was enriched by references to current problems of secular law. In analyzing the texts of Justinian, the professors would introduce legal questions of current practical significance and would analyze them in the light of the Roman texts as well as of the canon law.

Thus the revival of the study of the Roman law of an earlier time led to the analysis of current legal problems. Roman law served at first as an ideal law, a body of legal ideas, taken as a unified system ; current legal problems, previously unclassified and inchoate, were analyzed in its terms and were judged by its standards. In a sense, Roman law played a role for the medieval legal mind similar to that which legal history played for the modern Anglo-American legal mind from the seventeenth to the early twentieth century. It gave a perspective for analyzing prevailing laws, and it provided ideals for testing the validity of prevailing laws. This is not to say that Roman law was thought to be something other than prevailing law. It prevailed, alongside the newer laws, and in a sense over them. But it had a fundamental quality which they lacked. The newer laws were in the flux of becoming ; the rules of Roman law were present to be concorded.

Underlying the curriculum and the teaching methods of the law school at Bologna and of the other Western universities of the twelfth and thirteenth centuries was a new mode of analysis and synthesis, which later came to be called the scholastic method. This method, which was first fully developed in the early 1100s, both in law and in theology, presupposes the absolute authority of certain books which are to be comprehended as containing an integrated and complete body of doctrine. But, paradoxically, it also presupposes that there may be both gaps and contradictions within the text, and it sets as its main task the summation of the text, the closing of gaps within it, and the resolution of the contradictions. The method is called "dialectical," in that it seeks the reconciliation of opposites.

Both in law and theology, and later in philosophy, the scholastic mode of analysis and synthesis was promoted by the method of teaching in the university, particularly the method of "glossing" the text and posing "questions" for disputation. "The principal books of law and theology were the natural outgrowth of university lectures." In other words, science — scholarship — came from teaching, and not vice versa.

In law, the scholastic method took the form of analyzing and synthesizing the mass of doctrines, many of them in conflict with others, found in the law of Justinian as well as in the prevailing law and custom of ecclesiastical and secular authorities. As in the case of theology, the written text as a whole, the *Corpus Iuris Civilis*, like the Bible and the writings of the church fathers, was accepted as sacred, the embodiment of reason. But the emphasis on reconciliation of contradictions gave the twelfth-century Western jurist a greater freedom and flexibility in dealing with legal concepts and rules than his Roman predecessors had had. Like them, he was, to be sure, concerned, in Professor Dawson's words, with the "consistent and orderly treatment of individual cases." But he was also concerned, as they were not, with finding "elaborately reasoned justifications" and a "theoretical synthesis." And in seeking justifications and synthesis, he often sacrificed the narrower kind of consistency which the Romans prized.

The method of the twelfth-century European jurists was a transformation of the methods of dialectical reasoning characteristic of ancient Greek philosophy and of classical and postclassical Roman law. "Dialectic," in Greek, means "conversation" or "dialogue." Ancient Greek philosophers referred to the "art of conversation" (*tekhne dialektike)* as a method of reasoning ; indeed, Plato viewed it as the only sure method of arriving at knowledge of the truth. The Socratic dialogues reported by Plato involved several basic "dialectical" techniques : (a) the refutation of an opponent's thesis by drawing from it, through a series of questions and answers, consequences that contradict it or that are otherwise unacceptable ; (b) the deriving of a generalization — again, by questions and answers — from a series of true propositions about particular cases ; (c) the definition of concepts by the techniques of distinction, that is, repeated analysis of a genus into its species and the species into their subspecies, and synthesis, that is, repeated collection of species into their genus and the genera into larger genera. Through such reasoning Plato sought to achieve sure knowledge of the nature of Goodness, Justice, Truth, Love, and other "Forms" existing, as he thought, in the universe.

Aristotle greatly refined Plato's concepts of dialectical reasoning. He distinguished, first, between reasoning from premises that are known to be necessarily true (such as "all men are mortal" or "fire burns") and reasoning from premises that are generally accepted, or propounded by experts, but are nevertheless debatable (such as "man is a political animal" or "philosophy is desirable as a branch of study"). Only the latter kind of reasoning is dialectical, according to Aristotle, and since its premises are disputable it is not capable of arriving at certainty but only at probabilities. The former kind of reasoning, on the other hand, called "apodictic," is alone capable of demonstrating necessary truths since only from indisputable premises can indisputable conclusions be drawn.

In both apodictic and dialectical reasoning, Aristotle said, either inductive or deductive logic may be applicable. Nevertheless, in Aristotle's view inductive logic is to be preferred in dialectical reasoning, since it is clearer and more convincing to most people, whereas in apodictic reasoning deductive logic is appropriate to certain kinds of science (e.g., mathematics) but not to others (e.g., biology). Inductive logic moves from experience either to certainty or to probability, by finding the common element in the particular cases that have been observed.

The special distinguishing feature of dialectical reasoning, however, is not that it is partial to inductive logic, for, as Aristotle showed, apodictic reasoning also inclines toward the inductive method in many fields. Dialectical reasoning is distinguished above all by the fact that it does not start with "propositions," that is, with declarative statements that must be either true or false, but rather with "problems," or "questions," about which people may differ, although ultimately the disputed question will be resolved conclusively by a proposition, or first principle, in favour of one side or the other if valid methods of dialectial reasoning are used.

Aristotle's distinction between apodictic and dialectical reasoning was accepted by the Stoics of the third century B.C. and thereafter. However, the Stoics viewed dialectical reasoning not as a method of arriving at first principles but as a method of analyzing arguments and defining concepts by distinction and synthesis of genus and species. And they lacked Aristotle's overriding concern for systematic exposition ; dialectics now became an independent discipline, not essentially different from logic but with strong elements also of rhetoric and grammar.

It was in its Stoic form, with the writings of Plato and Aristotle in the background that Greek dialectic was imported into Rome in the Republican period (second and first centuries B.C.). There it was taken up among the educated classes, including the jurists, who applied it for the first time to prevailing legal institutions. However, the Roman jurists took an intensely practical approach to law. Their importation of Greek dialectical reasoning, although it was the first scholarly inroad into Roman law, was not the intermarriage of Roman law with Greek philosophy that took place over a thousand years later in the universities of Western Europe. The Roman jurists refused to adopt the Hellenistic system of education ; legal training continued to consist chiefly of very informal individual apprenticeship in the house of an older practitioner.

> The [Roman] jurisconsults did not discuss with their pupils basic conceptions like justice, law, or legal science, though to the Greeks these seemed problems of the highest, nay almost of sole importance. The student was plunged straight into practice, where he was faced with the ever-recurrent question : What, on the facts stated, ought to be done ?[7]

Nevertheless, it was in this period — before the great flowering of so-called classical Roman law in the first to third centuries A.D. — that jurists first attempted systematically to classify Roman law into its various kinds (genera and species) and with precision to define general rules applicable to specific cases.

Perhaps the earliest example of the systematic application of dialectical reasoning to law was the treatise on *ius civile* by the Roman jurist Q. Mucius Scaevola (d. 82 B.C.). In this work, which is said to have "laid the foundations not merely of Roman, but of European jurisprudence," civil law was classified into four main divisions : the law of inheritance, the law of persons, the law of things, and the law of obligations. Each of these was subdivided into two or three broad categories and the subdivisions themselves were further subdivided. Under the various genera and species, each characterized by its governing principles, legal materials were reproduced — above all, the decisions of praetors in particular cases, but also legislative enactments, authorities from older collections of documents, and also authorities from the oral tradition. The major task which the author set for himself was to present "definitions," as he called them, that is, precise statements of the legal rules implicit in decisions of cases.

In the work of Q. Mucius Scaevola, and of his fellow jurists of the second and first centuries B.C., not only the classification system but also the method of arriving at the formulation of specific rules was dialectical in the broad Greek sense. Questions were posed, various answers of jurists were collected, the author's own solutions were offered. For example, an earlier jurist had summarized various decisions concerning the scope of the law of theft by saying that one who borrowed a horse was guilty of theft if he took it to a place other than that agreed when he received it or if he took it further than the place agreed. Q. Mucius Scaevola reviewed the same decisions, and others, and achieved a broader, and at the same time a more precise, formulation : whoever receives a thing for safekeeping and uses it, or receives it for use and uses it for a purpose other than that for which he receives it, is guilty of theft. Here not only loans but deposits are included, and "thing" is substituted for "horse."

Professor Stein writes : "Following the Aristotelian techniques [Q. Mucius] saw his task as that of explaining what actually happened in legal proceedings."[8] He sought to achieve that task by subdivision of genera and species until he reached specific decisions which, having classified, he was able to explain by finding "a form of words which included all the relevant categories and excluded all others."[9] His aim, and that of other jurists who followed him was, as Professor Stein has said, to declare the preexisting law and to define its precise limits. One would not look to the Roman jurists of the republican period for a discussion of legal concepts ; "indeed the notion of a concept was not found in their mental equipment."[10]

Subsequently, in the classical and postclassical periods, the Roman jurists refined and developed the dialectical techniques that had been applied by their republican predecessors, without changing them fundamentally. There was a tendency toward somewhat greater abstraction. In the first part of the second century they began to speak expressly of "rules" (*regulae*), and not only of "definitions" (*definitiones*). The difference between the two terms is a subtle one. The "definitions" seem to have been more closely connected with the cases which they generalized. The "rules," though derived from cases, were capable of being considered separately. Sometimes they were collected in "books of rules" (*libri regularum*), which were especially useful to the numerous minor officials of the Empire. Also a few law schools were founded in this period, and although their orientation remained intensely practical, they undoubtedly contributed to a tendency to search for broader rules. Aristotelian concepts of the "nature" of a thing were used, for example, to summarize rules concerning what may be omitted from the express terms of agreements of purchase and sale : it was said that terms that "naturally belong" (*naturaliter insunt*) to the case require no express agreement. However, only one kind of term was given as "naturally belonging" to all types of purchase and sale — namely, that the vendor had title. Various other specific "implied warranties" (as we would call them today) for individual types of purchase and sale were then listed — for example, that an animal is healthy, or that a slave is not in the habit of running away. Sometimes common rules were developed to govern diverse types of contracts, such as sales and leases. Only occasionally would Roman jurists go so far as to postulate broad principles that seemed to embrace the entire law. Thus Gaius, the great jurist and law teacher of the middle second century, wrote that agreements concluded "against the rules of the civil law" are invalid, thereby implying, but only implying, what was first spelled out in the twelfth century by the scholastic jurists of the West : that the law forms a whole system, a whole "body."

This implication was also present in some very broad *regulae* which, when abstracted from the cases from which they were first generalized, have the form of succinct, epigrammatic statements of fundamental legal principles. In Justinian's Digest the concluding title 50.17, "Concerning various rules of the ancient law," collects 211 such broad rules. Examples are : "No one is considered to defraud those who know and consent," "In doubtful matters the more benevolent interpretations should always be preferred," "Good faith confers as much on a possessor as the truth, whenever the law (*lex*) offers no impediment." However, as Professor Stein has recently shown, these "legal maxims," as they came to be called in the twelfth century, have a wholly different meaning when taken as abstract principles from that which they had in the context of the types of cases in which they were originally uttered and which are generally reproduced in the earlier parts of the Digest itself. Thus the first of the "rules" quoted above originally referred to the case of one who acquires something from a fraudulent debtor with the consent of the creditors : the creditors may not later claim that they were defrauded. The second originally referred to legacies : the "more benevolent interpretations" are those that are more benevolent to legatees. The third originally referred to the good faith possessor of another's slave : if the slave stole from another, the victim has an action against the possessor. In 530 A.D. Justinian issued a constitution clarifying the older law on the subject. This constitution is the *lex* which is obliquely referred to in the concluding phrase of the *regula*.

The collection of 211 bare statements of abstract "rules" was not intended by Justinian to deceive anyone into believing that they had a meaning independent of the concrete situations to which they were originally applied. The very first *regula* presented in title 50.17 makes this clear : the jurist Paul is quoted as having said, "A rule is something which briefly relates a matter . . . [B]y means of a rule a short account of matters is passed on and . . . if it is inaccurate in any respect, it loses its effect." In other words, rules must not be considered outside the contexts of the cases which they summarize. This is also shown by the fact that each rule is preceded by a citation to its original context. Morever, except that the first one belongs where it is, they are arranged entirely unsystematically, and some of them are contradictory to each other. Justinian added the "*regulae* of the ancient law" partly, at least, as an ornamental index to his great collection. It is also likely that they were intended to be useful in argument, possible as presumptions that could be used to shift the burden of proof. Finally, they served a didactic purpose as an aid to memory of the vast text. But no Roman jurist treated them as abstract principles. Indeed, the entire title 50.17 of the Digest must have demonstrated beyond a doubt to the Roman lawyers of Justinian's time the validity of the famous "rule" of Javolenus, also contained in title 50.17 : "All rules [*definitiones*] in civil law are dangerous, for they are almost always capable of being distorted." That, too, was probably aimed at a specific "definition."

The classical and postclassical Roman jurists thought of a legal rule as a generalization of the common elements of decisions in a restricted, specified class of cases. Only by thus limiting the scope of legal rules did they hope to achieve their objective of using Greek methods of classification and generalization as a rational basis for deciding cases. The Greeks had never attempted any such rationalization of legal decisions and rules. For them, dialectical reasoning was a technique for deriving valid philosophical conclusions — "propositions" — from agreed-upon premises. The Romans converted the Greek dialectic from an art of discovery (*ars inveniendi*) to an art of judging (*ars iudicandi*).

It is important to distinguish Roman legal casuistry from the legal casuistry of the later Western European jurists of the eleventh and twelfth centuries and thereafter, as well as from the "case method" of analysis characteristic of the English and American common law to this day. On the one hand, the Romans did not use cases in order to illustrate principles, or to test them by going back a step, so to speak, in order to see their applications. On the other hand, they reduced their cases to bare holdings, without treating them in their fullness — without discussing ambiguities or gaps in their fact situations, alternative formulations of the legal issues involved, and the like. Max Weber undoubtedly went too far when he referred to the classical Roman jurists' use of rules as a "merely paratactic and visual association of the analogy." Yet their failure to articulate the assumptions and deeper reasons on which the analogies were founded, indeed, their failure even to define the most important legal terms, led to a narrowness, or woodenness, in case analysis — which is just what the Roman jurist wanted ! When Cicero argued for a more complex systematization of the law, with clear definitions and abstract legal rules, the jurists "answered these strictures by polite silence." They had no reason to try to transform the Roman genius for consistent adjudication into a philosophical system. They had every reason to be suspicious of the applicability of the higher ranges of Greek philosophy to the practical needs of adjudication.

The Western European jurists of the eleventh and twelfth centuries carried the Greek dialectic to a much higher level of abstraction. They attempted to systematize the rules into an integrated whole — not merely to define elements common to particular species of cases but also to synthesize the rules into principles and the principles themselves into an entire system, a "body" of law, or *corpus iuris.*

One of the techniques which the scholastic jurists used to achieve this objective was to treat the Roman *regulae*, found in title 50.17 of the Digest and elsewhere, as legal "maxims," that is, as independent principles of universal validity. The word "maxim" was drawn from Aristotelian terminology ; it referred to a "maximum proposition," that is, a "universal." The sixth-century Roman writer Boethius, from whose Latin translations and commentaries Western scholars from the sixth to the mid— twelfth centuries learned their Aristotle, wrote that Aristotle postulated certain self-evident propositions, and that from these "maximum, that is, universal . . . propositions . . . the conclusions of syllogisms are drawn." In the twelfth century, Peter Abelard, in his *Dialectica,* described such a maximum proposition as one that summarizes the meaning and the logic common to the particular propositions that are implied in it. For example, the propositions (a) that what may be said of a man may be said of an animal, (b) that what may be said of a rose may be said of a flower, (c) that what may be said of redness may be said of a colour, and other similar propositions, are summarized in the "maxim" that what may be said of a species may be said of a genus. "The maxim," Abelard wrote, "contains and expresses the sense of all such consequences and demonstrates the mode of inference common to the antecedents."[11] In the same way, the jurists of Bologna, contemporaries of Abelard, adduced universal principles from the implications of particular instances. This was just the opposite of the older Roman concept of a rule as merely "a short account of matters" ; now it was assumed that the whole law, the entire *ius,* could be adduced by synthesis from the common characteristics of specific types of cases.

It was this belief and this method that characterized the approach by which the scholastic jurists analyzed and synthesized the rediscovered texts of Justinian. This was Aristotelian dialectics — even before the translation of Aristotle's principal works on logic — carried over to law at a level of synthesis far higher than that of the Roman jurists whose writings were being studied.

Yet there was another side to it. Aristotle had denied the "apodictic" character of dialectical reasoning. It could not achieve certainty because its premises were uncertain. The twelfth-century jurists of Western Europe, on the other hand, used the Aristotelian dialectic for the purpose of demonstrating what is true and what is just. They turned Aristotle on his head by conflating dialectical and apodictic reasoning and applying both to the analysis and synthesis of legal norms. In contrast to the earlier Roman jurists and the earlier Greek philosophers, they supposed that they could prove by reason the universal truth and universal justice of authoritative legal texts. For them, the edicts and *responsa* of Roman law, taken both individually and as a whole, constituted what they certainly had not constituted in the minds of the Roman lawyers themselves — a written natural law, a *ratio scripta,* to be taken, together with the Bible, the patristic writings, and the canons of the church, as sacred. Since they were true and just, they could be reasoned from, apodictically, to discover new truth and justice. But since they contained gaps, ambiguities, and contradictions, they had to be reasoned from dialectically as well ; that is, problems (*quaestiones*) had to be put, classifications and definitions made, opposing opinions stated, conflicts synthesized. The scholastics added another methodological "topic" : where possible, legal maxims, the *brocardica,* were to be formulated as autonomous universal principles. Thus Aristotle's contradiction between dialectical reasoning and apodictic reasoning was itself resolved. The dialectical method became the scientific method in law — as it eventually became the scientific method in other branches of learning as well, including the natural sciences.

The scholastic jurists differed from the Greek philosophers not only in their belief that universal legal principles could be derived by reasoning from authoritative texts but also in their belief about the nature of such universal principles. Plato postulated that universals exist in nature — that the idea of justice or beauty, the idea of a triangle, the idea of colour, the idea of a rose, and other general ideas in people's minds are imperfect reflections of "paradigms," or "forms," that exist in external reality. Aristotle accepted this "Realist" view of universal ideas, as it was later called in the West (today we would call it "Idealist"), although he modified it somewhat, distinguishing universals that are self-evident maxims, and that form starting points for apodictic reasoning, from universals of a dialectical nature that are only probably true. In the West, Christian philosophers had raised some questions concerning the "reality" of universals, but the first sharp and systematic attack on the Realist position was taken in the eleventh and twelfth centuries, above all by — again — Peter Abelard. Abelard denied the external reality of the common characteristics that define a class of individual substances. He argued that only the individual substances exist outside the mind, and that universals are names (*nomina*) invented in the mind to express the similarities or relationships among individual things belonging to a class. Some "Nominalists" denied that universals have any meaning at all. Abelard, however, asserted that the names do have meaning, in that they characterize the individuals in the class, but that they do not "exist" except as they inhere in the individuals. Thus "goodness," or "society," or "colour," or "rose," are not to be found either in the physical world or in some ideal world of forms. They are simply general qualities that the human intellect attributes to good acts, or to individual people living in social relations with each other, or to particular pigments or individual roses.

Nominalism played an indispensable role in the movement to systematize law ; for Realism in the Platonic sense, however convincing or unconvincing it may be as metaphysics, was wholly alien to the effort of twelfth-century jurists to classify, divide, distinguish, interpret, generalize, synthesize, and harmonize the great mass of decisions, customs, canons, decrees, writs, laws, and other legal materials that constituted the legal orders of that time. To have postulated, in Platonic style, the external reality of justice, equality, consistency, procedural regularity, and other universal principles, and to have attempted to deduce from them specific legal rules and institutions, would have been a futile academic exercise. None of the emerging polities, ecclesiastical or secular, could have accepted or used such an abstract system. On the other hand, to have attempted to proceed by Aristotelian induction from the mass of existing legal institutions toward the same Platonic ideals would have also been misguided, since the existing legal institutions did not, in fact, necessarily imply those ideals.

What was needed was the Greek genius for classification and generalization but without the Greek belief that the classifications and generalizations reflect the realities of the external world — without, in short, Greek naturalism. In law, such naturalism could not go much beyond the casuistic *regulae* of the Roman jurists. The Nominalists, on the other hand, although they shared with the Realists (including Plato and Aristotle) a deep concern to establish general principles and to prove the validity of general concepts, nevertheless denied that such principles and concepts exist as such. For the Nominalists, universals are invented by the mind, by reason and will, and therefore can be revised by reason and will; at the same time, they inhere in the particulars that they characterize, and can therefore be tested by those particulars. Extreme Nominalism denies that "the whole is greater than the sum of its parts," but a more moderate Nominalism such as that of Abelard asserts that the whole is in the parts, holding them together, so that the parts taken in isolation from each other (rather than as "parts") are not as "great" as the parts taken in relation to each other. Thus the parts are not, strictly speaking, derived from the parts (induction), but rather the whole is the parts interacting with each other. Therefore Nominalism was congenial to the systematizing and synthesizing of law; for in law there can be no such separation of the whole and the parts, the general and the particular, the form and the substance, the ends and the means, as is inherent in both Platonic and (though to a lesser extent) Aristotelian philosophy.

The paradoxes implicit in the combining of universals and particulars were closely related to the paradoxes implicit in the combining of apodictic and dialectical reasoning. Both were closely related, in turn, to the paradoxes implicit in the scholastic synthesis of faith and reason. The scholastic dialectic was more than a method of reasoning and more than a way of organizing thought. Its criteria were moral as well as intellectual; it was a way of testing justice and not only truth. Thus the scholastic antitheses included not only general versus special, object versus subject, argument versus reply, but also strict law versus dispensation in exceptional cases, precept versus counsel, absolute rule versus relative rule, justice versus mercy, divine law versus human law. These and similar "oppositions" were used as a means of logical reconciliation of contradictory texts, but they were also used for shaping the legal institutions of both the church and the secular society in such a way as to manifest alternate values. For God himself was conceived to be a God both of justice and of mercy, both of strict law and of equity. The paradoxes of divine justice were now for the first time systematically applied to human laws. Thus "scholasticism" was not only a method but a jurisprudence and a theology.... [pp. 900-921]

The scholastic jurists created a legal science in the modern Western sense, rather than in the Platonic or Aristotelian senses. For Plato, "science" (*episteme*) was knowledge of the truth derived by deduction from the general to the particular. Although Aristotle recognized a whole series of separate and distinct sciences, all sharing in common the method of observation and hypothesis, he nonetheless focused on finding the true cause or necessity that produces a certain substance or conclusion. Thus, for Aristotle the ultimate model of science was geometry.

For modern Western man, however, the very certitude of mathematics, the fact that it is based on its own inner logic rather than on fallible human observation, makes it appear more like a language or a philosophy than a science. A science in the modern Western sense, unlike Aristotelian science, focuses on formulating hypotheses that can serve as a basis for ordering phenomena in the world of time, and hence in the world of probabilities and predictions rather than certitudes and necessities. The legal science of the scholastic jurists was just that kind of science. It used a dialectical mode of establishing general legal principles by relating them to particulars in predication. It was not, to be sure, an "exact" science, like modern physics or chemistry, nor was it susceptible to the kind of laboratory experimentation that is characteristic of many (though not all) natural sciences, although it did . . . utilize its own kinds of experimentation. Also it was concerned with constructing a system out of observed social phenomena — legal institutions — rather than observed phenomena of the world of matter. Nevertheless, like the natural sciences that developed in its wake, the new legal science combined empirical and theoretical methods.

A science, in the modern Western sense of the word, may be defined by three sets of criteria : (a) methodological criteria, (b) value criteria, and (c) sociological criteria. By all three sets of criteria, the legal science of the twelfth-century jurists of Western Europe was the father of the modern Western sciences.

A science in the modern Western sense may be defined in methodological terms as : (a) an integrated body of knowledge (b) in which particular occurrences or phenomena are systematically explained (c) in terms of general principles or truths ("laws"), (d) knowledge of which (that is, of both the phenomena and the general principles) has been obtained by a combination of (i) observation, (ii) hypothesis, (iii) verification, and (iv) to the extent possible, experiment. However, (e) the scientific method of investigation and systematization, despite these common characteristics, is not the same for all sciences but must be specifically adapted to the particular kinds of occurrences or phenomena under investigation by each particular science. [pp. 930-931]

NOTES

1. Harold J. Berman, "The Origins of Western Legal Science," *Harvard Law Review* 90 (1977) : 900-931.
2. S. Scott, Digest 42:16, in *The Civil Law* (1932), p. 308.
3. *Ibid.*
4. *Ibid*, p. 316.
5. J. Dawson, *The Oracles of Law* (1968), pp. 114-115.
6. *Ibid.*, pp. 116-117.
7. F. Schulz, *History of Roman Legal Science* (1946), pp. 57-58.
8. P. Stein, *Regulae Iuris* (Edinburgh : University Press, 1966), p. 37.
9. *Ibid.*, p. 41.
10. *Ibid.*, p. 48.
11. P. Abelard, *Dialectica*, ed. L.M. De Rijk (1956), p. 263, quoted in Stein, *op. cit.*, pp. 157-158.

THE HISTORY OF ENGLISH LAW[1]

Sir Frederick Pollock and Frederic Maitland

. . . Irnerius taught at Bologna. Very soon a school had formed itself around his successors. The fame of the four doctors, Bulgarus, Martinus, Jacobus, Hugo, had gone out into all lands ; the works of Placentinus were copied at Peterborough. From every corner of Western Europe students flocked to Italy. It was as if a new gospel had been revealed. Before the end of the century complaints were loud that theology was neglected, that the liberal arts were despised, that Seius and Titius had driven Aristotle and Plato from the schools, that men would learn law and nothing but law. This enthusiasm for the new learning was not soon spent ; it was not spent until the middle of the thirteenth century. Accursius had summed up its results in the *Glossa Ordinaria* and Azo of Bologna had taught Bracton what a law book should be.

The keenest minds of the age had set to work on the classical Roman texts and they were inspired by a genuine love of knowledge. Still they were far from regarding their study as mere historical research ; indeed for a critical examination of ancient history they were but ill prepared. The Roman law was for them living law. Its claim to live and rule was intimately connected with the continuity of the empire. A vast part, if not the whole, of the civilized world owed obedience to the Caesar for the time being. The German Henries and Fredericks were the successors of Augustus and the Antonines ; the laws of their ancestors had not been repealed and therefore were in force. Even in those kingdoms in which it was impossible to press the claims of a German prince, the king might theoretically be regarded as holding the place of an emperor. Our own Henry I, was he not Gloriosus Caesar Henricus ? But such theories apart, the Roman law demanded reverence, if not obedience, as the due of its own intrinsic merits. It was divinely reasonable. [pp. 111-112]

NOTE

1. Sir Frederick Pollock and Frederic Maitland, *The History of English Law*, 2nd ed., vol. 1 (Cambridge : Cambridge University Press, 1968), pp. 111-112.

ROMAN LAW AND ENGLISH JURISPRUDENCE YESTERDAY AND TODAY[1]

Peter Stein

In one of his conversations with Eckermann, Goethe is said to have likened the Roman civil law to a duck. Sometimes it is visible, swimming prominently on the surface of the water ; at other times it is hidden, diving amid the depths. But always it is there. This pervasiveness of Roman law, prominent at some periods and inconspicuous at others, is, I suggest, a feature of English legal thought, for Roman law has provided a fund of legal experience which, as I hope to show, has had a recurrent influence on English legal theory.

I will not be concerned with the influence of Roman law on the substantive common law. That topic has been discussed with great passion by legal historians on boths sides of the Atlantic and it is noticeable that American writers have been far readier to concede Roman influence than their English counterparts.

In the United States, particularly in the period immediately following the Revolution, legal publicists eagerly sought Roman models for common law institutions, since in that way they could emphasize the cosmopolitan character of the common law at a time when specifically English institutions had few claims to popularity. As late as 1832 President Quincy of Harvard asserted :

> It is an admitted fact, that a great proportion of the boasted wisdom of the English common law, was acquired by a silent transfer into it of the wisdom of the Roman law, through the medium of the courts of justice, and that thereby the English law was raised from its original state of rudeness and imperfection.

What President Quincy considered to be an admitted fact, however, has not been admitted by all English writers on the subject, many of whom seem to have regarded an admission that the common law had actually adopted an institution of Roman law rather in the way that a Scots presbyterian would regard an admission that episcopacy is an acceptable form of ecclesiastical polity.

The problem of Roman influence on English law has received much attention and aroused much emotion. The question of the influence of Roman law on English jurisprudence has received less attention and can be approached more calmly. I propose to treat it by a brief consideration of three key figures in the development of English legal theory : Henry of Bracton in the thirteenth century, Sir Matthew Hale in the seventeenth century and John Austin in the nineteenth century.

Bracton's work in *The Laws and Customs of England* is the earliest scientific exposition of the English common law and it opens with an extensive introduction drawn mainly from Azo's commentary on Justinian's Institutes and Code. But since the publication of Maitland's study of Bracton and Azo in 1895, the extent of Bracton's learning in Roman law has been a matter of controversy. At one extreme is the view that Bracton was an uninstructed beginner who used a few half-understood scraps of Roman law to give a veneer of superficial learning to his book. Others hold that he was a profound Romanist who had probably studied Roman and canon law at Oxford and so came to the common law with a solid base of civil law learning. The distribution . . . of the first two volumes of Professor Thorne's edition of Bracton has, I suggest, disposed forever of the former view. We now know that Bracton's Romanism was not limited to the incorporation of the numerous passages from contemporary glossators on Roman and canon law which have been identified in the last fifty years. Professor Thorne has shown that the first third of the work alone contains quotations from almost two hundred different sections of Justinian's Digest and that the Code too is well represented. These passages have lain unnoticed hitherto, because they are not cited formally with references, but are woven into the exposition quite naturally, thus showing that Bracton has made his Roman law part of his way of thinking as a lawyer. In countless passages, the language he uses is "the unmistakable technical vocabulary of the schools." Furthermore many of the apparent misunderstandings of Roman law to which earlier writers have drawn attention can now confidently be attributed to later editors.

Bracton realized at the outset that if he was to expound the laws and customs of England, as applied in the king's courts, in a manner at all coherent, he would need a minimal structure of general notions which was lacking in English law, and which was articulated only in Roman law. He could have set out the case law of England without the help of such notions. But his work would then have been a collection of writs and decisions which, in view of the range and complexity of the material, could not have been easily consulted or understood. Furthermore such a work would have done nothing to persuade foreigners that English law was worthy of consideration as a legal system, and one of Bracton's aims was to show that, despite its outlandish appearance, English law had an internal coherence and rationality comparable to that of other countries' laws. He tried to put English law in the perspective of the general jurisprudence of his time in a way that his predecessor Glanvill never attempted.

One of his main problems in this regard concerned the form of the law. The Roman law was set out in a series of fixed and unalterable texts, stamped with the authority of the Emperor Justinian. The *Corpus Iuris* was the authorized version of Roman law. The English law had no such authorized version. Already Glanvill had seen this difficulty and he and Bracton adopt a defensive attitude which suggests that some of the ecclesiastical colleagues, with a Bologna or Bologna-inspired education, had been sneering at their presumption in suggesting that English law was worthy of the title. It is true, they admit, that almost all countries have a written law (*ius scriptum*) and only England uses unwritten custom. But it will not be absurd (*non erit absurdum*) to use the term *leges* for the unwritten English rules. Bracton's book by presenting the common law in terms of the categories established by Roman law was a demonstration of this assertion. Just as an acquaintance with the Latin classics of antiquity was enabling the poets of northern Europe to follow through their native themes in a deeper and more coherent fashion, so his knowledge of the Roman civil law enabled Bracton to fashion the common law into a coherent system of principles and to expound it with a precise technical vocabulary, more sophisticated than that of the plea rolls.

Bracton's work may be looked at as a delayed reflection in the legal sphere of the twelfth century Renaissance. In the same way the lasting effects of the sixteenth-century Renaissance were not felt by English jurisprudence until the seventeenth century, and I suggest that they can be observed most conveniently in the work of Sir Matthew Hale.

It is generally agreed that Hale was able to make his unique contribution to English legal theory, precisely because he had prepared himself for the task by acquiring a knowledge of other sciences, particularly mathematics, and of other legal systems, particularly Roman law. His biographers agree that he often affirmed that "the principles of jurisprudence were so well delivered in the Digests that law could not be understood as a science without first resorting to them for information," and that he therefore lamented that Roman law was so little studied in England. This lament has, of course, been part of the stock in trade of Roman lawyers from the sixteenth century until today.

Hale's main contribution to English jurisprudence was the introduction of a historical conception of the growth of the common law. The medieval common law had received its greatest statement in the work of Sir Edward Coke at the beginning of the seventeenth century. Coke was a consummate master of the law contained in the old Year Books, but he was not interested in any law but that of the Year Books. He took it for granted that this law was the only law that had ever prevailed in England, that it was law because it was immemorial custom and that this kind of customary law constituted an artifical reason, which only the judges were capable of expounding. Coke ensured the continuity of the common law from medieval into modern times. But he also ensured that it would be a highly technical kind of law and highly resistant to change. Indeed those who wanted to do away with its antiquated technicalities had some cause to say Amen to the remark made by Lady Coke on her husband's death : "We shall never see his like again, praises be to God."

The idea that the law is essentially custom can produce two contrasting lines of thought, for custom can be treated either as something which has constantly been preserved as part of the heritage of the people, or as something which is continually being adapted to fit new social conditions. Coke stressed the first aspect and fostered a cult of the common law as something immemorial and unchangeable. Hale emphasized the other aspect. He had studied Roman law, as it was expounded by the Humanists. Unlike the Glossators of Bracton's time, who presented the Roman law dogmatically, with little regard to its historical development, the Humanists distinguished between the archaic law of the early Roman Republic, the classical law, and the law of Justinian. Hale proceeded to apply this kind of perspective to English law and so view its development in a new way. The common law, he asserted, was continually changing in response to circumstances and it was inevitable that it should grow more complex, as English society moved from a primitive to a more civilized state :

> In the first coalition of a people, their prospect is not great, they provide laws for their present exigence and convenience ; but in process of time possibly their first laws are changed, altered, or antiquated, as some of the laws of the Twelve Tables among the Romans were. But whatsoever be done touching their *old* laws, there must of necessity be provision of new and other laws successively, answering to the multitude of successive exigencies and emergencies, that in a long tract of time will offer themselves.[2]

This must have been the case in early Britain, he thought, but we cannot know for certain since it appears that in those early times, "the Britains were not reduced to that civilized estate as to keep the annals and memorials of their laws and government, as the Romans and other civilized parts of the world have done."

Clearly Roman law provided that basis of comparison which Coke lacked and which enabled Hale to see the development of the common law historically and write the first history of its evolution, from which these quotations are taken.

Apart from his interest in legal change, Hale felt that, in comparison with the civil law, the common law was badly arranged. Like his contemporary Lord Stair in Scotland, Hale was anxious to present his native system to outsiders, not as a mass of arcane mysteries, but as a rational discipline. Hale had been chairman of a committee of the Rump Parliament charged with reform of the law, and after the Restoration he continued his attempts to introduce some order and method into what his biographer Burnet calls "the indigestedness" of English law. Hale's learning and ability were such that he could have become the English Stair and produced Institutions of English law comparable to Stair's Institutions of Scots law. But this task would have been much harder — after all Stair had not been preceded by a Scottish Coke — and he refused to undertake it, on the ground that it was work not for one man but for a committee. He did produce a preliminary sketch, entitled "Analysis of the Civil Part of the Law," in which he adapted the scheme of Justinian's Institutes to the common law and grouped the law around the heads of persons, things, wrongs and remedies. In the following century Blackstone considered it the most scientific scheme that had yet appeared and adopted it in his Commentaries.

Roman law showed Hale both how to look at the common law historically and how to treat it more methodically, and he learned those lessons so well that Holdsworth calls him "the first of our great modern common lawyers."

I turn now to my third figure in the development of English jurisprudence, John Austin, but I need not labour his debt to Roman law, since it emerges clearly from even a cursory reading of his Lectures.

Austin was appointed to be the first Professor of Jurisprudence at University College London two years before he was to begin lecturing, and he spent much of this interim period studying at Bonn in Germany. His work shows many signs of the different trends in legal thought which he found there. The historical school, initiated by Gustav Hugo, was flourishing and, as we shall see, there is much more historical material in Austin's Lectures than is usually admitted. But the works of the Pandectists attracted Austin even more, because of their highly systematic structure and their rigorous analysis of legal institutions.

The rules of law contained in these treatises were Roman but the form in which they were cast owed little to that of Roman law. Paradoxically, in view of Austin's contempt for natural law, most of the formal structure of the Pandectist treatises was taken over from the systems of the eighteenth-century natural lawyers. Their generalized character made them a suitable model for the analytical part of Austin's Lectures, and in this part his method is often to set out the categories he found in the Pandectist treatises and see to what extent English law can be fitted into them. This kind of analysis set a pattern which dominated English legal thought for more than a century.

In each of the three cases I have cited, the English writer derived his knowledge of Roman law not from the original texts alone but from contemporary expositions. Bracton got his Roman law from the Glossators, Hale from the Humanists and Austin from the Pandectists. In each case the English writer was affected by the form and tendency of his source. Bracton found a legal grammar with which he was able to build up a picture of English law in substantive rather than in procedural terms. Hale found an account of the parallel development of law and society from a primitive to a sophisticated system. Austin found the categories and tools of analysis with which to test the scientific quality of the law against an external standard. In each case their study of Roman law, gave them more perspective and objectivity in facing the theoretical problems raised by the English law of their times. They could more easily see how far the problems could arise in any legal system and how far they were peculiar to English law. [pp. 3-13]

NOTES

1. Peter Stein, *Roman Law and English Jurisprudence Yesterday and Today* (Cambridge : University Press, 1969).

2. Sir Matthew Hale, *History of the Common Law of England*, 2nd ed. (1716), pp. 60-61.

ON THE LAWS AND CUSTOMS OF ENGLAND[1]

Bracton

The king has no equal within his realm. Subjects cannot be the equal of the ruler, because he would thereby lose his rule, since equal can have no authority over equal/ nor *a fortiori* a superior, because he would then be subject to those subjected to him. The king must not be under man but under God and under the law, because law makes the king,/Let him therefore bestow upon the law what the law bestows upon him, namely, rule and power./ for there is no *rex* where will rules rather than *lex*. Since he is the vicar of God,/And that he ought to be under the law appears clearly in the analogy of Jesus Christ, whose viceregent on earth he is, for though many ways were open to Him for His ineffable redemption of the human race, the true mercy of God chose this most powerful way to destroy the devil's work, he would use not the power of force but the reason of justice. Thus he willed himself to be under the law that he might redeem those who live under it. For he did not wish to use force but judgment. And in that same way the Blessed Mother of God, the Virgin Mary, Mother of our Lord, who by an extraordinary privilege was above law, nevertheless, in order to show an example of humility, did not refuse to be subjected to established laws. Let the king, therefore, do the same, lest his power remain unbridled./there ought to be no one in his kingdom who surpasses him in the doing of justice, but he ought to be the last, or almost so, to receive it, when he is plaintiff. If it is asked of him, since no writ runs against him there will [only] be opportunity for a petition, that he correct and amend his act ; if he does not, it is punishment enough for him that he await God's vengeance. No one may presume to question his acts, much less contravene them.... [p. 33]

No one may pass upon the king's act/or his charter/so as to nullify it, but one may say that the king has committed an *injuria*, and thus charge him with amending it, lest he/and the justices/fall into the judgment of the living God because of it. The king has a superior, namely, God. Also the law by which he is made king. Also his curia, namely, the earls and barons, because if he is without bridle, that is without law, they ought to put the bridle on him./That is why the earls are called the partners, so to speak, of the king.... [p. 110]

For the king, since he is the minister and vicar of God on earth, can do nothing save what he can do *de jure*,/despite the statement that the will of the prince has the force of law, because there follows at the end of the *lex* the words "since by the *lex regia*, which was made with respect to his sovereignty" ; nor is that anything rashly put forward of his own will, but what has been rightly decided with the counsel of his magnates, deliberation and consultation having been had thereon, the king giving it *auctoritas*./His power is that of *jus*, not *injuria*/ and since it is he from whom *jus* proceeds, from the source whence *jus* takes its origin no instance of *injuria* ought to arise, and also, what one is bound by virtue of his office to forbid to others, he ought not to do himself./as vicar and minister of God on earth, for that power only is from God,/the power of *injuria*, however, is from the devil, not from God, and the king will be the minister of him whose work he performs. Therefore as long as he does justice he is the vicar of the Eternal King, but the devil's minister when he deviates into injustice, For he is called *rex* not from reigning but from ruling well, since he is a king as long as he rules well but a tyrant when he oppresses by violent domination the people entrusted to his care. Let him, therefore, temper his power by law, which is the bridle of power, that he may live according to the laws, for the law of mankind has decreed that his own laws bind the lawgiver, and elsewhere in the same source, it is a saying worthy of the majesty of a ruler that the prince acknowledge himself bound by the laws. Nothing is more fitting for a sovereign than to live by the laws, nor is there any greater sovereignty than to govern according to law, and he ought properly to yield to the law what the law has bestowed upon him, for the law makes him king.[pp. 305-306]

NOTE

1. Bracton, *On the Law and Customs of England*, Samuel E. Thorne, trans., vol. 2 (Cambridge, Mass. : Harvard University Press, Belknap Press, 1968), pp. 305-306.

BRACTON ON GOVERNMENT[1]

Brian Tierney

. . . Are we after all to say that Bracton was a constitutionalist or that he was an absolutist ? A constitutionalist by temperament we may surely affirm, but one who was working with intractable materials. His work was essentially an attempt to fit a massive structure of English private law into a rather flimsy framework of Romanesque public law and naturally there are signs of strain. The figure of a king, half feudal lord half divine ruler, that he found in his plea rolls could not easily have been transformed into the first magistrate of a constitutional government even if Bracton had had any such conscious intention. It was indeed impossible to extract a theory of the constitutional state from the English materials because they simply lacked the idea of a state in the classical or modern sense. The writings of contemporary Roman and canon lawyers could have supplied that idea, but, while Bracton could deploy quotations from the more elementary Roman and canon law treatises competently enough, he had no sophisticated knowledge of contemporary jurisprudence in the two laws. His mind was formed by the law of England. The theories of Western constitutionalism did indeed eventually grow out of the encounter of minds shaped by a feudal age with classical and early Christian ideas of society and government that in the nature of things they could only half-understand. By the middle of the thirteenth century the materials were already at hand from which some genius — he would have had to be a polymath — might have constructed a theory of the constitutional state. Bracton was not sufficiently learned in the two laws, nor sufficiently imaginative nor, I am sure, sufficiently interested in this kind of problem, to achieve such a synthesis. [pp. 316-317]

NOTE

1. Brian Tierney, "Bracton on Government" *Speculum* (1963) : 295, in *Church Law and Constitutional Thought in the Middle Ages* (London : Variorum Reprints, 1979), iv.

JURISTIC OBSTACLES TO THE EMERGENCE OF THE CONCEPT OF THE STATE IN THE MIDDLE AGES[1]

Walter Ullmann

The question which has engaged the discerning historians of law no less than those of political ideas, is why the concept of the modern state did not find a habitat amongst the jurists of the Middle Ages. The less discerning historians, it is true, glibly, if not happily, operate with this concept, as if it were not only exactly the same concept with which we are familiar, but also one about the existence of which in the Middle Ages no doubt appears permissible; and they go even so far as to see a conflict between "the" State and "the" Church, again as if they were moving in the Bismarckian era or in France during the first decade of this century. Nevertheless, the repetition of this anachronistic view does not make it any the more acceptable, whilst the naked truth must still see the historical landscape of the Middle Ages unadorned with, and wholly devoid of, the concept of the state. What reasons can be adduced to demonstrate why this concept found it so hard to gain acceptance by the jurists? This question may also be put in a different way. How can one explain that despite the Aristotelian impact upon most departments of learning, the jurists remained so remarkably unresponsive to this influence that few traces of the Aristotelian concept of the state can be discerned amongst them? To read medieval jurists makes one feel transported to regions wholly uncontaminated with the doctrines of Aristotle relative to the concept of the state as an autonomous, indigenous, autogenous, independent corporation of citizens. There must quite obviously have been very pressing and cogent reasons for the tenacity, not to say, the stubbornness, of the juristic views. How does one account for them?

Here we can do no more than merely indicate the main lines of development. It would seem that there were three distinct channels of development which by the high Middle Ages had emerged into one broad stream. In themselves and still more in their totality these channels constituted practically insuperable obstacles to the recognition and hence to the emergence of the concept of the state. These obstacles mutually reinforced each other, so that when the convergence had taken place, they constituted in their aggregate a strong intellectual, doctrinal and also ideological barrier of resistance to any thesis or doctrine which rested on premises that had nothing in common with them. What is nevertheless interesting is that these three channels were entirely independent of each other. They may be classified (a) the ecclesiological; (b) the Germanic; and (c) the purely legal elements.

As regards the first two elements we can be brief. There is some justification for the brevity of treatment, because the substance of these two elements was, *stricto sensu,* only partially juristic.

The ecclesiological element (or obstacle to the emergence of the concept of the state) focused attention upon the church as the *congregatio* or *corpus fidelium.* The hallmark of this thesis was that the church was not a product of nature, was not the outcome of natural growth, but was founded by a specific act of divinity. It was to all intents and purposes a society which was brought into existence through the act of foundation by Christ. As such the church was neither autonomous nor had any powers which had not been specifically given to it: it derived its whole essence, its whole being, from the divine act of foundation. Consequently, whatever powers may be discerned within the body of the church, were not of its own making, but were given to it by superior authority. This latter was, within official precincts, the pope himself. The church did not confer any powers upon him and could not, therefore, take his powers away: from the fifth century throughout the Middle Ages and beyond there reverberates the statement *papa a nemine iudicatur.* In his function as gubernator, as a steersman, and as a successor of St. Peter the pope did not belong to the church, but stood outside and above it: the church was committed to him. The idea of the church having been committed to the pope — *ecclesia nobis commissa* — is a vital element in the chain of development which is pertinent to our examination. Associated with this element is another point : not only had the church as a corporation no autogenous powers and rights, no autonomy vis-a-vis the pope, but the individuals making up the corporation were as Christians similarly without these rights, at least as far as the public sphere went. What stands in the foreground is the idea of the *subditus*, of the *Untertan*, for which the Pauline views could be invoked as *pieces justificatives.*

Consequently, it was doctrinally impossible to construct within this scheme any thesis of a corporation which was to form, so to speak, an autonomous segment inside the body of Christians. In other words, on the premises of this theme no community, no corporation, no society could be constructed which could be said to have independent character : there was in logic as well as in theory no means of erecting a body, such as the state assuredly would have been within the society of Christians, so that it stood apart and aside. To realize this, needs no particular acumen or insight : a brief reflection suffices to show that, at any rate in Western Europe, during the Middle Ages, it was this all embracing, comprehensive ecclesiologically conceived unit which, in juristic terms, alone mattered. Departments within there certainly were, but they derived their being from superior authority and had no independent status. This juristic conception of the church militated *a priori* against the emergence of any autonomous unit — whether we call it state or give it some other name, makes no difference — and this ecclesiologically inspired pattern of thought left an indelible imprint upon the European Middle Ages.

Wholly independent of this substratum was the second channel, namely the Germanic element which in its essential features formed another barrier to conceptually recognizing the notion of a state, to wit, the *Munt (mundeburdium)* which had effectively favoured the relations between the strong and the weak in the primitive Germanic tribes and societies. Its essential feature consisted in that the more powerful members of society extended their protection over the less powerful. But the crucial point to be noted here is that with the development of social organization this relationship became institutionalized and thus emerged as an element which characterized early Frankish and later medieval society. Moreover, the protection afforded by the stronger — in practice the king — was not in any case one which the weaker members, the subjects, could demand as of right. This indeed was the pivotal point here : in strict analysis the protection contained in the *Munt* was a favour granted to the subjects : although they might ask for it or petition the king, there was, in law, no possibility of enforcing the demand. The king's protection was thoroughly and essentially autonomous. It was his own autonomous viewing of a situation — viewed, that is, from the vantage point of this superior position, symbolized by his sitting on the throne — which prompted him to grant or to withhold protection. The king as supreme protector extended his *Munt* when he himself considered it in the best interests of the subjects : the judge, however, when the latter's interests required or justified his intervention, was the king himself, and not the subjects in his care. Once more, one can say that the position of the king within the precincts of the *Munt* resembled that of a guardian who acted by legislation or other governmental means, in the interests of the people in his care.

It is now one of the most fascinating features to watch the confluence of the ecclesiological and the Germanic elements, a confluence that can clearly be witnessed, at the latest, by the second half of the eighth century. We find then not only the clear detachment of the king from the people — testified in the adoption of the king's title as *Rex Dei gratia* — but also the very adoption of the idea which we have seen characterized the ecclesiological substratum, namely the idea that the people were committed or entrusted to the ruler : *populus nobis commissus* or *Regnum nobis commissum*. The material ingredients of this ideology were in all essentials identical with those manifesting themselves in the corresponding ecclesiastical formula : *ecclesia nobis commissa*. This correctly understood theocratic standpoint makes it understandable why the people or the kingdom had nothing whatever to do with the king's office : it was an office laid up in heaven, and no member of the people or of the kingdom could in any way change it or interfere with it. The divine trust became juristically conceived, with the consequence that the individuals of the *populus* committed to his care, emerged as *subditi* in the proper legal meaning of the term. As far as public organization and their standing was concerned, they depended entirely upon the king's favours or his grace. The confluence of the ecclesiological and the Germanic elements created a most effective barrier to the recognition and consequent emergence of the idea of the state. Just as the church as the comprehensive unit of all Christians was not an autonomous body, so the kingdom as part of this unit, was not. Especially, when the so-called concession principle is brought to bear upon the analysis, it will be clear that — as the thousands of charters and diplomata abundantly prove — whatever rights the members of the kingdom had, they had as a result of a royal concession, structurally the exercise of the king's own grace or favour.

Turning now to the third channel or element, it may be as well to state in the beginning that the retarding effect of the Roman law and therefore of Roman medieval jurisprudence has not yet been recognized as an element which not only rather ostensibly prevented the recognition and emergence of the concept of the state, but which also appeared in a number of vital respects to provide the *piece justificative* for the other two obstacles. Both the Roman law and its expositors in the Middle Ages supplied first-class juristic ingredients for knitting the other two together. The result of this integration and combination was the growth of a doctrine which in its individual effects no less than in its cumulative weight, proved itself so strong a barrier and force inhibiting the realization of the idea of the autonomous state that even its conceptual emergence, let alone its practical application, was delayed far beyond the Middle Ages. Neither the ecclesiological nor the Germanic nor the combination of the two could in themselves have exercised that potent influence which the integration by the third force, the Roman law and medieval Roman (as well as canonistic) jurisprudence was to achieve. It is as well to draw attention to this unrecognized situation. And with every justification can one say that in this respect — perhaps the most important of all important topics belonging to medieval *Staatslehre* — we veritably move within the orbit of the *medio evo del diritto*.

There is here no need to go into any great detail concerning the Roman law itself, and it must suffice to point out that the Roman corporation — taking the term *largo sensu* — was considered to be incapable of expressing its will in a juristically relevant form. For instance, the jurist Paulus declared that the members of a corporation cannot give valid consent and Ulpian expressed exactly the same point of view, nor were they considered capable of acting "dolose." What is, however, immediately relevant, is that juristically no difference was made between the *collegium* or the *civitas* or the *curia* or the *populus.* Hence neither of these *corpora* was capable of expressing a legally relevant will, and the view prevailing in classical Roman law of putting the *civitas,* etc., on the same level as a *pupillus* and a *furiosus,* is indeed wholly understandable, because neither of them could be said to have the capability of expressing a legally valid will. This is exactly what Labeo laid down when he extended the Praetor's Edict (concerning the *restitutio in integrum*) to *furiosi, infantes* as well as *civitates.* And the further consequence that public bodies, such as municipalities and the like, in short the *respublica,* was, in law, treated on the same level as a minor under age, is not only logically defensible, but would also seem, from the Roman law point of view, the only sensible one. This was concisely and succinctly set forth by a rescript of Diocletian in the year 284 :

Res publica iure minorum uti solet,

and hence all the privileges appertaining to minors, notably the *restitutio in integrum,* were to be applicable to the former, which tallies with the other imperial enactment that the *respublica* was to be put on a level identical with the *pupillus.* It cannot be too strongly emphasized that this *equiparatio* of the *respublica* with a minor (the *pupillus*) was to become one of the most influential themes in medieval jurisprudence relative to our topic.

But since the public bodies were held incapable of formulating and expressing a will, they — in no wise different from an *infans* or a *furiosus* — needed in law a tutor to act for them. Here it is essential to point out that those whose affairs were in the hands of a tutor, were said to be *in aliena potestate.* The statement that tutorship consisted of the exercise of *vis ac potestas* entirely bears this conception out, and the consequence is equally noteworthy — noteworthy in view of the medieval doctrine concerning the relationship between the ruler and the kingdom (people) entrusted to him — that no contract between the tutor and the minor could be validly effected. Two observations are here in place. First, the close and intimate connection between the *tutela* and the *patria potestas* which clearly manifested itself in the *vis ac potestas* of the tutor over the minor. The *patria potestas* itself was in reality an offspring of the far more general power which the *manus* provided. And what is particularly relevant for our purposes, is that the term *manus* as well as its meaning and juristic connotations were exactly identical with the Germanic idea of the *Munt* and its juristic connotations. In this relationship of the Roman *tutela, patria potestas* and *manus* we may well detect one further reason why Roman law principles could with great facility be accommodated within the precincts of the thoroughly Germanic *Munt.*

The second observation concerns the functions and tasks of the tutor. His primary function was to supply what the minor could not give, was to supply the *auctoritas* and to act as the *auctor.* Now it is very likely that these two concepts stemmed from constitutional language and practice, and that their meaning in either camp was not essentially different, that is, the final guarantee, the final approval, the finality of the transaction, without which the latter would not have had any effects. The participation of the tutor was a necessary requirement : it was only through him that the minor entered into a legal nexus. Moreover, the tutor was to become active exclusively in the interests of the minor : the latter may well suggest certain actions, but the tutor is not bound by the minor's supplications or proposals : the consideration of the minor's interests is the vital element. Hence, the tutor could not be compelled by the praetor to exercise his *auctoritas* on behalf of the minor. This position and status of the tutor may well be considered one which approaches an autonomous status vis-a-vis the minor. Once again, one may say that in these maxims of the Roman law relative to the relationship of tutor and minor, a good many elements can be discerned which were to characterize the relationship of the medieval ruler to the people entrusted to him. The only material difference lay in the responsibility of the tutor and the ruler : in case of neglect the former had to face the *actio tutelae* (after the termination of the tutela), whilst in the case of the latter and within the theocratic precincts the only remedy lay in his awaiting judgment before divinity (which had appointed him). What however was common to both was the duty of protection, their sole *raison d'etre,* and the point of reference of protection was in each case the same : the well-being, the interests of the minor or the people entrusted to the tutor's (ruler's) care. [pp. 43-51]

NOTE

1. Walter Ullmann, "Juristic Obstacles to the Emergence of the Concept of the State in the Middle Ages," *Annali di storia del diritto (Studi in memoria Francesco Calasso)* 13 (1969) : 43, in *The Church and the Law in the Earlier Middle Ages* (London : Variorum Reprints, 1975), xii.

THE PRINCE IS NOT BOUND BY THE LAWS : ACCURSIUS AND ORIGINS OF THE MODERN STATE[1]

Brian Tierney

. . . Recent work on the political theories of the medieval glossators has been concerned as much with the constitutionalist as with the absolutist implications of their thought, and it has raised broad new problems for historians of Western institutions. To some scholars indeed it seems that the peculiar fusion of classical, Christian and feudal concepts which we encounter in the works of the thirteenth-century Roman and canon lawyers stimulated such far-reaching developments in the theory and practice of government as to make possible then for the first time the emergence of true constitutional status, and so the beginnings of a type of polity that, after centuries of vicissitudes and adaptations, has come to be characteristic of modern Western society. On this view the pattern of government that was emerging by the end of the thirteenth century in Europe was different in kind from that of any previous civilization ; different from the political organizations of primitive cultures because it did have written records, organized departments of state, the idea of legislation as a deliberate product of reason and will ; different from ancient empires (Wittfogel's "oriental despotisms") because of its constitutional limitations on monarchy ; different too from classical city-states because, for the first time, the techniques of representation and consent were so adapted as to make possible the practice of constitutional government throughout whole nations, over areas embracing many cities.

Not everyone would agree with this way of looking at things. No one indeed doubts that there were limitations on government in the Middle Ages ; the important question is whether there was really any state power to be limited. It has often been argued that in medieval times the rule was assumed to be "under the law," bound by a pre-existing fundamental law which had its roots in ancient custom, and that this presupposition stands in the sharpest contrast to the modern view that all law depends ultimately on the will of a sovereign legislator. This argument, in effect, treats medieval government as simply one additional specimen in a whole class of primitive legal systems. It has especial force when it cites by way of contrast the example of modern constitutional countries like England in which supreme power is vested in a sovereign legislature, untrammelled by any written constitution or enforceable precepts of natural law. (In our own subsequent argumentation we shall be concerned especially with this type of modern constitutionalism precisely because its underlying principles seem, at first sight, so remote from those of medieval constitutional law.) Many historians then, especially students of the Renaissance, would maintain that there is a radical discontinuity between medieval and modern concepts of government, that medieval kingdoms cannot properly be called "states" at all both because of their subordinate position in an international ordering of society and, what more particularly concerns us, because they lacked a concept of legislative sovereignty.

The arguments against this point of view rest largely on recent studies of medieval Roman and canon law. It is this situation that gives point to our enquiry. In the whole general debate concerning the influence of Roman law on medieval constitutional theory and the relationship of that theory to the modern concept of the state there is no particular topic more significant than the ideas on sovereignty associated with the principle *Princeps legibus solutus est* in the Middle Ages, and, among the medieval jurists, there is no one more important nor, from its point of view, more neglected than Accursius. His vast gloss (completed in its first recension c. 1228) synthesized and by so doing virtually superseded a century's work by the great line of glossators that stretches from Irnerius to Azo. It was used for centuries as a standard text in all the law schools of Christendom and its words were accorded an authority second only to those of the *Corpus Iuris Civilis* itself. The gloss of Accursius was not a work of profound originality, though throughout one has the impression of a formidable controlling intelligence at work in the selection of the comments and solutions of his predecessors that were chosen for emphasis. Its importance lies in the fact that, in an age when concepts of government were becoming permeated with the doctrines of Roman law, the Accursian gloss more than any other one work determined which interpretations of those doctrines would find general acceptance.

As we have indicated, the nature of this Roman law influence has become a matter of controversy among modern historians. An older school of thought, typified in the comments of Esmein, maintains that all Roman jurisprudence, civilian and canonist alike, was starkly absolutist in temper, and that consitutional government arose in spite of it from an original heritage of Teutonic liberty that was providentially preserved in England since there the sturdy growth of the common law excluded Roman influences. Although this view is still fairly widespread it has come under mounting criticism. Even before Esmein's paper A.J. Carlyle had suggested that "the conception of the revived study of the Roman law as unfavourable to the progress of political liberty . . . requires at least very considerable qualification,"[2] though he did not consider the implications of our "absolutist" text. C.H. McIlwain, when he wrote his admirable *Growth of Political Thought in the West,* could still refer to "the truly absolutist Roman doctrine of monarchy," but, a few years later, reconsidering the whole question at a time when events in contemporary Germany had produced a general scepticism about theories of innate Teutonic virtue, he strongly emphasized the contribution of Roman law to the growth of Western constitutionalism. . . .[3]

Thus two problems arise. The first, relatively straightforward, is to assess the significance of the constitutionalist elements in the medieval *Glossa Ordinaria* to the *Corpus* of Roman law. The second, extremely complicated, is to determine whether there really is any continuity between the underlying principles of medieval constitutionalism and those of the modern scholarship and in the nature of the source material itself which have impeded the development of any generally acceptable synthesis in this whole area of thought. (Not least important is the absence, among modern political scientists, of any universally accepted synthetic theory of law, sovereignty and the state.) At present a scholar who is disposed to find in the writings of the medieval civilians and canonists a significant contribution to the developing theory of the constitutional state finds himself obliged to argue on several different fronts at the same time. Against one established school of thought, which denies the very existence of the state in the Middle Ages (because then "all law was custom"), he must emphasize the broad legislative competence of the ruler which was already asserted in theory in the twelfth century and was being widely exercised in practice by the end of the thirteenth. But, in arguing against another traditional school of thought which sees medieval Roman jurisprudence as a mere apologia for absolutism, the same scholar must emphasize the limitations on the will of the sovereign that were implicit in medieval conceptions of the "rule of law." Finally, he has to show that, if there is a paradox involved in pursuing these two lines of argument simultaneously, it is a perennial one, that the tension between a concept of legislative sovereignty and a conviction that the sovereign should be in some meaningful sense "bound by the law" is not peculiar to the Middle Ages.

In fact, this tension arises in all modern constitutional countries that attribute sovereign power to a particular organ of government. We would maintain, therefore, that in discussing such matters the medieval jurists were not dealing with problems essentially alien to the nature of the modern state. On the contrary they were preoccupied with issues quite similar to those raised by contemporary constitutional lawyers who have tried to reconcile the theory of legislative sovereignty with the practice of constitutional government. The real persistence of this problem has sometimes been obscured in the past by the widespread acceptance (especially in England) of philosophies of sovereignty that really were incompatible with the principles of medieval constitutionalism. The point that has been becoming more and more apparent in recent years is that such philosophies are also incompatible with the practice of modern constitutional democracy. In the nineteenth century the two most influential doctrines were those derived from Austin, who treated law as positive command, and from Rousseau and Hegel, who treated it as a manifestation of general will. If the presuppositions of either system are accepted it is possible (in theory) to eliminate the "tension" to which we have referred. But both systems of thought are widely regarded as untenable or at least as quite inapplicable to Western constitutional states in the writings of contemporary jurists, philosophers, anthropologists and political theorists who have concerned themselves with the problems of law and sovereignty.

This rather obvious fact has not always been noticed sufficiently by historians who are interested in investigating the origins of the modern state. Too often, indeed, the argument that there was no really "modern" theory of sovereignty in the Middle Ages seems designed merely to prove that medieval ways of thinking about politics were different from those of Rousseau or Austin. Recently it has become more fashionable to maintain the opposite point of view, that those thinkers did have "precursors" in the thirteenth and fourteenth centuries and that, accordingly, a genuinely modern idea of the state did exist then. For a historian of constitutionalism the whole debate seems a singularly sterile one. The point is that the theories most favoured in the nineteenth century simply did not define adequately the characteristics of law and sovereignty as they actually exist in modern constitutional societies, and the fact is now widely recognized. In England legal complexities arising out of the enactment of the Statute of Westminster and the constitutional structure of the Commonwealth have begun to produce, among the more intelligent students of the common law, a certain disenchantment with the simplicities of Austinian theory, while the behaviour of modern totalitarian despotisms has rendered merely grotesque the view that organs of state necessarily pursue exalted ethical ends or translate into law the higher will of their citizens. Hence the cruder varieties of Hegelianism are happily unfashionable and there are relatively few simple unreconstructed Austinians left even in England. Recently, indeed, there have been most interesting attempts (to which we shall return), by writers working within the English common law tradition, to develop theories of law and sovereignty based on Kelsen's jurisprudence rather than Austin's, that is to say on a jurisprudence that treats legal systems as structures of interrelated norms rather than as mere collections of commands. The re-thinking concerning these questions that is going on in many quarters and from many points of view is healthy and welcome, but it is rendering obsolete a considerable body of historical writing which contentedly concludes to the existence or non-existence of a truly "modern" idea of sovereignty in the Middle Ages by demonstrating that a selected group of thinkers did or did not succeed in anticipating the ideas of Austin or Rousseau.

The difficulties of constructing a theory of sovereignty applicable to Western constitutional states are especially evident in discussions on the particular point to be investigated, the significance of our familiar phrase, the "rule of law," and the relationship of such a concept to that of legislative sovereignty. Dicey, a convinced Austinian, presented a famous definition of the rule of law which emphasized the exclusion of mere caprice from the exercise of governmental authority, "the absolute supremacy or predominance of regular law as opposed to arbitrary power." De Jouvenel has criticized this by calling attention to the wide discretionary powers of officials in modern states and has suggested instead that the rule of law can be said to exist only when the enacted laws themselves are in conformity with the deep-lying convictions shared by members of a political community.[4] It would seem that both points of view must be combined to achieve a satisfactory definition. However wide the discretionary powers of officials may be, the limits of those powers are defined by law in constitutional countries, and the courts would not uphold actions outside the defined limits. There could certainly be no rule of law if we ever abandoned the principle, "What is done officially must be done in accordance with law." At the same time we would not normally speak of the rule of law existing in a land where legislation was scrupulously enforced but the laws themselves were grossly unjust, imposed by a tyrant on unwilling subjects. In constitutional states the eliciting of a concensus is just as important as the exclusion of caprice. But this involves the further implication that, however great the power attributed to a sovereign govermnnent in a constitutional state, that power must be regarded as bound at least by the law that defines its own mode of functioning, and this in turn implies that the acts of such governments must themselves be regarded as justiciable at least in some exceptional circumstances. It is not only that orders of particular officials may contravene established laws, but also that situations can arise in which there is doubt whether a given decree emanating from a sovereign legislature has been duly promulgated in accordance with the rules specifying how laws may legitimately be enacted in a given society.

It was precisely this possibility of subjecting a sovereign government to any kind of legal limitation that Austin rejected as logically incompatible with his whole system of thought, for, he argued, if any rules existed specifying limits on the exercise of sovereign authority, those rules themselves could be abrogated at the pleasure of the sovereign. The absence of any tradition of formal judicial review in England made the argument acceptable to most common lawyers there until recently, but it seems most improbable that Austin himself was led to his conclusions by any profound meditations on the spirit and history of English law. On the contrary, it was the Roman Pandects that he studied during the years in Germany when he was preparing to take up his chair of jurisprudence at London. Moreover, his doctrine might well be regarded as a simple re-phrasing of our Roman law text, "The Prince is not bound by the laws" taken together with its well known counterpart, "What has pleased the Prince has the force of law." It would be no task at all to show that the medieval civilians had at their disposal the raw materials from which an Austinian theory of sovereignty could have been constructed. But, to repeat, if one is interested in investigating the origins of the modern Western state, the problem is not to find out how far medieval lawyers succeeded in anticipating the conclusions of Austin ; the more interesting question is how far they succeeded in avoiding them. We cannot hope to understand the origins of the constitutional state by seeking out medieval anticipations of nineteenth century aberrations from the Western constitutional tradition.

When one turns to the source material itself it is at once apparent that the texts of the *Corpus Iuris Civilis* are ambivalent. Some passages suggested that the emperor's power was of divine origin. Others asserted most explicitly that it came from the people.[5] At one point we find the simple statement that what has pleased the Prince has the force of law. At another a complex process of senatorial counsel and consent was laid down as necessary for an act of general legislation.[6] The maxim that we are especially concerned with, "The Prince is not bound by the laws" seems to have a precise antithesis in the *lex Digna* which asserted that "It is a statement worthy of the majesty of a ruler for the Prince to profess himself bound by the laws."[7] A modern student of classical Roman law would naturally and properly seek an explanation for these inconsistencies by investigating the historical development of the Roman constitution. The task for a medievalist is to discover what was made of them by jurists whose minds were saturated with the preconceptions of a feudal and Christian society and who were more at home with the techniques of dialectical argumentation than with those of historical research.

The very dialectical structure of the glossators' works has tended to discourage a systematic use of them by recent historians of political theory. Accursius did use the word state (*status*) and in something very like the modern sense of the term, but at no point did he offer a detailed explanation of his views on state sovereignty or on possible limitations of it. His glosses typically consist of a few words of comment surrounded by an intricate structure of cross-references to other sections of the *Corpus Iuris Civilis.* The substance of the argument can only be appreciated by checking all the contexts referred to. At those points one finds more glosses with further references. By exploring them in turn one is introduced to a whole network of texts, some of which seem to have little to do with one another at first glance, but which were all interconnected in the mind of the glossator and, indeed, were held to be fully intelligible only by virtue of their interconnections. It is much simpler to read John of Salisbury — and that presumably is why several widely used text book histories of political thought do not so much as mention the name of Accursius. On the other hand the labour involved in this kind of work is trivial compared with that of the glossators themselves who had to hew out, through the stubborn undergrowth of conflicting texts, the paths of argument that we can follow at leisure.... [pp. 378-387]

. . . [T]he traditional opinion expounded long ago by Esmein must evidently be abandoned. Accursius did not give an absolutist interpretation to constitutionalist maxims of Roman law. Rather he displayed considerable ingenuity in extracting a constitutionalist doctrine from a structure of texts that was originally intended to buttress Justinian's theocratic absolutism. The eventual divergence between the constitutional traditions of France and England is indeed a matter of great moment but it must be explained by legal and historical factors (and geographical ones) other than those discussed by Esmein, for the French constitutional lawyers of the sixteenth century whom he quoted were not reacting against the doctrine of the glossators, but were faithfully following the tradition of interpretation established by Accursius. Moreover there was no significant difference between England and France in the reception of these doctrines in the thirteenth century. On the contrary, Bracton took over from Accursius the whole structure of thought that we have been describing and incorporated it into his own treatise on the laws of England. Hence English common law lawyers were fortunate in having built into the foundations of their system the same structure of constitutional public law that the French exponents of limited monarchy strove to defend. After a century of Austinian aberration the most recent work of sovereignty in the common law tradition shows a refreshing return to the spirit of the founders. [p. 400]

NOTES

1. Brian Tierney, "The Prince Is Not Bound by the Laws : Accursius and Origins of the Modern State," *Comparative Studies in Society and History* 5 (1963) : 378, in *Church Law and Constitutional Thought in the Middle Ages* (London : Variorum Reprints, 1979), III.

2. R.W. and A.J. Carlyle, *A History of Mediaeval Political Theory in the West*, vol. 2, (Edinburgh, 1903-1936), p. 75.

3. C.H. McIlwain, *The Growth of Political Thought in the West* (New York, 1932), p. 383 ; *idem*, "Medieval Institutions in the Modern World," *Speculum* 16 (July, 1941) : 275-283 ; *idem*, "The English Common Law, Barrier Against Absolutism," *American Historical Review* 49 (Oct. 1943) : 23-31.

4. A.V. Dicey, *The Law of the Constitution*, 8th ed. (London, 1927), p. 198. De Jouvenel, *Sovereignty*, trans. J.F. Huntingdon (Cambridge, 1957).

5. E.g., on divine origin *Digest* Prologue (*Constitutio Deo Auctore*) and *Novels* 73.1 ; on popular origin *Institutes* 1.2.6., *Code* 1.17.1, *Digest* 1.4.1.

6. *Institutes* 1.2.6 and *Code* 1.14.8.

7. *Digest* 1.3.31 and *Code* 1.14.4.

COKE UPON LITTLETON[1]

For then only can we be said to know the law when we apprehend the reasons of it; that is, when we bring the reason of the law so to our own reason that we perfectly understand it as our own ; and then, and never before, have we such an excellent and inseparable property and ownership therein, as we can neither lose it, nor can any man take it from us ; and these reasons being fully apprehended in one case will direct us (the learning of the law is so chained together) in many other like cases. But if by your study and industry you make not the reason of the law your own it is not possible for you long to retain it in your memory.

NOTE

1. Coke, Sir Edward, *Coke Upon Littleton*, vol. 2 *Epilogus* [3946] (Philadelphia, Robert H. Small, 1853).

FUNDAMENTAL LAW IN ENGLISH CONSTITUTIONAL HISTORY[1]

J.W. Gough

One of the earliest of Coke's pronouncements was his judgment in the celebrated case of Dr. Thomas Bonham. This has been analyzed so often that one hesitates to add still further to the discussion of it, but as it is one of the most important and crucial elements in the situation we have under review, to do so is unavoidable. The case was an action for wrongful imprisonment brought by Dr. Bonham against the president and censors of the College of Physicians. The college was authorized by letters patent from Henry VIII to levy a fine of 100 shillings a month (half to the king, half to the president of the college) on anyone practising physic in the city of London without having been admitted to do so by the college. These letters patent were confirmed by statute, 14 & 15 Henry VIII, c. 5, the powers so conferred being subsequently confirmed and enlarged by a statute of Queen Mary. Dr. Bonham practised in the city without having being admitted by the college, and in 1606 he was summoned to appear before the president and censors, found "insufficient" to practise, and forbidden to do so. He nevertheless continued to practise for a month or more, and was then fined 100 shillings and enjoined, on pain of imprisonment, not to continue practising until found sufficient and admitted. He still continued to practise, and was later summoned again to appear before the authorities of the college. On his failure to appear he was ordered to pay a fine of £10, arrested, and delivered into custody. He subsequently appeared before the president and censors but refused to obey them, pleading that he was not insufficient to practise physic, for he had taken the degree of Doctor of Physic in the University of Cambridge, and he maintained that the act of Henry VIII confirming the powers of the college excepted graduates of Oxford and Cambridge from its control.

Coke found for Dr. Bonham, and in the course of his judgment he uttered these much quoted words : "And it appears in our books that in many cases the common law will control acts of parliament, and sometimes adjudge them to be utterly void : for when an act of parliament is against common right and reason, or repugnant, or impossible to be performed, the common law will control it, and adjudge such act to be void." Many of the commentators on Dr. Bonham's case have seen in these famous remarks evidence that Coke believed (or at any rate was asserting) that common law was fundamental, in the sense that acts of Parliament incompatible with it were invalid and could be set aside by the courts, and Sir Frederick Pollock felt "pretty sure" that this un-English doctrine came from Coke's study of the canonists. A number of American writers, lawyers, and historians, have judged Coke more sympathetically, because they have seen in his attitude an important and interesting forerunner of the principle of judicial review, which (the theory runs), though rejected in England, came to fulfilment in the United States. English lawyers, on the other hand, while accepting this interpretation of Coke's intention, have treated his efforts as an ill-judged excursus from the main current of English legal development, which fortunately came to nothing and left it to flow, majestic and unimpeded, to its predestined end in the modern doctrine of legislative sovereignty.... [pp. 31-32]

. . . [I]s it necessary to ascribe to Coke the belief in, or the attempt to construct, this theory of a fundamental common law which empowered the courts to nullify statutes ? Now, support for such an interpretation of Coke's view may be found, as for example in a work published in 1627 by Sir Henry Finch, sergeant-at-law, entitled *Law, or a Discourse thereof.* Here the opening chapters are devoted to "The Law of Nature," "The Law of Reason," etc., so that it is not until chapter six that he reaches "laws positive." All other laws are said to "receive their light" from the law of reason, "and hereupon are grounded . . . divers rules of reason, that everywhere go for undoubted oracles . . . : yea, such is their singular and incomparable use, that as Lords paramount they rule and overrule the grounds themselves. And rather than any of these . . . should fail, the very maxims and principles of the positive law will yield, as to a higher and more perfect law." Therefore, he continues, positive laws directly contrary to the law of reason "loose their force and are no laws at all . . . . It is truly said, and all men must agree, that laws indeed repugnant to the law of reason are as well void as those that cross the law of nature." It must be remembered, however, that this was an academic treatise which, while it indicates the atmosphere in which lawyers were educated in the seventeenth century, does not carry the authority of a judgment actually delivered in the courts.

A final answer to the question as to what Coke really meant cannot be given until we have examined his other sayings and writings, but it is worth noting here and now that his argument in Bonham's case is capable of a much less sweeping explanation, which can also be applied to treatises like Finch's. Sir

Carleton Allen concluded that Coke misunderstood Tregor's case, and that "all his remaining examples are cases merely of strict interpretation which seem to have produced a result other than that intended by the legislator," but none of them can be considered as in any way supporting a general doctrine that the courts have any power to "adjudge an act to be void." Holdsworth similarly considered that these cases amounted only to "decisions that the courts will . . . interpret statutes *stricti juris* . . . that is, so as to give them a meaning in accordance with established principle, and they cannot give any effect to them if they are meaningless. "These," he adds, "are principles of interpretation which would be accepted at the present day."[2] We can agree, but not with the inference that Coke has thus been proved to have failed in his purpose. It is more reasonable to suppose that this was exactly what he meant himself. Admittedly his phraseology was wide, but it is not necessary to suppose that he meant to claim for the courts general powers to declare statutes void on the ground of conflict with higher law. When he said that the common law would "control" an act of parliament he meant that the courts would interpret it in such a way as not to conflict with those same accepted principles of reason and justice which . . . were presumed to underlie all law. Similarly, when he spoke of adjudging an act to be void, he did not mean that the court could declare it to have been beyond the power of parliament to enact, but that the court would construe it strictly, if this were necessary in order to bring it into conformity with these recognized principles, either disregarding such part of it as affected the case being tried, or ruling that the case lay outside the scope of the statute, and that the statute was therefore inapplicable. [pp. 34-35]

NOTES

1. J.W. Gough, *Fundamental Law in English Constitutional History* (Oxford : At the Clarendon Press, 1955), pp. 31-35.
2. Holdsworth, Sir William S., *History of English Law*, vol. 2 (London : Sweet & Maxwell, 1956), p. 443.

BY COLOUR OF LAW[1]

Howard Nenner

The one element of constitutional continuity in seventeenth-century England was the acceptance by king and Parliament of a political rule of law. Law was the touchstone of politics. No matter how men might differ as to what the law said or what it might be made to mean, all were committed to a legal standard in the conduct of their political affairs. This is not to suggest that both king and Parliament adhered without exception to the substance of the law ; yet for each there was an unbroken reliance upon its structure, its arguments, its procedure, and its forms. The common law provided a constant conceptual framework for political action. Throughout the century virtually every important controversy was formulated, and every position justified, in legal language and common law paradigms. The law was the one constant in an era otherwise marked by constitutional uncertainty and political disarray. It afforded the one structure, both institutional and intellectual, which rendered the issues intelligible and which provided a forum for political debate. Never in question were the existence and utility of a rule of law. Law instead was an instrument and a prize ; he who would control the constitution would have first to control the law.

Historically, the instruments of legal control belonged predominantly, if not exclusively to the king. Law was the king's law, judges were the king's surrogates. Parliament existed only at the king's pleasure. As the century progressed, the place of law in politics became even more important. Force, as a lever of political control, no longer seemed to be a creditable option. It had been supremely difficult to lay two civil wars to rest and to restore a legitimate king to his rightful throne. A repetition of that process and of the mistakes that would make it necessary was almost unthinkable. It was thus that the fear of anarchy and the spectral horror of regicide were more than sufficient after 1660 to deter men from any course that might impel them once more to inconsiderate action. Political energies were now, more than ever before, to be concentrated upon the uses of the law and the opportunities for legal manipulation. This was as true of the crown as it was of Parliament. The attempt to suspend the law generally or to dispense with its effects in particular cases is evidence of Stuart legal sophistication. It is testimony to their imaginative and often effective use of the law rather than to their disregard of it.

The law was ready at hand. By the seventeenth century, England had developed a political culture completely comfortable with sophisticated legal concepts and no less at ease with the intricacies of legal form. Lawyers may have been mistrusted, but it was always a mistrust born of the practitioner's ability to convert the richness of the law to his own or his client's use. Law, in expert hands, was a powerful device, one that might also provide a paradigm for parliamentary politics. Crown and Parliament, both proficient in the legal craft, sought with consummate skill to control and to use the law. As a result, a legal disposition of mind which had been forged initially in the intricacies of the private law was being increasingly brought to bear upon political and constitutional problems. It conditioned men's thought and language and ultimately their actions. It found expression in every area of political life, and in 1688-89 it so determined the shape of events that revolution was made to seem respectable. What was to emerge was a revolution that was constitutionally palatable because of its overwhelming appearance of exacting legal form.

It was of little consequence that the law itself might sometimes be distorted. What was at the heart of constitutional development was this important matter of legal configuration. Substance, if necessary, could always be sacrificed to form, reality to fiction,and law to the "colour of law." In this effort the entire arsenal of the private law was brought to bear upon political issues ; and as long as political behaviour could find workable analogues in the law of contract, trust, real property, or inheritance, it would be able to claim a preeminent respectability.

In this way the law exercised a powerful hold over seventeenth-century constitutional politics, and it is for this reason that the culture, possibilities, and uses of the law need to be examined. Although we speak easily and correctly of the impact of the common lawyer upon the seventeenth-century constitutional crisis and of his role as an architect of the evolving seventeenth-century constitution, we need to know more of the impact upon politics of the common-law culture itself. To have been bred in that culture meant much more than having a knowledge of principles and rules. It meant having, as well, a ready-made vocabulary of political discourse and a particularized view of the political world. [pp. ix-xi]

NOTE

1. Howard Nenner, *By Colour of Law* (Chicago : University of Chicago Press, 1977), pp. ix-xi.

JAMES I ON MONARCHY : SPEECH TO PARLIAMENT 21 MARCH 1601[1]

The state of monarchy is the supremest thing upon earth ; for kings are not only God's lieutenants upon earth, and sit upon God's throne, but even by God himself they are called gods. There be three principal similitudes that illustrate the state of monarchy : one taken out of the word of God, and the two other out of the grounds of policy and philosophy. In the scriptures kings are called gods, and so their powers after a certain relation compared to the divine power. Kings are also compared to fathers of families, for the king is truly *parens patriae,* the political father of his people. And lastly, kings are compared to the head of this microcosm of the body of man.

Kings are justly called gods for that they exercise a manner or resemblance of divine power upon earth, for if you will consider the attributes to God you shall see how they agree in the person of a king. God hath power to create or destroy, make or unmake, at his pleasure ; to give life or send death, to judge all and to be judged accountable to none ; to raise low things and to make high things low at his pleasure ; and to God are both soul and body due. And the like power have kings : they make and unmake their subjects ; they have power of raising, and casting down ; of life, and of death, judges over all their subjects, and in all causes, and yet accountable to none but God only. They have power to exalt low things, and abase high things, and make of their subjects like men at the chess — a pawn to take a bishop or a knight — and cry up or down any of their subjects, as they do their money. And to the king is due both the affection of the soul and the service of the body of his subjects . . . .

But yet is all this power ordained by God, *ad aedificationem, non ad destrucionem.* For although God hath power as well of destruction, as of creation or maintenance, yet will it not agree with the wisdom of God to exercise his power in the destruction of nature, and overturning the whole frame of things, since his creatures were made, that his glory might thereby be the better expressed. So were he a foolish father that would disinherit or destroy his children without a cause, or leave off the careful education of them ; and it were an idle head that would in place of physic so poison or phlebotomise the body as might breed a dangerous distemper or destruction thereof.

But now in these our times we are to distinguish between the state of kings in their first original, and between the state of settled kings and monarchies that do at this time govern in civil kingdoms ; for even as God, during the time of the Old Testament, spake by oracles and wrought by miracles, yet how soon it pleased him to settle a church, which was bought and redeemed by the blood of his only son Christ, then there was a cessation of both, he ever after governing his people and church within the limits of his revealed will ; so in the first original of kings, whereof some had their beginning by conquest, and some by election of the people, their wills at that time served for law, yet how soon kingdoms began to be settled in civility and policy, then did kings set down their minds by law, which are properly made by the king only, but at the rogation of the people, the king's grant being obtained thereunto. And so the king became to be *lex loquens*, after a sort, binding himself by a double oath to the observation of the fundamental laws of the kingdom : tacitly, as by being a king, and so bound to protect as well the people as the laws of his kingdom, and expressly by his oath at his coronation. So, as every just king in a settled kingdom is bound to observe that paction made to his people by his laws, in framing his government agreeable thereto, according to that paction which God made with Noah after the deluge, "Hereafter seed time and harvest, cold and heat, summer and winter, and day and night shall not cease, so long as the earth remains" ; and therefore a king governing in a settled kingdom leaves to be a king, and degenerates into a tyrant, as soon as he leaves off to rule according to his laws. . . . As for my part, I thank God I have ever given good proof that I never had intention to the contrary, and I am sure to go to my grave with that reputation and comfort, that never king was in all his time more careful to have his laws duly observed, and himself to govern thereafter, than I.

I conclude then that this point touching the power of kings with this axiom of divinity, that as to dispute what God may do is blasphemy, but *quid vult Deus*, that divines may lawfully and do ordinarily dispute and discuss, for to dispute *a posse ad esse* is both against logic and divinity ; so it is sedition in subjects to dispute what a king may do in the height of his power, but just kings will ever be willing to declare what they will do, if they will not incur the curse of God. I will not be content that my power be disputed upon, but I shall ever be willing to make the reason appear of all my doings, and rule my actions according to my laws. [p. 12-14]

NOTE

1. J.P. Kenyon, ed., "James I on Monarchy : Speech to Parliament," in *The Stuart Constitution* (Cambridge : Cambridge University Press, 1966), pp. 12-109.

THE HIGH COURT OF PARLIAMENT[1]

Charles H. McIlwain

To those who believed in a fundamental law immutable, the present-day doctrine of legislative sovereignty seemed new and contrary to the spirit of English institutions. In the constitutional struggle of Charles I's reign the doctrine of parliamentary sovereignty came to men, as Mr. Figgis truly says, "with all the force of a discovery." It lent itself to the views of the more extreme on both the parliamentary and the royalist side, and its influence over men's minds since the days of Milton and Hobbes has become so complete that historians have well-nigh forgotten that any other theory ever existed.

The word of Parliament has come to carry with it the idea of a lawmaking assembly of the type described by Blackstone. Men in time became so familiar with that idea that they were not conscious of the great and unwarranted assumption they were making when speaking of Tudor and pre-Tudor times ; for

Parliament, up to the time of the Tudors was hardly thought of primarily or principally as a legislature : it was still in reality "The High Court of Parliament." That court then retained the varied functions of the old Curia, as Parliament now does ; but the judicial functions bulked larger in men's minds than the legislative. Parliament still seemed primarily a law-declaring machine. So long as the law was a thing fundamental and immutable, "a subject of science, capable of being learnt by special study, but not capable of being altered by the mere will of government," Parliament's functions must have been conceived to be in large part merely the enforcing and applying of this law : Parliament must have been thought of first as a court rather than as a legislature. This I believe to have been the view prevailing, among lawyers at least, as late as the assembling of the Long Parliament. The statement of James I and Bacon, that a judge's functions were rather *jus dicere* than *jus dare*, would have seemed as properly applicable to the High Court of Parliament, if not so fully, as to the courts at Westminster Hall. The prominence of the judicial character of Parliament in the minds of men of the medieval period is the normal and natural consequence of the prevailing view that law was fixed ; but it is at times surprising to find how late that idea has survived, how many of the characteristics even of the modern sovereign Parliament are due to it, and how many of the great parliamentary struggles of comparatively recent times have been influenced by the old conception of Parliament as a court. [pp. 109-110]

The events of the sixteenth and seventeenth centuries in England eventually did produce a theory of legislative sovereignty complete on both its negative and its positive side. Englishmen, after they had accepted the new theory, in their traditional manner began to search the records of their past to justify it. It was easy to fasten on such words as "absolute," "supreme," "transcendent," and interpret them in the new sense, and this was done with entire ingenuousness. In fact, it may be observed generally that this method of relying on precedents has been one of the mightiest factors in the development of the English constitution. Men cited as precedents for their actions or their views words and expressions that had grown up under different surroundings. The institutions had changed, the words had not. All unconscious of the change men still cited the old words, but to justify the new order. But for this, England would not have furnished the world the greatest example of the evolution of political institutions, coupled with a conservative temper in the people and a reliance upon precedent which is unexampled in European history. In the seventeenth century especially, the effect of this process upon England's development was very great. But what is admissible, it may be, in a judge, is not equally so in a critical historian. The stream of political thought in one sense is the converse of what we find in nature. As we follow it back toward its sources we find that instead of narrowing, it becomes ever wider. Institutions that are now narrow and definite become as we trace them back indistinguishable from others that we have always considered equally definite. To ignore this fact is fatal. To read the same definiteness into the earlier institutions is not necessarily to put words into men's mouths which they never uttered, but it is to put ideas into their heads that they never dreamed of. It is hardly going too far to say that the measure of our comprehension of the development of the institutions of central government in England in the seventeenth century is our ability to remake the historical "mistakes" of Sir Edward Coke. It is hardly necessary to add, however, that our attainments should not stop there.

Coke's words became in time of great service, when royal pretensions had to be met by parliamentary claims, and vice versa ; but notwithstanding it all, Coke himself "had not really grasped the conception of sovereignty." For him the High Court of Parliament was simply "absolute" and transcendent ; it was nothing more.

On any other interpretation it is impossible to reconcile Coke's words with his own statements made at other times. How, according to the prevailing interpretation, can Coke say that Parliament's power is absolute and transcendent, and at the same time hold, as he did in Dr. Bonham's Case, "that in many cases the common law will control acts of Parliament and sometimes adjudge them to be utterly void" ? The truth is that these two statements are not really contradictory : for the one is not an assertion of the legislative supremacy of Parliament ; the other is not a denial of it. Coke's actions may often have been capricious, as has been charged, but his legal and political theory was not so. Statements like the one in Bonham's Case were not, as has often been intimated, vagaries, due to caprice or temporary excitement, out of relation with his general teachings, isolated statements of a theory contrary to and incompatible with the generally accepted beliefs of the time. In reality, his statements were all of a piece and all easily reconcilable under the then prevalent theory of parliamentary "supremacy."

Evidence is found all through Coke's writings that the foregoing statements contain his true view of parliamentary institutions in England. He never recognized the antithesis between legislation and adjudication by which the moderns have interpreted him.

As the conflict between king and Parliament grew closer, statements of Parliament's supremacy became more frequent, but on the very eve of Parliament's great practical demonstration of its legislative sovereignty, and in fact long after that, men kept on citing the old precedents for judicial supremacy, and it is often clear that they themselves did not notice that the legislative power they were actually advocating was anything different from the old powers of the High Court of Parliament.... [pp. 145-148]

In England at the present day there seems little danger of encroachment by the courts upon the legislature, or vice versa. Their respective spheres have become pretty definitely marked. In a fairly recent decision it was said, "What is said or done within the walls of Parliament cannot be enquired into in a court of law." The antithesis here is sharp. There is nothing of Parliament and "other" courts, or Parliament and "any inferior court." Except in the well-defined cases of the Lords' judicature in cases of appeal or in the trial of peers, Parliament is now thought of and spoken of purely as a legislature, and even questions of privilege so far as they properly belong to the houses are hardly considered any longer as judicial. In a country where so much depends upon precedent as in England, it is impossible to say that new circumstances may not arise leading to furbishing of the old weapons, but it is safe to say that today the general idea of Parliament as a court is well-nigh forgotten.

"The separation of legislative and judicial functions is a refinement in the principles of political government and jurisprudence, which can only be the result of an advanced civilization." [pp. 165-166]

NOTE

1. Charles H. McIlwain, *The High Court of Parliament* (New Haven : Yale University Press, 1910), pp. 109-166.

PURITANS, LAWYERS, AND POLITICS IN EARLY SEVENTEENTH CENTURY ENGLAND[1]

J.D. Eusden

The story of the English revolt against the crown in the seventeenth century has been told many times. Once in the middle of the century and again near the end, the English people rose to assert principles of government which were to become the foundations of Western political life. The period between 1640 and 1660 has received probably more attention than any other part in the century. Concentration upon the first major climax of the 1660s, frequently known as the Puritan Revolution, is as it should be. This was the glorious age of John Pym, John Lilburne, Henry Ireton, Oliver Cromwell, and John Milton. During this period in England, particularly in the 1640s, modern democracy received form and substance. Indeed, continued research is needed before the significance of the Long Parliament, the Great Rebellion, the Commonwealth, and the Protectorate is fully revealed.

The author leaves this tumultuous age to those who have already demonstrated their competence to deal with it and to those who are yet to come. He would call attention to a less familiar part of the century, to the time just before new powers arose overnight as giants in the land to wage war, behead the king, and govern the country. The pre-1640 period lacks, perhaps, the colour and the sense of direction of the later years dominated by parliamentarian, Leveller, regicide, and lord protector. But the early seventeenth century made no less of a contribution to political history than the period succeeding....

In the early 1600s James I and Charles I faced a double-pronged opposition represented by the forces of religion and law. The leaders of this opposition were Puritans and common lawyers. A concern with the church placed the Puritans in the fore of the struggle, although there was seldom an issue of any kind on which they did not raise their voices. John N. Figgis writes that in the late medieval period "it is right to treat the growth of political ideas as a branch of ecclesiastical history."[2] The dictum is still applicable to the early seventeenth century in England when the Puritans steadily contended with the Stuart kings over the powers of the crown in the life of the church. The Puritan opposition to the throne is also marked by a challenge of the king's interference in the life of the universities. A true measure of the Puritan's animosity to the crown is found in James' characterization of these religious folk as "verie pestes in the Church and common-weale."[3]

The common lawyers rank as leading antagonists of the throne because of their defence of the law of the land in the face of Stuart absolutism. Attorney General Francis Bacon, that staunch and wily friend of the king, recorded the observation of James that "ever since his coming to the crown, the popular sort of lawyers have been the men, that most affrontedly . . . have trodden upon his prerogative...."[4] The lawyers concentrated on the common law courts, upholding their independence much as the Puritans did in regard to the church. Similarly, as the Puritans fought the crown over interference in the universities, so the lawyers opposed James and Charles for royal tampering with the Inns of Court. Early in his reign James came to know the common lawyers for what they were — legal thorns in the royal flesh. In a speech in the Star Chamber, he referred to the "sharp edge and vaine popular humour of some Lawyers at the Barre, that thinke they are not eloquent and bold spirited enough, except they meddle with the Kings Prerogative."[5]

The Puritans and lawyers were more than just institutional contenders with James and Charles, quarreling with the crown over church and courts, universities and Inns of Court. They went to the heart of the matter. Out of the Puritan insistence on divine sovereignty and the common law insistence on fundamental law came an explicit change to the whole idea of Stuart kingship. Throughout the pre-Civil War years, James and Charles were harried by these formidable contentious men of God and men of law.

Many others joined the Puritans and lawyers against the crown in the early part of the century. Together they lamented the end of happy Tudor days and looked forlornly at the Stuart age. There were the summer patriots who spoke fondly of good old Elizabethan times and now bemoaned the decline of the nation's power on the continent and overseas. The blame for the decay was placed squarely on the stumbling foreign policy of James and Charles. Certain university figures with pronounced democratic leanings were unalterably opposed to Stuart absolutism at home. And finally, there were the leaders of the rising middle class who sought to wrest financial independence from the crown. These were the folk who chafed under the restrictions created by the king's royal monopolies, patents, and impositions. All of these joined in the attack on the crown and made the early seventeenth century a time of vigorous opposition to the powers that be. We would explore two of the major strands in the opposition, the one religious and the other legal.

The French historian Paul Hazard has written about the years that lie just on either side of 1700 in *The European Mind : the Critical Years (1680-1715).* With Gallic *ravissement* the author says, "Never was there a greater contrast, never a more sudden transition than this ! An hierarchical system ensured by authority ; life firmly based on dogmatic principle — such were the things held dear by the people of the seventeenth century ; but these . . . were the very things that their immediate successors of the eighteenth held in cordial detestation . . . . One day, the French people, almost to a man, were thinking like Bossuet. The day after, they were thinking like Voltaire." British restraint is more in order when dealing with the early Stuart period, but there is no doubt that in England from 1603 to 1630, as in France from 1680 to 1715, matters of utmost significance for modern history were taking place. We Americans should take special notice, for we cannot understand ourselves or our country apart from our beginning in the England of the early 1600s. The words of Louis B. Wright, Director of the Folger Shakespeare Library, show perspicacity : "All the fundamental concepts which make us the kind of people we are today had their modern conception in the Tudor and Stuart periods. For us, that's the milk in the coconut."

The early seventeenth-century connection between England and America is particularly evident in regard to the subjects of this book. English Puritans contributed the ethos of American culture in the period of our country's settlement, a fact often recounted but never too often emphasized. Less well known is the

American indebtedness to English common law. With few exceptions, the law of the land for England became the law of the land for the colonies and later the states and the nation. The fathers of the American republic read Edward Coke and other English lawyers of the seventeenth century. They recrossed the Atlantic to study the common law at the Inns of Court and sent their sons to do the same. The Middle Temple became in a certain sense an American inn during the colonial period. The early seventeenth century left an enduring imprint on much of American life.

We are concerned chiefly with the political importance of the early 1600s as manifested in the struggle of the Puritans and common lawyers with James I and Charles I. The two groups roundly opposed the Stuart conception of the divine right of kings with theories that God and law ruled the world. Instead of a hierarchical arrangement of institutions with the king at the apex, the Puritans and lawyers saw all institutions, including the crown, standing independent of one another and responsible only to God and law. Authority had been "distributed" among the institutions of society according to specific laws, which were the marks of God's sovereignty and law's supremacy. There was interdependence among institutions, but no subordination of one to another. The Puritans and lawyers worked with the old idea of the limitation of power and applied it in a new political setting. In so doing, they fashioned one of the indispensable elements of contemporary democracy. Their concept of limited power takes a place alongside other contributions to modern political life. It ranks with the "rights of Englishmen" and the attendant conception of liberty which came out of the Puritan Revolution, and with the idea of equality found across the channel in France at the end of the next century.

The Puritan-common law adaptation of a medieval understanding of political power and authority was uniquely applied to Parliament, the new political force of the age. Puritans and lawyers brought to the House of Commons not only their grievances for redress but also their conception of authority. In later times, Parliament's exercise of the full powers of rule, once possessed by the crown, was tempered by the early seventeenth-century idea of authority. The influence of the Puritan-common law opposition was felt subsequently in the development of political sovereignty and the concept of the state. The Puritans and lawyers contributed a climate of opinion in which modern pluralism could flourish. Indeed, Anglo-American society has developed in its characteristically pluralist way because of theological and legal roots which reach down to the early 1600s in England.

Despite the importance of the Puritans and the lawyers, their political thought is elusive. It does not unfold as political *Weltanschauung,* but rather emerges in the course of a jumbled history. The stages of the history frequently do not even accord with each other. Puritan divines uphold a church established by the crown and yet attack James' exercise of ecclesiastical power. Sir Edward Coke seems to maintain now the supremacy of the judiciary in Dr. Bonham's Case, now the sovereignty of the king in the case of the *postnati,* and later the plenitude of Parliament's powers. One follows the course of Puritan and common law political thought much as one drives through a large city on a cross-country trip. The route signs are confusing or nonexistent in the urban maze, red lights impede progress, and streets entered prove to be one way in the wrong direction. The traveller need not, however, be confounded by the journey if he will always bear in mind the nature of the two groups. To treat the Puritans and lawyers as political theorists would be to view them as they refused to view themselves.

The subjects of our study were ministers of the Gospel and judges or practitioners of the common law. Politics was not their major concern ; the church and the law sufficed for the employment of their terrifying energy. Questions of political authority became important for them only when particular germane concerns were challenged by James and Charles. What resulted from the conflict was not a neat political theory but a loose-jointed conception of the meaning and application of political power. Despite their imprecision, the Puritans and the lawyers fashioned major determinants for Western political history.... [pp. 1-7]

For both Puritans and lawyers, government was a necessary good. It was quite another matter, however, to hold that king, or Parliament, or any other conceivable form of government deserved absolute obedience.

The issue of obedience is a helpful key to the political history of the time, but its promise fades when the word is applied solely to concrete authorities. For the Puritans and the lawyers, final loyalty was rendered to objects which no contemporary formulation of political power fully represented. Unqualified obedience could only be given to God and the law. Puritans swore allegiance to divine sovereignty and lawyers to fundamental law. When the judges refused to obey the king's commands, they did so partly on the basis of their oath to administer the law of the land. The order of the king to stay proceedings in the Case of Commendams in 1616 was held contrary to the judges' commission which bound them "upon their oaths, and according to their best knowledge and learning. . .to deliver the true understanding [of law] faithfully and uprightly." Likewise the Puritans were bound to obey God. There was no formal oath as in the case of the judges, but there was explicit opposition to any other sworn loyalty. Many Puritans were against all manner of oath taking. As with other groups in the history of the church, these men were determined to obey God even at the expense of disobeying men of high authority. One Puritan minister closed a sermon preached before the judges in Norwich at summer assizes in 1620 with this prayer : "Blesse the people, and teach them to obey for conscience sake ; and withall wisely to know where, and how it is better to obey thee, than [*sic*] man." God and law alone provoked ultimate loyalty. They alone could be obeyed unquestioningly.

The Puritans and lawyers were confident that God and law merited absolute obedience. For the Puritans, divine sovereignty was a matter to be reckoned with immediately in any question of loyalty. It was, as we have seen, the cornerstone of Puritan faith and morals. The rule of God was no temporary expediency created on the moment to deal with a particular situation. It had come into the world from without and had existed from eternity. The divine origin, comprehensiveness, and perpetuity of God's rule made it comparably superior to other forms of authority.

In a similar way the lawyers construed fundamental law. As "pure reason," or the perfection of reason, the logic and harmony of common law rules and statutes made them natural first sources of obedience. But there was more to commend the fundamental law than just reasonableness. The source of the ancient common law was somewhere in the dim beginnings of Anglo-Saxon history. Coke and others cleverly spun the tale of a law originating in the bliss of pre-

Norman times when all things existed in an uncontaminated state prior to the coming of William the Conqueror. Coke appropriated the Christian myth of creation and fall, even the motif of the Garden of Eden, in order to validate the superiority of the fundamental law. The ancient law of the land had a mystical aura, even a blessedness, which rightly called forth man's highest loyalty. The more extreme apologists among the common lawyers were not averse to pushing the matter all the way : The fundamental law was "grounded upon the law of God." Occasionally the lawyers' law of God was equated with the Bible ; the ancient common law rules were then seen to have their base in scripture. More often the law of God was cited as a vague foundation superior to other equally ill-defined bases, such as the law of nature or the law of nations. Particular laws constructed on this law of God were of greater worth than those built on lesser foundations. The absence of clarity and logic does not prevent the generalization that the lawyers honoured and revered their fundamental law. It was at least a "vital principle" to which early seventeenth-century judges and barristers were as attached as Puritan divines and teachers were to divine sovereignty.

For both Puritans and lawyers, the ultimate authorities had a direct relationship to the world of practical affairs. The relationship is indicated by the emphasis on "sovereignty" for God and "fundamental" for law. The omnipresence of fundamental law was a commonplace and demonstrable proposition for the lawyers. Common law rules and statutes were simply unavoidable when any practical questions or issues were raised.

How did divine sovereignty and fundamental law wield their ultimate authority in society ? In the practical world the sway of God and fundamental law, believed the Puritans and the lawyers, was shown forth through individual laws.

This conviction made our subjects legalists par excellence. Among both divines and barristers there was a marked disinclination to generalize about political authority. Rather there was a scurrying to respective law books to discover what was commanded by a particular legal norm, be it a common law rule, a biblical pronouncement, or a statute. No sweeping constitutional documents were produced by the Puritan-common law opposition in the prewar period. The heralded 1628 Petition of Right, for example, simply "placed on record the king's acceptance of the statement that according to these laws certain definite grievances were illegal... [it was] the recognition of a claim that every subject of the Crown had been wronged in certain specific matters, and that, in the future, in those matters, the laws would be observed."[6] The petition asked for no prohibition of the crown's financial impositions, save under the particular circumstances of the 1626 forced loan. In the ship money case of 1637 the whole issue of supply had to be fought through again, and a thorough examination of precedents was made once more by both sides.

The panegyric of a parliamentarian lawyer in the 1628 Parliament displayed the spirit of the age :

> Our Lawes, which are the rules of this Justice, they are the ne plus ultra to both the King and the Subject : and as they are Hercules Pillar, so they are the pillar to every Hercules, to every Prince, which he must not passe. Give me leave to resemble her to Nebuchadnezzar's tree : for she is so great, that she doth shade not onely the Pallace of the King, and the house of the Nobles, but doth also shelter the Cottage of the poorest beggar.[7]

As one scholar has written of the period before the Civil War, "Of legalism there is much; of political science, none."[8]

Arrogance often tinged the legalism of the Puritans and the lawyers. The divines wrestled with the laws of scripture and immodestly proclaimed their superiority in the interpretation of God's word. The lawyers argued that they alone possessed the knowledge needed for the understanding and application of the laws of the land. Unless one had studied the common law diligently, Coke told James in the prohibitions issue, the requisite "artificial reason" could not be acquired. The divines and barristers frequently represented themselves as unfailing experts in the multifarious laws of the time.

The law of the land did not have the sanction of scriptural law, for biblical commandments were fundamentally different from other laws inasmuch as they comprised the very word of God. But the common law rules and statutes had an authority which allowed them a station close to that held by scriptural law. One anonymous Puritan writer began his description of the laws of England with these words: "The Lawes of England which now wee enjoy, were not first framed and fashioned after the Lawes of the Romans & other Heathens which were in many things Corrupt & prophane; but after ye pure and undefiled Lawes of God; & are at this day more agreeable to ye Law of God than ye Civil or Cannon Lawes, or any other Lawes in ye World." As evidence of the agreeableness of England's laws with the law of God, the writer cited the origin of the former. The first English laws resulted from the promulgation of King Lucius acting on the advice of Eleutherius, a Christian bishop, who had urged that England's law be fashioned after God's law in the Bible. King Lucius heeded the advice of God's representative. Throughout English legal history, continued the author, the close accord of the common law with God's law was apparent. The writer never maintained that God had decreed the particulars of England's law of the land, but he did imply that the Almighty could not have done better if he had tried.

In order to establish similarity between the two kinds of law, the author used the common Puritan analogy of England as the new Israel. The meaning of the figure was not only that England and Israel were chosen lands, but that the laws by which the biblical and the British nation were governed were alike in origin and content. God had decreed laws for Israel throughout its life as a nation. These laws had a history, a development; they were an unfolding of God's will for his children, His ways of dealing with his Israel. Similarly God had treated England. As he had smiled on Israel through the laws of the Old Testament, so now he smiled on England through its common law rules and statutes. The laws of England comprised the story of God's dealing with his present chosen nation.

The Puritans went beyond both Wyclif and Calvin. Common law rules and statutes were not only necessary for political harmony. They had an even higher value inasmuch as they, like the laws of the Bible, were manifestations of God's rule. Puritans examined the fundamental law and saw there the guiding hand of the one God who rules everywhere.

The legalism of the lawyers was rooted in statutes and common law rules. Their professional lives were bound up with a never-ending study and exegesis of the particulars of England's legal tradition. But the legalism of the early seventeenth-century judges and barristers did not rest solely on acts of Parliament and ancient legal customs. The lawyers turned to Puritan norms, much as the divines had turned to the standards of the legal profession. Whenever a biblical saying could be found that corroborated the meaning of a common law rule or statute, it was eagerly seized upon.

In the 1628 Parliament, Sir Edward Coke spoke out against false imprisonment and summed up his argument thus : "I will conclude with the highest authority, that is, 25. chap. of the Acts of the Apostles, the last verse, where Saint Paul saith, *It is against reason to send a man to prison without shewing a Cause.*"[9] The great jurist could stay with the best of the divines on the authority of the Bible : "To those lawes which [the] holy church hath out of scripture, we ought to yield credit ; for that . . . is the common law, upon which all lawes are founded."[10]

Coke and his colleagues were hardly innovators, for repeated use of the Bible had been the practice of nearly every medieval commentator on the common law. Fortescue, the famed sage of the law in the fifteenth century, employed fifty-two biblical quotations in his short treatise *De Laudibus Legum Angiae.* The Bible supported, in the mind of the lawyers, the authority of ancient common law rules and parliamentary enactments and thus helped to effect the ultimate authority of fundamental law.

The legalism of the Puritans and the lawyers demonstrated once more an ideological parallelism. The Puritans held that divine sovereignty manifested its authority through particular laws. This is also what the lawyers believed about fundamental law. Actual reciprocity existed among the divines and the barristers, for they co-opted each other's particular laws. The Puritans found the whole common law tradition to be a part of God's extensive rule of the world, while the lawyers discovered that the Bible undergirded the authority of common law rules and statutes and thereby augmented the supremacy of fundamental law. Indeed, it might be said that the two groups possessed a mutual set of legal standards, consisting of the word of God in scripture and the word of fundamental law in ancient customs and parliamentary enactments.... [pp. 116-125]

NOTES

1. J.D. Eusden, *Puritans, Lawyers and Politics in Early Seventeenth Century England,* (New Haven : Yale University Press, 1958), pp. 1-125.
2. John N. Figgis, *Studies of Political Thought from Gerson to Grotius, 1414-1625* (Cambridge : University Press, 1907), p. 31.
3. "Basilikon Doron" in McIlwain, *James Works,* p. 24.
4. Basil Montagu, ed., *The Works of Francis Bacon,* vol. 2 (New York : Worthington, 1884), p. 494.
5. In McIlwain, *James Works,* p. 333.
6. E.R. Adair, "The Petition of Right," *History.* 5, No. 18 (July, 1920) : 102-103.
7. Fuller, *Prerogative,* p. 22.
8. William A. Dunning, *A History of Political Theories from Luther to Montesquieu* (New York : MacMillan, 1905), p. 194.
9. Fuller, *Prerogative,* p. 40.
10. *Institutes,,* 2d Pt., 2. Sec. VIII.

INTRODUCTION TO THE STUDY OF THE LAW OF THE CONSTITUTION[1]

A.V. Dicey

Foreign observers of English manners, such for example, as Voltaire, De Lolme, de Tocqueville, or Gneist, have been far more struck than Englishmen themselves with the fact that England is a country governed, as is scarcely any other part of Europe, under the rule of law ; and admiration or astonishment at the legality of English habits and feeling is nowhere better expressed than in a curious passage from de Tocqueville's writings, which compares the Switzerland and the England of 1836 in respect of the spirit which pervades their laws and manners.

"I am not about," he writes, "to compare Switzerland with the United States, but with Great Britain." "When you examine the two countries, or even if you only pass through them, you perceive, in my judgment, the most astonishing differences between them. Take it all in all, England seems to be much more republican than the Helvetic Republic. The principal differences are found in the institutions of the two countries, and especially in their customs (*moeurs*).

"1. In almost all the Swiss Cantons liberty of the press is a very recent thing.
"2. In almost all of them individual liberty is by no means completely guaranteed, and a man may be arrested administratively and detained in prison without much formality.
"3. The courts have not, generally speaking, a perfectly independent position.
"4. In all the Cantons trial by jury is unknown.
"5. In several Cantons the people were thirty-eight years ago entirely without political rights. Aargau, Thurgau, Tessin, Vaud, and parts of the Cantons of Zurich and Berne were in this condition. "The preceding observations apply even more strongly to customs than to institutions.
"i. In many of the Swiss Cantons the majority of the citizens are quite without taste or desire for self government, and have not acquired the habit of it. In any crisis they interest themselves about their affairs, but you never see in them the thirst for political rights and the craving to take part in public affairs which seem to torment Englishmen throughout their lives.
"ii. The Swiss abuse the liberty of the press on account of its being a recent form of liberty, and Swiss newspapers are much more revolutionary and much less practical than English newspapers.
"iii. The Swiss seem still to look upon associations from much the same point of view as the French, that is to say, they consider them as a means of revolution, and not as a slow and sure method for obtaining redress of wrongs. The art of associating and making use of the right of association is but little understood in Switzerland.
"iv. The Swiss do not show the love of justice which is such a strong characteristic of the English. Their courts have no place in the political arrangements of the country and exert no influence on public opinion. The love of justice, the peaceful and legal introduction of the judge into the domain of politics, are perhaps the most standing characteristics of a free people.
"v. Finally, and this really embraces all the rest, the Swiss do not show at bottom that respect for justice, that love of law, that dislike of using force, without which no free nation can exist, which strikes strangers so forcibly in England.

"I sum up these impressions in a few words. Whoever travels in the United States is involuntarily and instinctively so impressed with the fact that the spirit of liberty and the taste for it have pervaded all the habits of the American people, that he cannot conceive of them under any but a republican government. In the same way it is impossible to think of the English as living under any but a free government. But if violence were to destroy the republican institutions in most of the Swiss Cantons, it would be by no means certain that after a rather short state of transition the people would not grow accustomed to the loss of liberty. In the United States and in England there seems to be more liberty in the customs than in the laws of the people. In Switzerland there seems to be more liberty in the laws than in the customs of the country."[2]

De Tocqueville's language has a twofold bearing on our present topic. His words point in the clearest manner to the rule, predominance, or supremacy of law as the distinguishing characteristic of English institutions. They further direct attention to the extreme vagueness of a trait of national character which is as noticeable as it is hard to portray. De Tocqueville, we see, is clearly perplexed how to define a feature of English manners of which he at once recognizes the existence ; he mingles or confuses together the habit of self-government, the love of order, the respect for justice, and a legal turn of mind. All these sentiments are intimately allied, but they cannot without confusion be identified with each other. If, however, a critic as acute as de Tocqueville found a difficulty in describing one of the most marked peculiarities of English life, we may safely conclude that we ourselves, whenever we talk of Englishmen as loving the government of law, or of the supremacy of law as being a characteristic of the English constitution, are using words which, though they possess a real significance, are nevertheless to most persons who employ them full of vagueness and ambiguity. If therefore we are ever to appreciate the full import of the idea denoted by the term "rule, supremacy, or predominance of law," we must first determine precisely what we mean by such expressions when we apply them to the British constitution.

When we say that the supremacy or the rule of law is a characteristic of the English constitution, we generally include under one expression at least three distinct though kindred conceptions.

We mean, in the first place, that no man is punishable or can be lawfully made to suffer in body or goods except for a distinct breach of law established in the ordinary legal manner before the ordinary courts of the land. In this sense the rule of law is contrasted with every system of government based on the exercise by persons in authority of wide, arbitrary, or discretionary powers of constraint.

Modern Englishmen may at first feel some surprise that the "rule of law" (in the sense in which we are now using the term) should be considered as in any way a peculiarity of English institutions, since, at the present day, it may seem to be not so much the property of any one nation as a trait common to every civilized and orderly state. Yet, even if we confine our observation to the existing condition of Europe, we shall soon be convinced that the "rule of law" even in this narrow sense is peculiar to England, or to those countries which like the United States of America, have inherited English traditions. In almost every continental community the executive exercises far wider discretionary authority in the matter of arrest, of temporary imprisonment, of expulsion from its territory, and the like, than is either legally claimed or in fact exerted by the government in England ; and a study of European politics now and again reminds English readers that wherever there is discretion there is room for arbitrariness, and that in a republic no less than under a monarchy discretionary authority on the part of the government must mean insecurity for legal freedom on the part of its subjects.

If, however, we confined our observation to the Europe of today (1908), we might well say that in most European countries the rule of law is now nearly as well established as in England, and that private individuals at any rate who do not meddle in politics have little to fear as long as they keep the law either from the government or from any one else ; and we might therefore feel some difficulty in understanding how it ever happened that to foreigners the absence of arbitrary power on the part of the crown, of the executive, and of every other authority in England, has always seemed a striking feature, we might almost say the essential characteristic of the English constitution.

Our perplexity is entirely removed by carrying back our minds to the time when the English constitution began to be criticized and admired by foreign thinkers. During the eighteenth century many of the continental governments were far from oppressive, but there was no continental country where men were secure from arbitrary power. The singularity of England was not so much the goodness or the leniency as the legality of the English system of government. When Voltaire came to England — and Voltaire represented the feeling of his age — his predominant sentiment clearly was that he had passed out of the realm of despotism to a land where the laws might be harsh, but where men were ruled by law and not by caprice. He had good reason to know the difference. In 1717 Voltaire was sent to the Bastille for a poem which he had not written, of which he did not know the author, and with the sentiment of which he did not agree. What adds to the oddity, in English eyes, of the whole transaction is that the Regent treated the affair as a sort of joke, and, so to speak, "chaffed" the supposed author of the satire "I have seen" on being about to pay a visit to the prison which he "had not seen." In 1725 Voltaire, then the literary hero of his country, was lured off from the table of a duke, and was thrashed by lackeys in the presence of their noble master ; he was unable to obtain either legal or honourable redress and, because he complained of this outrage, paid a second visit to the Bastille. This indeed was the last time in which he was lodged within the walls of a French gaol, but his whole life was a series of contests with arbitrary power, and nothing but his fame, his deftness, his infinite resource, and ultimately his wealth saved him from penalties far more severe than temporary imprisonment. Moreover, the price at which Voltaire saved his property and his life was after all exile from France. Whoever wants to see how exceptional a phenomenon was that supremacy of law which existed in England during the eighteenth century should read such a book as Morley's *Life of Diderot.*The effort lasting for twenty-two years to get the *Encyclopedie* published was a struggle on the part of all the distinguished literary men in France to obtain utterance for their thoughts. It is hard to say whether the difficulties or the success of the contest bear the strongest witness to the wayward arbitrariness of the French government.

Royal lawlessness was not peculiar to specially detestable monarchs such as Louis the Fifteenth : it was inherent in the French system of administration. An idea prevails that Louis the Sixteenth at least was not an arbitrary, as he assuredly was not a cruel, ruler. But it is an error to suppose that up to 1789 anything like the supremacy of law existed under the French monarchy. The folly, the grievances, and the mystery of the Chevalier D'Eon made as much noise little more than a century ago as the imposture of the Claimant in our own day. The memory of these things is not in itself worth reviving. What does deserve to be kept in remembrance is that in 1778, in the days of Johnson, of Adam Smith, of Gibbon, of Cowper, of Burke, and of Mansfield, during the continuance of the American war and within eleven years of the assembling of the States General, a brave officer and a distinguished diplomatist could for some offence still unknown, without trial and without conviction, be condemned to undergo a penance and disgrace which could hardly be rivalled by the fanciful caprice of the torments inflicted by Oriental despotism.

Nor let it be imagined that during the latter part of the eighteenth century the government of France was more arbitrary than that of other countries. To entertain such a supposition is to misconceive utterly the condition of the continent. In France, law and public opinion counted for a great deal more than in Spain, in the petty States of Italy, or in the Principalities of Germany. All the evils of despotism which attracted the notice of the world in a great kingdom such as France existed under worse forms in countries where, just because the evil was so much greater, it attracted the less attention. The power of the French monarch was criticized more severely than the lawlessness of a score of petty tyrants, not because the French king rules more despotically than other crowned heads, but because the French people appeared from the eminence of the nation to have a special claim to freedom, and because the ancient kingdom of France was the typical representative of despotism. This explains the thrill of enthusiasm with which all Europe greeted the fall of the Bastille. When the fortress was taken, there were not ten prisoners within its walls; at that very moment hundreds of debtors languished in English gaols. Yet all England hailed the triumph of the French populace with a fervour which to Englishmen of the twentieth century is at first sight hardly comprehensible. Reflection makes clear enough the cause of a feeling which spread through the length and breadth of the civilized world. The Bastille was the outward and visible sign of lawless power. Its fall was felt, and felt truly, to herald in for the rest of Europe that rule of law which already existed in England.

We mean in the second place, when we speak of the "rule of law" as a characteristic of our country, not only that with us no man is above the law, but (what is a different thing) that here every man, whatever be his rank or condition, is subject to the ordinary law of the realm and amenable to the jurisdiction of the ordinary tribunals.

In England the idea of legal equality, or of the universal subjection of all classes to one law administered by the ordinary courts, has been pushed to its utmost limit. With us every official, from the prime minister down to a constable or a collector of taxes, is under the same responsibility for every act done without legal justification as any other citizen. The reports abound with cases in which officials have been brought before the courts and made, in their personal capacity, liable to punishment, or to the payment of damages, for acts done in their official character but in excess of their lawful authority. A colonial governor, a secretary of state, a military officer, and all subordinates, though carrying out the commands of their official superiors, are as responsible for any act which the law does not authorize as is any private and unofficial person. Officials, such for example as soldiers or clergyman of the established church, are, it is true, in England as elsewhere, subject to laws which do not affect the rest of the nation and are in some instances amenable to tribunals which have no jurisdiction over their fellow countrymen ; officials, that is to say, are to a certain extent governed under what may be termed official law. But this fact is in no way inconsistent with the principle that all men in England are subject to the law of the realm ; for though a soldier or a clergyman incurs from his position legal liabilities from which other men are exempt, he does not (speaking generally) escape thereby from the duties of an ordinary citizen.

An Englishman naturally imagines that the rule of law (in the sense in which we are now using the term) is a trait common to all civilized societies. But this supposition is erroneous. Most European nations had indeed, by the end of the eighteenth century, passed through that stage of development (from which England emerged before the end of the sixteenth century) when nobles, priests and others could defy the law. But it is even now far from universally true that in continental countries all persons are subject to one and the same law, or that the courts are supreme throughout the state. If we take France as the type of a continental state, we may assert, with substantial accuracy, that officials — under which word should be included all persons employed in the service of the state — are, or have been, in their official capacity, to some extent exempted from the ordinary law of the land, protected from the jurisdiction of the ordinary tribunals, and subject in certain respects only to official law administered by official bodies.

There remains yet a third and a different sense in which the "rule of law" or the predominance of the legal spirit may be described as a special attribute of English institutions. We may say that the constitution is pervaded by the rule of law on the ground that the general principles of the constitution (as for example the right to personal liberty, or the right of public meeting) are with us the result of judicial decisions determining the rights of private persons in particular cases brought before the courts ; whereas under many foreign constitutions the security (such as it is) given to the rights of individuals results, or appears to result, from the general principles of the constitution.

This is one portion at least of the fact vaguely hinted at in the current but misguiding statement that "the constitution has not been made but has grown." This dictum, if taken literally, is absurd. "Political institutions (however the proposition may be at times ignored) are the work of men, owe their origin and their whole existence to human will. 'Men did not wake up on a summer morning and find them sprung up. Neither do they resemble trees, which, once planted, are aye growing while men are sleeping.' In every stage of their existence they are made what they are by human voluntary agency."

Yet, though this is so, the dogma that the form of a government is a sort of spontaneous growth so closely bound up with the life of a people that we can hardly treat it as a product of human will and energy, does, though in a loose and inaccurate fashion, bring into view that fact that some polities, and among them the English constitution, have not been created at one stroke, and, far from being the result of legislation, in the ordinary sense of that term, are the fruit of contests carried on in the courts on behalf of the rights of individuals. Our constitution, in short, is a judge-made constitution, and it bears on its face all the features, good and bad, of judge-made law.

Hence flow noteworthy distinctions between the constitution of England and the constitutions of most foreign countries.

There is in the English constitution an absence of those declarations or definitions of rights so dear to foreign constitutionalists. Such principles, moreover, as you can discover in the English constitutions are, like all maxims established by judicial legislation, mere generalizations drawn either from the decisions or dicta of judges, or from statutes which, being passed to meet special grievances, bear a close resemblance to judicial decisions, and are in effect judgments pronounced by the High Court of Parliament. To put what is really the same thing in a somewhat different shape, the relation of the rights of individuals to the principles of the constitution is not quite the same in countries like Belgium, where the constitution is the result of a legislative act, as it is in England, where the constitution itself is based upon legal decisions. In Belgium, which may be taken as a type of countries possessing a constitution formed by a deliberate act of legislation, you may say with truth that the rights of individuals to personal liberty flow from or are secured by the constitution. In England the right to individual liberty is part of the constitution, because it is secured by the decisions of the courts, extended or confirmed as they are by the Habeas Corpus Acts. If it be allowable to apply the formulas of logic to questions of law, the difference in this matter between the constitution of Belgium and the English constitution may be described by the statement that in Belgium individual rights are deductions drawn from the principles of the constitution, whilst in England the so-called principles of the constitution are inductions or generalizations based upon particular decisions pronounced by the courts as to the rights of given individuals.... [pp. 184-198]

That "rule of law," then, which forms a fundamental principle of the constitution, has three meanings, or may be regarded from three different points of view.

It means, in the first place, the absolute supremacy or predominance of regular law as opposed to the influence of arbitrary power, and excludes the existence of arbitrariness, of prerogative, or even of wide discretionary authority on the part of the government. Englishmen are ruled by the law, and by the law alone; a man may with us be punished for a breach of law, but he can be punished for nothing else.

It means, again, equality before the law, or the equal subjection of all classes to the ordinary law of the land administered by the ordinary law courts; the "rule of law" in this sense excludes the idea of any exemption of officials or others from the duty of obedience to the law which governs other citizens or from the jurisdiction of the ordinary tribunals; there can be with us nothing really corresponding to the "administrative law" (*droit administratif*) or the "administrative tribunals" (*tribunaux administratifs)* of France. The notion which lies at the bottom of the "administrative law" known to foreign countries is, that affairs or disputes in which the government or its servants are concerned are beyond the sphere of the civil courts and must be dealt with by special and more or less official bodies. This idea is utterly unknown to the law of England, and indeed is fundamentally inconsistent with our traditions and customs.

The "rule of law," lastly, may be used as a formula for expressing the fact that with us the law of the constitution, the rules which in foreign countries naturally form part of a constitutional code, are not the source but the consequence of the rights of individuals, as defined and enforced by the courts ; that, in short, the principles of private law have with us been by the action of the courts and Parliament so extended as to determine the position of the crown and of its servants ; thus the constitution is the result of the ordinary law of the land. [pp. 202-203]

NOTES

1. A.V. Dicey, *Introduction to the Study of the Law of the Constitution,* 10th ed. (London : MacMillan & Co., 1959), pp. 184-203.

2. See de Tocqueville, *Oeures Completes,* 14th ed., vol. 8 (Melanges Historiques, 1864), pp. 455-457.

LETTERS OF THOMAS JEFFERSON

Letter written by Jefferson in his student days, to John Page, Dec. 25, 1762, while absent from his law studies during the Christmas holidays.[1]

And now although the picture be defaced, there is so lively an image of her imprinted in my mind, that I shall think of her too often I fear, for my peace of mind ; and too often, I am sure to get through old Coke this winter ; for God knows I have not seen him since I packed him up in my trunk in Williamsburg. Well, Page, I do wish the Devil had old Coke, for I am sure I never was so tired of an old dull scoundrel in my life.

A letter from Jefferson to Judge John Tyler on June 17, 1812, where he writes concerning Blackstone :[2]

. . .A student finds there a smattering of everything and his indolence easily persuades him that if he understands that book, he is a master of the whole body of the law. The distinction between these, and those who have drawn their stores from the deep and rich mines of Coke and Littleton, seems well understood even by the unlettered common people who apply the appellation of Blackstone lawyers to these ephemeral insects of the law.

Letter from Jefferson to Dr. Thomas Cooper, Jan. 16, 1814 :[3]

. . .But I am sure you join me in lamenting the general defection of lawyers and judges, from the free principles of government. I am sure they do not derive this degenerate spirit from the father of our science, Lord Coke. But it may be the reason why they cease to read him, and the source of what are now called "Blackstone lawyers."

Letter from Jefferson to James Madison, February 17, 1826 :[4]

. . .In the selection of our Law Professor, (for the University of Virginia) we must be rigorously attentive to his political principles. You will recollect that before the Revolution, Coke Littleton was the universal elementary book of law students, and a sounder Whig never wrote, nor of profounder learning in the orthodox doctrines of the British constitution, or in what were called English liberties. You remember also that our lawyers were then all Whigs. But when his black-letter text, and uncouth but cunning learning got out of fashion, and the honeyed Mansfieldism of Blackstone became the students' hornbook, from that moment, that profession (the nursery of our Congress) began to slide into Toryism, and nearly all the young brood of lawyers now are of that hue. They suppose themselves, indeed, to be Whigs, because they no longer know what Whigism or republicanism means. It is in our seminary that the vestal flame is to be kept alive ; it is thence it is to spread anew over our own and the sister states. If we are true and vigilant in our trust, within a dozen or twenty years a majority of our own legislature will be from one school, and many disciples will have carried its doctrines home with them to their several states, and will have leavened thus the whole mass.

NOTES

1. A.A. Liscomb, ed. *The Writings of Thomas Jefferson*, vol. 2 (Washington, D.C. : Thomas Jefferson Memorial Association of the United States, 1903-04) p. 3.
2. *Ibid.*, vol. 13, pp. 166-167.
3. *Ibid.*, vol. 14, p. 63.
4. Koch and Penden, eds., *The Life and Selected Writings of Thomas Jefferson* (New York : Modern Library, 1944).

DECLARATION OF INDEPENDENCE

July 4, 1776

The Unanimous Declaration of the Thirteen
United States of America

WHEN, in the course of human events, it becomes necessary for one people to dissolve the political bonds which have connected them with another, and to assume, among the powers of the earth, the separate and equal station to which the laws of nature and of nature's God entitle them, a decent respect to the opinions of mankind requires that they should declare the causes which impel them to the separation.

We hold these truths to be self-evident : that all men are created equal ; that they are endowed, by their Creator, with certain inalienable rights ; that among these are life, liberty, and the pursuit of happiness. That to secure these rights, governments are instituted among men, deriving their just powers from the consent of the governed ; that whenever any form of government becomes destructive of these ends, it is the right of the people to alter or to abolish it, and to institute a new government, laying its foundation on such principles, and organizing its powers in such form, as to them shall seem most likely to effect their safety and happiness. Prudence, indeed, will dictate, that governments long established, should not be changed for light and transient causes ; and accordingly all experience hath shown, that mankind are more disposed to suffer, while evils are sufferable, than to right themselves by abolishing the forms to which they are accustomed. But when a long train of abuses and usurpations, pursuing invariably the same object, evinces a design to reduce them under absolute despotism, it is their right, it is their duty, to throw off such government and to provide new guards for their future security. Such has been the patient sufferance of these colonies ; and such is now the necessity which constrains them to alter their former systems of government. The history of the present King of Great Britain is a history of repeated injuries and usurpations, all having in direct object the establishment of an absolute tyranny over these states. To prove this, let facts be submitted to a candid world.

ARTICLES IN ADDITION TO, AND AMENDMENT OF, THE CONSTITUTION OF THE UNITED STATES OF AMERICA, PROPOSED BY CONGRESS, AND RATIFIED BY THE LEGISLATURES OF THE SEVERAL STATES PURSUANT TO THE FIFTH ARTICLE OF THE ORIGINAL CONSTITUTION.

AMENDMENT I. Congress shall make no law respecting an establishment of religion, or prohibiting the free exercise thereof ; or abridging the freedom of speech, or of the press ; or the right of the people peaceably to assemble, and to petition the Government for a redress of grievances.

AMENDMENT IV. The right of the people to be secure in their persons, houses, papers, and effects, against unreasonable searches and seizures, shall not be violated ; and no Warrants shall issue, but upon probable cause, supported by Oath or affirmation, and particularly describing the place to be searched, and the persons or things to be seized.

AMENDMENT V. No person shall be held to answer for a capital or otherwise infamous crime, unless on a presentment or indictment of Grand Jury, except in cases arising in the land or naval forces, or in the Militia, when in actual service in time of War or public danger ; nor shall any person be subject for the same offence to be twice put in jeopardy of life or limb ; nor shall be compelled, in any criminal case, to be witness against himself ; nor be deprived of life, liberty, or property, without due process of law ; nor shall private property be taken for public use without just compensation.

AMENDMENT VI. In all criminal prosecutions, the accused shall enjoy the right to a speedy and public trial, by an impartial jury of the State and district wherein the crime shall have been committed, which district shall have been previously ascertained by law, and to be informed of the nature and cause of the accusation ; to be confronted with the witnesses against him ; to have compulsory process for obtaining Witnesses in his favour ; and to have the Assistance of Counsel for his defence.

AMENDMENT VIII. Excessive bail shall not be required, nor excessive fines imposed, nor cruel and unusual punishments inflicted.

AMENDMENT IX. The enumeration in the Constitution of certain rights, shall not be construed to deny or disparage others retained by the people.

AMENDMENT XIII, SEC. 1. Neither slavery nor involuntary servitude, except as a punishment for crime whereof the party shall have been duly convicted, shall exist within the United States, or any place subject to their jurisdiction.

AMENDMENT XIV, SEC. 1. All persons born or naturalized in the United States, and subject to the jurisdiction thereof, are citizens of the United States and of the State wherein they reside. No State shall make or enforce any law which shall abridge the privileges or immunities of citizens of the United States ; nor shall any State deprive any person of life, liberty, or property, without due process of law, nor deny to any person within its jurisdiction the equal protection of the laws.

AMENDMENT XV, SEC. 1. The right of citizens of the United States to vote shall not be denied or abridged by the United States or by any State on account of race, color, or previous condition of servitude.

AMENDMENT XIX. The right of citizens of the United States to vote shall not be denied or abridged by the United States or by any State on account of sex.

THE BILL OF RIGHTS[1]

Mr. Justice Hugo Black

What is a bill of rights ? In the popular sense it is any document setting forth the liberties of the people. I prefer to think of our Bill of Rights as including all provisions of the original Constitution and Amendments that protect individual liberty by barring government from acting in a particular area or from acting except under certain prescribed procedures. I have in mind such clauses in the body of the Constitution itself as those which safeguard the right of *habeas corpus,* forbid bills of attainder and *ex post facto* laws, guarantee trial by jury, and strictly define treason and limit the way it can be tried and punished. I would certainly add to this list the last constitutional prohibition in Article Six that "no religious Test shall ever be required as a qualification to any Office or public Trust under the United States...."

In applying the Bill of Rights to the federal government there is today a sharp difference of views as to how far its provisions should be held to limit the lawmaking power of Congress. How this difference is finally resolved will, in my judgment, have far-reaching consequences upon our liberties. I shall first summarize what those different views are.

Some people regard the prohibitions of the Constitution, even its most unequivocal commands, as mere admonitions which Congress need not always observe. This viewpoint finds many different verbal expressions. For example, it is sometimes said that Congress may abridge a constitutional right if there is a clear and present danger that the free exercise of the right will bring about a substantive evil that Congress has authority to prevent. Or it is said that right may be abridged where its exercise would cause so much injury to the public that this injury would outweigh the injury to the individual who is deprived of the right. Again, it is sometimes said that the Bill of Rights' guarantees must "compete" for survival against general powers expressly granted to Congress, and that the individual's right must, if outweighed by the public interest, be subordinated to the government's competing interest in denying the right. All of these formulations, and more with which you are doubtless familiar, rest, at least in part, on the premise that there are no "absolute" prohibitions in the Constitution, and that all constitutional problems are questions of reasonableness, proximity, and degree. This view comes close to the English doctrine of legislative omnipotence, qualified only by the possibility of a judicial veto if the Supreme Court finds that a congressional choice between "competing" policies has no reasonable basis.

I cannot accept this approach to the Bill of Rights. It is my belief that there are "absolutes" in our Bill of Rights, and that they were put there on purpose by men who knew what words meant, and meant their prohibitions to be "absolutes." The whole history and background of the Constitution and Bill of Rights, as I understand it, belies the assumption or conclusion that our ultimate constitutional freedoms are no more than our English ancestors had when they came to this new land to get new freedoms. The historical and practical purposes of a Bill of Rights, the very use of a written constitution, indigenous to America, the language the framers used, the kind of three-department government they took pains to set up, all point to the creation of a government which was denied all power to do some things under any and all circumstances, and all power to do other things except precisely in the manner prescribed.... [pp. 31-33]

The form of government which was ordained and established in 1789 contains certain unique features which reflected the framers' fear of arbitrary government and which clearly indicate an intention absolutely to limit what Congress could do. The first of these features is that our Constitution is written in a single document....

A second unique feature of our government is a Constitution supreme over the legislature. In England, statutes, Magna Carta, and later declarations of rights had for centuries limited the power of the king, but they did not limit the power of Parliament. Although commonly referred to as a constitution, they were never the "supreme law of the land" in the way in which our Constitution is, much to the regret of statesmen like Pitt the elder. Parliament could change this English "Constitution"; Congress cannot change ours. Ours can only be changed by amendments ratified by three-fourths of the states. It was one of the great achievements of our Constitution that it ended legislative omnipotence here and placed all departments and agencies of government under one supreme law.

A third feature of our government, expressly designed to limit its powers, was the division of authority into three co-ordinate branches,none of which was to have supremacy over the others. This separation of powers with the checks and balances which each branch was given over the others was designed to prevent any branch, including the legislative, from infringing individual liberties safeguarded by the Constitution.

Finally, our Constitution was the first to provide a really independent judiciary. Moreover, as the Supreme Court held in *Marbury v. Madison*, correctly, I believe, this judiciary has the power to hold legislative enactments void that are repugnant to the Constitution and the Bill of Rights. In this country the judiciary was made independent because it has, I believe, the primary responsibility and duty of giving force and effect to constitutional liberties and limitations upon the executive and legislative branches. Judges in England were not always independent and they could not hold parliamentary acts void. Consequently, English courts could not be counted on to protect the liberties of the people against invasion by the Parliament, as many unfortunate Englishmen found out, such as Sir Walter Raleigh, who was executed as the result of an unfair trial, and a lawyer named William Prynne, whose ears were first cut off by court order and who subsequently, by another court order, had his remaining ear stumps gouged out while he was on a pillory. Prynne's offences were writing books and pamphlets.

All of the unique features of our Constitution show an underlying purpose to create a new kind of limited government. Central to all of the framers of the

Bill of Rights was the idea that since government, particularly the national government newly created, is a powerful institution, its officials — all of them — must be compelled to exercise their powers within strictly defined boundaries. As Madison told Congress, the Bill of Rights' limitations point "sometimes against the abuse of the executive power, sometimes against the legislative, and in some cases against the community itself; or, in other words, against the majority in favour of the minority." Madison also explained that his proposed amendments were intended "to limit and qualify the powers of government, by excepting out of the grant of power those cases in which the government ought not to act, or to act only in a particular mode...." [pp. 36-37]

The First Amendment. . .reads :

> Congress shall make no law respecting an establishment of religion, or prohibiting the free exercise thereof; or abridging the freedom of speech, or of the press ; or the right of the people peaceably to assemble, and to petition the government for a redress of grievances.

The phrase, "Congress shall make no law" is composed of plain words, easily understood. The framers knew this. The language used by Madison in his proposal was different, but no less emphatic and unequivocal. That proposal is worth reading :

> The civil rights of none shall be abridged on account of religious belief or worship, nor shall any national rights of conscience be in any manner, or on any pretext, infringed.
>
> The people shall not be deprived or abridged of their right to speak, to write, or to publish their sentiments ; and the freedom of the press, as one of the great bulwarks of liberty, shall be inviolable.
>
> The people shall not be restrained from peaceably assembling and consulting for their common good ; nor redress of their grievances.

Neither as offered nor as adopted is the language of this Amendment anything less than absolute. Madison was emphatic about this. He told the Congress that under it, "The right of freedom of speech is secured ; the liberty of the press is expressly declared to be *beyond the reach of this Government....*" (Emphasis supplied in all quotations.) Some years later Madison wrote that "it would seem scarcely possible to doubt that *no power whatever* over the press was supposed to be delegated by the Constitution, as it originally stood, and that the amendment was intended as a *positive and absolute reservation of it.*" With reference to the positive nature of the First Amendment's command against infringement of religious liberty, Madison later said that "there is not a shadow of right in the general government to intermeddle with religion," and that "this subject is, for the honour of America, perfectly free and unshackled. The *government has no jurisdiction over it.*"

To my way of thinking, at least, the history and language of the Constitution and the Bill of Rights . . .make it plain that one of the primary purposes of the Constitution with its amendments was to withdraw from the government all power to act in certain areas — whatever the scope of those areas may be. If I am right in this, then there is, at least in those areas, no justification whatever for "balancing" a particular right against some expressly granted power of Congress. If the Constitution withdraws from government all power over subject matter in an area, such as religion, speech, press, assembly, and petition, there is nothing over which authority may be exerted.... [pp. 40-42]

For my own part, I believe that our Constitution, with its absolute guarantees of individual rights, is the best hope for the aspirations of freedom which men share everywhere. I cannot agree with those who think of the Bill of Rights as an eighteenth-century strait jacket, unsuited for this age. It is old but not all old things are bad. The evils it guards against are not only old, they are with us now, they exist today. Almost any morning you open your daily paper you can see where some person somewhere in the world is on trial or has just been convicted of supposed disloyalty to a new group controlling the government which has set out to purge its suspected enemies and all those who had dared to be against its successful march to power. Nearly always you see that these political heretics are being tried by military tribunals or some other summary and sure method for disposition of the accused. Now and then we even see the convicted victims as they march to their execution.

Experience all over the world has demonstrated, I fear, that the distance between stable, orderly government and one that has been taken over by force is not so great as we have assumed. Our own free system to live and progress has to have intelligent citizens, citizens who cannot only think and speak and write to influence people, but citizens who are free to do that without fear of governmental censorship or reprisal.

The provisions of the Bill of Rights that safeguard fair legal procedures came about largely to protect the weak and the oppressed from punishment by the strong and the powerful who wanted to stifle the voices of discontent raised in protest against oppression and injustice in public affairs. Nothing that I have read in the congressional debates on the Bill of Rights indicates that there was any belief that the First Amendment contained any qualifications. The only arguments that tended to look in this direction at all were those that said "that all paper barriers against the power of the community are too weak to be worthy of attention." Suggestions were also made in and out of Congress that a Bill of Rights would be a futile gesture since there would be no way to enforce the safeguards for freedom it provided. Mr. Madison answered this argument in these words :

> If they [the Bill of Rights Amendments] are incorporated into the Constitution, independent tribunals of justice will consider themselves in a peculiar manner the guardians of those rights ; they will be an impenetrable bulwark against any assumption of power in the legislative or executive ; they will be naturally led to resist every encroachment upon rights expressly stipulated for in the Constitution by the declaration of rights.

I fail to see how courts can escape this sacred trust.

Since the earliest days, philosophers have dreamed of a country where the mind and spirit of man would be free ; where there would be no limits to inquiry ; where men would be free to explore the unknown and to challenge the most deeply rooted beliefs and principles. Our First Amendment was a bold effort to adopt this principle — to establish a country with no legal restrictions of any kind upon the subjects people could investigate, discuss, and deny. The framers knew, better perhaps than we do today, the risks they were taking. They knew that free speech might be the friend of change and revolution. But they also knew that it is always the deadliest enemy of tyranny. With this knowledge they still believed that the ultimate happiness and security of a nation lies in its ability to explore, to change, to grow, and ceaselessly to adapt itself to new knowledge born of inquiry free from any kind of governmental control over the mind and spirit of man. Loyalty comes from love of good government, not fear of a bad one.

The First Amendment is truly the heart of the Bill of Rights. The framers balanced its freedoms of religion, speech, press, assembly, and petition against the needs of a powerful central government, and decided that in those freedoms lies this nation's only true security. They were not afraid for men to be free. We should not be. We should be as confident as Jefferson was when he said in his First Inaugural Address :

> If there be any among us who would wish to dissolve this Union or to change its republican form, let them stand undisturbed as monuments of the safety with which error of opinion may be tolerated where reason is left free to combat it. [pp. 47-48]

NOTE

1. Mr. Justice Hugo Black, "The Bill of Rights," in Irving Dilliard, ed., *One Man's Stand for Freedom* (New York : Alfred A. Knopf, 1963), pp. 31-48.

CONSTITUTION ACT, 1982

PART I

Canadian Charter of Rights and Freedoms

Whereas Canada is founded upon principles that recognize the supremacy of God and the rule of law :

1. The *Canadian Charter of Rights and Freedoms* guarantees the rights and freedoms set out in it subject only to such reasonable limits prescribed by law as can be demonstrably justified in a free and democratic society.

2. Everyone has the following fundamental freedoms :

(a) freedom of conscience and religion ;

(b) freedom of thought, belief, opinion and expression, including freedom of the press and other media of communication ;

(c) freedom of peaceful assembly ; and

(d) freedom of association.

3. Every citizen of Canada has the right to vote in an election of members of the House of Commons or of a legislative assembly and to be qualified for membership therein.

6. (1) Every citizen of Canada has the right to enter, remain in and leave Canada.

7. Everyone has the right to life, liberty and security of the person and the right not to be deprived thereof except in accordance with the principles of fundamental justice.

8. Everyone has the right to be secure against unreasonable search or seizure.

9. Everyone has the right not to be arbitrarily detained or imprisoned.

10. Everyone has the right on arrest or detention

(a) to be informed promptly of the reasons therefor;

(b) to retain and instruct counsel without delay and to be informed of that right; and

(c) to have the validity of the detention determined by way of *habeas corpus* and to be released if the detention is not lawful.

12. Everyone has the right not to be subjected to any cruel and unusual treatment or punishment.

15. (1) Every individual is equal before and under the law and has the right to the equal protection and equal benefit of the law without discrimination and, in particular, without discrimination based on race, national or ethnic origin, colour, religion, sex, age or mental or physical disability.

(2) Subsection (1) does not preclude any law, program or activity that has as its object the amelioration of conditions of disadvantaged individuals or groups including those that are disadvantaged because of race, national or ethnic origin, colour, religion, sex, age or mental or physical disability.

24. (1) Anyone whose rights or freedoms, as guaranteed by this Charter, have been infringed or denied may apply to a court of competent jurisdiction to obtain such remedy as the court considers appropriate and just in the circumstances.

(2) Where, in proceedings under subsection (1), a court concludes that evidence was obtained in a manner that infringed or denied any rights or freedoms guaranteed by this Charter, the evidence shall be excluded if it is established that, having regard to all the circumstances, the admission of it in the proceedings would bring the administration of justice into disrepute.

26. The guarantee in this Charter of certain rights and freedoms shall not be construed as denying the existence of any other rights or freedoms that exist in canada.

28. Notwithstanding anything in this Charter, the rights and freedoms referred to in it are guaranteed equally to male and female persons.

31. Nothing in this Charter extends the legislative powers of any body or authority.

33. (1) Parliament or the legislature of a province may expressly declare in an Act of Parliament or of the legislature, as the case may be, that the Act or a provision thereof shall operate notwithstanding a provision included in section 2 or sections 7 to 15 of this Charter.

(3) A declaration made under subsection (1) shall cease to have effect five years after it comes into force or on such earlier date as may be specified in the declaration.

(4) Parliament or a legislature of a province may re-enact a declaration made under subsection (1).

THE CONSTITUTION OF JAPAN, 1946[1]

CHAPTER III.
RIGHTS AND DUTIES OF THE PEOPLE

Article 11. The people shall not be prevented from enjoying any of the fundamental human rights. These fundamental human rights guaranteed to the people by this Constitution shall be conferred upon the people of this and future generations as eternal and inviolate rights.

Article 12. The freedoms and rights guaranteed to the people by this Constitution shall be maintained by the constant endeavor of the people, who shall refrain from any abuse of these freedoms and rights and shall always be responsible for utilizing them for the public welfare.

Article 13. All of the people shall be respected as individuals. Their right to life, liberty, and the pursuit of happiness shall, to the extent that it does not interfere with the public welfare, be the supreme consideration in legislation and in other governmental affairs.

Article 14. All of the people are equal under the law and there shall be no discrimination in political, economic or social relations because of race, creed, sex, social status or family origin.

(2) Peers and peerage shall not be recognized.

(3) No privilege shall accompany any award of honor, decoration or any distinction, nor shall any such award be valid beyond the lifetime of the individual who now holds or hereafter may receive it.

Article 15. The people have the inalienable right to choose their public officials and to dismiss them.

(2) All public officials are servants of the whole community and not of any group thereof.

(3) Universal adult suffrage is guaranteed with regard to the election of public officials.

(4) In all elections, secrecy of the ballot shall not be violated. A voter shall not be answerable, publicly or privately, for the choice he has made.

Article 16. Every person shall have the right of peaceful petition for the redress of damage, for the removal of public officials, for the enactment, repeal or amendment of laws, ordinances or regulations and for other matters, nor shall any person be in any way discriminated against for sponsoring such a petition.

Article 17. Every person may sue for redress as provided by law from the State or a public entity, in case he has suffered damage through illegal act of any public official.

Article 18. No person shall be held in bondage of any kind. Involuntary servitude, except as punishment for crime, is prohibited.

Article 19. Freedom of thought and conscience shall not be violated.

Article 20. Freedom of religion is guaranteed to all. No religious organization shall receive any privileges from the State nor exercise any political authority.

(2) No person shall be compelled to take part in any religious acts, celebration, rite or practice.

(3) The State and its organs shall refrain from religious education or any other religious activity.

Article 21. Freedom of assembly and association as well as speech, press and all other forms of expression are guaranteed.

(2) No censorship shall be maintained, nor shall the secrecy of any means of communication be violated.

Article 22. Every person shall have freedom to choose and change his residence and to choose his occupation to the extent that it does not interfere with the public welfare.

(2) Freedom of all persons to move to a foreign country and to divest themselves of their nationality shall be inviolate.

Article 23. Academic freedom is guaranteed.

Article 24. Marriage shall be based only on the mutual consent of both sexes and it shall be maintained through mutual cooperation with the equal rights of husband and wife as a basis.

(2) With regard to choice of spouse, property rights, inheritance, choice of domicile, divorce and other matters pertaining to marriage and the family, laws shall be enacted from the standpoint of individual dignity and the essential equality of the sexes.

Article 31. No person shall be deprived of life or liberty, nor shall any other criminal penalty be imposed, except according to procedure established by law.

Article 32. No person shall be denied the right of access to the courts.

Article 33. No person shall be apprehended except upon warrant issued by a competent judicial officer which specifies the offense with which the person is charged, unless he is apprehended, the offense being committed.

Article 34. No person shall be arrested or detained without being at once informed of the charges against him or without the immediate privilege of counsel ; nor shall he be detained without adequate cause ; and upon demand of any person such cause must be immediately shown in open court in his presence and the presence of his counsel.

Article 35. The right of all persons to be secure in their homes, papers and effects against entries, searches and seizures shall not be impaired except upon warrant issued for adequate cause and particularly describing the place to be searched and things to be seized, or except as provided by Article 33.

(2) Each search or seizure shall be made upon separate warrant issued by a competent judicial officer.

Article 36. The infliction of torture by any public officer and cruel punishments are absolutely forbidden.

Article 40. Any person, in case he is acquitted after he has been arrested or detained, may sue the State for redress as provided by law.

NOTE

1. Promulgated on November 3, 1946 ; Put into effect on May 3, 1947.

THE EUROPEAN CONVENTION ON HUMAN RIGHTS[1]

The Governments signatory hereto, being Members of the Council of Europe,

Considering the Universal Declaration of Human Rights proclaimed by the General Assembly of the United Nations on 10 December 1948 ;

Considering that this Declaration aims at securing the universal and effective recognition and observance of the Rights therein declared ;

Considering that the aim of the Council of Europe is the achievement of greater unity between its Members and that one of the methods by which the aim is to be pursued is the maintenance and further realization of Human Rights and Fundamental Freedoms ;

Reaffirming their profound belief in those Fundamental Freedoms which are the foundation of justice and peace in the world and are best maintained on the one hand by an effective political democracy and on the other by a common understanding and observance of the Human Rights upon which they depend ;

Being resolved, as the Governments of European countries which are like-minded and have a common heritage of political traditions, ideals, freedom and the rule of law to take the first steps for the collective enforcement of certain of the Rights stated in the Universal Declaration ;

Have agreed as follows :

Article I

The High Contracting Parties shall secure to everyone within their jurisdiction the rights and freedoms defined in Section I of this Convention.

Section I

Article 2

1. Everyone's right to life shall be protected by law. No one shall be deprived of his life intentionally save in the execution of a sentence of a court following his conviction of a crime for which this penalty is provided by law.

Article 3

No one shall be subjected to torture or to inhuman or degrading treatment or punishment.

Article 4

1. No one shall be held in slavery or servitude.

2. No one shall be required to perform forced or compulsory labour.

Article 5

1. Everyone has the right to liberty and security of person. No one shall be deprived of his liberty save ... in accordance with a procedure prescribed by law ;

Article 6

1. In the determination of his civil rights and obligations or of any criminal charge against him, everyone is entitled to a fair and public hearing within a reasonable time by an independent and impartial tribunal established by law....

2. Everyone charged with a criminal offence shall be presumed innocent until proved guilty according to law.

Article 9

1. Everyone has the right to freedom of thought, conscience and religion ; this right includes freedom to change his religion or belief, and freedom, either alone or in community with others and in public or private, to manifest his religion or belief, in worship, teaching, practice and observance.

2. Freedom to manifest one's religion or beliefs shall be subject only to such limitations as are prescribed by law and are necessary in a democratic society in the interests of public safety, for the protection of public order, health or morals, or for the protection of rights and freedoms of others.

Article 10

1. Everyone has the right to freedom of expression. This right shall include freedom to hold opinions and to receive and impart information and ideas without interference by public authority and regardless of frontiers. This article shall not prevent States from requiring the licensing of broadcasting, television or cinema enterprises.

2. The exercise of these freedoms, since it carries with it duties and responsibilities, may be subject to such formalities, conditions, restrictions or penalties as are prescribed by law and are necessary in a democratic society, in the interests of national security, territorial integrity or public safety, for the prevention of disorder or crime, for the protection of health or morals, for the protection of the reputation or rights of others, for preventing the disclosure of information received in confidence, or for maintaining the authority and impartiality of the judiciary.

Article 11

1. Everyone has the right to freedom of peaceful assembly and to freedom of association with others, including the right to form and to join trade unions for the protection of his interests.

2. No restrictions shall be placed on the exercise of these rights other than such as are prescribed by law and are necessary in a democratic society in the interests of national security or public safety, for the prevention of disorder or crime, for the protection of health or morals or for the protection of the rights and freedoms of others. This article shall not prevent the imposition of lawful restrictions on the exercise of these rights by members of the armed forces, of the police or of the administration of the State.

Article 13

Everyone whose rights and freedoms as set forth in this Convention are violated shall have an effective remedy before a national authority notwithstanding that the violation has been committed by persons acting in an official capacity.

Article 14

The enjoyment of the rights and freedoms set forth in this Convention shall be secured without discrimination on any ground such as sex, race, colour, language, religion, political or other opinion, national or social origin, association with a national minority, property, birth or other status.

Article 15

1. In time of war or other public emergency threatenting the life of the nation any High Contracting Party may take measures derogating from its obligations under this Convention to the extent strictly required by the exigencies of the situation, provided that such measures are not inconsistent with its other obligations under international law.

Section II

Article 19

To ensure the observance of the engagements undertaken by the High Contracting Parties in the present Convention, there shall be set up :

1. A European Commission of Human Rights hereinafter referred to as 'the Commission' ;

2. A European Court of Human Rights, hereinafter referred to as 'the Court' ;

NOTE

1. The European Convention was signed in Rome on 4 November 1950 and entered into force on 3 September 1953. Twenty States have ratified the Convention : Austria, Belgium, Cyprus, Denmark, France, Greece, Federal Republic of Germany, Iceland, Ireland, Italy, Luxembourg, Malta, Netherlands, Norway, Portugal, Spain, Sweden, Switzerland, Turkey and the United Kingdom.
Fourteen States have recognized the right of individual petition to the European Commission, and seventeen States have accepted the compulsory jurisdiction of the European Court of Human Rights.

GOVERNMENT UNDER LAW AND THE INDIVIDUAL[1]

Milton Katz

It was in the seventeenth and eighteenth centuries, in the aftermath of the Renaissance and Reformation, that the conceptions and institutions of government under law in Western society were moulded into the contours familiar today. From the idea of the sanctity of the individual human soul, there emerged the conception of the liberties of the individual and the rights of man. The medieval idea of the supremacy of law evolved into the modern principles of constitutionalism. The old pluralism of centres of power was vastly extended through the rise of parliamentary democracy, the development of Protestantism, and the expanding opportunities of the New World.

Through the nineteenth century and into the twentieth, the steady extension of suffrage, the expansion and invigoration of the middle class, the birth and growth of labour unions, and, in the United States, the widespread distribution of property ownership and widespread enjoyment of the fruits of increasing production have represented a continuing diffusion of power in Western society. The emergence of mass production and the accelerating consequences of modern technology, the rise of the modern corporation, and the effects of patterns of organization imposed on Western society by two world wars and by intensive preparations against the danger of a new war with nuclear weapons have represented reverse tendencies, toward the concentration of power. These developments have been attended by immense psychological processes in Western society, and a great variety of new legal and political arrangements. The implications for government under law remain to be evaluated. Perhaps they even remain to be seen. The prospect has been complicated within the past three decades by the threat of totalitarian doctrine and practice.

From a contemplation of the structure, processes, and animating ideas of European and American society, in the perspective of their long history, three elements, or groups of elements, tend to emerge as the essential components of government under law. They may be described, or at least their content may be suggested, in these terms :

The principle of substantive limitations upon the scope of governmental power, in the sense of a general acceptance that the individual has certain rights which are fundamental and may not be impaired by action of the government. Familiar illustrations are liberty of religion, of thought, of speech, of assembly.

The principle of procedural limitations upon governmental power, which apply even within the limits of its substantive scope. The government may not interfere with an individual except in accordance with a general law previously enacted or recognized as established through custom ; and the government may not apply sanctions against any individual even for violation of such a general law previously stated except in accordance with a just and orderly procedure. Familiar illustrations are the clause from Chapter 29 of Magna Carta, "nor will we not pass upon him nor condemn him but . . . by the law of the land" ; the protection against the deprivation of life, liberty, and property without due process of law ; the prohibition against *ex post facto* laws ; the prohibition against searches and seizures except under warrants issued upon probable cause ; the prohibition against cruel and unusual punishments.

The existence of effective institutions through which the foregoing principles may be vindicated. Familiar illustrations are an independent judiciary and judicial review of executive or legislative action.

These principles and institutions can only be understood in terms of their history and the endless variations of their actual application in practice. They merge into one another. In the United States, for example, it is only roughly true to say that the liberties of conscience and thought and speech represent substantive rights which the government may not destroy, for there is the possibility of constitutional amendment. A more accurate statement would be that the liberties of religion and thought and speech may not be nullified by an act of government, unless supported by two-thirds of each house of Congress and a majority in each of each of the legislatures of three-fourths of the states. In this aspect, the substantive limitations become procedural. Americans are prone to regard judicial safeguards against unconstitutional legislation as something solid and concrete and objective, in contrast with the vaguer protections of assumed parliamentary self-restraint upon which Englishmen rely. Yet judicial review would be meaningless if judges should lose their devotion to duty or their nerve ; if the executive should appoint judges who are supine or corrupt ; or if a reckless legislature should deliberately and consistently withhold appropriations for the compensation of judges and the conduct of the business of the courts. The ultimate reliance in the United States, as in England, is upon the values, customs, and frame of thought of the institutions involved — the courts, the congress or parliament, the presidency or cabinet or crown — and upon the patterns of thought, customs, and values of the societies within which these institutions are organic parts. In this aspect, the institutions relied on to vindicate concepts are seen to draw their vitality from concepts. This in no sense denies the force or dependability of these institutions. It merely reminds us that they are human.

The heart of the matter lies even deeper, in the factors which made possible the emergence of the principles and institutions that constitute the essential ingredients of the rule of law. In the evolution of government under law, the factors ultimately controlling have been a concept of the dignity of the individual ; a closely connected concept of the harmonious relationship of the individual to God or universal moral principle or truth or reason, depending upon whether the terms of statement have been religious or philosophical ; and an adequate diffusion of power. It may be anticipated that these factors will also control the future of government under law. [pp. 2-13]

NOTE

1. Milton Katz, *Government Under Law and the Individual* (American Council of Learned Societies, 1957), pp. 2-13.

2. Law and the Legitimacy of State Power

Emerging from the complex interplay between law and state are two kinds of law : judge-made law and legislation. If the state is justified in terms of the popular will or the right of a particular class to dominate, law is defined in terms of the will or command of the sovereign class, and the prevailing form of the law will be legislation. If the legitimacy of the state is grounded in its role as a protector of rights, then legislation will be made to accord with at least some fundamental principles of an autonomous body of law.

Theories of state legitimacy range from anarchism, which denies the right of state authority, to the ideology of the modern welfare states ; the "minimum state," and theories of separation of powers and judicial review lie somewhere in between. At the far end of the spectrum are the "Hegelian state" as the idealized form of community, and the Marxist-Leninist theories of the dictatorship of the proletariat. Each form of justification has implications for the law and the balance to be maintained between precedent and fiat.

Law's autonomy, either from the moral structures of age-old institutions such as the church, or from the bastions of state power, is not immediately obvious. Even though we might set out the conditions at the level of high theory of law's independence, the core values of the legal system and its ideologies of professionalism have neither in theory nor practice been safe from incursions. In actuality the law has served as a mediating force among various claims to authority and power emanating from church, economies, and political structures. The critical issue is whether law has managed, over time, to produce a set of principles distinct from political ideologies, and whether the procedures attached to law give it a set of criteria for adjudication which can be assessed as a closed system apart from other institutions. At various stages in the history of theory law has been confronted by critics who regard it as being a variable dependent on the will of the majority, that is expressed through concepts of community or state.

Even as an abstract set of precepts, law cannot remain totally isolated from the social community. In fact, the concept of rational law appears incomplete and elusive, as if to suggest that it can have no real suasion without being grounded in the conscious and habit-forming obedience of a politically defined citizenry. For this reason the covenantal community of ancient Judaism is attractive in its integration of its law with a congregation of persons committed to a personalized code of legal regulations and life-directives. For modern man the need for moral guidance is less pronounced at the conscious level and, if anything, his needs have suggested in the past few hundred years a scaling down of church and state interventions. In democratic societies this has resulted in a bold separation of church and state, and state and law. Yet, despite these historical movements, there is a disquieting aspect to man's contemporary legal predicament. For to operate according to rational law flies in the face of moral, emotional and political needs. There is a dialectical necessity that drives law back in the direction of the structures from which it was born and emancipated ; similarly, state theorists have looked to law for indigenous theories of justice and equality from which to glean political principles of legitimacy.

There is an affinity between the Marxist and positivist theorists who have reduced the law to a total dependency on economic or state power or, in the alternative, have qualified this harsh statement of affairs to see law as an instrument of state authority, which, if legitimated on the basis of some rudimentary notion of justice, makes law a necessary condition for realizing justifiable political ends.

The strong assumptions of Marxist and positivist thinking have receded and been replaced, both in liberal and socialist quarters, with attempts to rationalize claims of legal-moral autonomy. Since the Second World War the view that law is nothing other than the embodiment of naked political power has been found unsatisfactory. Even if we are prepared to admit that the legal system experiences many distortions and manipulations which find their seat in power, it may still be the case that the structures of legal rationality, infused with broad principles of adjudication and moral content, still represent the only credible alternative structure to the unpredictable forces of social discord.

There are those who are prepared to argue that the deep structure of law is so connected to the protection of property and contract, serving the purpose of the dominant power structures, that, unless we think of completely novel procedures and values, there is no chance for law to equip itself with the tools for an independent life apart from the state and class interest. The burden of recent liberal theory has been to make inroads into the nature of legal autonomy based on doctrines of fairness and justice which distinguish law from instrumentalist aims and mere utility.

In current Western liberal democratic theory there has been a tendency to bridge the moral gap between politics and law while maintaining the conditions for establishing law as an independent institution. This has demanded a laying out of a theory of rights, explaining the nature of legal principles, the limitations of judicial discretion, and a general theory of justice upon which the legitimacy of politics and law could be grounded.

IN DEFENCE OF ANARCHISM[1]

Robert Paul Wolff

Politics is the exercise of the power of the state, or the attempt to influence that exercise. Political philosophy is therefore, strictly speaking, the philosophy of the state. If we are to determine the content of political philosophy, and whether indeed it exists, we must begin with the concept of the state.

The state is a group of persons who have and exercise supreme authority within a given territory. Strictly, we should say that a state is a group of persons who have supreme authority within a given territory *or over a certain population.* A nomadic tribe may exhibit the authority structure of a state, so long as its subjects do not fall under the superior authority of a territorial state. The state may include all the persons who fall under its authority, as does the democratic state according to its theorists ; it may also consist of a single individual to whom all the rest are subject. We may doubt whether the one-person state has ever actually existed, although Louis XIV evidently thought so when he announced, "L'etat, c'est moi." The distinctive characteristic of the state is supreme authority, or what political philosophers used to call "sovereignty." Thus one speaks of "popular sovereignty," which is the doctrine that the people are the state, and of course the use of "sovereign" to mean "king" reflects the supposed concentration of supreme authority in a monarchy.

Authority is the right to command and, correlatively, the right to be obeyed. It must be distinguished from power, which is the ability to compel compliance, either through the use or the threat of force. When I turn over my wallet to a thief who is holding me at gunpoint, I do so because the fate with which he threatens me is worse than the loss of money which I am made to suffer. I grant that he has power over me, but I would hardly suppose that he has authority, that is, that he has a right to demand my money and that I have an obligation to give it to him. When the government presents me with a bill for taxes, on the other hand, I pay it (normally) even though I do not wish to, and even if I think I can get away with not paying. It is, after all, the duly constituted government, and hence it has a right to tax me. It has authority over me. Sometimes, of course, I cheat the government, but even so, I acknowledge its authority, for who would speak of "cheating" a thief?

To claim authority is to claim the right to be obeyed. To have authority is then — What ? It may mean to have that right, or it may mean to have one's claim acknowledged and accepted by those at whom it is directed. The term "authority" is ambiguous, having both a descriptive and a normative sense. Even the descriptive sense refers to norms or obligations, of course, but it does so by describing what men believe they ought to do rather than by asserting that they ought to do it.

Corresponding to the two senses of authority, there are two concepts of the state. Descriptively, the state may be defined as a group of persons who are acknowledged to have supreme authority within a territory — acknowledged, that is, by those over whom the authority is asserted. The study of the forms, characteristics, institutions, and functioning of *de facto* states, as we may call them, is the province of political science. If we take the term in its prescriptive signification, the state is a group of persons who have the right to exercise supreme authority within a territory. The discovery, analysis, and demonstration of the forms and principles of legitimate authority — of the right to rule — is called political philosophy.... [pp. 305]

The fundamental assumption of moral philosophy is that men are responsible for their actions. From this assumption it follows necessarily, as Kant pointed out, that men are metaphysically free, which is to say that in some sense they are capable of choosing how they shall act. Being able to choose how he acts makes a man responsible, but merely choosing is not in itself enough to constitute taking responsibility for one's actions. Taking responsibility involves attempting to determine what one ought to do, and that, as philosophers since Aristotle have recognized, lays upon one the additional burdens of gaining knowledge, reflecting on motives, predicting outcomes, criticizing principles, and so forth.

The obligation to take responsibility for one's actions does not derive from man's freedom of will alone, for more is required in taking responsibility than freedom of choice. Only because man has the capacity to reason about his choices can he be said to stand under a continuing obligation to take responsibility for them. It is quite appropriate that moral philosophers should group together children and madmen as beings not fully responsible for their actions, for as madmen are thought to lack freedom of choice, so children do not yet possess the power of reason in a developed form. It is even just that we should assign a greater degree of responsibility to children, for madmen, by virtue of their lack of free will, are completely without responsibility, while children, insofar as they possess reason in a partially developed form, can be held responsible (i.e., can be required to take responsibility) to a corresponding degree.

Every man who possesses both free will and reason has an obligation to take responsibility for his actions, even though he may not be actively engaged in a continuing process of reflection, investigation, and deliberation about how he ought to act. A man will sometimes announce his willingness to take responsibility for the consequences of his actions, even though he has not deliberated about them, or does not intend to do so in the future. Such a declaration is, of course, an advance over the refusal to take responsibility; it at least acknowledges the existence of the obligation. But it does not relieve the man of the duty to engage in the reflective process which he has thus far shunned. It goes without saying that a man may take responsiblity for his actions and yet act wrongly. When we describe someone as a responsible individual, we do not imply that he always does what is right, but only that he does not neglect the duty of attempting to ascertain what is right.

The responsible man is not capricious or anarchic, for he does acknowledge himself bound by moral constraints. But he insists that he alone is the judge of those constraints. He may listen to the advice of others, but he makes it his own by determining for himself whether it is good advice. He may learn from others about his moral obligations, but only in the sense that a mathematician learns from other mathematicians — namely by hearing from them arguments whose validity he recognizes even though he did not think of them himself. He does not learn in the sense that one learns from an explorer, by accepting as true his accounts of things one cannot see for oneself.

Since the responsible man arrives at moral decisions which he expresses to himself in the form of imperatives, we may say that he gives laws to himself, or is self-legislating. In short, he is autonomous. As Kant argued, moral autonomy is a combination of freedom and responsibility ; it is a submission to laws which one has made for oneself. The autonomous man, insofar as he is autonomous, is not subject to the will of another. He may do what another tells him, but not because he has been told to do it. He is therefore, in the political sense of the word, free.

Since man's responsibility for his actions is a consequence of his capacity for choice, he cannot give it up or put it aside. He can refuse to acknowledge it, however, either deliberately or by simply failing to recognize his moral conditions. All men refuse to take responsibility for their actions at some time or other during their lives, and some men so consistently shirk their duty that they present more the appearance of overgrown children than of adults. Inasmuch as moral autonomy is simply the condition of taking full responsibility for one's actions, it follows that men can forfeit their autonomy at will. That is to say, a man can decide to obey the commands of another without making any attempt to determine for himself whether what is commanded is good or wise.

This is an important point, and it should not be confused with the false assertion that a man can give up responsibility for his actions. Even after he has subjected himself to the will of another, an individual remains responsible for what he does. But by refusing to engage in moral deliberations, by accepting as final the commands of the others, he forfeits his autonomy. Rousseau is therefore right when he says that a man cannot become a slave even through his own choice, if he means that even slaves are morally responsible for their acts. But he is wrong if he means that men cannot place themselves voluntarily in a position of servitude and mindless obedience.

There are many forms and degrees of forfeiture of autonomy. A man can give up his independence of judgment with regard to a single question, or in respect of a single type of question. For example, when I place myself in the hands of my doctor, I commit myself to whatever course of treatment he prescribes, but only in regard to my health. I do not make him my legal counselor as well. A man may forfeit autonomy on some or all questions for a specific period of time, or during his entire life. He may submit himself to all commands, whatever they may be, save for some specified acts (such as killing) which he refuses to perform. From the example of the doctor, it is obvious that there are at least some situations in which it is reasonable to give up one's autonomy. Indeed, we may wonder whether, in a complex world of technical expertise, it is ever reasonable not to do so !...

The moral condition demands that we acknowledge responsibility and achieve autonomy wherever and whenever possible. Sometimes this involves moral deliberation and reflection ; at other times, the gathering of special, even technical, information. The contemporary American citizen, for example, has an obligation to master enough modern science to enable him to follow debates about nuclear policy and come to an independent conclusion. There are great, perhaps unsurmountable, obstacles to the achievement of a complete and rational autonomy in the modern world. Nevertheless, so long as we recognize our responsibility for our actions, and acknowledge the power of reason within us, we must acknowledge as well the continuing obligation to make ourselves the authors of such commands as we may obey. The paradox of man's condition in the modern world is that the more fully he recognizes his right and duty to be his own master, the more completely he becomes the passive object of a technology and bureaucracy whose complexities he cannot hope to understand. It is only several hundred years since a reasonably well-educated man could claim to understand the major issues of government as well as his king or parliament. Ironically, the high school graduate of today, who cannot master the issues of foreign and domestic policy on which he is asked to vote, could quite easily have grasped the problems of eighteenth-century statecraft.

The defining mark of the state is authority, the right to rule. The primary obligation of man is autonomy, the refusal to be ruled. It would seem, then, that there can be no resolution of the conflict between the autonomy of the individual and the putative authority of the state. Insofar as a man fulfills his obligation to make himself the author of his decision, he will resist the state's claim to have authority over him. That is to say, he will deny that he has a duty to obey the laws of the state simply because they are the laws. In that sense, it would seem that anarchism is the only political doctrine consistent with the virtue of autonomy.

Now, of course, an anarchist may grant the necessity of complying with the law under certin circumstances or for the time being. He may even doubt that there is any real prospect of eliminating the state as a human institution. But he will never view the commands of the state as legitimate, as having a binding moral force. In a sense, we might characterize the anarchist as a man without a country, for despite the ties which bind him to the land of his childhood, he stands in precisely the same moral relationship to "his" government as he does to the government of any other country in which he might happen to be staying for a time. When I take a vacation in Great Britain, I obey its laws, both because of prudential self-interest and because of the obvious moral considerations concerning the value of order, the general good consequences of preserving a system of property, and so forth. On my return to the United States, I have a sense of reentering my country, and if I think about the matter at all, I imagine myself to stand in a different and more intimate relation to American laws. They have been promulgated by my government, and I therefore have a special obligation to obey them. But the anarchist tells me that my feeling is purely sentimental and has no objective moral basis. All authority is equally illegitimate, although of course not therefore equally worthy or unworthy of support, and my obedience to American laws, if I am to be morally autonomous, must proceed from the same considerations which determine me abroad.

The dilemma which we have posed can be succinctly expressed in terms of the concept of a *de jure* state. If all men have a continuing obligation to achieve the highest degree of autonomy possible, then there would appear to be no state whose subjects have a moral obligation to obey its commands. Hence, the concept of a *de jure* legitimate state would appear to be vacuous, and philosophical anarchism would seem to be the only reasonable political belief for an enlightened man.... [pp. 12-19]

The solution which immediately springs to the fore is, of course, majority rule. Where the electorate are divided, take a vote ; give to each man one vote, and let the group as a whole be committed by the preponderance of voices. So widespread is the belief in majority rule that there is not a single variant of democratic theory which does not call upon it as the means for composing differences and arriving at decisions. Our task is to discover an argument which demonstrates that the autonomy of unanimous democracy is preserved in a democracy which is guided by the rule of the majority. In other words, we must inquire whether the members of a democratic polity are morally bound to obey the decisions of the majority and, if so, why.

The problem, of course, concerns those who find themselves in the minority on any question. The members of the majority bear the same relation to the law they have passed as to all the citizens in a unanimous democracy. Since the majority have willed the law, they are bound by it, and they remain autonomous in submitting to its authority. A member of the minority, however, has voted against the law, and he appears to be in the position of a man who, deliberating on a moral question, rejects an alternative only to find it forced upon him by a superior power. His readiness to deliberate, and to be committed by his decision, manifests his desire to be autonomous ; but insofar as he must submit to the will of the majority, it seems that his desire is frustrated.

One common justification of majority rule is that, on prudential or general moral grounds, it works better than any other system which has been devised. For example, it is said that democratic politics is a substitute for the rule of arms which prevails in lawless societies. Since the majority are, militarily speaking, likely to be the superior body, they must be allowed to rule by the ballot ; for otherwise they will resort to force and throw society back into chaos. Or, again, historical observation may reveal that rule by the majority tends to advance the general welfare better than any other system of government (such as rule by the wise or the powerful), since contrary to what Plato and others have supposed, the people know their own interest best. Majoritarian democracy, it is said, is therefore the most effective safeguard against the rule of a hypocritically self-interested elite. From the point of view of the individual, it might be urged that submission to the rule of the majority offers him the best chance, in the long run,for advancing his own interests, since by and large he will find himself in the majority as often as in the minority, and the benefit flowing from collective action will outweigh the losses suffered when his side loses.

All such defences, and others besides which might be based on considerations of interest or good consequences, are, however, strictly irrelevant to our inquiry. As justifications for an individual's autonomous decision to cooperate with the state, they may be perfectly adequate ; but as demonstrations of the authority of the state — as proofs, that is, of the right of the state to command the individual and of his obligation to obey whatever may be commanded — they fail completely. If the individual retains his autonomy by reserving to himself in each instance the final decision whether to cooperate, he thereby denies the authority of the state ; if, on the other hand, he submits to the state and accepts its claim to authority, then so far as any of the above arguments indicate, he loses his autonomy.

Indeed, the prudential and casuistical defences of democracy do not succeed in distinguishing it morally from any other form of political community. A man might find that his affairs flourished in a dictatorship or monarchy, and even that the welfare of the people as a whole was effectively advanced by the policies of such a state. Democracy, then, could claim to be no more than one type of *de facto* government among many, and its virtues, if any, would be purely relative. Perhaps, as Winston Churchill once remarked, democracy is the worst form of government except for all the others ; but if so, then the "citizens" of

America are as much subjects of an alien power as the Spaniards under Franco or the Russians under Stalin. They are merely more fortunate in their rulers.

A more serious case for majority rule can be founded on the terms of the contract by which the political order is constituted. According to many theorists of democracy, the transition from unanimous rule, as exemplified by the adoption of the social contract, to majority rule, on which the subsequent functionings of the society depend, is provided for by a clause in the original agreement. Everyone pledges himself henceforth to abide by the rule of the majority, and whenever a citizen objects to being required to obey laws for which he has not voted, he can be recalled to his promise. On that pact, it is asserted, rests the moral authority of a majoritarian state.

But this argument is no better than the previous one. A promise to abide by the will of the majority creates an obligation, but it does so precisely by giving up one's autonomy. It is perfectly possible to forfeit autonomy, as we have already seen. Whether it is wise, or good, or right to do so is, of couse, open to question, but that one can do so is obvious. Hence, if citizens contract to govern themselves by majority rule, they thereby obligate themselves in just the manner that they would be obligated by any promise. The state then has a right to command them, assuming that it is guided only by the majority. But the citizens have created a legitimate state at the price of their own autonomy ! They have bound themselves to obey laws which they do not will, and indeed even laws which they vigorously reject. Insofar as democracy originates in such a promise, it is no more than voluntary slavery, and the characterization which Rousseau gives of the English form of representation can as well be applied here.... [pp. 38-42]

We have come to a dead end in our search for a viable form of political association which will harmonize the moral autonomy of the individual with the legitimate authority of the state. The one proposal which appears genuinely to resolve the conflict, namely unanimous direct democracy, is so restricted in its application that it offers no serious hope of ever being embodied in an actual state. Indeed, since it achieves its success only by ruling out precisely the conflicts of opinion which politics is designed to resolve, it may be viewed as the limiting case of a solution rather than as itself a true example of a legitimate state....

Our failure to discover a form of political association which could combine moral autonomy with legitimate authority is not a result of the imperfect rationality of men, nor of the passions and private interests which deflect men from the pursuit of justice and the general good. Many political philosophers have portrayed the state as a necessary evil forced upon men by their own inability to abide by the principles of morality, or as a tool of one class of men against the others in the never-ending struggle for personal advantage. Marx and Hobbes agree that in a community of men of good will, where the general good guided every citizen, the state would be unnecessary. They differ only in the degree of their hope that so happy a condition can ever be realized.

Nor does our dilemma grow out of the familiar limitations of intellect and knowledge which afflict all but the most extraordinary men. It may be that in a technologically complex world only a few men can hope to master the major political issues well enough to have genuinely personal convictions about them. By positing a society of rational men of good will, however, we have eliminated such well-known obstacles to the fully just state. The magnitude of our problem is indicated by our inability to solve the dilemma of autonomy and authority even for a utopian society! By and large, political philosophers have supposed that utopia was logically possible, however much they may have doubted that it was even marginally probable. But the arguments of this essay suggest that the just state must be consigned the category of the round square, the married bachelor, and the unsensed sense-datum.

If autonomy and authority are genuinely incompatible, only two courses are open to us. Either we must embrace philosophical anarchism and treat all governments as non-legitimate bodies whose commands must be judged and evaluated in each instance before they are obeyed; or else, we must give up as quixotic the pursuit of autonomy in the political realm and submit ourselves (by an implicit promise) to whatever form of government appears most just and beneficent at the moment. (I cannot resist repeating yet again that if we take this course, *there is no universal or a priori reason for binding ourselves to a democratic government rather than to any other sort.* In some situations, it may be wiser to swear allegiance to a benevolent and efficient dictatorship than to a democracy which imposes a tyrannical majority on a defenceless minority. *And in those cases where we have sworn to obey the rule of the majority, no additional binding force will exist beyond what would be present had we promised our allegiance to a king!*)

It is out of the question to give up the commitment to moral autonomy. Men are no better than children if they not only accept the rule of others from force of necessity, but embrace it willingly and forfeit their duty unceasingly to weigh the merits of the actions which they perform. When I place myself in the hands of another, and permit him to determine the principles by which I shall guide my behaviour, I repudiate the freedom and reason which give me dignity. I am then guilty of what Kant might have called the sin of willful heteronomy.

There would appear to be no alternative but to embrace the doctrine of anarchism and categorically deny any claim to legitimate authority by one man over another. Yet I confess myself unhappy with the conclusion that I must simply leave off the search for legitimate collective authority. [pp. 69-72]

NOTE

1. Robert Paul Wolff, *In Defence of Anarchism* (New York: Harper & Row, 1970), pp. 3-72.

ANARCHY, STATE, AND UTOPIA[1]

Robert Nozick

The fundamental question of political philosophy, one that precedes questions about how the state should be organized, is whether there should be any state at all. Why not have anarchy? Since anarchist theory, if tenable, undercuts the whole subject of *political* philosophy, it is appropriate to begin political philosophy with an examination of its major theoretical alternative. Those who consider anarchism not an unattractive doctrine will think it possible that political philosophy *ends* here as well. Others impatiently will await what is to come afterwards. Yet, as we shall see, archists and anarchists alike, those who spring gingerly from the starting point as well as those reluctantly argued away from it, can agree that beginning the subject of political philosophy with state-of-nature theory has an *explanatory* purpose. (Such a purpose is absent when epistemology is begun with an attempt to refute the skeptic.)....

More to the point, especially for deciding what goals one should try to achieve, would be to focus upon a nonstate situation in which people generally satisfy moral constraints and generally act as they ought. Such an assumption is not wildly optimistic; it does not assume that all people act exactly as they should. Yet this state-of-nature situation is the best anarchic situation one reasonably could hope for. Hence investigating its nature and defects is of crucial importance to deciding whether there should be a state rather than anarchy. If one could show that the state would be superior even to this most favoured situation of anarchy, the best that realistically can be hoped for, or would arise by a process involving no morally impermissible steps, or would be an improvement if it arose, this would provide a rationale for the state's existence; it would justify the state.... [pp. 4-5]

The night-watchman state of classical liberal theory, limited to the functions of protecting all its citizens against violence, theft, and fraud, and to the enforcement of contracts, and so on, appears to be redistributive. We can imagine at least one social arrangement intermediate between the scheme of private protective associations and the night-watchman state. Since the night-watchman state is often called a minimal state, we shall call this other arrangement the *ultraminimal state.* An ultraminimal state maintains a monopoly over all use of force except that necessary in immediate self-defence, and so excludes private (or agency) retaliation for wrong and exaction of compensation; but it provides protection and enforcement services *only* to those who purchase its protection and enforcement policies. People who don't buy a protection contract from the monopoly don't get protected. The minimal (night-watchman) state is equivalent to the ultraminimal state conjoined with a (clearly redistributive) Friedmanesque voucher plan, financed from tax revenues. Under this plan all people, or some (for example, those in need), are given tax-funded vouchers that can be used only for their purchase of a protection policy from the ultraminimal state.

Since the night-watchman state appears redistributive to the extent that it compels some people to pay for the protection of others, its proponents must explain why this redistributive function of the state is unique. If some redistribution is legitimate in order to protect everyone, why is redistribution not legitimate for other attractive and desirable purposes as well? What rationale specifically selects protective services as the sole subject of legitimate redistributive activities?... [pp. 26-27]

A system of private protection, even when one protective agency is dominant in a geographical territory, appears to fall short of a state. It apparently does not provide protection for everyone in its territory, as does a state, and it apparently does not possess or claim the sort of monopoly over the use of force necessary to a state. In our earlier terminology, it apparently does not constitute a minimal state, and it apparently does not even constitute an ultraminimal state.

These very ways in which the dominant protective agency or association in a territory apparently falls short of being a state provide the focus of the individualist anarchist's complaint *against* the state. For he holds that when the state monopolizes the use of force in a territory and punishes others who violate its monopoly, and when the state provides protection for everyone by forcing some to purchase protection for others, it violates moral side constraints on how individuals may be treated. Hence, he concludes, the state itself is intrinsically immoral. The state grants that under some circumstances it is legitimate to punish persons who violate the rights of others, for it itself does so. How then does it arrogate to itself the right to forbid private exaction of justice by other nonaggressive individuals whose rights have been violated ? *What* right does the private exacter of justice violate that is not violated also by the state when it punishes ? When a group of persons constitute themselves as the state and begin to punish, *and forbid others from doing likewise,* is there some right these others would violate that they themselves do not ? By what right, then, can the state and its officials claim a unique right (a privilege) with regard to force and enforce this monopoly ? If the private exacter of justice violates no one's rights, then punishing him for his actions (actions state officials also perform) violates his rights and hence violates moral side constraints. Monopolizing the use of force then, on this view, is itself immoral, as is redistribution through the compulsory tax apparatus of the state. Peaceful individuals minding their own business are not violating the rights of others. It does not constitute a violation of someone's rights to refrain from purchasing something for him (that you have not entered specifically into an obligation to buy). Hence, so the argument continues, when the state threatens someone with punishment if he does not contribute to the protection of another, it violates (and its officials violate) his rights. In threatening him with something that would be a violation of his rights if done by a private citizen, they violate moral constraints.

To get something recognizable as a state we must show (1) how an ultraminimal state arises out of the system of private protective associations ; and (2) how the ultraminimal state is transformed into the minimal state, how it gives rise to that "redistribution" for the general provision of protective services that constitutes it as the minimal state. To show that the minimal state is morally legitimate, to show it is not immoral itself, we must show also that these transitions in (1) and (2) *each* are morally legitimate. In . . . this work we show how each of these transitions occurs and is morally permissible. We argue that the first transition, from a system of private protective agencies to an ultraminimal state, will occur by an invisible-hand process in a morally permissible way that violates no one's rights. Secondly, we argue that the transition from an ultraminimal state to a minimal state morally must occur. It would be morally impermissible for persons to maintain the monopoly in the ultraminimal state without providing protective services for all, even if this requires specific "redistribution." The operators of the ultraminimal state are morally obligated to produce the minimal state. . . . [W]e argue that no state *more* powerful or extensive than the minimal state is legitimate or justifiable.... [pp. 51-53]

The principle of compensation requires that people be compensated for having certain risky activities prohibited to them. It might be objected that either you have the right to forbid these people's risky activities or you don't. If you do, you needn't compensate the people for doing to them what you have a right to do ; and if you don't, then rather than formulating a policy of compensating people for your unrightful forbidding, you ought simply to stop it. In neither case does the appropriate course seem to be to forbid and then compensate. But the dilemma, "either you have a right to forbid it so you needn't compensate, or you don't have a right to forbid it so you should stop," is too short. It may be that you do have a right to forbid an action but only provided you compensate those to whom it is forbidden.... [p. 83]

A protective agency dominant in a territory does satisfy the two crucial necessary conditions for being a state. It is the only generally effective enforcer of a prohibition on others' using unreliable enforcement procedures (calling them as it sees them), and it oversees these procedures. And the agency protects those nonclients in its territory whom it prohibits from using self-help enforcement procedures on its clients,in their dealings with its clients, even if such protection must be financed (in apparent redistributive fashion) by its clients. It is morally required to do this by the principle of compensation, which requires those who act in self-protection in order to increase their own security to compensate those they prohibit from doing risky acts which might actually have turned out to be harmless for the disadvantages imposed upon them.

We noted . . . that whether the provision of protected services for some by others was "redistributive" would depend upon the reasons for it. We now see that such provision need not be redistributive since it can be justified on other than redistributive grounds, namely, those provided in the principle of compensation. (Recall that "redistributive" applies to reasons for a practice or institution, and only elliptically and derivatively to the institution itself.) To sharpen this point, we can imagine that protective agencies offer two types of protection policies : those protecting clients against risky private enforcement of justice and those not doing so but protecting only against theft, assault, and so forth (provided these are not done in the course of private enforcement of justice). Since it is only with regard to those with the first type of policy that others are prohibited from privately enforcing justice, only they will be required to compensate the persons prohibited private enforcement for the disadvantages imposed upon them. The holders of only the second type of policy will not have to pay for the protection of others, there being nothing they have to compensate these others for. Since the reasons for wanting to be protected against private enforcement of justice are compelling, almost all who purchase protection will purchase this type of protection, despite its extra costs, and therefore will be involved in providing protection for the independents.

We have discharged our task of explaining how a state would arise from a state of nature without anyone's rights being violated. The moral objections of the individualist anarchist to the minimal state are overcome. It is not an unjust imposition of a monopoly ; the *de facto* monopoly grows by an invisible-hand process and *by morally permissible means*, without anyone's rights being violated and without any claims being made to a special right that others do not possess. And requiring the clients of the *de facto* monopoly to pay for the protection of those they prohibit from self-help enforcement against them, far from being immoral, is morally required by the principle of compensation.... [pp. 113-115]

. . . What is the explanation of how a *minimal* state arises ? The dominant protective association with the monopoly element is morally required to compensate for the disadvantages it imposes upon those it prohibits from self-help activities against its clients. However, it actually might fail to provide this compensation. Those operating an ultraminimal state are morally required to transform it into a minimal state, but they might choose not to do so. We have assumed that generally people will do what they are morally required to do. Explaining how a state could arise from a state of nature without violating anyone's rights refutes the principled objections of the anarchist. But one would feel more confidence if an explanation of how a state *would* arise from a state of nature also specified reasons why an ultraminimal state would be transformed into a minimal one, in addition to moral reasons, if it specified incentives for providing the compensation or the causes of its being provided in addition to people's desire to do what they ought. We should note that even in the event that no nonmoral incentives or causes are found to be sufficient for the transition from an ultraminimal to a minimal state, and the explanation continues to lean heavily upon people's moral motivations, it does not specify people's objective as that of establishing a state. Instead, persons view themselves as providing particular other persons with compensation for particular prohibitions they have imposed upon them.... [p. 119]

NOTE

1. Robert Nozick, *Anarchy, State, and Utopia* (New York : Basic Books, Inc., 1974), pp. 4-119.

A THEORY OF JUSTICE[1]

John Rawls

The Main Idea of the Theory of Justice

My aim is to present a conception of justice which generalizes and carries to a higher level of abstraction the familiar theory of the social contract as found, say, in Locke, Rousseau, and Kant. In order to do this we are not to think of the original contract as one to enter a particular society or to set up a particular form of government. Rather, the guiding idea is that the principles of justice for the basic structure of society are the object of the original agreement. They are the principles that free and rational persons concerned to further their own interests would accept in an initial position of equality as defining the fundamental terms of their association. These principles are to regulate all further agreements ; they specify the kinds of social cooperation that can be entered into and the forms of government that can be established. This way of regarding the principles of justice I shall call justice as fairness.

Thus we are to imagine that those who engage in social cooperation choose together, in one joint act, the principles which are to assign basic rights and duties and to determine the division of social benefits. Men are to decide in advance how they are to regulate their claims against one another and what is to be the foundation charter of their society. Just as each person must decide by rational reflection what constitutes his good, that is, the system of ends which it is rational for him to pursue, so a group of persons must decide once and for all what is to count among them as just and unjust. The choice which rational men would make in this hypothetical situation of equal liberty, assuming for the present that this choice problem has a solution, determines the principles of justice.

In justice as fairness the original position of equality corresponds to the state of nature in the traditional theory of the social contract. This original position is not, of course, thought of as an actual historical state of affairs, much less as a primitive condition of culture. It is understood as a purely hypothetical situation characterized so as to lead to a certain conception of justice. Among the essential features of this situation is that no one knows his place in society, his class position or social status, nor does any one know his fortune in the distribution of natural assets and abilities, his intelligence, strength, and the like. I shall even assume that the parties do not know their conceptions of the good or their special psychological propensities. The principles of justice are chosen behind a veil of ignorance. This ensures that no one is advantaged or disadvantaged in the choice of principles by the outcome of natural chance or the contingency of social circumstances. Since all are similarly situated and no one is able to design principles to favour his particular condition, the principles of justice are the result of a fair agreement or bargain. For given the circumstances of the original position, the symmetry of everyone's relations to each other, this initial situation is fair between individuals as moral persons, that is, as rational beings with their own ends and capable, I shall assume, of a sense of justice. The original position is, one might say, the appropriate initial status quo, and thus the fundamental agreements reached in it are fair. This explains the propriety of the name "justice as fairness" : it conveys the idea that the principles of justice are agreed to in an initial situation that is fair. The name does not mean that the concepts of justice and fairness are the same, any more than the phrase "poetry as metaphor" means that the concepts of poetry and metaphor are the same.

Justice as fairness begins, as I have said, with one of the most general of all choices which persons might make together, namely, with the choice of the first principles of a conception of justice which is to regulate all subsequent criticism and reform of institutions. Then, having chosen a conception of justice, we can suppose that they are to choose a constitution and a legislature to enact laws, and so on, all in accordance with the principles of justice initially agreed upon. Our social situation is just if it is such that by this sequence of hypothetical agreements we would have contracted into the general system of rules which defines it. Moreover, assuming that the original position does determine a set of principles (that is, that a particular conception of justice would be chosen), it will then be true that whenever social institutions satisfy these principles those engaged in them can say to one another that they are cooperating on terms to which they would agree if they were free and equal persons whose relations with respect to one another were fair. They could all view their arrangements as meeting the stipulations which they would acknowledge in an initial situation that embodies widely accepted and reasonable constraints on the choice of principles. The general recognition of this fact would provide the basis for a public acceptance of the corresponding principles of justice. No society can, of course, be a scheme of cooperation which men enter voluntarily in a literal sense ; each person finds himself placed at birth in some particular position in some particular society, and the nature of this position materially affects his life prospects. Yet a society satisfying the principles of justice as fairness comes as close as a society can to being a voluntary scheme, for it meets the principles which free and equal persons would assent to under circumstances that are fair. In this sense its members are autonomous and the obligations they recognize self-imposed.

One feature of justice as fairness is to think of the parties in the initial situation as rational and mutually disinterested. This does not mean that the parties are egoists, that is, individuals with only certain kinds of interests, say in wealth, prestige, and domination. But they are conceived as not taking an interest in one another's interests. They are to presume that even their spiritual aims may be opposed, in the way that the aims of those of different religions may be opposed. Moreover, the concept of rationality must be interpreted as far as possible in the narrow sense, standard in economic theory, of taking the most effective means to given ends. I shall modify this concept to some extent . . . but one must try to avoid introducing into it any controversial ethical elements. The initial situation must be characterized by stipulations that are widely accepted.

In working out the conception of justice as fairness one main task clearly is to determine which principles of justice would be chosen in the original position. To do this we must describe this situation in some detail and formulate with care the problem of choice which it presents ... It may be observed, however, that once that principles of justice are thought of as arising from an original agreement in a situation of equality, it is an open question whether the principle of utility would be acknowledged. Offhand it hardly seems likely that persons who view themselves as equals, entitled to press their claims upon one another, would agree to a principle which may require lesser life prospects for some simply for the sake of a greater sum of advantages enjoyed by others. Since each desires to protect his interests, his capacity to advance his conception of the good, no one has a reason to acquiesce in an enduring loss for himself in order to bring about a greater net balance of satisfaction. In the absence of strong and lasting benevolent impulses, a rational man would not accept a basic structure merely because it maximized the algebraic sum of advantages irrespective of its permanent effects on his own basic rights and interests. Thus it seems that the principle of utility is incompatible with the conception of social cooperation among equals for mutual advantage. It appears to be inconsistent with the idea of reciprocity implicit in the notion of a well-ordered society. Or, at any rate, so I shall argue.

I shall maintain instead that the persons in the initial situation would choose two rather different principles : the first requires equality in the assignment of basic rights and duties, while the second holds that social and economic inequalities, for example inequalities of wealth and authority, are just only if they result in compensating benefits for everyone, and in particular for the least advantaged members of society. These principles rule out justifying institutions on the grounds that the hardships of some are offset by a greater good in the aggregate. It may be expedient but it is not just that some should have less in order that others may prosper. But there is no injustice in the greater benefits earned by a few provided that the situation of persons not so fortunate is thereby improved. The intuitive idea is that since everyone's well-being depends upon a scheme of cooperation without which no one could have a satisfactory life, the division of advantages should be such as to draw forth the willing cooperation of everyone taking part in it, including those less well situated. Yet this can be expected only if reasonable terms are proposed. The two principles mentioned seem to be a fair agreement on the basis of which those better endowed, or more fortunate in their social position, neither of which we can be said to deserve, could expect the willing cooperation of others when some workable scheme is a necessary condition of the welfare of all. Once we decide to look for a conception of justice that nullifies the accidents of natural endowment and the contingencies of social circumstance as counters in quest for political and economic advantage, we are led to these principles. They express the result of leaving aside those aspects of the social world that seem arbitrary from a moral point of view.

The problem of the choice of principles, however, is extremely difficult. I do not expect the answer I shall suggest to be convincing to everyone. It is, therefore, worth noting from the outset that justice as fairness, like other contract views, consists of two parts : (1) an interpretation of the initial situation and of the problem of choice posed there, and (2) a set of principles which, it is argued, would be agreed to. One may accept the first part of the theory (or some variant thereof), but not the other, and conversely. The concept of the initial contractual situation may seem reasonable although the particular principles proposed are rejected. To be sure, I want to maintain that the most appropriate conception of this situation does lead to principles of justice contrary to utilitarianism and perfectionism, and therefore that the contract doctrine provides an alternative to these views. Still, one may dispute this contention even though one grants that the contractarian method is a useful way of studying ethical theories and of setting forth their underlying assumptions....

The merit of the contract terminology is that it conveys the idea that principles of justice may be conceived as principles that would be chosen by rational persons, and that in this way conceptions of justice may be explained and justified. The theory of justice is a part, perhaps the most significant part, of the theory of rational choice. Furthermore, principles of justice deal with conflicting claims upon the advantages won by social cooperation ; they apply to the relations among several persons or groups. The word "contract" suggests this plurality as well as the condition that the appropriate division of advantages must be in accordance with principles acceptable to all parties. The condition of publicity for principles of justice is also connoted by the contract phraseology. Thus, if these principles are the outcome of an agreement, citizens have a knowledge of the principles that others follow. It is characteristic of contract theories to stress the public nature of political principles. Finally there is the long tradition of the contract doctrine. Expressing the tie with this line of thought helps to define ideas and accords with natural piety. There are then several advantages in the use of the term "contract." With due precautions taken, it should not be misleading....

The Original Position and Justification

I have said that the original position is the appropriate initial status quo which insures that the fundamental agreements reached in it are fair. This fact yields the name "justice as fairness." It is clear, then, that I want to say that one conception of justice is more reasonable than another, or justifiable with respect to it, if rational persons in the initial situation would choose its principles over those of the other for the role of justice. Conceptions of justice are to be ranked by their acceptability to persons so circumstanced. Understood in this way the question of justification is settled by working out a problem of deliberation : we have to ascertain which principles it would be rational to adopt given the contractual situation. This connects the theory of justice with the theory of rational choice.

If this view of the problem of justification is to succeed, we must, of course, describe in some detail the nature of this choice problem. A problem of rational decision has a definite answer only if we know the beliefs and interests of the parties, their relations with respect to one another, the alternatives between which they are to choose, the procedure whereby they make up their minds, and so on. As the circumstances are presented in different ways, correspondingly different principles are accepted. The concept of the original position, as I shall refer to it, is that of the most philosophically favoured interpretation of this initial choice situation for the purposes of a theory of justice.

But how are we to decide which is the most favoured interpretation ? I assume, for one thing, that there is a broad measure of agreement that principles of justice should be chosen under certain conditions. To justify a particular description of the initial situation one shows that it incorporates these commonly shared presumptions. One argues from widely accepted but weak premises to more specific conclusions. Each of the presumptions should by itself be natural and plausible ; some of them may seem innocuous or even trivial. The aim of the contract approach is to establish that taken together they impose significant bounds on acceptable principles of justice. The ideal outcome would be that these conditions determine a unique set of principles ; but I shall be satisfied if they suffice to rank the main traditional conceptions of social justice.

One should not be misled, then, by the somewhat unusual conditions which characterize the original position. The idea here is simply to make vivid to ourselves the restrictions that it seems reasonable to impose on arguments for principles of justice, and therefore on these principles themselves. Thus it seems reasonable and generally acceptable that no one should be advantaged or disadvantaged by natural fortune or social circumstances in the choice of principles. It also seems widely agreed that it should be impossible to tailor principles to the circumstances of one's own case. We should insure further that particular inclinations and aspirations, and persons' conceptions of their good do not affect the principles adopted. The aim is to rule out those principles that it would be rational to propose for acceptance, however little the chance of success, only if one knew certain things that are irrelevant from the standpoint of justice. For example, if a man knew that he was wealthy, he might find it rational to advance the principle that various taxes for welfare measures be counted unjust ; if he knew that he was poor, he would most likely propose the contrary principle. To represent the desired restrictions one imagines a situation in which everyone is deprived of this sort of information. One excludes the knowledge of those contingencies which sets men at odds and allows them to be guided by their prejudices. In this manner the veil of ignorance is arrived at in a natural way. This concept should cause no difficulty if we keep in mind the constraints on arguments that it is meant to express. At any time we can enter the original position, so to speak, simply by following a certain procedure, namely, by arguing for principles of justice in accordance with these restrictions.

It seems reasonable to suppose that the parties in the original position are equal. That is, all have the same rights in the procedure for choosing principles ; each can make proposals, submit reasons for their acceptance, and so on. Obviously the purpose of these conditions is to represent equality between human beings as moral persons, as creatures having a conception of their good and capable of a sense of justice. The basis of equality is taken to be similarity in these two respects. Systems of ends are not ranked in value ; and each man is presumed to have the requisite ability to understand and to act upon whatever principles are adopted. Together with the veil of ignorance, these conditions define the principles of justice as those which rational persons concerned to advance their interests would consent to as equals when none are known to be advantaged or disadvantaged by social and natural contingencies.... [pp. 11-19]

Two Principles of Justice

I shall now state in a provisional form the two principles of justice that I believe would be chosen in the original position. . . .

The first statement of the two principles reads as follows :

First : each person is to have an equal right to the most extensive basic liberty compatible with a similar liberty for others.

Second : social and economic inequalities are to be arranged so that they are both (a) reasonably expected to be to everyone's advantage, and (b) attached to positions and offices open to all....

By way of general comment, these principles primarily apply, as I have said, to the basic structure of society. They are to govern the assignment of rights and duties and to regulate the distribution of social and economic advantages. As their formulation suggests, these principles presuppose that the social structure can be divided into two more or less distinct parts, the first principle applying to the one, the second to the other. They distinguish between those aspects of the social system that define and secure the equal liberties of citizenship and those that specify and establish social and economic inequalities. The basic liberties of citizens are, roughly speaking, political liberty (the right to vote and to be eligible for public office) together with freedom of speech and assembly ; liberty of conscience and freedom of thought ; freedom of the person along with the right to hold (personal) property ; and freedom from arbitrary arrest and seizure as defined by the concept of the rule of law. These liberties are all required to be equal by the first principle, since citizens of a just society are to have the same basic rights.

The second principle applies, in the first approximation, to the distribution of income and wealth and to the design of organizations that make use of differences in authority and responsibility, or chains of command. While the distribution of wealth and income need not be equal, it must be to everyone's advantage, and at the same time, positions of authority and offices of command must be accessible to all. One applies the second principle by holding positions open, and then, subject to this constraint, arranges social and economic inequalities so that everyone benefits.

These principles are to be arranged in a serial order with the first principle prior to the second. This ordering means that a departure from the institutions of equal liberty required by the first principle cannot be justified by, or compensated for, by greater social and economic advantages. The distribution of wealth and income, and the hierarchies of authority, must be consistent with both the liberties of equal citizenship and equality of opportunity.... [pp. 60-61]

The Veil of Ignorance

The idea of the original position is to set up a fair procedure so that any principles agreed to will be just. The aim is to use the notion of pure procedural justice as a basis of theory. Somehow we must nullify the effects of specific contingencies which put men at odds and tempt them to exploit social and natural circumstances to their own advantage. Now in order to do this I assume that the parties are situated behind a veil of ignorance. They do not know how the various alternatives will affect their own particular case and they are obliged to evaluate principles solely on the basis of general considerations.

It is assumed, then, that the parties do not know certain kinds of particular facts. First of all, no one knows his place in society, his class position or social status; nor does he know his fortune in the distribution of natural assets and abilities, his intelligence and strength, and the like. Nor, again, does anyone know his conception of the good, the particulars of his rational plan of life, or even the special features of his psychology such as his aversion to risk or liability to optimism or pessimism. More than this, I assume that the parties do not know the particular circumstances of their own society. That is, they do not know its economic or political situation, or the level of civilization and culture it has been able to achieve. The persons in the original position have no information as to which generation they belong. These broader restrictions on knowledge are appropriate in part because questions of social justice arise between generations as well as within them, for example, the question of the appropriate rate of capital saving and of the conservation of natural resources and the environment of nature. There is also, theoretically anyway, the question of a reasonable genetic policy. In these cases too, in order to carry through the idea of the original position, the parties must not know the contingencies that set them in opposition. They must choose principles the consequences of which they are prepared to live with whatever generation they turn out to belong to.

As far as possible, then, the only particular facts which the parties know is that their society is subject to the circumstances of justice and whatever this implies. It is taken for granted, however, that they know the general facts about human society. They understand political affairs and the principles of economic theory; they know the basis of social organization and the laws of human psychology. Indeed, the parties are presumed to know whatever general facts affect the choice of the principles of justice. There are no limitations on general information, that is, on general laws and theories, since conceptions of justice must be adjusted to the characteristics of the systems of social cooperation which they are to regulate, and there is no reason to rule out these facts. It is, for example, a consideration against a conception of justice that in view of the laws of moral psychology, men would not acquire a desire to act upon it even when the institutions of their society satisfied it. For in this case there would be difficulty in securing the stability of social cooperation. It is an important feature of a conception of justice that it should generate its own support. That is, its principles should be such that when they are embodied in the basic structure of society men tend to acquire the corresponding sense of justice. Given the principles of moral learning, men develop a desire to act in accordance with its principles. In this case a conception of justice is stable. This kind of general information is admissible in the original position.... [pp. 136-138]

Background Institutions for Distributive Justice

The main problem of distributive justice is the choice of a social system. The principles of justice apply to the basic structure and regulate how its major institutions are combined into one scheme. Now, as we have seen, the idea of justice as fairness is to use the notion of pure procedural justice to handle the contingencies of particular situations. The social system is to be designed so that the resulting distribution is just however things turn out. To achieve this end it is necessary to set the social and economic process within the surroundings of suitable political and legal institutions. Without the proper arrangement of these background institutions the outcome of the distributive process will not be just. Background fairness is lacking. I shall give a brief description of these background institutions as they might exist in a properly organized democratic state that allows private ownership of capital and natural resources. These arrangements are familiar, but it may be useful to see how they fit the two principles of justice. Modifications for the case of a socialist regime will be considered briefly later.

First of all, I assume that the basic structure is regulated by a just constitution that secures the liberties of equal citizenship.... Liberty of conscience and freedom of thought are taken for granted, and the fair value of political liberty is maintained. The political process is conducted, as far as circumstances permit, as a just procedure for choosing between governments and for enacting just legislation. I assume also that there is fair (as opposed to formal) equality of opportunity. This means that in addition to maintaining the usual kinds of social overhead capital, the government tries to insure equal chances of education and culture for persons similarly endowed and motivated either by subsidizing private schools or by establishing a public school system. It also enforces and underwrites equality of opportunity in economic activities and in the free choice of occupation. This is achieved by policing the conduct of firms and private associations and by preventing the establishment of monopolistic restrictions and barriers to the more desirable positions. Finally, the government guarantees a social minimum either by family allowances and special payments for sickness and employment, or more systematically by such devices as a graded income supplement (a so-called negative income tax).

In establishing these background institutions the government may be thought of as divided into four branches. Each branch consists of various agencies, or activities thereof, charged with preserving certain social and economic conditions. These divisions do not overlap with the usual organization of government but are to be understood as different functions. The allocation branch, for example, is to keep the price system workably competitive and to prevent the formation of unreasonable market power. Such power does not exist as long as markets cannot be made more competitive consistent with the requirements of efficiency and the facts of geography and the preferences of households. The allocation branch is also charged with identifying and correcting, say by suitable taxes and subsidies and by changes in the definition of property rights, the more obvious departures from efficiency caused by the failure of prices to measure accurately social benefits and costs. To this end suitable taxes and subsidies may be used, or the scope and definition of property rights may be revised. The stabilization branch, on the other hand, strives to bring about reasonably full employment in the sense that those who want work can find it and the free choice of occupation and the deployment of finance is supported by strong effective demand. These two branches together are to maintain the efficiency of the market economy generally.

The social minimum is the responsibility of the transfer branch.... The essential idea is that the workings of this branch takes needs into account and assigns them an appropriate weight with respect to other claims. A competitive price system gives no consideration to needs and therefore it cannot be the sole device of distribution. There must be a division of labour between the parts of the social system in answering to the commonsense precepts of justice. Different institutions meet different claims. Competitive markets properly regulated secure free choice of occupation and lead to an efficient use of resources and allocation of commodities to households. They set a weight on the conventional precepts associated with wages and earnings, whereas the transfer branch guarantees a certain level of well-being and honours the claims of need. Eventually I will discuss these commonsense precepts and how they arise within the context of various institutions. The relevant point here is that certain precepts tend to be associated with specific institutions. It is left to the background system as a whole to determine how these precepts are balanced. Since the principles of justice regulate the whole structure, they also regulate the balance of precepts. In general, then, this balance will vary in accordance with the underlying political conception.

It is clear that the justice of distributive shares depends on the background institutions and how they allocate total income, wages and other income plus transfers. There is with reason strong objection to the competitive determination of total income, since this ignores the claims of need and an appropriate standard of life. From the standpoint of the legislative stage it is rational to insure oneself and one's descendants against these contingencies of the market. Indeed, the difference principle presumably requires this. But once a suitable minimum is provided by transfers, it may be perfectly fair that the rest of total income be settled by the price system, assuming that it is moderately efficient and free from monopolistic restrictions, and unreasonable externalities have been eliminated. Moreover, this way of dealing with the claims of need would appear to be more effective than trying to regulate income by minimum wage standards, and the like. It is better to assign to each branch only such tasks as are compatible with one another. Since the market is not suited to answer the claims of need, these should be met by a separate arrangement. Whether the principles of justice are satisfied, then, turns on whether the total income of the least advantaged (wages plus transfers) is such as to maximize their long-run expectations (consistent with the constraints of equal liberty and fair equality of opportunity).

Finally, there is a distribution branch. Its task is to preserve an approximate justice in distributive shares by means of taxation and the necessary adjustments in the rights of property. Two aspects of this branch may be distinguished. First of all, it imposes a number of inheritance and gift taxes, and sets restrictions on the rights of bequest. The purpose of these levies and regulations is not to raise revenue (release resources to government) but gradually and continually to correct the distribution of wealth and to prevent concentrations of power detrimental to the fair value of political liberty and fair equality of opportunity. For example, the progressive principle might be applied at the beneficiary's end. Doing this would encourage the wide dispersal of property which is a necessary condition, it seems, if the fair value of the equal liberties is to be maintained. The unequal inheritance of wealth is no more inherently unjust than the unequal inheritance of intelligence. It is true that the former is presumably more easily subject to social control; but the essential thing is that as far as possible inequalities founded on either should satisfy the difference principle. Thus inheritance is permissible provided that the resulting inequalities are to the advantage of the least fortunate and compatible with liberty and fair equality of opportunity. As earlier defined, fair equality of opportunity means a certain set of institutions that assures similar chances of education and culture for persons similarly motivated and keeps positions and offices open to all on the basis of qualities and efforts reasonably related to the relevant duties and tasks. It is these institutions that are put in jeopardy when inequalities of wealth exceed a certain limit ; and political liberty likewise tends to lose its value, and representative government to become such in appearance only. The taxes and enactments of the distribution branch are to prevent this limit from being exceeded. Naturally, where this limit lies is a matter of political judgment guided by theory, good sense, and plain hunch, at least within a wide range. On this sort of question the theory of justice has nothing specific to say. Its aim is to formulate the principles that are to regulate the background institutions.

The second part of the distribution branch is a scheme of taxation to raise the revenues that justice requires. Social resources must be released to the government so that it can provide for the public goods and make the transfer payments necessary to satisfy the difference principle. This problem belongs to the distribution branch since the burden of taxation is to be justly shared and it aims at establishing just arrangements. Leaving aside many complications, it is worth noting that a proportional expenditure tax may be part of the best tax scheme. For one thing, it is preferable to an income tax (of any kind) at the level of commonsense precepts of justice, since it imposes a levy according to how much a person takes out of the common store of goods and not according to how much he contributes (assuming here that income is fairly earned). Again, a proportional tax on total consumption (for each year say) can contain the usual exemptions for dependents, and so on ; and it treats everyone in a uniform way (still assuming that income is fairly earned). It may be better, therefore, to use progressive rates only when they are necessary to preserve the justice of the basic structure with respect to the first principle of justice and fair equality of opportunity, and so to forestall accumulations of property and power likely to undermine the corresponding institutions. Following this rule might help to signal an important distinction in questions of policy. And if proportional taxes should also prove more efficient, say because they interfere less with incentives, this might make the case for them decisive if a feasible scheme could be worked out. As before, these are questions of political judgment and not part of a theory of justice. And in any case we are here considering such a proportional tax as part of an ideal scheme for a well-ordered society in order to illustrate the content of the two principles. It does not follow that, given the injustice of existing institutions, even steeply progressive income taxes are not justified when all things are considered. In practice we must usually choose between several unjust, or second best, arrangements ; and then we look to nonideal theory to find the least unjust scheme. Sometimes this scheme will include measures and policies that a perfectly just system would reject. Two wrongs can make a right in the sense that the best available arrangement may contain a balance of imperfections, an adjustment of compensating injustices.

The two parts of the distribution branch derive from the two principles of justice. The taxation of inheritance and income at progressive rates (when necessary), and the legal definition of property rights, are to secure the institutions of equal liberty in a property-owning democracy and the fair value of the rights they establish. Proportional expenditure (or income) taxes are to provide revenue for public goods, the transfer branch and the establishment of fair equality of opportunity in education, and the like, so as to carry out the second principle. No mention has been made at any point of the traditional criteria of taxation such as that taxes are to be levied according to benefits received or the ability to pay. The reference to commonsense precepts in connection with expenditure taxes is a subordinate consideration. The scope of these criteria is regulated by the principles of justice. Once the problem of distributive shares is recognized as that of designing background institutions, the conventional maxims are seen to have no independent force, however appropriate they may be in certain delimited cases. To suppose otherwise is not to take a sufficiently comprehensive point of view.... It is evident also that the design of the distribution branch does not presuppose the utilitarian's standard assumptions about individual utilities. Inheritance and progressive income taxes, for example, are not predicated on the idea that individuals have similar utility functions satisfying the diminishing marginal principle. The aim of the distribution branch is not, of course, to maximize the net balance of satisfaction but to establish just background institutions. Doubts about the shape of utility functions are irrelevant. This problem is one for the utilitarian, not for contract theory.

So far I have assumed that the aim of the branches of government is to establish a democratic regime in which land and capital are widely though not presumably equally held. Society is not so divided that one fairly small sector controls the preponderance of productive resources. When this is achieved and distributive shares satisfy the principles of justice, many socialist criticisms of the market economy are met. But it is clear that, in theory anyway, a liberal socialist regime can also answer to the two principles of justice. We have only to suppose that the means of production are publicly owned and that firms are managed by workers' councils say, or by agents appointed by them. Collective decisions made democratically under the constitution determine the general features of the economy, such as the rate of saving and the proportion of society's production devoted to essential public goods. Given the resulting economic environment, firms regulated by market forces conduct themselves much as before. Although the background institutions will take a different form, especially in the case of the distribution branch, there is no reason in principle why just distributive shares cannot be achieved. The theory of justice does not by itself favour either form of regime. As we have seen, the decision as to which system is best for a given people depends upon their circumstances, institutions, and historical traditions.... [pp. 274-280]

. . . I now wish to give the final statement of the two principles of justice for institutions. For the sake of completeness, I shall give a full statement including earlier formulations.

First Principle

> Each person is to have an equal right to the most extensive total system of equal basic liberties compatible with a similar system of liberty for all.

Second Principle

Social and economic inequalities are to be arranged so that they are both :
(a) to the greatest benefit of the least advantaged, consistent with the just savings principle, and
(b) attached to offices and positions open to all under conditions of fair equality of opportunity.

First Priority Rule (The Priority of Liberty)

The principles of justice are to be ranked in lexical order and therefore liberty can be restricted only for the sake of liberty.
There are two cases :
(a) a less extensive liberty must strengthen the total system of liberty shared by all ;
(b) a less than equal liberty must be acceptable to those with the lesser liberty.

Second Priority Rule (The Priority of Justice over Efficiency and Welfare)

The second principle of justice is lexically prior to the principle of efficiency and to that of maximizing the sum of advantages ; and fair opportunity is prior to the difference principle. There are two cases :
(a) an inequality of opportunity must enhance the opportunities of those with the lesser opportunity ;
(b) an excessive rate of saving must on balance mitigate the burden of those bearing this hardship.

General Conception

All social primary goods — liberty and opportunity, income and wealth, and the bases of self-respect — are to be distributed equally unless an unequal distribution of any or all of these goods is to the advantage of the least favoured. [pp. 302-303]

NOTE

1. John Rawls, *A Theory of Justice* (Cambridge, Mass. : The Belknap Press of Harvard University Press, 1971), pp. 11-303.

TAKING RIGHTS SERIOUSLY[1]

Ronald Dworkin

Rights and the Right to Break the Law

There is a clear difference between saying that someone has a right to do something in this sense and saying that it is the "right" thing for him to do, or that he does no "wrong" in doing it. Someone may have the right to do something that is the wrong thing for him to do, as might be the case with gambling. Conversely, something may be the right thing for him to do and yet he may have no right to do it, in the sense that it would not be wrong for someone to interfere with his trying. If our army captures an enemy soldier, we might say that the right thing for him to do is to try to escape, but it would not follow that it is wrong for us to try to stop him. We might admire him for trying to escape, and perhaps even think less of him if he did not. But there is no suggestion here that it is wrong of us to stand in his way ; on the contrary, if we think our cause is just, we think it right for us to do all we can to stop him.

Ordinarily this distinction, between the issues of whether a man has a right to do something and whether it is the right thing for him to do, causes no trouble. But sometimes it does, because sometimes we say that a man has a right to do something when we mean only to deny that it is the wrong thing for him to do. Thus we say that the captured soldier has a "right" to try to escape when we mean, not that we do wrong to stop him, but that he has no duty not to make the attempt. We use "right" this way when we speak of someone having the "right" to act on his own principles, or the "right" to follow his own conscience. We mean that he does no wrong to proceed on his honest convictions, even though we disagree with these convictions, and even though, for policy or other reasons, we must force him to act contrary to them.

Suppose a man believes that welfare payments to the poor are profoundly wrong, because they sap enterprise, and so declares his full income-tax each year but declines to pay half of it. We might say that he has a right to refuse to pay, if he wishes, but the government has a right to proceed against him for the full tax, and to fine or jail him for late payment if that is necessary to keep the collection system working efficiently. We do not take this line in most cases ; we do not say that the ordinary thief has a right to steal, if he wishes, so long as he pays the penalty. We say a man has the right to break the law, even though the state has a right to punish him, only when we think that, because of his convictions, he does no wrong in doing so.

These distinctions enable us to see an ambiguity in the orthodox question : Does a man ever have a right to break the law ? Does that question mean to ask whether he ever has a right to break the law in the strong sense, so that the government would do wrong to stop him, by arresting and prosecuting him ? Or does it mean to ask whether he ever does the right thing to break the law, so that we should all respect him even though the government should jail him ?

If we take the orthodox position to be an answer to the first — and most important — question, then . . . paradoxes . . . arise. But if we take it as an answer to the second, they do not. Conservatives and liberals do agree that sometimes a man does not do the wrong thing to break a law, when his conscience so requires. They disagree, when they do, over the different issue of what the state's response should be. Both parties do think that sometimes the state should prosecute. But this is not inconsistent with the proposition that the man prosecuted did the right thing in breaking the law.

The paradoxes seem genuine because the two questions are not usually distinguished, and the orthodox position is presented as a general solution to the problem of civil disobedience. But once the distinction is made, it is apparent that the position has been so widely accepted only because, when it is applied, it is treated as an answer to the second question but not the first. The crucial distinction is obscured by the troublesome idea of a right to conscience ; this idea has been at the centre of most recent discussions of political obligation, but it is a red herring drawing us away from the crucial political questions. The state of a man's conscience may be decisive, or central, when the issue is whether he does something morally wrong in breaking the law ; but it need not be decisive or even central when the issue is whether he has a right, in the strong sense of that term, to do so. A man does not have the right, in that sense, to do whatever his conscience demands, but he may have the right, in that sense, to do something even though his conscience does not demand it.

If that is true, then there has been almost no serious attempt to answer the questions that almost everyone means to ask. We can make a fresh start by stating these questions more clearly. Does an American ever have the right, in a strong sense, to do something which is against the law ? If so, when ? In order to answer these questions put in that way, we must try to become clearer about the implications of the idea, mentioned earlier, that citizens have at least some rights against their government.

I said that in the United States citizens are supposed to have certain fundamental rights against their government, certain moral rights made into legal rights by the Constitution. If this idea is significant, and worth bragging about, then these rights must be rights in the strong sense I just described. The claim that citizens have a right to free speech must imply that it would be wrong for the government to stop them from speaking, even when the government believes that what they will say will cause more harm than good. The claim cannot mean, on the prisoner-of-war analogy, only that citizens do no wrong in speaking their minds, though the government reserves the right to prevent them from doing so.

This is a crucial point, and I want to labour it. Of course a responsible government must be ready to justify anything it does, particularly when it limits the liberty of its citizens. But normally it is a sufficient justification, even for an act that limits liberty, that the act is calculated to increase what the philosophers call general utility — that it is calculated to produce more over-all benefit than harm. So, though the New York City government needs a justification for forbidding motorists to drive up Lexington Avenue, it is sufficient justification if the proper officials believe, on sound evidence, that the gain to the many will outweigh the inconvenience to the few. When individual citizens are said to have rights against the government, however, like the right of free speech, that must mean that this sort of justification is not enough. Otherwise the claim would not argue that individuals have special protection against the law when their rights are in play, and that is just the point of the claim.

Not all legal rights, or even constitutional rights, represent moral rights against the government. I now have the legal right to drive either way on Fifty-seventh Street, but the government would do no wrong to make that street one-way if it thought it in the general interest to do so. I have a constitutional right to vote for a congressman every two years, but the national and state governments would do no wrong if, following the amendment procedure, they made a congressman's term four years instead of two, again on the basis of a judgment that this would be for the general good.

But those constitutional rights that we call fundamental like the right of free speech, are supposed to represent rights against the government in the strong sense ; that is the point of the boast that our legal system respects the fundamental rights of the citizen. If citizens have a moral right of free speech, then governments would do wrong to repeal the First Amendment that guarantees it, even if they were persuaded that the majority would be better off if speech were curtailed.

I must not overstate the point. Someone who claims that citizens have a right against the government need not go so far as to say that the state is *never* justified in overriding that right. He might say, for example, that although citizens have a right to free speech, the government may override that right when necessary to protect the rights of others, or to prevent a catastrophe, or even to obtain a clear and major public benefit (though if he acknowledged this last as a possible justification he would be treating the right in question as not among the most important or fundamental). What he cannot do is to say that the government is justified in overriding a right on the minimal grounds that would be sufficient if no such right existed. He cannot say that the government is entitled to act on no more than a judgment that its act is likely to produce, overall, a benefit to the community. That admission would make his claim of a right pointless, and would show him to be using some sense of "right" other than the strong sense necessary to give his claim the political importance it is normally taken to have.

But then the answers to our two questions about disobedience seem plain, if unorthodox. In our society a man does sometimes have the right, in the strong sense, to disobey a law. He has that right whenever that law wrongly invades his rights against the government. If he has a moral right to free speech, that is, then he has a moral right to break any law that the government, by virtue of his right, had no right to adopt. The right to disobey the law is not a separate right, having something to do with conscience, additional to other rights against the government. It is simply a feature of these rights against the government, and it cannot be denied in principle without denying that any such rights exist.

These answers seem obvious once we take rights against the government to be rights in the strong sense I described. If I have a right to speak my mind on political issues, then the government does wrong to make it illegal for me to do so, even if it thinks this is in the general interest. If, nevertheless, the government does make my act illegal, then it does a further wrong to enforce that law against me. My right against the government means that it is wrong for the government to stop me from speaking, the government cannot make it right to stop me just by taking the first step.... [pp. 188-192]

The individual rights that our society acknowledges often conflict... and when they do it is the job of government to discriminate. If the government makes the right choice, and protects the more important at the cost of the less, then it has not weakened or cheapened the notion of a right ; on the contrary it would have done so had it failed to protect the more important of the two. So we must acknowledge that the government has a reason for limiting rights if it plausibly believes that a competing right is more important.

May the conservative seize on this fact ? He might argue that I did wrong to characterize his argument as one that appeals to the general benefit, because it appeals instead to competing rights, namely the moral right of the majority to have its laws enforced, or the right of society to maintain the degree or order and security it wishes. These are the rights, he would say, that must be weighed against the individual's right to do what the wrongful law prohibits.

But this new argument is confused, because it depends on yet another ambiguity in the language of rights. It is true that we speak of the "right" of society to do what it wants, but this cannot be a "competing right" of the sort that may justify the invasion of a right against the government. The existence of rights against the government would be jeopardized if the government were able to defeat such a right by appealing to the right of a democratic majority to work its will. A right against the government must be a right to do something even when the majority thinks it would be wrong to do it, and even when the majority would be worse off for having it done. If we now say that society has a right to do whatever is in the general benefit, or the right to preserve whatever sort of environment the majority wishes to live in, and we mean that these are the sorts of rights that provide justification for overruling any rights against the government that may conflict, then we have annihilated the latter rights.

In order to save them, we must recognize as competing rights only the rights of other members of the society as individuals. We must distinguish the "rights" of the majority as such, which cannot count as a justifiction for overruling individual rights, and the personal rights of members of a majority, which might well count. The test we must use is this. Someone has a competing right to protection, which must be weighed against an individual right to act, if that person would be entitled to demand that protection from his government on his own title, as an individual, without regard to whether a majority of his fellow citizens joined in the demand.

It cannot be true, on this test, that anyone has a right to have all the laws of the nation enforced. He has a right to have enforced only those criminal laws, for example, that he would have a right to have enacted if they were not already law. The laws against personal assault may well fall into that class. If the physically vulnerable members of the community — those who need police protection against personal violence — were only a small minority, it would still seem plausible to say that they were entitled to that protection. But the laws that provide a certain level of quiet in public places, or that authorize and finance a foreign war, cannot be thought to rest on individual rights. The timid lady on the streets of Chicago is not entitled to just the degree of quiet that she now obtains, nor is she entitled to have boys drafted to fight in wars she approves. There are laws — perhaps desirable laws — that provide these advantages for her, but the justification for these laws, if they can be justified at all, is the common desire of a large majority, not her personal right. If, therefore, these laws do abridge someone else's moral right to protest, or his right to personal security, she cannot urge a competing right to justify the abridgement. She has no personal right to have such laws passed, and she has no competing right to have them enforced either.

So the conservative cannot advance his argument much on the ground of competing rights, but he may want to use another ground. A government, he may argue, may be justified in abridging the personal rights of its citizens in an emergency, or when a very great loss may be prevented, or perhaps, when some major benefit can clearly be secured. If the nation is at war, a policy of censorship may be justified even though it invades the right to say what one thinks on matters of political controversy. But the emergency must be genuine. There must be what Oliver Wendell Holmes described as a clear and present danger, and the danger must be one of magnitude.

Can the conservative argue that when any law is passed, even a wrongful law, this sort of justification is available for enforcing it ? His argument might be something of this sort. If the government once acknowledges that it may be wrong — that the legislature might have adopted, the executive approved, and the courts left standing, a law that in fact abridges important rights — then this admission will lead not simply to a marginal decline in respect for law, but to a crisis of order. Citizens may decide to obey only those laws they personally approve, and that is anarchy. So the government must insist that whatever a citizen's rights may be before a law is passed and upheld by the courts, his rights thereafter are determined by that law.

But this argument ignores the primitive distinction between what may happen and what will happen. If we allow speculation to support the justification of emergency or decisive benefit, then, again, we have annihilated rights. We must, as Learned Hand said, discount the gravity of the evil threatened by the likelihood of reaching that evil. I know of no genuine evidence to the effect that tolerating some civil disobedience, out of respect for the moral position of its authors, will increase such disobedience, let alone crime in general. The case that it will must be based on vague assumptions about the contagion of ordinary crimes, assumptions that are themselves unproved, and that are in any event largely irrelevant. It seems at least as plausible to argue that tolerance will increase respect for officials and for the bulk of the laws they promulgate, or at least retard the rate of growing disrespect.

If the issue were simply the question whether the community would be marginally better off under strict law enforcement, then the government would have to decide on the evidence we have, and it might not be unreasonable to decide, on balance, that it would. But since rights are at stake, the issue is the very different one of whether tolerance would destroy the community or threaten it with great harm, and it seems to me simply mindless to suppose that the evidence makes that probable or even conceivable.

The argument from emergency is confused in another way as well. It assumes that the government must take the position either that a man never has the right to break the law, or that he always does. I said that any society that claims to recognize rights at all must abandon the notion of a general duty to obey the law that holds in all cases. This is important, because it shows that there are no short cuts to meeting a citizen's claim to right. If a citizen argues that he has a moral right not to serve in the army, or to protest in a way he finds effective, then an official who wants to answer him, and not simply bludgeon him into obedience, must respond to the particular point he makes, and cannot point to the draft law or a Supreme Court decision as having even special, let alone decisive, weight. Sometimes an official who considers the citizen's moral arguments in good faith will be persuaded that the citizen's claim is plausible, or even right. It does not follow, however, that he will always be persuaded or that he always should be.

I must emphasize that all these propositions concern the strong sense of right, and they therefore leave open important questions about the right thing to do. If a man believes he has the right to break the law, he must then ask whether he does the right thing to exercise that right. He must remember that reasonable men can differ about whether he has a right against the government, and therefore the right to break the law, that he thinks he has ; and therefore that reasonable men can oppose him in good faith. He must take into account the various consequences his acts will have, whether they involve violence, and such other considerations as the context makes relevant ; he must not go beyond the rights he can in good faith claim, to acts that violate the rights of others....

Controversial Rights

The argument so far has been hypothetical : if a man has a particular moral right against the government, that right survives contrary legislation or adjudication. But this does not tell us what rights he has, and it is notorious that reasonable men disagree about that. There is wide agreement on certain clearcut cases ; almost everyone who believes in rights at all would admit, for example, that a man has a moral right to speak his mind in a non-provocative way on matters of political concern, and that this is an important right that the state must go to great pains to protect. But there is great controversy as to the limits of such paradigm rights, and the so-called "anti-riot" law involved in the famous Chicago Seven trial of the last decade is a case in point.

The defendants were accused of conspiring to cross state lines with the intention of causing a riot. This charge is vague — perhaps unconstitutionally vague — but the law apparently defines as criminal emotional speeches which argue that violence is justified in order to secure political equality. Does the right of free speech protect this sort of speech ? That, of course, is a legal issue, because it invokes the free-speech clause of the First Amendment of the Constitution. But it is also a moral issue, because, as I said, we must treat the First Amendment as an attempt to protect a moral right. It is part of the job of governing to "define" moral rights through statutes and judicial decisions, that is, to declare officially the extent that moral rights will be taken to have in law. Congress faced this task in voting on the anti-riot bill, and the Supreme Court has faced it in countless cases. How should the different departments of government go about defining moral rights ?

They should begin with a sense that whatever they decide might be wrong. History and their descendants may judge that they acted unjustly when they thought they were right. If they take their duty seriously, they must try to limit their mistakes, and they must therefore try to discover where the dangers of mistake lie.

They might choose one of two very different models for this purpose. The first model recommends striking a balance between the rights of the individual and the demands of society at large. If the government *infringes* on a moral right (for example, by defining the right of free speech more narrowly than justice requires), then it has done the individual a wrong. On the other hand, if the government *inflates* a right (by defining it more broadly than justice requires) then it cheats society of some general benefit, like safe streets, that there is no reason it should not have. So a mistake on one side is as serious as a mistake on the other. The course of government is to steer to the middle, to balance the general good and personal rights, giving to each its due.

When the government, or any of its branches, defines a right, it must bear in mind, according to the first model, the social cost of different proposals and make the necessary adjustments. It must not grant the same freedom to noisy demonstrations as it grants to calm political discussion, for example, because the former causes much more trouble than the latter. Once it decides how much of a right to recognize, it must enforce its decision to the full. That means permitting an individual to act within his rights, as the government has defined them, but not beyond, so that if anyone breaks the law, even on grounds of conscience, he must be punished. No doubt any government will make mistakes, and will regret decisions once taken. That is inevitable. But this middle policy will ensure that errors on one side will balance out errors on the other over the long run.

The first model, described in this way, has great plausibility, and most laymen and lawyers, I think, would respond to it warmly. The metaphor of balancing the public interest against personal claims is established in our political and judicial rhetoric, and this metaphor gives the model both familiarity and appeal.

Nevertheless, the first model is a false one, certainly in the case of rights generally regarded as important, and the metaphor is the heart of its error.

The institution of rights against the government is not a gift of God, or an ancient ritual, or a national sport. It is a complex and troublesome practice that makes the government's job of securing the general benefit more difficult and more expensive, and it would be a frivolous and wrongful practice unless it served some point. Anyone who professes to take rights seriously, and who praises our government for respecting them, must have some sense of what the point is. He must accept, at the minimum, one or both of two important ideas. The first is the vague but powerful idea of human dignity. This idea, associated with Kant, but defended by philosophers of different schools, supposes that there are ways of treating a man that are inconsistent with recognizing him as a full member of the human community, and holds that such treatment is profoundly unjust.

The second is the more familiar idea of political equality. This supposes that the weaker members of a political community are entitled to the same concern and respect of their government as the more powerful members have secured for themselves, so that if some men have freedom of decision whatever the effect on the general good, then all men must have the same freedom. I do not want to defend or elaborate these ideas here, but only to insist that anyone who claims that citizens have rights must accept ideas very close to these.

It makes sense to say that a man has a fundamental right against the government, in the strong sense, like free speech, if that right is necessary to protect his dignity, or his standing as equally entitled to concern and respect, or some other personal value of like consequence. It does not make sense otherwise.

So if rights makes sense at all, then the invasion of a relatively important right must be a very serious matter. It means treating a man as less than a man, or as less worthy of concern than other men. The institution of rights rests on the conviction that this is a grave injustice, and that it is worth paying the incremental cost in social policy or efficiency that is necessary to prevent it. But then it must be wrong to say that inflating rights is as serious as invading them. If the government errs on the side of the individual, then it simply pays a little more in social efficiency than it has to pay ; it pays a little more, that is, of the same coin that it has already decided must be spent. But if it errs against the individual it inflicts an insult upon him that, on its own reckoning, it is worth a great deal of that coin to avoid.

So the first mode is indefensible. It rests, in fact, on a mistake I discussed earlier, namely the confusion of society's rights with the rights of members of society. "Balancing" is appropriate when the government must choose between competing claims of right — between the southerner's claim to freedom of association, for example, and the black man's claim to an equal education. Then the government can do nothing but estimate the merits of the competing claims, and act on its estimate. The first model assumes that the "right" of the majority is a competing right that must be balanced in this way ; but that, as I argued before, is a confusion that threatens to destroy the concept of individual rights. It is worth noticing that the community rejects the first model in that area where the stakes for the individual are highest, the criminal process. We say that it is better that a great many guilty men go free than that one innocent man be punished, and that homily rests on the choice of the second model for government.

The second model treats abridging a right as much more serious than inflating one, and its recommendations follow from that judgment. It stipulates that once a right is recognized in clearcut cases, then the government should act to cut off that right only when some compelling reason is presented, some reason that is consistent with the suppositions on which the original right must be based. It cannot be an argument for curtailing a right, once granted, simply that society would pay a further price for extending it. There must be something special about that further cost, or there must be some other feature of the case, that makes it sensible to say that although great social cost is warranted to protect the original right, this particular cost is not necessary. Otherwise, the government's failure to extend the right will show that its recognition of the right in the original case is a sham, a promise that it intends to keep only until that becomes inconvenient.

How can we show that a particular cost is not worth paying without taking back the initial recognition of a right ? I can think of only three sorts of grounds that can consistently be used to limit the definition of a particular right. First, the government might show that the values protected by the original right are not really at stake in the marginal case, or are at stake only in some attenuated form. Second, it might show that if the right is defined to include the marginal case, then some competing right, in the strong sense I described earlier, would be abridged. Third, it might show that if the right were so defined, then the cost to society would not be simply incremental, but would be of a degree far beyond the cost paid to grant the original right, a degree great enough to justify whatever assault on dignity or equality might be involved.

It is fairly easy to apply these grounds to one group of problems the Supreme Court faced, imbedded in constitutional issues. The draft law provided an exemption for conscientious objectors, but this exemption, as interpreted by the draft boards, has been limited to those who object to *all* wars on *religious* grounds. If we suppose that the exemption is justified on the ground that an individual has a moral right not to kill in violation of his own principles, then the question is raised whether it is proper to exclude those whose morality is not based on religion, or whose morality is sufficiently complex to distinguish among wars. The Court held, as a matter of constitutional law, that the draft boards were wrong to exclude the former, but competent to exclude the latter.

None of the three grounds I listed can justify either of these exclusions as a matter of political morality. The invasion of personality in forcing men to kill when they believe killing immoral is just as great when these beliefs are based on secular grounds, or take account of the fact that wars differ in morally relevant ways, and there is no pertinent difference in competing rights or in national emergency. There are differences among the cases, of course, but they are insufficient to justify the distinction. A government that is secular on principle cannot prefer a religious to a non-religious morality as such. There are utilitarian arguments in favour of limiting the exception to religious or universal grounds — an exemption so limited may be less expensive to administer, and may allow easier discrimination between sincere and insincere applicants. But these utilitarian reasons are irrelevant, because they cannot count as grounds for limiting a right.

What about the anti-riot law, as applied in the Chicago trial ? Does the law represent an improper limitation of the right to free speech, supposedly protected by the First Amendment ? If we were to apply the first model for government to this issue, the argument for the anti-riot law would look strong. But if we set aside talk of balancing as inappropriate, and turn to the proper grounds for limiting a right, then the argument becomes a great deal weaker. The original right of free speech must suppose that it is an assault on human personality to stop a man from expressing what he honestly believes, particularly on issues affecting how he is governed. Surely the assault is greater, and not less, when he is stopped from expressing those principles of political morality that he holds most passionately, in the fact of what he takes to be outrageous violations of these principles.

It may be said that the anti-riot law leaves him free to express these principles in a non-provocative way. But that misses the point of the connection between expression and dignity. A man cannot express himself freely when he cannot match his rhetoric to his outrage, or when he must trim his sails to protect values he counts as nothing next to those he is trying to vindicate. It is true that some political dissenters speak in ways that shock the majority, but it is arrogant for the majority to suppose that the orthodox methods of expression are the proper ways to speak, for this is a denial of equal concern and respect. If the point of the right is to protect the dignity of dissenters, then we must make judgments about appropriate speech with the personalities of the dissenters in mind, not the personality of the "silent" majority for whom the anti-riot law is no restraint at all.

So the argument fails, that the personal values protected by the original right are less at stake in this marginal case. We must consider whether competing rights, or some grave threat to society, nevertheless justify the anti-riot law. We can consider these two grounds together, because the only plausible competing rights are rights to be free from violence, and violence is the only plausible threat to society that the context provides.

I have no right to burn your house, or stone you or your car, or swing a bicycle chain against your skull, even if I find these to be natural means of expression. But the defendants in the Chicago trial were not accused of direct violence ; the argument runs that the acts of speech they planned made it likely that others would do acts of violence, either in support of or out of hostility to what they said. Does this provide a justification ?

The question would be different if we could say with any confidence how much and what sort of violence the anti-riot law might be expected to prevent. Will it save two lives a year, or two hundred, or two thousand ? Two thousand dollars of property, or two hundred thousand, or two million ? No one can say, not simply because prediction is next to impossible, but because we have no firm understanding of the process by which demonstration disintegrates into riot, and in particular of the part played by inflammatory speech, as distinct from poverty, police brutality, blood lust, and all the rest of human and economic failure. The government must try, of course, to reduce the violent waste of lives and property, but it must recognize that any attempt to locate and remove a cause of riot, short of a reorganization of society, must be an exercise in speculation, trial, and error. It must make its decisions under conditions of high uncertainty, and the institution of rights, taken seriously, limits its freedom to experiment under such conditions.

It forces the government to bear in mind that preventing a man from speaking or demonstrating offers him a certain and profound insult, in return for a speculative benefit that may in any event be achieved in other if more expensive ways. When lawyers say that rights may be limited to protect other rights, or to prevent catastrophe, they have in mind cases in which cause and effect are relatively clear, like the familiar example of a man falsely crying "Fire!" in a crowded theatre.

But the Chicago story shows how obscure the causal connections can become. Were the speeches of Hoffman or Rubin necessary conditions of the riot? Or had thousands of people come to Chicago for the purposes of rioting anyway, as the government also argues? Were they in any case sufficient conditions? Or could the police have contained the violence if they had not been so busy contributing to it, as the staff of the President's Commission on Violence said they were?

These are not easy questions, but if rights mean anything, then the government cannot simply assume answers that justify its conduct. If a man has a right to speak, if the reasons that support that right extend to provocative political speech, and if the effects of such speech on violence are unclear, then the government is not entitled to make its first attack on that problem by denying that right. It may be that abridging the right to speak is the least expensive course, or the least damaging to police morale, or the most popular politically. But these are utilitarian arguments in favour of starting one place rather than another, and such arguments are ruled out by the concept of rights.

This point may be obscured by the popular belief that political activists look forward to violence and "ask for trouble" in what they say. They can hardly complain, in the general view, if they are taken to be the authors of the violence they expect, and treated accordingly. But this repeats the confusion I tried to explain earlier between having a right and doing the right thing. The speaker's motives may be relevant in deciding whether he does the right thing in speaking passionately about issues that may inflame or enrage the audience. But if he has a right to speak, because the danger in allowing him to speak is speculative, his motives cannot count as independent evidence in the argument that justifies stopping him.

But what of the individual rights of those who will be destroyed by a riot, of the passer-by who will be killed by a sniper's bullet or the shopkeeper who will be ruined by looting? To put the issue in this way, as a question of competing rights, suggests a principle that would undercut the effect of uncertainty. Shall we say that some rights to protection are so important that the government is justified in doing all it can to maintain them? Shall we therefore say that the government may abridge the rights of others to act when their acts might simply increase the risk, by however slight or speculative a margin, that some person's right to life or property will be violated?

Some such principle is relied on by those who oppose the Supreme Court's recent liberal rulings on police procedure. These rulings increase the chance that a guilty man will go free, and therefore marginally increase the risk that any particular member of the community will be murdered, raped, or robbed. Some critics believe that the court's decisions must therefore be wrong.

But no society that purports to recognize a variety of rights, on the ground that a man's dignity or equality may be invaded in a variety of ways, can accept such a principle. If forcing a man to testify against himself, or forbidding him to speak, does the damage that the rights against self-incrimination and the right of free speech assume, then it would be contemptuous for the state to tell a man that he must suffer this damage against the possibility that other men's risk of loss may be marginally reduced. If rights make sense, then the degrees of their importance cannot be so different that some count not at all when others are mentioned.

Of course the government may discriminate and may stop a man from exercising his right to speak when there is a clear and substantial risk that his speech will do great damage to the person or property of others, and no other means of preventing this are at hand, as in the case of the man shouting "Fire!" in a theatre. But we must reject the suggested principle that the government can simply ignore rights to speak when life and property are in question. So long as the impact of speech on these other rights remains speculative and marginal, it must look elsewhere for levers to pull.

Why Take Rights Seriously?

I said at the beginning of this essay that I wanted to show what a government must do that professes to recognize individual rights. It must dispense with the claim that citizens never have a right to break its law, and it must not define citizens' rights so that these are cut off for supposed reasons of the general good. Any government's harsh treatment of civil disobedience, or campaign against vocal protest, may therefore be thought to count against its sincerity.

One might well ask, however, whether it is wise to take rights all that seriously after all. America's genius, at least in her own legend, lies in not taking any abstract doctrine to its logical extreme. It may be time to ignore abstractions, and concentrate instead on giving the majority of our citizens a new sense of their government's concern for their welfare, and of their title to rule.

That, in any event, is what former Vice-President Agnew seemed to believe. In a policy statement on the issue of "weirdos" and social misfits, he said that the liberals' concern for individual rights was a headwind blowing in the face of the ship of state. That is a poor metaphor, but the philosophical point it expresses is very well taken. He recognized, as many liberals do not, that the majority cannot travel as fast or as far as it would like if it recognizes the rights of individuals to do what, in the majority's terms, is the wrong thing to do.

Spiro Agnew supposed that rights are divisive, and that national unity and a new respect for law may be developed by taking them more skeptically. But he is wrong. America will continue to be divided by its social and foreign policy, and if the economy grows weaker again the divisions will become more bitter. If we want our laws and our legal institutions to provide the ground rules within which these issues will be contested then these ground rules must not be the conqueror's law that the dominant class imposes on the weaker, as Marx supposed the law of a capitalist society must be. The bulk of the law — that part which defines and implements social, economic, and foreign policy — cannot be neutral. It must state, in its greatest part, the majority's view of the common good. The institution of rights is therefore crucial, because it represents the majority's promise to the minorities that their dignity and equality will be respected. When the divisions among the groups are most violent, then this gesture, if law is to work, must be most sincere.

The institution requires an act of faith on the part of the minorities, because the scope of their rights will be controversial whenever they are important, and because the officers of the majority will act on their own notions of what these rights really are. Of course these officials will disagree with many of the claims that a minority makes. That makes it all the more important that they take their decisions gravely. They must show that they understand what rights are, and they must not cheat on the full implications of the doctrine. The government will not re-establish respect for law without giving the law some claim to respect. It cannot do that if it neglects the one feature that distinguishes law from ordered brutality. If the government does not take rights seriously, then it does not take law seriously either. [pp. 193-205]

NOTE

1. Ronald Dworkin, *Taking Rights Seriously* (Cambridge, Mass. : Harvard University Press, 1977), pp. 188-205.

A CRITICAL EXAMINATION OF THE DECLARATION OF RIGHTS[1]

Jeremy Bentham

Article I

Men [all men] are born and remain free and equal in respect of rights. Social distinctions cannot be founded but upon common utility.

In this article are contained, grammatically speaking, two distinct sentences. The first is full of error, the other of ambiguity.

In the first are contained four distinguishable propositions, all of them false — all of them notoriously and undeniably false :

1. That all men are born free.
2. That all men remain free.
3. That all men are born equal in rights.
4. That all men remain (i.e., remain for ever, for the proposition is indefinite and unlimited) equal in rights.

All men are born free ? All men remain free ? No, not a single man : not a single man that ever was, or is, or will be. All men, on the contrary, are born in subjection, and the most absolute subjection — the subjection of a helpless child to the parents on whom he depends every moment for his existence. In this subjection every man is born, in this subjection he continues for years — for a great number of years — and the existence of the individual and of the species depends upon his so doing.

What is the state of things to which the supposed existence of these supposed rights is meant to bear reference : a state of things prior to the existence of government, or a state of things subsequent to the existence of government ? If to a state prior to the existence of government, what would the existence of such rights as these be to the purpose, even if it were true, in any country where there is such thing as government ? If to a state of things subsequent to the formation of government — if in a country where there is a government, in what single instance, in the instance of what single government, is it true ? Setting aside the case of parent and child, let any man name that single government under which any such equality is recognized.

All men born free ? Absurd and miserable nonsense ! When the great complaint, a complaint made perhaps by the very same people at the same time, is that so many men are born slaves. Oh ! but when we acknowledge them to be born slaves, we refer to the laws in being ; which laws being void, as being contrary to those laws of nature which are the efficient causes of those rights of man that we are declaring, the men in question are free in one sense, though slaves in another ; slaves, and free, at the same time : free in respect of the laws of nature, slaves in respect of the pretended human laws, which, though called laws, are no laws at all, as being contrary to the laws of nature. For such is the difference, the great and perpetual difference, betwixt the good subject, the rational censor of the laws, and the anarchist, between the moderate man and the man of violence. The rational censor, acknowledging the existence of the law he disapproves, proposes the repeal of it : the anarchist, setting up his will and fancy for a law before which all mankind are called upon to bow down at the first word ; the anarchist, trampling on truth and decency, denies the validity of the law in question, denies the existence of it in the character of a law, and calls upon all mankind to rise up in a mass, and resist the execution of it....

All men are born equal in rights. The rights of the heir of the most indigent family equal to the rights of the heir of the most wealthy ? In what case is this true ? I say nothing of hereditary *dignities* and *powers.* Inequalities such as these being proscribed under and by the French government in France are consequently proscribed by that government under every other government, and consequently have no existence anywhere. For the total subjection of every other government to French government is a fundamental principle in the law of universal independence — the French law. Yet neither was this true at the time of issuing this Declaration of Rights, nor was it meant to be so afterwards. The 13th article . . . proceeds on the contrary supposition : for, considering its other attributes, inconsistency could not be wanting to the list. It can scarcely be more hostile to all other laws than it is at variance with itself.

All men (i.e., all human creatures of both sexes) *remain equal in rights.* All men meaning doubtless all human creatures. The apprentice, then, is equal in rights to his master ; he has as much liberty with relation to the master as the master has with relation to him ; he has as much right to command and to punish him ; he is as much owner and master of the master's house as the master himself. The case is the same as between ward and guardian. So again as between wife and husband. The madman has as good a right to confine anybody else as anybody else has to confine him. The idiot has as much right to govern everybody, as anybody can have to govern him. The physician and the nurse, when called in by the next friend of a sick man seized with a delirium, have no more right to prevent his throwing himself out of the window than he has to throw them out of it. All this is plainly and incontestably included in this article of the Declaration of Rights : in the very words of it, and in the meaning — if it have any meaning. Was this the meaning of the authors of it — or did they mean to admit this explanation as to some of the instances and to explain the article away as to the rest ? Not being idiots, nor lunatics, nor under a delirium, they would explain it away with regard to the madman and the man under a delirium. Considering that a child may become an orphan as soon as it has seen the light and that in that case, if not subject to government, it must perish, they would explain it away, I think, and contradict themselves, in the case of guardian and ward. In the case of master and apprentice, I would not take upon me to decide : it may have been their meaning to proscribe that relation altogether ; at least, this may have been the case, as soon as the repugnancy between that institution and this oracle was pointed out ; for the professed object and destination of it is to be the standard of truth and falsehood, of right and wrong, in everything that relates to government. But to this standard, and to this article of it, the subjection of the apprentice to the master is flatly and diametrically repugnant. If it do not proscribe and exclude this inequality, it proscribes none : if it do not do this mischief, it does nothing.

So, again, in the case of husband and wife. Amongst the other abuses which the oracle was meant to put an end to, may, for aught I can pretend to say, have been the institution of marriage. For what is the subjection of a small and limited number of years in comparison of the subjection of a whole life ? Yet without subjection and inequality no such institution can by any possibility take place ; for of two contradictory wills both cannot take effect at the same time.

The same doubts apply to the case of master and hired servant. Better a man should starve than hire himself ; better half the species starve than hire itself out to service. For, where is the compatibility between liberty and servitude ? How can liberty and servitude subsist in the same person ? What good citizen is there, that would hesitate to die for liberty ? And, as to those who are not good citizens, what matters it whether they live or starve ? Besides that every man who lives under this constitution being equal in rights, equal in all sorts of rights, is equal in respect to rights of property. No man, therefore, can be in any danger of starving — no man can have so much as that motive, weak and inadequate as it is, for hiring himself out to service....

Look where I will, I see but too many laws, the alteration or abolition of which, would in my poor judgment be a public blessing. I can conceive some, to put extreme and scarcely exampled cases, to which I might be inclined to oppose resistance, with a prospect of support such as promised to be effectual. But to talk of what the law, the supreme legislature of the country, acknowledged as such, *can* not do ! To talk of a *void* law as you would of a *void* order or a *void* judgment ! The very act of bringing such words into conjunction is either the vilest of nonsense, or the worst of treasons : treason, not against one branch of the sovereignty, but against the whole : treason, not against this or that government, but against *all* governments.

Article II

The end in view of every political association is the preservation of the natural and imprescriptible rights of man. These rights are liberty, property, security, and resistance to oppression.

Sentence 1. The end in view of every political association is the preservation of the natural and imprescriptible rights of man.

More confusion, more nonsense, and the nonsense, as usual, dangerous nonsense. The words can scarcely be said to have a meaning : but if they have, or rather if they had a meaning, these would be the propositions either asserted or implied :

1. That there are such things as rights anterior to the establishment of governments : for natural, as applied to rights, if it mean anything, is meant to stand in opposition to *legal,* to such rights as are acknowledged to owe their existence to government, and are consequently posterior in their date to the establishment of government.

2. That these rights *cannot* be abrogated by government : for *cannot* is implied in the form of the word imprescriptible, and the sense it wears when so applied is the cut-throat sense above explained.

3. That the governments that exist derive their origin from formal associations, or what are now called *conventions* : associations entered into by a partnership contract, with all the members for partners, entered into at a day prefixed, for a predetermined purpose, the formation of a new government where there was none before (for as to formal meetings holden under the control of an existing government, they are evidently out of question here) in which it seems again to be implied in the way of inference, though a necessary and an unavoidable inference, that all governments (that is, self-called governments, knots of persons exercising the powers of government) that have had any other origin than an association of the above description, are illegal, that is, no governments at all ; resistance to them, and subversion of them, lawful and commendable, and so on.

Such are the notions implied in this first part of the article. How stands the truth of things ? That there are no such things as natural rights — no such things as rights anterior to the establishment of government — no such things as natural rights opposed to, in contra-distinction to, legal : that the expression is merely figurative ; that when used, in the moment you attempt to give it a literal meaning it leads to error, and to that sort of error that leads to mischief — to the extremity of mischief.

We know what it is for men to live without government and, living without government, to live without rights : we know what it is for men to live without government, for we see instances of such a way of life ; we see it in many savage nations, or rather races of mankind, for instance, among the savages of New South Wales, whose way of living is so well known to us : no habit of obedience, and thence no government ; no government, and thence no laws ; no laws, and thence no such things as rights ; no security ; no property : liberty, as against regular controul, the controul of laws and government — perfect ; but as against all irregular controul, the mandates of stronger individuals, none. In this state, at a time earlier than the commencement of history, in this same state, judging from analogy, we, the inhabitants of the part of the globe we call Europe, were ; no government, consequently no rights ; no rights, consequently no property ; no legal security ; no legal liberty : security not more than belongs to beasts — forecast and sense of insecurity keener — consequently in point of happiness below the level of the brutal race.

In proportion to the want of happiness resulting from the want of rights, a reason exists for wishing that there were such things as rights. But reasons for wishing there were such things as rights are not rights ; a reason for wishing that a certain right were established is not that right ; want is not supply ; hunger is not bread.

That which has no existence cannot be destroyed ; that which cannot be destroyed cannot require anything to preserve it from destruction. *Natural rights* is simple nonsense; natural and imprescriptible rights, rhetorical nonsense — nonsense upon stilts. But this rhetorical nonsense ends in the old strain of mischievous nonsense : for immediately a list of these pretended natural rights is given, and those are so expressed as to present to view legal rights. And of these rights, whatever they are, there is not, it seems,any one of which any government *can*, upon any occasion whatever, abrogate the smallest particle.... [pp 497-501]

Liberty, then, is imprescriptible — incapable of being taken away — out of the power of any government ever to take away : liberty, that is, every branch of liberty, every individual exercise of liberty ; for no line is drawn, no distinction, no exception made. What these instructors as well as governors of mankind appear not to know is that all rights are made at the expense of liberty — all laws by which rights are created or confirmed. No right without a correspondent obligation. Liberty, as against the coercion of the law, may, it is true, be given by the simple removal of the obligation by which that coercion was applied — by the simple repeal of the coercing law. But as against the coercion applicable by individual to individual, no liberty can be given to one man but in proportion as it is taken from another. All coercive laws, therefore (that is, all laws but constitutional laws, and laws repealing or modifying coercive laws), and in particular all laws creative of liberty, are, as far as they go, abrogative of liberty. Not here and there a law only, not this or that possible law, but almost all laws are therefore repugnant to these natural and imprescriptible rights : consequently null and void, calling for resistance and insurrection, and so on, as before.

Laws creative of rights of property are also struck at by the same anathema. How is property given ? By restraining liberty ; that is, by taking it away so far as is necessary for the purpose. How is your house made yours ? By debarring every one else from the liberty of entering it without your leave. [pp. 502-503]

NOTE

1. Jeremy Bentham, "A Critical Examination of the Declaration of Rights", in John Bowring, ed., *The Works of Jeremy Bentham* (New York : Russell and Russell, 1962), pp. 497-503.

AN INTRODUCTION TO THE PRINCIPLES OF MORALS AND LEGISLATION[1]

Jeremy Bentham

Nature has placed mankind under the governance of two sovereign masters, *pain* and *pleasure*. It is for them alone to point out what we ought to do, as well as to determine what we shall do. On the one hand the standard of right and wrong, on the other the chain of causes and effects, are fastened to their throne. They govern us in all we do, in all we say, in all we think : every effort we can make to throw off our subjection, will serve but to demonstrate and confirm it. In words a man may pretend to abjure their empire : but in reality he will remain subject to it all the while. The *principle of utility* recognizes this subjection, and assumes if for the foundation of that system, the object of which is to rear the fabric of felicity by the hands of reason and of law. Systems which attempt to question it, deal in sounds instead of sense, in caprice instead of reason, in darkness instead of light....

By the principle of utility is meant that principle which approves or disapproves of every action whatsoever, according to the tendency which it appears to have to augment or diminish the happiness of the party whose interest is in question : or, what is the same thing in other words, to promote or to oppose that happiness. I say of every action whatsoever ; and therefore not only of every action of a private individual, but of every measure of government.

By utility is meant that property in any object, whereby it tends to produce benefit, advantage, pleasure, good, or happiness (all this in the present case comes to the same thing) or (what comes again to the same thing) to prevent the happening of mischief, pain, evil, or unhappiness to the party whose interest is considered : if that party be the community in general, then the happiness of the community : if a particular individual, then the happiness of that individual.

The interest of the community is one of the most general expressions that can occur in the phraseology of morals : no wonder that the meaning of it is often lost. When it has a meaning, it is this. The community is a fictitious *body,* composed on the individual persons who are considered as constituting as it were its *members.* The interest of the community then is, what ? — the sum of the interests of the several members who compose it.

It is in vain to talk of the interest of the community, without understanding what is the interest of the individual. A thing is said to promote the interest, or to be *for* the interest, of an individual, when it tends to add to the sum total of his pleasures : or, what comes to the same thing, to diminish the sum total of his pains.

An action then may be said to be conformable to the principle of utility, or, for shortness sake, to utility, (meaning with respect to the community at large) when the tendency it has to augment the happiness of the community is greater than any it has to diminish it.

A measure of government (which is but a particular kind of action, performed by a particular person or persons) may be said to be conformable to or dictated by the principle of utility, when in like manner the tendency which it has to augment the happiness of the community is greater than any which it has to diminish it.

When an action, or in particular a measure of government, is supposed by a man to be conformable to the principle of utility, it may be convenient, for the purposes of discourse, to imagine a kind of law or dictate, called a law or dictate of utility : and to speak of the action in question, as being conformable to such law or dictate.

A man may be said to be a partisan of the principle of utility, when the approbation or disapprobation he annexes to any action, or to any measure, is determined by and proportioned to the tendency which he conceives it to have to augment or to diminish the happiness of the community : or in other words, to its conformity or unconformity to the laws or dictates of utility.

Of an action that is conformable to the principle of utility one may always say either that it is one that ought to be done, or at least that it is not one that ought not to be done. One may say also, that it is right it should be done ; at least that it is not wrong it should be done : that it is a right action ; at least that it is not a wrong action. When thus interpreted, the words *ought* and *right* and *wrong,* and others of that stamp, have a meaning : when otherwise, they have none.... [pp. 1-4]

Now an offence is an act prohibited, or (what comes to the same thing) an act of which the contrary is commanded, by the law : and what is it that the law can be employed in doing, besides prohibiting and commanding ? It should seem then, according to this view of the matter, that were we to have settled what may be proper to be done with relation to offences, we should thereby have settled every thing that may be proper to be done in the way of law. Yet that branch which concerns the method of dealing with offences, and which is termed sometimes the *criminal,* sometimes the *penal,* branch, is universally understood to be but one out of two branches which compose the whole subject of the art of legislation ; that which is termed the *civil* being the other. Between these two branches then, it is evident enough, there cannot but be a very intimate connection ; so intimate is it indeed, that the limits between them are by no means easy to mark out. The case is the same in some degree between the whole business of legislation (civil and penal branches taken together) and that of private ethics....

Ethics at large may be defined, the art of directing men's actions to the production of the greatest possible quantity of happiness, on the part of those whose interest is in view.

What then are the actions which it can be in a man's power to direct ? They must be either his own actions, or those of other agents. Ethics, in as far as it is the art of directing a man's own actions, may be styled the *art of self-government,* or *private ethics.*

What other agents then are there, which, at the same time that they are under the influence of man's direction, are susceptible of happiness ? They are of two sorts : 1. Other human beings who are styled persons. 2. Other animals, which, on account of their interests having been neglected by the insensibility of the ancient jurists, stand degraded into the class of *things.* As to other human beings, the art of directing their actions to the above end is what we mean, or at least the only thing which, upon the principle of utility, we *ought* to mean, by the art of government : which, in as far as the measures it displays itself in are of a permanent nature, is generally distinguished by the name of *legislation* : as it is by that of *administration,* when they are of a temporary nature, determined by the occurrences of the day....

As to ethics in general, a man's happiness will depend, in the first place, upon such parts of his behaviour as none but himself are interested in ; in the next place, upon such parts of it as may affect the happiness of those about him. In as far as his happiness depends upon the first-mentioned part of his behaviour, it is said to depend upon his *duty to himself.* Ethics then, in as far as it is the art of directing a man's actions in this respect, may be termed the art of discharging one's duty to one's self : and the quality which a man manifests by the discharge of this branch of duty (if duty it is to be called) is that of *prudence.* In as far as his happiness, and that of any other person or persons whose interests are considered, depends upon such parts of his behaviour as may affect the interests of those about him, it may be said to depend upon his *duty to others* ; or, to use a phrase now somewhat antiquated, his *duty to his neighbour.* Ethics then, in as far as it is the art of directing a man's actions in this respect, may be termed that art of discharging one's duty to one's neighbour. Now the happiness of one's neighbour may be consulted in two ways : 1. In a negative way, by forbearing to diminish it. 2. In a positive way, by studying to increase it. A man's duty to his neighbour is accordingly partly negative and partly positive : to discharge the negative branch of it, is *probity* : to discharge the positive branch, *beneficence.*

It may here be asked, How it is that upon the principle of private ethics, legislation, and religion out of the question, a man's happiness depends upon such parts of his conduct as affect, immediately at least, the happiness of no one but himself : this is as much as to ask, What motives (independent of such as legislation and religion may chance to furnish) can one man have to consult the happiness of another ? By what motives, or, which comes to the same thing, by what obligations, can he be bound to obey the dictates of *probity* and *beneficence* ? In answer to this, it cannot but be admitted, that the only interests which a man at all times and upon all occasions is sure to find *adequate* motives for consulting, are his own. Notwithstanding this, there are no occasions in which a man has not some motives for consulting the happiness of other men. In the first place, he has, on all occasions, the purely social motive of sympathy or benevolence : in the next place, he has, on most occasions, the semi-social motives of love of amity and love of reputation. The motive of sympathy will act upon him with more or less effect, according to the *bias* of his sensibility : the two other motives, according to a variety of circumstances, principally according to the strength of his intellectual powers, the firmness and steadiness of his mind, the quantum of his moral sensibility, and the characters of the people he has to deal with.

Now private ethics has happiness for its end : and legislation can have no other. Private ethics concerns every member, that is, the happiness and the actions of every member, of any community that can be proposed ; and legislation can concern no more. Thus far, then, private ethics and the art of legislation go hand in hand. The end they have, or ought to have, in view, is of the same nature. The persons whose happiness they ought to have in view, as also the persons whose conduct they ought to be occupied in directing, are precisely the same. The very acts they ought to be conversant about, are even in a *great measure* the same. Where then lies the difference ? In that the acts which they ought to be conversant about, though in a great measure, are not *perfectly and throughout* the same. There is no case in which a private man ought not to direct his own conduct to the production of his own happiness, and of that of his fellow-creatures : but there are cases in which the legislator ought not (in a direct way at least, and by means of punishment applied immediately to particular *individual* acts) to attempt to direct the conduct of several other members of the community. Every act which promises to be beneficial upon the whole to the community (himself included) each individual ought to perform of himself : but it is not every such act that the legislator ought to compel him to perform. Every act which promises to be pernicious upon the whole to the community (himself included) each individual ought to abstain from of himself : but it is not every such act that the legislator ought to compel him to abstain from.

Where then is the line to be drawn ? We shall not have far to seek for it. The business is to give an idea of the cases in which ethics ought, and in which legislation ought not (in a direct manner at least) to interfere. If legislation interferes in a direct manner, it must be by punishment. Now the cases in which punishment, meaning the punishment of the political sanction, ought not to be inflicted, have been already stated. If then there be any of these cases which, although legislation ought not, private ethics does or ought to interfere, these cases will serve to point out the limits between the two arts or branches of science. These cases, it may be remembered, are of four sorts : 1. Where punishment would be groundless. 2. Where it would be inefficacious. 3. Where it would be unprofitable. 4. Where it would be needless.... [pp. 309 — 314].

NOTE

1. Jeremy Bentham, *An Introduction to the Principles of Morals and Legislation* (New York : Hafner Publishing Co.), pp. 1-314.

JURISPRUDENCE[1]

John Austin

The matter of jurisprudence is positive law : law, simply and strictly so called : or law set by political superiors to political inferiors. But positive law (or law, simply and strictly so called) is often confounded with objects to which it is related by resemblance, and with objects to which it is related in the way of analogy : with objects which are also signified, properly and improperly, by the large and vague expression *law*. To obviate the difficulties springing from that confusion, I begin my projected course with determining the province of jurisprudence, or with distinguishing the matter of jurisprudence from those various related objects : trying to define the subject of which I intend to treat, before I endeavour to analyze its numerous and complicated parts.

A law, in the most general and comprehensive acceptation in which the term, in its literal meaning, is employed, may be said to be a rule laid down for the guidance of an intelligent being by an intelligent being having power over him. Under this definition are concluded, and without impropriety, several species. It is necessary to define accurately the line of demarcation which separates these species from one another, as much mistiness and intricacy has been infused into the science of jurisprudence by their being confounded or not clearly distinguished. In the comprehensive sense above indicated, or in the largest meaning which it has, without extension by metaphor or analogy, the term law embraces the following objects : laws set by God to his human creatures, and laws set by men to men.

The whole or a portion of the laws set by God to men is frequently styled the law of nature, or natural law : being, in truth, the only natural law of which it is possible to speak without a metaphor, or without a blending of objects which ought to be distinguished broadly. But, rejecting the appellation law of nature as ambiguous and misleading, I name those laws or rules, as considered collectively or in a mass, the *divine law*, or the *law of God.*

Laws set by men to men are of two leading or principal classes : classes which are often blended, although they differ extremely ; and which, for that reason, should be severed precisely, and opposed distinctly and conspicuously.

Of the laws or rules set by men to men, some are established by *political* superiors, sovereign and subject : by persons exercising supreme and subordinate government, in independent nations, or independent political societies. The aggregate of the rules thus established, or some aggregate forming a portion of that aggregate, is the appropriate matter of jurisprudence, general or particular. To the aggregate of the rules thus established, or to some aggregate forming a portion of that aggregate, the term law, as used simply and strictly, is exclusively applied. But, as contra distinguished to *natural* law, or to the law of nature (meaning, by those expressions, the law of God), the aggregate of the rules, established by political superiors, is frequently styled *positive* law, or law existing by position. As contra distinguished to the rules which I style positive morality, and on which I shall touch immediately, the aggregate of the rules, established by political superiors, may also be marked commodiously with the name of *positive law*. For the sake, then, of getting a name brief and distinctive at once, and agreeable to frequent usage, I style that aggregate of rules, or any portion of that aggregate, positive law : though rules, which are not established by political superiors, are also positive, or exist by position, if they be rules or laws, in the proper signification of the term.

Though *some* of the laws or rules, which are set by men to men, are established by political superiors, others are not established by political superiors, or are *not* established by political superiors, in that capacity or character.

Closely analogous to human laws of this second class, are a set of objects frequently but improperly termed laws, being rules set and enforced by *mere opinion*, that is, by the opinions or sentiments held or felt by an indeterminate body of men in regard to human conduct. Instances of such a use of the term *law* are the expressions "The law of honour," "The law set by fashion," and rules of this species constitute much of what is usually termed "international law."

The aggregate of human laws properly so called belonging to the second of the classes above mentioned, with the aggregate of objects improperly but by close analogy termed laws, I place together in a common class, and denote them by the term *positive morality*. The name morality severs them from positive law, while the epithet positive disjoins them from the law of God. And to the end of obviating confusion, it is necessary or expedient that they *should* be disjoined from the latter by that distinguishing epithet. For the name *morality* (or *morals*), when standing unqualified or alone, denotes indifferently either of the following objects : namely, positive morality *as it is*, or without regard to its merits ; and positive morality *as it would be* if it conformed to the law of God, and were, therefore, deserving of approbation....

Having suggested the purpose of my attempt to determine the province of jurisprudence : to distinguish positive law, the appropriate matter of jurisprudence, from the various objects to which it is related by resemblance, and to which it is related, nearly or remotely, by a strong or slender analogy : I shall now state the essentials of a *law* or *rule* (taken with the largest signification which can be given to the term properly).

Every *law* or *rule* (taken with the largest signification which can be given to the term properly) is a *command*. Or, rather, laws or rules, properly so called, are a species of commands.

Now, since the term command comprises the term law, the first is the simpler as well as the larger of the two. But, simple as it is, it admits of explanation. And, since it is the key to the sciences of jurisprudence and morals, its meaning should be analyzed with precision.

Accordingly, I shall endeavour, in the first instance, to analyze the meaning of "command" an analysis which, I fear, will task the patience of my hearers, but which they will bear with cheerfulness, or, at least, with resignation, if they consider the difficulty of performing it. The elements of a science are precisely the parts of it which are explained least easily. Terms that are the largest and, therefore, the simplest of a series are without equivalent expressions into which we can resolve them concisely. And when we endeavour to define them, or to translate them into terms which we suppose are better understood, we are forced upon awkward and tedious circumlocutions.

If you express or intimate a wish that I shall do or forbear from some act, and if you will visit me with an evil in case I comply not with your wish, the expression or intimation of your wish is a command. A command is distinguished from other significations of desire, not by the style in which the desire is signified, but by the power and the purpose of the party commanding to inflict an evil or pain in case the desire be disregarded. If you cannot or will not harm me in case I comply not with your wish, the expression of your wish is not a command, although you utter your wish in imperative phrase. If you are able and willing to harm me in case I comply not with your wish, the expression of your wish amounts to a command, although you are prompted by a spirit of courtesy to utter it in the shape of a request. "*Preces erant, sed quibus contradici non posset.*" Such is the language of Tacitus, when speaking of a petition by the soldiery to a son and lieutenant of Vespasian.

A command, then, is a signification of desire. But a command is distinguished from other significations of desire by this peculiarity : that the party to whom it is directed is liable to evil from the other, in case he comply not with the desire.

Being liable to evil from you if I comply not with a wish which you signify, I am *bound* or *obliged* by your command, or I lie under a *duty* to obey it. If, in spite of that evil in prospect, I comply not with the wish which you signify, I am said to disobey your command, or to violate the duty which it imposes.

Command and duty are, therefore, correlative terms : the meaning denoted by each being implied or supposed by the other. Or (changing the expression) wherever a duty lies, a command has been signified ; and whenever a command is signified, a duty is imposed.

Concisely expressed, the meaning of the correlative expressions is this. He who will inflict an evil in case his desire be disregarded, utters a command by expressing or intimating his desire : He who is liable to the evil in case he disregard the desire, is bound or obliged by the command.

The evil which will probably be incurred in case a command be disobeyed or (to use an equivalent expression) in case a duty be broken is frequently called a *sanction*, or an *enforcement of obedience.* Or (varying the phrase) the command or the duty is said to be *sanctioned* or *enforced* by the chance of incurring the evil.

Considered as thus abstracted from the command and the duty which it enforces, the evil to be incurred by disobedience is frequently styled a *punishment.* But, as punishments, strictly so called, are only a class of sanctions, the term is too narrow to express the meaning adequately....

It appears, then, from what has been premised, that the ideas or notions comprehended by the term command are the following. 1. A wish or desire, conceived by a rational being, that another rational being shall do or forbear. 2. An evil to proceed from the former, and to be incurred by the latter, in case the latter comply not with the wish. 3. An expression or intimation of the wish by words or other signs.

It also appears from what has been premised, that *command, duty,* and *sanction* are inseparably connected terms : that each embraces the same ideas as the others, though each denotes those ideas in a peculiar order or series.

"A wish conceived by one, and expressed or intimated to another, with an evil to be inflicted and incurred in case the wish be disregarded," are signified directly and indirectly by each of the three expressions. Each is the name of the same complex notion.

But when I am talking directly of the expression or intimation of the wish, I employ the term command : The expression or intimation of the wish being presented prominently to my hearer ; whilst the evil to be incurred, with the chance of incurring it, are kept (if I may so express myself) in the background of my picture.

When I am talking directly of the chance of incurring the evil, or (changing the expression) of the liability or obnoxiousness to the evil, I employ the term *duty,* or the term *obligation* : The liability or obnoxiousness to the evil being put foremost, and the rest of the complex notion being signified implicitly.

When I am talking immediately of the evil itself, I employ the term *sanction,* or a term of the like import : The evil to be incurred being signified directly ; whilst the obnoxiousness to that evil, with the expression or intimation of the wish, are indicated indirectly or obliquely.

To those who are familiar with the language of logicians (language unrivalled for brevity, distinctness, and precision), I can express my meaning accurately in a breath. Each of the three terms *signifies* the same notion ; but each *denotes* a different part of that notion, and *connotes* the residue.

Commands are of two species. Some are *laws* or *rules.* The others have not acquired an appropriate name, nor does language afford an expression which will mark them briefly and precisely. I must, therefore, note them as well as I can by the ambiguous and inexpressive name of "*occasional* or *particular* commands."

The term laws or rules being not unfrequently applied to occasional or particular commands, it is hardly possible to describe a line of separation which shall consist in every respect with established forms of speech. But the distinction between laws and particular commands may, I think, be stated in the following manner.

By every command, the party to whom it is directed is obliged to do or to forbear.

Now where it obliges *generally* to acts or forbearances of a class, a command is a law or rule. But where it obliges to a specific act or forbearance, or to acts or forbearances which it determines *specifically* or *individually,* a command is occasional or particular. In other words, a class or description of acts is determined by a law or rule, and acts of that class or description are enjoined or forbidden generally. But where a command is occasional or particular, the act or acts, which the command enjoins or forbids, are assigned or determined by their specific or individual natures as well as by the class or description to which they belong.

The statement which I have given in abstract expressions I will now endeavour to illustrate by apt examples.

If you command your servant to go on a given errand, or not to leave your house on a given evening, or to rise at such an hour on such a morning, or to rise at that hour during the next week or month, the command is occasional or particular. For the act or acts enjoined or forbidden are specially determined or assigned.

But if you command him simply to rise at that hour, or to rise at that hour always, or to rise at that hour till further orders, it may be said, with propriety, that you lay down a rule for the guidance of your servant's conduct. For no specific act is assigned by the command, but the command obliges him generally to acts of a determined class.

If a regiment be ordered to attack or defend a post, or to quell a riot, or to march from their present quarters, the command is occasional or particular. But an order to exercise daily till further orders shall be given would be called a general order, and might be called a rule.

If Parliament prohibited simply the exportation of corn, either for a given period or indefinitely, it would establish a law or rule : a kind or sort of acts being determined by the command, and acts of that kind or sort being generally forbidden. But an order issued by Parliament to meet an impending scarcity, and stopping the exportation of corn then shipped and in port, would not be a law or rule, though issued by the sovereign legislature. The order regarding exclusively a specified quantity of corn, the negative acts or forbearances, enjoined by the command, would be determined specifically or individually by the determinate nature of their subject.

As issued by a sovereign legislature, and as wearing the form of a law, the order which I have now imagined would probably be called a law. And hence the difficulty of drawing a distinct boundary between laws and occasional commands. [pp 86-93]

A law obliges generally the members of the given community, or a law obliges generally persons of a given class. A particular command obliges a single person, or persons whom it determines individually.

That laws and particular commands are not to be distinguished thus, will appear on a moment's reflection.

For, *first,* commands which oblige generally the members of the given community, or commands which oblige generally persons of given classes, are not always laws or rules.

Thus, in the case already supposed ; that in which the sovereign commands that all corn actually shipped for exportation be stopped and detained ; the command is obligatory upon the whole community, but as it obliges them only to a set of acts individually assigned, it is not a law. Again, suppose the sovereign to issue an order, enforced by penalties, for a general mourning, on occasion of a public calamity. Now, though it is addressed to the community at large, the order is scarcely a rule, in the usual acceptation of the term. For, though it obliges generally the members of the entire community, it obliges to acts which it assigns specifically, instead of obliging generally to acts or forbearances of a class. If the sovereign commanded that black should be the dress of his subjects, his command would amount to a law. But if he commanded them to wear it on a specified occasion, his command would be merely particular.

And, *secondly,* a command which obliges exclusively persons individually determined, may amount, notwithstanding, to a law or a rule.

For example, a father may set a *rule* to his child or children ; a guardian, to his ward ; a master, to his slave or servant. And certain of God's *laws* were as binding on the first man, as they are binding at this hour on the millions who have sprung from his loins.

Most, indeed, of the laws which are established by political superiors, or most of the laws which are simply and strictly so called, oblige generally the members of the political community, or oblige generally persons of a class. To frame a system of duties for every individual of the community were simply impossible : and if it were possible, it were utterly useless. Most of the laws established by political superiors are, therefore, general in a twofold manner : as enjoining or forbidding generally acts of kinds or sorts ; and as binding the whole community or, at least, whole classes of its members.

But if we suppose that Parliament creates and grants an office, and that Parliament binds the grantee to services of a given description, we suppose a law established by political superiors, and yet exclusively binding a specified or determinate person.

Laws established by political superiors, and exclusively binding specified or determinate persons, are styled, in the language of the Roman jurists, *privilegia*....

It appears, from what has been premised, that a law, properly so called, may be defined in the following manner.

A law is a command which obliges a person or persons.

But, as contradistinguished or opposed to an occasional or particular command, a law is a command which obliges a person or persons, and obliges *generally* to acts or forbearances of a *class*.

In language more popular but less distinct and precise, a law is a command which obliges a person or persons to a *course* of conduct.

Laws and other commands are said to proceed from *superiors*, and to bind or oblige *inferiors*. I will, therefore, analyze the meaning of those correlative expressions ; and will try to strip them of a certain mystery, by which that simple meaning appears to be obscured.

Superiority is often synonymous with *precedence* or *excellence*. We talk of superiors in rank ; of superiors in wealth ; of superiors in virtue : comparing certain persons with certain other persons ; and meaning that the former precede or excel the latter in rank, in wealth, or in virtue.

But, taken with the meaning wherein I here understand it, the term superiority signifies might : the power of affecting others with evil or pain, and of forcing them, through fear of that evil, to fashion their conduct to one's wishes.

For example, God is emphatically the superior of Man. For his power of affecting us with pain, and of forcing us to comply with his will, is unbounded and resistless.

To a limited extent, the sovereign One or Number is the superior of the subject or citizen : the master, of the slave or servant : the father, of the child.

In short, whoever can *oblige* another to comply with his wishes, is the superior of that other, so far as the ability reaches : The party who is obnoxious to the impending evil, being, to that same extent, the inferior.

The might or superiority of God is simple or absolute. But in all or most cases of human superiority, the relation of superior and inferior, and the relation of inferior and superior, are reciprocal. Or (changing the expression) the party who is the superior as viewed from one aspect is the inferior as viewed from another.

For example, to an indefinite, though limited, extent the monarch is the superior of the governed : his power being commonly sufficient to enforce compliance with his will. But the governed, collectively or in mass, are also the superior of the monarch, who is checked in the abuse of his might by his fear of exciting their anger and of rousing to active resistance the might which slumbers in the multitude.

A member of a sovereign assembly is the superior of the judge : the judge being bound by the law which proceeds from that sovereign body. But, in his character of citizen or subject, he is the inferior of the judge : the judge being the minister of the law, and armed with the power of enforcing it.

It appears, then, that the term *superiority* (like the terms *duty* and *sanction*) is implied by the term command. For superiority is the power of enforcing compliance with a wish : and the expression or intimation of a wish, with the power and the purpose of enforcing it, are the constituent elements of a command.

"That laws emanate from superiors" is, therefore, an identical proposition. For the meaning which it affects to impart is contained in its subject.

If I mark the peculiar source of a given law, or if I mark the peculiar source of laws of a given class, it is possible that I am saying something which may instruct the hearer. But to affirm of laws universally "that they flow from superiors," or to affirm of laws universally "that inferiors are bound to obey them," is the merest tautology and trifling.

Like most of the leading terms in the sciences of jurisprudence and morals, the term *laws* is extremely ambiguous. Taken with the largest signification which can be given to the term properly, laws are a species of commands. But the term is improperly applied to various objects which have nothing of the imperative character : to objects which are not commands and which, therefore, are not laws, properly so called... [pp. 95-98]

The science of jurisprudence (or, simply and briefly, jurisprudence) is concerned with positive laws, or with laws strictly so called, as considered without regard to their goodness or badness.

Positive morality, as considered without regard to its goodness or badness, might be the subject of a science closely analogous to jurisprudence . I say "might be" since it is only in one of its branches (namely, the law of nations or international law), that positive morality, as considered without regard to its goodness or badness, has been treated by writers in a scientific or systematic manner. For the science of positive morality, as considered without regard to its goodness or badness, current or established language will hardly afford us a name. The name morals, or science of morals, would denote it ambiguously : the name morals, or science of morals, being commonly applied (as I shall show immediately) to a department of ethics or deontology. But, since the science of jurisprudence is not unfrequently styled "the science of positive law," the science in question might be styled analogically "the science of positive morality...."

The science of ethics (or, in the language of Mr. Bentham, the science of deontology) may be defined in the following manner. It affects to determine the test of positive law and morality, or it affects to determine the principles whereon they must be fashioned in order that they may merit approbation. In other words, it affects to expound them as they should be ; or it affects to expound them as they ought to be ; or it affects to expound them as they would be if they were good or worthy of praise ; or it affects to expound them as they would be if they conformed to an assumed measure.

The science of ethics (or, simply and briefly, ethics) consists of two departments : one relating specially to positive law, the other relating specially to positive morality. The department which relates specially to positive law, is commonly styled the science of legislation, or, simply and briefly, legislation. The department which relates specially to positive morality is commonly styled the science of morals, or, simply and briefly, morals.... [pp. 172-173]

The superiority which is styled sovereignty, and the independent political society which sovereignty implies, is distinguished from other superiority, and from other society, by the following marks or characters. 1. The *bulk* of the given society are in a *habit* of obedience or submission to a *determinate* and *common* superior : let that common superior be a certain individual person, or a certain body or aggregate of individual persons. 2. That certain individual, or that certain body of individuals, is *not* in a habit of obedience to a determinate human superior. Laws (improperly so called) which opinion sets or imposes may permanently affect the conduct of that certain individual or body. To express or tacit commands of other determinate parties, that certain individual or body may yield occasional submission. But there is no determinate person, or determinate aggregate of persons, to whose commands, express or tacit, that certain individual or body renders habitual obedience.

Or the notions of sovereignty and independent political society may be expressed concisely thus. If a determinate human superior, not in a habit of obedience to a like superior, receive habitual obedience from the bulk of a given society, that determinate superior is sovereign in that society, and the society (including the superior) is a society political and independent.

To that determinate superior, the other members of the society are *subject* : or on that determinate superior, the other members of the society are *dependent.* The position of its other members towards that determinate superior, is *a state of subjection,* or *a state of dependence.* The mutual relation which subsists between that superior and them, may be styled *the relation of sovereign and subject,* or *the relation of sovereignty and subjection.*

Hence it follows, that it is only through an ellipsis, or an abridged form of expression, that the *society* is styled *independent.* The party truly independent (independent, that is to say, of a determinate human superior), is not the society, but the sovereign portion of the society : that certain member of the society, or that certain body of its members, to whose commands, expressed or intimated, the generality or bulk of its members render habitual obedience. Upon that certain person, or certain body of persons, the other members of the society are *dependent :* or to that certain person, or certain body of persons, the other members of the society are *subject.* By "an independent political society," or "an independent and sovereign nation," we mean a political society consisting of a sovereign and subjects, as opposed to a political society which is merely subordinate : that is to say, which is merely a limb or member of another political society, and which therefore consists entirely of persons in a state of subjection.

In order that a given society may form a society political and independent, the two distinguishing marks which I have mentioned above must unite. The generality of the given society must be in the habit of obedience to a determinate and common superior : whilst that determinate person, or determinate body of persons must not be habitually obedient to a determinate person or body. It is the union of that positive, with this negative mark, which renders that certain superior sovereign or supreme, and which renders that given society (including that certain superior) a society political and independent.

To show that the union of those marks renders a given society a society political and independent, I call your attention to the following positions and examples.

1. In order that a given society may form a society political, the generality or bulk of its members must be in a *habit* of obedience to a determinate and common superior.

In case the generality of its members obey a determinate superior, but the obedience be rare or transient and not habitual or permanent, the relation of sovereignty and subjection is not created thereby between that certain superior and the members of that given society. In other words, that determinate superior and the members of that given society do not become thereby an independent political society. Whether that given society be political and independent or not, it is not an independent political society whereof that certain superior is the sovereign portion.... [pp. 220-222]

Society formed by the intercourse of independent political societies is the province of international law, or of the law obtaining between nations. For (adopting a current expression) international law, or the law obtaining between nations, is conversant about the conduct of independent political societies considered as entire communities : *circa negotia et causas gentium integrarum.* Speaking with greater precision, international law, or the law obtaining between nations, regards the conduct of sovereigns considered as related to one another.

And hence it inevitably follows, that the law obtaining between nations is not positive law : for every positive law is set by a given sovereign to a person or persons in a state of subjection to its author. As I have already intimated, the law obtaining between nations is law (improperly so called) set by general opinion. The duties which it imposes are enforced by moral sanctions : by fear on the part of nations, or by fear on the part of sovereigns, of provoking general hostility, and incurring its probable evils, in case they shall violate maxims generally received and respected....

The definition of the abstract term *independent political society* (including the definition of the correlative term sovereignty) cannot be rendered in expressions of perfectly precise import, and is therefore a fallible test of specific or particular cases. The least imperfect definition which the abstract term will take would hardly enable us to fix the class of every possible society. It would hardly enable us to determine of every *independent* society, whether it were *political* or *natural.* It would hardly enable us to determine of every *political* society, whether it were *independent* or *subordinate.*

In order that a given society may form a society political and independent, the positive and negative marks which I have mentioned above must unite. The *generality* or *bulk* of its members must be in a *habit* of obedience to a *certain* and *common* superior : whilst that certain person, or certain body of persons, must *not* be habitually obedient to a certain person or body. [pp. 225-227]

NOTE

1. Robert Campbell, ed., *Austin on Jurisprudence*, vol. 1 (London : John Murray, 1885), pp. 86-227.

LAW IN THE PERSPECTIVE OF PHILOSOPHY : 1776-1976[1]

H.L.A. Hart

In *A Fragment on Government*, published four months before the Declaration of Independence, Bentham described the Principle of Utility as the fundamental axiom according to which "[i]t is the greatest happiness of the greatest number that is the measure of right and wrong." In Bentham's hands this maxim was to provide, among other things, the justification for the exercise of government of men by coercive laws and the justification both for obedience to laws and, when occasion required it, for withholding obedience. Utilitarianism thus became a justificatory theory of government and of the limits of government. In his contribution to *An Answer to the Declaration of the American Congress*, Bentham attacked the alternative justification for those things which was offered by the doctrine of inalienable rights of man. In so doing he fired the first light shots of destructive analysis which developed into a lengthy and heavy bombardment 17 years later when the doctrine reappeared in the French Declaration of the Rights of the Man and the Citizen.

With those two works, Jeremy Bentham opened in 1776 a whole epoch in that area of philosophy which is of peculiar relevance and concern to the lawyer. Moreover, even if in the narrow English style we conceive of jurisprudence as lying outside the scope of political philosophy or theory, it is true that in jurisprudence, Bentham's thoughts published just 200 years ago have been enormously influential and persistent. During the years since his death in 1832 much argument and counter-argument about the nature of law, about the relationship between law and morality, and about the forms of legal reasoning appropriate to legal adjudication have revolved around ideas found in Bentham's works. The most fundamental of these ideas is that law, good or bad, is a man-made artifact which men create and add to the world by the exercise of their will ; it is not something already in the world that men discover through the exercise of their reasoning powers. Bentham thought that there are indeed good reasons for having laws, but a reason for a law, even a good reason, is not a law any more than "hunger is bread." On this foundation rested the famous definition of laws as the commands, prohibitions, or permissions of a sovereign legislature, issued either explicitly and directly by the sovereign, or indirectly through subordinates whose mandates the sovereign explicitly authorizes or tacitly adopts.

With these fundamental ideas went the sharp severance which Bentham made in *A Fragment on Government* between law as it is and law as it ought to be (and between an analytical or, as he termed it, expository jurisprudence and a critical or censorial jurisprudence), and his insistence in the same work that the foundations of a legal system are not to be found in any moral or justificatory theory, but are properly described in the morally and evaluatively neutral terms of a general habit of obedience to a sovereign legislature. This cluster of ideas opened the long positivist tradition in English jurisprudence. Transmitted through the medium of John Austin's work, in a style more easily assimilable than Bentham's by lawyers who were not also philosophers, this tradition has of course profoundly and, as some think, disastrously, influenced English legal education and the English conception of the judicial function, leaving its profound imprint on English legal thought in general.

Even in the United States the leading themes of Benthamite jurisprudence have reverberated, although, to continue the musical metaphor, they have been transposed into another key with the American law-making court replacing the British sovereign legislature as the chief focus of attention. John Chipman Gray in *The Nature and Sources of the Law* explicitly endorsed and indeed applauded the Benthamite and Austinian distinction between law as "that which is" and law as an ideal of what ought to be, and Holmes, who had read with care and responded to much of Austin's work, finding its apparent toughness congenial to his temperament, advocated what was in essence the same distinction when he argued that the clear-minded jurist should wash the notion of legal obligation and duty in "cynical acid" so as to free law from a perennial and obscuring confusion with morality.

Such then were the leading ideas with which an epoch opened in both political and legal theory in 1776. But there are signs that this epoch may now be closing. Utilitarianism, which for long was regarded as the sober, workmanlike English manifestation of the European Enlightenment and which was certainly the fountain of great reforms of the archaic English legal system as well as the inspiration of progressive thought in England and elsewhere, is now seen by many thinkers to have a darker, more sinister side, licensing anything to be done to individuals, condoning any sacrifice, in the pursuit of the ultimate goal of maximizing the aggregate or average welfare of a community. Moreover, much of the most interesting current work among American political philosophers — and I am thinking here of John Rawls's *A Theory of Justice* and Robert Nozick's *Anarchy, State, and Utopia* — is not only frankly hostile to Utilitarianism but identifies as Utilitarianism's cardinal sin its failure to recognize that the division of humanity into separate individuals is a fact of great moral importance which confers on certain interests of individuals a title to inviolability to be maintained even where to maintain it may reduce the level of aggregate or average welfare below that which could otherwise be achieved. Plainly, a social philosophy in this temper has much affinity with the eighteenth century doctrines of the inalienable rights of man that were long thought to have succumbed to their great Utilitarian critic. As for jurisprudence, in suggesting that we may be at the end of an epoch and at the beginning of a new one, I am thinking of the work of my American successor in the Chair of Jurisprudence at Oxford, Professor Ronald Dworkin. The transition is marked not only by the same antipathy to Utilitarianism and the same insistence on the independent importance of individual rights, but also by a new form of the ancient theory that there are vital conceptual connections between law and principles of justice which justify the law, to which, it is said, positivism has been blind and has blinded its victims.

Of course, criticism of Bentham's form of Utilitarianism is no new thing. For a century at least in England and America there has been a stream of intermittent, unsystematic and piecemeal criticism of Bentham's legacy to political philosophy and jurisprudence. Until recently the criticisms had been absorbed as matters calling for refinement, qualification, or reinterpretation of the doctrines and not outright rejection, even if in the case of some of the reinterpretations — notably John Stuart Mill's distinctively libertarian and individualistic version of the notion of Utility — it might seem that the spirit of Bentham's doctrine was quite transformed and only the terminology in which it is formulated remains the same. But the three contemporary writers whom I have mentioned are different, and it is a phenomenon of importance that in spite of many differences of doctrine and political implications, the liveliest and most interesting modern writings in political and legal theory contain frank and fundamental challenges to Bentham's thought about law and politics. So in the remainder of this short presentation I shall take two examples of the new ideas and raise the question whether we should do well to regard them as disposing finally of Bentham's thought in these fields.

In his attack in 1776 on the Declaration of Independence, Bentham allows that the concept of a non-positive right — that is, one not created by the law or social custom — is coherent and not self-contradictory, though his own view was that it was indeed self-contradictory and a species of nonsense. Within the framework of this provisional concession Bentham focused his criticism of the Declaration of Independence on the absurdity of combining the assertion that there are inalienable rights with the assertion that government is necessary to protect them and legitimate when it does so. This combination was absurd in Bentham's view because the exercise of the necessary powers of any government must constantly restrict the exercise by the individual of his alleged inalienable rights :

> They see not, or will not seem to see that nothing that was ever called government ever was or could be in any instance exercised save at the expense of one or other of those rights : that (consequently) in as many instances as government is ever exercised some one or other of these pretended unalienable rights is alienated. . . . If the right of pursuit of happiness is a right unalienable . . .why (how) are thieves restrained from pursuing it by theft, murderers by murder, and rebels by rebellion . . . .[2]

Taken strictly as offering unqualified guarantees of certain liberties, the doctrine is essentially anarchical, and anarchists have not been slow to invoke it in support of their claim that the state is, morally speaking, illegitimate. Bentham insisted that no political principles with the rigidity of the doctrine of inalienable specific rights could have any application in the real world where men live their lives. Such principles belong to Utopia — that is, to Nowhere or to an imaginary world. Accordingly, he stigmatized the doctrine as the product not of reason but of mere imagination, complaining that such principles were "deaf, unyielding, and inflexible — principles [which] will hear of no *modification*, [which] will look at no *calculation* [which,] if instead of imagination, reason [were] consulted, would be necessary."

This form of criticism was amplified by Bentham when he came to deal with the French Declaration of the Rights of the Man and the Citizen by demonstrating that inalienable rights, construed as guarantees of specific liberties of action, were not only incompatible with government but were doomed to constant conflict with each other. Simple and crude as this form of criticism may seem, it became, and remained for decades, the standard objection to the doctrine of fixed natural rights. Indeed, its vitality is paradoxically confirmed by one of the works which I have already mentioned, Nozick's *Anarchy, State, and Utopia.*

For at the outset, Nozick raises precisely Bentham's question and asks "How much room do individual rights leave for government ?" What is astonishing is that Nozick also gives Bentham's answer : No room except in an imaginary world. That is the message of Nozick's infinitely ingenious and brilliant work. Thus, he argues that granted a set of natural rights — such as the right not to be killed, assaulted, coerced, not to have property taken or destroyed, and not to be limited in the use of property — only a minimal form of state, the so-called "nightwatchman" state, whose functions are limited to the punishment of violations of such rights, can be legitimate. Moreover, given those natural rights, even that minimal form of state could be justified only under certain conditions which Bentham never considered. Yet Bentham might be forgiven for failing to do so, for they are conditions produced out of Nozick's lively imagination which are highly unlikely to be satisfied in the real as contrasted with the imaginary world. The conditions in question are that the state should have arisen through individuals voluntarily joining a private protection association which might eventually achieve, without infringing any natural rights, dominance in a limited territory even if not everyone joined it. But all this seems indeed imaginary and irrelevant in a world where states do not arise in that way.

So Nozick's theory seems tailor-made for Bentham's accusation that talk of inalienable rights, taken strictly, belongs only to the world of the imagination. Of course, Bentham realized that defenders of the doctrine would disclaim such rigid unqualified interpretations of it and, while speaking of rights as "inalienable," would admit that limitations of scope, qualifications and exceptions as well as balancing of right against right and of right against the general welfare may be necessary. Bentham also realized that those defenders would even be content to view inalienable rights merely as ideal directions to governments to do the best they can for certain individual interests. But he claimed that the doctrine would then be nugatory. To support that claim he could have cited some famous — or infamous — examples from America, where express declarations of natural rights to liberty, incorporated into state constitutions, were held not to affect the slave owner's rights to property in his slaves. He depicted the French advocates of natural rights as on the horns of a dilemma between the impossible and the nugatory. In this I think he was wrong : there is certainly more to be said about the relationship between basic human rights and other values than he allows. But in spite of recent work, I do not think we yet have a satisfactory theory showing how respect for such rights is to be combined with the pursuit of other values. Some theories seem to me to throw out the baby — that is basic rights compatible with each other and with government — with the bathwater of excessive rigidity. Other theories — perhaps Professor Nozick's among them — do worse; they throw out the baby and keep the bathwater.... [pp. 538-545]

In my perspective for the future of law and philosophy, there is much unfinished business. At a time when . . . substantive issues of social policy are much discussed in terms of individuals' rights, we still need a satisfactory theory of basic human rights and their relationship to other values pursued through the law. So too, if positivism in jurisprudence is to be finally laid to rest, we still need a demonstration that an expanded concept of law, which includes for every legal system a unique set of justicatory principles as a reserve for the solution of hard cases, will illumine and not obscure the description and the performance of the judge's task. But judging from the work in progress, the prospects that we shall have at least some of these things are good. Certainly American philosophers are more likely than any others to provide them ; but let us hope it will not take them another 200 years. [p. 551]

NOTES

1. H.L.A. Hart, "Law in the Perspective of Philosophy : 1776-1976," 51 *New York University Law Review* (1976) : 538-551.

2. Bentham's letter in T. Sprigge, ed., *The Correspondence of Jeremy Bentham,* (1968), pp. 342-343.

PHILOSOPHY OF RIGHT[1]

Hegel

The state is the actuality of the ethical Idea. It is ethical mind *qua* the substantial will manifest and revealed to itself, knowing and thinking itself, accomplishing what it knows and in so far as it knows it. The state exists immediately in custom, mediately in individual self-consciousness, knowledge, and activity, while self-consciousness, in virtue of its sentiment towards the state finds in the state, as its essence and the end and product of its activity, its substantive freedom....

The state is absolutely rational inasmuch as it is the actuality of the substantial will which it possesses in the particular self-consciousness once that consciousness has been raised to consciousness of its universality. This substantial unity is an absolute unmoved end in itself, in which freedom comes into its supreme right. On the other hand this final end has supreme right against the individual, whose supreme duty is to be a member of the state.... [pp. 155-156]

The Idea of the state

(a) has immediate actuality and is the individual state as a self-dependent organism — the *Constitution* or *Constitutional Law* ;
(b) passes over into the relation of one state to other states — *International Law* ;
(c) is the universal Idea as a genus and as an absolute power over individual states — the mind which gives itself its actuality in the process of *World History.*

The state is the actuality of concrete freedom. But concrete freedom consists in this, that personal individuality and its particular interests not only achieve their complete development and gain explicit recognition for their right (as they do in the sphere of the family and civil society) but, for one thing, they also pass over of their own accord into the interest of the universal, and, for another thing, they know and will the universal ; they even recognize it as their own substantive mind ; they take it as their end and aim and are active in its pursuit. The result is that the universal does not prevail or achieve completion except along with particular interests and through the co-operation of particular knowing and willing ; and individuals likewise do not live as private persons for their own ends alone, but in the very act of willing these they will the universal in the light of the universal, and their activity is consciously aimed at none but the universal end. The principle of modern states has prodigious strength and depth because it allows the principle of subjectivity to progress to its culmination in the extreme of self-subsistent personal particularity, and yet at the same time brings it back to the substantive unity and so maintains this unity in the principle of subjectivity itself.... [pp. 160-161]

The state in and by itself is the ethical whole, the actualization of freedom ; and it is an absolute end of reason that freedom should be actual. The state is mind on earth and consciously realizing itself there. In nature, on the other hand, mind actualizes itself only as its own other, as mind asleep. Only when it is present in consciousness, when it knows itself as a really existent object, is it the state. In considering freedom, the starting point must be not individuality, the single self-consciousness, but only the essence of self-consciousness ; for whether man knows it or not, this essence is externally realized as a self-subsistent power in which single individuals are only moments. The march of God in the world, that is what the state is. The basis of the state is the power of reason actualizing itself as will. In considering the Idea of the state, we must not have our eyes on particular states or on particular institutions. Instead we must consider the Idea, this actual God, by itself. On some principle or other, any state may be shown to be bad, this or that defect may be found in it ; and yet, at any rate if one of the mature states of our epoch is in question, it has in it the moments essential to the existence of the state. But since it is easier to find defects than to understand the affirmative, we may readily fall into the mistake of looking at isolated aspects of the state and so forgetting its inward organic life. The state is no ideal work of art ; it stands on earth and so in the sphere of caprice, chance, and error, and bad behaviour may disfigure it in many respects. But the ugliest of men, or a criminal, or an invalid, or a cripple is still always a living man. The affirmative life subsists despite his defects, and it is this affirmative factor which is our theme here.

The state in its actuality is essentially an individual state, and beyond that a particular state. Individuality is to be distinguished from particularity. The former is a moment in the very Idea of the state, while the latter belongs to history. States as such are independent of one another, and therefore their relation to one another can only be an external one, so that there must be a third thing standing above them to bind them together. Now this third thing is the mind which gives itself actuality in world history and is the absolute judge of states. Several states may form an alliance to be a sort of court with jurisdiction over others, there may be confederations of states, like the Holy Alliance for example, but these are always relative only and restricted, like "perpetual peace." The one and only absolute judge, which makes itself authoritative against the particular and at all times, is the absolute mind which manifests itself in the history of the world as the universal and as the genus there operative.

The Idea of the state in modern times has a special character in that the state is the actualization of freedom not in accordance with subjective whim but in accordance with the concept of the will, i.e., in accordance with its universality and divinity. Immature states are those in which the Idea of the state is still veiled and where its particular determinations have not yet attained free self-subsistence. In the states of classical antiquity, universality was present, but particularity had not then been released, given free scope, and brought back to universality, i.e., to the universal end of the whole. The essence of the modern state is that the universal be bound up with the complete freedom of its particular members and with private well-being, that thus the interests of family and civil society must concentrate themselves on the state, although the universal end cannot be advanced without the personal knowledge and will of its particular members, whose own rights must be maintained. Thus the universal must be furthered, but subjectivity on the other hand must attain its full and living development. It is only when both these moments subsist in their strength that the state can be regarded as articulated and genuinely organized.

In the state everything depends on the unity of universal and particular. In the states of antiquity, the subjective end simply coincides with the state's will. In modern times, however, we make claims for private judgment, private willing, and private conscience. The ancients had none of these in the modern sense; the ultimate thing with them was the will of the state. Whereas under the despots of Asia the individual had no inner life and no justification in himself in the modern world man insists on respect being paid to his inner life. The conjunction of duty and right has a twofold aspect: what the state demands from us as a duty is *eo ipso* our right as individuals, since the state is nothing but the articulation of the concept of freedom. The determinations of the individual will are given an objective embodiment through the state and thereby they attain their truth and their actualization for the first time. The state is the one and only prerequisite of the attainment of particular ends and welfare.

In Plato's state, subjective freedom does not count, because people have their occupations assigned to them by the guardians. In many oriental states, this assignment is determined by birth. But subjective freedom, which must be respected, demands that individuals should have free choice in this matter.

The state, as mind, sunders itself into the particular determinations of its concept, of its mode of being. We might use here an illustration drawn from nature. The nervous system is the sensitive system proper; it is the abstract moment, the moment of being by oneself and so of having identity with oneself. But analysis of sensation reveals that it has two aspects and these are distinct in such a way that each of them seems to be a whole system by itself. The first is feeling in the abstract, keeping oneself self-enclosed, the dull movement which goes on internally, reproduction, internal self-nutrition, growth, and digestion. The second moment is that this self-related existence has over against it the moment of difference, a movement outwards. This is irritability, sensation moving outwards. This constitutes a system of its own, and there are some of the lower types of animals which have developed this system alone, while they lack the soul-charged unity of inner sensation. If we compare these natural features with those of mind, then the family must be paralleled with sensibility and civil society with irritability. Now the third is the state, the nervous system as a whole, something inwardly organized; but this lives only in so far as both moments (in this case family and civil society) are developed within it. The laws regulating family and civil society are the institutions of the rational order which glimmers in them. But the ground and final truth of these institutions is mind, their universal end and known objective. The family too is ethical, only its end is not known as such, while it is the separation between one man and another which makes civil society what it is. [pp. 279-281]

NOTE

1. T.M.Knox, trans., *Hegel's Philosophy of Right,* (London : Oxford University Press, 1942), pp. 155-281.

THE MATERIALIST CONCEPTION OF HISTORY[1]

Karl Marx

I was led by my studies to the conclusion that legal relations as well as forms of state could neither be understood by themselves, nor explained by the so-called general progress of the human mind, but that they are rooted in the material conditions of life, which are summed up by Hegel after the fashion of the English and French writers of the eighteenth century under the name civil society, and that the anatomy of civil society is to be sought in political economy. The study of the latter which I had begun in Paris, I continued in Brussels where I had emigrated on account of an expulsion order issued by M. Guizot. The general conclusion at which I arrived and which, once reached, continued to serve as the guiding thread in my studies, may be formulated briefly as follows : In the social production which men carry on they enter into definite relations that are indispensable and independent of their will ; these relations of production correspond to a definite stage of development of their material powers of production. The totality of these relations of production constitutes the economic structure of society — the real foundation, on which legal and political superstructures arise and to which definite forms of social consciousness correspond. The mode of production of material life determines the general character of the social, political, and spiritual processes of life. It is not the consciousness of men that determines their being, but, on the contrary, their social being determines their consciousness. At a certain stage of their development, the material forces of production in society come in conflict with the existing relations of production, or — what is but a legal expression for the same thing — with the property relations within which they had been at work before. From forms of development of the forces of production these relations turn into their fetters. Then occurs a period of social revolution. With the change of the economic foundation the entire immense superstructure is more or less rapidly transformed. In considering such transformations the distinction should always be made between the material transformation of the economic conditions of production which can be determined with the precision of natural science, and the legal, political, religious, aesthetic, or philosophical, in short, ideological, forms in which men become conscious of this conflict and fight it out. Just as our opinion of an individual is not based on what he thinks of himself, so can we not judge of such a period of transformation by its own consciousness ; on the contrary, this consciousness must rather be explained from the contradictions of material life, from the existing conflict between the social forces of production and the relations of production. No social order ever disappears before all the productive forces for which there is room in it have been developed ; and new, higher relations of production never appear before the material conditions of their existence have matured in the womb of the old society. Therefore, mankind always sets itself only such problems as it can solve ; since, on closer examination, it will always be found that the problem itself arises only when the material conditions necessary for its solution already exist or are at least in the process of formation. In broad outline we can designate the Asiatic, the ancient, the feudal, and the modern bourgeois modes of production as progressive epochs in the economic formation of society. The bourgeois relations of production are the last antagonistic form of the social process of production ; not in the sense of individual antagonisms, but of conflict arising from conditions surrounding the life of individuals in society. At the same time the productive forces developing in the womb of bourgeois society create the material conditions for the solution of that antagonism. With this social formation, therefore, the prehistory of human society comes to an end.... [pp. 51-53]

Since the state is the form in which the individuals of a ruling class assert their common interests, and in which the whole civil society of an epoch is epitomized, it follows that the state acts as an intermediary for all community institutions, and that these institutions receive a political form. Hence the illusion that law is based on will, and indeed on will divorced from its real basis — on *free* will. Similarly, law is in its turn reduced to the actual laws.

Civil law develops concurrently with private property out of the disintegration of the natural community. Among the Romans the development of private property and civil law had no further industrial and commercial consequences because their whole mode of production remained unchanged. Among modern peoples, where the feudal community was disintegrated by industry and trade, a new phase began with the rise of private property and civil law, which was capable of further development. The first town which carried on an extensive trade in the Middle Ages, Amalfi, also developed at the same time maritime law. As soon as industry and trade developed private property further, first in Italy and later in other countries, the perfected Roman civil law was at once taken up again and raised to authority. When, subsequently, the bourgeoisie had acquired so much power that the princes took up their interests in order to overthrow the feudal nobility by means of the bourgeoisie, there began in all countries — in France in the sixteenth century — the real development of law, which in all countries except England proceeded on the basis of the Roman Code. Even in England, Roman legal principles had to be introduced for the further development of civil law (especially in the case of movable property). It should not be forgotten that law has not, any more than religion, an independent history.... [p. 223]

In historical fact the theorists who considered force as the basis of law were directly opposed to those who saw will as the basis of law.... If force is taken to be the basis of law, as by Hobbes, law and legislative enactments are only a symptom or expression of other conditions upon which the state power rests. The material life of individuals, which certainly does not depend on their mere "will," their mode of production and their form of intercourse, which reciprocally influence each other, are the real basis of the state. This material life is, at every stage in which the division of labour and private property are still necessary, quite independent of the will of individuals. These real conditions are not created by the state power ; they are rather the power which creates it. The individuals who rule under these conditions, quite apart from the fact that their power has to constitute itself as a state, must give their will, as it is determined by these definite circumstances, a general expression as the will of the state, as law. The content of this expression is always determined by the situation of this class, as is most clearly revealed in the civil and criminal law. Just as the bodily weight of individuals does not depend upon their ideal will or caprice, so it does not depend on them whether they embody their own will in law, and at the same time, in accordance with individual caprice give everyone beneath them his independence. Their individual domination must at the same time form a general domination. Their individual power rests upon conditions of existence which develop as social conditions and whose continuance they must show to involve their own supremacy and yet be valid for all. Law is the expression of this will conditioned by their common interests. It is just the striving of independent individuals and their wills, which on this basis are necessarily egoistic in their behaviour to each other, which makes self denial through law and regulation essential, or rather self denial in exceptional cases and maintenance of their interest in general.... The same holds good for the subject classes, on whose will the existence of law and the state is equally little dependent. For instance, as long as the productive forces are insufficiently developed to make competition superfluous, with the consequence that competition is always reappearing, the subject classes would be willing the impossible if they "willed" to abolish competition and with it the state and law. Moreover, until conditions have developed to a point where they can produce this "will" it exists only in the imagination of the ideologists. Once conditions are sufficiently developed to produce it, the ideologist can imagine it as purely capricious and therefore conceivable at any period and under any circumstances. Crime, i.e., the struggle of the single individual against the dominant conditions, is as little the product of simple caprice as law itself. It is rather conditioned in the same way as the latter. The same visionaries who see in law the rule of an independent and general will see in crime a simple breaking of the law. The state does not rest on a dominating will, but the state which arises out of the material mode of life of individuals has also the form of a dominating will. If this will loses its domination this means not only that the will has changed but also that the material existence and life of individuals has changed despite their will. It is possible that law and legislation have an autonomous evolution but in that case they are purely formal and no longer dominating, as many striking examples in Roman and English legal history show. We have already seen how, through the activity of philosophers, a history of pure thought could arise by the separation of thought from the individuals and their actual relations which are its basis. In the present case, also, law can be separated from its real basis, and thereby we can arrive at a "ruling will" which in different periods has a different expression and which, in its creations, the laws, has its own independent history. By this means political and civil history is ideologically transformed into a history of the dominance of self-developing laws. [pp. 225-227]

NOTE

1. Karl Marx, "The Materialist Conception of History," in T. Bottomore, trans., *Karl Marx* (New York : McGraw-Hill Book Co., 1956), pp. 51-227.

ON THE JEWISH QUESTION[1]

Karl Marx

Security is the highest social concept of civil society, the concept of the police. The whole of society is merely there to guarantee to each of its members the preservation of his person, rights, and property. It is in this sense that Hegel calls civil society the "state of need and of reason."

The concept of security does not allow civil society to raise itself above its egoism. Security is more the assurance of egoism.

Thus none of the so-called rights of man goes beyond egoistic man, man as he is in civil society, namely an individual withdrawn behind his private interests and whims and separated from the community. Far from the rights of man conceiving of man as a species-being, species-life itself, society, appears as a framework exterior to individuals, a limitation of their original self-sufficiency. The only bond that holds them together is natural necessity, need and private interest, the conservation of their property and egoistic person.

It is already paradoxical that a people that is just beginning to free itself, to tear down all barriers between different sections of the people and form a political community, should solemnly proclaim (Declaration of 1791) the justification of egoistic man separated from his fellow men and the community. Indeed, this proclamation is repeated at a moment when only the most heroic devotion can save the nation, and is therefore peremptorily demanded, at a moment when the sacrifice of all the interests of civil society is raised to the order of the day and egoism must be punished as a crime (*Declaration of the Rights of Man. . . 1793*). This fact appears to be even more paradoxical when we see that citizenship, the political community, is degraded by the political emancipators to a mere means for the preservation of these so-called rights of man, that the citizen is declared to be the servant of egoistic man, the sphere in which man behaves as a communal being is degraded below the sphere in which man behaves as a partial being, finally that it is not man as a citizen but man as a bourgeois who is called the real and true man.

"The aim of every political association is the conversation of the natural and imprescriptible rights of man" (*Declaration of the Rights of Man. . .1791,* Article 2). "Government is instituted to guarantee man the enjoyment of his natural and imprescriptible rights" (*Declaration of the Rights of Man. . .1791,* Article 1). So even in the moments of youthful freshness and enthusiasm raised to fever pitch by the pressure of circumstances, political life is declared to be a mere means whose end is the life of civil society. It is true that its revolutionary practice is in flagrant contradiction with its theory. While, for example, security is declared to be a right of man the violation of the privacy of correspondence is publicly inserted in the order of the day. While the "unlimited freedom of the press" (Constitution of 1793, Article 122) is guaranteed as a consequence of the right of man to individual freedom, the freedom of the press is completely destroyed, for "the liberty of the press must not be permitted when it compromises public liberty" ("The Young Robespierre," in Buchez and Roux, *Parliamentary History of the French Revolution*, vol. 28, p. 159). This means then that the right of man to freedom ceases to be a right as soon as it enters into conflict with political life, whereas, according to the theory, political life is only the guarantee of the rights of man, the rights of individual man, and so must be given up as soon as it contradicts its end, these rights of man. But the practice is only the exception and the theory is the rule. Even though one were to treat the revolutionary practice as the correct version of the relationship, the riddle still remains to be solved of why, in the minds of the political emancipators, the relationship is turned upside down and the end appears as the means and the means as the end. This optical illusion of their minds would always be the same riddle, although it would then be a psychological and theoretical riddle.

The riddle has a simple solution.

Political emancipation is at the same time the dissolution of the old society on which rests the sovereign power, the essence of the state alienated from the people. Political revolution is the revolution of civil society. What was the character of the old society ? One word characterizes it. Feudalism. The old civil society had a directly political character. The elements of civil life, like, for example, property or the family or the type and manner of work, were, in the form of seignorial right, estates and corporations, raised to the level of elements of state life. They defined in this form the relationship of the single individual to the state as a whole, that is, his political relationship, the relationship of separation and exclusion from the other parts of society. For this sort of organization of the people's life did not turn property or work into social elements but completed their separation from the state as a whole, and made them into particular societies within society. But the vital functions and conditions of life in civil society was still political even though political in the feudal sense, that is, they excluded the individual from the states as a whole. They turned the particular relationship of the corporation to the totality of the state, into his general relationship to the life of the people, as it turned his particular civil occupation into his general occupation and situation. As a consequence of this organization the unity of the state — the mind, will, and authority of this state unity, the power of the state in general — equally appears necessarily as the particular affair of a lord and servants who are cut off from the people.

The political revolution overthrew this feudal power and turned state affairs into affairs of the people ; it turned the state into a matter of general concern, i.e., into a true state ; it necessarily destroyed all estates, corporations, guilds, privileges which were so many expressions of the separation of the people from the community. The political revolution thus abolished the political character of civil society. It shattered civil society with its simple parts, on the one hand into individuals, on the other hand into the material and spiritual elements that make up the life experience and civil position of these individuals. It unfettered the political spirit that had, as it were, been split, cut up, and drained away into the various cul-de-sacs of feudal society. The political revolution collected this spirit together after its dispersion, freed it from its confusion with civil life and set it up as the sphere that was common to all, the general affair of the people in ideal independence from the other particular elements of civil life. Particular professions and ranks sank to a merely individual importance. They were no longer the relationship of individuals to the state as a whole. Public affairs as such became the general affair of each individual and politics was a general occupation.

But the perfection of the idealism of the state was at the same time the perfection of the materialism of civil society. The shaking off of the political yoke entailed the shaking off of those bonds that had kept the egoistic spirit of civil society fettered. Political emancipation entailed the emancipation of civil society from politics, from even the appearance of a general content.

Feudal society was dissolved into its basis, into man. But into the man that was its true basis, egoistic man. This man, the member of civil society, is the basis, the presupposition of the political state. He is recognized by it as such in the rights of man.

But the freedom of egoistic man and the recognition of this freedom is the recognition of the unimpeded movement of the spiritual and material elements that go to make up its life.

Man was therefore not freed from religion ; he received freedom of religion. He was not freed from property ; he received freedom of property. He was not freed from the egoism of trade ; he received freedom to trade.

The formation of the political state and the dissolution of civil society into independent individuals, who are related by law just as the estate and corporation men were related by privilege, is completed in one and the same act. Man as a member of civil society, unpolitical man, appears necessarily as natural man. The rights of man appear as natural rights, because self-conscious activity is concentrated upon political action. Egoistic man is the passive, given result of the dissolved society, an object of immediate certainty and thus a natural object. Political revolution dissolves civil life into its component parts, without revolutionizing and submitting to criticism these parts themselves. Its attitude to civil society, to the world of need, to work, private interests, private law is that they are the foundation of its existence, its own presupposition that needs no further proof, and thus its natural basis. Finally, man as a member of civil society counts for true man, for man as distinct from the citizen, because he is a man in his sensuous, individual, immediate existence, while political man is only the abstract fictional man, man as an allegorical or moral person. This man as he actually is, is only recognized in the form of the egoistic individual, and the true man only in the form of the abstract citizen.

The abstraction of the political man is thus correctly described by Rousseau : "He who dares to undertake the making of a people's institutions ought to feel himself capable, so to speak, of changing human nature, of transforming each individual, who is by himself a complete and solitary whole, into part of a greater whole from which he in a manner receives his life and being ; of altering man's constitution for the purpose of strengthening it ; and of substituting a partial and moral existence for the physical and independent existence nature has conferred on us all. He must, in a word, take away from man his own resources and give him instead new ones alien to him, and incapable of being made use of without the help of other men."

All emancipation is bringing back man's world and his relationships to man himself.

Political emancipation is the reduction of man, on the one hand to a member of civil society, an egoistic and independent individual, on the other hand to a citizen, a moral person.

The actual individual man must take the abstract citizen back into himself and, as an individual man in his empirical life, in his individual work and individual relationships become a species-being ; man must recognize his own forces as social forces ; organize them and thus no longer separate social forces from himself in the form of political forces. Only when this has been achieved will human emancipation be completed. [pp. 104-108]

NOTE

1. Karl Marx, "On the Jewish Question," in David McLellen, ed. and trans., *Karl Marx Early Texts* (Oxford : Blackwell, 1971), pp. 104-108.

THE STATE AND REVOLUTION[1]

V.I. Lenin

The whole theory of Marx is the application of the theory of development — in its most consistent, complete, considered and pithy form — to modern capitalism. Naturally, Marx was faced with the problem of applying this theory both to the *forthcoming* collapse of capitalism and to the *future* development of *future* Communism.

On the basis of what *data*, then, can the question of the future development of future Communism be dealt with ?

On the basis of the fact that *it has its origin* in capitalism, that it develops historically from capitalism, that it is the result of the action of a social force to which capitalism *gave birth.* There is no trace of an attempt on Marx's part to conjure up a utopia, to make idle guesses about what cannot be known. Marx treats the question of Communism in the same way as a naturalist would treat the question of the development, say, of a new biological variety, once he knew that such and such was its origin and such and such the exact direction in which it was changing....

Marx writes :

> "Present-day society" is capitalist society, which exists in all civilized countries, more or less free from medieval admixture, more or less modified by the special historical development of each country, more or less developed. On the other hand, the "present-day state" changes with a country's frontier. It is different in the Prusso-German Empire from what it is in Switzerland, it is different in England from what it is in the United States. The "present-day state" is, therefore, a fiction. Nevertheless, the different states of the different civilized countries, in spite of their manifold diversity of form, all have this in common, that they are based on modern bourgeois society, only one more or less capitalistically developed. They have, therefore, also certain essential features in common. In this sense it is possible to speak of the "present-day state," in contrast with the future in which its present root, bourgeois society, will have died off.
>
> The question then arises : what transformation will the state undergo in communist society ? In other words, what social functions will remain in existence there that are analogous to present functions of the state ? This question can only be answered scientifically, and one does not get a flea-hop nearer to the problem by a thousandfold combination of the word people with the word state.[2]

Having thus ridiculed all talk about a "people's state," Marx formulates the question and warns us, as it were, that a scientific answer to it can be secured only by using firmly established scientific data.

The first fact that has been established with complete exactitude by the whole theory of development, by science as a whole — a fact that was forgotten by the utopians, and is forgotten by the present-day opportunists who are afraid of the socialist revolution — is that, historically, there must undoubtedly be a special stage or a special phase of *transition* from capitalism to Communism.

Marx continues :

> Between capitalist and communist society lies the period of the revolutionary transformation of the one into the other. There corresponds to this also a political transition period in which the state can be nothing but *the revolutionary dictatorship of the proletariat.*

Marx bases this conclusion on the analysis of the role played by the proletariat in modern capitalist society, on the data concerning the development of this society, and on the irreconcilability of the antagonistic interests of the proletariat and the bourgeoisie.

Previously the question was put in this way : in order to achieve its emancipation, the proletariat must overthrow the bourgeoisie, win political power and establish its revolutionary dictatorship.

Now the question is put somewhat differently : the transition from capitalist society — which is developing towards Communism — to a communist society is impossible without a "political transition period," and the state in this period can only be the revolutionary dictatorship of the proletariat.

What then, is the relation of this dictatorship to democracy ?

We have seen that the *Communist Manifesto* simply places side by side the two concepts : "to raise the proletariat to the position of the ruling class" and "to win the battle of democracy." On the basis of all that has been said above, it is possible to determine more precisely how democracy changes in the transition from capitalism to Communism.

In capitalist society, providing it develops under the most favourable conditions, we have a more or less complete democracy in the democratic republic. But this democracy is always hemmed in by the narrow limits set by capitalist exploitation, and consequently always remains, in reality, a democracy for the minority, only for the propertied classes, only for the rich. Freedom in capitalist society always remains about the same as it was in the ancient Greek republics : freedom for the slave-owners. Owing to the conditions of capitalist exploitation the modern wage slaves are so crushed by want and poverty that "they cannot be bothered with democracy," "they cannot be bothered with politics ;" in the ordinary peaceful course of events the majority of the population is debarred from participation in public and political life....

Marx grasped this *essence* of capitalist democracy splendidly, when, in analyzing the experience of the Commune, he said that the oppressed are allowed once every few years to decide which particular representatives of the oppressing class shall represent and repress them in parliament !

But from this capitalist democracy — that is inevitably narrow, and stealthily pushes aside the poor, and is therefore hypocritical and false to the core — forward development does not proceed simply, directly and smoothly towards "greater and greater democracy," as the liberal professors and petty-bourgeois opportunists would have us believe. No, forward development, i.e., towards

Communism, proceeds through the dictatorship of the proletariat, and cannot do otherwise, for the *resistance* of the capitalist exploiters cannot be *broken* by anyone else or in any other way.

And the dictatorship of the proletariat, i.e., the organization of the vanguard of the oppressed as the ruling class for the purpose of suppressing the oppressors, cannot result merely in an expansion of democracy, which *for the first time* becomes democracy for the poor, democracy for the people, and not democracy for the moneybags, the dictatorship of the proletariat imposes a series of restrictions on the freedom of the oppressors, the exploiters, the capitalists. We must suppress them in order to free humanity from wage slavery, their resistance must be crushed by force ; it is clear that where there is suppression, where there is violence, there is no freedom and no democracy.... [pp. 101-105]

"Equal right," says Marx, we indeed have here ; but it is *still* a "bourgeois right," which, like every right, *presupposes inequality.* Every right is an application of an *equal* measure to *different* people who in fact are not alike, are not equal to one another ; that is why "equal right" is really a violation of equality and an injustice. Indeed, every man, having performed as much social labour as another, receives an equal share of the social product (after the above-mentioned deductions).

But people are not alike : one is strong, another is weak ; one is married, another is not ; one has more children, another has less, and so on. And the conclusion Marx draws is :

> . . . with an equal performance of labour, and hence an equal share in the social consumption fund, one will in fact receive more than another, one will be richer than another, and so on. To avoid all these defects, right instead of being equal would have to be unequal.

Hence, the first phase of Communism cannot yet produce justice and equality : differences, and unjust differences, in wealth will still exist, but the *exploitation* of man by man will have become impossible, because it will be impossible to seize the *means of production,* the factories, machines, land, etc., as private property. While smashing Lassalle's petty-bourgeois, confused phrases about "equality" and "justice" *in general,* Marx shows the *course of development* of communist society, which is *compelled* to abolish at first *only* the "injustice" of the means of production having been seized by individuals, and which is *unable* at once to eliminate the other injustice, which consists in the distribution of articles of consumption "according to the amount of labour performed" (and not according to needs)....

Marx not only most scrupulously takes account of the inevitable inequality of men, but he also takes into account the fact that the mere conversion of the means of production into the common property of the whole of society (commonly called "Socialism") *does not remove* the defects of distribution and the inequality of "bourgeois right" which *continues to prevail* as long as products are divided "according to the amount of labour performed." Continuing, Marx says :

> But these defects are inevitable in the first phase of communist society as it is when it has just emerged after prolonged birth pangs from capitalist society. Right can never be higher than the economic structure of society and its cultural development conditioned thereby.

And so, in the first phase of communist society (usually called Socialism) "bourgeois right" is *not* abolished in its entirety, but only in part, only in proportion to the economic revolution so far attained, i.e., only in respect of the means of production. "Bourgeois right" recognizes them as the private property of individuals. Socialism converts them into *common* property. To *that extent* — and to that extent alone — "bourgeois right" disappears.

However, it continues to exist as far as its other part is concerned ; it continues to exist in the capacity of regulator (determining factor) in the distribution of products and the allotment of labour among the members of society. The socialist principle : "He who does not work, neither shall he eat," is *already* realized ; the other socialist principle : "An equal amount of products for an equal amount of labour," is also *already* realized. But this is not yet Communism, and it does not yet abolish "bourgeois right," which gives to unequal individuals, in return for unequal (really unequal) amounts of labour, equal amounts of products.

This is a "defect," says Marx, but it is unavoidable in the first phase of Communism ; for it we are not to indulge in utopianism, we must not think that having overthrown capitalism people will at once learn to work for society *without any standard of right* ; and indeed the abolition of capitalism *does not immediately create* the economic premises for *such* a change.

And there is no other standard than that of "bourgeois right." To this extent, therefore, there still remains the need for a state, which, while safeguading the public ownership of the means of production, would safeguard equality in labour and equality in the distribution of products.

The state withers away in so far as there are no longer any capitalists, any classes, and, consequently, no *class* can be *suppressed.*

But the state has not yet completely withered away, since there still remains the safeguarding of "bourgeois right," which sanctifies actual inequality. For the state to wither away completely complete Communism is necessary. [pp. 110-112]

NOTES

1. V.I. Lenin, *The State and Revolution* (Peking : Foreign Language Press, 1970), pp. 100-112.

2. See Karl Marx, "Critique of the Gotha Program, Karl Marx and Frederich Engels," in *Selected Works* vol. 2, Eng. ed. (Moscow, 1951), p. 30.

THE THEORY OF THE STATE AND LAW[1]

S.A. Golunskii and M.S. Strogovich

Sec. I. The State and Law. The state — an organization of the authority of the dominant class, . . . is a "complex machine," with whose aid the exploiter classes in exploiter society crush and oppress the toiling masses, and the proletariat in socialist society — effectuating its dictatorship — destroys exploitation and the exploiter classes, and builds socialist society. In all its activity, the state — realizing the *will* of the dominant class to which authority belongs — defends and guarantees the interests of that class. For this, the governing class requires that the mandates of its will be binding in society — that all citizens of the state be subject to, and observe them. To this end, the exploiter class forces its will upon the exploited — dictates its will to the people, subordinates the people to itself. In a socialist state, the will of the worker class, which has abolished exploitation — thereby expressing the interests of all the toilers — is binding upon all citizens, to the end of establishing and developing socialist relationships and building a classless, communist society.

Such an expression and realization of the will of the dominant class, to the end of establishing and strengthening social arrangements advantageous and agreeable to the dominant class, are attained with the aid of *law*, binding rules of conduct (chiefly in the form of legislation) established by the dominant class, which assures observance thereof by the entire force of its apparatus of constraint : the state. "Will, if it is the state's will, must be expressed as *legislation* established by *authority* — otherwise 'will' is an empty concussion of air by an empty sound." In the *Communist Manifesto*, Marx and Engels wrote of the bourgeoisie : "Your law is merely the will of your class, erected into legislation — a will whose content is defined by the material conditions of the existence of your class."

This proposition of the founders of Marxism revealing the class essence of bourgeois law — is the key to understanding the class essence of law of any sort, viz., the will of the dominant class elevated into legislation. This means that such will is precisely formulated and given universally binding force, becoming a rule of conduct binding upon all. The law of exploiter society always expresses the will of the class of exploiters — aided by law the exploiter classes impose their will upon the exploited popular masses. The law of socialist society likewise expresses the will of the dominant class, the worker class ; and — since exploiter classes have there been destroyed, and the worker class (to which the state guidance of society belongs) expresses the interests and aspirations of all the toiling people — socialist law is the will of the soviet people elevated into legislation — the will of the people who have built socialist society under the guidance of the worker class headed by the bolshevik party.

Lenin has pointed out that "without an apparatus capable of *compelling* the observance of legal rules the law is nothing," which solves also the problem of the relationship between law and the state. This problem is still unsolved in bourgeois legal theory — as is the controversy as to which has precedence. Is the state founded on law ? Or is law created by the state ? The most distinct expression of the idea that the law has precedence is by those who hold the contract theory of the origin of the state : viz., that the basis of the state is a contract between citizens and the state authority, and that the conditions of this contract — as well as "natural law" established by nature independently of the state — are binding upon the latter. In another form, the idea that law has precedence was expressed in the theory of the Rechtsstaat, which holds that the state itself is a purely legal concept. Other bourgeois theorists defend the view that the state has precedence — including those holding . . . the theory of violence — and that the state creates law. From the viewpoint of the Marx-Lenin theory of the state, each of these interpretations is incorrect. Law and the state are not two distinct phenomena — one preceding the other — but are two sides of one and the same phenomenon : class dominance, which is manifested (a) in the fact that the dominant class creates its apparatus of constraint (the state), and (b) in the fact that it expresses its will in the shape of rules of conduct which it formulates (law) and which — with the aid of its state apparatus — it compels people to observe.

As we have seen *supra*, law emerged jointly with the state, in consequence of the disintegration of the primordial-communal social order, the appearance of private property, and the division of society into classes. In class society antagonistic classes struggle *inter se* and the dominant class — aided by the instrument of constraint (the state) — holds the subordinate classes obedient, and — aided by *law* — dictates its will to them. Like the state, law is a historical phenomenon, emerging under the influence of the causes aforesaid, and — like the state — it will disappear with the disappearance of the causes which evoked it.

Sec. 2. Definition of Law. The study of any law — and even of individual juridic enactments — leads, first of all, to the conclusion that law is an *aggregate of the rules of human conduct.* Each enactment consists of rules regulating human conduct ; this is readily seen by reading any measure, for example the Civil Code — which establishes the rules for consummating various contracts and agreements (a loan, a sale, etc.) and thus regulates civil property relations ; and the Criminal Code which defines acts constituting crimes and the penalties applicable to persons who have committed them. These Codes are thus the aggregate of the rules of human conduct in different fields of life....

Law is thus composed of rules of human conduct. These are called norms in legal science — norm *meaning a rule, an order, a requirement.* Rules of conduct — norms — are distinguishable according to their character. Some — like the rules as to military duty — directly enjoin upon persons definite conduct. Others — like the norms of the criminal law (the Criminal Code) — forbid persons to commit certain acts ; still others — like most of the norms of the Civil law (the Civil Code) — grant citizens the opportunity to perform certain acts or establish the conditions requisite for their performance. But a legal norm — however formulated — always establishes a definite rule of human conduct. Consequently, as we survey the problem : what is law ? *we establish first of all, that law is an aggregate of the rules of human conduct (norms).*

This, however, does not completely define the concept. A multitude of rules (norms) existing and operative in society are not to be related to the category of law : laws of morality, first of all, defining human conduct in society from the dominant concepts of what is just or what is good ; or rules of decorum, of cultured behaviour as between citizens, or friendship and companionship, etc. While all these are rules of conduct, acts of this character are not regulated by law — the law intervenes in them only when moral requirements are at the same time legal requirements ; the law does not regulate the observance of the decencies except in cases where nonobservance takes on the character of conduct — such as hooliganism, which is punishable criminally.

Any legal norm is thus a rule of human conduct, but a rule of human conduct is not necessarily a legal norm. What rules of conduct are specifically referable to the category of law ? What are legal norms ? *Legal norms are those rules of human conduct established or affirmed by the state, whose coercive force guarantees their being put into operation.* The fact that state authority is the source of its force and binding character distinguishes a legal norm from a moral norm. If the fulfillment and observance of a rule of conduct is guaranteed by state authority — which compels fulfillment of the rule directly, or applies measures effective upon persons who break it — then we have a legal norm : a legal rule of conduct. If, however, a rule of conduct is guaranteed by measures of social cogency — but not by constraint upon the part of the state — we have norms of morality and rules of community living, but not legal norms.

A rule of conduct, therefore, becomes a legal norm only when the coercive force of the state guarantees its observance. This does not mean, however, that only direct constraint by the state effectuates — vitalizes — each legal norm : legal norms are in reality effected in most cases without the state's intervention. Thus in the Soviet socialist state, as the national masses becomes increasingly cultured and conscious, citizens give effect voluntarily to the overwhelming majority of legal norms in constantly greater degree by virtue of the authority of soviet legislation. However, if anyone permits a violation of law — fails to observe soviet legislation — the soviet state constrains the lawbreaker to submit to the law presently in force, acting through its organs (the court, the administrative organs). Hence it would be incorrect to say that a legal norm is *put into operation* coercively (by direct constraint on the part of the state) : the converse assertion would be correct : the coercive power of the state *guarantees* that legal norms are put into operation.

Law thus consists of rules of conduct whose observance is guaranteed by the coercive force of the state.

The state creates legal norms in different ways. It either (a) directly issues statutes or other legislative measures of state authority (establishing therein new rules of human conduct), or (b) gives binding force — that is to say, the character of a legal norm — to rules of community living or customs already existing in society, but not (prior to being affirmed by the state) legal norms. Their fulfillment was not guaranteed by the state, but they had the force of established practices, traditions, etc. Rules of conduct acquire the force of legal norms — their binding significance — in some manner from the state, which either establishes them itself, or approves (recognizes, gives binding significance to) rules of conduct already existing (which are not, however, legal norms without such affirmance).

Consequently, *law is the aggregate of the rules of conduct established or affirmed by state authority.*

Law, as we have seen, expresses *the will* of the dominant class, and so has a definite goal which the dominant class attains with its aid. It always regulates social relationships — systematizes and coordinates them, secures and defends them, and develops them conformably with the interests of the dominant class. It always comes as a regulation of social relationships employed by the dominant class, to strengthen its dominance, to guarantee its interests, and to resist encroachments upon that dominance and those interests. In his report at the Extraordinary VIII All-Union Congress of Soviets on the Draft of the U.S.S.R. Constitution, Stalin pointed out that in a bourgeois state "a constitution is necessary in order to make secure social arrangements agreeable and advantageous to the 'have' classes," whereas in the soviet state "a constitution is necessary in order to make secure social arrangements agreeable and advantageous to the toilers." These words, while referring directly to the Constitution — the fundamental law, establishing the basic legal norms of supreme importance — are completely applicable as well to the entire aggregate of laws presently in force in society : to all law.

Law thus consists of norms as to which state authority guarantees their being put into operation to the end of defending, securing, and developing legal relationships and arrangements agreeable and advantageous to the dominant class. Individual legal norms, therefore — individual rules of conduct — are not a fortuitous accumulation of heterogeneous demands upon people, but are penetrated by one and the same class content and are directed at the attainment of identical goals.

Summarizing the foregoing features and indicia of law, we may define it as follows : *Law is the aggregate of the rules of conduct (norms) established or approved (sanctioned) by state authority, expressing the will of the dominant class, as to which the coercive force of the state guarantees their being put into operation to the end of safeguarding, making secure, and developing social relationships and arrangements agreeable and advantageous to the dominant class.*

The regulation of human conduct by law is expressed in the form that legal norms grant to citizens definite rights and impose on them definite obligations. Every legal norm is created in order that it may be applied in practice, in the sense that — by its very grant of rights to individuals and organizations, and its imposition of obligations on them — the legal norm is directing civil activity. One to whom a legal norm grants a right can require that others (on whom corresponding obligations are imposed) carry out — or refrain from — definite actions indicated in the legal norm. The obligors must fulfill this requirement — otherwise the state will compel them to do so. It is thus through the rights and obligations which it creates for citizens that a legal norm becomes a living reality ; and in this connection the term "law" acquires two meanings, signifying (1) the rules of conduct themselves — the norms — expressed in statutes and other legislative measures of state authority, and (2) that a citizen or an organization can require definite acts on the part of other persons and of organs of authority. When we say that soviet socialist *law (pravo)* establishes the method and the measure of wages payable to workers and clerks, we have in mind law *(pravo)* as an aggregate of norms. But when one declares : "The law *(zakon)* grants me the right *(pravo)* to demand payment for work," this means that out of the norms of law *(pravo)* — definite rights which he can utilize are created in his behalf.

In bourgeois legal theory, legal norms regulating civil conduct are *law in the objective sense* ; and the civil rights emanating from legal norms are *law in the subjective sense,* or subjective law. This delimitation of legal concepts — accepted in bourgeois jurisprudence — is essentially incorrect. It is in human conduct — human actions and relationships — that the aggregate of the legal norms termed law in the objective sense is realized ; and to contrast legal norms (law in the objective sense) with civil rights creates the false idea that law exists objectively — independently of human actions and relationships, and independently of the social relationships which it regulates. Such a view has its inception in the fact that bourgeois legal science ascribes to law an independent existence unrelated to the reality of human life in society, and contemplates it rather as expressing eternal principles than as possessing the reality of social phenomenon which exists in definite social conditions. Obviously this bourgeois theory is based on the desire to conceal the class essence of law.

The same purpose is evidenced in the attempt to regard civil rights (law in the subjective sense) in isolation from the legal norms operative in the state, to the end of giving rights an independent character in the eyes of the people, and contemplating them as indefeasible attributes of persons — as "innate" rights, independent of the state which expresses the interests of the dominant class.

Such is the idea developed in the celebrated Declaration of Rights of Man and Citizen, adopted in France during the 1789 revolution. The Declaration asserts that there are eternal and inalienable rights belonging to man : freedom, (private) property, safety, etc.

As is evident from the definition of law given in the present text, the aggregate of legal norms (rules of human conduct, established and invested with authority by the state) is law in neither the objective nor the subjective sense, but in the *single* sense : *the expression of social class relationships* which are certain or capable of definition. Rules of conduct expressed in statutes and other legislative acts of state authority grant citizens definite rights and impose on them definite obligations. Civil rights, therefore, constitute the area, established by law, within which citizens may require — of each other and of all organs of authority — that their interests, insofar as these are safeguarded by legal norms, be observed.

It must be emphasized that civil rights cannot be isolated from civil obligations : a statute not only grants rights but also imposes certain obligations. In studying each legal norm, therefore, we must always ascertain both the rights it grants to citizens and the obligations it imposes upon them. This may be illustrated from any statute and from any legal norm....

Sec. 3. Law and Social Relationships. Law is an aggregate of the rules of human conduct — consequently it regulates human behaviour, human actions, the relationships of humans *inter se* and with organs of the state and with the state itself. Human relations in society are called social relations — it is these relations which are objects of regulation by law. At the same time, however, law itself issues out of definite social relationships which arise independently of law. Thus law — while it emanates from social relationships — regulates these social relationships as well. This dual bond between law and social relationships requires special clarification to the end that we neither dissociate law from social relationships nor ignore specific peculiarities of law which distinguish it from other sides of social life — from other social phenomena connected with it. The Marx-Lenin teaching is that social life is founded on production relationships : mutual relationships into which people enter during the production process. "The aggregate of these production relationships constitutes the economic structure of society — the true basis on which the juridic and political superstructure is raised, and with which definite forms of social consciousness correspond." These production-economic relations are therefore the foundation or basis, and law is a superstructure. Law emerges out of definite economic relationships. Thus, the emergence of private property — the relationships between persons, whereby specific things are in the exclusive possession of individuals — was due to the influence of expanded production forces. It was independent of law. When the development of private property attained definite limits — when all the basic means of production had passed into private property — those who had property were bound to defend it against encroachment by those who did not have property. Then arose *the law of private property* : legal norms requiring people to refrain from encroachment on the property of another. Fulfillment of these — as of all — legal norms was guaranteed by the coercive power of the state, the class organization of property owners. *The law of private property* thus originates in factual social relationships, which arose on the basis of private property —

wherefor the character of these social relationships defined as well the content of these legal norms. [pp. 365-373]

Sec. 4. Socialist Law Defined. Socialist law is a completely unique type of law, differing radically from all the species (slave-owning, feudal, and bourgeois) of exploiter law. It is unique in that it is the first law in the history of human society which is not exploiter law : it banishes exploitation, and gives expression to the interests and will of all the toiling people — of the socialist worker-peasant state. It differs in form and in substance from any law ever existing in any exploiter state. Being the aggregate of norms expressing the will and guaranteeing the interests of a people freed from exploitation — operating in a society wherein exploiter classes have been destroyed — socialist law is founded upon public socialist property (the indefeasible basis of the socialist social order) and not upon private property ; upon the principles of the proletarian dictatorship which is carrying into effect the state guidance of society. As the interests of the worker class in socialist society (wherein exploiter classes have been destroyed) reflect the interests of the entire people, the peasants and the intellectuals, so socialist law, too, expresses the will — and defends the interests — of all the toiling people.

Socialist law consists of the rules of conduct (norms) of socialist society. They express the will of the entire people. The coercive force of the socialist state guarantees their being applied. Socialist legal norms are established here in the form of legislation of the socialist state, or in the form of socialist customs and other rules of social life together, clothed with authority by the state.

Socialist law is thus, above all, an instrument with whose aid the socialist state guarantees the strengthening and the development of socialist social relationships, and destroys the survivals of capitalism in the economy, mode of life and consciousness of human beings.

As the socialist state organizes the future development of socialism in the direction of its higher stage — classless communist society — so socialist law serves the same end.

Applying the general definition of law to socialist legal norms, we may define socialist laws as follows : *soviet socialist law is the aggregate of rules of conduct (norms) established or approved by the state authority of the socialist state, and expressing the will of the worker class and of all the toilers ; the application of these rules of conduct is guaranteed by the coercive force of the socialist state to the end of defending, making secure and developing relationships and arrangements advantageous and agreeable to the worker class and to all the toilers, of destroying completely and finally the survivals of capitalism in the economy, mode of life and consciousness of human beings, and of building communist society.*

Socialist law is not a further development of bourgeois law, but a new type of law that has grown out of the socialist revolution of the proletariat. When it destroyed the bourgeois state, the Great October Socialist Revolution destroyed bourgeois law as well. In the revolution itself, the masses created new law. As early as 1906, Lenin — speaking of the appearances of mass revolution in 1905-1906 — pointed out that the mass of the people "itself and directly creates new revolutionary law." This direct revolutionary creation of law by the masses was organized by the proletarian dictatorship. Guided by the worker class and the communist party, the popular masses continued to create new, socialist law through its state organs : the soviets. [pp. 385-386]

NOTE

1. S.A. Golunskii and M.S. Strogovich, "The Theory of the State and Law," in H.W. Babb, *Soviet Legal Philosophy* (Cambridge : Harvard University Press, 1951), pp. 365-386.

THE LAW OF THE SOVIET STATE[1]

Andrei Vyshinsky, Editor

The nature of the state is the most important question in the science of public law. The theory of the state is the basis not only of the science of state law but also of law in general, inasmuch as a scientific understanding of law is impossible without a correct understanding of the state. Law and state cannot be studied separately and apart from each other. Law draws its force, and obtains its content, from the state.

"Law is nothing without a mechanism capable of compelling the observance of legal norms."

This fundamental precept of the Marxist-Leninist theory defines the relationship between law and state.... [p. 5]

The Marxist-Leninist doctrine of the state is not limited solely to an investigation of the nature of the origin and disappearance of the state, of its nature and characteristics. It also exhaustively elaborates and illuminates a series of other and most important questions connected with the state, on the one hand, and problems and interests of the proletarian battle for emancipation, on the other. Typical of such questions are those concerning the state of the period of transition from capitalism to communism, concerning the proletarian state as a state form of proletarian dictatorship, concerning the state and democracy in general, concerning the Soviet state and socialist democracy in particular, concerning the forms and methods of reinforcing the proletarian state, concerning communism and the state, and, finally, concerning the state's disappearance of "withering away" in the highest phase of communism, complete and fully developed.

Marxist-Leninism gives a clear definition (the only scientific definition) of the essence of law. It teaches that legal relationships (and, consequently, law itself) are rooted in the material conditions of life, and that law is merely the will of the dominant class, elevated into a statute. It starts from the proposition that political, legal, philosophical, religious, and literary development is defined by — and is a superstructure over — economics.

Law is one of the superstructures above the totality of production relationships forming society's economic structure. [p. 8]

NOTE

1. Andrei Vyshinsky, ed., *The Law of the Soviet State* (New York : MacMillan and Co., 1954), pp. 5-8.

THE GENERAL THEORY OF LAW AND MARXISM[1]

E.B. Pashukanis

In order that the products of human labour may be capable of being related to each other as values, people must be related to each other as independent and equal personalities. If one man is in the power of another — that is to say, if he is a slave — his labour ceases to create and to be the substance of value. The worker strength of a slave — on the same plane as the worker strength of a domestic animal — merely transfers into the product a definite part of the costs of its production and reproduction. On this basis Tugan-Baranovskii draws the conclusion that political economy can be comprehended only by one who starts from the guiding ethical idea of supreme value — and, therefore, of the equivalency — of human personality. Marx, as is well known, draws the opposite conclusion : He associates the ethical idea of the equivalency of human personality with the form of goods — that is to say, he infers that idea from the equalization *inter se* of all the species of human labour.

In reality, man as a moral subject — that is to say, as a personality possessing equivalency — is no more than a condition of exchange according to the law of value. Man as a subject of rights — that is to say, as a property-owner — is the same condition of exchange according to the law of value. Finally, both these definitions are most closely associated with a third, wherein man figures as an egoistic directive (managing) subject. None of these three definitions can be reduced to any other — they are even contradictory, as it were — and accordingly they reflect the totality of the conditions essential for realizing the value relationship : that is to say, the relationship wherein the association of persons in the process of labour appears as a material attribute of the products which are the subject of exchange.

If we disassociate these definitions from the real social relationship which they express and seek to develop them as independent categories — that is to say, by a process of pure reasoning — the result will be a tangle of contradictions and mutually destructive propositions. But in the real relationship of exchange these contradictions dialectically unite like something combined into a whole. The person taking part in exchange is bound to be an egoist — that is to say, he is bound to be guided by pure economic calculation — otherwise the value relationship cannot manifest itself as a relationship socially necessary. The person taking part in exchange is bound to be the bearer of a right — that is to say, it must be possible for him to form an autonomous decision — for the reason that *his will* "must be found in things." Finally, the person taking part in exchange embodies the element of the equivalency of human personality in point of principle — for the reason that all species of labour are equalized *inter se* in exchange and are reduced to abstract human labour.

These three elements : egoism, freedom, and the supreme value of personality — or principles as people formerly liked to term them — are thus indissolubly associated *inter se*, being in their aggregate the rational expression of one and the same social relationship. The egoistic subject, the subject of a right, and the moral personality are the three basic masks under which man emerges in a goods-producing society. The economics of value relationships provide the key to the understanding of the legal and moral structure : not in the sense of the specific content of norms of law or morality but in the sense of the form itself. The idea of the value and the equivalency of human personality as a matter of principle has its long history : through stoic philosophy it gained currency among Roman jurists and in the doctrine of the Christian church, and later in the natural-law doctrine. The existence of slavery in ancient Rome was no obstacle to Seneca's coming to the conclusion that "even if the body can be unfree and belong to the master, the spirit always remains *sui juris.*" Strictly speaking, Kant's advance over this formula was very slight — his autonomy of the personality as a matter of principle unites prettily with the views of serfdom itself as regards the relationships between masters and servants. In whatever garb this idea was dressed out, however, nothing could be disclosed therein other than an expression of the fact that these concrete species of socially beneficial labour come down to labour in general insofar as the products of labour begin to be exchanged as goods. In all other relationships, human inequality — inequality of sex, inequality of class, and so on — is so glaringly conspicuous as history stretches before us that we can only marvel, not at the wealth of arguments that its various opponents could advance against the doctrine of natural equality of human beings, but at the fact that down to Marx — and independently of Marx — no one concerned himself with the problem of the historical causes which contributed to the rise of this natural-law prejudice. For if over the ages human thought has so stubbornly returned to the thesis that people are equal and has worked it out in a thousand modes, it is clear that there must be some objective relationship concealed behind it. No doubt the concept of a moral or equivalent personality is an ideological elucubration, and as such is not adequate to reality. The egoistic, directive subject is not a whit less an ideological distortion of reality. None the less, both these definitions are adequate for one specific social relationship, and merely express it abstractly (and consequently unilaterally). Speaking generally, we have already had occasion to point out that the concept or word "ideology" should not hold us back from further analysis. To soothe oneself with the notion that man is equal to another man is to give birth to an ideology and to over-simplify the task. "Lower" and "higher" are merely concepts which express our "earthly" ideology. At their basis, however, lies the incontrovertible and factual reality of earthly gravitation ; and the moment man became cognizant of the actual cause compelling him to differentiate between lower and higher — that is to say, of the force of gravity directed to the centre of the earth — he comprehended the limited character of these definitions — and their inadequacy — as applied to all cosmic reality. The disclosure that the concepts were ideological was thus another aspect of disclosing their verity.

If moral personality is nothing but the subject of a goods-producing society, then the moral law must reveal itself as a rule of the intercourse of goods possessors. This inevitably attributes duality to the moral law : on the one hand, it must have a social character (and as such stand above individual personality) ; on the other hand, the goods possessor is by nature the bearer of a freedom (freedom to acquire and freedom to alienate), wherefore a rule of the intercourse of goods possessors must also be put in the spirit of each of them — and be the inner law of each. Kant's categorical imperative unifies in itself these conflicting requirements. It is supra-individual because it has nothing in common with any natural stimuli (fear, sympathy, pity, a feeling of solidarity, and the like). It does not terrify, it does not persuade, it does not flatter (as Kant expressed it). In general it is located outside all empirical motives — that is to say, outside all purely human motives. At the same time, it emerges independently of any sort of external pressure in the direct and crude sense of the word. It operates exclusively by virtue of the consciousness of its universality. Kant's ethics are the ethics most characteristic of a goods-producing society, while at the same time they are the purest and most complete form of ethics in general. To the form which bourgeois society —

resolved into atoms — sought to embody in reality, Kant gave an appearance logically complete : liberating personality from the organic bonds of the patriarchal and the feudal epochs.

The basic concepts of morality have therefore no meaning of any kind if they are dissociated from goods-producing society and sought to be applied to any other social structure. The categorical imperative is by no means a social instinct. It is fundamentally predestined to be operative where no natural, organic, supra-individual motivation of any sort is possible. Where there is a close emotional bond between individuals — effacing the boundaries of the individual ego — the phenomenon of a moral duty can have no place. To understand the category of moral duty, it is necessary to start from a condition of *disassociatedness,* and not from the organic bond existing, for example, between the mother and her young or between the clan (*gens*) and each of its members. Moral being is a necessary supplement of juridic being — each of them is a means of the intercourse of persons producing goods. The whole tragedy of Kant's categorical imperative comes down to the fact that man does "freely" — that is to say, in accordance with inner conviction — that which he was constrained to do on the plane of the law. The very examples cited by Kant to illustrate his thoughts are typical — they reduce completely to nothing more than a manifestation of bourgeois respectability. The framework of his categorical imperative has no place for heroism or for exploits. Self-sacrifice is not at all obligatory inasmuch as you do not require such sacrifice of another. "Senseless" acts of self-renunciation and self-forgetfulness in the name of fulfilling one's historical calling or one's social function — acts in which the highest tension of the social instinct is manifested — lie outside the fields of ethics in the strict sense of the word....

The only respect in which rationalist ethics is actually elevated above mighty and irrational social instincts is its applicability to all mankind. It breaks with the entire organic (and necessarily narrow) framework (*gens,* tribe, nation) and strives to become universal. Therein it reflects the definite material achievements of humanity : viz., the conversion of trade into world trade. "Neither Greek nor Jew" reflected an actual fact in the history of the peoples united by the power of Rome.

Inasmuch as the universalism of the ethical (and consequently of the legal) form (all men are equal, all men have the same "soul," all men may be subject of rights, and so forth) was bound up with the practice of commercial intercourse with foreigners (that is to say, with persons of foreign customs, language, and religion), so at the outset it was hardly — if at all — sensed as something positive, if only because it was associated with a renunciation of local and specific customs which were deeply rooted (love for *one's own* and disdain for another's). Thus, for example, Maine points out that *jus gentium* was itself the product of the disdain cherished by the Romans for foreign law, and of their unwillingness to grant the alien the advantages of their indigenous *jus civile.* In his judgment, the ancient Roman loved the *jus gentium* as little as he loved the foreigners for whose benefit it was ordained. The very word *aequitas* signified leveling ; at first it was probably given no ethical tinge whatsoever, nor is there reason to suppose that the proceeding designated by the expression aroused anything but aversion in the mind of the early primitive Roman.

Nevertheless, as matters develop, rationalist ethics represent the maximum attainment and the supreme cultural good for a goods-producing society —

whereof it is usual to speak only in tones of the loftiest ecstacy. It is sufficient to recall the well-known words of Kant : "Two things fill the soul with ever new and ever increasing amazement and reverence, the more frequently the more deeply we ponder upon them — the starry sky above my head and the moral law within me."

Meanwhile, when it is a matter of furnishing examples of the "free" execution of a moral duty, the same unvarying bestowal of alms upon a beggar or refusal to tell a lie in circumstances where one could lie with impunity, and the like trot out upon the stage. On the other hand, Kautskii is perfectly correct in observing that the rule : "regard another as an end in himself," has meaning where a man can practically be made an instrument for another. Moral pathos is indissolubly connected with — and is nourished by — the immorality of social practice. Ethical doctrines assume to change and to correct the world, whereas in reality they are a distorted reflection of only one side of that real world : that side where the relations of human beings are subject to the law of value. It must not be forgotten that moral personality is only one of the hypostases of the triune subject : man as an end in himself is another side of the egoistic directive subject. A measure — being the genuine and only real embodiment of the ethical principle — comprises within itself a negation of that principle. The big capitalist "in good faith" ruins the small capitalist without for a moment encroaching upon the absolute value of his personality. The personality of the proletarian is "in point of principle equivalent" to the personality of the capitalist : this finds expression in the fact of the "free" contract of hiring. Out of this materialized freedom itself, however, flows the possibility of a quiet death by starvation, for the proletarian.

This ambiguity of the ethical form is not something fortuitous — it is no external defect for which the specific shortcomings of capitalism are responsible : on the contrary it is an essential indicium of the ethical form as such. Elimination of the ambiguity of the ethical form means transition to a planned social economy, and this in turn means the realization of a social order in which people can form and apprehend their relationship by employing the simple and clear concepts of harm and advantage. To destroy the ambiguity of the ethical form in its most essential field — that is to say, in the field of the material existence of human beings — means the destruction of that form in general.

It is from this point of view of harm and advantage that pure utilitarianism — striving to dispel the metaphysical fog surrounding the ethical doctrine — approaches the concepts of good and evil. This of course simply destroys ethics — or rather tries to destroy and to vanquish ethics, for ethical fetishes can be completely overcome in reality only if the fetishisms of good and of law are vanquished at the same time. People whose conduct is guided by the clear and simple concepts of harm and advantage will not require that their social relationships be expressed either in terms of value or in terms of law. Until this historical stage of development is attained by mankind, however — that is to say, until mankind is rid of the inheritance of the capitalist epoch — the struggle of theoretical thinking can only anticipate this future emancipation without the capacity to embody it in practice. We must here recall Marx's words concerning goods fetishism : "the tardy scientific discovery that the products of labour expended on their production, constitutes an epoch in the history of human development ; but it is certainly far from destroying the material semblance of the social character of labour."

But it will be objected that the class morality of the proletariat is now already liberated from all fetishes. That which is morally due is that which is beneficial to the class. In this form, morality comprises nothing absolute — since what is beneficial today may cease to be beneficial tomorrow — and comprises nothing supernatural or wrapped in mystery, inasmuch as the principle of benefit is simple and a matter of reason.

There is no doubt that the morality of the proletariat — or rather of the advanced strata of the proletariat — loses its doubly fetishist character, being liberated, let us say, from religious elements. But morality — even morality which is completely free from an alloy of religious elements, remains morality all the same : that is to say, a form of social relationship in which as yet not everything is reduced to man himself. If the living link with the class is in reality so strong that the boundaries of the ego are effaced, as it were, and the benefit of the class actually merges with individual benefit, then there is no sense in talking about the fulfilment of a moral duty — in general the phenomenon of morality is then absent. Where such a merger has not taken place, an abstract relationship of moral duty — with all the consequences therefrom ensuing — inevitably arises. The rule : so act as to confer the greatest benefit on the class will sound like Kant's formula : so act that the maxim of your conduct may serve as a principle of universal legislation. The whole difference is this that in the former case we introduce a concrete limitation — we set a class framework for ethical logic. But within this framework it remains in full force. The class content of ethics does not *per se* destroy the form of ethics. We have in view the form of the actual manifestation, and not merely the logical form. Deep within the proletarian, that is to say, the class-collective, we observe the means of realizing that which is morally due — means which are in form identical and which take shape from two contrasting elements : (a) on the one hand, the collective does not renounce all possible means of exerting pressure upon its members to incite them to that which is morally due ; (b) on the other hand, the same collective classifies conduct as moral conduct only when this external pressure — as a motive — is concededly absent. It is for this very reason that morality and moral conduct are so closely bound up in social practice with hypocrisy. It is true that the conditions of the life of the proletariat include the prerequisites for the development of a new, loftier, and more harmonious form of the relationship between personality and the collective — as evidenced by the facts relating to the manifestation of the class solidarity of the proletariat. But the old continues to exist alongside the new. Side by side with the social man of the future, who merges his ego with the collective and finds therein life's highest satisfaction and meaning, the moral man continues to exist — bearing upon himself the weight of a more or less abstract duty. The victory of the first form has the force (a) of complete liberation from all the survivals of private-property relationships, and (b) of the final reeducation of mankind in a spirit of communism. Of course this is not at all a task purely ideological or pedagogic — the new type of relationship requires the creation and strengthening of a new material economic basis.

It must, therefore, be borne in mind that morality, law, and state are forms of bourgeois society. The fact that the proletariat may be compelled to use them by no means signifies that they can develop further in the direction of being filled with a socialist content. They have no capacity adequate to hold a socialist content and are bound to die out to the extent that it is brought into being. Nevertheless, in the present transition period, the proletariat must necessarily utilize in its class interest these forms which have been inherited from bourgeois society and thereby exhaust them completely. To this end, the proletariat must first and foremost have a notion of the historical origin of these forms which is perfectly clear and free from ideological haziness. Its attitude must be one of sober criticism not only as regards the bourgeois state and bourgeois morality, but also as regards its own state and its own proletarian morality — that is to say, it must comprehend the historical necessity alike of their existence and of their disappearance. [pp. 193-201]

NOTE

1. E.B. Pashukanis, in Hugh Babb, trans., "The General Theory of Law and Marxism," *Soviet Legal Philosophy* (Harvard University Press, 1951), pp. 193-201.

PASHUKANIS AND VYSHINSKY : A STUDY IN THE DEVELOPMENT OF MARXIAN LEGAL THEORY[1]

Lon L. Fuller

. . . Pashukanis' legal theory is founded on two principles well-established in the writings of the Soviet founding fathers : (1) law and the state are a superstructure reflecting the basic economic organization of society, and (2) in the socialist economy of the future, both law and the state will "wither away."

Proceeding from these premises, Pashukanis then expounds his own theory, which is briefly as follows : the basic institution of capitalism is *exchange*; all goods (including labour) are viewed as "commodities," that is, as destined for exchange on the market. In keeping with Marxist theory, therefore, we should expect bourgeois law to be permeated with the concept of exchange, and to take its origin in the act of trading or bartering.

This expectation is confirmed by history and sociology. The first appearance of the criminal law in its rudest form is in connection with bartering, that is, in the buying off of the blood feud. Throughout history the development of law has gone hand in hand with the development of trade.

Most definitions of law mistakenly try to make it equivalent to an authoritative ordering of social relations, but this does not expose its real essence. The ideal type of an authoritative ordering would be a military company marching in perfect step, ready to follow every command of its captain. Yet such a phenomenon is not only not legal in nature, but actually stands at the opposite pole from law. This is true generally of mere relationships of power. Slavery, for example, requires no legal form. If the relation of master and slave is in any sense legal, it is only because the master can exchange the slave for other goods, or because the law recognizes some semblance of a right in the slave against the master. Law appears as a distinct social phenomenon not when we have one man standing over another, but only when we have men standing toward one another with rights and duties.

The basic concept of law is, then, the legal subject, the possessor of rights and duties. The legal subject is, however, merely the economic trader seen in his juristic aspect. Take from the legal subject the power to settle or compromise his differences with his fellows by a process of barter and he ceases to be a legal subject. Legal rights wholly removed from the area of trade are not legal rights at all. Every legal subject is therefore a potential trader, and his capacity to possess rights and duties and to enter legal relations with others derives from this fact. The economic institution of exchange is accordingly presupposed in the conception of a legal right. The whole legal order, in turn, has its reason for being in the vindication of rights. The modern notion that the individual derives his rights from the law or from the state is the symptom of a decadent capitalism. When capitalism was itself a revolutionary force it was universally thought that law exists to protect rights, that rights precede law.

In modern criminal law, a first cousin of economic exchange appears in the notion of retribution. The criminal code is a kind of schedule of compositions, setting the price (in terms of punishment) appropriate for each crime. According to the principle of *nulla poena sine lege* the criminal must be given a chance to know in advance what the price of each kind of misconduct is. Advanced bourgeois criminologists have long condemned these conceptions as irrational. They continue, however, to be entertained by the bulk of society and to be applied by the courts. When the public follows a criminal trial in the newspapers it is not interested in learning whether the criminal can be rehabilitated, or whether he is maladjusted to social life, but whether he actually did what he is accused of doing and whether he is going to get what is coming to him. The attitudes engendered by an economy founded on exchange are too deeply rooted to be destroyed by learned treatises.

Though in bourgeois society, law is an instrument of domination by the ruling classes, it is so only in an indirect sense. To say that law is a means of domination or exploitation fails to reveal its essence. The domination of one class by another can exist without law, where, for example, it is founded on religious superstition or military power. The exploitation of the proletariat by the capitalist takes a special and peculiar form. On its economic side, it is primarily through the market; on the legal side, it is through the notion that the worker sets his legal relations with his employer through contract. It is an exploitation through exchange, and, in keeping with the Marxian theory of the primacy of the economic form, its essential nature is determined by this fact.

This analysis of law is not simply an analysis of bourgeois law, but of law generally. In truth, the only law is bourgeois law. To be sure, legal institutions in embryo can be found in a feudal or slave society, where they are intertwined with religious and military elements. Modern scholars are likely to misinterpret these rudimentary legal elements in pre-capitalistic society as the equivalent of modern law. Actually, these embryonic and undifferentiated legal elements are like the first tentative gropings toward a capitalistic organization that can be detected in even the most primitive societies. The full inner logic of the conception of law can assert itself only under capitalism. The ideal of law is realized at the same time as the ideal of the market; both present man as the trader, as an autonomous agent setting his relations with his fellows.

Not only is law founded on the concept of exchange, but the same thing may be said of morality. Morality has to do with conflicts of interests between individuals who are conceived to have it within their power to determine what they shall do or not do toward one another. Such individuals are simply economic traders seen in the light of ethics. Moral treatises lay down a kind of minimum standard of conduct designed to maintain the principle of reciprocity. They do not answer such questions as whether a man should volunteer on a suicide mission ; acts of heroism or of extraordinary devotion to the group fall outside the competence of ethical philosophy. Kant's conception that every man should be treated as an end in himself, as a *Selbstzweck*, implies a trading economy. Only in such an economy can a man who is conceived to be an end in himself be brought, through self-interest, to serve the ends of others — a result essential if any collective activity is to be achieved.

From these premises it follows that law and morality will disappear when, and only when, the last vestiges of the economic institution of exchange have been rooted out of society. The Soviet system still contains important elements of exchange. These exist not only in the area set aside for private trading, but in the relations of governmment corporations to one another, and in the payment of workers, who are compensated on the basis of work performed, in violation of the formula of mature communism, "From each according to his capacities, to each according to his needs."

On the other hand, when the notion of economic exchange has been completely eliminated in every form, then — with some allowance for a lag in time — the superstructure of law, the state, and morality will dissolve and disappear. Man will have become a "group-creature," no longer thinking of his own interest as something distinct from that of his fellows. The concept of justice and the notion of demanding measure for measure will have become as inapplicable to this situation as they now are, say, to a mother and child between whom there is a complete identity of interest. [pp. 1159-1162]

NOTE

1. L.L. Fuller, "Pashukanis and Vyshinsky : A Study in the Development of Marxian Legal Theory," *Michigan Law Review* 47 (1949) : 1159-1162.

3. Equality, Status, and Liberty in the Modern Industrial State

Increases in crime and widespread disrespect for legal institutions are the more obvious indications of the erosion of our social and legal fabrics. Solutions suggestive of harsher treatments, and even the more efficient delivery of justice, are unlikely to cure our deeper ills. Citizens across the globe observe the incapacity of governments to respond effectively to inflation, pollution, overpopulation, poverty, and ideological discord. Many persons lack confidence in the Western institutions of public order, and are questioning the existing Western forms of government. This crisis of belief in democratic institutions is also experienced in Third World countries, with the consequence that in the East and the West, both industrial and emerging nations have been turning with astonishing regularity to totalitarian solutions.

Western societies have passed through any number of ideological and economic revolutions. Structural tools have been placed at man's disposal to redefine his social and economic relations according to the rules of rational law, with such principles and rights as property, equality and liberty, but there is little evidence either in liberal democratic or socialist republics that the archetypal authority model of patriarchy has disappeared. On the contrary, there are transnational trends to replace monarchies with dictatorships, nationalism with tribalism, slavery with economic dependency, and aristocracies of blood with new elites who exercise power through political position, wealth, and the weaponry of modern technology. It is safe to venture that our cumulative historical record shows that the universal forms of Western law have been filled with patriarchal content.

It is necessary to confront the theoretical underpinnings of major economic theories such as capitalism and Marxism, to assess their applications in the light of historical developments, and the implications of their doctrines for a concept of human nature, and hence of law. The modern state, linked either to laissez-faire concepts of the market place with attendant notions of liberal values and individualism, or to state control and affirmation of collective interests, has threatened the ideal of both the free individual and an autonomous legal form. This challenge to human freedom has often been associated with monolithic or utopian visions of man's integration into an organic community.

If stable orders are to persist which protect and foster the rudimentary values of social liberal democracies, it must at the same time be shown that a legal structure has the capacity progressively to alter its content without doing havoc to the adjudicative process, representative of centuries of evolutionary growth. It was the assumption of Marxist theory that the contradictions of capitalism would always prevent the credible articulation of a just theory of distribution and equality. It has been the response of traditional common law and liberal democratic theorists that the reduction by Marxism of the legal form to alienated forms of human relationships, which mirror the material conditions of capitalism, necessarily downplays the potential of J autonomous law to serve as a corrective against authoritarian politics.

There are serious differences in Western society about how to create the conditions for a meaningful social revolution that will permit a fair distribution of wealth and power and include the preservation of the rule of law as we know it. Some believe that this can only be realized through equality before the law. This is disturbing, however, to those who observe the consistency of the rule of law with economic inequality. Others see a social equality which would result in a fairer distribution of economic wealth. Yet the pursuit of such equality appears to be inversely related to liberty in that such economic equality demands the accumulation of power in the hands of restricted numbers with the prospect of the loss of individual liberty. This raises the question of what the long term gain of economic equality is if such gain is at the price of political inequality.

Laissez-faire economics have encouraged and protected accumulations of capital with the consequent disproportionate power of the multinational corporations. The common law, which maintains a low profile in society, and responds cautiously to specific disputes, is favoured by those who believe in the possibility and attractiveness of a free market. Others, who are prepared to make sacrifices in personal freedom in order to structure a more economically just society, regard the power of the state as exercised through legislative social planning and regulations as the optimum form of social control and ordering.

The question before us is whether the legal forms with which we are familiar and the bonding values of the systems which emanate from century old sources in the Judeo-Christian and Greco-Roman cultures have given us the appropriate tools to meet the problems of industrialization. We are driven, therefore, to investigate the very roots of our social, political, and legal civilization. In the West, since the time of the Greeks, societies have built their institutions upon an assumed order and rationality in the universe, exemplified in man's nature as a rational being. In the twentieth century psychology has led us to reassess man in the light of his unconscious. Those who have resisted this exploration explain phenomena such as the horrors of the Nazi holocaust and other bizarre manifestations of evil on the basis of theories of politics or economy. Even though difficulties have been encountered in making lucid applications of psychological theory to politics and law, the magnitude and type of social disorders continue to move us in the direction of psychological explanations.

The political dynamics of social conflict such as the struggle for liberty, the maintenance of authority, the eradication of racism, and the preservation of ethnic cultural heritages probably are outward manifestations of an inner psychological conflict between the need for individuality and the need for community. The evolution of liberty may usefully be viewed as a part of the process of the evolution of human consciousness, and the reversion to patriarchal status as the product of unconscious drives to lose onself in the collective.

In awakening our psychological understanding of man's nature in relation to his legal ordering we are confronted with the reality that our Western patriarchal consciousness has affected and distorted even our preliminary investigations into the nature of female consciousness. It is premature for us to appreciate the terms and conditions of rapprochement between the masculine and feminine aspects of consciousness. At best we are operating in the foreground of discovery. Even the language of discourse is prejudiced by the patriarchal ethos. Androgeny is an ideal in our culture which meets with anger and resistance from many sectors.

Without knowing the ultimate demands to be placed upon it the law perseveres in employing its familiar tools. The final question is whether the deep structure of laws, procedures, and values is impounded by history to a patriarchal fate or, whether, either in a new form or in a dramatic shifting of its historical ground, law will be recognizable in the next millenium as an institution worthy of trust, re-emerging as the arbiter and spokesman for the highest values of the new age. Law has already experienced that role in every culture and society since the dawn of Western civilization. The ultimate challenge for law is to participate in the explorations of new forms of consciousness while never failing to remember the lessons of history.

THE NEW CLASS[1]

Milovan Djilas

The strength of Marxist philosophy did not lie in its scientific elements, but in its connection with a mass movement, and most of all in its emphasis on the objective of changing society. It stated again and again that the existing world would change simply because it had to change, that it bore the seeds of its own opposition and destruction ; that the working class wanted this change and would be able to effect it. Inevitably, the influence of this philosophy increased and created in the European working-class movement the illusion that it was omnipotent, at least as a method. In countries where similar conditions did not exist, such as Great Britain and the United States, the influence and importance of this philosophy was insignificant, despite the strength of the working class and the working-class movement.

As a science, Marxist philosophy was not important, since it was based mainly on Hegelian and materialistic ideas. As the ideology of the new, oppressed classes and especially of political movements, it marked an epoch, first in Europe, and later in Russia and Asia, providing the basis for a new political movement and a new social system.... [pp. 1-6]

Abstract logic would indicate that the Communist revolution, when it achieves, under different conditions and by state compulsion, the same things achieved by industrial revolutions and capitalism in the West, is nothing but a form of state-capitalist revolution. The relationships which are created by its victory are state-capitalist. This appears to be even more true because the new regime also regulated all political, labour and other relationships and, what is more important, distributes the national income and benefits and distributes material goods which actually have been transformed into state property.

Discussion on whether or not the relationships in the U.S.S.R. and in other Communist countries are state-capitalist, socialist, or perhaps something else, is dogmatic to a considerable degree. However, such discussion is of fundamental importance.

Even if it is presumed that state capitalism is nothing other than the "antechamber of socialism," as Lenin emphasized, or that it is the first phase of socialism, it is still not one iota easier for the people who live under Communist despotism to endure. If the character of property and social relationships brought about by the Communist revolution is strengthened and defined, the prospects for liberation of the people from such relationships become more realistic. If the people are not conscious of the nature of the social relationships in which they live, or if they do not see a way in which they can alter them, their struggle cannot have any prospect of success.

If the Communist revolution, despite its promises and illusions, is state-capitalist in its undertakings with state-capitalist relationships, the only lawful and positive actions its functionaries can take are the ones that improve their work and reduce the pressure and irresponsibility of state administration. The Communists do not admit in theory that they are working in a system of state capitalism, but their leaders behave this way. They continually boast about improving the work of the administration and about leading the struggle "against bureaucratism."

Moreover, actual relationships are not those of state capitalism ; these relationships do not provide a method of improving the system of state administration basically.

In order to establish the nature of relationships which arise in the course of the Communist revolution and ultimately become established in the process of industrialization and collectivization, it is necessary to peer further into the role and manner of operation of the state under Communism. At present, it will be sufficient to point out that in Communism the state machinery is not the instrument which really determines social and property relationships ; it is only the instrument by which these relationships are protected. In truth, everything is accomplished in the name of the state and through its regulations. The Communist

Party, including the professional party bureaucracy, stands above the regulations and behind every single one of the state's acts.

It is the bureaucracy which formally uses, administers, and controls both nationalized and socialized property as well as the entire life of society. The role of the bureaucracy in society, i.e., monopolistic administration and control of national income and national goods, consigns it to a special privileged position. Social relations resemble state capitalism. The more so, because the carrying out of industrialization is effected not with the help of capitalists but with the help of the state machine. In fact, this privileged class performs that function, using the state machine as a cover and as an instrument.

Ownership is nothing other than the right of profit and control. If one defines class benefits by this right, the Communist states have seen, in the final analysis, the origin of a new form of ownership or of a new ruling and exploiting class.

In reality, the Communists were unable to act differently from any ruling class that preceded them. Believing that they were building a new and ideal society, they built it for themselves in the only way they could. Their revolution and their society do not appear either accidental or unnatural, but appear as a matter of course for a particular country and for prescribed periods of its development. Because of this, no matter how extensive and inhuman Communist tyranny has been, society, in the course of a certain period — as long as industrialization lasts — has to and is able to endure this tyranny. Furthermore, this tyranny no longer appears as something inevitable, but exclusively as an assurance of the depredations and privileges of a new class.

In contrast to earlier revolutions, the Communist revolution, conducted in the name of doing away with classes, has resulted in the most complete authority of any single new class. Everything else is sham and an illusion.

Everything happened differently in the U.S.S.R. and other Communist countries from what the leaders — even such prominent ones as Lenin, Stalin, Trotsky, and Bukharin — anticipated. They expected that the state would rapidly wither away, that democracy would be strengthened. The reverse happened. They expected a rapid improvement in the standard of living — there has been scarcely any change in this respect and, in the subjugated East European countries, the standard has even declined. In every instance, the standard of living has failed to rise in proportion to the rate of industrialization, which was much more rapid. It was believed that the differences between cities and villages, between intellectual and physical labour would slowly disappear; instead these differences have increased. Communist anticipations in other areas — including their expectations for developments in the non-Communist world — have also failed to materialize.

The greatest illusion was that industrialization and collectivization in the U.S.S.R., and destruction of capitalist ownership, would result in a classless society. In 1936, when the new constitution was promulgated, Stalin announced that the "exploiting class" had ceased to exist. The capitalist and other classes of ancient origin had in fact been destroyed, but a new class, previously unknown to history, had been formed.

It is understandable that this class, like those before it, should believe that the establishment of its power would result in happiness and freedom for all men. The only difference between this and other classes was that it treated the delay in the realization of its illusions more crudely. It thus affirmed that its power was more complete than the power of any other class before in history, and its class illusions and prejudices were proportionally greater.

This new class, the bureaucracy, or more accurately the political bureaucracy, has all the characteristics of earlier ones as well as some new characteristics of its own. Its origin had its special characteristics also, even though in essence it was similar to the beginnings of other classes.

Other classes, too, obtained their strength and power by the revolutionary path, destroying the political, social, and other orders they met in their way. However, almost without exception, these classes attained power *after* new economic patterns had taken shape in the old society. The case was the reverse with new classes in the Communist systems. It did not come to power to *complete* a new economic order but to *establish* its own and, in so doing, to establish its power over society.

In earlier epochs the coming to power of some class, some part of a class, or of some party, was the final event resulting from its formation and its development. The reverse was true in the U.S.S.R. There the new class was definitely formed after it attained power. Its consciousness had to develop before its economic and physical powers, because the class had not taken root in the life of the nation. This class viewed its role in relation to the world from an idealistic point of view. Its practical possibilities were not diminished by this. In spite of its illusions, it represented an objective tendency toward industrialization. Its practical bent emanated from this tendency. The promise of an ideal world increased the faith in the ranks of the new class and sowed illusions among the masses. At the same time it inspired gigantic physical undertakings.

Because this new class had not been formed as a part of the economic and social life before it came to power, it could only be created in an organization of a special type, distinguished by a special discipline based on identical philosophic and ideological views of its members. A unity of belief and iron discipline was necessary to overcome its weaknesses.

The roots of the new class were implanted in a special party, of the Bolshevik type. Lenin was right in his view that his party was an exception in the history of human society, although he did not suspect that it would be the beginning of a new class.

To be more precise, the initiators of the new class are not found in the party of the Bolshevik type as a whole but in the stratum of professional revolutionaries who made up its core even before it attained power. It was not by accident that Lenin asserted after the failure of the 1905 revolution that only professional revolutionaries — men whose sole profession was revolutionary work — could build a new party of the Bolshevik type. It was still less accidental that even Stalin, the future creator of a new class, was the most outstanding example of such a professional revolutionary. The new ruling class has been gradually developing from this very narrow stratum of revolutionaries. These revolutionaries composed its core for a long period. Trotsky noted that in pre-revolutionary professional revolutionaries was the origin of the future Stalinist bureaucrat. What he did not detect was the beginning of a new class of owners and exploiters.

This is not to say that the new party and the new class are identical. The party, however, is the core of that class, and its base. It is very difficult, perhaps impossible, to define the limits of the new class and to identify its members. The new class may be said to be made up of those who have special privileges and economic preference because of the administrative monopoly they hold.

Since administration is unavoidable in society, necessary administrative functions may be coexistent with parasitic functions in the same person. Not every member of the party is a member of the new class, any more than every artisan or member of a middle-class party is a bourgeois.

In loose terms, as the new class becomes stronger and attains a more perceptible physiognomy, the role of the party diminishes. The core and the basis of the new class is created in the party and as its top, as well as in the state political organs. The once live, compact party, full of initiative, is disappearing to become transformed into the traditional oligarchy of the new class, irresistibly drawing into its ranks those who aspire to join the new class and repressing those who have any ideals.

The party makes the class, but the class grows as a result and uses the party as a basis. The class grows stronger, while the party grows weaker ; this is the inescapable fate of every Communist party in power.

If it were not materially interested in production or if it did not have within itself the potentialities for the creation of a new class, no party could act in so morally and ideologically foolhardy a fashion, let alone stay in power for long. Stalin declared, after the end of the first five year plan : "if we had not created the apparatus, we would have failed !" He should have substituted "new class" for the word "apparatus," and everything would have been clearer.

It seems unusual that a political party could be the beginning of a new class. Parties are generally the product of classes and strata which have become intellectually and economically strong. However, if one grasps the actual conditions in pre-revolutionary Russia and in other countries in which Communism prevailed over national forces, it will be clear that a party of this type is the product of specific opportunities and that there is nothing unusual or accidental in this being so. Although the roots of Bolshevism reach far back into Russian history, the party is partly the product of the unique pattern of international relationships in which Russia found itself at the end of the nineteenth and the beginning of the twentieth century. Russia was no longer able to live in the modern world as an absolute monarchy, and Russia's capitalism was too weak and too dependent on the interests of foreign powers to make it possible to have an industrial revolution. This revolution could only be implemented by a new class, or by a change in the social order. As yet, there was no such class.

In history, it is not important who implements a process, it is only important that the process be implemented. Such was the case in Russia and other countries in which Communist revolutions took place. The revolution created forces, leaders, organizations, and ideas which were necessary to it. The new class came into existence for objective reasons, and by the wish, wits, and action of its leaders.

The social origin of the new class lies in the proletariat just as the aristocracy arose in a peasant society, and the bourgeoisie in a commercial and artisans' society. There are exceptions, depending on national conditions, but the proletariat in economically underdeveloped countries, being backward, constitutes the raw material from which the new class arises.

There are other reasons why the new class always acts as the champion of the working class. The new class is anti-capitalistic and, consequently, logically dependent upon the working strata. The new class is supported by the proletarian struggle and the traditional faith of the proletariat in a socialist, Communist society where there is no brutal exploitation. It is vitally important for the new class to assure a normal flow of production, hence it cannot ever lose its connection with the proletariat. Most important of all, the new class cannot achieve industrialization and consolidate its power without the help of the working class. On the other hand, the working class sees in expanded industry the salvation from its poverty and despair. Over a long period of time, the interests, ideas, faith, and hope of the new class, and of parts of the working class and of the poor peasants, coincide and unite. Such mergers have occurred in the past among other widely different classes. Did not the bourgeoisie represent the peasantry in the struggle against the feudal lords?

The movement of the new class toward power comes as a result of the efforts of the proletariat and the poor. These are the masses upon which the party or the new class must lean and with which its interests are most closely allied. This is true until the new class finally establishes its power and authority. Over and above this, the new class is interested in the proletariat and the poor only to the extent necessary for developing production and for maintaining in subjugation the most aggressive and rebellious social forces.

The monopoly which the new class establishes in the name of the working class over the whole of society is, primarily, a monopoly over the working class itself. This monopoly is first intellectual, over the so-called bavant-gardee proletariat, and then over the whole proletariat. This is the biggest deception the class must accomplish, but it shows that the power and interests of the new class lie primarily in industry. Without industry the new class cannot consolidate its position or authority.

Former sons of the working class are the most steadfast members of the new class. It has been the fate of slaves to provide for their masters the most clever and gifted representatives. In this case a new exploiting and governing class is born from the exploited class.... [pp. 33-42]

As in other owning classes, the proof that it is a special class lies in its ownership and its special relations to other classes. In the same way, the class to which a member belongs is indicated by the material and other privileges which ownership brings to him.

As defined by Roman law, property constitutes the use, enjoyment, and disposition of material goods. The Communist political bureaucracy uses, enjoys, and disposes of nationalized property.

If we assume that membership in this bureaucracy or new owning class is predicated on the use of privileges inherent in ownership — in this instance nationalized material goods — then membership in the new party class, or political bureaucracy, is reflected in a larger income in material goods and privileges than society should normally grant for such functions. In practice, the ownership privilege of the new class manifests itself as an exclusive right, as a party monopoly, for the political bureaucracy to distribute the national income, to set wages, direct economic development, and dispose of nationalized and other property. This is the way is appears to the ordinary man who considers the Communist functionary as being very rich and as a man who does not have to work.

The ownership of private property has, for many reasons, proved to be unfavourable for the establishment of the new class's authority. Besides, the destruction of private ownership was necessary for the economic transformation of nations. The new class obtains its power, privileges, ideology, and its customs from one specific form of ownership — collective ownership — which the class administers and distributes in the name of the nation and society.

The new class maintains that ownership derives from a designated social relationship. This is the relationship between the monopolists of administration, who constitute a narrow and closed stratum, and the mass of producers (farmers, workers, and intelligentsia) who have no rights. But that is not all, since the Communist bureaucracy also has complete monopolistic control over material assets.

Every substantive change in the social relationship between those who monopolize administration and those who work is inevitably reflected in the ownership relationship. Social and political relations and ownership — the totalitarianism of government and the monopoly of ownership — are being more fully brought into accord in Communism than in any other political system.

To divest Communists of their ownership rights would be to abolish them as a class. To compel them to relinquish their other social powers, so that workers may participate in sharing the profits of their work — which capitalists have had to permit as a result of strikes and parliamentary action — would mean that Communists were being deprived of their monopoly over property, ideology, and government. This would be the beginning of democracy and freedom in Communism, the end of Communist monopolism and totalitarianism. Until this happens, there can be no indication that important, fundamental changes are taking place in Communist systems, at least not in the eyes of men who think seriously about social progress. [p. 44-46]

The heroic era of Communism is past. The epoch of its great leaders has ended. The epoch of practical men has set in. The new class has been created. It is at the height of its power and wealth, but it is without new ideas. It has nothing more to tell the people. The only thing that remains is for it to justify itself.

It would not be important to establish the fact that in contemporary Communism a new owning and exploiting class is involved, and not merely a temporary dictatorship and an arbitrary bureaucracy, if some anti-Stalinist Communists including Trotsky as well as some Social Democrats had not depicted the ruling stratum as a passing bureaucratic phenomenon because of which this new ideal, classless society, still in its swaddling clothes, must suffer, just as bourgeois society had had to suffer under Cromwell's and Napoleon's despotism.

But the new class is really a new class, with a special composition and special power. By any scientific definition of a class, even the Marxist definition by which some classes are lower than others according to their specific position in production, we conclude that, in the U.S.S.R. and Communist countries, a new class of owners and exploiters is in existence. The specific characteristic of this new class is its collective ownership. Communist theoreticians affirm, and some even believe, that Communism has arrived at collective ownership.

Collective ownership in various forms has existed in all earlier societies. All ancient Eastern despotisms were based on the pre-eminence of the state's or the king's property. In ancient Egypt after the fifeenth century B.C., arable land passed to private ownership. Before that time only homes and surrounding buildings had been privately owned. State land was handed over for cultivation while state officials administered the land and collected taxes on it. Canals and installations, as well as the most important works, were also state-owned. The state owned everything until it lost its independence in the first century of our era.

This helps to explain the deification of the pharaohs of Egypt and of the emperors, which one encounters in all the ancient Eastern despotisms. Such ownership also explains the undertaking of gigantic tasks, such as the construction of temples, tombs, and castles of emperors, of canals, roads, and fortifications.

The Roman state treated newly conquered land as state land and owned considerable numbers of slaves. The medieval church also had collective property.

Capitalism by its very nature was an enemy of collective ownership until the establishment of shareholders' organizations. Capitalism continued to be an enemy of collective ownership, even though it could not do anything against new encroachments by collective ownership and the enlargement of its area of operations.

The Communists did not invent collective ownership as such, but invented its all-encompassing character, more widely extended than in earlier epochs, even more extensive than in pharaoh's Egypt. That is all that the Communists did.

The ownership of the new class, as well as its character, was formed over a period of time and was subjected to constant change during the process. At first, only a small part of the nation felt the need for all economic powers to be placed in the hands of a political party for the purpose of aiding the industrial transformation. The party, acting as the *avant-garde* of the proletariat and as the "most enlightened power of socialism," pressed for this centralization which could be attained only by a change in ownership. The change was made in fact and in form through nationalization first of large enterprises and then of smaller ones. The abolition of private ownership was a prerequisite for industrialization, and for the beginning of the new class. However, without their special role as administrators over society and as distributors of property, the Communists could not transform themselves into a new class, nor could a new class be formed and permanently established. Gradually material goods were nationalized, but in fact, through its right to use, enjoy, and distribute these goods, they became the property of a discernible stratum of the party and the bureaucracy gathered around it.

In view of the significance of ownership for its power — and also of the fruits of ownership — the party bureaucracy cannot renounce the extension of its ownership even over small-scale production facilities. Because of its totalitarianism and monopolism, the new class finds itself unavoidably at war with everything which it does not administer or handle, and must deliberately aspire to destroy or conquer it.... [pp. 53-56]

The most important problem for Communism, in theory and practice, is the question of the state ; the question is a constant source of difficulties since it is such an obvious contradiction inside Communism.

Communist regimes are a form of latent civil war between the government and the people. The state is not merely an instrument of tyranny ; society as well as the executive bodies of the state machine is in a continuous and lively opposition to the oligarchy, which aspires to reduce this opposition by naked force. In practice, the Communists are unable to attain the goal of a state existing solely on naked force, nor are they able to subordinate society completely. But they are able to control the organs of force, that is, the police and party, which in turn control the entire state machine and its functions. The opposition of the organs and functionaries of the state to the "irrationalities" of the party and police, that is, of the political functionaries, is really the oppositon of society carried over into the state machine. It is an expression of dissatisfaction because of the oppression and crippling of society's objective aspirations and needs.

In Communist systems, the state and state functions are *not* reduced to organs of oppression, nor are they identical with them. As an organization of national and social life, the state is *subordinated* to these organs of oppression. Communism is unable to solve this incongruity, for the reason that by its own totalitarian despotism it inevitably comes in conflict with dissimilar and opposite tendencies of society, tendencies which are expressed even through the social functions of the state.

Because of this contradiction, and the unavoidable and constant need of the Communists to treat the state predominantly as an instrument of force, the Communist state cannot become a lawful state, or a state in which the judiciary would be independent of the government and in which laws could actually be enforced. The whole Communist system is opposed to such a state. Even if the Communist leaders wished to create a lawful state, they could not do so without imperilling their totalitarian authority.

An independent judiciary and the rule of law would inevitably make it possible for an opposition to appear. For instance, no law in the Communist system opposes the free expression of opinion or the right of organization. Laws in the Communist system guarantee all sorts of rights to citizens, and are based on the principle of an independent judiciary. In practice, there is no such thing.

Freedoms are formally recognized in Communist regimes, but one decisive condition is a prerequisite for exercising them : freedoms must be utilized only in the interest of the system of "socialism," which the Communist leaders represent, or to buttress their rules. This practice, contrary as it is to legal regulations, inevitably had to result in the use of exceptionally severe and unscrupulous methods by police and party bodies. Legal forms must be protected on the one hand while the monopoly of authority must be insured at the same time.

For the most part, in the Communist system, legislative authority cannot be separated from executive authority. Lenin considered this a perfect solution. Yugoslav leaders also maintain this. In a one-party system, this is one of the sources of despotism and omnipotence in government.

In the same way, it has been impossible in practice to separate police authority from judicial authority. Those who arrest also judge and enforce punishments, The circle is closed : the executive, the legislative, the investigating, the court, and the punishing bodies are one and the same.

Why does the Communist dictatorship have to use laws to the great extent that it does ? Why does it have to hide behind legality ?

Foreign political propaganda is one of the reasons. Another important one is the fact that the Communist regime must insure and fix the rights of those upon whom it depends — the new class — to maintain itself. Laws are always written from the standpoint of the new class's or party's needs or interests. Officially the laws must be written for all citizens, but citizens enjoy the rights of these laws conditionally, only if they are not "enemies of socialism." Consequently, the Communists encounter no end of trouble when forced to evade the laws which are of their own making. With the passage of time, they became familiar with this kind of difficulty, so they always leave loopholes and exceptions in their laws, in order to make evasion easier.

For instance, the Yugoslav legislative authorities stand on the principle that no one can be convicted except for an act which has been exactly formulated by the law. However, most of the political trials are held on the grounds of so-called "hostile propaganda," although this concept is purposely not defined but, instead, left up to the judges or secret police.

For these reasons political trials in Communist regimes are mostly prearranged. The courts have the task of demonstrating what the power-wielders need to have demonstrated ; or have the task of giving a *legal* cloak to the *political* judgment on the "hostile activity" of the accused.

In trials conducted by this method the confession of the accused is most important. He himself must acknowledge that he is an enemy. Thus, the thesis is confirmed. Evidence, little as there may be of it, must be replaced by confession of guilt.... [pp. 87-90]

The theory that contemporary Communism is a type of modern totalitarianism is not only the most widespread, but also the most accurate. However, an actual understanding of the term "modern totalitarianism" where Communism is being discussed is not so widespread.

Contemporary Communism is that type of totalitarianism which consists of three basic factors for controlling the people. The first is power ; the second, ownership ; the third, ideology. They are monopolized by the one and only political party, or — according to my previous explanation and terminology — by a new class ; and, at present, by the oligarchy of that party or of that class. No totalitarian system in history, not even a contemporary one — with the exception of Communism — has succeeded in incorporating simultaneously all these factors for controlling the people to this degree.

When one examines and weighs these three factors, power is the one which has played and still continues to play the most important role in the development of Communism. One of the other factors may eventually prevail over power, but it is impossible to determine this on the basis of present conditions. I believe that power will remain the basic characteristic of Communism.

Communism first originated as an ideology, which contained in its seed Communism's totalitarian and monopolistic nature. It can certainly be said that ideas no longer play the main, predominant role in Communism's control of the people. Communism as an ideology has mainly run its course. It does not have many new things to reveal to the world. This could not be said for the other two factors, power and ownership.

It can be said : power, either physical, intellectual, or economic, plays a role in every struggle, even in every social human action. There is some truth in this. It can also be said : in every policy, power, or the struggle to acquire and keep it, is the basic problem and aim. There is some truth in this also. But contemporary Communism is not only such a power ; it is something more. It is power of a particular type, a power which unites within itself the control of ideas, authority, and ownership, a power which has become an end in itself.

To date, Soviet Communism, the type which has existed the longest and which is the most developed, has passed through three phases. This is also more or less true of other types of Communism which have succeeded in coming in to power (with the exception of the Chinese type, which is still predominantly in the second phase).

The three phases are : revolutionary, dogmatic, and non-dogmatic Communism. Roughly speaking, the principal catch words, aims, and personalities corresponding to these various phases are : "Revolution," or the usurpation of power — Lenin, "Socialism," or the building of the system — Stalin. "Legality," or stabilization of the system — "collective leadership."

It is important to note that these phases are not distinctly separate from one another, that elements of all are found in each. Dogmatism abounded, and the "building of socialism" had already begun, in the Leninist period ; Stalin did not renounce revolution, or reject the dogmas, which interfered with the building of the system. Present-day, non-dogmatic Communism is only non-dogmatic conditionally : it just will not renounce even the minutest practical advantages for dogmatic reasons. Precisely because of such advantages, it will at the same time be in a position to persecute unscrupulously the minutest doubt concerning the truth or purity of the dogma. Thus, Communism, proceeding from practical needs and capabilities, has today even furled the sails of revolution, or of its own military expansion. But it has not renounced one or the other.

This division into three phases is only accurate if it is taken roughly and abstractly. Clearly separate phases do not actually exist, nor do they correspond to specific periods in the various countries.

The boundaries between the phases, which overlap, and the forms in which the phases appear are varied in different Communist countries. For example, Yugoslavia has passed through all three phases in a relatively short time and with the same personalities at the summit. This is obvious in both precepts and method of operation.

Power plays a major role in all three of these phases. In the revolution it was necessary to seize power ; in the building of socialism, it was necessary to create a new system by means of that power ; today power must preserve the system.

During the development, from the first to the third phase, the quintessence of Communism — power — evolved from being the means and became an end in itself. Actually power was always more or less the end, but Communist leaders, thinking that through power as a means they would attain the ideal goal, did not believe it to be an end in itself. Precisely because power served as a means for the Utopian transformation of society, it could not avoid becoming an end in itself and the most important aim of Communism. Power was able to appear as a means in the first and second phases. It can no longer be concealed that in the third phase power is the actual principal aim and essence of Communism.

Because of the fact that Communism is being extinguished as an ideology, it must maintain power as the main means of controlling the people.

In revolution, as in every type of war, it was natural to concentrate primarily on power : the war had to be won. During the period of industrialization, concentrating on power could still be considered natural : the construction of industry, or a "socialist society," for which so many sacrifices had been made, was necessary. But as all this is being completed, it becomes apparent that in Communism power has not only been a means but that it has also become the main, if not the sole, end.

Today power is both the means and the goal of Communists, in order that they may maintain their privileges and ownership. But since these are special forms of power and ownership, it is only through power itself that ownership can be exercised. Power is an end in itself and the essence of contemporary Communism. Other classes may be able to maintain ownership without a monopoly over power, or power without a monopoly over ownership. Until now, this has not been possible for the new class, which was formed through Communism ; it is very improbable that it will be possible in the future.

Throughout all three of these phases, power has concealed itself as the hidden, invisible, unspoken, natural and principal end. Its role has been stronger or weaker depending on the degree of control over the people required at the time. In the first phase, ideas were the inspiration and the prime mover for the attainment of power : in the second phase, power operated as the whip of society and for its own maintenance ; today, "collective ownership" is subordinated to the impulses and needs of power.

Power is the alpha and the omega of contemporary Communism, even when Communism strives to prevent this.

Ideas, philosophical principles and moral considerations, the nation and the people, their history, in part even ownership — all can be changed and sacrificed. But not power. Because this would signify Communism's renunciation of itself, of its own essence. Individuals can do this. But the class, the party, the oligarchy cannot. This is the purpose and the meaning of its existence.

Every type of power besides being a means is at the same time an end — at least for those who aspire to it. Power is almost exclusively an end in Communism, because it is both the source and the guarantee of all privileges. By means of and through power the material privileges and ownership of the ruling class over national goods are realized. Power determines the value of ideas, and suppresses or permits their expression.

It is in this way that power in contemporary Communism differs from all other types of power, and that Communism itself differs from every other system.

Communism has to be totalitarian, exclusive, and isolated precisely because power is the most essential component of Communism. If Communism actually could have had other ends, it would have to make it possible for other forces to spring up in opposition and operate independently. [pp. 166-170]

NOTE

1. M. Djilas, *The New Class* (New York : Holt, Rinehart and Winston, Inc. 1957) pp. 1-170.

WOMAN AND SOCIALISM[1]

August Bebel

We must therefore seek to bring about a state of society in which all will enjoy equal rights regardless of sex. That will be possible when the means of production become the property of society, when labour has attained its highest degree of fruitfulness by employing all scientific and technical improvements and advantages, and when all who are able to work shall be obliged to perform a certain amount of socially necessary labour, for which society in return will provide all with the necessary means for the development of their abilities and the enjoyment of life.

Woman shall become a useful member of human society enjoying full equality with man. She shall be given the same opportunity to develop her physical and mental abilities, and by performing duties she shall be entitled to rights. Being man's free and equal companion no unworthy demands will be made upon her. The present development of society is tending in this direction, and the numerous and grave evils incidental to this development necessitate the introduction of a new social order. [p. 232]

NOTE

1. August Bebel, *Woman and Socialism* (New York : Socialist Literature Co., 1910), p. 232.

ORIGIN OF THE FAMILY[1]

Frederick Engels

The history of the family is the progressive narrowing of the circle, originally embracing the whole tribe, within which the two sexes have a common conjugal relation. The continuous exclusion, first of nearer, then of more and more remote relatives, and at last even of relatives by marriage, ends by making any kind of group marriage practically impossible. Finally, there remains only the single, still loosely linked pair, the molecule with whose dissolution marriage itself ceases. This in itself shows what a small part individual sex-love, in the modern sense of the word, played in the rise of monogamy. Yet stronger proof is afforded by the practice of all peoples at this stage of development. Whereas in the earlier forms of the family men never lacked women, but, on the contrary, had too many rather than too few, women had now become scarce and highly sought after. Hence it is with the pairing marriage that there begins the capture and purchase of women — widespread *symptoms*, but no more than symptoms, of the much deeper change that had occurred. These symptoms, mere methods of procuring wives, the pedantic Scot, McLennan has transmogrified into special classes of families under the names of "marriage by capture" and "marriage by purchase." In general, whether among the American Indians or other peoples (at the same stage), the conclusion of a marriage is the affair not of the two parties concerned, who are often not consulted at all, but of their mothers. Two persons entirely unknown to each other are often thus affianced ; they only learn that the bargain has been struck when the time for marrying approaches. Before the wedding the bridegroom gives presents to the bride's gentile relatives (to those on the mother's side, therefore, not to the father and his relations), which are regarded as gift payments in return for the girl. The marriage is still terminable at the desire of either partner, but among many tribes, the Iroquois, for example, public opinion has gradually developed against such separations ; when differences arise between husband and wife, the *gens* relatives of both partners act as mediators, and only if these efforts prove fruitless does a separation take place, the wife then keeping the children and each partner being free to marry again.

The pairing family, itself too weak and unstable to make an independent household necessary or even desirable, in no wise destroys the communistic household inherited from earlier times. Communistic housekeeping, however, means the supremacy of women in the house ; just as the exclusive recognition of the female parent, owing to the impossibility of recognizing the male parent with certainty, means that the women — the mothers — are held in high respect. One of the most absurd notions taken over from eighteenth-century enlightenment is that in the beginning of society woman was the slave of man. Among all savages and all barbarians of the lower and middle stages, and to a certain extent of the upper stage also, the position of women is not only free, but honourable. As to what it still is in the pairing marriage, let us hear the evidence of Ashur Wright, for many years missionary among the Iroquois Senecas :

> As to their family system, when occupying the old long-families, it is probable that some one clan [*gens*] pre-dominated, the women taking in husbands, however, from the other clans [*gentes*]....Usually, the female portion rules the house.... The stores were in common ; but woe to the luckless husband or lover who was too shiftless to do his share of the providing. No matter how many children, or whatever goods he might have in the house, he might at any time be ordered to pick up his blanket and budge ; and after such orders it would not be healthful for him to attempt to disobey. The House would be too hot for him ; and ... he must retreat to his own clan [*gens*] ; or, as was often done, go and start a new matrimonial alliance in some other. The women were the great power among the clans [*gentes*], as everywhere else. They did not hesitate, when occasion required, " to knock off the horns" as it was technically called, from the head of a chief, and send him back to the ranks of the warriors.

The communistic household, in which most or all of the women belong to one and the same *gens*, while the men come from various *gentes*, is the material foundation of that supremacy of the women which was general in primitive times.... The reports of travellers and missionaries, I may add, to the effect that women among savages and barbarians are overburdened with work in no way contradict what has been said. The division of labour between the two sexes is determined by quite other causes than by the position of woman in society. Among peoples where the women have to work far harder than we think suitable, there is often much more real respect for women than among our Europeans. The lady of civilization, surrounded by false homage and estranged from the real work, has an infinitely lower social position than the hard-working woman of barbarism, who was regarded among her people as a real lady (lady, frowa, Frau-mistress) and who was also a lady in character.... [pp. 11-13]

In the great majority of cases today, at least in the possessing classes, the husband is obliged to earn a living and support his family, and that in itself gives him a position of supremacy, without any need for special legal titles and privileges. Within the family he is the bourgeois and the wife represents the proletariat. In the industrial world, the specific character of the economic oppression burdening the proletariat is visible in all its sharpness only when all special legal privileges of the capitalist class have been abolished and complete legal equality of both classes established. The democratic republic does not do away with the opposition of the two classes ; on the contrary, it provides the clear field on which the fight can be fought out. And in the same way, the peculiar character of the supremacy of the husband over the wife in the modern family, the necessity of creating real social equality between them, and the way to do it, will only be seen in the clear light of day when both possess legally complete equality of rights. Then it will be plain that the first condition for the liberation of the wife is to bring the whole female sex back into public industry, and that this in turn demands the abolition of the monogamous family as the economic unit of society. [p. 39]

NOTE

1. Frederick Engels, "Origin of the Family," in *The Woman Question* (U.S.A. : International Publishers Co., Inc., 1975), pp. 11-39.

WOMEN AND SOCIETY[1]

V.I. Lenin

Socialism and the Emancipation of Women

As long as women are engaged in housework their position is still a restricted one. In order to achieve the complete emancipation of women and to make them really co-equal with men, we must have social economy, and the participation of women in general productive labour. The women will occupy the same position as men. [p. 52]

NOTE

1. V.I. Lenin, "Women and Society," in *The Woman Question* (U.S.A. : International Publishers Co. Inc., 1975), p. 52.

POLITICS AND LAW : THE THEORY AND PRACTICE OF THE IDEOLOGY OF FEMALE SUPREMACY : OR, IT WASN'T GOD WHO MADE HONKY TONK ANGELS[1]

M.G. Lorenne Clarke

. . . Political theory up to our own time, and including Marx, is the ideology of the male, serving the interest of the dominant sex, whose dominance is likewise assumed, and asserted, to be "natural," the dominance of those who are naturally stronger, freer from the grinding necessities of biological reality, more aggressive, more contemplative, and rational.

The fundamental problem with which traditional political theory has failed to come to grips, indeed the fundamental reality politics was devised as an escape from, is reproduction. It is precisely because of this fact that politics represents a flight from reality, and why, stripped of its sexist assumptions, it is, as we know it, incapable of providing us with a set of workable social institutions guaranteeing equality to all regardless of sex. At its very heart politics assumes that reproduction is demeaning, that fundamental meaning and importance for man, and here I mean the term literally, cannot derive from the theory to support it, was born from a sense of the futility of the reproductive function. It was designed exclusively by men, exclusively for men, as an escape from the world of the household, the realm of the "merely" biological, of pure necessity.

But since reproduction is necessary if there is to be any continuing social unit at all, the rejection of it as a meaningful human activity and as the primary organizing principle of social life necessarily condemned women to carry on an indisputably necessary social function without any recognition whatsoever and without any power to shape other social institutions in ways which were compatible with this central process in individual and social life. The business of reproduction was carried on, one might say, *sub judice*. It took place outside the political sphere, not merely in the sense that it just happened to be a nonpolitical activity, but in the strong sense that it was declared by fiat not to be a political activity and not to have any significance within the political sphere. It was by definition, by arbitrary and deliberate convention, and not by mere historical accident, set apart from the political realm and declared to be of no political importance. It was a merely private matter, to be contained within the household walls well out of the public eye. The family was not, and is not, an acknowledged political institution so far as political theory has been concerned, and reproduction is not, and has not been, an activity of acknowledged political significance. And if women are assumed to be capable of being fitted into the ontology of politics — if "mankind" really is taken to be generic and to refer to both males and females — one central question remains glaringly obvious : who, then, is doing the reproductive work ?

But I am not asserting in what I have developed so far that reproduction is women's only, or even their primary, function, or that men have no reproductive function. That view is, indeed, a consequence of the ideology I am now attempting to explicate. It takes two human beings, a male and a female, to create new human life, and it ought, though it has not, at least as a general phenomenon, for some time been the case that men shared the reproductive function beyond the initial procreative stage. For the reproductive function is not simply the creation and birth of a new human individual. Creation and birth are but the first steps in the process. It is the whole process from conception through birth and subsequent development to a state of more or less independence that constitutes the reproductive process. The fact that women carry and give birth to the child is merely a differentiation of function, but does not make the whole process their single-handed function or responsibility. The view that it does, or that it should, is itself a product of the ideology of male supremacy and has no basis in fact or justification in logic.

In so far as politics, and political theory as we know it, assumes that reproduction is not a political activity, that it has no political and human value, and that it must lie outside the public realm, that politics and that theory must be rejected. As it stands, it reflects a rejection of the male role in reproduction and substitutes for that reality an image of man the producer, a creator of things rather than of persons.

As political theory developed, however, the paradoxes inherent in it because of its fundamental misconception about the role and value of reproduction, and its assumed but frequently unstated premise as to the inequality of the sexes, only became more apparent, though that did not, of course, mean that they were noticed. But starting as it did from the assumption that reproduction had no political value, it followed that it had no economic value either. This aspect of the paradox only shows up fully when we get to Marx, for of course Marxism is not less a part of this tradition than any other political theory. However, I would like to interject at this point that the critique of political theory that I and others are now engaged in does not falsify Marxist theory but merely shows it to be incomplete, at least in the sense in which it is supposed to provide a blueprint for the future. It is incomplete in the sense that the complete realization of the Marxist dialectic would not necessarily abolish inequality. However, I accept Marxism as providing a basically true description of society in so far as the relations of production and the development of inequality through the class structure is concerned. But the Marxist assumption that the fundamental determinant of any political system is the economic factor, and that the economic factor is the product of the relation between individuals and the modes of production posits an ontology of males who are the producers and an epistemology which cannot make truth claims of important sorts about women.

On the Marxist model as it stands, either women's ability to become producers will still somehow have to be fitted around their still-assumed-to-be-natural reproductive function, or the reproductive function will have to be eliminated. The fact that the latter is now a distinct possibility is what I find extremely frightening. To the extent that women become producers, they are desexed, at least in the sense that their reproductive abilities must be totally denied. This is to return to a point made earlier, that woman's visibility within a Marxist analysis requires the severance of her identity from her reproductive abilities. While no feminist wants her sexuality totally identified with her reproductivity, it seems too much to assume that her equality necessitates the abolition of her reproductive ability as any part of her identity. And this is a point of no small importance. With advances in technology, more and more of the reproductive function can in fact be transformed into a form of production. But to the extent that this is true, its logical outcome is the artificial production of children. Indeed, Firestone had already suggested that the complete equality of women can only be achieved once all babies are produced artificially. Only then will that part of the reproductive function which is irreducibly the ability of women, as opposed to men, become totally obsolete and the source of even the periodic invisibility of them and their unique labour. But why should the reproductive function have to be totally abolished in order to allow women to assume their equal place within society ? Surely this represents the complete victory of the dominant sex and of the values they have enforced, namely, the utter redundancy of the female in so far as she has a unique role in the reproductive process and the utter obliteration of the reproductive function as such. Production no longer presupposes reproduction and women no longer have a reproductive identity. Just as importantly, neither do men. Thus, full visibility within society, at least in so far as a Marxist analysis is genuinely descriptive of society, entails the destruction of our sexual difference and of at least that much of our sexual identity as rests on our differentiated reproductive abilities. [pp. 37-49]

NOTE

1. M.G. Lorenne Clarke, "Politics and Law : The Theory and Practice of the Ideology of Female Supremacy : Or, It Wasn't God Who Made Honky Tonk Angels," in D.N. Weisstub, ed., *Law and Policy* (Toronto : Osgoode Hall Law School, 1976), pp. 37-49.

VINDICATION OF THE RIGHTS OF WOMEN[1]

Mary Wollstonecraft

After considering the historic page, and viewing the living world with anxious solicitude, the most melancholy emotions of sorrowful indignation have depressed my spirits, and I have sighed when obliged to confess that either Nature has made a great difference between man and man, or that the civilization which has hitherto taken place in the world has been very partial. I have turned over various books written on the subject of education, and patiently observed the conduct of parents and the management of schools ; but what has been the result ? — a profound conviction that the neglected education of my fellow-creatures is the grand source of the misery I deplore, and that women, in particular, are rendered weak and wretched by a variety of concurring causes, originating from one hasty conclusion. The conduct and manners of women, in fact, evidently prove that their minds are not in a healthy state ; for, like the flowers which are planted in too rich a soil, strength and usefulness are sacrificed to beauty ; and the flaunting leaves, after having pleased a fastidious eye, fade, disregarded on the stalk, long before the season when they ought to have arrived at maturity. One cause of this barren blooming I attribute to a false system of education, gathered from the books written on this subject by men who, considering females rather as women than human creatures, have been more anxious to make them alluring mistresses than affectionate wives and rational mothers ; and the understanding of the sex has been so bubbled by this spacious homage, that the civilized women of the present century, with a few exceptions, are only anxious to inspire love, when they ought to cherish a nobler ambition, and by their abilities and virtues exact respect.

In a treasure, therefore, on female rights and manners, the works which have been particularly written for their improvement must not be overlooked, especially when it is asserted, in direct terms, that the minds of women are enfeebled by false refinement ; that the books of instruction, written by men of genius, have had the same tendency as more frivolous productions ; and that, in the true style of Mahometanism, they are treated as a kind of subordinate beings, and not as a part of the human species, when improvable reason is allowed to be the dignified distinction which raises men above the brute creation, and puts a natural sceptre in a feeble hand. [pp. 79-80]

In the present state of society it appears necessary to go back to first principles in search of the most simple truths, and to dispute with some prevailing prejudice every inch of ground. To clear my way, I must be allowed to ask some plain questions, and the answers will probably appear as unequivocal as the axioms on which reasoning is built ; though, when entangled with various motives of action, they are formally contradicted, either by the words or conduct of men.

In what does man's pre-eminence over the brute creation consist ? The answer is as clear as that a half is less than whole, in Reason.

What acquirement exalts one being above another ? Virtue, we spontaneously reply.

For what purpose were the passions implanted ? That man by struggling with them might attain a degree of knowledge denied to the brutes, whispers Experience.

Consequently the perfection of our nature and capability of happiness must be estimated by the degree of reason, virtue, and knowledge, that distinguish the individual, and direct the laws which bind society : and that from the exercise of reason, knowledge and virtue naturally flow, is equally undeniable, if mankind be viewed collectively.

The rights and duties of man thus simplified, it seems almost impertinent to attempt to illustrate truths that appear so incontrovertible ; yet such deeply rooted prejudices have clouded reason, and such spurious qualities have assumed the name of virtues, that it is necessary to pursue the course of reason as it has been perplexed and involved in error, by various adventitious circumstances, comparing the simple axiom with casual deviations.

Men, in general, seem to employ their reason to justify prejudices, which they have imbibed, they can scarcely trace how, rather than to root them out. The mind must be strong that resolutely forms its own principles ; for a kind of intellectual cowardice prevails which makes many men shrink from the task, or only do it by halves. Yet the imperfect conclusions thus drawn, are frequently very plausible, because they are built on partial experience, on just, though narrow, views. [pp. 91-92]

NOTE

1. Mary Wollstonecraft, *A Vindication of the Rights of Woman*, first published in 1792 Miriam Kramnick ed. (Pelican Books 1975), pp. 79-92.

WOMEN IN WESTERN POLITICAL THOUGHT[1]

Susan M. Okin

It must be recognized at once that the great tradition of political philosophy consists, generally speaking, of writings by men, for men, and about men. While the use of supposedly generic terms like "man" and "mankind," and of the allegedly inclusive pronoun, "he," might lead one to think that philosophers have intended to refer to the human race as a whole, we do not need to look far into their writings to realize that such an assumption is unfounded. Rousseau, for example, tells his reader at the beginning of the *Discourse on the Origins and Foundation of Inequality among Men* that "It is of man that I am to speak." It subsequently becomes very clear that it is only the inequality between males that is the subject of his investigation, and the inequality between the sexes is assumed in passing. Past and present feminists, only too aware of such practices, have pointed out the dangerous ambiguity of such linguistic usage in a patriarchal culture. For it enables philosophers to enunciate principles as if they were universally applicable, and then to proceed to exclude all women from their scope.

Even when philosophers have used words which in their respective languages refer unambiguously to any human being, they have felt in no way deterred from excluding women from the conclusions reached. Aristotle, for example, discusses at length what is the highest good for a human being (*anthropos*). He then proceeds to characterize all women as not only conventionally deprived of, but constitutionally unfitted for, this highest good. Again, Kant uses the most inclusive terms of all for the subjects of his ethical and political theory ; he even says that he is not confining his discussion to humans, but that it is applicable to "all rational beings." Subsequently, however, he proceeds to justify a double standard of sexual morality, to the extent that a woman is to be condoned for killing her illegitimate child because of her "duty" to uphold, at all costs, her "sexual honour." He also reaches the conclusion that the only characteristic that permanently disqualifies any person from citizenship in the state, and therefore from the obligation to obey only those laws to which consent has been given, is that of being born female. Thus, even words such as "person," "human," and "rational being," apparently, do not necessarily include women.

This phenomenon, made possible by the ambiguity of our language, is not confined to political philosophy. The grand statements of our political culture, too, such as the Declaration of Independence and the Constitution, are phrased in universal terms, but..., they have frequently been interpreted in such a way as to exclude women. Thus when the Founding Fathers declared it to be a self-evident truth that "all men are created equal," not only did they intend the substantial slave population to be excluded from the scope of their statement, but they would have been amused and skeptical (as indeed John Adams was to his wife's appeal that they not forget the ladies) at the suggestion that women were, and should be considered, equal too. Similarly, though the Constitution is phrased in terms of "persons," there was clearly no idea in its framers' minds that this word might be interpreted so as to include women on the same terms as men.

"Human nature," we realize, as described and discovered by philosophers such as Aristotle, Aquinas, Machiavelli, Locke, Rousseau, Hegel, and many others, is intended to refer only to male human nature. Consequently, all the rights and needs that they have considered humanness to entail have not been perceived as applicable to the female half of the human race. Thus there has been, and continues to be, within the traditions of political philosophy and political culture, a pervasive tendency to make allegedly general statements as if the human race were not divided into two sexes, and then either to ignore the female sex altogether, or to proceed to discuss it in terms not at all consistent with the assertions that have been made about "man" and "humanity." [pp. 5-6]

. . . [T]he most important factor influencing the philosophers' conceptions of, and arguments about, women has been the view that each of them held concerning the family. Those who have regarded the family as a natural and necessary institution have defined women by their sexual, procreative, and child-rearing functions within it. This has led to the prescription of a code of morality and conception of rights for women distinctly different from those that have been prescribed for men. The assumption of the necessity of the family leads the theorists to then regard the biological differences between the sexes as entailing all the other, conventional and institutional differences in sex role which the family, especially in its most patriarchal forms, has required.

Second, as a consequence of the above, the constricted role in which woman has been placed has been regarded as dictated by her very nature. Thus, where philosophers have explicitly discussed women, they have frequently not extended to them their various conceptions of "human nature." They have not only assigned women a distinct role, but have defined them separately, and often contrastingly, to men. They have sought for the nature of women not, as for the nature of men, by attempting to separate out nature from the effects of nurture, and to discover what innate potential exists beneath the overlay which results from socialization and other environmental factors. The nature of women, instead, has been seen to be dictated by whatever social and economic structure the philosophers favour and to be defined as whatever best suits her prescribed functions in that society. Philosophers who, in laying the foundation for their political theories, have asked "What are men like ?" "What is man's potential ?" have frequently, in turning to the female sex, asked "What are women *for* ?" There is, then, an undeniable connection between assigned "female nature" and social structure, and a functionalist attitude to women pervades the history of political thought.

The conclusions drawn here are, first, that women cannot simply be added to the subject matter of existing political theory, for the works of our philosophical heritage are to a very great extent built on the assumption of the inequality of the sexes. In the case of theorists for whom equality, in some form or other, is an important value, the unequal treatment of women tends to be concealed by the adoption of the male-headed family, rather than the individual adult, as the primary unit of political analysis. Indeed, the thoroughly equal treatment of women, involving far more than the right to vote, requires the rethinking of some of the most basic assumptions of political philosophy — having to do with the family and woman's traditionally dependent and subordinate role within it.

Second, as we examine some twentieth-century perceptions of women and analyze legal discrimination against women, it becomes clear that these findings should be of interest not only to historians or students of political theory. The functionalist treatment of women — the prescriptive view of woman's nature and proper mode of life based on her role and functions in a patriarchal family structure — is still alive and influential today. Giant figures in modern sociology and psychology present arguments about women that parallel those of Aristotle and Rousseau. Moreover, when we examine the opinions handed down by the highest courts of the land in cases involving sex discrimination, we find, here too, that judges have used functionalist reasoning of a strikingly Aristotelian character in order to justify their treatment of women as a class apart. Thus, there is no doubt that a thorough understanding of this mode of argument can help us to see why women, in spite of their political enfranchisement, are still second-class citizens. [pp. 8-9]

. . . Once one recognizes the existence of women as individuals in their own right, this assumption of the total unity of the family's interests becomes exposed for the myth that it always was. The clear constrast that has been pointed to by many philosophers between the altruistic, loving sphere of the family and the harsh, competitive world outside, is no longer as distinct. Perhaps this realization will result in a questioning of both sides of the exaggerated dichotomy — of the atomistic assumptions about the outside realm as well as the unrealistic degree of altruism that has been supposed to characterize family relationships. If, as seems likely, the assumed love and altruism of the family, founded as it is upon the radical inequality of women, has served to soften the full impact of a world of self-interested individuals, maybe one of the results of treating women as beings with their own personalities and interests will be to expose the full implications of a theory in which self-interest is assumed to be the norm for economic and political life. Without the total selflessness that was supposed to exist within families, the total self-interestedness that liberalism assumes exists outside of them may seem more in need of reconsideration.

It should by now be clear that it is by no means a simple matter to integrate the female half of the human race into a tradition of political theory which has been based, almost without exception, upon the belief that women must be defined exclusively by their role within the family, and which has thus defined them, and intrafamilial relationships, as outside the scope of the political. There is no way in which we can include women, formerly minor characters, as major ones within the political drama without challenging basic and age-old assumptions about the family, its traditional sex roles, and its relation to the wider world of political society.

Before we leave the subject of the adaptations to political theory that would be made necessary by the absolutely equal treatment of women, we should note one respect in which democratic theories would thereby be rendered more internally consistent. For any theorist who aims at genuine political equality, the transformation of the family into a more egalitarian group should be welcome for reasons affecting the health of the political community as a whole. If the family is to lose the last vestiges of its patriarchal character, and to become a democratically run institution in which the only differential in terms of authority is the temporary one of age, this will surely affect the potential of the family as a socializing agency for the wider political community. The patriarchalism of the seventeenth century is the clearest parallel that has been drawn by political theorists between familial and governmental structures of authority and obedience. Clearly, in the view of such theorists, the hierarchical nature of the family made it an exemplary socializing agent for the hierarchical world of king and subjects. For democratic or egalitarian political theorists, however, it would seem that a family structure that is as democratic and egalitarian as possible would best serve the function of preparing future citizens for a life of political participation and equality. [pp. 285-287]

. . . The scientific breakthroughs that have prolonged life, eradicated epidemics, and drastically reduced infant mortality, mean that there is now no need for women to spend more than a tiny fraction of their lives in bearing enough children to maintain the population level. Moreover, the provision by technology of increasingly reliable methods of birth control and increasingly safe methods of abortion means that each woman can choose both if and when she will bear children. Just as the characteristics of the means of production affect people's development and their nature, so do the characteristics of the means of reproduction.... By reasoning parallel to Marx's concerning the realm of production, women can achieve freedom and a fully developed human nature only when the reproduction and rearing of children becomes a freely chosen activity, and when it no longer dictates the entire mode of life of the female sex.

For these conditions to come about, however, more than a revolution in technology is required ; a revolution in conditions and ideas must occur with it, and although this has clearly begun, it is by no means completed. This latter revolution must accomplish two ends. First, it must make motherhood a freely chosen option for women. Contraception in itself, of course, does not make childbearing optional, if female socialization is overwhelmingly weighted toward motherhood, or if women are not reinforced or highly rewarded in other spheres of their lives. Second, the revolution must succeed in clearly separating out those aspects of reproduction which are biologically women's — necessarily, pregnancy, and if it is opted for, lactation — from all these long-term aspects of child-rearing which are not necessarily women's work, but have been made to seem so on account of the accepted structure of the family. As we have seen... some feminists as well as antifeminists have fallen into the trap of perceiving child-rearing as inseparable from childbearing, which means of course that as long as the latter is a female function, so must the former be.

Now that technology has given women the means of controlling reproduction (in principle, though by no means universally in practice), there is a far greater possibility of achieving a separation of functions. The fact that many women have now, and it is to be hoped all women will have in the future, complete freedom of choice as to whether to bear children at all, and when to bear those they choose to have, means that women's lives need not be perceived, by either themselves or society, as dictated by the physical demands of maternity.

As for the socialization of young children, while it is clearly of immense significance, there is no reason why it should be done by one woman, the biological mother. There is, indeed, no reason why it should be done by one person alone, or by women only. In this area, the structure of the family that has predominated throughout history must change radically if woman are to achieve equality with men....

We must aim toward a time when child-rearing will be equally shared between the sexes. This is essential, if women are to enjoy equality, for three reasons. First, the great majority of women, who are mothers, can never be men's equals in the work force or in any realm of activity outside the home while only their working lives are subject over a period of years to the effects of the total responsibility for child-rearing. Women presently are handicapped in the realm of work and public activity not only by the fact that most, by far, still actually do take a disproportionate amount of responsibility for housework and child-care, but also because, even if they do not, this is the expectation of the world in general — of employers, courts, voters, and other persons and institutions who have power over what women will be able to do in the outside world, and who discriminate against them to the extent documented above.

Second, only when men share equally in such tasks as housework and child-rearing will they come to be valued equally with those "masculine" tasks which society presently acknowledges to be productive and rewards with money, and sometimes with prestige. There will be no such thing as an inferior class of "women's work," and no relegation of women alone, in the work force as in the home, to nurturing, "expressive," supportive and under— or unpaid work.

Third, it is clearly by identification with the parents, ... that children learn traditional sex roles. Girls and boys will not grow up with open-minded ideas about themselves and the kinds of lives they want to lead until they perceive adults, and especially those closest to them — their parents — filling, and expressing themselves in, all types of roles. None of these three aims can be achieved until housework is shared and "parenting" takes the place of "mothering." [pp. 298-302]

NOTE

1. S.M. Okin, *Women in Western Political Thought* (Princeton : Princeton University Press, 1979), pp. 5-302.

PATRIARCHA AND OTHER POLITICAL WORKS OF SIR ROBERT FILMER[1]

Introduction
Peter Laslett, Editor

Now the social anthropologist classifies European culture of all periods, even in the present era of self-conscious rationalism, as markedly patriarchal. It is patriarchal in its family forms, it is patriarchal in its emotional attitudes : it is even patriarchal in its politics and economics. In none of these respects, of course, is it as extreme in its patriarchalism as are many other cultures, ancient or modern, primitive or advanced. The European cannot sympathize, for example, with contemporary Japanese society which builds its whole political philosophy on the Emperor as the literal ancestor of all the Japanese. Nevertheless we need go no further than our vocabulary of political and religious authority to see how closely we still associate all forms of power with the power of the father. God is still the Father, the Pope is still Papa, we still talk of paternal despots, even of paternal bureaucracies. In fact, in the view of the most influential school of social psychologists, the emotional attitude of the contemporary American to political authority is identical in character with his emotional attitude to the father of this family.

But it is in the economic field that the evidence for the survival of patriarchal institutions into present day European society is most marked. It is astonishing to realize that in this respect the Europe of today is almost exactly the same as the Europe of Sir Robert Filmer's generation. In all parts of the world where European law and culture prevail, with the exception of the areas which have adopted communism, there is a general presumption which favours of the inheritance of a father's property by his eldest son. There is also a tendency to subordinate the interests of women to men in the possession of property and above all there is an assumption that a man has a right before all other men to the possessions of his dead father. All these assumptions about the transference of property are the assumptions of patriarchalism. To patriarchalism is due the very possibility of a man's identifying himself with his posterity and so striving to build up his wealth for the benefit of his son and his son's son. In this form patriarchalism is readily recognized as an essential feature of the European tradition, and it is easy to see how differently modern society would have developed if the patriarchal rules of property had become as archaic as the patriarchal rules of politics. It is clear, for example, that patriarchalism has always been an essential, perhaps the essential, presupposition of capitalism. [p. 23]

NOTE

1. Peter Laslett, ed., *Patriarcha and Other Political Works of Sir Robert Filmer* (Oxford : Basil Blackwell, 1949), p. 23.

THE END OF IDEOLOGY[1]

Daniel Bell

The story of the rise and fall of social classes in Western society ... is that of the rise and fall of families. Without understanding that fact, as many American sociologists, accustomed to viewing class position in individualistic terms, have failed to do, one cannot understand the peculiar cohesiveness of dominant economic classes in the past, or the sources of the breakup of power in contemporary society today.

Capitalism is not only, as Marx saw it, an economic system with employer-worker relations and classes formed on strictly economic lines, but a social system wherein power has been transmitted through the family, and where the satisfactions of ownership lay, in part, in the family name, by which the business enterprise was known. (In Marcel Pagnol's *Fanny* the ecstatic hope of Panisse is to add the words "and Son" over the door of his shop, a practice long maintained by commercial enterprises.)

The social organization of the family rested on two institutions : property and the "dynastic" marriage. Property sanctioned by law and reinforced by the coercive power of the state, meant power ; the "dynastic" marriage was a means of conserving and, through inheritance laws, of transmitting property and so preserving, as the case might be, the continuity of family enterprise. (A classic instance of this process, perhaps, was the assumption of Gustav von Bohlen of the family name of Krupp when the line of the famous German steel company lacked male heirs.)

The relationship of property to family structure is one of the oldest institutions in Western society, reaching far back to the Roman law of land. Land, historically, was the oldest and most basic form of property and power. In Roman law, property did not inhere in a particular person, in the head of the family ; property inhered in the heir. And when the heir became head of the family, the property no longer belonged to him, but to his heirs. This "fiction," as Sir Henry Maine called it, regarding the ownership of property, was necessary to preserve its "inalienability," i.e., the fact that it could not be freely disposed of at will. The effort to freely dispose of land — to make it inalienable — to rid it of all entails, strict settlements, primogenitures, and the like was part of the effort to make property a free commodity. In English law, it was not until 1925, in fact, that all impediments to the alienability of property were completely removed.

In philosophical terms, the linked institutions of property and family were always seen as a necessary precondition to established society. When Godwin and Condorcet, at the turn of the nineteenth century, insisted that progress and freedom lay only in striking the bonds of marriage and sharing all property, they were answered for all bourgeois society by Parson Malthus, who insisted that without the restraints of family and property the "natural" instincts to lust and licentiousness would assert themselves so freely that population would break all bounds, outstrip the growth of resources, and result in privation and misery for the multitude rather than happiness. The *Essay on Population*, in fact, was not an exercise in demography, but a sermon in morals.

But more than economic or moral considerations were involved in the linkage of the family and property systems. Through the fusion of the two institutions, a class system was maintained : people met at the same social levels, were educated in common schools appropriate to their wealth, shared the same manners and morals, read the same books and held similar prejudices, mingled in the same milieus — in short, created and shared a distinctive style of life.

The singular fact is that in the last seventy-five years the old relation between the two institutions of property and family, which, Malthus maintained, represented the "fundamental laws" of society, has broken down. The specific reasons for this breakdown are too complex for a short sketch, but the process is clear. In bourgeois society, marriage was a means of keeping sex relations within bounds ; in bourgeois marriage, as Denis de Rougement wittily observed, every woman had a husband and desired a lover ; the great continental novels of the nineteenth century, Tolstoy's *Anna Karenina*, Flaubert's *Madame Bovary*, with their geometry of adultery, pointed up this paradox. The growth of romanticism, the high premium on individual attachment and free choice, the translation of passion into secular and carnal terms — all worked against the system of "dynastic" marriage. The emancipation of women meant, in one sense, the disappearance of one of the stable aspects of bourgeois society. If women could marry freely, crossing class lines if they so desired, then the economic enterprise with which the "dynastic" marriage was intertwined would lose some of its staying power.

But there are also reasons more indigenous to the nature of the economic system why the mode of family capitalism has given way. Some are general : the decline of the extended family or clan narrowed the choice of heirs competent to manage the enterprise ; the increasing importance of professional techniques placed a high premium on skill rather than blood relationships. These reasons apply largely to the United States, and principally to those corporate areas where managerial and technical skill refuse simply to be agencies of family domination and want to lead in their own right. Yet in Europe, as studies by David Landes, for example, have shown, the continuity of family enterprise has been remarkable. And the continuing existence of such family enterprises, with its caution, conservatism, and fear of allowing outside capital to enter into its affairs, argues Landes, is one of the chief reasons, until now, for the slow rate of economic growth on the continent.

The situation in America, from the start, has been somewhat different. One important reason is that title to almost all land in the United States has been held in fee simple, rather than entail as in Europe, and family founders have been comparatively unable to impose their wishes regarding the conservation of property upon successive generations. Another is that there has been in the United States, for a variety of complex reasons, a tradition — or at least a myth — whereby the son does not succeed the father but strikes out for himself. These two factors, historical and socio-psychological, have been distinctive elements which hindered the development of a full system of family capitalism in the United States.

Yet efforts to create such a system were constantly being made. As Bernard Bailyn has pointed out in his study of American merchants in the seventeenth century, the rise of business enterprise in the United States was due not to individual initiative but to family solidarity. The family was the source of initial capital, and from the extended family one could draw a variety of skills for the growth of the enterprise. Family enterprises were quite common along the eastern seaboard — particularly in the major cities of Boston, Philadelphia, and New York — in the post-colonial period, and "society" was made up of these leading family clans. The constant movement westward, the vast speculations, the wild economic swings, all acted as disruptive factors.

With the rapid industrialization after the Civil War, the new enterprises often began as family groups. In a capitalist society, control of money and credit, the sources of capital formation, is the fulcrum of power. Few of the companies that began were public corporations. They drew capital from family holdings and expanded by "self-financing". Most of the large "middle-sized" industries in the country have been typical family enterprises. This has been most true of textiles and brewing, but equally of others. International banking, characteristically, has been a "family" affair because of the "secret" nature of much of the business and the need for people one could trust to be placed in different parts of the world. The same reasons apply to shipping. Packing, for historical reasons, has been a closely held family set of enterprises, as have chemicals, soap, and newspapers. The big "names" in American industry began as "family" names : du Pont, Swift, Armour, Grace, Ford, Olin Chemical, Dow, etc. Even today, most major newspapers are family-owned, rather than being public corporations on the market.

The family system had a social counterpart as well : the domination, by the leading family, of the towns in which the family enterprise resided ; and, since most industrial enterprise, at least in the late nineteenth and early twentieth century were located in river valley areas, the stratification had a topographical correlate as well : the workers lived in the valley because the factory was located there, and the family owners lived "on the hill" because it had the commanding view.

However much family capitalism has entrenched itself in many middle-sized enterprises and left its mark on so many cities, it never succeeded in establishing its hegemony in the area of large-scale capital industries. For this, one has to look to the peculiar set of economic events which mark the crucial period of American capitalism, the period from 1890-1910.

The breakup of family capitalism began, roughly, around the turn of the century, when American industry, having overextended itself, underwent a succession of crises. At this point, the bankers, with their control of the money and credit market, stepped in and reorganized and took control of many of the country's leading enterprises. The great mergers at the turn of the century, typified by the formation of United States Steel, marked the emergence of "finance capitalism" in this country.

By their intervention, the investment bankers, in effect, tore up the social roots of the capitalist order. By installing professional managers — with no proprietary stake themselves in the enterprise, unable therefore to pass along their power automatically to their sons, and accountable to outside controllers — the bankers effected a radical separation of property and family.

The men who made the "modern" corporation were not family enterprisers. Nor were they just bureaucratic managers administering a finished set of routines. The "corporate organizers" were a special breed, often engineers, whose self-conscious task was to build a new economic form, and whose rewards were not primarily money — few accumulated the large fortunes made by Carnegie, a Rockefeller, a Harriman, or a Ford — but status achievements and, ultimately, some independent power of their own. Thus, T.N. Vail, who created American Telephone and Telegraph, Elbert Gary, who became the public relations face of U.S. Steel ("He never saw a blast furnace until he died," said Ben Stolbert once, bitterly), Alfred P. Sloan, who fashioned the decentralized structure of General Motors, Gerard Swope, who held together General Electric, Walter Teagle, who rationalized Standard Oil, left no personal dynasties, nor do the corporations bear their names ; but their imprint on American society is indelible. Following them, the "young men from the provinces," passing through the classrooms of the Harvard Business School, now had an avenue by which to ascend to high social as well as economic positions. Thus family capitalism gave way to social mobility.

In time, however, the power of the bankers, too, declined as the managers became able, especially in the last twenty years, to detach themselves from financial controls and win independent power in their enterprises. In some cases they were able to do this because they, the corporate engineers, were strong individuals ; even more important was the enforced separation, by the New Deal measures, of investment and banking functions, which limited the investment bankers' control of the money market ; but, most important of all, perhaps, was the fact that the tremendous growth of American corporations enabled them to finance their expansion from their own profits rather than by borrowing on the money market.

The breakup of family capitalism may explain, in part, the "dynamic" nature of modern American capitalism, for the establishment of independent managerial controls has produced a new impetus and new incentives. Unable to withdraw enormous sums of wealth from their corporations, as, say, Andrew Carnegie did from his steel company, the chief status drives of the managers have been performance and growth. Such aims, combined with the changed tax laws, have stimulated a high and constant degree of reinvestment of profits. Whereas only 30 per cent of corporate profits in 1929 were reinvested, about 70 per cent of corporate profits in the postwar years were plowed back for expansion.

The fact that the new managers have lacked a class position buttressed by tradition has given rise to a need on their part for an ideology to justify their power and prestige. In no other capitalist order, as in the American, has this drive for an ideology been pressed so compulsively. In other orders it was less needed. Private property was always linked, philosophically, to a system of natural rights ; thus, property itself provided a moral justification. But private productive property, especially in the United States, is largely a fiction, and rarely does one hear it invoked any longer as the moral source of the corporate executive's power. As we have had in the corporation the classic shift from ownership to managerial control, so, on the symbolic level, we have the shift from "private property" to "enterprise" as the justification of power. And, as with any ideology, the symbol itself sometimes becomes a propelling force, and "performance" for its own sake has become a driving motive of the American corporate head.

Sociologically, the breakup of family capitalism is linked to a series of shifts in power in Western society as a whole. No longer are there America's "Sixty Families" (or even "France's "Two Hundred"). Family capitalism meant social and political as well as economic dominance. It does so no longer. Many middle-sized enterprises are still family owned, with son succeeding father (e.g., breweries), and many towns, like St. Louis and Cincinnati, still reveal the marks of the old dominance by families, but by and large the system of family control is finished — so much so, that a classic study of American life like R.S. Lynd's *Middletown in Transition*, with its picture of the "X" family dominating the town, has in less than twenty years become a picture of the past rather than of contemporary society.

Two "silent" revolutions in the relations between power and class position in modern society seem to be in process. One is a change in the mode of access to power insofar as inheritance alone is no longer all-determining ; the other is a change in the nature of power-holding itself insofar as technical skill rather than property, and political position rather than wealth, have become the basis on which power is wielded.

The two "revolutions" proceed simultaneously. The chief consequence, politically, is the breakup of the "ruling class." A ruling class may be defined as a power-holding group which has both an established community of interest and a continuity of interest. Today, there is an "upper class" and a "ruling group." Being a member of the "upper class" (i.e., having differential privileges and being able to pass those privileges along to one's designees) no longer means that one is a member of the ruling group, for rule is now based on other than the traditional criteria of property ; the modern ruling groups are essentially coalitions, and the means of passing on the power they possess, or the institutionalization of any specific modes of access to power (the political route, or military advancement), is not yet fully demarked and established. [pp. 37-42]

NOTE

1. Daniel Bell, *The End of Ideology* (New York : The Free Press, 1962), pp. 37-42.

ECONOMIC POWER AND THE FREE SOCIETY[1]

A.A. Berle

The cycle of shift from individual possessory holdings into power systems, and from power systems back once more into possessory personal holdings, appears to be a kind of rhythm of history, especially in the West. As the feudal system merged into the king state, the revolutionary doctrine that there should be private property began to assert itself, reaching a high degree of philosophical justification in the middle of the eighteenth century, when the French physiocrats declared that if a man was to be free, able to speak his own mind, depict his own thought, and develop his own personality, he would have to have a base apart from one that was politically or ecclesiastically organized and controlled. The theory of private property as a part of freedom reached its culmination in the French Revolution and in the far slower and quieter industrial revolution in England.

No doubt the American system is the child of that revolution. Certainly the Jeffersonian ideal was a country in which everyone had private property, no one was very rich, no one was very poor. In order to make this sytem work, however, a companion theory was needed — that economics worked automatically. The self-interest of men levering against each other and controlling each other through competition resulted in a splendid ethical balance wheel, which was the open market. This leveled out inequalities, eliminated the inefficient, and through competition prevented an undue concentration of power.

Adam Smith's Wealth of Nations consecrated the theory. Smith said that this strange animal "the corporation" could never be a major factor in economics because in it men worked for other men, and obviously no man would ever pay as much attention to other men's affairs as he would to his own. Therefore, such a collective enterprise could never play a major role in society. Its inefficiency would always be such that the workings of the market would eliminate it. Thus, the corporation was merely an agency of the state for specialized purposes, and those suspect.

At the convention which met to draw up the Constitution of the United States the proposal was made that the federal government be given the power to incorporate. According to Madison's notes the answer was : No, a corporation prevented men from getting into action, and this is a dangerous power. A corporation had not merely the privilege of existence but other privileges as well, or if it did not have them it could get them. As a result monopolies would arise and dominate the United States. This should not be allowed.

So the federal government was specifically denied the power to create corporations. This was to be left to the states, and it was assumed that they would not exercise this power or, if they did, would exercise it only as a means of carrying on government. This doctrine survived less than fifteen years. By 1791 the federal government found it desirable to organize a corporation entitled the Bank of the United States, and in the 1819 Supreme Court case McCulloch v. Maryland Justice Marshall decided that the implied powers granted to the government of the United States included the power to form a corporation if it were opposite to the particular functions the government wished to perform. It is still true that the federal government can create corporations only for governmental or quasi-governmental purposes ; the states, on the other hand, have been allowed to create them as they would ; and as our technology developed corporations began to proliferate to such an extent that by 1835 our great-grandfathers felt that the situation called for a close look.

As we look back on their findings now, they made a surprisingly accurate prediction of the probable effects of an unlimited corporate life. (They were not so sound, perhaps, in their estimate as to whether it was desirable or undesirable.) For the next fifty years they used every known legal means to keep a corporation to a single defined and manageable enterprise. The corporation lawyer of the period spent most of his time on the law of ultra vires, which dealt with corporations that tried to transcend the limits that had been set out for them. These limits ordinarily were :

First, that they could only own a limited amount of property, frequently and especially only a limited amount of real property. The fear was they would start absorbing huge quantities of land.

Second, that they could indulge in only one type of business. If a corporation was organized to run a flour mill, it had to run a flour mill and nothing more.

Third, that they should last only for a defined period of time, twenty or thirty years or whatever the statutory limitation was.

Not infrequently there was a fourth limitation. This was that the corporation should be subject to continuous inspection. The courts could appoint a "visitor" — today he would be called an auditor. He was authorized to inspect and analyze the workings of a corporation and report to the judge, who, in turn, had an undefined power to say what should or should not be done.

A variety of other limitations were imposed from time to time, all of them representing attempts to prevent exactly what happened :

First, that a corporation would grow so large that its economic strength would vastly outweigh the strength of any individual enterprise

Second, that it would be able to rove the country, if not the world, at will and do what it wished in terms of economic enterprise

And third, that it would become a trust for perpetual accumulation ; that its assets, in so far as they were not distributed by way of dividends, would be permitted to pile up to unlimited amounts.

These three results have come about, of course. Corporations did do, have done, and are doing exactly what our forefathers worried about. Part of their fear stemmed from the belief that the corporation was only an artificial personality and therefore did not have a soul or a conscience. Lacking a conscience, it had no morals and was prima facie dangerous. This is why throughout our history, society has attempted to control and constrict the corporation.

The rise of the large contemporary corporation — the giant as we know it today, the true collectivism — began with the railroad systems. There were other large corporations, but the railroad systems were the ones that posed the real problems. They were the first to demonstrate the shift in the private property system that came about when we began to realize that there was no real way of constricting a corporation whose business the community needed. If its economic functions were necessary to the welfare of the community, the law somehow had to recognize that fact, however backhandedly. If a railroad needed to go through to the Pacific coast, the law had to find some way around the fact that the corporate power did not let it go that far.

A diagram of what was happening to private property while this was going on would look something like this :

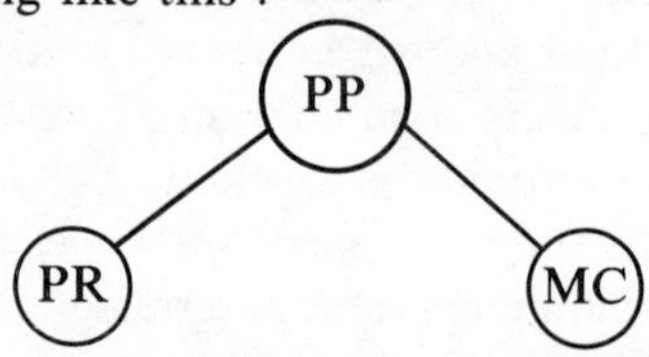

PP, or "possessory property," is where it all began in about 1810 or 1820. This is our great-great-grandfather's farm or forge, which he had not only created but owned and operated. This was the assumed unit of property at the beginning, and even today we still talk in those terms. This possessory property becomes incorporated as an enterprise and is immediately split into two functions. At the left is one function — PR, or "passive receptive." This is the receptive side of property, the stockholder's share. The shareholder cannot manage. Every corporation statute in the country says that the business of the corporation shall be managed by its directors, and almost every court has agreed that the director is not an agent of the stockholder and does not have to follow his instructions. So the right-hand side of the diagram is MC, or "managing and creating."

The business of stockholders is primarily to receive ; the business of management is primarily to manage and create. In the early days, when corporations were still small, the stockholder powerfully influenced the director, but today they are so far apart that the stockholder can hardly communicate with management even by megaphone. We go through the ancient forms, and it is good that we do so, but everyone knows that a stockholders' meeting is a kind of ancient, meaningless ritual like some of the ceremonies that go on with the mace in the House of Lords. The passive receptive side of the coporation, in short, is functionless.

The MC side looks better at first glance. But in any large corporation the management groups are actually as striated as it is possible to be. The president and the chairman of the board probably work together as the theoretically responsible officers, but they must operate through committees of officers — big officers, medium officers, and little officers, all divided in as many different ways as the management experts can invent. While the top officers officially have the right to enter upon the property and do things, even though they are not able to own it, the fact is that they have had to subdivide that right to such a degree that in practice the real possessor of a piece of property is the manager of the particular division or area of the property — and even he probably has to share his right with his plant manager, if he has got one. This is possession without right, just as on the passive receptive side there is right without possession.

As things look now, this imbalance is about to be redressed. Whether it will be good redressing is another matter. Theoretically, management got its legitimacy by the fact that it represented the will of the shareholders. This was a kind of quasi-amateur democratic legitimacy. However, on examination, it was found that although the stockholders theoretically chose the management, in fact they were completely unable to do so. The management would send out a proxy naming three agents whom the stockholders appointed to cast their vote at a meeting. In older days the management often did not even bother to say for what directors these proxies would cast their vote. Since the passage of Securities and Exchange Commission legislation, they have to do that ; but the corporation secretary who sent out the proxies was the man who really determined what happened for all practical purposes in the power relationship. The president or the directors could fire him, of course, so he did what they told him to do. When the directors wished to renominate themselves or to add to their number or to fill a vacancy, they did it. This is still the method by which the directors in a great corporation are chosen. This is an automatic self-perpetuating oligarchy.

These are a string of bad words. There was at least one court case in which it was held that a self-perpetuating oligarchy was illegal. This was the famous case in which a life insurance company in New Jersey purchased control of a trust company by buying a majority of shares. Thereafter it caused the trust company to purchase a majority of its shares. The result was an unbreakable ring. A New Jersey court said that this was illegal, created an oligarchy, and was contrary to the theory of New Jersey corporation laws.

However, thereafter, somebody asked whether corporations really should be run democratically. Should this group or that group or the other group campaign against each other, offering inducements to shareholders to vote for them instead of the other group ? Could corporations assimilate this kind of democratic government ? There was no answer. In fact, the choice of management depends not on an assent of balanced interest but on expert judgment of technical ability with a companion judgment of honesty and character. As a result, for all practical purposes, management controls the corporation unless it is itself controlled by another oligarchy with enough shares to dominate the situation at all times.

There is a good deal of loose thinking about this. It is commonly believed that the holder of 20 per cent or 25 per cent of a corporation's stock can control that corporation. This was the inference in the recent du Pont-General Motors case. This is not true. It is true that with 20 per cent of the stock-holders' list of a large corporation plus control of the directors it can be done. But if the directors of General Motors decided not to vote with du Pont, it is very doubtful whether the du Pont interest would be sufficient to go out and get the other 30 per cent of General Motors stockholders which it would need. This is not pure theory. When a certain gentleman ran Standard Oil of Indiana he did various things that induced the so-called controlling group to want a change. They canvassed the board of directors and asked whether they would not fire the man. The directors said they would not. Thereupon the controlling group went to work to try to win the next election. Between their own and allied holdings they had slightly over 20 per cent of the stock. They did control in the end, and the man was fired. But they achieved it only by spending $800,000 on a stockholders' campaign.

The control system in today's corporations, when it does not lie solely in the directors as in the American Telephone and Telegraph Company, lies in a combination of the directors of a so-called control bloc (a misnomer, incidentally) plus the directors themselves. For practical purposes, therefore, the control or power element in most large corporations rests in its group of directors and is autonomous — or autonomous if taken together with a control bloc. And inheritance tax distribution of stock being what it is, the trend is increasingly to management autonomy. This is a self-perpetuating oligarchy.

Meanwhile, the next phase has been emerging. It will stay with us, and it will be of some interest. This involves what are known as pension trusts — welfare funds and pension funds. A pension trust in most cases differs from an insurance trust in that it has an unlimited and indefinite obligation. It is there to pay pensions to X, Y, and Z which shall be a fraction of the salaries X, Y, and Z will have collected during the years of their tenure. The pension trust fund, if it is properly administered, has to think not merely of paying out a stated number of dollars in, say, 1980, as an insurance company does, but of having enough dollars to meet obligations later to be determined. No human being knows the future course of inflation of the dollar, prices, pay, and so forth. Nevertheless, although the payment period may be twenty or thirty years away, the pension trusts must keep abreast of inflation at least as it affects pay.

This suggests, of course, that they must invest in equities, whereas, classically, trust funds invested in fixed obligations. This is the sharp difference between the kind of burden resting on an honourable pension trustee and on the directors of, say, the New York Life Insurance Company, whose business is to provide a stated number of dollars against stated contracts to pay those dollars with interest later on. The pension trust funds, therefore, belong among the stockholders in the passive receptive column of our diagram because of their ownership of common stocks. The holdings of life insurance companies include less than 5 per cent in common stock equities ; in the pension trust funds equities are running close to 30 per cent of their assets and may be more. The total of pension trust funds at the moment is almost $31 billion. Roughly half of this is in the hands of insurance companies, which operate — perhaps erroneously — on the assumption that they have only another set of insurance policies. Ninety per cent of the remaining pension funds are in the hands of eight or nine New York banks, the largest single one being the pension trust fund of the American Telephone and Telegraph Company, which is worth about $2.2 billion so far and is operated by a committee through the Bankers Trust Company.

As a result of this broad-scale buying of equities the pension trusts are slowly "chewing up" control of those corporations which offer the best means of equity investment. These are voting equities. Thus far no attempt has been made to make use of this except in the case of the Sears, Roebuck pension trust fund which undertook to buy Sears, Roebuck stock and presumably now has a controlling interest in the company. As a result Sears, Roebuck is socializing itself via its own pension trust fund, and is discovering that it is running into the same difficulty which a socialist or any other form of oligarchic government has — it has self-contained control, and management is thus responsible to itself. Query : Does it continue to have "legitimacy" when the only mandate it can refer to is its own ?

The present $30 billion in the pension trusts of course is doomed to increase. These are compulsory savings, and the funds must continue to accumulate. They now cover only about half of the non-farm labour force ; they will undoubtedly soak up a considerable part of the balance before long, and must increase, particularly in view of the population rise. In addition, it will be another twenty or thirty years before this "levels off" ; that is, before the payment from the funds begins to balance the incoming. The pension trust funds will perhaps level out at somewhere in the vicinity of $70 to $80 billion, probably increased by the coefficient of the increase in population or the increase in the labour force within the population. This will mean that if the pension trusts continue to take the good equities, as they have been doing, they may well have the prevailing control-stockholding position and the capacity to make it absolute. They will have, say, 20 per cent to 30 per cent of the good equity stocks and the capacity to increase that to 40 per cent or 50 per cent (45 per cent for practical purposes is a majority at any big stockholders' meeting).

With the rise of the pension trusts into the passive receptive end of the corporation structure the old passive receptive stockholder is gradually disappearing. At best he is, shall we say, a pensioner. The last vestige of his power to legitimate a management by a vote is in the hands of the pension trustees. He has an expectation arising out of the fact that he may have performed a certain number of years of acceptable work and fulfilled a certain number of other conditions. But does he have any property right in the pension trust ? The courts say no. The power — what is left of it — lies in the trustees, or in those insurance companies which administer trusts.

When power is lodged in a particular group it has no choice except either to exercise it or to try to revolutionize the system. There is no way of avoiding power. If you take it and refuse to exercise it you suffer the fate of King Lear — the king who wanted to be king but did not want to be bothered. The trust funds admit they have it, but they have thus far refused to use it. This situation cannot last very much longer. Somebody is bound to use that power, of necessity. Pension trusts are so concentrated that a relatively small amount in equities outbalances any number of scattered holdings.

The private property system in production, which began with our great-grandfather's farm and forge, has almost vanished in the vast area of the American economy dominated by this system. Instead we have something which differs from the Russian or socialist system mainly in its philosophical content. Under a pure socialist or Communist system, in theory, every worker has an old-age pension at the end of his labours. We are developing the same thing by "socializing" property without a revolution. It is one of our more amazing achievements. Whether one likes it or not depend's on one's philosophy.

Possessory private property in this area has been metamorphosed. In its place is a power pyramid. At the moment, this is a management pyramid, but it is beginning to be balanced by a pyramid of men who have no possible property interest in the actual corpus but do have the power of choice — the pension trustees. These are naked power vehicles, with the "receptive" end so far dispersed that it cannot even be discerned. To make the joke complete, let us suppose that a pension trust liquidated itself tomorrow and satisfied its contract obligations. If it was a well-run trust, there would be a balance left over. That balance would very likely escheat to the state because there was no claimant to it left. In the most violently private-property-minded country in the world this is perhaps one of the most magnificent economic jests the world has seen.

None of this has come about as a result of the villainy of conspiring men. That might have been true in the freewheeling corporation days of a hundred years ago, but it would be as ridiculous an assumption today as is the basic assumption of the Supreme Court decision in the recent du Pont case. This decision apparently assumed that because du Pont bought 23 per cent of General Motors forty years ago, perhaps hoping that it could control General Motors, du Pont still holds to the intention of exercising this control. Actually, there has been a kind of continual biological progression over the years. Change is part of the progression. Bigger enterprise was needed to satisfy the desires of the population. In addition, the techniques which made it possible to satisfy certain necessities made it impossible to rely only on the individual. Consequently, organization and power, not ownership, had to meet the resulting problems. The progression has been natural.

Today approximately 50 per cent of American manufacturing — that is everything other than financial and transportation — is held by about 150 corporations, reckoned, at least, by asset values. If finance and transportation are included, the total increases. If a rather larger group is taken, the statistics would probably show that about two-thirds of the economically productive assets of the United States, excluding agriculture, are owned by a group of not more than 500 corporations. This is actual asset ownership. (Some further statistical analysis is called for if financial corporations are included, for these, of course, double up. One of the largest and most plainly oligarchically controlled corporations in the United States, the Metropolitan Life Insurance Company, duplicates assets because it holds securities of other corporations.) But in terms of power, without regard to asset positions, not only do 500 corporations control two-thirds of the non-farm economy but within each of that 500 a still smaller group has the ultimate decision-making power. This is, I think, the highest concentration of economic power in recorded history. Since the United States carries on not quite half of the manufacturing production of the entire world today, these 500 groupings — each with its own little dominating pyramid within it — represent a concentration of power over economics which makes the medieval feudal system look like a Sunday school party. In sheer economic power this has gone far beyond anything we have yet seen.

We can talk about the various alleged legal controls which somehow or other, when the chips are down, neither control nor even seek to control. We can point out the fear of "monopoly" and "restraint of trade" and say that from time to time this fear has checked the process. True, our law has prevented any one of these power groups from becoming a monopoly, but it has not seriously prevented the concentration of power as power, though it has prevented certain ultimate results. The question is then : Why has concentrated economic power in America not got completely out of hand ? Many of these corporations have budgets, and some of them have payrolls which, with their customers, affect a greater number of people than most of the ninety-odd sovereign countries of the world. American Telephone and Telegraph, for example, based on combined population and wealth, would be somewhere around the thirteenth state of the union in terms of budget, and certainly larger than many of the countries of South America. Some of these corporations are units which can be thought of only in somewhat the way we have heretofore thought of nations.

Whether we like it or not, this is what has happened. As noted, it is not the product of evil-minded men. I believe that we must try to work with the system. The dangers are obvious. But history cannot usually be reversed. Until engineers and economic forces give us a way by which a man can manufacture an automobile in his backyard we will continue to have organizations the size of General Motors or Ford — as long as people want Chevrolets or Fords. We will have railroads the length of the Union Pacific as long as people want to go across the continent by railroad. In other words, until a combination of technique and organization can be invented permitting *individuals* to do the job, we are bound to try to make the best we can out of the situation. To my mind most of the results are rather surprisingly good.

This does not mean, however, that I am not afraid. I am. I believe it is the *content* of these systems rather than their form that matters. Their power can enslave us beyond present belief, or perhaps set us free beyond present imagination. The choice lies with the men who operate the pyramids, and with the men affected who can demand what they really want. Our Anglo-Saxon democratic liberties, after all, were beaten out, not against the framework of the personal possessory property regime, but against the background of two of the most brutal despotisms in Western history. Both the Angevin dynasty in Normandy and the Tudor dynasty in England were rank despotisms. The content of our democratic liberties from Magna Carta down was pumped in by extraneous moral processes. Our institutionalized liberties present the case of an institution conscripted into utility, rather than something that emerged full-armed from the head of Jove. It was probably better that way ; the democracy of the Greeks did not work so very well.

We have to accept the power situation as, let us call it, a neutral mechanism subject to the control of the body politic as long as we keep it subject to that control. That control, I believe, will be essentially intellectual and philosophical, capable of being translated into legal rules when necessity arises. In that respect I make three points in summary :

1. The first is that whenever there is a question of power there is a question of legitimacy. As things stand now, these instrumentalities of tremendous power have the slenderest claim of legitimacy. This is probably a transitory period. They must find some claim of legitimacy, which also means finding a field of responsibility and a field of accountability. Legitimacy, responsibility, and accountability are essential to any power system if it is to endure. They correspond to a deep human instinct. A man desires beyond anything else to have someone give him the accolade of "Well done, thou good and faithful servant," thereby risking the condemnation of "You have been no good — get out." If he has to say it to himself, or hear it from a string of people whom he himself has hired or controls, he is apt to die a cynical and embittered man.

The medieval feudal power system set the "lords spiritual" over and against the "lords temporal." These were the men of learning and of the church who in theory were able to say to the greatest power in the world : "You have committed a sin ; therefore either you are excommunicate or you must mend your ways." The lords temporal could reply : "I can kill you." But the lords spiritual could retort : "Yes, that you can, but you cannot change the philosophical fact." In a sense this is the great lacuna in the economic power system today. In theory the stockholders can act as the lords spiritual through their vote. In fact they cannot, and they know they cannot. Are the pension trustees or their equivalent slowly emerging as the men who can ? They had not thought so — nobody had thought so. They have been essentially a method of transmission of choice and not much else. We are looking for the kind of thing that C. Wright Mills in his recent book on the American power elite rightly said did not exist. He wrongly concluded, therefore, that the system was a mess, which it obviously is not. We are, if you choose, searching for the pyramid on the other side of our diagram. But every time we have had the chance to construct that kind of elite we seem to have abandoned it, and chucked in an administrator instead.

2. My second summary point is that the sheer power of invading personality is great and that a doctrine is already at work which plays a second joke on our constitutional system. The United States began by saying that its federal government could not construct corporations and apparently by assuming that the states would not. Both have done so. It also said that corporations should be kept apart from governmental power. De facto, they have not been. We are now, in fact, beginning to converge on a doctrine which may well push right over the line when the next case comes up. This doctrine is that where a corporation has power to affect a great many lives (differing from the little enterprise which can be balanced out by the market) it should be subject to the same restraints under the Constitution that apply to an agency of the federal or state government. In that case, the Bill of Rights and the Fourteenth and Fifteenth Amendments would apply. At the moment this is one jump ahead of current law. Yet it seems probable that this will be the next phase — just as we already have the constitutional doctrine that under the Fifth Amendment you may not by private contract prohibit a Negro from buying land.

3. My third point is destined to be in infinitely greater controversy, and I do not know what the end of the controversy will be. Great corporate power is exercised in relation to certain obligations :

a. It should supply the want in the area of its production. Where the community has come to rely on a corporation for steel, oil, automobiles, or cigarettes, the corporation is obliged reasonably to meet that demand.

b. The price must not be considered extortionate. It must be "acceptable" — which does not necessarily mean fair or just.

c. It must provide at least some continuity of employment.

d. It must give a continuing attention to the technical progress of the art.

At every point in the individual history of large corporations there has been some moment of impact on the community when either the community felt the corporation was not fulfilling its obligations or, alternatively, the corporation realized it was up against a situation it could not handle. In every case the result has been either a friendly and orderly, or unfriendly and disorderly, hassle out of which a piece of planned economy emerged. Roughly two-thirds of American industry and much of American finance is now controlled by a formal or informal federal industrial plan. Here are two illustrations at each end of the cycle.

The oil industry claims to be the most non-socialist, free-wheeling, private business that ever was. But the fact is that after many vicissitudes it sought control by, and is controlled by, various acts of Congress. After orderly discussion certain laws were passed. Under these laws, first, the Bureau of Mines of the Department of Interior estimates the probable consumption month by month of gasoline and the chief oil products. Second, an interstate treaty exists among the oil-producing states, ratified by the Congress. Third, a Congressional act makes it illegal to transport oil in interstate commerce which has been produced in excess of a state allowable. This legislation might break down if it were not for the fact that because there is a relatively concentrated system in the oil industry the refineries will not buy "non-certified" oil anyway. As a result, the big companies do not violate the act ; the little ones cannot ; and the result is a planned oil economy by which supply is equated to demand and the oil industry from well to refinery to gas station is more or less geared to meet it.

Here is a disorderly example : Aluminum was manufactured by a monopoly which was ordered to be split up under an antitrust decree. By a combination of administrative orders entirely without administrative rationale but all working toward the same end the federal government used the aluminum plants it had itself created during World War II in order to set up two competitors to Alcoa. It likewise required Alcoa to sell its Aluminum of Canada shares. This was not enough by itself ; so the government for a period of years handled its defence orders in such a way that the new companies had adequate assurance of a market until they could get properly under way. The policy still is to make certain that the new companies, which can stay in business only by being assured a reasonable market, will get the extent of market they need. There was a stockpiling arrangement at one time, followed later by the release of part of the stockpiled aluminum. In a wholly disorderly way which only the American system could ever conceive, there arose the equivalent of a de facto planned economy in aluminum. At the moment this industry now sails away, freewheeling. But there is not the slightest doubt that if conditions required transition back into a planned economy it would happen.

These two illustrations could be multiplied. The point is merely that (1) through constitutionalization of the corporation some attention is being paid to the protection of the individual; and (2) through a slowly emerging, industry-by-industry, flexibly planned economy, some protection of the community is coming about.

Obviously a system like this is just as good as the ideas and strength of the body politic behind it. The same system in the hands, for example, of a Latin American dictator could produce terrible oppression.

There is a gradually growing feeling that pension trusts, for example, must be controlled. A pension trust ring could be something to bind a man beyond belief. It could bind him to his job, he could not change it without losing a substantial part of his life savings. He might be controlled in all sorts of ways. We are beginning to think even that the pension trust right which cannot be transferred to some other pension trust is suspect.

As men think, so they are. We are really seeking now a body of doctrine which will control power. I close by returning to my first point, which related to the desperate search for a field of responsibility and accountability referent to some point of view outside the system, that is, to some modern "lords spiritual." I suggest that the real purpose is to supply exactly that. [pp. 86-102]

NOTE

1. A.A. Berle, "Economic Power and the Free Society," in Andrew Hacker, ed., *The Corporation Take-Over* (New York : Doubleday, 1965), pp. 86-102.

THE CONSTITUTION OF LIBERTY[1]

Friedrich Hayek

Though freedom is not a state of nature but an artifact of civilization, it did not arise from design. The institutions of freedom, like everything freedom has created, were not established because people foresaw the benefits they would bring. But, once its advantages were recognized, men began to perfect and extend the reign of freedom and, for that purpose, to inquire how a free society worked. This development of a theory of liberty took place mainly in the eighteenth century. It began in two countries, England and France. The first of these knew liberty; the second did not.

As a result, we have had to the present day two different traditions in the theory of liberty : one empirical and unsystematic, the other speculative and rationalistic — the first based on an interpretation of traditions and institutions which had spontaneously grown up and were but imperfectly understood, the second aiming at the construction of a utopia, which has often been tried but never successfully. Nevertheless, it has been the rationalist, plausible, and apparently logical argument of the French tradition, with its flattering assumptions about the unlimited powers of human reason, that has progressively gained influence, while the less articulate and less explicit tradition of English freedom has been on the decline.

This distinction is obscured by the facts that what we have called the "French tradition" of liberty arose largely from an attempt to interpret British institutions and that the conceptions which other countries formed of British institutions were based mainly on their description by French writers. The two traditions became finally confused when they merged in the liberal movement of the nineteenth century and when even leading British liberals drew as much on the French as on the British tradition. It was, in the end, the victory of the Benthamite Philosophical Radicals over the Whigs in England that concealed the fundamental difference which in more recent years has reappeared as the conflict between liberal democracy and "social" or totalitarian democracy....

Though these two groups are now commonly lumped together as the ancestors of modern liberalism, there is hardly a greater contrast imaginable than that between their respective conceptions of the evolution and functioning of a social order and the role played in it by liberty. The difference is directly traceable to the predominance of an essentially empiricist view of the world in England and a rationalist approach in France. The main contrast in the practical conclusions to which these approaches led has recently been well put, as follows : "One finds the essence of freedom in spontaneity and the absence of coercion, the other believes it to be realized only in the pursuit and attainment of an absolute collective purpose" ;[2] and "one stands for organic, slow, half-conscious growth, the other for doctrinaire deliberateness ; one for trial and error procedure, the other for an enforced solely valid pattern."[3] It is the second view, as J.L. Talmon has shown in an important book from which this description is taken, that has become the origin of totalitarian democracy.

The sweeping success of the political doctrines that stem from the French tradition is probably due to their great appeal to human pride and ambition. But we must not forget that the political conclusions of the two schools derive from different conceptions of how society works. In this respect the British philosophers laid the foundations of a profound and essentially valid theory, while the rationalist school was simply and completely wrong.

Those British philosophers have given us an interpretation of the growth of civilization that is still the indispensable foundation of the argument for liberty. They find the origin of institutions, not in contrivance or design, but in the survival of the successful. Their view is expressed in terms of "how nations stumble upon establishments which are indeed the result of human action but not the execution of human design."[4] It stresses that what we call political order is much less the product of our ordering intelligence than is commonly imagined. As their immediate successors saw it, what Adam Smith and his contemporaries did was "to resolve almost all that has been ascribed to positive institution into the spontaneous and irresistible development of certain obvious principles, and to show with how little contrivance or political wisdom the most complicated and apparently artificial schemes of policy might have been erected."[5]

This "anti-rationalistic insight into historical happenings that Adam Smith shares with Hume, Adam Ferguson, and others"[6] enabled them for the first time to comprehend how institutions and morals, language and law have evolved by a process of cumulative growth and that it is only with and within this framework that human reason has grown and can successfully operate. Their argument is directed throughout against the Cartesian conception of an independently and antecedently existing human reason that invented these institutions and against the conception that civil society was formed by some wise original legislator or an original "social contract."[7] The latter idea of intelligent men coming together for deliberation about how to make the world anew is perhaps the most characteristic outcome of those design theories. It found its perfect expression when the leading theorist of the French Revolution, Abbe Sieyes, exhorted the revolutionary assembly "to act like men just emerging from the state of nature and coming together for the purpose of signing a social contract."[8]

The ancients understood the conditions of liberty better than that. Cicero quotes Cato as saying that the Roman constitution was superior to that of other states because it "was based upon the genius, not of one man, but of many : it was founded, not in one generation, but in a long period of several centuries and many ages of men. For, said he, there never has lived a man possessed of so great a genius that nothing could escape him, nor could the combined powers of all men living at one time possibly make all the necessary provisions for the future without the aid of actual experience and the test of time."[9] Neither republican Rome nor Athens — the two free nations of the ancient world — could thus serve as an example for the rationalists. For Descartes, the fountainhead of the rationalist tradition, it was indeed Sparta that provided the model ; for her greatness "was due not to the pre-eminence of each of its laws in particular . . . but to the circumstance that, originated by a single individual, they all tended to a single end."[10] And it was Sparta which became the ideal of liberty for Rousseau as well as for Robespierre and Saint-Just and for most of the later advocates of "social" or totalitarian democracy.

Like the ancient, the modern British conceptions of liberty grew against the background of a comprehension, first achieved by the lawyers, of how institutions had developed. "There are many things specially in laws and governments," wrote Chief Justice Hale in the seventeenth century in a critique of Hobbes, "that mediately, remotely, and consequentially are reasonable to be approved, though the reason of the party does not presently or immediately and distinctly see its reasonableness.... Long experience makes more discoveries touching conveniences or inconveniences of laws than is possible for the wisest council of men at first to foresee. And that those amendments and supplements that through the various experiences of wise and knowing men have been applied to any law must needs be better suited to the convenience of laws, than the best invention of the most pregnant wits not aided by such a series and tract of experience.... This adds to the difficulty of a present fathoming of the reason of laws, because they are the production of long and iterated experience which, though it be commonly called the mistress of fools, yet certainly it is the wisest expedient among mankind, and discovers those defects and supplies which no wit of man could either at once foresee or aptly remedy . . . . It is not necessary that the reasons of the institution should be evident unto us. It is sufficient that they are instituted laws that give a certainty to us, and it is reasonable to observe them though the particular reason of the institution appear not."[11]

From these conceptions gradually grew a body of social theory that showed how, in the relations among men, complex and orderly and, in a very definite sense, purposive institutions might grow up which owed little to design, which were not invented but arose from the separate actions of many men who did not know what they were doing. This demonstration that something greater than man's individual mind may grow from men's fumbling efforts represented in some ways an even greater challenge to all design theories than even the later theory of biological evolution. For the first time it was shown that an evident order which was not the product of a designing human intelligence need not therefore be ascribed to the design of a higher, supernatural intelligence, but that there was a third possibility — the emergence of order as the result of adaptive evolution.

Since the emphasis we shall have to place on the role that selection plays in this process of social evolution today is likely to create the impression that we are borrowing the idea from biology, it is worth stressing that it was, in fact, the other way round : there can be little doubt that it was from the theories of social evolution that Darwin and his contemporaries derived the suggestion for their theories. Indeed, one of those Scottish philosophers who first developed these ideas anticipated Darwin even in the biological field ; and the later application of these conceptions by the various "historical schools" in law and language rendered the idea that similarity of structure might be accounted for by a common origin a commonplace in the study of social phenomena long before it was applied to biology. It is unfortunate that at a later date the social sciences, instead of building on these beginnings in their own field, re-imported some of these ideas from biology and with them brought in such conceptions as "natural selection," "struggle for existence," and "survival of the fittest," which are not appropriate in their field ; for in social evolution, the decisive factor is not the selection of the physical and inheritable properties of the individuals but the selection by imitation of successful institutions and habits. Though this operates also through the success of individuals and groups, what emerges is not an inheritable attribute of individuals, but ideas and skills — in short, the whole cultural inheritance which is passed on by learning and imitation.... [pp. 54-59]

The great aim of the struggle for liberty has been equality before the law. This equality under the rules which the state enforces may be supplemented by a similar equality of the rules that men voluntarily obey in their relations with one another. This extension of the principle of equality to the rules of moral and social conduct is the chief expression of what is commonly called the democratic spirit — and probably that aspect of it that does most to make inoffensive the inequalities that liberty necessarily produces.

Equality of the general rules of law and conduct, however, is the only kind of equality conducive to liberty and the only equality which we can secure without destroying liberty. Not only has liberty nothing to do with any other sort of equality, but it is even bound to produce inequality in many respects. This is the necessary result and part of the justification of individual liberty : if the result of individual liberty did not demonstrate that some manners of living are more successful than others, much of the case for it would vanish.

It is neither because it assumes that people are in fact equal nor because it attempts to make them equal that the argument for liberty demands that government treat them equally. This argument not only recognizes that individuals are very different but in a great measure rests on that assumption. It insists that these individual differences provide no justification for government to treat them differently. And it objects to the differences in treatment by the state that would be necessary if persons who are in fact very different were to be assured equal positions in life.

Modern advocates of a more far-reaching material equality usually deny that their demands are based on any assumption of the factual equality of all men. It is nevertheless still widely believed that this is the main justification for such demands. Nothing, however, is more damaging to the demand for equal treatment than to base it on so obviously untrue an assumption as that of the factual equality of all men. To rest the case for equal treatment of national or racial minorities on the assertion that they do not differ from other men is implicitly to admit that factual inequality would justify unequal treatment; and the proof that some differences do, in fact, exist would not be long in forthcoming. It is of the essence of the demand for equality before the law that people should be treated alike in spite of the fact that they are different.

The boundless variety of human nature — the wide range of differences in individual capacities and potentialities — is one of the most distinctive facts about the human species. Its evolution has made it probably the most variable among all kinds of creatures. It has been well said that "biology, with variability as its cornerstone, confers on every human individual a unique set of attributes which give him a dignity he could not otherwise possess. Every newborn baby is an unknown quantity so far as potentialities are concerned because there are many thousands of unknown interrelated genes and gene-patterns which contribute to his makeup. As a result of nature and nurture the newborn infant may become one of the greatest of men or women ever to have lived. In every case he or she has the making of a distinctive individual.... If the differences are not very important, then freedom is not very important and the idea of individual worth is not very important."[12] The writer justly adds that the widely held uniformity theory of human nature, "which on the surface appears to accord with democracy . . . would in time undermine the very basic ideals of freedom and individual worth and render life as we know it meaningless."[13]

It has been the fashion in modern times to minimize the importance of congenital differences between men and to ascribe all the important differences to the influence of environment. However important the latter may be, we must not overlook the fact that individuals are very different from the outset. The importance of individual differences would hardly be less if all people were brought up in very similar environments. As a statement of fact, it just is not true that "all men are born equal." We may continue to use this hallowed phrase to express the ideal that legally and morally all men ought to be treated alike. But if we want to understand what this ideal of equality can or should mean, the first requirement is that we free ourselves from the belief in factual equality.... [pp. 85-87]

This spirit of the laws of free Rome has been transmitted to us mainly in the works of the historians and orators of the period, who once more became influential during the Latin Renaissance of the seventeenth century. Livy — whose translator made people familiar with the term "isonomia" (which Livy himself did not use) and who supplied Harrington with the distinction between the government of law and the government of men — Tacitus and, above all, Cicero became the chief authors through whom the classical tradition spread. Cicero indeed became the main authority for modern liberalism, and we owe to him many of the most effective formulations of freedom under the law. To him is due the conception of general rules or *leges legum*, which govern legislation, the conception that we obey the law in order to be free, and the conception that the judge ought to be merely the mouth through whom the law speaks. No other author shows more clearly that during the classical period of Roman law it was fully understood that there is no conflict between law and freedom and that freedom is dependent upon certain attributes of the law, its generality and certainty, and the restrictions it places on the discretion of authority.

This classical period was also a period of complete economic freedom, to which Rome largely owed its prosperity and power. From the second century A.D., however, state socialism advanced rapidly. In this development the freedom which equality before the law had created was progressively destroyed as demands for another kind of equality arose. During the later empire the strict law was weakened as, in the interest of a new social policy, the state increased its control over economic life. The outcome of this process, which culminated under Constantine, was, in the words of a distinguished student of Roman law, that "the absolute empire proclaimed together with the principle of equity the authority of the empirical will unfettered by the barrier of law. Justinian with his learned professors brought this process to its conclusions."[14] Thereafter, for a thousand years, the conception that legislation should serve to protect the freedom of the individual was lost. And when the art of legislation was rediscovered, it was the code of Justinian with its conception of a prince who stood above the law that served as the model on the continent.

In England, however, the wide influence which the classical authors enjoyed during the reign of Elizabeth helped to prepare the way for a different development. Soon after her death the great struggle between king and Parliament began, from which emerged as a by-product the liberty of the individual. It is significant that the disputes began largely over issues of economic policy very similar to those which we again face today. To the nineteenth-century historian the measures of James I and Charles I which provoked the conflict might have seemed antiquated issues without topical interest. To us the problems caused by the attempts of the kings to set up industrial monopolies have a familiar ring : Charles I even attempted to nationalize the coal industry and was dissuaded from this only by being told that this might cause a rebellion.

Ever since a court had laid down in the famous *Case of Monopolies* that the grant of exclusive rights to produce any article was "against the common law and the liberty of the subject," the demand for equal laws for all citizens became the main weapon of Parliament in its opposition to the king's aims. Englishmen then understood better than they do today that the control of production always means the creation of privilege : that Peter is given permission to do what Paul is not allowed to do.

It was another kind of economic regulation, however, that occasioned the first great statement of the basic principle. The Petition of Grievances of 1610 was provoked by new regulations issued by the king for building in London and prohibiting the making of starch from wheat. This celebrated plea of the House of Commons states that, among all the traditional rights of British subjects, "there is none which they have accounted more dear and precious than this, to be guided and governed by the certain rule of law, which giveth to the head and the members that which of right belongeth to them, and not by any uncertain and arbitrary form of government . . . . Out of this root has grown the indubitable right of the people of this kingdom, not to be made subject to any punishment that shall extend to their lives, lands, bodies, or goods, other than such as are ordained by the common laws of this land, or the statutes made by their common consent in Parliament."[15]

It was, finally, in the discussion occasioned by the Statute of Monopolies of 1624 that Sir Edward Coke, the great fountain of Whig principles, developed his interpretation of Magna Carta that became one of the cornerstones of the new doctrine. In the second part of his *Institutes of the Laws of England,* soon to be printed by order of the House of Commons, he not only contended (with reference to the *Case of Monopolies*) that "if a grant be made to any man, to have the sole making of cards, or the sole dealing with any other trade, that grant is against the liberty and freedom of the subject, that before did, or lawfully might have used that trade, and consequently against this great charter";[16] but he went beyond such opposition to the royal prerogative to warn Parliament itself "to leave all causes to be measured by the golden and straight mete-wand of the law, and not to the incertain and crooked cord of discretion."[17]

Out of the extensive and continuous discussion of these issues during the Civil War, there gradually emerged all the political ideals which were thenceforth to govern English political evolution. We cannot attempt here to trace their evolution in the debates and pamphlet literature of the period, whose extraordinary wealth of ideas has come to be seen only since their re-publication in recent times. We can only list the main ideas that appeared more and more frequently until, by the time of the Restoration, they had become part of an established tradition and, after the Glorious Revolution of 1688, part of the doctrine of the victorious party.

The great event that became for later generations the symbol of the permanent achievements of the Civil War was the abolition in 1641 of the prerogative courts and especially the Star Chamber which had become, in F.W. Maitland's often quoted words, "a court of politicians enforcing a policy, not a court of judges administering the law."[18] At almost the same time an effort was made for the first time to secure the independence of the judges. In the debates of the following twenty years the central issue became increasingly the prevention of arbitrary action of government. Though the two meanings of "arbitrary" were long confused, it came to be recognized, as Parliament began to act as arbitrarily as the king, that whether or not an action was arbitrary depended not on the source of the authority but on whether it was in conformity with pre-existing general principles of law. The points most frequently emphasized were that there must be no punishment without a previously existing law providing for it, that all statutes should have only prospective and not retrospective operation, and that the discretion of all magistrates should be strictly circumscribed by law. Throughout, the governing idea was that the law should be king or, as one of the polemical tracts of the period expressed it, *Lex, Rex.*

Gradually, two crucial conceptions emerged as to how these basic ideals should be safeguarded: the idea of a written constitution and the principle of the separation of powers. When in January, 1660, just before the Restoration, a last attempt was made in the Declaration of Parliament Assembled at Westminister to state in a formal document the essential principles of a constitution, this striking passage was included: "There being nothing more essential to the freedom of a state, than that the people should be governed by the laws, and that justice be administered by such only as are accountable for mal-administration, it is hereby further declared that all proceedings touching the lives, liberties and estates of all the free people of this commonwealth, shall be according to the laws of the land, and that the Parliament will not meddle with ordinary administration, or the executive part of the law : it being the principle [*sic*] part of this, as it hath been of all former Parliaments, to provide for the freedom of the people against arbitrariness in government."[19] If thereafter the principle of the separation of powers was perhaps not quite "an accepted principle of constitutional law,"[20] it at least remained part of the governing political doctrine.

All these ideas were to exercise a decisive influence during the next hundred years, not only in England but also in America and on the continent, in the summarized form they were given after the final expulsion of the Stuarts in 1688. Though at the time perhaps some other works were equally and perhaps even more influential, John Locke's *Second Treatise on Civil Government* is so outstanding in its lasting effects that we must confine our attention to it.

Locke's work has come to be known mainly as a comprehensive philosophical justification of the Glorious Revolution ; and it is mostly in his wider speculations about the philosophical foundations of government that his original contribution lies. Opinions may differ about their value. The aspect of his work which was at least as important at the time and which mainly concerns us here, however, is his codification of the victorious political doctrine, of the practical principles which, it was agreed, should thenceforth control the powers of government.

While in his philosophical discussion Locke's concern is with the source which makes power legitimate and with the aim of government in general, the practical problem with which he is concerned is how power, whoever exercises it, can be prevented from becoming arbitrary : "Freedom of men under government is to have a standing rule to live by, common to every one of that society, and made by the legislative power erected in it ; a liberty to follow my own will in all things, where that rule prescribes not : and not to be subject to the inconstant, uncertain, arbitrary will of another man."[21] It is against the "irregular and uncertain exercise of the power"[22] that the argument is mainly directed : the important point is that "whoever has the legislative or supreme power of any commonwealth is bound to govern by established standing laws promulgated and known to the people, and not by extemporary decrees ; by indifferent and upright judges, who are to decide controversies by those laws ; and to employ the forces of the community at home only in the execution of such laws."[23] Even the legislature has no "absolute arbitrary power,"[24] cannot assume to itself a power to rule by extemporary arbitrary decrees, but is bound to dispense justice, and decide the rights of the subject by promulgated standing laws, and known authorized judges,"[25] while the "supreme executor of the law ... has no will, no power, but that of the law."[26] Locke is loath to recognize any sovereign power, and the treatise has been described as an assault upon the very idea of sovereignty. The main practical safeguard against the abuse of authority proposed by him is the separation of powers, which he expounds somewhat less clearly and in a less familiar form than did some of his predecessors. His main concern is how to limit the discretion of "him that has the executive power,"[27] but he has no special safeguards to offer. Yet his ultimate aim throughout is what today is often called the "taming of power" : the end why men "choose and authorize a legislative is that there may be laws made, and rules set, as guards and fences to the properties of all the members of society, to limit the power and moderate the dominion of every part and member of that society."[28]

It is a long way from the acceptance of an ideal by public opinion to its full realization in policy ; and perhaps the ideal of the rule of law had not yet been completely put into practice when the process was reversed two hundred years later. At any rate, the main period of consolidation, during which it progressively penetrated everyday practice, was the first half of the eighteenth century. From the final confirmation of the independence of the judges in the Act of Settlement of 1701, through the occasion when the last bill of attainder ever passed by Parliament in 1706 led not only to a final restatement of all the arguments against such arbitrary action of the legislature but also to a reaffirmation of the principle of the separation of powers, the period is one of slow but steady extension of most of the principles for which the Englishmen of the seventeenth century had fought....

The second half of the eighteenth century produced the coherent expositions of the ideals which largely determined the climate of opinion for the next hundred years. As is so often the case, it was less the systematic expositions by political philosophers and lawyers than the interpretations of events by the historians that carried these ideas to the public. The most influential among them was David Hume, who in his works again and again stressed the crucial points and of whom it has justly been said that for him the real meaning of the history of England was the evolution from a "government of will to a government of law."[29] At least one characteristic passage from his *History of England* deserves to be quoted. With reference to the abolition of the Star Chamber he writes : "No government, at that time, appeared in the world, nor is perhaps to be found in the records of any history, which subsisted without the mixture of some arbitrary authority, committed to some magistrate ; and it might reasonably, beforehand, appear doubtful, whether human society could ever arrive at that state of perfection, as to support itself with no other control, than the general and rigid maxims of law and equity. But the Parliament justly thought that the king was too eminent a magistrate to be trusted with discretionary power, which he might so easily turn to the destruction of liberty. And in the event it has been found that, though some inconveniences arise from the maxim of adhering strictly to law, yet the advantages so much overbalance them, as should render the English forever grateful to the memory of their ancestors who, after repeated contests, at last established that noble principle."[30]

Later in the century these ideals are more often taken for granted than explicitly stated, and the modern reader has to infer them when he wants to understand what men like Adam Smith and his contemporaries meant by "liberty." Only occasionally, as in Blackstone's *Commentaries*, do we find endeavours to elaborate particular points, such as the significance of the independence of the judges and of the separation of powers, or to clarify the meaning of "law" by its definition as "a rule,not a transient sudden order from a superior or concerning a particular person but something permanent, uniform, and universal."[31]

Many of the best-known expressions of those ideals are, of course, to be found in the familiar passages of Edmund Burke. But probably the fullest statement of the doctrine of the rule of law occurs in the work of William Paley, the "great codifier of thought in an age of codification."[32] It deserves quoting at some length : "The first maxim of a free state," he writes, "is, that the laws be made by one set of men, and administered by another ; in other words, that the legislative and the judicial character be kept separate. When these offices are unified in the same person or assembly, particular laws are made for particular cases, springing often times from partial motives, and directed to private ends : whilst they are kept separate, general laws are made by one body of men, without foreseeing whom they may affect ; and, when made, must be applied by the other, let them affect whom they will . . . . When the parties and interests to be affected by the laws were known, the inclination of the law makers would inevitably attach to one side or the other ; and where there were neither any fixed rules to regulate their determinations, nor any superior power to control their proceedings, these inclinations would interfere with the integrity of public justice. The consequence of which must be, that the subjects of such a constitution would live either without constant laws, that is, without any known pre-established rules of adjudication whatever ; or under laws made for particular persons, and partaking of the contradictions and iniquity of the motives to which they owed their origin.

With the end of the eighteenth century, England's major contributions to the development of the principles of freedom come to a close. Though Macaulay did once more for the nineteenth century what Hume had done for the eighteenth, and though the Whig intelligentsia of the *Edinburgh Review* and economists in the Smithian tradition, like J. R. MacCulloch and N. W. Senior, continued to think of liberty in classical terms, there was little further development. The new liberalism that gradually displaced Whiggism came more and more under the influence of the rationalist tendencies of the philosophical radicals and the French tradition. Bentham and his Utilitarians did much to destroy the beliefs which England had in part preserved from the Middle Ages, by their scornful treatment of most of what until then had been the most admired features of the British constitution. And they introduced into Britain what had so far been entirely absent — the desire to remake the whole of her law and institutions on rational principles.

The lack of understanding of the traditional principles of English liberty on the part of the men guided by the ideals of the French Revolution is clearly illustrated by one of the early apostles of that revolution in England, Dr. Richard Price. As early as 1778 he argued : "Liberty is too imperfectly defined when it is said to be 'a Government of LAWS and not by MEN.' If the laws are made by one man, or a junto of men in a state, and not by common CONSENT, a government by them is not different from slavery."[33] Eight years later he was able to display a commendatory letter from Turgot : "How comes it that you are almost the first of the writers of your country, who has given a just idea of liberty and shown the falsity of the notion so frequently repeated by almost all Republican Writers, 'that liberty consists in being subject only to the laws ?'"[34] From then onward, the essentially French concept of political liberty was indeed progressively to displace the English ideal of individual liberty, until it could be said that "in Great Britain, which, little more than a century ago, repudiated the ideas on which the French Revolution was based, and led the resistance to Napoleon, those ideas have triumphed."[35] Though in Britain most of the achievements of the seventeenth century were preserved beyond the nineteenth, we must look elsewhere for the further development of the ideals underlying them. [pp. 166-175]

NOTES

1. Freidrich Hayek, *The Constitution of Liberty* (Chicago : The University of Chicago Press, 1960), pp. 54-175.
2. Talmon, *Origins of Totalitarian Democracy* (London, 1952), p. 2.
3. *Ibid.*, p. 71.
4. A. Ferguson, *An Essay on the History of Civil Society* (Edinburgh, 1767), p. 187.
5. Francis Jeffrey, "Craig's Life of Millar," *Edinburgh Review*, 9 (1807).
6. D. Forbes, "Scientific Whiggism," *Cambridge Journal*, 7 (1954) : 645.
7. L. von Mises, *Socialism*, new ed. (New Haven : Yale University Press, 1951), p. 43.
8. Quoted in Talmon, *op. cit.*, p. 73.
9. M. Tullius Cicero, *De Republica* ii, I, 2.
10. R. Descartes, *A Discourse on Method* ("Everyman" ed.) Part II, p. 11.
11. "Sir Matthew Hale's Criticism on Hobbes' Dialogue on the Common Law" reprinted as an appendix to W.S. Holdsworth, *A History of English Law*, vol. 5 (London, 1924), pp. 504-5.
12. Roger J. Williams, *Free and Unequal : The Biological Basis of Individual Liberty* (Austin : University of Texas Press, 1953), pp. 23 and 70.
13. *Ibid.*, p. 152.
14. F. Pringsheim, "Jus aequum und jus structum," *Zeitschrift de Savigny — Stifung fur Rechtsgeschichte*, 42 (1921) : 668.
15. Great Britain, Public Record Office, *Calendar of State Papers, Domestic Series*, July 7, 1610.
16. E. Coke, *The Second Part of the Institute of the Laws of England (1642)*, (London, 1809), p. 47.
17. *Ibid.*, p. 51.
18. F.W. Maitland, *The Constitutional History of England* (Cambridge : Cambridge University Press, 1909), p. 263.
19. F.D. Wormuth, *The Origins of Modern Constitutionalism* (New York, 1949), p. 71.
20. *Ibid.*, p. 72.
21. J. Locke, *The Second Treatise of Civil Government*, J.W. Gough ed. (Oxford, 1946), Sec. 22, p. 33.
22. *Ibid.*, Sec. 127, p. 63.
23. *Ibid.*, Sec. 131, p. 64.
24. *Ibid.*, Sec. 137, p. 69.
25. *Ibid.*, Sec. 136, p. 68.
26. *Ibid.*, Sec. 151, p. 75.
27. *Ibid.*, Sec. 159, p. 80.
28. *Ibid.*, Sec. 22, p. 107.
29. F. Meinecke, *Die Entstehung Deo Historismus* (Berlin, 1936), I, 234.
30. D. Hume, *History of England*, vol. 5 (London, 1762), p. 280.
31. Sir William Blackstone, *Commentaries on the Laws of England*, vol. 1 (London, 1765), 44.
32. D. Hume, *History of England*, vol. 5 (London, 1762), p. 280.
33. R. Price, *Two Tracts on Civil Liberty* (London, 1778), p. 7.
34. Price, *Observations on the Importance of the American Revolution* (London, 1785), p. 111.
35. W.S. Holdsworth, *A History of English Law*, *op. cit.*, vol. 10, p. 23.

LAW, LEGISLATION AND LIBERTY, VOL. I RULES AND ORDER[1]

Friedrich Hayek

There are two ways of looking at the pattern of human activities which lead to very different conclusions concerning both its explanation and the possibilities of deliberately altering it. Of these, one is based on conceptions which are demonstrably false, yet are so pleasing to human vanity that they have gained great influence and are constantly employed even by people who know that they rest on a fiction, but believe that fiction to be innocuous. The other, although few people question its basic contentions if they are stated abstractly, leads in some respects to conclusions so unwelcome that few are willing to follow it through to the end.

The first gives us a sense of unlimited power to realize our wishes, while the second leads to the insight that there are limitations to what we can deliberately bring about, and to the recognition that some of our present hopes are delusions. Yet the effect of allowing ourselves to be deluded by the first view has always been that man has actually limited the scope of what he can achieve. For it has always been the recognition of the limits of the possible which has enabled man to make full use of his powers.

The first view holds that human institutions will serve human purposes only if they have been deliberately designed for these purposes, often also that the fact that an institution exists is evidence of its having been created for a purpose, and always that we should so redesign society and its institutions that all our actions will be wholly guided by known purposes. To most people these propositions seem almost self-evident and to constitute an attitude alone worthy of a thinking being. Yet the belief underlying them, that we owe all beneficial institutions to design, and that only such design has made or can make them useful for our purposes, is largely false.

This view is rooted originally in a deeply ingrained propensity of primitive thought to interpret all regularity to be found in phenomena anthropomorphically, as the result of the design of a thinking mind. But just when man was well on the way to emancipating himself from this naive conception, it was revived by the support of a powerful philosophy with which the aim of freeing the human mind from false prejudices has become closely associated, and which became the dominant conception of the Age of Reason.

The other view, which has slowly and gradually advanced since antiquity but for a time was almost entirely overwhelmed by the more glamorous constructivist view, was that that orderliness of society which greatly increased the effectiveness of individual action was not due solely to institutions and practices which had been invented or designed for that purpose, but was largely due to a process described at first as "growth" and later as "evolution," a process in which practices which had first been adopted for other reasons, or even purely accidentally, were preserved because they enabled the group in which they had arisen to prevail over others. Since its first systematic development in the eighteenth century this view had to struggle not only against the anthropomorphism of primitive thinking but even more against the reinforcement these naive views had received from the new rationalist philosophy. It was indeed the challenge which this philosophy provided that led to the explicit formulation of the evolutionary view....

This "rationalist" approach, however, meant in effect a relapse into earlier, anthropomorphic modes of thinking. It produced a renewed propensity to ascribe the origin of all institutions of culture to invention or design. Morals, religion and law, language and writing, money and the market were thought of as having been deliberately constructed by somebody, or at least as owing whatever perfection they possessed to such design. This intentionalist or pragmatic account of history found its fullest expression in the conception of the formation of society by a social contract, first in Hobbes and then in Rousseau, who in many respects was a direct follower of Descartes. Even though their theory was not always meant as a historical account of what actually happened, it was always meant to provide a guideline for deciding whether or not existing institutions were to be approved as rational.

It is to this philosophical conception that we owe the preference which prevails to the present day for everything that is done "consciously" or "deliberately," and from it the terms "irrational" or "non-rational" derive the derogatory meaning they now have. Because of this the earlier presumption in favour of traditional or established institutions and usages became a presumption against them, and "opinion" came to be thought of as "mere" opinion — something not demonstrable or decidable by reason and therefore not to be accepted as a valid ground for decision.

Yet the basic assumption underlying the belief that man has achieved mastery of his surroundings mainly through his capacity for logical deduction from explicit premises is factually false, and any attempt to confine his actions to what could thus be justified would deprive him of many of the most effective means to success that have been available to him. It is simply not true that our actions owe their effectiveness solely or chiefly to knowledge which we can state in words and which can therefore constitute the explicit premises of a syllogism. Many of the institutions of society which are indispensable conditions for the successful pursuit of our conscious aims are in fact the result of customs, habits, or practices which have been neither invented nor are observed with any such purpose in view. We live in a society in which we can successfully orientate ourselves, and in which our actions have a good chance of achieving their aims, not only because our fellows are governed by known aims or known connections between means and ends, but because they are also confined by rules whose purpose or origin we often do not know and of whose very existence we are often not aware.

Man is as much a rule-following animal as a purpose-seeking one. And he is successful not because he knows why he ought to observe the rule which he does observe, or is even capable of stating all these rules in words, but because his thinking and acting are governed by rules which have by a process of selection been evolved in the society in which he lives, and which are thus the product of the experience of generations.

The constructivist approach leads to false conclusions because man's actions are largely successful, not merely in the primitive stage but perhaps even more so in civilization, because they are adapted both to the particular facts which he knows and to a great many other facts he does not and cannot know. And this adaptation to the general circumstances that surround him is brought about by his observance of rules which he has not designed and often does not even know explicitly, although he is able to honour them in action. Or, to put this differently, our adaptation to our environment does not consist only, and perhaps not even chiefly, in an insight into the relations between cause and effect, but also in our actions being governed by rules adapted to the kind of world in which we live, that is, to circumstances which we are not aware of and which yet determine the pattern of our successful actions.

Complete rationality of action in the Cartesian sense demands complete knowledge of all the relevant facts. A designer or engineer needs all the data and full power to control or manipulate them if he is to organize the material objects to produce the intended result. But the success of action in society depends on more particular facts than any one can possibly know. And our whole civilization in consequence rests, and must rest, on our *believing* much that we cannot *know* to be true in the Cartesian sense.... [pp. 8-12]

The characteristic error of the constructivist rationalists in this respect is that they tend to base their argument on what has been called the *synoptic delusion*, that is, on the fiction that all the relevant facts are known to some one mind, and that it is possible to construct from this knowledge of the particulars a desirable social order. Sometimes the delusion is expressed with a touching naivete by the enthusiasts for a deliberately planned society, as when one of them dreams of the development of "the art of simultaneous thinking : the ability to deal with a multitude of related phenomena at the same time, and of composing in a single picture both the qualitative and the quantitative attributes of these phenomena." They seem completely unaware that this dream simply assumes away the central problem which any effort towards the understanding or shaping of the order of society raises : our incapacity to assemble as a surveyable whole all the data which enter into the social order. Yet all those who are fascinated by the beautiful plans which result from such an approach because they are "so orderly, so visible, so easy to understand," are the victims of the synoptic delusion and forget that these plans owe their seeming clarity to the planner's disregard of all the facts he does not know.... [pp. 14-15]

The cultural heritage into which man is born consists of a complex of practices or rules of conduct which have prevailed because they made a group of men successful but which were not adopted because it was known that they would bring about desired effects.

Man acted before he thought and did not understand before he acted. What we call understanding is in the last resort simply his capacity to respond to his environment with a pattern of actions that helps him to persist. Such is the modicum of truth in behaviourism and pragmatism, doctrines which, however, have so crudely oversimplified the determining relationships as to become more obstacles than helps to their appreciation.

"Learning from experience," among men no less than among animals, is a process not primarily of reasoning but of the observance, spreading, transmission, and development of practices which have prevailed because they were successful — often not because they conferred any recognizable benefit on the acting individual but because they increased the chances of survival of the group to which he belonged. The result of this development will in the first instance not be articulated knowledge but a knowledge which, although it can be described in terms of rules, the individual cannot state in words but is merely able to honour in practice. The mind does not so much make rules as consist of rules of action, a complex of rules that is, which it has not made, but which have come to govern the actions of the individuals because actions in accordance with them have proved more successful than those of competing individuals or groups.

There is in the beginning no distinction between the practices one must observe in order to achieve a particular result and the practices one ought to observe. There is just one established manner of doing things and knowledge of cause and effect and knowledge of the appropriate or permissible form of action are not distinct. Knowledge of the world is knowledge of what one must do or not do in certain kinds of circumstances. And in avoiding danger it is as important to know what one must never do as to know what one must do to achieve a particular result.

These rules of conduct have thus not developed as the recognized conditions for the achievement of a known purpose, but have evolved because the groups who practised them were more successful and displaced others. They were rules which, given the kind of environment in which man lived, secured that a greater number of the groups or individuals practising them would survive. The problem of conducting himself successfully in a world only partially known to man was thus solved by adhering to rules which had served him well but which he did not and could not *know* to be true in the Cartesian sense.

There are thus two attributes of these rules that govern human conduct and make it appear intelligent which we shall have to stress throughout, because the constructivist approach denies implicitly that it can be rational to observe such rules. Of course in advanced society only some rules will be of this kind ; what we want to emphasize is merely that even such advanced societies will in part owe their order to some such rules.

The first of these attributes which most rules of conduct originally possessed is that they are observed in action without being known to the acting person in articulated ("verbalized" or explicit) form. They will manifest themselves in a regularity of action which can be explicitly described, but this regularity of action is not the result of the acting persons being capable of thus stating them. The second is that such rules come to be observed because in fact they give the group in which they are practised superior strength, and not because this effect is known to those who are guided by them. Although such rules come to be generally accepted because their observation produces certain consequences, they are not observed with the intention of producing those consequences — consequences which the acting person need not know.

We cannot consider here the difficult question of how men can learn from each other such, often highly abstract, rules of conduct by example and imitation (or "by analogy"), although neither those who set the examples nor those who learn from them may be consciously aware of the existence of the rules which they nevertheless strictly observe. This is a problem most familiar to us in the learning of language by children who are able to produce correctly most complicated expressions they have never heard before ; but it occurs also in such fields as manners, morals, and law, and in most skills where we are guided by rules which we know how to follow but are unable to state.

The important point is that every man growing up in a given culture will find in himself rules, or may discover that he acts in accordance with rules — and will similarly recognize the actions of others as conforming or not conforming to various rules. This is, of course, not proof that they are a permanent or unalterable part of "human nature," or that they are innate, but proof only that they are part of a cultural heritage which is likely to be fairly constant, especially so long as they are not articulated in words and therefore also are not discussed or consciously examined.... [pp. 17-19]

The study of spontaneous orders has long been the peculiar task of economic theory, although, of course, biology has from its beginning been concerned with that special kind of spontaneous order which we call an organism. Only recently has there arisen within the physical sciences under the name of cybernetics a special discipline which is also concerned with what are called self-organizing or self-generating systems.

The distinction of this kind of order from one which has been made by somebody putting the elements of a set in their places or directing their movements is indispensable for any understanding of the processes of society as well as for all social policy. There are several terms available for describing each kind of order. The made order... referred to as an exogenous order or an arrangement may again be described as a construction, an artificial order or, especially where we have to deal with a directed social order, as an *organization.* The grown order, on the other hand,... referred to as a self-generating or endogenous order, is in English most conveniently described as a *spontaneous order.* Classical Greek was more fortunate in possessing distinct single words for the two kinds of order, namely *taxis* for a made order, such as, for example, an order of battle, and *kosmos* for a grown order, meaning originally "a right order in a state or a community...."

It would be no exaggeration to say that social theory begins with — and has an object only because of — the discovery that there exist orderly structures which are the product of the action of many men but are not the result of human design. In some fields this is now universally accepted. Although there was a time when men believed that even language and morals had been "invented" by some genius of the past, everybody recognizes now that they are the outcome of a process of evolution whose results nobody foresaw or designed. But in other fields many people still treat with suspicion the claim that the patterns of interaction of many men can show an order that is of nobody's deliberate making ; in the economic sphere, in particular, critics still pour uncomprehending ridicule on Adam Smith's expression of the "invisible hand" by which, in the language of his time, he described how man is led "to promote an end which was no part of his intentions." If indignant reformers still complain of the chaos of economic affairs, insinuating a complete absence of order, this is partly because they cannot conceive of an order which is not deliberately made, and partly because to them an order means something aiming at concrete purposes which is, as we shall see, what a spontaneous order cannot do....

One effect of our habitually identifying order with a made order or *taxis* is indeed that we tend to ascribe to all order certain properties which deliberate arrangements regularly, and with respect to some of these properties necessarily, possess. Such orders are relatively *simple* or at least necessarily confined to such moderate degrees of complexity as the maker can still survey ; they are usually *concrete* in the sense just mentioned that their existence can be intuitively perceived by inspection ; and, finally, having been made deliberately, they invariably do (or at one time did) *serve a purpose* of the maker. None of these characteristics necessarily belong to a spontaneous order or *kosmos.* Its degree of complexity is not limited to what a human mind can master. Its existence need not manifest itself to our senses but may be based on purely *abstract* relations which we can only mentally reconstruct. And not having been made it *cannot* legitimately be said to *have a particular purpose*, although our awareness of its existence may be extremely important for our successful pursuit of a great variety of different purposes.

Spontaneous orders are not necessarily complex, but unlike deliberate human arrangements, they may achieve any degree of complexity. One of our main contentions will be that very complex orders, comprising more particular facts than any brain could ascertain or manipulate, can be brought about only through forces inducing the formation of spontaneous orders.

Spontaneous orders need not be what we have called abstract but they will often consist of a system of abstract relations between elements which are also defined only by abstract properties, and for this reason will not be intuitively perceivable and not recognizable except on the basis of a theory accounting for their character. The significance of the abstract character of such orders rests on the fact that they may persist while all the particular elements they comprise, and even the number of such elements, change. All that is necessary to preserve such an abstract order is that a certain structure of relationships be maintained, or that elements of a certain kind (but variable in number) continue to be related in a certain manner.... [pp. 36-38]

Legislation, the deliberate making of law, has justly been described as among all inventions of man the one fraught with the gravest consequences, more far-reaching in its effects even than fire and gun-powder. Unlike law itself, which has never been "invented" in the same sense, the invention of legislation came relatively late in the history of mankind. It gave into the hands of men an instrument of great power which they needed to achieve some good, but which they have not yet learned so to control that it may not produce great evil. It opened to man wholly new possibilities and gave him a new sense of power over his fate. The discussion about who should possess this power has, however, unduly overshadowed the much more fundamental question of how far this power should extend. It will certainly remain an exceedingly dangerous power so long as we believe that it will do harm only if wielded by bad men.

Law in the sense of enforced rules of conduct is undoubtedly coeval with society ; only the observance of common rules makes the peaceful existence of individuals in society possible. Long before man had developed language to the point where it enabled him to issue general commands, an individual would be accepted as a member of a group only so long as he conformed to its rules. Such rules might in a sense not be known and still have to be discovered, because from "knowing how" to act, or from being able to recognize that the acts of another did or did not conform to accepted practices, it is still a long way to being able to state such rules in words. But while it might be generally recognized that the discovery and statement of what the accepted rules were (or the articulation of rules that would be approved when acted upon) was a task requiring special wisdom, nobody yet conceived of law as something which men could make at will.

It is no accident that we still use the same word "law" for the invariable rules which govern nature and for the rules which govern men's conduct. They were both conceived at first as something existing independently of human will. Though the anthropomorphic tendencies of all primitive thinking made men often ascribe both kinds of law to the creation of some supernatural being, they were regarded as eternal truths that man could try to discover but which he could not alter.

To modern man, on the other hand, the belief that all law governing human action is the product of legislation appears so obvious that the contention that law is older than law-making has almost the character of a paradox. Yet there can be no doubt that law existed for ages before it occurred to man that he could make or alter it. The belief that he could do so appeared hardly earlier than in classical Greece and even then only to be submerged again and to reappear and gradually gain wider acceptance in the later Middle Ages. In the form in which it is now widely held, however, namely that all law is, can be, and ought to be, the product of the free invention of a legislator, it is factually false, an erroneous product of that constructive rationalism which we described earlier.

We shall later see that the whole conception of legal positivism which derives all law from the will of a legislator is a product of the intentionalist fallacy characteristic of constructivism, a relapse into those design theories of human institutions which stand in irreconcilable conflict with all we know about the evolution of law and most other human institutions.

What we know about pre-human and primitive human societies suggests a different origin and determination of law from that assumed by the theories which trace it to the will of a legislator. And although the positivist doctrine stands also in flagrant conflict with what we know about the history of our law, legal history proper begins at too late a stage of evolution to bring out clearly the origins. If we wish to free ourselves from the all-pervasive influence of the intellectual presumption that man in his wisdom has designed, or ever could have designed, the whole system of legal or moral rules, we should begin with a look at the primitive and even pre-human beginnings of social life.

Social theory has here much to learn from the two young sciences of ethology and cultural anthropology which in many respects have built on the foundations of social theory initially laid in the eighteenth century by the Scottish moral philosophers. In the field of law, indeed these young disciplines go far to confirm the evolutionary teaching of Edward Coke, Matthew Hale, David Hume and Edmund Burke, F.C. von Savigny, H.S. Maine and J.C. Carter and are wholly contrary to the rationalist constructivism of Francis Bacon or Thomas Hobbes, Jeremy Bentham or John Austin, or of the German positivists from Paul Laband to Hans Kelsen.... [pp. 72-74]

The distinct character of the rules which the judge will have to apply, and must endeavour to articulate and improve, is best understood if we remember that he is called in to correct disturbances of an order that has not been made by anyone and does not rest on the individuals having been told what they must do. In most instances no authority will even have known at the time the disputed action took place what the individuals did or why they did it. The judge is in this sense an institution of a spontaneous order. He will always find such an order in existence as an attribute of an ongoing process in which the individuals are able successfully to pursue their plans because they can form expectations about the actions of their fellows which have a good chance of being met.

To appreciate the significance of this it is necessary to free ourselves wholly from the erroneous conception that there can be first a society which then gives itself laws. This erroneous conception is basic to the constructivist rationalism which from Descartes and Hobbes through Rousseau and Bentham down to contemporary legal positivism has blinded students to the true relationship between law and government. It is only as a result of individuals observing certain common rules that a group of men can live together in those orderly relations which we call a society. It would therefore probably be nearer the truth if we inverted the plausible and widely held idea that law derives from authority and rather thought of all authority as deriving from law — not in the sense that the law appoints authority, but in the sense that authority commands obedience because (and so long as) it enforces a law presumed to exist independently of it and resting on a diffused opinion of what is right. Not all law can therefore be the product of legislation ; but power to legislate presupposes the recognition of some common rules ; and such rules which underlie the power to legislate may also limit that power. No group is likely to agree on articulated rules unless its members already hold opinions that coincide in some degree. Such coincidence of opinion will thus have to precede explicit agreement on articulated rules of just conduct, although not agreement on particular ends of action. Persons differing in their general values may occasionally agree on, and effectively collaborate for, the achievement of particular concrete purposes. But such agreement on particular ends will never suffice for forming that lasting order which we call a society. [pp. 94-95]

NOTE

1. Friedrich Hayek, *Law, Legislation and Liberty,* vol. 1 (Chicago : University of Chicago Press, 1973), pp. 8-95.

FROM CONTRACT TO COMMUNITY[1]

Christian Bay

My thought on contract versus community will proceed within the context, and is sustained by the experiences, of our post-industrial world. Let us very briefly consider four of its problematic aspects.

First, I say "post-industrial *world*" advisedly, even though I fully realize that much of the world today is not industrial yet, let alone post-industrial. But people all over the world are today at the mercy of those who control the corporations — the economic core of post-industrial life — which in turn control the bulk of the world's industry *and* agriculture. The 500 largest corporations in this country have in the last fifteen years increased their share of all U.S. manufacturing and mining assets from 40 percent to 70 percent of the total industrial and mining wealth of the nation.

Such immense concentrations of private power can make or break a lot of governments, and this renders the dream of achieving democracy anywhere in the "free world" today an illusion. The multinational corporations are beyond the reach of any national government as the U.S. government would quickly discover if it tried to tax some of them severely : They would soon relocate their operations elsewhere, or threaten to do so, with dire consequences for one or more U.S. states or cities. Even in the United States, private corporate power now largely determines what kinds of people are to achieve political influence, through its ability to hand out or withhold large sums of money and its control of many other kinds of favours. In short, private capitalism has spawned powerful international organizations that behave as if they were new states, although they are motivated by narrow economic interests rather than by political ideals or purposes. Their powers are enhanced, both internationally and within each non-Communist nation, by their tendency to form coalitions among themselves and with the governments in the rich nations, which in turn operate credit agencies like the World Bank and the International Monetary Fund in the interest of private corporate business.

Second, the concentration of corporate power in our post-industrial world has ideological as well as economic and political implications. Although the "free world" rhetoric has faded with the protraction of the shameful war in Indochina, the "free enterprise" ideology remains unchallenged in the context of practical politics in this country ; both political parties advocate this ideology and both take "free enterprise" to mean, not plenty of opportunity for the small businessman, but something like "plenty of elbowroom and privilege for private corporate power." Marcuse and Habermas have analyzed, as Marx did for an earlier stage of capitalist development, how the realities of power and profit are obfuscated and made palatable to many of the poor and exploited as well as the rich. Let me cite Gore Vidal's livelier prose : "Most Americans lack the words, the concepts that might help them figure out what has happened ; and it is hardly their fault. Simple falsities have been drummed into their heads from birth (Sweden = socialism = suicide) so that they will not rebel, not demand what is being withheld them...and that is not not rebel, not demand what is being withheld them...and that is not Nixon's elegant 'a piece of the action' but justice. Social justice."[2]

Organized labour in the rich nations, particularly in North America, has largely been co-opted, but not, as yet, the bulk of the Third World populations, whose privations have remained too extreme to permit co-optation. However, with a few notable exceptions, the peasantry and proletariats of poorer countries have been kept too miserable and too weak to struggle effectively for a better world.

A third aspect of the post-industrial world is the fact of permanent structural unemployment. The ultimate harm of man's alienation under liberal capitalism, in my view, resides not in exploitation as such, but in the combination of exploitation with the mentality of the Puritan work ethic, which induces the exploited to anchor their self-respect in "having a job," so that the grim fact of unemployment, for those affected, means psychological as well as economic debilitation. At the same time, objectively degrading jobs (like producing arms for oil sheiks), *any* jobs, are accepted with gratitude. Mankind's problem of industrial production appears to have been solved, but with a vengeance : Now we are faced with the reverse problem of destructive overproduction, and also with a progressively worsening condition of maldistribution, especially in a global context.

A fourth aspect of our post-industrial world is a situation that may prove to be too much of a challenge for liberal capitalism to cope with : that is, the fact of radically declining ecological resources, like clean air, water, food, energy, and wilderness space. Up to now a key argument of the liberal capitalist ideology has been that freedom for the energetic and strong will increase production to such an extent that even the weak and lazy will be better off in the long run. Although this argument may have been meritorious 100 years ago, today it has become palpable nonsense, considering the fact that the number-one problem for rich countries and corporations is no longer how to produce enough, but how to *sell* their products. The worst colonialism today, in Johan Galtung's phrase, is *colonialism in time*,[3] not imperialism or colonialism in space. At the present rate of our waste of the world's resources, we North Americans are destroying the basis of a viable life for our grandchildren and subsequent generations even more wantonly than we are exploiting the poor people in the Third World.

Having sketched some major features of contemporary social and political life, I want to examine briefly the historical development of the now conventional liberal ideology and mentality.

Modern liberalism is based on three principal ideas : the individualist contract theory ; the utilitarian principle ; and the assumption of equality. I shall limit my critique here to the first of the three, because it seems to me the most problematic. About the other two premises, let me only say that the notion of utility is compatible with any number of political positions, including the "communitarian" view to be developed later : *If* a simple substantive aim has been chosen, "utilitarian" means or policies are to be preferred as a matter of rational choice. Concerning egalitarianism, it is distressingly clear that liberals and many democratic socialists have tended to settle for the empty shell of "equality of opportunity" or "an equal chance" as distinct from demanding a society that promotes relatively egalitarian standards of life, in a sense of a minimum measure of substantive well-being and justice guaranteed to all.... [pp. 31-34]

Philip Slater in his *Pursuit of Loneliness*, subtitled *American Culture at the Breaking Point*, speaks of three human desires that are deeply and uniquely frustrated by American culture :

1. The desire for *community* — the wish to live in trust and fraternal cooperation with one's fellows in a total and visible collective entity.
2. The desire for *engagement* — the wish to come directly to grips with social and interpersonal problems and to confront on equal terms an environment which is not composed of ego-extensions.
3. The desire for *dependence* — the wish to share responsibility or the control of one's impulses and the direction of one's life.[4]

Slater sees our society's "uptightness" about challenges to our faith in rugged individualism as evidence that desires such as the three listed are an important part of our nature, persistently and yet precariously suppressed.

Every political culture in a sense cribs and confines our conscious desires and identities within its standardized conventions governing individual behaviours. American capitalist liberalism, Kenneth Keniston argues, has accentuated toughness and ego strength at the expense of emotional development, especially in the "red-blooded" North American male. Marcus Raskin lists four principal power hierarchies in our society — the military, the industrial and commercial, the educational, and the dream-manufacturing hierarchies — which between them control not only much of our working lives, but also our leisure, our dreams, and our personal life plans to a considerable extent.[5] All this domination occurs under the guise of the rugged-individualist ideology of traditional American liberalism. No wonder that our habitual cheering for individualistic values tends to be hollow at times.

Fresh insight is painful but useful, if we want to develop as human beings. No struggle for emancipation is possible before we begin to understand the reality of our need for community ; for this to happen, the liberal democratic make-believe must be exposed as the blindfold to social reality that it is. Let me now turn to a very different tradition from the contract legacy : that of communalism, which I find expressed in the writings of Aristotle, Rousseau, and Marx.

As is well known, Aristotle asserted that man is by nature a political animal and he added that "he who by nature or by mere accident is without a state, is either a bad man or above humanity." As he continued : "A social instinct is implanted in all men by nature, and he who first founded the state was the greatest of benefactors."[6] If we forget about the slaves, the women, and the barbarians, Aristotle's Athens — at least during the period of direct democratic government — was nearer to a natural community than any modern state can be. In the same context Aristotle observed that man, unlike other animals, "has a sense of good and evil, of just and unjust, and the like, and the association of living beings who have this sense makes a family and a state." The sense of justice emerges here from man's communitarian nature, in contrast to the modern conception of the "state of nature" where might makes right. It was because Hobbes had rejected this communitarian nature that he had to resort to the fiction of a social contract.

Hobbes and Locke chose to play down the communitarian aspects of man's nature — without which, as Aristotle saw, man will be "bad," that is, lacking in a sense of justice. Hobbes put his faith in an absolute power to hold the state together, whereas Locke chose a *quid pro quo* contract between all persons of property. Both contracts, by assuming "bad" men, that is, men content to take every legal advantage of one another, tended to make men worse and more callous and produced ruling classes that had no qualms, for example, about letting the poor starve to death or allowing colonial people to be captured for slavery, and all in the name of liberty and progress.

Although partially wedded to the contractual tradition, Rousseau preferred to emphasize man's communitarian instincts. In Sheldon Wolin's words, Rousseau proposed "a paradox : Let us create a society which causes men to grow closer to one another, to become so strongly solidary that each member will be made dependent on the whole society and, by that very fact, be released from *personal* dependencies.[7] Rousseau, it is true, thought good government to be possible only in small states, like his native Geneva ; he had little hope for large societies, because economic selfishness would weigh heavily with most people's "particular wills," and these would tend to drown out the "general will" as embodied in minorities of uncorrupted citizens. Rousseau's *Contrat Social* was a book about the eternal contest between man's "natural" communitarian "general will" and the crippling pathologies of behaviour that feudal as well as liberal capitalist structures of domination bring about — sycophancy under feudalism, and rootless individualism under capitalism....

Let us consider a portion of the argument in Marx's controversial essay "On the Jewish Question," which he wrote in 1843 at age twenty-five. In this essay he criticized the liberal ideology at its highest ground : the constitutional bills of rights. The burden of his argument is that bills of rights extol and protect individualistic, private man, while downgrading the citizen, the species-being, that is, man the community member. In Marx's words : "Liberty as a right of man is not founded upon the relations between man and man, but rather upon the separation of man from man. It is the right of such separation. The right of the *circumscribed* individual, withdrawn into himself." In practice this liberty focuses on property, which is associated with narrow self-interest : "It leads every man to see in other men, not the *realization,* but rather the *limitation* of his own liberty." Bourgeois political liberators, Marx continues,

> reduce citizenship, the *political community,* to a mere *means* for preserving these so-called rights of man ; and consequently, . . . the citizen is declared to be the servant of egoistic man, . . .the sphere of man as a species-being is degraded to a level below the sphere where he functions as a partial being, and finally . . . it is a man as a bourgeois and not man as a citizen who is considered the *true* and *authentic* man.[8]

In Marx's view, then, liberal bills of rights erect fences between people ; they reinforce egotistical individualism and rationalize the sanctification of property rights while sacrificing traditional citizen virtues, including the sense of justice that is man's attribute as a species-being and that, according to Aristotle, presupposes membership in a human community. Marx would have us aim at a new society, past the contractual arrangements of liberalism that suit private men with exclusive property rights. In the words of the *Manifesto* : "In place of the old bourgeois society, with its classes and class antagonisms, we shall have an association, in which the free development of each is the condition for the free development of all."[9]

In endorsing Marx's critique of liberal bills of rights I do not mean to abandon what I called the "human rights" approach in my own book, *The Structure of Freedom.*[10] Although couched largely in "liberal" terms in that earlier work, my value position has been and remains similar to Marx's. The "rights priorities" stipulated in that work were meant to correspond closely with priorities of human needs, on the principle that a more basic need always must take precedence over a less basic need, in accordance with a Maslovian scale of human needs. And I insisted then, as I do now, that the realization and protection of basic rights, including the right of health and freedom from debilitating poverty, must be in principle prior to all exclusive property rights and other privileges ; also, I construe the legitimating task of any state to be to promote freedom with justice, that is, with priority for the freedom of the least free, to the exclusion of *any other* task except the obvious concern with securing the achieved levels of freedom and well-being over time, for our generation and our successors.

Where my book fell short — in the same way as Rawls's work does — was in its lack of attention to critical social analysis, and particularly in its failure to recognize the harm that a liberal vocabulary can do in providing ideological support for the capitalist system : Even a radical reformulation that imbues reformist liberalism with socialist need priorities will all too readily suggest that radical changes can be brought about within an ostensibly democratic system, a system that in fact is invulnerable to any political challenge that accepts and strictly honours the system's constitutional rules. These rules have been developed, after all, largely for the purpose of maintaining illusions of freedom and democracy, and thus to protect the owners against democratic or socialist-type onslaughts.

Having said this, I must also put in a word in praise of our liberal representative institutions and the U.S. Bill of Rights : They make it possible to avoid much political violence for those who are working to overturn the exploitive economic system. With expanding political education it may become feasible some day to make our representative institutions more democratically meaningful. And they are lesser evils today than one-party dictatorships, even dictatorships in the name of the proletariat, certainly in our part of the world — although, to be sure, when balanced against the suffering that Western imperialism inflicts on the Third World, our liberal institutions can be viewed as conveniences that others are paying for in blood. These institutions do, after all, tend to legitimate imperialist foreign policies in the minds of many, perhaps most, liberals....

Obstacles to natural community are legion in a class-divided, elite-ridden society. As students of political psychology amply have demonstrated, many low-status people lack a sense of political competence, and will habitually take orders rather than assert themselves. We do know a great deal, however, about how families, schools and other institutions can nourish a sense of personal competence and worth in all of our young — which is the first prerequisite for developing our communitarian human nature and the natural communities that will sustain it. The second prerequisite is to debunk the false notion of obligation to the state that liberalism has fostered.... The third is to study specific strategies for social change, with a special focus on nonviolent (or minimally violent) approaches.

Beyond the natural local communities, there is one other kind of community that is natural only in the sense that it has existed in the political imagination of a great many public-spirited men and women through the ages. That is the community of humankind. In our shrinking interdependent world, I doubt that anyone capable of humane reflection needs to be convinced of the importance of soon achieving a "we-feeling" that embraces the whole human race, with all present and future members included.

Through building local communities of equals, in which we are free to develop more fully our natural solidarity feelings, I think we can learn to combat the arrogance of nationalism which, at least for the last centuries, has been one main obstacle to the growth of humanitarian internationalism. To the extent that, as community members, we have learnt to cooperate with one another and with other communities, in challenging the restrictive barriers of our nation-states, we may perhaps also learn to empathize with people and communities in other cultures, and come to extend our communitarian feelings to strangers as well as to our friends.

The urgent necessity of looking in common after the interests that are shared by all humanity should soon begin to recommend itself to most people, I would think, as we become free enough to be rational about our stake in an ecologically viable, just, and peaceful world. [pp. 37-43]

NOTES

1. Christian Bay, "From Contract to Community," in Fred R. Dallmayr, ed., *From Contract to Community* (New York : Marcel Dekker Inc., 1978), pp. 31-43.

2. Gore Vidal, "The State of the Union," 83 *Esquire*, no. 5 (May 1, 1975) : 61-68, 137.

3. See Johan Galtung's "Structural Pluralism and the Future of Human Society" in *Proceedings from the Second International Future Research Conference* (Tokyo : Kodansha, 1971).

4. Philip Slater, *Pursuit of Loneliness : American Culture at the Breaking Point* (Boston : Beacon Press, 1970), p. 5.

5. Marcus Raskin, *Being and Doing* (New York : Random House, 1971).

6. Aristotle, *Politics*, 1253a ; compare *Nicomachean Ethics*, 1076b.

7. Sheldon Wolin, *Politics and Vision* (Boston : Little, Brown, 1960), p. 371.

8. Reprinted in Robert C. Tucket, ed., *The Marx-Engels Reader* (New York : W.W. Norton, 1972), pp. 40-41. Italics in original.

9. Karl Marx, *The Communist Manifesto*, reprinted in *The Marx-Engels Reader*, *op. cit.*, p. 353.

10. Christian Bay, *The Structure of Freedom* (Stanford, Calif. : Stanford University Press, 1958, 1970).

HAYEK'S LIBERALISM : THE CONSTITUTION OF PERPETUAL PRIVILEGE[1]

Christian Bay

Hayek seems blissfully unaware of being, as he in fact is, a special pleader for a particular class interest. His special pleading is firmly wrapped into the definitions of his key terms — first of all in his definitions of "liberty," "coercion," and "privilege."

A cynical critic might well have accused Hayek of dishonesty when he writes as if his were the only or the conventional or the "natural" definitions, on the assumption that he should know better. My own interpretation is that an eminent pupil of Ludwig von Mises and other leading Manchester-liberal economists may have come to feel so certain of knowing the answers to all economic problems that radical reflection about ethical or political value postulates have seemed needless. Liberals, too, can have an armour that no unpalatable idea can penetrate, and Manchester liberals may be more exposed to this hazard than most other kinds of liberals. A commitment to an "open society" is no guarantee of an open mind. In fact, Hayek's commitment to *laissez-faire* and to the cluster of preferred liberties associated with this doctrine appears to be held with a complete sense of certainty, even though he is able to discuss rationally certain very limited functions that he would allow for government in economic life (for example, providing care for the indigent, or providing efficiency information to farmers). Any evidence that large-scale free enterprise does not exist, or cannot work, seems to be ruled out. Social miseries resulting from competitive corporate enterprise, or from the absence of adequate social welfare legislation, are made tolerable to Hayek by his great learning, it would seem ; and his ability to keep his humanitarian impulses in check reminds me of Rousseau's example of the philosopher who could go back to sleep after a murder had been committed under his window.

Now it is true of any closed system of thought, whether capitalist or socialist or vegetarian or what have you, that the key terms are chosen and defined shrewdly : in these definitions the seeds of the desired conclusions are not only planted but also safely sheltered from the winds of adverse facts. Mind you, this need not be a reflection on the shrewdness or the (dis)honesty of an individual writer. Most of us tend to gravitate toward the ideologies whose applications make us comfortable, or whose spokesmen we admire. It requires no base motives to be influenced by an eminent teacher, or to feel comfortable with an ideology that defends one's class interests. And so far I have not argued with the substance of Hayek's position ; my immediate objective is only to expose the loaded terms he uses ; and, further, his (objectively speaking) false pretense of presenting a *general* inquiry on liberty rather than one geared to special interests and to particularistic, not humanistic commitments.

"Freedom" and "liberty" are synonymous terms to Hayek. "Though I have a personal preference for the former, it seems that 'liberty' lends itself less to abuse." And he mentions Franklin D. Roosevelt's phrase "freedom from want" as an example of such abuse. A state of liberty or freedom, Hayek defines, is "that condition of men in which coercion of some by others is reduced as much as is possible in society."[2] The criterion of freedom is one person's degree of "independence of the arbitrary will of another." "In this sense freedom refers solely to a relation of men to other men, and the only infringement on it is coercion by men. This means, in particular, that the range of physical possibilities from which a person can choose at a given moment has no direct relevance to freedom.[3] The needy and the poor are free if they are blessed with living in "a free country," one may infer.

The only evil that can negate the positive value of freedom is *coercion*, subsequently defined as "such control of the environment or circumstances of a person that, in order to avoid greater evil, he is forced to act not according to a coherent plan of his own but to serve the ends of another."[4] Or, in a briefer formulation, coercion "occurs when one man's actions are made to serve another man's will, not for his own but for the other's purpose."[5]

We see right away an in-built preference for the demands of the strong, over the needs of the weak. Already Hayek's choice of definition of "freedom" (and of "coercion," its negation) makes it almost inevitable that he should consider the United States of today a country in which "the defence of the existing is often a defence of freedom." For an alternate view of America, which is based on a humanistic commitment, not a commitment to a parochial concept of freedom take a recent statement by Edgar Z. Friedenberg : "American society is not designed to respond to needs, which is what losers have. Instead, it responds to demands, which are what winners are in a position to make."[6] Now, there are mountains of evidence, I think, with which Friedenberg's observation can be substantiated. Does it still seem reasonable to defend most American institutions, and in the name of *freedom* ?

"Freedom" and "liberty" are emotion-packed words, and *The Constitution of Liberty* is presented as not just a scholarly treatise but also a plea to all academics, and those they can influence, to join in the noble crusade for liberty. The deception, of which the author is unaware, is manifest when "liberty" then is given a severely restricted definition, arbitrarily limited to liberties important mainly to those who are doing well within the system ; the classes of people who dread interference with their further plans and ambitions, not the classes of people who desperately could use a little "arbitrary interference" to keep their children alive and well.... [pp. 110-112]

Hayek's philosophy of maximal freedom for the affluent is developed on the basis of loaded definitions, we have seen. It is also based on a number of substantive assumptions, a few of which will be examined now ; assumptions about the nature of man and of social institutions and political processes.

About man's potentialities for generosity and individual responsibility Hayek takes, as also most conservatives do, a skeptical view. He is careful to distinguish, in Chapter 4, his kind of Burkean liberalism from the continental, rationalist school of liberalism based on a belief in the perfectibility of man. It is only within the framework of traditions, he asserts, "that human reason has grown and can successfully operate...."[7]

Institutions, like laws, reflect power structures and class interests ; those that serve the interests of the powerful have a survival chance far above and beyond those that might merely serve the interests of the oppressed, in any social order. Essentially a social Darwinist himself, Hayek nowhere in his long book entertains the thought that some institutions might be very stable and perhaps centuries-old and yet be thoroughly oppressive. Karl Marx has called religion "the opiate of the people" ; even those who hesitate to go that far might still concede that to praise traditions and to derogate the powers of reason of each new generation and of each individual is to blunt the cutting edge of every rebel's cry for an end to oppression and injustice.

Yet, Hayek goes further still, and insists, as we have seen, that unjust institutions are in the general interest, for "those lower down profit materially from the fact that others are ahead." Competition is the yeast of progress, he believes, and the only hope for a decent life for ordinary working people is in never-ending progress. He never, unfortunately , defines this key term, although he devotes his Chapter 3 to "the common sense of progress." The closest he comes to a definition is when he rejects "advance toward a known goal" and says he prefers "to think of progress as a process of formation and modification of the human intellect, a process of adaptation and learning in which not only the possibilities known to us but also our values and desires continually change. As progress consists in the discovery of the not yet known, its consequences must be unpredictable."[8]

What this view of progress amounts to, I think, is yet another line of defence against reason in politics. The "open society" is further fortified with "open criteria" for justifying whatever developments suit the country's economic rulers. Progress becomes, in effect, what is good for General Motors and GM's competitors and customers. It becomes a truism, then, rather than an empirical observation to state, as Hayek does, that the enjoyment of personal success for large numbers depends on rapid progress, while stagnation or decline will lead to deprivation.

Hayek may for all I know be a kindly man personally, but he could not care less, it would seem, about those in the third world who live in deepening poverty in a world dominated by the economic and military might of American capitalism. Human nature being what it is, Hayek writes, "we cannot feel [genuine concern] about the thousands or millions of unfortunates whom we know to exist in the world but whose individual circumstances we do not know."[9] Yet it is a political fact of life that the greater part of mankind "has only just awakened to the possibility of abolishing starvation, filth, and disease ...." What can we do about this ? "Our task must be to continue to lead, to move ahead along the path which so many more are trying to tread in our wake . . . even a small decline in our rate of advance might be fatal to us."[10]

On the issue of social justice the contrast between Hayek's position and mine is extreme. I incorporate the idea of social justice into my concept of freedom, by asserting the primacy of the freedom of the least free. Hayek, as we have seen, limits his conception of injustice to harm done by "the deliberate treatment of men by other men," and thus defines away any notion that contrasts in wealth or standards of living are as such unjust. His concept of justice has as little to do with degrees of human fortune or misery, then, as have his concepts of liberty and coercion. And it is made plausible that we should have as little government planning and indeed as little government as possible, to Hayek's followers at any rate, once the *problem* of social injustice, or justice, has been defined out of existence, almost, and the problem of coercion, or liberty, in effect has been *defined* as involving (mainly) governmental interference in the business world. So narrow is Hayek's conception of "justice," and yet so oblivious is Hayek to the possibility of any merit in alternate concepts of justice, that he is able to say that the principle favouring progressive taxation "cannot be defended on grounds of justice."[11] [pp. 122-123]

NOTES

1. Christian Bay, "Hayek's Liberalism : The Constitution of Perpetual Privilege," *The Political Science Reviewer* 1 (1971) : 110-123.
2. F. A. Hayek, *The Constitution of Liberty* (Chicago : University of Chicago Press, 1960), p. 11.
3. *Ibid.*, p. 12.
4. *Ibid.*, pp. 20-21.
5. *Ibid.*, p. 133.
6. "Bad Blood," a review of Richard M. Titmuss, *The Gift Relationship* (New York, 1971), in *New York Review*, May 20, 1971, p. 8.
7. Hayek, *op. cit.*, p. 57.
8. *Ibid.*, p. 57.
9. *Ibid.*, p. 84.
10. *Ibid.*, pp. 52-53.
11. *Ibid.*, p. 322.

LAW IN MODERN SOCIETY[1]

Roberto M. Unger

An understanding of liberal society illuminates, and is illuminated by, an awareness of that society's legal order and legal ideals. For the rule of law has been truly said to be the soul of the modern state. The study of the legal system takes us straight to the central problems faced by the society itself.

If this hypothesis, which underlies my argument, is correct, then any revision of the nature and uses of law will reveal changes in the basic arrangements of society and in men's conceptions of themselves. At the same time, whatever we can learn about these social changes will help us reinterpret the transformation of the legal order. In this spirit, I discuss on the following pages some aspects of the way certain countries, the Western capitalist social democracies, have become postliberal societies.

The characteristics of these societies undermine the rule of law and they strengthen tendencies in belief and organization that ultimately discourage reliance on public and positive rules as bases of social order. These startling trends will force us to reexamine our view of the situation and the prospects of postliberal societies. For my immediate purposes, it is enough to emphasize two commonly observed sets of features of this novel form of social life.

The first group of features refers to the overt intervention of government in areas previously regarded as beyond the proper reach of state action. The response to the problems of unjustified hierarchy, a response the rule of law failed to provide, is now sought from the government. The rank order itself increasingly moves to the centre of political debate and political action. As the state becomes involved in the tasks of overt redistribution, regulation, and planning, it changes into a welfare state.

The other notable set of attributes of postliberal society is but the reverse side of the events just enumerated : the gradual approximation of state and society, of the public and the private sphere. For one thing, the state's pretense to being a neutral guardian of the social order is abandoned. For another thing, private organizations are increasingly recognized and treated as entities with the kind of power that traditional doctrine viewed as the prerogative of government. People may become more conscious of what was always partly true, though perhaps less so in earlier periods : society consists of a constellation of governments, rather than an association of individuals held together by a single government. The state that has lost both the reality and the consciousness of its separation from society is a corporate state.

Now let us see how these welfare and corporatist tendencies affect the society's normative order.

Welfare state developments influence the legal order of postliberal society in a variety of ways. But two kinds of immediate influence seem particularly significant.

The first type of effect is the rapid expansion of the use of open-ended standards and general clauses in legislation, administration, and adjudication. For example, the courts may be charged to police unconscionable contracts, to void unjust enrichment, to control economic concentration so as to maintain competitive markets, or to determine whether a government agency has acted in the public interest. Such indeterminate prescriptions have always existed in the law, but they grow rapidly in prominence because of the transformations to which I refer.

The second major impact of the welfare state on law is the turn from formalistic to purposive or policy-oriented styles of legal reasoning and from concerns with formal justice to an interest in procedural and substantive justice. Before further discussion, these terms should be defined.

Legal reasoning is formalistic when the mere invocation of rules and the deduction of conclusions from them is believed sufficient for every authoritative legal choice. It is purposive when the decision about how to apply a rule depends on a judgment of how most effectively to achieve the purposes ascribed to the rule. The difference between these two types of legal reasoning is one between the criteria thought appropriate to the overt justification or criticism of official decisions ; it does not pretend to describe the actual causes and motives of decision.

An ideal of justice is formal when it makes the uniform application of general rules the keystone of justice or when it establishes principles whose validity is supposedly independent of choices among conflicting values. It is procedural when it imposes conditions on the legitimacy of the processes by which social advantages are exchanged or distributed. It is substantive when it governs the actual outcome of distributive decisions or of bargains. Thus, in contract law, the doctrine that bargains are enforceable given certain externally visible manifestations of intent exemplifies formal justice ; the demand that there be equality of bargaining power among contracting parties illustrates procedural justice ; and the prohibition of exchanges of two performances of unequal value, however value may be assessed, represents substantive justice.

A formal view of justice requires, to be coherent, a belief in the possibility of formalistic legal reasoning. And it is likely to be most persuasive in the realm of exchanges among individuals rather than in that of governmental distribution, which inevitably involves choices among conflicting interests. Thus, it tends to distinguish sharply between an impersonal justice of reciprocity that dispenses with distributive premises and an arbitrary justice of distribution whose pronouncements are never impartial and general enough to have anything more than the appearance of law.

Procedural or substantive notions of justice become important as purposive forms of legal reasoning are adopted, and they in turn give impetus to those varieties of argument. For policy-oriented legal discourse forces one to make explicit choices among values, and the pursuit of procedural or substantive justice requires that rules be interpreted in terms of ideals that define the conception of justice. Hence, every decision about the principles that govern exchange is seen to rest upon procedural or distributive premises and to have procedural or distributive consequences.

Postliberal society witnesses an escalating use of open-ended standards and a swing toward purposive legal reasoning and procedural or substantive approaches to justice. This is a change of emphasis rather than a sequence of clearly differentiated stages. In few societies have these shifts followed a line of uninterrupted progression. Periods of greater stress on formalistic legal reasoning and formal justice have followed eras of a more policy-oriented mode of legal discourse, as in nineteenth-century America. Even during the hegemony of formalism, there has often been a widespread awareness of the fact that the legal order was redistributing resources among groups and classes. Nevertheless, I shall argue later that present-day tendencies differ from their earlier counterparts not merely because of the more pronounced, persistent, and universal character of the contemporary developments, but, above all, because of the emergence in the welfare-corporate state of a unique relationship among problems of formality, equity, community, and equality in law.

The immediate causes of the postliberal moves toward purposive legal reasoning and procedural or substantive justice are directly connected with the inner dynamic of the welfare state. These moves appear as ways to deal with concentrated power in the private order or to correct the effects of a system of formal rules. As government assumes managerial responsibilities, it must work in areas in which the complexity and variability of relevant factors of decision seem too great to allow for general rules, whence the recourse to vague standards. These standards need to be made concrete and individualized by persons charged with their administrative or judicial execution.

The reasons for the greater emphasis on purposive legal reasoning and on procedural or substantive justice are more obscure and less amenable to a comprehensive interpretation. Changes in the theoretical understanding of language, in the character of common beliefs about the basis and scope of legitimate state action, and in the structure of the rank order all seem to play a part. Language is no longer credited with the fixity of categories and the transparent representation of the world that would make formalism plausible in legal reasoning or in ideas about justice. In the absence of belief in the naturalness of existing hierarchies of power or distribution, the legitimacy of governmental, including judicial, activity comes to depend increasingly on the welfare consequences of that activity. Finally, the vicissitudes of class struggle strip the state of every pretense to impartiality and transform it into an acknowledged tool of factional interest in a social situation in which the dictates of justice are still believed to be unknowable.

Whatever the causes of the trends I have described and however much they may vary from one country to another, their chief effects on the law seem clear. They repeatedly undermine the relative generality and the autonomy that distinguish the legal order from other kinds of law, and in the course of so doing they help discredit the political ideals represented by the rule of law.

Open-ended clauses and general standards force courts and administrative agencies to engage in ad hoc balancings of interest that resist reduction to general rules. One of the corollaries of generality in law is a severe limitation of the range of facts considered relevant to the making of official choices. If the number of pertinent factors of decision is too large, and each of them is constantly shifting, then categories of classification or criteria of analogy will be hard to draw and even harder to maintain. But the kinds of problems to which comprehensive standards characteristically apply tend to defy such limitations. They involve the conflict of numerous and inchoate interests against the background of a refusal to sacrifice any one of these interests completely to the others.

When attempts are made to codify standards, to reduce them to rules, their character is distorted. Either a large area of uncontrolled discretion and individualization subsists under the trappings of general norms, or the flexibility needed to make managerial decisions or to produce equitable results is lost. The same dialectic of illusion and petrification can be observed in the analagous processes by which Roman praetorian law was overtaken by imperial legislation, English equity lost out to common law, and the customary or sacred laws of non-Western societies were codified by colonial administrators.

Purposive legal reasoning and nonformal justice also cause trouble for the ideal of generality. The policy-oriented lawyer insists that part of interpreting a rule is to choose the most efficient means to the attainment of the ends one assigns to it. But as the circumstances to which decisions are addressed change and as the decisionmaker's understanding of the means available to him varies, so must the way he interprets rules. This instability of result will also increase with the fluctuations of accepted policy and with the variability of the particular problems to be resolved. Hence, the very notion of stable areas of individual entitlement and obligation, a notion inseparable from the rule of law ideal, will be eroded.

The quest for substantive justice corrupts legal generality to an even greater degree. When the range of impermissible inequalities among social situations expands, the need for individualized treatment grows correspondingly. No matter how substantive justice is defined, it can be achieved only by treating different situations differently. Thus, for example, it may become necessary to compensate for an existing inequality with a reverse preference afforded by the legal order to the disadvantaged group. Priorities among groups in turn shade imperceptibly into preferences among individuals and individual situations.

The history of the law of obligations and of liability rules in many Western social democracies illustrates another way in which the insistence on substantive justice enters into conflict with established notions of generality. Classic theories of contractual and delictual liability drew a sharp line between the allegedly impersonal justice of reciprocity ; with which they were concerned, and distributive justice, which, if it existed at all, was the province of politics and the marketplace. At the same time, they confined liability to areas of conduct that seemed amenable to general rules and they asserted its absolute character within those confines.

In the era of the welfare state and of policy-oriented legal discourse, there is a firmer recognition that exchange rules do have a distributive significance. Nonetheless, the attempt to take distributive criteria into account in an adjudicative setting unavoidably forces the courts into fields in which the complexity of relevant factors and the lack of widely shared standards of justice make generalization hard to come by and to stick with. The situation is aggravated by the impulse to extend liability, in response to equitable considerations, to areas where the same sorts of problems arise. And the difficulty is compounded still further by the willingness, in criminal as well as in private law, to admit a growing list of exculpatory conditions within this enlarged sphere of liability. For the granting of an excuse turns on judgments about particular persons and individual situations, judgments that resist statement as rules.

The same events that subvert the generality also tend to destroy the relative autonomy of the legal order in its substantive, methodological, institutional, and occupational dimensions.

Overarching standards invite their appliers to make use of the technician's conception of efficiency or the layman's view of justice. If, for example, one seeks to give content to the conception of good faith in contract law, one must go outside the narrow confines of lawyers' learning to consult the practices and enter into the thought patterns of a certain social group.

As purposive legal reasoning and concerns with substantive justice begin to prevail, the style of legal discourse approaches that of commonplace political or economic argument. All are characterized by the predominance of instrumental rationality over other modes of thought. Indeed, policy-oriented legal argument represents an unstable accommodation between the assertion and the abandonment of the autonomy of legal reasoning, just as a procedural justice mediates between formal and substantive justice.

The decline in the distinctiveness of legal reasoning is connected with the need administrators and judges have of reaching out to the substantive ideals of different groups, of drawing upon a conventional morality or a dominant tradition. These changes in the substance and method of law also help undercut the identity of legal institutions and of the legal profession. Courts begin to resemble openly first administrative, then other political institutions. Thus, the difference between lawyers and other bureaucrats or technicians starts to disappear.

The cumulative impact of the movements discussed in the preceding pages is to encourage the dissolution of the rule of law, at least insofar as that form of legality is defined by its commitment to the generality and autonomy of law. To be sure, autonomy and generality could never be meant as completely actualized descriptions of the legal order in liberal society ; they are no more than ideals which the liberal form of social life makes necessary to entertain and impossible to achieve fully. What distinguishes the law of the postliberal period is primarily the turning away from these ideals, a change of course that, despite its apparent insignificance, indicates important shifts in human belief and social order.

The corporatist tendencies of postliberal society have potentially an even more dramatic effect on the law than the welfare state trends. If the latter contribute to the disintegration of the rule of law, the former ultimately challenge the more universal and elementary phenomenon of bureaucratic law, law that is public and positive.

The spearhead of corporatism is the effacement both in organization and in consciousness of the boundary between state and society, and therefore between the public and the private realm. As the state reaches into society, society itself generates institutions that rival the state in their power and take on many attributes formerly associated with public bodies. It is doubtless true that much of the earlier separation of government and society may have been more a matter of vision than of reality. But here one must tread carefully. The images people hold of their social situation are an integral part of those situations ; indeed, they establish their specifically social meaning. Thus, a modest change of emphasis in forms of organization may be important if it is accompanied by a transformation of belief. The corporatist developments, like the welfare state ones mentioned earlier, seem to exemplify this principle.

Corporatism's most obvious influence on the law is its contribution to the growth of a body of rules that break down the traditional distinction between public and private law. Thus, administrative, corporate, and labour law merge into a body of social law that is more applicable to the structure of private-public organizations than to official conduct or private transactions. But though this development undermines the conventional contrast of public and private law, it does not necessarily destroy the broader difference between the law of the state and the internal, privately determined regulations of private associations. Insofar as private law is laid down by the state, it too is, in this more comprehensive sense, public.

The deepest and least understood impact of corporatism is the one it has on the very distinction between the law of the state and the spontaneously produced normative order of nonstate institutions. As private organizations become bureaucraticized in response to the same search for impersonal power that attracts government to the rule of law principle, they begin to acquire the features, and to suffer the problems, of the state. At the same time, the increasing recognition of the power these organizations exercise, in a quasi-public manner, over the lives of their members makes it even harder to maintain the distinction between state action and private conduct. Finally, the social law of institutions is a law compounded of state-authored rules and of privately sponsored regulations or practices ; its two elements are less and less capable of being separated. All these movements, which tend to destroy the public character of law, carry forward a process that begins in the failure of liberal society to keep its promise of concentrating all significant power in government.

The tendency of large corporate organizations to become bureaucratized and to produce a body of rules with many of the characteristics of state law should not be confused with an increasing regulation of the corporation by the state. In fact, quite the opposite may be true : the bureaucratization of corporate institutions may be associated with their ability to become relatively independent power centres with decisive influence over government agencies.

Corporatist tendencies are often associated with demands for the change of public and private organizations into democratic communities. These demands are still usually encountered as ideologies rather than as institutional realities. Nonetheless, they are just as much rooted in the structure of the postliberal order as the rule of law ideal is in the nature of liberal society.

Sometimes the communitarian aspirations are part of a radical attack on the corporate bodies. At other times, they present themselves under the guise of a reformist politics of participation. But whatever their immediate source or objective, they all betray a dissatisfaction with the nature of hierarchy and therefore of personal existence under liberalism. They all attempt to show how the fundamental experience of unjustified power and arbitrary consensus can be dealt with when the rule of law fails to dispose of it. And they all look for an alternative to the ideal of legality in the notion of a community bound together by a shared experience and capable of developing its own self-revising customs or principles of interaction. The profound and irreconcilable differences between rightist and leftist interpretations of the communitarian program have to do with the extent to which they envisage the community as arising from a preservation and strengthening, or from a destruction, of the rank system of liberal society.

An integral part of the search for community in both its conservative and its revolutionary variant is the aim of avoiding the manipulation of social life by imposed rules and of respecting the spontaneously produced internal customs of each communal group. This longing is heralded by the currents in social thought and jurisprudence that emphasize the "living" or "inner" law of associations in contrast to the made rules of the state. What is ultimately at issue is therefore the positive character of law itself : whether or not significant reliance will be placed upon made and articulated rules as opposed to immanent and implicit custom. And behind this conflict of types of law lies a more general antagonism between forms of social life — one for which order is a spontaneous byproduct of interaction ; another for which it represents authority imposed from above or outside. [pp. 192-203]

NOTE

1. R.M. Unger, *Law in Modern Society* (New York : The Free Press, 1976), pp. 192-203.

THE MYTH OF THE STATE[1]

Ernst Cassirer

... The modern politician has had to combine in himself two entirely different and even incompatible functions. He has to act, at the same time, as both a homo magus and a homo faber. He is the priest of a new, entirely irrational and mysterious religion. But when he has to defend and propagate this religion he proceeds very methodically. Nothing is left to chance ; every step is well prepared and premeditated. It is this strange combination that is one of the most striking features of our political myths.

Myth has always been described as the result of an unconscious activity and as a free product of imagination. But here we find myth made according to plan. The new political myths do not grow up freely ; they are not wild fruits of an exuberant imagination. They are artificial things fabricated by very skilful and cunning artisans. It has been reserved for the twentieth century, our own great technical age, to develop a new technique of myth. Henceforth myths can be manufactured in the same sense and according to the same methods as any other modern weapon — as machine guns or airplanes. That is a new thing — and a thing of crucial importance. It has changed the whole form of our social life. It was in 1933 that the political world began to worry somewhat about Germany's rearmament and its possible international repercussions. As a matter of fact this rearmament had begun many years before but had passed almost unnoticed. The real rearmament began with the origin and rise of the political myths. The later military rearmament was only an accessory after the fact. The fact was an accomplished fact long before ; the military rearmament was only the necessary consequence of the mental rearmament brought about by the political myths.

The first step that had to be taken was a change in the function of language. If we study the development of human speech we find that in the history of civilization the word fulfils two entirely different functions. To put it briefly we may term these functions the semantic and the magical use of the word. Even among the so-called primitive languages the semantic function of the word is never missing ; without it there could be no human speech. But in primitive societies the magic word has a predominant and overwhelming influence. It does not describe things or relations of things ; it tries to produce effects and to change the course of nature. This cannot be done without an elaborate magical art. The magician, or sorcerer is alone able to govern the magic word. But in his hands it becomes a most powerful weapon. Nothing can resist its force. "Carmina vel coelox possunt deducere lunam," says the sorceress Madea in Ovid's *Metamorphoses* — by magic songs and incantations even the moon can be dragged down from the heavens.

Curiously enough all this recurs in our modern world. If we study our modern political myths and the use that has been made of them we find in them, to our great surprise, not only a transvaluation of all our ethical values but also a transformation of human speech. The magic word takes precedence of the semantic word. If nowadays I happen to read a German book, published in these last ten years, not a political but a theoretical book, a work dealing with philosophical, historical, or economic problems — I find to my amazement that I no longer understand the German language. New words have been coined ; and even the old ones are used in a new sense ; they have undergone a deep change of meaning. This change of meaning depends upon the fact that those words which formerly were used in a descriptive, logical, or semantic sense, are now used as magic words that are destined to produce certain effects and to stir up certain emotions. Our ordinary words are charged with meanings ; but these new-fangled words are charged with feelings and violent passions.

Not long ago there was published a very interesting little book, *Nazi-Deutsch. A Glossary of Contemporary German Usage.* Its authors are Heinz Paechter, Bertha Hellman, Hedwig Paechter, and Karl O. Paetel. In this book all those new terms which were produced by the Nazi regime were carefully listed, and it is a tremendous list. There seem to be only a few words which have survived the general destruction. The authors made an attempt to translate the new terms into English, but in this regard they were, to my mind, unsuccessful. They were able to give only circumlocutions of the German words and phrases instead of real translations. For unfortunately, or perhaps fortunately, it was impossible to render these words adequately in English. What characterizes them is not so much their content and their objective meaning as the emotional atmosphere which surrounds and envelops them. This atmosphere must be felt ; it cannot be translated nor can it be transferred from one climate of opinion to an entirely different one....

In the last two hundred years our conceptions of the character of savage life, when compared to the life of civilized men, have completely changed. In the eighteenth century Rousseau gave his famous description of savage life and the state of nature. He saw in it a real paradise of simplicity, innocence, and happiness. The savage lived alone in the freshness of his native forest, following his instincts and satisfying his simple desires. He enjoyed the highest good, the good of absolute independence. Unfortunately the progress of anthropological research made during the nineteenth century has completely destroyed this philosophical idyll. Rousseau's description was turned into its very opposite. "The savage," says E. Sidney Hartland in his book, *Primitive Law,*

> is far from being the free and unfettered creature of Rousseau's imagination. On the contrary, he is hemmed in on every side by the customs of his people ; he is bound in the chains of immemorial tradition.... These fetters are accepted by him as a matter of course ; he never seeks to break forth.... To the civilized man the same observations may very often apply ; but the civilized man is too restless, too desirous of change, too eager to question his environment, to remain long in the attitude of acquiescence.[2]

These words were written twenty years ago ; but in the meantime we have learned a new lesson, a lesson that is very humiliating to our human pride. We have learned that modern man, in spite of his restlessness, and perhaps precisely because of his restlessness, has not really surmounted the condition of savage life. When exposed to the same forces, he can easily be thrown back to a state of complete acquiescence. He no longer questions his environment ; he accepts it as a matter of course.

Of all the sad experiences of these last twelve years this is perhaps the most dreadful one. It may be compared to the experience of Odysseus on the island of Circe. But it is even worse. Circe had transformed the friends and companions of Odysseus into various animal shapes. But here are men, men of education and intelligence, honest and upright men who suddenly give up the highest human privilege. They have ceased to be free and personal agents. Performing the same prescribed rites they begin to feel, to think, and to speak in the same way. Their gestures are lively and violent ; yet this is but an artificial, a sham life. In fact they are moved by an external force. They act like marionettes in a puppet show

— and they do not even know that the strings of this show and of man's whole individual and social life, are henceforward pulled by the political leaders.

For the understanding of our problem this is a point of crucial importance. Methods of compulsion and suppression have ever been used in political life. But in most cases these methods aimed at material results. Even the most fearful systems of despotism contented themselves with forcing upon men certain laws of action. They were not concerned with the feelings, judgments, and thoughts of men. It is true that in the great religious struggles the most violent efforts were made not only to rule the actions of men but also their consciousness. But these attempts were bound to fail ; they only strengthened the feeling for religious liberty. Now the modern political myths proceeded in quite a different manner. They did not begin with demanding or prohibiting certain actions. They undertook to change the men, in order to be able to regulate and control their deeds. The political myths acted in the same way as a serpent that tries to paralyze its victims before attacking them. Men fell victims to them without any serious resistance. They were vanquished and subdued before they had realized what actually happened.

The usual means of political oppression would not have sufficed to produce this effect. Even under the hardest political pressure men have not ceased living their own lives. There has always remained a sphere of personal freedom resistant to this pressure. The classical ethical ideas of antiquity maintained and strengthened their force amidst the chaos and the political decay of the ancient world. Seneca lived in the times and at the court of Nero. But this did not prevent him from giving, in his treatises and moral letters, an epitome of the loftiest ideas of Stoic philosophy, ideas of the autonomy of the will and the independence of the wise man. Our modern political myths destroyed all these ideas and ideals before they begin their work. They do not have to fear any opposition from this quarter. In our analysis of Gobineau's book we have studied the methods by which this opposition was broken down. The myth of the race worked like a strong corrosive and succeeded in dissolving and disintegrating all other values.

To understand this process it is necessary to begin with an analysis of the term "freedom." Freedom is one of the most obscure and ambiguous terms not only of philosophical but also of political language. As soon as we begin to speculate about the freedom of the will we find ourselves involved into an inextricable labyrinth of metaphysical questions and antinomies. As to political freedom all of us know that it is one of the most used and abused slogans. All political parties have assured us that they are ever the true representatives and guardians of freedom. But they have always defined the term in their own sense and used it for their particular interests. Ethical freedom is, at bottom, a much simpler thing. It is free from those ambiguities that seem to be unavoidable both in metaphysics and in politics. Men act as free agents not because they possess a *liberum arbitrium indifferentiae.* It is not the absence of a motive but the character of the motives that marks a free action. In the ethical sense a man is a free agent if these motives depend upon his own judgment and own conviction of what moral duty is. According to Kant freedom is equivalent to autonomy. It does not mean "indeterminism," it rather means a special kind of determination. It means that the law which we obey in our actions is not imposed from without but that the moral subject gives this law to itself.

In the exposition of his own theory Kant always warns us against a fundamental misunderstanding. Ethical freedom, he declares, is not a fact but a postulate. It is not *gegeben* but *aufgegeben* ; it is not a gift with which human nature is endowed ; it is rather a task, and the most arduous task that man can set himself. It is no datum, but a demand ; an ethical imperative. To fulfil this demand becomes especially hard in times of a severe and dangerous social crisis when the breakdown of the whole public life seems to be imminent. At these times the individual begins to feel a deep mistrust in his own powers. Freedom is not a natural inheritance of man. In order to possess it we have to create it. If a man were simply to follow his natural instincts he would not strive for freedom ; he would rather choose dependence. Obviously it is much easier to depend upon others than to think, to judge, and to decide for himself. That accounts for the fact that both in individual and in political life freedom is so often regarded much more as a burden than a privilege. Under extremely difficult conditions man tries to cast off this burden. Here the totalitarian state and the political myths step in. The new political parties promise, at least, an escape from the dilemma. They suppress and destroy the very sense of freedom ; but, at the same time, they relieve men from all personal responsibility.

That leads us to another aspect of our problem. In our description of the modern political myths one feature is still missing. As we pointed out, in the totalitarian states the political leaders have had to take charge of all those functions that, in primitive societies, were performed by the magician. They were the absolute rulers ; they were the medicine men who promised to cure all social evils. But that was not enough. In a savage tribe the sorcerer has still another important task. The *homo magus* is, at the same time, the *homo divinans.* He reveals the will of the gods and foretells the future. The soothsayer has his firm place and his indispensable role in primitive social life. Even in highly developed stages of political culture he is still in full possession of his old rights and privileges. In Rome, for instance, no important political decision was ever made, no difficult enterprise was undertaken, no battle was fought without the advice of the augurs and haruspices. When a Roman army was sent out it was always accompanied by its haruspices ; they were an integral part of the military staff.

Even in this respect our modern political life has abruptly returned to forms which seemed to have been entirely forgotten. To be sure, we no longer have the primitive kind of sortilege, the divination by lot ; we no longer observe the flight of birds nor do we inspect the entrails of slain animals. We have developed a much more refined and elaborate method of divination — a method that claims to be scientific and philosophical. But if our methods have changed the thing itself has by no means vanished. Our modern politicians know very well that great masses are much more easily moved by the force of imagination than by sheer physical force. And they have made ample use of this knowledge. The politician becomes a sort of public fortuneteller. Prophecy is an essential element in the new technique of rulership. The most improbable or even impossible promises are made ; the millennium is predicted over and over again.... [pp. 282-289]

Of all human idols the political idols, the idola fori, are the most dangerous and enduring. Since the times of Plato all great thinkers have made the greatest efforts to find a rational theory of politics. The nineteenth century was convinced that it had at last found the right path. In 1830 Auguste Comte published the first volume of his *Cours de philosophie positive.* He began with analyzing the structure of natural science ; he went from astronomy to physics, from physics to chemistry, from chemistry to biology. But according to Comte natural science is only a first step. His real aim and highest ambition was to become the founder of a new social science and to introduce into this science the same exact way of reasoning, the same inductive and deductive method as we find in physics or chemistry.

The sudden rise of the political myths in the twentieth century has shown us that these hopes of Comte and of his pupils and adherents were premature. Politics is still far from being a positive science, let alone an exact science. I have no doubt that later generations will look back at many of our political systems with the same feeling as a modern astronomer studies an astrological book or a modern chemist an alchemistic treatise. In politics we have not yet found firm and reliable ground. Here there seems to be no clearly established cosmic order ; we are always threatened with a sudden relapse into the old chaos. We are building high and proud edifices ; but we forget to make their foundations secure. The belief that man by the skilful use of magic formulae and rites can change the course of nature has prevailed for hundreds and thousands of years in human history. In spite of all the inevitable frustrations and disappointments mankind still clung stubbornly, forcibly, and desperately to this belief. It is, therefore, not to be wondered at that in our political actions and our political thoughts magic still holds its ground. Yet when small groups do try to enforce their wishes and their fantastic ideas upon great nations and the whole body politic, they may succeed for a short time, and they may even achieve great triumphs, but these must remain ephemeral. For there is, after all, a logic of the social world just as there is a logic of the physical world. There are certain laws that cannot be violated with impunity. Even in this sphere we have to follow Bacon's advice. We must learn how to obey the laws of the social world before we can undertake to rule it. [pp. 294-295]

NOTES

1. E. Cassirer, *The Myth of the State* (New Haven and London : Yale University Press, 1946), pp. 282-295.
2. E.G. Hartland, *Primitive Law* (London, Metheun & Co., 1924), p. 138.

PHILOSOPHY AND MYTH IN KARL MARX[1]

Robert Tucker

. . . Truly, Marxism may be seen as Hegelianism inverted. Speaking very broadly, the relation between them may be described as follows : Hegel represents the universe as a subjective process ; Marx, turning the system around, ends up by representing a subjective process as the universe — the social cosmos.

Having arrived at this point, Marx maintained that he had gone beyond philosophy, and in a very significant sense he was right. But beyond to what ? He claimed direct insight into "reality," and on this ground described his own representation of it as real positive science. Now it is quite true that he had an arresting vision of something real. Were this not so, incidentally, Marxism could scarcely have achieved any large influence in the world and drawn followers after the manner of religious movements from time immemorial. But the reality that Marx apprehended and portrayed was *inner reality.* The forces of which he was aware were subjective forces, forces of the alienated human self, conceived, however, and also perceived, as forces abroad in society. Insofar as this determined his thinking, it was not "real positive science" at which he had arrived out of Hegelianism. Instead, he had gone beyond philosophy into that out of which philosophy, ages ago, originated — myth. For this is the decisive characteristic of mythic thought, that something by nature interior is apprehended as exterior, that a drama of the inner life of man is experienced and depicted as taking place in the outer world.

In this modern instance of it, an historic sequence was reversed. Whereas philosophy had once arisen against a background of myth, here myth arose against a background of philosophy — the Hegelian philosophy. A phenomenology of spirit, in which the world was consciously represented as a subjective process of realization of a world-self, became first a new phenomenology in which Marx pictured the world as a process of realization of a human species-self. This was done consciously and without mystification, and original Marxism remained fundamentally on the ground of philosophical thought. At a decisive point in it, however, Marx made the transition to the mythic mode of thought. The subjective process of *Entfremdungsgeschichte* was embodied in an image of society. And Marx went on to elaborate *The Materialist Conception of History* as the doctrinal enclosure of a mythic vision in which the dualism of conflicting forces of the alienated self was apprehended as a dualism of social forces, a class struggle in society, a warfare of labour and capital. From this standpoint it might be said that mature Marxism is mystified original Marxism. The classic vehicle of this mystification is *Capital....* [pp. 118-119]

One of the characteristics of true mythic thinking is that the thinker is not aware of it as mythical. For him it is a revelation of what empirically *is.* The inner process that the myth represents as outer is actually perceived to be taking place in the outer world. It fills the field of mental vision as an overwhelmingly immediate and tangible presentation of external reality. To describe and depict it appears, then, as no more than the true empiricism, and to act in terms of it the utmost realism. So it was with Marx. Now that reality had been grasped, he said, philosophy — speculative thought — had lost its medium of existence. It had given way to "real positive science," which would consist in the transcription of the apprehended reality. The "reality" to which he referred was something that he actually saw in a vision of the kind just described.

What he beheld in the vision was a process or movement, a movement of the social world. In one place he called it "the real historical movement which is turning the world upside down." Elsewhere he described it as a "real social movement which already, in all civilized countries, proclaims the approach of a terrible upheaval." It must be emphasized that he was not using the term "movement" in the sense meant when we speak, for example, of communism as a world-wide movement. He was not referring to any such circumscribed sociopolitical fact as an organized mass movement of people to gain certain objectives. He was speaking of the process projected in *Capital,* the movement of a class-divided society to the final point of crisis and convulsion at which the Collective Worker would rise up in awful wrath and destroy My Lord Capital.

It was a visible presence before his mind. This is reflected in his continual references to it as a movement taking place "under our very eyes." The frequency with which this expression appears in his writings after 1844 is remarkable. In the *Manifesto* he speaks of "a historical movement going on under our very eyes." In *The Poverty of Philosophy* he says that socialists need not concern themselves with devising programmes for the future, but "have only to give an account of what passes before their eyes and to make of that their medium." Again, in *Herr Vogt* he writes that it "is not a matter of bringing some utopian system or other into being but of consciously participating in the historical revolutionary process of society which is taking place before our very eyes."

So overpoweringingly vivid and compelling was Marx's vision of the "real social movement" that he feared the final upheaval would come before he had completed the grand demonstration of it in *Capital.* "I am working like mad all through the nights at putting my economic studies together so that I may at least have the outlines clear before the deluge comes," Marx asserted to Engels on 8 December 1857. He was working like mad to forestall the world cataclysm with his book about it. He was afraid that the world would turn upside down before he had shown how and why it would happen. In a letter written in 1858, he said: "I have a presentiment that now, when after fifteen years of study I have got far enough to have the thing within my grasp, stormy movements from without will probably interfere. Never mind. If I get finished so late that I no longer find the world ready to pay attention to such things, the fault will obviously be my own." These statements, written in the relatively tranquil 1850's, tell little about the actual social world of Europe at that time. They reveal a great deal, however, about the inner world that Marx apprehended as outer. [pp. 224-225]

None of what has been said here is meant to deny that Marx's vision corresponds to certain socio-economic actualities of his time and after. Were that not so, it would be very hard to explain why the *Weltanschauung* of the *Communist Manifesto* and *Capital* has seemed to many people in different times and places to be relevant to social reality as given in their experience. In speaking of Marx's "myth of the warfare of labour and capital," I am not at all suggesting that there have been no class antagonisms in modern society, that strife between wage workers and capitalist employers is some sort of chimera. Manifestly, these things are facts of social history and contemporary life. Capital and labour have fought their battles in various forms and at different levels of intensity in all industrial societies. The argument of these pages is not that warfare between labour and capital is *per se* a myth, or that *Capital* lacked any meaningful resemblance to the society it purported to describe. It is, rather, that Marx projected upon the real conflicts of that society a conflict out of the inner life of man. His representation of this conflict was shaped by the whole preceding development of German philosophy as we have traced it and also, presumably, by his own experience as a person beset by acute inner conflict and tending unconsciously to seek some solution, such as by projection. The mythic quality of the resulting portrayal of capitalist society is more clearly seen in its dramatic character....

For the mythic thinker there is no problem of conduct in the sense in which the moral philosopher understands it. There is, in other words, no question of what manner of life is best for man to lead and why, and consequently no search for an ethical principle of conduct as the solution of the question. The proper and worthy mode of conduct is as overwhelmingly plain as the reality luminously present before his mind in the myth. The answer to the question as to what should be done is given in the vision of what is happening in the world.

This, as suggested above, is a vision of the inner as outer. A drama of the inner life of man is externalized and experienced as taking place in the outer world. The conflict of good and evil forces of the self, its constructive and destructive powers, appears to be resolving itself externally. For Marx the outer reality is social reality, and the conflict appears as a war of classes into which society has split. The contending forces of good and evil are respectively the productive powers, lodged in the proletariat, and the inhuman force of capital incarnate in the bourgeoisie, which is the collective *Personafikation des Kapitals* (to use Marx's own phrase).

Why the problem of conduct is resolved in the mythic vision itself, resolved without ever arising as a subject of inquiry, is obvious. The thinker himself is intensely involved in the drama that appears to be taking place in the world outside him. Were this not so, he would never have engaged in the myth-making act in the first place. Once he has done so, however, his involvement becomes an involvement in what is now apprehended as a world-conflict. The moral drama of the self has its locus for him in the movement of the world wherein it appears writ large. The whole world, or alternatively the world of society, has become the battlefield on which the war of the self is being waged, on which the good forces are fighting for their life against the evil ones. Since it is *his* conflict that is being enacted out there, the thinker naturally feels impelled to do his part, help the good forces along, urge them to battle, cheer their victories, bemoan their setbacks, and in general give them all manner of active support. He wants to join the fray, and bids others to do the same. The point is to *participate* in the action already going on, as he sees it, outside him.

This is the special logic (or "psycho-logic") of mythic thinking as it relates to practical action. The answer to the question as to what should be done is given in the mythic vision itself, and can be summed up in a single word : "Participate !" In so far as the mythic thinker gives any recognition at all to the problem of conduct, he answers immediately, emphatically and categorically in this vein. So Marx, as noted above, says that it is not a matter of bringing some utopian system or other into being (i.e., of defining a social goal and purposefully endeavouring to realize it) but simply of "consciously participating in the historical revolutionary process of society which is taking place before our very eyes." Here the participation takes the form of "revolutionary praxis." To engage in practical revolutionary action on the side of the proletariat is to promote, help along and accelerate the "real historical movement which is turning the world upside down." Moreover, since the theory of revolution is simply the "literary expression" of this movement, revolutionary praxis is the conscious enactment of the theory, and Marx is convinced that all "theoretical" problems have their solution in social praxis. This is his celebrated doctrine of the unity of theory and practice. Not pragmatism but mysticism is its foundation.

If the projection of an inner moral drama upon the outer world is the essence of myth, the urge and injunction to "participate" is the origin of ritual. Later the ritual activity may come to be performed as a merely symbolic reenactment of the events recounted in the mythic narrative. But it is not so in the beginning. Originally the call to participate expresses the mythic thinker's passionate felt need to accelerate the ongoing drama of events as he expereiences it in the vision. This imperative of participation is categorical. The mythic thinker cannot or will not reason with you about it. All he can do is to point to the world and say : "Can't you *see* what is happening ?" He knows that if you *do* see, you will, just as he does, act accordingly. Therefore, his supreme concern is just to make everybody see what is going on under their eyes, to communicate the vision in an image of the world-process, e.g., a *Capital*. This, he may feel, is the most effective way in which he himself can actively participate.

Thus, Marx sees his paramount practical task as that of making the good forces more fully conscious of the nature, conditions, and prospects of the conflict, more clearly aware of the total evilness of the evil forces against which they are pitted, more cognizant of the utter hopelessness of any compromise solution in terms of justice, which would imply a delimitation of mutual claims and a cessation of hostilities. He wants everybody on his side to understand that there is no substitute for unconditional victory of the good forces and total defeat of the evil ones. Anyone who takes the idea of justice at all seriously (Proudhon, for example) becomes the butt of his bitter abuse and invective. Further, he wants to buoy the good forces up with firm confidence in their ultimate triumph, and so concludes the *Communist Manifesto* by telling the proletariat that is has nothing to lose but its chains and a world to win. He wants to organize and direct these forces, to provide generalship for them in the ongoing conflict and impending final battle, and so helps found an International Workingmen's Association and immerses himself in the practical politics of world revolution. For it is "the practical and violent action of the masses alone by which these conflicts can be resolved." Only by a mass revolutionary praxis that consummates the historical movement of the world can the war of the self be won. For Marx, then, the active promotion of the inevitable found its rationale in the idea of shortening the "birth pangs" of a new state of the world that in turn meant to him a new *state of self*. And siding with the proletariat meant siding with the force in the world that was fighting *his war*. For him the proletariat remained always what he had once called it, the material weapon of philosophy or reality striving toward thought. But this was *his* thought.

The immense distance of the standpoint of the mythic consciousness from that of moral philosophy as an activity of free critical inquiry into values is perfectly plain. Not only are they far apart ; they are irreconcilably in conflict. Presupposing as it does a suspension of commitment in the matter of what is good and what is evil, moral philosophy *per se* bespeaks — the visionary Marx — a perverse blindness to what is happening in the world. No one who saw what he sees could possibly consider the problem of conduct to be intellectually problematic. Hence the very idea of moral philosophy became anathema to Marx. He could not abide it and displayed towards it an attitude of utter contempt. His cardinal concern, as a totally committed mythic thinker, was simply to elaborate the vision, to make others see what he saw. He knew that if he could only make them more "conscious" of it, then they too — or many of them — would participate more actively. There was no question whatever of propounding some normative principle of life and conduct. What Marx produced, therefore, in *Capital* was not a book of ethics but a book of revelation. As such, however, this bible of Marxism, as it is justly called, is moralistic from beginning to end.

Marx's mythic vision of the world movement died with him, although he attempted to perpetuate it in writings that were to become sacred texts of real social movements carrying on in his name. The story of the different interpretations of its meaning which have arisen within these movements would be the subject of an independent study. Suffice it to say that Marx's myth of the warfare of labour and capital has meant many things to many people. Some of the followers, contrary to all Marx's explicit statements on this point, assumed that the moral message had to do with justice and injustice. Others understood in various ways that it had to do with freedom and bondage. Finally, some among the literal-minded intellectuals of the movement, especially at the close of the nineteenth century, assumed that there was no moral theme in it at all. This is understandable when we consider that Marx offered the myth as real positive science, and economic science at that, and accompanied the statements of it with the most emphatic disclaimers of ethical purport.... [pp. 227-232]

NOTE

1. Robert Tucker, *Philosophy and Myth in Karl Marx,* 2nd ed. (Cambridge : Cambridge University Press, 1972), pp. 218-232.

A SEASON IN HELL[1]

George Steiner

The Books of the Prophets and the Sermon on the Mount and parables of Jesus which are so closely related to the prophetic idiom, constitute an unequaled act of moral demand. Because the words are so familiar, yet too great for ready use, we tend to forget or merely conventionalize the extremity of their call. Only he who loses his life, in the fullest sense of sacrificial self-denial, shall find life. The kingdom is for the naked, for those who have willingly stripped themselves of every belonging, of every sheltering egoism. There is no salvation in the middle places. For the true disciple of the prophets and of Jesus, the utmost ethical commitment is like common breath. To become man, man must make himself new, and in so doing stifle the elemental desires, weaknesses, and claims of the ego. Only he who can say with Pascal, "le moi est haïssable," has even begun to obey the Gospel's altruistic imperative.

That imperative was stated and restated innumerable times in the course of Western history. It is the staple of Christian ethics, of the Christian doctrine of right living. How many could hope to respond adequately ? In how many human careers were these prescripts of ascetic love, of compassion, of self-suppression, more than a Sunday tag ? Apologetics of practical life, the prodigal economics of repentance, and a "fresh start," papered over the deep cracks between secular existence and the eschatological demand. But the cracks would not mend. They opened explosively in the individual conscience (of Pascal, of Kierkegaard, of Dostoevski). By their simple presence, at every occasion of Christian worship, these fantastic moral requirements mock and undermine mundane values. They set anarchic love against reason, an end of time against history.

The result of this incessant dialectic was a profound unbalance at the pivot of Western culture, a corrosive pressure on the subconscious. Once again, as with abstract monotheism, men had enforced upon them ideals, norms of conduct, out of all natural grasp. And again, these challenges to perfection continued to weigh on individual lives, on social systems, in which they could not be honestly met.

The third confrontation between exigent utopia and the common pulse of Western life occurs with the rise of messianic socialism. Even where it proclaims itself to be atheist, the socialism of Marx, of Trotsky, of Ernst Bloch, is directly rooted in messianic eschatology. Nothing is more religious, nothing is closer to the ecstatic rage for justice in the prophets, than the socialist vision of the destruction of the bourgeois Gomorrah and the creation of a new, clean city for man. In their very language Marx's 1844 manuscripts are steeped in the tradition of messianic promise. In an astounding passage Marx seems to paraphrase the vision of Isaiah and of primitive Christianity : "Assume *man* to be *man* and his relationship to the world to be a human one : then you can exchange love only for love, trust for trust." When human exploitation is eradicated, the grime shall be scoured from the tired earth, and the world made a garden once more. This is the socialist dream and millenary bargain. For it generations have died. In its name falsehood and oppression have spread over a good deal of the earth. But the dream remains magnetic. It cries out to man to renounce profit and selfishness, to melt his personal being into that of the community. It demands that he break down the blackened walls of history, that he leap out of the shadow of his petty needs. Those who resist the dream are not only madmen and enemies of society ; they betray the part of light in their own humnaity. The god of utopia is a jealous god.

Monotheism at Sinai, primitive Christianity, messianic socialism : these are the three supreme moments in which Western culture is presented with what Ibsen termed "the claims of the ideal." These are the three stages, profoundly interrelated, through which Western consciousness is forced to experience the blackmail of transcendence. "Surmount yourself. Surpass the opaque barriers of the mind to attain pure abstraction. Lose your life in order to gain it. Give up property, rank, wordly comfort. Love your neighbor as you do yourself — no, much more, for self-love is sin. Make any sacrifice, endure any insult, even self-denunciation, so that justice may prevail." Unceasingly, the blackmail of perfection has hammered at the confused, mundane, egotistical fabric of common, instinctual behaviour. Like a shrilling note in the inner ear. Men are neither saints nor ascetics ; their imaginings are gross ; ordinarily, their sense of the future is the next milestone. But the insistence of the ideal continued, with a terrible, tactless force.

Three times it sounded from the same historical center. (Some political scientists put at roughly 80 percent the proportion of Jews in the ideological development of messianic socialism and communism.) Three times, Judaism produced a summons to perfection and sought to impose it on the current and currency of Western life. Deep loathing built up in the social subconscious, murderous resentments. The mechanism is simple but primordial. *We hate most those who hold out to us a goal, an ideal, a visionary promise which, even though we have stretched our muscles to the utmost, we cannot reach, which slips, again and again, just out of range of our racked fingers — yet, and this is crucial, which remains profoundly desirable, which we cannot reject because we fully acknowledge its surpreme value.* In his exasperating "strangeness," in his acceptance of suffering as part of a covenant with the absolute, the Jew became, as it were, the "bad conscience" of Western history. In him the abandonments of spiritual and moral perfection, the hypocrisies of an established, mundane religiosity, the Absences of a disappointed, potentially vengeful God, were kept alive and visible.

When it turned on the Jew, Christianity and European civilization turned on the incarnation — albeit an incarnation often wayward and unaware — of its own best hopes. It is something like this that Kafka meant in his arrogant humble assertion that "he who strikes a Jew strikes down man/mankind" (*den Menschen*). In the holocaust there was both a lunatic retribution, a lashing out against intolerable pressures of vision, and large measure of self-mutilation. The secular, materialist, warlike community of modern Europe sought to extirpate from itself, from its own inheritance, archaic, now ridiculously obsolete, but somehow inextinguishable carriers of the ideal. In the Nazi idiom of "vermin" and "sanitation" there is a brusque insight into the infectious nature of morality. Kill the remembrancer, the claim agent, and you will have canceled the long debt.

The genocide that took place in Europe and the Soviet Union during the period 1936-45 (Soviet anti-Semitism being perhaps the most paradoxical expression of the hatred which reality feels towards failed utopia) was far more than a political tactic, an eruption of lower-middle-class malaise, or a product of declining capitalism. It was no mere secular, socioeconomic phenomenon. It enacted a suicidal impulse in Western civilization. It was an attempt to level the future — or, more precisely, to make history commensurate with the natural savageries, intellectual torpor, and material instincts of unextended man. Using theological metaphors, and there is no need to apologize for them in an essay on culture, the holocaust may be said to mark a second Fall. We can interpret it as a voluntary exit from the Garden and a programmatic attempt to burn the Garden behind us. Lest its remembrance continue to infect the health of barbarism with debilitating dreams or with remorse.

With the botched attempt to kill God and the very nearly successful attempt to kill those who had "invented" Him, civilization entered, precisely as Nietzche had foretold, "on night and more night."

By the mid-1760's, after the *affaire Calas,* Voltaire and his informed contemporaries expressed the confident belief that torture and other bestialities practiced on subjects or enemies were passing forever from civilized society. Like the Black Death and the burning of witches, these somber atavisms from primitive and prerational ages would not survive the new temper of European enlightenment....

Today, exactly two hundred years later, we find ourselves in a culture in which the methodical use of torture towards political ends is widely established. We come immediately after a stage of history in which millions of men, women, and children were made to ash. Currently, in different parts of the earth, communities are again being incinerated, tortured, deported. There is hardly a methodology of abjection and of pain which is not being applied somewhere, at this moment, to individuals and groups of human beings. Asked why he was seeking to arouse the whole of Europe over the judicial torture of one man, Voltaire answered, in March 1762, "c'est que je suis homme." By that token, he would, today, be in constant and vain cry.

That this should be the case is catastrophic. The widescale reversion to torture and mass murder, the ubiquitous use of hunger and imprisonment as political means mark not only a crisis of culture but, quite conceivably, an abandonment of the rational order of man. It may well be that it is a mere fatuity, an indecency to debate of the definition of culture in the age of the gas oven, of the arctic camps, of napalm. The topic may belong solely to the past history of hope. But we should not take this contigency to be a natural fact of life, a platitude. We must keep in sharp focus its hideous novelty or renovation. We must keep vital in ourselves a sense of scandal so overwhelming that it affects every significant aspect of our position in history and society. We have, as Emily Dickinson would have said, to keep the soul terribly surprised. I cannot stress this enough. To Voltaire and Diderot the bestial climate of our national and social conflicts would have seemed a lunatic return to barbarism. To most intelligent men and women of the nineteenth century a prediction that torture and massacre were soon to be endemic again in "civilized" Europe would have seemed a nightmarish joke. There is nothing *natural* about our present condition. There is no self-evident logic or dignity in our current knowledge that "anything is possible." In fact, such knowledge corrupts and lowers the threshold of outrage (only Kierkegaard foresaw both the inchoate possibility and the corruption). The numb prodigality of our acquaintance with horror is a radical human defeat.

How did this defeat come about ? The subject is not only an ugly one ; it bristles with philosophic traps. [pp. 42-47]

It is to the ambiguous afterlife of religious feeling in Western culture that we must look, to the malignant energies released by the decay of natural religious forms.

We know from the plans of those who built them and from the testimony inmates, that the death camps constituted a complete, coherent world. They had their own measure of time, which is pain. The unbearable was parceled out with pedantic nicety. The obscenities and abjections practiced in them were accompanied by prescribed rituals of derision and false promise. There were regulated gradations of horror within the total, concentric sphere. *L'univers concentrationnaire* has no true counterpart in the secular mode. Its analogue is Hell. The camp embodies, often down to minutiae, the images and chronicles of Hell in European art and thought from the twelfth to the eighteenth centuries. It is these representations which gave to the deranged horrors of Belsen a kind of "expected logic." The material realities of the inhuman are detailed, endlessly, in Western iconography, from the mosaics at Torcello to the panels of Bosch ; they are prepared for from the fourteenth-century Harrowings of Hell to *Faust*. It is in the fantasies of the infernal, as they literally haunt Western sensibility, that we find the technology of pain without meaning, of bestiality without end, of gratuitous terror. For six hundred years the imagination dwelt on the flaying, the racking, the mockery of the damned, in a place of whips and hellhounds, of ovens and stinking air.

The literature of the camps is extensive. But nothing in it equals the fullness of Dante's observations. Having no personal experience of the *Arschloch der Welt* — that hideously exact and allegoric German term for Auschwitz and Treblinka — I can make only approximate sense of many of Dante's notations. But whoever can grasp, in canto 33 of the *Inferno*", the full meaning of

> The very weeping there forbids to weep,/And grief finding eyes blocked with tears/Turns inward to make agony greater.

will, I believe, have grasped the ontological form of the camp world. The concentration and death camps of the twentieth century, wherever they exist, under whatever regime, are *Hell made immanent.* They are the transference of Hell from below the earth to its surface. They are the deliberate enactment of a long, precise imagining. Because it imagined more fully than any other text, because it argued the centrality of Hell in the Western order, the *Commedia* remains our literal guidebook — to the flames, to the ice fields, to the meat hooks. In the camps the millenary pornography of fear and vengeance cultivated in the Western mind by Christian doctrines of damnation was realized....

In our current barbarism an extinct theology is at work, a body of transcendent reference whose slow, incomplete death has produced surrogate, parodistic forms. The epilogue to belief, the passage of religious belief into hollow convention, seems to be a more dangerous process than the *philosophes* anticipated. The structures of decay are toxic. Needing Hell, we have learned how to build and run it on earth. A few miles from Goethe's Weimar or on the isles of Greece. No skill holds greater menace. Because we have it and are using it on ourselves, we are now in a *post-culture*. In locating Hell above ground, we have passed out of the major order and symmetries of Western civilization. [pp. 53-56]

NOTE

1. George Steiner, *In Bluebeard's Castle : Some Notes Towards the Redefinition of Culture* (New Haven : Yale University Press, 1971), pp. 42-56.

ESCAPE FROM FREEDOM[1]

Erich Fromm

FREEDOM : A PSYCHOLOGICAL PROBLEM ?

Modern European and American history is centred around the effort to gain freedom from the political, economic, and spiritual shackles that have bound men. The battles for freedom were fought by the oppressed, those who wanted new liberties, against those who had privileges to defend. While a class was fighting for its own liberation from domination, it believed itself to be fighting for human freedom as such and thus was able to appeal to an ideal, to the longing for freedom rooted in all who are oppressed. In the long and virtually continuous battle for freedom however, classes that were fighting against oppression at one stage sided with the enemies of freedom when victory was won and new privileges were to be defended.

Despite many reverses, freedom has won battles. Many died in those battles in the conviction that to die in the struggle against oppression was better than to live without freedom. Such a death was the utmost assertion of their individuality. History seemed to be proving that it was possible for man to govern himself, to make decisions for himself, and to think and feel as he saw fit. The full expression of man's potentialities seemed to be the goal toward which social development was rapidly approaching. The principles of economic liberalism, political democracy, religious autonomy, and individualism in personal life, gave expression to the longing for freedom, and at the same time seemed to bring mankind nearer to its realization. One tie after another was severed. Man had overthrown the domination of nature and made himself her master ; he had overthrown the domination of the church and the domination of the absolutist state. The *aboli-*

tion of external domination seemed to be not only a necessary but also a sufficent condition to attain the cherished goal : freedom of the individual.

The World War was regarded by many as the final struggle and its conclusion the ultimate victory for freedom. Existing demorcracies appeared strengthened, and new ones replaced old monarchies. But only a few years elapsed before new systems emerged which denied everything that men believed they had won in centuries of struggle. For the essence of these new systems, which effectively took command of man's entire social and personal life, was the submission of all but a handful of men to an authority over which they had no control.

At first many found comfort in the thought that the victory of the authoritarian system was due to the madness of a few individuals and that their madness would lead to their downfall in due time. Others smugly believed that the Italian people, or the Germans, were lacking in a sufficiently long period of training in democracy, and that therefore one could wait complacently until they had reached the political maturity of the Western democracies. Another common illusion, perhaps the most dangerous of all, was that men like Hitler had gained power over the vast apparatus of the state through nothing but cunning and trickery, that they and their satellites ruled merely by sheer force ; that the whole population was only the will-less object of betrayal and terror.

In the years that have elapsed since, the fallacy of these arguments has become apparent. We have been compelled to recognize that millions in Germany were as eager to surrender their freedom as their fathers were to fight for it ; that instead of wanting freedom, they sought for ways of escape from it ; that other millions were indifferent and did not believe the defence of freedom to be worth fighting and dying for. We also recognize that the crisis of democracy is not a peculiarly Italian or German problem, but one confronting every modern state. Nor does it matter which symbols the enemies of human freedom choose : freedom is not less endangered if attacked in the name of anti-Fascism or in that of outright Fascism. This truth has been so forcefully formulated by John Dewey that I express the thought in his words : "The serious threat to our democracy," he says, "is not the existence of foreign totalitarian states. It is the existence within our own personal attitudes and within our own institutions of conditions which have given a victory to external authority, discipline, uniformity and dependence upon The Leader in foreign countries. The battlefield is also accordingly here — within ourselves and our institutions...."[2]

In addition to the problem of the economic and social conditions which have given rise to Fascism, there is a human problem which needs to be understood.... These are the outstanding questions that arise when we look at the human aspect of freedom, the longing for submission, and the lust for power : What is freedom as a human experience ? Is the desire for freedom something inherent in human nature ? Is it an identical experience regardless of what kind of culture a person lives in, or it is something different according to the degree of individualism reached in a particular society ? Is freedom only the absence of external pressure or is it also the *presence* of something — and if so, of what ? What are the social and economic factors in society that make for the striving for freedom ? Can freedom become a burden, too heavy for man to bear, something he tries to escape from ? Why then is it that freedom is for many a cherished goal and for others a threat ?

Is there not also, perhaps, besides an innate desire for freedom, an instinctive wish for submission ? If there is not, how can we account for the attraction which submission to a leader has for so many today ? Is submission always to an overt authority, or is there also submission to internalized authorities, such as duty or conscience, to inner compulsions or to anonymous authorities like public opinion ? Is there a hidden satisfaction in submitting, and what is its essence ?

What is it that creates in men an insatiable lust for power ? Is it the strength of their vital energy — or is it a fundamental weakness and inability to experience life spontaneously and lovingly ? What are the psychological conditions that make for the strength of these strivings ? What are the social conditions upon which such psychological conditions in turn are based ?

Analysis of the human aspect of freedom and of authoritarianism forces us to consider a general problem, namely, that of the role which psychological factors play as active forces in the social process ; and this eventually leads to the problem of the interaction of psychological, economic, and ideological factors in the social process. Any attempt to understand the attraction which Fascism exercises upon great nations compels us to recognize the role of psychological factors. For we are dealing here with a political system which, essentially, does not appeal to rational forces of self-interest, but which arouses and mobilizes diabolical forces in man which we had believed to be nonexistent, or at least to have died out long ago. The familiar picture of man in the last centuries was one of a rational being whose actions were determined by his self-interest and the ability to act according to it. Even writers like Hobbes, who recognized lust for power and hostility as driving forces in man, explained the existence of these forces as a logical result of self-interest : since men are equal and thus have the same wish for happiness, and since there is not enough wealth to satisfy them all to the same extent, they necessarily fight against each other and want power to secure the future enjoyment of what they have at present. But Hobbes's picture became outmoded. The more the middle class succeeded in breaking down the power of the former political or religious rulers, the more men succeeded in mastering nature, and the more millions of individuals became economically independent, the more did one come to believe in a rational world and in man as an essentially rational being. The dark and diabolical forces of man's nature were relegated to the Middle Ages and to still earlier periods of history, and they were explained by lack of knowledge or by the cunning schemes of deceitful kings and priests.

One looked back upon these periods as one might at a volcano which for a long time has ceased to be a menance. One felt secure and confident that the achievements of modern democracy had wiped out all sinister forces ; the world looked bright and safe like the well-lit streets of a modern city. Wars were supposed to be the last relics of older times and one needed just one more war to end war ; economic crises were supposed to be accidents, even though these accidents continued to happen with a certain regularity.

When Fascism came into power, most people were unprepared, both theoretically and practically. They were unable to believe that man could exhibit such propensities for evil, such lust for power, such disregard for the rights of the weak, or such yearning for submission. Only a few had been aware of the rumbling of the volcano preceding the outbreak. Nietzsche had disturbed the complacent optimism of the nineteenth century ; so had Marx in a different way.

Another warning had come somewhat later from Freud. To be sure, he and most of his disciples had only a very naive notion of what goes on in society, and most of his applications of psychology to social problems were misleading constructions; yet, by devoting his interest to the phenomena of individual emotional and mental disturbances, he led us to the top of the volcano and made us look into the boiling crater.

Freud went further than anybody before him in directing attention to the observation and analysis of the irrational and unconscious forces which determine parts of human behaviour. He and his followers in modern psychology not only uncovered the irrational and unconscious sector of man's nature, the existence of which had been neglected by modern rationalism; he also showed that these irrational phenomena followed certain laws and therefore could be understood rationally. He taught us to understand the language of dreams and somatic symptoms as well as the irrationalities in human behaviour. He discovered that these irrationalities as well as the whole character structure of an individual were reactions to the influences exercised by the outside world and particularly by those occurring in early childhood....[pp. 17-24]

The social history of man started with his emerging from a state of oneness with the natural world to an awareness of himself as an entity separate from surrounding nature and men. Yet this awareness remained very dim over long periods of history. The individual continued to be closely tied to the natural and social world from which he emerged; while being partly aware of himself as a separate entity, he felt also part of the world around him. The growing process of the emergence of the individual from his original ties, a process which we may call "individuation," seems to have reached its peak in modern history in the centuries between the Reformation and the present.

In the life history of an individual we find the same process. A child is born when it is no longer one with its mother and becomes a biological entity separate from her. Yet, while this biological separation is the beginning of individual human existence, the child remains functionally one with its mother for a considerable period.

To the degree to which the individual, figuratively speaking, has not yet completely severed the umbilical cord which fastens him to the outside world, he lacks freedom; but these ties give him security and a feeling of belonging and of being rooted somewhere. I wish to call these ties that exist before the process of individuation has resulted in the complete emergence of an individual "primary ties." They are organic in the sense that they are a part of normal human development; they imply a lack of individuality, but they also give security and orientation to the individual. They are the ties that connect the child with its mother, the member of a primitive community with his clan and nature, or the medieval man with the church and his social caste. Once the stage of complete individuation is reached and the individual is free from these primary ties, he is confronted with a new task : to orient and root himself in the world and to find security in other ways than those which were characteristic of his preindividualistic existence. Freedom then has a different meaning from the one it had before this stage of evolution is reached. It is necessary to stop here and to clarify these concepts by discussing them more concretely in connection with individual and social development.

The comparatively sudden change from foetal into human existence and the cutting off of the umbilical cord mark the independence of the infant from the mother's body. But this independence is only real in the crude sense of the separation of the two bodies. In a functional sense, the infant remains part of the mother. It is fed, carried, and taken care of in every vital respect by the mother. Slowly the child comes to regard the mother and other objects as entities apart from itself. One factor in this process is the neurological and the general physical development of the child, its ability to grasp objects — physically and mentally — and to master them. Through its own activity it experiences a world outside of itself. The process of individuation is furthered by that of education. This process entails a number of frustrations and prohibitions, which change the role of the mother into that of a person with different aims which conflict with the child's wishes, and often into that of a hostile and dangerous person. This antagonism, which is one part of the educational process though by no means the whole, is an important factor in sharpening the distinction between the "I" and the "thou."

A few months elapse after birth before the child even recognizes another person as such and is able to react with a smile, and it is years before the child ceases to confuse itself with the universe. Until then it shows the particular kind of egocentricity typical of children, an egocentricity which does not exclude tenderness for and interest in others, since "others" are not yet definitely experienced as really separate from itself. For the same reason the child's learning on authority in these first years has also a different meaning from the learning on authority later on. The parents, or whoever the authority may be, are not yet regarded as being a fundamentally separate entity ; they are part of the child's universe, and this universe is still part of the child ; submission to them, therefore, has a difference quality from the kind of submission that exists once two individuals have become really separate.

A remarkably keen description of a ten-year-old child's sudden awareness of its own individuality is given by R. Hughes in *A High Wind in Jamaica :*

> And then an event did occur, to Emily, of considerable importance, She suddenly realized who she was. There is little reason that one can see why it should not have happened to her five years earlier, or even five years later ; and none, why it should have come that particular afternoon. She had been playing house in a nook right in the bows, behind the windlass (on which she had hung a devil's-claw as a door knocker) ; and tiring of it was walking rather aimlessly aft, thinking vaguely about some bees and a fairy queen, when it suddenly flashed into her mind that she was she. She stopped dead, and began looking over all of her person which came within the range of her eyes. She could not see much, except a fore-shortened view of the front of her frock, and her hands when she lifted them for inspection ; but it was enough for her to form a rough idea of the little body she suddently realized to be hers.
>
> She began to laugh, rather mockingly. "Well !" she thought, in effect : "Fancy you, of all people, going and getting caught like this !— You can't get out of it now, not for a very long time : you'll have to go through with being a child, and growing up, and getting old, before you'll quit of this mad prank !
>
> Determined to avoid any interruption of this highly important occasion, she began to climb the ratlines, on her way to her favourite perch at the masthead. Each time she moved an arm or a leg in this simple action, however, it struct her with fresh amazement to find them obeying her so readily. Memory told her, of course, that

> they had always done so before : but before, she had never realized how surprising this was. Once settled on her perch, she began examining the skin of her hands with the utmost care : for it was hers. She slipped a shoulder out of the top of her frock ; and having peeped in to make sure she really was continuous under her clothes, she shrugged it up to touch her cheek. The contact of her face and the warm bare hollow of her shoulder gave her a comfortable thrill, as if it was the caress of some kind friend. But whether her feeling came to her through her cheek or her shoulder, which was the caresser and which the caressed, that no analysis could tell her.
>
> Once fully convinced of this astonishing fact, that she was now Emily Bas-Thornton (why she inserted the "now" she did not know, for she certainly imagined no transmigrational nonsense of having been anyone else before), she began seriously to reckon its implications.

The more the child grows and to the extent to which primary ties are cut off, the more it develops a quest for freedom and independence. But the fate of this quest can only be fully understood if we realize the dialectic quality in this process of growing individuation.

This process has two aspects : one is that the child grows stronger physically, emotionally, and mentally. In each of these spheres intensity and activity grow. At the same time, these spheres become more and more integrated. An organized structure guided by the individual's will and reason develops. If we call this organized and integrated whole of the personality the self, we can also say that the *one side of the growing process of individuation is the growth of self-strength.* The limits of the growth of individuation and the self are set, partly by individual conditions, but essentially by social conditions. For although the differences between individuals in this respect appear to be great, every society is characterized by a certain level of individuation beyond which the normal individual cannot go.

The other aspect of the process of individuation is *growing aloneness.* The primary ties offer security and basic unity with the world outside of oneself. To the extent to which the child emerges from that world it becomes aware of being alone, of being an entity separate from all others. This separation from a world, which in comparison with one's own individual existence is overwhelmingly strong and powerful, and often threatening and dangerous, creates a feeling of powerlessness and anxiety. As long as one was an integral part of that world, unaware of the possibilities and responsibilities of individual action, one did not need to be afraid of it. When one has become an individual, one stands alone and faces the world in all its perilous and overpowering aspects.

Impulses arise to give up one's individuality, to overcome the feeling of aloneness and powerlessness by completely submerging oneself in the world outside. These impulses, however, and the new ties arising from them, are not identical with the primary ties which have been cut off in the process of growth itself. Just as a child can never return to the mother's womb physically, so it can never reverse, psychically, the process of individuation. Attempts to do so necessarily assume the authority and the child who submits to it is never eliminated. Consciously the child may feel secure and satisfied, but unconsciously it realizes that the price it pays is giving up strength and the integrity of its self. Thus the result of submission is the very opposite of what it was to be : submission increases the child's insecurity and at the same time creates hostility and rebelliousness, which is the more frightening since it is directed against the very persons on whom the child has remained — or become — dependent.

However, submission is not the only way of avoiding aloneness and anxiety. The other way, the only one which is productive and does not end in an insoluble conflict, is that of *spontaneous relationship to man and nature*, a relationship that connects the individual with the world without eliminating his individuality. This kind of relationship — the foremost expressions of which are love and productive work — are rooted in the integration and strength of the total personality and are therefore subject to the very limits that exist for the growth of the self ....

The child becomes more free to develop and express its own individual self unhampered by those ties which were limiting it. But the child also becomes more free from a world which gave it security and reassurance. The process of individuation is one of growing strength and integration of its individual personality, but it is at the same time a process in which the original identity with others is lost and in which the child becomes more separate from them. This growing separation may result in an isolation that has the quality of desolation and creates intense anxiety and insecurity ; it may result in a new kind of closeness and a solidarity with others if the child has been able to develop the inner strength and productivity which are the premise of this new kind of relatedness to the world.

If every step in the direction of separation and individuation were matched by corresponding growth of the self, the development of the child would be harmonious. This does not occur, however. While the process of individuation takes place automatically, the growth of the self is hampered for a number of individual and social reasons. The lag between these two trends results in an unbearable feeling of isolation and powerlessness, and this in its turn leads to psychic mechanisms, which later on are described as mechanisms of escape.

Phylogenetically, too, the history of man can be characterized as a process of growing individuation and growing freedom. Man emerges from the prehuman stage by the first steps in the direction of becoming free from coercive instincts. If we understand by instinct a specific action pattern which is determined by inherited neurological structures, a clearcut trend can be observed in the animal kindgom. The lower an animal is in the scale of development, the more are its adaption to nature and all its activities controlled by instinctive and reflex action mechanisms. The famous social organizations of some insects are created entirely by instincts. On the other hand, the higher an animal is in the scale of development, the more flexibility of action pattern and the less completeness of structural adjustment do we find at birth. This development reaches its peak with man. He is the most helpless of all animals at birth. His adaptation to nature is based essentially on the process of learning, not on instinctual determination. "Instinct ... is a diminishing if not a disappearing category in higher animal forms, especially in the human."

Human existence begins when the lack of fixation of action by instincts exceeds a certain point ; when the adaptation to nature loses its coercive character ; when the way to act is no longer fixed by hereditarily given mechanisms. In other words, *human existence and freedom are from the beginning inseparable.* Freedom is here used not in its positive sense of "freedom to" but in its negative sense of "freedom from," namely freedom from instinctual determination of his actions.

Freedom in the sense just discussed is an ambiguous gift. Man is born without the equipment for appropriate action which the animal possesses ; he is dependent on his parents for a longer time than any animal, and his reactions to his surroundings are less quick and less effective than the automatically regulated instinctive actions are. He goes through all the dangers and fears which this lack of instinctive equipment implies. Yet this very helplessness of man is the basis from which human development springs ; *man's biological weakness is the condition of human culture.*

From the beginning of his existence man is confronted with the choice between different courses of action. In the animal there is an uninterrupted chain of reactions starting with a stimulus, like hunger, and ending with a more or less strictly determined course of action, which does away with the tension created by the stimulus. In man that chain is interrupted. The stimulus is there but the kind of satisfaction is "open," that is, he must choose between different courses of action. Instead of a predetermined instinctive action, man has to weigh possible courses of action in his mind ; he starts to think. He changes his role toward nature from that of purely passive adaptation to an active one : he produces. He invents tools and, while thus mastering nature, he separates himself from it more and more. He becomes dimly aware of himself — or rather of his group — as not being identical with nature. It dawns upon him that his is a tragic fate : to be part of nature, and yet to transcend it. He becomes aware of death as his ultimate fate even if he tries to deny it in manifold phantasies.

One particularly telling representation of the fundamental relation between man and freedom is offered in the biblical myth of man's expulsion from paradise.

The myth identifies the beginning of human history with an act of choice, but it puts all emphasis on the sinfulness of this first act of freedom and the suffering resulting from it. Man and woman live in the Garden of Eden in complete harmony with each other and with nature. There is peace and no necessity to work ; there is no choice, no freedom, no thinking either. Man is forbidden to eat from the tree of knowledge of good and evil. He acts against God's command, he breaks through the state of harmony with nature of which he is a part without transcending it. From the standpoint of the church which represented authority, this is essentially sin. From the standpoint of man, however, this is the beginning of human freedom. Acting against God's orders means freeing himself from coercion, emerging from the unconscious existence of prehuman life to the level of man. Acting against the command of authority, committing a sin, is in its positive human aspect the first act of freedom that is, the first *human* act. In the myth the sin in its formal aspect is the acting against God's command ; in its material aspect it is the eating of the tree of knowledge. The act of disobedience as an act of freedom is the beginning of reason. The myth speaks of other consequences of the first act of freedom. The original harmony between man and nature is broken. God proclaims war between man and woman, and war between nature and man. Man has become separate from nature, he has taken the first step toward becoming human by becoming an "individual." He has committed the first act of freedom. The myth emphasizes the suffering resulting from this act. To transcend nature, to be alienated from nature and from another human being, finds man naked, ashamed. He is alone and free, yet powerless and afraid. The newly won freedom appears as a curse ; he is free *from* the sweet bondage of paradise, but he is not free *to* govern himself, to realize his individuality.

"Freedom from" is not identical with positive freedom, with "freedom to." The emergence of man from nature is a long-drawn-out process ; to a large extent he remains tied to the world from which he emerged ; he remains part of nature — the soil he lives on, the sun and moon and stars, the trees and flowers, the animals, and the group of people with whom he is connected by the ties of blood. Primitive religions bear testimony to man's feeling of oneness with nature. Animate and inanimate nature are part of his human world or, as one may also put it, he is still part of the natural world.

These primary ties block his full human development ; they stand in the way of the development of his reason and his critical capacities ; they let him recognize himself and others only through the medium of his, or their, participation in a clan, a social or religious community, and not as human beings ; in other words, they block his development as a free, self-determining, productive individual. But although this in one aspect, there is another one. This identity with nature, clan, religion, gives the individual security. He belongs to, he is rooted in, a structuralized whole in which he has an unquestionable place. He may suffer from hunger or suppression, but he does not suffer from the worst of all pains — complete aloneness and doubt.

We see that the process of growing human freedom has the same dialectic character that we have noticed in the process of individual growth. On the one hand it is a process of growing strength and integration, mastery of nature, growing power of human reason, and growing solidarity with other human beings. But on the other hand this growing individuation means growing isolation, insecurity, and thereby growing doubt concerning one's own role in the universe, the meaning of one's life, and with all that a growing feeling of one's own powerlessness and insignificance as an individual.

If the process of the development of mankind had been harmonious, if it had followed a certain plan, then both sides of the development — the growing strength and the growing individuation — would have been exactly balanced. As it is, the history of mankind is one of conflict and strife. Each step in the direction of growing individuation threatened people with new insecurities. Primary bonds once severed cannot be mended ; once paradise is lost, man cannot return to it. There is only one possible, productive solution for the relationship of individualized man with the world : his active solidarity with all men and his spontaneous activity, love and work, which unite him again with the world, not by primary ties but as a free and independent individual.

However, if the economic, social and political conditions on which the whole process of human individuation depends, do not offer a basis for the realization of individuality in the sense just mentioned, while at the same time people have lost those ties which gave them security, this lag makes freedom an unbearable burden. It then becomes identical with doubt, with a kind of life which lacks meaning and direction. Powerful tendencies arise to escape from this kind of freedom into submission or some kind of relationship to man and the world which promises relief from uncertainty, even if it deprives the individual of his freedom. [pp. 39-52]

NOTES

1. Erich Fromm, *Escape from Freedom* (New York : Holt, Rinehart & Winston, Inc., 1969), pp. 17-52.

2. John Dewey, *Freedom and Culture* (New York : G.P. Putman's Sons, 1939).

THE FEAR OF FREEDOM[1]

E. R. Dodds

Our survey starts from an age when Greek rationalism appeared to be on the verge of final triumph, the great age of intellectual discovery that begins with the foundation of the Lyceum about 335 B.C. and continues down to the end of the third century. This period witnessed the transformation of Greek science from an untidy jumble of isolated observations mixed with *a priori* guesses into a system of methodical disciplines. In the more abstract sciences, mathematics and astronomy, it reached a level that was not to be attained again before the sixteenth century ; and it made the first organized attempt at research in many other fields, botany, zoology, geography, and the history of language, of literature, and of human institutions. Nor was it only in science that the time was adventurous and creative. It is as if the sudden widening of the spatial horizon that resulted from Alexander's conquests had widened at the same time all the horizons of the mind. Despite its lack of political freedom, the society of the third century B.C. was in many ways the nearest approach to an "open" society that the world had yet seen, and nearer than any that would be seen again until very modern times. The traditions and institutions of the old "closed" society were of course still there and still influential : the incorporation of a city-state in one or other of the Hellenistic kingdoms did not cause it to lose its moral importance overnight. But though the city was there, its walls, as someone has put it, were down : its institutions stood exposed to rational criticism ; its traditional ways of life were increasingly penetrated and modified by a cosmopolitan culture. For the first time in Greek history, it mattered little where a man had been born or what his ancestry was : of the men who dominated Athenian intellectual life in this age, Artistotle and Theophrastus, Zeno, Cleanthes, and Chrysippus were all of them foreigners ; only Epicurus was of Athenian stock, though by birth a colonial....

Certainly it is in this age that the Greek pride in human reason attains its most confident expression. We should reject, says Aristotle, the old rule of life that counselled humility, bidding man think in mortal terms ; for man has within him a divine thing, the intellect, and so far as he can live on that level of experience, he can live as though he were not mortal. The founder of Stoicism went further still : for Zeno, man's intellect was not merely akin to God, it *was* God, a portion of the divine substance in its pure or active state. And although Epicurus made no such claim, he yet held that by constant meditation on the truths of philosophy one could live "like a god among men."

But ordinary human living, of course, is not like that. Aristotle knew that no man can sustain the life of pure reason for more than very brief periods ; and he and his pupils appreciated, better perhaps than any other Greeks, the necessity of studying the irrational factors in behaviour if we are to reach a realistic understanding of human nature....

Aristotle's approach to an empirical psychology, and in particular to a psychology of the Irrational, was unhappily carried no further after the first generation of his pupils. When the natural sciences detached themselves from the study of philosophy proper, as they began to do early in the third century, psychology was left in the hands of the philosophers (where it remained — I think to its detriment — down to very recent times). And the dogmatic rationalists of the Hellenistic Age seem to have cared little for the objective study of man as he is ; their attention was concentrated on the glorious picture of man as he might be, the ideal *sapiens* or sage. In order to make the picture seem possible, Zeno and Chrysippus deliberately went back, behind Aristotle and behind Plato, to the naive intellectualism of the fifth century. The attainment of moral perfection, they said, was independent both of natural endowment and of habituation ; it depended solely on the exercise of reason. And there was no "irrational soul" for reason to contend with : the so-called passions were merely errors of judgement, or morbid disturbances resulting from errors of judgement. Correct the error, and the disturbance will automatically cease, leaving a mind untouched by joy or sorrow, untroubled by hope or fear, "passionless, pitiless, and perfect." [pp. 236-239]

Looking at the picture as a whole, an intelligent observer in or about the year 200 B.C. might well have predicted that within a few generations the disintegration of the inherited structure would be complete, and that the perfect Age of Reason would follow. He would, however, have been quite wrong on both points — as similar predictions made by nineteenth-century rationalists look like proving wrong. It would have surprised our imaginary Greek rationalist to learn that half a millennium after his death Athena would still be receiving the periodic gift of a new dress from her grateful people ; that bulls would still be sacrificed in Megara to heroes killed in the Persian Wars eight hundred years earlier ; that ancient taboos concerned with ritual purity would still be rigidly maintained in many places. For the *vis inertiae* that keeps this sort of thing going — what Matthew Arnold once called "the extreme slowness of things" — no rationalist ever makes sufficient allowance. Gods withdraw, but their rituals live on, and no one except a few intellectuals notices that they have ceased to mean anything. In a material sense the Inherited Conglomerate did not in the end perish by disintegration ; large portions of it were left standing through the centuries, a familiar, shabby, rather lovable facade, until one day the Christians pushed the facade over and discovered that there was virtually nothing behind it — only a faded local patriotism and an antiquarian sentiment. So, at least, it happened in the cities ; it appears that to the country folk, the *pagani* certain of the old rites still did mean something, as indeed a few of them, in a dim half-comprehended manner, still do.

A prevision of this history would have surprised an observer in the third century B.C. But it would have surprised him far more painfully to learn that Greek civilization was entering, not on the Age of Reason, but on a period of slow intellectual decline which was to last, with some deceptive rallies and some brilliant individual rear-guard actions, down to the capture of Byzantium by the Turks ; that in all the sixteen centuries of existence still awaiting it the Hellenic world would produce no poet as good as Theocritus, no scientist as good as Eratosthenes, no mathematician as good as Archimedes, and that the one great name in philosophy would represent a point of view believed to be extinct — transcendental Platonism.

To understand the reasons for this long-drawn-out decline is one of the major problems of world history. We are concerned here with only one aspect of it, what may be called for convenience the Return of the Irrational....

[A]fter the third century a different kind of interaction shows itself, with the appearance of a pseudo-scientific literature, mostly pseudonymous and often claiming to be based on divine revelation, which took up the ancient superstitions of the East or the more recent phantasies of the Hellenistic masses, dressed them in trappings borrowed from Greek science or Greek philosophy, and won for them the acceptance of a large part of the educated class. Assimilation henceforth works both ways : while rationalism, of a limited and negative kind, continues to spread from above downwards, antirationalism spreads from below upwards, and eventually wins the day.

Astrology is the most familiar example. It has been said that it "fell upon the Hellenistic mind as a new disease falls upon some remote island people." One may guess that its spread was favoured by political conditions : in the troubled half-century that preceded the Roman conquest of Greece it was particularly important to know what was going to happen.... But behind such immediate causes we may perhaps suspect something deeper and less conscious : for a century or more the individual had been face to face with his own intellectual freedom, and now he turned tail and bolted from the horrid prospect — better the rigid determinism of the astrological Fate than that terrifying burden of daily responsibility. Rational men like Panaetius and Cicero tried to check the retreat by argument, as Plotinus was to do later, but without perceptible effect ; certain motives are beyond the reach of argument.

Besides astrology, the second century B.C. saw the development of another irrational doctrine which deeply influenced the thought of later antiquity and the whole Middle Age — the theory of occult properties or forces immanent in certain animals, plants, and precious stones. Though its beginnings are probably much older, this was first systematically set forth by one Bolus of Mendes, called "the Democritean," who appears to have written about 200 B.C. His system was closely linked with magical medicine and with alchemy ; it was also soon combined with astrology, to which it formed a convenient supplement. The awkward thing about the stars had always been their inaccessibility, alike to prayer and to magic. But if each planet had its representative in the animal, vegetable, and mineral kingdoms, linked to it by an occult "sympathy," as was now asserted, one could get at them magically by manipulating these earthly counterparts. Resting as they did on the primitive conception of the world as a magical unity, Bolus' ideas were fatally attractive to the Stoics, who already conceived the cosmos as an organism whose parts had community of experience. From the first century B.C. onwards Bolus begins to be quoted as a scientific authority comparable in status with Aristotle and Theophrastus, and his doctrines become incorported in the generally accepted world picture....

All these developments are perhaps symptoms, rather than causes, of a general change in the intellectual climate of the Mediterranean world — something whose nearest historical analogue may be the romantic reaction against rationalist "natural theology" which set in at the beginning of the nineteenth century and is still a powerful influence today. The adoration of the visible cosmos, and the sense of unity with it which had found expression in early Stoicism, began to be replaced in many minds by a feeling that the physical world — at any rate the part of it below the moon — is under the sway of evil powers, and that what the soul needs is not unity with it but escape from it. The thoughts of men were increasingly preoccupied with techniques of individual salvation, some relying on holy books allegedly discovered in Eastern temples or dictated by the voice of God to some inspired prophet, others seeking a personal revelation by oracle, dream, or waking vision ; others again looking for security in ritual, whether by initiation in one or more of the now numerous "mysteria" or by employing the services of a private magician. There was a growing demand for occultism, which is essentially an attempt to capture the Kingdom of Heaven by material means — it has been well described as "the vulgar form of transcendentalism." And philosophy followed a parallel path on a higher level. Most of the schools had long since ceased to value the truth for its own sake, but in the Imperial Age they abandon, with certain exceptions, any pretence of disinterested curiousity and present themselves frankly as dealers in salvation. It is not only that the philosopher conceives his lecture-room as a new dispensary for sick souls ; in principle, that was nothing new. But the philosopher is not merely a psychotherapist ; he is also, as Marcus Aurelius put it, "a kind of priest and minister of the gods," and his teachings claim to have religious rather than scientific worth. "The aim of Platonism," says a Christian observer in the second century A.D., "is to see God face to face." And profane knowledge was valued only so far as it contributed to such aims. Seneca, for example, quotes with approval the view that we should not trouble to investigate things that it is neither possible nor useful to know, such as the cause of the tides or the principle of perspective. In such sayings we already feel the intellectual climate of the Middle Ages. It is the climate in which Christianity grew up ; it made the triumph of the new religion possible, and it left its mark on Christian teaching ; but it was not created by Christians. [pp. 243-249]

If future historians are to reach a more complete explanation of what happened, I think that, without ignoring either the intellectual or the economic factor, they will have to take account of another sort of motive, less conscious and less tidily rational. I have already suggested that behind the acceptance of astral determinism there lay, among other things, the fear of freedom — the unconscious flight from the heavy burden of individual choice which an open society lays upon its members. If such a motive is accepted as a *vera causa* (and there is pretty strong evidence that it is a *vera causa* today), we may suspect its operation in a good many places. We may suspect it in the hardening of philosophical specualtion into quasi-religious dogma which provided the individual with an unchanging rule of life ; in the dread of inconvenient research expressed even by a Cleanthes or an Epicurus ; later, and on a more popular level, in the demand for a prophet or a scripture ; and more generally, in the pathetic reverence for the written word characteristic of late Roman and mediaeval times — a readiness, as Nock puts it, "to accept statements because they were in books, or even because they were said to be in books."

When a people has travelled as far towards the open society as the Greeks had by the third century B.C., such a retreat does not hapen quickly or uniformly. Nor is it painless for the individual. For the refusal of responsibility in any sphere there is always a price to be paid, usually in the form of neurosis. And we may find collateral evidence that the fear of freedom is not a mere phrase in the increase of irrational anxieties and the striking manifestations of neurotic guilt-feeling observable in the later stages of the retreat. These things were not new in the religious experience of the Greeks : we encountered them in studying the Archaic Age. But the centuries of rationalism had weakened their social influence and thus, indirectly, their poser over the individual. Now they show themselves in new forms and with a new intensity.... Pagan and Christian alike prayed in the later Imperial Age for protection against invisible perils — against the evil eye and daemonic possession, against "the deceiving demon" or "the headless dog." One amulet promises protection "against every malice of a frightening dream or of beings in the air" ; a second, "against enemies, accusers, robbers, terrors, and apparitions in dreams" ; a third — a Christian one — against "unclean spirits" hiding under your bed or in the rafters or even in the rubbish-pit. The Return of the Irrational was, as may be seen from these few examples, pretty complete.

There I must leave the problem. But I will not end ... without making a further confession. I have purposely been sparing in the use of modern parallels, for I know that such parallels mislead quite as often as they illuminate. But as a man cannot escape from his own shadow, so no generation can pass judgement on the problems of history without reference, conscious or unconscious, to its own problems. And I will not pretend to hide from the reader that in writing these chapters, and especially this last one, I have had our own situation constantly in mind. We too have witnessed the slow disintegration of an inherited conglomerate, starting among the educated class but now affecting the masses almost everywhere, yet still very far from complete. We too have experienced a great age of rationalism, marked by scientific advances beyond anything that earlier times had thought possible, and confronting mankind with the prospect of a society more open than any it has ever known. And in the last forty years we have also experienced something else — the unmistakable symptoms of a recoil from that prospect. It would appear that, in the words used recently by Andre Malraux, "Western civilisation has begun to doubt its own credentials."

What is the meaning of this recoil, this doubt ? Is it the hesitation before the jump, or the beginning of a panic flight ? I do not know. On such a matter a simple professor of Greek is in no position to offer an opinion. But he can do one thing. He can remind his readers that once before a civilised people rode to this jump — rode to it and refused it. And he can beg them to examine all the circumstances of that refusal.

Was it the horse that refused, or the rider ? That is really the crucial question. Personally, I believe it was the horse — in other words, those irrational elements in human nature which govern without our knowledge so much of our behaviour and so much of what we think is our thinking. And if I am right about this, I can see in it grounds for hope. As these chapters have, I trust, shown, the men who created the first European rationalism were never — until the Hellenistic Age — "mere" rationalists : that is to say, they were deeply and imaginatively aware of the power, the wonder, and the peril of the Irrational. But they could describe what went on below the threshold of consciousness only in mythological or symbolic language ; they had no instrument for understanding it, still else for controlling it ; and in the Hellenistic Age too many of them made the fatal mistake of thinking they could ignore it. Modern man, on the other hand, is beginning to acquire such an instrument. It is still very far from perfect, nor is it always skillfully handled ; in many fields, including that of history, its possibilities and its limitations have still to be tested. Yet it seems to offer the hope that if we use it wisely we shall eventually understand our horse better ; that, understanding him better, we shall be able by better training to overcome his fears ; and that through the overcoming of fear horse and rider will one day take that decisive jump, and take it successfully. [pp. 252-255]

NOTE

1. E. R. Dodds, *The Greeks and the Irrational* (Berkeley : University of California Press, 1951), pp. 236-255.

AUTHOR INDEX

[References are to pages]

SUBJECT INDEX

[References are to pages]